M000209033

History of Warren County [N.Y.] With Illustrations and Biographical Sketches of Some of its Prominent men and Pioneers

You are holding a reproduction of an original work that is in the public domain in the United States of America, and possibly other countries.You may freely copy and distribute this work as no entity (individual or corporate) has a copyright on the body of the work.This book may contain prior copyright references, and library stamps (as most of these works were scanned from library copies).These have been scanned and retained as part of the historical artifact.

This book may have occasional imperfections such as missing or blurred pages, poor pictures, errant marks, etc. that were either part of the original artifact, or were introduced by the scanning process. We believe this work is culturally important, and despite the imperfections, have elected to bring it back into print as part of our continuing commitment to the preservation of printed works worldwide. We appreciate your understanding of the imperfections in the preservation process, and hope you enjoy this valuable book.

In Compliance with current
copyright law, Cornell University
Library produced this
replacement volume on paper
that meets the ANSI Standard
Z39.48-1992 to replace the
irreparably deteriorated original

1998

CORNELL
UNIVERSITY
LIBRARY

Abbie Washburn Kendrick
Glen's Falls 1885.

HISTORY

OF

WARREN COUNTY

*WITH ILLUSTRATIONS AND BIOGRAPHICAL SKETCHES
OF SOME OF ITS PROMINENT MEN AND PIONEERS*

EDITED BY
H. P. SMITH

SYRACUSE, N Y
D. MASON & CO, PUBLISHERS
1885

KC

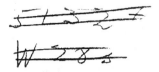

A768943

D. MASON & CO.,
PRINTERS AND PUBLISHERS,
63 WEST WATER STREET
SYRACUSE, N. Y

INTRODUCTORY.

WHILE it may seem to the uninitiated a task involving but little difficulty to prepare for publication a work no more comprehensive in character than this volume, and containing merely the history of a single county, still it is not out of place here to assure all such readers that the work is one demanding a vast amount of labor and research, watchful care, untiring patience and fair discrimination   This need not be said to any person who has had experience in similar work   In attempting the production of a creditable history of Warren county the publishers and the editor did not underestimate the difficulties of their task, and came to it fully imbued with a clear idea of its magnitude and determination to execute it in such a manner that it should receive the general commendation of all into whose hands it should fall.   It is believed that this purpose has been substantially carried out, and that, while a perfect historical work has never yet been published, this one will be found to contain so few imperfections that the most critical readers will be satisfied

It is a part of the plans of the publishers in the production of county histories to secure, as far as possible, local assistance, either as writers, or in the revision of all manuscripts; the consequence being that the work bears a local character which could not otherwise be secured, and, moreover, comes from the press far more complete and perfect than could possibly be the case were it entrusted wholly to the efforts of comparative strangers to the locality in hand   In carrying out this plan in this county the editor has been tendered such generous co-operation and assistance of various kinds that to merely mention all who have thus aided is impossible, the satisfaction of having assisted in the production of a commendable public enterprise must be their present

5

reward But there are some who have given so generously of their labor and time towards the consummation of this work, that to leave them unmentioned would be simple injustice First, perhaps, should be mentioned Dr. A W Holden, of Glens Falls, from whose excellent history of Queensbury we have been compelled to draw so liberally, to his generous co-operation we are also indebted for the chapter on the Medical Profession, the Press chapter, and other important work To the Hon Isaac Mott the work is indebted for the chapter on the Courts, the Beanch and Bar of the county Others, who have generously aided the work, are T. S. Ketchum, for labor on the Masonic Order, H. M Harris, of the Glens Falls *Republican*, and the press generally throughout the county, for use of files, etc , Henry Griffing, of Warrensburgh; David Noble, of Johnsburgh, D. Aldrich, of Thurman; George T Rockwell, of Luzerne, Daniel V Brown, county clerk; Professor Farr, of Glens Falls Academy, the town clerks of the county, and many others To all such the gratitude of the publishers and readers is extended.

With this word of introduction the work is commended to its readers by the publishers and

THE EDITOR

CONTENTS.

CHAPTER VIII

CONTINUATION OF FRENCH AND ENGLISH WAR.

CHAPTER IX

;EXTINCTION OF FRENCH POWER IN AMERICA.

CHAPTER X

EARLY SETTLEMENTS

CHAPTER XI.

FROM 1763 TO THE REVOLUTION

CHAPTER XII

FROM 1770 TO 1775

CHAPTER XIII

CLOSE OF 1776

CHAPTER XIV

TO THE CLOSE OF THE REVOLUTION

CHAPTER XV

FROM THE REVOLUTION TO 1815

CHAPTER XVI

TO THE PRESENT TIME

CHAPTER XVII

LAND TITLES

CHAPTER XVIII

WARREN COUNTY IN THE REBELLION

CHAPTER XIX

COUNTY BUILDINGS, SOCIETIES, ETC

CHAPTER XX.

THE COUNTY PRESS

CHAPTER XXI

INTERNAL IMPROVEMENTS

CHAPTER XXII

THE BENCH AND BAR OF WARREN COUNTY

CHAPTER XXIII

THE MEDICAL PROFESSION

CHAPTER XXIV.

SECRET SOCIETIES

CHAPTER XXV

CHAPTER XXVI

CHAPTER XXVII.

CHAPTER XXVIII.

CHAPTER XXIX

CHAPTER XXX

CHAPTER XXXI

CHAPTER XXXII.

CHAPTER XXXIII.

CHAPTER XXXIV

CHAPTER XXXV.

CHAPTER XXXVI

BIOGRAPHICAL.

ILLUSTRATIONS.

HISTORY

OF

WARREN COUNTY.

CHAPTER I

THE SUBJECT

The Historical Beginning — Formation of the County — Situation and Boundaries — Area, etc

WHILE the history of Warren county as a defined section of the State of New York extends into the past only to the year 1813, yet at that comparatively recent date much of the important history of the immediate region, of which the county now forms a part, had been enacted For how many years (or, possibly, centuries) before the locality was known to the white race who now possess it the beautiful waters, lovely valleys and rugged mountains were favorite resorts of the aborigines who have been driven from their domain, is a vexed question that has not been answered with any great degree of assurance, and probably never will be To these primitive inhabitants, well-known as their general characteristics now are, we shall devote a few pages herein, while to the sanguinary strife in which they were prominent actors and which for nearly two centuries made this region one great battlefield, must be given up a share of this work proportionate to the historical importance of those events The history of the territory now embraced within the boundaries of Warren county may, therefore, properly begin with the early years of the seventeenth century, at the time when Samuel de Champlain, with his party of northern Indians and two white attendants, came up Lake Champlain on a hostile incursion against the proud Iroquois [1]

---

[1] This name is used here and hereafter for convenience, although it had not yet, of course, been applied to these Indians The name was given to the Five Nations by the French, who also prefixed the name "Huron," because their language indicated the Hurons, who were seated on the shores of the Georgian Bay, as a branch of the Iroquois, and, like them, isolated in the midst of the Algonquins, when discovered by the French — LOSSING

2

From the date when Champlain entered the lake which bears his name
(July 4th, 1609) to the present time, the historic traces are generally clearly
defined, gradually broadening outward toward the present advanced state of
civilized occupation of this region, that event, approaching as it did, if not
actually embracing a visit from the great explorer, to places within the present
boundaries of this county, was the direct forerunner of the stirring era that
extended down to the close of the Revolutionary War

Warren county was formed from Washington county on the 12th of
March, 1813, and received its name in honor of General Joseph Warren, of the
Revolutionary army   It lies near the eastern boundary of the State, south
and west of Lake George   It contains nine hundred and sixty-eight square
miles, its population according to the census of 1880 was 25,180   It contains
eleven towns, with Caldwell as the county seat

Although the county was not formed until 1813, it may often become
necessary to speak of the inhabitants of the territory now embraced within the
county boundaries, and events occurring therein, previous to the actual formation and existence of the county as a civil organization   In doing so, allusion
may be made, for the sake of convenience and simplicity, to Warren county
before its actual creation

Such is a brief general reference to the subject of this history —a locality
which has been the theatre of events possessing great historic interest and importance, which is distinguished by some of nature's most marvelous works
and is surrounded with an atmosphere of romance

CHAPTER II

NATURAL CHARACTERISTICS [1]

General Topography — The Geological Survey — Description of the Five Mountain Ranges —
Recommendations to Lovers of Nature — Valleys of the County — Lakes and Ponds — Falls and Cascades — Geology — Granite — Serpentine — Potsdam Sandstone — Sand Rock — Black Marble — Trenton Limestone — Utica Slate

MOUNTAINS — When, by an act of the State Legislature, the geological
survey was commenced, the people at large looked upon it as a foolish
waste of money, but when Ebenezer Emmons submitted his report in 1842
for the survey of the second district, there was throughout the country a feeling of satisfaction, and particularly among men of scientific attainments, for

---

[1] This chapter was prepared by Homer D L Sweet, of Syracuse, N Y, a gentleman who is eminently qualified for the task, having been prominently connected with one survey of the greater part of
Northern New York, and with much other similar work

he had discovered mountains that were theretofore unknown, more than a mile in height, giving us, as a State, the right to use the "Great Seal" without inconsistency ; for the sun, as depicted on the shield, could rise from behind real mountains, and the legend underneath, "EXCELSIOR," was no longer a myth

Mr Emmons gave, in the early pages of his report, a very concise description of the five great mountain ranges that occupy the entire northeast quarter of the State, and which farther investigation has not materially changed in the last forty years , but when treating of these same ranges of mountains in Warren county, he has given to them different names from those applied in Essex county, and in treating of the same in the county of Essex, he has left out the third range entirely   It is by this discrepancy in his descriptions that much trouble has been occasioned, and differences of opinion among individuals have arisen   To some of these ranges he gave names, and to others none   James Johonnot, who had charge of the topographical features of French's *Gazetteer* in 1860, added names to those ranges that had not been named, changed Moriah range to Boquet range and Clinton to Adirondack   These changes were called for, because that portion of the Boquet range in Moriah was an insignificant portion only , whereas, by naming it from a river that bordered it on the north, the name rendered its location at once apparent   Changing the Clinton range to Adirondack was only in conformity to common usage, which in twenty years had become quite fixed in the minds of the people, and which twenty-five years additional has completely established

In writing of the topography of Warren county, to obtain a fair comprehension of the whole subject, it is easier and much more satisfactory to take it in connection with the surrounding territory, particularly in regard to the mountain ranges, for four of the five cross Warren, although they may have their rise or termini in other counties   A mountain range is as much determined by continuous valleys as by continuous peaks, and in the following descriptions I shall be as much governed by one as by the other   When Mr Emmons made his survey there was no map of the State that was at all creditable, very few of the mountains had a location on them and that few were no more correctly located than they are on the maps we have at present, which is bad enough.   Nothing but the trigonometrical survey of this entire region will ever place them absolutely in their right localities

The first, or Palmerton range of mountains, rises in the extreme south point of Warren county, where it is locally known as the Luzerne Mountain, with its main axis lying in a southwest and northeast direction   Proceeding in a general northeast course, it is divided by a lateral valley, through which the road runs from Glens Falls to Lake George.   Proceeding in the same general course, the next mass is known as French Mountain   Beyond this is a little valley in which is situated the hamlet of Harrisena   From this point the mountain ridge becomes more continuous, and occupies about all the territory between Lake George and Lake Champlain, with the same general course, with scarcely any thing like a lateral valley, receiving different names in different localities, and finally terminates at Mount Defiance, where it proudly overlooks old Fort Ticonderoga   This range is about fifty miles in length, from three to five miles in width, and extends through the towns of Luzerne and Queensbury in Warren county, Fort Ann, Dresden, and Putnam in Washington county, and a part of Ticonderoga in Essex county   The highest point is in Washington county, in Dresden, called Black Mountain, which is about 3,000 feet high. The sides of this range are steep and rocky, often precipitous, composed of primitive rock and but scantily covered with a thin, sandy soil   Viewed from the deck of a steamboat on either lake, this high ridge is the most attractive in the landscape

The second or Kayaderosseras range, rises in Montgomery county, a little north of Amsterdam, and taking the same general northeast direction, is not broken by any lateral valley till it reaches the Sacandaga River a little west of the village of Luzerne   North of the Sacandaga, and west of the Hudson, is a single mass, where the continuity is again broken by the Hudson   From this point it again assumes the full character of a continuous range for several miles, only partially cleft by a little valley, through which the road runs from Caldwell to Warrensburgh   Still continuing in the same general direction in a high rocky ridge for about twenty miles, it spreads out in several spurs in the vicinity of Brant Lake, and one of them culminates in Mount Pharaoh, which has an estimated altitude of 4,500 feet   From this region the ridges, which are spread to about fifteen miles in width, gradually approach each other, and finally terminate on Lake Champlain in Bulwagga Mountain, which has a precipitous face of about 1,200 feet

This range is some twenty to thirty miles longer than the first, and is flanked on both sides with outlying spurs, or isolated peaks, sometimes attaining a width of seven to ten miles in the southwest portion, but between the Hudson River and Lake George it is not more than four, farther north it occupies all the territory between Schroon Lake and Lakes George and Champlain   This mountain range takes a great variety of forms — sharp, steep and rocky on one side, and quite gradual in its slope on the other, is often precipitous, with bare and barren summits   In the southwest portion a very little arable land is found nestled in the coves and curves of either side, but as we proceed farther north the cultivated spots become less, and smaller, and finally die out altogether, until we reach the slope towards Lake Champlain, where the dairyman again assumes sway, and a little farther on the soil is in a good state of cultivation well up on to the sides of the mountain slopes   This range occupies parts of the towns of Edinburgh, Day and Hadley in Saratoga county, Luzerne, Caldwell, Bolton, Horicon and Hague in Warren county, Schroon, Ticonderoga and Crown Point in Essex county

The third, or Schroon, range rises north of Johnstown, where it is called the Mayfield Mountain, and forms for a considerable distance a continuous ridge The valley of the Sacandaga in the town of Hope, Hamilton county, completely dissevers it, but it soon assumes the full characteristics of a range, and for eight or ten miles lies nearly north and south, but finally bears off to the northeast again, and sends out a spur to the right, which is the culminating point of the range — Crane Mountain in Johnsburgh

The most continuous ridge is farther west and passes Schroon Lake on the west and, some miles farther north, forms the divide between the waters of the Hudson and the Boquet, where it bends again more to the east and finally terminates in Split Rock Point on Lake Champlain This range is about ninety miles in length, from three to five in width at the southern extremity, and about fifteen in width opposite Crane Mountain and quite narrow at its terminus In the widest part the masses are not very high, with the exception of Crane Mountain, which is, barometrically, 3,289 feet, and the slopes are quite gentle in some places, but farther north in Essex county (a few miles north of Schroon), the masses are high, sharp and angular, with deep narrow valleys or gorges between them This range occupies all the north part of Mayfield in Fulton county, the east part of Hope and Wells in Hamilton county, Thurman, Johnsburgh and Chester in Warren county, Minerva, North Hudson, Moriah, a corner of Elizabethtown and a part of Westport in Essex county The lateral valleys are very few, and the only ones are the Sacandaga before spoken of, and the northwest branch of the Hudson In its broadest portion there is very little arable land, for where it might be cultivated so far as the surface of the soil is concerned, it is covered by such quantities of boulders — brought down from farther north — that it is unprofitable to attempt the raising of but very limited patches of grain

The fourth, or Boquet, range rises at the Noses, on the east line of the town of Palatine, and pursues the same general northeast direction, through Palatine and Mohawk in Montgomery county; Ephrata, Johnstown, Caroga and Bleeker in Fulton county, Hope, Wells, Lake Pleasant and Indian Lake in Hamilton county, all the northwest part of Johnsburgh in Warren county, it enters Essex county in the southwest corner of Minerva, and, still continuing its course, it finally culminates in Dix's Peak, which is, barometrically, 4,916 feet above tide This point is in the town of North Hudson, and from there it loses its continuity as a range, being completely broken up into spurs and isolated masses in Keene, Elizabethtown and Lewis, finally it ends in the town of Willsborough, Essex county, and is the only range that does not end abruptly in a precipice on the shore of Lake Champlain. The continuity of this range is broken in its southern portion, where it is crossed by the two lateral valleys of the western branches of the Sacandaga River in Hamilton county, and again by the Hudson in the town of Minerva The borders of this range are not as well defined as in some of the others, it is broad where the third range is narrow, and narrow where the third range is broad   It is about one hundred and ten miles in length and from five to fifteen miles in width, its narrow portions being in the vicinity of Lake Pleasant, and near its culminating point, with three broad portions   one at the southern part, one in the vicinity of Indian Lake, and the third at the northern extremity.   Piseco Lake, Lake Pleasant, and Indian Lake farther north, lie upon the west side

In the vicinity of Dix's Peak are several remarkable mountains — high, sharp, conical peaks, with deep, narrow gorges between them , or very narrow, sharp ridges, which, plainly visible when viewed from one direction, are not recognized when viewed from another but slightly altered direction   The clefts between them are very narrow, almost chasms, with nearly perpendicular sides, ragged in the extreme.   This range has many outlying spurs, some of them rising into quite prominent peaks, that in any other portion of the State would be considered as objects of grandeur

The fifth, or Adirondack, range rises fairly south of the Mohawk River and crosses that stream at Little Falls   From this point it pursues the same general course with all of the others, occupying a portion of Manheim and Salisbury in Herkimer county, Morehouse, Arietta, Lake Pleasant and Indian Lake in Hamilton county, all of Newcomb, Keene, Jay and Chesterfield, with parts of Elizabethtown and Lewis in Essex county , and finally terminates at Trembleau Point on Lake Champlain, near Port Kent, at the mouth of the great Ausable River   The continuity of this whole range is only broken by two lateral valleys, the first, by the little branch of the Hudson, just west of Lake Sanford, in Newcomb, and again by the south branch of the Ausable in the town of Keene   This, principal of all the mountain ranges in the State, is one hundred and thirty miles in length from the Mohawk River to the lake at Trembleau Point, and from ten to twenty miles in width   It has many outlying spurs in its whole course, but around the highest portion are clustered a group of the most remarkable peaks in the United States east of the Mississippi River   Mount Marcy, the highest of all, is 5,344 feet above tide, and Mount McIntyre, a near neighbor, 5,112   In the immediate vicinity are several others that have an altitude of over 4,000 feet, and in the whole range there are perhaps fifty that have an altitude of over 3,000 feet   It has three outlying spurs to the north that culminate in three remarkable peaks · Emmons in Hamilton county, Seward in Franklin county , and Whiteface in Essex county   Emmons (or Blue Mountain) 3,762, Seward 4,384, and Whiteface 4,871 feet above tide, respectively   In the southern portion of this range the sides of the hills where they are not properly called mountains are susceptible of some cultivation, and farther north the dairyman finds pasturage for his herds , but after leaving the county of Herkimer, the soil is thin, sandy, and the entire absence of lime renders it unsusceptible of profitable cultivation   The sides of the mountains soon become steep and rocky, and the valleys filled with boulders, brought from the far north, which are too troublesome to contend with In the middle portion of the range, in Hamilton county, it is the broadest and to a great extent has not been explored in any scientific manner known to the writer, but in the northern part this has been done, and the mountain masses are between high, sharp, conical peaks, with deep, narrow defiles, gorges and chasms, in great variety The flanking spurs on either side are great mountains, nearly equal to the principal ones of the range, and cover a vast extent of territory, giving in this portion of the State the appellation of "The Switzerland of America" Northeast of the great group of mountains that gives this range its name, the "flankers" seem to withdraw from their skirmishing expeditions, the "pickets" are drawn in, and on approaching the lake the range modestly assumes the form of a respectable hill, and finally disappears in the rippling depths

Still farther to the northwest of all these mountains is another great range, called the Ausable, or broken range It occupies, with its spurs and isolated peaks, a territory of nearly a hundred miles in length, by from twenty to forty in width, embracing several hundred peaks of greater or less magnitude, a few of which only have been measured The highest portion is the southeast border, and some of the most prominent peaks are Mount St Louis in Herkimer county, 2,295, Owl's Head in Hamilton, 2,825, Graves in St Lawrence, 2,345; St Regis in Franklin, 2,888, De Bar in Franklin, 3,011, and Lyon Mountain in Clinton county, 3,809

From this elevated portion towards the northwest the whole country gradually sinks and loses its rough characteristics, and when within about twenty miles of the St. Lawrence River it entirely disappears, and a nearly level plain continues to the river This is not properly a range, but in treating it as such it occupies all of the territory lying to the northwest of the Fulton chain of lakes in Herkimer, Raquette and Long Lakes in Hamilton, the Saranacs and the Saranac valley continued to Lake Champlain This range is thickly interspersed with numerous lakes and ponds, besides those on the southeast side that define its boundaries and give to it that fascination and attraction to those who delight in visiting this region as a summer resort

Originally all of these mountain ranges were covered with a forest, and far up the slopes a heavy growth of timber of many varieties formerly existed, and in some instances to the very summits, but generally for not more than 2,000 feet was the timber of any great value, as above that in most instances it was dwarfed and useless except to retain moisture to supply the little rills that formed the rivers of the whole region. Some of the highest peaks were bald and barren, and this baldness and barrenness has been terribly increased by the forest fires and the woodman's axe, and the wildness, rockyness and barrenness revealed, where Nature, in her charity, has robed the deformity with a mantle of beauty.

Valleys — To the lover of nature in winter, Essex stands pre-eminently first in the magnitude and magnificence of its mountains, but in summer, Warren equally claims his admiration, in the verdant beauty of its valleys, and the loveliness of its lakes   The first valley (that is, the one between the first and second ranges of mountains), is occupied for at least three-fourths of its length by Lake George, while the valley continues on to the southwest to the great bend of the Hudson River, near Corinth in Saratoga county   The rise in this direction from the lake is quite gradual, and the valley has several little lakes in its length, this is the most natural continuance of the valley, rather than the one leading to Glens Falls   It is bordered by an almost continuous chain of mountains on both sides, and the little lateral valleys are hardly noticeable on either side   The one through which the road leads to Glens Falls is the only one of importance

The second valley extends from Luzerne northeasterly, and naturally follows the Schroon branch of the Hudson River, it is narrow in the southern portion, but widens out in the vicinity of Warrensburgh to several miles, gradually contracting again in the vicinity of Schroon Lake   The bordering hills and mountains wind and curve gracefully in the whole course, one little lateral valley only, on the east side, breaks the continuity, until the stream from Brant Lake is reached, which is so narrow as to be scarcely noticeable   On the west there are two or three breaks in the continuity of the mountain range before the valley of the northwest branch of the Hudson is attained, which is quite broad for some distance, and one other little break, where the stream comes in from Pottersville. These are the only continuous valleys in the county of any extent   The third valley, or the one between the third and fourth ranges of mountains, is simply a depression in the heights of the mountains, and is not occupied by any considerable stream   Its lowest depression is a little southeast of Gore Mountain, where North Creek falls into the Hudson and extends in the same southwest direction, and in its southern portion is occupied by the east branch of the Sacandaga River

The valley of the northwest branch of the Hudson cuts through the third range of mountains, it is wild and picturesque, and the only one of any consequence in the western part of the county   The valleys of the smaller streams are narrow, crooked, deep, wild, and rocky, and hardly one of them affords much opportunity for the cultivation of the soil   These hill and mountain sides are for the most part covered with the native forest, except where the fire has swept them bare, and even here they are gradually regaining their brightness and beauty   The broader valleys have but very little intervale land, but the slopes in many places are susceptible of cultivation   They are beautifully winding in their outlines, with an occasional rocky promontory, high, steep and covered with a great variety of foliage, which, in the autumn, cannot be surpassed for beauty in the wide world

Lakes, Streams, Drainage, etc — Lake George is the largest lake that is directly associated with the great wilderness region of northern New York It is thirty-six miles in length and nearly all lying in Warren county It varies in width from less than a quarter of a mile to about two miles and for a greater part of its entire length is beautified with many lovely islands These are said to number three hundred and sixty-five, and vary in size from a few square feet, to several acres A number of them are inhabited as summer resorts, having elegant residences, some are barren and others are covered with the native forest, embracing a great variety of species both deciduous and coniferous It is flanked on both sides with high, rocky, and precipitous mountains, clothed with dark forests, and picturesque in the highest degree

As seen from the deck of a steamboat in sailing its entire length, it gives the beholder a panorama of continual beauty, exciting always a lively interest, even to those who are familiar with its loveliness Travelers often compare it with the famous lakes of the old world — Scottish, Swiss, Italian, and usually with no disparagement to Lake George Than the beauty of the lake itself, without raising the eyes above their natural plane, there is nothing in the world more lovely In the height of the snow-capped mountains that surround it, Lake Luzerne (Switzerland) may bear off the palm Lakes Constance and Geneva have none of the beauty of its islands, Como and Maggiore in Italy, and Lomond in Scotland have nothing to compare with the variety of its verdure on the mountain sides, while in the purity of its waters all travelers acknowledge that it is no where equaled It is three hundred and forty-three feet above tide, and discharges its water north into Lake Champlain

A well known American writer [1] has thus beautifully pictured this lovely lake in language that has, no doubt, often been felt by other visitors without his poetic power of expression —

> I linger sadly, loth to say adieu
>   To that which of me forms so sweet a part,
> The crystal waters and the mountains blue,
>   Are mirrored deeply in my heart of heart,
> And lake and mountains, rocks and wooded streams,
> Now pass from pleasant seeing to my world of dreams
>
> Upon the lofty wooded mount I stand,
>   Where erst of old the simple huntsman stood,
> I see about me far and wide expand
>   The scene of lake and mountains, isles and wood,
> Like him I linger, loth to break the spell,
> That lives in one sad word, and vainly says, farewell
>
> Now like vast giants in their deep repose
>   These mountains rest beneath the autumn day,
> From early morn until the evening's close
>   The dreamy shadows on their summits play,
> While in the distance dim they catch the hue
> Of heaven, and melt in cloudland's deepest tint of blue

[1] DONN PIATT

I stood by lakes where peaks do pierce the sky,
  Snow-clad, and grand in rocky solitudes,
I saw the homes where round them living lie
  Tradition-haunted tales of love and feud,
Sweet human gossip chased the gloom so drear,
And gave to what was grand, humanity more dear

They had no beauty like to thine, Lake George,
  Where all that's grand, with all that's sweet, entwine,
I see thy fairy isles, while down each gorge
  The birch and maple tint the gloomy pine,
The mountain sides are forests wide and deep,
Where song birds nestle, and the eagles scream and sweep

And all is wild, as in that early day
  The nations found a highway on thy shore,
And meeting, battled for a world's wide sway,
  Thy mountains wakened to the mouthing roar
Of deadly cannon, while from each glen
Came back the doubled thunder to the strife of men

And all is wild, as when the solemn mind
  Of Cooper told its tale of savage war,
One was not startled in the wood to find
  The sage Mohican, or wild Iroquois,
The dusky shadows of those shadowy things
That will survive our life, in men's imaginings

Ah ! lovely lake, how do I long to dwell
  In humble quiet on thy fairy shore,
With rod and books, and those I love so well,
  Forgetting and forgot, live evermore
To float upon thy water's peaceful sheen
Where love is life and life a poet's happy dream

  *   *   *   *   *   *

Now dies apace the golden autumn day
  Now steal the ghostly shadows from the glen,
The stars are gathering in their glad array,
  And stillness falls upon the haunts of men,
Earth parts from me, and closing on my view,
Back to the busy world I go   Fair lake, adieu !

The western part of the county is thickly interspersed with little lakes and ponds that lie in the notches of the hills and mountains, deep, pure, and clear as crystal, usually surrounded with the native forest, these are the natural home of the trout, and consequently the enticing resort of the angler   Some of these are mere specks, as depicted upon the maps of this region, but are really large enough to thrill the visitor with their quiet beauty, to enrapture the poet, and captivate the painter.

Thirteenth Pond, which is more properly a lake, lies in the extreme north-west corner of the county   Loon Lake and Friends' Lake are considerable bodies of water in the north part of the county, and are very picturesque in all their surroundings   Besides these, there are many little ponds, some with

names, but more without, which add to the beauty of the scenery   Eleventh,
Mill Creek, Round, Wolfe, Lizzard, Indian, Puffer, are the principal ones, but
there are others that are equally as handsome, and in a piscatorial sense, quite
as important

In the extreme north part of the county is Schroon Lake, about half of
which lies in this county, it is one of the most attractive in the State   It re-
sembles those in the central counties of the State more than any other in this
region   Cultivated fields reach from the water's edge back to the hills, and the
contour of the shores has just enough of variety to keep the observer continuously on the watch for new beauties   It is eight miles long, and varies considerably in width, but averaging about a mile.   It is about eight hundred and
thirty feet above tide

Brant Lake, which lies between Schroon Lake and Lake George, is five miles
in length, and averages about half a mile in width, lying high up in the second
range of mountains   When first seen by the writer (1858) it was completely
surrounded by an unbroken wilderness   The pale blue of the water, the deep
blue of the sky, and the dark green of the forest between, brought to his mind
the familiar lines—

> " It was down by the dark tarn of Auber,
>   In the ghoul-haunted woodland of Wier "

The drainage of the entire county, with a little exception, is through the
Hudson River and its tributaries   Schroon Lake being considered as eight
hundred and thirty feet above tide, there is a fall of two hundred and ninety-four
feet between it and the mouth of the Sacandaga River   This gives a fall of about
eight and a half feet per mile in the distance of thirty-five miles, which causes
a strong and powerful current   The west or main branch of the Hudson must
have a very much more rapid current, for the fall from Lake Sanford to the
same place cannot be far from one thousand five hundred feet, and the distance about seventy miles   There is nothing that can be called a cascade or a
rapid in this whole distance, and consequently the descent must be very uniform   The tributaries of the Hudson on the west are all small, rapid streams,
rising high among the mountain peaks, and flowing in deep, narrow gorges
The watershed of Lake George is very limited, reaching scarcely more than a
mile from the shore in any place, the brooks are short and small   The immense flow of water from the outlet, that hardly varies an inch in a year, has
been computed as several times greater than is due to the rain-fall, and can
only be accounted for on the theory of great springs   In proof of this theory
the inhabitants say that the lake rarely freezes at the north end, and one of the
inducements offered by the proprietors of the water privileges, at the falls of
Ticonderoga, has ever been that the water is so warm in winter that the water-
wheels are never troubled by the formation of ice

Cascades — A few rods below the junction of the Sacandaga River with the
Hudson, at the village of Luzerne, their united waters plunge down a cascade

of considerable height, in a broken, foamy mass, rolling, boiling and tumbling in a most fantastic manner   This is locally known as Little Jessup's Falls, and were it not for the existence of one much larger in the immediate vicinity, would be considered one of the remarkable sights of this region

Jessup's, or High Falls, on the Hudson, are situated just below the great bend towards the east, at the extreme south point of the town of Luzerne, near the village of Corinth, in Saratoga county   The water flows in a series of rapids for three-fourths of a mile over a declining rocky bottom, and is then compressed into a narrow gorge for eighty rods, at the bottom of which it shoots down a nearly perpendicular descent of sixty feet   The gneiss ledge over which it falls is convex in form, and the water is broken into perfect sheets of snow-white foam   A few rods above the last leap of the water, and where it is rushing with the greatest velocity, the river can be spanned with a single plank thirteen feet in length

At Glens Falls the river flows over a shelving rock with a total descent of fifty feet   The fall is broken into three channels by natural piers of black limestone standing upon the brow of the precipice over which the water flows, forming a cascade of remarkable natural beauty

GEOLOGY

Primary Rock — Of the geology of Warren county, the most that we know is obtained from the reports of Ebenezer Emmons, on the Second District of the State, and made in 1842   From this source we have condensed portions of the following, modified by the discoveries of the past forty years and a few personal observations of the writer —

The principal portion of the county is composed of gneiss, granite, primitive limestone and serpentine appear as intruding rocks associated with the gneiss   The first range of mountains on the east is composed of gneiss; the second range is gneiss, with some granite and hornblende, the third range is gneiss and some decomposing granite near its culminating point in Johnsburgh. The fourth range is gneiss in its southern portion, and if hypersthene exists, as Mr Emmons supposed, it must be limited to the north extremity, on the borders of Essex county

There is no peculiar characteristic in this gneiss, it is all of the ordinary kind, with some intermixture of hornblende, that is common to other portions of the State   The general dip of the strata is westerly, and the strike obliquely across the main axis of the different ranges, in a direction more easterly than the general direction of the main chain.   In regard to imbedded minerals, there is, in fact, a lack of them, especially of the useful kinds   Iron ore of the magnetic kind is not infrequent, but it does not occur in considerable masses.

Granite — This rock, the next of any importance in extent in the county, is nearly all located in the valley between the second and third ranges of mountains   The most important mass is in the vicinity of Crane Mountain, in Johnsburgh   It is white, tolerably coarse and contains small particles of mica The feldspar decomposing rapidly forms the important material called porcelain clay   The precise extent of this material has not been determined, but it is known to extend, with little interruption, for about twenty miles

Primitive Limestone — This rock is of more frequent occurrence than granite; its beds, however, are generally quite limited in extent, but form quite a broad belt entirely across the county in the direction of the mountain ranges   It lies at their bases and forms low, inconspicuous hills, in the main valley   This belt, imperfect as it must be, passes through Stony Creek, Thurman, Johnsburgh, Warrensburgh, Chester and Horicon   It is one of the most important rocks in the county, as from it all the lime is obtained for building and agriculture When the stone is properly selected it makes the strongest lime, a bushel being worth as much as a bushel and a half of lime made from the transition limestone   This rock is not suitable for marble, in consequence of its liability to disintegrate

Serpentine — Associated with primitive limestone are extensive beds of serpentine, intermixed with carbonate of lime   This is usually called *verde antique ,* but this ancient and beautiful rock is composed of materials much harder and more valuable   It occurs in a great variety of colors, from a very dark green to a bright yellowish green   It has been discovered in a great many places, and for indoor work, mantels, table tops, etc , it would be very valuable

Potsdam Sandstone — This rock lies geologically next above the gneiss, or primary rocks, and is the first sedimentary rock in the New York sytem   At the High Falls on the Hudson at Corinth this rock appears about one hundred feet thick, the fall being occasioned by an uplift, and where the gneiss appears on one side of the river, and the sandstone on the other.   Here the strata of sandstone appear very nearly in a horizontal position, and apparently showing that it was deposited in the bottom of the ocean and has not been disturbed by any upheaval since   North of Glens Falls about five miles it appears again, and with a dip to the south and southwest   It forms a good building material in almost all the localities where found   A fact of importance to the geological student is, that at the falls in Corinth, the sandstone can be seen perfectly in place at its juncture with the primitive rock

Calciferous Sand Rock — This rock lies next above the Potsdam sandstone and may be observed in many places in the county   Diamond Island in Lake George is a good example, and is the usual form in which it appears   There are many varieties, but they still possess many characteristics in common About a mile northeasterly from Glens Falls it appears as an outcropping mass , it occurs in many places, at some of which it was quarried for locks on the Champlain Canal, and for other purposes   The beds are thick and blocks

of large size can be obtained, the stone is durable   This rock also appears.
at the falls, beneath the black marble, and is, we believe, the first rock that
shows the remains of any living animal

Black Marble, or Chazy Limestone — The stratum of limestone that is
quarried at Glens Falls, and sawed into marble, lies next above the calciferous
sand rock and corresponds with the marble of the Isle la Motte and the
Chazy limestone   By means of an uplift at the falls and the action of the
water, the three rocks have here been exposed and may be seen lying one
above another, on the Warren county side; on the Saratoga side is an additional stratum of slate above the Trenton limestone   The black marble of Glens
Falls is ten feet thick, and has now been quarried and manufactured for about
half a century.

Trenton Limestone — This rock lies next above the black marble and is
easily recognized by the geological student by its characteristic fossils   It occupies but a very little of the county and can only be examined with any degree of success in the limited chasm of the Hudson River below the falls.   The
gorge between Glens Falls and Baker's Falls gives the student a rare opportunity to study the different strata and obtain an exact knowledge of their situation, their fossils, and their superposition on one another

Utica Slate — The succeeding rock is Utica slate   In pursuing the course
of the river from Glens Falls either east or west for about a mile, this rock is.
seen resting on the Trenton limestone   It is a rock easily disintegrated by
the frost, very fragile, and never firm enough to use as a roofing slate   Its.
disintegration makes a slaty soil that time changes to a clayey one   It is of
no importance in this county except as being the highest rock, geologically.

In speculative geology, the student has an ample field in this county;
almost equal to that of Essex, and in some particulars, more than her equal
Although not so prolific in the mineral department, and not quite so interesting
in her great masses of mountains, there is a greater variety of rocks which show
in more places, with different characteristics and different associations, making
up what is lacking in one direction by going farther in another   Among minor
minerals, those of no particular importance in an economic or a commercial value, except magnetic iron ore, are pyroxene, hornblende, calcareous spar,
zircon, pyritous iron, pyritous copper, crystals of quartz, graphite, labradorite,
red oxide of titanium, tourmaline, sulphuret of iron, colophonite, scapolite and
manganese   The localities of these different minerals are in various parts of
the county, and since the geological survey was made their number has been
greatly increased   While in 1840 when there were not, probably, fifty men in
the State who were deeply interested in the geology of this or any other State,.
there are now probably five thousand who have made investigations in the Great
Wilderness of Northern New York, and could their researches be brought together at this day, and published, so that the knowledge that each has obtained.

would be combined and made useful to each and all, the knowledge of our State would greatly increased, and the science of geology made more popular with the great mass of the people

Soil. — Speaking in very general terms the soil of this county may be said to be composed mostly of thin, sandy loam. The declivities of the mountains particularly have a very thin soil and usually scant vegetation In the valleys clay is mixed with the sand to some extent which, with the disintegrated rock, forms a deep and generally excellent soil The level lands about Glens Falls are very sandy, and have been known as the "pine plains," from the fact of the locality having formerly been covered with a dense growth of heavy pine timber The soil of each town will be further described in the succeeding town histories

Forests — Most of the territory within this county was originally covered with a heavy growth of forest, much of which was valuable pine, such as we have mentioned as having covered the "pine plains " The cutting and marketing of these forests gave employment for many years to the early inhabitants and caused the erection of almost innumerable saw-mills wherever there was available water-power In some portions of the county the common varieties of hard timber were found — beech, maple, birch, oak, etc A large proportion of the mountainous portion of the county, which is not adapted to successful cultivation and which has been cleared of the primitive forest, has become more or less overgrown with a second growth of yellow pine and other varieties of wood, which in later years has furnished a supply of fuel Lumbering is still carried on in the northern and northwestern parts of the county, where there are still considerable areas of forest

---

CHAPTER III

INDIAN OCCUPATION

Original Possessors of the Soil — Relative Positions of the Algonquins and Iroquois — A Great Battle-Field — Evidences of Prolonged and Bloody Conflict — The Eastern Indians — Traditionary Origin of the Iroquois Confederacy — Peculiarities of the League — Personal Characteristics — Jesuit Labors among the Indians — Names of the Missionaries — Their Unselfish but Fruitless Work — The St Francis Indians — Indian Nomenclature

THE territory of which this work treats was probably never permanently occupied to any great extent by nations or tribes of Indians, that it formed a part of their hunting-grounds and was especially used as a highway between hostile northern and western nations is well settled At the time that

Samuel de Champlain made his memorable voyage up Lake Champlain and possibly penetrated to near the waters of Lake George (July, 1609), the territory now embraced in the northern part of the State of New York formed the frontier, the debatable ground, between the Algonquin (or Adirondack) Indians on the north, and the Iroquois on the south   Champlain found a tradition among the Indians along the St Lawrence that many years previously they possessed the territory far to the southward, but were driven out of it by the powerful Iroquois   The waters of Lake George, almost uniting with those of Lake Champlain, and extending almost from the doors of the " Long House " of the Iroquois to the St. Lawrence river, was doubtless the natural war-path between the northern Indians[1] and their powerful southern neighbors

To this latter-named nation (the Iroquois) belonged the territory now embraced in Warren county, at the advent of the whites, more than to any other division of the aborigines, and more particularly to the Mohawk tribe, the easternmost of the five composing the great Iroquois League   This was their hunting-ground, and later their memorable battle-field.   The waters of Lakes George and Champlain formed the natural war-path between the hostile savage elements north and south in their sanguinary incursions   Nature had given to much of the face of the country hereabouts a character so rugged and inaccessible, that it could not in any event have formed a chosen spot for the Indians permanently to occupy, which fact, added to the other still more forcible one, that it was the frontier, the fighting ground, between the hostile nations, sufficiently justify the belief that no permanent Indian settlement was ever made within the present boundaries of the county   Almost the whole of northeastern New York is a labyrinth of mountains, lakes and streams, once covered by an unusually heavy forest growth   It abounded in game and fish of all kinds, and may well have been the resort of the red man in his grand hunts; but as far as can be known, it offered him no permanent abiding-place, and many of the conflicts which have left their impress upon the history of the county since its discovery and occupation by Europeans, found hereabouts

---

[1] These northern Indians are known under the general national title of Algonquins; also as Hurons The name " Montagners " was applied, according to Dr O'Callaghan, to all the St Lawrence Indians, and was derived from a range of mountains extending northwesterly from near Quebec; but this must have been a local title   The name " Adirondack " is defined as meaning "wood, or tree, eaters " Its origin is ascribed to the Iroquois, who, after having conquered the former occupants of their territory and driven them northward, taunted them with no longer being brave and strong enough to kill game in the forests and they would, therefore, be compelled to "eat barks and trees "   Mr Lossing says, "the Algonquins were a large family occupying (at the advent of the Europeans) all Canada, New England, a part of New York and Pennsylvania, all New Jersey, Delaware, Maryland and Virginia, eastern North Carolina above Cape Fear, a large part of Kentucky and Tennesee and all north and west of those States and East of the Mississippi   They were the most powerful of the eight distinct Indian nations in possession of the country when discovered by the whites   Within the folds of this nation were the Huron-Iroquois, occupying a greater portion of Canada south of the Ottawa river and the region between Lake Ontario, Lakes Erie and Huron, nearly all of the State of New York and a part of Pennsylvania and Ohio, along the southern shore of Lake Erie."

their bloody theatre, and opened the way to the eventual triumph of the present occupants of the soil

"The evidences of these conflicts are found imbedded along the banks of every stream, and beneath the soil of every carrying-place from Albany to Montreal Arrow and spear-heads, knives, hatchets, gouges, chisels, amulets, and calumets, are, even to this late day, often found in the furrow of the plowman or the excavation of the laborer Few localities have furnished a more abundant yield of these relics than the soil of Queensbury. While gun-flints and bullets, spear-heads and arrow-points are found broadcast and at large through the town, there are places abounding with them Among the most noteworthy of these may be enumerated 'the Old Bill Harris's camp ground,' in Harrisena, the headlands around Van Wormer's, Harris's, and Dunham's Bays on Lake George, the Round Pond near the Oneida, the Ridge, the vicinity of the Long Pond, the banks of the Meadow Run and Carman's Neck at the opening of the Big Bend. This last was long noted as a runway for deer and traditions are handed down of grand hunting frolics at this point, where large quantities of game were hunted and driven within the bend, and while a small detachment of hunters served to prevent their retreat, the imprisoned game, reluctant to take the water down the precipitous bluffs, was captured or killed at their leisure At this point, and also in the neighborhood of Long Pond, fragments of Indian pottery, and culinary utensils of stone, have been found in such profusion, as to give coloring to the conjecture that large numbers of the natives may have resorted to these attractive spots, for a summer residence and camping-ground The old wilderness trails, and military thoroughfares, the neighborhood of block-houses, picket posts, garrison grounds, and battle-fields, in addition to their Indian antiquities have yielded many evidences of civilized warfare, in their harvests of bullets and bomb shells, buttons, buckles, bayonets, battered muskets and broken swords, axes and tomahawks of steel, chain and grape shot, coins, cob-money and broken crockery Such relics are often valuable as the silent witnesses to the truth of tradition, and the verification of history

"The eastern part of New York, at a period long anterior to the Iroquois ascendency, was occupied by a tribe variously known as the Ma-hick-an-ders, Muh-hea-kan-news, Mo-hea-cans, and Wa-ra-na-wan-kongs The territory subject to their domination and occupancy, extended from the Connecticut to the Hudson as far north as the southern extremity of Lake George. According to Schoolcraft, these Indians were among the tribes of the Algonquin stock At the period of their greatest power, their national council fire was held on the ground now covered by the city of Albany, which was then known to them by the name of Pem-pot-a-wut-hut, signifying the fireplace of the nation The word Muh-ha-a-kun-nuck, from which the word Mohican is derived, means a great water or sea that is constantly in motion, either flowing or ebb-

ing   Their traditions state that they originally came from a country very far to
the west, where they lived in towns by the side of a great sea   In consequence
of a famine they were forced to leave their homes, and seek a new dwelling
place far away to the east   They, with the cognate tribes of Manhattans,
Pequots, Narragansetts and Nipmucks, occupied the whole peninsula of New
England from the Penobscot to Long Island Sound   The Brotherton community, and the Stockbridge tribe, now constitute the sole remnant of this once
numerous people.   Previous to the establishment of the Dutch colonies in this
State the Mohicans had been driven eastwardly by the Iroquois, and, at the
time of their first intercourse with the whites, were found in a state of tributary
alliance with that fierce people.   The early attachment which was formed with
the first English colonists of Connecticut by the politic Mohicans, no doubt
contributed in a great measure to their preservation during the harassing wars
which prevailed through the colonial peninsula for the first fifty years of its
settlement

" The Schaghticoke Indians received their name from the locality where they
dwelt, derived, according to Spafford, from the Indian term Scaugh-wank, signifying a sand slide   To this, the Dutch added the terminal, cook   The evidences of the early Dutch occupancy exist to-day in the current names of the
tributaries of the Hudson as far up as Fort Edward Creek   The settlement of
this tribe was seated on the Hoosick River not far from the town bearing the
same name   The hunting grounds of this vicinity, as far north as Lake George,
for many years after the first white man had erected his rude habitation within
this disputed border, were occupied by the Schaghticokes, under permission
of the Mohawks, who owned the lands, and with whom they were upon friendly
terms " [1]

As we have intimated, at the time of the French discovery and occupation
of Canada, the Mohawks were in the ascendency in this region, and had, it is
believed, extended their dominion to the St Lawrence   They were the most
powerful and warlike of the Five Nations (Mohawks, Oneidas, Onondagas, Ca-
yuga and Senecas) composing the Iroquois Confederacy, which was located
across the State from east to west in the order here named.   The tradition of
the origin of this remarkable confederation ascribes it to Hiawatha, who was
the incarnation of wisdom, about the beginning of the fifteenth century   He
came from his celestial home to dwell with the Onondagas, where he taught
the related tribes all that was desirable to promote their welfare   Under his
immediate tutelage the Onondagas became the wisest counselors, the bravest
warriors and the most successful hunters   While Hiawatha was thus quietly
living, the tribes were attacked by a powerful enemy from the north, who laid
waste their villages and slaughtered men, women and children indiscriminately ;
utter destruction seemed inevitable   In this extremity they turned to Hiawa-

[1] HOLDEN's *History of Queensbury*

tha who, after thoughtful contemplation, advised a grand council of all that could be gathered of the tribes, saying, "our safety is not alone in the club and dart, but in wise counsels "[1] The counsel was held on Onondaga Lake and the fires burned for three days awaiting the presence of Hiawatha He was troubled with forebodings of ill-fortune and had resolved not to attend the council, but in response to the importunities of messengers, he set out with his beautiful daughter Approaching the council he was welcomed by all, who then turned their eyes upward to behold a volume of cloudy darkness descending among them All fled except Hiawatha and his daughter, who calmly awaited the impending calamity Suddenly and with a mighty swoop a huge bird, with long and distended wings, descended upon the beautiful maiden and crushed her to death, itself perishing with the collision For three days and nights Hiawatha gave himself up to exhibitions of the most poignant grief At the end of that period he regained his wonted demeanor and took his seat in the council, which, after some deliberation, adjourned for one day On the following day Hiawatha addressed the council, giving to each of the Five Nations its location and degree of importance, as we have already noted The advice of the venerable sage was deliberated upon until the next day, when the celebrated league of the Iroquois was formed and its details perfected

Whether or not there is any foundation in fact for this traditionary source of the confederacy, it grew into one of the most remarkable and powerful combinations known to history, a marvel to civilized nations and stamping the genius that gave it birth as of the highest order

The tradition further relates that Hiawatha now considered his mission on earth as ended and delivered to his brothers a farewell address, which concluded as follows "Lastly, I have now assisted you to form an everlasting league and covenant of strength and friendship for your future safety and protection If you preserve it, without the admission of other people, you will always be free, numerous and mighty If other nations are admitted to your councils they will sow jealousies among you and you will become enslaved, few and feeble Remember these words, they are the last you will hear from the lips of Hiawatha Listen, my friends, the Great Master of Breath calls me to go I have patiently awaited his summons I am ready, farewell " As his voice ceased the air was musical with sweet sounds, and while they listened to the melody, Hiawatha was seen seated in his white canoe, rising in mid air till the clouds shut out the sight, and the melody, gradually becoming fainter, finally ceased.[2]

---

[1] RUTTENBER

[2] Both reason and tradition point to the conclusion that the Iroquois originally formed one undivided people Sundered, like countless other tribes, by dissension, caprice, or the necessities of a hunter's life, they separated into five distinct nations —PARKMAN'S *Jesuits*

By the early French writers, the Mohawks and the Oneidas were styled the lower or inferior Iro-

Previous to the formation of the Iroquois confederacy each of the five nations composing it was divided into five tribes When the union was established, each tribe transferred one-fifth of its numbers to every other nation than its own The several tribes thus formed were named as follows: Tortoise, Wolf, Bear, Beaver, Deer, Potato, Snipe, Heron The Snipe and Heron correspond with the great and little Plover, and the Hawk with the Eagle of the early French writers Some authors of repute omit the name of the Potato tribe altogether These tribes were formed into two divisions, the second subordinate the first, which was composed of the four first named Each tribe constituted what may be called a family and its members who were all considered brothers and sisters, were also brothers and sisters of the members of all the other tribes having the same device It will be seen that an indissoluble bond was thus formed by the ties of consanguinity, which was still further strengthened by the marriage relation It was held to be an abomination for two persons of the same tribe to intermarry, every individual family must therefore contain members from at least two tribes The child belonged to the tribe, or clan, of the mother, not to the father, and all rank, titles and possessions passed through the female line The chief was almost invariably succeeded by a near relative, and always on the female side, but if these were unfit, then a council of the tribe chose a successor from among remoter kindred, in which case he was nominated by the matron of the late chief's household The choice was never made adverse to popular will Chiefs and sachems held their offices only through courteous, winning behavior and their general good qualities and conduct There was another council of a popular character, in which any one took part whose age and experience qualified him to do so, it was merely the gathered wisdom of the nation The young warriors also had their councils, so, too, did the women All the government of this "remarkable example of an almost pure democracy in government"[1] was exercised through councils, which were represented by deputies in the councils of the sachems In this peculiar blending of individual, tribal, national and federal interests, lay the secret of that immense power which for more than a century resisted the hostile efforts of the French, which caused them for nearly a century to be alike courted and feared by the contending French and English colonies, and enabled them to exterminate or subdue their neighboring Indian nations, until they were substantially dictators of the continent,[2] gaining them the title of "The Romans of the New World"

quois, while the Onondagas, Cayugas and Senecas were denominated the upper or superior Iroquois, because they were located near the sources of the St Lawrence.   *   *   *   To the Mohawks was always accorded the high consideration of furnishing the war captain, or "Tekarahogea," of the confederacy, which distinguished title was retained with them until the year 1814 —CLARK'S *Onondaga*

[1] LOSSING.

[2] The Iroquois league or confederacy was given an Indian name signifying, "They form a cabin," which was fancifully changed to "The Long House," the eastern door of which was kept by the Mohawks, and the western by the Senecas, with the great council fire in the center, with the Onondagas.

The military dominated the civil power in the league, and the army, which was supplied by volunteers, was always full Every able bodied man was subject to military duty, to shirk which was an everlasting cause of disgrace The warriors called councils when they saw fit and approved or disapproved of public measures But their knowledge of what is now considered military science, while vastly better than that of many of their neighbors, was insignificant, when viewed from a modern civilized standpoint They seldom took advantage of their great numbers and acted in concert as a great confederacy, but usually carried on their warfare in detached tribes or parties Their bravery, however, and their strategy in their peculiar methods of fighting, are unquestioned In the forest they were a terrible foe, while in an open country they could not successfully contend with European disciplined soldiery, but they made up for this to a large extent, by their self-confidence, vindictiveness and overwhelming desire for ascendency and triumph There is considerable difference in the writings of authors as to the true military status of the Iroquois [1]

The Iroquois lacked the great welding and cohesive power of a common language, all of the tribes having a distinct dialect, bearing a striking resemblance to each other, and evidently derived from a common root Of these the Mohawk was the most harsh and guttural, and the language of the Senecas the most euphonious In their ordinary conversation there was a great range of modulation in the inflections of the voice, while expressive pantomime and vehement gestures helped to eke out the meagerness of their vernacular on the commonest occasions Their proper names were invariably the embodiments of ideas, and their literature, as contained in their oft repeated legends, and the well remembered eloquence of their gifted orators, abounded with the most sublime imagery, and striking antitheses, which were drawn at will by these apt observers of nature, from the wild scenes, and picturesque solitudes with which they were most familiar

While the Iroquois Indians were superior in mental capacity and less improvident than the Algonquins and other nations, there is little indication that they were ever inclined to improve the conditions in which they were found by the Europeans They were closely attached to their warrior and hunter life, hospitable to friends, but ferocious and cruel to their enemies; of no mean mental capacity, but devoting their energies to the lower, if not the lowest, forms of enjoyment and animal gratification; they had little regard for the marriage tie and lasciviousness and unchastity were the rule, their dwellings, even among the more stationary tribes, were rude, their food gross and poor

[1] They reduced war to a science and all their movements were directed by system and policy They never attacked a hostile country till they had sent out spies to explore and designate its vulnerable points, and when they encamped they observed the greatest circumspection to guard against surprise. Whatever superiority of force they might have, they never neglected the use of stratagem, employing all the crafty wiles of the Carthaginians —DE WITT CLINTON

and their domestic habits and surroundings unclean and barbaric, their dress was ordinarily of skins of animals, until the advent of the whites, and was primitive in character, woman was degraded into a mere beast of burden, while they believed in a supreme being, they were powerfully swayed by superstition, incantations by "medicine men," dreams and the like, their feasts were exhibitions of debauchery and gluttony.

Such are some of the more prominent characteristics of the race encountered by Samuel Champlain when he floated up the beautiful lake that bears his name two hundred and seventy-five years ago and welcomed them with the first volley of bullets from deadly weapons—a policy that has been followed with faithful pertinacity by his civilized successors. These Indians possessed redeeming features of character and practice, but these were so strongly dominated by the barbaric way of living and their savage traits, that years of faithful missionary labor among them by the Jesuits and others, was productive of little good [1]

The Society of Jesus, or Jesuits, was founded in 1539 and planted the cross amid the most discouraging circumstances, overcoming almost insurmountable obstacles, in Europe, Asia, Africa and America. When Champlain opened the way for French dominion in the latter country, the task of bearing the Christian religion to the natives was assigned to this noble and unselfish body of devotees While their primary object was to spread the gospel, their secondary and scarcely less influential purpose, was to extend the dominion of France Within three years after the restoration of Canada to France in 1736, there were fifteen Jesuit priests in the province, and they rapidly increased and extended their labors to most of the Indian nations on the continent, including the powerful Iroquois

In 1654, when peace was temporarily established between the French and the Five Nations, Father Dablon was permitted to found a mission and build a chapel in the Mohawk Valley The chapel was built in a day "For marbles and precious metals," he wrote, "we employed only bark, but the path to Heaven is open through a roof of bark as through arched ceilings of silver and gold" War was again enkindled and the Jesuits were forced to flee from the Iroquois, but their labors never ceased while opportunity was afforded

There were twenty-four missionaries who labored among the Iroquois between the years 1657 and 1769 We are directly interested only in those who sought converts among the Mohawks. These were Isaac Jogues, the recital of whose career in the Indian country forms one of the most thrilling chapters of history He was with the Mohawks as a prisoner from August, 1642, to

---

[1] In 1712 Rev Wm Andrews was sent among the Mohawks by the society for propagating the gospel, to succeed Rev Thoroughgood Moor, but he abandoned the work in 1719, failing in it as his predecessor had Says Hammond's *History of Madison County*, "He became discouraged and asked to be recalled, saying, 'there is no hope of making them better—heathen they are and heathen they still must be'" This is but one example of most of the missionary efforts among the Indians

the same month of the next year, and as a missionary with the same nation in in 1646, in October of which year he was killed Simon Le Moyne was with the Mohawks about two months in 1655; again in 1656 and the third time from August, 1657 to May, 1658 He died in Canada in 1665 Francis Joseph Bressani was imprisoned by the Mohawks about six months in 1644 Julien Garnier was sent to the Mohawks in May, 1668 and passed on to the Onondagas and Senecas Jacques Bruyas came from the Onondagas to the Mohawks in July, 1667, left for the Oneidas in September and returned in 1672, remaining several years Jacques Frémin came in July, 1667, and remained about a year Jean Pierron was sent in the same year and also remained about one year Francis Boniface labored here from 1668 to 1673, when he was succeeded by Francis Vaillant de Gueslis

These faithful missionaries were followed in later years by such noble workers as Rev Henry Barclay, John Ogilvie, Revs Messrs Spencer, Timothy Woodbridge and Gideon Hawley, Rev Dr Eleazer Wheelock, Rev Samuel Kirkland, Bishop Hobart, Rev Eleazer Williams, Rev Dan Barnes (Methodist) and others of lesser note, all of whom labored faithfully and with varying degrees of perseverance, for the redemption of the Iroquois But all were forced to admit that their efforts as a whole were unsatisfactory and discouraging [1]

Later religious and educational work among the Indians, even down to the present time, while yielding, perhaps, sufficient results to justify its prosecution, has constantly met with most discouraging obstacles among the tribes themselves

The advent of European nations to the American continent was the forerunner of the downfall of the Iroquois Confederacy and doubtless the ultimate extinction of the Indian race The French invasion of 1693 and that of three years later, cost the confederacy half of its warriors , their allegiance to the British crown (with the exception of the Oneidas) in the Revolutionary War, proving to be an allegiance with a failing power, — these causes, operating with the dread of vengeance from the American colonists who had so frequently suffered at the hands of the savages, broke up the once powerful league and scattered its

---

[1] The Rev Mr Kirkland, who acts as missionary among the Oneidas, has taken all the pains that man can take, but his whole flock are Indians still, and like the bear which you can muffle and lead out to dance to the sound of music, becomes again a bear when his muffler is removed and the music ceases The Indians will attend public worship and sing extremely well, following Mr Kirkland's notes , but whenever the service is over, they wrap themselves in their blankets, and either stand like cattle on the sunny side of a house, or lie before a fire.— *Doc. History*

Mr Kirkland was one of the very ablest and most self-sacrificing of the missionaries, and what he could not accomplish in his work, it may safely be concluded others could not In reference to his labors, an anonymous writer in the *Massachusetts Historical Collection* (1792) says "I cannot help being of the opinion that Indians .   never were intended to live in a state of civilized society There never was, I believe, an instance of an Indian forsaking his habits and savage manners, any more than a bear his ferocity "

members to a large extent, upon the friendly soil of Canada, or left them at the mercy of the State and general government, which consigned them to reservations.

The St Francis Indians are, according to Dr Holden's work before quoted, descended from the once powerful Androscoggins, a branch of the great Abenakies, or Tarrateens, which at one time held sway over the entire territory embraced in the peninsula of Nova Scotia, Maine and Eastern Canada

Through the indefatigable efforts of Father Rasles, who dwelt among these tribes for more than twenty years, a flourishing mission was established in the early part of the eighteenth century, at Nar-rant-souk on the river Kennebeck This settlement speedily became the rallying point for the French and Indians in their descents upon the frontier settlements of New Hampshire and Massachusetts   The danger from this quarter at length became so imminent and pressing, that an expedition was finally planned for its destruction   A force of two hundred men, with a detachment of Indian allies, was fitted out in the summer of 1724, under the leadership of Captains Moulton and Harman of York   The village was invested   The attack was a surprise   Father Rasles and about thirty of the Abenaki warriors were killed, and the remainder dispersed. The survivers of this relentless massacre, with the remainder of the tribe, fled to the mission village of St Francis, situated upon the lake of that name at the head of the St Francis River   The frequent accessions of fugitives to their ranks, due to the active, aggressive policy of the English, so increased their numbers, that they soon became known as the St Francis tribe Under the training of their priests they speedily became a powerful ally of the French, co-operating with the predaceous bands of half savage habitants, kept the English border settlements in terror and trepidation for a space of twenty-five years   In the notable campaign of 1757 a large party of them accompanied Montcalm in his expedition against Fort William Henry, at the southern extremity of Lake George, and were participants in the fearful and fiendish massacre which followed the surrender of that fort   They were doomed, however, to a reprisal and vengeance, swift, thorough and effective   Immediately subsequent to the successes of General Amherst in 1759, the distinguished partisan, Major Robert Rogers, was dispatched with a force of two hundred picked men from his corps of rangers, to demolish the settlement, and chastise the tribe for its complicity in the frightful massacres of the three preceding campaigns   Proceeding with caution and celerity, the village was surrounded before an alarm was given, and after a brief, sharp contest, the place was reduced and the inhabitants, without respect to age or sex, were ruthlessly put to the sword   The dwellings and fortifications, together with a valuable church, fitted up with costly decorations and embellishments, were committed to the flames, and destroyed

In this connection may profitably be inserted the following Indian names and their meaning, that come within the range of this work, as obtained in the records of various authors —

Adirondack. — According to Schoolcraft this name signifies " Bark-eaters " It was a party from this tribe that accompanied Champlain upon his journey into the country of the Iroquois The name may be said to apply to the Indians who dwelt along the Canada shore of the St Lawrence River

Aganuschion — Black mountain range, as the Indians called this Adirondack group — LOSSING

Andiatorocte — The place where the lake contracts A name applied to Lake George — DR O'CALLAGHAN

Aquanuschioni — The united people A name by which the Iroquois designated themselves — Drake's *Book of the Indians*

Atalapose — A sliding place Roger's Rock on Lake George The Indians entertained a belief that witches or evil spirits haunt this place, and seizing upon the spirits of bad Indians, on their way to the happy hunting grounds, slide down the precipitous cliff with them into the lake where they are drowned — Sabattis in Holden's *History of Queensbury*

Ausable Forks — " Tei-o-ho-ho-gen," the forks of the river

Bald Peak — (North Hudson) " O-no-ro-no-rum," bald head

Cahohatatea — Iroquois for North or Hudson River — Dr Mitchell, *Annals of Albany.*

Canada — From Kanata, a village — DR HOUGH Drake gives one Josselyn, an early writer, as authority for its derivation as *Can*, mouth, and *Ada*, country Other derivations are also given

Caniaderi Guarante — A name given to Lake Champlain, meaning " The gate of the country."

Caniaderi-Oit — " The tail of the lake," *i e*, Lake Champlain This name has been applied to Lake George, and also to that portion of Champlain below Ticonderoga

Cancuskee — Northwest Bay, Lake George. So called on a map of the Middle British Provinces, 1776 — Holden's *Queensbury*

Cataraqui — Ancient name of Kingston — HOUGH The St Lawrence River, signifying a fort in the water — HOLDEN.

Champlain — " Ro-tsi-ich-ni," the coward spirit The Iroquois are said to have originally possessed an obscure mythological notion of three supreme beings, or spirits, the good spirit, the bad spirit, the coward spirit The latter inhabited an island in Lake Champlain, where it died, and from this it derived the name above given. — HOUGH

Chateaugay — This is by some supposed to be an Indian name, but it is French, meaning gay castle The St Regis Indians call it "O-sar-he-hon," a place so close or difficult that the more one tries to extricate himself the worse he is off This probably relates to the narrow gorge near Chateugay village

Cheonderoga — One of the several names applied to Ticonderoga   Signifies, three rivers

Chepontuc — A difficult place to climb or get around   An Indian name of Glens Falls — Sabattis, in Holden's *History of Queensbury*

Chicopee — A large spring   Indian name of Saratoga Springs. — *Ibid*

Conchsachraga — The great wilderness   An Indian term applied to the wild track north of the Mohawk and west of Lakes George and Champlain — Pownal's *Topographical Description*

Flume of the Opalescent River. — "Gwi-en-dau-qua," a hanging spear

Ganaouske — Northwest Bay, on Lake George — *Col Hist*   Judging from analogy, this should mean the battle place by the water side — Holden's *Queensbury*

Glens Falls — Mentioned on a French map published at Quebec, 1748, by the name of "Chute de Quatrevingt Pds" — *Doc Hist*

Hochelaga — This name was applied by the Algonquins to the site now occupied by Montreal, and also to the St Lawrence River   Hough suggests its derivation from Oserake, a beaver dam — *Hist St Lawrence and Franklin Counties*, p 181

Houtkill — Dutch name of Wood Creek — *Doc Hist of N Y*, vol II, p 300

Huncksoock — The place where everybody fights   A name given by the nomadic Indians of the north to the upper falls on the outlet of Lake George — SABATTIS

Kaniadarosseras — Hence Kayaderosseras, the lake country — *Colonial Hist. N Y*, vol. VII, p 436

Kaskongshadi — Broken water, a swift rapid on the Opalescent river — Lossing's *Hudson*, p 33

Kayaderoga — A name of Saratoga lake — Butler's *Lake George, etc*

Kayaderosseras — A name applied to a large patent or land grant, stream and a range of mountains in Saratoga county, N. Y   In the *Calendar of N Y Land Papers*, it is variously written Caniaderosseros, Caneaderosseras, Kanyaderossaros, Cayaderosseras, said to mean "The crooked stream"   Other authorities give its meaning as "The lake country"

Kingiaquahtonec — A portage of a stone's throw or two in length between Wood Creek and Fort Edward Creek, near Moss street in Kingsbury — Evans's *Analysis*, p. 19

Miconacook — A name of the Hudson river — SABELE

Mohawk, from Mauqua or Mukwa, a bear — Schoolcraft's *Notes on the Iroquois*, p 73

Mount Marcy — Tahawus, "He splits the sky"

Mount McIntyre — He-no-ga, "Home of the thunder"

Mount Colden — "On-no-war-lah," scalp mountain, from the baring of the rocky peak by slides

Mount Pharaoh —" On-de-wa," black mountain

Oiogue —The Indian (Mohawk) name of the Hudson north of Albany — *Hist of New Netherland*, II, 300

Oneadalote Tecarneodi —The name of Lake Champlain on Morgan's map

Onderiguegon —The Indian name for the drowned lands 'on Wood Creek near Fort Anne, Washington county, N Y It signifies conflux of waters — *From a Map of the Middle British Colonies* by T Pownal, M P , 1776

Ongwehonwe —A people surpassing all others The name by which the Iroquois designated themselves

Ossaragas —Wood Creek, emptying into the head of Lake Champlain — *Top Descrip of the Middle British Colonies, Map*, T Pownal, 1776

Oswegatchie, or Oghswagatchie with a dozen other different spellings — " An Indian name," the historian James Macauley, informed the author,"which signifies *going or coming round a hill* The great bend in the Oswegatchie river (or the necessity of it), on the borders of Lewis county, originated its significant name An Indian tribe bearing the name of the river, once lived upon its banks , but its fate, like that of many sister tribes, has been to melt away before the progression of the Anglo-Saxon "—*Simms's Trappers of N Y*, p 249, *note* According to a writer in the *Troy Times* of July 7th, 1866, it is a Huron word signifying black water Sabattis defined it as meaning slow and long

Oukorlah —Indian name of Mount Seward, signifying the big-eye —C F HOFFMAN

Ounowarlah —Scalp Mountain Supposed to refer to that peak of the Adirondacks known as Whiteface Mountain —C F Hoffman in *The Vigil of Faith*

Petaonbough —" A double pond or lake branching out into two " An Indian name of Lake Champlain, which refers probably to its connection with Lake George —R W Livingston, quoted in *Watson's Hist Essex Co , N Y*

Petowahco —Lake Champlain —SABELE

Raquette —" The chief source of the Raquette is in the Raquette Lake, towards the western part of Hamilton county Around it, the Indians in the ancient days gathered on snow-shoes in the winter, to hunt the moose then found there in large droves, and from that circumstance they named it Raquet, the equivalent in French, for snow-shoes in English This is the account of the origin of its name given by the French Jesuits who first explored that re- gion Others say that its Indian name Ni-ha-na-wa-le, means a racket or noise, noisy river, and spell it *Racket* But it is no more noisy than its near neighbor the Grass River which flows into the St Lawrence from the bosom of the same wilderness "—Lossing's *Hudson*, p 11

Rotsichini —An Indian name of Lake Champlain signifying the coward spirit An evil spirit, according to the legend, whose existence terminated on an island in Lake Champlain The name was thence derived to the lake

Santanoni —"Si-non-bo-wanne," the great mountain This name is also said to be a corruption or condensation of St. Anthony

Schroon —"Sea-ni-a-dar-oon," a large lake Abreviated first to Scaroon and then to Schroon This is a Mohawk word which appears in the old land papers, applied to Schroon Lake In addition, Ska-ne-ta-no-wa-na, the largest lake Also, Scarona, the name of an Indian girl who leaped over a precipice from her French lover and was drowned It has been alleged, on what seems a very slender foundation, that the name was conferred in the latter part of the 17th century by a wandering party of Frenchmen in honor of Madame de Maintenon the wife of the poet Scarron —HOLDEN

Schroon River —" Gain-bou-a-gwe," crooked river

Saratoga —*Vide* General Index to documents relating to the history of the State of New York for seventeen different spellings of this word See *Calendar of N Y Land Papers*, where it is found spelled Saragtoga, Saraghtoga, Saraghtogue, etc Morgan renders it on his map in *the League of the Iroquois* Sharlatoga Hough, in the *Hist of St Lawrence and Franklin Counties*, has it Saratake, while Ruttenber, in his *Indian Tribes of the Hudson*, on what authority is not stated, derives it from Saragh, salt, and Oga a place, though he adds that " the name was originally applied to the site of Schuylerville, and meant swift water " an assertion which greatly impairs the value of the preceding statement Gordon in his *Gazetteer of New York*, p. 671, derives the word from Sah-ra-kah, meaning the great hill side, and states that it was applied to the country between the lake and the Hudson river An anonymous writer in the *Troy Times* of July 7, 1866, defines it as a place where the track of the heel may be seen

Senongewok —A hill like an inverted kettle, familiarly known as " the Potash," on the east side of the Hudson river about four miles north of Luzerne village, Warren county, N Y —*Vigil of Faith* by C F Hoffman

Split Rock —" Re-gioch-ne," or Regio rock, or Regeo From name of Mohawk Indian drowned near the rock It denoted the boundary between the Iroquois and the northern Indians

Skanehtade —The west branch of the Hudson and the river generally — Morgan's Map in *The League of the Iroquois*

Takundewide —Indian name of Harris's Bay on Lake George So called on a map of the middle British provinces by T Pownal, M P , London, 1776

Tenonanatchie —A river flowing through a mountain A name applied to the Mohawk river by the western tribes —H R SCHOOLCRAFT

Teohoken —The pass where the Schroon finds its confluence with the Hudson river —*The Vigil of Faith* by C F Hoffman See also *Col. Hist N Y,* vol VII, p 10, where it is defined as the forks of a river

Ticonderoga —There are about twenty renderings of the orthography of this word, and wide differences of meaning assigned to it Those most worthy of acceptance are given herewith Tienderoga "The proper name of the fort between Lake George and Lake Champlain signifies the place where two rivers meet "—*Colden's Account of N Y, Col Hist N Y*, VII, 795 "Tiaontoroken, a fork or point between two lakes "—*Hough's Hist St Lawrence and Franklin Counties*, p 181 Morgan, on his map, frequently referred to herein, spells it "Je hone ta lo ga" Teahtontaloga and Teondeloga are both defined as "two streams coming together" The sound and structure of the three words are similar The definition given by Colden is doubtless correct

Tiasaronda —The meeting of the waters The confluence of the Sacandaga with the Hudson —*The Vigil of Faith* by C F Hoffman

Wawkwaonk —The head of Lake George, Caldwell —SABELE

Whiteface Mountain —" Thei-a-no-gu-en," white head, from the naked rocky peak

---

CHAPTER IV

EUROPEAN DISCOVERY AND OCCUPATION

First European Colonists — Discoveries by Columbus and His Successors— Competitors for the New World— Colonization of New France — Difficulties of the Scheme — Final Success — Champlain's Advent — His Enterprising Explorations — His Colony of 1608 — Expedition against the Iroquois — The First Battle — Henry Hudson and Dutch Colonization — English Colonies at Plymouth Rock and Jamestown — Claims of Three European Powers — Subsequent Career of Champlain

BEFORE entering upon the work of detailing the events more directly connected with the early settlement of the valley of Lakes Champlain and George, it may not be out of place to glance hastily over some of the more notable acts and movements of governments and men that had much to do in opening the way and leading up to the final occupation and settlement of the territory under consideration

It is not yet four hundred years since the day on which occurred the event that proved to be the first ray of light from the rising sun of civilization, whose beams were destined to penetrate and dissipate the clouds of barbarism that hovered over the untamed wilderness of the American continent, and during the ages that preceded that event, no grander country in all respects ever awaited the advance of civilization and enlightenment With climate and soil diversified between almost the widest extremes, with thousands of miles of ocean shores indented by magnificent harbors to welcome the world's commerce, with many of the largest rivers of the globe intersecting and draining its territory and forming natural commercial highways, with a system of lakes so grand in proportions as to entitle them to the name of inland seas; with mountains, hills and valleys laden with the richest minerals and almost exhaustless fuel, and with scenery unsurpassed for grandeur, it needed only the coming of the Caucasian to transform a continent of wilderness, inhabited by savages, into the free, enlightened republic which is to-day the wonder and the admiration of the civilized world

The first Europeans to visit America were Scandinavians, who colonized Iceland in 875, Greenland in 983, and about the year 1000 had pushed their discoveries as far southward as the State of Massachusetts. But it was towards the close of the fifteenth century before the country became known to Southern Europe, a discovery accidentally made in a quest of a westerly route to India and China. In 1492 the Genoese, Christopher Columbus, set out on a voyage of discovery under the patronage of the Spanish power, and in that and the two succeeding years made his tropical discoveries. The Venetian sailor, John Cabot, was commissioned by Henry VII, of England, in 1497, to voyage to the new territory and take possession of it in the name of England. He discovered New Foundland and portions adjacent. In 1500 the coast of Labrador and the entrance to the Gulf of St. Lawrence were explored by two brothers from Portugal, named Cortereal. In 1508 Aubert discovered the St. Lawrence, and four years later, in 1512, Ponce de Leon discovered Florida. Magellan, the Portuguese navigator, passed through the straits which now bear his name in 1519, and was the first to circumnavigate the globe. In 1534. Jacques Cartier explored the St. Lawrence as far as Montreal, and five years later Fernando de Soto explored Florida. In 1578 an English navigator named Drake discovered Upper California. These brief data indicate that not a century had passed after the discovery of Columbus, before the different maritime powers of Europe were in active competition for the rich prizes supposed to exist in the New World

While the Spaniards were pushing their acquisitions in the South, the French had gained a foothold in the northern part of the continent. Here the cod fisheries of New Foundland and the prospects of a more valuable trade in furs, opened as early as the beginning of the sixteenth century by Frenchmen, Basques, Bretons and Normans, held out the most glowing inducements. In 1518 Baron Livy settled there (New Foundland) and in 1524 Francis I, of France, sent thither Jean Verrazzani, a noted Florentine mariner, on a voyage of exploration. He sailed along the coast 2,100 miles in the frail vessels of the period and returned safely to his country. On his coast voyage he entered a large harbor which is supposed to have been that of New York, where he remained fifteen days; it is believed that his crew were the first Europeans to land on the soil of the State of New York. He proceeded north as far as Labrador and gave to the whole region the name of New France, thus opening the way for the future contest between France and England

In 1534 a French navigator named Jacques Cartier, born in St Malo in 1494, was commissioned by the same French king, Francis I, and put in command of an expedition to explore the New World   After celebrating impressive religious ceremonies, as was the custom at that period before beginning any important undertaking, on the 20th of April, 1534, Cartier sailed from St Malo with two vessels and with upwards of two hundred men   He touched first the coast of New Foundland, and then, sailing northward, passed through the Strait of Belle Isle, landing on the coast of Labrador, where he took formal possession of the country in the name of his sovereign   Continuing his voyage, he followed the coast of New Foundland, making landings at various points and holding friendly intercourse with the natives, at Gaspé Bay he persuaded a chief to permit his two sons to accompany him on his return to France, here also he planted a cross with the French arms upon it, and thence sailed northeast through the Gulf of St Lawrence and entered the river of that name north of what is now called Anticosti Island   As he sailed up the broad stream on St Lawrence day (August 10th), he applied to the river the name of the illustrious saint whose memory is perpetuated by that day   Here, unaware that he had discovered the mouth of a noble river, and anxious to avoid the autumnal storms, he turned his prow towards France, and on September 5th, 1534, entered the harbor of St Malo

The succeeding year, 1535, having under the command of the king, fitted up a fleet of three vessels and organized a colony, to a large extent composed of the younger members of the French nobility, Cartier again sailed from France, empowered by the authority of the king to occupy and colonize the country he had discovered, and to which he gave the name of New France

Arriving at the mouth of the St Lawrence in July, he sailed up its majestic course to where the St Charles (to which he gave the name of St Croix) enters it, near the present site of Quebec, and cast anchor on the 14th of September

Here he was entertained by Donnaconna, a prominent chieftain, with the utmost hospitality, and through the aid of the two young Indians who had returned with Cartier, was enabled to indulge in considerable conversation with the royal savage   From this point he made several expeditions, the most important one being up the river to a large Huron Indian town bearing the name of Hochelaga, on the site of the present city of Montreal   To a prominent eminence back of the town Cartier gave the name Mount Real (Royal Mountain), hence the name of the modern city.   This was the most important town of a large Indian population, they possessed the country for a long distance up and down the river from that point, and appeared to be a thrifty, industrious people, living at peace among themselves and with adjoining tribes   Cartier found them kindly disposed towards him, and received numerous substantial evidences of their hospitality and confidence, to the extent of being permitted to take away with him a little Huron girl, a daughter of one of the chiefs, who " lent her to him to take to France " [1]

Though their town was palisaded plainly for the purpose of protection against enemies, he saw before him the open fields covered with ripening corn, attesting alike the industry of the people and the fertility of the soil   His imagination reveled in dreams of conquest and power, as, standing on the lofty hill at the rear of the town, his gaze wandered along the majestic river, embosoming fruitful islands, and beyond over miles of forests, streams, and lakes to where the dim outlines of mountain tops were shadowed upon the southern horizon   This was during the delightful Indian summer time , the coming winter, with its storms and snows, was an unknown experience to the adventurers

Returning in October to the point where his vessels were moored, called by the natives Stadacona (now the site of Quebec), Cartier made preparations to spend the winter   The result of this decision brought with it extreme suffering from the rigors of a climate to which the new-comers were wholly unaccustomed, augmented by the affliction of the scurvy, from which disease twenty-five of his men died.   The bitter experiences of this winter of 1535–36 on the Isle of Orleans (where they had constructed rude barracks) dimmed the bright hopes of the colonists, and in the spring Cartier, finding one of his vessels unfit for sea, placed his men upon the other two, and prepared to return to France   Taking possession of the country with all the formal " pomp and circumstance " of the age, he and his discouraged companions abandoned the idea of colonization and on the 9th of May, 1536, sailed for France

The day before his departure Cartier invited Donnaconna and eight of his chiefs to partake of a feast on board his ship   The invitation was accepted, and Cartier, imitating the infamy of the Spanish conquerors of the southern part of the continent, treacherously sailed away with them to France as captives, where they all soon died with grief

No further efforts at colonization were undertaken until about 1540, when Francis de la Roque, Lord of Roberval, was commissioned by the king of France with vice-royal powers to establish a colony in New France   The king's authorization of power conferred upon De la Roque the governorship of an immense extent of teritory, shadowy if not illimitable in boundary, but extending in all directions from the St Lawrence and including in its compass all of what is now New England and much of New York   In 1541 he caused to be fitted out a fleet of vessels, which sailed from St Malo, with Cartier as captain-general and pilot   When, late in August, they arrived at Stadacona the Indians were overjoyed at their arrival, and poured on board the ships to welcome their chief whose return they expected, relying upon Cartier's promise to bring him back.   They

[1] LOSSING

put no faith in the tale told them that he and his companions were dead, and even when shown the Huron maiden, who was to be returned to her friends, they incredulously shook their heads, and their peaceful attitude and hospitality hour by hour changed to moroseness and gradually to hostility The first breach of faith had occurred, never to be entirely healed

Cartier made a visit to Hochelaga, and returned thence to Stadacona On the Isle of Orleans he erected a fort for protection during the approaching winter Patiently waiting and watching for De la Roque, who had promised to follow him early in the season, they saw the arrival of winter and the closing of the river by ice without the vision of the hoped-for vessels

In the spring following (1542) Cartier departed for France He ran into the harbor of St Johns, and there met De la Roque, who was on his way to the St Lawrence From Cartier the viceroy heard the most discouraging accounts of the country, with details of the suffering he and his men had endured during the preceding winter, both from the climate and from the hostility of the Indians, followed by the navigator's advice that the whole expedition return to France, or sail to some other portion of the continent This De la Roque declined to do, and ordered Cartier to return to the St Lawrence Cartier disobeyed this order, and sailed for France This was his last voyage, he died in 1555

De la Roque, after his separation from Cartier, pushed on and ascended the river to above the site of Quebec, where he constructed a fort in which he spent the succeeding winter, undergoing extreme suffering from the climate In the autumn of 1543 De la Roque returned to France, having accomplished nothing towards colonization, and learning but little of the country not already known

This was the final breaking up of French attempts at colonization at that time, and nothing more was done by that nation towards settling in the new country for nearly fifty years De la Roque, however, in 1549, with his brothers and a number of adventurers, again sailed for the St Lawrence, but as they were never heard of afterwards it was supposed they were lost at sea

History has demonstrated that the most successful attempts at colonization and settlement in new sections have been achieved by private enterprise, in many cases started and fostered by commercial undertakings The interest and spirit of individual energy has more often than otherwise accomplished greater results in subduing the wilds of nature and in planting and extending the benefits of civilization, than the most powerful and thoroughly organized expeditions sent out under governmental authority Too often in the latter case the personal aggrandizement of the leaders has overthrown the better motives and works of the masses composing the organizations

The efforts of the royal government of France in endeavoring to establish a foothold in the New World were no exception to this view, and it was not till the enterprise was undertaken by private individuals that anything like success followed 4

From 1600, and on for a few years, one M Chauvin, having obtained a broad patent which formed the basis of a trade monopoly, carried on an extensive fur trade with the natives, resulting in establishing numerous small but thrifty settlements, but the death of the organizer caused their abandonment.

The year 1603 was signalized by the initiatory steps that resulted in the final settlement of the French in the region of the St Lawrence. M Aylmer de Chastes, governor of Dieppe, stimulated by the commercial success that had followed the efforts of Chauvin and others, obtained a charter to establish settlements in New France and organized a company of Rouen merchants, the existence of which becomes of paramount historic importance as having introduced to the field of his later great work, Samuel de Champlain, discoverer of the lakes and the territory of which this history treats, and the real founder of New France, as well as the most illustrious of those who guided its destinies

" Champlain was born at Brouage, in 1567, a seaport situated on the Bay of Biscay   Addicted to an intercourse with the sea by the associations of his boyhood, near the most tempestuous waters of Western Europe, he gratified his instincts by a connection at an early age with the royal marine of his native country.   Although a Catholic by birth and sentiment, he followed in the civil wars of France the 'Banner of Navarre'   When that cause had triumphed he received a pension from the gratitude of his liberal but impoverished leader. Too active and ardent to indulge in the relaxations of peace, he conceived the design of a personal exploration of the colonial possessions of Spain, and to thus obtain a knowledge of their condition and resources, which was studiously vailed from the world by the jealous policy of that government   His scheme was sanctioned by the wise and sagacious head of the French administration. Through the influence of a relative in that service Champlain secured the command of a ship in the Spanish West India fleet   This singular position, not, perhaps, in perfect accordance with modern conceptions of professional honor, was occupied two years, and when he returned to France his mind was stored with the most valuable information and his journal, laded with the results of keen observation of the regions he had visited, was quaintly illustrated by his uncultivated pencil "[1]

Champlain must have been born with the uncontrollable instinct of investigation and desire for knowledge of the material world that has always strongly marked the great explorers   He made a voyage (1599), landed at Vera Cruz, penetrated to the city of Mexico and visited Panama   More, his journal shows that he conceived the idea of a ship canal across the isthmus by which " the voyage to the South Sea might be shortened by more than fifteen hundred leagues "

At the request of De Chastes, Champlain was commissioned by the king lieutenant-general of Canada (a name derived, it is supposed, " from the Huron

---

[1] WATSON'S *Essex County*

word Kan-na-ta, signifying a collection of cabins, such as Hochelaga " [1]) He sailed from the fort of Honfleur in March, 1603, in a single vessel, commanded by a skilled navigator named Pont-Grevé

They arrived at the mouth of the St Lawrence some time in May, and ascended the river as far as Stadacona, where they anchored From this point Champlain sent Pont-Greve upon an expedition up the river to above the La Chine Rapids At Hochelaga he found, instead of the palisaded city described by Cartier, nothing indicating that the locality had ever been thickly populated A few scattered bodies of Indians, of a different nation from those met by Cartier, who evinced the greatest wonder and interest in the new-comers, were all that he saw These natives gave Pont-Grevé much information relative to the regions on the south and west, and other intelligence of a nature to fill the mind of the explorer with the wildest dreams of conquest and empire

Without enacting more extended measures towards colonization and settlement than making a few brief expeditions of exploration, Champlain, in the autumn, returned to France, he found that in his absence his patron, De Chastes, had died, and that the concessions and privileges of the latter had been transferred to M Pierre de Gast, the Sieur de Monts Though a Protestant, the latter had secured additional favors from the royal hand, covering broad commercial rights, with vice-regal authority over a section of the new country extending from Philadelphia, or its site, on the south, to the forty-sixth parallel on the north, and from the sea-shore on the east to an indefinite limit on the west

Again, in the spring of 1604, Champlain sailed with De Monts with four vessels, bringing with them a number of people intended to colonize the grants They landed first at Nova Scotia, and remained there long enough to establish the beginning of a settlement, and, towards autumn, De Monts returned to France and left Champlain to explore the coast to the south as far his grant extended Champlain remained for some time at this point, pushing forward his settlement, and exploring the surrounding country, carrying out his employer's instructions to the extent of sailing along the coast as far south as Cape Cod In 1607 he returned to France

Expressing to De Monts his belief that the better site for establishing the seat of the proposed new empire would be a point on the St Lawrence River, some distance from the sea coast, he was sent with Pont-Grevé and a number of colonists, in 1608, to Stadacona, and there founded Quebec (a name of Indian derivation) There houses were built, and agricultural operations begun

In 1609 Champlain, who had secured the friendship of the Montagnais Indians, or Montagners, engaged to assist them in an expedition against their enemies, the Iroquois [2] It is probable that he was partly incited to his action

---

[1] LOSSING   [2] See note page 17

by desire to extend his knowledge of the country and to widen his sphere of influence   They were joined by a number of Hurons and Algonquins, and in May proceeded in canoes up the Sorel to the Chambly Rapids

The Indians had told Champlain that the country they wished to conquer was thickly settled; that to reach it they must pass by a waterfall, thence into another lake, from the head of which there was a carrying-place to a river, which flowed towards the sea coast   This course of their intended march is clearly understood to-day as leading up Lake Champlain to Ticonderoga, thence up the outlet of Lake George past the falls, thence through Lake George to the Hudson River

Pursuing their course up the Sorel, Champlain says in his journal, they reached "a great lake and gave it his own name"   Passing along the west side of the lake, he says of the country   "These parts, though agreeable, are not inhabited by the Indians, in consequence of their wars "

In proceeding up the lake it was the practice of the Indians to send three of their canoes in advance, as night approached, and if no enemy was discovered, to retire in peace   Against "this bad habit of theirs " Champlain expostulated, but to little purpose   In this manner "they proceed until they approach an enemy's country," when they advance "stealthily by night, all in a body except the scouts, and retire by day into picket forts where they repose " Thus the party proceeded up the lake to their landing-place, a full and graphic account of which journey is contained in Champlain's journal   Following is his vivid description of his meeting and battle with the Iroquois —

"Now on coming within about two or three days' journey of the enemy's quarters, we traveled only by night and rested by day   Nevertheless, they never omitted their usual superstition to ascertain whether their enterprise would be successful, and often asked me whether I had dreamed and seen their enemies.

" At nightfall we embarked in our canoes to continue our journey, and as we advanced very softly and noiselessly, we encountered a party of Iroquois, on the 29th day of the month, about 10 o'clock at night, at a point of a cape which juts into the lake on the west side.   They and we began to shout, each seizing his arms   We withdrew toward the water and the Iroquois repaired on shore, and arranged all their canoes, the one beside the other, and began to hew down trees with villainous axes, which they sometimes get in war, and others of stone, and fortified themselves very securely   Our party, likewise, kept their canoes arranged the one along side of the other, tied to poles so as not to run adrift, in order to fight all together should need be   We were on the water about an arrow shot from their barricade

" When they were armed and in order, they sent two canoes from the fleet to know if their enemies wished to fight, who answered they desired nothing else, but that just then there was not much light, and that we must wait

for day to distinguish each other, and that they would give us battle at sunrise
This was agreed to by our party   Meanwhile the whole night was spent in
dancing and singing, as well on one side as on the other, mingled with an infin-
itude of insults and other taunts, such as the little courage they had , how powerless their resistance against their arms, and that when day would break they
should experience this to their ruin   Ours likewise did not fail in repartee ,
telling them they should witness the effects of arms they had never seen
before , and a multitude of other speeches such as is usual at the siege of a
town

" After the one and the other had sung, danced and parliamented enough,
day broke   My companions and I were always concealed, for fear the enemy
should see us in preparing our arms the best we could, being, however, separated, each in one of the canoes of the savage Montaquars   After being
equipped with light armor we took each an arquebus and went ashore   I saw
the enemy leave their barricade , they were about 200 men, of strong and ro-
bust appearance, who were coming slowly towards us, with a gravity and assurance which greatly pleased me, led on by their chiefs   Ours were marching
in similar order, and told me that those who bore three lofty plumes were the
chiefs, and that there were but these three and they were to be recognized by
those plumes which were considerably larger than those of their companions,
and that I must do all I could to kill them   I promised to do what I
could, and I told them that I was very sorry that they could not clearly
understand me, so as to give them the order and plan of attacking their enemies, as we should undoubtedly defeat them all, but there was no help for that ,
that I was very glad to encourage them and to manifest to them my good
will when we should be engaged

" The moment we landed they began to run about two hundred paces toward their enemy, who stood firm, and had not perceived my companions, who
went into the bush with some savages   Ours commenced calling me in a loud
voice, and making way for me opened in two, and placed me at their head,
marching about twenty paces in advance until I was within thirty paces of the
enemy   The moment they saw me they halted, gazing at me and I at them
When I saw them preparing to shoot at us, I raised my arquebus, and aiming
directly at one of the three chiefs, two of them fell by this shot , one of their
companions received a wound of which he died afterwards   I had put four balls
in my arquebus   Ours on witnessing a shot so favorable for them, set up such
tremendous shouts that thunder could not have been heard , and yet there was
no lack of arrows on the one side and the other   The Iroquois were greatly
astonished seeing two men killed so instantaneously, notwithstanding they
were provided with arrow proof-armor,[1] woven of cotton thread and wood ,

---

[1] The allusion to this armor presents an interesting and suggestive inquiry   We know of the
product of no indigenous plant, which Champlain might have mistaken for cotton   He must have
been familiar with that plant   The fact he mentions implies either the existence of a commercial inter-

this frightened them very much   Whilst I was reloading one of my companions in the bush fired a shot, which so astonished them anew, seeing their chief slain, that they lost courage, took to flight and abandoned their fort, hiding themselves in the depths of the forest, whither pursuing them I killed some others   Our savages also killed several of them and took ten or twelve prisoners   The rest carried off the wounded   Fifteen or sixteen were wounded by arrows , they were promptly cured

" After having gained the victory they amused themselves by plundering Indian corn and meal from the enemy , also their arms which they had thrown away to run the better   And having feasted, danced and sung, we returned three hours afterward with the prisoners

" The place where the battle was fought is in forty-three degrees some minutes latitude, and I named it Lake Champlain "

This battle, the first of a long series that were to consecrate the locality with the blood of three contending powers, was doubtless fought near, if not directly upon the promontory afterwards occupied by Fort Ticonderoga This opinion is advanced by the best authorities   The plan of the campaign and the route to be traveled, as described to Champlain by his savage companions, led beyond question up the outlet from Lake Champlain to Lake George   Hence there is no reason for assuming that they followed further up the coast than Ticonderoga, and ample reason for believing that here would be their landing place.   The Indians had told Champlain that after traversing the lake they "must pass by a water-fall and thence into another lake three or four leagues long "   No clearer description of the route from one lake to the other can be written at this day

The Algonquin Indians, who had passed through a generation or more of warfare with the Iroquois and were generally getting the worst of the contest, now found themselves armed with a weapon with which they could, for a time, win victory on any field

Thus signalized the first hostile meeting between the civilized white man and the untutored Indian   Low as the latter was found in the scale of intelligence and terrible as were many of the subsequent bloody deeds of the Iroquois, it cannot be denied that their early treatment by the Europeans was scarcely calculated to foster in the savage breast any other feeling than bitterest hostility   It is like a pathetic page from a romance to read that " the Iroquois are greatly astonished, seeing two men killed so instantaneously," one of whom was their noble chief, while the ingenuous acknowledgment of Champlain, " I had put four balls in my arquebus," is a vivid testimony of how little mercy the Iroquois nations were to expect thenceforth from their northern

course between the natives of the North and South , or perhaps the Mohawks may have secured the cotton as a trophy in some of their southern incursions — WATSON'S *Essex County*

Without desiring to argue the question, it is still pertinent to state that is doubtful if the Indians could at that early date, have obtained cotton upon any southern incursion

enemies and the pale-faced race who were eventually to drive them from their domain

But it was an age in which might was appealed to as right oftener than in late years, and the planting of the lowly banner of the Cross was often preceded by bloody conquest   In the light of the prevailing customs in the Old World at that time, we must view the ready hostility of Champlain towards his helpless enemies

While the events above recorded were occurring under the leadership of Champlain, who was thus pushing southward from his embryo settlement on the St Lawrence, other explorations were being made from the sea coast northward, the actors in which were undoubtedly impelled by the same spirit of enterprise, but exemplified in a less belligerent manner   Prominent among these, and particularly noteworthy as opening the pathway of civilization leading to the same territory towards which Champlain's expedition tended, was the exploration of the noble river that now bears the name of its discoverer, Henry Hudson

Hudson was an Englishman, an expert navigator, and had made, in the interest of a body of English merchants, several voyages in search of a northeastern passage to India   Finally he, as well as his employers, became disheartened in attempting to force a way through the ice packs and floes between Spitzbergen and Nova Zembla, and Hudson went to Holland and offered his services to the Dutch East India Company, which were gladly accepted   He was put in command of the *Half-Moon*, a stoutly built vessel of ninety tons, and again, casting aside his previous disappointments, sailed for Nova Zembla But, as before, the fields of ice were a barrier too strong for even the staunch vessel commanded by Hudson, and he was forced to turn back   Determined not to return to Amsterdam without accomplishing something towards rendering his voyage fruitful, he directed his course towards Greenland, and sailed around the southern point thereof, taking the route that had already been pursued by others in search of a northwest passage   Baffled again by ice packs, he sailed southward, and discovered the American continent somewhere on the coast of Maine   Running into a harbor, he made necessary repairs to his battered vessel, and then followed down the coast as far as Virginia   Returning, he entered Delaware bay and made a partial examination of its shores, and in September, 1609, entered the present harbor of New York   He met and entertained the natives, and was hospitably received by them, but before his departure he conferred upon them experimental knowledge of the effects of intoxicating liquor — an experience perhaps more baneful in its results than that conferred by Champlain a hundred and fifty miles northward, with his new and murderous weapon   Hudson ascended the river to a point within less than a hundred miles of that reached by Champlain, and r turned to Europe, after having again sailed as far south as Chesapeake bay   " The unworthy monarch on

England's throne, jealous of the advantage which the Dutch might derive from Hudson's discoveries, detained him in England as an English subject; but the navigator outwitted his sovereign, for he had sent an account of his voyage to his Amsterdam employers by a trusty hand "[1] Through the information thus furnished was established a Dutch colony on the island of Manhattan, for which a charter was granted by the States-General of Holland, bearing date October 11th, 1614, in which the country was named New Netherland

It may not be out of place at this point to make brief mention of Hudson's subsequent career and sad ending In 1610 he made another and final voyage from England, sailing in April, and during the months of June and July discovered and navigated the great bay that bears his name It was his intention to winter there, but owing to scant provisions, a portion of his crew mutinied and compelled him to return On the way Hudson, his son, and seven of his crew who had remained faithful to him, were placed in an open boat, which was towed through the ice floes to the open sea, where it was cut adrift, and the unfortunate occupants were left to the mercy of the winds and waves His fate was afterwards revealed by one of the mutineers England sent an expedition in search of him, but not the slightest trace was found of him and his companions

Meanwhile, in 1607, the English had made their first permanent settlement at Jamestown, Virginia, and in 1620 planted a second colony at Plymouth Rock These two colonies became the successful rivals of all others of whatever nationality, in the strife that finally left them (the English) masters of the country

On the discoveries and the colonization efforts we have briefly noted, three European powers based claims to a part of the territory embraced in the State of New York England, by reason of the discovery of Cabot, who sailed under letters patent from Henry VII, and on the 24th of June, 1497, struck the sterile coast of Labrador, and that made in the following year by his son Sebastian, who explored the coast from New Foundland to Florida, claiming a territory eleven degrees in width and extending westward indefinitely France, by reason of the discoveries of Verrazzani, claimed a portion of the Atlantic coast, and Holland, by reason of the discovery of Hudson, claimed the country from Cape Cod to the southern shore of Delaware Bay As we have stated, the Dutch became, for the time being, the possessors of the region under consideration.

In concluding this chapter it will not be out of place to make a brief reference to the later career of Champlain, intimately associated as he was with the civilized knowledge of the beautiful waters of the lake that perpetuates his name, although the events noted are not directly connected with this history The year following his discovery of the lake, Champlain passed in France, but

[1] LOSSING

the opening season of 1610 found him again ascending the St Lawrence, and the same year he was wounded by an arrow in a fight with the Iroquois Again returning to France, at the age of forty-four years, he married a girl of twelve; and, in 1612 returned to Quebec, clothed with the power of sovereignty granted him by Prince de Conde, who had succeeded Count de Soissons, the successor of De Monts In the following year he ascended the Ottawa River in quest of a fabulous sea, of which he had heard tales, made successful arrangements for carrying on the fur trade with the Indians, fought a battle with the Onondagas, and, returning to France, organized a fur company in 1616 On his return to Canada he took with him several Recollet priests In 1620, the colony beginning to languish, a new viceroy was appointed, who made Champlain governor, with full powers, of the whole territory In 1628 and 1629 the English laid siege to Quebec, which Champlain was finally forced to surrender, and he was taken to England By treaty, in 1632, Canada was restored to France, and Champlain was reinstated governor, he returned the last time in 1633 to the state his wisdom and zeal had created, invested by Richelieu with all his former prerogatives Having suppressed the Indian excitement which had agitated his province, conciliated the jarring jealousies and angry feuds of mercenary traders and arbitrary officials, and amply asserted and perfected the dominion of his sovereign over a vast region, Champlain died in 1635, and is commemorated in the annals of the country he served so ably and with such fidelity as " the father of New France "

<hr />

CHAPTER V

FRENCH AND INDIAN WAR

Antagonism between the Northern Indians and the Iroquois — Lakes George and Champlain the Highways of Hostile Flements — End of the Dutch Régime — Expedition against the Mohawks under De Courcelles — The Peace of Breda — Continued Hostilities of the French and Iroquois — Invasion of the Country of the Senecas — Revenge of the Indians — Montreal Sacked — Return of Frontenac — Three English Expeditions — Schuyler's Expedition against La Prairie — Extracts from His Journal — Deplorable Condition of the French — Frontenac Marches against the Mohawks — Peace Treaty of Ryswick — Neutrality between the French and Iroquois — The English at last Rendered Desperate — Failure of their Plans — Treaty of Utrecht — Its Provisions Broken by the French — Fort St Frederic Built

FROM the date of the death of Champlain until the end of French domination in New France, the friendship established by that great explorer between the Northern Indians and the French was unbroken, while at the same time it led to the unyielding hostility of the Iroquois, and especially of the

Mohawks   If truces and informal peace treaties were formed between these antagonistic elements, they were both brief in tenure and of little general effect As a consequence of this and the fact that Lakes Champlain and George were the natural highway between the hostile nations, they became the scene of prolonged conflict and deeds of savage atrocity which retarded settlement and devastated their borders   The feuds of the peoples of Europe and the malignant passions of European sovereigns, armed the colonies of England and the provinces of France in conflicts where the ordinary ferocity of border warfare was aggravated by the relentless atrocities of savage barbarism   Each power emulated the other in the consummation of its schemes of blood and rapine. Hostile Indian tribes, panting for slaughter, were let loose along the whole frontier, upon feeble settlements, struggling amid the dense forest with a rigorous climate and reluctant soil for a precarious existence   Unprotected mothers, helpless infancy and decrepit age, were equally the victims of the torch, the tomahawk and scalping-knife   The two lakes formed portions of the great pathway (equally accessible and useful to both parties) of these bloody and devastating forays   In the season of navigation they glided over the placid waters of the lake, with ease and celerity, in the bark canoes of the Indians.   The ice of winter afforded them a broad, crystal highway, with no obstruction of forest or mountain, of ravine or river   If deep and impassable snows rested upon its bosom, snow-shoes were readily constructed, and secured and facilitated their march

The settlement made on Manhattan Island, the occupation of which followed Hudson's discovery and the granting of the charter of 1614 to the Dutch East India Company, progressed rapidly   A fort was built on the island, and also one on the site of Albany   In 1621 the Dutch West India Company was formed and, under their charter, took possession of New Amsterdam, as the fort with its surroundings was called   For fifteen years the most amicable relations existed between the Dutch and the Indians, but the harsh and unwise administration of William Kieft, who was appointed director-general in September, 1637, provoked the beginning of hostilities with the natives, which were kept up with more or less vindictiveness during the period of his administration   In May, 1647, Peter Stuyvesant succeeded Kieft as director-general or governor   He was the last of the Dutch officials in that capacity, and the firm and just course followed by him harmonized the difficulties with the Indians and also with the Swedes who had colonized in the region of the Delaware

On the 12th of March, 1664, Charles II, of England, conveyed by royal patent to his brother James, Duke of York, all the country from the river St Croix to the Kennebec, in Maine, also Nantucket, Martha's Vineyard and Long Island, together with all the land from the west side of the Connecticut River to the east side of Delaware Bay   The duke sent an English squadron, under Admiral Richard Nicolls, to secure the gift, and on the 8th of September following Governor Stuyvesant capitulated, being constrained to that course by the Dutch colonists, who preferred peace with the same privileges and liberties accorded to the English colonists, to a prolonged and perhaps fruitless contest Thus ended the Dutch régime The English changed the name of New Amsterdam to New York

The Dutch had, during their period of peace with the Iroquois, become thrifty and well-to-do through the energetic prosecution of their missionary work of trading guns and rum to the Indians, thus supplying them with a two-edged sword The peaceful relations existing between the Dutch and the Indians at the time of the English accession were maintained by the latter, but strife and jealousy continued between the English and French, the former steadily gaining ground, both through their success in forming and maintaining an alliance with the Iroquois and the more permanent character of their settlements

"The right of France to the country of the Iroquois, which embraced in part the valleys of Lakes Champlain and St Sacrament [George], was based on an established maxim existing among European nations, that the first discoverers who planted the arms of their government upon aboriginal soil acquired thereby the property of that country for their respective nations "[1]

About this time the French became possessed of the desire to control the Hudson River and the port of New York To carry out this purpose meetings of the cabinet council discussed plans, and measures were inaugurated Also, in the hope of avenging past injuries and to put an end to future incursions, the government of New France resolved, in 1665, to send against the Mohawks a force that would not return until their enemies were wiped from the face of the earth. On the 23d of March of that year Daniel De Runy, knight, Lord de Courcelles, was appointed governor of Canada, and in September of that year arrived with a regiment, several families and necessaries[2] for the establishment of a colony In June of the same year M de Tracy was appointed viceroy of the French Possessions in America, and brought with him to Quebec four regiments of infantry On the 9th of January, 1666, De Courcelles started with less than six hundred men on a long and perilous march of nearly three hundred miles in mid-winter when the snow was four feet deep "The governor caused slight sledges to be made in good numbers, laying provisions upon them, drew them over the snow with mastiff dogs "[3] The men traveled on snow-shoes, each carrying twenty-five to thirty pounds of biscuits "On the third day out many had their noses, ears, fingers or knees frozen, and some, wholly overcome by the cold, were carried to the place where they were

---

[1] BUTLER's *Lake George and Lake Champlain*
[2] It is recorded that the first horses were brought to Canada on this occasion
[3] Relations of the march, *Doc History*

to pass the night Still they pushed on, until, on the 9th of February, they arrived within two miles of Schenectady "[1] Here they learned that the greater part of the Mohawks and Oneidas had gone to a distance to make war upon the "wampum-makers" Watson says they "were only preserved from destruction by the active, though ill-requited beneficence of a small Dutch settlement, standing on the outer verge of civilization The potent influence and urgent intercessions of a prominent, although private citizen of Schenectady averted from the suffering and defenseless Frenchmen, the vengeance of the exasperated Mohawks" — (referring to Arent Van Corlear). His unselfish act was gratefully acknowledged by the colonial government, and De Tracy urged him to visit Quebec Corlear accepted this courtesy in the year 1667, and while making the passage of Lake Champlain was drowned "by a sudden squall of wind, in crossing a great bay " Deeming it "useless to push further forward an expedition which had all the effect intended by the terror it spread among all the tribes,"[2] Courcelles retraced his march

The magnitude of this expedition, although it resulted in no immediate disaster to the Iroquois, prompted them to sue for peace, and a treaty was concluded in May, June and July, 1666, by the Senecas, Oneidas and Mohawks, respectively Pending the negotiations, the Mohawks committed an outrage on the Fort St Anne garrison, and M de Tracy was convinced that the treaty would be rendered more stable if the Mohawks were further chastised Accordingly in September, at the head of six hundred troops and seven hundred Indians, he made an incursion into the Mohawk country only to find it deserted by the wily savages, after destroying their villages and crops, he returned

In the following year (July, 1667) was concluded the peace of Breda, between Holland, England and France This gave the New Netherlands to the English, and Acadia (Nova Scotia), with fixed boundaries, to the French But the period of quiet was of short duration, for in 1669 we find the French again at war with their old antagonists, the Iroquois Owing to the increasing hostilities the inhabitants found it difficult to harvest their crops in safety, suffering and consternation prevailed and many prepared to return to France But in April, 1672, Count de Frontenac was appointed governor and lieutenant-general of Canada, and under his efficient administration, confidence was restored and a treaty of peace again established in 1673 [3]

In 1684 another rupture occurred between the French and Iroquois M. de la Barre was then governor of New France, and Colonel Dongan governor of New York The Frenchman led an expedition against the Senecas, but

---

[1] BUTLER

[2] *Doc History*

[3] Count De Frontenac writes September 14th, 1674 "In spite of the efforts of the Dutch to get the Iroquois to make war on the French, the Iroquois came last year on solemn embassy to Montreal, brought eight children belonging to the principal families of their villages, and ratified the treaty made with them in 1673 " — *Colonial History of New York*

hearing that the latter would be reinforced by Dongan with "four hundred horse and four hundred foot," he gave up his purpose This pretentious expedition, which ended so ignominiously, subjected De la Barre to severe censure and in the following year he was superseded by the Marquis Denonville, who came over instructed to preserve a strict neutrality This he found to be impossible and so informed his sovereign Reinforcements were sent him for a determined attack upon the Senecas, and in the summer of 1687 an expedition of two thousand French and Indians was organized and marched against the enemy This large force impelled the Indians to adopt their customary tactics for self-preservation, and their villages were deserted, or nearly so After destroying everything of value, the expedition returned This bold incursion into the country of their strongest nation, alarmed the Iroquois and they applied to Governor Dongan for protection It was promised them, of course, with the accompanying advice that they should not make peace with the French , but Denonville called a meeting of chiefs of the Five Nations at Montreal to arrange a treaty, and they decided to send representatives Before this was consummated and on account of alleged treachery on the part of Denonville, the Iroquois became deeply angered against the French and burned for revenge In July, 1689, twelve hundred Iroquois warriors landed on the upper end of the Island of Montreal, burned houses, sacked plantations, massacred men, women and children and retired with twenty-six prisoners, most of whom were burned alive In October following they made a similar incursion at the lower end of the island, which was likewise devastated These successful invasions were of incalculable injury to the French interests, and becoming known to their Indian allies, already disgusted with De la Barre's failure, caused many of them to seek an alliance with the English and open trade with them "They would have murdered the whole French colony to placate the Iroquois, and would certainly have done it," says Colden, "had not the Sieur Perot, with wonderful sagacity and eminent hazard to his own person, diverted them "

The French colony was now in a pitiable condition, but an unexpected and welcome change was at hand The divided counsels of the English colonies, growing out of the revolution in the mother country resulting in the accession of the Prince of Orange to the throne, gave a new aspect to affairs The Count de Frontenac, whose previous administration had been wise and efficient, was again appointed governor May 21st, 1689, and arrived in October He had learned the futility of prosecuting a war against the Iroquois and made earnest efforts to negotiate a peace with them Failing, he determined to terrify them into neutrality For this purpose he fitted out three expeditions, one against New York, one against Connecticut and the third against New England. The first was directed against Schenectady, which was sacked and burned on the night of February 9th, 1690 A band of the French and Huron Indians, after a march of twenty-two days "along the course of West Canada creek" — a route the course of which is to-day shrouded in doubt, but probably west of the lake, through certain narrow valleys, where evidences of ancient pathways were visible but a few years since — fell upon the defenseless hamlet But two houses were spared, with fifty or sixty old men, women and children and about twenty Mohawks, "in order to show them that it was the English and not they against whom the grudge was entertained " The French made a rapid but disastrous retreat, suffering from the severe weather and the harassing pursuit of their enemies This and other assaults at other points so disheartened the people at Albany that they resolved to retire to New York; their course was altered only after a delegation of the brave Mohawks had visited them and reproached them for their supineness, urging them to a courageous defense of their homes This heroic conduct of the Iroquois challenges our admiration, notwithstanding French intrigues and Jesuitical influence, combined with exasperating English apathy which appeared willing to sacrifice these savage yet noble allies, they adhered to their early allegiance

Repeated incursions by the French and Indians at last awakened the English colonists to the conviction that they must harmoniously unite in their efforts against their enemies if they would succeed   A convention was accordingly held in New York in May, 1690, constituted of delegates from Massachusetts, Connecticut and New York, at which it was resolved to combine their strength for the subjugation of Canada Massachusetts engaged to equip a fleet and attack the French possessions by sea, while the other two States should assault Montreal and the forts upon the Sorel The land forces mustered at Lake George in formidable numbers, embarked in canoes and sailed to Ticonderoga Embarking again on Lake Champlain, but little progress was made when the expedition was abandoned through failure in supplies and dissensions in the force The failure of these efforts and the heavy expenses incurred, left the colonies in a more defenseless situation than before

In the same year, John Schuyler (grandfather of Philip Schuyler, of Revolutionary fame) organized a band of about one hundred and twenty "Christians and Indians" for an incursion into the French possessions He cautiously passed down Lake Champlain and landed in the vicinity of Chambly. Leaving his canoes in safety, he penetrated to La Prairie, far within the line of the French fortresses The unexampled bravery of the little force contributed largely to its remarkable success They fell upon the French colonists who were unsuspectingly engaged in their harvest, and in the savage spirit that then controlled such movements, committed young and old alike to slaughter. The " scalps of four women folks " were among the trophies

In the summer following (1691) Major Peter Schuyler collected a body of about two hundred and fifty whites and Indians, and taking the route followed by John Schuyler, made an attack upon the doomed settlement of La Prairie.

He states in his journal that he left Albany June 21st, and marched twenty-four miles to Stillwater   Halting till the 24th, on that day he proceeded to Saraghtoga, a distance of sixteen miles, on the 26th he marched to the first carrying-place (Fort Miller), and thence to the second carrying-place (Fort Edward)   On the 28th the march was continued to the last carrying-place, and there they began building canoes   July 1st they built eight canoes, capable of carrying from seven to twelve men   July 9th (quoting Schuyler's journal), "came Gerrard Luykosse and Herman Vedder, from a party of eighty Mohawks, at a lake right over Saraghtoga [Saratoga Lake], who went by the way of Lake St Sacrament,[1] and promised to meet us in six days at 'Chinandroga'" (Ticonderoga)   On the 14th "we removed to the Falls [Whitehall], distant sixteen miles, and then encamped"   On the 16th "moved from the Falls, and pitched our tents in the narrows of the drowned lands, twelve miles distant" Proceeding on the 17th they "advanced to Chianderoga, and two hours after met the Mohauques, eighty in number, after which we fell to making canoes, the Christians having broken two of theirs coming over the falls"

This is the first record known of a military expedition passing through Lake George

The party reached the objective point of their march, La Prairie, at dawn on the 1st of August   After "saying their prayers," they moved cautiously towards the fort   But, in passing a wind-mill, the miller fired a shot (killing an Indian), which was returned by one of Schuyler's white men, killing the miller in his own door   Before reaching the fort they were met by a party of militia, whom they repulsed, they next encountered a body of regulars, with whom they had a short but sharp engagement   Falling back a short distance, Schuyler drew up his men in a ditch or disused canal, forming an ambuscade into which the pursuing Frenchmen rushed, meeting with considerable loss, but escaping capture   While these movements were enacting, an officer with a force one-half as large as Schuyler's interposed between the latter and his boats   Forming his men and telling them it was either fight or die, Schuyler ordered an advance   The first volley from the French killed and wounded the greater part of those lost in the expedition.   But the case was a desperate one, and a vigorous charge dislodged the French from their position, and the men reached their boats, embarked and arrived at Albany on the 9th of August The losses were twenty-one killed and twenty-five wounded   The result of

---

[1] Saint Sacrament, literally the Lake of the Blessed Sacrament, which name it obtained in 1646, from Father Jogues, because he passed through it on the Festival of Corpus Christi —E B O'CALLAGHAN

The common impression that the name of the lake was suggested by the singular purity of its water, is erroneous   By the aborigines, it was in one dialect called Caniadere-Oit, or the Tail of the Lake, in reference to its relation to Lake Champlain — SPAFFORD'S *Gazetteer*

By the Iroquois it was named Andiatarocte, "There the lake shuts itself" — *Relations.*

"Horicon," although redolent with beauty, seems to be a pure poetical fancy   The various names attached, as well to tribes as to places, in the difficult Indian language, often lead to confusion and error — WATSON

the expedition was fruitless, except so far as it aided in keeping the French settlers in a state of terror

The Iroquois continued their incursions against the French and were, perhaps, more dreaded by the latter than the English   The French were prevented from tilling their lands and a famine ensued, " The poor inhabitants," says Colden, " being forced to feed the soldiers gratis, while their own children wanted bread "   The French fur trade was also nearly ruined by the Iroquois, who took possession of the passes between them and their western allies, and cut off the traders   These terrible incursions by the Five Nations exasperated Count de Frontenac, governor of New France, to the last extremity and he determined, if possible, to end them [1]   He planned an expedition against the Mohawks to be undertaken in midwinter of the year 1693   He collected a force of between six and seven hundred French and Indians, secretly passed Lake Champlain on the ice, descended into the Mohawk country and captured three of their castles, meeting with resistance only in the last   They retreated with about three hundred prisoners   Major Peter Schuyler, ever the firm friend of the Mohawks, hastily gathered a party of Albany militia and Indians to the number of five hundred, and started in pursuit   So prompt was their action that the fugitives were closely pressed and suffered greatly for food, being compelled " to eat the leather of their shoes "   They escaped, however, with a loss of eighty killed and thirty-three wounded

After vain efforts to negotiate peace with the Iroquois Frontenac made preparations for a still more formidable effort to coerce them into submission   In the summer of 1695 he sent a strong force to repair and garrison Fort Cadaraqui, which then took his name   On the 4th of July in the following year he embarked from the south end of the island of Montreal with all the militia of the colony and a large body of Indians, for a destructive incursion against the Onondagas   Although by far the most formidable invasion yet made into the Iroquois country, it was almost fruitless in results, other than the destruction of villages and crops

The treaty of Ryswick was concluded in September, 1697   While it established peace between the French and English, it practically left unsettled the status of the Iroquois   The French, while insisting on including their own Indian allies in the terms of the treaty, were unwilling to include the Iroquois, and made preparations to attack them with their whole force , but the English as strenuously insisted on extending the terms to their allies, and Earl Bellomont informed Count de Frontenac that he would resist with ,the entire force of his government, any attack on the Iroquois, if necessary   This put an end to French threats

---

[1] June 6, 1692, the Iroquois entered into a formal treaty of alliance and friendship with Major Richard Ingoldesby, who assumed the gubernatorial office of New York on the death of Col Henry Sloughter, in July, 1691   Ingoldesby was succeeded by Benjamin Fletcher in August, 1692.

For five or six years after the signing of the treaty at Ryswick quiet prevailed in the territory between Albany and Lake Champlain The breaking out of the war of the Spanish Succession, or, as it was called in America, Queen Anne's War, again plunged the colonies of the two countries into the caldron of contention Queen Anne ascended the English throne in 1702, and soon afterward found cause to declare war against France The Five Nations, by a treaty of neutrality with the French in Canada, made August 4th, 1701, became a barrier against the savages from the north But in the east the French induced the Indians to violate a treaty made with the colonists of New England, thus opening a new series of hostilities in that region that soon spread along the whole frontier For several years ferocious forays occurred in New England and elsewhere " Remote settlements were abandoned, and fields were cultivated only by armed parties united for common defense "[1] Finally this state of affairs became insupportable, and after several fruitless expeditions, fitted out chiefly by Massachusetts to chastise the French and their Indian allies for three or four successive seasons, in 1710 an armament of ships and troops sailed for Port Royal (Nova Scotia), which was captured Acadia was seized and annexed to the English colony The following year (1711) an English fleet and army arrived at Boston On the 15th of August fifteen men-of-war and forty transports, bearing an army of 7,000 men, partly composed of New England forces, sailed for the St Lawrence, under the command of Sir Hovenden Walker In the mean time Governor Nicholson had proceeded to Albany, where a force of about 4,000, partly composed of Iroquois Indians, had been concentrated Walker, inexperienced and " strong in his own conceit," declined to be advised by subordinates better versed, shipwrecked eight of the vessels of his fleet and lost 1,000 of his men on the rocks at the entrance of the St Lawrence Discouraged by this he ignobly turned his prow towards England, having first sent the New England men back to Boston Nicholson, who had begun his march towards Montreal, was overtaken with the news of Walker's disheartening failure, and immediately retraced his route to Albany. Thus ended another enterprise, planned upon a magnificent scale for those days, and mainly owing its disastrous failure to the policy of England of placing officials in command who were every way unfitted for the positions they held

Hostilities were now suspended, and the treaty of peace at Utrecht [2] between England and France (April 11, 1713) secured peace until 1744.

The Iroquois were now debarred from continuing their incursions upon the northern and western Indians, and their natural inclinations led them south-

[1] LOSSING

[2] This treaty " secured the Protestant succession to the throne of England, the separation of the French and Spanish crowns, the destruction of Dunkirk, the enlargement of the British colonies in America, and full satisfaction from France of the claims of the allies, England, Holland and Germany " This treaty terminated Queene Anne's War, and secured peace for thirty years

ward where they chastised their old enemies living in Carolina. While upon this expedition they adopted into their confederacy the Tuscaroras, of North Carolina, who became known as the sixth nation of the Iroquois. They were assigned territory west of and near to the Oneidas.

But in 1731, during this period of peace, M de Beauharnois, the French governor of the Canadian colony, by the authority of Louis XV, and in violation of the treaties of Ryswick and Utrecht, peoceeded up Lake Champlain and began fortifying Crown Point. As the work was first erected, it was a small wooden fort, scarcely strong enough to resist the weakest artillery, but it was added to and strengthened during the successive years, until, in 1755, it contained space and quarters for five or six hundred men. It was called by the French Fort St Frederic. Thirty men only formed the first French garrison at this point.

This movement startled New York and New England. The assembly of the former resolved that "this encroachment, if not prevented, would prove of the most pernicious consequence to this and other colonies." They sent notice of the encroachment to Pennsylvania, Connecticut and Massachusetts, and applied to the board of trade and plantations for aid. While that body would have granted the request, Robert Walpole counseled peace.

The French, upon their occupation of Crown Point, seemed to have anticipated the apathy of the English that actually followed. Three years later Beauharnois informed his government that he was "preparing to complete" his incipient fortifications. As late as 1747 it had not attained such strength or proportions as to induce the belief that it could not have been recaptured and the garrison with it, at any time since its occupation, by the efforts of any one of the English colonies, had England seen fit to sanction the movement.

To protect Canada from incursions by the Iroquois was the ostensible reason advanced by France for erecting the fortress at Crown Point. That there was a deeper purpose is too palpable to need demonstration. So ignorant, or indifferent, or both together, was the English government, to the real situation and its importance, that the lords of trade as early as December, 1738, confessed to Governor Clinton their ignorance of the location even of French fortifications on Lake Champlain. When, soon after, the attention of the French government was called to the violation of the treaty of Utrecht, the response was a denial of "all knowledge of the projected establishment," and the unavailing assurance that an inquiry on the subject would be made. Meanwhile France, in pursuit of its early policy, was consummating the establishment of trading posts from Canada to the gulf of Mexico.

CHAPTER VI

FRENCH AND ENGLISH RIVALRY

Declaration of War between France and England — Destruction of Saratoga — Indian and French Atrocities — English Apathy — Events of 1747 — Treaty of Aix-la-Chapelle — Operations by the English in 1754 — Hendrick's Speech — The Massachusetts Expedition — Braddock's Campaign — The Movement Against Crown Point — Ticonderoga — Arrival of Dieskau and Vaudreuil — Engagement between Johnson and Dieskau — English Victory — Ephraim Williams's Death — Building of Fort William Henry

AGAIN, in 1744, as the result of the rivalries and jealousies of the two nations, war was declared between England and France

At this time the French held possession of the Champlain valley, and had fortified Crown Point and Ticonderoga   In the fall of 1745 an expedition was fitted out at Montreal and placed under the command of M Marin   The expressed object of this enterprise was to attack and sack certain settlements on the Connecticut River, but it seems that on arriving at Crown Point, or Fort St Frederic, the party was met by Father Piquet, a French *préfet apostolique,* who induced M Marin to change his purpose   Accordingly they proceeded up "Lake Champlain to Wood Creek, crossed the country to the Hudson River, destroyed Lydius's lumber establishment on the site of Fort Edward, and approached the thriving settlement of Saratoga, which they utterly destroyed "[1]   In this massacre about thirty men and women were killed, and fifty or sixty prisoners were taken   But one family escaped   The fort was burned to the ground   The New York Assembly rebuilt it the next year (1746) and named it Fort Clinton   It was then one hundred and fifty feet in length by one hundred in breadth, with several wooden redoubts, which were used as barracks   Its armament consisted of twelve cannon, six, twelve and eighteen pounders

All through the summer of 1746 small detachments of French soldiers and their Indian allies were dispatched from Montreal, and, proceeding to Fort St Frederic, halted long enough to make the necessary preparations, and then set out upon the trails leading to the scattered English settlements in the vicinity of Albany and westward along the Mohawk River   When we consider the mercilessness and barbarous atrocities perpetrated by these prowling bands, acting under the direct control of the French commandants, and often accompanied by them, it is not to be wondered at that the American colonists looked upon Fort St Frederic as a constant menace, and the source from which the enemy were enabled successfully to send out its marauding parties , and all the time the inhabitants felt their inability to protect themselves against the forays, and burned with indignation against the English government for its

[1] LOSSING

apathy and dilatoriness in thus leaving them to suffer at the hands of the relentless foe   The following memoranda, from the original French documents preserved in the *Documentary History*, throws strong light upon the proceedings of the French at this time, and may be considered indisputable, as it is their own statement —

"March 29, 1746   A party set out, consisting of fourteen Indians   . who have been in the country, near Albany, and returned with some prisoners and scalps

"26th (April)   A party of thirty-five warriors belonging to the Soult set out   They have been in the neighborhood of Orange (Albany), have made some prisoners and taken some scalps

" 27th   A party set out consisting of six warriors, who struck a blow in the neighborhood of Albany

" May 7   Six Nepissings started to strike a blow near Boston and returned with some scalps

" 10th   Gatienonde, an Iroquois, who had been settled at the lake for two or three years, left with five Indians of that village and Lieutenant St. Blein, to strike a blow near Orange   They brought in one prisoner   The leader was killed

" 12th.   Ten Indians of the Soult set out towards Boston and returned with some scalps

" 22d   Nineteen warriors of the Soult St Louis have been equipped They have been made to strike a blow in the direction of Albany

" 24th   A party of eight Abenakis has been fitted out, who have been in the direction of Corlac [Schenectady] and have returned with some prisoners and scalps

" 27th   Equipped a party of eight warriors of Soult, who struck a blow near Albany, and brought back six scalps

" 28th.   A party of twelve Nepissings made an attack in the neighborhood of Boston, and brought away four scalps and one prisoner, whom they killed on the road, as he became furious and refused to march

" A party of Abenakis struck a blow near Albany and Corlac, and returned with some scalps.

"June 2d   Equipped twenty-five warriors, who returned from the neighborhood of Albany with some scalps

" 3d   Equipped a party of eighteen Nepissings, who struck a blow at Albany and Corlac

" 19th   Equipped a party of twenty-five Indians of the Soult, who struck a blow near Orange   One or two of these Indians were wounded   They brought away some scalps

" 20th   Equipped a party of nineteen warriors of the Soult, who went to Orange to strike a blow

"21st   Equipped a party of twenty-seven of the same village to go to Albany   Sieur De Carquiville, an officer, was of the party, which has brought in a prisoner that was on the scout to Saristeau [Saratoga], and some scalps

"August 10th   Chevalier De Repentigny arrived at Quebec and reported that he had made an attack near Corlac and took eleven prisoners and twenty-five scalps"

And so on, each succeeding week being but a repetition of the preceding one   The terms of the records are brief, but the miseries and horrors hidden behind the few tame words are more than mind can conceive, or pen can write without shuddering.   Cunning, cruel and stealthy, the unfeeling Indians were fit tools in the hands of their unscrupulous employers   It is no wonder that the almost powerless English settlers were driven to desperation, and to a thirst for vengeance.

In 1747 the same methods were employed by the French, only that each succeeding attack seemed to be actuated by a deeper intent of murder and rapine than the one preceding   The terms of the treaties of peace between the parties were utterly ignored, as well in Europe as in the colonies   The original and deep-rooted plan of the French to establish a chain of military posts from Canada to the Mississippi and thence to the Gulf of Mexico, was never relinquished by them, no matter to what extent the text of the treaties they had signed forbade such a proceeding   By all the devices known the Indians were worked upon to take up arms in their favor, and so successful were they in accomplishing this even questionable military measure, that it is told by writers of the time that the sound of the hammer and saw in the construction of fortifications mingled with that of the rifles of their dark-skinned allies in their murderous depredations against the English settlers

It was the expressed purpose of the expeditions fitted out by the French at Montreal to "harass, murder, scalp, burn and pillage, and this was what they called war."   No doubt by experience they had learned that small parties thus composed and equipped following one another at short intervals, had a greater terrorizing effect upon the stricken settlers, and accomplished greater ruin than would the same number of men consolidated into a single army   The apathy that, from the beginning of the settlement of the country, had characterized the English government in protecting its colonists probably had much to do in augmenting the effrontery and recklessness of the French officials ; certain it is, that none of the expeditions set on foot by the English succeeded in chastising the marauders to the extent justice demanded, although it is on record that in the colony of New York alone seventy thousand pounds were expended in one year in carrying out plans to punish the French and Indians for the depredations they had committed

During the season above mentioned (1747) more than thirty different attacks were made on the settlements between the head of Lake George and Albany   The torch and scalping-knife had driven the inhabitants to desperation, and, discouraged at the supineness of the government, they took the matter into their own hands   On the 4th of August Colonel Johnson had despatched a body of the Iroquois to Canada, divided into two parties, who made an attack on Chambly.   They inflicted sharp punishment upon that post, for all they were drawn into an ambush and suffered severe losses   Johnson made another attempt to reach Canada, but found so large a body of the enemy at Crown Point that he abandoned the enterprise

In December Governor Clinton announced that he had succeeded in raising twenty companies to engage in the expedition against Crown Point the coming season — an enterprise urged by all the leading provincials as the first step necessary towards liberating the settlers from the harassing incursions of the French and northern Indians   These twenty companies numbered about 1,000 men

About this time orders were given to burn Fort Clinton at "Saraghtoga," after removing the property therein   The reason assigned for this remarkable action was that the provincial assembly had failed to furnish troops and supplies sufficient to protect it from even the small marauding parties of the enemy

In October, 1748, the European powers signed a new treaty of peace at Aix-la-Chapelle, which it was hoped, would bring a lasting peace   Once more the hatchet was buried, and the settler felt safe in planting his crops, and harvesting the same without the accompaniment of his rifle.   Many who had been driven from their clearings to the larger settlements, returned to find but a blackened spot where their homes had stood, and that nature does not remain idle while men are spending their strength in war.   But the return of peace brought with it hope and faith, and the sturdy backwoodsman returned to his axe and plow trusting that he had reached the beginning of the era of his reward   But yet the strife was not ended

"'The peace secured by the treaty of Aix-la-Chapelle, hollow and insincere in the Old World, was scarcely observed in the New   The ashes of the frontier settlements had scarcely ceased smoking when the French resumed [1] their military operations " The Indians, far and near, by threats and caresses, presents, promises, and displays of force, were rendered tributary to their vast designs " [2]

Beginning in 1754, continued alarms and occasional attacks on the frontiers awakened the colonists to the fact that the fancied security arising from the peace treaty was but the lull before the storm   Measures were accordingly undertaken for a more vigorous defense than had before been made   When the New York Assembly met in the spring of 1754, Governor James De Lancey in his message called their attention to the recent encroachments of the

French and to a request by Virginia for aid   The assembly voted a thousand pounds and to bear its share in erecting forts along the frontier   By victories in western Pennsylvania in 1754, the French were left in undisputed possession of the entire region west of the Alleghanies   The necessity for concerted action by the English colonies was now too apparent to be overlooked; but the old sectional differences tended to prevent harmonious action   The Iroquois were also becoming, to some extent, alienated from the English, whose apathy and failures they did not relish   The English ministry had, therefore, advised a convention of delegates from all the colonial assemblies in an effort to secure the continued alliance of the Six Nations   This convention was held in Albany in June, 1754, Governor De Lancey was president, and he opened the proceedings with a speech to the Indian chiefs who were present   A treaty was renewed and the Indians left apparently satisfied [1]

It was upon this occasion that, in his final speech, Hendrick, the famous Mohawk chief, closed as follows   " Brethren, we put you in mind from our former speech, of the defenseless state of your frontiers, particularly of this city of Schenectady, and of the country of the Five Nations   You told us yesterday you were consulting about securing both   We beg you will resolve upon something speedily   You are not safe from danger one day   The French have their hatchet in their hands both at Ohio and in two places in New England   We don't know but this very night they may attack us   Since Colonel Johnson has been in this city there has been a French Indian at his house, who took measure of the wall around it, and made very narrow observations on everything thereabouts   We think Colonel Johnson in very great danger, because the French will take more than ordinary pains to kill him or take him prisoner, both on account of his great interest among us and because he is one of our sachems

" Brethren, there is an affair about which our hearts tremble and our minds are deeply concerned   We refer to the selling of rum in our castles   It destroys many, both of our old and young people   We are in great fears about this rum.   It may cause murder on both sides   We, the Mohawks of both castles, request that the people who are settled round about us may not be suffered to sell our people rum   It keeps them all poor, and makes them idle and wicked   If they have any money or goods they lay all out in rum   It destroys virtue and the progress of religion among us "

---

[1] It was on this occasion that the venerable Hendrick, the great Mohawk chieftain, pronounced one of those thrilling and eloquent speeches that marked the nobler times of the Iroquois   It excited the wonder and admiration of those who listened, and commanded the highest encomiums wherever it was read   In burning words he contrasted the supineness and imbecility of the English, with the energies of the French policy   His hoary head and majestic bearing attached dignity and force to his utterances   " We," he exclaimed, " would have gone and taken Crown Point, but you hindered us "   He closed his philippic with this overwhelming rebuke   " Look at the French, they are men   They are fortifying everywhere   But you, and we are ashamed to say it, you are like women, bare and open without any fortifications "

The governor promised satisfaction to this pathetic appeal, of course, gave the Indians thirty wagon loads of presents, and the civilized inhabitants went on selling their gallons of rum for beaver skins   And the Indians have often been cursed for their intemperance

Meanwhile at the suggestion of the Massachusetts delegates to this convention, a plan for the union of the colonies was taken into consideration   The suggestion was favorably received and a committee of one from each colony was appointed to draw plans for the purpose   Then the fertile mind of Benjamin Franklin, having already conceived the necessity of union and harmony, produced a plan which he had already prepared and which was adopted   It was the forerunner of our constitution , but the assemblies rejected it, deeming that it encroached on their liberties, while the ministry rejected it as granting too much power to the people

As one of the results of the convention, Massachusetts raised three regiments of infantry, one of which was placed under command of Ephraim Williams as colonel   As an element in the proposed campaign Colonel Williams was to co-operate with General William Johnson in an attack upon the posts the French had established along Lake Champlain, and was ordered to proceed to Albany for that purpose, along with other New England forces

Though England and France were nominally at peace,[1] the frontier was continually harassed by the Indians, fitted out and let loose by the French, and the colonists continued their appeals to the English ministry

On April 14th, 1755, a congress, composed of General Edward Braddock, Commodore Keppel, with the governors of Massachusetts, New York, Pennsylvania, Maryland and Virginia, was held at Annapolis, Maryland   Braddock had lately arrived as commander-in-chief of the British forces in America. Under instructions from the ministry he directed the attention of the colonial governors to the necessity of raising a revenue for military purposes.   The governors informed him of their strifes with their respective assemblies, and assured the British general that no such fund could be established without the first step being taken by parliament.   It was finally determined, however, to begin a campaign by organizing four separate expeditions   The first to effect the reduction of Nova Scotia, the second to recover the Ohio valley ; the third to expel the French from Fort Niagara and then form a junction with the Ohio expedition, and the fourth to capture Crown Point   The first of these expeditions was entirely successful , the second, under command of Braddock himself, was, chiefly through his folly, disastrous in the extreme   He failed to send out scouts, as repeatedly counseled by Washington, and when within a few miles of Fort Du Quesne, the army was surprised by the lurking foe and only saved from destruction by Washington, who, upon the fall of Braddock, as-

---

1 War was not formally declared in Europe till the following year (1756) by England on the 18th of May, and by France on the 9th of June following

sumed command and conducted the retreat   The expedition against Fort
Niagara was also unsuccessful   It was commanded by General Shirley, governor of Massachusetts, and many of his force deserted upon hearing of Braddock's defeat   Leaving a garrison at Oswego, he led the remainder of his
army to Albany and returned to Massachusetts

The army gathered for the capture of Crown Point was assembled at Albany and the command entrusted to General William Johnson   It comprised
the militia and volunteers from New York, Massachusetts, Rhode Island and
Connecticut   They came together fired with zeal and enthusiasm born of the
conviction that they were to fight for the safety of their firesides

"His army, fresh from the plow and the workshop, save a few who had been
engaged at the siege of Louisburg, were novices in the arts and services of war
The provincials, clothed in the home-spun garments woven by wives and mothers, armed only with their own rifles and fowling pieces, without bayonets, but
animated by the noblest impulses of patriotism and courage, and inspired by a
fervid religious enthusiasm, which kindled the faith that they were battling in
defense of the altars of Protestantism and for the subversion of idolatry   While
the preparations were in active, but to their impatient ardor, slow progress,
they were restive and impatient for the advance   On the Sabbath, in obedience
to their Puritan habits, they assembled to unite in prayer and to ' listen to the
word,' while their swarthy allies gravely hear the interpretation of a long sermon." [1]

In July General Lyman, of New Hampshire, with 600 men was sent forward to clear up the old military road along the Hudson, and rebuild the fort
at Lydius's Mills   Meantime Colonel Williams was sent to the "second carrying-place" on the Hudson, where he erected a block-house and entrenchments   The village of Fort Miller still perpetuates the name then given to
these defenses

The French were not idle and already their attention, or that of their engineers, was drawn to the bold and rocky cliffs at the confluence of Lake George
(known to the French as Lake St Sacrament[2]) and Lake Champlain, as an
excellent military stronghold   In the summer of 1755, Du Quesne had advised the construction of works at that point   The selection of the site and
the construction of the works were entrusted to Lotbinière, an engineer of the
province   The original fort (which was still unfinished a year later) "was a
square fort with four bastions, and built of earth and timber "[3]   In the same
year Johnson mentions Ticonderoga as an important but unoccupied position

---

[1] WATSON'S *Essex County*.

[2] Father Jogues   on his return to Canada   set out with some Indians for the
scene of his former sufferings in company with Sieur Bourdon, royal engineer, and arrived on the festival of Corpus Christi at Lake Andiatorocte, to which, in honor of the day, he gave the name of the
Lake of the Blessed Sacrament —O'CALLAGHAN

[3] *Documentary History*, x, 414.

Such was the inception of Fort Carillon,[1] about which was to center so much of military conflict and heroism. It is not now known when the imposing stone battlements were erected, whose picturesque ruins inform the beholder of to-day of their original strength In the year 1758 the French were energetically engaged in extending and strengthening the fortress; at that time Crown Point, on account of its less favorable position, and the falling walls of Fort St. Frederic, became of secondary importance to them

When the news of Braddock's movements reached France, a fleet bearing six battalions of regulars was dispatched to the aid of the troops in Canada With it came also Vaudreuil, governor-general of New France (the last one) and Baron de Dieskau as commander-in-chief of the colonial armies The latter laid his plans for the immediate capture of Oswego, when the govenor-general received the startling intelligence of Johnson's movement towards Ticonderoga and Crown Point Dieskau was, therefore, hurried to the defense of Lake Champlain

All the preparations for the campaign having been completed at Albany in the early part of August, the main body of the troops began its slow and tedious march along the old military road up the Hudson, General Johnson following immediately after with the artillery, stores and baggage On the 14th of August Johnson reached the " great carrying-place," when he reported to Governor De Lancey that his whole force did " not exceed 2,850 men fit for marching to Crown Point " One regiment was left behind to guard the wagons and bateaux

While awaiting the arrival of his stores and implements of war, General Johnson began an addition to the defenses at this point, to which was given the name of Fort Lyman, in honor of Major-General Phineas Lyman,[2] of the Connecticut troops, who had charge of its erection It was soon after changed to Fort Edward, as a compliment to Edward, Duke of York, brother of George III

On the 15th a council was called by Johnson, at which resolutions were passed asking for reinforcements from the governors of New York and Connecticut; and requesting the governor of Massachusetts to make a diversion in his favor by sending a detachment down the Chaudière River to attack the

---

[1] Mr Watson says the name "Carillon seems to bear the same signification as the Indian name, "The-Onderoga," the original of Ticonderoga, meaning noise-chimes, in allusion, doubtless, to the brawling waters

[2] General Lyman was a graduate of Yale College, and a lawyer by profession He commanded the Connecticut troops in this movement, under Johnson, and when the latter was wounded at the battle of Lake George, the command devolved upon him He participated in later campaigns, under Abercrombie, Lord Howe, and Amherst In 1763 he was sent to England as agent to receive prize moneys due him and other officers, and as agent for a company soliciting a grant of lands on the Mississippi, and there wasted eleven years of his life, being deluded by idle promises until his mind sank to imbecility. In 1774 his wife sent his second son to bring him home. About this time the petitioners received their grant of land, when he and his eldest son embarked for the Mississippi, and died on the way in West Florida in 1755.

French posts in that vicinity. Later in the month he reported to Governor De Lancey that "the road is now making from this place to Lake St Sacrament where I propose to build magazines and raise a defensible fortification," and adds, "I propose to march to-morrow or next day with the first division of about fifteen hundred men, and some Indians, and a few field pieces "[1]

The following detailed and trustworthy account is taken from Holden's *History of Queensbury* It is based upon early documents, and is considered a valuable historical statement —

"Awaiting developments, General Johnson established a camp at the head of the lake, and under the immediate supervision of Col Williams, a large clearing was made on the headland afterward covered by the intrenchments of Fort William Henry

"In a communication to the board of trade dated 3d Sept, 1755, General Johnson states as follows 'I am building a fort at this lake where no house ever before was built, nor a rod of land cleared, which the French call Lake St. Sacrament, but I have given it the name of Lake George, not only in honor to His Majesty but to ascertain his undoubted dominion here When the battoes (certain small boats so called) are brought from the last fort caused to be built at the great carrying-place ab^t 17 miles from hence, I propose to go down this lake with a part of the army, and take part of the end of it about fifty miles from hence at a pass called Tionderogue ab^t 15 miles from Crown Point, there wait the coming up of the rest of the army, and then attack Crown Point '

"On Sunday, the seventh, the camp was hushed to listen to the first Christian services and sermon held on this spot of which there is record The venerable and Reverend Stephen Williams, of Longmeadow, Mass, a near relative of Col Williams, and chaplain of his regiment, preached in camp from the prophetic words of Isaiah, 'which remain among the graves and lodge in the mountains ' The forces gathered here now numbered nearly five thousand, and the want of transportation, coupled with the intelligence received from his trusty scouts and runners, that the French were in possession of the passes at the north dissipated the plan for any further advance

"In the mean time the enemy, more active and aggressive, had dispatched three thousand men to the frontier post of St Frederic, early one-third of these veterans from the fields of France, the remainder consisting of Canadians and Indians They were joined on the seventeenth by the Baron de Dieskau, a brave and experienced officer, who had been assigned to the command of the expedition For the following fifteen days he was encamped under the entrenchments of that fort, maturing his plans — sending out scouts for intelligence and harmonizing disagreements among the intractable savages who constituted so large a part of his following On the second of September he

[1] *Documentary History of N. Y.*, II, p 682

reached the lower fall on the outlet of Lake George, whence he sent out a small scouting party, and bivouacked for a couple of days at what is now known as the fort ground of Ticonderoga On the 4th M de St. Pierre was sent forward with the Canadians and Indians, who were to sleep that night on the side of the great marsh near Whitehall General Dieskau made the great mistake of leaving the bulk of his force, viz 1800 men, at Carillon, and with a flying corps of six hundred Canadians, as many Indians, and three hundred regulars, he reached the head of South Bay, on Lake Champlain, on the 5th, and set forward on his march to Fort Lyman Continuing the march on the 6th, about noon the detachment encamped beyond the mountains. Here small scouting parties were sent off in the direction of Fort Lyman and the head of Lake George One of these returning the same night discovered and reported thick smoke seen in the direction of Johnson's camp On the 7th the army, preceded by scouts, again set forward About two o'clock of that day the scouts, who had been sent to reconnoiter in the vicinity of Fort Lyman, rejoined the main body, with the information that there were about fifty tents outside of the fort, upon which Dieskau decided to attack it Pushing forward he reached that night the banks of the Hudson River about one league from the fort, where he encamped for the night [1]

"At daybreak on the 8th the Indians fired at and killed a courier galloping towards the fort. On his person was found a dispatch to the officer in command of the garrison at that place advising him of Dieskau's approach, with a large force of Frenchmen, Canadians, and Indians, and cautioning him as to the proper disposition of the provisions and ammunition. Twelve wagons shortly after passed in the same direction, from which Dieskau only obtained two prisoners, from whom he obtained tolerably accurate information as to the condition and disposition of the English forces at the head of the lake The garrison at Fort Lyman consisted of only about three hundred troops from the New Hampshire levies under Col Blanchard It was the baron's original intention, after learning the weakness of the latter place, to move forward with celerity, assault and carry it by storm 'The Iroquois refused point blank to march to attack the fort' Dieskau in his account of the affair says: 'I was to arrive at nightfall at the fort and rush to the attack, but the Iroquois, who took the lead on the march, under the pretense of zeal, caused a wrong direction to be taken; and when I was informed of the circumstance, it was no longer time to apply a remedy, so that at nightfall I was yet a league from that fort on the road leading from it to Lake St Sacrament'

"M de St Pierre who, by the baron's orders, had consulted the chiefs of the different natives, and communicated to them his intention of attacking the camp at the head of the lake, under the alluring representation 'that the more English there were, the more of them he would kill,' reported that the Indians

---

[1] Probably on the flat at the foot of Sandy Hill

would submit to his pleasure , and should he succeed at Lake St Sacrament, they would accompany him to the fort

"After daybreak on the morning of the eighth, Dieskau commenced his march along the newly made road so recently traversed by Johnson and his army His force was disposed in five columns, marching at a distance of thirty paces apart. The regular troops forming the center were led by the Baron, in person, while on either flank was a column of Canadians and another of Indians The latter were obliged, in order to maintain their front, to wade morasses and streams, thread the tangled underbrush of the forest and climb the hills on their route Nevertheless the for ce moved with considerable celerity, reaching the heights just north of Brown's Half-way House, at about eight o'clock in the morning Here he was met by some scouts who brought in two English prisoners, from whom he derived the intelligence that General Johnson had fortified and entrenched the English camp, that he was in possession of twelve cannon from thirty pounders down And, 'that a large body of English and Indians were following them on their way to reinforce Fort Lydius' In consequence of this information, a halt was ordered, the Canadians and Indians deposited their packs, and in light marching order were instructed to place themselves in ambush on the side hill west of the road, which was occupied by Dieskau with his regular troops

"In the mean time an express arrived at the English camp with the intelligence that he had seen a large body of the enemy, a few miles to the north of Fort Lyman In the morning following a council of war was held to determine a plan of procedure, at which it was resolved to send out a small party to reconnoitre and harass the enemy's flanks as they approached King Hendrick, the celebrated chief of the Mohawks, being asked for his opinion, replied 'If they are to fight they are too few, if they are to be killed they are too many' It was subsequently proposed to divide the party into three detachments The brave old sachem remonstrated, and forcibly illustrated the folly of the suggestion by picking up three sticks and binding them together saying 'You see now that these cannot easily be broken , but take them one by one, and you may break them at once The council of war adopted in part the chief's advice, and one thousand men, under the command of Col. Ephraim Williams, of the Massachusetts levies, and two hundred Mohawks, led by King Hendrick, the sachem of the upper castle of that tribe, were detailed for this service Before starting King Hendrick mounted a gun carriage and addressed his followers in a strain of thrilling eloquence, that at once aroused their courage, and kindled their ferocious passions for the approaching fray An eye-witness, who did not understand a word of what was said, described it as the most affecting speech he ever heard

"The road recently made followed the course of a ravine extending from the head of the lake nearly due south for a distance of several miles The detachment headed by Colonel Williams took this route at nine o'clock in the morning, and in consequence of the intelligence received at midnight, supposed the enemy to be still in the vicinity of Fort Lyman; and probably moved forward with less precaution than he would have done, if he had supposed the enemy nearer   At a point about two miles south of the encampment, near a place now known as Hendrick's Spring, he halted, and was joined by the detachment of Mohawks, who, with their chief, passed to the front, and at ten o'clock resumed the march   King Hendrick was mounted on a small horse, loaned for the occasion by his friend the general   Flanking parties were now thrown out, which advanced, cautiously beating the dense woods on the right and left.

"About one-third of a mile south of Bloody Pond the ravine, through which Williams's detachment proceeded, is narrowed by the abrupt shoulder of a hill projecting from the west, while on the east the sharp acclivity and rugged sides of French Mountain abut the narrow defile   At its base creep the shimmering waters of a rivulet known as Rocky Brook.   When within a short distance of the ambush, a herd of deer, probably driven forward by the French advance, rushed violently down the defile, and effected their escape by breaking through the ranks of the advancing party   Still, no apprehensions were entertained of the proximity of the enemy, and they continued to advance in fearless confidence, the entire command marching in double files along the road, until entered some distance within the jaws of the ambuscade, when, reaching a small eminence, the keen sighted Hendrick suddenly halted and exclaimed to Williams who was near him   ' I scent Indians '   A few Mohawks pushed out into the thick undergrowth of bushes, and the detachment moved cautiously forward for a short distance, when one of the French allies called out, 'Whence come you?' 'From the Mohawks,' was the reply   'Whence come you?' returned Hendrick to which was answered, ' Montreal,' accompanied with a few scattering shots, followed shortly by the terrific Indian war-whoop, and a destructive volley of musketry from the woods and rocks on the right   Shortly afterward a heavy fire was poured in by the Canadians on the left   King Hendrick's horse was killed by the first fire, and he was soon after dispatched with a bayonet. The advancing files of provincials, wholly unprepared for the unexpected encounter, made but a feeble resistance, while at the first alarm the Mohawks took promptly to cover

"Colonel Williams, perceiving the firing to be the heaviest from the ascent to the right, ordered his troops to charge up the the hill with the hope of turning the enemy's flank, and gaining a more elevated and commanding position. This was attempted, but they had no sooner changed front and advanced, than a destructive volley was poured in upon them from the thickly guarded summit, and the thinned ranks, stunned, swayed backward, closed up in a confused mob and fled panic stricken from the scene of action   Colonel Williams fell

dead at the head of his column [1] The command now devolved upon Lieutenant Colonel Whiting, who, after a while, succeeded in restoring a degree of
order among the fugitives

[1] Colonel Ephraim Williams was born at Newtown, Mass , February 24th, 1715 His ancestors
were of Welsh stock, having immigrated to America in 1630 The surroundings of his youth must
have had a controlling influence in the formation of his character Newtown at the time of his birth
was on the extreme frontier, and exposed to all the horrors of rapine and massacre by the savages that
were the invariable accompaniment of first settlements elsewhere in the new country His early association with peril and privation tended to the formation of a character noted for its firmness, keen
conception, bravery and honor His parents died while he was quite young, and he was placed in the
care of a grandfather, who was engaged in mercantile pursuits In his grandfather's employ he made
several voyages to foreign ports, spending some time in the different countries with which the colonists
were in communication, thereby adding to his knowledge and broadening his mind with information
gleaned by the way At the beginning of the French war he was selected as a proper person to com
mand the troops of that section, and he was accordingly commissioned as captain, and was afterwards
(in 1754) promoted to colonel Until August, 1746, he was in command of Fort Massachusetts "which
stood not far from the northeastern end of Saddle Mountain, within the present township of Adams, and
on the eastern border of Hoosac river " At that date he marched at the head of the Massachusetts
levies to join Governor Clinton at Albany, in the proposed invasion of the French settlements in Canada While he was absent Fort Massachusetts was captured by the French under Vaudreuil and its
garrison taken prisoners to Canada In 1748 he was again in command of Fort Massachusetts, which
had been rebuilt and garrisoned with one hundred men In August of that year the fort was attacked
by a force of two hundred French and Indians Although drawn into an ambush in a successful sally
for the rescue of four of his men who were returning from a scout, by intrepidity and brilliant maneuv-
ering he escaped the clutches of the wily foe and escaped to the fort with the loss of but one man In
the campaign of 1755 he was ordered with his command to Albany While awaiting here the movement of the troops he made his will, in which, after making certain bequests to relatives, he devised the
remainder of his property to the establishment of a free school The terms of his will being carried
out and the school proving a success, the Legislature in 1793, erected it into a college, by the name of
Williams College

All trustworthy statements regarding the death of Colonel Williams show that he fell at the head
of his troops at the beginning of the battle Dr Holden says "He was shot through the head,
and fell dead upon the spot His body was hidden by two of his comrades, near the rock which bears
his name, to prevent its mutilation by the savages After the action it was buried by the side of the old
military road at the foot of a pine tree This place was originally designated by a small granite slab
marked E W

"About forty years since, Dr William H Williams (nephew of the colonel), of Raleigh, N C ,
exhumed the skull, and carried it off The statement that the entire remains were subsequently removed is doubtless an error The pine has fallen, but two thrifty scions, till within a few years,
shaded the grave where the warrior sleeps.

"When the monument was put up, the grave was refilled and a pyramidal boulder still remaining, placed upon it, bearing the plain inscription E W 1755 In the year 1854, a plain marble shaft
was placed by the alumni of Williams College upon the rock which bears his name It contains the
following inscriptions —

EAST SIDE

To the memory of COLONEL EPHRAIM WILLIAMS
A native of Newtown, Mass , who, after gallantly defending the frontiers of his native State, served under
General Johnson against the French and Indians, and
nobly fell near this spot in the bloody conflict of Sept
8th, 1755, in the 42d year of his age

NORTH SIDE

A lover of peace and learning, as courteous and gene-

"A temporary stand was made at the Bloody Pond behind which the troops rallied, and the French were held in check for several minutes by the determined and resolute bravery of the provincials   Compelled at length from the numerical superiority of the enemy to give way, they resumed their retreat, constantly holding the pursuers in check by a scattering but well aimed fire from every cover which could be made available on the route   The echoes of the protracted firing had been heard with gradually approaching nearness at the head of the lake, and hurried preparations were made for placing the camp in a defensible condition, for as yet no line of entrenchments had been thrown up, or any cover, redoubt, rifle pit or fortification constructed to retard the progress of the enemy   The trunks of the trees, already fallen, were hastily piled up as a sort of rude breastwork in front, while the flanks and rear were protected by seven field pieces and two mortars   The roadway was also commanded by four large cannon advantageously posted   While these dispositions were being made Lieutenant Colonel Cole was dispatched with three hundred men to the assistance and relief of the defeated detachment   He met the flying troops a little north of the Bloody Pond, and checked, by a well-timed volley, the pursuit of the enemy and covered the retreat of the fugitives into camp.   So furious and disastrous had been this brief engagement that on reaching camp, the numbers of the French were greatly magnified by the terrified survivors, while, as usual on such occasions, their own powers and achievements were greatly exaggerated

"Thus terminated the battle long known in fireside story and oral tradition as the bloody morning scout, which resulted in disaster and humiliation to the English cause, and well nigh terminated the fortunes of the day "

The losses of the English were severe, especially among the officers   The total loss of the whites was two hundred and sixteen dead and ninety-six

---

rous as he was brave and patriotic, Col Williams sympathized deeply with the privations of the frontier settlers, and by his will, made at Albany, on his way to the field of battle, provided for the founding among them of an institution of learning, which has since been chartered as Williams College

WEST SIDE

Forti ac magnanimo EPH. WILLIAMS, Collegii Gulielmi Conditori , Qui in hostibus patriae repellendis, prope hoc saxum cecidit , grati alumni posuetunt, A D 1854

SOUTH SIDE

This Monument is erected by the alumni of Williams College, the ground donated by E H ROSEKRANS, M W PERRINE, J HAVILAND

"This monument and the scenes around it are now classic ground to every educated American, and are annually visited by hundreds, eager to pay the tribute of a pilgrimage to the shrine of a hero and a patriot "

wounded, and of the Mohawks thirty-eight were killed and twelve wounded
The death loss is convincing evidence of the close range and fierceness of the
action, evidence strengthened by the fact that few prisoners were taken, nearly
all, as soon as fallen, being dispatched by the tomahawk and scalping-knife

The Mohawks deeply mourned the death of their beloved chief, and it was
with difficulty they were restrained from wreaking their vengeance upon the
few captives taken

The impetuous Dieskau, whose motto was, " Boldness wins," did not stop
to reconnoitre, but started at the head of the French and Indians in rapid pursuit of the retreating English   He hoped thus to enter and capture an unfortified camp   But Johnson and his skillful woodsmen from New England had
not been idle   Trees were felled and hasty breastworks constructed, behind
which a few cannon that were hurried from the lake were placed   When the
Indians heard the roar of the guns, they again thwarted Dieskau's designs by
"stopping short," and he also soon saw the Canadians "scattering right and
left " [1]

This defection forced Dieskau to make a brief halt near the works, which
was of great advantage to his enemy   The second struggle of the battle now
waged hotter than before and continued for more than four hours — the blood-
iest and most obstinately contested the New World had yet witnessed   A vigorous assault on the center by Dieskau's regulars was " thrown into disorder
by the warm and constant fire of the artillery and colonial troops "   He then
assailed the left, was again repulsed and in a last desperate effort hurled his decimated force upon the right, but in vain, only a bloody repulse awaited him.
The French regulars fought with great heroism, but were unequal to their undertaking   The Canadians and Indians were of but little assistance and "were
dispersed by a few shots thrown into their midst "

The French general was wounded and disabled, but bravely refused to be
carried from the field, and ordered his subordinate, Montrueil, to assume the
command and make the best retreat possible   Two Canadians came to the relief of Dieskau, but one of them was shot and fell directly across the legs of the
general, " to his great embarrassment," as he expressed it   While supporting
himself against a tree here amid a hail of bullets, a refugee Frenchman came
upon him and fired a bullet through both his hips, causing a wound which resulted in his death twelve years later   He was left by his king to suffer as a
prisoner, neglected by his country, until the peace of 1763

The French army was now broken and scattered, and a routed party of
about three hundred were encountered by a body of provincials under McGinnis, of New Hampshire (who was killed in the action), and Folsom, of New
York   The Frenchmen were put to flight in such confusion that all their baggage and ammunition was left behind for the victors

[1] *Documentary History*

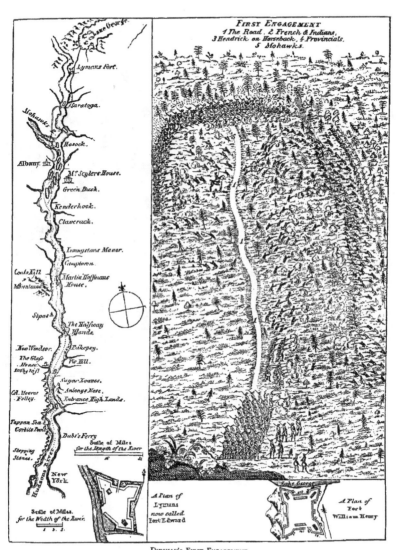

DIESKAU'S FIRST ENGAGEMENT.

From Butler's "Lake George and Lake Champlain."

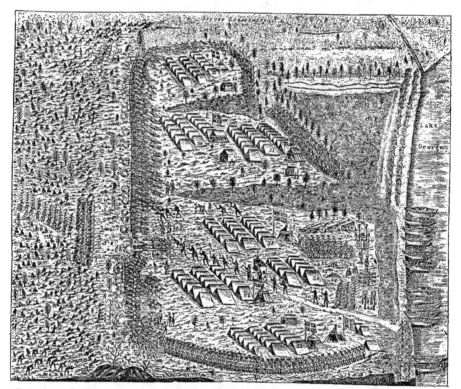

Explanation:—6. Canadians and Indians. — 7. French regulars attacking the center. — 8. The road. — 9. Provincials in action posted in front. — 10. The trees felled for the breastworks. — 11. Cannon. — 12. A cannon posted "advantageously" on the eminence. — 13. Place where Dieskau fell. — 14, 15. Canadians' attack. — 16. The man that shot Dieskau. — 17. Reserves. — 18. Woods and swamps. — 19. Murass. — 20. Cannon defending the flank. — 21. Baggage wagoos. — 22, 23, 24. Stores and ammunition. — 25. Mortars. — 26. Road to the Lake. — 27, 28, 29. Storehouse. — 30. Mohawks. — 31. Gen. Johnson's tent.— 32. Lyman's regiment. — 33. Col. Harris' company. — 34. Col. Cockroft. — 35. Col. Williams. — 36. Col. Ruggles. — 37. Col. Titcomb. — 38. Col Guttridge. — 39. Officers.

DIESKAU'S SECOND ENGAGEMENT.

From Butler's "Lake George and Lake Champlin."

The losses were about equal on both sides, amounting to four hundred and fifty of the French, and something less by the English and Mohawks Decisive victory rested with neither The British were prevented for the time from the conquest of Lake Champlain, an object of no small advantage to the French But the colonists achieved an actual triumph of arms which, following closely upon the disasters of Braddock, filled the land with rejoicing The French and Canadians were taught that in the New England colonies was growing an element of military strength and heroism that could not be lightly encountered — an element that in later days was to win freedom for the country

" Dieskau appears not to have been adapted by temperament or manners to conciliate the attachment or to command the confidence of his savage allies Instead of indulging in familiar intercourse and yielding to their habits and peculiarities, he maintained with them — and equally with his subordinates and the Canadians—the stately German style of seclusion and exclusiveness This course destroyed the influence and devotion, which could only be exerted over their rude and capricious nature, by controlling their impulses and affections "

Johnson was wounded early in the battle and turned the command over to General Lyman,[1] of the Massachusetts division His enthusiastic soldiers and the impetuous Mohawks would have pursued the fleeing French and Canadians, but Johnson, either through over-cautiousness or timidity, restrained them, and the French continued their retreat unmolested to Carillon A vigorous prosecution of the campaign as originally planned was urged by the people of the colonies The French were partially paralyzed by the defeat , the walls of St Frederic were crumbling, and the fortress at Ticonderoga was still unfinished But Johnson neglected what was undoubtedly his great opportunity and spent the remainder of the season in erecting Fort William Henry at the head of Lake George , the Mohawks returned to their homes

---

CHAPTER VII

FRENCH AND ENGLISH WAR

Plans of the Campaign — Apathy and Indecision of the English — Brilliant Deeds of the Rangers — Arrival of Montcalm — Capture of Oswego — Campaign of 1757 — Marin's Operations — Montcalm's Preparations for the Capture of Fort William Henry — Council with the Indians — March of De Levis — Condition of the Fort — Webb's Pusillanimous Conduct — Details of the Massacre

AFTER the hostilities above described, strange as it may appear, it was not till the following year, as hereinbefore mentioned, that a formal declaration of war was proclaimed between England and France In the year 1756 an-

---

[1] Johnson's conduct seems to have been neither just nor magnanimous He ascribed all the glory of the event to himself, Lyman was not named in his report, and but slight mention was made of other officers Yet Johnson was rewarded with a baronetcy, £5,000 and the appointment of superintendent of Indian affairs, which was wrung from the pittance allowed the colonies for their burdens

other force was organized for an attack upon Crown Point   Sir Charles Hardy, who arrived as governor of New York in September, 1755, had delegated most of his civil duties to De Lancey, and in 1757 resigned   The campaign of 1756, as planned, comprised movements against Fort Niagara with six thousand men, Fort Du Quesne with three thousand men and Crown Point with ten thousand, while two thousand were to advance on the French settlements on the Chaudière and to Quebec — a campaign of sufficient magnitude surely   The population of the province of New York was then 96,775   The expedition against Crown Point was entrusted to General John Winslow, but lacking confidence in the number of his force, he awaited reinforcements from England   Lord Loudoun had recently been appointed commander-in-chief and governor of Virginia, with General Abercrombie second in command   Late in June the latter arrived with troops to reinforce General Winslow, but he at once blighted all prospects of success in the field, by placing regular officers above the provincial officers of equal rank   Many men deserted and officers threatened to relinquish their commissions   This difficulty was finally adjusted by an agreement that the regulars should be assigned to garrison duty, the provincials to take the field   But through the dissensions, incapacity and apathetic indecision of the English commander, little was accomplished of an offensive character against the French during the year, other than the often brilliant exploits of the American rangers, commanded by Rogers, Stark and others   In the language of Mr Watson, " Rogers, the gallant ranger, was particularly conspicuous in these wild and daring adventures   Sometimes stealing under the cover of night by the forts in canoes, he lay in ambush far down the lake, surprised and captured boats laden with supplies, which, unsuspicious of danger, were proceeding to relieve the garrisons   Frequently he approached the forts by land, and prowling about them with Indian skill and patience, until he ascertained the intelligence he was ordered to collect, he captured prisoners, shot down stragglers, burnt dwellings, and slaughtered cattle feeding around the works, and then defying pursuit, retreated in safety   In one of these bold incursions, which signalized the opening of the next year, Rogers and Stark had penetrated with a force of less than eighty men, to a point between the French fortresses, near the mouth of a stream, since known as Putnam's Creek, and there in ambush awaited their victims   A party of French are passing in gay and joyous security on the ice towards Ticonderoga   Part are taken, the rest escape and alarm the garrison   The rangers attempt to escape, pressing rapidly along the snow path, in Indian file, as was their custom, but on ascending the crest of a hill they receive the fire of an overwhelming force, posted with every advantage to receive them   A fierce and bloody conflict ensued, protracted from near meridian until evening   The rangers retreating to a hill, are protected by the covert of the trees and there gallantly sustain the unequal conflict   Rogers, twice wounded, yields the command of the little band to Stark, who, with infinite skill and courage, guides the battle, repulses the foe, with a loss far exceeding his entire force, and at night conducts a successful retreat to Lake George This courageous band, reduced to forty-eight effective men, with their prisoners effected a retreat to Fort William Henry in safety "

A similar brilliant movement was attempted in the ensuing February, by the French and Canadians to the number of fifteen hundred, led by Vaudreuil They traversed the ice and snow of Lakes Champlain and George, more than one hundred miles in an effort to surprise and capture Fort William Henry But the vigilant garrison successfully defended the works, although the little fleet of bateaux and the huts of the rangers were destroyed

The Marquis de Montcalm was made the successor of Dieskau in command of the French and their allies, and succeeded, even to a greater extent than had his predecessors, in winning the confidence and utilizing the power of the Indians[1] They were the most dreaded opponents and formidable enemies to the brilliant and heroic operations of the rangers under Rogers, Stark and Putnam.

Montcalm[2] arrived at Quebec in May, 1756, and immediately made himself acquainted with the condition and prospects of his forces, and he found the situation anything but encouraging He visited Carillon (Ticonderoga) where he had given but one day to inspection and consultation, when he was recalled by Vaudreuil Early in August he had organized at Frontenac a force of about five thousand men, with which he rapidly advanced upon Oswego Abercrombie was informed at Albany of the contemplated attack, but the characteristic apathy of the English at that period prevented the necessary immediate action, instead of which Abercrombie and Loudoun began deliberate preparations for a descent upon Ticonderoga and Crown Point Reinforcements were sent to Forts Edward and William Henry The opportunity for relieving Oswego was lost After a brief defense the fort at that point capitulated (August 11th, 1756) and turned over to Montcalm sixteen hundred men, one hundred cannon, a large quantity of stores, and the vessels then in the harbor Even the fall of Oswego did not awaken the energies of Loudoun An attack was, however, made by the English, with a fleet of boats upon the outworks and flotilla at Ticonderoga, but Montcalm had proceeded thither and the attack was repulsed with severe loss

---

[1] The French, far more than the English, were successful in conducting military operations in association with their savage auxiliaries More flexible in their own feelings, they were more yielding and tolerant towards the peculiar habits and temperament of the Indians Coercion and reason were powerless with such allies They were often the most valuable auxiliaries, and achieved victory upon more than one important field, but always unreliable, no safe calculations could be placed upon their services, their fidelity or constancy Montcalm pronounced them inestimable as scouts and spies — WATSON

[2] He was of noble birth and thorough education, and entered the French army at fourteen, distinguished himself in the war of the Austrian succession in Germany, and gained the rank of colonel for his conduct in the battle of Piacenza, in Italy, in 1746 His career in the New World was marked by skill, heroism and humanity

For the campaign of 1757 Loudoun made requisition for four thousand troops from the northern colonies, which were furnished, as was supposed for the reduction of Crown Point and Ticonderoga, but the incapable official again disappointed them, and in June made an ineffectual effort to capture Louisburg This futile and impracticable scheme left the frontier colonies open and unprotected The vigilant and sagacious enemy, from their watch-towers at Carillon, saw the error and prepared promptly to seize the advantage

In July Marin[1] left Carillon with a small party of Indians and surprised and attacked near Fort Edward two detachments, which suffered severely at his hands His retreat, made in the face of superior numbers, was successfully conducted He brought in thirty-two scalps In the same summer a party of three hundred and fifty English provincials, who were proceeding down Lake George, were surprised by a force of Ottawa Indians, under Corbière, at Sabbath-day Point Only two boats and fifty men escaped

It had now become a cherished purpose with Montcalm to destroy Fort William Henry, which was a source of constant anxiety to the Canadian government, and he resolved to make the effort The Indian warriors were summoned and responded in such numbers, from Lake Superior to Acadia, that Montcalm was constrained to write, " I have seized their manners and genius " This able general, with rare intuitiveness, mingled with the savages and took part in their ceremonies, made them liberal gifts, and then excited their passions with visions of rich plunder and revenge The French and Canadian forces were rapidly assembled at Crown Point and Carillon, where they were joined by the Indians The latter came up the lake in two hundred canoes, accompanied by the priests, the war chants blending with missionary hymns Across the portage of about three miles to Lake George, two hundred and fifty bateaux and two hundred canoes were transported, a work of great magnitude, and performed witout the aid of horses or oxen The following day Montcalm called a council of his Indian allies It should be understood that at this time large numbers of the Five Nations had become settled in Canada, or had joined the French cause from other points, chiefly on account of the success of the French arms and the apathy of the English On the occasion in question these Iroquois warriors acted the host and received the other tribes with hospitality To the Iroquois Montcalm presented the " great belt of two thousand beads, to bind the Indians to each other and all to himself" He then unfolded to them his plans De Levis, with twenty-two hundred French and Canadians, started two days in advance, under escort of six hundred Indians, with the purpose of traversing the mountain track on the west side of the lake, leaving his baggage to come by water On the first of August the

---

[1] Marin was formerly connected with the French navy, but while yet young he was allured by the promised romance and daring of the border warfare in New France and joined the irregular forces of Indians and Canadians His deeds were valorous, often sanguinary, but sometimes redeemed by generous acts

remainder of the force embarked in the bateaux   After severe trials De Levis reached his destination and signaled the fact to Montcalm by means of fires at Ganaouské   On the same evening Montcalm marched towards the fort. Montcalm's force comprised about five thousand five hundred effective men and sixteen hundred Indians

The fort was garrisoned by five hundred men, under the gallant veteran, Colonel Munro, and supported by seventeen hundred troops in an entrenched camp   General Webb was at Fort Edward, only fifteen miles distant, with four thousand men   Colonel Munro felt strong in his position under these favorable circumstance   Webb had visited Fort William Henry just before Montcalm's investment, escorted by a body of rangers under Putnam   The latter, in making a reconnaissance down the lake, discovered the approach of the French, which fact he immediately communicated to Webb and urged him to oppose their landing   Instead, he ignobly enjoined secrecy upon Putnam and hastily returned to Fort Edward   Learning of the movements of Mont-calm, Johnson had already marched to Fort Edward with a force of militia and Indians, reaching there on the second day of the siege   For six days the siege was continued, during which almost daily appeals were sent to Webb for aid   None was sent   He finally consented that Johnson should march with the militia and rangers to the relief of the beleaguered fortress, but he was peremptorily recalled after he had proceeded about three miles   Webb sent a letter[1] to Munro advising surrender   It is clear that poltroons sometimes reach high station in the military as well as in civil life   Montcalm was fortunate On the same day he received from France dispatches promising royal favors to the army and conferring upon himself the red ribbon with the rank of com-mander of St Louis   The army was inspired to added enthusiasm

Webb's letter to Munro was intercepted by Montcalm, who forwarded it to the fort, with a demand for its instant surrender   Further resistance was use-less, and with his ammunition nearly exhausted and half his guns useless, Munro was forced to hang out a flag of truce   Montcalm agreed to honorable terms, one stipulation being that the English troops should march out of the fort " with their arms and other honors of war, and receive an escort to Fort Edward   The following night was spent by the Indians in their customary orgies in celebration of a victory , but they were disappointed that they could

---

[1] This letter was written by an aide-de-camp, who says   " He [General Webb] has ordered me to acquaint you that he does not think it prudent (as you know his strength at this place) to attempt a junction or to assist you, till reinforced by the militia of the colonies, for the immediate march of which repeated expresses have been sent   One of our scouts brought in a Canadian prisoner last night from the investing party, which is very large, and have possessed all the grounds five miles on this side of Fort William Henry   The number of the enemy is very considerable, the prisoners say eleven thou-sand, and have a large train of artillery, with mortars, and were to open their batteries this day (Aug 4th)   The general thought proper to send you this intelligence, that in case he should be so unfort-unate, from the delays of the militia, not to have it in his power to give you timely assistance, you might be able to make the best terms in your power," etc

not glut their vengeance with more blood, and a most horrible and disgraceful atrocity followed As the garrison was marching from the works early in the morning, the Indians gathered about and began robbing and insulting the prisoners, brandishing their tomahawks and amusing themselves with the terror inspired in their victims Personal encounters ensued and with the first flow of blood the savages seemed transformed into demons Slaughter began on all sides and the dismayed prisoners fled in confusion At this juncture Montcalm and other French officers rushed upon the scene, bared their breasts and 'by threats, prayers, caresses and conflicts with the chiefs, arrested the massacre'[1] 'Kill me,' cried Montcalm, 'but spare the English, who are under my protection' Over one-half the English reached Fort Edward in broken squads, four hundred were rescued with their property and restored under the capitulation of Montcalm and many others, through his solicitation, were ransomed from the Indians by Vaudreuil About thirty were killed outright

Montcalm has been impassionately charged with complicity in this outrage, but it must be confessed that a calm review of the subject does not warrant such a charge[2]

Fort William Henry was totally destroyed and all its stores and munitions captured And all this was effected with a loss to the besiegers of only fifty-three men. General Webb sent his personal baggage to a place of safety and prepared to retreat from Fort Edward to the Hudson The reduction of this fortification and the possible capture of Albany had been a part of the plans of Montcalm, but for sufficient reasons (chief among which was the required presence of his Canadian soldiers in their harvest fields in order to avert a famine) he retired satisfied with his success and glory Meanwhile Loudoun had taken his position on Long Island, the English had been driven from the Ohio and Montcalm had placed the valley of the St Lawrence under the dominion of France Great Britain and her colonies were humiliated and fearful for the future

A detailed account of the massacre of Fort William Henry, published by Dr Holden in his *History of Warren County*, as an extract from a now very rare work, namely, "Travels in North America, by Jonathan Carver, captain of the Provincial troops in North America," cannot fail to be of interest to the people of Warren county Dr Holden says that it has long been the basis from which the various accounts of the affair have been prepared, and as an offset to the French account, is of value to the historian —

---

[1] *Doc History*

[2] Such atrocities were utterly incompatible with his high character as a Christian noble, a gallant soldier, and a refined scholar, whose sensibilities had been purified and elevated by communion with the poets and philosophers of antiquity But it (history) can never exonerate his fame from the imputation of criminal negligence and a reckless disregard to the safety of those confided to his honor and protection by the most solemn act known to warfare A moral responsibility rests upon those who set in motion a power, which they know they have no ability to guide or control — WATSON

"As a detail of the massacre at Fort William Henry, in the year 1757, the scene to which I refer cannot appear foreign to the design of this publication, but will serve to give my readers a just idea of the ferocity of this people I shall take the liberty to insert it, apologizing at the same time for the length of the digression, and those egotisms which the relation renders unavoidable.

"General Webb, who commanded the English army in North America, which was then encamped at Fort Edward, having intelligence that the French troops under Mons Montcalm were making some movements towards Fort William Henry, he detached a corps of about fifteen hundred men, consisting of English and provincials, to strengthen the garrison In this party I went as a volunteer among the latter

"The apprehensions of the English general were not without foundation ; for on the day of our arrival we saw Lake George (formerly Lake Sacrament), to which it lies contiguous, covered with an immense number of boats, and in a few hours we found our lines attacked by the French general, who had just landed with eleven thousand regulars and Canadians, and two thousand Indians Colonel Monro, a brave officer, commanded in the fort, and had no more than two thousand three hundred men with him, our detachment included

"With these he made a gallant defense, and probably would have been able at last to preserve the fort had he been properly supported and permitted to continue his efforts On every summons to surrender sent by the French general, who offered the most honorable terms, his answer repeatedly was, that he yet found himself in a condition to repel the most vigorous attacks his besiegers were able to make, and if he thought his present force insufficient, he could soon be supplied with a greater number from the adjacent army

"But the colonel, having acquainted General Webb of his situation, and desired he would send him some fresh troops, the general dispatched a messenger to him with a letter, wherein he informed him that it was not in his power to assist him, and therefore gave him orders to surrender up the fort on the best terms he could procure This packet fell into the hands of the French general, who immediately sent a flag of truce, desiring a conference with the governor

"They accordingly met, attended only by a small guard, in the center between the lines, when Mons Montcalm told the colonel that he was come in person to demand possession of the fort, as it belonged to the king, his master The colonel replied that he knew not how that could be, nor should he surrender it up whilst it was in his power to defend it

"The French general rejoined, at the same time delivering the packet into the colonel's hand, ' By this authority do I make the requisition.' The brave governor had no sooner read the contents of it, and become convinced that such were the orders of the commander-in-chief, and not to be disobeyed, than he hung his head in silence, and reluctantly entered into a negotiation

" In consideration of the gallant defense the garrison had made, they were permitted to march out with all the honors of war, to be allowed covered wagons to transport their baggage to Fort Edward, and a guard to protect them from the fury of the savages

" The morning after the capitulation was signed, as day broke, the whole garrison, now consisting of about two thousand men, besides women and children, were drawn up within the lines, and on the point of marching off, when great numbers of Indians gathered about and began to plunder We were first in hopes that this was their only view, and suffered them to proceed without opposition Indeed it was not in our power to make any, had we been so inclined , for though we were permitted to carry off our arms, yet we were not allowed a single round of ammunition In these hopes, however, we were disappointed , for presently some of them began to attack the sick and wounded, when such as were not able to crawl into the ranks, notwithstanding they endeavored to avert the fury of their enemies by their shrieks or groans, were soon dispatched.

" Then we were fully in expectation that the disturbance would have concluded, and our little army began to move , but in a short time we saw the front divison driven back, and discovered that we were entirely encircled by savages We expected every moment that the guard, which the French by the articles of capitulation had agreed to allow us, would have arrived and put an end to our apprehensions , but none appeared The Indians now began to strip every one without exception of their arms and clothes, and those who made the least resistance felt the weight of their tomahawks

" I happened to be in the rear division, but it was not long before I shared the fate of my companions Three or four of the savages laid hold of me, and whilst some held their weapons over my head, the others disrobed me of my coat, waistcoat, hat and buckles, omitting not to take from me what money I had in my pocket As this was transacted close by the passage that led from the lines on to the plain, near which a French sentinel was posted, I ran to him and claimed his protection , but he only called me an English dog, and thrust me with violence back again into the midst of the Indians.

" I now endeavored to join a body of our troops that were crowded together at some distance , but innumerable were the blows made at me with different weapons as I passed on, luckily, however, the savages were so close together that they could not strike at me without endangering each other Notwithstanding which, one of them found means to make a thrust at me with a spear, which grazed my side, and from another I received a wound with the same kind of a weapon in my ankle At length I gained the spot where my countrymen stood, and forced myself into the midst of them But before I got thus far out of the hands of the Indians the collar and wristbands of my shirt were all that remained of it, and my flesh was scratched and torn in many places by their savage grips

"By this time the war-whoop was given, and the Indians began to murder those that were nearest to them without distinction It is not in the power of words to give any tolerable idea of the horrid scene that now ensued, men, women and children were dispatched in the most wanton and cruel manner and immediately scalped Many of these savages drank the blood of their victims as it flowed from the fatal wounds

"We now perceived, though too late to avail us, that we were to expect no relief from the French, and that, contrary to the agreement they had so lately signed to allow us a sufficient force to protect us from these insults, they tacitly permitted them, for I could plainly perceive the French officers walking about at some distance, discoursing together with apparent unconcern For the honor of human nature I would hope that this flagrant breach of every sacred law proceeded rather from the savage disposition of the Indians, which I acknowledge it is sometimes almost impossible to control, and which now might have unexpectedly arrived to a pitch not easily to be restrained, than to any premeditated design in the French commander An unprejudiced observer would, however, be apt to conclude that a body of ten thousand Christian troops had it in their power to prevent the massacre from becoming so general But whatever was the cause from which it arose, the consequences of it were dreadful, and not to be paralleled in modern history

"As the circle in which I stood enclosed by this time was much thinned, and death seemed to be approaching with hasty strides, it was proposed by some of the most resolute to make one vigorous effort, and endeavor to force our way through the savages, the only probable method of preserving our lives that now remained This, however desperate, was resolved on, and about twenty of us sprang at once into the midst of them

"In a moment we were all separated, and what was the fate of my companions I could not learn till some months after, when I found that only six or seven of them effected their design Intent only on my own hazardous situation, I endeavored to make my way through my savage enemies in the best manner possible And I have often been astonished since when I have recollected with what composure I took, as I did, every necessary step for my preservation Some I overturned, being at that time young and athletic, and others I passed by, dextrously avoiding their weapons, till at last two very stout chiefs of the most savage tribes, as I could distinguish by their dress, whose strength I could not resist, laid hold of me by each arm, and began to force me through the crowd

"I now resigned myself to my fate, not doubting but that they intended to dispatch me, and then to satiate their vengeance with my blood, as I found they were hurrying me towards a retired swamp that lay at some distance But before we had got a great many yards an English gentleman of some distinction, as I could discover from his breeches, the only covering he had on, which were of fine scarlet velvet, rushed close by us   One of the Indians instantly relinquished his hold, and, springing on this new object, endeavored to seize him as his prey, but the gentleman, being strong, threw him on the ground and would probably have got away, had not he who held my other arm quitted me to assist his brother   I seized the opportunity and hastened away to another party of English troops that were yet unbroken, and stood in a body at some distance   But before I had taken many steps I hastily cast my eyes towards the gentleman, and saw the Indian's tomahawk gash into his back and heard him utter his last groan, this added both to my speed and desperation

"I had left this shocking scene but a few yards when a fine boy about twelve years of age, that had hitherto escaped, came up to me and begged that I would let him lay hold of me, so that he might stand some chance of getting out of the hands of the savages   I told him that I would give him every assistance in my power, and to this purpose bid him lay hold, but in a few minutes he was torn from my side, and by his shrieks I judge was soon demolished   I could not help forgetting my own cares for a minute to lament the fate of so young a sufferer, but it was utterly impossible for me to take any methods to prevent it

"I now got once more into the midst of friends, but we were unable to afford each other any succor   As this was the division that had advanced the furthest from the fort, I thought there might be a possibility (though but a bare one) of my forcing my way through the outer ranks of the Indians, and getting to a neighboring wood, which I perceived at some distance   I was still encouraged to hope by the almost miraculous preservation I had already experienced

"Nor were my hopes in vain, or the efforts I made ineffectual   Suffice it to say that I reached the wood, but by the time I had penetrated a little way into it my breath was so exhausted that I threw myself into a brake and lay for some minutes apparently at the last gasp   At length I recovered the power of respiration; but my apprehensions returned with all their former force when I saw several savages pass by, probably in pursuit of me, at no very great distance   In this situation I knew not whether it was better to proceed, or endeavor to conceal myself where I lay till night came on, fearing, however, that they would return the same way, I thought it most prudent to get further from the dreadful scene of my distresses   Accordingly, striking into another part of the wood, I hastened on as fast as the briars and the loss of my shoes would permit me, and after a slow progress of some hours, gained a hill that overlooked the plain that I had just left, from whence I could discern that the bloody storm raged with unabated fury

"But not to tire my readers, I shall only add that, after passing three days without subsistence, and enduring the severity of the cold dews for three nights,

I at length reached Fort Edward, where with proper care my body soon recovered its wonted strength, and my mind, as far as the recollection of the late melancholy events would permit, its usual composure

" It was computed that fifteen hundred persons were killed or made prisoners by these savages during this fatal day   Many of the latter were carried off by them and never returned. A few, through favorable accidents, found their way back to their native country, after having experienced a long and severe captivity

" The brave Colonel Monro had hastened away soon after the confusion began to endeavor to procure the guard agreed by the stipulation ; but his application proving ineffectual, he remained there till General Webb sent a party of troops to demand and protect him back to Fort Edward   But these unhappy occurrences, which would probably have been prevented had he been left to pursue his own plans, together with the loss of so many brave fellows, murdered in cold blood, to whose valor he had been so lately a witness, made such an impression on his mind that he did not long survive   He died in about three months, of a broken heart, and with truth it might be said that he was an honor to his country

" I mean not to point out the following circumstance as the immediate judgment of heaven as an atonement for this slaughter, but I cannot omit that very few of those different tribes of Indians that shared in it ever lived to return home   The small-pox, by means of their communication with the Europeans, found its way among them and made an equal havoc to what they had done   The methods they pursued on the first attack of that disorder rendered it fatal   Whilst their blood was in a state of fermentation, and nature was striving to throw out the peccant matter, they checked her operations by plunging into the water , the consequence was that they died by hundreds   The few that survived were transformed by it into hideous objects, and bore with them to the grave the deep indented marks of this much-dreaded disease   .   Mons   Montcalm died soon after on the plains of Quebec

" That the unprovoked cruelty of this commander was not approved by the generality of his countrymen I have since been convinced by many proofs. One only, however, which I received from a person who was a witness to it shall I at present give : A Canadian merchant, of some consideration, having heard of the surrender of the English fort, celebrated the fortunate event with great rejoicing and hospitality, according to the custom of that country , but no sooner did the news of the massacre which ensued reach his ears, than he put an immediate stop to his festivities, and exclaimed in the severest terms against the inhuman permission , declaring at the same time that those who had connived at it had thereby drawn down on that part of the king's dominions the vengeance of heaven   To this he added that he much feared the total loss of them would deservedly be the consequence   How truly this prediction has been verified we well know "

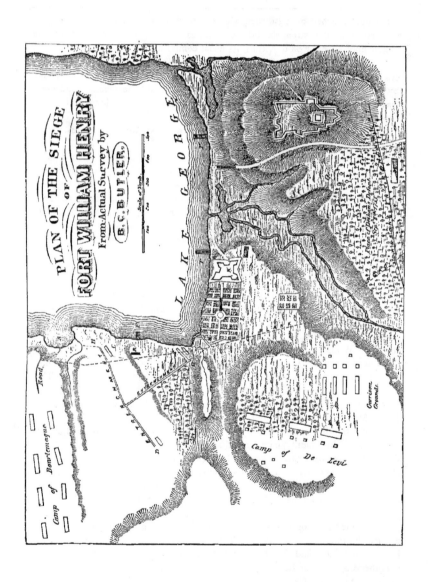

PLAN OF THE SIEGE
OF
FORT WILLIAM HENRY
From Actual Survey by
B. C. BUTLER.

Scale of Yards

LAKE GEORGE

Road.

Camp of Bourlemaque

ENTRENCHMENTS

Camp of De Levi

Garrison Grounds.

Referring to the scourging of the Indian tribes in the service of the French
by small-pox, Carver says they contracted the disease "by means of their communication with the Europeans" In the *Journals of Major Robert Rogers* he
says in a foot note "My brother, Captain Richard Rogers, died with the
small-pox a few days before this fort [Fort William Henry] was besieged; but
such was the cruelty and rage of the enemy after their conquest, that they dug
him up out of his grave, and scalped him"

Pouchot, in his *Memoirs of the War of* 1756–60, mentions an instance of
disinterment of the dead — perhaps the same as that of Richard Rogers above
noticed, and relates the consequences as follows "The Indians as they set
out to return to their country, carried with them a disease of which many died
Some of them, seeing new graves, disinterred the dead to take their scalps, but
unfortunately found that they had died of small-pox, and the infection was
thus given to the Indians The Poutéotames nation, one of the bravest
and most strongly attached to the French, almost entirely perished of this
epidemic"

CHAPTER VIII

CONTINUATION OF FRENCH AND ENGLISH WAR

Prospects for Campaign of 1758 — Discouragement in New France — England's Preponderance —
Rogers's Rangers and their Deeds — Putnam — Three Expeditions by the English — Fall of Louisburg
and Du Quesne — March against Ticonderoga — Howe's Death — The French Position — Assault
by the English on the French Lines — A Bloody Battle — Abercrombie's Headquarters — Victory of
the French — Engagement at Half-Way Brook — Three Military Posts within the present limits of
Warren County

WHEN the reader of to-day reflects upon the relative situations of France
and England in the New World at the beginning of the year 1758, he
finds it difficult to believe that the latter government would submit to five
years more of destructive war upon the colonies before establishing her dominion over the territory south of the St. Lawrence The vast disproportion
in their material resources and military strength became constantly more ob-
vious and decisive The opening of the year named found Canada threatened
with a famine The harvest of the previous year was a failure, and the home
government found it difficult to transmit supplies across an ocean thronged
with the enemies ships. Montcalm wrote the French minister, "The article
of provisions makes me tremble" The fact is a scarcity of provisions followed
which caused many deaths by starvation The population of Canada was estimated at only eighty-two thousand, from which Montcalm relied upon drawing about seven thousand men, a force which he could support with nearly four

thousand regulars These troops were "suffering and impoverished," while fortunes awaited the corrupt high officials, frauds were perpetrated upon the king of such a flagrant character that they demanded investigation at the close of the war, and numerous other embarrassments crippled the energies and chafed the gallant spirit of Montcalm

On the other hand, although the recent campaign had been one of disaster to the English, that fact seemed to infuse a little spirit into the English ministry which found public expression chiefly from the gifted statesman, William Pitt A million and a half of people inhabited the British colonies and an army of some fifty thousand men was subject to the commands of Abercrombie Commercial intercourse with the mother country was almost untrammeled, and there seems no sufficient reason why the French power should not have been extinguished by one grand movement

But this predominance of the English was considerably modified by the facts that France had gained far stronger influence over the Indians than had the English, the Canadian population was more concentrated, and above all, the French cause was kept under command and direction of far the most brilliant and able men Britain sent to her colonies effete generals, bankrupt nobles, and debauched parasites of the court France selected her functionaries from the wisest, noblest and best of her people, and therefore her colonial interests were usually directed with wisdom and sagacity

English hostilities began in December, 1757 with brilliant deeds by the rangers under Rogers and Putnam, which could not, however, seriously influence the general campaign On the 17th of that month, Rogers, in pursuance of orders issued by Lieutenant-Colonel Haviland, who was in command of the English forces at Fort Edward, marched thence with one hundred and fifty men to reconnoitre Ticonderoga, or Carillon The following account of the expedition we take from *Rogers's Journal*, and serves to illustrate the character of this feature of the war, and of the men engaged in it —

On the 17th "we marched six miles and encamped, the snow being then three inches deep, and before morning it was fifteen, we however pursued our route

"On the 18th in the morning, eight of my party being tired, returned to the fort, with the remainder I marched nine miles further, and encamped on the east side of Lake George, near the place where Mons Montcalm landed his troops when he besieged and took Fort William Henry, where I found some cannon balls and shells, which had been hid by the French, and made a mark by which I might find them again

"The 19th we continued our march on the west side of the lake nine miles further, near the head of the northwest bay

"The 21st so many of my party tired and returned as reduced our number to 123, officers included, with whom I proceeded ten miles further, and en-

7

camped at night, ordering each man to leave a day's provisions there till our return

"The next day we marched ten miles further, and encamped near the great brook that runs into Lake George, eight miles from the French advanced guard

"The 23d we marched eight miles, and the 24th six more, and halted within six hundred yards of Carillon fort   Near the mills we discovered five Indians' tracks, that had marched that way the day before, as we supposed, on a hunting party   On my march this day between the advanced guard and the fort, I appointed three places of rendezvous to repair to, in case of being broke in an action, and acquainted every officer and soldier that I should rally the party at the nearest post to the fort, and if broke then to retreat to the second, and at the third to make a stand till the darkness of the night would give us an opportunity to get off   Soon after I halted I formed an ambush on a road leading from the fort to the woods, with an advanced party of twenty men and a rear guard of fifteen   About eleven o'clock a sergeant of marines came from the fort up the road to my advanced party, who let him pass to the main body, where I made him prisoner   Upon examination he reported 'that there were in the garrison 350 regulars, about fifty workmen, and but five Indians; that they had plenty of provisions, &c , and that twelve masons were constantly employed in blowing up rocks in the entrenchment, and a number of soldiers to assist them, that at Crown Point there were 150 soldiers and fourteen Indians, that Mons Montcalm was at Montreal, that 500 Ottowawas Indians wintered in Canada, and that 500 Rangers were lately raised in Canada, each man having a double-barrelled fuzee, and put under an experienced officer, well acquainted with the country, that he did not know whether the French intended to attack any of the English forts this winter or not, but that they expected a great number of Indians as soon as the ice would bear them, in order to go down to the English forts, and that all the bakers in Carillon were employed in making biscuit for the scouts above mentioned '

"About noon a Frenchman, who had been hunting, came near my party in his return, when I ordered a party to pursue him to the edge of the cleared ground, and take him prisoner, with this caution, to shoot off a gun or two, and then retreat to the main body, in order to intice the enemy from their fort, which orders were punctually obeyed, but not one of them ventured out

"The last prisoner, on examination, gave much the same account, but with this addition, 'that he had heard the English intended to attack Ticonderoga as soon as the lake was froze so as to bear them

"When I found the French would not come out of the Fort, we went about killing their cattle, and destroyed seventeen head, and set fire to the wood which they had collected for the use of the garrison, and consumed five large piles, the French shot off some cannon at the fires, but did us no harm   At eight o'clock at night I began my march homewards, and arrived at Fort Edward with my prisoners on the 27th "

In a document entitled *Journal of Occurrences in Canada*, 1757–58, printed with the *Paris Documents*, under date of January 2d, 1758, occurs the following entry "A courier from Carillon reports that the English showed themselves there on Christmas eve to the number of 150, with the design of setting fire to the houses under the curtain of the fort, that the cannon prevented them from doing so ; that they killed some fifteen beeves, to the horns of one of which the commander had affixed a letter couched in these words ·

"'I am obliged to you, sir, for the repose you have allowed me to take I thank you for the fresh meat you have sent me I will take care of my prisoners I request you to present my compliments to the Marquis de Montcalm

"'(Signed) ROGERS,

"'Commander of the Independent Companies '"

It seems strange that the English did not immediately, even if in midwinter, precipitate an attack upon these two important French strongholds, when it was shown that the forces that occupied them were so small

Again in March Rogers left Fort Edward with one hundred and eighty men to reconnoitre the vicinity of Ticonderoga, when near the foot of the lake they encountered a body of about a hundred Canadians and Indians These were dispersed and the march continued until the English were suddenly confronted with a large force in ambush A desperate conflict followed, the rangers fighting with a valor born of their knowledge that it was a question of life or death Nearly the entire detachment was slain and one hundred and forty-four scalps were carried to Montcalm Rogers, with a few of his men escaped This bloody affray was fought near the rock bearing Rogers's name, in the northeast corner of Warren county The battle was probably fought on snow-shoes, amid the rugged rocks and defiles of the mountains

Another heroic incident may be related here Major Putnam was employed early in the campaign in protecting the English communications and was stationed in a commanding position at a point near Whitehall, where he lake makes a sharp angle, now known as Fiddler's Elbow He was in command of thirty-five rangers, and on the eastern cliffs he built a stone breastwork, which he disguised with green boughs Here he patiently waited four days until, on the evening of the fourth day, his scout announced the approach of a flotilla Clear moonlight revealed every movement on the water When the foremost boats had passed the barricade the rangers poured destructive volleys upon them in rapid succession An attempt by part of the French to land was repulsed by twelve of the little band As dawn appeared Putnam found his ammunition expended and was forced to retire His only loss was two men wounded The location is still known as Put's Rock

In March Rogers was ordered to Albany for recruiting purposes, and met with a friendly reception from Lord Howe, who was then at Albany, organizing an army with which to begin operations as soon as practicable   Howe granted Rogers permission to visit New York, where he waited upon General Abercrombie, who had succeeded Lord Loudoun as commander-in-chief   Abercrombie commissioned Rogers major, his commission placing him at the head of all the scouts and rangers in that vicinity   On his return to Albany he reported to Lord Howe, who gave him his instructions, when he hurried on to Fort Edward, and resumed command of his celebrated corps

Three formidable expeditions were planned for this year   The first against Louisburg, the second against Fort Du Quesne, the third contemplated the clearing of the Champlain valley of French occupation

Admiral Boscowan, with twenty ships of the line and fifteen frigates, together with twelve thousand men under General Amherst arrived before Louisburg on the 3d of June   A vigorous siege was begun, which lasted until the 26th of July, when the French surrendered the position

The expedition against Du Quesne was commanded by General John Forbes, through whose dilatory action it came very near being disastrous and abandoned   After months of wasted time, Washington was sent forward and when within a day's march of the fort they were discovered by some Indians, who carried the news of their approach to the garrison   There were then but five hundred men in the fortification, and they on the 24th of November set it on fire and fled down the Ohio River

The capture of Ticonderoga and a descent upon Montreal was the more important, indeed it was the vital, point in the plans of the campaign   A force of about seven thousand regulars, nearly nine thousand provincials and a heavy train of artillery was assembled at the head of Lake George by the beginning of July   This was the finest army yet organized on the western continent, but unfortunately its command was given to General James Abercrombie   Judging well of his incapacity, Pitt sought to avert the probability of failure by the selection of Lord Howe, who was given the rank of brigadier-general and made the controlling spirit of the undertaking

At dawn on the morning of the 5th of July this splendid army embarked on Lake George in nine hundred bateaux and one hundred and thirty-five whale boats, the artillery being transported on rafts   It was an imposing fleet, such as had not before been seen on American waters   A halt was made at Sabbath-day Point for rest and refreshment just before evening, and at ten o'clock the army was again under headway   Early on the morning of the 6th a landing was made on the west side of the lake at a point which still bears the name of General Howe   Howe and Stark lay upon the same bear skin the previous night and discussed the situation at Carillon, a feeling of mutual regard sprang up between them

De Boulamarque had been stationed at the foot of the lake with three regiments, to oppose the landing of the English, but on their approach in such overwhelming numbers, he retreated to the fort, burning both the bridges across the outlet of Lake George, compelling Abercrombie to pursue his march through the pathless forest on the west side of the stream He left his baggage and stores at the deserted camp of De Boulamarque and took up the march directly for the French works, but the intricacy of the forest and the roughness of the ground soon broke up the columns While in this state of confusion they encountered a body of three hundred and fifty French and Indians, who had been detached under De Trèpesée, and had been for twelve hours endeavoring to tread their way through the almost impenetrable woods A skirmish ensued in which the French soldiers displayed great heroism, despite their exhausted condition, but were nearly all slain It proved a disastrous event to the English, for the gallant Lord Howe,[1] upon whom, as it developed, the success of the expedition depended, fell at the first fire The British regulars were appalled at the death of Howe and, unused to forest fighting, faltered and broke, but were gallantly sustained by the provincials The French general was also mortally wounded and almost the entire detachment slain or captured, with insignificant loss to the English [2]

With the death of Howe fled the hope of a successful campaign The chronic imbecility and apathy of the English returned and the army of sixteen thousand men, their only immediate enemy being four thousand under Montcalm, was withdrawn to Lake George on the morning of the 7th Bradstreet took possession of the saw-mill at the Falls about noon, rebuilt the bridges, and in the evening the army took up its position at that point, about two miles from the fort During this valuable period the French were strengthening their defenses The French position is thus described by Mr Watson "The promontory held by Montcalm was a narrow and elevated peninsula, washed on three sides by deep waters (see engraving), with its base on the western and only accessible side On the north of this base access was obstructed by a wet meadow, and on the southern extremity it was rendered impracticable to the advance of an army by a deep slope, extending from the hill to the outlet The summit between these two points was rounded and sinuous with ledges and elevations at intervals Here and about half a mile in advance of the fort Montcalm traced the line of his projected entrenchment It followed the sinuosities of the land, the sections of the works reciprocally flanking each other "

[1] This noble and brave officer being universally beloved by both officers and soldiers of the army, his fall was not only sincerely lamented, but seemed to produce an almost general consternation and languor through the whole — Hough in Rogers's Journal

[2] If the British army narrowly escaped by this panic a renewal of the bloody scenes on the Monongahela, it is equally probable, if Howe had lived, and a rapid and vigorous advance been made after the annihilation of Trèpesée's party, that the imperfect entrenchments of the French might have been entered and captured in the disorder and alarm of the moment But the bugle of Abercrombie sounded the retreat, and the opportunity was lost — Watson

The entrenchment, which was about an eighth of a league in length, was constructed by Dupont Le Roy, an accomplished engineer   " It was formed by
falling trunks of trees, one upon the other, and others felled in front, their
branches cut and sharpened produced the effect of a *chevaux de frise* "[1]   The
abatis was about one hundred yards in width   The entire day of the 7th was
spent by the French in energetic labor on this effective entrenchment, their
flags flying along the line and music playing, until the line arose to a height
of from eight to ten feet its entire length

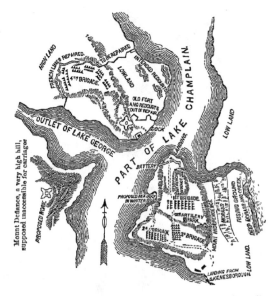

TICONDEROGA AND ITS DEPENDENCIES, AUGUST, 1776, FROM A PLAN DRAWN BY
COL. JOHN TRUMBULL

De Levis, who had organized an expedition against the Mohawk Valley,
was recalled to reinforce Ticonderoga, which was reached on the night of the
7th, by his four hundred veterans, he following at five o'clock the next morning, accompanied by the gallant De Senezergues   At about the same hour
Johnson joined the English camp with three or four hundred Mohawks

It is well settled that at this time it was Montcalm's intention to evacuate
Ticonderoga ; to the experienced military eye it must have seemed untenable,
and it is claimed that he did not decide upon a vigorous defense until the

---

[1] MONTCALM'S Report   Rogers says   " We toiled with repeated attacks for four hours, being
greatly embarrassed by trees that were felled by the enemy without their breastwork "

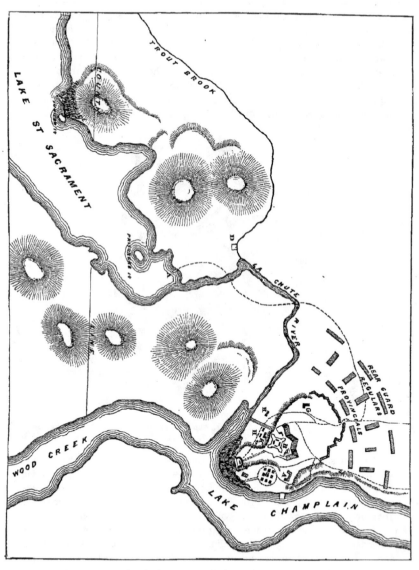

MAP OF THE OUTLET OF LAKE ST. SACRAMENT, TO ILLUSTRATE ABERCROMBIE'S ATTACK ON CARILLON.

From Butler's Lake George and Lake Champlain.

morning of the attack   His force on that day amounted to three thousand and six hundred men, four hundred and fifty of whom 'were irregular troops   The number of fighting men was two thousand nine hundred and ninety-two   The troops were called to the lines at daybreak and assigned their positions for the day and then returned to improve the precious hours on the entrench-ments   The meadow on the right, in front of which was a slight abatis, was occupied by the irregular troops   The fort guns commanded this opening as well as the slope on the extreme left   De Levis was placed on the right with three regiments   De Boulamarque held the left with an equal force, while Montcalm occupied the center with two battalions and pickets   The declivity towards the outlet was guarded by two companies   Behind each battalion was stationed in reserve a company of grenadiers   At the preconcerted signal (an alarm gun) the troops left their labors on the lines and were at their re-spective stations under arms just as the advance of the British appeared

Abercrombie was misled to the belief that reinforcements were on their way to Montcalm   This fact, with the added opinion of his engineer, Clarke, that the French lines were vulnerable to infantry (although the practiced eye of Stark saw otherwise and so reported), prompted Abercrombie to an im-mediate attack before the arrival of his powerful artillery

The imposing advance was made in three columns   First, rangers, bateau men and light infantry, next the provincials marched with wide openings be-tween the regiments, behind these openings were the regulars in columns, the New Jersey and Connecticut levies formed the rear   Johnson was posted with his force of Indians on Mount Defiance, then known as Sugar Loaf Hill He took little part in the battle.

The regulars rapidly advanced between the provincial regiments and hurled themseleves with intrepid bravery and great determination upon the abatis in front of the French   Two columns attacked the right, another the center, and a fourth was thrown upon the left   But when the almost insurmountable barrier was reached, its impenetrable thicket broke up all military order, while from be-hind the works came terrible volleys with murderous effectiveness   More he-roic valor or greater individual bravery has seldom been shown in battle than was exhibited by the British veterans, and seldom has the great advantage of even temporary entrenchments been more clearly established   The deadly fire of the French soldiers, protected by their abatis, and the cannonade from the howitzers posted at intervals along the line, told with fearful effect upon the assaulting army; but they heard no command to retreat, they had re-ceived their orders to advance, and although they could not surmount the works of the enemy, they could die in front of them   The fire of the provin-cials and their marksmen was perhaps more effective than the volleys of the regulars;[1] as Montcalm referred to " their murderous fire "

---

[1] "Their fire greatly incommoded those in the entrenchments." — POUCHOT

The details of this sanguinary battle need not be further pursued, they are emblazoned on the pages of many a history   The assault was hopeless from the beginning, and while its bloody scenes were being enacted under the watchful eye of the brilliant French general, Abercrombie looked after the welfare of his noble person amid the security of the saw-mills, two miles from the battle-field   All day long the battle raged, and between the hours of six and seven the heroic columns still continued to charge upon the French lines   But the time for retreat had arrived, it should have arrived earlier, and regiment after regiment, weary and decimated and without any general order, retired to the camp, their retreat covered by the provincials   Then followed one of those strange panics to which armies, made up of the bravest material, have often been subject   From some influence that is difficult to comprehend, a feeling of terror spead through the ranks, and a wild flight ensued   Nothing but the prompt firmness of Bradstreet prevented further sacrifice   That immediate pursuit did not follow was due only to the comparative feebleness of the enemy and the impracticability of traversing the forest without Indian guides   De Levis went over the track of Abercrombie's army on the morning of the 10th and found only the vestiges of a routed host, and before that hour the English general had dishonorably placed the length of Lake George between him and his conquerors

Abercrombie admitted the loss of about two thousand men, but the French placed it much heavier, claiming their own to be less than five hundred   Boulamarque was severly and Bougainville slightly wounded

This terrible and probably unnecessary catastrophe was partially offset by the successful siege of Frontenac, which capitulated to Bradstreet on the 26th of August, but the while Abercrombie dallied in helpless indecision, Montcalm, reinforced on the 12th of July by the younger Vaudreuil with three thousand Canadians, and by six hundred Indians on the 18th,[1] was vigilant and persistent, striking wherever and whenever he could detect a vulnerable point

" On Friday, the 20th of July, succeeding this event," says Holden, in his *History of Queensbury*, " a detachment of four hundred men, consisting of Canadians and Indians, under the command of M de Luc la Corne, a colonial officer, attacked an English force of one hundred and fifty men, consisting of teamsters and an escort of soldiers, while on their way from the station at the Half-way Brook, to the camp at the head of the lake   The account here given is as nearly as can be remembered in the language of a Mr. Jones, of Connecticut, who was a member of Putnam's company which arrived on the ground soon after the affray took place   In the year 1822 he related the circumstances as here recorded to the late Herman Peck, esq, of this place, while on a visit to Connecticut   It is from Mr Peck that I obtained the narrative,

---

[1] Abercrombie uses the fact of the arrival of these reinforcements to justify himself for attacking the French before the arrival of his artillery

which corresponds so completely with the French version of the affair that there can be no question whatever as to its general accuracy and reliability

" A baggage train of sixty carts, each cart drawn by two or three yoke of oxen, accompanied by an unusually large escort of troops, was dispatched from Fort Edward to the head of Lake George with supplies for the troops of General Abercrombie, who lay encamped at that point with a force of twelve thousand men   This party halted for the night at the stockade post at the Half-way Brook   As they resumed their march in the morning, and before the escort had fairly cleared the picketed enclosure, they were suddenly attacked by a large party of French and Indians which lay concealed in the thick bushes and reeds that bordered the stream, and lined the road on both sides along the low lands between the block-house and the Blind Rock

" The night previous to this ambuscade and slaughter, Putnam's company of rangers, having been to the lake to procure supplies, encamped at the flats near the southern spur of the French Mountain   In the early morning they were aroused from their slumbers by the sound of heavy firing in a southerly direction, and rolling up their blankets they sprang to their arms and hastened rapidly forward to the scene of action a distance of about four miles.   They arrived only in time to find the slaughtered carcasses of some two hundred and fifty oxen, the mangled remains of the soldiers, women and teamsters, and the broken fragments of the two-wheeled carts, which constituted in that primitive age the sole mode of inland transportation

" The provisions and stores had been plundered and destroyed   Among the supplies were a large number of boxes of chocolate which had been broken open and their contents strewed upon the ground, which, dissolving in the fervid heat of the summer sun, mingled with the pools and rivulets of blood, forming a sickening and revolting spectacle   The convoy had been ambushed and attacked immediately after leaving the protection of the stockade post, and the massacre took place upon the flats between the Half-way Brook and the Blind Rock, or what is more commonly known at the present day as the Miller place

"Putnam, with his command, took the trail of the marauders, which soon became strewed with fragments of plunder dropped by the rapidly retreating savages

" They were followed to Ganaouske Bay, on the west side of Lake George, where Putnam arrived only in time to find them embarked in their canoes, at a safe distance from musket shot, on the waters of the lake, and their discovery was responded to by insulting and obscene gestures, and yells of derision and defiance   The provincials returned immediately to the scene of the butchery, where they found a company from Fort Edward engaged in preparing a trench for the interment of the dead

" Over one hundred of the soldiers composing the escort were slain, many of whom were recognized as officers, from their uniform, consisting in part of red velvet breeches   The corpses of twelve females were mingled with the dead bodies of the soldiery   All the teamsters were supposed to have been killed   While the work of burial was going forward the rangers occupied themselves in searching the trails leading through the dense underbrush and tangled briars which covered the swampy plains   Several dead bodies were by these means added to the already large number of the slain   On the side of one of these trails, the narrator of these events saw a new unhemmed bandana handkerchief fluttering from the twigs of an old tree that lay among the weeds near the brook   This he found perforated with a charge of buck shot, part of which remained enveloped in its folds

"Following up the trail, he soon found the corpse of a woman which had been exposed to the most barbarous indignities and mutilations, and fastened in an upright position to a sapling which had been bent over for that purpose   All of the bodies had been scalped, and most of them mangled in a horrible manner

"One of the oxen had no other injury than to have one of its horns cut out, it was still alive and bellowing with agony   This they were obliged to kill

"Another ox had been regularly scalped   This animal was afterwards driven to the lake, where it immediately became an object of sympathy and attention of the whole army   By careful attendance and nursing, the wound healed in the course of the season   In the fall the animal was driven down to the farm of Colonel Schuyler, near Albany, and the following year was shipped to England for exhibition as a curiosity   Far and wide it was known as the scalped ox   The bodies of the dead were buried in a trench near the scene of massacre, a few rods east of the picketed enclosure   The French version of the affair states 'the oxen were killed, the carts burnt, the property pillaged by the Indians, one hundred and ten scalps were secured, and eighty-four prisoners taken, of these twelve are women and girls   The escort which was defeated consisted of forty men commanded by a lieutenant who has been taken   The remainder who were killed or taken prisoners consisted of wagoners, sutlers, traders, women and children   The English 'tis known feel this loss very sensibly   Some baggage and effects belonging to General Abercrombie, as well as his music, were among the plunder   On the news of this defeat, the English general sent a very considerable force in pursuit, under the command of the partisan Robert Rogers, but he was too late   He was on the point of returning, when, on the advice of a colonial gunner, a deserter, he received orders to lay in ambush to surprise a third detachment which the Marquis de Montcalm had just dispatched under the orders of M Marin, a colonial officer of great reputation   This detachment was composed of fifty regulars, one hundred Canadians, and one hundred and fifty Indians   That of the enemy, of about seven hundred men   They met in the woods, about seven o'clock in the morning of the eighth of August, and in spite of superior numbers, M. Marin made his arrangements to fight the enemy

" He forced them to waver by two volleys, which killed a great many , but having been supported by the regulars, they rallied, and the firing was brisk on both sides for nearly an hour   M Marin, perceiving that they were receiving a reinforcement, and that the Indians, who feared that they would not be able to carry off some wounded, demanding to retire, he was obliged to think of retreating, which he did in good order, and without being pursued, after having, for an hour longer kept up a fire with such picked men as he had, who performed prodigies of valor   The Indians, in general, have also behaved well; but of one hundred Canadians, more than sixty deserted M Marin, no one knows wherefore, at the very moment when the English were wavering   The English loss is reported in this account at upwards of two hundred killed and two officers taken prisoners   The French loss is stated at ten killed and eleven wounded   The scene of this engagement was near Fort Anne ' Rogers's journal estimates the French loss at one hundred and ninety-nine "

Putnam and a few others were cut off from the main body   The men were slain, and Putnam captured and securely bound to a tree   As the changes of the battle surged around him, he was placed at times between the fire of the contending parties and his garments torn by the shots, alike by friend and foe. While in this helpless condition, a young Indian approached and amused himself with the strange pastime of hurling his tomahawk at the prisoner, practicing how near he could approach without hitting the mark   A still more savage Canadian presented his gun at Putnam's breast, but it missed fire   He then indulged his fierce passions by inflicting upon the prisoner several severe wounds with the butt of the weapon   When the French were repulsed and commenced their retreat, his Indian captor released Putnam and extended to him that mysterious tenderness and care with which the Indians treat their victims destined to the torture   The savages encamped at night, and then the strange motive that actuated this kindness was revealed   Putnam, stripped of his clothing, was again tied to a sappling; dried fagots were piled about him, the torch applied, and while the smoke and crackling flames began to ascend, the thoughts of the brave ranger dwelt upon his happy home and prattling children When the agony of death in this frightful form was almost passed, the generous Marin, who had learned of his peril, rushed to the spot, and bursting through the circle of shouting savages, scattered the firebrands and rescued the victim In the ensuing autumn Putnam was exchanged and returned to new fields of glory, but to none of such appalling horror

About this time there were three picketed forts or stockades constructed along the line of the old military road   One was "on what was then called Picket Brook, a small rivulet which crosses the plank road about one-eighth of a mile south of the upper toll-gate by Brown's Half-way House (at French Mountain), and empties into a stream known in the earlier annals of the town as Hampshire Creek or Rocky Brook, but now called Trout Brook   This fortification was erected on the south side of the rivulet, to which led a covered way, even now to be distinctly traced   It was called Fort Williams "[1]   One was at Half-way Brook, and was used as a depot for provisions and stores   A third, " capable of accommodating about three hundred men was built somewhere near the site of Richards's steam saw-mill, on the berme side of the Glens Falls feeder, and east of the bridge on the road leading to Sandy Hill

.   Connected with this fort was a burial ground which has been in use so lately as since the Revolutionary war " [2]

.

CHAPTER IX

EXTINCTION OF FRENCH POWER IN AMERICA

Continuation of the Famine — Exigencies of the French — Montcalm's Prophecies — Pitt's Zeal and its Effect — The Proposed Campaign — Abercrombie's Recall and Amherst's Appointment — His Extensive Military Preparations — Assembling His Army — Montcalm Asks to be Recalled — Capture of Ticonderoga and Crown Point by Amherst — Fort Gage — Destruction of the Indian Village of St Francis — Rogers's Wonderful Expedition — Amherst's Fleet and its Operations — Gen Wolfe before Quebec — Fall of the City — Montcalm and Wolfe killed — Strengthening of Crown Point and Ticonderoga — Campaign of 1760 — Extinction of French Power in the New World

WHILE the events recorded in the preceding chapter would seem to indicate an early approaching triumph of the French cause in America, the reverse was the fact   Canada was suffering the actual horrors of famine and was almost depopulated of males who had reached maturity, to swell the ranks of the military   The ocean teemed with British ships, rendering it practically impossible for France to grant the appeal   " We want provisions, we want powder, and France should send ten thousand men to preserve the colony "   For three years, against odds that would, in any other hands than those of the incompetent English commanders, have crushed him in a single campaign, the brave Montcalm had preserved the French possessions, but in the spring of 1759 he wrote the government minister   " If the war continues, Canada will belong to England, perhaps this campaign or the next "   And then referring to the gross corruption, jealous wrangles and insolence of the French officials towards the Canadians, added in the same letter   " If there be peace the colony is lost unless the entire government is changed "   Moreover, a feel-

---

[1] HOLDEN's *History of Queensbury*   [2] Ibid

ing of jealousy and ill-will had grown up between Montcalm and Vaudreuil and was fostered by the brilliant military exploits of the former, while the latter, from his position of authority, carried to the throne imputations against Montcalm of insubordination, neglect of instructions, lack of adaptation to the command in Canada, and a personal deportment that alienated the alliance of the Indians This spirit was reflected upon and infused into the army, while the savages, although still professing fealty, failed to rally to the French cause as they had formerly done A large body of warriors had been promised Montcalm at Ticonderoga, with the aid of which he felt that he could have successfully pursued and overwhelmed Abercrombie The warriors did not appear until too late, when they were rebuked by Montcalm [1] The chiefs complained to Vaudreuil and he promptly carried their complaints to Versailles

While this untoward state of affairs with the French was growing worse, the zeal of Pitt was stirring the sluggish British to action The proposed campaign involved, besides the conquest of Ticonderoga, the capture of Fort Niagara and the siege of Quebec. On the 27th of July General Prideaux, who was joined by Johnson at Oswego, appeared before Niagara, but the siege had scarcely begun when he was slain Johnson then assumed command and the siege continued On the 24th a large body of French and Indians attempted to raise the siege A sharp conflict ensued and the effort was defeated The garrison surrendered the next day.

With the fall of Louisburg, as already recorded, General Amherst embarked four or five regiments and hurried to Boston, whence he marched across the country for Lake George, reaching there in October (1758) Abercrombie had already been recalled (September) and Amherst given the command of all the forces in North America, which he assumed in November [2]

Amherst [3] began at once his preparations for an active campaign He proved to be the right man for the emergency, and the colonies had need of all their confidence in him and his proposed measures, for he called for more than seventeen hundred recruits, a number that appalled them, coming as an addition to their already heavy sacrifices But inspired by the enthusiasm of Pitt and relying on the genius of Amherst, the colonies yielded up their men and means

Rogers, with an augmented force of rangers, under Stark and other Indian

---

[1] When the chiefs proposed to take the war path toward Fort Edward, Montcalm told them to "go to the d—l "

[2] Abercrombie returned to England, evaded censure, was gladdened by promotion, and lived to vote as a member of Parliament for the taxation of a country, which his imbecility might have lost, and which was always the object of his malignant aspersions — BANCROFT

[3] Amherst, without any claim to brilliancy or genius, was calculated to command success by the excellence of his judgment, his prudent circumspection, and persevering firmness His character and policy had secured to him the respect and confidence of the colonies His measures were not stimulated by the arrogance of Braddock, nor trammeled by the feebleness and indecision of Abercrombie, nor dishonored by the pusillanimity of Webb — WATSON

veteran fighters, was constantly on the move, harassing the enemy's outposts, capturing prisoners, sometimes singly and often in considerable numbers, but always enduring the severest hardships and occasionally suffering defeat   The shores of Lake George and the upper end of Lake Champlain constituted the field of operations, and there was hardly a mile contiguous to the banks of either from Fort George to Crown Point that was not the scene of some thrilling incident connected with the war

"General Gage, who was a prominent officer in Amherst's campaign, being assigned to leading and important duties, with a strong detachment was sent forward in advance of the main army, and taking position at the head of the lake, proceeded to the erection of some temporary defenses on a commanding eminence, spoken of as Element Hill in one of the soldier's journals, to the west of the old Fort William Henry, to which was given the name of Fort Gage,[1] in honor of its builder   Gage was soon after joined by Stark with three companies of rangers   Rogers, with the other three companies, remained at Fort Edward, engaged in frequent scouts and reconnaissances, under the immediate supervision of Amherst in person"

Continuing our extract from Dr Holden   "The main body of the army was put in motion in the early part of June, and after three days' march General Amherst encamped with his entire force at Fort Edward   Here the troops were again placed under a rigid system of discipline, exercise, and drill to prepare them for their coming duties   The raw and inexperienced provincials who composed the greater portion of the army, unused to the irksome and rigid requirements of stern military rules, soon manifested a disposition to return to the homes from which they had been so unceremoniously torn   Wearied and heartsick of the monotonous camp duties assigned them, with a certain prospect of a dangerous march and a sanguinary battle-field before them, the spirit of insubordination[2] and desertion spread to an alarming extent ; the provincials by twos, threes and even whole platoons stealing off to the woods, despite the most exacting vigilance, and animated appeals to their patriotism and courage   At length Amherst found it necessary to resort to the terrible death penalty to stay the progress of the alarming defection in his fast dwindling

---

[1] HOLDEN in his *History of Queensbury*, from which the above extract is taken, says, in a foot-note, concerning this fort that he "has sought diligently for some account or description of this fortification, whose name and site, tradition has preserved for more than a century, but none has been found   It is on the authority of the late Hon William Hay, of Saratoga Springs, that the period above named is given as the date of its construction   It was probably little more than a redoubt, and intended as a flank support to the main fortifications now known as the ruins of Fort George"

[2] Thomas Burk, waggoner, tryed by a court martiall of the line for abusing and offering to strick his officer at Half-way brook, is found guilty of the crime laid to his charge, and sentenced to receive four hundred lashes   The general approves of the above sentence, and orders that the said Thomas Burk is marched to-morrow morning at 5 o'clock by the provost guard, regiment to regiment and that he receives 30 lashes at each of the four regular regiments, beginning at Forbse's and so on to the right   That he also receives 30 lashes each at the head of 8 provincial regiments, and 40 at the head of Schuyler's —WILSON'S *Orderly Book*

army Four deserters, Dunwood, Ward, Rogers and Harris by name, were apprehended, and after a trial by court martial, were shot in the sight of the whole army, which was drawn out in battle array to witness the execution This stringent measure had the desired effect in stopping the progress of desertion "[1]

"Towards the close of June, the army, amounting to six thousand men, preceded by Rogers's rangers, advanced in two colums to the head of Lake George, where they erected their camp, very nearly on the ground occupied by Abecrombie the year before On the following day Amherst traced a plan for a fortification near the camp ground, which was soon afterwards constructed, and whose ruins are now crumbling in massive piles upon the shrub-grown eminence to the east of the village of Caldwell While the army remained posted at this position several days elapsed in bringing up, from the various posts below, the artillery, heavy stores, boats and baggage, necessary for prosecuting the siege of Forts Carillon and St Frederic

"During this time the corvette, *Halifax*, which had been sunk at the head of the lake after Abecrombie's retreat the preceding year, was raised and refitted, together with several bateaux, and a large floating battery, in which labor Captain Loring of the English navy, lent his most efficient aid In the mean time several skirmishes both by land and water occurred between the scouting parties of the opposing forces, in the majority of which the French were triumphant "

During the ensuing month Amherst's army was swelled to more than eleven thousand effective men, and on the 21st of July, 1759, the bosom of Lake George was again the scene of a gorgeous array of boats bearing this army towards their enemies A landing was made on the eastern shore, nearly opposite Howe's Cove, whence he was prepared for his successful march against Ticonderoga

The unhappy condition of the French had already impelled Montcalm to ask repeatedly for his own recall, a request that was as often endorsed by Vaudreuil, but the home government appreciated the genius of the general at its true value and sent him the following dispatch · " You must not expect to receive any military reinforcements, we will convey all the provisions and ammunition possible, the rest depends on your wisdom and courage and the

---

[1] Of the severity of the discipline followed in this campaign, the following is an illustration
                                                    "TICONDEROGA, 3d August, 1759.
   "George Edwards a deserter from the 17th regiment is to suffer death The Picquits of the line to assemble immediately in front of Montgomerys The commanding officer of Forbes will order that regiment to erect a gallows imediately on the battery in front of Montgomerys, where the prisoner, George Edwards is to be hanged in his French coat, with a libble on his breast, *Hanged for deserting to the French* He is to be hanging all day and at the retreat beating he is to be buried very deep under the gallows, and his French coat with him This to be put in execution instantly and if the provost martiall does not find a hangman, the commanding officer of the Picquitts will order that provost martiall does it himself "—WILSON's *Orderly Book*, p 113

bravery of your troops" Our sympathy must go out to the gallant officer who was constrained to turn his thoughts from his family and his wasting estate and give up his life for a falling fabric. He wrote a friend in France. 'There are situations where nothing remains for a general but to die with honor "

Amherst arranged his forces in four columns, the center ones consisting entirely of regulars, and led by himself while the two flanking columns, composed mainly of provincial troops, were commanded by General Gage His whole force numbered eleven thousand eight hundred and thirty-three men, with a section of the royal artillery and fifty-four guns of various calibre

On the 21st of July the army landed and bivouacked at the same point where Abercrombie had camped the year before. The next day they reached the foot of the lake and disembarked Rogers with his rangers pushed forward across the mountain ridge, and took possession of the bridge and sawmills at the lower falls On what is now known as Mount Hope they were met by a squad of French and Indians and a skirmish followed The latter were readily dispersed and retreated hastily to the fort That night Amherst with his whole force occupied the heights around the fort, resting upon their arms

The next morning the rangers were pushed forward to a point on the shore of the lake partly flanking the enemy's batteries, while a force attacked the works in front, carrying the first entrenchment and forcing the enemy inside the fort While these preliminary operations were going on the provincials were engaged in hauling the artillery and ammunition over the "carrying-place" from Lake George As soon as the artillery was in position and his lines formed Amherst moved forward to make the final assault To his surprise he found the entrenchments almost unoccupied The circumstances surrounding the abandonment of the post by the French, as narrated in Holden's *History of Queensbury*, were as follows —

"The defense of the frontier of Lake St Sacrament and fortress of Carillon was entrusted at this time to M de Boulemarque, an officer of distinguished ability, who for two campaigns had served with great success in this vicinity The garrison consisted of one battalion of the regiment of La Reine, two battalions of the regiments of Berry, one hundred and fifty soldiers detached from the other five battalions, an equal number of soldiers of the marine, and eight hundred provincial militia, making an aggregate of two thousand three hundred men His instructions, based upon dispatches recently received from the court of France, were not to hazard an engagement but to fall back before the advance of the English army, and take position upon an island in the river St John which was judged to be the post best adapted to protect the frontier The main body of the French and Canadian forces were at this time drawn away by Montcalm to the north for the defense of the almost impregnable stronghold of Quebec, which was being threatened by the veteran brigades under the command of the daring Wolfe

8

" M de Boulemarque, finding the English army too well prepared for an attack, and he being too circumspect to trust the event of a siege, prudently resolved to act in conformity with his instructions and abandon the fortress to its inevitable fate. Accordingly preparations were made for a retreat, and during the night of the 23d the main division of the army filed noiselessly out and retired to their boats The final defense of the post was committed to the care of Captain d'Hébecourt and four hundred men During the retreat of the main body the attention of the British army was diverted by the assault of this small force upon the entrenchments. This threw the English lines into such confusion that they fired upon each other, thus enabling the assaulting party to retire in safety to their defenses In this affray the English lost sixteen men During the next three days the fire from the French batteries was maintained with great activity and effect holding the English well in check Among the killed in these discharges was Colonel Townsend, assistant adjutant-general, an officer of great ability and universally beloved throughout the army

" During this period the English engineers were busily engaged in planting siege batteries, while a portion of the army was employed in preparing fascines At the same time a portion of the rangers was dispatched on a scout to Crown Point To Major Rogers was entrusted the important duty of cutting away a large boom which the French had built across the narrow part of the lake, opposite the fort, to obstruct the navigation   .

" On the evening of the 26th some deserters brought to the English camp intelligence that the French had abandoned the fort, and that, in expectation of an assault from the besieging army, a slow match had been left burning which connected with the magazine and battery, every gun of which was loaded to the muzzle with grape, canister and chain shot In addition to this, several mines charged with the most destructive missiles were sprung beneath the fortifications This timely notice saved the English forces At ten o'clock at night, in the sight of th · whole British army, which was drawn out in anticipation of the spectacle, the most terrific explosion took place Running along the cleft chasms in the rocky ground the yellow fire rushed, greedily lapping with the forked tongues of its lambent flame the gaping crevices in the massive masonry, that trembled, reeled and fell, while the solid earth for many rods shook as with the throes of an earthquake One after another the guns of the fortress flashed out from the sulphurous glow that invested the ruined pile, and their sharp reports were slowly answered by long, dull echoes from the deep caverns beneath Bombs, grenades and rockets, booming and whirring through the heavy night air, exploded in every direction, trailing earthward long and glittering lines of various colored light Soon, through the dim haze of smoke and vapor the glaring red light of the barracks and woodwork of the fortress burst forth, revealing through the veil of surrounding gloom, the ruined wrecks hurled in unsightly piles along the line of fortification, while here and there a long gaping fissure in the smoking earth exhibited the direction of the mines, and the tremendous agencies which had toppled down the massive ramparts and towering bastions from their rocky bases."[1]

General Amherst, mistaking the then inevitable current of events and consequently magnifying the importance of Ticonderoga and Crown Point after their capture, began the work of erecting a new fortress near the site of St Frederic but of vastly greater strength and magnitude   The conquest of Canada left the fortification useless and unfinished after an expenditure of more than ten million dollars   He also began the vigorous construction of a naval flotilla for Lake Champlain which should permanently secure its conquest While this work was progressing two measures of considerable importance were ordered by Amherst   The first was the construction of a military road from Crown Point to Charlestown on the Connecticut River   This was an improvement of great value at that time and opened up a large territory to settlement earlier than would have been the case without it   It is said that the remains of this work may still be traced   The other measure contemplated the destruction of the Indian village of St Francis on the river of that name about midway between Montreal and Quebec   Rogers was selected for the undertaking and given command of one hundred and forty-two men   He descended the lake with caution and on the tenth day concealed his boats at the foot of Missisqui Bay, leaving two Indians to watch them   Two days later he was overtaken by the Indians with the information that he was followed by the French, who had captured his boats and were in ambush awaiting his return In this emergency he conceived the bold and hazardous design of prosecuting his original purpose, after which he would march through the wilderness to the "Cohase Intervales," a point sixty miles north of Charlestown on the Connecticut River, and the northernmost English post on that stream   He immediately dispatched eight of his men under Lieutenant McMullin through the wilderness to Crown Point with a request to Amherst to send the necessary supplies to meet him at the designated point on the Connecticut   On the evening of the twenty-second day of their march the little band reached the vicinity of the Indian village, which was carefully reconnoitered   At dawn the next morning they fell upon the unsuspecting savages, of whom few escaped, about two hundred were killed   Daylight revealed to the victors the sight of more than six hundred English scalps of both sexes and all ages floating from the lodge poles of the Indians   If this massacre of the village seems a cold and blood-thirsty deed, the finding of these dread trophies of savage atrocities against helpless Europeans must modify our deprecation of it   Rogers loaded his men with what plunder they could carry and started for the Connecticut   He was pursued by a body of Indians who hung upon his rear, repeatedly attacking

[1] HOLDEN's *History of Que nsbury*

him   He was finally forced to divide his party in order to more readily procure subsistence, which policy left him still more exposed to the assaults of the
Indians, who killed many and captured a number of prisoners.   Rogers and the
remainder of his men reached the appointed place on the Connecticut after
much hardship, only to find it deserted by the men who had been sent by
Amherst with supplies   Rogers then took with him one ranger and an Indian
youth and started to descend the river on a raft , the journey was at last accomplished after the most perplexing trials and inflexible determination, and
supplies were forwarded to the waiting rangers   Rogers returned to Crown
Point on the 1st of December, and when the scattered parties were reassembled
he reported a loss of three officers and forty-six privates

Meanwhile the construction of Amherst's navy was progressing under direction of Captain Loring, and by the 11th of October there were finished a
sloop carrying sixteen guns, a brigantine and radeau mounting six cannon of
large calibre   Under escort of these vessels, Amherst embarked his army on
bateaux and sailed down the lake on his long deferred expedition towards
Quebec   On the following day twelve of his boats were foundered in a gale
and the remainder of the fleet sought shelter in lee of the western shores [1]
Loring took the brigantine and sloop, continued on down the lake and forced
the French to destroy two of their vessels in a bay on the northeast of Valcour
Island , a third was sunk, and one schooner only was saved by seeking shelter
under the guns of Isle aux Noix   It is believed that Amherst's extreme caution more than the exigencies of the situation, caused him to return to Crown
Point after an absence of ten days, instead of pressing on to the relief of Wolfe

This brave but fated officer found himself before Quebec in June, with
eight thousand men in transports under convoy of twenty-two line-of-battle
ships   He landed his men on the Isle of Orleans, three miles below the town,
and on the 30th seized Point Levi, opposite the city, on which he erected batteries   Several unsuccessful efforts were made to cut out and destroy the
French shipping, and two months passed during which little progress had been
made towards the capture of the city   Neither had any intelligence been received from Amherst other than report by the enemy that he had retreated
General Wolfe was prostrated by sickness and the future looked gloomy, but

---

[1] Mr. Watson in his *History of Essex County* concludes that Amherst probably advanced under his
adverse circumstances to the vicinity of Valcour Island and there on the mainland formed an encampment   In support of this conclusion he quotes as follows from the writings of Alvin Colvin, esq   "I
adopt this conclusion from the language of an English writer of the period, and from the popular traditions of the region   Those are still living who recollect an opening on the pine bluffs, south of the
Ausable River and directly upon the boundary line between Clinton and Essex counties, which, in the
early part of the century, was known as Amherst's encampment.   It exhibited vestiges of extensive
field-works, the habitual caution of Amherst would have led him to erect, and also the remains of tar
manufactories, formed in the primitive manner of the pioneers   It is a singular coincidence that the
tar and pitch used in the equipment of Macdonough's fleet more than fifty years afterwards, were made
on the same ground and by a similar process."

a council of officers called at his bedside decided to scale the heights of Abraham from the St Lawrence and assault the town Feeble as Wolfe was, he resolved to lead the attack The camp below the Montmorency was broken up on the 8th of September and Montcalm's attention was diverted from the real movement by seeming preparations to attack his lines On the 12th the vessels bearing the army moved up the stream above the intended landing place At midnight the troops left the ships and proceeded in flat boats and with muffled oars to the landing, where a ravine led up to the plains In early morning the entire English force had reached the destination and were ready to attack the works

Meanwhile Montcalm saw the coming doom and on the 24th of August wrote with realistic forecast " The capture of Quebec must be the work of a *coup de main* The English are masters of the river They have but to effect a descent on the bank on which this city, without fortification and without defense, is situated, and they are at once in condition to offer me battle which I cannot refuse and which I ought not to be permitted to gain In fine, Mr Wolfe, if he understands his business, has but to receive my first fire, to rush rapidly upon my army, to discharge his volley at close quarters, and my Canadians, without discipline, deaf to the call of the drum and trumpet, and thrown into disorder by this assault, will be unable to recover their ranks. They have no bayonets to meet those of their enemy, nothing remains for them but flight, and I am routed irretrievably "

" Mr Wolfe ' understood his business This plan of assault, so clearly practicable to the experienced eye of the French general, was substantially carried out and after a sanguinary battle (the details of which are beyond the province of this work) the victory was won, with a thousand prisoners and five hundred French killed, among whom was the brave Montcalm The English loss was six hundred killed and wounded, among the former being the gallant Wolfe, who received three wounds early in the attack, the third one being mortal General Townsend now prepared to besiege the city itself "Threatened famine within aided him," and five days after the death of Wolfe (September 18, 1759), Quebec with its fortifications, shipping, stores and people was surrendered to the English General Murray, with five thousand troops, took possession, and the fleet with the sick and prisoners sailed for Halifax

For the fall of Quebec Montcalm was largely held responsible and was even charged with deliberately sacrificing it to gratify his jealousy of Vaudreuil, but a calm view of the situation in the brilliant light of his previous heroic services will hardly substantiate such charges Vaudreuil returned to France after the capitulation, and he also became an object of persecution and unjust censure

A period of quiet followed these events, during which Amherst devoted his energies to the extension of the works at Ticonderoga, the erection of the great fortress at Crown Point, and began the building of Fort George [1]

A comparative brief campaign in 1760 completed the conquest of the French in the New World De Levis made a heroic effort to recapture Quebec in the battle of Sillery, in which Murray suffered a disastrous defeat, but it came too late to permanently re-establish the fortunes of France Amherst's plans for the year 1760 embraced his own advance upon Montreal by way of Oswego and the St Lawrence, for which purpose he reserved for himself by far the strongest column of the army, numbering about ten thousand men With this invincible force he moved with his accustomed deliberation and caution and appeared before Montreal on the 6th of September Haviland was left in command of the fortresses on Lake Champlain, from which locality several successful incursions were made against Canadian settlements under command of Rogers, while awaiting the deliberate movements of Amherst On the 16th of August the last military pageant of this war left Crown Point and sailed down the lake It comprised about three thousand regulars and provincials under Haviland, who were embarked in bateaux under convoy of four war vessels, with an equal number of radeaux bearing heavy armaments Bougainville occupied the Isle aux Noix, which he had strengthened by anchoring a fleet of small vessels on his flank He had sixteen hundred men Haviland reached the main land opposite the island without opposition, where he erected batteries The vessels of the French were dispersed or captured and on the night of the 20th they abandoned the position The fortifications at St Johns and Chambly were evacuated at the same time, the garrisons falling back towards Montreal Meanwhile Murray had ascended the river from Quebec and joined Amherst before Montreal, where Haviland formed a junction on the 7th of September Here was gathered all that remained of the chivalry of France in the New World, with their allies, to oppose the last attack, the success of which would drive them from the country forever However honorable to the French arms, the struggle was hopelessly unequal and

---

[1] Concerning the erection of this fort Dr. Holden, in his *History of Queensbury*, says " The plan of Fort George was marked out by Colonel James Montressor, chief engineer on General Amherst's staff, on the 22d of June, 1759 It was laid out on an elevation situated about six hundred yards south from the head of the lake, and about the same distance easterly from the site of old Fort William Henry It was known in colloquial parlance as ' Montressor's Folly ' The only portion of the fort ever com pleted was the southwest bastion A temporary stockaded post was built within its protection, also officers' barracks, soldiers' barracks, guard-room, kitchen and store-houses A saw mill in the swamp, southwest from the fort, furnished a great portion of the material for these buildings An irregular wall to the northeast, whose ruins are still partly visible, enclosed a space devoted to gardening purposes In 1776 there were erected for hospital use two buildings, one on the flat below the fort, and the other, of considerable dimensions, near the former site of Fort William Henry, which were used for the accommodation of General Schuyler's army, then lying at Fort Edward To these were probably added others, for in the army correspondence of those days we learn that over three thousand troops were invalided here with the small-pox   . At the time it was taken possession of by Burgoyne's advance there were fourteen pieces of artillery here, only two of which were mounted "

on the 8th of September Vaudreuil capitulated and New France, with all of its dependencies, fell into the hands of the British Amherst made terms of generous magnanimity and the details were soon agreed upon, while England sent up a national shout of exultation Although hostilities between the two nations ceased, a formal peace was not established until 1763, when, on the 10th of February, the treaty of Paris was signed, by which France ceded to Great Britain all her possessions in Canada

On the 30th of July, 1760, Governor De Lancey, of New York, suddenly died and the government passed into the hands of Cadwallader Colden, who was commissioned lieutenant-governor in August, 1761 In October of that year General Robert Monkton was appointed governor of New York

CHAPTER X

EARLY SETTLEMENTS

Pioneers of Northern New York — Governor De Lancey's Proclamation — Its Effect on Settlements — Jeffrey Cowper — Queensbury Surveyed — Abraham Wing's Advent — His Family — The Queensbury Patent — Names of the Original Proprietors — Their Early Meetings and Action — Division of Lots — Steps toward Permanent Settlement

THE tumult of the war we have attempted to describe had scarcely ceased and the new reign of peace begun in the land, before the adventurous pioneer found his way into the wilderness of Northern New York in quest of a home where he and his descendants could enjoy the fruits of his labor The territory known as the New Hampshire grants, over which there had been so much strife, was already echoing with the sounds of the settler's axe From Charlestown, No 4, in that territory John Goffe, in charge of eight hundred levies, cut the road already alluded to through the wilderness to Crown Point, where he joined Colonel Haviland in his expedition against Montreal , and through the lands of Queensbury hunters and trappers made their trails and disbanded soldiers explored among the often trod battle-fields for eligible sites for homes on lands given to them under military grants There were small clearings about the three picketed forts which have been mentioned as erected during the French war along the line of the old military road , beyond these almost the entire territory was unbroken wilderness Northward from Albany the only settlements were a small hamlet at Fort Edward and a still smaller one at Stillwater, and the tide of immigration soon to begin its flow northward had not yet set in But while the smoke of battle had but just disappeared and there still lingered possible danger to the exposed northern frontier, already repeatedly devastated by the hand of war, it was felt that there was a necessity for taking steps that would lead to its settlement by a class of inhabitants peculiarly adapted to withstand any incursion from hostile forces   In pursuance of this action Lieutenant-Governor De Lancey issued the following proclamation · —

" By the Honorable James De Lancey Esq , His Majesty's Lieutenant Gover-
          nor and Commander-in-chief in and over the province of New
[L S]   *York and the territories depending thereon in America*

A PROCLAMATION

" Whereas from the Success of His Majesty's Arms, in the reduction of the important Fortresses at Ticonderoga and Crown Point, and the Very Strong Works erecting at the latter, the whole Country along Hudson's River down to Albany, will for the future be so effectually covered and secured from the Ravages of the Enemy, that the Inhabitants may return to their settlements and abide there with safety to their Persons, Families and Estates , in confidence of which many have already returned to their Habitations   And whereas the Fortress now erecting at Crown Point is in great forwardness, and His Excellency, Major-General Amherst hath assured me, that he is determined it shall be so far finished before the Troops go into Winter Quarters, as to answer the purpose of covering and protecting the country, and as an encouragement to Settlers, he has desired that I would make known that those who with the leave of this Government shall now choose to go and settle between Lake George and Fort Edward, will there find, three Several Spots of cleared Ground, two of them capable of containing half a dozen Families each, and the other not less than twelve , on which shall be left standing for their Convenience the Wooden Hutts and Coverings of the Troops that have been posted there since the Beginning of the Campaign, which from the footing we have now at Crown Point, will be no longer necessary, and will be evacuated and left for the use of those who shall become Settlers   The first of the said Spotts is situated four miles above Fort Edward , The Second at the Half-Way Brook , and the other three miles from Lake George   The Soil good and capable of improvement, and all three well watered   The Half-Way Brook being the Spott sufficient for a dozen families   I have therefore thought fit by and with the Advice of His Majesty's Council to issue this Proclamation Hereby inviting the Inhabitants who formerly abandoned their Dwellings to return to their Settlements, and improve the advantages offered to them under the Protection and Cover of the important Posts and Strong Fortresses above mentioned   And as an inducement to such as shall be inclined to settle on any or either of the three Spotts of ground above described , I do hereby promise his Majesty's Grant thereof to any persons who shall apply for the same, on condition of immediate settlement thereof in the form of a Township with a sufficient quantity of woodland adjoining for that purpose ; and that I will use my Endeavors to ob-

tain for the Grantees an Exemption from the Payment of Quit Rent for such
a number of years as His Majesty shall be pleased to indulge therein

"Given under my Hand and Seal at Arms at Fort George in the city of
New York the 21st day of September, 1759, in the thirty-third year of the
Reign of our Sovereign Lord George the Second, by the Grace of God of
Great Britain, France and Ireland King, Defender of the Faith and so forth

"JAMES DE LANCEY

"By his Honour's Command,

"G W BANYAR, D Sec'y.

"God save the King"

This proclamation had the desired effect and led to the immediate application of Daniel Prindle and others for a patent for a township of twenty-three
thousand acres, lying upon the Hudson river and embracing within its limits
the three clearings mentioned   Previous to this however the buildings at
Half-way Brook were occupied by Jeffrey Cowper, or Cooper (the name being spelled both ways), who was, without doubt, the first white inhabitant to
make a permanent residence in the town   In regard to him Sir Jeffrey Amherst wrote in a letter to a Mr Sharpe, dated New York, 20th of October,
1762, as follows   "The permit to Jeffrey Cooper to occupy the small Post at
Half-way Brook between Fort Edward and Lake George, was only intended
for the preservation of the barracks, etc, that had been erected there, and for
the convenience of Passengers, as I judged it unnecessary after the reduction
of Canada, to leave a Garrison at that Post"

Little is known of Cooper's life, but it has been conjectured that he was a
seafaring man, from the fact that in the "Calendar of English Manuscripts" in
the Secretary of State's office is filed a petition by "Ephraim Cook, owner of
the *Snow Cicero*, thirty-four guns," in which he applies "for a commission, and
in case of his death, to his first lieutenant, Richard Harris, and Jeffrey Cowper, his second lieutenant to command said *Snow Cicero*"   His name appears
in the town records for the year 1766 only, and in April of the year preceding
he stands charged in the account book of Abraham Wing[1] with one hundred
pounds of pork and seven pounds of nails

It is supposed that the permit to Cooper was granted as early as 1759 or
1760, while Amherst was in that vicinity

In the summer of 1762 the survey of the town plot of Queensbury was in

---

[1] All of the extracts from what we call the Wing papers that appear in this work, are from Dr. A
W Holden's admirable *History of Queensbury*, published in 1873   A few years prior to that date the
late Abraham Wing gave Dr Holden access to family books, papers, etc, which had descended
through three generations of the family, from which he obtained much material that was almost invalu-
able in the preparation of his work   It was most fortunate that this work was performed when it was,
for a little later when the great fire of 1864 destroyed the greater part of the village of Glens Falls,
those books, papers, etc., were burned

progress by Zaccheus Towner, who was accompanied to the region by Abraham Wing, as appears in the following journal —

"August 23d day, 1762   Then set out for Queensbury township from home early in the morning, and dined at Nehemiah Merritts   Then set off for our journey and lodged at Esquire Castle's that night   The 24th traveled to Livingstone's manor, the 25th traveled to Greenbush and lodged at Captain Dows   The 26th we passed the ferry and eat breakfast in Albany and got our stores and traveled to Stillwater and lodged at Millerd's that night   The 27th was a rainy morning, but we traveled on to Bemises and there we eat breakfast, and waited there a little while, then went forward and eat dinner at Moores, and traveled that night to Fort Miller and stayed there that night   The 28th we set forward, being a showery day, made a short stop at Fort Edward where we were obliged to show our pass, and then set forward and arrived at the Half-way Brook about the middle of the day, where we were doubtful of some trouble   We had not been there in the tavern many minutes before the question was asked of the tender, whether we should have the liberty of a room to put our stores in, and so told our business   He replied, there is room enough, and after a short consideration, he replied, if we would go with him, he would show us a room, and accordingly we cleared out our house, put in our stores, and went to surveying the town plot   The 29th, being the first day of the week, set forward early in the morning"

This was the first visit of Mr Wing to the scenes of his subsequent labors, and it is to be regretted that the journal must be abruptly concluded with the above entry   The town plot alluded to as such by him is elsewhere described as the originally proposed site of the village

The Wings of this country, as far as known, are descended from John Wing, who settled in Sandwich, where, as appears by the records, he had three sons, Daniel, John and Stephen   These accepted the Quaker beliefs, and their descendants became scattered through different parts of the country   Daniel was the eldest son and had a son of the same name, who was born November 28th, 1664, and married Deborah Dillingham, of Sandwich, in 1686   His oldest son, Edward, was born July 10th, 1687   He had three wives, the first, Desire Smith, November, 1713, of Dartmouth, whither he removed, second, Sarah Tucker, June 1st, 1714, third, Patience Ellis, October, 1728   Abraham Wing, the pioneer of Warren county, was the son of Edward and Sarah (Tucker) Wing, and was born at Dartmouth, Bristol county, province of Massachusetts Bay, on the 4th of August, 1721   Sometime previous to 1745 he removed to "The Oblong," Duchess county, the precise date not being now known   He married Anstis Wood, supposed to be the daughter of William Wood, of Dartmouth   Following is the family record —

Phebe, b 5th of 3d month, 1742, m Nehemiah Merritt, jr ⎫
Sarah, b 7th of 12th month, 1743, m Ichabod Merritt ⎬ brothers
Hannah, b 28th of 12th month, 1745, m Daniel Merritt ⎭

Benj , b 18th of 9th month, 1748, m Thankful Lockwood, d 19th June, 1824
Deborah, b 6th of 7th month, 1750, m Daniel Jones
Patience, b 6th of 9th month, 1751, m Phineas Babcock
Content, b 11th of 4th month, 1755, m $\left\{\begin{array}{l}\text{Jacob Hicks}\\ \text{James Higson}\end{array}\right.$
Abraham, b 29th of 6th month, 1757, m Mary McKie
Mary, b 9th of 11th month, 1760, m Andrew Lewis

On the 29th of May, 1762, the patent of Queensbury was granted to twenty-three petitioners, as will presently be further alluded to , in the month of June following Abraham Wing, of the Oblong, purchased of several of the patentees for a nominal sum all their right, title and interest in this grant   In August following the official survey of the town was made by Zaccheus Towner, as mentioned in Mr Wing's diary, divided into sections , these were distributed by lot at a meeting of the proprietors, and subsequently deeds of partition were executed, giving each one his title   In this allotment Abraham Wing came into possession of two sections, upon which the principal portion of the village of Glens Falls[1] is built   He was subsequently granted by the proprietors as a free gift, a lot of ten acres of land on the left bank of the river, embracing the valuable water privileges, in consideration of his erecting a saw-mill and grist-mill at that point   In 1765 he removed with his dependents and laborers and began a settlement , three log houses were put up that fall and winter, one of which stood back of the old McDonald mansion, near the railroad , the second at the old Buckbee place on the Sandy Hill road, and the third near Duncan McGregor's residence   In the spring of 1766 their families were removed hither and in May the first town meeting was held, at which Mr Wing was elected supervisor, a position which he held until after the close of the Revolutionary War   During that period he was the foremost man in the little community — " the merchant, the lawyer, the minister and the innkeeper united in one "[2] He, with his sons-in-law and others, suffered heavy losses during the war, for which he was never adequately remunerated   He was, like most of the early settlers in this region, a member of the society, or sect, of Friends (Quakers) and consistently followed and adhered to this simple religious faith to the end of his life   His remains repose, with those of many other early settlers, in the burial ground by the Half-way Brook, where the old Quaker church stood

The granting of the Queensbury patent was preceded by various preliminary applications dating from January, 1760, ending with the application dated March 31st, 1762, by Daniel Prindle, Elihu Marsh, Thomas Hungerford, Samuel Hungerford, John Buck, Daniel Tryon, Amos Leach, Benjamin Seelye,

---

[1] In this work the present customary spelling of the name of the village will be followed, unless in case of quotations from old documents   The name has passed through several phases of orthography, such as "Glenns Falls," "Glenn's Falls," "Glen's Falls,' and the present better style

[2] HOLDEN's *History of Queensbury*

Anthony Wanser, Jonathan Weeks, John Page, Elihu Marsh, jr, Abraham Wanz(s)er, Benjamin Elliot, John Seeley, Aaron Prindle, Thomas Northrop, Ezekiel Pain, Jedediah Graves, David Cummins, Ebenezer Preston, David Preston and Joshua Agard for twenty-three thousand acres of land [1] This application was made to the provincial council of New York, presided over by the Hon Cadwallader Colden, lieutenant-governor of the province, for land lying on the Hudson River west of lands then recently surveyed for James Bradshaw,[2] and others. called Bradshaw's Township, and named in the patent the Township of Kingsbury These twenty-three thousand acres embraced a territory six miles square, besides allowances for numerous ponds, for highways to be constructed and a due regard for "the profitable and unprofitable acres," so that the actual area of the township probably reached thirty thousand acres or more

The application having been favorably received, the patent was duly granted on the 20th of May, 1762, it being in the second year of the reign of George III, the name "Queensbury" was given in honor of his then lately wedded consort The grant was then included in the county of Albany, the undefined boundaries of which embraced all the northern part of this State and nearly all the western part of the State of Vermont This grant was made subject to all the royal quitrent provisos, as also the annual payment of two shillings and six pence sterling for every hundred acres therein It reserved to the crown all mines of gold and silver, and also all white or other pine trees fit for masts, of the growth of twenty-four inches diameter and upwards at twelve inches from the earth It is very doubtful whether the crown ever profited by these reservations, although the entire township was covered with a heavy growth of timber, the principal part of which was valuable yellow pine of magnificent dimensions Among the conditions of the patent was the stipulation for the erection of the town into a body politic, providing for the annual election by the inhabitants of one supervisor, two assessors, one treasurer, two overseers of the highway, two overseers of the poor, one collector and four constables, the election to take place on the first Tuesday in May, at the most public place in the town, which was forever thereafter to be the place for such elections The patent was also to be vacated in case three of every one thousand acres should not be planted or placed under cultivation within three years from the termination of the war then in progress between France and England.

Following is given a copy of the original patent of the town of Queensbury, which was carefully compared with the transcript on file in the office of the Secretary of State, for Dr Holden · —

---

[1] To prevent monopoly of the then wild land in the province, His Majesty had restricted individual grants of land to one thousand acres to each *bona fide* grantee

[2] James Bradshaw was a resident of New Milford, Litchfield county, Conn, which place was also the home of the greater portion of the applicants for the Queensbury patent, and contiguous to Quaker Hill, Beekman precinct, and the Oblong, whence most of the early settlers of Queensbury emigrated.

Copy of the original patent of the town of Queensbury

Compared and corrected with the copy on file in the Secretary of State's office at Albany

"GEORGE the Third, by the Grace of God of Great Britain, France and Ireland King, defender of the faith and so forth   To all to whom these presents shall come GREETING   WHEREAS our loving subjects Daniel Prindle, Elihu Marsh, Thomas Hungerford, Samuel Hungerford, John Buck, Daniel Tryon, Amos Leach, Benjamin Seeley, Anthony Wanser, Jonathan Weeks, John Page, Elihu Marsh, Junior, Abraham Wanzer, Benjamin Elliot, John Seeley, Aaron Prindle, Thomas Northorp, Ezekiel Pain, Jedediah Graves, David Preston, and Joshua Agard, did by their humble petition presented unto our trusty and well beloved Cadwallader Colden Esquire, our Lieutenant Governor and Commander-in-chief of our Province of New York and the territories thereon depending, in America in council on the thirty-first day of March now last past humbly pray our Letters Patent granting to each of the said Petitioners respectively and to their respective heirs, the quantity of One Thousand Acres of a certain Tract of Land in the said Province vested in the Crown that had been surveyed and laid out for the said Daniel Prindle and his associates above named of the contents of six miles square adjoining to the lands intended to be granted to James Bradshaw and others between Fort Edward and Lake George under the Quit Rent provisoes, Limitations and restrictions directed and prescribed by Our Royal instructions together with the like privileges of a Township (as were lately granted to Isaac Sawyer and others) by the name of Queensbury Township   WHICH PETITION having been then and there read and considered of our said council did afterwards on the fifteenth day of April now last past humbly advise our said Lieutenant Governor and Commander-in-Chief to grant the prayer thereof   WHEREFORE in obedience to our said Royal Instructions our commissioners appointed for the setting out all lands to be granted within our said province have set out for the petitioners above named, ALL that certain Tract or Parcel of Land situate lying and being in the county of Albany on the north side of Hudson's river between Ft Edward and Lake George BEGINNING at the north-west corner of a certain Tract of land surveyed for James Bradshaw and his associates and runs from the said north-west corner, north twenty-seven chains, then west five hundred and thirty-five chains, then south five hundred and thirty-six chains to Hudson's river, then down the stream of said River as it runs to the west Bounds of said Tract surveyed for James Bradshaw and his associates, then along the said West Bounds North to the place where this tract first began containing after deducting for sundry ponds of water lying within the above mentioned Bounds Twenty-three thousand acres of land and the usual allowances for Highways   AND in setting out the said Tract of Land the said commissioners have had regard to the profitable and unprofitable acres, and have taken care that the length thereof does not extend along the Banks

of any other River otherwise than is conformable to our said Royal Instructions for that purpose as by a certificate thereof under their hand bearing Date
the Twenty-first Day of April now last past and entered on Record in our Secretary's Office in our City of New York may more fully appear   Which said
Tract of Land set out as aforesaid, according to our said Royal Instructions,
We being willing to grant to the said petitioners their heirs and assigns forever,
with the several privileges and powers hereinafter mentioned   Know Ye that
of our especial grace certain knowledge and meer motion We have given
granted ratified and confirmed and DO by these presents for us our Heirs and
successors give grant retify and confirm unto them the said Daniel Prindle,
Elihu Marsh, Thomas Hungerford, Samuel Hungerford, John Buck, Daniel
Tryon, Amos Leach, Benjamin Seeley, Anthony Wanser, Jonathan Weeks,
John Page, Elihu Marsh Junior, Abraham Wanser, Benjamin Elliot, John See-
ley, Aaron Prindle, Thomas Northorp, Ezekiel Pain, Jedediah Graves, David
Cummins, Ebenezer Preston, Daniel Preston and Joshua Agard their Heirs and
Assignees for ever ALL THAT the aforesaid Tract or parcel of Land set out
abutted bounded and described in Manner and Form as above mentioned together with all and singular the Tenements, Hereditaments Emoluments and
Appurtenances thereunto belonging or appertaining, and also all our Estate,
Right, Title, Interest, Possession, Claim and Demand Whatsoever of in and to
the same Lands and Premises and every part and parcel thereof and the Reversion and Reversions Remainder and Remainders, Rents, Issues and profits
thereof and of every part and parcel thereof, EXCEPT and always reserved
out of this our present GRANT unto us our Heirs and Successors for ever all
mines of Gold and Silver and also all White and other sorts of Pine Trees fit
for masts of the Growth of Twenty-four Inches Diameter and upwards at twelve
Inches from the Earth, for Masts for the Royal Navy of us our Heirs and Successors TO HAVE AND TO HOLD one full and equal Three and Twentieth
part (the whole into Twenty-three equal parts to be divided) of the said Tract
or parcel of Land, Tenements, Hereditaments and Premises by these Presents
granted, ratified and confirmed, and every part and parcel thereof with their
and every of their appurtenances, (except as is herein before excepted) unto each
of them our Grantees above mentioned their Heirs and Assignees respectively
TO then only proper and separate use and Behoof respectively for ever as Tenants in common and not as joint tenants   TO BE HOLDEN of us, and
Heirs and Successors in fee and common socage as of our Manor of East
Greenwich in our County of Kent within our Kingdom of Great Britain,
YIELDING, rendering, and paying therefore yearly and every year forever
unto us our Heirs and Successors at our Custom House in our City of New
York, unto our or their Collector or Receiver General therefore the time being
on the Feast of the Annunciation of the blessed Virgin Mary commonly called
Lady day the yearly rent of two shillings and six pence Sterling for each and

every Hundred Acres of the above granted lands and so in proportion for any
less in quantity thereof saving and except for such part of the said Lands allowed for Highways as above mentioned in Lieu and stead of all other Rents,
Services, Dues, Duties, and Demands whatsoever for the hereby granted Land
and Premises, or any part thereof AND WE DO of our especial Grace certain knowledge and meer motion, create, erect and constitute the said Tract or
parcel of Land hereby granted and every part and parcel thereof a Township
for ever hereafter to be, continue, and remain and by the name of QUEENS-
BURY Township for ever hereafter to be called and known AND for the better
and more easily carrying on and managing the public affairs and Business of
the said Township our Royal will and pleasure is and we do hereby for us our
Heirs and Successors give and grant to the inhabitants of the said Township
all the Powers, Authority, Privileges and Advantages heretofore given and
granted to or legally enjoyed by all, any or either our other Township within
our said Province AND we also ordain and establish that there shall be forever
hereafter in the said Township One Supervisor, Two Assessors, One Treasurer,
Two Overseers of the Highways, Two Overseers of the Poor, One Collector
and four Constables elected and chosen out of the Inhabitants of the said Township yearly and every year on the first Tuesday in May at the most publick
place in the said Township, by the majority of Freeholders thereof

[End of contents of first piece of parchment]

"THEN and there met and assembled for that purpose, hereby declaring
that wheresoever the first Election in the said Township shall be held the future
Elections shall forever thereafter be held in the same place as near as may be,
and giving and Granting unto the said officers so chosen, power and authority
to exercise their said several and respective offices, during one whole year from
such election, and until others are legally chosen and elected in their room and
stead, as fully and amply as any the like officers have or legally may use or
exercise their offices in our said Province AND in case any or either of the
said officers of the said Township should die or remove from the said Township
before the Time of their Annual service shall be expired or refuse to act in the
Offices for which they shall respectively be chosen, then our Royal Will and
pleasure further is and we do hereby direct ordain and require the Freeholders
of the said Township to meet at the place where the annual election shall be
held for the said Township and chuse other or others of the said Inhabitants
of the said Township in the place or stead of him or them so dying removing or refusing to act within Forty days next after such contingency
AND to prevent any undue election in this case, We do hereby ordain and
require, That upon every vacancy in the office of Supervisor, the Assessors,
and in either of the other offices, the Supervisor of the said Township shall
within ten days next after any such vacancy first happens appoint the Day for
such Election and give public Notice thereof in Writing under his or their

Hands by affixing such Notice on the Church Door, or other most public place in the said Township, at the least Ten days before the Day appointed for such Election, and in Default thereof we do hereby require the Officer or Officers of the said Township or the Survivor of them, who in the order they are hereinbefore mentioned shall next succeed him or them so making Default, within ten days next after such default to appoint the day for such election, and give notice thereof as aforesaid, HEREBY Giving and Granting that such person or persons as shall be so chosen by the majority of such of the Freeholders of the said township as shall meet in manner hereby directed, shall have, hold, exercise and enjoy the Office or Offices, to which he or they shall be so elected and chosen from the Time of such Election until the first Tuesday in May then next following, and until other or others be legally chosen in his or their place and stead as fully as the person or persons in whose place he or they shall be chosen might or could have done by virtue of these presents   AND WE do hereby will and direct that this method shall for ever hereafter, be used for the filling up all vacancies that shall happen in any or either of the said Offices between the annual Elections above directed, PROVIDED always and upon condition nevertheless that if our said Grantees, their heirs or assigns or some or one of them shall not within three years next after the conclusion of our present war with France settle on the said Tract of Land hereby granted so many families as shall amount to one Family for every thousand acres thereof OR if they our said Grantees, or one of them, their or one of their heirs, or assigns shall not also within three years to be computed as aforesaid plant and effectually cultivate at the least three acres for every fifty acres of such of the hereby granted Lands as are capable of cultivation, OR if they our said Grantees or any of them or any of their heirs or assigns, or any other person or persons by their or any of their previty consent or procurement, shall fell, cut down or otherwise destroy any of the Pine Trees by these Presents reserved to us our heirs and successors or hereby intended so to be, without the Royal license of us, our heirs or successors for so doing first had and obtained, that then and in any of these cases this our present Grant and every Thing therein contained shall cease and be absolutely void, and the Lands and Premises hereby granted shall revert to and vest in us, our heirs and successors, as if this our present Grant had not been made, anything hereinbefore contained to the contrary thereof in any wise notwithstanding PROVIDED further and upon condition also nevertheless, and we do hereby for us, our heirs and successors direct and appoint that this our present Grant shall be registered and entered on Record within six months from the date thereof in our Secretary's Office in our City of New York in our said Province in one of the Books of Patents there remaining and that a Docquet thereof shall be also entered in our Auditor's Office there for our said Province and that in default thereof this our present Grant shall be void, and of none effect any Thing before in these Presents contained to the contrary thereof in any wise notwithstanding AND WE DO moreover of our Grace certain knowledge and meer motion consent and agree that this our present Grant being registered, recorded and a Docquet thereof made as before directed and appointed shall be good and effectual in the Law to all Intents, Constructions and Purposes whatsoever against us, our heirs and Successors notwithstanding any Misreciting, Misbounding, Misnaming or other Imperfection or Omission of, in, or in any wise concerning the above granted or hereby mentioned or intended to be granted Lands, Tenements, hereditaments and premises or any part thereof IN TESTIMONY whereof we have caused these our Letters to be made patent and the Great Seal of our said Province to be hereunto affixed WITNESS our said trusty and well beloved Cadwallader Colden, Esquire, our Lieutenant Governor and Commander in Chief of our Province of New-York and the Territories depending thereon in America At our Fort in our City of New-York the Twentieth day of May in the year of our Lord One Thousand Seven hundred and Sixty-two and of our Reign the second (First Skin Line 31 the word *of* interlined line 47 the words *any or* wrote on an erasure and Line 49 the word *the* interlined

"CLARKE"[1]

Endorsements on the back of the parchment skin No 1

"Secretary's Office 25th May, 1762, The Within Letters Patent are Recorded in Lib Patents No 13, Pages 478 to 483"

"Geo Banyar D Sec'y"

"New York Auditor Generals Office 1st June, 1762 The within Letters Patent to Daniel Prindle and others are Docqueted in this office"

"Geo Banyar Dept Auditor"

Endorsement on the back of parchment skin No 2

"Letters Patent 20th May, 1762

"To Daniel Prindle, and others for 23000 acres of land in the county of Albany"

Attached to these parchments, was the great seal of the province, a fac-simile of which may be found in the fourth vol of the *Doc'y Hist of N Y*

The fact that this patent was granted on the 20th of May and that at a proprietors' meeting held on the 18th of June following the ownership of the patent had nearly all changed hands, would indicate that such a transfer had been contemplated by the original applicants, who, being men of influence, lent their names to secure the grant for the benefit of those whose purpose it was to become actual settlers At this last mentioned meeting a vote was passed authorizing Abraham Wing to keep and preserve the certificate and patent of the township for the benefit of the proprietors; these are still in the possession of his descendants

---

[1] One of the members of the council

9

The following names are recorded as proprietors at this meeting · John Dobson, Nehemiah Merritt, Abraham Wing, Daniel Merritt, John Lawrence, Henry Haydock, Wm. Smith, Benjamin Ferriss, John Burling, John Akin, Thomas Dobson, Reed Ferriss, George Bowne, Ichabod Merritt, Elihu Marsh, jr, John Farrington, Haydock Bowne, Nathaniel Hazard, John Rapelje, Samuel Bowne, Benj'n Seeley, John Carmon, Jacob Haviland, Samuel Hungerford, Joseph Pursell, John Hadok, Edward Burling, Elihu Marsh, Wm Haviland, Nathaniel Stevenson, Isaac Mann

Thirty-one names in all, and of the entire number not over half a dozen of them who ever became actual residents, although from time to time their descendants appear among the records of the township

Another meeting of proprietors was held on the 10th of July following at the shop of Nehemiah and Daniel Merritt (sons-in-law of Mr Wing) on the Oblong, at which a vote was passed that the town lots in said township be drawn by lot on the 24th inst, at the same place, that Daniel Case and Thomas Aiken should perform the drawing and that John Gurney should make the proper record of such distribution   The survey by Zaccheus Towner, "of New Fairfield, Connecticut, surveyor for the proprietors," was begun on the 29th of August, 1762, and finished before the following November   In this survey the village was located at the Half-way Brook, at the crossing of the military road, where there were a few buildings and a clearing   The town plot at this point was run out into forty-eight ten acre lots, six lots deep from north to south and eight lots deep from east to west, forming an oblong tract which was intersected through the center in each direction by a highway eight rods wide, and two four-rod roads between the tiers of lots to the east and west of the main road, the whole plot to be surrounded by a four rod road   The center lots were reserved for public buildings   The remainder of the township was run out into one hundred and one two-hundred-and-fifty-acre lots, as nearly as possible   At the drawing Abraham Wing was so fortunate as to secure lots numbers 29, 36 and 37, which, as before intimated, became among the most valuable in the town, embracing the greater part of the site of Glens Falls village

On the 8th of November another proprietors' meeting was held (their number now increased to thirty) at the same place, when deeds of partition were issued to the individuals for the lots drawn by each   At this meeting it was also voted that Daniel Chase and William Haight be appointed to draw lots for the balance of the survey not then appropriated   In this second partition several of the great lots were subdivided by lines drawn from east to west, and renumbered

On the 23d of February, 1763, the proprietors met at the building before mentioned, in Beekman precinct, Duchess county, and appointed William Smith, Nehemiah Merritt and Abraham Wing, trustees to partition out the remaining undivided lands

In the course of the summer of this year (1763) a little progress was made towards the first permanent settlement of the town, as fully appears in the history of Queensbury in later pages of this work—progress that was destined ere long to be disastrously interrupted by the clash of arms and the din of battle in the Revolutionary struggle, previous to the triumph of liberty and the reign of peace that followed

These pioneers who penetrated the wilderness where fields were still reeking with the signs of recent bloody strife may well be counted among the early heroes of their country, and their heroism was yet to be tested and honorably sustained before their descendants could peacefully enjoy their possessions

---

CHAPTER XI

FROM 1763 TO THE REVOLUTION

The New Hampshire Grants Controversy —English Oppression of Colonists—The Sons of Liberty —The Stamp Act—Its Repeal—Obnoxious Parliamentary Action—The Liberty Pole Assault—Signals of the Revolution

LET us now return to the important events occurring elsewhere in the country between the peace of 1763 and the outbreak of the great struggle that gave America her independence   In the year just mentioned the boundary line between New York and New Hampshire became the subject of much controversy   The territory in dispute was what is now comprised in the State of Vermont, lying between the Connecticut River and Lake Champlain   Controversies had previously arisen growing out of the indefinite character of their charters, between New York, Massachusetts and Connecticut, but the boundaries were finally adjusted by negotiation and compromise   The line between these States was fixed upon as extending north and south twenty miles east of the Hudson River   New Hampshire, regardless of justice or title, insisted upon a continuation of this line as her western boundary, and by the year 1763 her governor had issued one hundred and thirty-eight townships in grants to settlers   Against all this New York entered vigorous protest, and in December, of the year named, Governor Colden issued a proclamation claiming jurisdiction to the Connecticut River and commanded the sheriff of Albany county to return the names of all persons who, by virtue of the New Hampshire grants had taken possession of lands west of the Connecticut River   This was followed by a counter proclamation by the governor of New Hampshire   In the following year the question was referred to the crown and a decision rendered that the Connecticut River should form the boundary between New York and New Hampshire   Thereupon the government of New York declared the grants by New Hampshire illegal, and insisted that the settlers on those grants should either surrender or repurchase the lands. This demand was opposed by the settlers, whereupon the New York government granted the lands to others, who obtained judgments in their favor by bringing ejectment suits in Albany.

Although carrying us out of chronological order in recording events, the conclusion of this controversy may as well be detailed here. The civil officers of New York were opposed by force in their attempts to eject the settlers and the New York Assembly passed an act declaring such resistance to be felony. A proclamation was issued, also, by Governor Tryon, who succeeded Lord Dunmore (Colden's successor) in 1771, offering a reward for the apprehension of Ethan Allen and other conspicuous offenders. This was followed by a burlesque proclamation offering a reward for the arrest of the governor of New York. The matter neared a crisis in the spring of 1775, when New York sought to establish courts in the disputed territory, the officers were prevented from entering the court-house, upon which they collected a force, fired into the building, killing one man and wounding others. Some of the officers were then arrested and lodged in jail. The Revolutionary outbreak caused a cessation of these disputes, but in 1777 the inhabitants of the disputed territory held a convention at Windsor and declared the "grants" an independent State with the name of Vermont. They at the same time addressed a petition to Congress setting forth their motives for action and asking admission to the confederacy of independent states and seats for delegates to Congress. This petition was disposed of by resolutions, one of which declared "that the independent government attempted to be established by the people styling themselves the inhabitants of the New Hampshire grants can derive no countenance or justification from the act of Congress declaring the united colonies to be independent of the crown of Great Britain, nor from any other act or resolution of Congress." The discord was revived and so antagonistic to New York and the colonial authorities at large did the settlers on the grants become, that it is believed they secretly negotiated with the British to become a colony under the crown, this feature of the controversy will be hereafter alluded to. After the ratification of the Articles of Confederation in 1781, Congress offered to admit the new State, but with curtailed boundaries, this offer was rejected and for ten years it remained outside of the Union. Finally on the 10th of January, 1791, a convention at Bennington adopted the National constitution, and Vermont, having agreed to pay to the State of New York $30,000 for territory claimed by that State, was admitted to the Union.

During the progress of these events and those described in Chapter IX the British parliament continued its arbitrary and oppressive course towards the American colonists. But the time arrived when unquestioning submission to such measures could no longer be exacted. The people were heavily burdened with the expenses of the late war, the results of which gave to England a large extent of territory, yet, almost before the smoke of the battles had cleared away, the English ministry began devising plans to tax them for a revenue without their consent   In 1764 a proposition was submitted to the House of Commons for raising revenue in the colonies by the sale of stamps   Contrary to promises the stamp act was passed in March, 1765   By its provisions no legal or commercial documents were valid unless made upon stamped paper, upon which a price was placed according to the nature of the document   This act was bitterly denounced throughout the colonies and particularly in New York, and resistance determined upon   The "Sons of Liberty"[1] were organized and meetings held to devise plans of opposition to the obnoxious act   On the 7th of October a convention of delegates from the different colonies was held in New York city and continued in session two weeks   A declaration of rights was adopted and petitions and memorials sent to parliament, in which the principles that governed the colonies during the Revolution were clearly foreshadowed

The stamp act was to take effect on the 1st of November, but as the date drew near, excitement increased, and on that day flags hung at half mast, bells were tolled and other funereal demonstrations made   Governor Colden became alarmed and refused to issue any of the stamped paper, leaving the ugly duty to his successor, Sir Henry Moore, then on his way from England   The new governor soon saw the folly of attempting to oppose the will of the people in that direction   The final result was the destruction of a large quantity of the odious paper by the Sons of Liberty, and the repeal of the stamp act in March, 1766   This action was not, however, due to the good will of parliament, nor to the appeals of the colonists, but to the solicitations of London merchants who had been deprived of their American trade through a union of colonial merchants who pledged themselves to cease importations from England

" From the time of the stamp act riots, occasional gatherings of Whigs assembled at Fort Edward among whom were numbered such representative and influential names as the Bradshaw, Moss, Baker and High families of Kingsbury; the Bitleys, Sherwoods, and Durkees, of Fort Edward, the Paynes, Parkes and McCreas of the yet unnamed district on the west side of the Hud-

---

[1] In 1735 the radical opponents of the royal governors were called Sons of Liberty, but the name was not often heard until after Colonel Barré made his memorable speech in the House of Commons (1765)   In reply to an assertion by Charles Townshend that the colonies had been nurtured into strength by the indulgence of the home government, Barré made a scornful denial, saying that the only care that had been exercised had been in sending weak and unfit men to rule over them — "men whose behavior on many occasions had caused the blood of those *sons of liberty* to recoil within them "   The organization was composed chiefly of ardent young men, who had nothing to lose by their course, with whom people of consideration did not affiliate, though they generally favored the acts of the Sons. They finally spread over the colonies from Massachusetts to Georgia, and became the most radical leaders in the growing quarrel with England, and promoters of the war that followed.

son ; so that when the beacon fires of the Revolution burst forth, the lines of political opinion were sharply drawn and defined and it was known at the outset through a wide range of neighborhood, who were the friends as well as foes of the general opposition to and uprising against British misrule "[1]

Rejoicing over the repeal of the stamp act had scarcely died away, when Parliament again stirred up discontent among the colonists by other unjust and oppressive acts   The Assembly was called upon by the governor to concede to the demands of the ministry in furnishing supplies for the soldiers in New York city , this created a good deal of animosity and led to hostility between the Sons of Liberty and the troops   The Assembly, moreover, subsequently refused to comply with the request of the ministry to make provision for the soldiers, for which action parliament declared the legislative powers of the Assembly annulled

In 1767 a bill was passed by parliament imposing a duty on tea, glass, lead, paper, and painter's colors imported into the colonies   This action caused renewed excitement and in the following year the Assembly of Massachusetts addressed a circular to the other colonies soliciting their co-operation in defending the common liberties   This so offended the ministry that a letter was sent to the colonial governors forbidding their assemblies to correspond with that of Massachusetts   This mandate was absolutely opposed and disobeyed, with declarations on the part of the New York Assembly of its inherent rights in the case, denunciations of parliament and other evidences of refraction , the Assembly was thereupon dissolved by the governor   But the people sustained their representatives and returned most of them to the new Assembly of 1769

The English merchants, who were suffering from the non-importation agreement of the American dealers, now joined their petitions to those of the colonists for the repeal of the obnoxious custom-house act   A circular letter assured the people in response that the duties should be removed at the next session of parliament on all articles except tea   This was something, but the principle of the right of the mother country to tax the colonies remained, and the promises of parliament were far from satisfactory   Animosity and hostility, moreover, continued between the soldiery and the Sons of Liberty   Arrangements having been perfected by which the soldiers' supplies were guaranteed, coming, too, largely from the resources of the colonists, the troops still did not hesitate to make manifest their disdain for, and hostility towards the people   On the evening of the 2d of January, 1769, they made their second assault on the liberty pole of the Sons of Liberty in New York, and charged upon the opposing citizens, drove a party of them into a tavern which was a popular resort, and broke in the windows and destroyed the furniture   On the evening of the 16th they sawed down the pole, cut it in pieces and piled them in front of the obnoxious hotel   A resolution of the citizens followed, to the effect that

[1] HOLDEN'S *History of Queensbury*

all soldiers found in the streets after roll-call should be dealt with as enemies to the peace of the city   This resolution was ridiculed in handbills posted by the soldiers, and two or three of the latter were arrested in the act of posting them   While conducting the soldiers to the mayor's office the citizens were attacked by a party of twenty troops and a skirmish ensued in which several citizens, some of whom had not participated in the mêlée, were wounded Other affrays occurred the next day in which the soldiers generally got the worst of it   The mayor then issued a proclamation forbidding them to leave their barracks unless in company of a non-commissioned officer, and order was partially restored

It is commonly held that the battle of Lexington was the first conflict of the Revolutionary struggle   But, although this skirmish in the streets of New York may be looked upon as a comparatively insignificant affair, still there was bloodshed, and it was the actual beginning of the great conflict, five years before the guns of Lexington were heard

---

CHAPTER XII

FROM 1770 TO 1775

Governor Colden's Successor — Old Troubles Renewed — A large Cup of Tea — Congress and its Declaration of Rights — Impending War — The British March to Lexington — Paul Revere's Ride — The Battle on the Green — Retreat of the British — Preparations for the Capture of Crown Point and Ticonderoga — Ethan Allen's Command — Arnold's Arrival and its Consequences — Plan of the Expedition — Capture of Ticonderoga — Surrender of Crown Point — Reassembling of Congress — Congressional Vacillation — Allen and Arnold's Naval Exploit — Indian Action in the Revolution — The Canadian Invasion — Montgomery's Initial Movements — Allen's Capture — Carleton's Plan for Relief of St Johns — Its Failure — Capture of St Johns and Montreal by Montgomery — Arnold's Wonderful Expedition — Montgomery before Quebec — Demand for its Surrender and the Reply — Montgomery's death and Failure of the Attack — A Disastrous Retreat — Charlotte County Created — Militia Affairs

IN October, 1770, Lord Dunmore succeeded Colden as governor and brought with him royal approval of the act authorizing the issue of colonial bills of credit   The duties had, meanwhile, been removed from all articles except tea   Colonial affairs were going on more smoothly   On the 18th of July, 1771, William Tryon was commissioned governor and Lord Dunmore transferred to Virginia   The old differences finally again came to the surface. The East India Company, having suffered severely through the imposition of the American duty on tea, petitioned Parliament in 1773 to abolish the tax, offering at the same time to submit to double the amount of that duty as an exportation tariff   This was refused, but, instead, the ministry agreed to favor the company by a special act allowing them to ship their teas to the American colonies free of duty as an export, while still enforcing the importation duty, in other words the determination was clearly shown that the assumed right to tax the colonists in any way, or all ways, was not to be relinquished under any circumstances   The India company now loaded their ships with teas, appointed consignees for their reception and expected a ready sale at the low prices that could now be made   Their reckoning failed   The Sons of Liberty met and resolved that the obnoxious article should not be landed in the province under any pretense   The tea commissioners, in submission to the popular will, resigned   The first cargo arrived off Sandy Hook in April, 1774, whence the pilot, acting under his instructions from the vigilance committee, refused to bring the ship to port.   In the mean time Captain Chambers, of another vessel, a professed patriot, sailed his ship into the harbor   When threats were made of a purpose to search his cargo, he admitted that he had tea on board which he had brought over as a private venture   His chests were thereupon hoisted on deck and given a salt water plunge bath   The vessels were sent on return voyages   In the mean time a cargo of tea had arrived in Boston harbor ; the vessel was boarded by the patriotic sons of that city and the chests emptied into the sea

The English ministry were now so enraged at the outcome of the tea tariff, in connection with other measures of resistance, or disloyalty, as it was there termed, that they resolved to at once subjugate the country   One of the steps towards this end was the adoption of the infamous " Boston port bill," the purpose of which was to practically close the Boston harbor and thus destroy the trade of the city   The people throughout the colonies were in earnest sympathy with their Massachusetts friends, aware that similar ruinous measures might be in store for themselves   Public meetings were held for the consideration of the common grievances and among movements for protection the restoration of the non-importation agreement was urged and the assembling of a colonial congress

A congress was called and met on the 5th of September, 1774, adopted a declaration of rights, and agreed upon a petition to the king and an appeal to the people of Great Britain and Canada.   An adjournment was then taken until the following May   The New York Assembly was the only one that did not sanction these congressional proceedings, but instead, addressed a remonstrance to parliament, which was, of course, treated with disdain [1]   The New York Assembly adjourned on the 3d of April, 1775, and never met again   Its refusal to appoint delegates to the congress gave much dissatisfaction and a

[1] On the 12th of January, 1775, at a cabinet council, it was declared there was nothing in the proceedings of Congress that afforded any basis for an honorable reconciliation   It was therefore resolved to break off all commerce with the Americans, to protect the loyalists in the colonies, and to declare all others to be traitors and rebels — LOSSING

provincial convention of county representatives was called by the people to perform that duty.

The Americans had long felt their critical condition and foresaw that an appeal to arms must, doubtless, follow   A quantity of military stores had been collected by them at Concord, Mass   To destroy these, General Gage sent a detachment of British regulars on the 18th of April, 1775, from Boston, where he had between three thousand and four thousand troops   But Paul Revere made his famous ride to Concord and aroused the people to the menaced incursion, and when, early on the following morning, the detachment reached Lexington, they found the militia drawn up on the public green. The British officer ordered them to disperse, but the order was not heeded, and the regulars fired   Eight of the "minute men" were killed and several wounded, the remainder were dispersed and the British pressed on to Concord   There the militia had gathered from all directions, the stores were secreted and the invaders were given a warm reception, causing them to retreat   As they fell back towards Lexington they were disastrously harassed by the colonists, who killed many of their number, shooting from behind fences, buildings and trees   It is probable that the whole detachment might have been cut off, but for the fact that reinforcements met them near Lexington, but the retreat was continued and many more regulars fell by the sharp shooting of the citizens   The whole country was aroused and the revolution was begun in earnest

The next event of importance, and one that bears more directly upon the history of Warren county and vicinity was the capture of Ticonderoga and Crown Point   According to Dr Holden, "After the close of the French war, or at least as early as the year 1767, the fort at the head of Lake George was partially dismantled, and abandoned as a military post, the forts at Ticonderoga and Crown Point being of more massive character, were considered an adequate protection on a frontier no longer threatened by the annual incursion of the savages   At this time the only occupants of this post were a retired invalid officer of the British army, Captain John Nordberg and two men supposed also to have belonged to the army, and who were possibly pensioners of the crown   There are reasons for supposing that one of these was John McComb, and the other Hugh McAuley whose name subsequently appears in the records, and who was the ancestor of the McAuley family, of the town of Queensbury "[1]   General Frederick Haldimand had been left in command on Lake Champlain   He had already announced to the British government in 1773 that the fort at Crown Point was entirely destroyed, while that at Ticonderoga was in a "ruinous condition," and that both could not "cover fifty men in winter"   Ethan Allen, who had been conspicuous in his opposition to New York in the New Hampshire grants trouble, and was declared an outlaw and

---

[1] *History of Queensbury*

a hundred and fifty pounds offered for his arrest, was one of the brave spirits who first took up arms against the oppression of Great Britain   He was found at Bennington by the force which had been collected in Connecticut and Massachusetts with the design of descending upon the works at the two fortified points on Lake Champlain   The expedition numbered about forty volunteers when it reached Bennington, where Allen's powerful influence and enthusiastic assistance were secured   On the 7th of May a band of brave men numbering two hundred and seventy (all but forty-six being " Green Mountain boys," as Allen's followers were termed) had assembled at Castleton   At this inopportune time Benedict Arnold appeared on the scene, bearing a commission from the Massachusetts committee of safety, dated May 3d, clothing him with authority to effect the same purpose for which the other force was destined   A conflict for the command ensued, which was finally terminated by the refusal of the volunteers to march except under the command of Allen   Arnold reluctantly accompanied the expedition as second in command

Noah Phelps, one of the Massachusetts committee, entered the fort at Ticonderoga in pretended quest of a barber, and thus gained definite knowledge of its condition   Captain Herrick was ordered to Skenesborough, whence, after the capture of the younger Skene and the stores there accumulated, he was to join Allen at Ticonderoga   Douglass was ordered to Panton to secure boats for transportation of the force   The committees of Albany and New York appear to have declined any part in these operations

Allen's force marched with as much secrecy as possible to the eastern shore of the lake, posted pickets on all roads leading to Ticonderoga, to cut off possible conveyance to the fort of intelligence of the movement, and there waited a day and a night for the arrival of the boats   Finally with the few boats that were at hand Allen resolved to attempt the passage, and on the night of the 10th eighty-three men embarked at Hand's Point and landed about a mile north of the fort   Dawn was approaching and the commander realized to the fullest the importance of prompt action   He had been furnished with a guide in the person of young Nathan Beman, son of a patriot of Shoreham, who had a perfect knowledge of the works gained during his boyhood.

Allen, in a low and earnest voice, addressed his little band, inspiring them with the importance of their mission and the glory of its success, and then told them that all who accompanied him must go voluntarily, and ordered all who were ready to poise their firelocks   Every musket was instantly raised   After again pacifying Arnold, who assumed to the leadership, by agreeing that they should advance together, Allen and Arnold took the lead, with young Beaman, and the column filed up to the sallyport of the fortress   The sentinel snapped his gun as they approached and retreated through the covered way, closely followed by the Americans, who drew up on the parade in two lines, each facing the barracks   Their shouts awakened the garrison and Captain de la

Place came forth from his quarters clad only in his night apparel   He was
confronted by Allen with a peremptory summons to surrender   When he requested to know by what authority the demand was made, Allen uttered his
immortal response, " By the authority of the Great Jehovah and the Continental
Congress ! "

Allen says, in his own graphic account of the event   " The authority of
the Congress being very little known at that time, he began to speak again,
but I interrupted him, and with drawn sword over his head again demanded
an immediate surrender of the garrison, with which he then complied, and
ordered his men to be forthwith paraded without arms, as he had given up the
garrison   In the mean time some of my officers had given orders and in consequence thereof sundry of the barrack doors were beat down, and about one-
third of the garrison imprisoned, which consisted of the said commander, a Lieutenant Feltham, a conductor of artillery, a gunner, two sergeants, and forty-
four rank and file, about one hundred pieces of cannon, one thirteen-inch mortar, and a number of swivels   This surprise was carried into execution in the
gray of the morning of the 10th of May, 1775   The sun seemed to rise on
that morning with a superior lustre, and Ticonderoga and its dependencies
smiled to its conquerors who tossed about the flowing bowl and wished success
to Congress and the liberty and freedom of America   Happy it was for me,
at that time, that those future pages of the book of fate, which afterwards unfolded a miserable scene of two years and eight months imprisonment, were
hid from my view "

Allen's well planned measures were all successful   Crown Point surrendered on the following day, with its entire armament and its small garrison of
twelve men   Herrick made his capture of Skenesborough, with Skene and
his forces, besides several boats and a trading schooner   This success was
crowned by the capture of two dispatch boats by Baker, which had been sent
from Crown Point with news of the fall of Ticonderoga   Amos Callandar was
detached with a party to the fort at the head of Lake George, whence he soon
after conducted the prisoners to Hartford.

Although, when viewed from certain standpoints, this event was not one
of great magnitude, yet it was, at that particular time, one upon the success
or failure of which depended momentous issues, and its success caused a thrill
of joy and astonishment to pervade the country   The men who were most
prominent in its brave deeds became the possessors of high military distinction
before the close of the Revolution — distinction won by their own efficient
heroism

New York was slow to acknowledge the importance of Allen's victory, or
to profit by it   The Albany Committee, to whom John Brown bore Allen's
letter of particulars of the event, with a request for such reinforcements as would
prevent the recapture of the fortifications, merely forwarded the letter to the

New York Committee They also refused to act in the matter and in turn forwarded the dispatches to the Congress in Philadelphia. Brown was already there and gave the August body an account of the brilliant event. Their reception of it shows that they were still uncertain and vacillating in attempting to decide what were to be the future relations of America and Great Britain, whether it might not still be the best policy not to arouse the mother country to unconditional hostility While Congress privately exulted over Allen's conquest, it hesitated to publicly and directly assume the responsibility of it. Instead, it recommended the New York and Albany Committees to immediately remove the armament and stores at the two forts on Lake Champlain to the head of Lake George, and "indirectly counseled the establishment of a strong post at that point" As an indication of the uncertainty just alluded to, Congress also recommended "that an exact inventory of them [the armament and stores] should be taken, in order that they might be safely returned when the restoration of the former harmony between Great Britain and the colonies, so ardently wished for by the latter, should render it prudent and consistent with the overruling law of self-preservation "

To this response Allen, as well as Connecticut and Massachusetts at large, manifested the most earnest opposition, and the plans were abandoned. When, a few months later, Washington at Boston was in sore need of artillery,[1] the immense value of the victory won by Allen and his men at Ticonderoga and Crown Point became apparent Henry Knox, the young Boston bookseller (afterwards a brigadier-general in the American army), transported fifty heavy guns from Ticonderoga to Washington's camp in the mid-winter of 1775–76 This enterprise was one of almost unparalleled toil, the work being accomplished by numerous teams of oxen, and the journey entending through two hundred miles of wilderness The procession was received with an ovation

The Continental Congress had reassembled and organized on the 10th of May, the day on which Allen captured Ticonderoga Almost its first labors were in the direction of raising an army for general defense New York was ordered to raise three thousand volunteers A Provincial Congress of New York convened on the 22d of May, authorized the raising of troops, encouraged the manufacture of powder and muskets in the province, and projected fortifications on the Lower Hudson

The capture of the fortifications on Lake Champlain opened the way for an invasion of Canada, which, at that time and amid the then prevailing spirit of the Canada soldiers and people, could scarcely have failed Canada was in a peculiarly defenseless condition, many of her troops having been withdrawn to Boston, and it was believed that a large portion of her people would assume the

---

[1] The whole train of artillery possessed by the colonies when the war for independence broke out, was composed of four field pieces, two belonging to citizens of Boston, and two to the province of Massachusetts — LOSSING

cause of America in the event of an invasion promising success   But Congress hesitated, and although Allen had, in a communication of June 7th, declared that "with fifteen hundred men I could take Montreal," that body was averse to an act involving possibilities of apprehension in the minds of many citizens of the colonies, and so thoroughly offensive in its character against the mother country

Soon after the capture of the forts fifty men who had been enlisted by Arnold arrived at Ticonderoga   An armed schooner was then lying in the Sorel River near St Johns   Her capture would secure the naval supremacy of the lake, and Arnold and Allen resolved upon the attempt   Arnold took his fifty recruits and manned the schooner captured at Skenesborough, and on the fifth day after the surrender of the fort sailed for St Johns   Allen accompanied him with one hundred and fifty men in bateaux   Favorable winds enabled Arnold to distance the bateaux   Arriving within thirty miles of his destination, a calm overtook him, but he was not disposed to share with Allen whatever honor might be forthcoming, and accordingly embarked thirty-five men in two boats, hastened forward, surprised and captured the fort, with its guard of twelve men, and seized the schooner, making a successful retreat with his prize   Returning he met Allen and acquainted him with intelligence he had received of an approaching detachment of troops towards St Johns, but Allen pushed on and landed   The presence of a large force with artillery compelled him to return [1]

"Among the military personages to whom the emergencies of the hour gave special prominence,' says Dr Holden, "was Colonel Bernard Romans

He was a soldier by training, a gentleman by birth and culture and an accomplished scholar"   That he was connected with the capture of Skenesborough is an undisputed fact, but under whom or by whose orders no record exists to show, it is only known that he took possession of Fort George on the 12th of May (1775), as the following petition of John Nordberg, a British officer on half pay who, as his petition states, was living in or near Fort George at the time —

---

[1] Following is Arnold's own subsequent estimate of the importance of these captures   "We were now masters of Lake Champlain, and the garrisons depending thereon   This success I viewed of consequence in the scale of American politics, for, if a settlement between the then colonies of Great Britain had soon taken place, it would have been easy to have restored these acquisitions, but viewing the then future consequences of a cruel war, as it has really proved to be, and the command of that lake, garrisons, artillery, etc, it must be viewed to be of signal importance to the American cause, and it is marvelous to me that we ever lost command of it   Nothing but taking a Burgoyne with his whole British army could, in my opinion, atone for it, and notwithstanding such an extraordinary victory, we must be obliged to regain the command of that lake again, be the cost what it will, by doing this Canada will easily be brought into union and confederacy with the United States of America   Such an event would put it out of the power of the western tribes of Indians to carry on a war with us, and be a solid and durable bar against any further inhuman barbarities committed on our frontier inhabitants by cruel and blood-thirsty savages, for it is impossible for them to carry on a war, except they are supported by the trade and commerce of some civilized nation, which to them would be impracticable did Canada compose a part of the American empire "

"CAPTAIN NORDBERG TO THE NEW YORK PROVINCIAL CONGRESS.

"The most respectable Gentlemen Provincial Congress in New York   I beg leave to represent to the most respectable congress this circumstance

"I am a native of Sweeden, and have been persecuted for that I have been against the French faction there.   I have been in his Brittannick Majesty's service since January, 1758

"I have been twice shot through my body here last war in America, and I am now 55 years old, reduced of age, wounds, and gravels, which may be seen by Doctor Jones certificate

"[In] 1773, I got permission in Jamaica to go to London, where I petition to be an Invalid officer, but as a foreigner, I could not enjoy a commission in England or Ereland   His Majesty was graciously pleased to give me the allowance for Fort George, 7 shillings sterling per day, with liberty to live where I pleased in America, *because the Fort has been abandoned this 8 year and only 2 men remain there for to assist any express going between New York and Canada* I arrived here in New York last year in September, with intention to live in New York, as I heard nothing els than disharmony amongst Gentlemen which was not agreeable to my age, I resolved to go to Fort George, and live there in a little cottage as a Hermit where I was very happy for 6 months

"The 12th of May last Mr Romans came and took possession of Fort George, Mr Romans behaved very genteel and civil to me, I told that I did not belong to the army, and I may be considered as half pay officer or invalid, and convinced him that I was plagued with Gravell, Mr Romans gave me his passport to go to New Lebanon for to recover my health, and he told me that in regard to my age I may go where I pleased

"As I can't sell any bill for my subsistence, and I can't live upon wind and weather, I therefore beg and implore the most respectable Congress permission to go to England, and I entend to go to my native country   I could have gone away secret so well as some others have done, but I will not upon any account do such thing

"I hope the most respectable will not do partially to refuse me, because Major Etherington, Captain Brown, Captain Kelly, which is in the army have been permitted to go to England, and it may happen they return here again on actual service, which old age and infirmities render me incapable off

"As it is the custom amongst the Christian Nations and the Turks, that they give subsistence to every Prisoner according to their rank, should the most respectable Congress have claim upon me to be a prisoner here, I hope they will give me my subsistence from the 12 May last, according to my rank as captain   I implore the favour of the most respectable Congress, answer   I have the honor to remain with great respect, Gentlemen, Your most obedt servant,

"JOHN NORDBERG

"New-York, december, 1775"

In June Arnold turned over his command to Colonel Benjamin Hinman, who was stationed at Ticonderoga with about five hundred troops of the 1,000 he had brought from Connecticut   Soon after this, through an understanding with General Washington and by direction of Congress, General Schuyler assumed the general command of all the northern troops   On the 1st of July following Schuyler, in his returns to Congress, reported the following troops under his command, and their disposition   At Ticonderoga, 495, at Crown Point, 302, at Lake George Landing, 102, and at Fort George 104, all belonging to Colonel Hinman's force of Connecticut troops, and of the Massachusetts troops there were at Ticonderoga 40, at Crown Point, 109, at Fort George, 25; of New York soldiers there were 205 at Fort George [1]

Lossing, in his *Life of Schuyler*, quotes from a letter of Schuyler to General Washington the following not encouraging report of the discipline in force at Ticonderoga upon his arrival at that post   " About ten last night, I arrived at the landing place, the north end of Lake George, a post occupied by a captain and one hundred men   A sentinel, on being informed that I was in the boat, quitted his post to go and wake the guard consisting of three men, in which he had no success   I walked up and came to another, a sergeant's guard   Here the sentinel challenged, but suffered me to come up to him, the whole guard, like the first, being sound asleep "

The course pursued by the Indians early in the Revolutionary struggle was the cause of much anxiety to the colonists and opened the way to the bloody deeds that followed their alliance with the English and their association with the Tories   The alarming encroachments of the white settlers upon the domain of the Iroquois undoubtedly had its influence in producing this deplorable result   Sir William Johnson, England's Indian agent, died in 1774, but much of his great influence over the Six Nations descended to his successor, an influence that was potent in withholding the Iroquois power from alliance with the French in the earlier war   The successor was Sir Guy Johnson, a nephew of Sir William   Upon the breaking out of the Revolution it became the policy of the Americans to secure simply the neutrality of the Indians (which policy was successful as far as the Oneidas were concerned), while the British made undisguised efforts to effect their close alliance to the royal cause   La Corne St Luc, a bitter partisan, had declared, "We must let loose the savages upon the frontier of these scoundrels to inspire terror and to make them submit · In the spring of 1777 Governor Tryon wrote to Germain that he and the partisan named were perfectly agreed as to the employment of Indians in the war   Brant, the great Mohawk chief, had already been taken to England (1775–6), was shown marked favor by the government and employed to lead all who would follow him against the colonists   Against this inhuman policy Pitt hurled his bitterest invective and in 1777, when the policy was thus defended by one of the secretaries of state, in parliament: "It is perfectly justifiable to use all the means that God and nature have put in our hands," Pitt replied. "I know not what idea that lord may entertain of God and nature, but I know that such abominable principles are equally abhorrent to religion and humanity" He called upon the bishops to disavow such principles and "to vindicate the religion of our God" But his appeals were in vain, and the colonial secretary (Germain) gave special instructions to employ Indians "in fighting Republicans"

At length, late in the season of 1775, the Congress began to see the importance of an invasion into Canada It had, apparently, become a necessary measure for self-protection, as Governor Carleton (of Canada) had received a commission authorizing him to muster and arm the people of the province, and to march them into any province of America and arrest and put to death, or spare "rebels" and other offenders Major-General Philip Schuyler had been appointed to the command of the northern department (which included all of New York) with Richard Montgomery as his chief lieutenant An army of three thousand men was concentrating at Ticonderoga for the proposed expedition, while Carleton, apprised of the movement, made preparations to oppose it by creating a naval force competent to maintain supremacy on the lake To defeat this design Montgomery took the small force already assembled and rapidly descended the lake and seized the position at the Isle aux Noix There he was joined by Schuyler and an address of conciliation was made to the Canadians, which had the effect of partially influencing the people to maintain neutrality towards the Americans At the same time Carleton's efforts to enlist the general populace were almost unsuccessful, they would not join in active aggression against their neighbors across the border

A council had already been held at Montreal by the chiefs and warriors of the Iroquois, Guy Johnson and Brant both taking part Here the savages swore fealty to the king, the first act in the long catalogue of slaughter and devastation that followed

As the first step towards the invasion the Americans, 1,000 strong, made a demonstration against St Johns, during which they were attacked by a body of Indians who were repulsed After erecting a slight breastwork near the fort, Schuyler fell back to his original position and erected a *chevaux de frise* in the Sorel, obstructing navigation into the lake by Carleton's vessels, then in progress of construction at St Johns Schuyler was now called to Albany and was there detained by sickness, leaving the command in the efficient hands of Montgomery. He soon adopted aggressive measures St. Johns was then occupied by a garrison of 700 men under Major Preston, and was looked upon as the key to Canada This position was considered impregnable to the force at Montgomery's command, and he resolved to assault the works at Chambly, a few miles below It was accomplished in the night (Oct 19th), after feeble defense by the small garrison, and placed in Montgomery's possession several heavy guns, a large quantity of powder and other stores, all which he was in extreme need of This success turned the scale of Canadian sympathy more towards America and large numbers joined the army , which spirit was fostered by Montgomery, who sent detachments of his soldiers in different directions through their country for that purpose Two of these parties, under Allen and Brown, respectively, approached Montreal, and without order and with apparent injudiciousness, resolved upon capturing the island Brown failed to cooperate with Allen, as arranged, and the latter with his party was captured after gallant fighting [1]

Carleton's success over Allen and Brown now led him to attempt the relief of St. Johns His plans embraced a conjunction with Colonel McLean who was stationed with a corps at the mouth of the Sorel Carleton started with a force of about 1,000, mostly Canadians and Indians, to make the passage of the river from Montreal to Longueil , but Seth Warner had already occupied the eastern bank of the river with his Green Mountain boys, and apprehending Carleton's movements, he fortified his position with a few pieces of artillery and awaited the fleet Carleton was welcomed by Warner with a terrible fire of musketry and grape shot, which sent his undisciplined troops flying back to the island McLean also retreated to his former position and at this time through an intercepted letter from Arnold to Schuyler, learned that a formidable force was descending the valley of the Chaudière to assault Quebec ; he accordingly hastened, with such force as he could collect, to occupy that place Montgomery immediately occupied the position from which McLean had fallen back, erected works at the confluence of the St Lawrence and Sorel and, further aided by floating batteries, completely controlled both streams, cutting off Montreal and the fortifications on the upper waters of the river and lakes from communication with Quebec and the sea This well conceived action forced Preston to surrender St Johns, after which Montgomery marched against Montreal and that city also surrendered without making defense Carleton relinquished the command at Montreal to Prescott before Montgomery's arrival, and escaped in disguise in the night down the river past the American batteries

Meanwhile Washington had planned one of those remarkably bold and original movements for which he was famous, with the capture of Quebec as its object This was no less than the march of a thousand men from Cambridge, by way of Kennebec River, through the untrodden wilderness between that stream and the Chaudière, and the descent of the latter to Quebec

Had it been possible for human sagacity to foresee the almost insurmount-

---

[1] Allen was taken a prisoner to 'England, where he was held nearly three years, and persecuted with all manner of indignities in loathsome prisons At the end of his imprisonment he was exchanged and received with honors by his country

able obstacles and hardships to overcome in this then unparalleled expedition, it would in all probability have been so directed as to have been entirely successful   But as it proved the heroic troops and their officers were buried in the depths of the wilderness for thirty-two days, suffering the horrors of starvation, tempestuous weather and freezing floods in the streams they were forced to ford, before reaching the Chaudière   Here actual starvation threatened, and it was still seventy miles to the nearest French settlement   Arnold, therefore, left the main body of his troops and, taking with him fifty-five men, started down the river for food   The settlement was reached and Indians sent back with supplies and to guide the troops down the river.   This was all accomplished, but it took time, and it was nearly two months from the date of leaving Cambridge before they reached the St Lawrence opposite Quebec (November 9th), decimated to 750 strong [1]

It is more than probable that this expedition, bold, hazardous, and secret as it was, would have secured the prize for which it was planned, but for the intercepted letter before alluded to.   The alertness of McLean saved the city from capitulation.   Four days Arnold was prevented from crossing the river, at the end of which, on the night of the 13th of November, he embarked 550 men in bark canoes and landed them at Wolf's Cove, whence they ascended to the Plains of Abraham   Here he ordered his men to give three cheers, in the hope of thus calling the garrison out to attack him, upon which it was his purpose to rush through the open city gates, call around him the sympathizers he believed to be in the city and hold the situation   The regulars did not come out   Arnold was joined by the 200 men left on Point Levi across the river, and he now spent a few days in issuing proclamations and arrogantly demanding the surrender of the city   Little attention was paid to him or his movements by the enemy   Learning that Carleton was coming down the river and that the garrison was preparing for a sortie that might overwhelm his really insignificant force, he prudently retreated to Point aux Trembles, twenty miles above, and awaited instructions from Montgomery   The latter had left Montreal in charge of a force under General Wooster, and on the 3d of December reached Arnold and his " shivering troops "   With the clothing he brought the complaining soldiers were reclad and then the combined force, still less than 1,000 strong, outside of 200 Canadians who had volunteered under Colonel James Livingstone, pressed forward and halted before Quebec on the 5th of December   A demand for the surrender of the city was made on the following morning but the flag sent was fired upon, and in response to a letter from

---

[1] Their sufferings from cold and hunger had been extreme   At one time they had attempted to make broth of boiled deer skin moccasins to sustain life, and a dog belonging to Henry (afterwards General) Dearborn made savory food for them   In this expedition were men who afterwards became famous in American history — Aaron Burr, R. J Meigs, Henry Dearborn, Daniel Morgan and others — Lossing

Montgomery to Carleton, the latter said he would hold no communication with
" a rebel general "

Preparations were now made to assault the city   Colonel Lamb had brought
six twelve-pounder guns which were mounted upon a redoubt built of ice, and
from a few mortars stationed in the lower town, shells were thrown into the
city, by which a few buildings were set on fire   But Lamb's ice battery was
destroyed by well-directed cannonade from the citadel and he was forced to
withdraw   Clearly, this course would not succeed, and Montgomery waited
two weeks in vain for reinforcements   His soldiers, many of whom had left
him before his departure from Montreal, upon expiration of their terms, were becoming dissatisfied ; the small-pox broke out among them and to make matters worse, Arnold, always dictatorial and obstinate, quarreled with other officers and thus further alienated some of the troops

At last and almost in desperation, Montgomery determined upon an attempt to carry the city by a direct assault at two points, one division to be led
by himself and the other by Arnold   On the first stormy night Arnold was to
attack the lower town, set fire to the suburb of St Roque, while the main body
should make an assault from the St Lawrence River side under Montgomery
A snow storm began on the 30th of December , sickness, desertion and expiration of enlistment terms had dwindled the force to seven hundred and fifty effective men, but the movement was carried forward   While Arnold led his
three hundred and fifty men to the assault on the St Charles side, Livingston
made a feint upon the St Louis gate and Major Brown menaced the Cape Diamond bastion   At the same time Montgomery descended to the St Lawrence
and made his way along the narrow shore at the foot of the cape   The whole
plan had been revealed to Carleton by a Canadian deserter and the garrison
was prepared for the assault   A battery was placed at the narrow pass on the
St Charles side and a block-house with masked cannon occupied the narrow
road at the foot of Cape Diamond   Montgomery approached this block-house,
where all was still   Believing his presence was not known he shouted to the
companies of Captains Mott and Cheesemen, near him, " Men of New York,
you will not fear to follow where your general leads , push on, my brave boys
and Quebec is ours !"   At this moment a charge of grape shot from a single
gun, which, tradition says, was fired by a drunken sailor (the last of the block-
house garrison, the remainder having fled at the approach of the Americans),
swept through the narrow path with terrific destructiveness   Montgomery
fell, pierced though the head and both legs; his dying form was caught in the
arms of Burr   Cheeseman and McPherson, aids, and ten others were killed
The assault was doomed , the fall of the brave leader overwhelmed the troops,
and Montgomery's division, now in command of Colonel Campbell, hastily
withdrew.

Meanwhile Arnold's band was marching through blinding snow and heavy drifts, in single file, up the defile that led to his point of attack This could be raked by the guns of the battery and swept by the musketry from the garrison walls   Lamb had left his artillery as useless, and joined Arnold   The city bells began ringing and drums beating   Fire was opened on the narrow pass and Arnold fell wounded and was borne from the field   Morgan took command and amid desperate fighting a battery was captured with a number of the guards and its barricades scaled with ladders   The commander was the second man to cross the works   With the aid of Colonel Green and Majors Bigelow and Meigs he succeeded in gathering around him two hundred of the troops, covered with snow and ice and suffering with the cold , but as day dawned they were imbued with renewed enthusiasm and called on their brave commander to lead them against a second battery mounted beyond the angle of a street   The advance was quickly made, but turning the angle they were met by a body of troops under Captain Anderson , the latter called on Morgan to surrender and was immediately shot by him   The Americans now rushed ahead, planted ladders against this barricade and mounted to the top   Here they saw before them two lines of British regulars, the butts of their muskets on the ground and their bayonets towards the summit of the barricade   Many of the Americans retreated into the stone houses whence they could maintain their fire, and the conflict continued   But Carleton was enabled, through the failure of the other assaults, to throw his entire force against Morgan   After several hours of resistance and waiting in vain for aid from the other detachments, the brave band was compelled to surrender after a loss of a hundred men   Thus ended the siege   .

The entire loss of the Americans in killed wounded and prisoners, was about four hundred   The British lost about twenty killed

Upon the death of Montgomery Arnold took the command and retired with the remainder of the troops to Silllery, three miles up the river, where he blockaded Quebec during the remainder of the winter   His position and his prospects were not encouraging   The troops were insubordinate and the Canadian people, prompted by the priests, were becoming disaffected towards the Americans, while at the same time disease was rampant among the troops. Arnold was relieved in April by General Wooster and a month later General Thomas took command   Arnold was transferrsd to Montreal, where " he revealed the cupidity and rapaciousness, which, in after years, and on another stage deformed and debauched his whole character " [1]

The approach of three British ships that had forced their way up the river, conveying troops and supplies, coupled with his own almost helpless situation, impelled Thomas to begin a retreat, which was done on the 5th of May   The order was for such immediate movement that most of the sick and wounded and the stores were abandoned   The retreat itself was a long series of hard-

---

[1] WATSON'S *Essex County*

ships, struggles with sickness and hunger and general suffering   At Sorel
General Thomas fell a victim to the prevailing epidemic and was succeeded by
General Sullivan   This officer's subsequent conduct of the retreat showed the
highest generalship and was formally recognized by Congress   The capture
of the post at the Cedars, on the St Lawrence, by the Canadians and Mohawks, and the sanguinary disaster at the Three Rivers, only served to hasten
Sullivan's retreat, and he arrived at Crown Point in June, with the remnant of
a conquered army

CHAPTER XIII

CLOSE OF 1776

The Canadian Mission — Its Failure — Hostilities near New York — Battle of Long Island —
Small-Pox at Crown Point — Carleton's Pursuit of the Americans — Dr Thacher's Journal — Building
a British Fleet for Lake Champlain — Counter-Action by Arnold — Sailing of the British Fleet — Respective Positions of the American and British Vessels — The Engagement — Retirement of the Americans — Rapid Pursuit — Arnold's Bravery — Burning of a Portion of the Fleet — Escape of the Remainder to Crown Point — The British Retire to Canada for the Winter — Campaign of 1777 — Burgoyne's Operations — Assault upon and Evacuation of Ticonderoga — The Jane McCrea Incident — Burgoyne's Surrender

THE country was now fully ablaze with the Revolution, and the remainder
of the year 1776 witnessed some important occurrences   The month of
March, while Arnold was yet in command at Montreal, had witnessed the failure of the commission appointed by Congress, consisting of Benjamin Franklin,
Samuel Chase and Charles Carroll, to proceed to Canada and induce the people
to establish a free government and join the confederated colonies   Hostilities
were for the time being transferred to New York and vicinity and the battle of
Long Island, disastrous to the Americans, was fought and New York was evacuated in September, while other occurrences of moment were taking place in
the northern department, with which we are more directly interested

When the retreating army had reached Crown Point, as detailed at the close
of the preceding chapter, it mustered about five thousand men, but more than
half of these were helpless in sickness, chiefly from the terrible scourge, small-
pox   For ten days the troops remained there, suffering much from exposure,
during which brief period three hundred deaths occurred   What would have
happened had not Sullivan, in his wisdom, destroyed everything in his track
that could have aided the British in their pursuit, may be imagined   When
they arrived at Champlain their progress was stayed for want of shipping   The
naval supremacy of the lake now became of perhaps greater moment than ever

before Carleton immediately began the construction of boats in the Sorel, and six large vessels, which had been built in England, were taken apart below the Chambly Rapids and conveyed to St Johns, where they were again rebuilt in the utmost haste   The 1st of October found him with a fleet of thirty-one vessels all armed with from one to eighteen guns and manned by several hundred seamen and a corps of artillery

Congress had not been idle   Here Arnold found a field for the exercise of his indomitable energy, and he saw the construction, directly from the forest trees, and equipment of fifteen vessels, armed in the aggregate with fifty-five guns and manned by three hundred and fifty men, men, however, with little experience in naval affairs

A short period of repose followed, but neither antagonist was idle   Carleton strengthened the forts at St. Johns and Isle aux Noix and gathered a land force of seven thousand troops to march against his enemy when the lake was conquered, and Arnold cruised the lake in defiance of the foe, perfected his plans for the expected contest, and drilled his men

Meanwhile General Gates had, through intrigue, displaced General Schuyler in command of the northern army, and concentrated his forces at Ticonderoga [1]

Dr James Thacher joined the American forces that marched to Ticonderoga from Boston   He was an intelligent man and kept a journal from 1775 to 1783, which proved of great historic value   He writes of Ticonderoga and the events about to occur in that vicinity with such clearness and evident sincerity and judgment, that we are fully justified in quoting as follows : —

August 20th, 1776 — "Having recovered my health and being prepared to follow my regiment, I am this day to bid adieu to the town of Boston, where I have resided very pleasantly for the last five months   I am destined to a distant part of our country, and know not what sufferings and hazards I shall be called to encounter, while in the discharge of my military duty. I shall commence my journey in company with Lieutenant Whiting and fourteen men who were left here as invalids

" September — We took our route through Worcester, Springfield, Charlestown, in New Hampshire, and over the Green Mountains to Skeensboro, which is the place of rendezvous for the continental troops and militia destined to Ticonderoga   Here boats are provided at the entrance of Lake Champlain, which are continually passing to and from this place   We embarked on the

---

[1] Gates at first established his headquarters at Crown Point, but soon afterward withdrew his forces from that post and fell back upon Ticonderoga. This step was taken by the advice and concurrence of a board of general officers but contrary to the wishes of the field officers   The commander-in-chief was exceedingly dissatisfied with this movement of Gates, believing that the relinquishment of that post in its consequences would be equivalent to an abandonment of Lakes George and Champlain, and all advantages to be derived therefrom — STONE'S *Life of Brant*, with reference to Washington's letter to Gates.

6th instant, and with good oarsmen and sails we arrived the same day, and joined our regiment here, a distance of thirty miles

"10th — Ticonderoga is situated on an angle of land forming the western shore of Lake Champlain, or rather what is called South Bay, being the inlet into the lake   It is about twelve miles south of the old fortress at Crown Point, and about one hundred and ten miles north of Albany   This point of land is surrounded on three sides by water, and on the northwest side it is well defended by the old French lines and several block-houses   On the east side of South Bay, directly opposite to Ticonderoga, is a high circular hill, on the summit of which our army has erected a strong fort, within which is a square of barracks   This is called Mt Independence   A communication is maintained between the two places by a floating bridge thrown across the lake, which is about four hundred yards wide.   The army stationed at this post at present is supposed to consist of about eight to ten thousand men, and Major General Gates is commander-in-chief   We have a naval armament[1] on Lake Champlain, below this garrison, which is commanded by the intrepid General Arnold, General Waterbury is second in command   The British have also a naval armament[2] of superior force, at the head of which is the celebrated Sir Guy Carleton "

Carleton and Arnold's Naval Battle — " Preparations are making on both sides for a vigorous combat to decide which power shall have dominion on the lake   Should Sir Guy Carleton be able to defeat our fleet, it is supposed that he will pursue his victorious career by an attempt to possess himself of this garrison , and our troops are making the utmost exertion to put our works in the best possible defense   Each regiment has its alarm post assigned, and they are ordered to repair to it, and to man the lines at day light every morning   Among our defensive weapons are poles, about twelve feet long, armed with sharp iron points, which each soldier is to employ against the assailants when mounting the breast works

"10th [3] — By intelligence from our fleet, on the lake, we are in daily expectation of a decisive naval action, as the British are known to have a superior force , our officers here, I understand, are full of anxiety respecting the important event   Great confidence is reposed in the judgment of General Arnold, whom General Gates has appointed to command our fleet

"15th — I have now to recount an account of a naval engagement between the two fleets on Lake Champlain [4]   The British under command of Sir Guy Carleton, advanced on the 11th instant, and found our fleet in a line of

---

[1] Built and equipped by Arnold at Ticonderoga and Crown Point, as already described

[2] Built at St. Johns and navigated by seven hundred veteran seamen

[3] Without doubt, October 10th

[4] This engagement occurred in the strait between Valcour Island and the western shore, just north of the mouth of the Ausable   Its history cannot be omitted in the sketch of Fort Ticonderoga, because the American vessels were built and manned there

battle prepared for the attack   A warm action soon ensued, and became extremely close and severe, with round and grape shot, which continued about
four hours   Brigadier-General Waterbury, in the *Washington Galley*, fought
with undaunted bravery, till nearly all his officers were killed and wounded,
and his vessel greatly injured, when General Arnold ordered the remaining
shattered vessels to retire up the lake, towards Crown Point, in order to refit.
On the 13th they were overtaken by the enemy, and the action was renewed,
in which was displayed the greatest intrepidity on both sides   The *Washington Galley* being crippled in the first action, was soon obliged to strike and
surrender   General Arnold conducted during the action with great judgment,
firmness, and gallantry, obstinately defending himself against a superior force,
both in numbers or weight of metal   At length, however, he was so closely
pressed that his situation became desperate and he run his own vessel, the
Congress Galley, on shore, which with five gondolas were abandoned and blown
up   Out of sixteen of our vessels, eleven were taken or destroyed, five only
arrived safely at this place   Two of the enemy's gondolas were sunk by our
fleet, and one blown up with sixty men   Their loss in men is supposed to be
equal to our own, which is estimated at about one hundred "

   Preparations to Receive an Attack — " A large number of troops were on
board the British fleet, consisting of regulars, Canadians and savages, which
have been landed on each side of the lake, and it is now expected that Sir Guy
Carleton, at the head of his army, reported to be about ten thousand strong,
will soon invest this post   By order of General Gates, our commander, the
greatest exertions are constantly making, by strengthening our works, to enable us to give them a warm reception, and our soldiery express a strong desire to have an opportunity of displaying their courage and prowess; both
officers and men are full of activity and vigilance

   " 18th — It is now ascertained that the British army and fleet have established themselves at Crown Point, and are strengthening the old fortifications
at that place   Some of their vessels have approached within a few miles of
our garrison, and one boat came within cannon shot distance of our lower battery, in order to reconnoitre and sound the channel, but a few shot having
killed two men, and wounded another, soon obliged her to retire   All of our
troops are to repair to their alarm posts, and man the lines and works, every
morning our continental troops are advantageously displayed on the ramparts,
and our cannon and spears are in readiness for action

   " 20th — Ever since the defeat of our fleet we have been providentially
favored with a strong southerly wind, which has prevented the enemy's advancing to attack our lines, and afforded us time to receive some reinforcements of militia, and to prepare for a more vigorous defense   It seems now
to be the opinion of many of our most judicious officers, that had Sir Guy
Carleton approached with his army immediately after his victory on the lake,

the struggle must have been most desperate, and the result precarious, but we now feel more confidence in our strength"

Carleton Retires to Canada — "November 1st — The enemy remain at Crown Point, and evince no disposition to molest our garrison, having probably discovered that our means of defense are too formidable for them to encounter   General Gates has now ordered a detachment of troops to march towards Crown Point, to reconnoitre their position, or to attack them   A report was soon returned that the whole fleet and army have abandoned Crown Point, and retired into Canada, where they will probably occupy their winter quarters in peace, and it is not probable that Sir Guy Carleton intends to invest our garrison, at this advanced season, unless, however, he should attempt it by marching his army over the ice when the lake is frozen, which will probably be very practicable"

Winter Life in the Barracks — "15th — Ticonderoga is in about latitude forty-four degrees   I have no means in possession of ascertaining the precise degrees of cold, but we all agree that it is colder here than in Massachusetts at the same season   The earth has not yet been covered with snow, but the frost is so considerable that the water of the lake is congealed, and the earth is frozen   We are comfortably situated in our barracks, our provisions are now good, and having no enemy near enough to alarm and disturb us, we have nothing of importance to engage our attention   Our troops are quite healthy, a few cases of rheumatism and pleurisy comprise our sick list, and it is seldom that any fatal cases occur"

Such was the sagacious physician's description of the most important naval engagement on Lake Champlain and other contemporaneous events   General Carleton was harshly and unjustly censured for his retirement to Canada   He realized the strength of the garrison at that time and properly estimated the hazards of an approaching winter which would cut him off from rapid transportation to Canada

While the garrison was "comfortably situated" in the barracks as chronicled by Thacher, Washington was retreating in gloom across the Jerseys, closely pursued by Cornwalis, Forts Washington and Lee had fallen into the hands of the enemy, the militia had shown little of that heroism that was expected of them, and the tory spirit was rife in New York and New Jersey, the American cause seemed in desperate straits   But the spirits of Washington rose to the emergency and before the close of the year he won the battle of Trenton (December 26), which, with Carleton's departure from Lake Champlain, revived the depressed spirits of the colonists

For the campaign of 1777 the English made the most thorough preparation in the north, where General Burgoyne had succeeded Carleton   A large and fully equipped army was gathered in Canada and placed under his command, with which it was intended to crush the insurgent colonies   The force designed for the enterprise numbered more than seven thousand men, besides about two hundred and fifty Canadians, to which were added some four hundred Indians and a large park of artillery   The forces, with the exception of the Indians, assembled at St Johns and Isle aux Noix   Its command, under Burgoyne, was entrusted to such brave and skillful officers as Generals Phillips, Frazer, Powell and Hamilton, of the British troops, and Riedesel and Specht of the hired Germans   Early in June this splendid army left St Johns in boats and reached the banks of the Boquet, where it halted ten days, to enable the commander to make a reconaissance of Ticonderoga, drill his boatmen and hold his notorious conference with the Indians, in which they were deliberately employed to glut their savage passions upon the Americans   This conference was held on the 21st   Burgoyne made a stirring speech to the Indians who pledged themselves to carry out his behests against the colonists   There will always, doubtless, be differences of opinion as to how far Burgoyne went in this bargain and to what extent he inflamed the savages, but the fact must remain that he knew the character of the Indians and their mode of warfare; he knew also, that the Americans had not sought their alliance, desiring only their neutrality, hence the bloody scenes that followed directly upon this bargain between him and the six nations must, in a measure, be accredited to him [1]

The plans of the English for the campaign embraced the cutting off of New England from the Middle States by the opening of communication between New York and Canada   This was to be accomplished by Burgoyne, in co-operation with General Clinton, whose operations were to be carried on down the Hudson   At the same time Sir Wm Howe, with an army of 16,000 men, was to withdraw from New Jersey and move simultaneously around to the Chesapeake and take possession of the Middle States

Unfortunately for the Americans, these plans were hidden and mystified to such an extent that the commanding officers were in great perplexity in devising measures of opposition.   It was the general impression that Burgoyne contemplated a movement against Boston and that Sir Wm Howe was to cooperate in the subjugation of the hot-bed of rebellion, New England   Even after Burgoyne descended from the north, General Howe's movements were misunderstood by Washington, his uncertainty being strengthened by a feigned dispatch sent by Howe to Burgoyne upon the subject of ascending the Hudson, this dispatch was purposely allowed to fall into the hands of the Ameri-

---

[1] "It is but just to this gallant but unfortunate officer, however, to state, that he did all in his power to restrain the excesses and barbarities of the Indians   At the council and war feast, which he gave them near Crown Point, he endeavored to explain to them the laws of civilized war, and charged them that they must only kill those opposing them in arms, that old men, women and children, and prisoners, must be held sacred from the knife or hatchet, even in the heat of battle   But it did no good "— STONE'S *Life of Brant*   The question will, doubtless, be asked whether Burgoyne should not have known, or did not know, at the time that it would "do no good "

can commander, who was thereby impelled to remain inactive and to withhold reinforcements from the northern department As late as July 2d, Washington wrote the Congress, "If we were certain General Burgoyne were approaching Ticonderoga with his whole army, I should not hesitate a moment in concluding that it is in consequence of a preconcerted plan with General Howe, and that the latter is to co-operate with him by pushing his whole force up the North River" And July 22d he wrote, "I cannot give you any certain account of General Howe's operations His conduct is puzzling and embarrassing beyond measure; so are the informations I get At one time the ships are standing up toward the North River, in a little while they are going up the sound, and in one hour after they are going out of the hook" This to General Schuyler In reality the fleet sailed for the Virginia capes on the 23d of July

The command of the northern department was again, by the vacillation of Congress, placed in the hands of General Schuyler, only to deprive him of it the second time on the first of the following August The immediate command of Ticonderoga and its dependencies was given to General Arthur St Clair, an officer of ability and experience, but destined to misfortune Here should have been concentrated an army of ten thousand men, yet Schuyler could muster but half that number in his whole department, while but three thousand were given to St Clair But the works were vastly stronger than when they were so heroically defended by Montcalm The old lines had been fortified by the erection of a block-house, and new works erected at the sawmills and the Lake George landing, all of which were, however, only occupied by feeble detachments A small fort was erected on Mount Hope, while Mount Independence, on the eastern shore of the lake, directly opposite the main fort, was effectively fortified by a star fort enclosing barracks, the base of the hill and its sides were entrenched and supplied with artillery. Ticonderoga and Mount Independence are about fifteen hundred yards apart. Let us quote a little further from the journal of Dr Thacher. —

"According to authentic reports, the plan of the British government for the present campaign is that General Burgoyne's army shall take possession of Ticonderoga, and force his way through the country to Albany, to facilitate this event, Colonel St Leger is to march with a party of British, Germans, Canadians and Indians, to the Mohawk River, and make a diversion in that quarter The royal army at New York, under command of General Howe, is to pass up the Hudson River, and calculating on success in all quarters, the three armies are to form a junction at Albany Here, probably, the three commanders are to congratulate each other on their mighty achievements, and the flattering prospects of crushing the rebellion This being accomplished, the communication between the Southern and Eastern States will be interrupted, and New England, as they suppose, may become an easy prey

"Judging from the foregoing detail, a very active campaign is to be expected, and events of the greatest magnitude are undoubtedly to be unfolded.

"The utmost exertions are now making to strengthen our works at Ticonderoga, and, if possible, to render the post invulnerable Mt Independence, directly opposite to Ticonderoga, is strongly fortified and well supplied with artillery On the summit of the mount, which is table land, is erected a strong fort, in the center of which is a convenient square of barracks, a part of which are occupied for our hospital The communication between these two places is maintained by a floating bridge, which is supported on twenty-two sunken piers of very large timber The spaces between these are filled with separate floats, each about fifty feet long and twelve feet wide, strongly fastened together with iron chains and rivets A boom composed of large pieces of timber, well secured together by riveted bolts, is placed on the north side of the bridge, and by the side of this is placed a double iron chain, the links of which are one and a half inch square The construction of this bridge, boom and chain, of four hundred yards in length, has proved a most laborious undertaking, and the expense must have been immense It is, however, supposed to be admirably adapted to the double purpose of a communication and an impenetrable barrier to any vessels that might attempt to pass our works

"July 1st — We are now assailed by a proclamation of a very extraordinary nature, from General Burgoyne [1] The militia of New England are daily coming in to increase our strength , the number of our troops and our ability to defend the works against the approaching enemy, are considerations which belong to our commanding officers One fact, however, is notorious, that when the troops are directed to man the lines, there is not a sufficient number to occupy the whole extent It appears, nevertheless, so far as I can learn, to be the prevalent opinion, that we shall be able to repel the meditated attack and defeat the views of the royal commander , both officers and men are in high spirits and prepared for the contest "

In spite of the conclusions of this eye witness, it is clear that St Clair was in no condition to repel an assault from such a force as that under command of Burgoyne He knew this to be the fact On the 25th of June he communicated to Schuyler the perilous circumstances by which he was surrounded and the inadequacy of his resources , but he was given no alternative other than to hold the position to the last, when an early evacuation might have averted the misfortune that overtook him The commander-in-chief and Congress were still clinging to the belief and hope that Burgoyne's movements were pretexts

---

[1] Let not people consider their distance from my camp, I have but to give stretch to the Indian forces under my direction — and they amount to thousands — to overtake the banded enemies of Great Britain If the frenzy of hostility should remain, I trust I shall stand acquitted in the eyes of God and man in executing the vengeance of the State against the wilful outcasts — *From Burgoyne's Proclamation*

to cover other operations   Mt Defiance, the real key to success in operations against Ticonderoga, was still unfortified and unoccupied [1]

On the first of July Burgoyne's army appeared before Ticonderoga   The small garrison at Crown Point had fallen back to this point, and Burgoyne established there a hospital, magazine, store-house and base of supplies   He disposed his forces with light infantry, grenadiers, Canadians, Indians and ten pieces of artillery, under command of General Frazer, on the west side of the lake at Putnam's Creek   This force was moved up to Five Mile Point   On the east side of the lake were the Germans, under Riedesel and Breyman , they were moved up to a point nearly opposite, while the remainder of the army were on board of the gunboats and the frigates *Royal George* and *Inflexible*, under the immediate command of Burgoyne himself   This fleet was anchored between the wings of the army and just out of cannon shot from the fort

On the second the right wing of the British was extended on the flank, threatening St Clair's outposts, whereupon the small force on Mt Hope and at the landing was ordered to burn the mills and the public property and fall back within the American lines   Mt. Hope was immediately seized by the British and, it is said, received its name from General Phillips, as expressive of his feelings at that time   St Clair's communications with Lake George were now severed and the eminence was at once further fortified and artillery conveyed to its summit by almost incredible toil, which operations were carried on under a cannonade from St Clair's guns   During these operations Burgoyne's engineer, Lieutenant Twiss, reconnoitered what was then called "Sugar Loaf Hill," the lofty eminence rising seven hundred and fifty feet from the confluence of Lake Champlain and the outlet and directly commanding both Ticonderoga and Mt Independence   The engineer reported, in accordance with his belief, that the eminence was not only unoccupied, but could be reached by a road for transportation of cannon in twenty-four hours   This road was cut out during the night of the fourth, the sound of the choppers' axes being drowned by a cannonade from Mt Hope, the Americans remaining in blissful ignorance of the operation   Before morning several pieces of artillery, which had been landed from the *Thunderer*, were transported to the top of the mountain   Holes were drilled directly into the rocks to which the guns were chained, [2] they comprised eight pieces, twelve pounders and eight-inch howitzers   When the sun rose on the fifth, the British looked down on the strongest fortress of the Americans, confident that they could destroy its garrison and demolish its walls with the plunging shots from their guns   They thereupon, as it is said, called the eminence Mt Defiance, the name it still bears

---

[1] The imagined impregnability of these works would at once fail, in the event of this eminence being occupied by a hostile battery   St Clair had been apprised of this momentous fact by the examination of the preceding year   Pont Le Roy, the engineer of Montcalm, evidently referred to it   And we cannot doubt that the possession of Ticonderoga during more than eighteen years, had disclosed the military value of this position to the British commanders — WATSON

[2] These holes are still visible

The astonishment and anxiety of the Americans when the morning mists swept back from the mountain and revealed the battery almost over their heads, may be imagined   St Clair saw that the position was doomed.   A council of officers was called, but there could be but one decision, if the army was to be saved — evacuation

Even this alternative was threatened with disaster, as General Riedesel was menacing the only avenue of escape by stretching his force around Mount Independence to command the narrow water passage towards Skenesborough Situated, as they were, in full view of the British on Mount Defiance, it was clear that the retreat must be made in the night, and preparations were at once begun   At dusk a heavy cannonade was opened from the outer lines to cover their movements while the garrison gathered stores of all kinds, which, with the sick and wounded, were placed in two hundred boats, with a guard of six hundred men and embarked for Skenesborough, in charge of Colonel Long and accompanied by five armed vessels   At three o'clock on the morning of the 6th the troops began to cross the bridge   At this juncture, and in contradiction of express orders, a building was set on fire on Mount Independence by General De Fermoy   The brilliant illumination spread over the entire scene, the British were aroused and preparations for immediate pursuit begun   St Clair had not the time to destroy the bridge which had cost so much money and labor, and Frazer hurried across it with a strong detachment in pursuit of the fleeing Americans   Within the next few hours Burgoyne so broke up the bridge as to admit the passage of two ships and several of his gunboats, which were crowded on after the American flotilla   Of the moonlight voyage of the latter, Dr Thacher vividly wrote as follows: —

"At about twelve o'clock on the night of 5th instant I was urgently called from sleep, and informed that our army was in motion, and was instantly to abandon Ticonderoga and Mount Independence   I could scarcely believe that my informant was in earnest, but the confusion and bustle soon convinced me that it was really true, and that the short time allowed demanded my utmost industry   It was enjoined on me immediately to collect the sick and wounded and as much of the hospital stores as possible, and assist in embarking them on board the bateaux and boats at the shore   Having with all possible dispatch completed our embarkation, at three o'clock in the morning of the 6th, we commenced our voyage up the South Bay to Skeensboro, about thirty miles   Our fleet consisted of five armed galleys and two hundred bateaux and boats, deeply laden with cannon, tents, provisions, invalids and women   We were accompanied by a guard of 600 men, commanded by Colonel Long, of New Hampshire

"The night was moonlight and pleasant, the sun burst forth in the morning with uncommon lustre, the day was fine, the water's surface serene and unruffled   The shore on each side exhibited a variegated view of huge rocks, caverns and clifts, and the whole was bounded by a thick, impenetrable wilderness.   My pen would fail in the attempt to describe a scene so enchantingly sublime   The occasion was peculiarly interesting, and we could but look back with regret and forward with apprehension   We availed ourselves, however, of the means of enlivening our spirits   The drum and fife afforded us a favorite music, among the hospital stores we found many dozen bottles of choice wine, and, breaking off their necks, we cheered our hearts with the nectarous contents

"At three o'clock in the afternoon we reached our destined post at Skeensboro, being the head of navigation for our galleys   Here we were unsuspicious of danger, but, behold! Burgoyne himself was at our heels   In less than two hours we were struck with surprise and consternation by a discharge of cannon from the enemy's fleet, on our galleys and bateaux lying at the wharf.   By uncommon efforts and industry they had broken through the bridge, boom and chain, which cost our people such immense labor, and had almost overtaken us on the lake, and horribly disastrous indeed would have been our fate   It was not long before it was perceived that a number of their troops and savages had landed, and were rapidly advancing towards our little party   The officers of our guard now attempted to rally the men and form them in battle array, but this was found impossible, every effort proved unavailing; and in the utmost panic they were seen to fly in every direction for personal safety   In this desperate condition, I perceived our officers scampering for their baggage; I ran to the bateaux, seized my chest, carried it a short distance, took from it a few articles, and instantly followed in the train of our retreating party   We took the route to Fort Anne, through a narrow defile in the woods, and were so closely pressed by the pursuing enemy, that we frequently heard calls from the rear to 'March on, the Indians are at our heels'

"Having marched all night we reached Fort Anne at five o'clock in the morning, where we found provisions for our refreshment   A small rivulet called Wood Creek is navigable for boats from Skeensboro to Fort Anne, by which means some of our invalids and baggage made their escape, but all our cannon, provisions, and the bulk of our baggage, with several invalids, fell into the enemy's hands"

While Burgoyne was engaged in these successful operations St. Clair pursued a forced and disorderly march towards Castleton, which he reached in the following night   The three regiments constituting the rear guard of the Americans, under Warner, Francis and Hale, halted at Hubbardton to reorganize and collect the stragglers who had fallen out on the hurried retreat   They occupied a favorable position and there awaited an expected attack   Frazer was near at hand, having lain on his arms the preceding night, and, without waiting for the expected arrival of Riedesel, attacked the American

lines with vigor   Frazer had but eight hundred and fifty regulars, while the
opposing force numbered about thirteen hundred , but this disparity was soon
equalized by the retreat of Hale's regiment [1]   A long and bloody engagement
followed, in which victory seemed alternately to belong to either side   Francis
fell at the head of his regiment   Warner succeeded in joining Schuyler at
Fort Edward   Six miles from this battle-field lay St Clair with his detachment, the co-operation of which might have turned defeat into victory   That
he did not move for that purpose is attributed by his apologists to the fact that
his militia refused to march

The capture of Ticonderoga caused deep consternation and regret throughout the colonies and general rejoicing in England. It had been looked upon as
an impregnable stronghold, and to see it fall without a battle filled the Americans with despondency and gloom   Charges of baseness and treachery were
freely indulged in towards St Clair and Schuyler, and the latter was again
superseded   Even the serene mind and cool judgment of Washington was
disturbed [2]   The truth is, the actual force and condition of St Clair's army
had been over-estimated, both by army officers at a distance and the general
public

Burgoyne's advance was temporarily checked at Fort Anne by Colonel
Long, but the latter was forced to retreat , setting fire to the fort, he fled to
Fort Edward   Here was General Schuyler, his provisions nearly exhausted
and with little ammunition   Being in no condition to offer effective resistance,
the whole force was compelled to fall back to Albany   It was in this crisis
that the soul of Washington arose to that height of hopefulness, patience and
calm strength so seldom reached   Said he in a letter to Schuyler, " This stroke
is severe indeed, and has distressed us much   But, notwithstanding things at
present have a dark and gloomy aspect, I hope a spirited opposition will check
the progress of General Burgoyne's army, and that the confidence derived
from his success will lead him into measures that will, in their consequences be
favorable to us   We should never despair, our position has before been un-
promising, and has changed for the better , so, I trust, it will again "

It is not out of place here to digress from our general subject to mention
an incident that occurred about this time — an incident whose terrible details

---

[1] Hale's regiment was largely composed of sick and convalescent soldiers, and after a sharp skirmish continued the retreat to Castleton , but he was intercepted by a British detachment and himself and
nearly his whole regiment captured.   Hale has been charged with misconduct on this occasion, but the
testimony of those who were present in the engagement and of other patient investigators is to the effect that his action was justified by the circumstances by which he was surrounded

[2] The evacuation of Ticonderoga and Mt Independence is an event of chagrin and surprise, not apprehended nor within the compass of my reasoning   I know not upon what principle it was founded,
and I should suppose it still more difficult to be accounted for, if the garrison amounted to five thousand
men, in high spirits, healthy, well supplied with provisions and ammunition, and the eastern militia
marching to their succor, as you mentioned in your letter on the 9th to the council of safety of New
York — *Washington to General Schuyler, July* 15, 1777

carried a shock of horror to the hearts of all men, whether royal or provincial, while on the part of the latter a feeling of indignation was engendered that no excuses could calm   While Burgoyne was slowly making his way to the Hudson, Jane McCrea, an attractive young woman, was visiting friends at Fort Edward   While her friends were staunch defenders of freedom, she was so much of a royalist as to have become the betrothed of a young tory whose home was in the vicinity of Fort Edward, but who, at this time, was with Burgoyne's forces   When the army of Burgoyne had reached a point near Fort Edward, a squad of Indians, who were scouting in advance of the troops, entered the house of her friends and seized Miss McCrea, and, placing her on a horse, attempted to take her to Burgoyne's camp   As soon as information of the abduction reached the fort, a detachment was started off to rescue her. The Indians with their captive were soon overtaken, but instead of turning to fight, they made the best speed possible to escape   This brought a volley of bullets from their pursuers, one of which struck the poor girl and she fell dead to the ground   Before the Americans could reach them, the Indians, seeing that she was killed, scalped her and bore her sunny lock to the British camp as a trophy.   Her lover was so shocked by the deed that for a time his reason tottered , he finally, after securing by purchase the mournful relic of her death, went to Canada, where he lived alone, a melancholy man, to his death at an advanced age   Miss McCrea's body was buried near Fort Edward, whence, a few years since, it was removed to a cemetery between Fort Edward and Sandy Hill.   Many wild and romantic versions of the atrocious deed have been written, but this is the true one   At the time the story, being repeated from mouth to mouth, became enlarged and distorted to one of abduction and cold murder and raised in the bosoms of hundreds of young men a burning indignation against the British, and Burgoyne in particular, for employing the merciless savages to fight against their countrymen, and caused many to join the army with a determination to avenge the bitter wrong

Contemporaneously with Burgoyne's operations thus far described, was Colonel Barry St Leger's march from Montreal to Oswego, to form a junction with the Indians and tories collected under Johnson and Brant, whence they hoped to penetrate to the Mohawk River by way of Oneida Lake and Wood Creek, with the ultimate view of joining Burgoyne at Albany   To the office of general history must be resigned the details of this unsuccessful campaign, the failure of which formed a part of the general calamity that was to overtake Burgoyne

Gates was now again at the head of the northern military department   General Stark was at Bennington, with part of a brigade   At this point the Americans had collected a large quantity of stores, which Burgoyne, finding himself short of provisions, determined to capture, and at the same time secure loyalist volunteers   An expedition was fitted out for this purpose, under com-

11

mand of Colonel Baume, about the middle of August. On the 14th they approached the American position and entrenched   Stark had collected a large number of fugitives from the Hubbardton disaster and Warner joined him on the 15th   The next day Stark made a brilliant attack on the British and the ensuing battle of Bennington ended with a loss of less than one hundred Americans, while the Hessians lost in killed, wounded and prisoners nearly a thousand

Burgoyne's progress was slow, harassed as he was by the desolation Schuyler had wisely left in his way and continued attacks by the Americans. Gates formed a fortified camp on Bemis's Heights, on the Hudson, where he was attacked by Burgoyne September 19th   The battle was indecisive, the British retiring to their camp on Saratoga Heights (now Schuylerville), to await the hoped for approach of Sir Henry Clinton from the south   The latter captured the fortifications on the Hudson Highlands and burned Kingston. Burgoyne now again attacked Gates at Bemis's Heights, but was defeated and again retired to his camp   Here, harassed by defeat on all sides, his supplies failing and finding it impossible to move forward and equally impossible to make a successful retreat, he surrendered his entire army on the 17th of October   At the opening of the campaign Burgoyne's army numbered nine thousand two hundred and thirteen men   When he laid down his arms, his Indians having already abandoned him, he surrendered five thousand, seven hundred and fifty-two [1]

While Burgoyne was proceeding southward, as detailed, Lincoln was engaged in collecting a force of four thousand militia at Manchester, Vt, by which the flank of the British army was seriously menaced   A portion of this force was then detailed for an important movement which was intended should sever Burgoyne's communications and possibly seize Ticonderoga   Colonel Johnson, with a party of about five hundred men was detached and sent against Skenesborough and Fort Edward, and with the special object of covering the retreat of the other detachments   One of these was commanded by Brown (about the same strength as the first named), and was ordered to proceed to the landing on Lake George and rescue the prisoners held there, which accomplished he was to act upon his best judgment   Crossing Lake Champlain at the narrows above Ticonderoga, his band marched all night, kept together by signals imitating the hooting of owls and after severe toil among the rugged fastnesses of the mountains that separate the two lakes for a distance of fourteen miles, he fell upon the enemy by a complete surprise just as day was breaking   Three hundred British troops were captured without resistance, with the works on Mount Hope and at the landing, two hundred bateaux, an armed

---

[1] "It was, perhaps, no fault of General Gates that he had been placed in command at the north just at the auspicious moment (August 1st, joining the army the 19th) when the discomfiture of Burgoyne was no longer problematical   He was ordered by Congress to the station, and performed his duty well   But it is no less true that the laurels won by him ought to have been harvested by Schuyler "

sloop and a number of gunboats stationed here to protect the landing   One hundred American prisoners were liberated, which was the primary object of the expedition   Captain Ebenezer Allen was detached by Brown with a small force to assail the works on Mount Defiance   The precipitous acclivity was scaled and the battery captured without firing a gun   Early the following morning Colonel Johnson joined Brown before Ticonderoga   These united forces invested the fortress and called on the commander, General Powell, to surrender   A defiant reply was returned and after cannonading the works for four days, the attack was abandoned, the walls being impregnable to the small guns in possession of the Americans   At the landing Brown embarked a body of troops in the captured boats and ascended Lake George, with the design of seizing Diamond Island, where Burgoyne had deposited a quantity of stores

When the tidings of Burgoyne's surrender reached Ticonderoga the small garrison dismantled and evacuated the works and started upon a stealthy flight down the lake , but they were not permitted to escape unscathed, for Allen intercepted them near the site of the village of Essex, cut off and captured several of the rear boats and seized about fifty prisoners, with stores, cattle, etc

CHAPTER XIV

TO THE CLOSE OF THE REVOLUTION

Effects of Burgoyne's Defeat—The Gates-Conway Cabal — Appointment of Lafayette to Command of the Northern Department—Closing Events of the Revolution — An Insult to General Schuyler — Garrisons at Fort Edward and Vicinity — Events of 1778-79 — Sir John Johnson's Invasion —The Sammons Incident—Capture of Fort Anne—Attack upon Fort George—A Bloody Engagement—Evacuation of Fort Edward—The Vermont Mystery—Close of the Revolution

AFTER Burgoyne's surrender all the forts and posts held by the British were evacuated and as far north as Crown Point the country was relieved of the invaders   Even the Tories, many of whom had taken an active part in Burgoyne's advance, seemed to be suddenly impressed with the idea that Canada was a good place to live in, and, leaving lands and houses, sought sympathy and homes across the northern border among their royalist friends

A few families had remained in the vicinity of Lake George during the exciting weeks preceding Burgoyne's futile march, and all had suffered more or less at the hands of the invaders for their temerity   But the literal wiping out of the enemy was hailed with nearly as much joy as would have been a proclamation of peace by those who had sought safety in flight, and with cheered hearts they returned to their homes, often to find them sacked or burned

It was during this autumn that the famous " Gates-Conway cabal " came near to disrupting Congress and, perhaps, ruining all that had been gained in the cause of liberty   The jealous, intriguing disposition of Gates was the prime cause of the trouble   He sought to fill the place held by Washington and believed that the powerful influence of his friends in Congress, who composed nearly all of the eastern delegates, would place him there, and to accomplish this end he himself left no effort untried   He found a willing and capable tool for his purpose in General Thomas Conway, who threw his whole energy and ability into the dirty work, even stooping to writing anonymous letters to members of Congress filled with vile insinuations against Washington, and forging others as from the pen of Washington   But though feeling ran high in Congress regarding the matter and many eminent and true patriots used strong language against Washington and in favor of Gates, the conspiracy was finally headed off   One of the insults of this disgraceful affair was the appointment by Congress of Lafayette to the command of the northern department, unbeknown to General Washington, at whose request or through whose orders alone it properly should have been done   But the generous commander-in-chief overlooked the insult from Congress, and lent the young ally his best aid in making preparations for an invasion in Canada — another undertaking ordered by Congress without consulting Washington   But like many another attempt of this kind by legislatures and governments, it was given up for the reason that the ordering power failed to furnish men and means for carrying out its own plans   Consequently comparative quiet existed in the northern part of New York, and particularly so in the vicinity of Lake George   The subsequent events of the Revolutionary struggle bore not so directly upon the history of Lake George and its environs, as those which have been briefly detailed   The year 1777 had been fruitful in military events of a minor character, which are beyond the province of this work, yet all influencing to some degree the fortunes of the great contest   Among these were the battle of Brandywine, fought in September, ending in at least partial defeat to the Americans ; the massacre at Paoli ; the battle of Germantown, October 4th, claimed as an American victory , the effort of Congress to secure the neutrality, at least, of the Six Nations, December 3d, an effort which was once more repeated only to fail on both occasions   But the discouraging character of most of these operations was happily overshadowed by the successes of the North, as already described

The opening of 1778 was signalized by a treaty of alliance with France, which was the source of renewed confidence throughout the colonies, but though the year was, like the preceding one, filled with stirring events, nearly all of them occurred far beyond the province of this work to record   The historic invasion and massacre at Wyoming, the battle of Monmouth, at first disastrous to the Americans, but saved to them by the genius of Washington ; the destruction of the settlement at the German Flats, and the bloody massacre at Cherry Valley, were among the more prominent events of the year, which closed without important or decisive advantage to either army

Much complaint had been made in Congress concerning the administration of the northern department, no doubt generated by Gates and kept in brisk activity by his friends in Congress A committee was appointed by Congress to investigate the subject, which finally reported in February following (1778), recommending the ordering of a court-martial to try General Schuyler for general neglect of duty The court was organized with General Lincoln as president and John Laurens as judge advocate, at Pawling, Duchess county, and the trial lasted thirty-five days, when he was acquitted " with the highest honor " The verdict was afterward confirmed by Congress, to which body Schuyler had been elected before the verdict was made public

So entirely had Burgoyne's disastrous campaign crushed the war spirit and depleted the material of the English in the North, that all the American troops were withdrawn to Washington's aid in the more exciting and stirring scenes farther South, except a very few small detachments, which were left more to care for the fortifications they occupied than to repel an expected or possible attack of the enemy.

At Fort Edward a few men were retained , this post for some time was the most northern one occupied by the Americans in the valleys of Lakes George and Champlain It was even contemplated closing this fort, judging from the following extract from a letter from General Washington to General Stark, written in October, 1778 " I would not have you build barracks at Fort Edward The troops now there may winter at Saratoga, where are good barracks for three hundred men "[1]

In fact, nearly all the great military operations for the succeeding two years took place on the southern boundary of the State and along the sea coast In June, however, a company of Tories who had fled to Canada with Sir John Johnson, to the number of one hundred or more, made a rapid and stealthy march through Fonda's Bush to the Sacandaga, where they embarked and " descended twenty-five miles to the Hudson, and thence by the way of Lakes George and Champlain, proceeded to St Johns in safety This foray may have awakened its commander to a sense of the exposed condition of the northern department, for we learn from Stark's *Memoirs* that late in the fall small detachments of soldiers were stationed at Fort Edward, Fort Schuyler, and other points, in expectation of further raids In November of this year a large British force and several armed British vessels advanced to Ticonderoga and completed the devastation that had been begun on both sides of the lake — a course that was, perhaps, justified by the rules of warfare, but one that worked little good to the English cause, while it needlessly caused much private suffering The year 1778 thus closed, neither side appearing anxious or

---

[1] *General Stark's Memoirs*

able to disturb the other.   Only bands of marauding Indians were to be looked for on the part of the Americans, while the Indians themselves cared but little for any injury the impoverished and harassed settlers could do them in return

The year 1779 witnessed the attempt of the British to secure the alliance of the neutral Oneidas, an attempt that did not succeed   It also saw the remarkable expedition of Sullivan and Clinton into the heart of the domain of the Six Nations and the destruction of many of their most important villages; but the general progress of the war was marked with but few signal actions, it was rather a continuation of the predatory warfare that had already distinguished much of the British arms   The struggle had now been continued for five years, but the settlers of New York State were destined to still further suffering

In March, 1779, a band of Indians made an attack upon the settlement of Skenesborough   But three lives were lost by this incursion, but every building in the place was burned to the ground, and all property that was transferable was borne away by the captors, who, as usual, loaded it upon the backs of their prisoners, who comprised nearly every inhabitant of the settlement These prisoners were afterwards transferred to the British at Montreal for the sum of eight dollars each, and were finally exchanged, after suffering two years' imprisonment

In the spring of 1780, Sir John Johnson came up Lake Champlain to Crown Point, at the head of a force of five hundred men, composed of British troops, a detachment of his own Royal Greens, and about two hundred Indians and Tories   From Crown Point he made his way through the forest to the Sacandaga River, and at midnight entered the north part of Johnstown so stealthily that the sleeping inhabitants were entirely unaware of his proximity. He divided his force into two bodies that they might cover more territory, and then ensued a catalogue of barbarous atrocity almost too cold-blooded and ruthless to live in history.   Families of men, women and children were brutally slaughtered, their dwellings burned and their property destroyed   Incidents almost without number occurred, the recital of which has brought the blush of anger to the cheek of honorable manhood and filled the childish breast with horror for a century   The Mohawk valley was devastated in the track of the barbarous horde   The immediate object of this cowardly invasion was the recovery of some valuable plate which had been buried at the time of Johnson's flight in 1776   Since that time it had been faithfully watched over by a former slave of Johnson's, who, with the aid of four soldiers, disinterred the silver and laid it at his master's feet   It was divided among forty soldiers for transportation to Montreal   Common humanity will find it difficult to find in the quest of his property, justification for the inhuman accompaniments of the expedition   At the time of this invasion Governor Clinton was at

Kingston He hastened to Albany when the first intelligence reached him, collected such militia as he was able and marched to Lake Géorge to intercept Johnson Colonel Van Schaick with seven hundred men followed the invaders by way of Johnstown, in the event of their going in the direction of Oswegatchie Descending Lake George to Ticonderoga, the governor was joined by a body of militia from beyond the lake, but it was all to no purpose and Johnson escaped, taking to his bateaux, probably at Crown Point, whence they proceeded down the lake to St Johns Their captives, among whom were Jacob and Frederick Sammons, were thence transferred to the fort at Chambly These two of the forty prisoners resolved upon escape and the thrilling story of the attempt is of such interest and so nearly relates to Lake Champlain, that we quote it as given in Stone's *Life of Brant* —

"On the day after their arrival Jacob Sammons, having taken accurate survey of the garrison and the facilities of escape, conceived the project of inducing his fellow prisoners to rise upon the guards and obtain their freedom The garrison was weak in number, and the sentinels less vigilant than is usual among good soldiers The prison doors were opened once a day, when the prisoners were visited by the proper officers, with four or five soldiers Sammons had observed where the arms of the guards were stacked in the yard, and his plan was, that some of the prisoners should arrest and disarm the visiting guard on the opening of the door, while the residue were to rush forth seize the arms, and fight their way out The proposition was acceded to by his brother Frederick, and one other man named Van Sluyck, but was considered too daring by the great body of the prisoners to be undertaken It was therefore abandoned, and the brothers sought afterward only for a chance of escaping by themselves Within three days the desired opportunity occurred, viz , on the 13th of June The prisoners were supplied with an allowance of spruce beer, for which two of their number were detached daily to bring the cask from the brew-house, under a guard of five men, with fixed bayonets Having reason to suppose that the arms of the guards, though charged were not primed, the brothers so contrived matters as to be taken together to the brewery on the day mentioned, with an understanding that at a given period they were to dart from the guard and run for their lives — believing that the confusion of the moment, and the consequent delay of priming their muskets by the guards, would enable them to escape beyond the ordinary range of musket shot The project was boldly executed At the concerted moment the soldiers sprang from their conductors and stretched across the plain with great fleetness The alarm was given, and the whole garrison was soon after them in hot pursuit Unfortunately for Jacob, he fell into a ditch and sprained his ankle Perceiving the accident, Frederick turned to his assistance , but the other generously admonished him to secure his own flight if possible, and leave him to the chances of war Recovering from his fall, and regardless of the accident, Jacob sprang forward again with as much expedition as possible, but finding that his lameness impeded his progress, he plunged into a thick clump of shrubs and trees, and was fortunate enough to hide himself between two logs before the pursuers came up   Twenty or thirty shots had previously been fired upon them, but without effect   In consequence of the smoke of their fire, probably, the guards had not observed Jacob when he threw himself into the thicket, and supposing that, like his brother, he had passed around it, they followed until they were fairly distanced by Frederick, of whom they lost sight and trace   They returned in about half an hour, halting by the bushes in which the other fugitive was sheltered, and so near he could distinctly hear their conversation   The officer in command was Captain Steele   On calling his men together, some were swearing, and others laughing at the race, and the speed of the 'long-legged Dutchmen,' as they called the flying prisoners   The pursuit being abandoned, the guards returned to the fort

"The brothers had agreed, in case of separation, to meet at a certain spot at 10 o'clock that night.   Of course Jacob lay ensconced in the bushes until night had dropped her sable curtains, and until he supposed the hour had arrived, when he sallied forth, according to the antecedent understanding   But time did not move as rapidly on that evening as he supposed   He waited upon the spot designated, and called aloud for Frederick, until he despaired of meeting him, and prudence forbade his remaining any longer   It subsequently appeared that he was too early on the ground, and that Frederick made good his appointment

"Following the bank of the Sorel Jacob passed Fort St Johns soon after daybreak on the morning of the 14th   His purpose was to swim the river at that place, and pursue his course homeward through the wilderness on the eastern shore of Lake Champlain, but just as he was preparing to enter the water, he descried a boat approaching from below, filled with officers and soldiers of the enemy   They were already within twenty rods   Concealing himself again in the woods, he resumed his journey after their departure, but had not proceeded more than two or three miles before he came upon a party of several hundred men engaged in getting out timber for the public works at the fort   To avoid these he was obliged to describe a wide circuit, in the course of which, at about 12 o'clock, he came to a small clearing   Within the enclosure was a house, and in the field were a man and boy engaged in hoeing potatoes   They were at that moment called to dinner and supposing them to be French, who he had heard were rather friendly to the American cause than otherwise — incited, also, by hunger and fatigue — he made bold to present himself, trusting that he might be invited to partake of their hospitality   But, instead of a friend, he found an enemy   On making known his character, he was roughly received

"'It is by such villians as you are,' replied the forester, 'that I was obliged to fly from Lake Champlain' The rebels, he added, had robbed him of all he possessed, and he would now deliver his self-invited guest to the guard, which, he said, was not more than a quarter of a mile distant Sammons promptly answered him that that was more than he could do The refugee then said he would go for the guard himself, to which Sammons replied that he might act as he pleased, but that all the men in Canada should not make him again a prisoner

"The man thereupon returned to the potatoe field, and resumed his work, while his more compassionate wife gave him a bowl of bread and milk, which he ate sitting on the threshhold of the door, to guard against surprise While in the house he saw a musket, powder-horn and bullet-pouch hanging against the wall, of which he determined, if possible, to possess himself, that he might be able to procure food during the long and solitary march before him On retiring, therefore, he traveled only far enough into the woods for concealment — returning to the woodman's house in the evening, for the purpose of obtain- ing the musket and ammunition But he was again beset by eminent peril Very soon after he entered the house, the sound of approaching voices was heard, and he took to the rude chamber for security, where he lay flat upon the irregular floor, and, looking through the interstices, saw eleven soldiers en- ter, who, it soon appeared, came for milk His situation was now exceedingly critical The churlish proprietor might inform against him, or a single move- ment betray him But neither circumstance occurred The unwelcome vis- itors departed in due time, and the family all retired to bed, excepting the wife who, as Jacob descended from the chamber, refreshed him with another bowl of bread and milk The good woman earnestly entreated her guest to surren- der himself, and join the ranks of the king, assuring him that his majesty must certainly conquer in the end, in which case the rebels would lose all their prop- erty, and many of them be hanged into the bargain But to such a proposi- tion he of course would not listen Finding all her efforts to convert a Whig into a Tory fruitless, she then told him, that if he would secrete himself two days longer in the woods, she would furnish him with some provisions, for a supply of which her husband was going to the fort the next day, and she would likewise endeavor to provide him with a pair of shoes

"Disinclined to linger so long in the country of the enemy, and in the neighborhood of a British post, however, he took his departure forthwith But such had been the kindness of the good woman, that he had it not in his heart to seize upon her husband's arms, and he left this wild scene of rustic hospital- ity without supplies, or the means of procuring them Arriving once more at the water's edge at the lower end of Lake Champlain, he came upon a hut, within which, on cautiously approaching it for reconnaisance, he discovered a party of soldiers all soundly asleep Their canoe was moored by the shore, into which he sprang, and paddled himself up the lake under the most encouraging prospect of a speedy and comparatively easy voyage to its head, hence his return home would be unattended with either difficulty or danger But his pleasing anticipations were extinguished on the night following, as he approached the Isle aux Noix, where he descried a fortification and the glitter of bayonets bristling in the air as the moon-beams played upon the burnished arms of the sentinels, who were pacing their tedious rounds. The lake being very narrow at this point, and perceiving that both sides were fortified, he thought the attempt to shoot his canoe through between them rather too hazardous an experiment His only course, therefore, was to run ashore, and resume his travels on foot. Nor, on landing, was his case in any respect enviable Without shoes, without food, and without the means of obtaining either — a long journey before him through a deep and trackless wilderness — it may well be imagined that his mind was not cheered by the most agreeable anticipations But without pausing to indulge unnecessarily his 'thick-coming fancies, he commenced his solitary journey, directing his course along the eastern lake shore toward Albany During the first four days of his progress he subsisted entirely upon the bark of the birch — chewing the twigs as he went On the fourth day, while resting by a brook, he heard a rippling of the water caused by the fish as they were stemming its current He succeeded in catching a few of these, but having no means of striking a fire, after devouring one of them raw, the others were thrown away

"His feet by this time were cut, bruised, and torn by thorns, briars, and stones , and while he could scarcely proceed by reason of their soreness, hunger and fatigue united to retard his cheerless march On the fifth day his misery was augmented by the hungry swarms of mosquitoes, which settled upon him in clouds while traversing a swamp On the same day he fell upon the nest of a black duck — the duck sitting quietly upon her eggs until he came up and caught her The bird was no sooner deprived of her life and her feathers, than he devoured the whole, including the head and feet. The eggs were nine in number, which Sammons took with him, but on opening one he found a little half-made duckling, already alive Against such food his stomach revolted, and he was obliged to throw the eggs away.

"On the tenth day he came to a small lake His feet were now in such a horrible state, that he could scarcely crawl along Finding a mitigation of pain by bathing them in water he plunged his feet into the lake, and lay down upon its margin For a time it seemed as though he could never rise upon his feet again Worn down by hunger and fatigue — bruised in body and wounded in spirit — in a lone wilderness, with no eye to pity, and no human arm to protect — he felt as though he must remain in that spot until it should please God in his goodness to quench the dim spark of life that remained Still, he was comforted in some measure by the thought that he was in the hands of a being without whose knowledge not a sparrow falls to the ground.

"Refreshed, at length, though to a trifling degree, he resumed his weary way, when, on raising his right leg over the trunk of a fallen tree, he was bitten in the calf by a rattlesnake Quick as a flash, with his pocket knife, he made an incision in his leg, removing the wounded flesh to a greater depth than the fangs of the serpent had penetrated His next business was to kill the venomous reptile, and dress it for eating, thus appropriating the enemy that had sought to take his life, to its prolongation His first meal was made from the heart and fat of the serpent Feeling somewhat strengthened by the repast, and finding, moreover, that he could not travel further in his present condition, he determined to remain where he was for a few days, and by repose, and feeding upon the body of the snake, recruit his strength Discovering, also, a dry fungus upon the trunk of a maple, he succeeded in striking a fire, by which his comforts were essentially increased Still he was obliged to creep upon his hands and knees to gather fuel, and on the third day he was yet in such a state of exhaustion as to be utterly unable to proceed Supposing that death was inevitable and very near, he crawled to the foot of a tree, upon the bark of which he commenced inscribing his name — in the expectation that he should leave his bones there and in the hope that, in some way, by the aid of the inscription, his family might ultimately be apprised of his fate While engaged in this sad work, a cloud of painful thoughts crowded upon his mind, the tears involuntarily stole down his cheeks, and before he had completed the melancholy task, he fell asleep

"On the fourth day of his residence at this place, he began to gain strength and as a part of the serpent yet remained, he determined upon another effort to resume his journey But he could not do so without devising some substitute for shoes For this purpose he cut up his hat and waistcoat, binding them upon his feet — and thus he hobbled along On the following night, while lying in the woods, he became strongly impressed with the belief that he was not far distant from a human habitation He had seen no indications of proximity to the abode of man, but he was, nevertheless, so confident of the fact, that he wept for joy Buoyed up and strengthened by this impression, he resumed his journey on the following morning, and in the afternoon, it being the 28th of June, he reached a house in the town of Pittsford, in the New Hampshire grants — now forming the State of Vermont He remained there for several days, both to recruit his health, and, if possible, to gain intelligence of his brother But no tidings came, and as he knew Frederick to be a capital woodsman, he of course concluded that sickness, death or re-capture, must have interrupted his journey Procuring a conveyance at Pittsford, Jacob traveled to Albany, and thence to Schenectady, where he had the happiness of finding his wife and family "

The adventures of the brother were scarcely less thrilling, but this one must suffice as an example of many similar ones happening on the frontier

Frequent forays of Indians and Tories continued, accompanied, as always, with murder, torture and rapine, throughout the summer In October, 1780, a force of eight hundred British regulars and three or four hundred Indians and Tories, commanded by Major Christopher Carleton, came up Lake Champlain with eight vessels and twenty-six boats, and made a landing on the shore of South Bay From here a portion of the party was detached to return to Ticonderoga (which had been occupied in July by the English), with the view of moving across the carrying-place to Lake George, thence proceeding up the west side, in order to co-operate with the main force in an attack upon the forts at its head Captain Sherwood was in command of a force of about seventy-five men at Fort Anne, mostly undisciplined recruits The enemy demanded the surrender of the fort, which, in consideration of the smallness of the force occupying it, and a limited supply of ammunition, was conceded, the one stipulation that the women and children within the fort should be safely conducted to their homes, being the only conditions insisted upon This fort was burned and the invaders continued their march, burning and destroying as they went

The main body, under Carleton in person, marched across the country to Fort George, where Captain John Chipman was stationed with two companies of Colonel Warner's regiment Early in the month his scouts had brought him advices of the approach of the enemy, having seen the arrival of their vessels at Crown Point, which information he had forwarded to headquarters of the northern department On the morning of the 11th a detachment was sent to Fort Edward for provisions From this body a messenger soon returned with the information that he had seen a party of Indians near Bloody Pond Being unaware that these Indians were Carleton's advance Captain Chipman deemed it best to send out a party of sufficient strength to put the Indians to flight ; and he was probably further incited to that by the fact that he was short of ammunition, and believed that an attack by an overwhelming number would make the action shorter He therefore dispatched all his force except fourteen men The following quaint order was issued to Captain Thomas Sill, who commanded the party —

"Oct'br 11, 1780

" Sir , as it is reported to me that there is a small party of savages near Bloody pond, you will immediately take Forty Eight men, officers included and proseed on the main road, until you make discoveries of them, keeping a Suffiscient advance and Flank gards in Such a manner as to prevent being surrounded If you find a large party you will Emmediately Retreat to the fort except they be savages only, in which case you will attack and immediately Charge upon them   JOHN CHIPMAN, Capt Com'd' "

In carrying out his orders, Captain Sill made the mistake of passing by the enemy, and the first view he had of them disclosed the fact that they were be-

tween him and the fort   Had his force been larger and the fort's defenders
less few in number, this position would not have been the unenviable one it
really was   But there was no chance for retreat, and the action that followed
his discovery by the enemy was short and bloody   It took place between
Bloody Pond and Gage's Hill   One officer and fourteen men, becoming separated from the main body during the action, escaped capture   The victors
immediately invested the fort, which was obliged to capitulate   Fort George,
in reality but one angle of a bastion, was destroyed

The Tories and Indians continued their depredations to the south, burning
and destroying everything that came in their way belonging to the patriots, as
far as Stillwater   Fort Edward was evacuated after the removal of the stores

The peculiar exemption of the territory of Vermont on this and subsequent
occasions, attracted attention and leads us to the consideration of the equivocal
position of that territory during parts of the years 1780–81   We have already
reviewed the trouble growing out of the New Hampshire grants   The people of
these grants had formally declared their independence in 1777, and under the
name of "Vermont" had assumed to themselves the attitude and prerogatives of a
sovereign state; they were filled with bitter hostility towards New York, growing
out of the firm conviction that her claims were unjust and that Vermont had endured great wrong   In a message from Governor Clinton to the New York Legislature, he communicated important information respecting the designs of the
Vermont people, foremost among whom was Ethan Allen , this information
was derived from two prisoners who had escaped from Canada   The substance
of their statements was that several of the leading men of the grants were forming an alliance with the British officers in Canada , that mutual consultation
had been held at Castleton and in Canada , that the grants were to furnish fifteen hundred or two thousand men under command of Allen, etc   Color was
given to these statements by the fact that the two prisoners had not been together in Canada and had escaped by different routes   By later information
the governor learned further details of the purposes of the disaffected people
By this information it appeared that the territory claimed by the inhabitants of
Vermont was to be formed into a distinct colony , that the government thereof
should be similar to that of Connecticut except that the nomination of the governor should be vested in the crown , that they should be allowed to remain
neutral unless the war should be carried into their own territory , that they
should raise two battalions to be in the pay of the crown, but not to be called
to service except in defending the colony ; and that they should enjoy free
trade with Canada   General Haldimand was in command at Ticonderoga, and
would not assume the responsibility of deciding such important issues, but transmitted them to England

Such was the purport of Governor Clinton's information, and so powerful
was the weight of testimony that he did not hesitate to assert that they " proved

a treasonable and dangerous intercourse and connection between the leaders of the revolt in the northeastern part of the State and the common enemy." Aware of the feeling in Vermont, Colonel Beverly Johnson wrote Ethan Allen in March, 1780, the letter being personally delivered by a British soldier in disguise, this letter was not answered and a second was sent in February, 1781, which, with the first, was enclosed to Congress by Allen in the following month, accompanied by a letter from himself in which he plainly claimed the right of Vermont to agree to a cessation of hostilities with Great Britain, provided its claims as a State were still rejected by Congress   In April and May following the governor of Vermont commissioned Ira Allen, a brother of Ethan, to proceed to the Isle aux Noix to settle a cartel with the British in Canada, and also, if possible, to negotiate an armistice in favor of Vermont, only eight persons were admitted to the secret design of this expedition   Allen and a small party made the journey and remained for a considerable time in consultation with the British officers, and many confidential consultations were held   From the beginning it seems to have been perfectly understood by both parties that they were treating "for an armistice, and to concert measures to establish Vermont as a colony under the crown of Great Britain"[1]   Allen stated that "the people of Vermont were not disposed any longer to assist in establishing a government in America which might subject them and their posterity to New York whose government was more detested than any other in the known world"   This sentiment was gratifying to the British officers, and the cartel was arranged and a verbal armistice established to continue until after the next session of the Vermont Legislature, or longer if the prospects warranted it to the commander-in-chief in Canada   As Vermont had then extended her unjust claim over the territory of New York to the Hudson River, that also was included in the terms of the armistice   During the continuance of the armistice British officers were to have free communication through the State, while the inhabitants were to be gradually prepared for the change of government"[2]

But the suspicions of the people were aroused and the earnest Whigs became alarmed   When the Legislature met, the apprehensive ones gathered in large numbers to learn of the situation, but the adroit dissimulations of those in the secret quieted the suspicions of their neighbors, and "the Allen's and their co-operators held communication with the enemy during the entire summer"[3]   In September negotiations were renewed, the representatives of both parties meeting at Skenesborough. But Sir Frederick Haldimand became impatient and efforts were made to induce Vermont to make an open declaration, but the Vermont Commissioners pleaded for more time in which to prepare the public mind for the change, and asked that the matter might go

---

[1] *Political History of Vermont*, published by Ira Allen in London, 1798
[2] ALLEN'S *Political History of Vermont*.
[3] STONE'S *Life of Brant*

over the winter   It was, however, stipulated that a British force might ascend
the lake with proclamations offering to confirm Vermont as a British colony
if the people would return to their allegiance   The Legislature of the grants
assembled at Charlestown in October   General St Leger, in consonance with
the arrangement alluded to, ascended the lake to Ticonderoga with a strong
force   To continue an appearance of hostility to this movement the Vermont
people posted a military force on the opposite shore, under General Enos, to
whom the secret was confided   Scouts and patrols were sent out in alleged
mimicry of hostile preparations, but with no real intention of offering injury to
each other   But on one of these occasions shots were exchanged and a Vermont sergeant was killed   His men retreated   St Leger saw that the body
was properly buried and returned the uniform to General Enos, accompanied
by a letter of apology and regret   This letter was unsealed and its contents
became known   General suspicion was again aroused and a messenger was
dispatched to Governor Chittenden at Charlestown, he, unsuspicious of the
true situation, proclaimed the incident of the killing of the sergeant and St
Leger's remarkable letter   The consequence was general excitement and dis-
trust at Charlestown   Major Runnels confronted Ira Allen and demanded to
know why St Leger was filled with regret for the death of the American sergeant   An evasive reply was returned   An altercation ensued, which gave
the now alarmed board of war time to prepare a document embodying certain
portions of General Enos's dispatches which would best serve their purpose,
to be read to the Legislature and the people   This action had the desired effect and the excitement was allayed

Meanwhile the progress of the great contest in other parts of the country
led up to the latest scenes, and the news of the surrender of the great army of
Cornwallis, which virtually closed the war, reached the North   The effect of
the first intelligence upon the people was such as to induce Allen and his co-
operators to write the British Commissioners that it would be imprudent to
promulgate the royal proclamation at that particular time, and urging delay
The bearer of this dispatch had not been an hour at the headquarters of St
Leger in Ticonderoga when an express confirmed the intelligence of the surrender of Cornwallis on the 19th of October   The effect was electric   All
idea of further operations in that quarter, hostile to the American cause, was
instantly abandoned   Before evening of the same day St Leger's troops and
stores were re-embarked, and before a fair wind he sailed for St Johns   Ticonderoga and the lake were at peace for a third of a century [1]

[1] This version of these remarkable events is based upon the testimony of Ira Allen, as before noted,
and is the one adopted by many able writers   On the other hand, historians of equal ability and judgment take the high ground that all the apparently disloyal movements described were actuated for the
sole purpose of deceiving the enemy and thus escaping the destructive effects of war upon their own
soil, that the people of Vermont never entertained the idea of returning to the allegiance of Great
Britain   Stone says in a foot note in his *Life of Brant*   "Sparks, adopting the view of early writers,

Whatever may be the reader's judgment upon this case, the early patriotism of the men connected with it can never be doubted nor the value of their services diminished If they hoped to escape domestic tyranny, or what they considered such, even by equivocal action, it is equally true that they hated foreign tyranny and promptly came forward to aid in putting it down , and whatever may have been the designs of the leaders, the masses of the people of Vermont amply vindicated their loyalty to their country through all the afflicting scenes and events of the Revolution

During the early months of 1782 Sir Frederick Haldimand made efforts towards a renewal of the negotiations which had been so suddenly terminated , but his advances were received with the utmost coolness by the people of Vermont The intervention of peace relieved this region from all danger of further British invasion

From this time on to the 19th of April, 1783, no active military operations were carried on in the northern department General Stark had been placed in command of the division in June, 1781, with his headquarters at Saratoga But, aside from the rumors of expeditions growing out of the Vermont " conspiracy " above described, comparative peace reigned The whole section, however, was infested with lawless robbers, nearly always in small bands, who, royalists at heart as well as by profession, did not scruple to pillage defenseless members of the same political faith, booty being their chief object

But on the date above given — April 19th, 1783 — by order of General Washington a proclamation announcing a close of hostilities with England was read in all the camps of the patriots The war had ceased, although the formal ratification of the treaty of peace did not occur till September 3d of that year

With the close of the war the Iroquois Indians, dreading the possible vengeance of the whites, took refuge in Canada, with the exception of the Oneidas and Tuscaroras Their lands, with the exception of certain reservations, passed to the possession of the State

Almost immediately after the declaration of peace, those who had been absent in the ranks of the army returned to their homes Town organizations that had been more or less broken up by the war, were renewed, and the first fruits of settled peace began to appear Details of these beginnings of a lasting progress will be found in the town histories hereinafter

has noticed the case in this favorable aspect in his *Sketch of the Life of Ethan Allen* The author certainly agrees with Mr Sparks in the opinion that 'there was never any serious intention on the part of the Vermontese to listen to British proposals.' But with great deference, after a full examination of the case, the same cannot be said of the *leaders* of the Vermontese *They* had determined that New York should be dismembered , and if they could not force themselves into the confederation as a State, were willing to fall back into the arms of Great Britain as a colony "

CHAPTER XV

FROM THE REVOLUTION TO 1815

Advancement of Civil Government — Political Divisions — Renewed Difficulties with England — The Non-Intercourse Act — Its Repeal — Troubles Relative to Impiovements — Declaration of War — Offensive Measures — Canada to be Invaded — Three Movements and the Results Thereof — The Northern New York Measures — Naval Operations on Lake Ontario — Attack on Sackett's Harbor by the British — Battle of Plattsburg — American Victory — Close of the War

WHILE the young nation was making rapid strides of recovery from the baneful effects of the Revolution, the period between the treaty of 1783 and 1812 was pregnant with the discussion and settlement of several important civil matters, and the inauguration of new and untried measures of government   It was a day when statesmanship was developed, and the best intellects were called into the field of action and their powers brought to a crucial test in dealing with questions of State evolved by the generation of plans of government yet unproved

It was but natural, while peace was hailed by all as a blessing, that the new era should give birth to parties influenced by strong motives and actuated by deep feeling   While the defense of their rights had been the common purpose of the patriotic people during the war, no sooner were those rights secured to them by the peace that followed, than the enjoyment and administration of those rights became the potent elements in the formation of political parties   Added to this cause was the old bitterness of feeling engendered by the difficulties between England and France, each country having its ardent sympathizers and supporters in the new republic

The Democratic party, from the time of its organization, had maintained only feelings of bitter hostility to England, and those of warm friendship towards France   Its opponent in the political arena, the Federalist organization, detested France and every thing French, while they sought to be on good terms, at least, with England   Many national, and often local questions, for some few years, prevented thorough party organization , nevertheless, political sentiment was active, and, by 1811, resulted in the drawing of firm party lines. Each party was headed by able men, who, we believe, were actuated by honorable principles, and labored for what they believed was best for the country's good

For many years from a date soon after the close of the Revolution, the "insolence and aggressions of ever insolent and aggressive England" in maintaining what she was fain to consider her undoubted position as "mistress of the seas," added to her continued attempts to incite the savages of Canada and the

12

Northwest into a war of extermination against the Americans on the northern and western borders of civilization, in order that the valuable trade with the Indians might be diverted into the hands of the English and retained by them, had demonstrated to those of clear foresight and political knowledge that ultimately nothing but war between the two nations could settle the troubles

The United States had maintained a strict neutrality during the progress of the Napoleonic war with Great Britain, but our rights as a neutral nation had been totally disregarded   The embargo act, passed December 22d, 1807 — an attempt to compel two belligerent nations to respect the rights of neutrals in refusing intercourse with the world — proved so disastrous to commercial pursuits that it was repealed March 1st, 1809, and a non-intercourse act passed in its stead.   In April, 1809, the English ambassador at Washington opened negotiations for the adjustment of existing difficulties, and consented to the withdrawal of the obnoxious "orders in council," as far as they effected the United States, on the condition that the non-intercourse act should be repealed   This was agreed upon   The president issued a proclamation announcing that on the 10th of June trade with Great Britain might be renewed   But when official intelligence of this action reached England that government refused to ratify the proceedings, and the minister was recalled   The president's proclamation was therefore revoked, and the previous relations between the two countries were resumed

Aside from all other causes of complaint against Great Britain the one around which, irrespective of politics, the greater portion of the people of the United States gathered in unanimity, was that of impressment   Beside the insult of England's claim to the right to search American vessels for supposititious English sailors, gross outrages were perpetrated, and for which it seems there was no relief   Lord Castlereagh, British minister of foreign affairs, admitted on the floor of the House of Commons that, at the beginning of 1811, there were sixteen hundred *bona fide* American sailors serving under compulsion in the British navy   Add to this that the captain of every British merchantmen claimed and exercised the right to impress from weaker American vessels such seamen as he desired, it is but little wonder that a feeling of indignation filled the breast of every honest American against the insolent tyranny of the government that upheld such a disgraceful and unlawful custom

The Democratic party, which was in the ascendant, was known as the *War party* and the Federalists as the *Peace party*   The president and a majority of his cabinet, though Democrats, were opposed to a declaration of war   But the strength of the party in Congress and the rising storm of expressed indignation on the part of the people, brought about a determination that war should be declared at an early day, as all attempts at a pacific adjustment of the differences had signally failed, Great Britain arrogantly refusing to concede her "rights" to impress seamen from American vessels, and insisting upon other as audacious privileges

On the 19th of June, 1812, President Madison formally declared war against Great Britain The Federalists, in their apathy and sometimes antagonistic actions, were a paralyzing influence at the very beginning upon the aims and proceedings of the Democrats or War party Nevertheless, active measures were inaugurated, and, too, upon no insignificant scale The results of these plans can be but briefly reviewed, as but little occurred in the vicinity of War-ren county in consequence of the war

For nearly two years the United States attempted to carry on the war on the offensive plan , but owing to various causes, the attempt was unsuccessful upon the whole The entire sea coast was alive with British cruisers, and every port was menaced Consequently the people of each of the sea-board cities sought their own protection, and devoted their attention to arranging for the defense of their own towns While in nearly every naval contest between the English and Americans the latter were victorious, the former, possessed of a much larger fleet, were enabled to terrorize the whole coast

One of the early war measures entertained, like many undertaken during the Revolution, was an invasion of Canada Steps were taken to gather forces along the frontier of Northern New York and thence westward to Michigan These were arranged in three divisions The northwestern division assembled at Detroit , the central, under command of General Stephen Van Rensselaer, had its headquarters at Lewiston, on the Niagara River , while the eastern made its rendezvous on the western shore of Lake Champlain, in the vicinity of Plattsburg A naval force was also placed upon the lakes

The first of the three attempts resulted in the disastrous expedition of Hull to Detroit, ending in the surrender of the post with all its troops and stores, to the enemy, on the 16th of August, 1812 General Hull, who had been a Rev-olutionary officer, and was governor of the Territory of Michigan at this time, was severely criticised and condemned for his course He was afterwards tried by court-martial and condemned to be shot, but on account of his age and the services he had rendered during the Revolution, his sentence was commuted to dishonorable discharge from the army Before he died, however, in 1825, he so far vindicated his course by his own statements and with the help of those who were with him, and whose judgments and criticisms had become merciful under cooler consideration of his offense, that the people looked upon his error more with compassion than indignation "To-day the character of General William Hull, purified of unwarranted stains, appears in history without a blem-ish in the history of just appreciation " [1]

The results of the efforts of the second division of the invading army, while not burdened with success, were far more encouraging than those of the Detroit

[1] LOSSING

campaign   On the 9th of August, 1812, General Dearborn, commanding the
third invading wing at Plattsburg, had signed an armistice with Sir George
Provost, governor-general of Canada, in consequence of negotiations for a suspension of hostilities between the contending powers then proposed   The
armistice was rejected by the United States government, but Dearborn continued it until the 29th of August, on the ground that by doing so he was aided
in forwarding stores to Sackett's Harbor   This armistice so delayed the preparations for invasion on the Niagara frontier that General Van Rensselaer, who
commanded at that post, found himself on the 1st of September at the head of
only seven hundred men   After the armistice was suspended troops, both regulars and militia, gathered on the frontier, along the river from Lewiston to
Buffalo, to the number of six thousand   In the early morning of October 12th,
Colonel Solomon Van Rensselaer crossed the river with a portion of his force,
and after a sharp contest captured Lewiston Heights   Emboldened by their
success, the assailants, reinforced with a small detachment of regulars under
Captain (after General) John E Wool, pressed the British back and finally
gained possession of Queenstown Heights.   Colonel Van Rensselaer, as well
as Captain Wool, had been wounded, but the latter refused to leave the command until the arrival of Lieutenant-Colonel Chrystie   At Fort George, seven
miles below Queenstown, General Brock, who had heard the firing, pushed
hastily, with his staff, to the scene of action   He found the little fortress in the
possession of Captain Wool, who, though wounded, still remained with his men.
General Brock gathered a body of the defeated British and attempted to drive
Wool from his post, but unsuccessfully   A second assault was made, in which
General Brock fell mortally wounded, and Wool was left master of the Heights
Lieutenant-Colonel Chrystie, who had arrived soon after the last assault, was
followed by General Wadsworth, of the New York militia ; he took the chief
command   The British General Sheaffe, who succeeded Brock, once more rallied the scattered English troops   Lieutenant-Colonel Winfield Scott (afterwards well known as the commander-in-chief of the army), having arrived as
a volunteer, at the request of General Wadsworth, took the active command
Soon after noon, under the lead of the Mohawk chief, John Brant, his savage horde fell with a rush and war-whoop upon the outer American lines
The militia wavered and were about to break into retreat, when the stentorian
voice of Scott arrested their flight   He urged them to turn upon the savages,
which they did to such purpose that the barbarians fled in terror to the woods
General Stephen Van Rensselaer, who had come over to ascertain the state of
affairs, hastened back to Lewiston to send over more militia   But the latter
refused to go, claiming that they were not obliged to leave the soil of their
own country   General Sheaffe, who had received reinforcements from Fort
George, pressed forward with overwhelming numbers (the Americans on the
heights did not number more than nine hundred), and compelled the plucky

Americans to surrender — a needless sacrifice, had their cowardly comrades on the other side of the river hastened to their assistance when ordered by General Van Rensselaer The militia were paroled, but the regulars were held as prisoners Had the commanding general been possessed of a sufficient number of boats to have transported his whole force across the river in the morning, at the time the first attack was made, no doubt final success would have been the award of their bravery As it was, while the expedition as a whole was disastrous, the brave militia who had earned victory under their spirited officers, felt no shame at their defeat — excepting the cowardly majority who refused their aid when needed

The third element in the plan of invasion was the division of Northern New York About the first of September, 1812, General Bloomfield had collected a force of about 8,000 men, composed of regulars, militia and volunteers, at Plattsburg , in addition a few scattered detachments were stationed at advanced points along the lake and at Chazy Major-General Henry Dearborn arrived later and assumed command of the department, and on the 16th of November moved with 5,000 troops towards Canada He reached the La Colle, a small stream emptying into the Sorel, where he met a considerable force of British and Canadian troops and Indians, commanded by an energetic British officer, Lieutenant-Colonel De Salaberry At early dawn on the 20th Colonel Zebulon Pike crossed the La Colle and surrounded a block-house A body of New York militia sent to support him were seen approaching, and, in the dim light, were supposed to be British , fire was opened upon them, and they, equally mistaken in believing the fire to be from a sallying party from the block-house, returned it, and for half an hour a sharp engagement was maintained. Finally when the error was discovered, De Salaberry was seen approaching with an overwhelming force, cutting off their only path of escape The Americans made a fierce attack upon the advancing columns, hoping to make an opening for retreat ; in this they succeeded, but at the cost of leaving their dead and wounded on the field This unpropitious opening of the campaign disheartened the army, and it returned to Plattsburg Dearborn was charged with incompetency, and in June of the next year, he was superseded He asked in vain for a court of inquiry   .

Thus ended for the year the grandly-planned invasion of Canada Nothing was gained to the Americans, while its losses in men and material far exceeded that of the British

One of the first warlike measures undertaken by the Americans before hostilities actually began on the northern frontier, was the construction of the brig *Oneida*, of sixteen guns, at Sackett's Harbor. She was launched in 1809, and was intended to serve the two-fold purpose of enforcing the revenue laws under the Embargo Act, and to defend American property on the lake in case of a war with England, of which ominous mutterings even then were heard all

over the country   The first duty of the *Oneida* occurred in 1812, while under
the command of Lieutenant Woolsey   A schooner, the *Lord Nelson*, owned
by British subjects at Niagara, was on her way, laden with flour and other
merchandise, to Kingston, where she was captured by the *Oneida* and condemned as a lawful prize   The *Oneida* captured several other vessels, which
were condemed under the revenue laws

Early in July a rumor reached Sackett's Harbor that the *Oneida* had been
captured by the British, and that a squadron was on the way from Kingston
to recapture the *Lord Nelson*, which lay at Sackett's Harbor   The rumor was
false , but eighteen days after five British vessels, carrying an aggregate of
eighty-two guns, commanded by Commodore Earle, of Canada, appeared off
the town   Earle communicated to Colonel Bellinger, commanding the militia
at Sackett's Harbor, that all he wanted was the *Oneida* and *Lord Nelson*, and
that in case resistance was made the town would be destroyed   The *Oneida*,
failing in an attempt to run by the approaching fleet into the lake, anchored off
Navy Point in position to use her broadside of nine guns on the nearing vessels   The remainder of her guns were taken out and placed in battery on the
shore   An iron thirty-two pounder, which had been lying in the sand on the
shore, whereby it gained the name of the " Old Sow," was placed in battery on
a bluff with three other heavy guns   A company of artillery also had four
guns   With this inadequate supply of artillery the Americans proposed to defend the place   The fleet slowly entered the harbor, and were fired upon by
the Americans, whose shots fell so far short of their object, that shouts of
laughter and ridicule were heard on board the British vessels by the people on
shore   For about two hours a lively cannonading was kept up, the vessels
standing off and on, but keeping out of range of the Americans' smaller guns
Finally a thirty-two pound shot from one of the vessels struck the ground,
plowed a furrow, and stopped near the battery wherein the " Old Sow " was
placed   Sergeant Spier caught up the shot and ran with it to Captain
Vaughn, an old sailing-master who was in charge of the battery, saying . " I
have been playing ball with the redcoats and have caught them out   See if
the British can catch it back again "   The *Royal George*, the larger vessel of
the fleet, at that moment was nearing to deliver a broadside   The captured
ball was immediately sent back by Captain Vaughn's " Old Sow " with such
force and accuracy that it crushed through the stern of the *Royal George*,
raked her decks to the stem, sending splinters as high as her mizzen topsail,
killing fourteen men and wounding eighteen   She had already received a shot
between wind and water and been pierced by another, which forced her to signal retreat   The whole squadron sailed out of the harbor to the strains of
" Yankee Doodle," played by the fifes and drums of the defenders   The
Americans received no injury

About the first of October, 1812, General Jacob Brown was sent to Ogdensburg to garrison old Fort Presentation or Oswegatchie, to repel a threatened invasion by the British in that quarter   On the second of October the British left Prescott, immediately opposite Ogdensburg, with a flotilla of two gunboats and twenty-five bateaux, and 750 armed men for the purpose of capturing Ogdensburg

Brown had about twelve hundred men in the village, and company of riflemen encamped on the bank of the river near Fort Presentation   The latter were stationed in line of battle upon the river bank to dispute the landing of the invaders   Brown had but two field-pieces, and when the approaching flotilla had reached the middle of the river the two guns were operated with such effect that the enemy retreated with the utmost alacrity   This repulse reflected much credit upon Brown

In October, 1812, Lieutenant Jesse D Elliott, then but twenty-seven years of age, was in command of an incipient dockyard which had been established by the government at Black Rock, two miles below Buffalo   On the morning of the 8th two British vessels, the *Caledonia* and the *Detroit* (the latter had been the *John Adams* and was taken at the surrender of Hull and its name changed), had anchored off Fort Erie.   Elliott conceived a plan for their capture, which, with the aid of a squad of seamen just arrived from New York, fifty artillerymen, and several sailors and citizens from Buffalo, was successfully carried out on the morning of the 9th at one o'clock   The vessels and their men were made captives in less than ten minutes   A battery at Fort Erie was brought to bear upon the vessels before they could be got away, and a severe struggle for their possession ensued   The *Detroit* was finally burned, but the *Caledonia* was got away   She proved a rich prize, her cargo being worth $200,000   The Americans lost one man killed and five wounded

In February, 1813, the British again attacked Ogdensburg   On the 22d about eight hundred British, commanded by Colonel McDonell, appeared in front of the village on the ice in two columns   Colonel Forsyth, with his riflemen, were stationed at Fort Presentation, and against them moved one column, three hundred strong   Awaiting the near approach of the British, Forsyth's men attacked them vigorously with rifle and the two field-pieces that had done such effective service in the hands of General Brown   The attacking column was repulsed with considerable loss, and retreated to the opposite side of the St Lawrence   While this was going on the second column of five hundred had entered the town and captured a twelve-pound cannon and the gunners   The invaders supposed their conquest complete, but were soon confronted by two pieces of artillery under Captain Kellogg and Sheriff York   The gun of the former becoming disabled, he and his men crossed the Oswegatchie and joined Colonel Forsyth, leaving York to fight the battle alone, the latter was soon compelled to surrender   McDonell then proceeded to dislodge Forsyth, and demanded his surrender, in these words   "If you surrender it shall be

well, if not, every man shall be put to the bayonet " " Tell ¡Colonel Mc-
Donell," replied Forsyth, " that there must be more fighting done yet " But
an assault by an overwhelming force compelled the spirited commander, after
he had thrown them once into disorder with grape and canister, to order a retreat, and he and his little force made their way to Black Lake, nine miles
distant The town was plundered by the Indians and camp-followers of both
sexes, who came over from Canada After burning the barracks and two
schooners fast in the ice, and sacking every house but three, the British and
their tribe of marauders returned to Prescott.

In May, 1813, the British, hearing that Chauncey and Dearborn had depleted the forces at Sackett's Harbor to strengthen the expedition for the capture of York, determined to attack the place It was then the chief place of
deposit of the goverment military stores, and its possession by the British was
desirable On the evening of the 27th rumors reached Sackett's Harbor that
Sir James Yeo had sailed from Kingston with a formidable squadron Colonel
Backus was in command of the forces at the Harbor. General Jacob Brown,
who was at his home a few miles from Watertown, had promised to take chief
command in case of an attack, he was therefore summoned, and on the morning of the 28th was in Backus's camp He immediately summoned all the
militia in the vicinity to the field, and as fast as they arrived they were armed
and sent to Horse Island, where the lighthouse now stands This island was
connected with the mainland by an isthmus covered with water of fordable
depth, here it was expected the British would attempt to land About noon
of the 28th six vessels and forty bateaux, carrying over one thousand British
land troops, appeared off the town They were under command of Governor-
general Sir George Provost The troops were embarked in the bateaux but
were soon ordered back, and the whole squadron went out on the open lake
Sir George had been frightened by the appearance outside the harbor of a
flotilla of American gunboats that were bringing part of a regiment from Oswego to aid the post at Sackett's Harbor As soon as Sir George discovered
the weakness of this force he returned, and on the morning of the 29th landed
a considerable force with artillery and muskets on Horse Island. The militia had
been withdrawn behind a gravel ridge on the mainland They fled at the first
fire of the British General Brown vainly attempted to rally the fleeing militia,
while Colonel Backus, with his regulars and Albany volunteers, contested the
ground, inch by inch, with the enemy, and a heavy gun at Fort Tompkins sent
its missiles among the British ranks At this moment a dense smoke was
seen rising in the rear of the Americans The storehouses with their valuable
contents, and a ship on the stocks, had been fired by the officers in charge,
who, upon seeing the flying militia, believed the fort would be captured. For
a moment Brown, who supposed the British to be the incendiaries, was disheartened, but when he learned that the destruction was the act of an over-

zealous and unwise friend, he redoubled his exertions to make an effective defense   He finally succeeded in rallying the militia, and was returning with them in good order to the field, which led General Prevost, who, perched upon a stump, discerned them with his field-glass, to believe that the Americans had received reinforcements   Without taking further measures to prove the truth of his surmise, he sounded a retreat, which soon turned to a disorderly rout, and left his dead and wounded where they fell   By noon the whole fleet had left the harbor   The fired ship was saved, but the stores, to the amount of half a million dollars, were destroyed   For this gallant defense General Brown was made a brigadier in the regular army

These few detailed accounts are given that an idea may be formed of the nature and results of the conflict on the northern border   Almost invariably the Americans, in defending their positions, were successful, when acting on the offensive, seldom so

The brilliant victories of the navy, both on the lakes and the ocean, served to encourage and strengthen the Americans, and to fill with bitterness the English heart that had always been firm in the belief of the invulnerability of its navy   On the land in other parts of the country occurred engagements of more or less importance in their results, particularly the burning of the public buildings at Washington and the defense of Fort McHenry at Baltimore

But on the northeastern frontier nothing of note occurred until the summer of 1814, when the attack upon and successful defense of Plattsburg brought the war so near to the residents of Warren county, that every inhabitant was charged with its excitement

The British plans for the campaign of 1814 on the northern New York frontier resembled closely those made for Burgoyne in 1777   The programme involved the invasion of the State, the possession of Lakes Champlain and George, the penetration of the country to Albany and below, and by the co-operation of a land and naval force, the capture of New York, and, by holding the Hudson River, separate by military posts the New England States from the remainder of the Union   It was expected that the downfall of Napoleon would release a large number of troops, and allow them to be sent to America to aid in crushing the Americans   This prospect gave joy to the "Peace party," who did not hesitate to openly flaunt their joyful hopes in the faces of the patriots, who felt at times that the struggle against their fireside foes, though bloodless, was far more bitter than the armed war against their foreign enemy   The crushing of Napoleon did release many British troops on the Continent, and several thousands of them were immediately sent to Canada to reinforce General Prevost   They arrived in July and were immediately pushed forward to Montreal   In the mean time Prevost had been engaged in extensive preparations for invading New York, increasing his flotilla of vessels in the Sorel, and otherwise strengthening his force   Early in May General George Izard was put in command of the right division of the army of the North   On the 19th of that month he was informed that the the enemy below were approaching   Captain Pring, commanding the British flotilla, moved up the Sorel, and on the 13th attacked the American flotilla under Lieutenant Thomas Macdonough, then lying at Vergennes, Vt , at the head of navigation on Otter Creek   Macdonough, having been apprised of the movement, sent a party to reinforce a detachment of light artillery who had a small battery at the mouth of the creek   Governor Chittenden, of Vermont, also ordered out some militia to assist in repelling the expected attack   On the morning of the 14th Pring's boats and a bomb sloop anchored off the mouth of the creek, where they met a warm welcome from the little battery   For an hour the cannonade continued, when Pring found it necessary to retreat   He then crossed the lake and passed a short distance up the Boquet River for the purpose of destroying a quantity of flour stored there   On his return he was assailed by a number of militia, who had gathered at the mouth of the river. Many of the British were killed and wounded   Meeting with stern repulse in each attack, Pring returned to the Sorel, a wiser man , for he had learned that the people of Vermont were ready to fight, even if their governor was opposed to the war   A few days after Macdonough sailed out of Otter Creek and anchored in Plattsburg Bay

All through the month of May both parties were making additional preparations to settle the question of the supremacy of Lake Champlain and the route to the Hudson   Both sides were reinforced with men and material

General Izard, contrary to the orders of the secretary of war, erected a battery of four eighteen-pounders at Cumberland Head, instead of at Rouse's Point at the mouth of the Soul, where the secretary, urged by Major Totten, chief engineer, ordered it placed

In June General Izard made preparations for an offensive movement into Canada   He sent General Smith with about fourteen hundred men to occupy Champlain, five miles below the Canada line   He had eight hundred men at Chazy under Colonel Pearce, and about twelve hundred occupied the peninsula at Plattsburg between the lake and Saranac River, the works on Cumberland Head, and a position on Dead Creek, two miles below Plattsburg   Macdonough was below Cumberland Head, watching the British flotilla, which lay at the Isle aux Têtes   The British had a force of five thousand five hundred men, with a reserve of two thousand at Montreal

Frequent skirmishes occurred along the border, each side exhibiting a continued restlessness, and apparently anxious to draw out the other   But no movement of great moment occurred till late in July, when General Macomb's brigade embarked at Cumberland Head for Chazy Landing at the mouth of Chazy Creek   At the same time Bissell's brigade started by land for Chazy village While the removal of these troops depleted the force at Plattsburg, the enemy was continually growing stronger During July and August not less than fifteen thousand men, chiefly veterans from Wellington's armies, arrived at Montreal All but one brigade of these forces were held to participate in the invasion of New York

Soon after the advance of the Americans to Champlain and Chazy, General Prevost arrived at Isle aux Noix, where he had sent a large body of veterans, and took the command in person It was plainly evident that the British commander was contemplating a speedy invasion of Northern New York, and yet, with full information of the circumstances, the United States government ordered Izard to march a larger part of his force westward to co-operate with the army of Niagara The army and the people were astonished at the order, it was an open invitation to invasion The disappointed Izard could suppress his indignation, but wrote the Secretary of War, saying ' I will make the movement you direct, if possible but I shall do it with the apprehension of risking the forces under my command, and with the certainty that every thing in this vicinity but the lately erected works at Plattsburg and Cumberland Head will, in less than three days after my departure, be in possession of the enemy." But while continuing to protest, he obeyed orders. Though short of means of transportation, he soon put four thousand men in motion by way of Lake George, Schenectady and the Mohawk valley, and arrived with them at Sackett's Harbor in September He left but twelve hundred effective men to garrison Plattsburg and Cumberland Head, and made a requisition upon General Mooers for the available militia of the district to assemble at Chazy The command was left to Brigadier-General Alexander Macomb, with headquarters at Plattsburg

Macomb used every available method to increase his force At the end of August he had about three thousand four hundred troops; but these were in a weak condition, full fourteen hundred of them being invalids or non-combatants, the ordnance and stores were in confusion, and the works of defense were all incomplete Yet Macomb, concentrating all his forces at Plattsburg, worked with energy on preparations for defense

On the 29th of August, the day Izard left his camp at Champlain, General Brisbane crossed the line with a considerable body of British troops and occupied the village, and on the 3d of September full fourteen thousand more assembled in the vicinity, Prevost being in command, assisted by General De Rottenburgh The governor-general issued a proclamation announcing that he intended to take possession of the country, and inviting the inhabitants to throw off their allegiance to the Union, and furnish him with supplies On the following day they moved to Chazy, and on the 5th they were encamped at Sampson's, eight miles north of Plattsburg The British squadron at the same time moved up the lake and anchored off Isle la Motte, and on the west side

of that island erected a battery to cover the landing of supplies for Prevost's.
army

Meantime Macomb, by working his men day and night, succeeded in erecting three redoubts   Remains of these works are still visible   Also two block-
houses were built on the Saranac, and at the mouth of the river stood a heavy
stone mill   Macomb divided his forces into detachments, holding each responsible for the work assigned to it.

When the British advanced to Chazy Macomb sent out troops to meet them.
On the morning of the 5th the initiatory skirmish of the battle of Plattsburg
occurred between Major John E Wool, at the head of two hundred and fifty
regulars, and the advance of the British   The fight was short but sharp   Wool
could not withstand the onslaught of the heavy column, and fell back to within
a mile and a half of Plattsburg.   There he was joined by Captain Leonard, with
two pieces of artillery, with which fearful execution was done upon the advancing columns of the enemy, the balls cutting open lanes through the moving
mass   Finally a charge of the enemy compelled Leonard and Wool to retreat
across the Saranac, taking their guns with them   Other outlying detachments
had been driven, though in each case with greater loss to the enemy than to
the retreating bodies   When all had crossed the Saranac, the planks from the
bridges were removed

When the British reached Plattsburg and found the bridges destroyed,
they made preparations to encamp in order that measures might be undertaken
to force a passage at the fords   Several sharp skirmishes took place, with no
advantage to the enemy, and he was even forced to withdraw from a number
of buildings he had occupied along the river, driven out by fire communicated
by hot shot thrown by the Americans   Thus, on the evening of the 6th of
September, Prevost was aware that the task before him was not a light one,
though he had at his command an overwhelming force with ample munitions
of war

During the time from the 7th to the 11th Prevost brought up his batteries
and stores, and threw up several works, commanding the river, town and bay
Meantime the Americans were not idle   They strengthened such fortifications
as they had, and concentrated their forces at those points where they would
probably be most needed

While these operations were being carried on on the land, the opposing
forces were making preparations for a battle on the water.   As before stated,
Captain Pring, with the larger part of the British flotilla, had advanced to Isle
la Motte, where the remainder of the squadron joined him, and Captain George
Downie, of the royal navy, took the chief command   Macdonough still lay at
anchor in Plattsburg bay   For the five days during which Prevost was making
his preparations for the attack, the seamen were awaiting his signal to also begin   During this time several affairs of minor importance occurred between

the land troops, one in particular, in which fifty men under Captain McGlassin crossed the river and captured one of Prevost's redoubts, occupied by three hundred men, who fled to the main body, leaving the Americans to spike the guns, destroy the carriages, and return to their quarters, to the discomfiture of General Prevost

Early in the morning of the 11th the British land and naval forces were under motion for the attack The Americans were on the alert, and though threatened with overwhelming numbers, prepared to meet the onslaught pluckily

We cannot go into the details of the engagement for want of space, though their interest would warrant us in doing so The engagement was opened on the lake When Macdonough saw the British vessels approaching in line of battle, he cleared his ship for action, and calling his officers and men around him, knelt upon the deck and in a few simple words prayed the Almighty God for aid, and left the issue in His hands

The naval action was severe and continuous, for two hours and twenty minutes the battle raged, while the thunder of cannon, the hiss of rockets, the scream of bombs and the rattle of musketry were heard on the shore The fight was characterized by a vigor and destructiveness not excelled by any during the war The force of the American squadron was eighty-six guns and eight hundred and eighty-two men, while that of the British was ninety-five guns and a little more than one thousand men But even with this difference in his favor, the enemy was forced to lower his flag to the young lieutenant who publicly asked the Almighty's assistance before opening fire Immediately after receiving the surrender of the British vessels, Macdonough sent the following dispatch to the Secretary of the Navy —

"Sir—The Almighty has been pleased to grant us a signal victory on Lake Champlain, in the capture of one frigate, one brig and two sloops of war of the enemy"

The entire loss of the Americans was one hundred and ten, fifty-two of whom were killed The British loss was was more than two hundred, including Captain Downie

According to an arrangement with Captain Downie, Prevost was to put his troops in motion when the topmasts of the fleet came into his view around Cumberland Head When the first gun was fired on the lake, the British land batteries opened, and under cover of the shot and shell therefrom, Prevost advanced to attack the Americans in three columns At the lower bridge the attack was sharply repulsed At the upper bridge the enemy met an obstinate resistance, and failed in forcing a passage At the upper ford the column was more successful, there, under Generals Mooers and Wright, was stationed the militia of Essex and Clinton, after two or three repulses a few companies of the British succeeded in crossing and forcing the militia from their position

Supports, including a piece of artillery, coming up at this time, stimulated the fleeing militia to the rallying-point, when they turned and vigorously assaulted the pursuing enemy   At this moment Mooer's adjutant-general, Walworth (late chancellor of New York), dashed up, his horse flecked with foam, and announced that the British fleet had surrendered   The enemy must have obtained this information at the same time, for they turned their backs to the cheers of their opponents, and dashed back across the Saranac

Thus ended the battle of Plattsburg.   Sir George Prevost, a coward in danger, according to English historians, became terribly alarmed, and experienced, as he said, " extreme mortification to hear the shout of victory from the American works, when the fleet surrendered, and decided him that " further prosecution of the service was become impracticable "

Before morning the British commander and his army were ten miles on the way to Canada, having left his sick and wounded and a vast quantity of munitions of war behind him   Troops were sent in pursuit, but the flight of the enemy was too rapid, and he reached Montreal without further chastisement His losses were not far from two thousand men, while that of the Americans was less than one hundred and fifty

This victory called forth acclamations of joy throughout the country, and generous honors were awarded the leaders therein   Congress voted the thanks of the nation, and to Macdonough, Macomb and others gold medals were presented   Honorable burial was accorded Captain Downie and other British officers   They were buried in a beautiful cemetery near Plattsburg.

Almost simultaneous with this victory came the repulse of the British at Fort Erie, their expulsion from Baltimore, and the closing scenes of their operations on the New England coast

There are no available records of the part taken by the inhabitants of Warren county in this late struggle with Great Britain , only a few scattered items can to-day be gathered.   In the *Warren Republican*, of December 13, 1813, says Dr Holden, appears the following notice

" TO YOUNG MEN OF ZEAL AND HONOR,

" *To those who feel for the abused rights of their beloved country*

"Every able-bodied man between the age of 18 and 45 years, who is willing to serve his country during the present war, or five years (as he may choose), shall receive TWENTY DOLLARS IN CASH DOWN, and TWENTY DOLLARS more when he shall be mustered, or join his regiment   He shall also receive neat and handsome clothing of all kinds immediately   Eight dollars per month and his rations   He shall furthermore receive and have guaranteed to him 160 acres of excellent land, to be laid out and located at the public expense—or if he should die in the service, his heirs or representatives shall be entitled to the same , and three months additional pay, beyond his term of service   For further particulars, please call at the Rendezvous now opened at A Emmons' Inn, at Glens Falls

" CHARLES HARRISON, *Lieut*

" 13*th Regiment U S Infantry* "

This is certainly evidence that volunteers were called for, if not that they were forthcoming, which latter is more than probable, if the following statement in Palmer's *History of Lake Champlain* is a criterion of the patriotism of the people of the young country .—

" When Major-General Mooer's orders were received for the militia of Warren and Washington counties to assemble *en masse*, and march to the frontier, there appeared, under arms, two hundred and fifty men *more* than had ever mustered at an inspection or review "

Dr Holden says that " of the male citizens of Warren and Washington counties, but few were left behind.   The towns of Athol, Luzerne, Warrensburg and Chester were almost depopulated "   A company from Luzerne, under Captain Gideon Orton, was attached to the Saratoga regiment   Queensbury sent its quota of two companies , the one from Glens Falls being commanded by Lieutenant Royal Leavens   Caldwell and Bolton sent a rifle company under the command of Halsey Rogers   There was also a squadron of cavalry raised chiefly in the towns of Kingsbury and Queensbury, of which Daniel W Wing was lieutenant commanding , but it was not ordered out in time to take part in the battle of Plattsburg

During the latter part of December, 1814, General Andrew Jackson was completing preparations for the defense of New Orleans, and at the same time was frequently engaged with the enemy, who was making strenuous efforts to gain a foothold on the coast, thereby enabling him to more effectually blockade the port of New Orleans   Repeated engagements occurred, some of them very severe, resulting on the whole in favor of the Americans

On the 8th of January, 1815, the contest culminated in the battle historically known as that of New Orleans, in which Jackson signally defeated Packenham, the latter losing two thousand six hundred men, killed and wounded, including the commander, while the former's force suffered by the loss of only eight men killed and one hundred wounded   This brilliant action, as a finishing stroke of repeated successes of the American arms, brought joy and rejoicing to the country.

The treaty of Ghent was completed December 24, 1814, and was ratified by the Prince Regent on December 28th, and by the United States Congress on February 17th, 1815   While it secured many advantages to the Americans, the principle for which they went to war, namely, immunity from search and impressment, was not secured them   The Americans had fought their last battle with a foreign foe

A general conviction prevailed after the declaration of peace that the

United States would not again become involved in war   It had twice defeated one of the strongest nations of the earth, and the feeling grew in strength
that foreign powers would hesitate long before provoking the republic to hostility   This condition of the public mind exerted a widespread and beneficial
influence upon the progress of settlement in all new localities, which had been
seriously impeded by the war   The people of Warren county, many of
whom did valiant service in the struggle just ended, returned to their homes
and engaged, with confidence and renewed energy, in the arts of peace and
progress

CHAPTER XVI

TO THE PRESENT TIME

]° Ɱ Early Settlement — Subdivision of Albany County — Formation of Charlotte County — Change
of Name — Formation of Towns within Present Limits of Warren County — Pioneer Experiences —
Warren County Organized — Boundaries — County Seat, Buildings, etc — The " Cold Summer " —
Schools and Churches — Internal Improvements — Financial Crisis 1837–38 — State Legislation Referring to Warren County — Political Campaign — The Leather Industry — Civil List

W E have in Chapter X described the circumstances surrounding the granting of the Queensbury Patent in 1762 and the first attempts made towards the permanent settlement of the territory within the present limits of
Warren county   While many of the early proprietors of the original Queensbury Patent retained their ownership and a few spent the greater part of their
time on their possessions until the close of the Revolutionary War, by far the
larger number were driven away to the more peaceful localities where they
had previously dwelt, by the excitement and danger of conflict along the
northern frontier   With all the details of the early settlements in what is now
the town of Queensbury, as well as in the other towns of the county, the reader
will be made familiar in the subsequent town histories

With the dawn of peace following the Revolution the pioneers of the
county again turned their faces towards the wilderness and were rapidly followed by many others, who resolutely began the task of making for themselves and their posterity attractive and valuable homes where had recently
stood the primeval forest   We have seen in the preceding chapter how the
inhabitants of Warren county sprang to arms for the last time in nearly half a
century, in the War of 1812, to aid in convincing the mother country that the
reign of liberty was to be permanent in the land

Previous to this event occurred the subdivision of Albany county, by which all that portion which included the colonial settlements to the west and south-west of Schenectady was set off and named Tryon county, in honor of William Tryon, then governor of the province   Charlotte county was formed on the 12th of March, 1772, and embraced the territory now comprised in Washington, Warren, Essex and Clinton counties in New York, and part of Bennington, Rutland, Addison, Chittenden and Franklin counties in Vermont   This county was named in honor of the Princess Charlotte of Mecklenburgh-Strelitz   After considerable strife the county seat of Charlotte county was located at Skenesborough (now Whitehall), provided Major Skene should furnish for public use a tract of land   On the 18th day March, 1772, the legislative council passed an act, "to enable the inhabitants of the county of Charlotte to raise and defray the public and necessary charges of the said county, and to choose county officers"   In September, 1773, an ordinance was issued by the governor with the advice of the Council, "establishing a Court of Common Pleas and a Court of General Sessions of the Peace to be held annually in the county of Charlotte"   The name of this county was changed in 1784 to Washington, and on the 10th of April, 1792, the town of Luzerne was set off from Queensbury under the name of "Fairfield," which name was changed April 6th, 1808; a strip one mile wide was taken from this town March 30th, 1802, and given to Queensbury   On the same date with the formation of Luzerne, the original town of Thurman was formed   On the 25th of March, 1799, the towns of Bolton and Chester were formed from Thurman and the town of Hague was set off from Bolton February 28th, 1807, under the name of "Rochester," which name was changed April 6th, 1808   Johnsburgh was formed from Thurman April 6th, 1805, and Caldwell from Queensbury, Bolton and Thurman March 2d, 1810   February 12th, 1813, just previous to the county organization, Warrensburgh was formed from Thurman   Settlements in all of these towns was begun long before their formation as civil divisions of the county, as detailed in the subsequent town histories   These settlements contributed a class of pioneers of exceptionally energetic, persevering and moral character, men who came into the wilderness thoroughly imbued with a determination to leave not only good homes to their children, but names untarnished by evil report   Log houses sprang up in the forests, to be followed at a date much earlier than was the case in many localities by neater frame cottages, the building of which was rendered possible by the early establishment of the numerous saw-mills

The building of a log house in pioneer days was often a scene of neighborly gathering and festivity, intermingled with the most energetic and rapid work, to which the old inhabitants have always loved to turn their thoughts. It was the first earnest work of the pioneer   If he found a few neighbors within a circle of as many miles, he was generously and willingly aided in the task, if not, he must do the best he could with the aid of his brave-hearted

13

wife and his boy, if he had one In such cases the dwelling often scarcely rose to the dignity of a house, it was more frequently a mere cabin Where a few settlers formed what might, by a broad rendering of the term, be called a neighborhood, the incoming pioneer always received a warm welcome. His arrival meant the clearing of another farm; another social neighbor near at hand, another strong and willing pair of hands for all good work and another friend in case of adversity. Then the building of the log house became, not a tedious and toilsome task, but a mere occasion for a day's social gathering of neighbors, a scene of festivity, mingled with a little labor For such an event the summons went out for a house-raising on a specified day, and when a dozen or more willing men had congregated, every one of them unsurpassed in dexterity with the axe, down fell the tall, straight trees, the logs were cut and drawn together by the oxen, four of the most active and expert of the men, schooled by many a similar experience, were placed at the corners of the foundation to cut and shape the ends of the logs, and long before night the walls were raised to a height of six or eight feet, the rafters were put in place, and the dwelling was soon ready for its pioneer occupants On these occasions the hard-working men were usually cheered in their labor by a passing whisky jug, for within a short time after the first settlement it was a cold day when a jug of whisky could not be found in almost any neighborhood The finishing work was put on the house by the owner at his leisure; but there was no delay in beginning "to live" in those days, the house which was embodied in standing trees in the morning, sheltered the happy pioneer and his wife at the supper table in the evening on the same day

In these dwellings, although "house-keeping" was begun under many adverse circumstances, who shall say that there were not as warm hearts, as true domestic devotion and sympathy and as pure contentment and peace as ever existed in the palaces of the world Here the pioneer and his family began life with faith in their Creator and faith in themselves — a life that was to carry them from their present condition of trials and privations onward to the comforts of civilization His house once built, the early settler found ample work for his hands in felling the forest trees, in the "logging bees" by which fields were cleared in a day by the union of many hands, in planting a little corn or wheat, in sugar-making in the spring, in caring for his limited stock and in supplying his household with venison and other game from the forest

The forests in the region of which this work treats abounded, not only with game that was a heaven-sent boon to early settlers, but with wild beasts which ravenously preyed upon the scanty flocks and sometimes imperiled the lives of the people Long after they ceased to cause any apprehensions to the settlers themselves, these wild beasts, especially the wolves, were a constant source of annoyance, and every man's hand was raised against them for their extermination This work was encouraged by the offer of generous public bounties   Under such efforts, and the gradually increasing population, the forests were cleared of these foes to man and his civilizing work

One of the brightest features of pioneer life and one to which the writer may always turn with gratification, was the general spirit of fraternity and sociability and mutual helpfulness which pervaded the young communities. Most of the early settlers stood upon the same plane of life, held the same hopes and aspirations, born of poverty and nurtured in privation, which were common to all   Each felt an impulse, dictated by the humanity that was sure to develop amid such surroundings, to assist his neighbor whenever and wherever assistance was needed, realizing that he might any day become the grateful recipient of similar service   That social ostracism engendered by caste, a relic alike of ignorance and barbarism, which it is the mission of the genius of American institutions to eradicate, and which inexorably separates the individual members of a community at the present day, was then unknown They mingled freely with each other, and shared each other's joys and sorrows

On the 12th of March, 1813, Warren county was set off from Washington county, receiving its name in honor of General Joseph Warren, of the Revolutionary army   The boundaries of the new county were thus defined —

" All that part of the State bounded northerly by a line running a due west course from the northwest corner of the county of Washington so as to strike the most northerly point of the rock commonly called Rogers's Rock, on the west side of Lake George, and continued west until intersecting a line drawn from the Mohawk River, where the northeast corner of the tract of land granted by letters patent to George Ingoldsby and others touches the Mohawk, north one degree and twenty-five minutes west , westerly by the line just mentioned intersecting a west line drawn from Fort George, near Lake George , by that line until it strikes the north branch of the Hudson River, and by the middle of said branch and of the main stream to the southeast corner of Queensbury ; north along the east line of that town to Lake George , thence north along the west line of the towns of Fort Ann and Putnam to the north bounds of the county "

William Robards was elected the first judge of the new county and held the office until 1820   Robert Wilkinson was the first surrogate , Henry Spencer, sheriff, John Beebe, county clerk , and Michael Harris, treasurer   The county seat was established at Caldwell, where it has ever since remained, in spite of numerous energetic attempts to secure its removal to Glens Falls, as narrated in a later chapter   An act passed March 12th, 1813, established a Court of Common Pleas and General Sessions of the Peace to meet three times a year   The courts, meetings of the supervisors and other public gatherings were, for a few years, held in the old Lake George Coffee-House, on the site of the present Lake House in the village of Caldwell   On the first of March, 1816, an act was passed providing that the county clerk's office was to be kept within one-half mile of the Lake George Coffee-House, and the mileage to be computed from there   The new county buildings were erected and ready for occupation by the county officials in 1817, in which year the supervisors' meeting was held in the court-house   The details of the construction of these and other county buildings are given in later pages

It was the month of June, 1813, that saw the issue of the initial number of the first newspaper published in Warren county — an event always of much significance in any locality   The young pioneer journal bore the name of the *Warren Republican*, and was published at Glens Falls   Of course it was a small affair, but its birth marked an era in the growth of the county   (See chapter on the county press)

Much of the attention of pioneers in any locality and of early public officials has always been devoted to the laying out and opening of highways   One of the most important of the early thoroughfares in this section of the State is what is still known as the old State Road   Its opening was authorized early in the century and it runs from Sandy Hill northward through the present towns of Queensbury, Caldwell, Warrensburgh and Chester, and on northward across Essex and Clinton counties to the Canada line   Platt Rogers was conspicuous in opening this highway and received large grants of public land in Essex county for his services in this capacity   The State Road involved a heavy outlay in its construction and large sums have since been expended in its maintenance , but it has always been kept in very good repair and was, from the first, of great utility to the inhabitants of the territory contiguous to its course   Another prominent highway, which was opened at an early day, was that running from the State Road near the foot of Schroon Lake northwesterly across the town of Chester and the southwest corner of Essex county and into Hamilton county

The inhabitants of Warren county suffered considerably from the effects of what is remembered as the cold summer, in the year 1816, although its effects were not so deplorable as those of the succeeding summer, when the scarcity caused by the failure of the crops of the preceding year was most seriously felt   Perhaps the cases of actual suffering in this county were less numerous than in many other localities, as the inhabitants were a little less dependent upon the actual products of the land from year to year , but there were many in the rural districts who felt the pinch of want and were hard pressed to provide actual necessities for their families   The season was a most remarkable one and has not had a parallel since   The sun seemed bereft of his power to give out heat to the freezing earth , ice formed in many localities every month in the year , snow fell in this county in June and crops could not grow and ripen except in the most favored localities   Those who were successful in raising crops to any considerable extent, felt the extreme need of saving them for the next year's seed time, while many who possessed the means of relieving the less fortunate, declined to do so except at such exorbitant rates as to practically shut out the poor   A season of this character might occur at the present day without causing even a scarcity in the thickly populated communities of the country.   If crops fail in one section they succeed in another, and even if it is remote, even if the ocean roll between the favored and unfavored localities, modern rapid transportation is adequate to adapt the supply to the demand in all sections, while the wealth of one region rarely rests idle in these later days, another one wants   Hence, it is difficult for the reader of to-day to realize and appreciate the fact that their ancestors of only two or three generations ago saw "the wolf at their doors" in the great Empire State, because a cold season cut off most of the crops   But the fact remains, and is vividly remembered by old residents of the county

But the privations and hardships of the pioneers of the county soon began to be mitigated by the advancing march of civilization, the introduction of public improvements, the influx of settlers, the opening of roads, the establishment of schools and churches and the increasing productiveness of the farms

In the early days of the settlement of the county the productions of the soil were limited almost exclusively to the necessities of the inhabitants   If a surplus was raised there was little market for it, except at a great distance. Money was scarce, very scarce, and most exchanges were made by bartering one commodity for another   Almost every dwelling had its loom, boots and shoe were made largely by itinerant mechanics, while the actual food necessities were raised from the ground   Had it been otherwise in these respects, the scarcity of money would have been felt in a much greater degree than it was

The early settlers of the county, in common with those of most other localities in the country, no sooner became located in their humble homes, than they set about providing means for the education of their children, and rustic school-houses were soon scattered — often very widely scattered, to be sure — through the wilderness.   But in these pioneer schools and under the most discouraging circumstances were laid the foundation of education and character which enabled the growing youth to enter upon life as they found it, armed with all the necessary elements of success   Churches, too, were organized, the primitive school-houses commonly sufficing for some years as places for religious worship, and the spread of the gospel was none the less rapid and permanent because the prayers of the people went up from very humble temples

The region of Northern New York of which this county forms an important part, was vastly benefited in its material interests by the opening of the Champlain canal in 1823, and to a greater degree, particularly the locality of which we are writing, by the completion of the Glens Falls feeder which was made navigable for boats in 1832   The lumber interest, the manufacture of lime and, in short, every branch of industry in the county was given an impetus by these improvements, the effects of which are still felt   Railroad agitation also began as early as 1831–32, in which year the Warren County Railroad Company was organized and incorporated for the avowed purpose of building a road from Glens Falls to Caldwell, with the privilege of extending the line to Warrensburgh Application was made to the Legislature early in 1831 for the incorporation of a company comprising John Baird, Peter D Threehouse and associates, as a company to build a railroad from Saratoga to Glens Falls , but it was many years before these projects were consummated   The details of the internal improvements in the county are given in a later chapter

On the 26th of May, 1836, the towns of Chester, Johnsburgh, Warrensburgh, Athol, Caldwell and Queensbury were taxed $3,000 for the improvement of the State road, with John Richards, Allen Nelson and Ezra B Smith as commissioners.   In March of the following year another sum was taxed for a similar purpose

The memorable financial crisis of 1837–38, from which the entire country suffered, was severely felt in this county   The newspapers of the period teem with accounts of failures, losses and suffering which have since been without a parallel   Money was extremely scarce and the ordinary necessaries of life were difficult to obtain without ready pay   One item in a local paper states that "a man floated a raft of lumber worth $5,000 into the port of Bangor, Me , for which he was unable to obtain a single barrrel of flour   The lumber would not sell and the flour could not be bought except for cash "   Many in this county lost their all in the general panic , but the energy of the people and the advantages of the locality in a business sense, enabled them to quickly recover from the blow

We have before in this work alluded to the prevalence of wild animals in this region and the part they played in the food supply of the pioneers   Down to even comparatively recent times, the remote parts of the county have been the home of several varieties of the early forest denizens   It is not very many years since the larger wild animals were quite frequently killed in the county and were even viewed as a public nuisance   In the *Spectator* of August 11, 1837, appears the following item · "Destruction among panthers — There was an old panther and two young ones killed by a party of hunters one day last week in the town of Johnsburgh, in the northern part of the county.   The old one measured eight feet in length , the others were some somewhat smaller." It was not far from the same date that Samson Paul killed a large panther with a fishing spear on the shore of Lake George in the town of Bolton   Still later, according to Dr Holden, one of the grandsons of Sabele, the Indian, killed one with a pitchfork in a barn in Johnsburgh.   These animals, with bears, deer and wolves, have been known to frequent the county at much later times than those referred to, and bounties were offered in most of the towns for their extermination

State legislation having direct reference to this county has not been extensive nor very important in character, having for its chief objects the authorization of roads, bridges, the improvement of the streams, and kindred topics.
On the 20th of April, 1836, an act was passed appropriating $4,000 to build a
bridge at the junction of the Schroon and middle branches of the Hudson
River, between the towns of Athol and Warrensburgh George Pattison and
Stephen Griffin, of Warrensburgh, and Richard Cameron of Athol, were the
commissioners On the 27th of April, 1841, John Richards, jr, of Warren
county, and Ezra Thompson and George Parburt, of Hamilton county, were
by law appointed a commission to lay out and make a road four rods wide,
" commencing on the State road near the mills of Elias P Gilman, town of Gilman, Hamilton county, and thence in the most direct line to Johnsburgh " On
the 26th of May of the same year $4,000 was appropriated for the repair of
the State road from Glens Falls to Chesterfield, in Essex county On the 2d
of May, 1844, an act was passed appointing James D Weston, of Luzerne,
John J Harris and Abraham Wing, of Queensbury, commissioners to locate
and superintend the building of a bridge over the Hudson River at Johnsburgh They were authorized to borrow $2,500 on the credit of the county
for that purpose May 12th, 1846, Abraham Wing and Cyrus Burnham, of
Warren county, and Clark Rawson, of Essex county, were appointed by law
as commissioners to lay out roads and expend the highway moneys in the counties of Warren, Essex and Hamilton On the 31st of January, 1849, an act
was passed authorizing the purchase of the toll bridge at Jessup's Little Falls,
the comptroller being allowed to loan $1,200 to the counties of Saratoga and
Warren, out of the common school fund The purchase to be made of George
T Rockwell, Jeremy Rockwell and Betsey Rockwell, executors of the estate
of Jeremy Rockwell In the year 1849 considerable appropriations were
made for the improvement of the channels of streams in the county, for the fa-
cilitating of the rafting business Ten thousand dollars were appropriated towards improving the upper waters of the Hudson, with Jacob Parmeter, of
Essex, Daniel Stewart, of Warren, and Jeremy Rockwell, of Saratoga county, as
commissioners Two thousand dollars appropriated "to clear the rafting channel
from the foot of the rapids at the head of the Glens Falls feeder pond to Hadley's Falls " Fifteen hundred dollars appropriated for clearing the rafting
channel between Phelps Bay to Barber mill dam Four thousand dollars appropriated for clearing the rafting channel at and above Jessup's Little Falls,
including the Schroon and the west branches of the said river April 9th, 1853,
William Hotchkins, of Chester, Jonas Ordway, of Johnsburgh, Thomas Barnes,
of Minerva, Essex county, were by law appointed a commission to superintend
the construction of a bridge in Johnsburgh three-fourths of a mile from North
Creek; the State appropriated $2,000 On the 25th of April, 1866, Henry
Crandell, Joel Green and Benjamin C Butler were appointed commissioners

to " lay out a road for wagons from Hudson River near Roblee's Hotel in Johnsburgh, up through the town of Indian Lake to the Carthage road near the head of Long Lake, Hamilton county "

In the year 1848 the plank road was built from Glens Falls to the village of Caldwell, an improvement that was of much benefit to the northern part of the county ; this utility was still further enhanced when the road was continued to Warrensburgh a few years later

The formation of the town of Horicon took place March 29th, 1838, when it was set off from Bolton and Hague, and November 13th, 1852, the town of " Athol," which had been formed from the original town of Thurman at the the time of the formation of Warrensburgh, February 12th, 1813, was divided into the present town of Thurman and Stony Creek, completing the town organization of the county.

There have been several notably exciting political campaigns in Warren county, although as a general rule political antagonism and animosity cannot be said to have run as high as in many localities   During the anti-Masonic period much feeling was awakened and considerable excitement followed.   In 1826–27, also, when William Hay and Norman Fox were the opposing candidates for the Assembly, a very stirring campaign was carried on   Joseph W Paddock came into the field as a " Jackson man," and by the aid of influential political friends was run as an " independent " candidate   Hay was elected on the then so-called " Republican " side, and his victory was celebrated in political campaign songs, etc   Personal rivalry ran so high as to lead to libel suits, which, however, did not result seriously to any one   The campaign of 1844 was one of unusual interest in this section   The Glens Falls *Republican*, started the year previous, espoused the cause of the Democracy and made its influence felt from the first   That party was then largely in the ascendant in the county. Since the organization of the Republican party Warren county has uniformly given majorities for the candidates of that political faith, although many Democrats have been elected to offices of importance, through their individual popularity and worth

The growth of Warren county, after its organization, has been rapid and healthful   It presented to settlers attractions in its water power, its vast and valuable forests and its other natural advantages not offered by many other sections, and a sturdy and energetic population sought its borders, secured the lands and many of them entered largely into the lumber business when it was about the only means, or at least the most available one, of securing a livelihood and ready return for labor   There were many mills within the present limits of the county before the beginning of the present century, and the number rapidly multiplied after that date, until they were scattered over all parts of the region, many of them erected in later years of enormous capacity, and the lumber interest became and long continued of paramount importance   In the year

1877 Dr A W Holden furnished to Franklin B Hough the following details and statistics of the lumber interest as applicable to Warren county, which we are amply justified in placing in these pages —

"The lumber business on the Hudson River dates back to an early period in the history of the country Mrs. Grant in her *Memoirs of an American Lady*, speaks of timber rafts being floated down to Albany as far back as 1758 Saw-mills were erected at Glens Falls in 1770, and from that time to the present the manufacture and export of timber has constituted one of the most important industries But the once heavily-timbered pine forests have receded before the axe of the lumberman, until far away among the sources of the mountain rivulets at the north there is only left here and there a scattered remnant of those towering and stately ornaments of the woods Since 1850 the manufacture of pine timber has formed but an inconsiderable item in the product of the Hudson River mills In addition to the destructive fires which, from time to time, have devastated the mountains and cleared the forests along the line of the border settlements, the death of the spruces from some mysterious cause has stripped the forest of its evergreens and in many instances necessitated the in-gathering of thousands of logs to save them from becoming a loss through natural decay Nevertheless, as fifty spruce trees to the acre is considered a liberal estimate and the surrounding woods are often so heavily timbered with other growths as to make it difficult to fall the spruces without lodgement, the clearing away of the dead-wood makes but little difference in the general aspect or density of the forest On the southeast side of the great Adirondack plateau the hemlock-producing belt extends but little if any north of the Warren county line A few isolated clumps, a gnarled and dwarfed specimen at widely recurring intervals are but the exceptions which establish the rule The consumption of the deciduous forest trees within the lumber district proper has not yet entered as a factor in the lumber product . The relatively few dock-sticks, spars and pieces of round timber which find their way to market down the river, or by the Glens Falls feeder, are nearly or quite all obtained at points within the range of settlements and south of the wilderness border. The lumber region tapped by the Hudson and its affluents is relatively small, as compared with the vast water-shed drained by the Raquette and its tributaries, to say nothing of the Black, the Oswegatchie, the Grass and the St Regis Rivers, all of which contribute to swell the majestic flood of the St Lawrence And yet along the ponds and marshes and headwaters of the Schroon, the Sacandaga, the North, Boreas, Indian, Cedar and Rock Rivers are to be found extensive and untouched tracts of timber of as good quality as any ever brought to market

"It is worthy of mention that while of the second growth of white pine the quality is greatly inferior to that of 'the forest primeval,' the same is not true of either the spruce or the hemlock, the younger and newer trees being preferable as

producing the strongest, soundest and most desirable grades of lumber   Another interesting fact in this connection is that considerable tracts of territory
on the borders of, and within, the great wilderness which have been cleared by
the axe of the settler, or denuded by destructive fires, are again covered with
a dense second-growth of trees , and it is confidently asserted by those whose
judgment should be competent, that there is to-day a larger area of forest in
'the great North Woods' than there was twenty-five years ago, and that this
condition is relatively increasing, notwithstanding the enormous consumption of
the lumber-producing evergreens   It is a mistake to suppose that the Adirondack wilderness is being cleared up

"River-driving is a feature in the lumber business which came in vogue
about fifty years ago   Previous to that time the practice prevailed of erecting
small mills of feeble capacity and primitive machinery on brooks, rivulets, or
by the aid of wing dams, on the banks of rivers near the sources of supply
This system was attended with great waste of labor and material   As the
growth of our cities and the demands of commerce increased, mechanical in-
ventions multiplied, the economies of manufacture were studied, extensive mills
with all the adjuncts of machinery were constructed at central points, and logs
were drawn or floated to the mills from the ponds above   As the cost of production increased and material receded, combinations of operators were organized, river-driving became systematized and manufacturing at the great centers
of the lumbering business steadily increased

"This mode of operating necessitated the accumulation at seasons of high
water of large quantities of logs for the year's supply   At this day the points
of supply and consumption are so remote that one and often part of two years'
stocks, representing from three-fourths to a million of dollars, are constantly
afloat   A system of booms was devised in order to retain and convey the
logs to the points where they were to be sawed   But it was found that enormous losses frequently resulted from freshets   Once in four or five years,
sometimes oftener, a tremendous spring flood would occur, which no amount
of precaution or care could (or did) prevent from bearing off on its resistless,
turbulent and turbid waters, the gathered harvest of an entire year's work in
the woods, leaving the mills idle for the want of stock, and the employees,
thus thrown out of their regular work, were forced to seek in other fields of industry a scanty and precarious employment

"To remedy these evils, 'the Hudson River Boom Association was formed
about the year 1849   This combination included all the mill owners below the
great falls on the Hudson River (Jessup's Falls), together with many log owners who had their lumber made at their mills   At great expense a substantial
series of piers and system of chain booms was constructed at the foot of the
Big Bend, about four miles above Glens Falls, which, strengthened and improved from time to time, has never failed to accomplish the work for which it

was designed and to withstand the pressure of the heaviest freshets   In order to equalize the annual expenses attendant upon the management of the boom and the reception and discharge of the logs, a record of the number delivered and sworn to by each contributor to the drive had to be kept by the Boom Association, and thus we are enabled through the courtesy of its secretary, Mr William McEachron, of Glens Falls, to present in a tabulated form the number of logs received for the last twenty-five years, with the exception of three years, which are estimated   It is premised that each unit of the count here given is a *market log*, viz   a log thirteen feet long and nineteen inches in diameter in the clear at the smaller end   Such a log, calculated as a cylinder, contains 25 6 cubic feet and practically represents about two hundred feet of lumber, board-measure   As the average of stock runs in the boom, including logs of all sorts, each market log will represent two pieces by count and the actual number of logs delivered to the various drives is obtained by multiplying the numbers of the table by two

"The amount of lumber carried to market by rail is very inconsiderable and scarcely worth mentioning   By estimates it would not exceed one per cent The number of market logs manufactured at points above the Big Boom is roughly estimated at twenty-five thousand, representing 5,000,000 feet of lumber per annum —

Market Logs Received at the Big Boom from the time of its Construction in 1851 to the Present Time

YEARS	MARKET-LOGS
1851	132,500
1852	345,400
1853	303,000
1854	297,000
1855	302,500
1856	292,500
1857	298,000
1858	332,000
1859	400,000
1860	353,000
1861	300,000[1]
1862	300,000[1]
1863	310,000
1864	279,000
1865	292,000
1866	507,000
1867	832,000
1868	600,000
1869	543,000
1870	687,000
1871	551,000
1872	1,069,000
1873	824 000
1874	446,000
1875	563,000
1876	575,500
1877	575,000[1]
Total	12,309,500[2]"

[1] No report, estimated

[2] Equal to 2,461,800,000 feet of lumber in twenty-seven years, or 91,180,741 feet on general average per annum

The conditions of the lumber interest in the county have not materially changed from those above described in 1877. It is still the leading industry, but must soon decline with the gradual disappearance of the great forests upon which it has fed and grown. The great mills, principally located in the town of Queensbury, the lumber companies, and other features of the business are treated in the history of that town, as also is the manufacture of lime, one of the prominent industries of the county.

WARREN COUNTY CIVIL LIST.

Representatives in Congress — 1823–25, John Richards; 1835–37, Dudley Farlin; 1845–47, Joseph Russell; 1849–51, John R. Thurman; 1851–53, Joseph Russell; 1867–69, Orange Ferris; 1869–71, Orange Ferris.

Delegates to Constitutional Conventions — Oct. 13 to Oct. 27, 1801, John Vernor, Queensbury; Aug. 28 to Nov. 10, 1821, John Richards, Johnsburgh; June 1 to Oct. 9, 1846, William Hotchkiss, Chester; 1868, Andrew J. Cherritree, Luzerne.

Presidential Electors — 1808, Micajah Pettit (appointed), Chester; 1816, Artemus Aldrich (appointed), Thurman; 1832, Dudley Farlin (elected), Warrensburgh; 1840, Keyes P. Cool, (elected), Queensbury; 1848, Billy J. Clark, (elected), Queensbury; 1860, N. Edson Sheldon (elected), Queensbury; 1864, Alonzo W. Morgan (elected), Queensbury.

State Senators — 1839–42, Bethuel Peck, Queensbury; 1854–55, George Richards, Warrensburgh; 1856–57, William Hotchkiss, Chester; 1862–63, Russell M. Little, Glens Falls; 1878–79–81–82, William W. Rockwell, Glens Falls.

Assemblymen — 1786–87–88–89, Peter B. Tearse, Queensbury; 1800–02, Micajah Pettit; 1800, John Thurman, Johnsburgh; 1800–01, Seth Alden, Queensbury; 1805, James Starbuck, Chester; 1807, William Robards, Queensbury; 1812, Halsey Rogers, Caldwell; 1812–13, John Beebe, Caldwell; 1814, Charles Starbuck, Chester; 1814–15, John Richards, Johnsburgh; 1816, Michael Harris, Caldwell; 1817, William Cook, Hague; 1818, Duncan Cameron, Thurman; 1819–20, Norman Fox, Chester; 1821, James L. Thurman, Warrensburgh; 1822, Duncan Cameron, Thurman.

Prior to the erection of Warren county, and until 1822, this portion of the Assembly District, which embraced Warren county, was frequently represented. The district sent from three to six members, according to the ratio of representation. The above names are among the list. Since 1822 the county has formed a separate Assembly District, entitled to send only one member.

Assemblymen — 1822, William McDonald; 1823, William McDonald; 1824, Dudley Farlin; 1825, William Cook; 1826, Norman Fox; 1827, William Hay, jr.; 1828, Truman B. Hicks; 1829, William McDonald; 1830, Norman Fox; 1831, Samuel Stackhouse; 1832, Allen Anderson; 1833,

Nicholas Roosevelt, jr ; 1834, Thomas Archibald, 1835, Truman B Hicks, 1836, William Griffin, 1837, Walter Geer, jr, 1838, Thomas A Leggett, 1839, William Griffin; 1840, Joseph Russell, 1841, George Sanford; 1842, Benjamin P Burhans, 1843, Pelatiah Richards, 1844, John F Sherrill, 1845, James Cameron; 1846, Winfield S Sherwood, 1847, John Hodgson, 2d, 1848, Albert N Cheney, 1849, Reuben Wells; 1850, Cyrus Burnham, 1851, David Noble, 2d, 1852, George Richards, 1853, Richard P Smith, 1854, David Noble, 2d; 1855, Reuben Wells, 1856, Thomas S Gray; 1857, Samuel Somerville, jr, 1858, Alexander Robertson, 1859, Elisha Pendell, 1860, Benjamin C Butler, 1861, Walter A Faxon, 1862, Thomas S Gray, 1863, Newton Aldrich, 1864, Robert Waddell, 1865, Jerome Lapham, 1866, David Aldrich, 1867, Columbus Gill, 1868, Nicholas B La Bau; 1869, Nicholas B. La Bau, 1870, Godfrey R Martine, 1871, Duncan Griffin, 1872, Joseph Woodward, 1873, James G Porteous, 1874, Austin W Holden, 1875, Stephen Griffin, 2d, 1876, Robert Waddell, 1877, Robert Waddell, 1878, Alson B Abbott, 1879, Barclay Thomas, 1880, Henry P Gwinup; 1881, Benjamin C Butler, 1882, Nelson W. Van Dusen, 1883, Lorenzo R Locke, 1884–85, Frank Byrne

Justices of the Supreme Court —1855, Enoch H Rosekranz, 1863, Enoch H Rosekranz

County Judges — 1813, William Robards, 1820, Halsey Rogers, 1823, Silas Hopkins, 1827, Joseph W Paddock, 1829, Horatio Buell, 1832, Seth C Baldwin, 1837, Hiram Barber, 1845, Halsey R Wing; 1847, Enoch H Rosekranz, 1851, Orange Ferris, 1863, Stephen Brown; 1871, Isaac J Davis, 1882, Andrew J Cherritree

Surrogates — 1813, Robert Wilkinson, 1815, Thomas Pattison, 1819, Joseph W Paddock, 1820, John Beebe, 1823, Allen Anderson, 1827, Abraham Wing, 1832, Stephen Pratt, 1835, Seth C Baldwin, 1840, Orange Ferris, 1845, Thomas S Gray; County Judge since 1847

District Attorneys — 1818, Ashael Clark, 1821, Horatio Buell; 1823, Seth C Baldwin, 1825, William Hay, jr ; 1827, Seth C Baldwin, 1835, Enoch H Rosekranz, 1845, Alfred C Farlin, 1847, George Richards, 1850, Levi H Baldwin, 1853, Stephen Brown, 1856–59–62–65, Isaac Mott, 1868; Freedom G Dudley, 1871, Andrew J Cherritree, 1873, Isaac Mott, 1873, Melville A Sheldon, 1876, Charles M. Mott, 1879, Henry A Howard ; 1882, Henry A Howard, 1884, Henry A Howard

Sheriffs — 1813, Henry Spencer; 1815, Joseph Tefft, 1817, Artemus Aldrich, 1818, James L Thurman, 1820, Pelatiah Richards, 1821, Dudley Farlin, 1822, Dudley Farlin, 1825, Henry Spencer, 1828, Dudley Farlin, 1831, James I Cameron, 1834, Joseph Russell; 1837, Timothy Bowman, 1840, Steven Griffin, 1843, Timothy Bowen, 1846, James Lawrence, 1849, Luther Brown, 1852, King Allen, 1855, Lewis Pierson; 1855, Daniel Ferguson, 1858, Stephen Starbuck; 1861, Daniel V Brown, 1864, Lewis Pierson, 1867, Westel W Hicks, 1870, John Loveland, 1873, Gideon Towsley; 1876, John Loveland, 1879, Richard P Smith, 1882, Truman N Thomas

County Clerks — 1813, John Beebe, 1815, William Smith, 1817, Myron Beach, 1820, Seth C Baldwin, jr, 1821, Thomas Archibald, 1822, Thomas Archibald, served forty years, 1861, Westel W Hicks, 1864, George P Wait; 1873, Albert F Ransom, 1876, W Scott Whitney, 1879, Daniel V Brown, 1882, Daniel V Brown

County Treasurers. — 1813–20, Michael Harris; 1820-32, Thomas Pattison, 1832–45, Charles Roberts; 1848, Frederick A Farlin; 1851, Westel W Hicks, 1857, Samuel T Richards, 1869, Daniel Peck; 1873, Miles Thomas; 1879, Emerson S Crandall, 1882, Emerson S Crandall

School Commissioners — 1856, Andrew J Cherritree, 1858, M Nelson Dickinson; 1861-64, Luther A Arnold, 1867, Theodore Welch, Adam Armstrong, jr, Daniel B Ketchum, Randolph McNutt, Adam Armstrong, jr.

County Superintendents of Common Schools — By an act passed April 17, 1843, the Boards of Supervisors of the several counties were directed to appoint county superintendents of common schools The office was abolished March 13th, 1847. During the existence of the law the following were appointed. 1843, Seth C Baldwin; 1843–44, Halsey R Wing, 1844–45, Lemon Thompson, 1846–47, Austin W Holden

CHAPTER XVII

LAND TITLES [1]

Causes Leading to Applications for Land Patents — Difficulties in Locating Many Early Patents — Conditions of Grants of Land to Officers and Privates — The Great Dellius Grant — Map of the Same — Alphabetical List of Land Patents within the present Warren County — The Glen Tract — Other Tracts and Patents — Map Making in the County

THE establishment of the military posts of Fort George on the lake and Fort Edward on the Hudson had as much to do, perhaps, with the early settlement of the present county of Warren as any other one circumstance It was the only way that civilization could be advanced in those days, for but very few people could be induced to try to establish a home beyond the sound of the gun of the fort, and when the terms of enlistment expired, either of officers or privates, they usually applied for a little tract of land Sometimes

[1] This chapter was prepared by Homer D L Sweet, of Syracuse, N Y, except those portions credited to Dr Holden's *History of Queensbury*, and has involved extensive research among the records in Albany, added to a large general knowledge of the subject

this was done by individuals, but generally in squads of from four to a dozen or more, probably with the idea of founding a nucleus for a little community, in which mutual aid and protection was their first consideration, and second the quality of the soil

One thing that tended to make small communities in this region was the small quantity of arable land that was scattered in little patches among the mountain ranges, and would not profitably admit of any large accumulation of agricultural inhabitants   The distance to market was not taken into account as at the present day, as the officers and garrisons were for many years the only non-producers in a vast region   Had any community raised more than was needful for home consumption, the facilities for getting it to market were of the rudest kind, for in the early days the water ways were the only available means of transportation, and the falls in the Hudson, at Luzerne, Corinth, Glens and Baker's, rendered that stream almost, if not entirely, unnavigable Those inhabitants that had mechanical trades almost invariably had a little farm attached to their other calling, but when nine-tenths of the heads of families had been soldiers, but very few had any mechanical trades with any degree of perfection

That these men, educated as they had been in the art of war, born in a foreign land, on a fruitful soil with a different climate, should *fail* in this region is not surprising, and this circumstance alone may be the excuse we have to make for many, very many, who had patents granted to them, and where it is easily ascertained that in a few years the same land was re-conveyed to other parties   Sometimes when this occurred, before the Revolutionary War, we attribute the cause to non-occupancy, or a neglect to record the patent, but after that period, we often attribute the cause to a disloyalty to the new government, or adherence to the old   Some patents were granted whose boundaries depended on other and older patents, perhaps, but when these were escheated, or confiscated, it is impossible for the writer to locate them without the original maps   There are quite a number of these in the county that apparently are wiped out of existence, as completely as they are rendered obsolete on the maps, but they are usually very small and appear to be covered by larger tracts, both of alluvial and mountain land, which have taken their places Most of the patents in the county are for small alluvial tracts on both sides of the Hudson, and on the west side of Lake George, and were granted to officers and soldiers who served in the French and Indian War   Other patents were granted to what professed to be actual settlers, and to no man more than a thousand acres

The quantity of the British grants contemplated by the proclamations was the concession of five thousand acres to a field officer, to a captain three thousand acres, to a subaltern staff officer two thousand acres, to a non-commissioned officer two hundred acres, and to a private fifty acres   These grants were

conferred by parchment patents, under the great seal of the colony and impressed with the royal arms   They reserved to the king "all mines of gold
and silver, and all pine trees fit for masts of the growth of twenty-four inches
diameter and upwards at twelve inches from the earth "   These grants were
held for ten years "in free and common socage exempt from all quit rents,
and after the expiration of that term, rendering and paying in the custom
house in New York, at Lady Day, the yearly rent of two shillings and sixpence
sterling, for each and every hundred acres of the granted land "   The farther
conditions imposed the settlement "of as many families on the tract as shall
amount to one family on every one thousand acres thereof," and "to cultivate
at least three acres for every fifty acres susceptible of cultivation "   Both of
these conditions were to be performed within three years from the date of the
grant   "No waste was to be committed on the reserved timber; the grant to
be registered at the secretary's office and docketed at the auditor's office in
New York "   A neglect to perform either of these conditions worked a for-
feiture of the grant   We may trace in the land papers serious consequences
resulting from these delinquencies   The council seems to have possessed certain powers to control the nature and form of these proceedings   In February, 1765, it adopted a rule, that no soldier was entitled to a grant "unless
disbanded on the reduction of the regiment"   By minutes in 1770, 1771, it
required grants to be taken out in three months after the petition had been presented, and in the last date ordered names of delinquents to be stricken from
the list of grants   Most of these grants were located in the vicinity of Lake
Champlain, and a large proportion upon the eastern side, upon what is now
the territory of Vermont   In the confusion of the agitated period that preceded the Revolution, numerous cases of these petitions remained in an in-
choate condition ; and in others, although the proceedings had been regular
and ample, were not consummated by patents from the colonial government
In most of these instances the succeeding State government refused to ratify the
proceedings of the claimants, and large estates were lost   The State constitution of 1777, by a provision which has been incorporated in the constitutions
of 1821 and 1847, abrogated all royal grants after October 14th, 1775

As appropriately introducing descriptions of the various patents granted
for lands within the present county of Warren, we quote the following relative
to the old Dellius Grant, from Dr Holden's work on Queensbury ·—

"Following in the wake of the Van Rensselaers, the Lansings, the Bay-
ards, and Van Courtlandts, the Rev Godfrey Dellius, the Dutch minister at
Albany, who had the address and influence to secure the appointment as one
of the commissioners of Indian affairs, made use of his position to obtain the
conveyance from the Indians and a subsequent confirmation by patent of two
large wilderness tracts, bordering upon Lakes George and Champlain and the
east banks of the Hudson as far south as the Battenkill.   To quote the lan-

guage of the early historian of the province,[1] he had fraudulently obtained
the Indian deeds according to which the patent had been granted.   *   *

"One of the grants included all the land within twelve miles on the east
side of the Hudson River, and extended twenty miles in length, from the
north bounds of Saratoga. Another statement says the patent was made

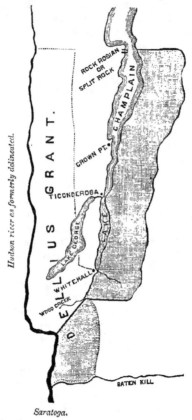

Saratoga.

under the great seal of the province, bearing date September 3d, 1696, and
embraced the territory "lying upon the east side of the Hudson River, between the northernmost bounds of Saratoga and the Rock Rossian,[2] contain-

[1] *Smith's History of New York,* p. 159.

[2] "At this period, the country on both sides of the Hudson was called Saratoga. The Rock Rossian is in Willsborough, Essex county, and is now called Split rock."—*Macauley's Hist. of N. Y.,*
vol. II, p. 412, *note.*

14

ing about 70 miles in length and 12 miles broad, subject to a yearly rent to the crown of one hundred raccoon skins ! "[1]

This patent was issued under the great seal of the province, by Col. Fletcher while acting as governor in 1696, and included the greater portion of Essex, Warren and Washington counties   This with other patents was vacated at the instance of Lord Bellamont, at the session of the provincial assembly, which was organized March 21st, 1699   Notwithstanding this fact, Dellius still asserted his claim and right to the territory in question, and on his return to Holland is commonly stated to have disposed of his interests therein to his successor in the ministry at Albany, the Rev John Lydius [2]

Nearly all the earlier writers concur with singular unanimity in making this statement, and are endorsed by such later writers as Gordon, Fitch and Lossing

" In a pamphlet exposition of the title of Lydius, printed at New Haven in 1764, doubtless by his authority, he says nothing about the Dellius grant, but claims under an Indian deed in language as follows

" ' The father of the present Colonel Lydius, being a minister of the gospel at Albany, was well known to have taken much pains with the Mohawk Indians for a series of years, in which (on his decease) he was succeeded by his son aforesaid, who (though not a clergyman) still continued their instruction, till he so far ingratiated himself into their favor, that on the first day of February, 1732, he obtained a deed of the heads of that nation, for two certain tracts of land lying on Otter Creek and Wood Creek, and bounded as follows   Beginning at the mouth of Otter Creek, where it empties into Lake Champlain and runs easterly, six Dutch miles (equal to twenty-four English), then runs southerly to the uppermost falls on Otter Creek, being about fifteen Dutch miles, be the same more or less, then westerly six Dutch miles, and thence northerly to the place of beginning   The other on Wood Creek beginning two Dutch miles and a half due north of the place called *Kingequaghtenock,* or the falls on Wood Creek, and thence runs westerly to the falls on Hudson River, going to Lake St Sacrament, thence down said river five Dutch miles, and thence running easterly five Dutch miles, thence southerly three Dutch miles and a half, thence easterly five Dutch miles, and thence northerly to the place of beginning '

" The pamphlet then states that his title by the Indian deed was confirmed

---

[1] *Munsell's Annals of Albany,* vol I, p 95   *Macauley's Hist of N Y,* vol II, *ut supra*

[2] Lydius was not the immediate successor of Dellius. In August, 1683, the Reformed Dutch church of Albany took measures for determining the salary of the newly arrived pastor from Holland, the Rev Godefridus Dellius   On the 12th of May, 1699, he was deposed by act of general assembly "from the exercises of his ministerial function in the city and county of Albany, for the illegal and surreptitious obtaining of said grants "   Having ten months in which to procure his reinstatement, the Rev John Peter Nucella occupied the pulpit as a temporary supply until the 20th of July, 1700, when he was succeeded by the Rev John Lydius, whose ministry terminated with his death 1st March, 1709 —*Munsell's Annals of Albany,* vol I, pp 82-88, 95

and declared valid by Governor Shirley of Massachusetts, in obedience to the special command of his majesty The Indian deed to Lydius, as well as the confirmation of it, if they ever existed, were both doubtless founded in fraud But the description of the land claimed by Lydius, as well as the title under which he professes to derive it, seems to exclude any idea that it had any connection with the previous grant to Dellius [1]

"On the strength of this claim Mr John Henry Lydius, son of the minister, erected a block-house on the south side of Fort Edward Creek and a trading post on the site of old Fort Nicholson, which had been built as early as 1709, built mills, supplied with water from a a wing dam extending from the main land to the island opposite the village, put up a number of log dwellings, introduced a small colony of dependents, and for a period of ten years maintained a considerable state of establishment, claiming for himself the title of Governor of Fort Edward, in his majesty's dominions of North America [2] He was familiar with many of the Indian dialects, was often consulted by Sir William Johnson in reference to Indian affairs, and was, to some extent, the rival of the astute baron in the influence and regard of the wandering tribes who enjoyed his hospitality, accepted his gifts and looked up to him as their father His little settlement and fort, which was named for him, were once or twice made the subject of incursions by the savages in 1745, when the improvements were utterly destroyed and the inhabitants driven off They were afterwards rebuilt and reoccupied to some extent, and Lydius is supposed to have acquired a handsome property in the prosecution of his traffic with the Indians After the outbreak of the last French war he held for a year or more some subordinate position in connection with the public service, but falling into disagreement with his superiors, he afterwards returned to Europe and disappeared from public view He died at Kensington, near London, in the spring of 1791, at the advanced age of ninety-eight"

The great patent of Queenbury was granted May 20th, 1762, for twenty-three thousand acres This will be noticed more at length in an appropriate place in the history of that town

Abeel — James Abeel obtained a patent for three thousand one hundred and fifty acres lying on the east side of the northeast branch of the Hudson River, next to Hill Mitchell, on the 14th of August, 1786 This seemed to take the place of several small patents that had, perhaps, been confiscated He at a later day obtained another grant for eight hundred acres lying east of the first tract, which overlapped the Northwest Bay tract The first patent

[1] Dr Hall, in number 5, vol III, *Historical Magazine* for 1868, p 310 It will be perceived by the above defined boundaries, that the greater portion of the town of Queensbury was included in the Lydius claim

[2] "Lydius soon after built a stone trading-house upon the site of Fort Edward Its doors and windows were strongly barred, and near the roof the walls were pierced for musketry It was erected upon a high mound and palisaded as a defense against enemies "—*Lossing's Hudson*, p 74

will be found in *Patents*, Vol XIX, page 146, and the second in *Patents*, XXIII, page 10   These are both located in the present town of Bolton

Adams — On a little tract, called Sabbath-day Point tract, the maps in the Surveyor-General's office have the name of Andrew Adams   Whether it be an old or a new name we cannot tell   It lies in the town of Hague

Barber — There is a small tract on the map in the Surveyor-General's office, next north of Hitchcock's and Smith's, marked J Barber   It is in Bolton on Northwest Bay

Caldwell— James Caldwell was granted a patent for four tracts of land on the west side of Lake George on the 29th of September, 1787, at a point called at that time McDonold's Bay   The first for three hundred and sixty acres, the second for four hundred and eighty-five acres, the third for one hundred and fifty-five acres, and the fourth for one thousand acres   This last one began at the most northerly corner of the first — *Patents*, Vol XX, page 48 to 51

He was granted a patent for six hundred acres opposite a small island, near Rogers's Rock, on the 11th of October, 1791, and another tract in the same patent for eight hundred acres, which began on the north bounds of the first, and probably is in the county of Essex

Mr Caldwell obtained other tracts by purchase or otherwise around the head of Lake George, and the foot-note in French's *Gazetteer*, page 673, is an error, for those lands described are easily located in a patent given to himself and others, at a later date

Campbell —A patent was granted to John Campbell and seven others for four hundred acres on the 30th of May, 1771   The description began at the northwest corner of a tract granted to John Watts, which we conclude was confiscated, and regranted to James Abeel   It is in the town of Bolton, north of Abeel, and south of Oglevie. — *Military Patents*, Vol II, page 606

Christie — A patent was granted to William Christie, for two hundred acres, on the east bank of the Hudson River, on the 18th of July, 1770.   It lies north of Jessup's second tract and west of the third, in the town of Luzerne. — *Military Patents*, Vol II, page 364.

Dartmouth Township. — A patent was granted to Jeremiah Van Rensselaer and James Abeel, with forty-five others, for eighteen thousand and thirty-six acres, being a part of forty-seven thousand acres petitioned for on the 4th of October, 1774   This tract was granted with the usual rights and privileges of those great quit-rent provisos, and with the usual organization of a township, precisely the same as in the Queensbury patent — *Patents*, Vol XVI, page 452, etc

On the same day a patent was granted to the same parties for twenty-eight thousand acres lying next north of the first purchase, which was to be divided into forty-seven equal parts   Both of these tracts were bounded on the west by Palmer's purchase   These patents lie partly in Stony Creek and partly in Thurman — *Patents*, Vol XVI, page 462, etc

Davies — A patent was granted to Thomas Davies, which began in the north bounds of Thomas Roberts and eleven others, and at the southwest corner of Randall's   This tract must have reverted, or the name has become obsolete — *Military Patents*, Vol II, page 611

Douglass — Wheeler Douglass obtained a patent for two tracts on the west side of Lake George, on the 18th of April, 1794   The first tract, which included Green Island, contained five hundred acres, and the second was south of the first and, exclusive of the waters of Trout Lake, contained two thousand five hundred acres   These two tracts lie in the town of Bolton — *Patents*, Vol XXIII, page 367

Ford — Thomas Ford and seven others obtained a patent for a tract of land on both sides of Beaver Brook, which empties into Northwest Bay, for one thousand six hundred acres, on the 7th of October, 1769   This little, narrow, crooked tract was intended to cover about all of the arable land between two great mountains   It lies partly in Bolton and partly in Hague — *Military Patents*, Vol II, page 297

Friend — I have not found any map that showed Friend's patent, but, judging from the name of Friend's Point on the lake, have concluded that that must be its locality   It is in the town of Hague

Garland — A tract of one thousand acres was granted to Peter Garland and nineteen others, next north of a tract surveyed for John Hamilton and nineteen others, on the 28th of March, 1771   The land surveyed for Hamilton and others was afterwards patented to Crane Brush   It lies in Bolton — *Military Patents*, Vol II, page 374

Goldthwaite — A patent was granted to Joseph Goldthwaite on the 25th of March, 1775, for two thousand acres   This was granted with the usual allowance, but the dimensions on the map, when computed, amount to two thousand one hundred acres actually granted   This patent is in Warrensburgh, next to the town of Luzerne — *Military Patents*, Vol III, page 49

Glen — " Among the ancient landmarks connected with the survey of this tract " (the Kayaderosseras tract), says Dr Holden in his *History of Queensbury*, " were a rock on the west side of the river near the foot of Baker's Falls, a point near the Big Falls in the town of Luzerne, Warren county, and a towering pine, whose lofty crest is at all seasons of the year conspicuous from the summit of the Palmertown Mountain, about two miles north from Doe's Corners in the town of Wilton   The swerve of the river out of its general direction from the Queensbury west line to Baker's Falls, left a gore containing upwards of two thousand acres between the north line of the Kayaderosseras patent and the Hudson River at and below Glens Falls   This tract afterwards became known as the Glen patent, it was at one time petitioned for, as appears by documents on file in the Secretary of State's office at Albany, by Simon and John Remsen, on the 14th of September, 1769, and an order was issued in council for its conveyance on the 29th of September, 1770   In the mean time, however, other claims were asserted as appears by the following —

" ' We the undermentioned subscribers do hereby certify that we, being associates in a certain purchase made from the Indians of the Mohawk Castle by John Glen, jr , Philip Van Petten, Simon Schermerhorn, for all the vacant lands lying between Sacondago, Kayaderosseras and the river to the third falls,[1] we hereby allow and agree, that John Glen, jr ,[2] is to have that part lying near the third falls on Hudson's River, containing about fifteen hundred acres, we hereby allow, and agree with the said John Glen, jr , that he may take out a special patent for the said tract of land [3]

" ' Seymen Schermerhorn,	Philip V Van Petten,
" ' Cornelius Cuyler,	Johannis Schermerhorn,
" ' John Cuyler, jr ,	Ryckart Vanfranken,
" ' Cornelius Glen,	John Roseboom,
" ' Henry Glen,	Chris Yates, for myself and Jellis Fonda,
" ' Abrm C Cuyler,	Harms H Wendell,
" ' Seymon Joh's Veeder,	Aaron Van Petten,
" ' Deryk V franken,	Reyier Schermerhorn '

" This petition was endorsed as having been granted on the request of Peter Remsen, in his own behalf and for Simon and Peter A Remsen, and was succeeded by the following application · —

" ' To the Honorable Cadwallader Colden, esq , lieutenant-governor, and commander-in-chief in and over the province of New York, etc , etc , etc   In council, Humbly showeth That your Petitioner and associates have made a purchase of all the vacant lands lying between the patents of Kayaderosseras, Sacondago, and Hudson's River to the third falls on said river, your petitioners therefore Humbly Pray your Excellency will be pleased to grant them a patent for a small part thereof   Beginning at the third falls on Hudson's River, and so up the river till it joyns the line of Kayaderosseras Patent and so along the line thereof to the third falls aforesaid, being the place of beginning, together with all the islands in the said river opposite   And your Petitioners shall ever pray

" ' JOHN GLEN, JR
" ' HENRY GLEN '

---

[1] Baker's Falls on the Hudson River   A long and costly law suit, in the early part of the century, hinged upon the question whether the third fall on the Hudson River applied to Baker's Falls or the falls at Fort Miller   The question was ultimately decided to apply to the former, an opinion abundantly corroborated by all the earlier maps and surveys

[2] For ancestry, etc , of Glen, see succeeding history of Queensbury and Glens Falls village

[3] This tract had been petitioned for by John Glen and others as early as May 6th, 1761, thus taking precedence in priority of the Queensbury patent — *Vide Calendar of N Y Land Papers*, p 303

" The Burnham family of Glens Falls have, in their possession, a lease en-
grossed on parchment, in which, on the 5th of February, 1772, John Glen
conveys to Christopher Yates, the use for one year of part of two islands in
the Hudson River and a tract of land on the west side of Hudson River, the
same being a part, as the instrument states, of a patent granted to John Glen
and Henry Glen   The islands referred to are those lying near the eastern
boundary of the town of Queensbury, and elsewhere referred to as owned first
by the Jessups and afterwards by Daniel Jones "

Dr Holden adds the observation that " more space is here devoted to the
consideration of the Glen tract than would otherwise be given it, from the fact
that the name of Glens Falls is derived from one of the patentees, the circumstances connected with which have been presented to the public in such distorted shape, as to require a new and thorough explanation "   This statement
gives ample reason for the insertion of the full explanation herein

Glen — The records show that there were four patents granted to Jacob
Glen on the 6th of March, 1790, for one thousand one hundred acres in the
aggregate   These little tracts were just west of Queensbury patent   Two of
these tracts are in Queensbury, and two in Luzerne — *Patents* Vol XXII,
page 199

Harris — On the 22d of April, 1788, there was granted to Joshua Harris
four small patents of two hundred acres each, between Queensbury patent and
Lake George   These lie in the town of Queensbury — *Patents*, Vol XX,
pages 293 to 296

Harris — On the border of the county next to Washington are several
patents that were granted to Moses Harris, according to the small map of the
Lake George tract, through which the county line runs

Houghton — A tract around the head of Lake George, and reaching as far
south as Queensbury patent, was granted to Robert Harpur, of King's College,
New York, and eighty-six others, " Protestants and dutiful subjects of the
North of Ireland " for three thousand seven hundred acres, with 31,015 acres
lying between Wood Creek and Lake George, together with Long Island in
Lake George, on the 22d of May, 1765   In this patent was granted the rights
and privileges of a township named Harpurville, precisely as in the case of
Queensbury   Why this patent reverted would be of interest to know, as the land
that was covered by the patent has been resurveyed in other tracts, and the
original boundaries become obsolete   A small part of this original grant, lying
around the " garrison grounds " at Caldwell, and reaching south to Queensbury patent in a very small point, was granted to William Houghton on the
3d of July, 1770, containing two thousand acres   The commencement of this
survey is identical with the first and so are several of the courses, and distances
The first grant is in *Patents*, Vol XIV, page 78, etc , and the second *M P*,
Vol II, page 479   It lies in the town of Caldwell

Hyde Township — This township was granted to Edward and Ebenezer Jessup and thirty-eight others, with all the rights and privileges of a township, the same as Queensbury   The tract was to contain forty thousand acres, but in reality contains a great deal more, even allowing for the usual five per cent. for highways   Patent dated September 10th, 1774 — *Patents*, Vol XVI, page 410, etc   It lies in Warrensburgh and Thurman

Hitchcock — Zina Hitchcock and Philip Smith were granted a patent for one thousand and eighty-one acres on the 15th of August, 1795   It lies next north of Wheeler Douglass in Bolton, and is marked " Smith," on Burr's Atlas. — *Patents*, Vol XIII, page 407

Jessups — Ebenezer Jessup and fourteen associates petitioned for fifteen thousand acres of unoccupied land on the east side of the Hudson River   As they could not find enough to suit them in a body, they were content to take it in several places   The first tract, which is the one lying farthest north was granted on the 20th of May, 1768, and contained seven thousand five hundred and fifty acres, which was to be divided into fifteen equal shares — *Patents*, Vol XIV, page 270 etc

The second tract was patented on the 21st day of May, 1768, to the same parties, and contained four thousand one hundred acres   It is on this second tract that the village of Luzerne stands — *Patents*, Vol XIV, page 276, etc

The third tract was located between these two, and only granted to Ebenezer and Edward Jessup   It was patented on the 10th of April, 1772, and contained two thousand acres.   This patent was bounded on the west by Watcock, Quinn and Christie — *Patents*, Vol XVI, page 208

Jones — John Jones, who is described as "barrack-master," was granted two hundred acres on the west side of Lake George, which embraced the site of the village of Caldwell   The grant was made in June, 1785   This tract was conveyed to Udney Hay, who re-conveyed it to Mr Caldwell   (See history of the town of Caldwell)

Kennedy — Robert Kennedy was granted a patent for two thousand acres, on the west side of Lake George, north of the site of Caldwell village   The date was October 1st, 1774   The original grant is in the Warren county clerk's office

Kayadcrosseras Patent — Of this patent Dr Holden writes as follows in his *History of Queensbury*. —

" We next come to the consideration of the Kayaderosseras patent, whose north line cuts through the west and southwest portions of the town, and from the beginning has given rise to almost interminable litigation.   The early law reports of the century are loaded with these cases, whose various points and issues have hardly yet been completely tested.   One of the more recent cases was tried in 1857, being brought by Thomas B Bennett, who claimed under the Kayaderosseras patent, against Abraham Wing and others, who also claimed under the same patent but from a different deed Bennett's action being founded on a supposition that Wing would claim under the Queensbury patent, he was defeated with costs It is proper to state however, that there were other points in issue

"The great Kayaderosseras patent was founded on a grant obtained in 1702 from two Mohawk sachems named Ter-jen-nin-ho-ge, or Joseph, and De-han-och-rak-has, or Hendrick The grantees were Robert Livingston and David Schuyler; and the consideration, sundry goods, wares and merchandise It was soon afterwards alleged that the purchase was fraudulent, the chiefs signing the deed being intoxicated for that purpose, and in no way authorized by their tribe to dispose of the lands embraced in the purchase, and that much more territory was claimed and subsequently granted by patent than was embraced even by this fraudulent conveyance For upwards of sixty years, this transaction was a prolific source of anxiety to the Indians, and of reproach and trouble to the whites At a council held with the lower castle of the Mohawks at Albany, Thursday, June 27th, 1754, Lieutenant Governor James De Lancy presiding, the speaker in behalf of the Indians said —

" ' Brother, we are told a large tract of land has been taken up called Kayaderosseras, beginning at the half moon, and so along up the Hudson River, to the third fall and thence to the Cacknowaga or Canada Creek which is about four or five miles above the Mohawk, which, upon enquiry among our old men, we can not find was ever sold, and as to the particular persons, many of them live in this town,[1] but there are so great a number we cannot name them '

" This purchase was confirmed by letters patent from the crown in 1708 to thirteen patentees and contained by estimation about eight hundred thousand acres lying between the Hudson and Mohawk Rivers A great proportion of the land titles in Saratoga county, as also the western part of Warren county, are predicated upon this grant [2] The points in controversy were amicably settled in 1768, by the recession to the natives of a portion of the disputed territory lying near the Mohawk River,[3] and the payment by the proprietors of $5000 for the remainder, extending on the Hudson (with the exception of two small patents previously issued) to the falls at Sandy Hill "

Copy of a description of the Kayaderosseras Patent from the Wing MSS

"Kayaderosseras alias Queensbury, granted by Queen Anne, the 2d day of November, 1708, beginning at a place in Schenectady River about three miles distant from the southwesterly bounds of Nistigione, the said place being

---

[1] Albany, where the council was being held

[2] In one of the road surveys for the town of Queensbury, for 1820, the north boundary of the Kayaderosseras patent is made the line of a newly relaid road — *Town Records*, p 210

[3] " On the 15th of Jan'y, 1793, the legislature of this State appointed a commission consisting of Egbert Bensen and Peter Curtenius of Dutchess, Samuel Jones of New York, Jesse Woodhull of Orange and Cornelius Schoonmaker of Ulster counties, to ascertain and settle the boundaries of the patent of Kayaderosseras and Half Moon "

the southwesterly corner of the patent then lately granted to Nanning Harmanse, Peter Fauconier, and others, thence along the said Schenectady River westerly to the southeasterly corner of a patent lately granted to William Apple, thence along the easterly, northerly and westerly lines of the said William Apple's patent down to the above said river, thence to Schenectady bounds, or the southwesterly corner of the said patent on the said river, so along the easterly northerly and westerly bounds thereof down to the said river again, thence along the said river up westerly to the southeasterly bounds of a tract of land then lately granted to Ebenezer Wilson, and John Abeel, and so along the patent round to the southwesterly corner thereof up the said Schenectada river then continuing to run westerly up said Schenectada river to a place or hill called Tweetonondo being five miles distant or thereabouts from the southwesterly corner of the Wilson and Abeel's patent, thence northerly to the northwesternmost head of a creek called Kayaderosseras about fourteen miles more or less, thence eight miles more northerly, then easterly or northeasterly to the third falls on Albany river about twenty miles, more or less thence along the said river down southerly to the northeasterly bounds of Saratoga thence along the said Saratoga northerly, westerly and southerly bounds on the said river, thence to the northeasterly corner of Anthony Van Schaik's lands on the said river, so northerly and westerly along the said Van Schaik's patent to the northeast corner of the above said patent granted to Nanning Harmanse, Peter Fauconier and others thence along the northerly and westerly bounds thereof down to the above said river of Schenectada it being the place where it first began, which said tract of land we have divided into twenty-five allotments viz   Allotment No 3, 4, 7, 8, 9, 10, 21, 22, 23, 24, and 25, are controverted, and the remaining allotments, viz . Allotment No 1, 2, 5, 6, 11, 12, 13, 14, 15, 16, 17, 18, 19, and 20, are not controverted, also the lots No 1 and 2, distinguished in the map by the red stain, which together contain 21,350 acres we have set apart for defraying the charges of the partition "

                                                              (Not signed)

Lawrence — There is quite a tract marked on the map of French Mountain tract, as belonging to John Lawrence, but whether it was patented to him or not we did not succeed in finding out   It is in Queensbury

McCauley — There is a small patent nearly south of the village of Warrensburgh, and marked Auley on Burr's atlas (which ought to be Hugh McAuley)   We failed to find further records of it   It lies in the town of Caldwell

McClay — There is another small patent marked on the map of Warrensburgh tract, " D McClay," of which we have failed to find any record   It lies in the town of Warrensburgh in the extreme southwest corner

Laws — A patent of about fifteen hundred and fifty acres lies in the town of Hague, on the lake shore, on which the village of Hague stands, of which we obtained no definite trace

McClallen — A large tract of twenty-two thousand one hundred acres in the north part of Hague, and in the south part of Ticonderoga, was granted to Robert McClallen, James Caldwell and Robert Cochran, and a second tract south of the first, of seventeen thousand six hundred acres, on the 3d of March, 1795   In the description of the boundaries of these two tracts, there is mention made of the patents of Samuel Deal, John Stoughton, Jonathan Mathews, John Lee, James Stevenson, Theopilact Bache, George Robinson, James Scott, William Friend, besides several patents that were granted to James Caldwell. — *Patents*, Vol XVIII, page 56, etc

McDonold — Niel McDonold, with seven others, was granted a patent for sixteen hundred acres on the 28th of March, 1771   It lies next north of Peter Garland and among the names is William Nowland, which may account for the name on the map in Burr's atlas, as Norman   We find no such name in the Indexes   The patent is in the town of Bolton — *Military Patents*, Vol II, page 578.

Mitchell — Hill Mitchell and fifteen others obtained a patent for eight hundred acres next north of David Smith, and twelve others on the 5th of April, 1771   It lies in the extreme north point of Caldwell — *M P*, Vol II, page 584

Porter. — Thomas Porter and twenty-seven others were granted a patent for fifty-six hundred acres lying next north of Niel McDonold, on the northeast branch of the Hudson River (or what is now known as the Schroon branch), on the 8th day of March, 1771   It is in Horicon — *M P*, Vol II, page 541

Oglevie — Alexander Oglevie and others were granted a patent for six hundred acres bounded on the south by John Campbell and west by the river   This patent lies in the town of Bolton — *Military Patents*, Vol II, page 604

Queensbury — See later pages

Quinn — Edward Quinn and six others obtained a patent for three hundred and fifty acres next north of Christie's, bounded on the east by Jessup's third tract   It is in the town of Luzerne   Dated July 18th, 1770 — *M P*, Vol II, page 262

Robinson — George Robinson and others obtained a patent for a narrow strip of land on both sides of Beaver Brook, and north of Ford's patent, in the town of Hague

Ross — James Ross obtained a patent for two thousand acres on the 10th of April, 1775   It lies next north of Goldthwaite's patent in the town of Warrensburgh — *M P*, Vol III, page 50

Roberts — Thomas Roberts and eleven others obtained a grant for six hundred acres next north of Thomas Porter, on the 8th of March, 1771   This lies almost all in the town of Horicon — *M P*, Vol II, page 538

Rogers — Platt Rogers obtained a patent for a large tract lying on both sides of Schroon River, as compensation for building roads   This patent, known as the Road patent, is in the towns of Horicon and Chester.

Smith — David Smith and twelve others obtained a grant for a tract of two thousand six hundred acres, next south of Mitchell's opposite Warrensburgh village, on the southwest side of the northeast branch of the Hudson River, in Caldwell, on the 5th of April, 1771 — *M P*, Vol II, page 582

Watcock — Richard Watcock and six others had a patent of three hundred and fifty acres next south of Quinn, on the east bank of the Hudson River in the present town of Luzerne — *M P*, Vol II, page 361.

By an examination of a quantity of old maps obtained in various places, for the construction of French's map of the State, we have found names that we do not find on any of the engraved maps   Three little tracts marked E Dunham, on Tongue Mountain tract; David McClay, on Warrensburgh tract, James Robertson, James Mountfort, and William Brown, on the Luzerne tract; Charles Sheriff, James Parkinson, James Panton, and Jesse Chidester, on the north of Hyde township, Andrew Gowdy, F Turner, James Randell, south of Brant Lake tract   N Gardinier, just south of Platt Rogers's Road tract, on the same map   On the other hand there are in the Indexes at Albany the names of many persons that are indexed to various parts of this county that it is now impossible to locate

Large Tracts — Besides these, and those that we have failed to find the record of, and others where we have found the record and have not found a place on the map in which to locate them, there are several large tracts that were surveyed at a later date, and sold by the State to individuals, and although they obtained patents for their purchases, it did not change the name of the tract   Hague tract lies in the west part of Hague, and reaches north into Ticonderoga   Brant Lake tract lies next west of Hague, and covers most of the town of Horicon   South of these lies Northwest Bay tract, in Bolton, and Tongue Mountain tract partly in Bolton and partly in Hague.   Warrensburgh tract lies in the southwest corner of that town, and Luzerne tract is nearly all in the east part of that town   French Mountain tract lies in the northeast point of Queensbury   Totten and Crossfield purchase covers all the northwest corner of the county, all of Johnsburgh and a part of Chester.   The rear division of Palmer's purchase lies mostly in Stony Creek, with a small portion in Thurman   The twenty-fifth division of the Kayaderosseras lies south of Luzerne tract and Queensbury patent, in the towns of Luzerne and Queensbury   The rear division of Palmer's purchase was sub-divided by the heirs of Thomas Palmer, Philip Livingstone, Peter Remsen and Dirck Lefferts

When application was made to the colonial government for a tract of land the signers of the petition usually affirmed that they were true and lawful subjects, and desired the land for actual settlement, and it would be a curious question to answer by the historian in how many cases the land was actually occupied by the petitioners The small patents were usually granted to the officers, non-commissioned officers and privates of the British army that were garrisoned at Fort George, Fort Edward, Fort Lyman, or Fort William Henry A glance at the map, and a comparison of the dates of their respective patents, will convince the reader that the county was sparsely settled long before the Revolutionary war, if those only who took patents actually occupied them, yet it is a difficult matter to trace the correct history of occurrences back to that period There *may* be a history of any of the great tracts, equal to that available of Queensbury, if we only knew where to find it, but we do not, even if it exists

Map — To arrange these patents, grants and large tracts in their proper places in order to project a map of the county is one of those tasks that never has been done and never will be until the Trigonometrical Survey of the State has been completed. The causes that combine to defeat anything like accuracy are, first, the variation of the magnetic needle by which all these were located ; second, the errors in chaining over mountains and streams , third, the allowances that surveyors made for rough land and for highways , and, fourth, the laps and gores, or the interference of patent lines and the spaces between patents

Beside the annual and ever increasing variation of the magnetic needle, the local attractions were very prominent in many portions of this county This cause alone was sufficient to disarrange any survey made in that manner, but frequently the surveyor, in correcting up his latitude and departure, would rely on his needle and not on the chain, and plot his courses so as to balance, making his distances agree to a single link Surveyors of the present day know that this is utterly preposterous, and when they have the least suspicion, invariably rely on the chain Frequently in the returns of the surveyor to the land commissioners, he would say in his survey-bill, "as the needle pointed " in some previous year, and particularly when he was following an old line , but when he began to run a new line in the wilderness, he would invariably run as the needle happened to point at that time Thus lines that were intended as parallel on the ground, and were so, would have a variation on the map of several degrees

The difficulties in chaining over mountains, precipices, lakes and chasms, and getting the distances correct, is apparent to any intelligent man , but to make this look particularly absurd, in common chain surveying, we give an incident of a State Deputy Surveyor who measured a gore between the Old Military tract and the Refugee tract, in Clinton county. This strip of land was quite narrow, but very long, reaching from Dannemora to the Canada line He passed over three mountain chains, two large rivers, several precipices and a chasm three hundred feet deep , and yet his distances invariably balance Besides this impossible feat, he made the Canada line at right angles to his

north and south lines   When absolute accuracy is desired, it is safe to say that
no two men can chain a mile and then chain it back again, and find the two
measurements agree

It was the invariable rule in the early surveys, to make the "usual allowance for roads"   This was in many instances known to be five per cent , but
if the patent was for a specified number of acres, the returns of the surveyor
would make the distances in his return, and the map also, to cover the precise
quantity   This five per cent might be added to the side or to the end of a
patent, and to this day which course was adopted, no one can tell   Besides
this discrepancy in the measurement, the Commissioners of the Land Office
would often say in the patent, "in setting out this grant we have made due allowance for the profitable and unprofitable acres," and this may have added to
a confusion already badly confounded.

The laps, or the interference of patent lines that must have necessarily
followed such a style of surveying, were not known sometimes until many
years had elapsed   The starting points were often ill-defined and a malicious
person could, with an axe, destroy them in a few minutes   These interferences
were necessarily settled in the courts, and there is hardly a map in the archives
of the State to show such records   The gores that have been discovered by
later surveyors have invariably been applied for, the tracts surveyed and patents granted   Some of these were discovered in the early part of the century,
and some as late as 1855   These laps and gores alone are enough to destroy
the accuracy of Burr's atlas and, in a great degree, all that has since been published   The writer had practical experience in plotting Warren county and
brief details of the work may not be uninteresting here

The county line on the north, as surveyed by Joseph L Harris, was the
base line for the plot, and from this was projected on the south all of the different tracts, as he had indicated them   But as there was no certainty that he
had laid down the lines of the lots, the patent or tract lines correctly, everything that could be obtained in the offices of the Secretary of State and the
Surveyor-General, and all that could be obtained on the ground of local
surveyors was brought to bear on the case, and all known authorities
were consulted   The measurements governed where they agreed, or very
nearly, and the course of the lines were left to vary as the measurements should
prove them to be   The Hague tract was first plotted, then the Northwest Bay
tract, then the Luzerne tract, which gave a strip nearly across the county north
and south, and on which the measurements were supposed to be quite accurate,
as no account had to be taken for "the usual allowance"   From these as a
base we could plot to the east and west, and by careful work bring all of the
little patents into their respective places   These usually did not agree with the
dimensions as given in the patents, or as designated on the maps, but when
the shore line of Lake George was drawn, according to a very finely made

map of the lake by Aug F Dalton (1855), it was ascertained that they
agreed in very many nice particulars   In plotting west from the large tracts
mentioned, the position of the confluence of the Sacandaga River with the
Hudson was obtained, and then to lay out the Dartmouth patent and Hyde
township was undertaken   This brought trouble and confusion, as the northwest corner of Hyde township must be a right angle, and the northwest line
would strike the Hudson River too far south   Finally the townships of Totten
and Crossfield were plotted and the southwest line of Hyde township made to
agree with townships 12 and 14, and the space that was left was assigned to
Hyde township, let it be more or less   From this line the Dartmouth patent
was plotted, and Palmer's purchase, according to the decision of the court in
a great law suit where the patents were said to interfere   From the Luzerne
tract to the east there was no trouble in plotting Queensbury and the French
Mountain tract, and the work was completed   In all this labor the greatest
care had to be taken, and the longest lines drawn first   To make sure that the
surveyor was pretty nearly correct, we invariably added his dimensions of the
lots, to see if they agreed with the length given on the outside lines, and as
often the different dimensions of the little patents adjoining   When they dis-
agreed to any considerable extent, the latest measurement was adopted
When we consider that hardly a mile of any of these lines was originally run
on level land, and some of them over very high mountains, steep, rocky, and
covered with a dense growth of forest, it is surprising that anything like accuracy could be obtained

.

CHAPTER XVIII

WARREN COUNTY IN THE REBELLION

Patriotic Action of the County — The First Recruiting Officers — Two Companies Raised — The
Twenty-second Regiment — Company Officers — Rosters — The Ninety sixth Regiment — Company I
— Company K, One Hundred Fifty-third Regiment — The Ninety-third Regiment — Warren County
Enlistments — The One Hundred Eighteenth Regiment — Second Veteran Cavalry — Statistics

THE news of the outburst of "the great Rebellion," in April, 1861, was
borne through the rugged wilds and hills of Warren county with a celerity
like that of the "fiery cross," which in past generations gathered the clans of
Scotland to the call of their chieftains

In less than three days after the fall of Sumter, applications were addressed
to the adjutant-general's office, in Albany, for authority to procure enlistments

On the morning of Thursday, the 18th of April, handbills were posted

throughout the village of Glens Falls, containing a call, signed by over forty of
the leading citizens of the place, for "a meeting to sustain the government"
At this meeting, which was held the same evening, and which was largely attended, several spirited addresses were made The national flag was brought
in and displayed amidst the wildest enthusiasm, and a series of patriotic resolutions adopted, from which the following extract is taken as a sample of their
purport and spirit. —

"*Resolved*, That the village of Glens Falls will not be behind any of her sister villages in contributing the men and the means necessary to defend the
government, and to maintain the permanency of our beloved institutions ; and
that, as our fathers who established the Union pledged 'their lives, their fortunes, and their sacred honors,' to gain our independence, so will we pledge all
we possess to cherish and protect the work of the illustrious men of the past,
and to transmit unimpaired to our descendants the noble institutions given
to us

"*Resolved*, That to the end we are for maintaining this Union undivided,
and, whatever may be the consequences, sacrifice of property or life itself —
everything but loss of honor — we will stand by the stars and stripes until the
last faint echo in the expiring gale wafts our dying prayer heavenward, in behalf of our country, its institutions, and humanity "

On the succeeding Saturday the first recruiting office was opened by Dr
A W Holden, and during the following week Captain George Clendon, jr ,
was similarly authorized to raise another company, both of which were designed
to apply on the quota of New York to fill the first call for troops

At this early period in the war, no other town in the county had as yet undertaken to raise a company The hardy and adventurous youth and patriotic
manhood of its northern towns were not, however, to be repressed Day by
day they poured in at the recruiting stations, and, in many instances, impatient
of the tardy process of enlistment, pushed on to the cities and enlisted in companies and regiments already formed, and ready for departure to the scene of
hostilities

The two companies above mentioned were soon filled, and were accepted
into the State service on the 6th and 7th of May following, and on the 9th were
ordered into quarters—one into the barracks at Troy, the other at the Albany
depot The latter was at a later period sent to Troy, and the two afterwards
joined together in the formation of the New York Twenty-second Volunteers,
of which regiment a sketch is given in this chapter Companies G and I of
the same command also received considerable accessions from Warren county

Contemporaneously with the organization of these companies a relief fund
was raised by voluntary subscriptions, in the town of Queensbury alone,
amounting to $11,243, for the aid and support of the families of such mem-
bers of these companies as were needy or destitute Another fund, the

amount of which is unknown, was applied to defray the expenses of subsistence during the progress of enlistment

For the disbursement of the first named fund a committee was appointed, and assessments made from time to time, as occasion required The total amount of collections from this source up to June, 1863, when these companies were finally mustered out of service, was $3,260 47, which was apportioned among twenty-nine different families

The preceding paragraphs are the language used by Dr Holden in introducing his sketch of the military work of the town of Queensbury, in his history of that town, and serves to properly introduce the following accounts of the various organizations to which companies from this county were contributed:—

The Twenty-second Regiment [1] — This regiment was enlisted and mustered in 1861, under the call of the president for 75,000 men for two years' service, issued on the 15th of April This proclamation was followed by an act of the Legislature, passed April 17th, authorizing the creation of a volunteer force sufficient to fill its quota Thirty-eight regiments were raised under this act It was only cities and densely populated towns which were able to supply complete regiments to the service In thinly settled regions and agricultural districts three, and sometimes more, counties combined to make up a battalion More frequently still, the military board, to meet the exigencies of government, consolidated companies and formed regiments irrespective of personal interests and local prejudices

At an early period in the formation of the companies composing the Twenty-second Regiment conferences were held, at which it was resolved to organize a regiment representing the old congressional district of Essex, Warren and Washington counties Applications to the executive and also to the military board, with the same intent, received a favoring response A formal petition, signed by nearly if not quite all the line officers subsequently embraced in this command, desiring to be associated together as a regiment, being forwarded to the military board, was ordered to be held at Stanwix Hall, Albany, on the evening of the 14th of May, 1861 This meeting was presided over by Brigadier-General Rathbone, and resulted in the election (nearly unanimous) of the following field officers, viz —

Colonel, Walter Phelps, jr, of Glens Falls, Warren county; lieutenant-colonel, Gorton T Thomas, of Keeseville, Essex county; major, John M'Kie, of Cambridge, Washington county It will be perceived that each section of the district was thus represented in the election

These officers had all been military men connected with the old State militia organization, which, poor as it was (for there were none so abject as to

1 This sketch of the Twenty-second Regiment was largely made up from newspaper correspondence from the pen of Dr A. W Holden

do it reverence), supplied a large proportion of the officers, and a goodly number of the men, who filled this first installment of the mighty armies of the North. By special favor from the military board the regiment was permitted to go into barracks at the fair grounds of the Rensselaer County Agricultural Society, near the city of Troy, although Albany had been officially designated as the military depot for that section of the State. Here commenced the first experiences of that rigid discipline so necessary to the formation of the thorough soldier. Here was first tasted that bitter cup to the volunteer soldier, the restriction of personal liberty by sentries and guard lines. Although accepted and mustered into the State service, some of the companies, through dissatisfaction with their officers and various other causes, became rapidly reduced by desertion. Prompt steps were taken to supply the unwelcome deficit at this critical moment, for it was still obligatory to come up to the prescribed standard of "seventy-five men," neither more nor less, before the companies could be mustered into the United States service. Recruiting officers from nearly every company were dispatched home for fresh volunteers, and the regiment was thus increased by over a hundred. About this time it became necessary to disband the Whitehall company, through an embittered state of feeling which had grown up between the men and its officers, and also, as was alleged, from the failure of the home committee to support the families of the enlisted men agreeably to the understanding had when they enlisted. There may have been still other causes, but these were the leading ones. Most of the men re-enlisted, some in one company, some in another. The commissioned officers being left without a command, of course resigned. Upon the feeble *debris* of the company left a new one was soon afterward organized, nearly all the companies in the barracks contributing their surplus men for the purpose, the new captain, Benjamin Mosher, soon after increasing the number by a fresh importation of recruits from Whitehall and vicinity.

About the 20th of May the staff appointments were made and announced, and for the first a complete roster was made.

Following is a roster of the officers of the Twenty-second Regiment on the 1st of June, 1861. The commissions are all dated May and June, 1861.

Field and Staff — Colonel, Walter Phelps, jr., Glens Falls.

Lieutenant-colonel, Gorton T Thomas, Keeseville.

Major, John M'Kie, Cambridge.

Adjutant, Edward Pruyn.

Quartermaster, Henry Woodruff, Troy.

Surgeon, J B Atherly, Albany.

Assistant surgeon, W F Hutchinson, Sandy Hill.

Chaplain, Rev H H Bates, Glens Falls.

Paymaster, Benjamin C Butler, Luzerne.

Non-Commissioned Staff — Sergeant-Major, John F Towne, Sandy Hill.

Quartermaster-sergeant, Jeremiah W Fairbanks, Cohoes

Commissary-sergeant, Charles Bellamy, Glens Falls

Hospital steward, David H King, Fort Edward

Drum-major, John Scott, Hebron

Fife-major, John Wright, Glens Falls

Color-sergeant, James Johnson, Glens Falls

Right general-guide, Malachi Weidman, Waterford

Left general-guide, John J Barker, Glens Falls

Line Officers — Company A. — Captain, J L Yates, Cohoes, first lieutenant, Jas H Bratt, Waterford, second lieutenant, Hiram Clute, Cohoes

Company B — Captain, Robert McCoy, Fort Edward, first lieutenant, Duncan Lendrum, Fort Edward, second lieutenant, James W McCoy, Fort Edward

Company C — Captain, O D. Peabody, Keeseville, first lieutenant, C D Beaumont, Keeseville, second lieutenant, C B Piersons, Albany

Company D. — Captain, H S Milliman, Cambridge, first lieutenant, T B Fisk, Cambridge, second lieutenant, R A Rice, Cambridge

Company E — Captain, Geo Clendon, jr, Glens Falls, first lieutenant, John S Fassett, Glens Falls, second lieutenant, G H Gayger, Glens Falls

Company F — Captain, A W Holden, Glens Falls, first lieutenant, Wm H Arlin, Glens Falls; second lieutenant, O. B Smith, Glens Falls

Company G — Captain, Benj J Mosher, Whitehall, first lieutenant, Duncan Cameron, Glens Falls, second lieutenant, Henry C Hay, Glens Falls

Company H — Captain, T J Strong, Sandy Hill, first lieutenant, W A Pierson, Sandy Hill, second lieutenant, M S Teller, Sandy Hill

Company I — Captain, Lyman Ormsbee, Schroon, first lieutenant, J R Seaman, Schroon, second lieutenant, D Burgey, Schroon

Company K — Captain, Miles P S Caldwell, Port Henry, first lieutenant, E F Edgerly, Moriah, second lieutenant, C W Huntly, Bridgeport, Vt

On the 6th of June the band of the regiment was mustered into the service by Captain Frank Wheaton, of the regular army, much to the pleasure and satisfaction of the entire organization It was under the leadership of Asa Patten.

While encamped at Troy the time was busily improved by the regiment in the daily drill which is necessary to efficiency in any military organization On Monday, June 20, the regiment was ordered to Albany, where it occupied quarters at the Industrial barracks, quarters which were vastly inferior to those left On the following day the men received their first pay as soldiers, covering the time passed in the service of the State While in Albany the regiment received its first equipment of arms, the guns being the old pattern of smooth-bore Springfield musket, this arm gave considerable dissatisfaction, and at a subsequent date, through the exertions of Colonel Phelps and Quartermaster Schenck, the Springfield rifle was substituted

June 27th the regiment received marching orders, and on the following day, under escort of Captain Ainsworth's Albany Zouaves, marched through the principal streets to the steamer   The band played national airs and the troops were cheered and greeted by waving banners and handkerchiefs from many windows   Embarking in two barges and a steamer, the trip down the Hudson was made and the next day the Dey street dock was reached in New York city   The same evening the regiment was transferred to a steamer and taken to Elizabethport, N J, where for the first time hard tack and raw meat were issued to the men   It was an unwelcome and radical change from the sumptuous Albany rations and gave a foretaste of what was to come   About midnight the regiment embarked on freight cars and the journey to Baltimore was safely made, with but one untoward incident   Joseph Pero and Frederick Minne, of Company C, were knocked from the car by coming in contact with a footbridge   They were severely injured, but finally recovered   Pero was killed in the Second Bull Run battle

As the regiment approached Baltimore the men were deeply imbued with the expectation of an attack by the mobs that had but a few weeks previously so ruthlessly attacked the Massachusetts troops   The regiment left the cars about 8 o'clock P M, and was drawn up in line   The following description of the passage through the city was written by Dr Holden in 1862.   " The men who had been previously furnished with six rounds of cartridges were now ordered to load   Although the dun clouds which shrouded the sun's golden setting had veiled the stars with a filmy haze, the evening was still calm, beautiful and serene   Just as the long rows of gas lights came flashing into existence, we were ordered to wheel into column by platoons, and then we commenced our march   Never did those glorious old national anthems speak more thrillingly to the heart than on the occasion now described   The proud patriotism which animated every heart in the line prepared each one then and there to become martyrs if need be for our country's welfare.   It was Sunday night, an ' evening calm and cool,' when all were at leisure, and nothing prevented the gathering of a mob   The bold, martial strains of a military band, especially of a Sunday night, were a novelty to the citizens of Baltimore, for since the occurrence of the riot and massacre of the Massachusetts troops on the 17th of April, all of the national troops had been hurried through the city without ceremony, regardless of military display, and some of that dignity which should always attend a preponderating armed force   Our advent and transit was at first met with a dubious welcome, and as we occasionally turned a street corner, with a few faint-hearted cheers   In one or two instances bouquets were flung in our midst by true-hearted, loyal women who dared to be patriotic, against the pretensions of class and the exclusiveness of caste, at a period when slave aristocracy was combining its fairest energies to rule or ruin   As we passed the heart of the city and approached the suburbs on the opposite side, the gathering hostile elements became rapidly apparent, and cheers for 'Jeff Davis,' and groans, execrations, anathemas and maledictions for 'Abe Lincoln,' became painfully distinguishable above the noise of the music, and the steady tramp of our advancing column As we drew near the Camden depot at the Washington extremity, the shouts and clamor increased in frequency and volume, while the walks and streets were thronged with the populace eagerly hurrying along upon our flanks Then came the order 'by the right flank, by file left, march,' and soon the head file of the column entered the depot The band continued playing until it reached the opposite end of the building when the line was 'halted,' brought to the 'front face' and 'dressed' Companies B and G, on the extreme left, were still outside the building A sergeant was entering the building, he stumbled and fell, and his musket (being loaded and capped), as it struck heavily on the floor, exploded, the discharge wounding a citizen, standing near by, in the foot This was followed by three or four scattering shots, apparently from the roof of the building, which was succeeded by a fusilade partly on the right and partly in the center of the regiment At this juncture all the gas lights in the building were suddenly extinguished as though by a preconcerted signal At the same instant a flash as of thirty or forty pieces was seen from the side of the building towards which the line was faced, and similar flashes appeared as though from the roof, towards which a scattered and irregular fire was kept up through the line At this stage of affairs the commanding voices of Colonel Phelps and Lieutenant-Colonel Thomas were heard through the line above the din and roar of musketry Their self-possession, aided by the efforts of the line officers, soon restored order and quiet through the ranks Major M'Kie, in consequence of an injury received while landing from the boat at Elizabethport, N J, had been left behind and did not rejoin the regiment until the following day During the tumult, one of the privates from Company F mounted the shoulders of a comrade and endeavored to light one of the gas burners with a match, but could not, thus showing conclusively that the gas had been turned off at the meter Shots were also distinctly seen by those standing outside the building, fired towards the regiment from the windows of the adjacent houses As soon as order was restored the employees of the building rekindled the lights, and the startling word was passed through the line that one of our brother soldiers was killed and another seriously wounded, with other vague conjectures and rumors that an organized attack was being made upon us by the notorious and infamous 'plug-uglies' of Baltimore A portion of this intelligence was alas, too true, and as later acquired knowledge would seem to justify the opinion, probably all of it Edward Burge, a private belonging to Company I, whose home was in Pottersville, Warren county, was found dead—shot through the head, by the testimony of the regimental surgeon in a subsequent investigation of the affair,—the ball entering the skull from above and passing out below near the jaw-bone   The wounded man belonged to Company H, of Sandy Hill   His name was Lorenzo Palmer   Police officers were soon on the ground inquiring into the details of the affair, and seemed anxious to get rid of us as quickly as possible   In a short time the regiment was shipped aboard of a train of cars and was rattling on its way to Washington   Before we left assurances were received that all the forces in the adjacent fortifications, numbering eight regiments, were already on their way to our assistance   The following morning the arrest of Marshal Kane and other arch conspirators in that hot-bed of secession did something towards checking that rampant hostility towards the northern soldiery then pouring in daily by regiments to the national capitol   A new system was speedily inaugurated   The old police force was disbanded, many being placed under summary arrest, some of whom were no doubt participants in the April riots "

Whether or not this occurrence was the result of preconcerted plans for assaulting the regiment is even yet a question of dispute   A court of inquiry was held and the people of Baltimore exonerated, the cause of the whole affair being attributed to the first accidental discharge of one musket and the succeeding firing by the troops without orders , but there are others still living who were participants in the affair, and take a different view of the matter

The regiment reached Washington about midnight, where the men saw the dead body of a picket brought in, one who had recently been shot while on duty   This incident — a trifle in the red annals of the war — and the sight of camp-fires in all directions, with other unmistakable indications, told the regiment in no uncertain tones that they had almost reached the theatre of their future struggles   A portion of the regiment was quartered in the Washington Assembly Rooms and the remainder in the Baptist Church on Fifth street   On the following day the lamented Burge was buried in one of the city burial grounds.   The next day, July 1st, the regiment was marched up Seventh street to the neighborhood of the Soldiers' Retreat, about two and a half miles northeast of the city, to the grounds vacated by the Fourteenth (Brooklyn) New York State Militia, where it went into camp   Here, in the beautiful Virginia summer days, the regiment enjoyed a period of pleasant camp life, varied only by the part it took in the remarkable celebration of July 4th which took place in Washington   Again we quote from Dr Holden his description of the occurrences of the next few weeks   " The fortnight following the review was a busy time in Washington, for preparations were being actively made for an attack upon the rebel force assembled at Manassas Plains   The battle was fought ; — fought bravely and well for comparatively raw troops   Its general results were soon known far and wide, and the whole affair has now become a part of the history of the war   The cannonading of the 17th (Thursday), as well as the 21st, was distinctly heard in our camp, and while speculation was rife as to its causes and results, we were in the interval momentarily expecting

to move over the river and participate in the action   We were happily spared
both its dangers and glories   On Sunday morning, July 21st (the day of the
famous First Bull Run fight), just as the regiment had been drawn up in line for
religious services, a courier dashed up to headquarters on a gallop with a message which proved to be 'marching orders' for Harper's Ferry   The regiment
was ordered to be in readiness to move at twelve o'clock M , at which hour the
order was countermanded   The same evening at 'dress parade' orders were
received to march immediately across the river   The line was dismissed and
the boys with a cheer set hastily to work to make the necessary preparations,
which included the distribution of cartridges and the preparation of two days'
rations   Within an hour to the inspiriting rattle of the 'long roll,' the men
were again in line in 'light marching order'   We were instructed to leave our
tents standing and our baggage packed behind us   The men moved buoyantly
forward down South street, to the exhilarating music of our band   As the
head of our column wheeled into the avenue, dense crowds of anxious-looking
people thronged the sidewalks, who hailed our advent with prolonged and repeated cheers   The bad news was just coming in from Bull Run   As we
reached the eastern extremity of the Long Bridge, we were directed to 'halt,'
'stack arms,' and 'rest'   While awaiting further orders at this point, scattering
and fleet-footed fugitives from the scene of conflict came cantering hurriedly
across the bridge   Among the number was the famous correspondent
of the *London Times*, quite extensively known by the *sobriquet* of 'Bull
Run Russell'   Of his interview with our regiments at that time, he makes the
following mention in his published 'diary.' 'At the Washington end of the
bridge I was challenged again by the men of a whole regiment, who, with piled
arms, were halted on the chaussie, smoking, laughing, and singing   " Stranger
have you been to the fight ? "   " I have been only a little beyond Centerville "
But that was quite enough   Soldiers, civilians, and women who seemed to be
out unusually late, crowded around the horse, and again I told my stereotyped
story of the unsuccessful attempt to carry the Confederate position, and the retreat to Centerville to await better luck next time   The soldiers alongside me
cheered, and those next them took it up, till it ran through the whole line, and
must have awakened the night-owls   After remaining about two hours, orders
came, and the men in a very despondent, dissatisfied sort of a way, resumed their
arms, and we retraced our steps in silence and gloom, only broken by the monotonous tramp, tramp, of many feet   The next day was a gloomy one for the
city and the government   It rained heavily, and stragglers wet, dispirited and
demoralized, thronged the thoroughfares, while the wounded came in like the
waves of a flood-tide, filling up all the temporary makeshifts dignified by the
name of hospitals, which was the best that could be done at the time, no doubt
The Second New Hampshire Volunteers, whose camp adjoined ours, and whose
tents had been left standing, suffered severely in the engagement, and all day

long their wounded and stragglers came droopingly along by ones, twos, and threes—a sorry but impressive sight, enabling us all to appreciate to some degree the terrors, the terrible realities of war   Fragments of regiments but lately exultant with swollen ranks and brave bearing, came creeping along to the slow tap of the drum, while knots and gangs of stragglers assailed every guard line and camp for food, shelter, and drink   The army, by general order was declared demoralized, and stringent orders were speedily promulgated, that all stragglers and soldiers without properly authenticated passes, should be arrested and sent to their respective commands   It was not permitted to harbor or refresh them under penalty, — seemingly a rash rule, but really just and proper, contributing largely to the restoration of discipline and good order among them   It will also be borne in mind that with the few exceptions of sick and lame, it is the poorest and most cowardly, and not the bravest and best soldiers, who straggle from their commands "

The remainder of our account of this regiment is gathered in disconnected details from portions of the annual reports of the Chief of the Bureau of Military Statistics and from the vivid recitals of passing events written home by soldiers at the time of their occurrences

The next day the regiment went into camp on Arlington Heights   General McDowell commanded the division   On the route, after crossing to Alexandria, the march was conducted between almost unbroken lines of troops, among which were the New York Twenty-first, Twenty-third, Twenty-fourth and Twenty-fifth Volunteers, and the Fourteenth Chasseurs from Brooklyn, who, in the engagement at Bull Run, had seven times attacked the enemy's batteries and were seven times repulsed with deadly loss   All along the lines were visible the pavilioned fields of the Union patriots, giving encouraging evidence that the government deemed it necessary to make this important post as nearly impregnable as possible, for from the heights rising just across the river from Washington, the city could be easily bombarded and destroyed   At this time the soldiers were in a general state of discouragement   The adverse turn which affairs had taken at Bull Run, the disheartening disparity in the numbers and equipment of the men from the South and the boys from the North, and the greater fatigue necessarily falling to the lot of the invading forces, united in augmenting the already thickening gloom of war   Notwithstanding this discouraging state of affairs the men of the Twenty-second bore up with praiseworthy stoicism   In a letter written by an officer of this regiment from Arlington Heights, July 29th, 1861, is the following description of the march from Washington —

" Our regiment received the order on Wednesday afternoon last to march across the Potomac, forty minutes after notice the men were moving in column towards the Long Bridge, which they crossed between seven and eight o'clock   They carried their muskets, cartridge-boxes and haversacks, with rations for thirty-six hours   As the tents and other camp equipage were left in charge of a guard at the old encampment, of course the soldiers had to rough it a little.   They slept on the ground in the open air, and on their arms, prepared to turn out at a moment's warning to receive the enemy, an attack from whom was not entirely unexpected   Indeed, the long roll was once sounded and the whole regiment turned out and marshaled for an attack, but the alarm was happily unfounded   Located as we now are, not far from the rebel outposts, a night onset on our sentinels, or even an attempted surprisal of our camp, might at any hour of darkness be looked for

"Our regiment was to-day paid off from the first of June—the day on which they were mustered into the United States service—to the first of July Hitherto the government has paid its soldiers only once in two months , but a bill is before Congress, which has already passed the House, to pay the men monthly   This bill will pass the Senate, as it ought, and under it our men will in a few days receive another month's pay now almost due "

Until September 28th the regiment remained at the Heights performing camp, guard and fatigue duties, and on that day was in the reconnaissance to Upton's Hill, and took up camp there for the winter

About ten o'clock in the evening of March 10th. 1862, the troops were notified that orders had been issued for the advance, early on the following morning, of the entire army.   The march was commenced as ordered, and a little after noon on the 11th took the Twenty-second to Fairfax Court House, Va., about three miles from Centerville   On the 13th they advanced to Centerville   On the 15th the regiment returned to Alexandria by a march of twenty-one miles through a drenching rain, and across streams almost destitute of bridges   On the next day it removed to its old camp on Upton's Hill

The regiment entered upon the campaign of 1862 on the 4th of April, by breaking camp and marching to within four miles of Fairfax, where, near Annandale, it bivouacked   On the 5th camp was pitched four miles beyond Centerville   The next day it marched about four miles beyond Manassas Junction, near Bristow Station, camped, and remained through a severe storm of rain and snow until the 15th, when, between the hours of 6 and 10 P M, it marched to near Catlett's Station on Cedar Run   At half-past six on the morning of the 17th the march was resumed, and continued, with occasional brief intermissions, until nine o'clock that evening , on the 18th, after a march was begun which occupied the energies of the regiment from two o'clock in the morning until nine, and Falmouth, opposite Fredericksburg, on the Rappahannock River, was reached   During the entire marching the retreating enemy was in the front engaging in occasional skirmishes with our cavalry advance, and finally receding to Fredericksburg and burning the bridge across the Rappahannock   At this encampment the regiment remained until the 25th of May, with varied camp and patrol duties   It participated in the grand review by the president on the 23d   On the 25th it crossed the river, moved about six miles below Fredericksburg and bivouacked near the Massaponax Between this time and the 15th of June the regiment was kept moving.   At Massaponax, the order to advance being countermanded, the regiment, on the 29th of May, retraced its steps to within eight miles of Fredericksburg, reached Catlett's Station on the 31st (*enroute* for Manassas Gap), there took the cars and after riding all night reached Front Royal   Being unable to cross the Shenandoah, by reason of the destruction of the bridge, it returned to Haymarket, June 6th   On the 15th of June, it passed successively from bivouac to bivouac, through Warrenton, Warrenton Junction, to Elk Run Crossing At this encampment the men were chiefly occupied with camp duties and details on the railroad bridge   Field duties were not resumed until the 5th of August   After returning from a reconnaissance south of Fredericksburg it left that place on the 10th and after repeated marches attended with all the ludicrous and tragical concomitants of an army in motion, reached the vicinity of the Cedar Mountain battle-field August 9th   Thence it passed to Cedar Mountain, to the neighborhood of Rappahannock Station on the Orange and Alexandria railroad, and, on the 20th, across the Rappahanock   Here the rear guard went through the initiatory experience of an engagement, being attacked by the enemy, and the regiment participated, on the three succeeding days, in a series of engagements, and repulsed the efforts of the enemy to cross the river.   At 9 o'clock on the evening of August 23d the regiment reached Warrenton   On the 29th it was engaged at Manassas Plains (second Bull Run), and fell back to Centerville at night with only one captain and four lieutenants out of twenty-five officers who had accompanied the regiment to the battle-field, and two hundred and four enlisted men present for duty   The fight lasted two days   On both days the men, it is said, were sacrificed, led into an ambush and subjected to a terrible enfilading fire on the left, front and rear   The men stood under this fire until their ammunition was gone, and then threw stones at the enemy !

On the second of September the remnant of the regiment reached their old encampment at Upton's Hill, and on the sixth entered upon the Maryland campaign   It took an active part in the battles of South Mountain and Sharpsburg (Antietam)   At the former engagement the advance was made under hot fire, to close quarters.   The enemy were found posted behind a fence and were charged and routed with a heavy loss on both sides, and the position held for half an hour   A regiment of Patrick's Brigade then relieved the Twenty second, which, however, remained on the field during the night   About twenty-five per cent of this regiment were lost in this battle   A description of the battle of Antietam, contained in a report of an officer present at the scene, is substantially as follows   On Tuesday night (the 16th) the men slept on their arms At half-past five in the morning of the 17th the Twenty-second was ordered

to the support of Gibbon's Brigade which had advanced to attack the enemy
It moved by the flank through an open field in which Campbell's battery had
taken position, and passed into a cornfield in line of battle to support Gibbon's
Brigade   The direct and cross artillery fire from the enemy's batteries playing
on this field was very heavy, but the brigade containing the Twenty-second
Regiment was moved without loss to a position some ninety paces in advance
of Campbell's battery, where a column was deployed, and in line of battle
moved steadily forward to about fifty paces in the rear of Gibbon's infantry,
who at this time had not engaged the enemy, but were cautiously advancing
through the cornfield   At length the engagement began, the enemy being
posted in the road behind a line of fence and sheltered by woods   The
Twenty-second, in company with the other regiments in the same brigade,
moved forward, halted about twenty-five paces in rear of Gibbon's line, and
lay down in preparation for the support   After severe fighting and considerable loss this brigade fell back to the rear of the cornfield   When they again
faced the front they had scarcely enough men to bear the colors   In the engagement Lieutenant Charles Cushing, of Glens Falls, was killed   The total
loss was a fraction over forty-three per cent of those engaged

The regiment marched on the 19th to within a mile and a half of the Poto-
mac, where it remained encamped until October 20th   Between that time
and the 11th of November it passed through Bakersville, South Mountain,
Birketsville, Petersville, camped near Harper's Ferry, after crossing into Virginia on a pontoon bridge, marched in and through Purcellsville, Bloomfield,
Rectortown, Warrenton, Fayetteville, and thence on the last named date to
Falmouth   In the battle of Fredericksburg, which occurred on the 13th of
December, 1862, it was on the extreme left of Franklin's Corps, remained
under fire for three days, and lost seven wounded   It returned to its old
camping-ground on the 15th, participated in the well-named "mud march"
of January, 1863, and then took up winter quarters at Belle Plain   The regiment crossed the Rappahannock on boats (April 28th, 1863), soon after the
enemy had been driven from their rifle-pits   On the following day it was
joined by the rest of the division, and was marched to the bank of the river
to protect the detail engaged in launching the boats, where it was exposed to
a galling fire of musketry, which, during that day, wounded eleven of the men
It manœuvred about here until the 4th of June, when it returned to this State
Two days afterward it was received with appropriate ceremonies at Fort Edward, Sandy Hill and Glens Falls, and on the 19th was mustered out of service at Albany

*Roster with Dates and Appointments of the Field, Staff and Line Officers
of the Twenty-second N Y Volunteers to March 20th, 1863* — Walter Phelps,
jr , colonel, May 16th, 1861, on detached service in command of brigade
Gorton T Thomas, lieutenant colonel, May 16th, 1861, died of wounds re-

ceived August 30th, 1862   John M'Kie, major, May 16th, 1861, promoted *vice* Thomas, died of wounds, September 3d, 1862   John M'Kie, lieutenant colonel, August 30th, 1862, resigned from wounds and ill-health, February 13th, 1863   George Clendon, jr, major, August 30th, 1862, promoted from captain (Co E) *vice* M'Kie promoted   Edward Pruyn, adjutant, May 16th, 1861, resigned January 18th, 1862   John S Fassett, adjutant, January 18th, 1862, transferred from Company E, *vice* Pruyn resigned   Henry D Woodruff, quartermaster, May 16th, 1861, resigned from ill-health March 1st, 1863. James W Schenck, jr, quartermaster, September 5th, 1861, *vice* Woodruff promoted on de ached service, brigade quartermaster   Joseph B Atherly, surgeon, May 16th, 1861, died of typhoid fever at Falmouth, Va , August 12th, 1862   William F Hutchinson, assistant surgeon, May 16th, 1861, promoted *vice* Atherly deceased   William F Hutchinson, surgeon, August 12th, 1862, dismissed the service November 20th, 1862   Austin W Holden, assistant surgeon, August 24th, 1862, transferred from company F, *vice* Hutchinson promoted   Miles Goodyear, second assistant surgeon, September 22d, 1862, resigned from physical disability January 24th, 1863   Elias S Bissell, surgeon, November 20th, 1862, *vice* Hutchinson dismissed   Henry H Bates, chaplain, May 16th, 1861

Non-commissioned Staff — John F Towne, sergeant-major, May 16th, 1861, transferred and promoted to first lieutenant Company G, March 1st, 1862. Jeremiah Fairbanks, quartermaster-sergeant, May 16th, 1861, discharged   Charles B Bellamy, commissary-sergeant, May 16th, 1861   David H King, hospital steward, May 16th, 1861   John Scott, drum major, May 16th, 1861, discharged by general order   John Wright, fife-major, May 16th, 1861, transferred to band   Malachi Weidman, sergeant-major, March 1st, 1862, *vice* Towne promoted   Daniel Thomson, quartermaster-sergeant, March 1st, 1862, *vice* Fairbanks discharged   Levi J Groom, fife-major, *vice* Wright transferred, resigned, ill-health   George Crandell, fife-major, *vice* Groom discharged by general order   Malachi Weidman, adjutant, February 27th, 1863, *vice* Fassett resigned   Henry Barton, sergeant-major, March 22d, 1863, from sergeant Company A, *vice* Bellamy promoted   George Torrey, commissary-sergeant, March 22d, 1863, from sergeant Company B, *vice* Weidman, promoted

Line Officers — Company A — Jacob L Yates, captain, May 8th, 1861, resigned, ill-health, March 1st, 1863   James H Bratt, first lieutenant, May 8th, 1861, resigned December 21st, 1861   Hiram Clute, second lieutenant, May 8th, 1861, promoted *vice* Bratt resigned   Hiram Clute, first lieutenant, December 21st, 1861, died September 28th, 1862, of wounds received August 30th, 1862   Addison L Estabrook, second lieutenant, December 21st, 1861, from first sergeant *vice* Hiram Clute promoted   Addison Estabrook, first lieutenant, September 28th, 1862, *vice* Hiram Clute deceased.   Amos T Calkins, second lieutenant, September 28th, 1862, *vice* Estabrook promoted from first sergeant

Company B — Robert E M'Coy, captain, May 10th, 1861, killed in action August 29th, 1862   Duncan Lendrum, first lieutenant, May 10th, 1861, missing, probably killed in action August 30th, 1862   James W M'Coy, second lieutenant, May 10th, 1861, promoted   James W M'Coy, captain, August 29th, 1862, *vice* Robert E M'Coy, killed in action. William H Hoysradt, first lieutenant, August 30th, 1862, *vice* Lendrum, missing, from first sergeant   Charles H Doubleday, second lieutenant, November 16th, 1862, promoted and transferred from Company H, *vice* M'Coy, promoted

Company C — Oliver D Peabody, captain, June 1st, 1861. Carlisle D Beaumont, first lieutenant, June 1st, 1861, killed in action August 29th, 1862   Charles B Piersons, second lieutenant, June 1st, 1861, died September 7th of wounds received in action, August 30th   Gorton T Thomas, second lieutenant, September 7th, 1862, *vice* Piersons, died of wound   Gorton T Thomas, first lieutenant, February 1st, 1863, *vice* Beaumont, killed in action   James Valleau, second lieutenant, February 1st, 1863, from first sergeant *vice* Thomas promoted

Company D — Henry S Milliman, captain, June 1st, 1861, died September 10th, 1862, of wounds received in action August 30th   Thomas B Fish, first lieutenant, June 1st, 1861, discharged on surgeon's certificate October 22d, 1862   Robert A Rice, second lieutenant, June 1st, 1861, resigned December 14th, 1861   William T Beattie, second lieutenant, December 14th, 1861, from first sergeant *vice* Rice resigned, killed in action August 30th, 1862   Lucius E Wilson, captain, September 10th, 1862, transferred from company G, *vice* Milliman, died of wounds   Henry B Cook, first lieutenant, October 23d, 1862, from first sergeant *vice* Fish, discharged   Charles H Aiken, second lieutenant, August 30th, 1862, from second sergeant *vice* William T Beattie, killed in action

Company E — George Clendon, jr , captain, May 7th, 1861, promoted to major August 30th, 1862   John Fassett, first lieutenant, May 7th, 1861, transferred to regimental staff January 8th, 1862   G Horton Gayger, second lieutenant, May 7th, 1861, resigned October 3d, 1861   William T Norris, second lieutenant, October 3d, 1861, *vice* Gayger resigned   William T Norris, first lieutenant, January 8th, 1862, *vice* Fassett transferred, missing and probably killed in action August 30th, 1862   Charles Cushing, second lieutenant, January 8th, 1862, *vice* Norris killed, fell in action September 7th, 1862   Warren Allen, second lieutentant, September 18th, 1862, *vice* Charles Cushing killed in action, from first sergeant   Daniel Burgey, captain, February 25th, 1862, transferred and promoted from Company I, *vice* Clendon, promoted

Company F — Austin W Holden, captain, May 8th, 1861, transferred to medical staff August 16th, 1862   William H Arlin, first lieutenant, May 8th,

1861, resigned January 8th, 1862   Orville B Smith, second lieutenant, May 8th, 1861, promoted to first lieutenant, *vice* Arlin, resigned   Orville B Smith, first lieutenant, January 8th, 1862, promoted to captain, *vice* Holden transferred   Fred E Ranger, second lieutenant, January 8th, 1862, *vice* Smith, promoted   Orville B Smith, captain, August 24th, 1862, *vice* Holden, transferred, resigned November 5th, 1862   Fred E Ranger, first lieutenant, August 24th, 1862, *vice* Smith, promoted   James H Merrill, second lieutenant, August 24th, 1862, from first sergeant, *vice* Ranger, promoted   Fred E. Ranger, captain, November 5th, 1862, *vice* Smith, resigned   James H Merrill, first lieutenant, November 5th, 1862, *vice* Fred E Ranger, promoted   Salmon D Sherman, second lieutenant, November 5th, 1862, from second sergeant, *vice* Merrill, promoted

Company G — Benjamin Mosher, captain, June 6th, 1861, resigned February 28th, 1862   Henry Hay, first lieutenant, June 6th, 1861, resigned June 12th, 1861.   Horrace W Lucca, second lieutenant, June 6th, 1861, resigned February 28th, 1862   Duncan Cameron, first lieutenant, June 15th, 1861, *vice* Hay, resigned   Duncan Cameron, captain, March 1st, 1862, *vice* Mosher, resigned   John F Town, first lieutenant, March 1, 1862, *vice* Cameron promoted, resigned July 23d, 1862   Lucius E Wilson, second lieutenant, March 1st, 1862, *vice* Lucca resigned, from first sergeant   Lucius E Wilson, first lieutenant, July 21st, 1862, *vice* Town resigned, promoted and transferred to Company D   Lester A. Bartlett, second lieutenant, July 21st, 1862, *vice* Wilson promoted, transferred from Company I   Asa W Barry, first lieutenant, September 11th, 1862, from first sergeant, *vice* Wilson transferred

Company H — Thomas J Strong, captain, May 8th, 1861   William A. Pierson, first lieutenant, May 8th, 1861, discharged on surgeon's certificate August 31st, 1862   Mathew S Teller, second lieutenant, May 8th, 1861, first lieutenant, August 31st, 1862, *vice* Pierson resigned   A Halleck Holbrook, second lieutenant, August 31st, 1862, from sergeant, *vice* Teller promoted

Company I — Lyman Ormsbee, captain, May 9th, 1861   Joseph R Seaman, first lieutenant, May 9th, 1861, resigned February 22d, 1862   Daniel Burgey, second lieutenant, May 9th, 1861   Daniel Burgey, first lieutenant, February 22d, 1862, *vice* Seaman resigned, transferred to Company E   Lester A Bartlett, second lieutenant, February 22d, 1862, *vice* Burgey promoted, transferred to Company G   Benjamin Wickham, second lieutenant, July 21st, 1862, *vice* Bartlett transferred, from first sergeant   Benjamin Wickham, first lieutenant, September 3d, 1862, *vice* Burgey transferred   George Wetmore, second lieutenant, September 3d, 1862, from sergeant, *vice* Wickham promoted

Company K — Miles P Caldwell, captain, May 9th, 1861, killed in action August 30th, 1862   Edward F Edgerly, first lieutenant, May 9th, 1861.

Clark W Huntley, second lieutenant, May 9th, 1861, resigned in consequence of wounds, February 6th, 1863   Edward F Edgerly, captain, August 31st, 1862, *vice* Caldwell killed in action   Clark W Huntley, first lieutenant, August 31st, 1862, *vice* Edgerly, promoted   John J Baker, second lieutenant, August 31st, 1862, from first sergeant, *vice* Huntley promoted   John J Baker, first lieutenant, February 6th, 1863, *vice* Huntley resigned   Charles Bellamy, second lieutenant, February 6th, 1863, from commissary-sergeant, *vice* Barker promoted

Register of Fatalities in the Twenty-Second Regiment from the time of its Organization to March 20th, 1863 — Field and Staff — Joseph B Atherly, surgeon, typhoid fever, August 12th, 1862, at Falmouth, Virginia   Gorton T Thomas, lieutenant-colonel, wounds, September 2d, 1862, at Washington

Company A — Timothy B Vandecar, third sergeant, typhoid fever, September 26th, 1861, at Georgetown, D C   John H Vanderworken, private, typhoid fever, July 6th, 1862, at Eckington, D C   Hiram Clute, first lieutenant, wounds, September 18th, 1862, at Washington   John Murray, private, wounds, September 23d, 1862, Frederick, Maryland   Chauncey F. Van Dusen, private, fell in action, August 30th, 1862, at Bull Run   Leonard G Fletcher, corporal, fell in action, August 30th, at Bull Run   Jonathan G Porter, private, fell in action, September 14th, 1862, at South Mountain   John Wright, private, fell in action, September 14th, 1862, at South Mountain

Company B — William Baker, private, pneumonia, February 11th, 1862, at Upton's Hill, Virginia   Edward Cromwell, corporal, wounds, 1862, at Upton's Hill   Gurdon F Viele, private, wounds   Robert E McCoy, captain, fell in action August 29th, 1862, at Groveton   Charles E Mills, first sergeant, fell in action August 30th, 1862, at Bull Run   Patrick Mehan, private, fell in action August 30th, 1862, at Bull Run   Charles E Stickney, second sergeant, fell in action September 14th, 1862, at South Mountain   Oliver L Lackey, private, fell in action September 14th, 1862, at South Mountain   Duncan Lendrum, first lieutenant, missing August 30th, 1862, at Bull Run   Charles H Reed, private, missing August 30th, 1862, Bull Run

Company C — Charles Piersons, second lieutenant, wounds, September 7th, 1862, at Washington   Carlysle D Beaumont, first lieutenant, fell in action August 29th, 1862, at Groveton   James Murray, private, fell in action August 29th, 1862, at Groveton   Henry N Dunckly, private, fell in action August 29th, 1862, at Groveton   Joseph Pero, private, fell in action August 30th, 1862, at Bull Run   Henry W Hathaway, third sergeant, fell in action September 14th, 1862, at South Mountain

Company D — James Stalker, private, inflammation of brain, July 17th, 1861, at Washington   Charles J Eaton, third sergeant, typhoid fever, May 18th, 1862, at Washington   Henry S Milliman, captain, wounds, September 10th, 1862, at Washington   William T Beattie, second lieutenant, fell in action August 30th, 1862, at Bull Run

Company E — John M'Auley, private, typhoid fever, September 14th, 1861, at Arlington, Virginia   Rollin F Austin, private, typhoid fever, April 10th, 1862, at Alexandria   Timothy Bradley, private, diarrhœa, October 16th, 1862, Smoketown, Maryland   Byron G Charette, private, wounds, September 13th, 1862, at Washington   Charles Goolah, private, wounds, September 22d, 1862, at Washington   Frank Aubin, private, wounds, 1862, at Frederick, Maryland   Joseph Whitford, private, wounds, 1862, in field hospital.   Jacob Ross, private, wounds, October 14th, 1862, at Smoketown, Maryland   Wilber F Buswell, private, fell in action September 14th, 1862, at South Mountain   Charles Cushing, second lieutenant, fell in action September 17th, 1862, at Antietam   Patrick Johnson, private, missing August 29th, 1862, Groveton   Nelson Ross, private, missing, August 29th, 1862, Groveton   William T Norris, first lieutenant, missing, August 30th, 1862, Bull Run

Company F — Emanuel Noel, private, typhoid fever, November 24th, 1861, Georgetown   Lyman Ward, private, small-pox, January 17th, 1862, in hospital   Titus L West, private, typhoid fever, May 13th, 1862, at Alexandria   Rufus N Barto, private, wounds, October 18th, 1862, Colt's hospital   John E Benjamin, private, wounds, September 11th, 1862, at Fairfax   Allen Sherman, private, wounds, October 9th, 1862, at Frederick, Maryland   De Witt C. Barton, private, killed April 5th, 1862, at Centerville, Virginia   Willard Combs, private, fell in action August 30th, 1862, at Bull Run   Andrew La Point, private, fell in action August 30th, 1862, at Bull Run   Daniel Pendell, fifth sergeant, fell in action September 14th, 1862, at South Mountain.   Benjamin F Hendricks, private, missing, August 30th, 1862, Bull Run   William O Jackson, corporal, missing, August 30th, 1862, Bull Run   Archibald Ramsey, private, missing, August 30th, 1862, Bull Run

Company G — Nelson Hastings, private, consumption, July 16th, 1861, at Washington.   Cornelius White, private, typhoid fever, October 26th, 1861, at Upton's Hill   William Washburn, private, typhoid fever, December 13th, 1861, at Upton's Hill   John Constantine, private, wounds, September 15th, 1862, at Washington   Rufus K Verrill, private, wounds, September 8th, 1862, at Washington   Ansel Taft, private, wounds, September, at Alexandria   Thomas Whitton, private, wounds, September, 1862, at Alexandria   Lewis T Johnson, corporal, fell in action August 30th, 1862, at Bull Run.   Thomas Moore, private, fell in action August 30th, 1862, at Bull Run   William Riley, private, fell in action August 30th, 1862, at Bull Run   Lewis Fenix, private, fell in action August 30th, 1862, at Bull Run   John Necson, private, fell in action September 14th, 1862, at South Mountain   James Connell, private, fell in action September 17th, 1862, at Antietam   George F Cleveland, private, missing, August 30th, 1862, at Bull Run

Company H — Edward Blanchard, private, typhoid fever, November 14th, 1861, at Colt's hospital   Lyman Chamberlain, private, typhoid fever, April

19th, 1862, at Bristol Station   Charles H Bowen, private, pneumonia, June
20th, 1862, at Carver Hospital   Stephen Podwin, private, wounds, September
3d, 1862, at Washington   James Wythe, private, fell in action August 29th,
1862, at Groveton   Rollin C Wyman, private, fell in action August 30th, 1862,
at Bull Run   Selden L Whitney, private, fell in action September 14th, 1862,
at South Mountain   George W Miner, private, missing, August 30th, 1862,
at Bull Run

Company I — Edward Burge, private, killed June 30th, 1861, in Baltimore
Thomas Crawford, fifth sergeant, fell in action August 30th, 1862, at Bull Run
Joseph W Booth, private, fell in action August 30th, 1862, at Bull Run   Syl-
vanus A Durkee, private, fell in action August 30th, 1862, at Bull Run
Ephraim J Smith, private, fell in action August 30th, 1862, at Bull Run
James Dignan, private, fell in action September 17th, 1862, at Antietam

Company K — Timothy D Murray, private, wounds, October 15th, 1862,
Harwood Hospital   Henry Sumner, private, fell in action August 29th, 1862,
at Groveton   Miles P Caldwell, captain, fell in action August 30th, 1862, at
Bull Run   Daniel McCartey, private, fell in action August 30th, 1862, at Bull
Run   James Gleason private, fell in action August 30th, 1862, at Bull Run
James Evans, third sergeant, fell in action September 14th, 1862, at South
Mountain [1]

The Ninety-sixth Regiment — One full company (Co I) of this regiment
was recruited in Warren county in the fall of 1861, almost entirely by and at
the expense of C H Burhans, now of Warrensburgh, who went out as its captain   Following are the names of its officers and members, as given on the
records —

Captain, Charles H Burhans, first lieutenant, Gerard L M'Kenzie; second
lieutenant, Emory M Lyon   Sergeants, Thomas W Sutton, John G Joslin,
of Warrensburgh, Warren Luce and Levi Hill, of North River, Mortimer
Allen, of Athol   Corporals, William Beadnell and Peter Allard, of Potters-
ville, Paul Declane, Abial Fuller, Thomas Short, Augustus Stone and George
Pelton, of Warrensburgh   Musician, Peleg Barton, of Athol   Wagoner,
John McMillen, of North River   Privates, John B. Allard, Isaac Archibald,
Edward Archibald, William Ausmeut, John Baker, James W Bennett, John
C Bennett, Augustus Bennett and Levi Bennett, of Warrensburgh, Theophile
Beaudry, North River, William B Blany and George Brown, Warrensburgh;
Benjamin L Cady, Pottersville, Charles Combs and Francis Darrell, of War-
rensburgh; Barney Davar and Ed F Densmore, of Pottersville; Ebenezer L
Farrar, Ed S Fuller, Joseph Genier, Antoine Gerouse, Jamon Harrington,
Myles Hewett, James Hill, of Warrensburgh, John H Ingraham, Pottersville,
John Keys and Charles Lamb, of Warrensburgh, Michael Lynch and Edward
McDonnell, of Pottersville, William B Morrill and Samuel B Moses, of War-

rensburgh ; Levi Olden, Pottersville , Chauncey F Perry, Oscar F. Perry, Dan-
iel O Porter, Edward Porter, La Fayette Scripten and Jesse N. Seseton, of
Warrensburgh , Cornelius Sherman, of Pottersville , George W Stearns, War-
rensburgh , Eli Streeter, Pottersville , Samuel J Taylor, Warrensburgh , James
Tucker and Giles Vanderwarker, of Pottersville ; Daniel Vaughn and Paul
Vigean, of Warrensburgh , Nathan Wallace, Pottersville , Henry F Wright,
Warrensburgh

This regiment was entirely enrolled in Northern New York and earned a
most gallant record   One of its companies (G) was from Essex county and
was commanded by Captain Alfred Weed, it having been principally raised in
the town of Ticonderoga   This fact led to the preparation by Winslow C
Watson, esq , of Plattsburg, of a detailed history of the organization, which
was printed in his valuable *History of Essex County,* published in 1870, when
data for military history was much more accessible than at the present time.
From his work we condense the following account —

"The regiment was organized at Plattsburg, and departed for the field
March, 1862, under the command of James Fairman, colonel, Charles O Gray,
lieutenant-colonel, and John E Kelley, a veteran of the regular army, major
Nathan Wardner, of Jay, was appointed chaplain of the organization, John H
Sanborn, quartermaster, and Francis Joseph D'Avignon, of Ausable Forks,
surgeon   The Ninety-sixth, in the early stages of its services, was severely
depressed, through the unfavorable auspices by which it was surrounded, but
after the brave and accomplished Gray was placed in command, the regiment
rapidly attained a very high reputation   It had been precipitated by ill-ad-
vised councils into active service without the advantages of any adequate drilling, and was hurried into the peninsula campaign before the habits of the troops
were adapted to field duty, and while they were yet unacclimated   From this
cause and some dissensions among officers the efficiency of the regiment was
much impaired for a period

" Major Kelley was killed in a picket skirmish immediately before the battle of Fair Oaks   In that action the losses of the Ninety-sixth regiment were
extremely severe. The services of the regiment, throughout the peninsula
campaign were marked by great perils and hardships, and elicited from General Peck, the commander of the division, warm and unusual encomiums   It
was afterwards ordered to Suffolk, enduring all the trials and sufferings of that
field, and was subsequently engaged in the North Carolina expedition, and
gallantly participated in all the hard services of that vigorous campaign   In
the battle of Kingston, December 14th, 1862, Colonel Gray, who had already,
although a youth of twenty-four, achieved a brilliant fame, was killed while
charging at the head of the regiment over the bridge on the Neuse, and in the
act of planting its standard upon the enemy's works   Three weeks before in
presenting a new flag to the Ninety-sixth, he had uttered a glowing and elo-

quent tribute to the old flag, and now this enveloped his coffin, as the remains were borne from his last battle-field to its resting place among his familiar mountains That venerated flag is deposited in the Military Bureau After this event the Ninety-sixth was for a short term under the command of Colonel McKenzie A A Fuller and J C Bennett, Company I, were wounded in this battle

" Early in 1864 the regiment was transferred to the Army of the James before Petersburg, and attached to the same brigade with which the One Hundred and Eighteenth was connnected It was incorporated with the Eighteenth and afterwards with the Twenty-fourth Corps The Ninety-sixth was engaged in all the subsequent operations of the Eighteenth Corps At Cold Harbor, and the assault on Fort Harrison, the Ninety-sixth and the Eighth Connecticut formed the assaulting columns, with the One Hundred and Eighteenth New York, and Tenth New Hampshire on their flanks as skirmishers The division approached the works in close order, and in a distance of fourteen hundred yards was exposed to a plunging and galling fire of artillery and musketry

" It steadily advanced to the base of the hill, which was crowned by the enemy's work Here the column, exhausted by its rapid progress, paused The enemy perceiving the point of attack were meanwhile pouring reinforcements into the menaced works The crisis was imminent, and General Stannard commanding the division sent an earnest order for an instant assault The head of the column charged up the hill, and scaling the parapet, drove the enemy from their guns Sergeant Lester Archer of the Ninety-sixth and the color bearer of the Eighth Connecticut simultaneously planted their respective regimental flags upon the ramparts The Rev Nathan Wardner, chaplain of the Ninety-sixth, charged with his regiment in the advancing columns, prepared to administer spiritual consolation on the very field of carnage The captured guns of the fort were turned upon the retreating enemy with terrible effect The Ninety-sixth were conspicuous in opposing the repeated, resolute and desperate attempts of the rebels to recover this important position

" The Ninety-sixth continued near Fort Harrison, in camp with its brigade, after the capture of that work, until the 24th of October, when the entire division marched against Fort Richmond at Fair Oaks It bivouacked that night, about three miles from the fort While the skirmishing party of the One Hundred and Eighteenth was engaged in the perilous and hopeless assault of the enemy's line, the next morning the Ninety-sixth, in common with the remainder of the division, stood idle spectators of the slaughter of those troops, although little doubt now exists, that a combined and energetic attack of the fort, when the One Hundred and Eighteenth advanced and while it was occupied by a force wholly inadequate to its defense, would have secured a glorious success A designed feint had been converted into a real and sanguinary assault, and the character of this bloody field, conspicuous for its profitless and murderous losses, was only redeemed by the valor of the troops

"For two long and trying hours, after the repulse of the One Hundred and Eighteenth the residue of the division stood under arms, in front of the enemy's lines, with no orders, either to advance or retreat, while the rebels were observed eagerly rushing troops into the fort, on foot and upon horseback Horses were constantly perceived hurrying up at their highest speed, bearing three riders, and as they approached the works, two leaping from the horse would enter the fort, while the third returned at the same speed, to bear back another freight of defenders   At length, when the lines by this delay had been rendered impregnable to an attack, the division was madly hurled upon the works   It was bloodily repulsed   The casualties of the Ninety-sixth were in the highest degree severe

"The ground upon which these unfortunate operations occurred had been signalized by the sanguinary battle of Fair Oaks, during the peninsula campaign   The works erected by McClellan were still discernible, and as the Federal troops moved to the assault, they disturbed and trampled upon skulls and bones and other ghastly memorials of the former conflict   The Ninety-sixth participated in the brilliant closing scenes of the war around Richmond and its final consummation"

After paying a glowing and deserved tribute to Dr Francis Joseph D'Avignon, surgeon of the Ninety-sixth, Mr Watson concludes his sketch with the following: —

Officers of the Ninety-sixth mustered out with the Regiment, February 6th, 1866 — Colonel, Stephen Moffitt, brevet brigadier-general U S V ; lieutenant-colonel, George W. Hinds, brevet colonel N Y V , major, Courtland C Babcock, brevet lieutenant-colonel N Y. V , quartermaster, Allen Babcock, surgeon, Robert W Brady, chaplain, Nathan Wardner   Captains — Earl Peirce, Moses Gill, Moses E Orr, Henry C Buckham, brevet major N Y V , William B Brokaw, brevet major N Y V , Merlin C Harris, brevet major N Y V., Thomas E Allen, Oscar B Colvin   First lieutenants — William B Stafford, Thomas Burke, Charles H Hogan, Orlando P Benson, Lyman Bridges, George J Cady, Lucien Wood, Alexander M. Stevens, Alonzo E Howard   Second lieutenants — Washington Harris, Stanford H Bugbee, Alexander McMartin, Charles Sharron, Amos S. Richardson, Silas Finch, Judson C Ware

Enlisted Men of the Regiment to whom Medals of Honor have been Awarded by the Secretary of War. — Sergeant Lester Archer

The archives of the State present the following brilliant record of the services of the Ninety-sixth   Gainesville, Second Bull Run, South Mountain, Antietam, Mine Run, Fredericksburg, Chancellorsville, Gettysburg, Wilderness, North Anna, Mattapony, Spottsylvania, Bethesda Church, Petersburg, Weldon

Railroad, Chapel House, Hatcher s Run, Yorktown, Williamsburg, Fair Oaks, Seven Days' Battle, Blackwater, Kingston, Whitehall, Goldsboro', Siege of Newbern, Drury's Farm, Port Walthall, Coal Harbor, Battery Harrison, Charles City Road

One Hundred and Fifty-third Regiment — One company (K) of this regiment was raised in Warren county, largely in the town of Queensbury, and principally by Frederick J P Chitty, who served as its captain Philip H Fitzpatrick, first lieutenant, and C H Pike, second lieutenant, were from Clinton county The regiment was recruited for three years' service and organized at Fonda The other companies were from Fulton, Montgomery, Saratoga, Clinton and Essex counties It was mustered into the service of the United States October 18th, 1862, and was mustered out at the expiration of term of service, October 2d, 1865 The principal engagements in which the regiment took part were those at Sabine Cross Roads, Pleasant Hill, Marksville, Cane River, Mansura, and Alexandria, La , as given in the reports

Captain Chitty has kindly furnished us with the enrollment papers, containing endorsements of the fate of the members of the company, from which the following list is made up —

George Albro, mustered out with regiment, Mark A Allen, died in Richmond as a prisoner, Amos Baker, jr, died in hospital, Amyel Baker, mustered out with regiment, Stephen J Beadleston, mustered out with regiment; Franklin Benman, mustered out with regiment, Robert Blackburn, discharged for disability, Benjamin Brown, mustered out with regiment, John M Crossett, died in hospital, Lemuel Davis, mustered out with regiment, Leonard N Foster, deserted, George Harris, died in hospital at Alexandria, December 1st, 1862, William Hillis, died in hospital, Philander Hurd, died in hospital, Anson Jones, rejected at Fonda; Charles La Point, mustered out with regiment, Frank La Point, mustered out with regiment, Cass La Point, Joseph Luther, mustered out with regiment, Jacob F Miller, mustered out with regiment, Charles W Morgan, mustered out with regiment, Daniel R Moss, died in hospital, Thomas Robinson, mustered out with regiment, Anson A Scovill, discharged from hospital, William H Sheffer, mustered out with regiment; Seneca B Smith, mustered out with regiment, William H Stevenson, mustered out with regiment, Henry A Swan, mustered out with regiment, William Sullivan, transferred to veteran reserve corps, Thomas Taylor, discharged for disability, Allen S Underwood, mustered out with regiment as first lieutenant (in command of the company much of the time of its service), Weston J Wilkie, discharged for disability; James M Walkup, died from disease

The following brief account of the career of this regiment is also from Watson's *History of Essex County* —

"The regiment immediately after its organization was ordered to Alexandria, and subsequently at Washington was employed in provost duty   Early in 1864 the One Hundred and Fifty-third was transferred to Louisiana and incorporated with the Nineteenth Army Corps   It was engaged in the Red River expedition and participated in all the hardships and disasters of that campaign   When the Union forces, after the battle of Sabine Cross Roads, fell back, Company I (of Essex) was the rear company in the retreat of the army The Nineteenth Corps sailed from New Orleans on the 3d of July with sealed orders, but its destination proved to be the Chesapeake   The One Hundred and Fifty-third, and four companies belonging to other regiments, the advance of the corps, on the arrival at Fortress Monroe were instantly ordered, without disembarking, to the defense of Washington, then menaced by Early's incursion   These troops were hastened through the city amid the deep excitement and alarm of the people to a position at Fort Stevens, where they went into immediate action   After the repulse of the rebels, the One Hundred and Fifty-third joined in their pursuit across the Potomac into the Shenandoah Valley, but was suddenly recalled to the vicinity of the capital, to oppose another apprehended advance of the enemy   The regiment was soon after engaged in the battle of Winchester, and it participated in the engagement at Fisher Hill and in the pursuit of the Confederates from that field   The Nineteenth Corps was at Cedar Creek and suffered heavy losses incident to the surprise and early catastrophies of that eventful day   The One Hundred and Fifty-third formed part of the picket line that enveloped Washington after the assassination of Mr Lincoln, and discharged guard duty at the arsenal on the military trials that succeeded   In June, 1865, the regiment was ordered to Savannah, where it performed provost duty until its discharge   In the succeeding October the One Hundred and Fifty-third was mustered out at Albany "

In this connection the following brief sketch of the career of Captain Chitty, embodying military history, will be of interest: He was born in Birmingham, England, in April, 1824, and is by profession a druggist   He was mustered in as Captain of Company K, One Hundred and Fifty-Third Regiment, October 12th, 1862   In April, 1863, the One Hundred and Fifty-Third, then doing duty in Alexandria, Va , he was detached by order of Brigadier-General J P Slough, Military Governor, as Provost Marshal of the city, remaining in that position until the following August, when the regiment was removed from the command   Accompanying the order relieving him was a complimentary letter from the general, thanking him for the very efficient manner in which he had discharged the duties of his office, and regretting that a military necessity compelled his return to the regiment   Captain Chitty, in command of the guard of his regiment, removed the first lot of rebel prisoners (five hundred in number) from the Old Capitol prison in Washington to Point Lookout in Maryland, and in command of a battalion of his regiment escorted the remains of General Cochrane through the city of Washington on their way to New York for interment   In February, 1864, the One Hundred and Fifty-Third was assigned to duty in the Department of the Gulf, and in March Captain Chitty was appointed Acting Assistant Inspector-General of the First Brigade, First Division, Nineteenth Army Corps, on the staff of Brigadier-General William Dwight, and remained in that position through the Red River expedition and until the Nineteenth Corps was removed to Washington, D C , in July, 1864, when the city was threatened by the rebel General Early   General Dwight then being assigned to the command of the First Division, Captain Chitty was removed to the Division Staff as Inspector-General ' of the First Division, serving as such through General Sheridan's Shenandoah campaign , but on the removal of the division to Washington, immediately after the lamented Lincoln's assassination, he was assigned to duty at Camp Stoneman as Provost Marshal of the post, at that time the camp of organization for Hancock's Veteran Corps, and in a very demoralized condition.   Captain Chitty, however, went to Savannah, Ga , with his division in June, and the organization then being broken up, he was assigned to duty on the staff of Major-General I M Brennan, on the order of Major-General Steadman, commanding the Department of Georgia, as Inspector-General of the District of Savannah, First Division Department of Georgia, remaining in that position until the following October, when his term of service having expired he was ordered to Albany, N Y , and there mustered out of the service October 20th, 1865, having served full three years and participated in all the engagements on the Red River expedition and those of Hunter and Sheridan in Virginia in the summer and fall of 1864 , never having been in a fight but what the gallant First Division came out victorious

The Ninety-third Regiment — This regiment was recruited in the counties of Albany, Alleghany, Rensselaer, Washington and Warren, nearly half of its members being from the last-named county   It was mustered into service in October, 1861, for three years   At the expiration of its term of service the organization returned to New York two hundred and sixty strong, February 28th, 1864, all of whom re-enlisted and were retained in service until June 29th, 1865, when they were finally mustered out

Following are the names of the officers of the regiment, with the memoranda of the career of each as far as obtained, and the names of recruits in the different companies from Warren county, as given in the records · —

Field Officers — Colonel, John S Crocker, discharged September 19th, 1864 , lieutenant-colonel, Benjamin C Butler, then of Luzerne, mustered out February, 1865 , adjutant, Haviland Gifford , surgeon, Strobridge Smith, of Glens Falls, mustered out with the regiment . major, Ambrose L Cassidy , Chaplain, Christopher H Edgerton, of Johnsburgh, resigned May 2d, 1862

Company A — Captain, Orville L Colvin, of Chester, dismissed May 25th,

1863, first-lieutenant, Henry C Newton, then of Glens Falls and now of Moreau, promoted to captain July 20th, 1863, discharged May 15th, 1865 ; second lieutenant, James M Southwick, died of disease May 4th, 1862 , sergeants (1st to 5th, inclusive) — Danford R. Edmonds, John D Nutting, Oscar B Ingraham, promoted to second lieutenant , David Burnham, Queensbury, promoted to second lieutenant June, 1862, and resigned March 2d, 1863 , Frederick J Thompson   Corporals (1st to 8th, inclusive) — James W Nutting of Chester, promoted to second lieutenant September 30th, 1864, mustered out with regiment, Charles A Culver, Obed A Brooks, Charles Finch, Rufus D Hastings, Eldridge Fletcher, Joseph M Wood, Philetus Bump   Privates, Alexander Anderson, George Algier, Sheldon Austin, Nathaniel Albro (transferred to Captain Charles F Barnes's company), Rufus Bump, Henry A Brooks, Jeremiah Bennett, Joel Benjamin, Daniel Benjamin, Joseph C Carpenter, Benjamin Cleveland, Calvin Clemens, Franklin Colt, Almer Conklin, James M Cowles, Chauncey Davis, Augustus Davis, Jeremiah Driscoll, Andrew J Dickens, Orvis Fish (died in hospital December 21st, 1861), Daniel Farr, Louis Frederick, Franklin G Gatchell, George W Greene, Dallas M Gurney, Isaiah Gifford, Patrick Hurson, Norman Hitchcock, John Haverty, John W Hays, Edgar Inlay, Henry Johnson, Lewis Jenks, Samuel Jackson, Aaron Knowlton, Jerry M King, Allen P Lillebridge, Adolphus La Point, James Lowe, Andrew J Merithen, Peter McGown, John McMahon, John Mauller, Samuel Murdock, Marvin E Orlon, James Pollard, Loland Page, Henry Porter, Francis Quinn, Orlin M Russell, George B Rogers (died is hospital December 25th, 1861), Lewis Robbins, William G Russell, Orville Ross, Charles D Roberts, Nelson Rhodes, Elisha Randall, Franklin D Smith, Charles Smith, Bethuel Smith, Cyrenus Sprague, Moses Sherman, James Scribner, James H Stewart, Asa Swarz, Elijah Taft, John T Turner, Lorenzo Underwood, Jay Vandusen, Wesley Wood, George Williams, Simon Welch, George Youngs, Anson M Pettys, John Pettys

This company was nearly or quite all recruited from Warren county, but we have no means of crediting them to their respective towns   Below are given the Warren county credits to the other companies of the regiment, with data of such promotions of Warren county men as we have been able to collect —

Company B, Nathaniel Albro, corporal (promoted from private), James Barney, Charles Cowles, Charles Fish, Oris H. King, Elijah Rider, James Ross, Elijah Robbins, Lewis Taber, George Taber, Henry C Taber, Andrew J Smith

Company C, William W Clark and Ambrose Spencer, sergeants , James H Lawrence, corporal ; Abraham Austin, Martin B Clemens, William C Fuller, Samuel Galusha, Thomas J Hays, Charles Ramsey, Truman M Stewart, Henry E Whitmore

Company F, Edward A Tanner and Fayette Selleck, sergeants , Abram

Austen, Daniel Bennett, Thomas Bemis, Jonathan Brown, jr, Elnathan Bristol, Samuel B Cutts, James I Darling, Patrick Ford, James H Gray, Lewis Hamlin, Robert Martin, George McDonald, Edward Story, Wesley Scofield, Jesse B. Thompson, Francis L Tanner, Joseph Woodman, Hough Wells.

Company G, James H Morehouse, James F Rowe

Company H, Captain, Hiram S Wilson, of Bolton, died March 24th, 1864, of disease First lieutenant, Edson Fitch, of Warren county, promoted to captain December 1st, 1863, mustered out on expiration of term Sergeant, Charles F Brown Corporals, Charles Cleveland and Charles Roberts Privates, Owen Allen, Avery Allen, Fayette Bush, Franklin Brese, Rolland Balcom, Murray Bentley, Benjamin Clark, Thomas D Clark, John Calihan, David H Decker, John Dean, Ira Duell, 2d, Joseph Duell, Martin J Eastwood, Warren Emerson, Norman F Eldridge, Johnsburgh, promoted to second lieutenant May 25th, 1863, and to first lieutenant, July 20th, 1863, killed in action in the Wilderness, May 6th, 1864, Horace P Eldridge, Sidney Fuller, Thomas Fitch, Montgomery Fish, Harley Finkle, George French, William J Griffin Henry Goodwin, Samuel G Goodman, Ashel Granger, Loren S Gibson, Almon B Griffin, M C Holcomb, Perry G Hammond, Hialmer P Hammond (musician), Artemus A Hastings, Nicholas Hartman, Daniel T Hicks, Homer Hammond, Charles H Hall, Josiah F Lovett, Andrew Lord, Warren Mead, Sylvester McCauley, E McDonnell, Philander Norton, Ira Ogden, Leroy Potter, Oliver Pratt, Stephen M Pratt, Luther W Peck, Robert Ramsey, Andrew Ryan, Clark Shaw, Russell Streeter, William Sexton, Julius P Sexton, Leander Sherman, George Smith, George Sweet, Isaac Threehouse, Erskine Truesdell, Dallas M Vernam, Sidney B Viele, Alfred L Wescott, Moses Wright, Ephriam T Weeks commissioned second lieutenant January 30th, 1862, resigned January 12th, 1863, David Bushaw, James Barnes, Otis Beswick, Chauncey Bullard, Isaac Bentley, Philander Bartlett, Leander Bartlett, George Lake, Charles Larose, Joseph Larkin, James McCabe, DeWitt Munger, John Austin, Isaac R Knapp, Bernard Murray

Company I, Bethuel Comstock, George Cleveland, Stephen Monthoney, Stephen F Monthoney

Company K were all credited to Troy, N Y

During its term of service and upon the re-organization of the Ninety-third after the expiration of its first term of service, as above alluded to, there were other enlistments, appointments and promotions from Warren county, among which were those of Joseph S Little, now of Glens Falls, who was promoted to first lieutenant July 20th, 1863, and lost a leg in battle, Daniel W Thompson, commissioned as first lieutenant January 30th, 1865, but not mustered under the commission, Oscar B Ingraham, commissioned first lieutenant September 16th, 1864, but not mustered under the commission; Lewis W Hamlin, then of Queensbury, now of Moreau, commissioned second lieutenant January 30th, 1865, and mustered out with the regiment, John Bailey, of Stoney Creek, commissioned captain July 20th, 1863, was killed in action May 5th, 1864. There may be others who deserve mention under this feature of the records, but if so, we have been unable to obtain them

The Ninety-third regiment has a noble record, and it is to be regretted that a more explicit account of its valorous deeds in the field and the individual acts of heroism on the part of many of its members cannot be given at this late day It bears upon its banners a list of engagements embracing Yorktown, Williamsburg, Fredericksburg, Chancellorsville, Antietam, Wilderness, Coal Harbor, Spottsylvania, North Anna, Tolopotomoy, Petersburg, Strawberry Plains, Deep Bottom, Poplar Spring Church, and Boydton Road—a series of battles through which no regiment could pass and come out without leaving a large portion of its members either dead on southern soil, or wounded in many hospitals We find the following brief sketch of the regiment in a Glens Falls paper of a date not long before its return to New York, in 1864 —

"This remarkably fine regiment was raised in the fall and winter of 1861, in the counties of Washington, Warren, Essex and Alleghany, and took its departure from the State in March, 1862, one thousand strong, of whom but two hundred and sixty now remain It formed part of Palmer's Brigade, of Casey's Division, in Keyes's Corps, and went down to the peninsula with the rest of McClellan's army In the advance from Fortress Monroe, in April, the Ninety-third formed the extreme left of the army and was encamped near the the mouth of Warwick River, where they took part in many skirmishes and reconnaissances and performed much severe labor While here Colonel Crocker and Major Cassidy were taken prisoners within our own lines, through the negligence of the officer of the picket, and until their exchange several months later, the command of the regiment devolved upon Lieutenant-Colonel Butler

" At the battle of Williamsburg the Ninety-third was the only regiment of the brigade that arrived on the field during the action and was highly complimented by General Keyes for its promptness and energy.

" Soon after the battle of Williamsburg General McClellan ordered the regiment to be detailed as guard at general headquarters of the army—a high testimonial to its drill, discipline and *morale* General Burnside, on assuming command of the army, retained the Ninety-third at his headquarters, as did also General Hooker and General Mead, all of whom spoke of it in the highest terms In drill, discipline, and *morale*, it is surpassed by no regiment in the army of the Potomac and none can better perform the duties of the position Noble, pure-minded General Patrick greatly admires it, and declares it shall remain at headquarters as long as he does "

One Hundred and Eighteenth Regiment — This regiment was organized at Plattsburg, N Y, for three years' service. It was recruited entirely in the Sixteenth Senate District, comprising the counties of Clinton, Essex and Warren, companies A, D, and G, being from the last named county It was mustered into service on the 30th of August, 1862 Following are the names of the regimental officers at the organization of the regiment —

Field Officers — Colonel, Samuel T Richards, resigned July 8th, 1863 Lieutenant-colonel, Oliver Keese, jr, promoted to colonel July 31st, 1863, and resigned September 16th, 1864 Major, Geo F Nichols, promoted to lieutenant-colonel August, 1863, and to colonel November 28th, 1864, mustered out with the regiment Adjutant, Charles E Pruyn, promoted to major August, 1863, and killed in action June 13th, 1864 Quartermaster, Patrick Delaney, resigned August 19th, 1864 Surgeon, John H Mooers, resigned April 4th, 1864 Assistant surgeon, James G Porteus, promoted to surgeon Forty-sixth New York Volunteers, November 12th, 1864 Chaplain, Charles S Hagar

Following are the officers and members of Companies A, D, and G, raised in Warren county, with considerable details of promotions, etc . —

Company A, captain, Josiah H Norris, of Glens Falls, resigned January 1st, 1864 First lieutenant, Edward Riggs, of Glens Falls, promoted to captain January 12th, 1863, resigned August 5th, 1863 Was drowned while on his way South, in 1865, to procure substitutes to apply on the Queensbury quota (See biography of Daniel V Brown, in later pages of this work) Second lieutenant, Simon E Chamberlain, promoted to captain Twenty-fifth New York Cavalry, May 19th, 1864 Sergeants (first to fourth inclusive), Edgar Comstock, James Kendall, Orange A Cowles, Michael Reynolds, commissioned second lieutenant April 13th, 1864, killed in action near Coal Harbor, June 2d, 1864, these all from Queensbury Corporals (first to eighth inclusive), Amos B Haviland, James Goodwin, Gustus C Sherman, Charles A Grace, commissioned second lieutenant May 11th, 1865, mustered out with the regiment , Samuel Van Tassell, Cass C La Point, Edward E Clute, George H Wing, all from Queensbury William E Hall, drummer, Carlos M Brainerd, wagoner , Clark Arnold, Adelbert Andrews, William H Allen, Henry Andrews, Charles C Bennett, Royal Bullion, William Bullock, Edward Brownse, Andrew J Brummagim, John Balfour, jr Adolphus P Burkhart, William A Coffee, Martin Chamberlain, Abner Croff, Charles F Copeland, Abner B Crannell, John Clute, John M J Crannell, Joseph Doket, Marquis Davis, Hosea Day, Robert K Evans, Edward B Fish, Franklin Foster, Isaac Gilman, William H Groom, Norman H Gourlay, Hubbard W Goodrich, Adolphus Guyat, Joseph Granger, Joseph Herbert, William Hartman, John H Hall, Henry L Hall, Allen D Hubbell, Alonzo S Hopkins, Clifford Hubbard (of Glens Falls, commissioned second lieutenant November 30th, 1864, and made adjutant, May 11th, 1865 , mustered out with the regiment) , Eber F Irish, John Jordon, Franklin Jandro (awarded medal of honor by the Secretary of War) , De Estaing Johnson, Stephen B Little, Mahlon Lord, Levi

Ladao, Joseph Morrison, Henry M Mellis, Arad B Mickle, William Mallery, Clark N Northrup, Daniel Norlon, Ira Norlon, Franklin T Paige, William D Palmer, George A Potter, Mandeville Potter, William H Potter, Isaac Philo, jr, Henry W. Persons, John C Robillard, Theophile Rienvielle, Silas Randall, Addison L Stoddard, Alanson D Simpson, Frederick W Shaw, Janurius Surprenant, John S Shippy, Wells E Stone, James R Tillotson, William W Thayer, James Van Wagoner, Albert Wilson, Duane Williams, Holdridge H Whipple, Abraham White, Charles C Wright, Amos Ward, Edgar M Wing, (Glens Falls, commissioned second lieutenant January 12th, 1864, died May 16th, 1864), Benoni T Wert, George Wescott, Hiram Yetto   This company was raised largely in the town of Queensbury

Company D, captain, Richard P Smith, Horicon, resigned December 10th, 1862   First lieutenant, Cyrus O Burge, Chestertown, resigned November 24th, 1863   Second lieutenant, John H Smith, jr, commissioned first lieutenant, June 12th, 1863, but not mustered, resigned January 16th, 1863   Sergeants (first to fifth inclusive), Elisha M Baxter, Horicon, James M Colony, Ebenezer N. Jenks and Warren S Wickham, of Chester; Joseph A Hastings, Horicon   Corporals (first to eighth inclusive), Samuel Sherman, Horicon, commissioned second lieutenant March 17th, 1863, and promoted to first lieutenant April 13th, 1864, discharged October 19th, 1864, George B Green, Ebenezer M Sexton, William C Duel, C Brown, of Horicon, Reuben W Mead and Charles H Osborn, of Chester, William Cox, Johnsburg   Alfred H Holley, Horicon, drummer, Eli Pettys, Chester, wagoner.   Privates, David Austin, Johnsburg, Lorenzo J Barton, Chester; John Bolton, Royal Z Bennett, Washington Baker, Lewis Bartlett, Hiram Brown, Joel Brown, Benjamin Baker, Enos Brown and Lemuel Bentley, of Horicon, Jeremiah Bennett, Johnsburgh, John Calkins, Hague (commissioned second lieutenant September 16th, 1864, and promoted to first lieutenant May 11th, 1865, mustered out with the regiment), Michael Cummings, Johnsburgh, Henry D Coville, Hiram Drake, Reuben J Davis, James P Davis, of Chester; Oscar O Duel, Richard Dycher and Patrick H Dugan, of Horicon, James H. Dingman, Luzerne, Edmond Eldridge and James D. Flansburgh, Johnsburgh, George Frazier, Horicon, William Frazier, Levi Fuller and Henry Flansburgh, of Johnsburgh, Emory Gregory, Horicon, James Hughes, Alfred Hotchkiss and Charles W Higley, of Chester, James Hastings, Amasa Hill, Timothy Hill and Thomas J Hays, of Horicon, Ira Hill, Chester; Tarquin Ingram, Horicon, Hollis Johnson, Irwin Johnson, Norman W King and John E King of Chester, Daniel King and Norman J King, of Horicon, Napoleon Laperarie, Johnsburgh, James Lamb, Horicon, Horace P May, Chester, Russell McCauley, Horicon, James McCormick and Frank Potter, of Johnsburgh; Dalhousie Priestley and David G Perry, of Chester, Lewis Pilotts, Adam Putnam and Jeffreys Prichard, of Horicon, Henry R Putnam, Johnsburgh, Michael Rattigan, Chester, Orange Remington, Martin Russell, Benager Robbins and Solomon Robbins, of Horicon, Rodney Ross, Johnsburgh, William W Stannard, Chester, Toner Smith, Horicon, Thomas Simmons, Samuel Smith and George W Sherman, Horicon, George Sturgis, Johnsburgh, Charles C Smith, Alva B Taylor, Oscar Tyrrell and Daniel R Taylor, of Chester, Lorenzo D Tripp, Mallory Tripp, Alonzo Tyrrell and George W. Tyrrell, of Horicon, Charles Underwood, Chester, Josiah D Waldron, Richard S Waters and Henry A Wood, of Horicon, Job A Wilcox, Luzerne

Company G — Captain, Dennis Stone, of Warrensburgh, resigned May 26th, 1865 First lieutenant, Stephen H Smith, Horicon, resigned November 23d, 1862 Second lieutenant, M Nelson Dickinson, Warrensburgh, promoted to first lieutenant June 12th, 1863, resigned May 3d, 1865 Sergeants (first to fifth inclusive), Henry P Grump, Luzerne, B P Dean, Stony Creek; Bennett J Leonard, Johnsburgh, Truman N Thomas, Bolton, discharged November 20th, 1863, George W Carnes, Warrensburgh Corporals (first to eighth inclusive), Thomas H Tripp, Stony Creek, George W Fuller, Johnsburgh, David W Bartlett, Bolton, Charles A Lincoln, Warrensburgh, Roswell Walsh and George Murray, Stony Creek, Henry S Perkins, Warrensburgh, Orlando J Brown, Johnsburgh

J W Odell, musician, Stony Creek, Calvin G Wood, musician, Warrensburgh, D M Woodward, wagoner, Warrensburgh Privates, Lewis Aldrich, Luzerne, Edgar Burnett, Johnsburgh; Sewell P Braley, Bolton, John Beswick, John Burnett, Johnsburgh, Robert Boyd, Bolton, Royal Bates, Caldwell, Nathan Beswick, Bolton, John H. Bennett, Warrensburgh; William J. Barber, Luzerne, George Casey and George H Clark, Johnsburgh, Martin V B Coon, John Dawson and William N Dingman, Stony Creek, Charles Fenton, Warrensburgh, William Freeborn and Darius Fuller, Johnsburgh; John J Flanders, Luzerne, William Goodnow, Stony Creek, Martin Gardner, Johnsburgh, John A Grimes, Warrensburgh, Lemuel Griffin, Bolton, Parley Gray, jr, and William Gamble, Stony Creek, William H Gates and Hiram B Gates, Johnsburgh, Edmond Gibo, Joseph H Higgins and Jasper Harvey, Johnsburgh, Harrison Hall, Luzerne, G H Hall, Johnsburgh, Valentine Hoyle, Luzerne; John Jones, Johnsburgh; James A King, Stony Creek, Edgar E Lincoln, Johnsburgh, William Latham, Warrensburgh, William H Layway, Bolton, James McCarthy, Warrensburgh, Benjamin F. W Monroe, Johnsburgh, Samuel Maxim and William Morehouse, Warrensburgh, Sylvester McDonald, Stony Creek, A J Myers, Warrensburgh, Joseph L Norton, Johnsburgh, Jonathan Nolton and Benjamin F. Nolton, Stony Creek, Truman H Parke, Warrensburgh, Dudley R Peabody, Luzerne, Alfred S Purver, Warrensburgh; William R Perkins, Stony Creek; William H Parkiss, Warrensburgh, Benjamin B Perry, Caldwell, Delius Rist, Johnsburgh, Rufus Randall, jr, Aaron G Randall and Selah Randall, Bolton, Joseph Reed, Stony

Creek, Henry Shaw, Luzerne, George Sanders, Johnsburgh, Ransom H. Stanton and Joel Streeter, Warrensburgh, Sidney Smith, Johnsburgh; Sylvanus H Smith, Bolton, Elias K Sargent, Johnsburgh; H O Shedel, Bolton; Elihu Stevens and William C Stevens, Stony Creek, Wilson Smead, Luzerne; Charles C Sexton and James E Sexton, Bolton, Edward Tucker, Warrensburgh, Richard H Turner, Johnsburgh, James Tucker, Warrensburgh, William S Taylor, Luzerne, Merritt Vermun, Warrensburgh, Garry Vandenburgh, George Williams and William H Washburn, Johnsburgh, Franklin L Weaver and Joshua Carnes, Warrensburgh.

Three of the companies of this regiment were from Essex county (C, E, and F), and a part of Company K, which fact rendered it incumbent upon Mr Winslow C Watson, in the writing of his history of that county, some ten years ago, and from which we have already made extracts in this connection to give an account of its career, from his sketch, revised and corrected by several living officers, we condense the following —

"The regiment, with great appropriateness called the Adirondac, was mustered into the service the 29th of August, 1862 By the successive resigna_ tions of Colonel Richards and Lieutenant-Colonel Keese, as above noted, Major Nichols was promoted to the command of the regiment, and led it with distinguished skill and courage. John L Cunningham, then of Essex, and now of Glens Falls, went out as first lieutenant of Company F, of which Robert W Livingston, now the veteran journalist of Essex county, living at Elizabethtown, was captain Lieutenant Cunningham was promoted to captain of Company D, of Warren county, September 4th, 1863, and to major November 28th, 1864, he was also brevetted lieutenant-colonel, and mustered out with the regiment James S Garrett, now of Glens Falls, was promoted from sergeant to second lieutenant, December 9th, 1862, and to first lieutenant March 8th, 1864, he was brevetted captain and mustered out with the regiment

"The One Hundred and Eighteenth entered the service with an aggregate of nine hundred and eighty-three men, it was re-enforced at intervals by three hundred and fifty recruits, but returned from the field at the expiration of its term with only three hundred and twenty-three in its ranks, both officers and privates Immediately upon joining the army the regiment began a series of active and incessant duties It formed a part of Peck's force, in the memorable defense of Suffolk, and was employed in the arduous raids along the Black River It was warmly engaged through two days and often under heavy fire, in a continued skirmish with the rebel sharp-shooters near Suffolk, and participated in a diversion to the northward of Richmond, to attack Lee or a portion of his army from Pennsylvania, in June, 1863 The brigade to which the One Hundred and Eighteenth Regiment was attached was in the advance, and the regiment was ordered to destroy parts of the Richmond and Fredericksburg railroad While the regiment was engaged in executing this service, two companies, A, Captain Norris, and F in the absence from sickness of Captain Livingstone commanded by Lieutenant Cunningham, were advanced as skirmishers along the railroad, towards the South Anna River, and after cautiously proceeding about one mile came in contact with the rebel pickets   The command continued to advance in line under a sharp and constant fire, the enemy slowly retiring, and speedily in addition to small arms they opened a fire on the Union troops from batteries in front commanding the line of railroad and on a flank   The companies under this concentrated fire were compelled to retreat and fell back in order, assuming a strong position in a wood, behind a ditch with an open field in front   During this movement, Lieutenant Cunningham received a painful wound from a spent ball, but did not leave the field Major Nichols soon after appeared on the ground with two fresh companies, D, Captain Riggs, and a company of the Ninety-ninth New York   These companies deployed on either side, and the line thus formed made a rapid advance A warm action ensued in which the command was subjected to a heavy fire of mingled bullets, shot and shells   The enemy were at length driven back along their whole front, except at one point in their position, which was obstinately maintained and appeared to be fortified   This point, which proved to be a breastwork of plank, Lieutenant W H Stevens of Company F proposed to capture ; and calling for volunteers for the service, selected five of the first who offered   He rapidly advanced in the dark behind a screen of bushes, which flanked the rebel's position on the right, and with fixed bayonets and loaded guns rushed upon the breastwork with a wild shout   Although surprised, the enemy attempted a resistance, but the gallant Stevenson killed one with his revolver, wounded a second and captured the remainder of the party consisting of thirteen men, who were brought into the Federal lines   The constancy and resolution of the regiment was first tested on this occasion, and the conduct of the officers engaged and the steadiness and discipline of the troops received the highest encomiums.

"The One Hundred and Eighteenth continued attached to the column of the James until the spring of 1864, and was engaged in operations near Norfolk and at or near Bermuda Hundred, and in February it advanced to Bolton's Bridge from Williamsburg, in an attempt on Richmond , and in operations near Norfolk and at or near Bermuda Hundred   It at this time constituted a part of the Second Brigade, First Division of the Eighteenth Corps   General W F Smith commanded the corps, Brooks the division, and Burnham the brigade All these officers were eminently distinguished by their fighting qualities and high reputation   Early in May the army marched upon the ill-omened expedition against Fort Darling on the James, which was terminated by the fatal results at Drury's Bluff   This march from its commencement to its disastrous issue was a constant scene of fighting and skirmishes   On the tenth, companies D, F, and K. were advanced in a skirmishing line, the last held in reserve, while the remainder of the regiment was deployed   The coolness and bearing of Lietenant Stevenson of F, and Kellogg of Company D, were conspicuous, and the steadiness of the whole line was eminently distinguished. The One Hundred and Eighteenth four days after captured with small loss a series of rifle pits, redoubts and batteries, which formed a strong advance line of the enemy   This work from the form of its construction offered no protection to the Federal troops   The enemy occupied a short distance in front far more formidable works mounted with heavy guns, and during the whole day the Second Brigade was exposed to a severe fire of shells from this work   One of the missiles crushed the head of Sergeant Place of Company K, a brave and intelligent soldier   Throughout Sunday the 15th the brigade maintained this exposed position, which was soon to acquire a dread and bloody prominence in one of the darkest pages of the war   Heckman's Brigade, lying to the right of the second, formed the extreme right of the army line   Between Heckman's Brigade and the James there was an interval of a mile in length, which was left unoccupied, except by a few feeble and scattering posts of colored cavalry   No entrenchment had been constructed either in front of the Union lines or on the flank , excepting such as were hastily thrown up under the direction of commanders of particular brigades or regiments   The ground had been previously occupied by the Confederates, by whom scattered and irregular redoubts, trenches and rifle pits were constructed , but these were so arranged that they afforded no protection to the Union troops in their present position.   The line held by the Second Brigade stretched along a deep excavation which had been made by the rebels and at this time was filled with water   A standing place was formed for the brigade by leveling a narrow space, between this ditch and the embankment created by the earth thrown up at its construction   Slight bridges were at short intervals thrown across the trench   These precautions proved a few hours later of infinite importance   The embankment was thus converted into an important defense which in the subsequent action afforded great protection to the troops   General Brooks conceived the novel and happy idea of extending a telegraph wire in front of the brigade , but unfortunately Heckman's Brigade was without even this feeble protection and lay totally exposed to the assault of a vigilant foe

" At three o'clock on the morning of the 16th, the One Hundred and Eighteenth was aroused and at its post, in conformity to special orders, or its established practice   The air was loaded with a thick, dank fog, which the opening dawn but slightly dissipated   As sun-rise approached, the advance or movement of troops was noticed in front, but in the obscure light the color of their uniform could not be distinguished, nor their evolutions determined   A few shots from Belger's artillery in front of the brigade, were thrown into the ravine along which these troops were advancing and they were seen to halt and lie down   A staff officer who at that moment appeared on the field, pro-

nouncing them to be Federal pickets retiring and ordered the firing to cease
Small white flags or signals were distinctly discerned waving in the mist, and
voices shouted from the obscurity, 'Don't fire on your friends' The musketry had already become sharp on the right, but the Second Brigade had received no orders of any kind   There was a period of fearful suspense and
hesitation   Captain Ransom of Company I, unable to restrain his impatience,
leaped upon the embankment and firing his revolver, exclaimed   'This is my
reception of such friends   The last chamber was scarcely exploded when he
fell, pierced by a ball that passed through his body, and shattered an arm
Doubt no longer existed of the character or purpose of these troops, and the
One Hundred and Eighteenth instantly poured a volley into the advancing line
The front rank of the enemy now rushed impetuously forward, and in the dimness
of the light stumbled over the wires, and those in the rear pressing after them all
were hurled together in a promiscuous mass, their ranks broken and thrown
into inextricable disorder   Many of the enemy involved in the confusion threw
down their arms and surrendered, and were sent to the rear.   Up to this point
the One Hundred and Eighteenth had achieved a success   It was vigilant and
the contemplated surprise had been defeated, but Heckman's Brigade had been
surprised and nearly flanked from the undefended space on its right   It had
fallen back and at one time the whole brigade were prisoners, but in the tumult and amid the dense mist and smoke escaped   The Eighth Connecticut,
next on the right of the One Hundred and Eighteenth, was attacked in flank,
doubled up and disappeared from the field   The One Hundred and Eighteenth
was now exposed to a crushing fire in front and upon the right flank   The
extemporaneous traverses which it had constructed at this crisis were most
effective, affording a partial protection, and for a while the resistance of the regiment appeared to be successful, but it was enveloped by an overwhelming
force, and a sanguinary conflict ensued   In this desperate aspect of the battle
each man was directed to gain the rear without regard to discipline   A few
embraced the opportunity to retreat, others still sustained the fight, while the
wounded implored their comrades not to abandon them, and more than one
noble life was sacrificed to preserve these sufferers from the horrid calamities
of a hostile prison house   The regiment was soon after rallied and made a
gallant stand, but was compelled to fall back, again advanced a short space
and ultimately retreated in order   Captain Dominy, the senior officer, succeeded to the temporary command of the regiment on the disability of Colonel
Nichols

"The dire aceldama was ennobled by deeds of daring heroism, and instances of exalted devotion   An intrepid young lieutenant, Henry J Adams,
of Elizabethtown, at the moment the regiment was breaking seized a standard
and shouting the words so familiar to scenes of home and festive joyousness
'Rally around the flag, boys,' attempted to arrest the retreat, and essentially
17

aided in rallying the troops Captain Robert W Livingston of Company F, early in the action moved from the cover of the enbankment in order to communicate with Colonel Nichols, and while standing a moment exposed was was struck down by a frightful wound in the shoulder His gallant young lieutenant, W H Stevenson, who was behind an enbankment and in a situation comparatively secure, saw him fall and calling on the men to bring in their captain, rushed out to Livingston's assistance, accompanied by four of the company Livingston admonished them of the great exposure they incurred and urged that he might be left, but Stevenson persisted in his generous purpose and in a moment after fell dead at his commander's side, a sacrifice to duty and friendship Livingston, as he was borne from the field, was struck by another shot that terribly lacerated his foot and leg He languished in great suffering fourteen months in a hospital before his severe wounds permitted a return to his home, a mutilated and disabled soldier

" The regiment was not pursued by the severely punished enemy and was immediately rallied by its own officers It maintained a bold and defiant attitude until most of its wounded were borne from the field In that conflict, scarcely extending over the space of half an hour, the One Hundred and Eighteenth, out of the three hundred and fifty men engaged, lost one hundred and ninety-eight privates and thirteen officers in killed, wounded and prisoners Amid all these disasters and sacrifices the regiment had captured and secured two hundred prisoners, a greater number than it retained men fit for duty Among the killed on this fatal day was Captain John S Stone, of Company K Lieutenant Stevenson was killed and Lieutenant Edgar A Wing, Company E, a youth of high promise who had been promoted to the company only a few days before, was mortally wounded, taken prisoner and died the next day Lieutenant-Colonel Nichols was slightly wounded in the side and hand, from which his sword was stricken by a shot, and his clothing, as was that of several other officers, was riddled by bullets Adjutant John M Carter lost an arm and was captured, Captains Livingston and Ransom were severely wounded, Lieutenants Treadway and Sherman were wounded, and Captain Dennis Stone, Company A, and James H Pierce, Company C, taken prisoners The army on the same day fell back to Bermuda Hundred and fortified, but the stricken and fragmentary One Hundred and Eighteenth were exempted from the toil of entrenching

" On the 29th of May the Eighteenth Corps, embracing the One Hundred and Eighteenth, embarked in transports, and passing down the James, ascended the Pamunky and landed at the White House Directly upon disembarking it was rushed to the front, and on the 1st of June it joined the army of the Potomac On that day near Coal Harbor commenced a battle which continued until the 3d, and was one of the most severely contested and sanguinary engagements of the war, but its incidents and results have been singularly veiled from the public eye   The Eighteenth Corps occupied a position in front of the Union army   The One Hundred and Eighteenth was engaged in the bloody scenes of these conflicts, but not unconnected with its corps   Its casualties were extremely severe   At times exposed to a heavy fire in front, and enfiladed by a battery and rifle pits, to escape annihilation the troops were compelled to lie prone upon the earth, while a tempest of minnie balls, shot and shells, hurtled just above them   The dead could neither be removed nor buried, and their corpses were thrown upon the breastwork, with a slight covering of earth strewn upon them, and thus their decaying bodies aided to form a bulwark for the protection of their living comrades   The taint from the decomposing mass became almost insufferable before the corps was withdrawn from the trenches   The sufferings of the regiment through the trying ordeal of those eight days were extreme   It lost at Coal Harbor seventy men and officers   Among the casualties were Lieutenant Michael Reynolds, of Company A, killed, and Captain Jacob Parmerter, of Company E, severely wounded with the loss of a leg

" An impregnable line in front arrested all advance by the Union army, but the enemy was held in an equally tenacious and unyielding grasp   The Eighteenth Corps sustained its exposed position, and in the end formed a curtain behind which, on the 12th, General Grant accomplished his perilous and memorable flank movement which effected the change of his base   When this bold and remarkable operation had been accomplished, the Eighteenth also hastily abandoned its entrenchments and fell back unopposed to White House, and returned to its previous field of duty   On the 15th of June the One Hundred and Eighteenth was engaged in the attack on Petersburg   Here it suffered a heavy loss in the death of Major Charles E Pruyn, who was in temporary command of the regiment   While standing in an exposed position, and in the act of surveying the works he was preparing to assault, he was struck and horribly mutilated by a shell   He had acted as adjutant in the organization of the regiment, and its singlar proficiency and high discipline were chiefly imputed to the skill and assiduity of his services, sustained by the field officers, pre-eminently by the military attainments and persistent zeal of Colonel Keese   Lieutenant Rowland C Kellogg was also wounded by the explosion of a shell   Captain Levi S Dominy of Company B succeeded to the immediate command of the regiment

" The fierce and protracted siege of Petersburg exacted from the One Hundred and Eighteenth the most arduous and exhaustive duties   Night succeeded the day, days rolled into weeks, and the weeks formed months, but their toils had no mitigation, while their endurance and dangers were perpetual   Now exposed to the burning sun and breathing the arid sand, and now struggling in mud and water , often suffering for drink, seldom able to wash, and never changing their clothing for rest   Constantly shelled and frequently enfiladed by new batteries, burrowing in the earth to escape projectiles, against which ordinary entrenchments afforded no protection, the troops were yet joyous, patient, enduring and full of hope   Amid all these exposures and suffering, after it had recovered from an almost universal prostration by chills and fever at Gloucester Point, and altogether moving in a malarious region, the One Hundred and Eighteenth was always vigorous and healthy   The rigorous ordeal to which it was now subjected continued with brief relief until the 29th of July, when the regiment was withdrawn to aid in the support of the storming column, which was designed to assail the enemy's works, on the explosion of the long projected mine   They witnessed in sadness and humiliation the disastrous failure of that magnificent experiment   On the 27th of August, after a term of two months, the Second Brigade was relieved from its arduous trench duties   During the long period of one hundred and thirteen days the One Hundred and Eighteenth had marched and toiled and endured, with no enjoyment of quiet repose, and almost incessantly subjected to the fire of the enemy

" A single month the One Hundred and Eighteenth was permitted to repose, after its prolonged and severe service, in a pleasant encampment near the southern banks of the James   In that interval the Ninety-sixth had been attached to the Second Brigade   This brigade, by the proficiency of its drill, its exact discipline, and general efficiency, had become conspicuous and universally esteemed second to no other in its distinguished corps   On the 27th September, every indication presaged the renewal of active duty   Rations for two days were ordered prepared   An unusual earnestness and activity were manifested by the generals and their staffs   The next night the tattoo, suggestive of repose, had scarcely sounded, when the brigade was ordered to move promptly and in profound silence, leaving their tents standing   Previous to breaking camp, the One Hundred and Eighteenth and the Tenth New Hampshire had by a special order exchanged their Enfield guns for the Spencer repeating rifle, a tremendous weapon in the hands of resolute and expert marksmen   This selection by the corps commander was a distinguished recognition of the efficiency of the preferred regiments   At three o'clock on the morning of the 29th, the division led by the second brigade, was passing over the James upon a pontoon bridge, which had been completed the same hour   The sound of the movement was suppressed by earth or other substances strewn upon the bridge   On reaching the north bank of the river, the One Hundred and Eighteenth and Tenth New Hampshire were thrown out as skirmishers and flankers, while the remainder of the command was advanced along the road in column   Soon after daybreak a brisk fire was opened by the enemy's pickets which fell back on their reserves, and the whole were forced rapidly back through a dense wood, for the distance of more than two miles, when the Union column entered upon open ground   A strong earth work was now revealed in front, and mounted with heavy guns This formidable work, was Fort, or rather Battery Harrison, and General Stannard instantly ordered Burnham to take it by assault The Ninety-sixth and Eighth Connecticut forming the storming column were supported by the First and Third brigade of the division with the One Hundred and Eighteenth New York, and Twelfth New Hampshire as skirmishers on their flank The column rushed impetuously forward, along the open space, met by a furious, plunging fire from the enemy's lines When it reached, after this rapid advance along the distance of nearly three-fourths of a mile, the base of the eminence upon which the works were erected, the column breathless and exhausted, paused in a position comparatively protected As we have already seen, the enemy was hastening re-enforcements to the point of attack, and the commander both of the division and brigade, alarmed at the posture of affairs, sent a member of his staff to order an instant assault Lieutenant George F Cambell, Company C, One Hundred and Eighteenth, aid to General Burnham, dashed across the plains exposed to the whole range of the enemy's fire and unhurt communicated the order The two regiments impetuously scaled the hill, mounted the parapet, and their gallant color-bearers planted simultaneously their flags upon the works The enemy precipitately abandoned the lines, falling back to other works, while their own guns were turned upon them with deadly effect In the act of training one of these guns upon the fugitives, General Burnham was mortally wounded and died in a few minutes after

"While these events were in progress in the center, the skirmishing support had approached the fort, and used their rifles in picking off the gunners in the works, and demoralizing the defense Lieutenant-Colonel Nichols, with the One Hundred and Eighteenth, after being distinguished 'for cool conduct on the skirmish lines in the general assault, captured two redoubts on the right of the fort, during the main assault Surgeon F G Porteous, of the One Hundred and Eighteenth, was officially noticed with strong recommendations for bravery and attention to duties, being the only surgeon in the brigade advancing with his regiment in the charging column ' The Second Brigade now moved upon two intrenchments in front, and captured them successfully, driving the enemy back upon their third and last defense on this line of works Fort Harrison had thus been snatched from the jaws of the Confederate army, which lay in great force immediately contiguous, and was too important a position to be relinquished without a desperate struggle The last line captured by the Union troops was exposed to the fire of the enemy's gun-boats and to assault, and it was deemed expedient to fall back upon Fort Harrison The enemy vigorously pursued, and in this movement both Colonel Donohoe and Lieutenant-Colonel Nichols were severely wounded The night and the succeeding morning were assiduously employed in extending and strengthening the works, which now acquired the form and strength of an enclosed fortifica-

tion   A second and third time the onset was repeated, and met in the same
corageous spirit, and with similar results   On the last assault, those of the
assailants who survived the withering fire of the Federal troops, threw down
their arms and surrendered   About noon the next day rebel troops had been
massed in three heavy columns, and covered by two batteries, rushed upon the
new Federal lines with heroic impetuosity   The One Hundred and Eighteenth
and Tenth New Hampshire were stationed at salient points in the works, and
the fatal power of their new weapons was frightfully demonstrated upon the
Confederate ranks   Gun-boats were constantly, but with trifling effect, shell-
ing the Union position   This formidable assault was repulsed by musketry
alone, and the rebels falling back to cover, abandoned their numerous dead
and wounded upon the field   Besides Lieutenant-Colonel Nichols, Captain
Dobie and Lieutenant Treadway of the One Hundred and Eighteenth were
wounded

"The One Hundred and Eighteenth moved with its division from the
quarters near Fort Burnham where it had remained since the capture of that
work, on the 26th of October, to a position within about three miles of Fort
Richmond, erected on the former battle-ground of Fair Oaks   The regiment
at that time was composed of two hundred and five men for duty including
supernumeraries. At dawn the succeeding morning it advanced. That part
of the regiment embracing more than half which was armed with the Spencer
rifles, was thrown in front as skirmishers, and the remainder held in reserve
Passing a covert of woods, the skirmishers entered upon a cleared field which
extended to the fort, a distance of about one-fourth of a mile   Over this space
they made a rush upon the work, in the face of a terrible fire, and succeeded
in approaching it within about one hundred yards   The enemy's lines at this
moment were only slightly manned, but the entrenchment was heavy and
formidable, and wholly unassailable by the feeble skirmishing force   Major
Dominy, an officer conspicuous for his fighting qualities, commanded the regiment, and at this time passed an order for the troops to lie down, seeking any
cover that presented itself, for protection against the irresistible tempest of
shot and balls that was hurled upon them   Soon after they were directed to
fall back singly to an excavation on a road in the rear   The regiment made no
further advance, but after the repulse of the assaulting column mentioned in
the notice of the Ninety-sixth Regiment, retreated to its former encampment
The losses of the regiment were greater in proportion to its strength than on
any previous occasion   The skirmishing party entered into action with nine
officers   three of these, Major Dominy, Lieutenants McLean and Gibbs returned in safety, but Captain J R Seaman, Company A, was seriously wounded
Lieutenant M J Dickinson was wounded and taken prisoner, with Lieutenants
Saunders, Potter, O'Connor, and Bryant   Captain M V B Stetson in the reserve was also wounded while aiding to remove Colonel Moffitt of the Ninety-

fifth from the field When the regiment reached its former quarters scarcely forty men had gathered to its standard, but others returned until the aggregate was increased to nearly one-half the number who had marched out the day preceding The One Hundred and Eighteenth remained in camp through the winter, and on the march upon Richmond the ensuing spring, its relics were engaged on picket duty and advanced as skirmishers, covering the Third Division of the Twenty-fourth Corps It was the first organized Federal regiment that entered Richmond The One Hundred and Eighteenth bore the noble inscription upon its national flag ' Suffolk—South Anna—Coal Harbor—Fort Harrison—Bermuda—Swift Creek—Petersburg—Fair Oaks—Drury's Bluff —Crater—Richmond ' This attests its military glory, but its high moral qualities are still more illustrated by the remarkable fact, that not a single member of this regiment was known to have deserted to the enemy In more authoritative language than I can use, General Devens, in recapitulating its services, pronounces this eulogium upon the One Hundred and Eighteenth at Drury's Bluff: ' This regiment distinguished itself for great valor and pertinacity, and won the reputation it has since enjoyed, of being one of the most resolute regiments in the service,' He adds ' With this weapon (the Spencer rifle) they will return to your State armed, and it is a most appropriate testimonial of their efficiency ' " [1]

Officers of the One Hundred and Eighteenth Regiment, when mustered out of the service, June 13th, 1865 — Colonel, George F Nichols, brevet general U S V, lieutenant-colonel, Levi S Dominy, brevet colonel N Y V, major, John L Cunningham, brevet lieutenant-colonel U S V, surgeon, William O Mansfield, assistant surgeon, J C Preston, chaplain, Charles L Hagar, adjutant, Clifford Hubbard, quartermaster, Henry J Northrup, brevet captain N Y V

Company A — Captain, Joseph R Seaman, brevet major U S V, first lieutenant, J W Treadway, brevet captain N Y V, from Company E

Company B — Captain, George H Campbell, brevet major N Y V·, from Company C, first lieutenant, James A Garrett, brevet captain N Y V, from Company A; second lieutenant, Merril Perry, brevet captain N Y V, from Company A

Company C — Captain, C W Wells, brevet major N Y V, from Company K, first lieutenant, L S Bryant; second lieutenant, N. H Arnold, from Company E

Company D — Captain, John W Angell, from Company E, second lieutenant, Philip V N McLean, from Company K

Company E — Captain, Henry S Graves, from Company I, first lieuten-

---

[1] Mr Watson acknowledges assistance in preparing this sketch to a series of articles in the Glens Falls *Republican*, to several officers of the regiment and to official documents In our work we must give credit for valuable aid to Captain Livingston, of Elizabethtown, and Colonel J L Cunningham, of Glens Falls

ant, George H Potter, from Company A, second lieutenant, William T Bidwell, late hospital steward

Company F — Captain, Robert W Livingstone, brevet major N Y V, first lieutenant, Daniel O'Connor, assistant hospital steward, second lieutenant, Charles A. Grace, from Company A

Company G — First lieutenant, James H Pitt, from Company H

Company H — Captain, David F Dobie, brevet major N Y V, first lieutenant, F Saunders

Company I — Captain, Martin V B Stetson, major N Y V, first lieutenant, Nelson J Gibbs, brevet captain N Y V, from Company F

Company K — Captain, John Brydon, brevet major N Y V, first lieutenant, John W Calkins, from Company K, second lieutenant, George Vaughan, from Company I

In this connection we deem it most important to append the following chronological record of the movements of the One Hundred and Eighteenth, as furnishing ready means of reference, which has been kindly transcribed for us by Colonel Cunningham —

September 1st, 1862, left Plattsburg   3d, in New York   4th, reached Baltimore   5th to 12th, at Camp Hall, Baltimore and Ohio Railroad, near Elkridge, Md   To October 23d, Camp Wool, near Relay House, Md   October 24th to February 12th, 1863, camp near Fort Ethan Allen, Virginia   February 12th to April 20th, Camp Adirondack, near Findley Hospital, north of the capitol, Washington   April 20th to 22d, en route to defense of Suffolk, Va   22d to 29th, Camp Nansemond, Suffolk defenses   29th to May 1st, camp near Fort McClellan, Suffolk defenses   May 1st to 14th, camp near Fort Union, Suffolk defenses   14th to June 18th, camp near Seaboard and Roanoke Railroad, Suffolk defenses   While in this camp the following expeditions were participated in   May 20th to 26th Blackwater raid and destruction of railroad, and June 12th to 17th reconnaissance toward Petersburg, Va   June 18th, 19th, en route for Yorktown, Va, by railroad and transport   19th to 26th, camp at Yorktown.   26th, en route by transport to White House, Va   26th, 27th, camp at White House   27th to July 1st, beyond Pamunky River in detachments as advance pickets on different roads   July 1st to 4th, on the march with General Dix's expedition to the north of Richmond, sometimes called the "Blackberry Raid"   4th, battle of South Anna   July 5th to 10th, on return march to Yorktown   10th to 13th, camp at Yorktown   13th to October 2d, in garrison at Fort Keyes, Gloucester Point, Va   2d, 3d, en route for Norfolk, Va, by transport   3d, in Camp Barnes, near Norfolk   11th, Companies E, G, I and K ordered to Portsmouth, Va   November 6th, Companies C and H joined the Portsmouth detachment, and A, B, D and F went into the entrenched camp about two miles from Norfolk   November 4th to December 12th, whole regiment quartered at Portsmouth   December 12th to

January 21st, 1864, in camp at Newport News, Va   21st to 23d, on march to Williamsburgh, Va   23d to February 6th, in camp near Fort Magruder, Williamsburgh   6th to 9th, on the expedition against Richmond, *via* Bottom's Bridge and the Chickahominy   9th to 13th, camp near Union Cemetery, Williamsburgh   13th to 15th, marched to Newport News, thence by transport and railroad to Getty's Station, Va   15th to March 12th, in camp near Getty's Station   While here, March 1st to 9th, on expedition to Deep Creek to resist raid of the enemy and pursuing raiders to Ballyhack, on the Dismal Swamp Canal   Part of the time while here, Companies B, H and K were stationed at Magnolia Station   March 12th to April 19th, camp at Bowers's Hill, Va , near Dismal Swamp   From this camp several expeditions and raids were made , the most important, April 13th, 14th, across the Nansemond, through the Chucatuck country   April 19th to 21st, *en route* by transport to Newport News, and march *via* Big Bethel to Yorktown, Va   21st to May 4th, in camp at Yorktown   May 4th to 6th, on transport up the James River   May 6th, landed at Bermuda Hundred, Va , and marched to near Point of Rocks on the Appomattox   7th, 8th, engaged with enemy near Richmond and Petersburg Pike and Railroad   9th, 10th, skirmishing and destroying railroad , battle of Swift Creek on 9th   11th, resting in entrenchment near Point of Rocks   12th to 14th, fighting and skirmishing along the Richmond and Petersburg Pike and in action at Warebolton Church and Proctor's Creek   15th, holding captured works near Drury's Bluff   16th, battle of Drury's Bluff   17th to 19th, slashing timber, entrenching, skirmishing and meeting attacks at various points along the Bermuda front   29th, 30th, on transports *via* James, York and Pamunkey Rivers to White House, Va   30th and June 1st, on march to Cold Harbor   June 1st to 11th, battle of Cold Harbor and in trenches and advanced rifle-pits there.   12th, marched to White House   13th, 14th, on transports back to Bermuda Hundred   15th, crossed the Appomattox , battle of Petersburg Heights , Major Pruyn killed   15th to August 27th, in and about the trenches and rifle-pits in the siege of Petersburg, variously stationed near corps headquarters, near Beasley House, among the pines, near Mortar Battery (called the "Petersburg Express"), in ravine, at the battle of the Mine, etc.   August 27th to September 28th, on Bermuda front, near south bank of the James   September 28th, marched at night across the James River and received new armament, the Spencer repeating rifle   29th, battle of Chapin's Farm and capture of Fort Harrison , brigade commander, General Burnham, killed   30th, battle of holding the fort against three charges of the enemy   30th to October 27th, in vicinity (and in entrenchments) of the captured fort, now called Fort Burnham.   October 27th, marched to Seven Pines   28th, battle of Second Fair Oaks   29th to November 3d, in vicinity of Fort Burnham, in trenches   November 3d, marched to Aikens's Landing, following orders which were revoked there   November 4th

to 7th, in reserve near Fort Burnham   7th, marched to Deep Bottom against
expected attack   8th to April 3d, 1865, in camp in vicinity of the New
Market Road at the front   April 3d, entered Richmond   4th to June 14th,
in camp near Manchester, Va   June 14th, down the James *en route* for home
17th, in New York city   19th, reached Plattsburg   June 16th, mustered
out

The foregoing pages of military history embrace the record of the services
of all the full companies that went from Warren county, but it falls far short
of comprehending all of the enlistments in the county, statistics of which, as
far as available, will be found a little further on   The county was most honorably represented by numerous enlistments, besides those already noted, in
the Ninety-first, Ninety-third, Thirtieth, One Hundred and Fifteenth, One
Hundred and Twenty-fifth, One Hundred and Twenty-sixth, One Hundred
and Fifty-sixth, One Hundred and Sixty-ninth and One Hundred and Ninety-second regiments, and the Second Veteran Cavalry, the Sixteenth Heavy
and the Twenty-third Light Artillery, while many other organizations contained scattering recruits from here   It is impossible at this time to give even
statistical details of all these enlistments, the records in existence not being
perfect by any means, and the space at our disposal being entirely inadequate
in which to cover so broad a ground   The Thirtieth regiment, organized at
Albany to serve for two years, was raised in the counties of Columbia, Duchess, Rensselaer, Saratoga, Washington and Warren, containing a considerable
number of recruits from the latter   It was mustered into the service June 1st,
1861, and was honorably engaged at Gainesville, Groveton, South Mountain,
Antietam and Fredericksburg   It was associated with the Twenty-second,
Twenty-fourth and Eighty-fourth regiments, forming the honorable "Iron
Brigade," a title which it won in the first advance upon Fredericksburg in the
spring of 1862   At the expiration of its term of service most of the men re-
enlisted for three years and were transferred to the Seventy-sixth New York
Regiment   Dr Francis L R Chapin, now of Glens Falls, was surgeon of this
regiment

The Second Veteran Cavalry — This organization was recruited largely
from the "Iron Brigade," to which allusion has been made, some three hundred or more of its members being from Warren county   The brave Captain
Duncan Cameron, who went out in the Twenty-second regiment and lost an
arm, raised a company mostly in Glens Falls, and William H Arlin, then of
Glens Falls, raised the greater part of another company   The regiment was
organized at Saratoga, to serve for three years, and was recruited in the counties of Saratoga, Schenectady, Montgomery, Clinton, Essex, Warren, Albany,
Rensselaer and Columbia   It was mustered into the service from August 16th,
to December 30th, 1863, and mustered out November 8th, 1865   It went out
commanded by Colonel Morgan H Chrysler, with Asa L Gurney, of Queens-

bury, as lieutenant-colonel, Duncan Cameron, of Glens Falls, as major, John S Fassett, of Glens Falls, who was instrumental in recruiting for the organization, was also commissioned major, and both he and Major Cameron were brevetted lieutenant-colonel, adjutants, Michael A Stearns, Henry W Heartt, and Robert Barber, the latter of Glens Falls Among the captains of this organization from Warren county were Smith J Gurney, of Queensbury, William H Arlin, of Glens Falls, Mason W Covell, of Queensbury, and Israel Litno, of Horicon Thomas Ledwick, Augustus Higby, Miles T Bliven and Mason W Covell, all of Glens Falls, held commissions as first lieutenant Thomas Ledwick, Enoch H Gurney, Albert W Thompson, Harrison P Kingsley, Henry M Bailey, W. Scott Whitney, and Albert Case held commissions as second lieutenants

This regiment performed noble service and bears an honorable record It made its first rendezvous after leaving the State, at Giesborough, Md, and thence went by transport to New Orleans in February, 1864, to join Banks's army of the Red River, Department of the Gulf It was next transferred to Brashear City and thence to Alexandria, La, being engaged in skirmishes and other active field service on the way It then accompanied General Banks's army to Pleasant Hill, participating in the engagement at that point, and others at Grande Cour and Cane River Crossing, the latter a severe engagement The regiment was then transferred to Canby's command and stationed at Morganzia, La, during the winter of 1864, its principal duty was in quelling guerilla raids and in opposition raiding on its own part After the somewhat noted Mississippi raid, it crossed the river at Baton Rouge and proceeded into Mississippi to distract the enemy from possible opposition to Sherman's march to the sea A detachment of the regiment was sent out fifty miles in advance to destroy the trestle work and tear up the track of the Mobile and Ohio railroad The enemy was encountered at McLeod's Mills, a short distance from the railroad, about a thousand strong; the force was charged, a number killed and several prisoners captured This event occurred December 10th, 1864, and the force was commanded by Colonel A L Gurney The detachment numbered two hundred and fifty Lieutenant Harrison P Kingsley was wounded, taken prisoner and afterward died from his injuries The raid was entirely successful The regiment was with Canby and participated honorably in the capture of Fort Blakeley and Mobile After these events it was ordered to Talladega, Ala, where it was mustered out

Statistics — The following valuable and interesting records were furnished to the Bureau of Military Statistics by Frederick A Johnson, of Glens Falls, county correspondent of the bureau, under date of January 1st, 1864 —

Up to the date named Warren county had furnished one thousand two hundred and twenty-five men for the war, of whom two hundred and seventy were enlisted for two years and the remainder for three years Of the latter three hundred and thirty men enlisted between July 1st, 1863, and January 1st, 1864 The regiments into which these men entered were as follows : — Twenty-second (two years), from Washington, Warren, Clinton, Essex and Rensselaer counties Colonel Walter Philips, jr , two entire companies from Warren county, viz . Company E, Captain George Clendon, jr , one hundred and forty men , Company F, Captain A W Holden, one hundred and fifty men

Seventy-seventh Regiment, chiefly from Saratoga county, known as the "Bemis Heights Regiment," in companies not known, twenty-five men

Ninety-third Regiment, from Washington, Warren, Essex and Clinton counties, three companies from Warren county· Company A, Captain Orville L. Colvin, one hundred men , Company H, Captain Hiram S. Wilson, one hundred men, Lieutenant P P Eldridge, twenty-five men.

One Hundred and Eighteenth Regiment, from Clinton, Essex, Warren and Franklin (chiefly from Sixteenth Senatorial District) Company A, Captain J. H Norris, one hundred and ten men (The reader has learned of the two other companies which went out in this regiment, but which do not appear in Mr Johnson's report)

One Hundred and Twenty-third Regiment, raised chiefly in the Twelfth Senatorial District Company A, Captain George B Warren, fifty men , Captain Coleman, fifty men

One Hundred and Fifty-third Regiment, Washington, Saratoga, Warren and Hamilton counties (Fifteenth Senatorial District) Company K, Captain F. J P Chitty, fifty men (The muster rolls and the enrollment papers furnished us by Colonel Chitty and herein given, report but thirty-three men)

One Hundred and Sixty-ninth Regiment, chiefly from Twelfth Senatorial District James Brice fifty men

In Independent Cavalry, William H Orton, fifty men enlisted since July 1st, 1863 For Second Veteran Cavalry, Company A, Captain Duncan Cameron, one hundred men , Company F, Captain J S. Fassett, one hundred men ; Company K, Captain William H. Arlin, one hundred men, and fifty in other companies

Supplementary to this report, we find a statement, evidently made up with care, which gave the number of volunteers from ten towns, which reported (exclusive of Caldwell, which did not report) as two hundred and twenty-eight to the first thirty-eight regiments organized in the State ; five hundred and twenty-three between the last of those regiments to which Warren county contributed and the president's call for six hundred thousand troops, and under that call, five hundred and seventy, making a total of one thousand four hundred and twenty-one men The same statement gives the amount of money raised in the country to promote enlistments as $30,082, and the amount raised by individual subscription as $15,575 The amount of money raised by Warren county for bounties to her soldiers, in the respective years 1861, 1862, 1863 and 1864, was as follows —

The distribution of the above totals among the towns of the county is shown in the following table —

	RATE	1862	RATE	1863	RATE	1864	TOTAL
Bolton	$ 50	$ 50 00	$300	$4,500 00	$644	$21,900 00	$26,450 00
Caldwell	53	106 00	250 } 350 }	3,900 00	1,000	18,000 00	22,006 00
Chester				800 00	400 } 800 }	48,039 22	48,839 22
Hague						8,293 56	8,293 56
Horicon					600 } 800 }	28,645 62	28,645 62
Johnsburgh	50	1,200 00	300	11,000 00		28,802 00	41,002 00
Luzerne		225 00		130 71		16,185 00	16,540 71
Queensbury	50 } 100 }	8,292 00	100 } 300 }	8,804 02	300 } 800 }	116,360 09	133,456 11
Stony Creek¹...							
Thurman	50	500 00	300	5,000 00	800	20,000 00	25,500 00
Warrensburgh ..	50	900 00	300		800	21,700 00	23,400 00
Total		$11,273 00		$34 134 73		$327,925 49	$373,333 22

From the foregoing pages, imperfect as the record undoubtedly is, the reader will have correctly inferred that the county of Warren was in no respect behind any other locality in her promptness of action, liberality in the expenditure of money, and patriotism in enlistments As the various calls of the president for troops in the closing years of the Rebellion were issued, and the State Legislature made it possible for counties to pay generous bounties for the more rapid filling of the different quotas, the Board of Supervisors of Warren county held numerous special meetings, the representatives of the several towns being fully authorized by their constituents, and bounties proportionate with those paid in other localities were promptly offered and enlistments were made as required to fill the quotas In the succeeding history of the town of Queensbury, the reader will find still further details of the action in that town throughout the Rebellion, as given in Dr Holden's valuable history

---

¹ No bounties paid

CHAPTER XIX.

COUNTY BUILDINGS, SOCIETIES, ETC.

Where Early Public Business was Transacted — The County Seat — The First County Courts — First Steps Towards Erecting County Buildings — The First Buildings — Changes in Court Terms — Burning of the County Buildings —'Erection of New Ones — Attempts to remove the County Seat — Reconstruction of Buildings — The County Almshouse — Warren County Agricultural Society.

COURT-HOUSE, Jail, and County Clerk's Office — From the earliest recorded date the public business of the county, the supervisors' meetings, sessions of courts, accumulation of title deeds and involuntary congregation of convicted criminals, have been respectively transacted, held and permitted to take place in the village of Caldwell in the town of the same name, at the head of Lake George   This was the county seat when the old county of Washington was divided and Warren county formed in 1813   An act passed March 12th of that year did not mention the place, but established a Court of Common Pleas and General Sessions to meet three times a year, the terms commencing as follows   on the second Tuesday in September, 1813, the third Tuesday of January, 1814, and the second Tuesday in May, 1814   These original courts, as well as the annual meetings of the supervisors, were held at the old Lake George Coffee House on the site of the present Lake House, until 1817.   On July 7th, 1815, a committee appointed by Governor Tompkins to find a suitable site for the erection of county buildings and composed of Salmon Child, Alexander Sheldon, and Charles E Dudley, reported as follows   "Having examined and explored said county do agree and determine that the most suitable and proper place for said buildings is in the town of Caldwell at the head of Lake George, on a piece of ground north of the Lake George Coffee House, lying between the highway and said lake, and within fifteen rods of a great white oak tree standing between said Coffee House and the church "

This was undoubtedly a description of the site of the present county buildings, and was the initial step towards the erection of the first buildings for county purposes   On the first of March, 1816, a law was passed providing that the county clerk's office was to be kept within one-half mile of the Lake George Coffee House, and the mileage to be computed from there, in this way attesting that whatever the progress of the building of the new structures, the public business was still transacted in said Coffee House   The court-house was certainly ready for use soon after, for the annual meeting of the Board of Supervisors for 1817 was held in the new court-house   It was not, however, entirely completed, for during that very session the supervisors passed a resolution that $1,050 be raised " to finish the court-house and gaol "   Notwithstanding these effectual measures, the need was felt of a safer and more commodious clerk's office In April, 1818, another act was passed directing the supervisors of Warren county to raise the sum of six hundred and fifty dollars (with five cents on the dollar for collector's fees), to build a fire-proof clerk's office on a part of the lot occupied by the court-house, and the clerk was directed to remove all the books, records and documents to the new office as soon as it was completed The necessary measures were at once adopted and the office ready for occupancy in the following year Everything began to take its proper place, and business became routine until April 8th, 1824, when the January term of the Court of Common Pleas and General Sessions was abolished, and two terms only appointed to be held, viz commencing respectively on the third Tuesday in April and the third Tuesday in October of each year This is evidence that the litigation of the new county did not assume the enormous proportions expected On January 24th, 1827, the Legislature further changed the time of holding the October term of court from the third to the first Tuesday of October in each year In 1828 this last act was repealed In 1829 the October term was abolished and the third Tuesday of each September constituted the opening day of the succeeding fall terms This was evidently the tentative period of the courts In April, 1833, the April terms were changed to the second Tuesday and the September terms to the second Tuesday of that month in each year, and additional terms established to commence the second Tuesday of February and the last Tuesday of June On January 23d, 1838, the summer terms of the Circuit Court and Court of Oyer and Terminer, which had theretofore been held on and after the third Monday in June, were changed to the third Tuesday in May, and on the 27th of the same month the beginning of the spring terms of the Court of Common Pleas and General Sessions was changed from the second to the third Tuesday in April In April, 1842, the December term of the Circuit Court and Court of Oyer and Terminer was abolished and an October term established in its place These perpetual alterations of terms of courts are undoubtedly more or less indicative of corresponding changes in the business of the county, an increase of the terms following an increase of the litigation and other court business, and *vice versa*

The county buildings having been finished by 1819, nothing was left excepting to keep them in repairs until the exigencies consequent upon the growth of the county, and the accumulation of business, should necessitate the construction of new and larger buildings in their place Accordingly, we find, in 1835, that three hundred dollars were ordered raised to repair the county clerk's office, and John Richards, Thomas Archibald and Timothy Bowen, of Caldwell, were appointed commissioners to superintend the work On the 26th day of October, 1843, the court-house and clerk's office were destroyed by fire The loss to the county was very great, although most of the records were saved In the following year the supervisors appointed Roswell Judson and John Tracy, of Chenango county, and F B Jewett, of Onondaga county, commissioners to locate the site for new buildings   They selected the old site, and the work of erecting the buildings was immediately begun, and completed in 1845   These structures served the purpose of their erection until 1862, when material alterations were made on the upper floor of the court-house   At a supervisors' meeting held in 1868 a committee consisting of George P Wait, F B Hubbell, and Alphonso Brown was appointed to procure plans and specifications for the building of cells, and otherwise repairing, enlarging and improving the court-house and jail   E Boyden & Son, of Worcester, Mass, who were then at work on the Fort William Henry Hotel, made two plans, No 1 providing for building an addition to the present court-house, in front, thirty by seventy feet, and two stories in height, and lengthening the court-room twelve feet, No 2 providing for building the same addition in front, raising the existing court-house another story, and using a portion of the court-room for cells, and the rest for the jailor's family, the court-room to be on the second floor, and the front room on the first floor to be left for the clerk's office   At an evening session of the same meeting a resolution was offered that the county treasurer be authorized to secure a loan of the comptroller for $11,900 for the purpose of repairing the court-house, jail and clerk's office, payments to be made in three equal annual installments, interest payable annually; that a committee of three be appointed to build according to plan No 2, and that proposals be advertised for, and contracts made with the lowest bidder at a consideration not exceeding $12,000   This was adopted, and Jerome Lapham, George P. Wait, and F B Hubbell were appointed the building committee   They were subsequently restricted to $20,000, and instructed to find the cost of widening the court-room and rear building eight feet

At this time an organized effort was made to remove the county seat from Caldwell to Glens Falls, and seemed to contain all the elements of success   A citizens' meeting was held in Glens Falls, December 28th, 1868, at which Judge Rosekrans offered a resolution in brief that Queensbury would furnish a site and build a good court-house, jail and clerk's office at a cost of not more than $50,000, as an inducement to the removal   It was adopted and Stephen Brown, Isaac Mott, Jerome Lapham and Aug Sherman were appointed to present the proposition to the supervisors   Following this proposition was a resolution adopted by the Board of Supervisors at an adjourned meeting, to the effect that in the estimation of the board the site should be changed and a petition signed by the whole board presented to the Legislature for an act authorizing the change   A final resolution was put before adjournment that no repairs be made at Caldwell   Notwithstanding all this passing of preliminary resolutions nothing further was done towards the proposed removal   In the following year a resolution was offered at a meeting of the supervisors that $18,000 be raised by tax to improve the buildings according to Boyden's plan

It was laid on the table   The matter reached the Legislature in 1872, when an act was passed authorizing the raising of $5,000, payable in five equal annual installments, to "build a court-house, jail and clerk's office" at Caldwell   It seems that nothing came of this   In 1877 the supervisors adopted a resolution which proved effectual, viz   That Thomas Cunningham, T N Thomas, and James C Eldridge be appointed to take into consideration the whole matter of enlarging, improving or remodeling the jail, enlarging the court-house, erecting a sheriff's house, and a building for lunatics at the poor-house   In their report this committee recommended that the jail, sheriff's departments and court-house be rebuilt, changed and enlarged as per the plan presented, that the additions be of brick   The estimated cost of the reconstruction was $10,000, and $500 for furniture and $500 for water   Thomas Fuller, of Caldwell, was their architect   The plan was changed to Boyden's plan No 2, and with this alteration the report was unanimously accepted   The last measure before the repairs which made the buildings what they now are, was a resolution adopted with but one dissenting voice, March 7th, 1877, providing that $11,000 be raised to rebuild the court-house, etc, the amount to be paid in two annual installments   The building committee was Thomas Cunningham, J M Coolidge and Jerome N Hubbell   The contract was to be let to the lowest bidder, the committee being endowed with discretionary powers   The work thenceforward rapidly progressed and by the following year the buildings were completed in their present form, with the exception of the clerk's office, which is, at the time of the writing of this work, in process of rebuilding of brick   These buildings are now well adapted to their various purposes and a credit to the county

Warren County Alms-house — This institution is located in the town of Warrensburgh, on the west bank of the Schroon River, the farm being partly in this town and partly in the town of Bolton, on the opposite side of the river The land was purchased by the county in the year 1826, and embraces two hundred acres, seventy of which were purchased of James Durham at a cost of $950, and one hundred and thirty of Halsey Rogers for $450, it is the latter named tract that is located in the town of Bolton   About forty acres are under cultivation at the present time, the remainder being pasture and woodland   Buildings sufficient for the limited number of inmates were erected directly after the purchase of the lands   By 1860 the old county-house was found by reason of its limited capacity to be wholly inadequate to meet the necessities of the county poor, and the Board of Supervisors passed a resolution providing in its terms that $2,500 be raised to "build a plain, substantial and convenient county-house, at or near the old house on said farm," to be paid by tax, and in five installments   David Aldrich, Daniel Stewart and E. B Miller were appointed the building committee   The present stone portion of the poor-house was thereupon erected by Peter Bewel at the cost estimated,

18

viz , $2,500   Before this addition was made the building was in a very dilap-idated condition   At that time the annual revenue from the farm was about $800, and the average number of inmates was fifty-four, who were supported at a weekly expense of ninety cents each   This arrangement sufficed for a few years, and in 1868 other measures were deemed necessary   In 1868 a committee was appointed by the supervisors to see about the purchase of a farm , but, although the committee reported in favor of the Jonathan Potter farm three miles north of Glens Falls, the purchase was not effected   Such abortive measures not being calculated to enlarge or render more commodious the then existing capacity of the buildings, the demand for some decisive action grew more and more imperative until 1877, when a committee was appointed to investigate and report upon the most feasible way of answering this need and making a place for lunatics   The report read to the effect that the most practicable method would be to remove the old wood building (66 by 30 feet) and rebuild in wood on the same site   This would effectuate the object of ac-commodating more persons and providing for lunatics   The estimated cost was $1,900   Operations were spun out to 1883–84   At that season the ad-dition was completed   The superintendent of the poor is Alexander T. Pasko   The present keeper is George Bowen (chosen 1885)   He was preceded by Sylvester Hays, and the consecutive predecessors of Hays in the inverse order of their service have been   James Fowden, T N Thomas, Elbridge G Hall. Asa Smith, Nathaniel Smith, —— Stebbins, James Collins, Aaron Varnum The report of the superintendent, A T Pasko, for the year ending October 31st, 1884, shows that the house and out-buildings are in good repair   The average number of inmates for the year was sixty-six and one-half, and the expense per week for each was about one dollar and fifty-four cents   He esti-mated that it would be necessary to raise the sum of $8,500 for the support of the poor for the year following his report   The keeper, Sylvester Hays, reported that there were sixty-three inmates remaining under the charge of the county, Octocer 31st, 1884

Warren County Agricultural Society — During the summer and fall of the year 1856 the prominent men of the county discussed the feasibility of organ-izing an agricultural society, and on the 27th of December of that year a number of those most interested met at the house of Charles Rockwell, in Luzerne, and took preliminary measures toward the formation of such a so-ciety.

Benjamin C Butler, presiding, referred in his remarks to the important farming interests of the town and county, and the advantages the proposed organization would be to the inhabitants   He therefore urged its immediate formation   The organization was perfected and during the meeting it was resolved, " that to make it a condition of membership to said society, such members pay one dollar annually to the treasurer, to be expended in accordance with the constitution and by-laws of said society "

Charles Rockwell, the chosen secretary, was appointed to draft a constitution, and Benjamin C Butler to arrange the order of business, to be submitted at the next meeting appointed to be held in the M E Church, Thursday, January 1st, 1857

The first day of the year proved an inauspicious one, and only a small number were in attendance, and an adjournment was voted to Monday, January 5th, 1857, at the house of G T Rockwell   At this meeting the following gentlemen became the pioneer members of the organization   Benjamin C Butler, Luzerne, Charles Rockwell, Hadley, William W Rockwell, Hiram J Rockwell, George J Rockwell, Jeremy Leavins, Morgan Burdick, Orison Craw, Calvin C Lewis, and John C Beach, all of Luzerne

At the next meeting, on January 27th, 1857, the following names were added to the foregoing   Reuben Wells, James Lawrence, Sylvanus C Scoville, Andrew J Chentree, John H Wagar, William H Wells, and Charles Schemerhorn

February 17th, 1857, at a meeting for the election of officers, the following were chosen   President, Benjamin C Butler, vice presidents, Wertel W Hicks, Caldwell, William Hotchkiss, Chester, Samuel Richards, Warrensburgh, Samuel Somerville, Johnsburgh, John Clendon, Queensbury, William Griffin, Thurman, corresponding secretary, Rev C H Skillman, recording secretary, A J Chentree, treasurer, William H Wells, directors, Reuben Wells, W W Rockwell, Charles Schemerhorn, John C Beach, Orison Dean, George T Rockwell

The organization now being fully completed, it remained to adopt necessary measures to fulfil the purpose of the institution   It was, therefore, at a meeting on the 6th of April, 1858,

Resolved, That the next annual fair be located in that town which shall first raise a sum of not less than one hundred and fifty dollars, from fees of life members or in other ways (not including the regular annual dues of members), to be expended at the discretion of the executive committee in preparing and inclosing the Fair Grounds, or for such other purposes as they may direct

From the beginning until 1861 the fairs and meetings were held at Luzerne, the town in which the movement first assumed definite shape   In 1862 an arrangement was made with George Brown, of French Mountain, by which grounds near his " Half-way House " were prepared for the use of the society, and the annual meetings were thereafter held at that place until 1868

As the farming interests of the county developed each year, and the society became richer and more numerous, the boundaries at French Mountain were found to be too narrow, and the Agricultural Society availed itself of the offer of the " Glens Falls Citizens' Association," at Glens Falls, of the use of their grounds   Since that time the yearly meetings have been held there   Necessary buildings have been constructed as occasion required, viz   the " Home

Industrial," "Agricultural," "Mechanics," and "Floral" Halls among these
In the summer of 1883 a grand stand was built which will seat about two
thousand persons

The "Glens Falls Park, ' as the grounds are called, contains twenty-eight
acres of land owned by a stock company   The Agricultural Society has the
use of the grounds one week each year for fair purposes, the conditions being
that the stock company receive the amount collected on the grounds for food
and drink.

Several thousand dollars have been expended by the Agricultural Society
in the construction of buildings and other improvements, and the citizens of
Glens Falls have contributed by subscription about $1,500 toward beautifying
and improving the grounds

Since the infancy of the organization the cash premiums paid have been
satisfactory   In 1857 the amount of cash premiums was $10 00, in 1862 they
were increased to $221 50, in 1869 to $657, and in 1873 to $1,492 50   In
1885 they were $1,008 50

Following is a list of the presidents of the society, together with the present
officers, and one or two incidental happenings connected with the history of
the society legislation, etc

1859 to 1861 inclusive, B C Butler, president; 1862, William H Rockwell, 1863, Quartis Curtiss, 1864, Abraham Wing, 1865–66, B C Butler,
1867 to 1872 inclusive, Henry Griffing, of Warrensburgh, 1873–74, D S
Haviland, of Queensbury; 1875, Jerome Lapham, Queensbury   At the annual
meeting held on February 2d, of this year, the secretary, A. Newton Locke,
of Glens Falls, presented his report in verse   It was most ingeniously executed   1876–77, Jerome Lapham, president; February 12th, 1878, the constitution was revised and amended to meet the requirements of legislation subsequent to 1876, Joseph Haviland was elected president and served three
years   1881 to 1884 inclusive, A B Abbott

On the 20th of January, 1884, in the parlors of the Rockwell House at
Glens Falls, the following officers were elected for the ensuing year   president, T S. Coolidge; first vice-president, W. E Spier; second, D S Haviland,
third, Edward Vaughn; fourth, E. W Goodman, fifth, Lewis W Hamlin,
sixth, Ed Harrigan, secretary, T. K Locke, treasurer, H S Crittenden
The present directors are   C H Green and J W Morgan for 1886, W F.
Bentley and W J Potter, 1878; H R Leavens and P. T Haviland, 1888.

CHAPTER XX

THE COUNTY PRESS [1]

Early Papers — The First Publication in the County — The Warren *Republican* and its Career — The *Lake George Watchman* — The Glens Falls *Observer* — The Warren County *Messenger* and its Immediate Descendants — The Glens Falls *Spectator* — The Glens Falls *Gazette* — The Glens Falls *Clarion* — Another *Republican* — The *Rechabite and Temperance Bugle* — Glens Falls *Free Press* — The Warrensburgh *Annual* — Glens Falls *Advertiser* — The American *Standard* — The Warren County *Whig* — The Present *Messenger* — Daily Press — The *Daily Times* — The *Morning Star*

WARREN COUNTY does not possess a long or exciting newspaper history The sparse population of the county at large, and with the exception of Glens Falls, the absence of any large villages, have operated against the establishment of public journals, and have been the prime cause of the premature decay and death of many papers from which their learned editors expected fame and fortune It is a very sterile and thinly populated district in this great country of ours where at least one man cannot be found who believes himself born to be a journalist, and nothing can ever dispel this prevalent belief but the hard lesson of experience Hence the number of newspapers that have been started in the county, insignificant as it may seem when compared with those of other larger fields, cannot be counted on one's fingers and toes, and those that have survived the struggle for existence have been and are a credit to the county and to their editors, and have wielded a vast influence in the communities, and no little power in the politics of the State

In the fall of 1812 John Cunningham, of New England, accompanied by Eben Patrick, a journeyman, and Eliezer Wheelock, an indented apprentice, removed from Windsor, Vermont, to Glens Falls They brought with them an ample supply of type and an old-fashioned press Cunningham being taken sick on the way was obliged to defer his coming until the following spring, but the others continued their journey and opened a job office in a building on the corner of Ridge and Glen streets In April, 1813, Cunningham came on with his family, and in the succeeding month issued a prospectus written by William Hay On Thursday, the 16th of June, 1813, the first number of the first paper issued in Warren county, was published under the name of *The Warren Republican* It was a journal but little larger than a "common spelling book," so folded as to make twelve pages to each number, and was nearly half filled with advertisements This sheet was devoted to the interests of the dominant party and existing administration, and until the close of the war was well stocked with the exciting reports of domestic and foreign battles and *coups d'états*, which have since become matters of history After

---

[1] Largely prepared from newspaper sketches published some years since by Dr A W Holden

the publication of a few numbers the office was removed to the rooms long afterwards occupied by George Vanderheyden, where it was continued until the completion of the " long building," erected in 1813 by John A Ferris The *Republican* office was soon after removed to one of the upper rooms of this building

The name of the *Warren Republican* was changed to that of the *Warren Patriot* in 1815 by Linus J Reynolds, who had purchased it from Cunningham The paper was then enlarged from its duodecimo size and double column to a demy sheet with four columns In about a year Reynolds sold back to Cunningham, who associated with himself Adonijah Emmons The office was removed to an upper room in the north end of Emmons's house Cunningham, though a man of refined tastes and brilliant parts, was addicted to intemperate habits, and his prosperity was not commensurate with his enterprise or deserts The paper, therefore, in 1819, fell into the hands of the Hon William Hay, who assumed its publication on the 5th of February On the 16th of the following April it reverted to Cunningham The journal lingered along until the following year, and then died

The second newspaper published in the county was unquestionably the *Lake George Watchman*, started about the year 1816 by Timothy Haskins, of Salem, Washington county, N Y, with the assistance of Oliver Lyons, formerly of the *Troy Budget* Haskins soon transferred his interest to Storer, and Storer to one Cushman, who conducted the paper until 1820, under the name of *The Guardian* At that time it was again sold, and the name changed to the *Warren Recorder* It was ably conducted, but met with indifferent success, and the interest was soon disposed of to William Broadwell, who continued its publication at Caldwell in 1822–24 It was then removed to Glens Falls, and with a view to increasing the circulation of the paper and extending its patronage, Broadwell sent post-riders through all the surrounding country The expense was greater than the return, and Broadwell becoming bankrupt, and the paper went over to the majority In 1826 the press and its appurtenances were bought by Edwin Galloway Lindsay On the first Monday in January, 1827, he issued the third newspaper in the county under the style of *The Glens Falls Observer* Lindsay being a thoroughly educated printer, edited the paper with extraordinary ability for two years, when the publication ceased

On the first of January, 1829, was issued the first number of the *Warren County Messenger*, conducted by Abial Smith, who had formerly been employed with Broadwell and Lindsay The paper had a good circulation and support In January, 1831, the name was changed from *Warren County Messenger* to *Warren Messenger*, and the heading enlarged The publication day was also changed from Thursday to Saturday, and in the following year to Friday In 1834 the paper changed hands again Zabina Ellis, who had commenced his apprenticeship with Adonijah Emmons in the office of the *Sandy Hill Sun*, in 1825, and worked as "jour" for Abial Smith on the *Messenger*, bought the property, and changed the name of the sheet to *Warren Messenger and Glens Falls Advertiser* In September of that year the office was removed "to the building heretofore occupied for that purpose, directly over C L Brown's fancy store, and a few doors north of the Glens Falls Hotel " The next change occurred in May, 1835, when the *Messenger and Advertiser* was discontinued, and the press and type were leased by H B Ten Eyck The new proprietor resumed the publication of the paper under the old name of the *Warren Messenger*, and continued at its head for two years When he ceased in May, 1837, the press and type reverted to Zabina Ellis, who immediately issued the first number of the *Messenger's* successor under the title of the *Glens Falls Spectator* In his salutatory which accompanied the first number of the new paper Mr Ellis said —

"In presenting to the public the first number of the *Glens Falls Spectator*, we feel it incumbent upon us to state at least the general course we shall pursue in its future publication Our political views are in accordance with those of the present administration [Van Buren] whose measures we shall support so far as we shall deem them consistent with the best interests of the community A portion of our columns will be devoted to literary, miscellaneous, foreign, domestic, agricultural, and such other objects as are calculated to disseminate general intelligence, and will at all times be open for communications upon such subjects as may be of public interest We shall on all occasions tender a proper respect to those opinions which may be at variance with our own A well conducted periodical has been long desired in this county, and whether ours shall merit this distinction we leave to the discerning public to decide To the people of this county we look for a generous patronage We have before been the recipients of their favor, and, we humbly trust, no omission of duty on our part will forfeit a continuance of them "

On the 16th of November, 1839, the last number of the *Glens Falls Spectator* was published In the same month the type, furniture and presses were purchased by George Cronkhite and Dr Bethuel Peck, with a view to the publication of an anti-administration paper On Wednesday, December 3d, 1839, was published the initial number of the *Glens Falls Gazette* The new editor was Warren Fox, a son-in-law of Mr Cronkhite The *Gazette* was immediately recognized as the organ of the Whig party, at that time largely in the majority in this town The paper was the same size as the *Spectator*, but, though more elaborate as to its editorial department, had deteriorated in typographical and mechanical beauty and arrangement Meanwhile Zabina Ellis, having purchased an entire new outfit of type, and new furniture and cases, and procured the use of the old Ramage press used in the publication of the *Warren Recorder*, made arrangements to start a competing journal, and on the 18th of December,

1839, published, in continuation the 28th No, 30th Vol of the *Glens Falls Spectator*   This continued to be the organ of the administration, and for the first time in the history of the county, two papers were published contemporaneously, and assumed that active partisan character which has ever since distinguished the press of this part of the State   About this time, too, sprang up a corps of newspaper correspondents that kept the papers constantly supplied with contributions and original matter   After about eighteen months of journalistic warfare, the interest of Mr Ellis in the *Spectator* was purchased by Winfield Scott Sherman, who formed copartnership relations with Warren Fox, and consolidated the two presses into one concern   The new paper was entitled the *Glens Falls Clarion*, and was ostensibly neutral in politics and religion   In December, 1841, Hon A N Cheney purchased Fox's interest, and the joint editorship thereafter was W S Sherwood and George W Cheney   In May, 1842, the irrepressible Zabina Ellis bought out Mr Sherwood and the firm name was Cheny & Ellis   After the lapse of a year Ellis retired from the firm, and left Cheney to conduct the paper alone until January 1, 1851

Meanwhile newspaper enterprise seemed to be increasing   In September, 1843, two brothers, Marcellus and Thomas J Strong, practical printers, bought out the press and type of the *Literary Pearl*, a sheet which had been started by Newton M Curtis, and which had died after the fitful fever of a short life, and issued a paper under the name of the *Glens Falls Republican*   This sheet, besides containing the usual literary and miscellaneous matter of a country paper, ardently espoused the principles of the Democratic party, which, being then in the ascendent in Warren county, gave it at once an extended and liberal patronage   The circulation soon reached five hundred greater than had previously been attained by any paper   During the year following, September 23d, 1846, Dr A W Holden, the author, subsequently, of a valuable history of the town of Queensbury, and a coadjuter in the preparation of this history, was associated with T J Strong in the publication of the *Republican*   During the political canvass of 1844 the *Clarion*, which had claimed to be a neutral paper, came out vigorously for the Whigs   A campaign sheet called *The Whig Reveille* was published at the *Clarion* office, and another called *The Hickory Leaf* at the office of the *Republican*

But political newspapers are not the only kind which constitute the history of the county   During the temperance agitation which began about 1845, the object of which was to procure the enactment of a law restricting the sale of intoxicating drinks to specific and manifestly necessary cases, a small semi-monthly publication was started at Glens Falls, devoted to the principles of the agitators, and laboring under the euphonious title of *The Rechabite and Temperance Bugle*   The date of the first issue was July 29th, 1847, and the names of its editors, for it had two, were Marcellus and Thomas J Strong.   The intensity of the interest in the movement may be inferred from the circulation (1,500) which this paper soon attained, and the evanescence of the same from the rapid falling off from this encouraging number until the enterprise was pronounced a failure In August, 1848, while its prosperity was most flattering, the issue was made weekly On the 29th of November, 1849, T. J Strong purchased the entire interest and led it through its feeble career to the close, in May, 1853 In 1845–46–47, an annual, or occasional paper, called *The Token*, was published by the pupils of the Glens Falls Academy

Zabina Ellis reappears in January, 1851, as the purchaser of the *Clarion* Installing his brother-in-law, William Rogers, in the editorial department, and changing the name of the paper to the *Glens Falls Free Press*, Ellis consecrated the regenerated sheet to the interests of the Whig party At the end of the year Rogers, who had conducted the editorial work with signal ability, was superseded by Ellis himself In 1854 the paper wheeled into the ranks of the new Know Nothing party, and remained its champion while the party remained a palpable fact

The next effort at attaining newspaper fame in Warren county was made in 1859 by John A Bentley, a young lawyer, who hired the press and type of the *Glens Falls Free Press*, and with Edwin Pike for publisher, issued No 1, Vol 1, of a politico-religious paper called the *Free Press* Four numbers of this paper were published, and Zabina Ellis resumed the management

The *Free Press* establishment burned in the great fire of 1864 Mr Ellis, having enlisted in the Twenty-second Regiment and been transferred to the Seventy-sixth, he was not at the time of the fire acting as its editor The paper was never resuscitated

On January 1st, 1847, the *Warrensburgh Annual* was first published at Saratoga Springs, under the editorial management of William B Farlin B C. Butler, the founder of the Warren County Agricultural Society, was the leading spirit of this new enterprise, but Dudley Farlin was the responsible editor It was short-lived

Returning to the *Republican*, we find that in May, 1853, William Tinsley and his two sons, William T, and James H Tinsley, purchased the effects of the office, and took possession in the following July The paper was then a six column sheet, but in September was enlarged by the addition of a column to a page, and a proportionate increase in length The interest of James H Tinsley was bought in April, 1855, and the firm name changed from William Tinsley & Sons to William Tinsley & Son In the succeeding March the establishment was sold out to Hillman A Hall and Meredith B Little for $1,100, who continued the publication under the firm style of Hall & Little During the next two years the proprietorship passed from Hall & Little to Harris & Hall, Little's interest being purchased by H M Harris Next it became Harris & Little, Hall's interest passing to the latter, and finally, Mr Harris became the sole editor and proprietor. He has ever since retained his interest and made his paper one of the leading Democratic journals of the State and a power in the party Mr Harris is a clear and incisive writer, and from his stock of broad information on general matters, gives his paper an unusually interesting character

H M Harris, proprietor of the *Republican*, was born in Schenectady on the 12th of May, 1833 He began his apprenticeship as a printer in the office of the Granville *Telegraph*, a weekly published at Granville, Washington county, in 1849; this paper was the especial organ of the Washington County Mutual Insurance Company, then doing the largest business of any insurance company in the world, issuing as many as one thousand policies a week He remained there two years and in January, 1851, came to Glens Falls and finished his apprenticeship on the Glens Falls *Free Press*, under Zabina Ellis The next year Mr Harris proceeded to New York for the purpose of perfecting himself in the art of job printing, and assisted in the publication of a political campaign paper in Brooklyn in the Scott and Pierce campaign Returning to Glens Falls after an absence of two years, he became foreman for Messrs Hall & Little, on the *Republican*, which he soon after purchased, as above narrated Under his administration of nearly thirty years the *Republican* has been remarkably successful, it was enlarged in June, 1873, to its present handsome proportions The establishment passed through the great fire of 1864, and did not lose an issue In an editorial in a number succeeding the fire, Mr Harris wrote as follows

"Like the *Messenger*, our material, presses, etc , were nearly all destroyed, but the next day after the fire an extra was issued by the *Republican* from the Sandy Hill *Herald* office, and two or three numbers succeeding were issued from the same office." The new material was at once purchased and the paper re-established as previous to the fire

This was an era of ephemeral journals In 1853 a single edition of 3,000 copies of a paper called the *Glens Falls Advertiser* was issued from the office of the *Free Press* for George C Mott & Co It was an advertising sheet containing some original literary and historical matter and an exposition of the business interests and resources of Glens Falls Jackson & Seymour, under their firm name, issued a similar paper in 1854 In October, 1853, the first number of a literary monthly called *The American Standard*, was issued from the *Republican* office. It was edited by Holdridge & Wait, but was not a pecuniary success, and died with the eighth number In 1855 the Hon A N Cheney purchased a new font of type and a press for James Kelley, who began the publication of the *Warren County Whig* The paper soon collapsed

On January 2d the following year the Rev A D Milne, who for some months had been engaged in the publication of a Baptist monthly called *The Star of Destiny*, purchased the *Whig* office and started the *Glens Falls Messenger* Mr Milne was of Scotch descent, and possessed more than ordinary ability as an effective author, preacher and writer. He wrote a temperance book which was published in an illustrated edition by Shepard & Co, New York, and had an unprecedented sale in this country and Europe, receiving high commendation from the press. He was an easy and vigorous writer, and started the *Messenger* as a paper "devoted to subjects of a moral and religious character, with the intention of having nothing to do with politics except so far as they may have a direct bearing upon the destinies of the great brotherhood of man." But being a strong temperance and anti-slavery advocate, the paper in a few months naturally drifted into the support of the Republican nominee for president, John C Fremont. Since that date the *Messenger* has been an unwavering Republican paper. In the issue dated April 8th, 1858, Mr Milne, in a valedictory, stated that "feeble health has admonished us for some time that our labors as a publisher and editor must cease," and introduced L A Arnold as the future editor, who had associated with him Norman Cole, to superintend the mechanical part of the business. Arnold acted as editor and Cole as publisher. It was announced Nov 25th, 1863, that Norman Cole had purchased Arnold's interest and assumed the duties of both publisher and editor. On the last day of May, 1864, the paper was greatly crippled and its office completely consumed in the great fire which swept so disastrously through the village. It immediately sprang from the ashes, but did not emerge from the dark war cloud, which at that time hung over the land, nor did it appear in its full proportions until the 16th of September, when its new cylinder press arrived and the arduous work of publishing and editing so large a country newspaper was fully resumed. Not an issue was lost, however, although the copies intervening between the last of May and the 16th of September were of a smaller cast and different form. A copy of what was called the "Phœnix Edition" of the *Messenger*, which is herein printed, explains itself, and illustrates the condition of the village after the fire of 1864, the difficulties which the publishers encountered in continuing the publication without the loss of an edition, and the style of the paper itself. The copy is as nearly as possible a *fac-simile* of the original. That issue was printed from type borrowed of the Sandy Hill *Herald* office, on a little hand press saved from the *Messenger* office during the fire, the work being done in the editor's corn-house.

Glen's Falls Messenger.

PHENIX EDITION.

Vol 9   GLEN'S FALLS, N Y, FRIDAY, JUNE 3, 1864   No 23.

A GREAT FIRE!—One of the most destructive fires that ever happened in any village in the Northern States, visited Glen's Falls on Thursday last, May 31st, consuming the entire business portion of the village and sweeping away the wealth and accumulations of years The central part of the place is one mass of ruins Only three stores remain All the printing offices were destroyed—we saved our little Card Press, but not enough type to set a card —The morning after the fire we received the following from the Editor of the Sandy Hill Herald, to whose kindness we are indebted for type and ink to print this paper —

"FRIEND COLE My office is at your disposal   E D BAKER"

The following account is mainly taken from the Republican extra, issued from the Herald office —

About 3 o'clock the flames were first seen bursting through the roof of the Glen's Falls Hotel kitchen The alarm was instantly given, Engines, Firemen and Citizens sprang as if by magic to the threatened spot, but owing to a high wind and scarcity of water the flames rapidly spread, in a few moments enveloping the main portion of the Hotel, and from thence to the Commercial Bank, Rich's Jewelry Store, the Centre House, Glen's Falls Bank, Weed & Sherman's store, law office of Davis and Harris, Keenan & Wing's office, Wing's dry goods store, Ranger's book store, Republican printing office, Harris' Boot

and Shoe store, Peat's tailoring establishment and the Mansion House

Above the Glen's Falls Hotel, the fire had spread to Smith & Ambler's, DeVol's and Hubbard's clothing stores, Sheldon's drug store, Fonda's, Lasher & Frehgh's, Rice's and Cowles & Co's dry goods stores, Sisson's drug store Messenger office, Leavens' store, Goodman's marble shop, Bolles' book store and Colvin's cabinet store Crossing Glen street the fire first attacked Brown & Byrne's grocery store, and Vanderheyden's building with Bassinger's jewelry store and Clements' restaurant, and from thence ran rapidly to Ide & Co's boot and shoe store, Farrington's liquor store, the fruit stand of Bevins, Smith's boot and shoe store, Tearse's grain store—finally arrested by almost superhuman exertion at the residence of Mr. Samuel Ranger

On the west side of Ridge street, the warehouse of Brown & Byrne, Norris' wagon shop, and two dwelling houses were soon enveloped in flames On the east side the fire communicated with D H Cowles & Co, Clendon's drug store, Conkey's daguerrean rooms, internal revenue office, gas office, dentist's office, etc, driving with demoniac fury to the Post Office, Ferriss' law office, Seaman & Richards' candy establishment, Mrs Brydon & Whiting's millinery store, Traphagan's harness shop, and from thence to the fine residence of Mr Ezra Benedict, attacking at the same time the dwellings of A W Flack and Mr. Ketchum

Arrested by the solid stone dwelling owned by Mrs William Peck, on Ridge street, the flames swept down on both sides of Warren st, destroying in their rapid course Vanderheyden's brick building, Kenworthy's hardware store, C & D Peck's grain store and lumber yard, DeLong and Co's hardware store, the dwellings of Harmon Peck, Doct N E Sheldon, Mrs Rogers, Methodist, Presbyterian and Universalist churches, Engine House, Fonda's Masonic Block, in which were Vermilha's meat market, Hine & Bartlett s grocery store, the Free Press office, Buswell's gun shop, Senate Masonic Lodge, &c Onward rushes the devouring element to Baldwin's cabinet shop, the dwellings of Mr Kellogg, Rev Mr Fennel and Abraham Wing, Starbuck & Sanford's wagon shop, the dwellings of Seth Sprague, L A Arnold, Mrs Ray, E T Johnson, Alvin Cool, M B Little, J Johnson, Doct Patterson, David Roberts—destroying everything, arrested again, the flames shoot across three buildings, one of which is the old Furnace, and alight upon the dwellings of Mrs Hawkins and Mrs Lapham, burning both to ruins

Down Glen street, on the east side, commencing at the clothing store of Albert Hall, the sea of fire hurls its red and hissing billows, engulfing the entire row to the open space half way down the hill, destroying Hall's clothing store, Mrs Williams' millinery shop, Starbuck's express office, Ferguson's liquor store, Keeffe & Briggs' store, Bush's meat market, Kelley's grocery, Numan's large hall, a new dry goods store just opened, Austin's paint shop, S Carpenter's saloon, Staples' meat market, Crossett's vegetable store, Potter's boot and shoe store, A N Cheney's residence, H Wing's store, Bennett's building, Wilmarth's cabinet shop, Farmer's Hotel, Mechanics' Place, Burdick's planing

mill, Geo Cronkhite's and L B Barnes' dwellings, Rappe's dwelling and grocery.

At this time, about 6 o'clock P M , the centre of the village for blocks was one sea of livid flames. The hurrying to and fro of excited and almost despairing people, men, women and children, the crackling, seething fire, the wild attempts to save property, the hoarse commands of the firemen, mingled with the sound of falling buildings, formed a picture which we hope never to look upon again The main losses, as near as can be estimated, naming each sufferer as far as it is possible at the early hour of going to press, are as follows

Exchange Building, goods and building, loss $25,000—insured for $8,000

Charles Rice, store and goods, $30,000 —insured 10,000

Geo W Sisson, store and goods, 30,-000—insured 12,000

Messenger office, printing material and stock, over 2,000—insured 1,000

Lasher & Freligh, store and goods, 20,-000—insured 10,000

W A Fonda, house, store and goods, 20,000—insured 5,000.

N E Sheldon, store, goods and house, 10,000—insured 6,000

Hawley's store, goods and house, $3,-000—insured 1,000

Mansion House and the Glen's Falls Hotel, 20,000—insured 15,000

M C Rich, 3,000 to 4,000—insured 1,000

Commercial Bank, 4,000—insured 2,000

Rosekrans building and contents, 4,000 —no insurance

Glen's Falls Bank Building, 6,000—insured 4,000

Ezra Benedict, store and house, 8,000 —insured 2,000

Republican office, printing material, 1,-000—insured 800

H M Harris, boot and shoe store, 600 —no insurance

A N Cheney, house and contents and store, 8,000—insured 6,000

Ira Green, 500—no insurance

Doct M R Peck, store and goods, 3,-000—insured 2,300.

A E Smith, store and goods, 3,000— insured 1,500

J K Farrington, store and goods, 5,000 —insured 3,000

Geo Bassinger, 1,500—insured 1,900
Brown & Byrne, 40,000—insured 8,000
J H Norris, 6,000—insured 2,000
W H Gayger, 2,000—insured 1,500
E B Richards, 2,000—insured 1,500
Miss Mott, 1,000—insured 800
Mrs Martin, 1,500—no insurance
J T B Traphagen, 2,000—ins 2,000
A W Flack, 1,000—no insurance
Seaman & Richards, 1,009—no ins
D H Cowles & Co , 40000—ins 11,000
Vanderheyden, 5,000—insured 2,500
S Benedict, 3,000—insured 1,000
J L Kenworthy, 4,000—insured 2 800
Wm Cronkhite, 2,000—no insurance
C & D Peck, 20,000—insured 3,000
H Peck and DeLong & Son, 25,000—insured 6,000
M E Church, 5,000—no insurance
Firemen's Hall, 2,000—no insurance
E H Rosekrans, 1,000—no insurance
Universalist Church, 3,000—no ins
Albert Hall, 5,000—insured 2,000
John Ferguson, 1,000—fully insured
Keeffe & Briggs, 2,000—insured 5,000
Mr Benedict 1,000—insured 200
Mrs Grace, 500—no insurance
J B Cool, 500—fully insured
D Peck, 1,000—insured 600
Mr Staples, 2,000—insured 1,000
Wm Crosoett, 1,500—no insurance
Bennett's building, 4,000—ins 3,000
M L Wilmarth, 4,000—insured 2,000
Farmer's Hotel, 2,000—insured 1,000
Mechanics' Place, 2,000—insured 1,000
Wm Rappe, 1,500—insured 500
Masonic Block, 20,000—insured 7,000
Numan's Hall, 3,000—insured 1,000
Widow Peck, 2,000—no insurance
Presbyterian Church, 12,000—ins 5,000
Allen Burdick, 5,000—no insurance
A J Fennel, 2,000—insured 1,000
Abraham Wing, 8,000—no insurance
Starbuck & Sanford, 2,000—ins 1,000
C B. Sprague, 2,000—insured 1,500
Miss Ray, 1,500—insured 800
D Norris, 1,500—insured 600
Miss Mary Hunt, 2,000—insured 1,200
J Johnson, 1,000—no insurance
M B Little, 2,200—insured 2,000
Doct Patterson, 1,500—insured 1,200
Mrs Hawkins, 1,000—no insurance
Mrs Lapham, 1,000—no insurance

The entire loss will reach nearly to one million dollars

—The insurance is being promptly paid by the different companies, their agents, arriving here soon after the fire, are rapidly settling claims The loss is as follows

Home, New York	$65,000
Hartford, Conn	40,000
City, Albany	16,500
Dividend Mutual, Glen's Falls	22,000
Glens Falls Co	3,000
City Hartford, Ct	5,000
Massasoit, Springfield, Mass	5 900
Liverpool and London	5,000
Phœnix, Brooklyn	2,200
Security, New York	8,300
North American, Hartford	1,400

The total loss on buildings has been footed up to $260,000, and on merchandise at $300,000 About one hundred and twelve buildings were burned, including some sixty stores, &c

☞ At an adjourned meeting of the citizens of this village held this afternoon a committee of five was appointed to make equitable distribution among the sufferers by the late disastrous fire, of such contributions as have been and may be made for their relief That committee consists of Col A W Morgan, Jerome Lapham, Stephen L Goodman, Walter A Faxon and Enoch H Rosekrans A further committee of nine, of which A Sherman is chairman, was appointed to consult with property owners in regard to the time and mode of rebuilding upon the burnt district, and endeavor to secure a uniform style of building, as far as practicable, which shall be both substantial and ornamental

The citizens of this place are very grateful to the Firemen of Sandy Hill and Fort Edward who came as it were on the wings of the wind to our assistance, and who with our own "Defiance" and "Cataract," nobly fought the devouring element Had it not been for their aid, much greater would have been the ruin

☞ The citizens of Troy have contributed and sent up over eighteen hundred dollars towards relieving the greatest sufferers by the fire, with word that "more will be sent" The recipients will be exceedingly grateful to the donors

At the time the fire broke out, we were printing the first side of the Messenger, which was all destroyed, with press, and nearly everything else in the office

—The Messenger office was insured for $1,000, which has been promptly paid There was a mortgage on the office of $500, after paying this with interest, we have left, out of the insurance, only four hundred and sixty-eight dollars and thirty-three cents Those who are indebted to the Messenger will see that we need all that is our due, and we trust they will promptly respond, that we may be enabled to procure material for printing the Messenger on a larger sheet than this With our next issue we propose to send bills to all subscribers in arrears, and all others who feel disposed to aid us in getting a new press, may pay in advance, for as long a period as they can afford, and they will be credited with the amount and the paper sent the full time—or paid in advertising—if it be for a thousand years, Providence permitting Money may safely be sent by mail

—Already "shanties ' are being built along the streets, and quite a number of our dealers have resumed business The funds and valuables in the Banks came out all right The Commercial Bank is now located in the insurance building, to which the Internal Revenue Collector's office has also been removed The Glen's Falls Bank is in the brick dwelling house nearly opposite the American Hotel The post office occupies the place formerly known as Judge Hay's office, on Park St G W Sisson's drug store is opposite the American Hotel, on Bay St The MESSENGER office is now operating in a cornhouse, one mile north of the old place, on the Lake George road

☞ All property taken from the fire, the owners of which have not been found, should be left at the new stone church on Glen St, where it may be identified

Our files of the Messenger were burned, and we will be thankful for back numbers returned to us

—Hardly room enough this week for the letter just received from the 118th Regiment

—Gen Grant is pounding away at the very doors of Richmond

MARRIED – In Greenwich, May 23d, by Rev Mr Abbott, Mr Wesley Allen, of this village, to Miss Abbie White, of Sandy Hill

SUPREME COURT—The Dividend Mutual Insurance Company against Albert N Cheney, George W Cheney and Lucinda Cheney, his wife

Notice is hereby given that in pursuance and by virtue of a judgment of foreclosure and sale rendered in the above entitled action on the 22d day of April, 1863, the judgment roll whereof was filed and the judgment entered in the Warren County Clerk's office on the 10th day of May, 1864, I shall expose for sale and sell at public auction to the highest bidder, as the law directs, at the Glen's Falls Hotel in Glen's Falls, Warren County, New York, on the 25th day of June, 1864, at ten o'clock A M, the premises and property described in said judgment as follows

All that certain piece or parcel of land situate lying and being in the village of Glen s Falls aforesaid and bounded as follows to wit Beginning in the center of the Plank Road leading from Glen s Falls to Lake George and at the southwesterly corner of Orville Cronkhite's land" [now owned by the Glen s Falls Insurance Company], ' and running thence north sixty-six degrees east along said Cronkhite's land eleven chains and eighty-three links to James Sisson s land, thence south along said Sisson s land two chains and sixty-one links, thence south sixty-six degrees west ten chains and eighteen links to the centre of said Plank Road, thence north twenty-nine degrees west along the centre of said Plank Road two chains and thirty-seven links to the place of beginning, be the same more or less "

Dated May 10th, 1864
D V BROWN, Sheriff
By WM COSGROVE, Deputy
S BROWN, Plff's Att'y, Glen's Falls, N Y

EXECUTORS' NOTICE —Notice is hereby given to all persons having claims against Benjamin S Thompson, late of the town of Chester in the County of Warren, deceased, that they are required to exhibit the same with the vouchers thereof to the subscribers, Henry Thompson, one of the executors of the last will and testament of said deceased, at his dwelling-house in said town of Chester, on or before the 4th day of September next

Dated March 3d, 1864
HENRY THOMPSON,
ISAAC TOWSLEY,
n11m6   Executors

During the following ten years it prospered so well that it was encouraged to celebrate the 4th of July, 1873, by still another enlargement of an additional column on each page. On the 2d of July, 1875, it celebrated the advent of the grand water system of this village by first running its presses by hydraulic power On the 1st day of February, 1882, Mr Cole associated with himself F A Bullard, the firm name being Norman Cole & Co. — a relation and style which still exists On the 7th of July, 1882, the *Messenger* was again enlarged to thirty-six columns In an editorial of that issue, after a succinct retrospect, the purpose of the paper is set forth in the following language —

" We shall aim to make the *Messenger* the most reliable and the best newspaper in the county, by constantly guarding its columns and keeping out false reports and sensational and degrading matter that floods upon the press from every direction, and by sifting out and printing that which is good and true We shall endeavor to so condense the news as to give a faithful weekly summary of the important events of the world, paying especial attention to home matters and all that interests or affects our town, county, state or nation " It is only fair to say that the purpose of the publication as above expressed has been faithfully adhered to, and is the leading characteristic of the paper today

Norman Cole, at present at the head of the firm publishing the *Messenger*, was born in the town of Queensbury near Glens Falls, June 1st, 1835 His father, Levi Cole, and his grandfather Isaac, were both blacksmiths and remembered as noted for good honest work. When Norman was eight years old his father died, leaving a widow with four children of whom Norman was the oldest The limited means left was soon absorbed, except the homestead of ten or twelve acres of land, on which he had to labor o his utmost for the support of the family Three months of schooling in the winter of each of several years constituted the public educational advantages of the boy , but he studied, read and thought a good deal outside of his school days, which, with the careful and intelligent training of his mother, gave him a solid foundation of character as well as the basis of a fair education It was contemplated finally that Norman should learn a trade, but his mother could not entertain the thought of his leaving home ; neither did he incline towards any of the various occupations mentioned, until printing was mentioned, which, as he now expresses it, came to him like an inspiration, and he resolved to learn that profession He did not begin the attractive handiwork until the December following his twentieth birthday, but he was armed with a wonderful determination to master it, and of course success awaited him. He has risen to an honorable position in the great field of journalism and can look back upon his life, as far as it has passed, as one well spent

On the 17th of January, 1878, the Warrensburgh *News* was started by G

A Morris and Son (A H. Morris) In January, 1881, the establishment was purchased by L C Dickinson, who is present editor and proprietor, with C E. Cole as assistant It is a handsome country journal of eight pages, six columns to the page and independent It is very ably conducted.

The thrift and energy of the village of Glens Falls is particularly manifested by the fact that although as yet but a village, it possesses two daily newspapers It is a sign of enterprise and prosperity, and of that spirit which is the most distinguishing characteristic of modern times, especially in the United States It is the spirit, become a habit, with which a business or professional man, or an artisan sits down to his breakfast, paper in hand, and, learning of the movements of foreign armies, of the dissensions in the English House of Commons or the German Reichstag, and of the measures proposed and adopted or rejected by the Legislature of his own State and country, as well as the rumors of gossip and the reports of crime and casualties the world over, finds argument for the reflections of a day The daily press disseminates intelligence, while the weekly press and more deliberate publications give utterance to the prophecies which wise and experienced men deduce from the significant happenings of the times

The *Glens Falls Daily Times*, a handsome, eight-column sheet, was started June 21st, 1879 It was at the beginning but a 16x10 paper, printed on a quarto-medium Gordon press, one side at a time· The first proprietor was A B Colvin On January 1st, 1883, John H Burnham bought a half interest in the business and has been associated with Mr Colvin ever since The *Glens Falls Weekly Times* was first published in the spring of 1880, by Mr Colvin The editorial rooms are situated in the Times building in Glen street The paper is ably edited both with reference to its mechanical appearance and the editorial expressions of its proprietors Five libel suits have been brought against it, none of which terminated in a judgment for the plaintiff, a fact which is most significant as revealing at once the fearless aggressiveness and fidelity to truth and justice of those who are responsible for the utterances of the paper

The Morning Star, published daily excepting Sundays, was started on the 2d day of April, 1883, by its present proprietors, J C Mahoney, T. J Lord, B. W Sprague and A L McMullen, who compose the Star Publishing Company. In August, 1883, they began the issue of their weekly papers. The office is on the corner of Glen and Ridge streets The paper is a world of methodical mechanical arrangement and neatness, and contains always a full and complete account of the local, State, national and foreign news of the day Its editorial expressions are judicious and impartial These qualities conspire to increase its circulation and value as an advertising medium, and augment the encouraging prosperity of the enterprise

19

CHAPTER XXI

INTERNAL IMPROVEMENTS.

Reminiscences — Early Lumber Operations — Incipient Commercial Operations — The Canal and Feeder — Early Railroad Agitation — The Warren County Railroad Company — Navigation Projects — Other Railroad Enterprises — The Railroad Between Fort Edward and Glens Falls

THE early history of Warren county affords a striking example of the impossibility of thickly populating a region not easily traversable by commerce of some kind or other   Prior to the construction of the Champlain Canal and the opening of the Glens Falls Feeder, and of course long prior to the laying of a railroad track in the county, the time and means and labor expended in the transportation of exports and imports rendered the most comfortable life a series of anxieties and hardships which can scarcely be conceived by the more luxurious children of these latter days   The pioneers who immigrated hither, mostly from New England, at the beginning of the present century, would scarcely have been willing to suffer the toil, exposure and privation necessarily incident to the life they led, had they not been allured by the hope, often delusive, of amassing a fortune   This came, not for ease, but profit   *Otium cum dignitate* was a motto which if they ever heard they completely ignored and contemned   Almost without exception their ambition, the inducement to their coming, was to fell the splendid forests which mantled the mountain and darkened the depths of the valleys, and drive the logs down the Schroon and Hudson Rivers to the mills for the lumber markets of Albany and Troy. The most prominent, probably, of these early lumbermen was Abraham Wing The excellent water power at Glens Falls occasioned the building of huge sawmills at that place, more especially after the opening of the canal and feeder In 1860 one mill at the State dam had twelve gates and two hundred and fifty saws   Days and often weeks were consumed in getting this lumber and the other products of the county to their destination, and in bringing back the goods which necessity compelled the people to import   The primitive road was a scarcely discernible trail whose route was indicated by blazed trees , the primitive bridge was simply two logs thrown parallel across a stream, connected by a roadway of loose planks , the primitive vessel was a scow , and the primitive railway a horse   Of course the lapse of a few years witnessed a material amelioration of this condition of things   But the roads which, outside of the lumber interest, were the most important media of communication were indifferent until the plank road era between 1840 and 1850   Before this, however, the Champlain Canal had been opened (1823), an event which gave the lumber business of the entire region a new and lasting impetus

The Glens Falls Feeder — In about this same year of 1823 the Glens Falls Feeder, that important tributary of the Champlain Canal, was surveyed and commerce of all kinds began to grow more brisk   In 1824 the feeder was dug through, but was not made navigable to canal boats until its final completion in 1832   It extends a distance of seven miles from a point in the Champlain Canal at a summit level, a mile and a half northeast of Fort Edward to a point three miles above Glens Falls, where there is a State Dam across the Hudson seven hundred and seventy feet long and twelve feet high   When it was first built it was not wide enough for boats to pass except at the turn outs dug here and there along the channel   The opening of this feeder to boats is a most important event in the commercial history of the county   Caldwell had theretofore been the most thriving village in the county, but the commercial avenues which had formerly converged at that village were diverted to Glens Falls   From that time to the present the lumber business has been the most extensive interest of the county   The feeder was further enlarged about 1845 [1]

Navigation Projects —That the inhabitants of this northern region understood the necessity of opening thoroughfares of commerce between the natural avenues afforded by the lakes and rivers is manifested by the organization of navigation companies with projects more or less chimerical   While the pioneers of Warren county were struggling for existence in the wilderness, men all about them, impelled by motives of self-interest, were forming into companies for the purpose of building canals and dams and of improving the navigation of rivers and lakes   Plans for improving the navigation of the Mohawk River to the west were prepared as early as 1725, though nothing was done to this end till March 30th, 1792, when the " Western Inland Navigation Company " was incorporated, with powers to improve the channel and build canals and locks to Lake Ontario and Seneca Lake   At the same time the "Northern Inland Navigation Company " was formed, its object being to connect the waters of the Hudson River with Lake Champlain, work since accomplished by the Champlain Canal   This company made some progress, and began work to a limited extent, but failed for want of funds to carry out its plans

Railroads — Subsequent to the mania for building canals, when the fever had subsided, the county suffered in common with the rest of the civilized world from the perpetual agitation of schemes for the construction of railroads   There had been, it is true, some agitation of the kind as early as 1832   On April 17th of that year the " Warren County Railroad Company " was incorporated   The proposed route was to extend from the Champlain Feeder, at or near the village of Glens Falls, to the village of Caldwell, with the privilege of prolonging the road to the town of Warrensburgh

The commissioners were as follows   John Baird, Dudley Farlin, John

---

[1] The success of this enterprise was due largely to the efforts of William McDonald in the Legislature

Osborn, Pelatiah Richards, William McDonald, Alonzo W Morgan, Duncan McMartin, Halsey Rogers, Robert Gilchrist, William Caldwell, Jesse Buell, Peter Smith, Jerad H Coster, James B Murray, Russel H Nevins, and John C. Stevens But this scheme died a natural and an early death.

Several years previous to 1860 a company called the Sackett's Harbor and Saratoga Railroad Company projected a scheme for building a railroad through the county along the west side of the Hudson The Lake Ontario and Hudson River Railroad Company subsequently (before 1860) laid out the road and did a part of the grading, but were forced at last to abandon the project

Many of the inhabitants of Warren county were much elated about 1860–63 by the prospect of a railroad proposed to be built from Saratoga or Glens Falls northward across Warren and Essex counties to Plattsburg, and, by connections, to the St Lawrence The agitation of this enterprise, interrupted by the War of the Rebellion, was renewed at the close of that conflict, and for quite a period its consummation was confidently predicted Meetings were held and a partial survey of the route was made The rock upon which the enterprise finally foundered was the refusal of those controlling the great Moriah iron interests of Essex county to co-operate with other towns in any proposed railroad, the line of which did not extend along the western shores of the lake This enterprise owed its conception and incipient progress largely to T J Durand, who subsequently became the controlling power in the Adirondack Railroad Company, the line of which now ends at North Creek in this county, with a prospect of reaching up into Essex county sometime in the future A line of stages formerly ran over portions of this proposed route from Schroon Lake to Keeseville

The Adirondack Railway Company is really the offspring of a company formed in August, 1860, under the name of the "Adirondack Estate and Railroad Company," although a movement had years before been organized to construct a road between Saratoga Springs and Sackett's Harbor, and proved abortive as before stated The Adirondack Estate and Railroad Company controlled and held under contracts for the purchase of 800,000 acres of land in the northern wilderness of New York English capitalists were here in 1861 with funds to promote the opening of this region, but were precluded from consummating their project by the breaking out of the Civil War Soon after this legal proceedings were instituted, by virtue of which all the lands and other effects of the company went into the hands of Albert N Cheney Thomas C Durant then purchased the entire property of Mr Cheney, and under an act of the Legislature passed April 27th, 1863 (Chap. 236), formed the Adirondack Railway Company. Under that law the new company became possessed of all the rights, privileges and franchises of the old company The organization was completed by the signing of articles of association on October 15th, 1863 Amended articles, defining the present route of the road, were filed March 1st, 1871   The grading which had been barely begun by the old company was then finished, and the sixty miles of track now used was at once laid

The present officers of the company are as follows   President, Thomas C. Durant, secretary, William M Durant, general superintendent, C E Durkee; roadmaster, Charles R Eastman [1]

The railroad now composing one of the branches of the Delaware and Hudson Canal Company's lines was opened from Fort Edward to Glens Falls on the 4th day of July, 1869   It was arranged to be built by Glens Falls, Sandy Hill and Fort Edward   The cost of construction was to be $140,000, of which Glens Falls was to pay $100,000, Sandy Hill $25,000 and Fort Edward $15,000   The latter sum was never paid   The first president was John Keenan, and the first Board of Directors Jerome Lapham, Jeremiah Finch, Charles Hughes and Orson Richards   The opening of the road was a festive occasion A train of eleven coaches made eleven trips from Fort Edward to Glens Falls, and were crowded to their utmost capacity with free passengers, many of whom, it is said, took their lunches and road all day   In a short time after it was opened the Rensselaer and Saratoga Railroad Company took it from the Board of Directors, whose plans of running the road were frustrated by want of funds, and agreed to start and operate it   George H Cramer then became president.   The Rensselaer and Saratoga Company kept the road but two or three years, and then leased it to the Delaware and Hudson Canal Company   The road was extended to Caldwell in 1881, and the extended portion opened for business in June of the ensuing year   Fort Edward suffered materially by the opening of the road, while Glens Falls, from the same cause, the diversion of commerce, was greatly benefited

It was in the year 1869, also, that a great scheme was inaugurated for the construction of a road from Oswego, N Y, to Portland, Me, to pass through Warren county   The inhabitants of this county were greatly interested in the project   A railroad conference was held at Saratoga for a number of days, and was largely attended from all the interested sections   For want of vitality, means and harmony, the plan was abandoned and the road has never been built

---

[1] The information for the above sketch was kindly furnished by George F Fowler, esq, of Saratoga Springs, the attorney for the company

CHAPTER XXII

THE BENCH AND BAR OF WARREN COUNTY [1]

WARREN county was organized in 1813 from a portion of Washington county

The first Court of General Sessions of the Peace for the county was held in the Lake George Coffee House at Caldwell on the 2d Tuesday of September, 1813   Court organized as follows   William Robards, esq , presided as first judge , Michael Harris, judge ; David Bockes and Jeremiah Russell, esqs , justices of the peace

The following grand jurors appeared and were sworn, to wit : —

Halsey Rogers, foreman, Dilivan Gardner, John Darby, Roger Haviland, Thomas Tilford, John H Hitchcock, Benjamin Wing, jr , Elisha Folger, John S St John, Benjamin Barret, Edward Cornwell, John Lindsey, David Alden, Luther Stebbins, James Ware, Nathan Goodman, Obadiah Knapp, James L Throman, Herman Hoffman, James Archibald, Solyman B Fox, Thomas M Wright

The grand jury presented to the court seven indictments, four for assault and battery, one for assault and battery with intent to murder, and two for forgery

Mr Russell having been appointed district attorney, acted as such at this court   The first criminal action tried in the county was The People vs John Harrison for an assault and battery upon the body of Isaac Farr, before the following grand jurors : Nehemiah Wing, David Havilan, Jonathan Pitcher, Obadiah Mead, Frederick Hubbell, Nathanial Tripp, Orson Mead, O Taylor, Reuben Smith, Solomon Moon, Reuben Green, Isaac Washburn

David Sisson and Andrew Parsons were sworn as witnesses on the part of the people, and Isaac Farr was sworn as a witness on the part of the defendant

The jury, after being charged by Judge Robards, retired and rendered a verdict against the defendant of guilty of the assault and battery as charged in the indictment

Whereupon, on motion of Mr Russell, district attorney, the Court ordered " that the said John Harris for the offense aforesaid be imprisoned in the gaol of the county of Washington in close confinement for the space of two months "

At this court a second indictment against the same party for an assault and battery on the body of Daniel Sisson was tried and the defendant found guilty , and this entry on the records of the court made · " *Ordered the like sentence as in the last preceding cause* "

---

[1] Prepared by Hon Isaac Mott, of Glens Falls

The first Court of Common Pleas held in the county of Warren was held at the Lake George Coffee House in the town of Caldwell on the second Tuesday of May, 1813, and organized as follows —

William Robards, esq, first judge, Kitchel Bishop, Michael Harris, esqs, judges, Jeremiah Russell, esq, assistant justice, John Beebe, clerk; William Peffer, appointed crier

The following named persons were on motion admitted as attorneys and counselors, to wit —

Robert Wilkinson, Roswell Weston, Asahel Clark, Henry C Martindale, Lawrence T Vankleek, Royal Leavens, William Hay, jr, Horatio Buell and Christian Sacknder

The following orders were entered —

" *Ordered*, That the rules of the Court of Common Pleas of the County of Washington as those adopted the 12th day of March, 1808, be, and they are hereby adopted as the rules of this court in all cases where they will consistently apply

" *Ordered*, That every attorney of this court residing without the county (except attorneys residing in Sandy Hill in the county of Washington), shall appoint an agent who shall be an attorney of this court and who shall reside at Queensbury or Caldwell, which appointment shall be in writing signed by the attorney and filed in the clerk's office, and the clerk shall constantly have the names of the several agents of the respective attorneys appointing them, and the latter in alphabetical order, entered on a list to be kept in his office, and all notices and pleadings served on or delivered to such agent shall be good service upon the attorney on record, and in default of such appointment (except as aforesaid), the opposite attorney may proceed as in case when no attorney is employed "

Whereupon the court adjourned

At a Court of Common Pleas held at the Lake George Coffee House in the town of Caldwell on the 2d Tuesday of September, 1813, by William Robards, first judge, Michael Harris, esq, judge, Jeremiah Russell, David Boches, esqs, assistant justices

Archibald Noble, Edward Noble, Duncan McEwan, Duncan Cameron, James I Cameron, John Doig, Thomas Norman, Eliza Martha Norman, Robert Simpson, and James Dow were naturalized and declared citizens of the United States

The first civil cause tried in this court was Hannah Austin, administratrix, and Samuel Andrews, administrator, of the estate of Phineas Austin, deceased, vs James Divine and John Divine

Mr Wilkinson, attorney for plaintiffs

Judgment rendered for plaintiffs for $78 56 damages and six cents costs

Of the members of the Warren county bar, the name and fame of Enoch

H Rosekrans occupies the most prominent place   E H Rosekrans was born at Waterford, New York, October 16th, 1808   His preparatory education was acquired at the Lansingburgh Academy   He entered Union College, and graduated in July, 1826, with honors   Studied law with his uncle, Judge Samuel S Huntingdon, and after admission to the bar, in 1829, he became and continued the law partner of the latter gentleman for about two years; came to Glens Falls in 1831, and was married to Cynthia Beach, of Saratoga Springs, in 1832, and received the appointment of Supreme Court Commissioner, and Master in Chancery the same year.   In 1867 the degree of LL D was conferred upon him by Union College, was elected judge of the Supreme Court in 1854 and again in 1863, and continued to discharge the duties of that position until his term of office expired in 1871   He sought a renomination but failed to obtain it   His practical retirement from the bar soon followed, and although frequently consulted on important matters, he did not enter upon any active practice in court   Attorneys and clients, at times, found occasion to criticise his rulings from the bench as hasty and arbitrary   He was prompt to decide, and expeditious in the transaction of business, his language was concise and pointed, and his written opinions evinced an extensive knowledge and clear conception of the law seldom surpassed in the annals of the Supreme Court He died May 1st, 1877, mourned by a large circle of private and professional friends

Halsey R Wing was born at Sandy Hill, Washington county, N Y   He entered Middlebury College, Vermont, and graduated therein in 1832   His legal studies were pursued in the office of Hon Samuel Cheever   He served for a brief period as assistant district attorney of Albany county   In 1835 he was married to Harriet N Walton, of Montpelier, Vt.   He came to Glens Falls in 1841, in which year he was admitted as counselor at law, and the following year as solicitor in the United States Courts, and counselor in Chancery In 1845 he became the first judge of the county, having previously been elected to the office of justice of the peace and inspector of common schools   In 1851 he entered into partnership in an already established business, the celebrated Jointa Lime Company, consisting of himself and Mr. John Keenan, and continued a member of the successful firm up to the time of his death.   After entering the Jointa lime firm he gradually withdrew from the practice of law and did not again appear as an active practicing attorney in court   Afterwards Mr. Wing became largely connected with many other important and successful industries of Glens Falls, and was always respected by his associates for his uncompromising honesty and faithful performance of every duty which he was called upon to discharge   A careful, discreet, pains-taking, honest lawyer, a wise and prudent counselor, a faithful husband, loving father, and generous, trusting friend, he will be remembered for his progressive usefulness and virtuous manliness as one of the noble characters who has left his imprint on the

HALSEY R. WING.

" sands of time," and made the world brighter and better by the force of character and the virtue of good example

Orange Ferris was born at Glens Falls in 1814   His elementary education was received in his native village.   His collegiate course was pursued at the University of Vermont   He studied law in the office of Hon William Hay, of Glens Falls, and was admitted to the bar in 1840   The following year he was appointed surrogate of the county, in which position he served for four years   In 1851 he was elected county judge and surrogate, was re-elected in 1855 and again in 1859, thus serving in that capacity for twelve consecutive years   In 1865 he received the appointment of provost marshal for the Sixteenth Congressional District, but declined to serve   In 1866 he was elected to Congress, and was re-elected the succeeding term   In 1871 he was appointed commissioner of the Court of Claims, and in 1873 was reappointed for four years to the same position   In May, 1880, he was appointed second auditor of the treasury department, a position which he occupied until removed by the Democratic administration of President Cleveland   Whether acting as judge, congressman, commissioner, or auditor of the treasury, Judge Ferris has always maintained a spotless character which has commanded universal respect A sound lawyer, an impartial judge, a faithful executive, sincere friend, and honest man, he lives loved and respected by his friends and neighbors, hale and hearty for his advanced life, with many years of usefulness yet before him.

Isaac J. Davis was born at Castleton, Vt , in 1831   His education was chiefly acquired at the common schools   He came to Glens Falls in 1851 and commenced reading law in the office of L H Baldwin   Taught a district school the following winter, and in the spring renewed his legal studies with Henry B Northup, of Sandy Hill, where he remained one year   He then returned to Glens Falls and finished his studies in Baldwin's office   He was admitted to the bar in 1853, and immediately opened an office   From 1854 to 1857 he was a law partner of Halsey R Wing   He was the Democratic candidate for district attorney in 1859 and in 1863 for senator, was defeated, although running ahead of his party ticket in both instances   He was elected county judge in 1871 and again in 1877   He was twice married, to Miss Gray, of Arlington, Vt , in 1857, and to Miss Williams, of Schuylerville, N Y , in 1865   The latter lady survives him   Judge Davis was emphatically democratic in make up and manner, rarely lost an opportunity to make a new acquaintance, and as a consequence was more generally known through the county than any man that had ever lived in it   As a friend, counselor, and peacemaker Mr Davis was very generally sought, and whenever an amicable adjustment was reached without service of legal papers, he invariably rendered his services free of charge, laughing as he would sometimes remark, " Oh, never mind, let it go, that is all right "   Generous beyond the capacity of his purse, never refusing to buy a book, feed a pauper, or feast a prince, he became the idol of the populace, was cheered in every assembly, feasted at every board, and irresistible at the hustings, defeating Isaac Mott for the county judgeship in 1871 by seventy-three, and A J Cheritree in 1877 by four hundred and eighty-seven majority He possessed a clear, sound, legal mind, and when pressed into service was eloquent and effective with judge and jury, and not unfrequently converted defeat into victory by his earnestness and honesty of purpose Careless and indifferent by nature to the acquirement of this world's goods, he could never learn to say no, and was a prey to the greed and selfishness of real and fancied friends Dilatory and procrastinating in his practice, his wealthy clients were not numerous or his income large, and when death came, if poverty is a passport to eternal bliss, for kind hearted, good natured Davis, the gates stood ajar Judge Davis died in 1881, respected and esteemed by the entire community, as an upright judge, honest lawyer, good neighbor and faithful friend , peace and farewell

William Hay was born in Cambridge, Washington county, N Y , in 1790 About the year 1800 Mr Hay came with his family to Glens Falls and received only a limited school education, from the scanty opportunities afforded in the unsettled condition of the county in those early years of our history In 1808 we find him pursuing the study of law in the office of Henry C Martindale In 1813 he opened an office for the practice of law at the head of Lake George In 1817 he was married to Miss Paine, of Northumberland, Saratoga county In 1819 he became the proprietor and publisher of the *Warren Patriot*, the first and only newspaper published at Lake George In 1822 he removed to Glens Falls and resumed the practice of law In 1827 he was elected to the Assembly from Warren county In 1837 he removed to Ballston, retaining a branch office at Glens Falls In 1840 he transferred his residence to Saratoga Springs, where he continued to live up to the time of his death. He was a man of broad views, of extensive and varied information, and endowed by nature with great intellectual qualifications, which were always used for the improvement and advancement of human thought and progress With a heart as gentle as a girl's, he was a man among men, a philosopher among philosophers, and may be justly regarded as one of the bright spirits who adorned every walk of life, always defending the right fearless of consequences, dying as he had lived, esteemed and venerated by all who knew him

Stephen Brown was born in Massachusetts, and came to Glens Falls in 1852 By persistent industry and close attention to the duties of his profession he soon acquired an extensive and lucrative practice He served most acceptably as county judge from 1863 to 1871 The law firm of Brown & Sheldon, dissolved a few years since, was one of the best known in Northern New York during the several years of their copartnership Judge Brown is yet in active practice, deservedly holds a prominent position before the bar, and is always discreet, able and eloquent

Isaac Mott.

Andrew J Chentree, the present county judge, was born in Greene county, N Y, in 1830; came to Warren county in 1854, was supervisor of the town of Luzerne for several years, was appointed provost marshal at the close of the War of the Rebellion, served as school commissioner for about two years, and was subsequently appointed collector of internal revenue, was elected district attorney in 1871 without opposition, and county judge in 1882 by a large majority   Judge Chentree has justly earned a reputation for integrity and ability before the bar and on the bench which points to a wider field of usefulness in the not distant future

Isaac Mott [1]— The levity and brevity of human life with its innumerable train of fleeting ambitions, are but as the faint reflection of a passing shadow, which may be tinged with prismatic beauty and leave its imprint for a brief space of time upon the collective susceptibility of human nature, speaking to the senses through the beautiful in poetry, music and art   Or, it may be the more bold and picturesque shadow of tyrannic power and decorated pomp marching in triumph o'er "the purple flood" of human hopes and universal slaughter   The pyramids which have endured the wreck of time and the shock of worlds, are but ghastly spectacles of the whirling sands and red simoon of the desert, which have consigned to oblivion the kingly names vain glory designed to perpetuate

The imperial tyrant of Persia, with his myriads of desecrating vassals, live only in the hated recollection of Greece's proud, but melancholy history, which portrays Xerxes as the most tyrannic monster before whom an awed world ever bowed in abject submission   Earth, from pole to pole, resounded with the name and fame of Alexander who wept for other worlds in which ambition might revel in triumphal conquest   Caesar, Hannibal, Charlemagne, Napoleon, alternately saint and sinner, emblazoned their lurid pathways, and sailed in tempest down the stream of life amid the meteoric splendor of marvelous achievements

> "And now, a single spot
> Where oft they triumphed is forgot"

Passing away is written upon the brow of man and the face of nature   Philosophical reflection and Christian resignation, views with smiling complacency the brevity of human ambition   Spring and summer, ere long give place to autumn, when we that are now must take our destined places in the silent cavalcade ever moving to that mystical realm where no wave of trouble breaks upon the silent shore, where no echo of joy or sadness disturbs eternal repose, or everlasting gladness   Calmed by the elysian reveries of hope, imagination wings its flight beyond the shining stars and finds there written in legends of eternal light, this golden motto, "'Tis only truly noble to be truly good"

---

[1] Contributed to the chapter by a friend

From this atmosphere of moral purity, we may pursue with pleasure and profit the subject of our present sketch who was born in the town of Moreau, Saratoga county, New York, September 25th, 1818   His parents, James Mott and Anstis Merritt, were among the early settlers of Saratoga county and were blessed with a family of fourteen children, nine sons and five daughters. Isaac, the fifth son, "worked on the farm" and attended the "district school" until about the age of sixteen years, at which time he attended the schools at Glens Falls, where he obtained a good English education and the higher branches of mathematics   In 1836, a young man just from school, he was engaged as civil engineer on the New York and Erie R. R   The financial crisis of 1837 led to a suspension of the work and the young engineer was thrown out of employment, an incident which probably changed the entire current of his life   About this time he was offered a lucrative position on the State works, but declined, anticipating the continuance of the work on the Erie R. R   The summer of 1837 was devoted to the study of mathematics and traveling, and the following winter was profitably spent in teaching school in Washington county   In the spring of '38 he commenced the study of law in the office of Hon William Hay at Glens Falls, and continued his studies for several years, occasionally teaching school in the winter   Was admitted to the bar in 1844 and commenced at once the practice of his profession at Schuylerville, Saratoga county   In 1847 Mr Mott was married to Miss Mary A Cox, of Schuylerville, by whom he has had three sons, Charles M , Abram C and Edward P , and a daughter, Alice E   Charles M Mott, now of Dakota Territory, was one of the youngest and brightest ornaments of the Warren county bar   Genial of nature, happy of thought, pleasing in conversation, a safe counselor and honest friend , the happy possessor of every quality that endears, and every virtue that ennobles, he is a valuable acquisition to his new home, and will be admired and respected most by those who know him best Abram C is extensively engaged in the iron trade, and is president of the Abram Cox Stove Company of Philadelphia   Edward P Mott is manager of a branch house of the latter company at Chicago   Alice E , a most estimable and talented lady, is the wife of Edward E Hazlett, M D , an eminent young physician now practicing in Kansas

In the fall of 1847, Mr Mott, then but little known in the legal profession, moved to Glens Falls, N Y., where he formed a law partnership with Allen T Wilson and in a few months succeeded to the extensive law practice of Mr. Wilson, who moved to California   In 1850 Mr Mott was elected superintendent of public schools for the town of Queensbury, a position which he most satisfactorily discharged for six successive years   In 1856 he was elected district attorney for the county of Warren and discharged the duties of this position with marked ability, tact, wisdom, prudence and economy, which merited and won universal respect, and as a consequence retained possession of the office for twelve successive years

So generally was the ability, talent and sterling honesty of Mr Mott recognized by the community that he was nominated on the Republican ticket for the position of county judge in 1871, and under many adverse circumstances and a pernicious system of electioneering practiced by the opposition which Mr Mott could not and would not practice, was, after a most brilliant run, defeated by a small majority   In 1872 he was elected presidential elector on the Republican ticket and voted for General Grant at the electoral college of that year

Mr Mott is of long-living Quaker stock, and, although advanced in years, is hale and hearty in body and mind , possessing a fine person, pleasing features, a most agreeable manner of address, and a peculiar manliness and grace which art cannot teach or method imitate   Honesty, candor, moderation, is the golden tie running through the pearl-chain of his every day duty

<blockquote>
"These shall resist the empire of decay,
When time is o'er, and worlds have passed away "
</blockquote>

Feeling from his youth that the fundamental principles of moral and political philosophy are realities of the grandest and greatest importance, he never has fallen into the indolent and popular habit of declaiming about them as if they were nonentities incapable of being seen or understood.   He therefore never hesitates to frankly express his views on important subjects when the occasion demands it   Ardently devoted to home and family he naturally prefers an atmosphere superlatively pure and calm, to the more turbulent and tumultuous channels of life, where lives are wrecked and hopes are blighted Whole-souled and generous to a fault, his theology is tinged with the same characteristic generosity   A believer in a Supreme overruling power, yet absolutely without "ism " and therefore free from the distorted vision, cramped views, clouded understanding, illiberal opinions, and restless melancholy so frequently the prey and pride, the glory and shame of the narrow and contracted mind   Evidently believing with the poet,

<blockquote>
" If there is another world, I'll live in bliss,
If not I've made the best of this "
</blockquote>

Respected by his neighbors, and admired by his friends , a successful lawyer, a kind husband and prudent father   No sentiments can embellish, no words can add to the worth and importance of a life of usefulness devoted to honest and successful effort for nearly a half century

<blockquote>
" To guild refined gold, to paint the lily,
To throw a perfume on the violet,
To smooth ice or add another hue
Unto the rainbow, or with taper light
To seek the beauteous eye of heaven to garnish
Is wasteful and ridiculous excess "
</blockquote>

From Holden's *History of the Town of Queensbury*, to which we are largely indebted for much of the information contained in this sketch, we find that Seth C Baldwin, Hiram Barber, Horatio Buell and William Robards were judges of this county for terms varying from three to eight years

Melville A Sheldon, for fourteen years a partner of Judge Brown's, was born in Essex county, N Y, in 1829, was admitted to the bar in 1852 Came to Glens Falls in 1868, has been president of the village of Glens Falls, district attorney for three years, and is now a member of the board of education of the Union Free School As a lawyer Mr Sheldon is conceded to be without a superior in Northern New York, is a man absolutely without hypocritical polish, sham or pretense, a man eminently worthy of respect and confidence and an honor to the profession and the community in which he lives Seemingly reserved and distant in manner, yet possessing a heart kind, generous and sympathetic as could bless man

Emery D Harris, for many years a law partner of the late Judge Davis, was born in Washington county, N Y, in 1837, was admitted to the bar in 1861, was the Democratic candidate for district attorney in 1868, making a remarkable run under adverse circumstances, and coming within thirteen votes of an election Genial and warm hearted by nature, generous to a fault, possessed of a bright, clear, perceptive intellect, widely known and very popular, a good lawyer and devoted friend, he has passed quietly away in the morning of his manhood, a victim of the fatal malady of consumption, loved and esteemed most by those who knew him best

> " Green be the turf above thee, friend of my better days,
> None knew thee but to love thee, or named thee but to praise "

In addition to the above mentioned, the following gentlemen constitute the members of the Warren county bar admitted to practice in the Supreme Court —

A B Abbott, Eugene L Ashley, Louis S Brown, J H Bain, W M Cameron, Henry A Howard, W A Holman, D F Keeffe, H Prior King, Charles F King, Calhoon S Enches, Charles M Mott, James J Mead, Charles R Patterson, Edwin R Safford, Edward L Sterns, Frank H Streeter, Royal L Davis, of Glens Falls, H P Gwinup, Abram Newcomb, of Luzerne, Thomas Cunningham, L C Aldrich, of Warrensburgh, Adam Armstrong, Charles P Coyle, Stanly H Bevins, of Chester, C F Aldrich, L H Aldrich, of Thurman

Within the recollection of the writer many bright and noble spirits, ornaments of the Warren county bar, and the pride of the community in which they lived, have fallen by the wayside to appear before the final tribunal, where the costs are fixed by statute, where motions for new trials will not be heard, proceedings stayed, or appeal possible

In conclusion it is but just to say, that the Warren county bar has furnished its full quota of distinguished men to the legal profession, men who have swam to triumph on the crest of fortune, to pass away down the receding slope of years, leaving behind them sunny recollections and noble aspirations with those who in their turn shall obey the command of Nature and pass away

> " Thus the multitude goes like the flowers and the weeds,
> The multitude goes to let others succeed."

CHAPTER XXIII

THE MEDICAL PROFESSION [1]

Early Medical Legislation — Organization of the State Society — The County Society — Loss of Records — First Members — Early Delegates to the State Society — List of Officers of the Warren County Society — Biographic Sketches of Prominent Members of the Profession

UNFORTUNATELY for a correct and authentic account of the Warren County Medical Society, the records of that association were burned about the year 1858 Anterior to that period we are indebted chiefly to such brief mention as may be found in the transactions of the State Society for any reliable information concerning it

By an enactment of the New York Legislature, passed on the 4th of April, 1806, authority was given for the organization of medical societies for the purpose, as therein stated, of "regulating the practice of physic and surgery"[2] In accordance with this statute the Medical Society of the State of New York was duly organized on the first Tuesday of February, 1807 The county of Warren was not set off from the county of Washington, of which it formed an integral part, until March 12, 1813, hence it is manifest there could not have been a County Medical Society prior to this date

The first record that has been found of the existence of a county society is dated February, 1814, which states as follows "The following gentlemen presented their credentials from their respective county societies [viz, to the State Society] and were duly admitted as delegates" Then, among other names, follows that of Dr Asa Stower

The society (as is learned from the present record book, which was re-written as well as possible after the destruction of the original records on the 2d day of October, 1858) was formed by the following named members Asa Stower, of Queensbury, Zephaniah Tubbs, of Caldwell, John P Little, of Chester, Reuben C Gibson, of Bolton, Thomas Pattison, of Warrensburgh, Darius Hewitt, of Queensbury, Chester Thomas, of Chester, and Harmon Hoffman, of Warrensburgh The organization took place some time in the year 1813

There afterwards, and previous to 1858 (when the records were destroyed), joined the society the following named physicians Martin Jillett, Johnsburgh, Truman B Hicks, Caldwell, John S St John, Luzerne, Paul More, Bolton,

---

1 Prepared by Dr A W Holden, of Glens Falls

2 Prior to this time a most remarkable provision for licensure of candidates existed, by virtue of an act passed March 23d, 1797, which authorized "the chancellor, a judge of the Supreme Court or Common Pleas, or a Master in Chancery, to license physicians and surgeons on receiving evidence of their having studied two years," etc

Zerah Cushman, Chester, Nathan Tubbs, —— Kelley and Benjamin Dean, Chester; Lemuel Bugbee, Bolton, George Andrews, Athol, Fletcher Ransom, Queensbury, Nathaniel P Seaver, Bolton, Wm Wilson, Johnsburgh, —— Fuller, and Nathan P Colvin, Bolton, Wm N Edgerton and Oliver Strong, Warrensburgh, Alfred Mallory, Chester, James Lawrence, Luzerne, Bethuel Peck, Glens Falls, Ira Clement, Athol, Eliakim W Howard, Warrensburgh, Louis Charette, Bolton, Morgan W Pritchard, Chester, Hiram McNutt, Warrensburgh, Samuel H Hooker, Chester, Austin W Holden, Glens Falls, John B Burneson, Luzerne; Marshall Littlefield, Glens Falls, James Cromwell, Queensbury, James Ferguson, Glens Falls [1]

In addition to the above list (which may be more or less incorrect) the records show the following named physicians to have joined the society, the dates being given in some cases: Godfrey R Martine (then of Johnsburgh), D B Howard, Warrensburgh, F L R Chapin, Glens Falls; M R Peck, Glens Falls, John T Parker, Thurman, James G Porteous, Luzerne, N. E Sheldon, Glens Falls; Wm D Aldrich, 1872, Warrensburgh, Hiram E McNutt, 1872, Warrensburgh, R J Eddy, 1875, B G Streeter, 1876, and Benjamin C Senton, 1876, Glens Falls, W R Adamson, 1877, Lake George, G. H Aldrich, 1878, Stony Creek; W W Aldrich, 1878, Weavertown, F E Aldrich, 1879, W W McGregor, 1879, Glens Falls, Fred B Streeter, 1879, Glens Falls, A O Ameden, 1880, Glens Falls; Jno C Wall, 1880, Olmsteadville, Essex county, Adam Weston, 1880, Glens Falls, Chas F C Weston, 1880, Glens Falls; W S Robinson, 1878, Schroon Lake, S J Murray, 1881, Glens Falls, J B Washburne, 1882, Caldwell, Edward S. Coyle, 1882, Chester; Cassius J Loggins, 1882, Chester; C A Foster, 1882, Glens Falls, Chas. F Aldrich, 1882, Thurman, Chas S Barney, 1882, Glens Falls, E J. Dunn, 1882, Pottersville, F H Stevens, 1882, Lake George

In the annual reports of proceedings of the society we find in addition to the above the names of W C B Stewart, John Cady, A Irving Sternberg, and D P Kaynor among those admitted to membership

In 1817 the Warren County Society was represented at the State meeting by Dr John S St John, then practicing at Glens Falls The county does not appear to have been represented in the State Society again until the year 1822, and there was considerable irregularity in sending delegates until comparatively recent years In 1822 the name of Truman B Hicks appears as delegate, he then resided and practiced in Luzerne and was for many years, subsequent to 1820, president of the County Society He was also delegate to the State meetings in the years 1823, 1824, 1826, 1827, and was present in several other years, but not as a delegate. In the years 1829, 1830 and 1831 the County Society was not represented

The first meeting held after the records were destroyed was on January

---

[1] The spelling of these names is as given in the record.

A. W. Holden, M. D.

19th, 1859, at which were present Doctors Bethuel Peck, Alfred Mallory, E W Howard, Louis Charette, Hiram McNutt, Marshall Littlefield, M R Peck, N E Sheldon and James Ferguson

New by-laws were ordered drawn and other routine business transacted Doctor M Littlefield was elected president for the ensuing year, and Doctor Charette, vice-president, with Doctor James Ferguson secretary; and M R Peck, treasurer Doctor H McNutt was appointed delegate to the State Society

Since that date the following physicians have held the offices of president, vice-president and secretary of the County Society and delegates to the State Society —

1860, Louis Charette, president, Alfred Mallory, vice-president, H McNutt, secretary, James Ferguson, delegate

1861–62, no record

1863, H McNutt, president, James Ferguson, vice-president, L Charette, secretary

1864, A Mallory, president, L Charette, vice-president, A Irving Sternberg, secretary E W Howard was elected delegate to the American Medical Association

1865, L Charette, president, James Ferguson, vice-president, E W Howard, secretary, H. McNutt, delegate to American Association

1866, A I Sternberg, president, H McNutt, vice-president, D B Howard, secretary

1867, G R Martine, president, F L R Chapin, vice-president, D B Howard, secretary; M R Peck, delegate to American Association

1868, F L R Chapin, president, J G Porteous, vice-president, D B Howard, secretary, M R Peck, delegate to American Association Doctor H McNutt was sent as delegate to the State Society

1869, M R Peck, president, G R Martine, vice-president, D B Howard, secretary, F L R Chapin, delegate to American Association

1870, Alfred Mallory, president, J G Porteous, vice-president; D. B Howard, secretary

1871, J G Porteous, president, Louis Charette, vice-president, D B Howard, secretary

1872. Alfred Mallory, president, Louis Charette, vice-president, D B Howard, secretary

1873–74, no record

1875, James Ferguson, president, Louis Charette, vice-president, D. B Howard, secretary

1876, E W Howard, president, G R Martine, vice-president; R J Eddy, secretary. Doctor Chapin was elected delegate to the State Society and Doctor Louis Charette to the American Association

20

1877, B G Streeter, president, William Aldrich, vice-president; R. J. Eddy, secretary

1878, William D Aldrich, president, W R Adamson, vice-president, R J Eddy, secretary

1879, W. R Adamson, president, W W McGregor, vice-president, R J. Eddy, secretary D B Howard, delegate to State Society, L Charette, to American Association

1880, R J Eddy, president; F E Aldrich, vice-president, E W. Hill, secretary

1881, W. W McGregor, president, W R Adamson, vice-president, F B. Streeter, secretary, G H Aldrich, delegate to American Association

1882, L Charette, president, F E Aldrich, vice-president; F B Streeter, secretary, W D Aldrich, delegate to American Association

1883, D B Howard, president; ————, vice-president, F B Streeter, secretary

1884, C S Barney, president, F. H. Stevens, vice-president; W D Aldrich, secretary

The new by-laws were adopted at the second meeting, as was also a code of ethics, the latter being drawn by Doctors James Ferguson, Hiram McNutt and A W Holden, as committee

In the year 1875 a committee embracing Doctors F L R Chapin, R J Eddy, M R Peck, Louis Charette and D B Howard, was appointed to revise the by-laws This was done, but no changes of great importance were made. Another revision was made in 1881

———

Herewith we give in brief the statistics of the medical profession in Warren county, so far as they could be ascertained by diligent and persistent research through town, county, family and society records Old residents have been consulted, correspondence instituted with those far away, and every available source of information sought out in order to make this chapter creditable alike to the subject, to the individuals memorized, to the work itself, and to the compiler as well The results are unsatisfactory Considering, however, the many difficulties in the way, the long time which has elapsed since many of the actors in this field of science have " passed over to the great majority," it is not surprising that so many of the pioneers of medical practice should be passed by with the mere mention of a name This, however, does not excuse or apologize for those who, still living, have declined or neglected to avail themselves of the opportunity to place themselves fairly and squarely on the record, a chance that is not likely to occur again in many years Following we give life sketches of such individuals of the profession as we have been able to procure sufficient data .—

"Dr Seth Alden, son of Seth, was born probably at Shaftsbury, Vt , in 1749, died at Caldwell (head of Lake George) 30th July, 1809 We have no account of his early life, but that he was a man of some note in his profession is evident from the fact that in 1783 he was requested by Colonel Ethan Allen to visit his daughter in consultation with Doctor Hutton, his family physician, at the distance of some forty miles From Shaftsbury he removed to Caldwell, N Y , where he continued to reside until the time of his death " In a letter from Judge Hay I find the following " I have heard old James Caldwell speak of clearing and laying out the site for the Lake House, Caldwell , the first occupant I knew was Doctor Alden Before the Lake House was erected, the old hospital, or long house, had been used for a tavern "

He married first, Priscilla Cole, who died 20th of November, 1798, and second, Keziah Beach on the 1st of March, 1800, who died 10th October, 1810, æt 51 His two eldest daughters were married successively to John A Feiriss, a prominent merchant and business man of this place Doctor Alden was of the fifth generation in direct descent from John Alden of *Mayflower* memory, and was the grandfather of Hon O Ferriss The late Mr Ralph Stebbins, of Caldwell, informed me that Doctor Alden removed from Lake George to Fort Edward in 1809, and died the same year or the year following

---

Asa Stower was a native of Massachusetts, born as nearly as can be determined in one of the western border towns of the State His early childhood was passed at or near New Lebanon, N Y While yet a small boy his father embraced the Shaker faith and joined the society at that place, removing his family among them He soon afterward died of small-pox, when the mother, who still retained her religious views (being a Presbyterian), took her children and went back to live on their farm, for which they were still considerably in debt, but, with the help of the boys, after a few years finished paying for their home

Asa with his elder brother was allowed to attend the district school, and possessing a laudable ambition with a studious turn of mind, acquired a fair knowledge, not only of the rudimentary branches of learning there taught, but applying himself at leisure hours to the pursuit of the more recondite departments of science, evincing a special aptitude and taste in the direction of botany, a study then but little pursued in this country, and still in its infancy His inclination in this direction doubtless determined the choice of a profession, and at the age of eighteen he commenced the study of medicine, which he steadily prosecuted with such aid as his mother in her straitened circumstances could afford At the age of twenty-one he had completed his studies, and with a horse, saddle and bridle, and a pair of saddle bags filled with medicine, the parting gift of his mother, he started out to seek his fortune What led him to Queensbury is not known, but certain it is he came as the pioneer of the medical profession in Warren county, according to a statement of the late Dr Bethuel Peck, in the year 1788 or 1789, armed with a judge's certificate of ability to practice. He first made his home with William Robards, esq, who lived in a dwelling subsequently burned, not far from the residence of John M Haviland near the Ridge   Here he commenced his life work, and here he remained for a number of years, supplying a circle of country, thinly settled but very sickly, many miles in extent   Being economical, plain in his tastes and inexpensive in his habits, he soon acquired a competency   One of his first purchases was the farm at the Ridge now owned and occupied by Joseph Haviland, disposing of which he bought the farm where Anson Staples now lives, where he passed the remainder of his days in works of kindness and usefulness   In those early days, when the facilities for education were not as plentiful or accessible as at present, his office was the resort of medical students, who almost from the commencement of their studies were enabled to pay their way and acquire practical with theoretical knowledge by assisting the doctor in his long and laborious rides   Among the number who thus graduated from his office and supplied the adjacent country in the years following, were Dr Lemuel C Paine, Dr Nathan Tubbs, Dr Seneca Wing, two brothers and a cousin by the name of Dean, Dr Durfee and others whose names are forgotten or not readily recalled to mind

In a communication to the author in 1870, the venerable Dr Paine speaks of him as follows   " Dr Asa Stower was held in high repute all over the country   He was a great reader and had a retentive memory, but I think he was more diffuse than profound in his reading, and was far from being a scientific man in his profession   He was strictly a physician of the old school, but by reading and observation he had acquired a stock of medical information and experience which made him truly a successful and useful physician   He was a bachelor and a little singular in his manners and habits, by some he would be deemed a little odd, at least not exactly Chesterfieldian in his address and manners, especially among the ladies "   He acquired during his long practice a handsome property, owning real estate in various parts of the town   One of the last acts of his life was to order his accounts against the poor to be destroyed in order that they might not be distressed to make their payments

Of an estate, whose final adjustment realized upwards of twenty thousand dollars, not enough was left, by the greed of his heirs at law, to pay for a gravestone   Among his old neighbors a subscription was taken up sufficient to pay for a plain marble slab, on which is engraved the following simple inscription, a touching memorial of the evanescent character of all earthly things .—

"DR ASA STOWER,
Died May 25, 1848,
Aged 79 Years.
He lived respected in society "

Jared Hitchcock, son of Elijah and Sarah Hitchcock, was born in the town of Palmer, Mass, on the 11th of August, 1778 His elementary and professional education were obtained in that State, where, as the writer has been informed, he also received the degree of doctor of medicine, and practiced for a number of years. He removed to Glens Falls in the month of November, 1819 The following year his wife was thrown from a wagon near the residence of Truman Hamlin, in the town of Moreau, and killed By her he had four children He married for his second wife Caroline Stickney, who bore him six children In 1821 he removed to Sandy Hill, N Y, and from thence in 1828 to Galway, Saratoga county He afterward went to West Troy, and thence in 1840 to Glens Falls, where he died March 26th, 1846 Dr Hitchcock was a man of considerable erudition and a good practitioner He invented a remedy which attained considerable local repute and celebrity under the name of Hitchcock's pills He also left a medical treatise containing an exposition of his peculiar views as to theory and practice, but which never came to print

Billy J, son of Ithamar and Sarah (Simonds) Clark, was born at Northampton, Mass, on the fourth of January, 1778

About the year 1784 his parents removed to Williamstown, Mass, where, for three or four years, he enjoyed the benefits of that public school founded by the munificence of Col Williams, who fell in action at "the bloody morning scout" At the age of ten he removed with his parents to Pownal, Vt, where his youth, up to the time of his father's death, was passed in the varied avocations of farm boy, clerk and bar-tender His medical studies were commenced at the age of seventeen in the office of Dr Gibbs, of Pownal, where he was soon characterized as a pains-taking, indefatigable student In 1797 he removed to Easton, Washington county, N Y, where his studies were continued in the office of Dr Lemuel Wicker, a practitioner at that time of extensive repute and practice

Having obtained the requisite testimonials and passed the necessary examinations, he obtained a license from the county judge of Washington county to practice medicine He commenced his life work in the town of Moreau, Saratoga county, N Y, in 1799, where, for forty years, he was the only physician, and supplied a radius of country nearly twenty miles in extent, following the humanities of his calling, achieving a well earned reputation for usefulness, and that by the popularly appreciated gauge of success, a substantial competency

Dr Clark's name will be famous through all time as the originator of the first temperance organization that ever existed The date of this important event was in the early part of April, 1808 In this field of philanthropy the doctor was an ardent and efficient laborer all his life He represented his county in the Assembly in 1820, and was a member of the New York Electoral College in 1848   He died in this village on the 20th of September, 1866

Through his energy and perseverance, a special act of legislature was obtained, incorporating the Saratoga County Medical Society, the first organization of the kind in the State

---

Dr John Perrigo, of Queensbury   In Judge Robard's docket, under the date of April 30th, 1803, appears a record of more than forty summonses issued in Dr Perrigo's favor against parties residing mostly in Queensbury   There is but little authentic information to be obtained concerning him at this late date   It is believed that he came to this place about the year 1800 and resided during his stay here at a humble dwelling, subsequently known as the O'Flanagan house, the site of which is now registered No 17 Elm street.   He was then in the decline of life, and of somewhat dissipated habits, and his brief stay here was neither a professional or pecuniary success   It has been stated that he was a brother of Robert Perrigo, of Whipple City, later known as Union Village and now called Greenwich, of Washington county, N Y   Dr Perrigo at first settled at Kingsbury street in Bradshaw's patent, in the adjoining town of Kingsbury.   He was one of the three or four pioneers of the medical profession in this region of country, and at one time bore the reputation of a skillful and successful practitioner   It is said that he was the first to introduce to the attention of the profession and public at large the prophylactic and curative properties of the rattle-snake weed (*Prenanthes Serpentaria*), and its use as a prompt and efficient antidote to the poison of the *Crotalus horridus* and its cognate species, with which terrible pests in that early period of our history the swamps, morasses, ledges, cliffs and mountain sides of this region of the country were infested,[1] and some of the islands and promontories of Lake George are to the present day   This knowledge was in all probability derived

---

[1] The *Crotalus durissus* is the species more commonly encountered nowadays   In regard to this reptile we find the following interesting incident recorded in Anbury's *Travels*, vol 1, p 387, (Lieutenant Aubury being an officer in Burgoyne's army) —

"This island (Diamond) as well as the one that is close to it, formerly was so over-run with rattlesnakes that persons when they passed the lake seldom or never ventured on them

"A batteaux in sailing up it, went near Diamond Island, and among other things it contained several hogs, which swam to the shore as did the Canadians who were rowing it up, the latter, in apprehension of rattle-snakes, climbed up trees for the night, and the next morning observing a batteaux, they hailed the people in it, who took them in, and conveyed them to Fort George.

"Some time after, the man owning the hogs, being unwilling to lose them, returned down the lake and with some comrades ventured a search   After traversing the island a considerable time, they at last found them, but so prodigiously fat that they could scarcely move, and, in the search, only met with one rattle-snake, which greatly surprised them, as the island was reported to abound with them.   Their wonder, however, was not of long duration, for, being short of provisions, they killed one of the hogs, the stomach of which was filled with rattlesnakes "

It may with truth be stated, *currente calamo*, that to the same cause may be attributed the extinction of the reptile from the quarries and ledges, and rocky cliffs at Glens Falls and neighborhood

from the Indians, who, in his day, still lingered around their ancient hunting grounds, and made their summer camps by our rivulets, ponds, lakes and hill-sides

Dr Perrigo finally removed to Burlington, Vt, where he died and was buried, as the writer of this sketch has been credibly informed

---

Dr Thomas Pattison was born at Stillwater, Saratoga county, N Y, on the 24th of November, 1781 He was the son of Thomas Pattison of that place, and a near relative of the Pattison families of Troy and Fort Miller, N Y. His opportunities for an education were limited to the common schools of that day, when a fair knowledge of arithmetic with the ability to read fluently and write readily were considered sufficient for all practical purposes His course of medical studies was pursued in the office of Dr Potter, an eminent and successful practitioner of that day, who resided at Waterford, N Y Having obtained his license to practice from a judge of the Court of Common Pleas, he removed in 1803 to the town of Athol, in what was then known as "Thurman's Patent," and commenced the practice of medicine He boarded in the house of Richardson Thurman, whose daughter Elizabeth he married on the 4th of February, 1810, by whom he had eight children, four sons and four daughters The following year he removed to Warrensburgh, and settled upon the farm on Schroon River road near the lower borough now owned and occupied by John and James McGann Here he lived the remainder of his days in the faithful and industrious discharge of his professional duties, his practice extending in every direction, over rough bye-ways and forest paths, through a sparsely settled and heavily wooded country abounding in wild animals and game, and not over-productive in the comforts and necessities of life In 1820 he was appointed county treasurer by the Board of Supervisors, in the place of Michael Harris, deceased, and continued in the discharge of the duties of that office until 1832

Dr Pattison possessed the elements of a strong character ˉ To a sound judgment and close observation were added sterling probity, industrious application and a wonderful self-reliance In regard to practice he followed in the beaten track of his predecessors, making no hazardous venture, being at all times a safe, prudent, and careful, as well as a successful practitioner He died of cystitis, at his home, on the 6th of February, 1867

From an autobiographic sketch furnished by Dr Lemuel C Paine some years ago, we condense the following. —

"I am a descendant of a very ancient family in Barnstable county, Mass, and my line of descent is as follows I am the son of Ichabod S Paine, who was the son of Dr Ichabod S Paine, who was the son of Joshua Paine, who was the son of Thomas Paine, jr., of Eastham, Mass, who was the son of

Thomas Paine, sen., of Eastham, Mass, who was the son of Thomas Paine, of Yarmouth, Mass, the two latter came from Kent county, England, to Plymouth in New England, in 1621, and the former of the two, of Yarmouth, was the first representative from that town in the General Court of Plymouth Colony, in 1639

" My grandfather, Dr Ichabod S Paine, was an early settler in Shaftsbury, Bennington county, Vt, and died there when only twenty-nine years of age, in the year 1765 My father was born there about the time of the death of his father, but was brought up in the family of his uncle, Judge Ephraim Paine, in what is now called Amenia, Dutchess county, N Y My father on reaching his majority married and settled on some lands left by his father in Shaftsbury, and I was born there November 9, 1787 After living here a short time, and in Orwell and Benson, Rutland county, in the same State, he finally came down into 'York State,' and purchased a tract of land near the 'Round Pond,' in the vicinity of 'Sugar Loaf Mountain,' in the west part of Westfield, now Fort Ann, Washington county, N Y, in 1793   *   *   *   "

After several removals the practical results of which were unfortunate, Dr. Paine's father located soon after 1800 in Plattsburg, where he died of consumption in 1807 A portion of the previous years he had lived in the town of Queensbury After narrating his experience in securing a fair education by persevering study, "without a master," the autobiography states that Dr Paine paid a visit to his uncle and aunt, Eli Pierson and his wife, at Fort Ann, and continues —

" After some consultation it was made up between uncle and aunt Pierson and myself that if equitable arrangements could be made I should commence the study of medicine with Dr Asa Stower, of Queensbury, and commence immediately This arrangement was easily made, with some offers on his part for the future which were deemed at the time highly favorable, but which were never realized For a time I boarded with Mr Pierson, then taught school awhile on the Ridge, and then near Mr Pierson's in Fort Ann again, and so on during my studies, sometimes teaching and sometimes living and boarding with Dr Stower In May, 1811, having finished the legal term of study, I passed examination before the Censors of the Medical Society of Washington county at Cambridge   I formed a partnership with Dr. Stower, first for six months and afterwards for an indefinite period, which continued till the spring of 1816, and afterwards I continued alone in Queensbury and Kingsbury till about the close of 1817 when I left that part of the country Thus it will be perceived that in all, first and last, my residence in the town of Queensbury and its vicinity amounted to about eleven years

" In the autumn of 1811 I married Miss Cornelia Osborn, daughter of David Osborn, of Kingsbury, and commenced house-keeping in the winter following in a part of Stower's house, on Sandford's Ridge, Queensbury   I lived here and hereabouts, a part of the time in Queensbury and a part of the time in Kingsbury, in rather an unsettled state until the close of 1817, when, as intimated above, I closed my business here and sought my fortune elsewhere

"At the time of my debut as a physician, the physicians in practice in that vicinity were Dr Asa Stower, of Sandford's Ridge, Dr Israel P Baldwin, of Glens Falls, Drs Zina Hitchcock and Russell Clark, of Sandy Hill, Drs. Adolphus Freeman and —— Barnum, of Kingsbury, Drs Isaac Sargent and Roderic Roe, of the village of Fort Ann, Dr Liberty Branch, of West Fort Ann, Dr Joel Tubbs, of Warrensburgh, and Dr Reuben C Gibson, of Bolton"

Here follows brief sketches of the physicians named, which we insert only as far as they lived in this county Of Dr Asa Stower we have already given a sketch —

"Of Dr Israel P Baldwin (I am not sure I have given his first name correctly, but I believe so) I knew but little I met with him often and I believe he was a reputable practitioner of medicine I remember I visited him in his last sickness, which I think was consumption, when he advised me to get out of the country as soon as I could, where I could have a more compact practice and better pay He said I was doing just as he had done, riding over the mountains, hills and forests of Luzerne and the surrounding country, night and day, summer and winter, wet and dry, with hard fare and poor pay This was probably an epitome of the experience of Dr Baldwin

"Of Dr Joel Tubbs I remember but little more than his name, though I think I used to meet with him occasionally at Caldwell and in the town of Warrensburgh

"Dr Reuben C Gibson, the last in the list of names which occurs to my memory, resided for a time at what was then called Brown's Landing in the town of Ballston Dr Stower and myself used occasionally to ride into that town and it was there that I became acquainted with him, though he afterwards, about the time I left that county, moved to Sandy Hill and went into the druggist or some kind of mercantile business, I believe We were intimate friends and I respected him very much though I have little knowledge of his medical attainments.

"I cannot say but Dr Rugg, of Glens Falls, was in practice a short time before I left, and I think I signed his diploma as secretary of Warren County Medical Society Dr Peck, I think, was licensed afterward

"In the professional line the few living who know me, or knew me, must speak for me. I only say that while I remained I had as much practice as I could do My greatest fault was, my ambition in other matters was greater than my means, and my inexperience led me into pecuniary embarrassments which the hard times for money in that county just after the close of the War of 1812, completed my overthrow and made it necessary for me, if I would pay

my debts, to remove to another place   I did so and saved myself and my cred-
itors too, I have since been more fortunate   In politics I was always active and as such I was somewhat distinguished when I was young"

Here follows an extended account of the various political offices held by
Dr Paine, which we need not reproduce; the list embraces the offices of clerk
of elections (1809), town clerk of Queensbury (1812), justice of the peace, master in chancery, etc   The autobiography then concludes as follows —

"In the spring of 1813, in consequence of the death of my father-in-law,
David Osborn, I moved from the Ridge to his place, just beyond the town and
county line into Kingsbury, and remained here till the spring of 1815, when I
moved back to the Ridge again and remained about one year and then back
to Kingsbury again   I cannot say with certainty that the Medical Society of
the county of Warren was organized in this time, but I think it was   I recollect well of attending a meeting, I think about the beginning of 1816, at the
Lake George Coffee House   Dr Stower read an article on the great epidemic
of 1813-14 at this meeting, and I was elected secretary, and I believe a censor
of the society

"Having moved back into Kingsbury again, as above stated, I was again
appointed a justice of the peace, and a master in chancery, an office in those
days corresponding with a commissioner of deeds in later times, which I held
till I moved from the county in December, 1817"

Dr Paine died in Albion, N Y, about the year 1875.

Bethuel Peck was born at Sand Lake, Rensselaer county, N Y, on the
16th of June, 1788. His father, Daniel Peck, who was originally from New
Hampshire, was a soldier in the War of the Revolution   His mother was Me-
hitabel Harvey, of Marlborough, N H   His grandfather, Ichabod Peck, of
Cumberland, R I, was a lieutenant-colonel in the War of the Revolution   He
was wounded in action, and died in consequence of his wounds   His wife was
Lydia Walcott, of the same place   His father and grandfather both also bore
the name of Ichabod   The latter was the son of Jathniel, the son of Joseph,
jr, who was born in England and baptized there August 23d, 1623, came over
to the new world with his father in the ship *Diligent*, of Ipswich, John Martin
master, and settled at Hingham, Mass, in 1638, from which place they both
removed, about seven years later, to Seekonk, now Rehoboth, Mass — *Peck
Genealogy*

It is not known with certainty what causes led the subject of this sketch to
Glens Falls, but it is believed that he was brought along by some of the return
gangs of raftsmen who, in the early days of the settlement here, rafted their
lumber to market down the Hudson River   He at first found employment as
a stable boy at the old Glens Falls Hotel   Subsequently he secured a position
as an office boy for Dr Levi Rugg, with whom he commenced the study of

medicine, paying his way with his own earnings from a practice which he rapidly picked up and afterwards retained He subsequently attended medical lectures at the Medical College of Fairfield, N Y, from which institution he at a later period received his diploma He married Jerusha Winston, by whom he had one child that died in infancy She survived him a few years and died at Chicago, Ill, whence her remains were removed and deposited by the side of her husband in the village cemetery As will be seen by a reference to the civil list, he was elected for a term of four years to the State Senate He was a partner for a number of years with the late Billy J Clark in a drug and medicine establishment on the site now covered by Vermillia's market After his return from the Senate he erected the brick building to which he gave the name of the Glens Falls Druggist, on Glen street Here, in conjunction with Dr M R Peck, he carried on the drug business for a number of years As a medical man Dr Bethuel Peck was a close observer and good diagnostician, following in the broad beaten pathway of the schools, he was a safe and successful practitioner His air in the sick-room was well calculated to inspire trust and confidence, for besides his genial and sympathetic manner, he always contrived to leave the impression that what he didn't know about the case was hardly worth knowing He acquired in the practice of his profession and the the judicious investment of his resources what was considered in those days a handsome fortune He was for many years a leading and influential politician of the place He died on the 11th of July, 1862

Dr Penfield Goodsell came to the town of Bolton anterior to the year 1805 from Connecticut He had a wife, and also a son named after himself, but never brought them to Bolton to live He was the first physician who settled in the town to practice medicine He was respectable and highly esteemed, and for a time had a widely extended practice After a few years he became insane and a wretched, aimless wanderer, up and down, to and fro through the earth for many years After the establishment of the county poor-house he was removed thither, and was an inmate there for several years At length, having been restored to reason, he left and returned to a former home in Vermont, where he died

The next physician who settled in Bolton after Dr Goodsell was Dr Reuben C. Gibson He resided and practiced there somewhere between the years 1813 and 1825 In 1814 he was allowed pay by the Board of Supervisors for medical services rendered to paupers He was one of the physicians who assisted in organizing the County Society in 1813 He subsequently went to Sandy Hill and embarked in the mercantile business In this he acquired some property, and afterward removed to Michigan, where he died.

During the period indicated in the two preceding paragraphs a Dr John Stanton settled at Bolton for the practice of medicine In the winter of

1814–15 he was attacked by the epidemic (spotted fever) which prevailed that season through the Northern and Eastern States with such fatal virulence, and died   His remains were buried in Bolton

Dr Stanton was succeeded by a Dr Paul More (or Moore, as it is variously written), who settled in Bolton about this time   Of him but little is known, except that he is recorded as a member of the Warren County Medical Society. In 1827 Dr Elisha Moore was allowed by the Board of Supervisors an account for professional services rendered to prisoners at the county jail   Could it have been the same man ?

About the same time there came to Bolton a Dr Samuel Buckbee, or Bugbee, who it is stated was a man of superior ability and attainments   He is also recorded as a member of the County Medical Society   He built up a somewhat extensive business, traveling far and near in the practice of his profession   The supervisors' records show that he was allowed compensation for professional services rendered to prisoners and paupers in the years 1827, 1829, 1830, 1831, 1835 and 1836   In 1830 he was appointed county physician by the Board of Supervisors

At a very early date Dr Herman Hoffman settled in practice at Warrensburgh   He represented his town in the Board of Supervisors in the years 1814 and 1815   It appears from a record at hand that he was allowed a claim of ten dollars by the Board of Supervisors of Washington county in 1805   He was also one of the physicians who assisted in organizing the County Medical Society in 1813

Dr Nathan North, the only record of whom may be found in the town books, in which it is stated that in February, in the year 1817, he made a present to the overseers of the poor of Queensbury, a bill amounting to $28 40, for professional services

Dr Zephaniah Tubbs resided near the Baptist Church in the north part of Caldwell   He was one of the pioneers of the profession in this county, and assisted in the organization of the County Society in 1813   His practice, if we may judge from the records, was extensive and remunerative.   He was allowed claims by the Board of Supervisors in the years 1824, 1825 and 1831   He was the father of Dr Nathan Tubbs, who subsequently practiced medicine in Warrensburgh, Chester and Glens Falls   He finally removed to Pennsylvania, where he died   The following obituary notice appears in the *Warren County Messenger and Advertiser* for Friday, February 6th, 1835 —

"DIED — In Caldwell, on the 29th ult , Dr Zephaniah Tubbs, in the 72d year of his age."

Nathaniel Edson Sheldon was the youngest of ten children, the offspring of Job and Joanna C (Trippe) Sheldon, who migrated from Cranston, R I , to

Barnet, Vt , where the subject of this sketch was born on the 28th of September, 1804   While in early youth, Dr Sheldon's father removed to Delhi, Delaware county, N Y   Here he received the advantages of a good common school education, and being baptized and confirmed in the Episcopal Church, commenced studying for orders in that communion   We are not advised as to the causes which led to a change of pursuit in life, but shortly after we find him prosecuting the study of medicine with Dr Lang in the city of New York, in one of whose colleges he graduated about the year 1831   After receiving his diploma, he was appointed ward physician in one of the worst and hardest districts of the city   During the cholera season of 1832 he saw and reported the first case of that terrible scourge in the city   His superiors scouted the idea   The next morning seven more were down with the disease and three dead bodies in the building   A medical commission which had been dispatched to Canada to investigate the disease, on examination confirmed his diagnosis, and he was awarded the credit due to his discrimination and good judgment   At the end of the season he was presented with a massive silver pitcher, which remains as an heir-loom in the family, upon which is engraved the following inscription —

" Presented by the Board of Health of the city of New York to N Edson Sheldon, M D , for professional services gratuitously rendered to the poor of the Second Ward during the prevalence of the cholera, A D 1832 "

The following year he removed to Glens Falls and embarked in practice, and notwithstanding a sharp and sometimes acrimonious competition, he soon succeeded in acquiring a fair proportion of the patronage , the population of the village and town being less than one-fourth what it is to-day   For nearly twenty years, and until his voluntary retirement from professional cares, he held the position of a first-class practitioner, and the reputation of more than ordinary success   Even later his professional brethren, in token of respect, elected him president of the County Medical Society

While pursuing his medical studies, a young English lady, named Elizabeth Goodwin Olive, stopped for a few days' visit at his preceptor's while on her way with an uncle, a clergyman of the church of England, to Canada   A romantic attachment sprung up between them, and in May, 1834, they were married   She died on the 30th of December, 1840   On the 3d of October, 1842, he was again married to Abigal T , daughter of the late John A Ferriss, esq   Soon after, he engaged in the drug and medicine trade, and by strict attention and assiduity he built up a large and remunerative business   For a large proportion of his life, Dr Sheldon was known as an active and influential politician   Originally a Democrat, he with many others came out in 1838 in opposition to that party, and for many years his office was the rallying place and centre where politicians arranged the local affairs of both the Whig and Republican parties   In the exciting and important campaign of 1860, whose events culminated in our late civil war, he was chosen one of the electors of the Empire State, and cast his vote for the first term of service of the martyred and lamented Lincoln

In 1866 he was appointed by the governor one of the Board of Trustees of the New York State Institution for the Blind at Batavia In the exciting campaign of 1872 he was nominated and elected county treasurer, a position which his failing health compelled him to resign early in the succeeding year

Dr Sheldon was public-spirited, and always contributed to the development and advancement of the place He was from the first a stockholder and director in the Glens Falls and Lake George Plank Road Company, and for many years its secretary He was also for a long time one of the trustees of the Glens Falls Academy Conspicuous, however, above all other traits of character, was his sterling honor and integrity In the language of one who knew him intimately and well, " He would not have done an unjust, dishonest or fraudulent act to save his life " He died suddenly at his residence in Glens Falls, on the 3d of July, 1873

Dr Eliakim W. Howard, was born the 2d of January 1808, at Fort Ann, Washington county, N Y, being the son of Eliakim and Anna (Williams) Howard, and received his preparatory education at the common and graded schools of that vicinity He began the study of medicine in the month of April, 1830, with Dr Nelson Porter of Fort Ann In the winter of 1832 he taught school at Doe's Corners, and continued his studies with Dr H Reynolds. Beginning with the fall of 1830, he attended three courses of medical lectures at the Vermont Medical College at Castleton, and graduated from that institution, December, 1833 In the summer of 1832, and the following winter his studies were profitably pursued in the office of Dr Fletcher Ransom, a physician of growing repute, of Glens Falls Immediately after graduating he commenced practice in a settlement known as " the Oneida," a hamlet in the north part of Queensbury, N Y, five miles north of Glens Falls, at that time boarding at a public house kept by Harvey Low In April, 1837, he removed to Warrensburgh He resided the first year in a house on the south side of the Schroon River, on the road to the town of Thurman The following year he moved to the upper borough and lived for thirty years in the house now occupied by Captain F A Farlin At the end of that time he removed to his present residence on the north side of the main street, and about midway of the two villages

On the 22d of September, 1835, he married Rebecca Brown, of Queensbury, by whom he had four children, two sons and two daughters, a son and daughter now living She died in 1869 On the 31st of July, 1871, he married his second and present wife, then Mrs Adelia (*nce* Cameron) Fenton.

Dr Howard for many years has had a laborious and extensive ride reaching from Cedar River, in Hamilton county, to the southern extremity of Warren. Notwithstanding his advanced years he is still hale, active and vigorous, and attends to his professional calls with the same alacrity, zeal and interest that he did forty and fifty years ago, and gives promise of many years of usefulness yet to come   He was appointed an examining surgeon for the pension office before the close of the war, and has acted in that capacity ever since

Dr James Cromwell was born at Carlisle, Schoharie county, N Y, on the 27th of September, 1811   He was a direct descendant of Oliver Cromwell, so famous in English history as the stern puritan, regicide and ruler of the English commonwealth

His early educational advantages were restricted, with the exception of a single year's academic instruction at Schenectady, N Y, to the scanty and often interrupted opportunities afforded at the district school of his neighborhood   Nevertheless, by great diligence and application, he succeeded in acquiring a thorough knowledge of the ordinary English branches, and also a fair understanding of the rudiments of Latin and chemistry

When he had attained the age of eighteen he commenced the study of medicine with a young, and subsequently eminent, practitioner, then residing in his native place   For two years or more his studies were thus pursued with advantage and satisfaction, when the removal of his preceptor broke up his plans and barred his further progress   At this time, also, it became necessary to seek the means of self-support in the acquirement of a trade   This was followed for four years and upwards, when an opportunity was gladly improved to resume his studies   He succeeded in obtaining a position as a prescription clerk in the city of New York, which familiarized him with the character, composition and properties of drugs and medicines, and their recent method of combination, preparation and administration   A position afterward obtained in the old City Hospital during the year 1835 gave him ample field for observation and practical experience in both surgery and medicine   During the terms of 1837–38, 1838–39, he attended full courses of lectures at the Medical College at Fairfield, N Y, pursuing his studies meanwhile at the office of a prominent firm of medical practitioners at Albany

On the 10th of February, 1839, he was married to Miss Sarah C Bradshaw, of Mechanicsville, Saratoga county, N Y, a union which for a lifetime has proved of perfect harmony and accord

An eligible opportunity presenting for embarking in practice, he removed in the month of June following to Mantua, Portage county, Ohio, where for six years he found in a wide and constantly extending field of patronage, ample employment for himself and an assistant   He then returned to the east, and, with a view to graduating, attended an additional course of lectures at the Albany Medical College, pursuing his practice during the interim at Mechanicsville, N Y Four years after receiving his diploma he removed to the settlement known as " The Oneida," in the northern part of the town of Queensbury, where he practiced his profession for several years Here his attention was first called to the then new system of practice, which was beginning to find scattering adherents here and there throughout the country Pursuing his investigations carefully, he at length became a believer in its efficacy, a convert to its law of cure and adopted it as his mode of practice He soon after (in May, 1848) removed to the village of Caldwell, at the head of Lake George, so long and favorably known to the traveling public as an attractive resort, and fashionable watering-place Here Dr Cromwell's eminent abilities and marked success speedily placed him in the possession of an exclusive and wide-spread practice Here, surrounded by influential patrons, and an ever increasing circle of trusting friends, the doctor completed his life-work and ended his days During his career he was scrupulous and respectful in his relations to the profession, and invariably recognized the claims of suffering humanity upon his ability and skill, whenever opportunity offered He associated himself in the various organizations of the faculty, serving as president of the Warren and Washington County Homœopathic Medical Society, and also of the Society of Northern New York He was also a member of the State Homœopathic Medical Society

At the fall election preceding his demise he was elected one of the coroners of Warren county by a gratifying majority Like most men of marked character, Doctor Cromwell's friends were fast, zealous and warm , his enemies bitter and unforgiving His death, which occurred on the 7th of December, 1875, has proved a serious loss to the community in which he lived, and where he was held in universal esteem The following testimonial forms a fitting close to a long career of usefulness

At a special meeting of the vestry of St James's Church, Lake George, N. Y , held at the rectory on Saturday evening, December 11th, 1875, the following minute was unanimously adopted

Forasmuch as it hath pleased Almighty God, in his infinite wisdom, to remove from his labors in the church militant, our beloved associate and Senior Warden, James Cromwell, M D , we, the rector, surviving warden and vestrymen of St James's Church, do hereby express our high appreciation of his faithful services as warden of this church for twenty years past, since its organization in 1855, and of his uniform bearing as a Christian gentleman, consistent churchman and devoted servant of the Lord And we record, with sincere feeling, our affectionate remembrance of his companionship, and of the kindly disposition which endeared him to all, and secured the respect of the entire community

And we further desire most feelingly to tender to his widow and children our sympathy and sincere condolence in this the time of their sorrow, commending them to Him, the dear Lord, who comforteth those that are cast down

And it is hereby ordered that a copy of the foregoing be presented to the family of the deceased, entered on the parish record, and its publication asked in the Glens Falls papers CHARLES H LANCASTER, *Rector*

S R ARCHIBALD, *Clerk*

Samuel Jenkins, M D , of Queensbury. Dr Jenkins was born in the town of Queensbury on the 19th of October, 1815 He was a descendant of one of the earliest settlers of the town, and the family of which he was a conspicuous and honored member was one of the most prominent and respected in that portion of the town in which he was raised His early education was such as could be derived from the better class of our public schools, later on, his advantages being of a superior order, he graduated at the Clinton Liberal Institute in 1840, and was for a considerable period professor of languages at that institution

In 1842 he was, after a course of preparatory study, ordained a minister of the Universalist Church On the 12th of September, 1843, he was united in marriage with Almaria, daughter of Rufus and Sarah Anderson, who, with two sons, viz Lyman and Palmer B , still survive The same year he was called to and accepted the charge of the Universalist Church at New Market, N. H. In 1844 he commenced the study of eclectic medicine, under the tutelage of Mark Anthony Cushing, M D , of Glens Falls, N Y , and from the period of his graduation forward, continued the practice of medicine (except at Huntingdon, L I), in connection with his ministerial duties

In 1844 he was called to the pastorate of the Universalist Church at Utica, N Y , at Lee Center, N Y , in 1845–46, at East Medway, Mass , in 1847–48, at Rochester, N Y , in 1850, at which place on the 10th of February, 1851, he received his degree of M D from the Rochester Medical College For the six years following, namely, until 1857, he was in charge of the Universalist Church at Schenectady, N Y From 1857 to 1860 he was pastor of the Universalist Church at Huntingdon, L I , and again in 1860 at Schenectady From the later city he removed to his birthplace at the north part of Queensbury. where he remained in the successful practice of medicine, supplying an extended radius of rich farming country with his professional services, until the time of his death, which occurred on the 20th of December, 1873

Joseph L Stodard was born in the town of Moreau, Saratoga county, N Y , in the year 1817 His education was acquired in the common schools of his native place, the circumstances and condition of his parents being such as to preclude the opportunities for a higher grade of education In youth, how-

21

ever, he foreshadowed some of those qualities which in after life contributed largely to a career of usefulness   In character he was diffident, retiring, sedate, candid and industrious   But small portions of his time, even in boyhood, were passed in the sports and pastimes, fun and frolic usually characterizing that active and formative period of life   Assiduous and attentive to his studies, and improving to the utmost the scanty opportunities, he laid broad and deep the foundations of future character and intellectual culture yet to be achieved by his own personal endeavors

While yet a lad of immature age he was apprenticed to learn the trade of cabinet-making, in the village of Palmyra, Wayne county, N. Y , in which pursuit he, in the course of his apprenticeship, became a skilled and accomplished workman   At the age of eighteen years he was assailed by a chronic gastric disease, which, for a time, crippled his energies, and from which he never fairly recovered   For two years he was under medical treatment, and during this period commenced the investigation and study of topics relating to medical science

His health being partially restored, and lacking the means to further pursue his medical studies, he in 1838 removed to Glens Falls and opened a cabinet ware-room   Renewed application to his trade soon brought on a return of his disease, and thus being crippled in health and ability to work, he speedily became embarrassed in his pecuniary condition and circumstances , and soon his business venture proved a failure

This was indeed a dark and gloomy period of his life   To add to his trials, a prolonged fit of illness ensued which greatly prostrated his system and sapped the vital forces   This was in the year 1847

During his convalescence he began the regular course of study, adopting the Hahnemannian system, of which he had already acquired a partial knowledge   He soon after embarked in practice, and notwithstanding the hostility and opposition of the other school of medicine, he built up a substantial and paying practice among an intelligent and appreciative portion of the community in which he lived   For twelve years and more he maintained his position, constantly increasing in the confidence of the community, until he was again assailed by the disease, whose insidious approaches gradually sapped the fountains of life, and he died on the 9th of April, 1860

Marvin Russell Peck, son of Joel and Hannah (Baldwin) Peck, was born at Sand Lake (or rather that portion of it which has since been set off under the name of Poestenkill, in Rensselaer county, N Y), on the sixteenth of July, 1822.   His early education was received at the common schools of the neighborhood where his father resided, working on his father's farm summers, and going to school, as opportunity offered, winters   As a somewhat characteristic incident, illustrating his tenacity of purpose, he followed a teacher (whose superior acquirements and ability rendered his instruction desirable) to Wynantskill, a distance of six miles, and during a winter of considerable severity made his way on foot morning and night to and from the school whatever the weather, and whatever the traveling, as long as the school continued   After this he had the advantage of a select school one season   He came to Glens Falls on the last day of the year 1842, literally to seek his fortune   That winter and the summer following he attended the Glens Falls Academy   In the September succeeding he was taken in as office boy and clerk in the drug and medicine business   Here he acquired the repute of being one of the steadiest young men of the place   Two years later he was admitted as an equal partner in the same business   At about the same period he commenced his medical studies, which were prosecuted under peculiar embarrassments and difficulties, at such scanty intervals as could be snatched from the cares and anxieties of business   He had in the interval of student life the advantage of a large practice   He entered the Albany Medical College in the winter of 1848–49 and graduated, after attending three courses of lectures, with great credit in the class of 1851   After this he remained three or four years in partnership with his uncle, assisting him in his practice, and then sold out to him   He was married on the 9th of September, 1853, to Miss Marcia L , daughter of Thomas H and Eliza (Miller) Bemis, of New York city   He settled down to the practice of his profession, commanding a fair share of the public patronage and esteem   Two years later he bought out the old doctor, as his uncle was often called, and resumed the drug business in connection with his practice   Subsequent to the death of his uncle he bought of the executors the building used as his store and office   Was burned out in the great fire of 1864   Rebuilt the same year, materially enlarging the size of the building   He closed out the drug business in 1869 to Messrs Pettit & Fennel, after which time he devoted his attention exclusively to the practice of his profession

Dr Peck was a physician of more than ordinary acumen and discrimination , as a surgeon he had few, if any, superiors outside of the cities   He performed several capital and important operations, and a more than average amount of success attested his judgment and skill   He died on Friday the 4th day of April, 1884

———

Uberto Crandell, of Warrensburgh, studied with his uncle at Scipio, N Y , entered Union College, sophomore class, and graduated at the age of eighteen , studied medicine with Dr William U Edgerton two years , attended one course of medical lectures at Geneva, N Y , and died about 1846, as supposed from blood poisoning, the result of a dissecting wound

———

Buel Goodset Streeter was born 25th July 1832 at Warsaw, Wyoming county, N Y   His father's name was Joab Streeter   His mother's name was

Sophia Wheat   His father was a Methodist preacher   He was one of Bishop
Philip Embury's first class of converts in Hampton, Washington county   He
began preaching when he was about twenty years of age, first at home as a local
preacher, from which he moved to the tract called "The Holland Purchase,"
about the year 1828, and filled the position of traveling preacher until the time
of his death which occurred in 1868, at Carlton, Orleans county, N Y, aged
seventy-two years

The subject of this sketch at the time of his mother's death, which occurred
when he was nine years old, was thrown as a waif upon the mercies of a heartless
world — thenceforth destined to carve out his own career, working as a chore-
boy wherever he could get a job of work and receiving such chance advantages as were to be obtained by an irregular attendance upon the public schools
until he was sixteen years of age, when for two winters he became a teacher himself   He all this time lived in and about Warsaw   When eighteen years of age
(1850) he moved to West Poultney, Vt, where he entered the Troy Conference
Academy, where he remained for a year, and at the same time commenced
and prosecuted the study of medicine under the tutelage of Dr Wm H. Miller,
a young physician of promise and ability, who had then but recently settled
there, and who afterward completed his life work at Sandy Hill, N Y, where
he died about the year 1873   In 1852 he entered Castleton Medical College,
from whence he graduated at the end of a second term, 4th of November, 1853
He was married soon after to Lizana Hotchkiss, daughter of Captain Hiram
Hotchkiss, of Hampton, Washington county   He embarked in the practice
of medicine in Hampton, where he remained until about the year 1858 when
he moved to Granville (Bishop's Corners), and resumed the general practice
of his profession   At the breaking out of the Rebellion, moved by the same
patriotic impulses which actuated so many of the brave and daring spirits of
the North, he tendered his services and was commissioned assistant surgeon of
the Ninth N Y Cavalry, June 25th, 1862   His command was attached to
Siegel's celebrated corps, then operating in front of the defenses of Washington, and was in action at the battle of Cedar Mountain and the second battle
of Bull Run   The ensuing fall Siegel's command was turned over to the Army
of the Potomac, and constituted the Eleventh Corps under the command of
General O O Howard   During this period, preceding Burnside's famous
"mud march," the Ninth Cavalry was detached and incorporated with other
regiments of that arm of the service into the cavalry corps of the Army of the
Potomac under the command of Major General George Stoneman   During
this period the battle of Chancellorsville occurred, in which this brigade was a
participant, acting as provost guard, the remainder of the corps being detached
on a raid to the rear of the rebel lines   General Stoneman was superseded
soon afterward by Major General Alfred Pleasanton, under whose leadership
the subject of this sketch was promoted to the position of surgeon, and trans-

B. G. Streeter, M. D

ferred to the Fourth N Y Cavalry in the same brigade On the 9th of June, 1863, the entire corps was ordered to make a reconnaissance in force across the Rappahannock from the vicinity of Stafford C H , and in discharging that duty struck the right flank of the rebel army under General Lee at Brandy Station, where a severe all-day action occurred, resulting in being driven back across the Rappahannock, two heavy skirmishes having taken place previously at Beverly's and Kelly's Fords From opposite Brandy Station—the two armies moving in parallel lines down the Shenandoah Valley, and a spur of the Blue Ridge—the corps was ordered to make a reconnaissance through Ashby's Gap to determine the enemy's strength and location, here at Aldie on the 17th the corps encountered a division of Jeb Stuart's cavalry and had a severe engagement in which the colonel, Louis P Di Cesnola, was wounded and taken prisoner The rebels were driven through and beyond Middleburg on the Little Valley Pike where they remained until the 19th, the interval being devoted to bringing up the supplies and caring for the wounded, then moving forward encountered the enemy again a little beyond the town where another severe action took place, resulting in again driving the enemy On the 21st another encounter took place at Upperville, which resulted in the dispersion of the enemy in the direction of their main army. During these various actions, casualties to the number of several hundred occurred which kept the medical force in general, and Dr Streeter in particular, in active employment, engaged in amputations and superintending the removal of the wounded Here it was definitely ascertained that the enemy had determined upon invading the Union territory, and the cavalry corps, acting as an army of observation, retired slowly before the enemy's advance until the famous battle-field of Gettysburg was reached, when the division of General Gregg, in which the Fourth N Y Cavalry was included, was stationed to guard the right flank of the Union army and protect the immense trains of supplies and stores in the rear After the defeat of the rebels at Gettysburg this division was dispatched in pursuit of the retreating army, with the rear guard of which they had an active engagement at Falling Waters From this time forth Dr Streeter's regiment participated in all the active movements of the cavalry corps of the Army of the Potomac until the close of the campaign and then went into winter quarters at Culpepper Court House In the following May, 1864, the Army of the Potomac, being under the leadership of General Grant, and the command of the cavalry having been transferred to General Sheridan, this force crossed the Rapidan at Germania Ford and participated in the series of engagements known in history as the battle of the Wilderness After the action of Todd's Tavern (one of the series), Dr Streeter was ordered to take a large ambulance train of wounded and medical supplies and establish a hospital for the care of the wounded and sick of the cavalry corps, numbering about 2,000 Of this he had charge from two to three weeks, his time being fully occupied in the cares and duties devolving upon so important a responsibility   At the end of this period the hospital was broken up and the sick and wounded placed on transports and sent to Washington, the doctor being ordered to rejoin his regiment, which he found stationed at Whitehouse Landing   Crossing the James River with his regiment, he remained with the Army of the Potomac until Washington was again threatened by the invasion of Early from the valley, when two divisions of the cavalry (including the doctor's brigade) were dispatched to the relief of the national capital, under the command of General Sheridan, whose name is now a household word in every hamlet of the North.   The enemy speedily retired up the valley followed sharply by Sheridan's troopers, and in a sanguinary engagement at Newton, something like 200 men being wounded, the doctor was ordered to remove the disabled and wounded to Winchester and thence to Washington so soon as the railroad, which had been torn up by the vicissitudes of war, was reconstructed, he was afterward ordered to rejoin his regiment In this attempt, after having discharged the duty assigned him, he was captured by Mosby's guerilla band near Kernstown, four miles above Winchester He was sent to Richmond and confined in Libby prison for twelve days, and was finally released through the kindness and intervention of Captain Semple, of the rebel army and inspector of rebel prisons, who had previously, when wounded and a prisoner, received many kindnesses and attentions at the hands of the doctor, and through his agency and instrumentality the latter was released unconditionally and sent forward to the Union lines, reaching his regiment at Charleston Heights on the 12th of September, 1864.   Here the doctor resigned his commission as regimental surgeon to accept the position of acting staff-surgeon of the U S army, having a commission from the general government, and was at once assigned to duty as surgeon-in-chief of Powell's Division of Cavalry, in the cavalry corps of the Shenandoah Valley   On the 15th of November following (1864) he was assigned to duty as medical director of the cavalry corps of the Army of the Shenandoah, on the 10th of January following he was assigned to duty as medical director of the Army of the Shenandoah, in which capacity he served until July 1st, 1865, when he with the army was mustered out by general orders, and he returned to his home at Granville, where he remained in practice until April 1st, 1867, when he removed to Glens Falls.   He has been elected coroner two terms, and served as trustee of School District No 2 from 1872 to 1881, when, upon the consolidation of five of the village districts into the Union Free School No 1, of Glens Falls, he was elected one of the board of directors, and holds that position at the present time   The doctor feels justly proud of his relations to our public schools, and has, during his extended term of service, proved an energetic, faithful, and efficient officer.   Upon the organization in January last, in Glens Falls, of a board for the examination of pension claimants, he was appointed a member and elected treasurer of the same, positions which he now holds   In his profession, the doctor has earned a wide-spread reputation as a skillful surgeon and successful practitioner of medicine He is still in the prime and vigor of an active manhood, and gives promise of many coming years of activity and usefulness

———

Godfrey R Martine, son of James J Martine, of Caldwell, Warren county, was born in the city of Troy, N Y, on the 27th day of April, 1837 He came to Warren county when a lad of eight years and received his general education principally at the Warrensburgh Academy under different instructors, notably among whom was O E Babcock, afterwards General Babcock, conspicuous for his connection with General Grant The subject of this sketch pursued his Latin course under the direction of Rev R C Clapp, of Chestertown, and attended the Normal School in Albany, receiving a teacher's State certificate He afterwards taught in several of the towns of Warren county and was for a few terms principal of the Warrensburgh Academy He then entered the medical department of the University of Vermont for the study of his chosen profession, in which he continued until he graduated in June, 1862 Immediately after graduating he returned to Warren county and commenced the practice of medicine in Warrensburgh, afterward in Johnsburgh, and has practiced more or less in all the towns of Warren county and in all the adjoining counties In 1882 he removed to Glens Falls, where he has attained an enviable position in his profession.

Dr Martine was married on the 9th of September, 1869, to Mary Woodward, of Warrensburgh, a lady of well-known attainments and refinement They have one child, Byron A Martine, born April 8, 1883 Politically, Dr Martine has been a life-long Democrat, and in 1866 he was the nominee of that party for county school commissioner He represented the town of Johnsburgh on the Board of Supervisors from 1866 to 1870 inclusive In the fall of 1869 he was elected Member of the Assembly In these positions of trust his excellent natural and acquired qualifications and unflinching integrity enabled him to discharge his duties to the eminent satisfaction of his constituents

It may not be out of place here to state that the present popularity of the grand and beautiful Blue Mountain Lake region is due almost solely to the foresight and energetic efforts of Dr Martine In the year 1875, when that section was an unknown wilderness, he purchased the site and erected the Blue Mountain Lake House, a splendidly located hotel, accommodating 250 guests, inclusive of ten or twelve cottages which have been gradually added to the grounds Roads were opened and this famous region has become one of, if not the most popular resort in the great Adirondack wilderness It is to-day acknowledged by those best able to judge, that Dr Martine's perseverance and faith in this enterprise were the means of saving the Adirondack Railroad from an early decline The lasting benefits thus conferred upon the people of that section and the public at large, can never be properly estimated

Dr Martine is a Fellow of the New York State Medical Association, and one of its original members, has been president of the Warren County Medical Society, member of the American Medical Association, to which he has been several times elected delegate, and is now secretary of the Pension Board of Examining Surgeons, at Glens Falls   With the exception of a short term of volunteer service in the hospital at Annapolis, Md, during the War of the Rebellion, Dr Martine's labors in the medical profession, now extending over more than a quarter of a century, have been confined to Warren county and its surroundings, and his record throughout this whole section is that of a faithful and reliable physician

---

Dr. Fletcher Ransom came to Glens Falls in the year 1824   His office was in a framed building, subsequently occupied by Billy J Clark as a drug store, which stood on the site now occupied by Albert Vermillia as a meat-market   He was born in West Townshend, Windham county, Vt, in the year 1801, and graduated at the Vermont Medical School at Castleton, Vt., a short time previous to his removal to Glens Falls   He married the daughter of John Noyce, esq, of Putney, Vt, who died about the year 1849 at their home in Michigan   In 1830, according to the supervisors' record, he was allowed a claim for treating paupers   Dr Ransom was an enthusiast in his profession, and shortly gathered about him a number of young, ardent and aspiring students of medicine.   In furthering their purposes, and in perfecting his own knowledge of anatomy, it is stated that he sent below for subjects for dissection and practiced his anatomical researches, in company with his students, as opportunity presented   As this became gradually known to the public it met with popular disfavor and dislike.   Whether owing to this or other causes is not known to the writer, but at all events he suddenly decided to remove from the place, and in the spring of 1835 he, in company with A. T Prouty and Colonel Fred Curtenius, removed to Kalamazoo, Mich., where it is understood he abandoned the practice of his profession, and settled down to a farmer's life and all its peaceful, prosperous, and uneventful details, until the time of his death, which took place on the 2d of June, 1867

Truman Barney Hicks was born in the town of Sunderland, Bennington county, Vt, on the 8th of January, 1785   He was the son of Simeon and Molly (Barney) Hicks   Simeon Hicks was a soldier in the War of the Revolution and with that galaxy of Vermont patriots present in action at the battle of Bennington

Dr Hicks's educational advantages were only such as could be obtained in the very common schools of a border settlement   He attended lectures and graduated at the Medical College at Fairfield, N Y   One of the professors of this institution was named Westch Willoughby, for whom he formed so warm

G. R. Martine, M. D.

and durable a friendship as in later years to name for him his youngest son.
In 1810 he commenced practice at Wilton, Saratoga county, N Y. His first
wife was a Miss Barbara Hays, of Rutland, Vt, by whom he had three children, two sons and one daughter   From Wilton he moved to Hadley in the
same county, and later on to Luzerne, where he resided for many years   Here
he married for his second wife, Charlotte B, daughter of Judge Jeremy Rockwell, of Hadley   By her he had one son, already referred to in a preceding
paragraph   Dr Hicks was a man of unusual ability, good judgment and fair
attainments   He was a rugged, manly type of the hardy Green Mountain
Boys, such as Ethan Allen, Remember Baker, and Seth Warner, of Revolutionary memory, and of whom his father was another kindred spirit   Jovial
and rollicking, self-reliant, ready for any emergency, he had many fast and
warm friends and but few foes   In his practice he had few equals in this section of country   He was often called either in counsel or for professional services for distances of thirty or forty miles, and in his prime his activity and
endurance were something wonderful   From Luzerne Dr Hicks removed to
Caldwell at the head of Lake George where he passed the remainder of his
days   In the course of his life he filled many positions of honor and trust
He served seven months in the American army in the last war with England,
was commissioner of highways, colonel of militia, associate judge of the Warren
County Court of Common Pleas, coroner in the year 1827, and member of Assembly for Warren county in the years 1828 and 1835   In 1846 he received
the honorary degree of Doctor of Medicine from the Regents of the University
of the State of New York   In 1847 he was elected a permanent member of
the State Medical Society, in which body he had for many years represented
the county of Warren

    He died at Caldwell, Warren county, N Y, on the 16th of September,
1848, after an illness of about two weeks' duration   His remains were removed
to the town of Wilton, Saratoga county, N Y, for burial

    Marshall S Littlefield was born in the year 1804, in the town of Arling-
ton, Vt   He was the son of Simeon and Lydia Littlefield   His early education was acquired in the common schools of his native town   He studied medicine with his father, who was also a physician of considerable note and ability,
and had an extended ride through the rough mountainous region which envi-
roned his home.   After passing through two or three courses of lectures at
the Vermont Medical College at Castleton, the subject of this memoir received
his diploma from that institution in due course   He at first located at Caven-
dish, Vt, where he embarked in practice and remained about two years   At
the end of this period he returned to Arlington and married a Miss Hoyt, and
remained in practice there until her death, which occurred in something less
than two years   In 1830 he removed to the hamlet known as Pattin's Mills in

the north part of the town of Kingsbury Here he speedily became popular and built up an extensive and lucrative practice During his sojourn at this point he joined the Methodist Church, of which he remained a consistent and exemplary member to the day of his death In 1838 he removed to Glens Falls and opened an office for the practice of medicine In the fall of the same year he was united in marriage with Miss Catharine Buckbee, formerly of Clinton, Duchess county, N Y He continued in the flood-tide of remunerative and successful practice up to within a few days of his demise He was a kind and indulgent husband and father. Genial, sunny, and self-possessed in the sick-room, always well dressed, neat, cleanly and tidy in his personal appearance, his general air and manner were prepossessing and assuring to his patients and friends, who looked up to him as an oracle He died of typhoid fever, but notwithstanding the deadly contagion working in his system and slowly sapping the fountains of life, he bravely kept at his professional duties up to within five days of the time of his death, and retained his mental faculties nearly to the last On his gravestone is the following inscription " Dr Marshall S Littlefield, died Nov 20, 1863, aged 59 years " He was buried after the formula and ritual of the Masonic fraternity

CHAPTER XXIV

SECRET SOCIETIES

The First Lodge of Free Masons in Warren County — Glens Falls Chapter — Warrensburgh Lodge — Odd Fellows — Horicon Lodge No 305 — Horicon Lodge No 349 — Riverside Encampment — Other Lodges

WARREN county has been represented by the ancient and honorable Order of Free and Accepted Masons since early in the century, a Chapter having been formed in Glens Falls four years before Warren county was organized Since that date lodges have been instituted elsewhere in the county, the following account of which has been kindly furnished for this work by T S Ketchum, esq , of Glens Falls —

Glens Falls Chapter No 55 Royal Arch Masons — On the 29th of April, 1809, Ezra Ames, Grand High Priest of the Grand Chapter of Royal Arch Masons of the State of New York, granted a dispensation to John A Ferris, Israel P Baldwin and Hanmer Palmer to hold a Mark Lodge at Queensbury, under the name of Felicity Mark Lodge This body kept its organization until February 6th, 1817, when the same Grand High Priest recommended to the Grand Chapter that a warrant be issued to Asahel Clark, Charles White and Warren F Hitchcock to hold a chapter at Glens Falls under the name of Glens Falls Chapter No 55 This was done by the Grand Chapter on the same day, and the charter issued at that time now hangs in the rooms of the Chapter at Glens Falls The following list gives the names of the different ones who held the office of High Priest in the years indicated 1819-20, Royal Leavens, 1821, Charles White, 1822, Asahel Clark, 1823-24, James White, 1825, James Hay, 1826-27, James White, 1828, Henry G Brown, 1829, James White, from 1830 to 1854, no record whatever exists

On the 21st of March, 1855, John S Perry, Grand High Priest, granted a dispensation to A C Tiffany, Enoch Ellis and Samuel Ranger to re-organize the Chapter under the same name, and numbered 154 1856, 1857, 1858, A C Tiffany; 1859, F J J Kerney, 1860, 1861, 1862, M R Peck, 1863, 1864, 1865, 1866, G T Lewis, 1867, E R Lake, 1868, Jos Mead, 1869, 1870, M R Peck, 1871, 1872, 1873, 1874, J S Garrett, 1875 1876, T S Ketchum, 1877, W. H Van Cott, 1878, 1879, 1880, 1881, 1882, T S Ketchum, 1883-84, C H Hitchcock, 1885, W S Whitney

On the 6th of February, 1861, Dr M R Peck, then High Priest, secured the passage of a resolution in the Grand Chapter, changing the number from 154 to the original number 55

In 1864 the Chapter was burned out in the great conflagration of May 31st, losing many valuable records and nearly all of its paraphernalia In 1874 the Chapter inaugurated a movement by which the different Masonic bodies secured the lease of the present Masonic Hall in Sherman building on Glen street, which is claimed to be one of the most convenient, pleasant and finely furnished lodge rooms in the State outside of the large cities This body has among its members some of the most prominent men in town and is in a flourishing condition,

Warrensburgh Lodge. — This lodge, known as Warrensburgh Lodge No 425, was instituted August 27th, 1857. with the following as charter members: —Lewis Persons, Pelatiah Richards Benjamin P Burhans, Joseph Russell, Asa Crandall, M Nelson Dickinson, John A Russell, Hiram McNutt, J G McNutt.

The first officers of the lodge were as follows —Lewis Persons, W M , Hiram McNutt, S W , John A Russell, J W , Asa Crandall, treasurer, Edgar W Burhans, secretary, M N Dickinson, S D , Alfred Emerson, J D , C R Hawley, chaplain, J C Heath, tiler

The officers for the year 1884-85 are as follows: — John G Smith, W M., Albert H Thomas, S W , Lester C Dickinson, J W , Alexander T Pasko, treasurer, Thomas H Crandall, secretary, Daniel B Howard, S D , Louis Weinman, J D , Frederick Loveland, Thomas J Smith, M of C , Miles Thomas, chaplain, F O Burhans, marshall; M N Dickinson, Miles Thomas, Louis Charette, trustees; M N. Dickinson, N J Sharp, O F Hammond, standing committee; Eleazer Herrick, organist, Alexander Smith, tiler

ODD FELLOWS

The first lodge of Odd Fellows in Warren county was Horicon Lodge No. 305, which was instituted July 20th, 1847, with George W Vanderhuyden, E. C Hall, Walter Geer, jr., Robert R Tearse, William R Locke, Albert Vermillia, A W Holden and Stewart Brown as members   The lodge continued in successful working for nearly twenty years, but suspended during the late war

The new Horicon Lodge No 349 began work under dispensation February 19th, 1873, and its charter was granted on the 21st of August of the same year   The charter members were Stephen Starbuck, M M Taft, C C La Point, Franklin Winship, Andrew Lennox, L T Bullard, Sanford Duel, and Seymour Hawks   The first officers were as follows . Andrew Lennox, N G , C C La Point, V G , Seymour Hawks, secretary, M Hughes, P S , Stephen Starbuck, treasurer

The present officers of the lodge are as follows · Sanford Martindale, N. G , Frederick Chambers, V G , George W Capron, recording secretary, E. H Gates, financial secretary ; A Bloats, warden ; M G Crannell, conductor ; John Hill, inside guardian , J R Kee, treasurer

Riverside Encampment No 62 — This encampment was originally located at Sandy Hill, but in 1874 steps were taken looking to its removal to Glens Falls   This measure was finally accomplished and the first meeting here was held November 8th, 1875   Since that date the encampment has continued in a flourishing condition   Following are the present officers   J P. Wilcox, chief patriarch , M J Crannell, senior warden , E. H Gates, junior warden , Willard Monroe, high priest , Frederick Chambers, scribe , N L Nelson, treasurer ; R. Hopkins, inside sentinel

Lodges have been instituted within the past two years in Warrensburgh and Chester which are in a flourishing condition

---

CHAPTER XXV

HISTORY OF THE PATENT AND TOWN OF QUEENSBURY

WITH the stirring events of a military character which were enacted within and near to the boundaries of the present town of Queensbury down to the close of the Revolutionary War, we have endeavored to make the reader familiar in preceding chapters of this work   Previous to that memorable struggle for liberty, settlement had progressed on the original Queensbury patent to the proportions of a considerable community , but its peaceful thrift and progress were disturbed and interrupted by the Revolution, and most of the settlers were prompted by prudence to desert the homes they had reared, or were driven forth by war's stern necessities When they, or their successors, returned at the end of the conflict, they found little but general desolation and the partial re-establishment of Nature's supremacy over the soil, but the arts of peace were resumed and prosecuted with vigor by the pioneers, and ere many years had passed the foundations of the present prosperous and intelligent communities were broadly and deeply laid It remains for us to note the progress of those early settlements, the public civil acts of the inhabitants, and the later growth of the town and its institutions

Immediately following the granting of the Queensbury patent, its survey and partition among the proprietors early in the year 1763 (as detailed in previous pages), the infant settlement was begun [1] Abraham Wing and Ichabod Merritt came in from Duchess county in the summer of the year named and made an opening in the wilderness The first building erected was a log dwelling, which stood on the Sandy Hill road near the site of the residence occupied in late years by Charles Parsons Here Abraham Wing and his family lived for a time Mr Merritt and his family, it is believed, temporarily occupied the block-house in the neighborhood of Charles Green's steam saw-mill The second house was built in 1764 by Abraham Wing, who gave up the first dwelling to his son, this was also a log structure and stood a few rods in rear of the site of the old McDonald mansion, now owned by Gurdon Conkling The third building was a log house erected by Abraham Wing, jr, and stood on the site of Kenworthy's crockery and variety store

The valuable water power in this vicinity very naturally attracted the early attention of the pioneers and steps were taken in 1764 to improve it On the 9th day of July in that year an agreement was entered into between Moses Clement and Moses Phillips, by which the latter agreed to build a mill for Clement, working for "7s per day, Jos Taylor, his journeyman at 5s and John his prentice at 2s per Day" In the final account rendered Mr Clement was credited by Phillips with "£9 12 0 for Boarding, Drinking, Washing and Lodging," with other items A dispute arose over the contract and suit was brought (probably in Albany) to recover payment for building the mill, this occurred in March or April, 1765 The result of the action is not recorded, and it is of importance only that it was probably the first law-suit arising in the community

The location of the mill can only be conjectured, but is supposed to have been near the mouth of Cold Brook, at the eastern boundary of the town, the

---

1 It is stated on tradition, that at the time of the division and drawing of the town lots, one John Buck drew a lot now partly embraced within the limits of the corporation of Glens Falls, and when the surveyor's bill was presented, being unable to meet his assessment, he sold or offered his interest for a peck of beans — HOLDEN'S *History of Queensbury*

power being supplied by a wing dam extending across the island near the left bank of the river

There must have been a saw-mill in operation here previous to the erection of the one just described Whether it was built by Mr Wing alone, or in connection with his son-in-law, Nehemiah Merritt, or by the John Bracket alluded to, is not known The fact is amply substantiated, however, by the following document found by Dr Holden among the Wing manuscripts —

"CITY AND COUNTY ⎱ ss
   OF ALBANY,   ⎰

"The deposition of Simeon Chandler taken upon oath before me Patt Smyth Esq , one of his Majesty's Justices of the Peace, for the county aforesaid etc That in the year 1763, James Bradshaw did in my hearing, agree with Mr Abraham Wing, and Mr Nehemiah Merritt, for as many planks and boards as should be wanted for the work necessary to be done for the said mill in Kingsbury, in said year 1763, and on said Wing, and said Merritt departure from Queensbury, said Bradshaw did desire the above said Wing and Merritt would give orders that said Chandler should have what was then wanted for said work and said Wing and said Merritt did send a token to John Bracket to saw what planks were wanted for the work aforesaid

"The above is a true copy of what was wrote by the hands of Simeon Chandler the 18th day of Dec , 1763

" PATT SMYTH, Justice."

In the year 1765 the interest of Nehemiah Merritt in a mill here was transferred by the document quoted below to Abraham Wing , this mill, it appears, was built by those two men and may be identical with the one above described. Following is the assignment by Merritt. —

" Know all men by these presents that I Nehemiah Merritt, of Beekman's precinct in Dutchess county, and province of New York, gentlemen, for and in consideration of the sum of five shillings current money of New York, to me in hand paid by Abraham Wing of Beekman's precinct in Dutchess county and province of New York aforesaid, have and by these presents do for me and my heirs, remise, release, and forever quit claim unto him, the said Abraham Wing, his heirs and assigns in his peaceable and quiet possession, now being all that one full and equal half of all that saw-mill on the great fall in Queensbury township in Albany county and province of New York aforesaid which we the said Merritt and Wing in joint partnership built together, as likewise furnished said mill with utensils necessary, likewise the dwelling house standing a little northward about ten rods from said mill

" Now therefore, what is herein contained and intended is that I the said Nehemiah Merritt for me, my heirs and assigns will and hereby do release and forever quit claim unto him the said Abraham Wing his heirs and assigns, the one full and equal half of all that mill, dwelling house and utensils belonging

to said mill, and furthermore the one equal half of the water, and water course
to said mill, as likewise the equal half of said mill-dam, raceway, logway, and
all other privileges advantages and profits thereunto belonging, unto him the
said Abraham Wing his heirs and assigns forever

"In witness whereof, I the said Nehemiah Merritt to this my release have
set my hand and seal this seventh day of the tenth month in the year of our
Lord one thousand, seven hundred and sixty-five

"NEHEMIAH MERRITT [Seal]

"Sealed and delivered in the presence of

"Benjn Ferris junr

"Reed Ferris"

This mill stood, according to Dr Holden, near "the site of the old Spencer
tavern, or Glen House, under the hill"

Early log dwellings other than those mentioned were built at various points,
among them being one at the Butler Brook on the plank road, another on the
brow of the hill near the present residence of Duncan McGregor, and still another near the residence of Henry Crandell

It was about this period that the proprietors of Queensbury deeded to
Abraham Wing a section of thirty acres of unappropriated land immediately
at the falls, in consideration of his having been to the trouble and expense of
building a saw-mill and grist-mill for the accommodation of the inhabitants
The instrument by which this act was effected is as follows

"To the honorable proprietors and owners of Queensbury township in Albany county, your humble petitioner showeth —

"That Abraham Wing, late of Dutchess county, now resident of the above
said township have at a great cost and charge built mills in and on a small
tract of undivided land in the above said township to the great encouragement
for settling ye above lands which is and must be an advantage to the owners

"Wherefore in consideration for such cost and encouragement, I desire ye
owners of said lands on which the mills stand will convey the same to me as is
underwritten, etc

"This indenture made this seventh day of March in the year of our Lord
one thousand seven hundred and sixty-six by and between we the subscribers
of the one part, and Abraham Wing late of Dutchess county, now resident in
Queensbury township, Albany county and province of New York of the other
part witnesseth, that we the subscribers for divers good causes and considerations us hereunto moving, the receipt whereof we do hereby acknowledge, have
granted, bargained, quitclaimed and confirmed, and by these presents do grant,
bargain, quitclaim, alien, and confirm unto the said Abraham Wing his heirs and
assigns forever, all the right, title, interest, claim and demand that we now have,
ever had, or ought to have in that certain tract or parcel of undivided land in
the township of Queensbury in Albany county and province above said situ-

ate lying on the Great falls by Hudson's river in the above township, bounded to the east by lands of Nathaniel Stevenson and William Haviland, to the north and west by lands of Abraham Wing, and to the south on Hudson's river, containing about thirty acres of land, be the same more or less, and also all trees, wood, underwood, water, water courses, profits, commodities, advantages, hereditaments whatsoever to the said messuage and undivided land above mentioned belonging or in anywise appertaining, and also the reversion and reversions of every part thereof, and also all our estate, right, title, interest, claim, and demand whatsoever to him the said Abraham Wing, his heirs and assigns forever, to have and to hold the above granted, bargained and quit-claimed premises above mentioned and every part thereof to the only proper use and behoof of the said Abraham Wing, his heirs and assigns forever. And we the subscribers for ourselves, our heirs and assigns will warrant and forever defend from any claiming from or under us by these presents   In witness whereof to these presents we have hereunto subscribed our names and affixed our seals the day and year above written

" BENJAMIN SEELYE,	[L S]
" JOHN AKIN,	[L S]
" REED FERRISS,	[L S]
" NATHANIEL STEVENSON,	[L S]
" JACOB HAVILAND,	[L S]
" WILLIAM HAVILAND,	[L S]

" Sealed and delivered in the presence of
   " Reed Ferriss,
   " Matthew Franklin,
   " Gaius Talcott,
   " Judah Handy,
   " Jacob Hicks,
   " Eliezer Herrick "

These early mills were of the greatest importance to the settlers, they are the first necessity in all new communities   They were far different from the mammoth establishments that now occupy the vicinity, but they sufficed to supply rough lumber from the magnificent pines which abounded in the immediate locality, and were the beginning of the subsequent great lumber interest in which the early inhabitants engaged and which added largely to the thrift of the town, while the grist-mills were a still greater accommodation in giving the families facilities for grinding their grains, which they otherwise would have had to transport long distances

The need of transportation across the river was felt at an early day and a ferry was established about the period under consideration, which, according to Dr Holden, extended " from the upper rollway across to the head of Water street descending to the river from the old Folsom house, on the south side of

the falls   The old road followed the course of the ravine leading from the canal basin to Park street   This ferry was continued with little interruption up to
the close of the century   The first ferry house was a log building on the south
side of the river, and on its bank a few rods above the dam, and was occupied
by one of the Parks family   The cellar is even now visible   The house was
burnt during the Revolution   The second, which was in use subsequent to
the Revolution, was built on this side the river near the rollway "

These various early improvements aroused the apprehensions of the Indians, particularly the Mohawks, who complained and protested to Sir William
Johnson, then superintendent of Indian affairs for the northern department
The Indians witnessed the encroachments and improvements of the whites
with jealous eyes, but the wise jurisdiction of the superintendent and their
confidence in him prevented any outbreak, and their claims were subsequently
amicably adjusted.

The first white child born in the town was a son of Ichabod Merritt; this
child became the grandfather of Isaac Mott, now living at Glens Falls and a
prominent attorney of the county

On Tuesday, the 6th day of May, 1766, the first town meeting was held
in the town of Queensbury, when the following officers were chosen —

Abraham Wing, moderator; Asaph Putnam, town clerk; Abraham Wing,
supervisor, Jeffrey Cowper, assessor, Ichabod Merritt assessor, Asaph Putnam, constable, Ichabod Merritt, collector, Benajah Putnam, pathmaster,
Truelove Butler, pound-keeper, Abraham Wing, overseer of the poor, Caleb
Powell, overseer of the poor

Here were eleven officers and only seven men to fill them, those seven
without doubt, constituted the entire population eligible to office, and of the
seven, only two were proprietors of land   The modern scramble for political
station was then unknown, and it was not much of a man who could not have
two or three offices if he was ambitious in that direction

It now becomes incumbent to mention with more or less detail some of
the earliest settlers in the town, besides Abraham Wing, sen , and Jeffrey Cowper, who have been alluded to   While the latter was, probably, the first man
to locate permanently on the patent, it does not appear that he was a person
of any considerable prominence in the community   The three Merritt
brothers, Nehemiah, Daniel and Ichabod, married the three eldest daughters
of Abraham Wing, the pioneer   The first two never removed to Queensbury,
but Ichabod and his wife Sarah did, and his name appears above in the list of
town officers for 1766   The oldest son of Ichabod and the first white child
born in the town, was named Joseph, who was born December 17th, 1766.
From Ichabod Merritt are descended the numerous families of Motts and
Carys in this and the adjoining town of Moreau   He held other offices in the
town and is said to have erected the first frame-house in Queensbury; it was

22

situated on one of the town plot sections near the Half-way Brook and was burned during Burgoyne's advance, together with the mills at the Falls and several other dwellings In the early part of the Revolutionary War the family returned to Duchess county, whence Joseph removed to the town of Moreau where he died in 1826

Daniel Jones was one of the earliest settlers of Queensbury and was a brother of David Jones, whose fame rests upon his having been the betrothed of the hapless Jane McCrea The family, consisting of the widow and six sons, settled in Kingsbury, having removed from Leamington, N J After Daniel came to Queensbury he became one of the foremost in developing its water power and was interested in the first saw-mill and grist-mill built at Glens Falls, they were located just above the bridge He married Deborah Wing, sixth child of Abraham and Anstis (Wood) Wing He also bought the islands in the river of the Jessups of Luzerne, which he afterwards conveyed to Abraham Wing, one of them still bears the name of Wing's Island At the outbreak of the Revolution he adhered to the king and fled to Canada His lands here that had not been previously disposed of were confiscated and sold after the war At the time of Carleton's invasion in 1780, his house was burned by the invaders His wife died in Montreal March 28th, 1782, in childbed, which fact he communicated to her father in a feeling letter After the war he settled in Brockville, Upper Canada, where he received a large grant of land in consideration of his losses here In latter years the heirs endeavored to recover the value of the lands from the State, but were unsuccessful

Zachariah Butler was in Queensbury previous to the Revolution, and also adhered to the cause of the king He secreted his effects, burying some of them in the cellar, and fled to Canada His dwelling, on the Bay road, was burned by the invaders under Carleton, and Butler never returned It is believed that Butler Brook, a small affluent of Half-way Brook, and consisting of three small streams rising in the swamps west of the village, received its name from him It was at the northernmost of the three branches that Washington and his staff stopped to drink while on their way to Crown Point in 1783

Jacob Hicks was a son-in-law of Abraham Wing, having married Content, the seventh child of Mr Wing, when she was but fourteen years of age She was born the 11th of April, 1755 His name frequently occurs among the Wing manuscripts of an early date In a statement of account dated Albany 22d May, 1773, rendered by James Dole, merchant, of that city, for £68, 16s 8¾ d, as quoted by Dr Holden, the latter is credited by boards, plank, etc , and Daniel Jones's bond, together with cash nearly sufficient to cancel the same The conclusion reached by this is, that Hicks probably had the management of Jones and Wing's saw-mill at the falls Among the Wing papers is a receipt, dated 7th July, 1774, given by David Dickinson at Stillwater, for thirty-one shillings in full of all demands in favor of " John Hix, Deseest " In another receipt given for payment of a bill of goods sold Jacob Hicks, 5th Aug, 1772, the paper bearing date 7th May, 1774, Benjn Wing is named as executor   These data leave the inference quite probable that Hicks died in the latter part of 1773, or the early part of 1774   Two daughters, Sarah and Anstis, were the fruit of this marriage   Both survived and both married and raised large families

The family and descendants of Abraham Wing, the pioneer, demand much more extended reference than we have accorded them in an earlier chapter, in referring merely to the first settlement of the Queensbury patent in its chronological order with contemporaneous events   It is believed that Mr Wing's circumstances in the latter years of his life were considerably straitened, owing largely to his losses from the war   The following extract from his last will, furnished Dr Holden by Judge Gibson, of Salem, N Y, throws some light upon the extent of his estate —

"Wing, Abraham, of Queensbury, Wash Co, last will and testament dated '20 day of 9 month' 1794   Give to my wife *Anstis* the sole use of my house and farm containing about 342 acres and all my stock, farming utensils and household furniture during her natural life   To my son *Benjamin* and to his heirs, etc, the above homestead with stock, etc, on farm at death of my wife, to my grandson *Russell Lewis* at my and his G mother's decease, if he shall live with us till that time or when he shall be of age one yoke of oxen and two good cows, to the remainder of my children and G children, viz Abraham Winge, Phebe Merritt, Patience Babcock, Content Hixon, Mary Lewis, Grd children, Joseph, Mary and Deborah Merritt, Richard and Mary Jones, Russell Lewis and Willett Wing all the rest of my estate, viz 50 acres of land at the meadow, rear of first Division lots No 87, 86, 85, 37, 19, 17, and half of 10 and 4, to divide among Abraham, Phebe, Patience, Content, Mary, Joseph, Mary, Deborah, Richard, Mary, Russell and Willett, and if any or either of Grd children should die without a lawful heir, then their shares among the survivors   Appoints his wife *Anstis* exx and his son Abraham, and friend Elisha Folger exrs   *Witnesses*· Warren Ferriss, John A Ferriss, Reed Ferriss   Proved before the surrogate of Wash Co, 27 May, 1795, and the same by Abraham Wing, qualified as exr"

Among the children of Abraham Wing, sen, was Abraham, jr, who was the youngest son   He was born on the "29th of 6th month, 1757, and married Mary McKie"   They had seven children, the youngest of whom was born in Glens Falls on the 17th of August, 1791, and was also named Abraham The little settlement was then known as Wing's Falls   Mr Wing secured the elements of a sound business education and joined the late Josiah L Arms in mercantile business in the town of Wilton, Saratoga county   He was subsequently associated with several of the leading business men of Glens Falls in various enterprises   Upon the opening of the northern canal Mr Wing saw his opportunity and engaged heavily in the lumber business The extensive pine region in the Brant Lake Tract passed to the possession of parties in Troy, who sought out Mr Wing to manage their extensive business   " To his sagacity and clear-sighted judgment," wrote Dr Holden, " do we owe the present system of river-driving and booming which annually replenishes our mills, furnishes employment to a vast array of labor and which has substantially helped in building up our village to its present urban proportions '   When he assumed this responsibility the lumber business in this vicinity was looked upon as nearly exhausted, and the water power here as nearly worthless , no one thought the extensive forests to the far northward would ever become tributary to this immediate vicinity But Mr Wing instituted a new order of things and gave a vigorous impulse to the entire lumbering business on the Hudson River and its tributaries He soon became a partner in the business and ultimately sole proprietor of this and other large lumber interests, and accumulated a great fortune He was thrice married , first, to Abigail Barnard, of Townsend, Vt , second to Angeline B (Vail), widow of Alexander Robertson, of New York , third, to Mrs Frances A Glass (*née* Bowman) He had children only by his first wife, and two daughters only reached adult age He died in the entire respect of the community on the 13th of June, 1873

Daniel Wood Wing was the second child of Abraham jr , and Polly Mc-Kie Wing, and was born on the 25th of July, 1780, at the paternal homestead, the log dwelling before mentioned, that stood in rear of the old McDonald mansion In October, 1780," the year of the burning," as it was afterwards called in fireside story, while he was still a tender babe in his mother's arms, she fled at the approach of Carleton's marauding expedition and took refuge in the friendly recesses of the big Cedar swamp, that still borders, with its dense undergrowth and tangle of luxuriant vegetation, the eastern boundaries of the village The night following she lay concealed near the spring at the foot of Sandy Hill It is said of her that she emigrated to this country when she was but seventeen years of age She was a woman, if all accounts be true, of fine presence and rare personal attractions , of undoubted courage and heroism, well adapted to the rude times and rough border scenes of danger and peril in which she lived It is stated that in the early days of the settlement, while living in the old log tavern on the site of Kenworthy's hardware and variety store, she killed a large rattlesnake which she found coiled by a spring of water, still in existence under Vermillia's market, whither she had gone for her daily supply The rocks and ledges by the river banks, and the numerous swamps and swales of the neighborhood, afforded shelter and refuge in those days to vast numbers of rattlesnakes, and their extermination is believed to be due chiefly to the active agency of swine running at large, rather than any other cause [1]

---

[1] HOLDEN'S *History of Queensbury*, p 82.

The records show that in 1802 Mr Wing was keeping a tavern in the village of Glens Falls on the corner of Ridge and Warren streets, where he probably remained for a number of years as a landlord and merchant In 1809 he was in Sandy Hill keeping a tavern and in 1814 was again in Queensbury Not long after this date he removed to Fort Edward where he carried on mercantile and lumbering business and amassed a fortune He married first, July 25th, 1803, Rhoda Stewart, of Kingsbury, and second, August 18th, 1825, Almira Higby He died May 25th, 1856

Other descendants of Abraham Wing and the prominent part taken by them in the building up of the town will be mentioned in the proper place a little further on

Phineas Babcock was one of the earliest immigrants to this town and it is thought accompanied Abraham Wing when he made his first settlement here. He married Patience Wing, daughter of Abraham, and raised a large family He held most of the town offices, and that of supervisor several times He suffered heavily from the war and received therefor little or no compensation He resided at one period at the head of the lake Not far from the year 1790 he removed to St Albans, Vt, and located about a mile west of the site of that village There he erected the first framed house in that vicinity

"Here," to quote the language of a member of the family, "by the practice of frugality, and cheered by the consolations of religion, he pleasantly passed the remainder of his days in the bosom of his devoted family, and literally amidst the fragrance and beauty of surrounding shrubs and flowers planted by the hands of his affectionate companion, a woman of elevated aspirations, and refined taste and culture "

He died about the year 1820 His wife survived him about fifteen years She died at the house of her son-in-law, Willard Jewell, esq, St Albans, Vt, in the month of February, 1836, aged eighty-four years

The name of Truelove Butler appears as having been chosen to the office of pound-keeper at the first town meeting (1766) Of him Dr Holden says. "The only information the author has succeeded in obtaining in regard to this personage, is derived from the following, which is a copy of a paper contained in the Wing manuscripts

"'Memorandum this Ninth day of November in the year 1769, that I Jemima Butler widow, formerly wife to John Butler Deceased formerly both of Beekman's Precinct in Dutchess County and Province of New York Did Put and bind By Indenture our Son Truelove Butler an Apprentice to Abraham Wing him faithfully to Serve During the time the S^d Indentures specifyed which was about thirteen years and that time Being Expired ye S^d Apprentice is free and We the Said Butlers Did take and Receive an indenture of Abraham Wing, According to Custom and form obligating the Said Wing to Preform Sundry Duties and Preformances and Payments to our S^d Son, at the end of his Apprentice, which the S^d Abraham Wing has faithfully, honestly, and Compleatly fulfilled payed and don according to the Indenture, and our Satisfaction, and the Indentures which we had Being Not to be found and Lost, We the Subscribers Do By These Presents Acquit, Release and for Ever Discharge the S^d Abraham Wing from all agreements Promises Covenants and Payments in S^d Indenture Contained whatsoever   As Witness our hands the Day and Year above Written

"'JEMIMA ⨯ BUTTLER,
her
mark

"'TRUELOVE BUTTLER

"'Witnesses.
  "'John Smith Jr,
  "'Aron Butteler,
  "'Reed Ferriss'"

Andrew Lewis was another of the several sons-in-law of the founder of Queensbury   He came hither from New Milford, Conn, and married Mary Wing, the youngest daughter of the family, sometime previous to the Revolution   He became a resident of the island at the falls, known as Wing's Island   He was twice made a prisoner during the Revolution, and taken to Canada   On the first occasion he was one of a fishing party at the head of Lake George at the time of the capture of Fort Anne, on the second occasion he was captured during Carleton's invasion and remained in Canada until the close of the war   Descendants of Mr Lewis still live in Warren county   He held the office of constable in 1775 and down to 1780

James Higson (spelled "Hixon" in Mr. Wing's will) came to Queensbury previous to the Revolution   His name appears in the records as having held the office of assessor for nine years between 1777 and 1800   On the 18th of January, 1777, he advertised that he had taken it upon himself to act as the "executor to the estate of Jacob Hix, [Hicks] deceased, in place of Ichabod Merritt"   "It is presumed from this, and other circumstances" says Dr Holden, "that he had married a year or two previously, and perhaps longer, Content, the daughter of Abraham Wing, and the widow of said Hicks, who had died about the year 1774   Higson was taken prisoner together with Andrew Lewis, his brother-in-law, and William Robards, while hunting strayed cattle or horses near the Blind Rock at the time of Carleton's raid, in 1780   Another version of the affair states that they were preparing to go a fishing near East Creek, on Lake George, one of the number being engaged in chopping; the noise of which attracted the enemy, and they were surprised and captured   They were all taken to Canada, and after running the gauntlet, were rescued from the savages, and confined in prison   Robards afterwards escaped   The other two remained until the close of the war, being provided for to some extent, and probably kindly treated through the influence of some of their kinsmen who were refugees in Canada at that time After his return Higson built upon and occupied the land known as the Rosa farm, about one mile north of the village on the Ridge road. On the authority of the late Mr McDonald, Higson's wife was an intimate friend and confidant of Jane McCrea, they often exchanged visits, and after the atrocious massacre, the Indians exhibited Jenny's scalp, with its long tresses of golden hair, at her father's house near the lower freight house, back of the McDonald mansion Higson had three children, two daughters and a son John The latter removed west From Betsey the second child, are descended the Burnhams of this village "

William Robards, who was born in Canaan, Conn , February 10th, 1749, and married Phebe Fuller in 1774, came to Queensbury before the Revolution and probably soon after his marriage His name appears in the records in 1786 and from 1790 to 1794, in which years he held the office of supervisor He purchased a valuable farm on the Ridge and was a large land owner in other parts of the town Dr. Holden writes of him as follows . " He was merchant, farmer, manufacturer and magistrate , a man of large influence and wide popularity During the war he was twice made a prisoner and conveyed to Canada The first time was in 1777 at the date of Burgoyne's advance, when, with his wife's brother, Andrew Fuller and two of Wing's sons-in-law, Andrew Lewis and James Higson, a flying party of Tories and Indians made them prisoners, and conveyed them to Montreal, where they all had to run the gauntlet Robards, being fleet of foot, made his escape, but was afterwards recaptured He afterwards succeeded in escaping again from his prison house by breaking through the windows and scaling the wall, and after terrible exposures and sufferings reached his home He was again made prisoner while hunting for stray horses in the neighborhood of the Blind Rock at the time of Carleton's advance and was exchanged at the end of the war." He died August, 9th, 1802, and was buried in the family burying ground by the Round Pond at the Oneida.[1]

Asaph Putnam was a pioneer of Queensbury and must have immigrated very soon after Mr Wing's advent It is thought he was related by marriage to Mr Wing He held the office of town clerk from the year 1766–1777 inclusive, and was, like most of the pioneers, a member of the Society of Friends. While he resided here he lived in a log house which faced South street, on the estate of the late Roger Haviland, near the big dam

The preceding personal sketches embrace most of the pioneers of Queensbury who settled here prior to the breaking out of the Revolutionary War, as far as records are now accessible They came here and labored in the wilderness, hopeful and confident of the future, to build for themselves and their

---

[1] What was known as " Oneida Village " as early as 1818, and as " The Oneida " in later years, was a settlement on the Ridge road about five miles north of Glens Falls. It derived its name from Tom Hammond, a half-breed Oneida Indian, who kept a store here prior to and during the last war with Great Britain

posterity homes which they believed would rapidly increase in value and advance in attractiveness under the shelter of the peace then resting on the country   How these illusions were disturbed we shall endeavor to describe

Of the region of Queensbury as found by these pioneers, it may be said that it presented an undulating surface of wilderness, which was, in the language of Dr Holden, " but slightly broken by the numerous streams and ponds within its circuit, whose volume has been greatly diminished by the clearing up of the forests and swamps from whence they derived their supplies

"Three small clearings at the three picket forts previously named barely served to break the monotony of the old military road which led from near the intersection of Glen and Warren streets, in an almost direct line to the lot well known in the early part of the century as the Mallory place   The banks of the river, fringed with forest verdure, the island, the falls, then appeared in their native and undisturbed grandeur   The site of the village was broken by three deep gullies, or ravines, stretching for some distance from, and running at right angles with the river   One of these ravines now forms the principal sewer of the village, running down past the old foundry, and in that early day opening upon the river precisely at the point occupied by the Glens Falls Company's grist-mill   In the upper part of this ravine John A Ferriss constructed a fish pond of considerable size, which in 1802 was well stocked with trout, and was then considered one of the ornaments of the place   The second ravine may to this day be distinctly traced, commencing at Cross street and running parallel with Elm, crossing Park street, reissuing through the old Berry estate, and finding its outlet in the river just at the head of the falls   At a later period Judge Hay built a fish pond in this ravine, and Mr Cushing erected a diminutive water power in connection with the old red market, on the old Spencer place   The third followed the course of Basin street, and after effecting a junction with two small rivulets at the basin, opened on the river nearly opposite the steam saw-mill   Each of these ravines were in those primeval days the channels of rivulets, which, fed by springs, and supplied by the wash and drainage of the adjacent table lands, lent their constant supply to feed the waters of the Hudson "

With the exception of Jeffrey Cowper, as previously mentioned, the first settlers of Queensbury were members of the Society of Friends, or Quakers, and after the little community was established, one of the first acts of the inhabitants was the inauguration of religious services after the simple forms of that faith.   These services, it is supposed, were first held in the humble dwelling of the founder, Abraham Wing; later the old log Quaker church was erected on the south side of Half-way Brook, on the west side of the Bay Road Following is a copy of the first permit —

" Minute of a monthly meeting held at Nine Partners in Dutchess county and Province of New York the 19th of the 3d month, 1767

"At this meeting Abraham Wing in behalf of friends at Kingsbury [1] and Queensbury (and by way of Oblong preparative meeting) requested liberty to hold a meeting for worship there once a week, and its allowed at present to be held each first day at twelve o'clock And said Abraham Wing and James McKenney are appointed to have some care and oversight thereof and make report to this Monthly Meeting once in three months, or as often as they can, how the meeting is kept up and conducted, and what satisfaction they have in meeting together in that G R E A T, and necessary duty

"True Copy,
"Pr ZEBULON FERRIS, Clerk "

The old town records for the year 1767 bear the following record ·—

"At the annual town meeting held in Queensbury on Tuesday, ye 5 day of May, 1767, for the township of Queensbury

1 voted, Abraham Wing, Moderator
2 voted, Asaph Putnam, Town Clerk
3 voted, Abraham Wing, Supervisor
4 voted, Abraham Wing, and Asaph Putnam, Assessors
5 voted, Asaph Putnam, Constable
6 voted, Ichabod Merritt, Collector
7 voted, Benager Putnam, Pathmaster.
8 voted, Benjamin Wing, Pound-keeper
9 voted, Abraham Wing and Ichabod Merritt, Overseers of the Poor
10 voted, Benjamin Wing and Phineas Babcock, Fence-viewers '

The town records of olden times contain not alone matters of importance to the historian, but many entries so quaint in themselves as to render them worthy of transcription and preservation Under date of May 5th, 1772, we find that it was voted that "a Pound be Built about 10 rods North East from the house of Abraham Wing and to meet at the house of s'd Wing on monday the first day of June at Eight o'Clock in the fore Noon to Build said pound on the penalty of Six Shillings each man for non-appearance "

Again, in 1786, it appears that another pound was needed in another locality, the entry concerning which reads "Voted that their shall be a pound built west of the brig [bridge] over the half-way brook near the publick road on the forty acres left for such purposes to be built on Saturday the third day of June next Ensuing, each man to pay six shillings for his nun appearance on said day "

Scarcely less quaint is the following entry made in the next year "Voted that hogs shall be Free Commoners by warein a yok the debth of the Neck

---

[1] James Bradshaw and other petitioners for and settlers of the Kingsbury patent, were residents of New Milford, in the colony of Connecticut, whence, also, some of the patentees and first settlers of Queensbury also came In both of these towns the Quaker element was originally very strong, and in the latter for many years predominant; spreading hence to various parts of Warren county —HOLDEN's *History of Queensbury*

above the neck and half the depth blow, and the Cross peace twice the Length of the thickness of the Neck "

In the same year it was " Voted that there be a bounty of Forty Shillings For Cilling each wolf killed in The Town of Queensbury, To be paid by the Town Treasurer if it be collected before the seting of the assessors, otherwise to be maid in a Tax "

The prevailing absence of fences and the difficulty of keeping domestic animals sufficiently within control to even enable their owners to recognize his own without distinguishing marks, is indicated by the numerous entries in the records describing " ear-marks," as they were generally called   There is a quaintness and flavor of unintentioned humor about some of these that is enjoyable

In the year 1792 is noted, " Shadrack Hubble's ear-mark," which is tersely described as " a Crop in the Rite ear and a hole in the same "   " David Sealye's ear mark, a Crop of the left ear and two half pennyes the under side of the same "   Other marks were " a swallow fork of the right ear," " a slantin crop of the upper side of the left ear," " a double U in the end of the left ear," etc

The same absence of fences mentioned led to the annual recording of numerous stray animals, a practice which came down to as late as 1850 in some parts of the town   In 1802, according to the records, there " came into the inclosure of the subscriber about the 1st of Jan inst a redish brindle Cow with a bell on a white spot in her pate, on her left side behind her fore shoulder is a large white spot, all her feet white, some white under her belly, about three or four years old   WM ROBBARDS "

One more of these entries which occurs in the year 1833   " The undersigned whose place of residence is in said town has on his enclosed lands in said town, one Stray Cow, and the following is a description of the colour and marks natural and artificial of the said stray, a Red and white cow with a white spot in her fore-head and the ends of her horns sawed off, four years old

" ISAAC FLEWELING "

In 1770 the enterprise of Abraham Wing prompted him to the erection of better facilities for sawing lumber and he entered into a contract with Daniel Jones, of Fort Edward for the erection of what they termed a Dutch saw-mill, with fourteen saws, which was the joint property of the two men   The original contract was preserved among the Wing papers   The first clause of the contract was as follows —

" Whereas, the said Daniel Jones and Abraham Wing, are this day become joint owners and proprietors of a certain fall or stream of water and a saw mill with ten acres, two quarters and fifteen rods of ground adjoining the same with their appurtenances by deeds between them this day executed, and, whereas it is proposed that the said Daniel Jones shall erect and build another saw mill little below the said saw mill there already standing, for the joint use and benefit of them the said Daniel Jones and Abraham Wing their executors, adm'rs and assigns "

Other provisions of the contract were to the effect that the parties and their assigns should " at all times hold and keep or cause to be holden and kept in good, proper and sufficient repair the said two saw mills with their sluices, dam and appurtenances at their equal and joint costs and expense " The parties bound themselves to the fulfillment of the contract " in the penalty of the sum of one thousand pounds lawful money of New York " The saw-mill to be built was forty-seven feet in length and eighteen feet in width The contract was witnessed by Chris Yates and John Glen

Previous to the erection of the grist-mill at the Falls (a date which is not definitely known), the settlers were forced to go to Stillwater for their grinding , that place was reached partly by boat and partly by the old military road which was constructed ten or twelve years previously

The date of erection of the first grist-mill is placed previous to 1771 by the following document, also, which indicates that Samuel Brownson was a partner to some extent in the business of Abraham Wing —

" Queensbury the 4th day of February, 1771 We the subscribers have this day settled all our accounts on book excepting the saw mill and grist mill affairs and there remains due to Abraham Wing to balance book account, nine pounds, fifteen shillings York currency as witness our hands

" SAMUEL BROWNSON,
" ABRAHAM WING

"Witness

    " Asaph Putnam,
    " Job Wright "

Samuel Brownson, named above, must be classed with the pioneers who came to Queensbury prior to the Revolution , he held the office of fence-viewer in 1769 The changes in the town officers were for several years and down to the breaking out of the war but slight ; accessions to the settlement were few and consequently the same men had to be repeatedly chosen In 1770 Job Wright was elected to several of the offices and Ebenezer Fuller was chosen pound-keeper. In 1771 Daniel Jones, before mentioned, was made pound-keeper, and Benjamin Hix (or Hicks) was elected assessor The next year Nehemiah Seelye was placed in this office He was the ancestor of the Seelye families now living in this vicinity At the same election Ichabod Merritt and Jacob Hicks were chosen " firemen," — the first incident connected with the establishment of a fire department in Warren county Just what the duties of the office were at that time, is not now known During this year Albany county was divided That portion embracing the settlements to the west and southwest of Schenectady was set off and called Tryon county and

Charlotte county, set off March 12th, 1772, embraced the territory now comprised in Washington, Warren, Essex and Clinton counties, and part of Bennington, Rutland, Addison, Chittenden and Franklin counties, in Vermont. This county was so named in honor of the Princess Charlotte of Mecklenburgh-Strelitz, the consort of King George the III   Considerable strife ensued over the location of the county seat, Crown Point, Skenesborough (Whitehall), and Fort Edward contending for the honor   The latter place triumphed and on the 8th of September, 1773, an ordinance was issued by the governor with the advice of the council, " establishing a Court of Common Pleas and a Court of General Sessions of the Peace to be held annually in the county of Charlotte, at the house of Patrick Smith, Esquire, near Fort Edward, on the third Tuesday in the months of October and May "   The first court in pursuance of this order was held on the 19th of October of that year, with William Duer and Philip Schuyler as presiding justices

In the town records of 1773 we find the names of David Buck and Benedick Brown added to the civil list, the former as constable and the latter as overseer of the poor   Benedick Brown was the ancestor of the Brown families now living in the town and probably came hither in 1772, settling at the outlet of Long Pond, then often called French Pond ; mills were built at that point at a very early date   (See biographies of George and Daniel V Brown, herein)   The Harris and Brayton families came to Queensbury about this time and settled near the southern part of Fort Anne, then known as the Artillery Patent, or Westfield township, which included that portion of the town of Queensbury now known as Harrisena and embracing all that portion of the present town of Queensbury north and east of the bounds of the original patent   Zachariah Butler's name appears as a pathmaster in 1774, we have already referred to him and his career

The pioneers found several small Indian settlements in this vicinity, to which a few families came during the summer and autumn months for hunting and fishing, and occasionally in winter for trapping ; these settlements were at Harrisena, Dunham's Bay (at the southern extremity of Lake George), at the outlet of the Long Pond, at the Big Bend (the sweeping curve of the Hudson about three miles above Glens Falls), and at the foot of the Palmerton Mountain on the south side of the river   They still claimed these localities as their hunting grounds, enjoyed them without disturbance and maintained the most peaceful relations with the families of the pioneers

At the expiration of the first decade of settlement improvement had progressed to an encouraging extent, besides the mills and other industries described, twenty or more clearings had been made, each containing its humble log dwelling   Previous to settlement a frequently followed trail of the Indians was a portage of less than a mile between Fort Edward Creek near Moss street, and Wood Creek, leading past Fort Anne, the remainder of the route being

made by canoe   Within ten years after settlement began in Queensbury three
or four corduroy wilderness roads were opened, one leading to the Ridge, another towards Dunham's Bay, one across by the outlet from the upper picket
fort to Harrisena and thence to Fort Anne, the old military highway from
Fort Edward to the head of the lake, and a cross road along the north line of
the town plot   There was also a bridle path through the plains to the Big
Bend, and the old well-trodden Indian trail leading along the east side of the
town and connecting Wood Creek to the outlet of the Big Cedar swamp

It is believed, according to Dr Holden, that anterior to the Revolution, and
certainly at a very early period, a somewhat pretentious log dwelling was
erected on what is now the corner of Ridge and Warren streets, in Glens Falls
This structure was originally occupied by Abraham Wing for the double purpose of a store and an inn, where the few adventurous spirits who were drawn
hither found primitive accommodations, and the pioneers such goods as could
then be had in the wilderness   Here, says Dr Holden, "according to the
Wing papers, hundreds of pounds worth of liquor of various kinds was brought
from Albany, Montreal, and on one occasion from Nova Scotia   Here the
Jessups, Hugh Munro, Capt Bradshaw and the neighbors with but few exceptions, held high revel and ran up bar bills of lusty proportions   And hence
from the location of this tavern the little settlement soon became known, in
addition to its proper name of Queeensbury Patent, and its foster name of
Wing's Falls, as Wing's Corners, and finally The Corners"

The reader will be able to picture in his mind the appearance and condition
of the settlement of Queensbury as it existed at the time that the country was
about to be overwhelmed by the momentous outbreak of the struggle for
American liberty   The clearings, burned and blackened, dotted with stumps
and surrounded with rude fences; the surrounding unbroken expanse of heavy
forest, through which deer, moose, elk, wolves, lynx, panthers, wild cat and
bears in great numbers roamed, the incipient efforts of the inhabitants to develop the resources of the locality, the meager beginnings of mercantile business; the primitive inns — all this was but a repetition of the experiences of
American pioneer settlements made just before or soon after the Revolutionary
War   The settlers all suffered and enjoyed in similar ways, their enjoyment
lying less in the present and its rude surroundings, than in the fond hope of
future plenty and content

Cattle and sheep had been brought to the settlements in limited numbers,
contributing to the food supply of the community and giving an air of peaceful
civilization to the clearings in the forest   The settlers sometimes found it no
easy task to obtain their current food supply, and it was often even more difficult to procure sustenance for their stock   This might have been actually impossible but for the two large beaver meadows, one of which was on the Five-
mile Run (so-called from its being about that distance from the head of Lake

George), which was on this account given the name of Meadow Run, and the other on the outlet of the Big Cedar swamp on the east side of the town, this stream ran through Great Lot No 3, owned in early days by Reed Ferriss, and came to be known as Reed's Meadow Creek   Cattle were also driven to the woods to browse in winter, thus eking out the scanty supply of hay   During one winter of extreme severity, it is related that the cattle could not be driven to the swamp as usual, and the settlers were compelled to feed them with salted fish, trout and suckers, which had been caught in the fall and with which all the streams abounded   One of the early settlers brought in, with great trouble, a small flock of sheep, which he placed in a log pen near the house, for security from wolves   During the night the ravenous beasts thrust their noses between the logs and succeeded in killing all but two of the flock   Those two were killed the next day, *to save them*

While the families we have mentioned were struggling in the wilderness, with peace for their handmaid, public events were rapidly approaching the crisis that could end only in war   The "Sons of Liberty," determined, watchful and alert, were organizing in every center along the seaboard, and preparations were made for the oncoming struggle that was felt by the wisest counselors of the nation to be imperative   At the same time the authorities of New York and New Hampshire engaged in the prolonged civil strife known as the New Hampshire grants controversy, which has been described, while a plan was also laid, the details of which are not well understood, for erecting a new province comprising all of the Northern New York and the New Hampshire grants (the western part of the present State of Vermont)   Philip Skene[1] was to be the governor of the province, with the seat at Whitehall   The plan was frustrated by the breaking out of the war two years later and the capture of the ambitious Skene, his estates were confiscated at the close of the war

The principal events of a military character in the long and bitter struggle between Great Britain and her colonies have been described in early chapters of this work, with many of these the settlers of Queensbury were intimately associated, not as participators in the strife of battle to any great extent, on account of their religious belief, which precluded such acts, but as sufferers from

[1] In 1761 Philip Skene, an English major under half pay, who had been with Amherst in 1759, established a large colony near the mouth of Wood Creek   In the autumn he accompanied an expedition against Havana, and on his return, in 1763, found the settlement reduced to fifteen persons   He immediately set about re-establishing the colony, and in 1765 obtained patents for twenty-five thousand acres of land lying on and near the creek   Here he built a stone mansion forty feet by thirty, and two stories and a half in height   In 1770 he erected a large stone building one hundred and thirty feet long, which was used for a military garrison and depot   He also built at this place a stone forge of about the same dimensions as his house, where he commenced the manufacture of iron   This was the first forge erected on the borders of the lake   Skene owned a sloop, with which he kept up a regular communication with Canada, and at his own expense he cut a road through the wilderness as far as Salem, a distance of about thirty miles, from which point it was continued by others to Bennington   This road was used during the season when the navigation on the lake was closed by ice.   In 1773 Skenesborough contained a population of 379 — PALMER'S *History of Lake Champlain*, p 95

the devastation and destruction that alway follows in the track of war Early in the struggle the fort at Ticonderoga was captured by Ethan Allen and his men, an event which was soon followed by the seizure of the partially dismantled fortification at the head of Lake George (Fort George) by Colonel Romans, Daniel Parke[1] (or Parks) With the seizure of this post it is not probable that the peacefully-inclined inhabitants of Queensbury were directly connected except as here stated

The Revolution grew apace The "rebels," as they were termed by the British, seemed to almost spring up out of the earth on all sides, military organizations were perfected and the country was ablaze with preparations for war The territory with which we are here concerned was directly affected by this situation of affairs The eastern towns of Charlotte county were the very homes of the rebels who had captured Ticonderoga and Crown Point, and it was seen at once that hereabouts must, in the natural course of events, be enacted some of the stirring and bloody scenes anticipated by the people William Duer, a gentlemen of prominence residing in this vicinity, wrote to the Committee of Safety early in 1775, that certain lawless persons, mostly debtors, were assembling at Fort Edward to break up the courts of justice Captain Edward Motte, then on his way from Ticonderoga to Albany, reached there at this opportune time, and by his presence during a session of the court, prevented further disturbance

The first colonial assemblage convened in Albany and organized on the 22d of May under the name of the Provincial Congress The minutes of its journal show that John Williams and William Marsh, from Charlotte county, appeared with their certificates of appointment as delegates

The campaigns of 1775 and 1776 comprised a series of military events of great importance to the American cause, with the details of which the reader has been made familiar Notwithstanding the general uprising throughout the colonies against the tyranny of England, there was still a strong feeling in many sections of adherence to the royal cause, both with individuals and in the public

---

[1] It is related by the descendants of the Parke family, that Elijah Parke was the original settler in this region, locating on the south side of the river, opposite the site of Glens Falls Daniel Parke was a son of Elijah and began a settlement where South Glens Falls is built and erected the first mills at that point Dr Holden copied the following inscription from the Parks family Bible some years ago —

"I, S Parks and Susannah my wife was married in 1789, May I was 24 years old March 5, 1789 I was born in the town of Half-Moon now in the village of Waterford, when I was 2 months old my father moved his family to the town of Sharon in the St of Connecticut We lived there until 1773 and May the 10 and then my father moved his family to what was then called Wing's falls and now called Glen's falls and there built the first mills that was ever built there And we suffered a great deal in that struggle for liberty we lost our lives and property and became poor and weak S PARKS"

The mills mentioned were destroyed in the Revolutionary War and rebuilt after the close of that contest by Colonel John (Johannes) Glen, who purchased the estate of Parke and from whom the villages are named Daniel Parks died March 3, 1818, at the age of seventy-eight years, and was buried in the family lot opposite Sandy Hill His tombstone bears the following inscription "One of the veterans of the Revolutionary War, he was the man who took the key from the British officer at Lake George in 1775"

councils This feeling gave birth and strength to the bands of Tories who became, perhaps, the most dreaded enemies of the colonial armies. It is also further shown by the passage of the following resolution by the Congress —

"*Resolved*, That it is the opinion of this Congress, that none of the people of this colony have withdrawn their allegiance from His Majesty, or desire to become independent of the crown of Great Britain, or to change the ancient form of government, under which this colony hath grown up from its infancy to its present state "

This proceeding occurred as late as December 13th, 1775

The position and circumstances of the belligerents in the region with which we are here particularly interested, at the beginning of 1776, may be noted as follows Arnold was before Quebec with a force of about two thousand, not nearly all of which was effective ; the intermediate posts were all in possession of the Americans In addition to the garrisons at Crown Point, Ticonderoga and Fort George, a small earthwork was constructed at Summer-house Point on the Sacandaga River, where part of a regiment of Continentals was stationed , this post was abandoned in the following summer

Steps were now taken to organize the county militia, as will be seen by the following document —

" *To the Honor'l Members of the Provincial Congress*

" GENTLEMEN . Having received the Resolves relating to the Rules and Orders for Regulating the Militia in this Colony, we thought proper to carry it into Execution with all Convenient Speed, and ordered a meeting of the County Committee Immediately

" There being a Contention of part of this County in regard to Title of Land [the New Hampshire grants], And it was thought proper by the Committees on the Grants to divide the County into two Parts, as they Do no Choose to joyn the other part of the County , which was agreed to by the other Committees , And Each part of the County to form One Regiment, and Recommend their Field Officers to you, desiring you will remit their commissions with all Convenient Speed, so that the Regiment may be formed as soon as Possible, In Case any Incursions may be made from Canada, as we are much Exposed to that Country

" The following Gentlemen we recommend for Commissions, they being Friends to the present Cause and have signed the General Association ·

" Dr John Williams, Colonel,   Platt Smith, Esq , Lieut Col ,
" Messrs Nathan Hawly and   Mr John Jones, Adjutant,
" Hamilton McColister, Majors,   Mr Seth Sherwood, Quarter Master.
" Likewise the names of the inferior Officers in each district

" *District of White Creek*

" Ebenezer Clark, Esq , Captain,   Edward Savage, 2d Lieut ,
" Charles Hutchinson, 1st Lieut ,   Daniel McClary, Ensign

"*Argyle* ·

"Alex[r] Campbell, Capt,   Peter Gilchrist, 2d Lieut,
"Sam[l] Paine, 1st Lieut,   John McDougall, Ensign

"*Scheensburgh District*

"Jerem[h] Burroughs, Capt,   Elisha Tousea, 2d Lieut,
"Levi Stockwell, 1st Lieut,   Silas Granger, Ensign

"*Black Creek District.*

"Alex[r] Webster, Capt,   George McKnight, 2d Lieut,
"John Hamilton, 1st Lieut,   Samuel Crosett, Ensign

"*Kingsbury District*

"Asa Richardson, Capt,   Nehem[h] Sealey, 2d Lieut,
"Adiel Sherwood, 1st Lieut,   Samuel Harris, Ensign [1]
    "Signed by order of Committee,

          "SETH SHERWOOD, Chairman
" COUNTY CHARLOTTE, DORSETT, 21st Sept, 1775
    " Commissions issued Sept 29th, 1775
" In addition to the foregoing, warrants were issued on the 29th of June to [2]
    " Joseph McCracken, Capt,   John Barnes, 2d Lieut,
      " Moses Martin, 1st Lieut "

On the 25th of January, 1776, at a general meeting of the county committee of Charlotte county it was unanimously agreed that Dr John Williams be recommended to the Provincial Congress of New York for the command of the First Battalion of the militia of the county, Alexander Campbell, of Argyle, for lieutenant-colonel, Messrs Timothy Bewell, of Fort Miller, and Alexander Webster, of Black Creek, for adjutants, and Mr Samuel Fuller, of Skenesborough, quartermaster At the same time and place it was unanimously agreed that Dr John Williams, and Mr Alexander Campbell should represent the county of Charlotte in Provincial Congress till the second Tuesday in May next

During the progress of the campaign of 1776 the inhabitants of Queensbury began to feel the blows of the hand of war, property was taken with all the ruthlessness that characterizes the progress of armies, necessary though it may be, destruction followed the track of irresponsible bands of soldiery, and in various ways which we shall indicate, the settlers were called upon for sacrifices which they were illy prepared to make, and for which, as a rule, they could obtain no redress From among the Wing manuscripts Dr Holden secured and printed in his valuable work various statements of these losses, which possess a peculiar and important interest; quaint as many of them are,

---

[1] *Calendar of N Y Hist MSS. Rev Papers,* vol I, p 148 Sealey and Harris are supposed to have been residents of Queensbury
[2] *Idem*, p 106
23

in character, language and orthography, they still tell the story of devastation with simple eloquence   Following are the earliest of these documents

Paper No 1

Endorsed, "Capt Lammar's Account,
        and account of things his company stole"
"1776   Stolen, taken and carried out of my house, March 11th, by Capt. Lammar's company

	£	s	d
"One blue Broadcloath Jactcoat.............at	2	—	—
"One blue quilted petticoat................at	—	14	—
"One woolen checked shirt................at	—	$17\frac{1}{2}$	—
"One silk handkerchief.....................at	—	5	—
"One pewter basin ....at	—	4	—
"13 Dunghill fowls...... ....at	—	18	—
"One short stag goad.....................at	—	4	—

£ 5. 2 6

"Capt Lammar,   Dr ⎫
   "To one pleasure slay steel shod, painted green ⎪ £ 7
outside, red inside, which he carried away with him ⎬
and never returned   ⎭ ABRAHAM WING"

Paper No 2

Containing Capt Lamar's receipt, and Abraham Wing's affidavit in relation thereto

"I hereby certify that Mr Abraham Wing's slay was hired for the use of my company from the 13th of March to the first of April, 1776, when the ice-breaking up, I was obliged to leave her in the care of Mr Belton at Willsborough on Lake Champlain   MARIEN LAMAR
                                    "Capt 1, P B"

"I do most solemnly affirm that I never received the slay mentioned within, which was taken from me by Capt Lamar for the use of the army, nor have I ever received any compensation for the same, or any other person whatever on my account, and that the slay was worth at that time in hard cash, seven pounds   ABRAHAM WING,
                          "6th March, 1786

"Washington ⎫
   County ⎬
   "This day the above signed Abraham Wing appeared before me and affirmed to the truth of the same   ADIEL SHERWOOD, Jus Pe"

Paper No 3

Being a military order and receipt for the delivery of certain property, on a requisition

"To Mr Wyng·

"Sir, Plese deliver that gang of saws to the bearer, to be forwarded to Chesyrs,[1] and take his receipt therefor, on the back of this order

"Fort George, July ye 18th, 1776   NATH'L BUELL,

"Ast D Qr Mr Gen'l "

Endorsement

"July the 8th   Received the full contents of the within order, being 15 saws, with their stearups on   EBEN'R ASHUMN "

"Receive pr me

"1776 "

The town records of Queensbury for the year 1776 show but little change in the officers of the preceding year. Following is a transcript from the records. —

"At an annual town meeting held in Queensbury on Tuesday ye 2nd day of May, 1776, for the township of Queensbury   Then followed a list of the officers voted in as here given —

"Abraham Wing, Moderator, Asaph Putnam, Town Clerk, Abraham Wing, Supervisor, Asaph Putnam, Constable, Nehemiah Sealey, Constable, Daniel Jones, Constable, Ebenezer Fuller, Constable, Nehemiah Sealy and Benjamin Wing, Assessors, Abraham Wing, Path Master, Benedict Brown, Path Master, Ichabod Merritt and Nehemiah Sealy, Overseers of the Poor, Benjamin Wing, Collector, Abraham Wing, Town Treasurer, Abraham Wing, Keeper of the Pound, Ichabod Merritt, and Asaph Putnam, viewers of fence and prisers of damage, Abraham Wing, Asaph Putnam and Nehemiah Sealy, are appointed to enspect all persons that shall hunt the Deer in Queensbury, for the year ensuing "

"Voted that any person that shall harbor or entertain or assist any person or persons from any County to hunt or kill any fawn, buck or deer in Queensbury, in ye year ensuing shall Forfeit and pay to the treasury the Sum of five Pounds "[2]

The Daniel Jones mentioned above as having been made a constable was

---

[1] Cheshire's mill to which these saws were removed, it is supposed was situated on Fort Edward Creek in Kingsbury In a communication from General Gates to General Waterbury dated Ticonderoga, July 15th, 1776, he says   If we make our stand at the place proposed, it is essential that the road from *Cheshire's* to Fort Edward be immediately repaired and rendered easy for carriages * *— FORCE'S *American Archives*, fifth series, vol I, p 358

"You will also post three companies of a regiment, with a field officer at *Cheshire's mill* "

"Agreeably to your directions, I have ordered Captain *Veeder* and his company at the saw mill at *Cheshire's* "—*Richard Varick to General Gates, Albany, Oct* 14, 1776 —*Idem*, vol II, p 1037

Dr Holden has in his possession evidence that Cheshire's mill was situated at Kane's Falls on what is now called Half-way Brook (formerly Scoon Creek) This statement is in correction of that embodied in the first paragraph of this note which was taken from Dr Holden's *History of Queensbury*, and written upon the best information then obtainable by him

[2] The orthography of names in our extracts from records, ancient documents, etc, is according to the originals, though known in many instances to be either inaccurate or not according to present custom

a brother of David Jones, already spoken of as the betrothed of the hapless Jane McCrea   The brothers were, according to Dr Holden's *History of Queensbury* (p 412-13), mill-wrights and the family was quite prominent in early days among the settlers on the Kingsbury patent; their large posses-sions were afterward sequestrated by the Commission of Forfeitures   Their house was for a short time the headquarters of Burgoyne in the following year   Daniel Jones was a son-in-law of Abraham Wing, who, with others of his family, was an undoubted patriot, while the Jones family were bitter loyal-ists   This is an example of the family disunions and feuds that were prevalent in the great struggle in many localities   The family of Mr Wing, as well as those of all the prominent settlers of " the Corners," never took arms on either side

The campaign of 1776, as we have seen, was peculiarly disastrous to the American arms, and the cause was but little better served during the succeed-ing year   A policy of vacillation and general weakness characterized the councils of the colonies, preventing the degree of success that was warranted by the capacity of officers and bravery of soldiers   The beginning of the year found General Schuyler in charge of the northern department, and to his wise administration may be credited the first real successes of the war   In the course of the campaign the territory within and immediately surrounding the Queensbury Patent was the scene of many stirring events and felt the terrible effects of the war to a grievous extent   Ticonderoga was recaptured by the British, Fort Anne was evacuated after stubborn resistance, and other important military operations were carried on in various parts of the province.   Mean-while General Schuyler gathered the resources of the country surrounding his jurisdiction   On the 10th of July he announced by dispatch to General Ten Broeck that he had already saved about forty pieces of cannon and fifteen tons of gunpowder by removing them from Fort George; and a few days later he wrote, " If the enemy will permit me to pass unmolested three days longer to Fort George, I shall be able to bring away all the stores from thence and then draw off the few troops we have there "   Of this situation of affairs Burgoyne wrote to Lord George Germaine as follows.   " The enemy are laboring to re-move the magazines from Forts George and Edward, and everywhere destroy-ing the roads and preparing to drive and burn the country towards Albany "

Several important personal incidents in which residents of Queensbury were chief participants, occurred during this campaign, to which we must allude. In one of these William Robards was a conspicuous figure   He was a brother of the Ezekiel Robards[1] and has already been mentioned herein   Dr Holden

---

[1] The following paper is on file in the archives of the State   " Ezekiel Roberts of Saratoga district, states that in August, 1776, he engaged as sergeant in Capt Baldwin's Company of Rangers, was taken prisoner 19th May, 1777, and remained until December (when he was paroled and sent home with other prisoners by Governor Carleton)   In May, 1780, was informed by Gov Clinton that he was ex-changed and discharged from his parole   Went over Lake George by order of his excellency in pur-

gives the following account of his capture (*History of Queensbury*, p 421)
" He with Andrew Fuller, his wife's brother, and James Higson, an uncompromising Whig and son-in-law of Abraham Wing, were captured while preparing to go fishing on Lake George

" They were carried to Canada and imprisoned   While in jail Robards
was visited by some gentlemen, who wished him to give his parole that he
would not escape and they would give him the jail liberties   He refused, saying that his family needed his services, and if there was any chance of his getting home he should make the attempt   In consequence of this declaration he
had a strict guard placed over him, being confined in a room with another, a
British deserter, and through the day an armed sentry was stationed in the room
to watch their movements   The gentlemen who visited Robards were so well
pleased with his spirit and nice sense of honor, that they frequently sent him
wine and delicacies from their tables   While the sentry was out to his meals,
the prisoners being in some way cognizant or suspicious that a window was
boarded up in the room, amused themselves by throwing sticks of firewood
against the walls until the locality of the window was determined, and it was
shortly ascertained also that there was no intervening bars or bolts to prevent
their escape   Taking turns night after night in cutting away the boards cautiously and carefully, with which the window was ceiled, secreting and disposing of the chips and shavings thus made, they at length achieved their purpose,
and one day, while the guard was at dinner, the boarding was removed and
the deserter first clambered out   Robards being lithe, supple, and active,
jumped from the window, clearing the stockade which surrounded the building, and alighted in one of the streets of the French city of Montreal, where
they had been imprisoned   They were fired at by the guards on duty as they
ran, the Canadians on the street cheering and swearing to encourage the fugitives   The guards had to go around on the opposite side of the building, and
open the gates before they could follow in pursuit

" In the mean time, guided by some sympathizing spectators, Robards and
his companion ran along through the suburbs, gaining the city wall, which
they scaled at a favoring point, and made their escape to the woods   The deserter soon gave out, grew sick and tired of the adventure, and concluded to
return and surrender himself, leaving Robards to make his way alone   He
traveled by night, guiding his course by the stars, and lay secreted by day
At length he came to a place by the shore of the lake where a rock jutted out
above the water, having a cave or recess beneath   Here he took refuge and
rested a day or two   During this interval, he was suddenly aroused from a

suit of Sir John Johnson, and soon after appointed lieutenant in the State Levies, and again taken prisoner when under the command of Capt Sherwood at Fort Ann, 10th Oct , 1780, remained two years
in confinement, and then made his escape   Has a wife and two children for whose support he was
obliged to contract debts   Is now destitute of every thing   Prays for relief in a petition to the Legislature, January 20th, 1783 "

deep sleep by an Indian yell, and, apprehending pursuit, he sprang out from his place of concealment, and looking up, saw an Indian standing on the cliff above him, making signals to a companion standing on a point of land in the distance on the other side of the lake   Fortunately the savages did not discover him   At length, after many nights' wandering, he was fortunate enough to come across a canoe and a pair of paddles, which he unhesitatingly appropriated, and from that time forth his progress was more rapid and satisfactory

"One day his brother, Ezekiel Robards, then living in Queensbury, proposed to one of his neighbors to go up to Lake George for the purpose of fishing, and also to take a sharp look, to see if any Tories or Indians were about   While fishing near the mouth of Van Wormer's Bay, they saw a small object in the distance on the lake, which approaching them, gradually became more thoroughly defined, and, as it drew near, Ezekiel exclaimed, ' It's William I know by his motions ' And so it proved   They returned together without any long delay, and, as they neared their home, Ezekiel told William to stay back in the edge of the woods, while he went forward and broke the news to his wife   The latter was carrying a plate of butter from the spring house, or out-door cellar, and as Ezekiel approached he accosted her, saying, 'Phebe, I've got good news for you, I've heard from William ' She staggered back with the shock of emotion as if she had been struck, exclaiming, ' If you have heard from him you have seen him ,' and sank to the ground in a dead faint "

The Parks narrative is even more interesting, and is handed down in traditions that are strongly corroborated by concurrent events, the connection of the family with the original Glen patent, and other testimony which is considered by most persons conversant with the early history of the locality as quite conclusive   The account was furnished to Dr. Holden by Daniel E Parks, of Sandy Hill, N Y

"There was, in the British army, a captain by the name of Daniel Parks," says the narrative, "who took an active part in quelling and keeping in subjection, the savage, original inhabitants of the American continent long before the Revolution, who lived and died in some one of the Southern States, probably in Virginia, and who had a son by the name of Daniel Parks. The latter removed and settled in Salisbury, Conn , where he resided till within a few years of the Revolution, when he emigrated to Glens Falls, where he purchased a tract of eight hundred acres of land, situated along the south bank of the Hudson's River, and settled and built the first mills at that place   About the year 1777, while the Revolutionary War was in progress, and the country was swarming with marauding bands of savages and Tories, his house was attacked at night by a band of Tories, who demanded the keys to his desk, which contained his papers, etc , which the old man refused to deliver up   Thereupon one of the band clinched him, at which a scuffle ensued, which resulted in get-

ting the old man down, when one of the party drew up and shot him   He was
supposed at that time to be about seventy-five years of age, and died in defending himself from British aggression

" Among the band was a man by the name of Richardson,[1] who lived in
that vicinity, and who had purchased of the old man a piece of land containing
about one hundred acres, for which Parks held his obligation, and it is confidently believed that the murdering wretches were incited to the commission
of this act of barbarism by a desire to get possession of Richardson's obligation,
and thus leave his land free from incumbrance

" Elisha and Isaac Parks, sons of the old man above mentioned, resided
with their father, but the attack of the Tories was so sudden that they, not
being near at hand, were unable to render the old man any assistance, and
when they arrived they found their father dead, and his murderers apparently
gone[2]   Elisha, a young married man, went to the door to make a reconnaissance, and while doing so, held a light in his hand, it being then dark   This
attracted the attention of some of the Tories who were lying in ambush, and
made a good mark for their rifles, which they took advantage of, and shot him
through the bowels, his wife then standing beside him   Placing his hand over
the wound, he at once fled down the river, to the house of his brother, Daniel
Parks, who lived a mile below, and notified him of the presence of the Tories
and what had happened   Daniel at once took down his gun and proposed to
repair to the scene of action, but, upon the entreaties of Elisha, who represented that he could not contend against so many, and would only endanger
his life in a fool-hardy manner, he was prevailed upon to stay and secure his
family   This was done by removing them across the river in canoes   Elisha
proposed to remain at his brother's house, but Daniel would not listen to the
proposition   Yielding to the entreaties of the latter, he was conveyed across
the river, where they took refuge in the grist-mills[3] at Sandy Hill, where he
died the same night or early the following morning   His remains, and those

---

[1] All I know of Richardson, I learned from the Parks family   He was ringleader of the Tories,
who murdered the father of that family   He had some claim or title to the South Glens Falls water
power, and to obtain the Parks title papers, is supposed to have been the principal purpose of the expedition   Old Mr Parks saw through a window Richardson and Ferguson (a Tory tavern keeper at
the Bend) looking at the Parks papers, went into the house, and was immediately killed by a gun
breech blow on the head — *Letter to Dr Holden from the late Judge Hay*   In another account of the
affair, it is stated that the Tory party found rest and refreshments at the house of one Ferguson, a Tory
at the Bend   He had pretended to be a Whig, had attended their meetings and signed their articles of
association, and up to this time was supposed to be a zealous patriot   Sending out scouts in the direction of Lake George, and keeping a watchful outlook on the movements of the Parks family, the party
lurked around for a week or more, until Ferguson, in the expressive language of my informant, " was
eaten out of house and home "—HOLDEN'S *Queensbury, p* 425

[2] Ephraim Parks, a brother of Daniel, with his brother-in-law, Lewis Brown, lived in a double log
house, situated on the cliff just above the site of the paper mill   They were made prisoners, but Brown
afterwards escaped, as appears in the narrative —*Idem*

[3] Probably a mistake, for after diligent inquiry, the author failed to receive any evidence that a grist
mill was built at Sandy Hill before the year 1795

of his father, were buried at Sandy Hill, on the site now covered by the Presbyterian Church   Two rude slabs of stone, which originally marked the place of sepulture, it is said, were incorporated into the foundation of the edifice, whose fane shades the resting place of the martyrs

"Isaac, the other son, was taken prisoner and carried to Quebec, from whence he escaped three times, and was as often retaken, and ultimately exchanged   The third time he escaped in company with five others, who, after they had traveled through the wilderness a length of time sufficient to exhaust all of their provisions, and were in a famished condition, it was proposed to cast lots to see which should be sacrificed to serve as food for the remainder A vote being taken, three were for, and three against the proposition, Isaac Parks being among the latter   The fugitives then separated, those voting with Parks going in one direction, and the remainder in another   The Parks party was soon visited by a dog supposed to belong to some Indians scouting near This was killed and eaten, and they were afterwards driven to the extremity of roasting and eating their shoes   They at length became so utterly exhausted that they were unable to ascend a hill without help from each other, and whenever an elevation interrupted their progress, they were able to surmount it only by crawling on their hands and knees

"One day, while they were ascending a hill in this manner, they were discovered and retaken by a party of Indians, who displayed the usual terrific exultation on the seizure of a captive, and prepared to inflict the customary tortures and death   In some way Parks and his fellow sufferers succeeded in satisfying their captors that they were Tories and friends escaping from imprisonment by the Whigs   Under the promise of a guinea each, the Indians were induced to escort them back to the Canada border   Crossing the St Lawrence River they were recognized as escaped prisoners by some of the Indians there, and they would have been dispatched, but for the timely interference of some British soldiers.

"We supplement this narrative with the following relation made by a grand-daughter of Albert Baker, one of the first settlers at Sandy Hill.

"At the time when the Parkses were killed, the old lady and the rest of the women, running out of the back door of their homes,[1] escaped down the river, and crossing over, went directly to Albert Baker's house (near where Mr Nelson Wait now lives), in the dead of the night   The family were aroused by the hysteric sobs, shrieks and moans of the old lady

---

[1] Another account says, the women of the household at the first alarm made for the woods and escaped   They had with them a lad of thirteen or fourteen years of age, whom they bundled up with clothing to screen him from observation   On their way they were met by two or three Indians, who asked them where they were going and what they were doing with the boy

With great readiness of mind in the terrible emergency, one of them replied, that the boy had the small-pox and they were taking him away, so that the rest of the family should not catch the disease The Indians immediately dropped further inquiries, and hastened away from the supposed danger of infection, the entire party of fugitives, boy included, making their way to the woods and finally escaping to Fort Edward

"At this time Major Thomas Bradshaw,[1] son of James Bradshaw, one of the original patentees and proprietors of the towhship of Kingsbury, had a small reserve of militia posted at Bradshaw's farm, on Wood Creek, since known as the Bond place, between Smith's Basin and Dunham's Basin, on the northern canal

"Of the neighbors who came in as soon as the news of the massacre became known, none were found willing to go for help, until Albert Baker, jr, the narrator's father, and Rianaldo Burden Phillips, two stout, well grown lads, hardly appreciating the dangers, volunteered for the service When they reached the Bradshaw place, they found no one, but a Tory family living in the neighborhood directed them to the barn, where they found the major alone, his militia having scattered to their homes in the vicinity, and before he could rally them together the marauders were so far away on their retreat that pursuit was useless

"The alarm reaching Fort Edward,[2] on the following morning a party was soon made up to start in pursuit of the assassins On the way they were joined by Daniel Parks, and his brother-in-law, Lewis Brown, who, in the confusion of his capture, had managed to make his escape On reaching the scene of the massacre, they only found the smoking embers of the mills and the old man's house The other dwelling on the cliff above the mill was not disturbed It is stated that the Indians and Tories tried to reach the dwelling of Andrew Lewis, son-in-law of Abraham Wing, who then lived on the island, but were prevented by the absence of any boat

"The pursuers, taking the trail, followed the fugitives with considerable celerity, hoping to overtake them before reaching Lake Champlain, where their escape would be facilitated by canoes concealed somewhere along its shores Hastening up the west side of the Hudson, crossing the Sacandaga at its mouth, they proceeded as far as Stony Creek, a small creek in the town of that name in the western part of Warren county Here the fleeing party, finding they were pursued, took the bed of the stream, and made their way for many miles The pursuers were in consequence thrown off the trail, and the chase was abandoned

"The fruitless result of this expedition was doubtless fortunate for the few captives carried off, who were threatened with immediate death, if they were

---

[1] Thomas Bradshaw, a son of James Bradshaw, was a major in the American service but for some reason never succeeded in obtaining a pension — *Relation of Mrs Rachel Clary.*

Among the Wing papers was found the following memorandum, without date —

"The expenses of the men of the guard, amount to the sum of two pounds, (£2,00), for 6 eating and drinking,

"To Capt Richardson,   THOMAS BRADSHAW, Sarg't "

[2] Near the top of the hill above Fort Edward, not far from the site now occupied by the Grove House, there was a tavern kept by one Bell, a Tory It was a place of considerable note, a favorite resort of loyalists, where many a scheme of rapine, violence and outrage was concerted and matured — *Communication of the late Judge Hay to Dr Holden.*

overtaken by the pursuing party   The effect of this raid was to break up for the time being the settlement known as the Parks Mills   Daniel on the following morning procured a team and removed his family and such effects as could readily be transported within the protection of the military force at Fort Edward, and when that post was abandoned he retreated with the American army to Bemus's Heights, where he participated in that memorable action, which resulted in the surrender of one of the largest and best appointed British armies which had yet taken the field against the rebellious colonies   After the termination of the war he returned to rebuild the house, which he occupied with his family up to the time of his death   In the lapse and changes of years a large proportion of the Glen patent passed into the hands of various descendants of Daniel Parks

"Solomon Parks, then but a mere stripling, was among the militia stationed at Fort Anne under the command of Colonel Long in 1777.   About two weeks prior to Burgoyne's advance, and the capture of that post, Solomon with others was detailed to escort the inhabitants of the region to a place of safety   All the horses and oxen of the neighborhood were seized upon for that purpose, and most of the women and children of the threatened frontier were removed to join their friends in Duchess county and the adjacent county in Connecticut   At a later period these flittings and returns became so frequent, that in the language of one octogenarian, whose memory reverted back to those early days, 'they had little to carry or lose'   But with all their losses and sufferings, their unconquerable energy, perseverence and love of home were sufficient to bring them back to their desolated possessions."

Queensbury was afflicted in a particularly unfortunate degree by bands of Indians and Tories, the locality seeming to be a sort of headquarters for the latter   Dr Holden makes the statement that "there was probably nowhere in this vicinity a stronger Tory nest than that existing across the West Mountain, some ten miles distant from Queensbury settlement, under the favor and encouragement of the brothers, Ebenezer and Edward Jessup"   They had secured patents to various tracts of land both within the present town of Luzerne and also the Totten and Crossfield purchase, so-called   It is stated on the authority of Butler's *Hand-book of the Adirondack Railway*, that Totten and Crossfield were put forward in the securing of this enormous grant, merely as a cover to the operations of Ebenezer Jessup   He came into the wilderness about the year 1770, and built a spacious log dwelling, and there until after the beginning of the Revolutionary war, he lived in comparatively opulent style for those times   It is traditionally stated that in his house numerous hospitable entertainments were given, amid the surroundings of elegant furniture and costly paintings, where tables were laden with splendid settings and rare linen. All of this interior splendor was plundered and carried off at a later date   Scattered through this region were many other prominent Tories, among whom are mentioned John Howell, who lived up the Sacandaga River in the direction of Johnstown   Six brothers named Lovelace, descendants of Governor Lovelace, who resided at different points on the opposite side of the river, and one of whom was, in one of the late years of the war, executed as a spy by order of General Stark, after trial by drum-head court-martial   Another was Jacob Salisbury, who was captured in a cave known to this day as the Tory house There were also several members of the Fairchild family living a few miles farther down the river   "According to the tradition, in the month of April or May, 1777, Indian runners came and notified these families of Burgoyne's intended approach, and probably with some suggestions in regard to their co-operation with certain bands of Tories gathering in the lower part of the Saratoga district "[1]

In any event notice of their intentions was received and a party of Whigs started in pursuit   So hot became the chase that, it is said, one of the Jessups (Edward, if either, as Ebenezer was at this time in Canada, where he was given a command in Burgoyne's army) could escape only by jumping across the river at the Little Falls   Thence he hurried across the town of Queensbury to Skenesborough and joined Burgoyne's army at Willsborough Falls

In the course of Burgoyne's campaign of 1777, as we have incidentally mentioned, occurred the evacuation of Fort George and the removal of the stores; the fort was destroyed on the 16th of July   About this time a large fortified encampment was established on the high ground now occupied by South Glens Falls village, while Colonel John Ashley was in command of a military station at the Five-mile Run in the town of Queensbury

Previous to Burgoyne's advance it became known to the Committee of Safety that a regular system of communication was maintained between the British leaders at the North and South   It was of the utmost importance to the American cause that these dispatches should be intercepted and the system broken up   General Schuyler was, therefore, instructed to make careful inquiry for a shrewd, intelligent and courageous man, of well-known fidelity to the cause, who would volunteer upon the dangerous duty of acting as a double spy   This resulted in the recommendation to him of Moses Harris, of Duchess county, a young man of education, resources and great personal courage   As the settlement of that portion of the present town of Queensbury known as "Harrisena " was intimately connected with this man and his descendants, it becomes us to note something of his career [2]   One of the earliest settlers on

---

[1] HOLDEN's *History of Queensbury*

[2] In a foot note in his *History of Queensbury*, Dr Holden writes as follows · —

Moses Harris, jr , whose name frequently appears in the town records of Queensbury after the close of the Revolutionary War, was a surveyor by profession, and a large per centage of the early road surveys of the town were made by him   A monument to his memory (erected by his grandson, the late John J Harris) stands in the rural burial ground attached to the Episcopal Church at Harrisena, on which are engraved the following inscriptions —

the Bradshaw patent was Gilbert Harris   He owned what was familiarly known as "The Thousand Apple-tree Farm," which embraced a square mile of the fertile land in the north part of the town of Kingsbury   He was an uncompromising royalist and an efficient secret agent of the British in obtaining and transmitting intelligence through the American lines   This man was uncle to Moses Harris   Previous to the war they had been on friendly terms   To him Moses proceeded and,[1] " securing his confidence, gave him to understand that he had changed his views, that he was tired of the troubled and disturbed state of the country, and dissatisfied with the course pursued by the Whigs, and, believing that the Rebellion would be crushed out sooner or later, he had about come to the conclusion to join the British army, unless some more congenial employment was offered   At this stage of affairs the notorious Joseph Betteys seems to have been consulted, and to have completed the negotiations and arrangements by which Harris was to act as a courier in conveying dispatches between this point and Albany   He was conducted to a Tory rendezvous on the Halfway Brook, in the vicinity of the settlement now known as Tripoli,[2] where, in an underground apartment, amply furnished with arms, ammunition and provisions, he was sworn to secrecy and fidelity, and the dispatches here concealed were delivered to him for transmission to one William Shepherd, a Tory, who occupied, by arrangement, an old tenement on the Patroon's Creek, near the old Colonie in Albany, and who in turn, was to forward them to their destination for the British authorities down the river   The route pursued by Harris took him at night to the house of Fish, in Easton (the man who had recom-

West Side
MOSES HARRIS
DIED
Nov 13, 1838
Aged 89 years,
11 Mo's and 24
Days

North Side
In June, 1787, I moved with two of my brothers, William and Joseph Harris, on to the John Lawrence Patten, as you may see by the records in the Living's office of the county at that age in 1786 But now I am done with this world and race, and none but God shall say, where shall be my abiding place

South Side.
He was a man that was true to his friends and his country.   He was the man that carried the package for General Schuyler and from General Schuyler to General Washington   It went, and without doubt was the instrument that put General Burgoyne's journey to an end   He it was that bought the Patten 'granted to John Lawrence and others when wild, and settled the same, being two thousand acres, to the benefit of his children and grandchildren   For which I think I ought to do something to his memory — Y J H , *Grandson*

[1] From HOLDEN's *Queensbury*, communicated to him (1850) by Moses Harris, a son of the spy, and supplemented by information from Judge Hay

[2] In an article written by William L Stone, of Sandy Hill, and published in the *Magazine of American History*, July 1, 1878, a slightly different version is given, but we regard Dr Holden's as more authentic

mended Harris to General Schuyler), who lived about two miles from the river
Here the papers were transferred to Fish, who hastened with them to Albany,
where they were submitted to General Schuyler when present, and to his private secretary when absent, by whom they were carefully opened, examined,
transcribed, sealed up and returned to Harris, who then resumed his journey,
and deposited the papers in Shepherd's hands, receiving at the same time his
return message when there was one   Harris, in the mean time, by his uncle's
advice, stopped for refreshments at a tavern in the city, where he was on the
best of terms with the partisans of freedom

"This system was followed up for several weeks, when the British leaders,
finding their plans discovered and thwarted, suspicion fell upon Harris, and he
was arrested at his uncle's house, taken to another of the secret rendezvous of
the royalists, on an island in the big swamp east of Sandy Hill, where he was
charged with his treachery and his life threatened , but his cool self-possession
never for a moment forsook him, and he succeeded in persuading them that
they had done him a great injustice, after which he resumed his duties

"On another occasion, by previous arrangement and understanding with
General Schuyler for the purpose of averting suspicion, he was arrested and
thrown into jail in Albany, where he remained for several days, whence by
collusion with the keeper who had his private instructions, he was permitted to
escape, and went to Canada, where he was handsomely rewarded and made
much of by the authorities and renegade Tories

"On this occasion he communicated false and deceptive intelligence,
agreed upon in Albany, and which was near bringing him into trouble   On
his return from St Johns he was again entrusted with dispatches, which, in consequence of the sickness of Fish, he was obliged to take to Schuyler in person,
and thence by his orders to General Washington   Whether he was dogged
by spies or by reason of previous suspicions, Shepherd attempted to poison
him for his defection , and Jo Betteys, having entrapped him, he was obliged
to flee for his life   He at this time took refuge with one Dirk, or Diedrich
Swart, a Whig living at Stillwater, a friend of General Schuyler, who had requested him to afford Harris aid and protection in case of trouble   To com-
plicate his dangers at this time, Swart informed him that one Jacob Bensen, a
Whig, had threatened to 'put a ball through the cussed Tory' under the supposition that he was a loyalist, and that he was lying in wait for him for that
purpose in the adjacent woods   Another danger almost as formidable arose
from competition among the Tories for the position of spy and messenger,
and the enhanced pay that went with it, together with the consequence and
consideration that the position gave   Among the rivals floated to the surface
by the turbid current were two loyalists named Caleb Closson and Andrew
Rakely living in Kingsbury, and David Higginbottom, who had been a sergeant in the 31st British regiment.   On his last excursion he was weakened by

a wound he had received in one of his adventures, and exhausted by the pain and fatigue, he was forced to halt at brief intervals, stopping first with one Humighaus, a Tory living on the south line of Fort Anne, and next at the house of Peter Freel at Fort Edward. From here he proceeded toward Fort Miller, but on the way was pursued by a scouting party of Whigs, and compelled to seek safety in flight across the river, and shelter in the house of Noah Payn, a Whig who resided opposite to the block-house at Fort Miller His danger was so imminent that he was obliged to make known to the latter his relations to General Schuyler and the American army His secret was faithfully kept, and Payn afforded him the needed protection and rest, and assisted him on the way to Easton, giving him at the same time a letter of recommendation to General Putnam, a former townsman, neighbor, and friend of Payn

"After the battle of Stillwater, and Burgoyne's surrender, Harris received (so runs the family tradition) a purse of one hundred guineas from General Schuyler for services, and after the close of the war a pension of ninety-six dollars per annum was awarded him by the government After the war he returned to his favorite hunting haunts in the vicinity of Lake George, where he purchased a tract of two thousand acres of land [1] to which, and the adjacent territory, the name of Harrisena was given, where the remainder of his life was passed amidst the tranquillity of peaceful scenes, and where many of his descendants still reside

"In a communication from Gouverneur Morris at Saratoga dated July 17th to the Council of Safety, he says 'I left Fort Edward with General Schuyler at noon, and shall return thither some time to-morrow morning Fort George was destroyed yesterday afternoon, previous to which the provisions, stores, batteaux, &c , were removed, and this morning at ten o'clock the last of them passed us about three miles to the northward of Fort Edward, at which place all the troops from the lake have arrived, and these, together with some others, form an advanced post towards Fort George , about twelve hundred, perhaps more, are somewhat further advanced upon the road to Fort Anne The enemy have not yet made any motion that we know of, nor indeed can they make any of consequence until they shall have procured carriages, and then they may find it rather difficult to come this way, if proper care be taken to prevent them from procuring forage For this purpose I shall give it as my opinion to the general, whenever he asks it, to break up all the settlements upon our

---

[1] "Mr Benjamin Harris states that there were 21 corners to this lot, that he bought of Lawrence, Boel and Tuttle, who had a king's patent, which was surveyed by him in 1775. The three brothers, Moses, Joseph and William, came to settle on this tract in 1786. In the *Calendar of N Y Land Papers* there is a record of 16 certificates of location for about 5000 acres of land in small parcels — adjoining the other main tract , all in favor of Moses Harris, jr , occurring from 1786 to 1789 In the same authority, p 506, there is a return of survey Oct 12, 1770, for two tracts of land of 3000 acres each within the bounds of the Robert Harpur patent, surrendered to the crown, lying partly in Queensbury and partly in Fort Anne, to John Lawrence, Henry Boel and Stephen Tuttle "

northern frontier, to drive off the cattle, secure or destroy the forage, etc ,
and also to destroy the saw mills

" ' These measures, harsh as they may seem, are, I am confident, absolutely
necessary   They ought undoubtedly to be taken with prudence, and temper-
ately carried into execution   But I will venture to say that if we lay it down
as a maxim never to contend for ground but in the last necessity, to leave
nothing but a wilderness to the enemy, their progress must be impeded by obstacles which it is not in human nature to surmount , and then, unless we have,
with our usual good nature, built posts for their defense, they must at the approach of winter retire to the place from whence they at first set out   The
militia from the eastward come in by degrees, and I expect we shall soon be
in force to carry on the *petite guerre* to advantage, provided always, Burgoyne attempts to annoy us, for it is pretty clear that we cannot get at him '

" At the near approach of the enemy, the women and children had been
collected under escort, and sent forward within the American lines to places of
quiet and security for protection   Most of the residents of Queensbury, who
desired to avail themselves of the privilege, took refuge in Duchess county
Some few remained behind, depending for safety upon their principles of non-
resistance and their faith and reliance in God's protection   The scene of this
general flitting, expedited by the frequent appearance of small bands of armed
savages, is thus graphically portrayed by another —

" ' The roads were filled with fugitives , men leading little children by the
hand, women pressing their infant offspring to their bosoms, hurrying forward
in utmost consternation from the scene of danger   Occasionally passed a cavalcade, two and even three mounted on a single steed, panting under its heavy
load , sometimes carrying a mother and her child, while the father ran breathless by the horse's side   Then came a procession of carts drawn by oxen,
laden with furniture hastily collected , and here and there, mingling with the
crowd of vehicles, was seen many a sturdy husbandman followed by his household and driving his domestic animals before him ' "[1]

Following the engagement at and evacuation of Fort Anne, an interval of
nearly three weeks elapsed before Burgoyne began his advance to Fort Edward   This short period was fatal to his success and opened the way for his
overwhelming defeat, as chronicled in our earlier chapters

The first great blow for freedom was struck and the entire country drew a
breath of relief, but the desolated hearthstones of Queensbury told plainly of
the terrors of the struggle   A few families remained here during all of this
struggle, and with the promise of peace now held out, the scattered and fugitive settlers returned to rebuild their shattered homes and resume the avocations of peace.[2]

---

[1] WILSON's *Life of Jane McCrea*, p 80   HOLDEN's *History of Queensbury*, p 450

[2] The two following extracts from the Wing manuscripts go to show the continued occupancy of the
settlement —

The Wing papers, as drawn upon in Holden's *History of Queensbury*, show further losses by the war, additional to those already detailed   It will be seen that they amount in the aggregate to large sums in value, particularly those borne by Mr Wing · —

No 1

Affidavit of Abraham Wing relating to losses incurred during the retreat of the American army at the time of Burgoyne's advance towards Saratoga

" In the month of July, 1777, the under-mentioned cattle were taken from me by General Orders and Converted to the use of the Continental Army, for which I have never received any compensation, vizt —

" 1 Red Sorrel Horse aged 7 years and worth..........£25 ,, 00 ,, 0
" 1 Large Mare aged 2 years worth................. 20 ,, 00 ,, 0
" 1 Mare and her colt worth...................... 18 ,, 00 ,, 0
" 1 Cow five years old worth... .... 8 ,, 00 ,, 0
" 2 large fatt Calves worth when taken............. 3 ,, 00 ,, 0
" 11 Best Sheep worth two Dollars each............. 8 ,, 16 ,, 0

"£83 ,, 16 ,, 0

" And in the month of July, 1777, my mills were dismantled of 25 Saws, 2 Rag-Wheels, Gudgeons, Hoops, Bands, Hoggles, Roundsills, Hands, Dogs, Barrs & all other utensills necessary for two Mills in Compleat Repair, for none of which articles I have ever received any compensation whatever

" These Mill Irons were carried off in two waggons on the retreat of the Continental army from Fort George and were worth at least one Hundred and Twenty Pounds

" ABRAHAM WING

" Washington }
    County }   6th March, 1786

" This Day personally appeared the above named Abm Wing and made affirmation to the truth of the above before me

" ADIEL SHERWOOD, Jus Pe "

I NOTICE *of a Friend's Meeting with visitors from abroad —Extract from Abraham Wing's Pocket Memorandum*

3d mo 6, 1778

George Dillwyn from Burlington in West Jersey accompanied by Edward Hallock, Isaac Vail and Paul Upton of the Nine Partners monthly meeting, were here and had a meeting

II MEMORANDUM *concerning some horses left with Abraham Wing.*

Lake George the 12th Day of June A D 1778

Mr Abraham Wing I Cant have my Horses carried to Ticonderoga at Present and If you will Keep 2 Horses for me until the Hurry is over and then will send them up to Leonard Joneses and Desire him to send them to Ticonderoga and send me an account What the cost is I will send you the money or cum this way & Pay you If I may leave it at Leonard Joneses it will be the Handiest for me   I shall be glad to have them have good Pasture   This from yours to sarve

to mr Abraham Wing   &C DAVID WELCH

No 2

Affirmation of Abraham and Benjamin Wing, concerning grain and hay converted to the use of the Continental Army

"We do hereby most solemnly affirm that in the month of July, 1777, the undernamed grain was taken from us for the use of the Continental Army on their retreat from Fort George for which we have Never received any Compensation in any Manner & grane, and the Quantity was apprised by Morgan Lewis and the price affixed by Phineas Babcock, Andrew Lewis and James Higson, viz

" 16 Bushels Oats	
" 18 Bushels rye	
" 30 Bushels of Oats	Valued at forty-three
" 66 Bushels of Corn	pounds five shillings
" 36 Bushels of Wheat	ABRAHAM WING
" 3 tons of hay	BENJAMIN WING

"Washington ⎰ 6th March 1786
    County   ⎱   This day personally appeared the above Signers and Solemnly affirmed in the presense of Almighty God that they had not received any compensation for the above articles

"ADIEL SHERWOOD, Juss Peice"

No 3

Certificate of the Quartermaster General to the receipt of grain and hay for the use of the Continental Army

" 60 Bushels Potatoes	
" 80 Skipples Wheat	Abm Wing
" 5 Tons Hay	
" 16 Busls Oats	
" 18 Do Rye	
" 30 Do Oats	Benjn Wing
" 66 Do Corn	
" 36 Do Wheat	
" 3 Tons Hay	

"The above is agreeable to appraisement made by order Maj'r Gen'l Schuyler   M LEWIS,
   "9 May 1778   D Q M G"

No 4

Affidavit relating to the same

"We do hereby solemnly swear that to the best of our knowledge the different articles as certified by Morgan Lewis which were taken from Abraham and Benjamin Wing by the Continental Army were worth vizt.:

24

"from Abraham Wing   amount
"60 Bushels potatoes worth 2s 6d per Bushell.........£7 ,, 10 ,, 0
"80 Skipples Wheat 4s 6d per Skipple.............. 18 ,, 00 ,, 0
" 5 Tons Hay 60s per Ton....................... 15 ,, 00 ,, 0

                                                    £40 ,, 10 ,, 0
                "From Benjn Wing
"16 Bushell Oats worth 2s 6d per Bushell   .... £2 ,, 00 ,, 0
"18 Bushell Rye 5s per Bushell.................... 4 ,, 10 ,, 0
"30 Bushell Oats 2s 6d per Bushell................. 3 ,, 15 ,, 0
"66 Bushell Corn 4s per Bushell.......... ....13 ,, 4 ,, 0
"36 Bushell Wheat 6s per Bushell.................. 10 ,, 16 ,, 0
" 3 Tons Hay at 60s per Ton..................... 9 ,, 00 ,, 0

                "Amount of the whole   £43 ,, 5 ,, 0
"PHINEHAS BABCOCK
"JAMES HIGSON
"ANDREW LEWIS
"Washington County, 6th March 1786
"This day personally appeared before me the above signers and made
Solemn Oath in the presence of Almighty God the above estimation was to
the best of their knowledge
                                    "ADIEL SHERWOOD, Jus"
                        No 5

The following memorandum of account fixes the date of the foregoing
"The Public
"1777   To Abraham Wing   Dr
"July 16th To 60 Bushels at 6s ... .£18 ,, 00 ,, 0
        "   80 Skipples Wheat at 15s .... 45 ,, 00 ,, 0
        "   5 Tons Hay at £6,.................... 30 ,, 00 ,, 0"
                        No 6

            Affidavit of Andrew Lewis,— relating to loss of horses
"I do hereby most solemnly Swear that on the retreat of the Continental
Army from Fort George, there was a black mare taken from me by order of
Major General Schuyler, by a party Commanded by Col Morgan Lewis, which
mare was worth at least Twelve pounds in Gold or Silver & under nine years
of age   ANDREW LEWIS

"Washington } 6th March, 1786
  County   }
"This day personally appeared before me Andrew Lewis the signer of the
above and made solemn oath to the truth of the above.
                                    "ADIEL SHERWOOD, Jus"

No 7

Benjamin Wing's affirmation respecting the loss of cattle, etc

"I do hereby most solemnly affirm that in the Month of July 1777, the under-named Cattle were taken from me by order of Major General Schuyler for the Use of the Continental army on their retreat from Fort George, vizt

"1 Large Young Horse worth...	£26–0–0
"1 Large Ox worth........	10–0–0
"1 Bull worth...................................	5–0–0
"3 Milch Cows worth £7 Each...................	21–0–0
"2 Large fatt Heifers worth.....................	12–0–0
"3 Calves worth..............................	3–0–0
	"£77–0–0

"which Cattle I do solemnly affirm were worth at Least Seventy-seven pounds in Gold or Silver, when taken from me, & for which I never have received any Compensation myself nor no other person on my account   BENJ WING

"Washington ⎱ 6th March 1786
 County ⎰

"This Day personally appeared before me the above signer Benj Wing and affirmed in the presence of Almighty God that the above act is True for which he had received no Compensation   ADIEL SHERWOOD, Jus"

No 8

Phinehas Babcock's affidavit concerning losses

"I do hereby most Solemnly Swear that on the retreat of the Continental Troops from Fort George

"Captain Lyman & a party of Solders took from me one Milch Cow value ⎱ £6–0–0

"Capt Whitcomb & a party of Soldiers took from me 10 Sheep value 10s ⎱ 5–0–0

"Lieut Howard & a party of Soldiers took from me 1 yoke of oxen valued at £20
"1 Mare 3 years old value 10 ⎰ 30–0–0

 £41–0–0

"Amounting in all to forty-one pounds, for which no compensation whatever has been made to me or any other person on my behalf & I do further most solemnly swear that the above Cattle were worth the above valuation of forty-one pounds, in Gold or Silver, when taken from me for the use of the Continental Army—   PHINEHAS BABCOCK

"Washington ⎱ 6th March 1786
 County ⎰

"This Day personally appeared before me the above Signer Phinehas Babcock Made Solemn Oath in the presence of Almighty God that the above Estimation was true and that he had not received any pay or Compensation for any of them ADIEL SHERWOOD Jus."

No 9

In addition to the cattle heretofore enumerated were a number of milch kine which were returned to the owners pursuant to the following order of Maj Gen Schuyler

"Sir A number of Milch Cows have been brought down from beyond our lines some of which belong to Mr Abraham Wyng and his family and as he is so situated that he cannot move I have permitted him to remain and consented that he should take back eight of his cows You will therefore please to deliver them to him "I am Sir

"Your Hu Sert
"PH · SCHUYLER

" Head Quarters July 26 1777

" To Major Gray

"D Commissary "

No 10

James Higson's affidavit respecting losses

"In the month of July 1777, the Undermentioned articles were taken from me for the use of the Continental Army By General orders & delivered to Brigadier Genl Larned, vizt

" One Large Bay Mare value......................	£20–0–0
" One Large Bay Mare value	15–0–0
" Two very Large Milch Cows....................	16–0–0
" 1 Large Heifer...............................	4–0–0
" 2 Store Calves..............................	3–0–0

"£58–0–0

" For the above cattle which when taken were worth in Specie ,fifty-eight pounds I do solemnly swear that I never received any compensation nor any person on my behalf

" I do most solemnly Swear that in the month of July 1777, a quantity of corn as appraised by Col Lewis & others to four acres, a Quantity of oats as appraised by Col Lewis & others to three acres & Potatoes appraised by the same to one half acre were taken from me for the use of the Continental Army, for none of which I have received any compensation, nor any person on my behalf JAMES HIGSON

" Washington }
County } this day personally appeared before me James Higson and made oath in the presence of Almighty God that the above act was Just and True

" Fort Edward 6th March, 1786 ADIEL SHERWOOD Jus "

No 11

Permit from Col Yates to Abraham Wing, jr, to keep a horse

"Saratoga, Nov 17th, 1777

"I have considered about your Sons Horse and give him Leave to keep the Same until some higher Power shall order it otherwise I also grant you Leave to keep a hunting gun in your house and forbid any one to take the same without orders from the general I am Sir

"Your friend & hu Servt

"A true copy   CHRIS YATES

"To Abraham Wing "

Fortunately for the inhabitants of Queensbury, the important military operations of the next two years occurred farther to the southward along the seaboard, giving them and their property, which had not already been taken or destroyed, a little immunity from the effects of the war A small garrison was retained at Fort Edward, which was for several months the frontier post on the northern military route

The town book shows the results of the usual spring election in the following record —

"At an annual town meeting held in Queensbury on Tuesday ye 5 Day of May 1778 for the Township of Queensbury ·

"1 voted Abraham Wing, Moderator

"2 voted. Benjamin Wing, Town Clerk

"3 voted Abraham Wing, Supervisor

"4 voted James Higson, Constable

"5 voted John Graves, Constable

"6 voted Ebenezer Fuller, Phinehas Babcock and Nehemiah Sealey, Assessors

"7 voted Ebenezer Fuller, Pathmaster

"8 voted Nehemiah Sealey and Benjamin Wing, Overseers of the Poor

"9 voted Phinehas Babcock, Collector

"10 voted Abraham Wing, Town treasurer

"11 voted Abraham Wing, Jur, Pound keeper

"12 voted Nehemiah Sealey and Benjamin Wing, Viewers of fence and prizers of Damage "

With the opening of the spring campaign of 1778 General John Stark was placed in command of the northern department The year was locally signalized by bitter strife among the Tories and their loyal neighbors The former element had reached a position of defiance, maliciousness and cruelty, and it was determined to put them down at whatever cost In June Serenus Parks, a Tory residing near the Harris settlement in the north part of the town, was arrested, as appears by the following letter found among the Wing papers ·—

" Stillwater, 18th of June, 1778

" Sir we have Received yours of the 16th Inst in which you have sent us mr Parks & Jackson's Crime as Pr Complaint, we let you know that our Next meeting will be at the house of James Swarts at Saratoga on Thursday the 26th Inst. and as by order of Convention we are the Proper Judges of Persons of our own district in actions cognizable before a Sub Committee we therefore demand that the Sd Parks & Jackson shall be forthwith delivered to the Custody of Ensign Isac Doty—who is hereby authorized to Receive them in order that they may be caused to appear before us at the time and Place above mentioned when the Complainants may have opportunity to Produce their Evidence and proceed to tryal   By order of Committee,

" GEORGE PALMER, Chairman "

It was in this season, also, that Levi Crocker was taken prisoner by a band of Tories, of which some were neighbors and supposed friends Crocker was at work in his field when taken, and he received such abuse, indignity and insult, that he said to one of his captors, " Tom, there will come a time when I will make you bite the dust for this!" After some months' incarceration he was fortunate enough to escape from his prison, and return to his home at Fort Miller in safety One day a member of the family discovered the offending Tory, making his way across the lower end of their garden Crocker, who happened to be in the house, was immediately notified and, taking down his gun, which was always loaded in those exciting times, he stepped to the door and deliberately shot him While writhing in his death agony, Crocker walked to his side and reminded him of his treachery, and his own well-executed threat

" Among the pioneer settlers of the Bradshaw patent was Moses Harris, father of the spy whose exploits have already been in part narrated Like his brother Gilbert,[1] the Tory, he was also a militia man at the time of the capture of Port Royal In consequence of this service he became entitled to bounty-land, and it was probably while endeavoring to locate his scrip, that he settled in the northwestern part of Kingsbury He was arrested about the time of the occurrence of the events just narrated, at the house of his brother Gilbert The latter, well knowing that Moses was fully cognizant of his evil doings, insisted that he should be taken into Canada as a prisoner, even if he died on the route, he being not only advanced in years, but in feeble health at that time, but Andrew Rakely (or Rikely), who was in charge or command of the party of Tories, resolutely opposed the proposition, saying, ' He is an old man, and if he goes the exposure and fatigue will kill him ' To this Gilbert unfeelingly responded, ' Let him die then ' The matter was finally compro-

---

[1] Old Gil Harris found Kingsbury an unhealthy neighborhood to live in after the war was ended He removed, it is said, to Bolton, and died and was buried somewhere in the vicinity of Basin Bay on Lake George

mised by Moses taking an oath not to reveal anything, so long as the war lasted, which would prejudice Gilbert's interests or bring him into disrepute with
his Whig neighbors After the war, Joseph Harris, Moses's son, out of gratitude for this unusual act of kindness, sent word to Rakely in Canada, that if
he would come down and settle on it, he would give him one hundred acres of
as good farming land as this section of country afforded

"About the same time a lad by the name of Oliver Graham, being with
a party of three or four others on their way from Fort Edward, was shot at and
wounded by a party of Tories concealed on the route, of whom Gil Harris was
one One of the number exclaimed as he was about to fire, 'Why that's little
Oliver Graham, don't kill him,' to which Harris savagely replied, "Yes, damn
him ! let's kill all ' The poor fellow, on finding himself wounded, jumped from
the roadway into the woods on the opposite side from which the gun was
fired, and fell into the hands of another party in ambush, by whom he was
taken a prisoner to Canada, where he remained a prisoner until after the close
of the war, when he returned again to Sandy Hill "[1]

In short, anarchy reigned supreme, brother was often arrayed against
brother and father against son, few knew who could be trusted, the soldiery
assumed a license[2] to which they were not entitled, and justice, when it did
overtake the enemies of the country, was often prompt in obtaining satisfaction The following extract from a letter written by General Stark in June to
the president of the New Hampshire Congress is a vivid and blood-chilling
comment upon the general condition of affairs. —

"They [the people] do very well in the hanging way They hanged nine
on the 16th of May, on the 5th of June nine, and have one hundred and
twenty in jail, of which, I believe, more than one-half will go in the same way
Murder and robberies are committed every day in this neighborhood So
you may judge of my situation, with the enemy on my front, and the devil at
my rear "

On the 8th of June there were only twenty men left at Fort Edward, and
there is no mention of any force at Fort George or the smaller posts between

The events of the year 1778, as far as relates to this section, were closed
by a Tory raid by the way of Lake George and the Sacandaga, which is thus
described in Stone's *Life of Brant*. —

"Much has been said in the traditions of Tryon county, and somewhat,
also, in the courts of law, in cases involving titles to real estate formerly in the
family of Sir William Johnson, respecting the burial of an iron chest, by his
son, Sir John, previous to his flight to Canada, containing the most valuable

---

[1] These incidents are thus related in HOLDEN's *History of Queensbury*.

[2] In a letter from General Stark to Colonel Safford, dated at Albany, May 1st, he says "Doctor
Smith complains that the troops at Fort Edward are turning out the inhabitants and destroying the
buildings at that place I should be glad that such disorders should be suppressed, and the inhabitants' property secured "

of his own and his father's papers Late in the autumn of the present
year, General Haldimand, at the request of Sir John, sent a party of between
forty and fifty men privately to Johnstown, to dig up and carry the
chest away The expedition was successful, but the chest not being sufficiently tight to prevent the influence of dampness from the earth, the
papers had become mouldy, rotten and illegible when taken up The information respecting this expedition was derived in the spring following, from
a man named Helmer, who composed one of the party, and assisted in dis-
interring the chest "

The reader is already familiar with the events of the year 1779, few of
which bore important relation to the district under our present consideration
Skenesborough was burned in March by the infamous Joe Betteys and a party
of one hundred and thirty Indians, some of the inhabitants killed and the remainder made prisoners, Fort Anne was thus left as the frontier post on the
north

The town record book shows the usual election for 1779, with no change
of importance, except the substitution of Phineas Babcock for supervisor in
place of Abraham Wing In 1780 the following record appears —

"At an annual town meeting held in Queensbury on Tuesday ye 2 Day
of May, 1780, For the Township of Queensbury

"Voted, Abraham Wing, Moderator

"Voted, to Return this to Fort Miller, at Duer's big house, the Eight of
this instant at 9 in the Morning.

"Fort Miller ye 8 AD 1780, — The Meting mett, and opened according
to appointment "

The election of the following officers is then recorded, Benjamin Wing,
town clerk, Phineas Babcock, supervisor, James Higson and Andrew Lewis,
constables; Ebenezer Fuller, James Higson and Andrew Lewis, assessors,
Abraham Wing, pathmaster; Abraham Wing and Benjamin Wing, overseers
of the poor, Silas Brown, collector, Abraham Wing, town treasurer, Abraham Wing, jr., pound-keeper; Pardon Daly and James Higson, fence viewers
and appraisers of damages

The reason for adjourning this town meeting to Fort Miller is presumed to
have been the fear of some Tory irruption from Canada like that already related,
of which there were several more in the course of the season

Nearly or quite all of the families that have been mentioned as settlers in
Queensbury, and others (the Seelyes, the Fernsses, Merritts, Browns, Odells,
Braytons, Harrises, Parkses, Havilands, Griffings, Folgers, etc, who have been
conspicuous in the history of the town), were from Duchess county. There
they had been neighbors and friends for many years, and the trying experiences to which they were subjected on the scene of their new homes only
welded closer the bonds of friendship among them Most of them belonged

to the religious sect known as Friends, or Quakers,[1] and were on that account opposed to the war, consequently they took no part in it, and as year after year of the contest passed and their own immediate locality was threatened, they at various times gathered hastily movable property and precipitately retreated to their old homes in Duchess, to return again when the danger was passed These flittings were so frequent that, in the language of one of the old residents, "It soon got to be very easy to go, for they had but little to move" But, notwithstanding these hardships and periods of absence, the existence of the settlement was maintained with persistent energy, and with the exception of the last year of the war, the inhabitants did not fail to meet annually and elect their town officers, as we have seen

The following additional records complete the statements of losses by the inhabitants of Queensbury, as recorded in the Wing manuscripts —

No 1[2]

"Memorandum of Account of Outlays, Expenditures and losses by Abraham Wing:

"Time expended in Search of my Iron which was con-
sealed by Sargent Williams & Company June the 20
Day 1778 6 men and myself 1 Day..............£8 „ 8 „ 0
"2 cwt of Nails ....60 „ 00 „ 0
"To 3 journies to Fort Stark in the Summer in pursuit
of sd iron.................................. 3 „ 12 „ 0
"2 days at Court ....2 „ 8 „ 0
"2 large Carpenters Sledges or Mawls,............9 „ 12 „ 0
"8 ax „ 2 Iron wedges ....6 „ 8 „ 0

"ABRM WING"

No 2

Statement of losses by one Jacob Ferguson

"Capt moss I understand by Cornal mcCray that you had wheat from my fathers plase with others ond as it was one third part mine please to pay Abraham Wing the money for what you Had and you will oblige your Friend

"Queensbury the 4 of February 1780 JACOB FERGUSON"

"Capt putnam I understand by Cornal mcCray that you had sum wheat from my Fathers plase which wheat was one third part mine please to pay Abraham Wing for the Same and you will oblige your friend to sarve

"Queensbury the 4 february 1780 JACOB FERGUSON"

---

1 In the year 1813 the following named persons were returned from Queensbury as Quakers, subject to military duty, and refused Solomon Haviland, Dilwin Gardner, Joseph Haviland, Stephen Brown, Jonathan Brown, Henry Brown, Isaac Fancher, William Sisson, Nathaniel Sisson, jr, Daniel Sisson, Jonathan Dean, David Dean, Joseph Dean, David Brown, Benjamin Lapham Each of these was assessed four dollars in lieu of the year's military duty

2 HOLDEN'S *History of Queensbury*

No. 3.

Affidavit of Samuel Younglove relating to the destruction of property in Queensbury in 1780

" County of } ss Personally before me Albert Baker one of the Justices for said
Washington }   County Samuel Younglove of Lawfull age deposeth and saith
that he saw James Stinslor take out of the house of Abram Wing in the year
one thousand seven hundred and eighty to the amount of about one hundred
panes of glass with the sashes or near there abouts and saw him have five saw-
mill saws and sundry other articles which the said Stinslor told the deponent
he had taken from the said Wing, and the deponent further declares that the
said Stinslor told him the deponent that he had got to the amount of between
forty and fifty pounds from old Wing   farthermore deponent saith not

"Sworn before me this 11th June, 1787   SAML YOUNGLOVE "

          " ALBERT BAKER J Peace "

No 4

Affidavit concerning cattle seized in 1780

" Washington County State of New York ss

" Personally appeared before me John Williams one of Judges of the Court
of Sessions & common pleas for the said County John McCrea of said County
of lawful age who being duly sworn on the holy Evangelists of Almighty God
deposeth and saith that in the month of October in the year of our Lord one
thousand seven hundred and eighty that the Garrison stationed at Fort Edward were destitute of provisions and that the Commissary then at that post
was directed to get Cattle where they might be had for the support of the
Troops by order of General Schuyler Jonathan Jillet the then Commissary ap-
plyed to this deponent who had a pair of fatt oxen which he received and killed
at the post that this deponent applied to the commissary for payment who gave
this deponent a certificate for said Cattle which afterwards was destroyed with
the buildings of this deponent by the enemy that he the said Commissary left
the parts immediately after the Campaign ended so that this deponent could
not obtain any relief in the premises & has made application to the Legislature
of this State but did not receive any neither has he at any time or in any manner received any kind of restitution for said Cattle and further he this deponent
has not assigned or made over said certificate to any person or persons whatever and that the certificate which this deponent received for said oxen from
said Commissary was for fourteen hundred weight of Beef as near as this deponent recollects and further this deponent saith not   .

"Sworn before me this } JOHN WILLIAMS JUD CURIA "
   25th december 1790 }

No 5

Official certificates in favor of Abraham Wing and son

" No 416 I do hereby acknowledge myself indebted to Abraham Wing in

the Sum of Two Hundred dollars As Witness my hand this 11 Day of May
1780   MORN LEWIS D Q M G "

" This Certifies that Mr Abraham Wing hath supplied the Publick with 150
Plank and 50 Boards Price not known of the above Boards

"JONATHAN NICKLISON "

" This Certifies that Abraham Wing hath Supplied the Public with Two
tuns of Hay at One hundred and Sixty five Dollors pr tun Amounting to One
Hundred and Thirty two Pounds for Which Sum this Shall be a Sufficient
voucher Given under my hand and Seal————of September 1780   £132–0

"CHRIS YATES D Q M G

" FORT GEORGE 22d march 1780"

" These to Certify

" That abraham Wing Jun hath been two days Imployed in Public services
at the garrison at fort George with a sleigh and two Yoke of Oxen one day and
with one Span of Horses the other Day for which he hath Recd no pay

" To Whom it may ⎱   pr WM MOULTON Captn Commandt "
   Concern   ⎰

No 6

Deposition of James Higson concerning two oxen, the property of Benjn Wing
—taken for the public service in 1781

"The Peblic to Benjn Wing Dr 15th May 1781

" To Two Oxen Taken from Fort Miller by Lieut Bagley, by order of Lt
Col Vandike

" Washington ⎱   This Day personly appeared Before me James Higson of
   County   ⎰ Lawfull age and made solomn oath in the presence of Almighty God, that he Saw the above [named 'Lt Bagley Take the Oxen from
Fort Miller with a party of Soldiers and said he had orders from Col Van Dicke
to Do So, and that he the sd Deponant knew the oxen to be the property of
the above named Benjamin Wing   JAMES HIGSON

" Sworn before me at Fort Edward this 6th Day of March, 1786

" ADIEL SHERWOOD Jus Peace

" We Do hereby Solemnly Sware that to the best of our knowledge the
Two oxen above specified which were taken from Benjn Wing for the use of
the Continental Army, were worth at that time in specie Thirty pounds york
money

" PHINEHAS BABCOCK
" ANDREW LEWIS
" JAMES HIGSON

" Washington ⎱
   County   ⎰   this Day personly appeared before me the above Phis
Babcock, Andrew Lewis and James Higson and made oath to the same

" Fort Edward 6th March 1786   ADIEL SHERWOOD, Jus Peace

" 6th March 1786, this day personly appeared before me Benjn Wing and

Most Solemnly affirmed in the presence of Almighty God that he had not received any Compensation for the within mentioned oxen.

"ADIEL SHERWOOD, Jus Peace."

It is presumed that no part of these claims was ever adjusted

Queensbury was destined to still further devastation before the triumph of liberty was secured. The Tory element in this section continued to increase in numbers and vindictiveness, and the annals of the times are filled with thrilling incidents in which they and their loyal neighbors were the chief participants. The Sacandaga River and Lake George, with frequent forays into Queensbury, were the favorite routes for the incursions of the Tory bands It was early in this season (1780) that Justus Seelye (according to the narrative of his son given to Dr Holden), then a small boy and later a resident of this town, was smuggled into a neighbor's house at Fort Miller, where a meeting of Indians, as supposed, was held, and to whose consultations and proceedings he thus involuntarily became a witness After they left he escaped to his home and related the events and conversation of the evening A party was immediately organized in pursuit, which overtook and captured them, when one of them was discovered to be a neighbor and a Tory painted up in the fitting semblance of a savage He with the rest of his party, all Tories, were sent to Albany and imprisoned, tried by court martial and hung

In the autumn of the same year, when Captain John Chipman was in command at Fort George and Captain Adiel Sherwood at Fort Anne, both of these posts were captured by the British and the latter named unimportant fortification burned, the details of which, with those of other operations and the sanguinary engagement at Bloody Pond, have been given in an earlier chapter. The prisoners taken at the two forts were conveyed by way of Lake Leorge and transferred to the vessels on Lake Champlain, and Fort George was destroyed The detachment of Tories and Indians that proceeded south from Fort Anne hastened on through Kingsbury street, burning and destroying as they went In local traditions this year has ever since been termed "the year of the burning "

Of the incidents bearing a local interest and connected with these events, Dr Holden notes the following in his work on Queensbury "Among the number comprising this expedition [against the two forts] was a former resident of Sandy Hill named Adam Wint, who, espousing the royal cause, went to Canada in the early part of the war He with another Tory from the same neighborhood acted as guides to a party of Indians to whom was assigned the incendiary work of destruction At this time Albert Baker, sr ,[1] was attending

---

[1] The Bakers were of Scotch or North English origin For political reasons the original or pioneer emigrant of the name was obliged to flee his country, and seek refuge in this country, during Cromwell's protectorate Albert Baker, jr , was born 10th November, 1765 When he was four years of age his father moved to Sandy Hill Caleb Baker, son of Albert, was the first child born of white parents in the town of Kingsbury. Albert, jr , was sent to school at Glens Falls before there was any school at Sandy Hill He boarded at Abraham Wing's

court in the eastern part of the county   While his sons and hired men were at work, a part of them in the barn and the rest in the fields near by, a neighbor by the name of Thomas Lyon came rushing by exclaiming, 'Boys what are you about?   Don't you see that all Kingsbury's ablaze?   You'd better be getting out of this!'   After warning the family, the boys hitched up two yokes of oxen to a cart, and loading it hastily with what few things came readily to hand they made their escape by the way of Fort Edward   Even then the Tories had formed their ambuscade by the road side, for Gil Harris, who was one of the party, with others lay concealed behind a log on the route between Sandy Hill and Fort Edward, afterwards told Mrs Baker that he saw her passing with a tea-kettle in her hand, and that she would have been taken a prisoner to Canada had it not been from a fear of being pursued by the soldiers at Fort Edward

" A portion of the same party followed down the river on the west side as far as Stillwater, burning and destroying as th y went   The fugitive settlers from Kingsbury and Queensbury are said to have been guided on their retreat by the blaze of the burning buildings

" A widow Harris, who kept tavern nearly opposite the Baker house, had a little daughter captured by the enemy, but they shortly let her go again and she returned to her mother , home she had none, for it was burned   There were seventeen families living in Kingsbury at this time   Of all the buildings and betterments everything was destroyed but two

" At this time Queensbury was abandoned by its inhabitants, its dwellings and improvements were again burnt and destroyed and the settlement remained deserted for the next fifteen months, during which no record exists of town meetings, nor is there any other evidence of occupancy '

Of the situation after the era of destruction in Queensbury we have a vivid picture in the *Travels in North America*, by the Marquis de Chastellux, under date of December 30th, 1780, wherein he says   " I had scarcely lost sight of Fort Edward, before the spectacle of devastation presented itself to my eyes, and continued to distress them as far as the place I stopped at   Peace and Industry had conducted Cultivators amidst the ancient forests [who] were content and happy, before the period of this war   Those who were in Burgoyne's way alone Experienced the horrors of his Expedition ; but on the last invasion of the Savages, the desolation has spread from Fort Schuyler (or Stanwise) even to Fort Edward , I beheld nothing around me but the remains of conflagrations , a few bricks, proof against the fire, were the only indication of ruined houses , whilst the fences still entire, and cleared out lands, announced that these deplorable habitations had once been the abode of riches and happiness '

" Among the prisoners taken at this time by a party of savages and Tories accompanying the expedition to Fort George, were Eben Fuller (brother-in-law to William Robards, before mentioned) and his son Benjamin, Andrew

Lewis, who was held a prisoner in Canada to the close of the war, James Higson, soon afterward liberated through the intercession of his brother-in-law, Daniel Jones, Moses Harris the elder and his son William

"The morning following the surrender of the fort, the dwelling where they lived was surrounded by the invading party, and before they could make any preparations either for defense or escape, they were made prisoners   The elder Harris was treated with uncalled for severity and harshness   His shoes and stockings were taken off, and he was loaded with a heavy pack of plunder, with which, after his house and out buildings were burned, he was compelled to travel the rough road which led along the western banks of Lake George to a point on Lake Champlain north of Ticonderoga, probably Bulwagga Bay [1] The son begged the privilege of carrying his father's pack, and also to allow the old gentleman the use of his shoes and stockings, while he would go barefoot. Through the malignity of one of the Tories, who had an old grudge to revenge, this request was denied, and the old man's trail might, for many miles, have been traced by his bloody foot-prints   After reaching Lake Champlain the party, consisting of eighteen prisoners with their captors, were embarked in boats and bateaux, which had been concealed at that place on their way up, and after many privations, hardships and indignities, were finally landed at Quebec

"Here the captives were ransomed from the savages, and became prisoners of war   For a period they were held in close confinement, but after awhile the rigor of their discipline was somewhat relaxed, and the old man was permitted to follow the occupations of farming and also of dressing and tanning deerskins, with which he was familiar   In due course of time, he with other prisoners was sent to Halifax and exchanged, after which he returned to his former home in Duchess county.   The younger Harris, with thirteen other prisoners, through the same Tory influence that had made both his march and imprisonment of unusual rigor and severity, was placed for more perfect security where they were guarded by a patrol of soldiers and kept at work   With the opening of spring a yearning for freedom possessed the hearts of the prisoners, and they concerted a plan for escape, which was afterward matured and carried into effect as follows   A boat from the main land furnished them daily with pro-

---

[1] " It is proper to state," says Dr Holden in a foot note, p 485, " that this narrative and the other Harris traditions were taken down by the author about the year 1850 from the relation of Moses Harris, nephew of William, the principal actor in this life drama, by whom my informant had heard the events related many times   In one respect, and perhaps without sufficient cause, I have varied my account from the original version as given to me, which made the date of the capture of the Harrises and other prisoners at the time of Burgoyne's advance, which the following reminiscence would seem to confirm ; for William's son Benjamin informed me that his father's name was afterwards found on the muster and pay rolls in Sherwood's possession, as one of the militia drafted for that emergency, and that he was present in the fort as a soldier, and was made a prisoner at the time of the surrender of Fort Anne   It is gratifying, also, to record his justification of the surrender, inasmuch as, according to his judgment, the fort was wholly untenable against any considerable force

visions and such necessary supplies as their condition required   From these
supplies, they commenced saving up from their daily rations such portions as
could be most easily preserved, until they had accumulated sufficient to last
them for three days   When the critical moment of departure arrived, however,
only seven of the fourteen could be prevailed upon to undertake the perilous
journey   The most the others would do was to take a solemn oath not to
make any disclosure or raise any alarm which would lead to their apprehension,
until the evening following, when the sentries were changed, and the discovery
would be inevitable   They seized the boat which brought their provisions in
the morning and made their escape during the forenoon, landing upon the
south shore of the St Lawrence, on the borders of the vast wilderness stretching toward the New England colonies   Harris, being an excellent woodsman,
here took the lead, and they struck boldly into the wilderness, pursuing their
way southward for several days and nights with but little rest and scant refreshment, husbanding their slender stock of provisions to the utmost   These
soon gave out and they were obliged to depend upon such chance fare as the
forest afforded   At length, utterly worn out with fatigue they made a halt,
and to avoid the intolerable annoyance of the mosquitos and flies, it was proposed to build a fire, or more properly a *smudge*, as it is called in woodman's parlance   Harris opposed the project and endeavored to dissuade them from it,
on the ground that it would inevitably lead to their discovery and recapture, if
they were pursued, which was exceedingly probable   He was overruled, however, by the majority, and a place was selected on a low marshy spot of ground,
where the fire was started and then smothered with damp, rotten wood, which
prevented it from blazing and made a dense, heavy smoke which kept off the
insects   Around this they camped for the night, and exhausted with the protracted march and unwonted fatigue the entire party was very shortly buried
in a profound sleep   About midnight they were aroused from their slumbers
by a volley of musketry, by which one of their number was killed outright, and
two others were desperately wounded   Harris, who was a large, muscular man,
with limbs powerfully knit together, and of herculean proportions and strength,
arose in time to parry a blow from a tomahawk, which was aimed by a gigantic
savage at one of his companions   The Indian immediately grappled with him,
and after a struggle for some minutes Harris succeeded in throwing him upon
the now brightly blazing fire, when putting his feet upon his neck he pressed
the savage's head beneath the flames   At this juncture, a near neighbor and
former friend of Harris before the war, a Tory by the name of Cyrenus Parks,
approached him with his musket, clubbed, and ordered him to release the savage [1]   This he refused to do, and as he drew back to strike him, Harris ex-

---

[1] Cyrenus Parks had a brother named Joseph, who, after the war, lived on his brother's place, near
neighbor to William   As he was a Whig and patriot in sentiment, he and the Harrises were very amicable in their relations, until a misunderstanding arose between them in regard to some business transaction, when a gradual coolness ensued, which, for a while, estranged them   One morning Joseph

claimed, 'You won't kill an unarmed man will you, Parks, and an old neighbor too?'" Parks made no reply, nor for an instant wavered in his fell purpose, and the blow descended   Harris warded it off as well as he could with his arm, which was broken by its force, the remainder of the blow falling upon his head, the lock of the gun cutting a large gash through the scalp, down the sides of the head to the ear

"Harris fell stunned and remained insensible for many hours   When he awoke to consciousness he found another gash on the opposite side of his head, caused by the blow of a tomahawk, two wounds upon his forehead caused by the muzzle of a musket, jammed down with considerable force with the intent of dispatching him, and a bayonet thrust in the chest, which had been given to see if he was still alive.   All his companions were gone, as well as his coat, shoes and knapsack, which he had taken off the evening before, and which had served him as a pillow during his fatal sleep   He staggered to his feet, dressed his wounds as well as he could, slung his broken arm through his neck hand-kerchief, and, maimed and crippled, resumed his slow and toilsome progress towards home   He subsisted upon roots, leaves and herbs, such as he could find suitable for the purpose upon his route, and an occasional frog dressed with his remaining hand, aided by his teeth, and eaten raw

"At length he came out on the bank of a stream   While standing upon the gravelly beach, looking around for materials with which to construct a raft, the stream being deep and rapid, and he unable to swim, he suddenly caught sight of two men cautiously reconnoitering from some distance above him   He immediately concealed himself among the thick bushes and rank vegetation along the stream and crept back into the woods to an old tree top, which had been his place of concealment and lodging the night before   After waiting some time, and reflecting that his situation could be made but little worse even by a return to captivity, he resolved to go back and surrender himself to the lurking foe   He accordingly went back and again discovered the two men cautiously peering at him through the brushwood   Stepping boldly out in sight, he beckoned them to approach, when, to his great joy, he found that they were two Dutchmen from the Mohawk Valley, comrades of his, who had also escaped on the night of the attack   They dressed his wounds, which

called upon William, manifesting a disposition to conciliate and make friends again   In great good h mor he related several anecdotes and border adventures, until he thought his listener had reached a genial frame of mind, when, leading his way quietly and gradually to the subject, he asked William if he would not be willing to overlook the past and forgive his brother Cyrenus, if the latter would make a suitable acknowledgment and ask his forgiveness   Springing from his seat in a tempest of rage, the old scout replied with an oath   "No, he tried to kill me in cold blood, and if I ever get a chance I'll shoot him "   Joseph still pressed and argued the matter until Harris's suspicions were aroused, and he exclaimed   "Joseph, Cyrenus is at your house, and if he wants to live he had better keep out of my way "

The next night Cyrenus made his escape to Canada.   The popular tradition that Harris tracked him to the St. Lawrence River and shot him as he was crossing that stream, is declared by the family to be without warrant, and untrue

were found in a putrid condition and swarming with maggots They also adjusted his broken arm, dressing it with splints prepared from barks of trees and bound it together with his handkerchief The next day they constructed a raft and crossed the stream Fortunately, Harris had a hook and a line in his pocket, and coming to a good sized brook, they encamped and caught a fine string of trout, which they cooked and ate, the first warm meal they had enjoyed since they left the island

"Continuing their journey they came, after some days' travel, upon a small clearing and log house One of the three went forward, after carefully and cautiously reconnoitering to see that no enemy was around, and begged of the woman of the house She proved to be French They were still in Canada She gave the messenger to understand that she had no food to give, that her husband was away from home, and that their place was visited almost daily by armed bands of Indians and Tories A loaf of corn bread baked in the ashes was, after some search, discovered carefully hidden away, which the fugitive eagerly seized and carried to his companions They made what haste they could to get out of the dangerous locality After many more days' wandering they came out upon the settlements of the Lower Goos, now Bellows Falls, on the Connecticut River Here the trio parted, the two Dutchmen proceeding to Cherry Valley by way of Albany, and Harris repaired to New Perth, now Salem, in Charlotte county, where his wounds were first regularly and properly dressed by Dr Williams, then member of the Colonial Legislature, and colonel of militia His wounds were a long time in healing After his recovery it is stated that he served as a minute man, or one of the reserve militia, until the close of the war "[1]

During the two years following the occurrence of the events narrated, the history of Queensbury remains a blank, so far as local records are concerned It was practically wiped out of existence as a settlement Our early chapters have chronicled the public operations in this region which came down to the spring of 1783, when on the 19th of April (the day which completed the eighth year of the war), the cessation of hostilities and the triumph of the colonists was announced throughout the country No sooner was peace restored than the proprietors of Queensbury again entered upon their duties On Tuesday, May 6th, of that year the town meeting was held and the following officers elected —

Moderator — Abraham Wing

Town Clerk — Benjamin Wing.

Supervisors — Nehemiah Seelye, and Phineas Babcock

Constables — William Robards, and David Buck

Assessors — David Bennett, Wm Robards, and James Higson

Pathmasters — Benjamin Wing, and Silas Brown

---

1 This narrative is given in DR HOLDEN's *History of Queensbury,* p 485, etc

25

Overseers of the Poor — Abraham Wing, and Benedick Brown

Collector — Nehemiah Seelye

Treasurer — Abraham Wing

Fence Viewers — Phineas Babcock, David Bennett, and Jeremiah Briggs

In July of this year the locality was visited by General Washington and a portion of his staff (probably on the 19th or 21st of the month) on their way to inspect the posts at Lake George, Ticonderoga and Crown Point. On this occasion the party halted, and calling Walter Briggs, who was at work in an adjoining field, he came and helped them to water from the upper branch of the Butler Brook.

With the advent of peace came all of the beneficent influences that soon lifted the country from the terrors and depression of a long and destructive war to the plane of prosperity — a transition that was nowhere else more welcome than to the harrassed and distressed inhabitants of the region with which this history is most concerned.

This portion of our work may be appropriately closed with the following description of Queensbury and Glens Falls, as they appeared to the Marquis de Chastellux at the end of the year 1780 : —

"   On leaving the valley, and pursuing the road to Lake George, is a tolerable military position which was occupied in the war before the last, it is a sort of entrenched camp, adapted to abatis, guarding the passage from the woods, and commanding the valley.   Arrived at the height of the cataract, it was necessary to quit our sledges and walk half a mile to the bank of the river. The snow was fifteen inches deep, which rendered this walk rather difficult, and obliged us to proceed in Indian file. In order to make a path, each of us put ourselves alternately at the head of this little column, as the wild geese relieve each other to occupy the summit of the angles they form in their flight. But had our march been still more difficult, the sight of the cataract was an ample recompense. It is not a sheet of water as at *Cohos*, and at Totohaw; the river confined, and interrupted in its course by different rocks, glides through the midst of them, and precipitating itself obliquely, forms several cascades. That of *Cohos* is more majestic, this, more terrible, the Mohawk River seemed to fall from its own dead weight; that of the Hudson frets, and becomes enraged, it foams, and forms whirlpools, and flies like a serpent making its escape, still continuing its menaces by horrible hissings. On their return, the party stopped again at Fort Edward to warm by the fire of the officers who command the garrison. They are five in number, and have about one hundred and fifty soldiers. They are stationed in this desert for the whole winter."

Mention has been made in another chapter of the settlement of Jacob Glen on the south side of the river, where he obtained, according to traditions of the Parke family, his title of Elijah Parke, the original settler in that neighbor-

hood After the Revolutionary War Glen rebuilt the mills destroyed during
the struggle, manufactured lumber and passed some weeks every summer at
a cottage originally built by one of the Parke family and standing on the hill
overlooking the present paper-mill site Here he lived in what was grand
style for that period It was during one of these visits, as related by Dr Holden, that, " in a convivial moment, it was proposed by him to pay the expenses
of a wine supper for the entertainment of a party of mutual friends if Mr Wing
would consent to transfer his claim and title to the name of the falls Whether
the old Quaker pioneer thought the project visionary and impracticable, or
whatever motive may have actuated him, assent was given, the symposium
was held, and the name of Glens Falls was inaugurated [1]

" Mr Glen hastened to Schenectady and ordered some hand-bills printed,
announcing the change of name These were posted in all the taverns along
the highway and bridle paths from Queensbury to Albany, and the change of
name was effected with a promptitude that must have been bewildering to the
easy-going farmers of the town in those days The following letter, written
in elegant running hand, and still existing among the Wing MSS , is believed
to determine the date of this enterprise ·[2] —

" ' Mr Glen's compliments to Mr Wing, and requests the favor of him to
send the advertisement accompanying this by the first conveyance to his friends
at Quaker Hill

" ' Mr Glen hopes Mr and Mrs Wing and the family are all well

" ' Glen's Falls, April 29th, 1788 '

" Superscribed,   ' Mr Wing, Queensbury ' "

After the Revolution — Pioneer settlement had long been delayed in
Queensbury , but when a permanent peace was firmly established it was among
the first localities to feel its effects, as shown by a gradual influx of population,
increased cultivation of lands and a general aspect of thrift A writer over
the signature " Harlow " stated in the *Warren Messenger*, February, 1831,
that " the first clearing [at Glens Falls] was limited to the hill which rises from
the falls, and in the year 1783 presented only a wheat field, with a solitary
smoke on its border, and two other dwellings in the vicinity of the forest
These houses were built after the architecture of the first settlers, of a few
rough logs, placed one upon another, the interstices filled with straw and mix-

---

[1] The name of the village has passed through several changes of orthography, and is found printed
as "Glens," "Glenns," in each instance both with and without the indication of the possessive case,
and has finally, in recent years, settled down to the common usage adopted in this work — "Glens
Falls "

[2] " Colonel Johannes Glen, after whom the village was named, was the son of Jacob, who was the
son of Johannes, jr , who was the son of Jacob, the eldest son of the original immigrant, and brother
of Captain Johannes Glen, of Schenectady According to Professor Pearson's record, he was born 2d
of July, 1735, and baptized in Albany, where his father lived and died His mother's maiden name
was Elizabeth Cuyler He was quartermaster in the French and Revolutionary Wars, stationed at
Schenectady , in 1775 bought lands on the Hudson, above Fort Edward, of Daniel Parke, which tract
was afterwards called *Glens* Falls "

ture of mud and clay   But in the year 1784 an individual by the name of
Haviland [Abraham, a blacksmith by calling] erected, to use a graphical expression, a small framed house, near the hotel in the upper part of the village,[1]
which was soon followed by that now occupied by Mr Royal Leavins,[2] completed upon the model of an old-fashioned Massachusetts country house,
which two buildings were consequently the first of the kind which graced our
landscape." [3]

On the 26th of January, 1784, the inhabitants of Fort George were annexed to the Queensbury district by a vote of the inhabitants, and in the same
year, by act of Legislature, the name of Charlotte county was changed to
Washington county   The "inhabitants of Fort George," as appears in the
New York legislative papers, are embraced in the following. —

" The Petition of Jonathan Pitcher, Gurdon Chamberlin, Wyatt Chamberlin and Isaac Doty, residing on a tract of land at the South end of Lake George
commonly called Garrison Land, humbly sheweth, That your Petitioners,
some time since, being desirous to emigrate from the Old Settlements, and to
fix ourselves on the Frontier of the State, did obtain, from the Surveyor Genl
of the state, leases of the Lands whereon we now reside, which Leases being
only for the Term of One Year, induceth us to address Your Hon'ble Body on
the Subject   Your Petitioners having removed our families to this place at
great Expense from a very considerable distance, ardently wish to continue on
the same, and do most humbly pray that our leases may be renewed for as
long a Term of time as your Hon'ble Body shall deem most eligible, or that
any other mode may be adopted, whereby your petitioners may be allowed to
occupy the premises —Lake George, De 30, 1783 "

Dr. Holden adds upon this subject   " Jonathan Pitcher then kept a sort of
rude tavern at the head of the lake   Hugh McAuley was also another inhabitant of Lake George at that time   Robert Nesbit, who was in trade there
for several years, did not come until June, 1785 "

---

[1] Corner of South and Glen streets

[2] The dwelling lately owned and occupied by J W Finch

[3] The same writer continues as follows   "As early as 1786–87 the fruit of their reflections was
seen, a small, rudely constructed school-house, now the residence of Mrs Flannagan [Now the site
of Dr Holden, 17 Elm street]   .

" The village of Glens Falls was formerly known by the name of Wing's Falls, a name probably
derived from Mr Abraham Wing, one of the first emigrants to this place, who lived in a log building
which occupied the spot of Mr. L. L Pixley's store   .   .

" Then followed the dams, the one above, and the other below the falls, and the mill seats afforded
by them, owned and occupied by Mr Benjamin Wing, and General (Warren) Ferriss   Only one of
these dams is still remaining — that at the head of the rapids, now a bank of five feet high, and about
600 broad, over which the river pours its waters in one unbroken sheet   An Indian, for a
trifling reward, paddled his canoe to the brink of the precipice, and then shot like lightning into the
gulf to disappear forever, and the same is related of many others who dared the fury of the cataract

" But it is safe to leap from any of the rocks, at the southern point of the island or as far west as
the bridge   This was fully attested by Cook, who jumped three successive times from the old king-
post, into the water beneath (the gulf at the foot of the arch), and returned, exclaiming like Patch,
'There's no mistake'"—HOLDEN's *History of Queensbury*, p 498

James Stevenson came into the town in 1785, when, as stated by members of his family, there were but eighteen families in the whole town   The mills had been destroyed during the war and the inhabitants were forced to go to Jessup's Falls or Fort Miller for their grinding   Joseph Varney, son of Josiah Varney (a pioneer who married a daughter of Benedick Brown), told Dr Holden in 1868, that " Uncle " Silas Brown used to back grists over the mountain by a line of blazed trees, afterwards a bridle-path, to Jessup's grist-mill, in what is now Luzerne, during and after the Revolution

About this time the first house of worship was erected in the town — conclusive evidence that the inhabitants felt a degree of peaceful security in their homes to which they had theretofore been strangers   It was built by the Society of Friends on the south side of the Half-way Brook, adjoining the west side of the road leading to Dunham's Bay   The structure was of logs and about 20 by 30 feet dimensions   It stood within the limits of a small enclosed parcel of ground, used even to the present day as a place of burial   It has been described by those remembering it, as a long, low building, roughly ceiled on the inside, divisible by a movable or sliding partition into two parts, and provided by rough benches for seating the congregation   It had two entrance doors and was lighted by small windows placed high up towards the roof Here the first and second generations of the Friends of Queensbury met and worshiped, and in the limits of that field their remains repose without a monument or mark to designate their resting place from the common earth by which they are surrounded   Here, too, was kept the first school in the town, and the first burial ground where the founders of the town were laid to rest

Among the arrivals about the year 1785 was the Peck family, of whom Peter Peck, father of Reuben, Daniel and Edmond, was the head   They came from Litchfield, Conn   According to the family tradition they were two weeks on the way, the boys trudging along on foot, driving two yokes of oxen, with heavy, rude wagons laden with their effects, while the father rode on horseback   At that time there were only three dwellings at Glens Falls, a foot path to the Ridge and a rough wagon road up Bay street as far as the Quaker Church   Dr Holden gives the following details of the settlement of this family   Mr Peck purchased a large farm, or rather tract of wilderness, stretching from the Big Cedar Swamp on the east, to the road leading to Dunham's Bay on the west   A family named Varney then occupied a log house situated just north of the Half-way Brook, on the west side of the Bay road. Peck made it his home with these people for a short time, and was persuaded by them to build his house at a point nearly half way between the Ridge and Bay roads, they representing it, probably for the sake of having nearer neighbors, to be the most eligible and desirable point on his tract for that purpose He accordingly commenced his clearing, dug a well, but finding the land too low for a dwelling, abandoned the improvement and erected a substantial log house on the Ridge road, then called the new road, on the site of the brick house now owned by Mr Amos Graves. His nearest neighbor north lived in a log house situated to the east of the old Roger Haviland farm house The spot it occupied is now part of an open, cultivated field   There was another log dwelling on the ground now covered by the Reuben Numan residence   There was also one or two other log houses in the neighborhood, which comprised all that portion of the then existing settlement to the south of what was subsequently designated as Sanford's Ridge   The road was then newly cut through the the forest, the stumps still remaining, with fallen trees, decayed logs and rubbish lying across   It was hardly a respectable bridle path, and the unbroken wilderness stretched away from it on either hand for miles and miles save the three or four small clearings around the buildings above mentioned

" During the summer of 1786 Peck, accompanied by his youngest son, Edmund, then a lad five or six years old, started on horseback for the purpose of assisting to secure the harvest of a neighbor, David Ferriss, who lived in a small house on the side-hill just south of the Half-way Brook — on the east side of the road now leading to the Oneida   At nightfall he started on his return with his little boy seated before him on the horse   The dense forest soon shut in the last faint light of day, and he was obliged to stumble forward in the dark as best he might, trusting mainly to the sagacity of his horse for keeping in the road   At length, in endeavoring to guide his horse around the upturned roots of a large fallen tree which obstructed the way, he found to his consternation that he had lost the path   After spending some considerable time in a fruitless effort to regain the road, groping his way from tree to tree in the thick darkness, the thought occurred to him that a loud outcry might arouse the family he had just left and that some one would come to his assistance with lanterns or torches   He accordingly commenced shouting at thr top of his voice, and presently fancied he heard the call returned   He called again, and the answer was repeated more distinctly   The calls and answers were repeated in rapid succession, until he discovered to his horror that it was no human voice which responded to his alarm, but that of the dreaded panther   With an alacrity inspired of terror, Peck dismounted, and feeling his way rapidly along, at length he came to a large tree with low branching boughs to one of which he fastened his horse, and climbing the tree, found a refuge for himself and boy, on a large projecting limb   Through the entire length of that long and dreary night, the panther prowled around this retreat, at one moment threatening an attack upon the frightened horse, and at another stealthily rustling through leaves of the adjacent tree tops, awaiting an unguarded moment to make his fearful spring   A few raps with a stout cudgel on the trunk of the tree, from time to time, served to deter the brute from making his attack, until the morning light made its most welcome appearance, when the ferocious monster with low growls slunk away towards the recesses of the Big Cedar Swamp   As soon as the light became distinct enough to enable the benighted traveler to find his way, he descended from his perch, and to his great satisfaction discovered the road at no great distance, and, remounting the horse with his boy, soon after reached his home in safety   On his way he saw another huge panther apparently asleep in the top of a high tree, but on his return with a rifle the animal was gone   It had very probably made its way back to the big swamp, which for a long period afterward afforded a safe covert for these and other ferocious denizens of the forest "

Before tracing further the progress of settlement in the town, the following record of an election registry of 1786 will be of value in determining who were the residents of the town at that time and entitled to vote for senators and assemblymen , the registry embraces thirty-six voters, showing that the increase of settlement since the close of the war had been encouragingly rapid .—

" Att an Election held in Queensbury, May the 2 by an adjournment

| 1786 | Candates for Sinnet | | | | Candates for Assemblymen | | | |
Electors Names	Alexr Webster	John Williams	Peter B Tearse	Adiel Sherwood	Albert Baker	Edward Savage	Nehemiah Seelye	Seth Sherwood
Abrom Wing...........	I		I	I	I	I		I
William Tripp..........	I		I	I	I			I
David Seelye...........	I		I	I	I			I
David Bennett.........	I		I	I	I			I
Thomas Tripp..........	I			I	I		I	
Elisha Folger..........	I		I	I	I			I
Bennedick Brown.......	I		I	I	I			I
Justice Brown.........	I		I	I	I		I	
Volentine Brown.... ..	I		I	I	I			I
Ebenezar Buck........	I		I	I	I			I
Howgal Brown.........	I		I	I	I			I
Jeremiah Briggs........	I		I		I			I
Silas Brown............	I		I	I	I			I
James Tripp............	I		I	I	I			I
Jonathan Tripp.........	I		I	I	I			I
James Stevenson.......	I		I	I	I			I

Josi Varney	1		1	1	1	1
Hosea Howard	1		1	1	1	1
James Butler	1		1	1	1	1
Richard Bennet		1	1			1
William Guy	1		1	1	1	1
Walter Briggs	1		1		1	1
John Martin		1	1	1		1
David Bennet	1		1	1		1
Edward Fooller	1		1		1	1
Nathaniel Odle	1	1	1	1		1
Nathaniel Varney	1		1	1	1	1
Jonathan Hubbel	1		1	1	1	1
Stephen Lapham	1		1	1	1	1
Jonathan Pitcher	1		1	1	1	1
Henry Martin	1		1	1	1	1
Benjamin Wing	1		1	1	1	1
Phinhehas Babcock		1	1	1	1	1
James Hixen	1		1	1	1	1
Stephen Howard	1		1	1	1	1
Miles Washborn	1		1	1		1 "

These inhabitants, or such of them as had suffered losses during the war, pleaded their inability to pay the quit-rents and arrearages on their lands which now, through the change of government, lapsed to the State   To these the abatement and liquidation of all just indebtedness and future claims was awarded on the number of acres as given below, respectively, with the auditor's certificate as follows —

"Auditor's office, New York, 10th December, 1789   I do hereby certify that I have receiv'd Sundry Certificates signed by Ebenezer Russell, Judge for Washington county setting forth that the following persons were possessed of the number of acres set opposite their respective names in a Patent granted Daniel Prindle & others 29th May, 1762, and that on account of the war they were oblig'd to quit their Farms viz —

ACRES

Lot 29, Abraham Wing Junr............................150
" 29 & 32, Nath Babcock, Willlett & Daniel Wing......450
" 102, Asa & Parks Putnam...........................250
" 31, Daniel Hull....................................150
" 23 & 29, Charles Lewis.............................150
" 7, Ebenezer and Nathaniel Fuller...................250
" 22 & 23, Russell Lewis.............................150
" 37, Anstice & Sarah Hicks..........................250

Carried forward........ 1800

	ACRES
Brought forward	1800
" 36 & 29, Mary Lewis	.160
" 103, Howgil & Timothy Brown	250
" 39, Silas Brown	150
" 37, Truelove Butler	150
" 77, William Roberts Junr, & Ebenr Roberts	250
" 26 & 27, William Roberts	116
" 82 & 20, 35, 36, & 40 William Wing	90
" 36, Andrew Lewis	150
" 38, Benedick Brown	150
" 23, James Higson	.150
" 22, Abraham Wing	150
" 15, Benjamin & Nehemiah Wing	250
" 2, Reed Ferriss & Caleb Powel	250
	4066

"And I further certify that the above mentioned Persons are thereby discharged from paying all past and future Quit Rents for the Quantity of acres set opposite their respective names amounting in the whole to four thousand and Fifty Six acres in the above Pattent

"PETER S CURTENIUS, State Audr"

Proceedings identical with these were entered into between the State auditor and the following named persons, releasing them on the number of acres attached to their names, on the 28th day of December, 1791 :—

PROFESSORS' NAMES	NO ACRES	NO LOTS
Valentine Brown	150	41
Schuyler Brown	100	41
Phebe Robberds	145	26
Joseph Hepburn	150	49
Ebenezer Fuller Junr	150	50
Benjamin Fuller	100	50
Edward Fuller	125	38
Patrick Hepburn	150	48 & 57
Matthew Fuller	125	33
Justus Brown	125	39
John Akin	150	84
Albro Akin	100	84
Sarah Akin	150	84
Thomas Worth	125	51
Barsilla Worth	125	51

Carried forward 1970

POSSESSORS' NAMES	NO ACRES	NO LOTS
Brought forward 1970		
John Toffy............ 150		44
Hulet Toffy...................... 100		44
James Ferriss.......... . ... --- 150		57
Nathaniel Taber........................ 100		57
William Taber............... 100		3
Ephrahim Woodard...................... 150		3
David Ferris...................... ... 100		12
Benjamin Collins....................... 100		12
Ichabod Merritt,........................ 150		1
Joseph Merritt... 100		1
James Stephenson....................... 125		88
Jacob Stephenson...................... 150		90
Stephen Stephenson................. ... 100		90

3545

Again on the 1st of April, 1790, the following were released in a similar manner —

POSSESSORS' NAMES	NO ACRES	NO LOTS
Peter Peck....................... 130		25 & No 3 Town Plot
Reuben Peck.................... 125		30
William Tripp................... 125		11
Jonathan Tripp................ 125		11
Jeremiah Briggs................. 150		31
Nathaniel Varney............... 160		30

805

An account in settlement with the auditor also appears in the records, wherein Reed Ferriss is credited with eighteen pounds nineteen shillings and four pence for the release of 510 acres in one tract, and Enoch Hoag with seventeen pounds, three shillings on 250 acres

It will have been observed that among these names appear several the details of whose settlements have already been given, others will be noted in succeeding pages

Town Formation — Queensbury is one of the original towns erected by act of Legislature on the 7th of March, 1788, and its boundaries were defined as follows: "All that part of the said county of Washington, bounded easterly by Westfield and Kingsbury, and separated from Westfield by a line beginning at the northwest corner of the town of Kingsbury and running in the direction of Kingsbury west bounds till it strikes the water of Lake George, westerly by Fairfield, northerly by Lake George and a line running from the mouth of McAuley's Creek near the south end of said lake direct to the north-

east corner of the town of Fairfield, and southerly by the bounds of the county,"
(namely the Hudson River, which at this point runs nearly a due easterly
course) "shall be, and continue a town by the name of Queensbury"

The town then embraced the territory which in the year 1813 (according
to Spafford's *Gazetteer of New York*, published in that year) comprised the
towns of Bolton, Caldwell, Chester, Hague, Johnsburgh, Luzerne, Queensbury,
and Thurman, being all that part of the county of Washington lying west of
Kingsbury and Lake George, in other words, more than the entire present
county of Warren

An act of the Legislature of April 6th, 1808, changed the name of the town
of Westfield to Fort Ann, and that of Fairfield to Luzerne, for the very good
reason of the "considerable inconvenience which results from several of the
towns in this State having the same name"

On the 22d of October, 1798, the division line between the towns of Westfield (Fort Ann) and Queensbury was run out by the supervisors of the two
towns, assisted by Aaron Haight, surveyor, and "that portion of the town of
Queensbury usually called Harrisena" was annexed and erected into a separate road district   About the same time a strip of territory one mile wide
was taken from the eastern limits of the town of Fairfield (Luzerne) and annexed to the western side of Queensbury.   Following are the present boundaries of the town as provided by law —

"The town of Queensbury shall contain all that part of said county bounded
southerly and easterly by the bounds of the county, (viz 'by the middle of
the said [north] branch and of the main stream of the said [Hudson's] river,
until it reaches the southeast corner of the patent of Queensbury, with such
variations as may be necessary to include the whole of every island, any part
whereof is nearer to the north or east shore of the said river than to the south
or west shore thereof, and to exclude the whole of every island, any part whereof is nearer to the said south or west shore than to the north or east shore aforesaid, and easterly by the east bounds of said patent, and the same continued
north to Lake George,') westerly by Luzerne, and northerly by a line beginning at the southwest corner of Caldwell and running thence easterly and northerly along the bounds of Caldwell to Lake George, and then along the east
shore of Lake George to the bounds of the county"

Natural Features, Localities, etc — The natural characteristics of the town,
names of localities, etc, are thus clearly described by Dr Holden [1] "The
eastern and northern portions of the town are rolling and hilly, while the western part is one extended sandy plain, originally covered with a densely timbered pine forest, which for the first half century gave employment to a large
per centage of the population and to the numerous saw-mills which were erected
in the early days of the settlement on nearly every brook and rivulet in the

---

[1] *History of Queensbury*, p. 144, etc

town   Since then, and long within the memory of many living, these extensive pine plains have been periodically cropped of the second growth yellow
pine to supply the increasing demand for fuel   Now there is less than five
hundred acres of woodland all told between the village and the mountain, and
under a more thorough and intelligent system of agriculture these barren sand
plains are rapidly being reclaimed and becoming the most remunerative of our
farming lands

"The western part of the town is bordered by the Palmertown Mountains,
an outlying ridge of the great Adirondack range, whose beginning is at the
village of Saratoga Springs, and whose termination is at Harrington Hill in
Warrensburgh   At the north, lying partly in this town and partly in the town
of Caldwell, is the abrupt acclivity known as French Mountain, some sixteen
hundred feet in height, whose sharp promontory projects for several miles into
the head waters of Lake George   On the northeast the Dresden chain of
mountains throws out three considerable elevations called the Sugar Loaf, Deer
Pasture, and Buck Mountains, the last two of which slope down to the very
verge of the lake, and are still the home of the deer and the rattlesnake, with
which all this region once abounded

"This township, occupying a plateau on the great water-shed between the
Hudson and St Lawrence Rivers, its numerous streams, brooks, ponds, and
rivulets, and its surface drainage as well, find widely diverging outlets; that
from the northern and central parts of the town making its way to the Half-
way Brook and thence through Wood Creek to Lake Champlain and the St.
Lawrence, while the rivulets and marshes of Harrisena empty into Lake George,
and those of the west, south and eastern parts of the town are tributary to the
Hudson   It is noteworthy that the volume of all the streams, the river included,
has materially diminished within the memory of the oldest inhabitant, while a
few, by drainage and exposure to the sun and air, have ceased to exist   The
same remark holds true of several swamps and marshes, which in the early days
of the settlement were the lairs and coverts from which wild beasts issued in
their predatory attacks upon the stock of the pioneers   Wild Cat Swamp,
lying upon the western borders of the village, has been almost entirely reclaimed, while a large portion of the Big Cedar Swamp, stretching away for
two miles from its eastern boundary, is now under successful cultivation.
Among the numerous brooks, ponds and streams, with which the surface of
the town is diversified, the following are considered worthy of mention   Cold
Brook, which for a small portion of its extent forms a part of the eastern
boundary of the town and county, runs southwardly and empties into the Hudson immediately opposite an island, which in 1772 was deeded by one of the
Jessups of Tory memory to Daniel Jones   This brook and the flat adjacent
was the scene of a terrible massacre during the French War, which is elsewhere
recorded   Reed's Meadow Creek, the outlet of the Big Cedar Swamp above

referred to, flows east and southeasterly, and after receiving various accessions in its somewhat tortuous route it becomes Fort Edward Creek, and debouches into the Hudson at the southern extremity of the village of Fort Edward Its name is derived from Reed Ferriss, one of the early proprietors here, and one of the commissioners appointed by the proprietors to apportion the undivided sections of the township, two of which were included within the limits of the swamp Setting back from this outlet was a beaver dam, marsh and meadow, where the first settlers supplied themselves with hay The Meadow Run derived its name similarly from a large beaver meadow, which was almost the only resource of the inhabitants at the Corners for the sustenance of their stock during the long and vigorous winters of this latitude In some of the military reports and narratives it was called the Four Mile Run, it being about four miles miles distant from the military post at the head of Lake George This stream has its origin in the Butler Pond, on a summit of a spur of the Palmertown Mountains, in the west part of the town A neighboring elevation has, from the earliest days, been known as Hunting Hill, from the abundance of game once gathered there An adjoining eminence is the seat of a rich vein of iron ore, which, three years since, was successfully worked under the auspices of the Corning Iron Company, a body of Albany capitalists

"The Meadow Run, after passing through an expansion of its waters called Mud Pond, winds around the base of a series of knolls, and is received at the head of Long Pond not far from the outlet of Round Pond, another small sheet of water lying among the hills a few rods to the south A canal was cut by Dr Stower from one of these ponds to the other some years ago, for lumbering purposes, but was never completed or put in operation There are two or three extensive peat beds in this neighborhood, one of which, at the head of an estuary stretching westwardly through the marsh which makes back from Long Pond, has been extensively worked during the past few years by the Albany company above referred to There is at present a saw-mill in successful and remunerative operation near the head waters of the Meadow Run

"Rocky Brook, designated in the early road surveys and records of the town as Hampshire Creek, is a bright, sparkling mountain stream, leaping and flashing along the ravine at the western base of French Mountain, propelling two saw-mills on its route, and winding along through meadow, woodland and marsh, empties into the Meadow Run about twenty rods above the head of Long Pond On the flat west of its banks, was one of the three picket posts referred to in Governor Colden's proclamation, elsewhere quoted, and which is designated on one of the early maps as Fort Williams

"In the western part of the town, having its rise in the mountain ridge which separates it from Luzerne, is the once famous trout stream variously known as the Pitcher, the Ogden, and the Clendon Brook, deriving these names from persons once living in its vicinity In former years it furnished the motive power for a number of saw-mills, whose decaying debris encumber its banks at varying intervals with their unsightly accumulations Still further west, on the confines of the town, Roaring Brook, bounding from crag and cliff, pours its cold and foaming waters fresh from their mountain sources into the Hudson near the reefs

"The waters of Long Pond are discharged through the Outlet, a stream which, flowing eastwardly, effects a junction with the Half-way Brook at a settlement called Jenkins or Patten's Mills, near the eastern boundary of the town This brook supplies the power for several saw-mills, a grist-mill, a cider-mill, and a woolen factory

"The Half-way Brook, which was noted in the early colonial times as a halting-place and rendezvous for the troops and convoys of supplies in their transit between the great military posts at Fort Edward and the head of Lake George, is situated nearly midway between these points, and hence derives its name [1]

"The Half-way brook has its source in the same mountain range, and but a short distance west from the head waters of its sister stream, the Meadow Run Near the foot of the mountain, and nearly encircled by hills, is a natural basin, which, a few years since, was artificially enlarged, and cleaned, and a massive wall of masonry thrown across its outlet, for the formation of a reservoir to supply the Glen's Falls Water-works, a public and much needed improvement, which has been but recently completed at a cost of about eighty thousand dollars The surplus and waste water is directed back to its wonted channel immediately below the reservoir Running a tortuous course southeastwardly across the plains, the Half-way Brook expands into the Forge Pond, a small sheet of water, about one and a half miles west of Glen's Falls, and for a long period the favorite resort of the disciples of the gentle Isaac Walton, in pursuit of the speckled trout which once abounded in this stream At this point, as far back as the year eighteen hundred and eleven, a forge and trip hammer shop were erected by an enterprising pioneer named Johnson At the same time a saw mill was built which is still in operation, and which for years supplied the neighborhood and sent to market the products of the neighboring forests The manufacture of iron for some cause did not prove remunerative, and the enterprise, after languishing a few years, was finally abandoned, leaving its name, however, to the pond as a parting legacy, and a reminder of the old French proverb, that 'it is only success that succeeds' About a mile below, and nearly opposite to the garrison ground already referred to, is an enlargement of the Half-way Brook called Briggs's Pond, at the foot of which stands a dam and race way, affording water power Here at the close of the last century stood a saw-mill, while across the flat, some forty or

[1] It was on the banks of this famous stream that were erected two of the picketed enclosures about the middle of the last century, as described in an earlier chapter

fifty rods further west, in a ravine, partly natural, but enlarged by the hand of art, stood a large grist-mill, carried by water conducted by a canal artificially constructed, and leading from the pond above named These mills were owned and run by Walter Briggs, and were resorted to by the inhabitants and farmers from far and near, at a period when there was no grist-mill at Glens Falls The buildings have long since been torn down or removed, but the embankments of the canal, and the foundations of the mill are still conspicuous in the green meadow From this point the Half-way Brook bears northeastwardly through a continuation of swale, marsh, and meadow, creeping sluggishly along at the base of the ridge, and passes the Kingsbury town line in the neighborhood of a settlement bearing the euphonious name of Frog Hollow A basin among the hills, half a mile to the west of the settlement called the Oneida, contains a circular sheet of water, a few acres in extent, known as the Round Pond Here was built among the pines, on its shore, the first Baptist Church of Queensbury A small enclosure near by contains one of the oldest burial places in town

"Butler's Brook, near the north bounds of the corporation limits of Glen's Falls, has its source in three small brooks, one of which receives the drainage of the Wild Cat Swamp and west part of the village, the second crosses the plank road at the old Mallory place, and the third has its source in a swale a little north of the Warren county fair grounds It was on this branch, tradition informs us, that in the year seventeen hundred and eighty-three, while on his way to visit and inspect the fortifications at Lake George, Ticonderoga and Crown Point, General Washington and his staff halted to slake their thirst, and were waited upon with a cup and pail and a supply of water from the brook by Jeremiah Briggs, who was at work in a neighboring field This stream derived its name from one of the earliest settlers who lived in its vicinity Espousing the royal cause, at or during the war, he buried such of his effects as he could and fled to Canada His house shared the fate of most of the buildings in this vicinity at that time, being burnt by the savages and Tories in one of their numerous eruptions The Butler Brook after the confluence of its branches winds around the cemetery grounds and unites with the Half-way Brook about two miles north of Glens Falls, midway between the Ridge and Bay roads

"These ponds and streams during the early days of the settlement were abundantly stocked with trout, which, with the game then so plentiful in the surrounding forests, constituted a large portion of the resources of the inhabitants It was related to me by one of the patriarchs of the town that in a winter of uncommon severity, some of the families in Harrisena carried through their stock of cattle on a supply of salted fish, of which they had secured a large quantity the preceding season Until the erection of dams and mills shad ran up in the spring as far as the Falls, where they were caught in considerable quantities, and were to some extent an article of commerce

"The original survey of the township contemplated the location of the village at the Half-way Brook, where the existing clearings and buildings offered a strong inducement to the first settlers to locate their houses   Here the town plot was laid out, ranging due north and south   The lots were of ten acres each and forty-four in number, beside the road ways four rods in width, surrounding the whole an eight rod road in each direction, bisecting the plot into four equal sections   Four central lots at these angles were reserved for church and school purposes and for public buildings   Either half to the east and west was also divided by a north and south road four rods in width

"It is needless to say that no settlement was ever established here, and that Champlain's tannery, and the Pitcher tavern occupying the site just north of the Half-way Brook, upon which a brick house now stands, are the nearest approach to public buildings erected on the site of the projected village, after the original survey by Zaccheus Towner in 1762   The old Pitcher tavern was a place of considerable note in those days when every log hut was an inn, and every framed dwelling a hotel   It was kept by Jonathan Pitcher, whose name frequently appears in the town records, chiefly in connection with matters pertaining to the excise law, on two occasions he being excused by a vote of the people from paying his license

"Harrisena is a neighborhood at the north part of the town, and derives its name from the original founders of the settlement   The region comprising this somewhat vaguely defined locality includes some of the most fertile and productive farming lands in the county of Warren   The Harrisena Patent proper embraced two thousand acres of land, and was originally conveyed to Robert Harpur and others, but the grant for some cause was surrendered to the crown and reissued in 1772 to John Lawrence, Henry Boel and Stephen Tuttle, who relinquished or sold their title to Moses Harris   He, with another brother, settled upon it in 1787, and in the following January obtained certificates of location of the same, with several other rights or claims, embracing in all a territory of between three and four thousand acres   At about the same time Joshua Harris secured certificates of location for four lots of two hundred acres each in the same vicinity   These lands have mostly remained in the hands of the Harris family and their descendants to the present day   The first house erected here was a log tenement, built near a spring about ten rods southeast of the Rufus Harris place   Joseph Harris was the first settler, and moved here about the year 1784   The next was a framed house and was built for Moses Harris by John Phettyplace   It stood near the site occupied by the Henry Harris homestead   This wealthy and thriving agricultural district has in the course of years become thickly and compactly settled, for a farming region, possessing admirable public schools, two churches, one of which has a settled pastor; its ailments cared for by a resident physician, many of its wants provided for and supplied by home mechanics, while bordering upon the bays and points jut-

ting in and out around the head of Lake George are several pleasant and attractive places of resort, where travelers, invalids, pleasure seekers, business
men, worn out with the wearying and incessant round of business cares, repair
year by year in constantly increasing numbers, for that rest and recuperation
so difficult to find among the hot, crowded thoroughfares of our fashionable resorts and summer watering places.

" Five miles to the north of the village of Glens Falls, on the road to Harrisena, is situated a small settlement, which, for upwards of fifty years, has borne
in local colloquial phrase the name of the Oneida The attempt has been made to
call it Northville and Middleville, but no effort to shake off the former appellation has been successful About the time of the last war with England this
was a place of considerable importance, having two good sized and well patronized inns, three stores doing a quite extensive trade, a large lumbering business, in connection with adjacent mills, various mechanic shops, and a Baptist
church and society Here two noted justices of the peace, Dan D Scott and
James Henderson, held their weekly and august tribunals, at which as many
as one hundred and seventy summonses, besides criminal processes and subpœnas have been made returnable in one day Every Saturday, sometimes
oftener, from fifty to two hundred people assembled here to listen to the encounter of argument, the brilliant collision of wit and repartee, and the splendid oratory of that gifted and eloquent array of legal talent which then graced
the bar of Warren and Washington counties

" The first house at the Oneida was erected by Joshua Chase about the year
1793 The name was derived from a half-breed Oneida Indian by the name
of Thomas Hammond He, with his sister Dinah, were brought up by Capt
Green, of Whipple City, now Greenwich, Washington county, N Y Some
little time previous to the outbreak of the war he removed to Queensbury, and
opened a store of general merchandise in a building which is still standing on
the corner opposite and fronting the old tavern stand , and here, for a number
of years, he was engaged in carrying on a considerable trade, mixed up to
some extent with the lumbering business From the oft repeated expressions,
' Let's go up to the Oneida's,' ' I bought this at the Oneida's,' ' We must send
down to the Oneida's,' was derived the name which through the vicissitudes
of half a century has clung like a burr to the settlement Hammond married
Keziah, a sister of James Reynolds, of Caldwell Pursued by the red man's
curse, an unappeasable appetite for the terrible fire-water, he finally failed in
business, removed to French Mountain, and died an inebriate and outcast
Since then the magnificent pine forests which once stretched their serried ranks
across plain and hill side, from the lake to the Kingsbury line, have been cut
down, the local traffic has diminished, and the importance of the settlement
decreased

" The Ridge, or Sanford's ridge, is a name applied to a thickly settled farm-

26

ing district, stretching a distance of three or four miles along a crest of rich, arable land beginning about two miles north of Glens Falls village, and terminating beyond the town line on the east   Toward the close of the last century this was a settlement of greater size and importance than the village at the Falls   At that time there were two stores, a tavern, several mechanic shops and two physicians   In the year 1800 the Quaker church was built on the corners two miles north of the village   The first settler at the Ridge was Elijah Bartow who plied his trade as a blacksmith on what is known as the Gould Sanford farm   He lived in a log house near by   One of the first framed houses in the neighborhood was built and occupied by James Tripp on the site now covered by the residence of Joseph Haviland   Abraham Tucker about the same time built on the farm southwest of the Quaker church   This neighborhood derived its name from David Sanford, esq , who, in 1795, removed from the town of New Milford, Conn , to Queensbury and established himself in trade at this point   For the next ten years he was prominently identified with the business interests of the town, and the development of its resources He was frequently chosen to office, and up to the time of his death was a man of mark and consideration "

Returning now to the subject of the early settlements in the town and the incidents and enterprises connected therewith, we may properly first make further mention of Benedick Brown, who was one of the original settlers and probably came into the town as early as 1772, as his name appears in the records as overseer of the poor in 1773   He had a family, the sons being named Valentine, George, Justus, Howgill, Silas, and Timothy   They were Quakers and at one period the descendants of the family were so numerous in the town that a settlement between the outlet of Long Pond and Glens Falls was locally known as " Brown-town "   Valentine Brown built the first saw-mill north of Glens Falls   He was grandfather of George Brown, now of Lake George (Caldwell)   In this family was also Daniel V Brown, a descendant in the fourth generation from Bededick ; he was sheriff in the county from 1861 to 1864, previous to which date he had been supervisor   He was a prominent business man of Glens Falls and an active Democratic politician   He was drowned on the steamer *Melville* on the 8th of January, 1865, while on his way with Edward Riggs to South Carolina to procure volunteers or substitutes for the Queensbury quota in the anticipated draft   (See biography herein)

Reed Ferriss, of Duchess county, was an early and intimate friend of Abraham Wing, the founder of Queensbury, and purchased a large tract in the original patent   One of his lots was upon the eastern border of the town   Mr Ferriss was the founder of Ferrissbury, Vt , according to Dr Holden   The outlet of the Big Cedar Swamp derived its name from him, being called in the early survey and records, Reed's Meadow Creek. After the Revolutionary War Mr Ferriss came up the river every season to look after his interests here and in Vermont   His eldest son was named Edward, was a hatter, and removed to Glens Falls about the year 1794, bringing with him about $500 in cash   At that time this was quite a fortune, and he was offered in exchange for it great lot number 29, of the original survey, now embracing the most thickly settled and valuable portion of the village of Glens Falls, and the offer was declined   Soon after his arrival here he bought the lot next north of the present Glens Falls Insurance building, on the rear of which he erected a hat shop, where he carried on business for a number of years, he also built other structures and gave considerable impetus to the early growth of the place   In 1798 he erected a tavern on the site of the present dwelling owned by A Newton Locke, and in 1802 he began building the old Glens Falls Hotel on the site of the present Rockwell House   A year or two later he diverted the springs of water and the rivulet on the side-hill, now covered by the Glens Falls Opera House, into a shallow reservoir, making a fish pond in the rear of Albert Vermillia's market building, this was, for a period, one of the attractions of the place   Early in the century he erected the long known structure on Warren street, now owned by Mrs Dr Holden, which was subsequently variously designated as Ferriss's Row, the Tontine, the Long Row, Hemlock Row,' and McGregor's Row   This structure was burned in 1856   Mr Ferriss married first Parthenia, daugher of Dr Seth Allen, and second, her sister Hannah

John A Ferriss was a son of Edward and one of the leading men of Glens Falls   He was the first postmaster of the village, was president of the village in 1839 and held other positions of trust   He formerly carried on business on the corner of Warren and Glen streets, on the site of what is now the Holden block, and was recognized throughout the county as public-spirited and enterprising, commanding the respect of all. He died in 1840   Hon Orange Ferriss, of whom a brief sketch is given in the chapter devoted to the legal profession, was a son of John A Ferriss

David Ferriss was an early settler in the town, but little is now known of him   According to Dr Holden, " while yet there was little more than a bridle path from Glens Falls, then known as the Corners, to the Ridge, he settled on the farm now occupied by Isaac Mosher a little south of the Half way Brook on the road to the Oneida, where he built him a log house, which he not long afterwards abandoned, and being of an adventurous turn, went west, where, after various adventures, he was finally accidentally drowned in the Mississippi, while running a raft of timber down that stream   The name of Widow Ferriss appears recorded on the town book for the year 1792 "

Of the Gilchrist families of Glens Falls and Fort Edward the same writer says that "the ancestor of the American branch came to this country shortly prior to the Revolution, and was the head of this which, among many Scotch families, in those early days, took up tracts of land in and about Argyle, Hebron and Fort Edward The heir in the direct line failed for want of issue something over forty years ago During Burgoyne's advance in the Revolution, and while his force lay encamped at Kingsbury street, the Gilchrist homestead with its family bible and records was burned by a party of marauding Indians Other outrages and atrocities were perpetrated in the same neighborhood by the same gang A single link in the chain of evidence necessary to establish the proof of heirship was thus destroyed, and so the estate with its immense revenues lapsed to the crown, and Queen Victoria makes it her summer residence A striking instance of the value of a perfect family record "

In the year 1795 David Sanford, son of Zachariah and Rachel Sanford, removed to Sanford's Ridge, in this town He was born in 1769 At Sanford's Ridge he engaged in mercantile business in which he was very successful His name appears as town clerk in the years 1802–3 He received the deed of lot No. 12 of the orignal survey, from George Southwick and Justus Brown Mr Sanford married Amy Hartwell, and was the father of George Sanford, who was born at Sanford's Ridge in 1805 The father died when George was but seven years old, but he assumed at an early age the management of the homestead and the care of his mother and several sisters When he became of age he formed a co-partnership with Orlin Mead, his brother in-law, in the lumber business, while that traffic was in its infancy, the firm also carried on a large mercantile trade in Glens Falls He was an active politician, held the office of supervisor and represented the county in the Legislature in 1841 He was one of the founders of the Glens Falls Academy, and one of its earliest trustees, also one of the corporators of the Episcopal Church in the village, in 1840. In 1850 he removed to Ballston Spa, and a few years later to Syracuse, where he died in 1862

Peter B Tearse, whose name appears as Assemblyman from 1786 to 1789, then a resident of Fort Edward, and who was town moderator of Queensbury in 1795, was a man of prominence in the Revolution ; he was adjutant while stationed at Fort Edward at the time of Burgoyne's advance, and major in the regiment of Colonel Marinus Willet in 1777 Soon after the Revolution he settled at Fort Edward and married Polly Hunter, granddaughter of Mrs McNeil, who owned an immense landed property valued even in those days at more than eighty thousand dollars In 1798 Mr Tearse was chosen one of the town assessors and also held other minor offices About the beginning of the century he removed to the head of Lake George, and erected the first building on the site now occupied by the stone store in Caldwell Here he carried on a trade in general merchandise. He also owned an ashery for the manufacture of potash at the foot of the hill near his store and on the bank of the lake at the north side of the brook His success was not commensurate with his enterprise, which was at least half a century in advance of the age in which he lived Attracted by the newly discovered mineral waters of Ballston, he removed thither, where he soon after died (in the year 1802), and where his remains now lie buried in an unknown and unhonored grave

John Vernor's name appears frequently in the town records from 1795 to 1802   He was a merchant and inn-keeper at the head of Lake George early in the century and probably before that date, as it is on record that he was chairman of a public meeting of the citizens from various towns of Washington county, held at the house of Colonel Joseph Caldwell, of Kingsbury, on the 25th of February, 1793, at which Dr Zina Hitchcock was nominated as the Federal candidate for the Senate   He was one of the earliest commissioned magistrates in the county, having been appointed February 24th, 1791   He was quartermaster in the Thirteenth Regiment from the Saratoga district, of which John McCrea was colonel, all of whose officers were commissioned October 20th, 1775   John Vernor died December 1st, 1825, at the age of eighty His son, John, jr , died in 1822, aged fifty-one

One of the leading men of the town in early times was William Hay, born in Cambridge, Washington county, in the year 1790   He was related to Colonel Udney Hay, who was prominent in the Revolution. About the beginning of the century his father, also named William, came to Glens Falls, embarked in the lumber business and erected a store, the first building on the corner of Glen and Warren streets, now occupied by the Holden block   For a time he was very successful, but ultimately met with reverses and his property passed into the hands of others   During these reverses the son succeeded in acquiring an education, and in 1808 was studying law in the office of Henry C Martindale, in this village   In 1812–13 he opened a law office at the head of Lake George   He raised a rifle company and in 1814 proceeded to Plattsburg, but did not arrive in time to take part in the battle   In 1819 he became the publisher of the *Warren Patriot*, the first and only regular newspaper ever published at Lake George   In 1822 he removed to Glens Falls and resumed the practice of law   In 1827 he was elected to the Assembly   In 1837 he removed to Ballston and three years later to Saratoga Springs, where he died a few years later   He held the office of district attorney of Warren county in 1825–27 and was otherwise honored by his fellow citizens   He was possessed of fine literary abilities, broad general information and was a deep student

Adonijah Emmons was a pioneer of the town and held the office of postmaster at Glens Falls in 1816, he also practiced law and was an active and influential politician   He subsequently removed to Sandy Hill and published a partisan paper, the *Sandy Hill Sun*   He died in 1843 in Detroit, whither he removed his family in 1838   Halmer H Emmons was his son—a man of eminence in the legal profession, and United States Circuit judge in 1870

The name of William McDonald occupies a conspicuous place in the annals of the town   He was born in New Milford, Conn , in 1784   His mother was Mary, sister of David Sanford, before mentioned Mr McDonald came to the town when he was eight years old, but returned to New Milford to secure a business education He again came to Queensbury in 1799 and entered the employ of his uncle, David Sanford, as bookkeeper and accountant and soon had the full management of the large mercantile business About 1805 he purchased his uncle's interest in the store and continued trade until 1808, when he removed to Waterford Here he carried on a large business until 1820, when he returned to the Ridge and resumed trade at the old place. Three years later he disposed of his stock, removed to Glens Falls and soon afterward bought the old Wing farm, he enlarged and rebuilt the unfinished dwelling, making a spacious mansion, which he occupied until his death, September 11th, 1870 Mr McDonald held the office of town clerk as early as 1802-3, in 1821 he was nominated for the Assembly and overcame by his personal strength and popularity the opposition candidate, Asahel Clark, a man of great prominence. In the succeeding session Mr McDonald was chiefly instrumental in securing a survey and appropriation for the Glens Falls feeder He was elected the next year, only seventeen votes being cast against him, and was again elected in 1828 He was the first president of the old Commercial Bank, vestryman of the Episcopal Church at its formation, and received many other evidences of the confidence of the community

Among other prominent early settlers of whom our mention here must be brief, was Dr Seth Alden, of Shaftsbury, Vt, where he was born as early as 1749 He died at Fort Edward in 1809, or 1810, having removed there just previously He practiced at Caldwell from the date of his removal from Shaftsbury (now unknown, but very early) until he left for Fort Edward, and was eminent in the profession He is said to have been the first occupant of the old Lake House at Caldwell [1]

Dr Asa Stower, of Massachusetts, the pioneer of the medical profession in the country, came here in 1780, first making his home with William Robards at the Ridge. He subsequently bought a farm, lately occupied by Joseph Haviland, and later sold it and purchased the one now occupied by Anson Staples, where he passed the remainder of his days He died May 25th, 1848 [1]

Two brothers, John and Robert Moon, emigrated to this town from Rhode Island about 1783, but little is known of the former, but Robert settled on the outlet of Long Pond, where he built a saw-mill and the first grist-mill in use in the town after the Revolutionary War He had three sons, Solomon, Robert and Benjamin, who lived near each other and carried on the mills and farming business after their father's death

Parsons Ranger was here before the beginning of the century, his son, Samuel Ranger, was born in the town in 1796 He built the first Presbyterian

---

[1] See chapter on the medical profession.

Church in the town in 1806–8, the original subscription paper for which remains in the hands of his descendants (See history of the Presbyterian Church and original subscription list, presumably embracing most of the residents of the vicinity at the beginning of the century)

Stephen Stephenson came into this town about the year 1785 and settled on the Dunham's Bay road, where he made a small clearing and erected a log house At that time there were only eighteen families residing in the whole town His daughter Emma became the wife of John Goss

Phineas Austin was a very early settler, and father of John D Austin, who was born here in 1786 John Austin, now a resident of the town, is a son of John D His grandmother died here in 1856, at the age of one hundred and two years

Josiah Burnham settled in Moreau in 1784, and subsequently came to this town He was in the War of 1812 and drew a pension for his services He married a granddaughter of the elder Abraham Wing His son was Cyrus Burnham, who was the father of Glen F and Julius R Burnham, at present residing in the town.

Reuben Numan came to the town with his parents when he was fourteen, (1792), and located at the Ridge Charles P Numan, a farmer in the town, is a son of Reuben

The Haviland families have been identified with the history of the town from early years, and descendants now occupy prominent positions, business and otherwise, in the community Roger Haviland settled here as early as 1795, when he occupied a house which stood facing the south street at the turn of the road leading to the big dam, this house was burned about 1858 Roger Haviland afterward removed to the Ridge Abraham Haviland was a resident of the town, also, previous to the beginning of the century, and had a blacksmith shop on the site of George Ferguson's store in Glens Falls He had a son named John G Haviland, who had a son, John M The latter was father of John G Haviland, now a member of the firm of Havilands & Gilbert The elder Roger Haviland had sons named David, Solomon, Joseph and Roger A son of the latter, also named Roger, was father of C W Haviland, of the firm just named Four branches of the family, all descended from Roger, the pioneer, are represented in the town

John Vanduzen came to the town in 1785 Robert Vanduzen, now living near French Mountain, at the age of ninety-four years, with his son Ransom, is a son of John

Augustin Odell was the pioneer of the families of that name in this town. His name appears first in the town records in 1788

Other early settlers were Job Beadlestone, who came during the Revolutionary War and located near Harrisena His daughter, Phebe Ann, married Veniah Harris, the latter was a grandson of Moses Harris, the pioneer, and

son of Henry Harris   Palmer B Jenkins settled in the town before the beginning of the century, coming with his father, Simeon   Gamaliel Jenkins, of
Harrisena, is a son of Palmer B   Jonathan Crandell came in at about the beginning of the century   Isaac Crandell, the florist at Glens Falls, is a grandson of Jonathan   Col A W Morgan came to the town in 1813 and learned
the harness-maker's trade with Judge Henry Spencer   In 1835 he purchased
eleven acres of land, covering the central part of the site of the village of Glens
Falls, for $800, this he laid out into lots and sold, continuing the real estate
business until 1870   He laid out several of the village streets   He now lives
on a farm two miles north of Glens Falls

The names of many other early settlers and prominent men of this town
will appear in succeeding pages, in connection with the professional, mercantile and manufacturing interests of the county

A conspicuous figure among the early settlers and one well remembered
by them was that of the Indian preacher known as Father Paul   According
to tradition he was a pure blooded Mohican, a connection of the great Indian
preacher, Sampson Occum, and a pupil of the Rev Eleazer Wheelock.   Father
Paul came to Queensbury soon after the close of the Revolutionary War, removed to Caldwell, and later to Bolton, the "principal theatre of his ministerial
labors"   He had six children   James, Phebe, Jonathan (called Daunt), Benoni,
Henry, and Sampson   The children were all a dissipated, worthless set, scof-
fers at religion and social restraints, " given over to reprobate minds "   Sampson Paul's name appears in Judge Robard's docket, in 1802, as defendant in
a lawsuit, and Anthony Paul himself is recorded as defendant in a suit March
18th, 1805, in which David Osborn, jr, merchant, is plaintiff   Father Paul
was duly licensed to preach, and being the only person thus qualified who had
then made a home with the settlers hereabouts, he was invited to address them
on the Sabbaths on the themes of religion   He did so and they were edified
He shared with them their joys, he buried their dead, and consoled them in
their afflictions, but the appetite which had wrought its evil work upon his
race was the subject of his indulgence and effected his ruin   He became a
confirmed drunkard, he was, consequently, discarded as a public teacher, and
departed with so little regret to the neighborhood that no record is left of his
decease   He is described by one who saw him before his downfall as being
universally beloved and deserving it   " His broad, high-cheeked, copper-col-
ored face was spread over with an habitual smile of benevolence, and when, at
times, lit up with zeal, he opened his mouth with words of kindness, and
showed a broad row of beautiful teeth, the whole countenance was actually
beautiful   He had his weakness and we know it, but he was good to us, and
so he got his daily bread among us and ministered from house to house and
on the Sabbath in holy things, etc etc   At length Father Paul went from us,
whether falling a victim to his debasing habit, dying in a poor-house, or escap-

ing in some distant haunt among his countrymen, I could never learn   The
general belief was that he died alone, that he built a hut far down the lake,
just below The Narrows, and where the beetling cliffs of Tongue Mountain
almost shut up the passage, and there subsisted by fishing and hunting, until
a kind Providence granted him his release"

We have already alluded to the settlement in Queensbury of William Robards   His son, William, jr, was for a number of years early in the century
in the Commission of the Peace and later was promoted to the bench   The
following list of marriages performed by him throws considerable light upon
the residents of this region in early days   We give merely the names of the
contracting parties, without the often quaint accompanying remarks found in
the docket —

November 19th, 1801, George Bates and Mary Beadleston   December
30th, 1801, Reuben Seelye and Cynthia Odel, both of Queensbury   May 2d,
1802, Waterbury Gray and Betsy Stone, "Betsy of Queensbury and Gray
of Westchester county"   September 5th, 1802, John Goss and Emma Stevenson, Goss was from Fort Ann, (Westfield)   September 21st, 1802, John A
Ferriss and Hannah Alden   October 31st, 1802, Jonathan Strickland and
Katy Hubbel   November 16th, 1802, John Amiden and Rachel Sumner
January 2d, 1803, William D Harris and Sina Chandler   August 12th, 1803,
Luke Dalrymple and Susanna Jenkins, married at the house of Joseph Jenkins,
in Queensbury   August 14th, 1803, Azel Stevens and Polly Tyrrell, married
at Peter Peck's, Queensbury   August 28th, 1803, Seneca Lapham and Rachel
Allen   September 11th, 1803, Dexter Whipple and Rebecca Danforth, mar-
ried at Joshua Danforth's   October 23d, 1803, Enoch Haskins and Anna Hill,
married at Anson Comstock's, Queensbury   October 28th, 1803, Joseph Jenkins and Judah Bailey, "married at my house, Free Agents."   November 20th,
1803, Edmund Peck and Sally Ranger, "was then married at Person Ranger's"
November 24th, 1803, Jeremiah Tubbs and Sybil Odel   May 21st, 1804, Isaac
Hollibird and Charlotte Parks   May 25th, 1804, Henry Harris and Margaret
Brown   June 24th, 1804, Benjamin Seelye and Anna Haight   July 4th, 1805,
Schuyler Brown and Lydia Simpson, married at the house of Elnathan San-
ford   August 18th, 1805, Samuel Sherman and Peggy Thompson, married at
the house of Samuel Thompson   September 8th, 1805, Joseph Winslow and
Polly Wells   November 24th, 1805, William Tripp and Hannah Mead   March
26th, 1806, Thomas Hammon and Keziah Reynolds, married at the house of
Solomon Reynolds   May 10th, 1806, James Robertson and Martha Van Kleek
September 21st, 1806, Amos Irish and Vina Harris· and Daniel Peck and Tenty
Sisson, married at the house of N. Sisson   September 12th, 1807, Jacob Odel,
jr, and Phebe Brown, and Clark Jenkins and Rebekah Smith, at the same
time and place

It is probable that this list embraces a large majority of the marriages in the town during the period referred to, and most of the parties were among early residents of Queensbury, and many of them became prominent   William Robards, jr, died March 27th, 1820, at the age of forty-two years   He is buried in the little enclosure at the Round Pond   In his docket is a record which goes to show that he looked with little favor upon the evil of intoxication It reads as follows —

"Washington county   Be it remembered that on the 10th day of September in the year of our Lord 1805 * * * was convicted before me Wm Robards one of the Justices of the Peace in and for the County aforesaid on my view for being drunk in the town of Queensbury in said county on the day aforesaid   Given under my hand and seal the day and year above written"

This was followed by other entries of a similar character   The convictions become of some importance when we remember that they were adjudged at a time when intoxication was not considered the exception to general good conduct, as at the present time

It will have been seen by the foregoing pages that with the opening of the century, settlement had rapidly progressed in this town, and before the end of the first decade, the tide had turned to a great extent from the flat, alluvial lands of the "Genesee country," which were gaining a reputation for unhealthiness, northward along the old military road and the newer forest pathways, where not half a century before armies were marching and countermarching, leaving battle-fields behind them as mementoes of their sanguinary strife   Glens Falls was then a thriving hamlet and settlers had located in many other parts of the town, while the sites of the now populous cities of Syracuse, Rochester, Cleveland and Cincinnati were almost uninhabited wastes   The vast pine forests hereabouts offered irresistible attractions to hardy lumbermen, and the almost unlimited water power turned the numerous wheels of mammoth saw-mills on every hand [1]   Spafford's *Gazetteer of New York*, published in 1813, says in reference to Glens Falls at that time   "On the north shore [of the Hudson] are 2 saw-mills, the one a gang mill with 21 saws, a trip hammer, and a very valuable grain mill, with 4 running stones is now building on the site of the old one, by Gen Pettit, the enterprising proprietor of the other mills" And the same work further says upon this topic, that there were twenty-three saw-mills in active operation in the town of Queensbury in 1810, six of which were located on the outlet of the "Great Pond"   Large quantities of lumber were also manufactured at that date in Luzerne and Hadley, which was drawn around the "Big Falls," rafted down to the Bend, taken out and drawn over-

---

[1] Rev Dr Dwight traveled through this region in 1798, and thus expressed himself   "Thursday, Oct 4, 1798, we left Sandy Hill, and rode two miles and a half up the Hudson, to see the cataract, called from a respectable man living in the neighborhood, Glen's Falls   .   Almost immediately above the cataract is erected a dam eight or ten feet in height for the accommodation of a long train of mills on the north, and a small number on the south bank'   In contrast with this is what the same observer wrote in 1811   "At Fort Edward, Sandy Hill and Glen's Falls, there are three handsome villages, greatly improved in every respect since my last journey through this region"

land to Fort Edward, where it was again made into rafts and floated to market, all of this created an era of activity unusual in settlements no older than this

In all new communities the principal business of town officers is the laying out of roads and improving those already opened. Highways are almost the first and prime necessity of the pioneers The town records of Queensbury for the first quarter of a century after its existence as a town are largely comprised of road statistics — too voluminous for us to attempt their reproduction Reference has already been made to the several earliest roads In 1796 we find record of a "road beginning at the north end of a piece of land sold by James Ferriss to Nehemiah Platt, beginning upon the town line between Kingsbury and Queensbury, and running south," etc In the same year is recorded the opening of a "road beginning at the center of what is called the four corners by Benjamin Wing's store, and running," etc This was surveyed by Reuben Beck Another began "at the crotch of the roads south of Josiah Vernor s store " In 1806 the road districts were somewhat altered by Joel Winship and Henry Spencer, as commissioners, and a new district formed Three new roads were opened in that year, while in the year 1802 there were about twelve roads laid out, in 1803 fifteen, and so on In 1808 there were twenty-seven road districts; in 1842 thirty-nine

In 1813 the first newspaper in Warren county, always the accompaniment of industrial enterprise and vigorous growth, was started at Glens Falls, as the reader has already learned in the pages devoted to the press of the county In that year the county was organized, and general prosperity and thrift prevailed on every hand Other industries sprang into existence, a cotton factory was established, of which John A Ferriss and a Mr Gould, of Albany, were proprietors Here cotton yarn was merely spun at first and distributed to the busy housewives, who wove it into cloth With the war prices of that period, "factory cloth " commanded from fifty to seventy-five cents a yard About 1830 looms were introduced and cloth was made for exportation The factory, which stood on the south side of the river, was burned in 1832 Dr Bethuel Peck had charge of this business for a number of years [1]

A distillery, also, was in operation at this early day It was run by a man named Pease, who subsequently removed to Vermont, according to the memory of early inhabitants Such an establishment was needed in olden times, when whisky was consumed in a large majority of families, and no public occasion was considered as properly conducted without a supply of spirits

[1] Bethuel Peck was son of Daniel Peck, who was originally from New Hampshire and was a Revolutionary soldier. Dr Holden says "It is not known with certainty what causes led the subject of this sketch to Glens Falls, but it is believed that he was brought along by some of the return gangs of raftsmen, who, in the early days of the settlement here, rafted the lumber to market down the Hudson River He acted for a time as office boy for Dr Levi Rugg, with whom he then continued the study of medicine, and after attending lectures at Fairfield, N Y , he received his diploma He was elected to the State Senate in 1839 for a term of four years He afterwards erected a brick building in Glens Falls, to which he gave the name of 'the Glens Falls Druggist,' and, associated with Dr Mr R Peck, carried on that business for a number of years He died July 11th, 1862 "

Wool-carding and cloth-dressing were carried on "on the east side of the north end of the bridge," by Forbes & Gookin, Messrs White & Winston being proprietors

All this indicates clearly the general thrift and progress, when the country was again stirred by mutterings of war It was but natural that this region should be affected by the approaching struggle, and enlistments began in the county, while general industrial progress and the advancement of settlement was for a time checked

A fac simile of one number of the early newspaper mentioned is in existence. It consists of four pages, each about four by seven inches The subscription price was $1 50 a year In this number (dated September 23d, 1813) is a call for volunteers (as detailed in the preceding general county history of that period); a sheriff's writ against the personal property and title to lot 19, in the town of Athol, belonging to David Cook, the announcement that the first and second squadrons of cavalry (Seventh Regiment) would parade at Fort Miller Falls on the 28th, the marriage notice of Jonathan M'Comber, of Queensbury, and Lydia Newton, of Kingsbury, by Daniel D Scott, esq, and several advertisements Miss Rice returns thanks for the liberal support of her school at Glenns Falls and announces its removal to the second floor of the academy "Terms of tuition, two dollars per quarter" Forbes & Gookin advertise "cotton carding done at the cloth factory of White & Winston, on the east side of the bridge at Glenns Falls" Avery Benedict advertises his drug store, and adds that "Saratoga and Ballston Mineral Waters are constantly kept" The regular meeting of the Mechanical Association is announced to be "held at John Derby's hotel, H Spencer, 2d, secretary" Other marriages noticed were those of Joseph S Winston to Jane Ann Lewis, William Tierce to Sally Stewart, John Velie to Hannah Brown, and Joel Dean to Susan Brown The only editorial is devoted to a bitter criticism of the war. The following is a characteristic extract from it —

"What then is at this moment our real situation? At the end of two campaigns, which have been attended with an expense of more than $80,000,000, and of more than 10,000 lives, at the expiration of two years of war — of a war whose avowed object was the conquest of the Canadas, of a Country containing less than one-fourteenth our population, we find ourselves, through the valor of our generous seamen, in possession of Lake Erie and of two inconsiderable forts"

Notwithstanding "war prices" and the general effects of a war era, local improvements were not neglected and settlement soon regained its former activity The lumbering interest was developed to a marvelous business and furnished a majority of those who became prominent and wealthy citizens with the means for their material advancement Mercantile establishments multiplied and domestic manufactures increased as the demands of the town grew in extent, and few localities in the State gave better promise for the future   At the time when the resources of the State were so materially advanced through the building of the Erie and the Northern, or Champlain, Canals Glens Falls was one of the most populous and thrifty villages in northern New York, and the town at large partook of the same prosperity   The construction of the Glens Falls Feeder was a source of congratulation and satisfaction not only in this town, but throughout the county, it brought cheap and convenient means of transportation directly to the doors of the village and gave an impetus to all industries   Boats passed through the feeder in 1830, but it was not finished in its present dimensions until 1832 [1]

So important was this water-way considered that weekly arrivals and departures of boats were chronicled in the press, and there was a general feeling of relief from the former restricted commercial situation   Transportation companies were formed and a heavy business transacted in this line

It was about this time, also, that the inhabitants of the county first had their hopes raised by the project of building a railroad from Saratoga Springs to Glens Falls   It is quite probable that this enterprise was a direct result of the building of the feeder, one successful project of this character is very apt to lead to others   Under date of January 25th, 1831, the following notice appeared in the *Messenger* —

"Notice of application to Legislature to incorporate the subscribers and their associates as a company to make a railroad from Saratoga Springs to Glens Falls with the privilege of extending the same to the head of Lake George and also from the outlet of Lake George to Lake Champlain

" JOHN BAIRD,

" PETER B THREEHOUSE "

It was more than thirty-five years later before Warren county was given railroad communication with the distant world, but the community was continually awakened during that period with announcements similar to the above   In the absence of swifter transportation, a line of stages was put on about this time to run between Glens Falls and Troy   The stages made trips on alternate days for some time

During this same period and, indeed, for some years later, wolves and panthers were still being slain within the limits of the county, if not in this town   The newspapers chronicled in 1837 the destruction of an old panther and two

---

[1] " It affords us much gratification to announce to the inhabitants of this county, that a canal boat passed safely through the thirteen locks in the Glens Falls Feeder, a number of gentlemen from Sandy Hill and this place availed themselves of a passage on the boat, to witness a sight which had long been desired but which they had almost relinquished the hope of beholding.   The prospect of this work being finished cannot fail of proving a matter of much rejoicing to this county, as a navigable feeder is of deep importance to its present as well as its future prosperity   From an examination of the locks we confidently expect in a few days to have the pleasure of announcing an uninterrupted passage from and to this place, which, if finally accomplished, cannot but reflect credit on Colonel Sherwood, under whose superintendence it has been effected '—*Warren County Messenger*, Nov 4, 1830

young ones in Johnsburgh, and another was killed on the shore of Lake George in Bolton about the same time

The financial crisis in 1837 was greatly felt in this region and many were brought from wealth to penury, through the weakness of commercial credit and general depreciation of every kind of security   Prices of the necessaries of life advanced enormously, money was very scarce and a period of financial distress ensued from which recovery was the process of several years

From this time on to the present, the annals of the town reflect a steady, healthful growth in all material directions, as will be seen, with only the shadow of the great Rebellion, which for five years overwhelmed the entire country Of this momentous struggle we have given a general account, as it relates to the county at large, and fortunately, before it became impossible, Dr Holden accumulated most valuable statistics of the part taken in the war by the town of Queensbury, which here find their appropriate place

"With the tidings of the fall of Fort Sumter, a call was made, numerously signed by citizens of the village, irrespective of party, for a public meeting at Numan's Hall, a building which stood on what is now mostly a vacant space, between Cosgrove Music Hall, and the Glens Falls Opera House   A large and enthusiastic meeting, presided over by the Hon. Keyes P Cool, resolved that this community should do its share and be fully represented in the coming struggle Two persons, namely, the writer of this book[1] and Mr George Clendon received authorizations from the adjutant-general of the State to raise companies in response the first call of the president for volunteers   The ranks were speedily filled and the companies mustered for service by Colonel H K Colvin of the Thirty-first New York Militia   They were joined by another company (I) of stalwart men from the north part of Warren and Essex counties   These three companies received the honors of an ovation given them by the citizens of the village, a purse was made up and given to each company, and they were escorted to Fort Edward by the fire department of the place   The same day they reached the military rendezvous at Troy, where in due time they consolidated, as Companies E and F, with other companies from the neighborhood and formed the Twenty-second Regiment N Y Vols under the command of Colonel Walter Phelps, jr, of Glens Falls   It subsequently formed a part of the famous Iron Brigade of the First Division, and First Army Corps [2]   (See military chapter for history of the Twenty-second Regiment)

" From that time forward, scattering recruits from Queensbury were con-

---

[1] Dr A W Holden

[2] " With the first enlistment of two years' volunteers, as there was no bounty, either local, State or general, offered, recruits were backward in offering their services, until guarantees were given that in case of their death or disability their families should be provided for   This assurance was met by two subscription papers amounting to about ten thousand dollars each   Of this sum nearly one-half was collected and disbursed, the bounty system then coming in, dispensed with the need of any further assessments or collections. "

tinually pouring to the front, filling the ranks of the regular army, supplying deficient quotas from other sections of the State and county at large

"With the progress of the war,[1] and its prospective continuance, new calls were made, new levies demanded   The question was no longer one of patriotism, the claim was obligatory, its effect compulsory, month by month new regiments were raised, and new companies furnished   Nearly an entire company of Glens Falls boys was recruited for a District of Columbia regiment

"The Ninety-first, Ninety-third, Ninety-sixth, One Hundred and Fifteenth, One Hundred and Eighteenth, One Hundred and Twenty-fifth, One Hundred and Fifty-third, One Hundred and Fifty-sixth, One Hundred and Sixty-ninth and One Hundred and Ninety-second Regiments were represented by companies or detachments of Glens Falls volunteers, while scattering representatives might have been found in half the regiments of the State, and every branch of the service   After the boys in blue began to return home from expired enlistments, many of them re entered the army, resolved to see the thing through   In this way what was known as the veteran regiments were speedily filled out and returned to do good service in the war   In this way the Second New York Veteran Cavalry, and Sixteenth New York Heavy Artillery received large accessions from this vicinity

"The volunteer system of 1861 was found on brief trial to be entirely inadequate to the exigencies of the war   It took, however, a long time before all the machinery incidental to a new and hitherto untried system worked itself into thorough and harmonious operation   No quotas were assigned, and no records, coming within the scope of this article, were kept either by the State, or general government in that or the following years   It was not until March, 1863, that the general government made an enrollment, and through

---

[1] "One of the early efforts of the war was the issue of vast volumes of paper currency which speedily became known as greenbacks   A counter result was the almost immediate withdrawal from circulation of the specie of the country even to the copper and nickel issue   The consequence was, a great temporary distress for the want of small change   The country was flooded in a few weeks with a bogus brass currency, composed of tradesmen's cards   Postage stamps for large and small amounts were temporarily used, and one enterprising manufacturer of nostrums went so far as to enclose them in metallic cases bearing the stamped names of the remedies   In this emergency, the corporate authorities of Glens Falls issued in the fall of 1862, what were known as corporation shinplasters, to the amount of $5,000, in denominations of fifty twenty-five, ten and five cents   With the issue of postal currency by the general government, came a general law forbidding corporations or individuals from circulating such money, so it was called in and cancelled the following year "

Statement (October 20th, 1864) of the amount of fractional currency issued and redeemed by the village of Glens Falls and the expenses incurred in issuing the same —

Whole amount of fractional currency issued		$5 129 10
Interest accrued and deposits .... · .... ·		74 30
		$5,203 40
Bills redeemed	$4,703 05	
Expense printing, etc ...... · · .... · ·	390 15	5,193 20
Balance .... ·		$ 101 20
Leaving unredeemed ...... · · .. .. · ... $ 326 05		

its provost marshal in each Congressional District began its assignment of quotas
The following statistics appear on the files of the adjutant-general's department
at Albany for the year 1862 —

Population of the town of Queensbury 7,146
Number enrolled liable to military duty 1,107
Number of exempts embraced in above return................   86
Number liable to draft............................... 1,021
Quota of Queensbury under the calls of July and August, 1862,[1] 221
Number furnished to fill quota as above 208
Deficit carried forward.............   13

" During that dark period of the Rebellion which preceded the emancipa-
tion proclamation, Governor Morgan appointed in each Senatorial District a
committee of three gentlemen, who, in conjunction with sub-committees designated by them in each county, were known as the war committee, whose business seems to have been, without any specifically defined duties, to assist in
making up the complement of troops required of each locality   The late Halsey R Wing was the member who represented Queensbury on that committee,
and very efficiently and patriotically did he discharge that duty, for, besides
his time, his labor and his money, he gave his two sons, Edgar Murray and
George Henry, as an offering upon the altar of his country

" There at length came a time in our history when money had to be raised
to pay bounties, in order to save the trouble and reproach of a draft   A special
town meeting for this purpose was called on the 26th of July, 1864 (less than
three months after the great fire which had burned out the heart of our village,
and destroyed upwards of one million dollars worth of property) at which
one hundred thousand dollars were voted to pay the volunteers [2]   Bonds were

---

[1] " The call in July was for three hundred thousand three years' men   The call in August was for
three hundred thousand nine months' men   These two amounts were consolidated in one assignment
and equalized, so that an enlistment for three years represented and was equivalent to four enlistments
at nine months   There were but very few nine months' troops mustered from this State   The large
proportion were three years' men "

[2] Of this amount the Glens Falls Bank took shares amounting to $13 225, the Commercial Bank
$16,400   The balance was taken by private parties, the Hon Jerome Lapham alone bearing upwards
of ten thousand dollars of the amount   The bonds were so apportioned that an equal proportion matured each year until they were all cancelled

" Besides the amount already specified other sums were appropriated during the same year as appears by the following resolutions passed at the annual town meeting

" 'Resolved, That there be raised $109 60 for to pay expenses in recruiting Capt Fassett's com-
pany

" 'Resolved, That there be raised $108 87 to pay expenses in recruiting Capt Arlin's company

" 'Resolved, That there be raised $106 42 to pay expenses in recruiting Capt D Cameron's com-
pany

" 'Resolved, That there be raised $109 80 to pay George Conery and William Cosgrove for taking
up a note drawn by M W Coville for recruiting purposes

" 'Resolved, That there be raised $1,354 73 to pay a note dated Dec 20, 1862

" 'Resolved, That there be raised $7,015 to pay a note drawn for bounty money

" 'Resolved, That there be raised $1,890 12 to pay a note held by Jerome Lapham issued representing this sum, and twice to its credit be it said, that these securities were all quickly taken at home, and have long since been canceled At the town meeting referred to, the following gentlemen were chosen as a permanent war committee of the town, whose services, onerous, arduous and responsible, were continued to the end of the war, viz Jerome Lapham, Halsey R Wing, William A Wait, I J. Davis, George Conery, Lifelet Harris, F A Johnson, jr., Stephen Brown, R M Little

" Most of these gentlemen gave a large per centage of their time to this undertaking They offered bounties, and expended money to pay volunteers, sent agents both north and south to procure substitutes and fill the quotas required by the draft , looked after the soldiers' families at home, and superintended the investment and liquidation of the town bonds

Statement of the quotas assigned to Queensbury, Warren Co , 16th district of New York, and the credits applied thereon, under calls for troops

	Credits	Quotas
Quota under call of February 1, 1864		149
" " " March 14, 1864		62
		211
Credits by new recruits.........	179	
" " veteran volunteers . ..	13	
" " draft of 1863.....	46	238
" " surplus June 30th, 1864		27
Quota under call of July 18th, 1864......		128
Credits by new recruits....	157	
" " veteran volunteer ...	1	158
" ' surplus on call of July 18th, 1864..		30
Quota under call of December 19th, 1864		46
Credits by new recruits....	36	
" " " regular army ..	3	
" " draft	4	43
Deficiency on call Dec 19th, 1864 .		3

War Dept , Adjt General's office,
    Washington, D C., February 9th, 1874
           (Official)   THOMAS M VINCENT,
                          Assist. Adjutant General

Adj Gen 's office,
    Albany Feb 12th, 1874,
        Official copy,
           J B STONEHOUSE,
             Asst Adj Gen

" '*Resolved*, That there be levied and raised $4,845 to pay note in the Commercial Bank drawn by citizens for bounty of $300 each

" '*Resolved*, That there be raised $612 32 to pay note given to pay expenses of reception of 22d Regiment '

" At a special town meeting held December 19th, 1864, the following resolutions were passed

" '*Resolved*, That the sum of $30,000 be raised by the town for the purpose of paying bounties into the military and naval service of the United States

" '*Resolved*, That this money be collected in five equal installments of $6,000 each with the amount of interest unpaid thereon

" '*Resolved*, That $2,467 76 be raised for the purpose of paying bounties ' "

" At the termination of the war there remained a considerable balance in the treasury, and chiefly through the active agency of the late Halsey R Wing, it was decided after due deliberation to appropriate it to the erection of a soldiers' monument   The subject was submitted to the action of the annual town meeting held 6th March, 1866, when the following resolutions were submitted to the people and adopted —

" *Resolved,* That to commemorate the services and sacrifices of the soldiers of Queensbury, who during the war of 1861–65 fell in battle or died from wounds received or disease contracted in defense of the Union, and in memory of our late fellow citizens Daniel V Brown and Edward Riggs, who, while going to South Carolina as agents of the town under the directions of the town war committee, were lost at sea on the eighth day of January, 1865, the sum of eight thousand dollars be and the same hereby is appropriated by this town meeting, towards defraying the expense of erecting a suitable monument or cenotaph in such appropriate place as can be procured in or near the village of Glens Falls

" *Resolved,* That the sum of five thousand two hundred and sixty-four dollars and thirty-nine cents, military funds, in the hands of the supervisor, be appropriated toward the monument

" *Resolved,* That Jerome Lapham, R M Little, Wm A Wait, Lifelet Harris, Stephen Brown, I J Davis, George Conery, H R Wing, the members of the town war committee now residing in town, and M B Little in place of F A Johnson, jr, no longer a resident here, be and they are hereby appointed a committee to receive the said funds and according to their discretion disburse the same for the purpose of this appropriation

" *Resolved,* That the Legislature be and hereby is requested to legalize by law the appropriation made by the foregoing resolutions and that a copy of them be transmitted by the town clerk to our Member of Assembly, the Hon David Aldrich, for presentation to the Legislature

" *Resolved,* That there be raised two hundred and sixty dollars and seventy-eight cents to indemnify the loss of Edward Riggs to be paid to his sister Ellen Riggs

" *Resolved,* That there be raised three hundred and twenty-nine dollars and five cents to indemnify Daniel V. Brown for the loss of his private property, the same to be paid to Mrs D V Brown

" *Resolved,* That there be raised one hundred and twenty-five dollars to indemnify William Cosgrove for a gold watch, lost with D V Brown at the time of his death.

" The committee above named, after examining several designs and exerting careful and mature deliberation in the premises, adopted a plan (with some alterations) which was submitted by R T Baxter, at that time a resident of the village, a dealer in and manufacturer of marble and monumental work and entirely familiar with the business in all its details, and having made his specification and propositions, he was at length commissioned to erect the monument He at once embarked in the enterprise *con amore*, traveled far and wide to secure durable and suitable stone for the work, and employed special first-class workmen, part of whom were hired from the cities at great expense, to execute its finer details The work was commenced in the spring of 1867

" The foundation or substructure is fourteen feet square, and eight feet deep, built of massive blocks of marble from our own quarries, embedded in cement, and whose interstices are filled with grout and cement Upon this is laid a base of Sprucehead granite from Maine This is ten feet square, cornered, and eighteen inches thick

" Upon this rests a plinth sixteen inches in thickness, eight feet square and cornered This in turn supports a moulded plinth whose height is eighteeen inches and whose diameter each way is six feet and six inches, and also cornered, as is the entire shaft in all its pieces and additions to the capstone The second plinth is surmounted by a die five feet and six inches square, with four raised tablets, one upon each face Upon three of these are inscribed the roll of honored dead The remaining face, together with a raised wreath of oak and laurel on the die above, contains the dedicatory inscription

" On the corners of the lower die are wrought out in relief four cannon The material of the entire monument, above the granite base, is Dorchester freestone, fine in grain, dark brown in color, obtained at great cost from New Brunswick Upon the lower die rests a moulded cap eighteen inches in thickness, and six feet six inches square, which supports the upper die or shaft proper, one of whose faces has already been described

" On the north and south aspects of this die are niches, containing statues life size, cut from the same material that composes the monument, representing the one an officer, the other a soldier in the attitude of reversed arms Next follows four sections of the shaft, all gradually tapering toward the top which is twenty-two inches in diameter The three lower of these contain raised bands with the names of battle fields, chiseled in relief

" On the corners of each section also appears a star cut in relief The whole is surmounted by a capstone, cut from a block five feet square and three feet thick, representing the American flag drooping in graceful folds, upon which rests an eagle, in the art of springing into flight The spread of the eagle's wings is about five feet

" The entire monument is estimated to weigh about one hundred tons It was completed at a cost of about twelve thousand dollars, of which amount its unfortunate, though public-spirited architect, was left to meet and make up an unprovided deficit of about four thousand dollars "

The monument was dedicated with suitable and impressive services, attended by a large concourse of citizens, on Decoration day, May 30th, 1872

TOWN OFFICERS.

Following is the list of moderators, supervisors, justices and town clerks of the town of Queensbury from the first settlement to the present time —

Moderators —Warren Ferris, 1793, '97, '98, 1803, Augustine Odell, 1789, William Robards, 1796, '99, 1800, Peter B. Tearse, 1795, John Vernor, 1801, '02, Job Wright, 1770, '01, Abraham Wing, 1766–'69, '72–80 '83–'88, '90–'94

Supervisors.—Phineas Babcock, 1779, '80, '83, '84, '86, Daniel V Brown, 1859, Keyes P Cool, 1855; Benjamin Cornell, 1802, '04, J M Coolidge, 1876–78, H Crandell, 1879; Quartus Curtis, 1850–52, David M Dean, 1833, '39–41, Z I Delong, 1874, '75, George Ferguson, 1861–'63, John A Ferriss, 1813, '27–29, David Ferriss, 1785, Warren Ferriss, 1795–97, James C Finch, 1854; Dilwin Gardner, 1823–25, Charles M Gilchrist, 1869–73, S L Goodman, 1882, '83; Bartholomew Griffin, 1843–44, John J Harris, 1842, Jerome Lapham, 1857, '58, '64, '65, John Mallory, 1810–12; Alonzo W Morgan, 1834, '36, '46, '47, '66, '67, John Murray, 1791, Augustine Odell, 1788, '89, William Peck, 1848, Micajah Pettit, 1803, Walter Phelps, 1860, Alfred Pitcher, 1817, William Robards, 1786, '90–94, William Roberts, 1805–07, '09, Alexander Robertson, 1853, '68, George Sanford, 1837, '38, Nehemiah Seelye,[1] 1783, '84, James Sisson, 1849, Asa Stower, 1798–1801, '08, '15, '16, '18–22, '26, '30–'32, '35, Charles B Thompson, 1880, Nelson Van Dusen, 1881–84, James Vaughn, 1814, Abraham Wing, 1766–78, '85, '87

Justices of the Peace — Morville Baker, 1856, Hiram Barber, 1827–31, Stephen Beadlestone, 1821, '22; Horatio Buell, 1815, '16, George W Cheney, 1852–55, '58–73, Benjamin Cornell, 1801–04, George Curtis, 1865, David F Dickinson, 1817, '18, Isaac E Dutton, 1855, Enoch Ellis, 1822–26, Judiah Ellsworth, 1856, '57, Adonijah Emmons, 1816, 17, Calhoun S Enches, 1877–80, Orange Ferriss, 1838–41, '45–48, Warren Ferriss, 1795–1804, Horace Forbes, 1817, '18, Alanson Fox, 1812, '13; Dilwin Gardner, 1813–16, '20–23, Amos Green, 1819, '20, Walter Geer, jr, 1821-26, Bartholomew Griffin, 1827–34, 37–53, Joseph N Gurney, 1852, William B Gurney, 1880–82, and at present, Michael Harris, 1806–09, Elias Hawley, 1818, '19, William Hay, 1821–24, James Henderson, 1815–17, Hermon Hoffman, 1804-07; William Hotchkiss, 1859–76, De Witt C Jenkins, 1874–78; Gamaliel Jenkins, 1857–62; Lyman Jenkins, 1864–73, '79–82, and at present; Palmer B Jenkins, 1842–45, Ransom Jenkins, 1834–39, '70, Royal Leavens, 1813–15,

---

1 No lists of town officers are contained in the town records for the years 1781 and '82 It is therefore inferred that, in consequence of the unsettled state of the country, and the continuance of the war, the inhabitants had fled back to old Duchess county for safety and that no town meetings were held in these years

In the years 1783 to 1786 two supervisors had been elected, who appeared to act jointly in discharging the duties of that office

William McDonald, 1821, John Mallory, 1817, '18, Carlos Morgan, 1861–68; Ira A Paddock, 1825–28, '48–51, Elnathan Parsons, 1815, '16, Daniel Peck, 1807–13, Eli C Peirsons, 1835, '36; Joseph S Perine, 1848–56, Micajah Pettit, 1802–05, Nathan A Philo, 1829–32, Alfred Pitcher, 1823–25, Fred E Ranger, 1874–76, '78 to present time, Asa Ripley, 1820, James Ripley, 1817–20, William Roberts, 1795–1809; William Robinson, 1851–59, Daniel D Scott, 1812–15, James Sisson, 1848, Samuel G Skinner, 1823, 24, Henry Spencer, 1807–10, 18–21, 32–39, Edward L Stearns, 1881, '82, and at present, Robert Stewart, 1860–79, Asa Stower, 1817, '18, Samuel S Tallmadge, 1827–31, 36–43, Herman Vantassel, 1839–50; James Vaughn, 1811–14, '17–26, John Vernor, 1796–1803, Halsey R Wing, 1844–47; Nehemiah Wing, 1863.

Town Clerks — Phineas Babcock, 1786, Israel P Baldwin, 1813, Hiram Barber, 1826, Louis Brown, 1885, Keyes P Cool, 1831, Daniel H Cowles, 1847, John Derby, 1816; George Ferguson, 1854–60, John A Ferriss, 1796–1804, Warren Ferriss, 1795, Dilwin Gardner, 1815, Daniel B Ketchum, 1861–72, Orlin Mead, 1834–35, Lemuel C Paine, 1812, Elnathan Parsons, 1823–25, Charles Peck, 1848–53, Daniel Peck, 1805–11, Hermon Peck, 1830, William Peck, 1836–38, Micajah Pettit, 1814, Lewis L Pixley, 1827; John E Potter, 2d, 1873–84, Asaph Putnam, 1766–77, Ezra Ranger, 1832; David Sanford, 1802–03, Allen T Seaman, 1833, James Sisson, 1841–46, Henry Spencer, 1817–22, Samuel S Tallmadge, 1828–29, James Wells, 1839–40, Benjamin Wing, 1778–80 and '83–94

MUNICIPAL HISTORY

Glens Falls — This village is beautifully situated on the north bank of the Hudson River near the extreme southeast corner of the county   With the early settlement of this historic locality the reader has already been made familiar   The place was known in the first years of its settlement as the " Four Corners," which title, so familiar to hamlets in different parts of the State, it received from the corners now fronting the Rockwell House   It was given the name of " Glenville," also, as appears from early books of travel in this region   A little later and for a number of years in the early part of the century, a persistent attempt was made to fasten the name of ," Pearlville," or " Pearl Village," upon the place; for what reason does not appear   Fortunately, the effeminate and inappropriate title was displaced by the present name

It has already been discovered that this point was adapted by nature for the site of a ponderous business and manufacturing center, and its selection by the early pioneers as the site of a hamlet is proof of their sagacity   The region immediately surrounding the falls cannot be excelled for building purposes, while the unlimited water power gave promise of great value to those who might avail themselves of its use   The manufacture of lumber was the first industry to engage the energies of the inhabitants, and it has always been an industry of great importance   Before the War of 1812 put a temporary check upon the growth of the village, there were between twenty and thirty saw-mills in operation in the town, many of which were near Glens Falls, and there were thirty buildings constituting the village, they were all wood   Of these the principal ones were "The Tontine," before alluded to, the Glens Falls Hotel, a wooden structure erected by John A Ferriss, in 1808–10, and kept by John Derby in 1813, the New Union Church, and a large, unfinished two-story house built by General Warren Ferriss on Park street (burned in 1818) The mercantile interests of the village when the first number of the *Warren Republican* was issued, in 1813, comprised the drug store of Daniel Peck, on the site occupied in later years by his son Charles, the general store of John A Ferriss, and that of Micajah Pettit in the same line, which was in a small wooden structure in rear of the old stone store under the hill, where he had traded since 1793; Roberts & Goodman's store, "under the hill;" L I Van Kleeck's store, of which his announcement says he "kept an assortment of dry goods, groceries, hardware, and crockery in the building near the meeting house" (this was on the site now occupied by William Cronkhite & Son); and a store kept by the firm of Fox & Little   This shows that at that early date Glens Falls, or "Pearl Village," as it was called, was already the center of considerable trade   And there were other mercantile establishments in the town then and for many years previously.   David Sanford kept a store at Sanford's Ridge before 1810, which he subsequently sold out to John H. Hitchcock. Thomas Hammon had a store at the Oneida in 1808, and a few years later William McDonald established his prosperous mercantile business at the Ridge, on the site now occupied by Harris Haviland, and what was known as Osborne's store (1797) was also at the Ridge   Robert Wilkinson, William Hay, L I Van Kleeck and Abraham L Vandenburgh, attended to the legal business of the place, and Dr Levi Rugg was the leading physician, with Dr Asa Stower in the north part of the town

As we have already said, the early manufacturing interests, both at the village and throughout the town, was comprised largely of saw-mills   Some of the first ones were that of Thomas Scribner, which was probably located on the Big Pond Outlet, and as early as 1786; on the same stream Phineas Austin had a mill in 1808, and the Moon brothers, elsewhere mentioned, had both a saw-mill and a grist-mill there at about the same period, the remains of their grist-mill were visible down to a few years ago, one Odell, also, had a saw-mill before 1810, on the Outlet, Micajah Pettit had a saw-mill near his store on the west side of the road near the river bridge, in 1802; these mills rapidly increased in number until at the opening of the War of 1812 there were nearly thirty in the town, and at least six on the Outlet of Long Pond   Other manufactures of the first decade in the century embraced a tannery at the bridge,

Lewis L. Arms

which was conducted by a Mr Kimball, it stood near the site of the present school-house, a distillery, operated by one Pease, who came here from Poultney, Vt., which, it is said, did a good business, he also kept a tavern where the Glen House afterward stood, an ashery worked by David Sanford, at the Ridge, and perhaps other minor industries Abraham Haviland carried on blacksmithing on the site of the George Ferguson store as early as 1795

For the lumber business and what other carrying trade was connected therewith, Glens Falls was the outlet, this fact was the cause of the establishment of numerous taverns of all grades of importance, these old county inns have nearly all disappeared before the oncoming railroads, which enable the traveler who leaves the great hotel of one city or village in the morning to take his next meal in a similar house at his next stop, taverns where travelers could obtain rest and refreshment, with the unfailing accompaniment of ardent spirits, followed close upon the heels of settlement in all new communities, not only in the young villages and hamlets, but at intervals on the country roads; and these were sufficiently patronized to make them not an unprofitable investment We find that John Mallory kept a tavern in 1802 on the site of the present Glen Park Hotel at the corner of what was called in the early surveys, "The New Road" Peer's Tavern was a wayside inn about two miles north of the village at an early day Jonathan Pitcher kept a tavern in a log building at Halfway Brook, which was known as the Pitcher Tavern, and others were soon opened in various parts of the town In 1812 the old Union Hotel was built by Dr D McNeill; it originally consisted of a story and a half lean-to and adjoined the Henry Crandell premises For a long time a swing sign bearing the legend, "Coffee House — 1812," commemorated the date of its erection This original structure was enlarged to a commodious hotel, in 1814, by Samuel G Skinner, who kept it for many years as a popular house John A. Ferriss then kept the Glens Falls Hotel (built in 1802), on the site of the Rockwell House, and considerable rivalry existed between the two houses At the time Skinner opened his reconstructed house, a sort of an "infair" was held, and in order to surpass any and all efforts of a similar nature that ever had been or were likely to be made in the future by the rival house, Mr Skinner sent to Albany for a professional cook The entertainment is said to have been a sumptuous one and was remembered by old inhabitants for many years This house was kept soon after 1834 by Porter S Chapman, and burned about the year 1842 The Glen House was also a popular hostelry of a somewhat later period which stood just north of the La Point saloon, under the hill, it was burned in 1867, while being conducted by Russell Barber In 1815 Marmaduke Stevenson kept a tavern on the plank road two miles north of Glens Falls

The little hamlet grew apace and during the ten years succeeding the close of the War of 1812 took on the aspects of a thriving village The lumber interest was greatly developed, and minor manufacturing establishments were founded as the needs of the inhabitants demanded   The first bridge across the river at this point was built before 1795   In 1804 Warren Ferriss was awarded a grant by the Legislature to build a toll bridge, which was done   That bridge stood until 1832–33 when it was displaced by a free bridge, the latter was erected by C P and H J Cool, and James Palmeter, under the supervision of the commissioner of highways of the town   The *Warren Messenger* of January 25th, 1833, says : " The new free bridge across the Hudson at this place is already in a considerable state of forwardness   We understand that the contractors will commence raising it in the course of the week "

By the year 1823 the town was divided into twenty school districts, number twenty including the village of Glens Falls   In that year a resolution of the town authorities provided for the raising of money to build a school-house in Glens Falls   A resolution was passed as follows   " Resolved, That the site be near the burying ground at the crotch of the road leading from S G. Skinner's to Luzerne, on the east side of said burying-ground "   Here the old school-house was erected and used until 1863

From numbers of the Glens Falls *Observer*, published by E Galloway Lindsey in 1827–28, a glimpse of those business interests whose proprietors had sufficient faith in printer's ink to advertise, is obtained   Wing & Geer had a general store and announced " seasonable goods which will be sold cheap for cash, lumber or country produce "

Philo & Ferguson also advertised a general store, " on the corner nearly opposite Samuel G Skinner's coffee-house "

Miron Beach informed the public that he had started the manufacture of " fancy, Windsor and common chairs," a few doors east of the Glens Falls hotel, " all kinds of country produce taken in exchange "   A T Prouty also carried on cabinet-making, and G G Dickinson was the village tailor Hyman ·J Cool advertised cabinet-making " near the bridge " and Charles Spencer's card announces him as a shoemaker   Estabrook & Adams's advertisement reads, " To farmers —Ground Plaster for sale at our mills at Glens Falls at $7 50 per ton   Cash or grain taken in payment "   J Sisson carried on a druggist store, and Roswell Bacon erected tombstones over the departed John A Ferriss was prominent·among the advertisers, with a general stock, and S Burt did watchmaking   Such were the chief business interests of the village at that period

The opening of the canal in 1823 gave a mighty impetus to the village and caused a development of the lumber business that was almost marvelous ; while the same effects were produced upon the villages of Sandy Hill and Fort Edward, causing them for a period to even outstrip in rapidity of growth the village of Glens Falls, but a few years later (1830) the Feeder was opened to the latter village and inaugurated an era of growth and improvement which has continued to the present time   With the beginning of navigation in the following year (1831) the *Messenger* gave the following exhibit of the condition of the village —

"Our village at this time contains a population of about one thousand inhabitants   We have four lawyers, three physicians and one minister   Among our mechanics are to be found the shops of two cabinet-makers, five blacksmiths, two hatters, three wagon-makers, one chair-maker, four shoemakers, one book-binder, three tailors, one stone cutter, one cooper, three saddle and harness makers, one painter, five carpenters, three masons and one baker, and also four milliners   (In the issue of the paper for the following week the addition was made of one watch-maker and two tinners)   We have nine mercantile stores, two druggists do, a post-office, surrogate's office, three inns,[1] one cotton factory, one clothier's shop, one printing-office and book-store, two grist-mills, three saw-mills, one marble factory, one plaster-mill, three lime-kilns, a medical school,[2] an academy, a Methodist and a Presbyterian church

This statement gives a clear idea of the growth of the village down to that date, it also indicates that the young village was in a thriving condition and possessed all the establishments common to such communities

The decade following the opening of the Glens Falls Feeder was one of continued and increasing prosperity and growth in the village, and many improvements were made, chiefly in the direction of extending and perfecting the streets and supplying facilities for the extinguishment of fires

The following glimpse of the village industries is given in an article published in the *Messenger* by Dr Holden, as they appeared to him in 1836, in which year he made his acquaintance with the place   There were "the Glens Falls Hotel, kept by P D Threehouse, L L Pixley's store, on the corner of Ridge and Warren streets, D H Cowles & Co's store, K P & H J Cool's store, J A Deforest's store, in the stone building under the hill, H B Ten Eyck's store, books and stationery, James Sisson, Daniel Peck and Clark & Peck (Drs Billy J Clark and Bethuel Peck, who had bought out Dr Ransom), in the drug business, E H Rosekrans, Wm Hay, J L Curtenius, counselors and attorneys at law and solicitors in chancery, A T Prouty, cabinet-maker, D & J H Hitchcock, tin and hardware and general merchandise, A T Seaman, tailor, Dilwin Gardner, boots and shoes, A W Flack, grocery, and Philo & Ferguson, store"   Besides these there were then ap-

---

[1] These were the Glens Falls Hotel, then kept and owned by P D Threehouse, the Union Hotel (or Skinner's tavern), then conducted by Edmund B Richards, and the Glen House, under the hill, kept by the Widow Ray

[2] Of this school Dr Holden wrote about twenty years ago as follows   "The medical school referred to was kept by Dr Fletcher Ransom, whose office and drug store was in the building since burnt, on the site now occupied by Fonda and Numan's 'Masonic Block,' He had several students and legends of the dissecting room and stolen bodies are yet preserved in the memories of the older inhabitants   Dr Ransom came from Brattleboro, Vt, and removed to Kalamazoo, Mich. He abandoned the practice of medicine on removing to the west"

pearing on the signs in various parts of the village the names of Berry, Arms, Lapham, Ranger, Gillespy, Leavens, Tallmadge, Blakesly, Coffin, Geer, Haviland, etc   At that time the principal business of the place, and indeed the larger part of the entire village, was situated on the principal streets leading away to neighboring towns   Glen and Warren streets, Ridge (then called Quaker street), Bay, Park, Jay, Lime, Canal, Water, South and West streets, so much of Elm street as is embraced between Park and South streets, Exchange street and so much of Church street as extends from Warren to Canal streets, comprised the entire catalogue of streets at that time   In the ensuing summer John A. Ferriss opened that part of Maple street between Ridge and Bay streets, and Sidney Berry constructed the culvert, filled up the ravine and laid out and filled up Berry street   He also erected the Female Seminary, which was subsequently sold to district number 19, and used as a school-house

The village evidently suffered to some extent from the epidemic of small-pox, which swept over the country in the year 1832, as well as on several later occasions   In the year named vigilant measures were adopted for the protection of the community and the ravages of the disease reduced to the minimum   In 1844, again, a small-pox panic attacked the people of the town, and resolutions were passed ordering vaccination and the removal of all infected persons outside of the corporation limits   Such removals were placed in the hands of King Allen

Five years later (1849) another scare is remembered, which called forth the appointment in January of Drs B Peck and J L Stodard to see that every person in the corporation was vaccinated, to report cases of small-pox and varioloid, etc   The cholera appeared in the country during the summer, and in June resolutions were passed to have the streets thoroughly cleaned and make all necessary preparations to combat the disease   A Board of Health was appointed, consisting of Henry Spencer, Isaac Knapp and David M Dean

In 1861 (to dispose of the small-pox question) another panic occurred   Some cases of a disease appeared which entirely mystified some of the local medical faculty, and considerable discussion and antagonism ensued   To settle the matter Dr Swinburne, of Albany, was called to decide upon the character of the disease   In his report he said " That the disease which is now depopulating the fairest portion of West and Canal streets and causing the farmers to go to Sandy Hill with their 'apple sass' and potatoes, and the good denizens of the village to fight like cats on a rainy night, is pure and unadulterated small-pox, without the slightest doubt, that vaccination is the best and only preventive "   Prompt and sufficient action saved the community from a general spread of the loathsome disease   The village was again visited by the pestilence in 1881, and nearly twenty deaths followed, but better sanitary arrangements, more efficient action and thorough knowledge of requirements confined the disease to restricted limits

From notes printed in the *Messenger* in 1873, prepared by the Rev Ephraim H Newton, a more detailed account of the industries of the village can be given, as they existed in July, 1835   For example, on the south side of Washington street, leading east from the village, were Dwight Hitchcock's general store, Peter Pelkey, shoemaker; Drs Peck & Clark's drug store, a livery stable, kept by Enoch Ellis, James Parmeter's wagon shop, and Thomas Ramsey s stone-cutting establishment   On what is now Jay street (then called "The Lane") were John R Wilson's blacksmith shop, Charles Cleveland in the same business, Elnathan Parsons's tannery   On the north side of Washington street Lewis L Pixley kept a general store, Felix M Duffie had a barber shop, Elnathan Parsons a shoe store and shop, Sheldon Benedict a saddlery and harness shop, Peter Powell & Company, general store, drugs, etc, Daniel Peck & Son, druggists and general stock, Harmon Peck, stoves, iron and tinware   On what was then Pleasant street, leading north from the center of the village, on the east side were Pixley's store, already mentioned, Nehemiah Sheldon's tailor shop, and Lewis Numan's general store, on the west side were James Sisson's store, with a general stock, and Amarillis S Lindsley's millinery shop   On the east side of River street, leading south from the Glens Falls Hotel, were the post-office, with Jabez Briggs as postmaster, and his grocery, A N Cheney's grocery; Allen T Seaman's shop and clothing store, K P & H J Cool's store and cabinet shop, Dilwin Gardner's shoe store, currier shop and tannery, Henry Spencer's livery and tavern stables, John G Spencer's grocery; then there were the lime kilns, quarries, lumber yards, etc, with De Forest & Freeman's store, Butler & Putnam's blacksmith shop, William Williams's woolen factory, Hawley & Arms's saw-mills   On the west side of this street were the Glens Falls Hotel, then kept by Rogers & Brown, James Wells's tailor shop, Roswell Bacon's marble cutting shop, James H Comstock's hat store, Robert Dixon Barber, book binder, William Robinson's grocery, Rodgers & Cowles's general store, Calvin Robbins's stone blacksmith shop (then building), James F Kelly's grocery, David Johnson's office and lumber yard, A W Flack's grocery, the Glen House, Putnam & Prouty's wagon shop, A J Everett's blacksmith and forging shop, Abraham Wing's saw-mills, Jonathan Whitman's shingle-mill, J W Freeman's saw-mill, William Nunn's saw-mill, a stone structure which was burned in 1835, J W Freeman's gypsum-mill, Adams & Cronkhite's gristmill   On Warren street, west side, were George G Hawley's store, John A Ferriss's hat store, J. W Willson's grocery and meat market, the *Messenger* printing office, E Williams's store, Samuel S Tallmadge's store   On the east side of this street were James Sisson's store, William Fowler's shoe store, the Misses Ranger, milliners, P S Chapman's tavern

The foregoing embraces all or nearly all of the business industries of the village at that date   The stores and shops on several of the streets, which are now entirely given up to traffic, were then interspersed with dwellings   Drs Bethuel Peck, Billy J Clark and N E Sheldon looked after the bodily ills of the community, while the quarrels of the vicinity were adjusted in a legal manner by William Hay, John L Curtenius, E H Rosekrans and Ira A Paddock. The lumber and lime business were then the chief industries of the place

In this connection it will not be uninteresting to quote the following scheme for the development and improvement of Glens Falls which was evolved by E. H Newton . —

" In July, 1835, I, E H Newton, formed the following visionary scheme for the improvement of the village of Glens Falls, viz : That some one man of capital or company of men of ability and enterprise in the first place purchase all the lands and real estate which Micajah Pettit, of Sandy Hill, owns or holds in this village , also the Glen House or tavern stand and all the real estate appertaining thereto, in possession of Henry Spencer, esq , also the tanyard and the lands and buildings thereto attached, owned by Dilwin Gardner, esq , then run a straight line from or near the southwesterly corner of the said Gardner's tanyard to Calvin Robbins' stone dwelling house, and throw the whole of the land south of the line into a sidewalk, street, wharfs and lumber yards   Then commencing on the corner of the street which I shall now call Canal street and the street running from the Hudson River bridge to Peter Threehouse's Glens Falls Hotel, which I shall call River street, and erect a line of elegant stores, shops, offices, etc , with a finish of stone-pillared fronts, of three or more stories high and with cellars running into the bank in the rear, and the whole founded upon a rock   Then under or near Drs Peck & Clark's drug store build a reservoir holding not less than 1,000 hhds of water, and let this water be conveyed in aqueducts to this range of buildings, and the head will be sufficient to carry it to every apartment and the roofs thereof   Let the buildings be of stone, the fronts of the 2d and 3d stories with a finish of marble-hewn, sawn, cut-brick This street will be spacious, the centre of business and wealth, accessible to every species of trade and art   The Glen House to be rebuilt, finished and furnished with splendid accommodations for travelers and visitors of the Falls of the Hudson   This will prepare the way to throw the residue of the Pettit land into the market at a great advance   The scheme is grand in theory, but will be grander if carried into effect   So says   EPHM H NEWTON "

The financial crisis of 1837–38 came on and Glens Falls suffered heavily, in common with all other localities, but the tide of progress was not permanently staid, the village was controlled in its business relations by men of energy and ability, whose influence and determination were sufficient to inspire the entire community with courage

Incorporation — The subject of incorporation of the village had often been discussed, and on the 8th of December, 1838, a notice of application to the Legislature for the passage of an act of incorporation of the village of Glens

Falls appeared for the first time in the *Glen's Falls Spectator* The act of incorporation was passed in April, 1839 The corporation as then defined contained a population of 1,270 whites, 621 of whom were males and 649 females, and nineteen colored persons The first election of village officers was held on the 4th of June, resulting as follows —

John A Ferriss, Calvin Robbins, John W Willson, George Cronkhite and James Sisson, trustees, James Palmeter, Dwight Hitchcock and Henry Ferguson, assessors; William Peck, treasurer, Orange Ferriss, clerk; Hazzard Green, constable, and Ira Green, collector S S Tallmadge and Orange Ferriss were then justices of the peace of the town At the initial meeting of the board, four days after the election, the trustees chose John A Ferriss for president and adjourned This custom of allowing the trustees to elect a president continued in vogue until 1874, since then the people have voted direct for that officer The clerk was for many years elected by the people instead of being appointed by the trustees as at present

The village boundaries, as given in the act of incorporation, are as follows. " All that part of the town of Queensbury, in the county of Warren, contained within the following bounds, namely Beginning at the north bank of the Hudson River at low water mark, under the center of the bridge which crosses said river at Glen's Falls, running south seventy-six degrees thirty minutes west, along said river at low water mark, five chains and eight links, thence south forty-one degrees west, along said river at low water mark, eight chains, thence south twenty-six degrees west, along said river at low water mark, three chains, thence west twenty-eight chains and fifty links to stake standing on the westerly side of the Haviland road, thence north thirty minutes west, seventy-six chains, to a stake standing in the highway in front of Henry Philo's house, in range with the north line of lot number twenty-nine of the first division of lands in the town of Queensbury, thence east a part of the way on the north line of said lot number twenty-nine, eighty chains to a stake standing on the land of William McDonald; thence south thirty minutes east, eighty-two chains to the said Hudson River, at low water mark, thence north forty-two degrees west, along said river, at low water mark, twelve chains; thence north sixty-nine degrees west along said river at low water mark, ten chains; thence north eighty degrees west along said river at low water mark, twenty-two chains to the place of beginning, shall hereafter be known and distinguished by the name of the village of Glen's Falls, and the freeholders and inhabitants residing in said village, are hereby constituted a body corporate, by the name of the trustees of the village of Glen's Falls "

A code of by-laws and ordinances was passed upon by the new board and the village government was established on a firm basis The trustees were also empowered to act as excise commissioners, and the first year granted one tavern license and five to " groceries, " no saloons are mentioned in the records [1]

---

[1] These licenses were granted to Alanson Dixon, for a tavern, and to John W Willson, A W Flack,

The receipts from this source were $30   The clerk was paid $25 for his year's
service and the treasurer $3 25

Simultaneously with the application to the Legislature for the incorporation of the village, as before mentioned, a notice appeared in the same sheet
that application would be made to the Legislature for an act of incorporation
embracing the right to construct a toll bridge across the river at this place;
this notice was followed in the same month by three others similar in character   It appears that this project was looked upon as one the franchise for
which would be very valuable; but it was destined to fail at that time, and in
January, 1839, a notice was published in the *Spectator* to the effect that application would be made to the Board of Supervisors for a meeting of the board
"to be held at the house of A B Tubbs," on Wednesday, February 20th, to
levy a tax upon the several towns for the purpose of "repairing the present
bridge or constructing a new one across the Hudson River at this place, and
to construct other bridges in said county if deemed necessary"   This notice
was signed by A W Morgan, Keyes P Cool, Walter Geer, jr , B J Clark,
Orlin Mead and William McDonald [1]

In spite of the depression in financial affairs, another notice appeared at
the time under consideration announcing application for a charter of incorporation of a company "with banking powers" to "improve the navigation of the
upper portion of the Hudson River, either by canal or slack water navigation"
Of this scheme Dr Holden afterwards wrote   "This is memorable for more
reasons than one   Firstly, because of the banking clause and its insertion at a
period soon after the passage and repeal of the odious small bill law   (In that
connection, the older residents may remember the twenty-five cent "shinplasters" issue by Mead & Sanford, and imitations subsequently thrown into
circulation by Underwood, and which were made payable in White Pine Butts
at Wing's saw-mill, or new rum at Richard's tavern)   Secondly, the presentation of this petition originated a commission and appropriation for one of the
most thorough topographical surveys and elaborate reports ever made in the
State   Surveyors, engineers, chain-bearers, axe-men and pack-carriers accompanied by that gifted and sad-fated child of song, Charles Fenno Hoffman,
threaded our northern forests, taking elevations and channeling out the grim
old forest in tracks which can yet be seen   It was in one of these dim, green
alleys of the 'forest primeval' where was to be the canal to the Great Bear
Lake, 'a project that seems to have been a pet at one time'"

'The banking scheme alluded to again came before the public early in the
year 1839, when the following appeared in an editorial —

James Morgan Chris Shaw and Hazzard Green, as grocers   In 1841 the trustees refused to grant
licenses to grocers to sell liquors in quantities less than five gallons

[1] In February, 1841, the county of Warren was loaned $2,500 by act of Legislature, out of the
common school fund, to build a bridge over the Hudson at Glens Falls   A W Morgan, Daniel Roberts and George G Hawley, of Queensbury, were appointed commissioners under the act

"A meeting of the subscribers to the Glens Falls Banking Association is to be held at the Glens Falls Hotel on the 2d day of February next for the purpose of choosing thirteen directors and other preparations necessary to go into operation as soon as possible There is not a better location for a bank north of Troy than this" The project was not consummated for some undefined reason, and Glens Falls was without a bank for more than ten years afterwards, as will appear further on

While the newly incorporated village was enjoying its era of prosperity consequent upon the construction of the canals, and men were constantly coming hither who subsequently became instrumental in adding greatly not only to their own wealth, but to the general activity and growth of the place, educational and religious institutions increased in number and influence We have already alluded to the old academy, built in 1814, which had a useful career A village library was founded in 1835 which became a popular and beneficial institution for a number of years, and soon afterward the Female Seminary was built by Sidney Berry The *Spectator* of May 19th, 1837, contained a very eulogistic notice of the annual examination which had just been held The seminary was then under the direction of Miss Lucy Harris as principal, the institution passed to the direction of Miss Downs and her sister in 1849 and became quite prosperous In the latter part of the year 1839 a Lyceum was organized The following expression relative to this institution is found in the notice in the *Spectator* calling for a meeting of organization "That a positive benefit is the certain result to our village from a well-conducted and well-sustained Lyceum, no person can doubt, and as it is a matter of public profit, it should also be a matter of sufficient public interest to elicit a full house and efficient measures"

The principal business of the village authorities for a number of years was the improvement of streets, making additions to the facilities for extinguishing fires and auditing the limited number of accounts against the corporation The first practical steps toward protecting the village from fire were taken in the latter part of 1841, when a resolution was passed "that Henry Spencer be appointed to procure such hooks and ladders as may be necessary for the use of the village, and to secure a permanent place of deposit for the same" In the next year measures were adopted for the purchase of an engine and other apparatus, as will hereafter appear

Henry Spencer was president of the village for the year ending in May, 1843, and at the annual meeting for the election of officers he was voted twenty-five dollars for his services in that office This action established the precedent which has since been followed, of awarding the successive presidents an annual salary

The trustees were extremely solicitous in early years for the good looks of the streets and made some stringent regulations in regard to keeping them free

from incumbrances Even a pair of hay scales which D H Cowles, a prominent business man, began erecting in 1843 on the Warren street side of his
block, were vetoed as an incumbrance and contrary to the village by-laws He
was, however, permitted to place them on the Ridge street side of the block

Perhaps we shall be able to give our readers a tolerably clear idea of the
business interests of the village in the period between 1850 and 1855, by again
appealing to the advertising columns of the local newspapers In a number
of the Glens Falls *Free Press* of April 15th, 1854, we find it announced that
Cowles & Co , have just removed their stock of goods to the store of A Sherman on Glen street The copartnership of Morgan & Lapham was then just
dissolved , the firm having been engaged in a general mercantile business
The new firm to continue the business was composed of James Morgan, Jerome
Lapham and Charles Corliss George C Mott and Dr A. W. Holden carried
on the drug business, Dr N. E Sheldon also sold drugs, and M C Rich announced himself as a jeweler, "two doors north of Cronkhite Bros., Glen
street" J C Higby was prepared to rehabilitate gentlemen in fashionable
tailoring, ready-made clothing and furnishing goods in a new establishment
at the " north end of the Glens Falls Hotel," after which they could go to Carlos Morgan, "two doors north of Glens Falls Bank," or to Edwin O Peck,
artist in daguerreotype, "one door west of M C Rich's jewelry store," and have
their pictures made Hermon Peck, on " Warren street, sign of the big pad-
lock," and Noble Peck & Co (Noble Peck and J L Kenworthy), "Sandy
Hill Street, a few doors north of the Glens Falls Hotel," supplied the community
with hardware, stoves, etc Sheldon Benedict announced his abandonment
of building to engage in the saddlery and harness trade, " at his old stand
between Vaughn's and Peck's stores,' and Bennett & Traphagan (C R Bennett,
J T B Traphagan) carried on the same business at the " third door above Glens
Falls Bank " E Benedict & Co (from which firm William Dunning had just
withdrawn) were engaged in boot and shoe trade, which line was shared by A
F Smith on Exchange street The firm of Cool & Hall (H J Cool, E C
Hall) had recently dissolved, and the sale of hats and caps continued by the
senior member The Harris Lime Company, in " the old stone store near the
canal bridge," offered flour and groceries generally, and J D Cornell & Co
were engaged in the same line Among other business establishments at that
date were George C Mott & Co , hats and caps; William Peat, fashionable
tailor, James E Mart & Co. , J S Ladow, and Hopkins & Dix, machinists,
Cool & Robinson, Nova Scotia and western plaster, etc , J B Cool & Bros ,
salt, etc , and Briggs & Lapham, makers of endless chain pumps

From the Warren county *Whig* of about a year later we gain additional
information of other business establishments in the village, of which the following is a brief summary Fred E Ranger, bookseller, No 3 Merchants' Row ,
John H Martin, jeweler, No. 2 Exchange , W R Winchell, clothing and

furnishing goods, " north end of Carpenter's new hotel, Glen street ," Drs B & M R Peck, druggists, John N Clements, jewelry and musical instruments, two doors north of Rich's jewelry store, Glen street, J S Van Winkle, confectioner, James E Martin & Co, general store, "a few doors north of the Glens Falls Hotel," J C Johnson & Co, hardware, wines and liquors, groceries, etc, Glen street, J E & G W Dean, marble, Exchange building, S W Holdredge, musical merchandise, "No 2 Cowles's new building, up stairs," F Smith & Co, "respectfully announced the opening of a new clothing store in Cowles's new building," Henry Wing, general store in the "Brick Row," Cheney, Arms & Co, "new plaster-mill, adjoining the grist-mill," (South Glens Falls), George Clendon, jr, manufactured soap and candles, corner of Glen and Pine streets, and Daniel Benedict made brick one mile north of Glens Falls, E M Forbes was insurance agent, J S Perine, justice of the peace, and E B Cowles, architect and builder Wood sawing and turning was carried on at South Glens Falls by Gardner T Lewis, and Eastwood & Carpenter had a market on Glen street

From this date to the present the growth of Glens Falls has been steady and healthful, as will be seen in succeeding pages, and the public spirit of its citizens has kept pace with it in the establishment of all needed public institutions. The ordinances had already, in 1841, been amended and considerably extended, mainly in the direction of keeping the streets in order and free from roving animals

The building of the plank road from Glens Falls to Caldwell in the year 1848, was an improvement of great utility and added to the general development of the place through more rapid and easier transportation southward from the interior of the county

Coming down to the end of the first decade of the existence of the village as a corporation, we find that there were then twenty-five streets in the place, a number that has since grown in about thirty-five years to nearly eighty, and the general business interests of the village had increased to the satisfaction of the most hopeful

The lack of sufficient water supply for the village had been felt for some years, and in April, 1848, a project was agitated for bringing a supply of pure water to the village in pipes For this purpose Daniel G Harris was given permission to lay pipes, with the stipulation by the authorities that he should leave the streets in as good condition as he found them. For adequate reasons the scheme was never consummated, and the old wells and cisterns, to which frequent additions were made, furnished the only water supply for many years and until the inauguration of the present complete system

In 1853 the Glens Falls Cemetery was established upon lands purchased of Andrew Porteous Patrick Johnson was appointed as the first sexton, in April, 1855

28

In 1854 the first movement was made towards introducing illuminating gas into the village In April of that year Messrs. Sabbaton & Merrifield, of Albany, were given the exclusive privilege for two years of laying pipes in the streets for this purpose, provided they began the construction of works within four months and prosecuted the same to completion   The pipes were laid and in April, 1856, the trustees authorized the erection of a gas lamp post at each of the town pumps (where the fountain and the soldier's monument now stand)   For the succeeding three years these two lamps supplied all the light the village had, in 1859 six more lamps were added, and this number has been increased until now about one hundred and thirty lamps of gas and naphtha illuminate the streets

The year 1863 saw the erection of the brick school-house in the village At a special meeting held January 20th, of that year, the trustees were directed to purchase the old building and lot in front, in district No 20, for which purpose they were directed to raise by tax $350   They were also directed to purchase of Thomas Kirkham land enough to make a lot equal to the extent of the former lot, on South and West streets, at a cost not exceeding $200 George Conery was directed to prepare a plan for a school-house   The building was erected of brick, 70 by 35 feet, costing $1,400

There is little of importance to record in the general history of the village from the period last considered down to the breaking out of the war   Glens Falls then became the headquarters for a large district surrounding, and during the years of the great struggle, the village partook of the military character 'prevailing throughout the country, while business activity was greatly enhanced   In patriotic endeavor to respond to the different calls of the government for men and means, as well as in their determination that Queensbury soldiers and their families should not needlessly suffer, the inhabitants of Glens Falls and the town at large were not outdone by those of any community in the State   The details of the events of this period have already been given to the reader

Before the close of the war, and on the 31st of May, 1864, the village was the scene of an appalling calamity   A fire so destructive as to nearly wipe out the business portion of the place swept over the village, leaving but three of the numerous stores and but little of the manufacturing portion of the village The loss reached about half a million dollars   For a full account of this conflagration, the reader is referred to the chapter on the press of the county, where will be found a fac simile of the first issue of the *Messenger* after the fire, in which is printed a detailed account of the event

There were not wanting among the inhabitants of Glens Falls those who looked upon this disastrous fire as a blessing disguised ; such was the case even among some enterprising men who were actual heavy losers in dollars and cents   A large number of buildings were destroyed which were anything but an ornament to the place, and which otherwise would have stood for years, these were succeeded by the handsome structures of the present day, many wooden buildings being displaced by substantial brick structures, and the general appearance and character of the business portion of the village was vastly improved   The leading and most energetic men of the place came to the front and building after building arose in rapid succession, while business was carried on in the mean time by the most ingenious make-shifts   In short the disaster which, in a less enterprising community would have paralyzed the industries of the place, seemed here only to fire anew the energetic people and general prosperity was scarcely interrupted

Within a few years after the close of the war railroad agitation began, resulting in the building of the road connecting the village with Fort Edward and the outer world, which gave an added impetus to the growth of the place, this was supplemented at a later date by the extension of the road to Lake George, as elsewhere described

From the era of rebuilding after the great fire, the growth of Glens Falls has been uninterrupted to the present time, to-day it is one of the most thrifty, enterprising and rapidly growing villages in the State, while in its just claims to natural and artificial beauty, it is not often surpassed   Its population, exclusive of its suburbs, is about 7,000, and with the natural suburb of South Glens Falls (connected with this village by the bridge across the Hudson) and other surroundings that may almost be considered as belonging to the place, the number of inhabitants approaches ten thousand   The succeeding description of the present manufacturing and mercantile interests and other institutions will give the reader an intelligent idea of the village in all of its various aspects   Some of the men who have been most conspicuous in contributing to the growth and prosperity of Glens Falls have already been mentioned in these pages, but many have not, nor can all be in any detail, but it will not be out of place to speak of a few of the most prominent   Such are Augustus Sherman, Halsey R Wing, John Folsom, William McDonald and his son, L G. McDonald, John Keenan, Jonathan M and Thomas S Coolidge, Daniel Peck, Jerome Lapham, Rev R M Little, Samuel Pruyn, James and A W Morgan, William W Rockwell, William McEchron, William H Gayger, the several Haviland families, Fred A Johnson, Keyes P Cool, Hon E H Rosekrans, W E Spier, and a host of younger men now engaged in mercantile business or manufacturing, and professional men whose labors in other directions have been no less potent for the general good of the community

Following is a list of the presidents of the village from its incorporation to the present time, embracing the names of many men additional to the above, whose energies and influence have contributed substantially to the growth and welfare of the place · —

Ezra Benedict, 1857; William Briggs, 1845, '48, Daniel V Brown, 1861,

Stevens Carpenter, 1846, James C Clark, 1853, George Conery, 1864; Jonathan M Coolidge, 1883, Daniel H Cowles, 1859, Zopher I Delong, 1863, James Ferguson, 1862, '66, John A Ferriss, 1839, Henry E Fickett, 1858, Stephen L Goodman, 1865, George G Hawley, 1849, Richard W Higby, 1850–52, Frederick A. Johnson, jr, 1870, John Keenan, 1871, '76, '77, '84, S D Kendrick, 1880, '81, '85, Jerome Lapham, 1867, '74, William McEachron, 1872, Joseph Mead, 1869, Alonzo W Morgan, 1854; James Palmeter, 1840; S A Parks, 1877, Daniel Peck, 1868, Hiram Roberts, 1860, E H Rosekrans, 1855, James W Schenck, 1856, Melville A Sheldon, 1873; Henry Spencer, 1841, '42, '44; William E Spier, 1881; Samuel S Tallmadge, 1843, Jarvis A Underwood, 1878, Abraham Wing, 1847

Following is a list of the clerks of the corporation from its formation to the present time —

Adam Armstrong, jr, 1868, Louis M Brown, 1885, Alvin R Carpenter, 1869, George W Cheney, 1865, Isaac J Davis, 1856, '59, '60, C J Delong, 1878–80; A Hackley Fennel, 1867, Orange Ferriss, 1839–42, Emery D Harris, 1861–66, Henry C Hay, 1858, D F Keefe, 1876, Isaac Mott, 1849–54, J. F Patterson, 1874, 75, Charles R Patterson, 1884, Charles Peck, 1843, '45; Joseph S Perine, 1855, Ira A Perrin, 1843, Frederic E Ranger, 1857, E R Safford, 1881–83; John A Sheldon, 1870–73, Allen T Wilson, 1846–48

The following list gives the names of all who have held the office of village trustee and embraces a large majority of the prominent men of the place since the incorporation. Ezra Benedict, 1850, 51, '57, Wm Briggs, 1845, '46, '48, 57, Erastus Bronson, 1840, '41, Wm C Bronson, 1843, Daniel V Brown, 1850–52, '61, '69, Cyrus Burnham, 1844, H H Bush, 1878, '79, James Buswell, 1853, Charles R Cameron, 1866, '68, '75, '76, A R. Carpenter, 1877, '78, Stevens Carpenter, 1846, Albert N Cheney, 1846, James C Clark, 1848, '53, Sanford Coffin, 1880, Thomas Coffin, 1845; George Conery, 1861, '62, '64, '68, Joseph B Cool, 1855, Keyes P. Cool, 1840; Thomas S Coolidge, 1870; William Cosgrove, 1868, Daniel A Cowles, 1863, 59, H. S Crittenden, 1874, Henry Crandell, 1874, George Cronkhite, 1839, '44, Wm Cronkhite, 1858, Enos C Crosby, 1847; David M Dean, 1843, '48, C J Delong, 1875, Theodore S Delong, 1869, Zopher I Delong, 1862, '63, '73, Martin Eastwood, 1850; Enoch Ellis, 1842; Henry Ferguson, 1844, '50–52; James Ferguson, 1858, '61, '62, '66, John A Ferriss, 1839, Henry E Fickett, 1858, James C Finch, 1856, Joseph Fowler, 1879, Stephen L Goodman, 1865; Stephen Goodspeed, 1842, Enoch Gray, 1860, Joel B Green, 1863, '66, Hiram M Harris, 1871, '72, Ezra Hartman, 1876, '77, George G Hawley, 1849, '54, John C Higby, 1847, Richard W. Higby, 1847, '50, '51, '52, S W Higgins, 1882, '83, Alfred Hitchcock, 1858; A F Hitchcock, 1879, '80, C H Hitchcock, 1883' '84, Dwight Hitchcock, 1841,

'42, Dewitt C Holman, 1865, '82, Ezekiel Holman, 1846, William Hoskins, 1864, Theodore Hotchkiss, 1870, Edwin Hubbard, 1855, Frederick A Johnson, jr, 1870, Daniel F Keefe, 1869, John Keenan, 1863, '66, '71, '72, John L Kenworthy, 1853, Ruliff Kipp, 1864, '70, Isaac Knapp, 1849; Hiram Krum, 1863, '77, '78, Benjamin F Lapham, 1865; Henry G Lapham, 1873, Jerome Lapham, 1851, 57, '71, 72, Harmon R Leavins, 1869, '71, '72, '79, '80, Gardiner T Lewis, 1863, Meredith B Little, 1865, '73, Ira Locke, 1855, Leonard G McDonald, 1857, William McDonald, 1843, William McEachron, 1867, '71, '72, A McMullen, 1876, '77, Donald McNeil, 1847, Joseph Mead, 1867, '69, Alonzo W Morgan, 1841, '48, '54, '70, Isaac Mott, 1859, Henry Nesbitt, 1868, Josiah Norris, 1849, George Norton, 1861, '62, '75; Daniel Numan, 1861, '62; James Palmeter, 1840, Bethuel Peck, 1843, Charles Peck, 1848, Daniel Peck, 1864, '67, '68, '84, William Peck, 1845, '49, Walter Phelps, jr, 1858, Samuel Pruyn, 1874, Marquis C Rich, 1859, '60, Calvin Robbins, 1839, David Roberts, 1840, '41, David G Roberts, 1845, '66, '75, 76, Hiram Roberts, 1856, '60, '64, Frederic W Robinson, 1854, Enoch H Rosekrans, 1855, James W Schenck, 1852, '56, Nathaniel Shaw, 1846, Nehemiah Shaw, 1847, Melville A Sheldon, 1873, George Shippey, 1856, George W Sisson, 1865, James Sisson, 1838, '44, '45, '52, '56, O C Smith, 1883, '84, John Somers, 1854, Henry Spencer, 1841, '42, '44, Benjamin C Starbuck, 1855, Samuel S Tallmadge, 1843, Archibald C Tearse, 1857, '59, '60, '64, '67, Berry Thompson, 1842; George J. Tillotson, 1853, William Wait, 1873, James Wells, 1840, Martin L Wilmarth, 1859, '60, '80, John W Wilson, 1839; L G Wilson, 1882, '83, Abraham Wing, 1847

Following are the village officers for the year 1885   President, S D Kendrick, trustees, Daniel Peck, Daniel Corbet, John B De Long, and Merchant H Bradt; treasurer, Stowell B Whitney, collector, Edward Dougherty, Assessor, Charles Parsons

Post-offices — The first post-office was established at Glens Falls on the first of January, 1808   Previous to that time the nearest office was at Sandy Hill and the inhabitants at this place were compelled to go there for mail privileges   The list of postmasters at Glens Falls was furnished to Dr Holden by a friend in Washington, as they appear below, and with the list he enclosed the following information —

"In examining the old books some doubt has arisen whether 'Glenville' was not the original name; but, as no change of name is found, it is presumed that Glens Falls was established, or commenced rendering 1st January, 1808 Unfortunately, the fire which destroyed the building in 1836 consumed three of the oldest books, which makes it difficult to trace the exact date of many of the old offices, but this is believed to be correct"

Dr Holden adds that this statement is corroborated by the recollection of several persons, among whom may be mentioned the late Abraham

Wing and Judge Hay   The first post-office was established
building, the first structure erected on the southeast corner of Glen
ren streets   Judge Hay, whose father erected the building, wrote Dr
that "at the time of Emmons's appointment (1816), James Henderson
postmaster at the Oneida, but whether he was the first one appointed th
know not"

Following are the successive postmasters at Glens Falls John H Ferriss
1808, Adonijah Emmons, 1816, Horatio Buell, 1818, John A Ferriss, 1823,
Ira A Paddock, 1829; Jabez Briggs, 1835; Jonathan W Freeman, 1841,
Henry Philo, 1843, James Palmeter, 1845, Eleazer S Vaughn, 1848, Stephen
I Williams, 1849, William Peck, 1853; Daniel Peck, 1856, Hiram M Harris,
1860, John L Kenworthy, 1861, Carlos Morgan, 1863; W H Van Cott,
1881, H S Crittenden, the present incumbent, appointed 1885

Present Attorneys — In the preceding pages of the present chapter, and in
the earlier chapter devoted to the Bench and Bar of the county, the reader has
already become familiar with the names and careers of the members of the
legal profession who have at various times engaged in the counsels and forensic
contests of Glens Falls   The present attorneys of the place are E L Ashley,
J H Bain, Stephen Brown, L M Brown, William M Cameron, A J Chentree, C S Enches, H A Howard, Daniel F Keefe, Charles F King, H P
King, J J Mead, Isaac Mott, Charles R Patterson, E R Safford, M A
Sheldon, E L. Stearns and F H. Streeter

The attorney of longest standing in the village is Isaac Mott, who came
here in January, 1850   He began the study of law in Glens Falls with Judge
William Hay in 1838, was admitted to practice in 1844, at Utica, and practiced
in Schuylerville until 1849   He was obliged, with others, to compete with
Stephen Brown several years later   Mr Brown was graduated at the Ballston
Law School a short time before he opened an office in Glens Falls   H A
Howard was admitted at Albany in May, 1867, after passing the necessary
period of clerkship in Windsor, Vt , and completing a course of study at the
Albany Law School   Immediately after his admission to practice he came here
and has practiced with distinguished success ever since   He is now serving the
county in a second term as district attorney. M A Sheldon was admitted
at Lake George in 1852   He began his law studies at the Ballston Law School
a number of years before, and passed his clerkship in the office of Judge A C
Hand, of Elizabethtown   He practiced in Ticonderoga from 1852 to January
1st, 1868, at which time he removed to Glens Falls   Judge Andrew J Chentree was born in Greeneville, Greene county   He received his early education
in the Greeneville Academy, studied law in the office of Abraham Becker, in
South Worcester, Otsego county, was admitted at Morrisville, Madison
county, in 1852, came to Luzerne, in this county, in 1854   From there he
removed to Glens Falls in 1869   He is now, and since 1882 has been county

and surrogate of Warren county, and for nine months preceding the
..ion in 1882, held the position under the appointment of the governor.
..niel F Keefe was admitted at Schenectady in 1869, after taking the pre-
..ribed course of study in the office of Davis & Harris, in Glens Falls He
commenced practicing here in the spring of 1870 Edwin R Safford graduated
at the Albany Law School in June, 1874 For the first five or six years he
practiced as clerk in the office of Brown & Sheldon, of this place Since leaving them he has continued his practice alone Calhoun S Enches has practiced here since his admission in January, 1876. Previously he had read with
Armstrong & Keefe, and with Judge Davis H Prior King, after reading law
at Warrensburgh and with Judge Davis at Glens Falls, was admitted at Albany
in January, 1878 He has practiced here ever since J H Bain was admitted
in 1873 at Iowa City, Ia , after completing a course of study in the law department of the University of Iowa He practiced four years in West Liberty,
Iowa, and then, in 1878, removed to Glens Falls Charles R Patterson divided
his clerkship between R C Kellogg, of Elizabethtown, and Hon Warren S
Kelly, of Albany, and was graduated at the Albany Law School in May, 1878.
He then practiced in Elizabethtown until February, 1879, when he came to
Glens Falls E L Stearns passed the examination at the General Term of the
Supreme Court held in Saratoga in September, 1879 He had previously
studied with H A Howard, of this place In 1881 he was elected justice of
the peace and was re-elected in the spring of 1885 Frank H Streeter was
admitted at Albany in 1880, since which time he has been in practice in Glens
Falls. J J Mead read law in the office of Isaac J Davis, of Glens Falls, and
was graduated from the legal department of Union University, May 25th, 1883
He came here at once and opened an office After studying law with Brown
& Sheldon, and subsequently with Stephen Brown, L M Brown was admitted
at Saratoga in September, 1883 Since his admission he has practiced in company with his father, under the firm name of S & L M Brown Charles F.
King was admitted in the same class with Mr Brown He had previously
studied with Thomas Cunningham, of Warrensburgh, and later with Stephen
Brown. He is now clerk in the office of S & L M Brown William M Cameron was admitted in the fall of 1884 at Saratoga He passed his clerkship
with A Dallas Wait, ex-judge of Washington county He came to Glens Falls
in the spring of 1885 Eugene L Ashley passed a clerkship with M A Sheldon, of this place, and was admitted in January, 1885

Present Physicians — The introductory remark concerning the early history of the legal profession in Glens Falls will apply in this division, the early,
physicians having been properly referred to in the previous pages of this chapter and in the general chapter on the medical fraternity The physicians at
present practicing in the village are Drs A. O. Ameden, C S Barney, David Bullard, F L R Chapin, H W Coffin, R J Eddy, James Ferguson, D.

J Fitzgerald, C A Foster, W Garfield, A W Holden, Hamilton Holliday, G W Little, Godfrey R Martine, G W Nyce, Buel G Streeter and Fred B. Streeter Dr James Ferguson is a graduate of the medical college formerly situated at Castleton, Vt, which endowed him with a degree in 1841 From then until 1852 he practiced at Schoharie, N Y, and at the latter date removed to Glen Falls He owned the Prospect Mountain House at Caldwell, which was burned in 1880, and rebuilt as the Ferguson Mountain House Dr David Bullard was graduated at the Albany Medical College in 1849 In 1856 he was converted to the principles of the Homœopathic school. He practiced in Fulton county until 1860, the date of his arrival at Glens Falls. Dr F L R Chapin was graduated from the Albany Medical College in 1851. He practiced in Albany until 1865 (excepting two years in which he was in the war) and from 1853 to 1861 was demonstrator of anatomy in the college of which he is a graduate In 1865 he came to Glens Falls where he has continued to the present. (See biography herein) Dr Buel G Streeter was graduated at the Medical College at Castleton, Vt, in 1853, and located at Granville, Washington county, N Y He took an active part in the Rebellion, and filled a number of prominent medical and surgical positions After the war he came to Glens Falls (See biographical sketch herein.) Dr R J Eddy was graduated at the medical department of the University of Vermont at Burlington, in 1868 He first practiced in Salisbury, Vt, then at Bristol in the same State, and came to Glens Falls in 1872 Dr A O Ameden also received his medical education at the medical department of the University of Vermont He first practiced at Patten's Mills in Washington county about three years, he then passed over nine years at Ticonderoga He came here in January, 1878 He is a native of Queensbury, and was born in this town on the 21st day of October, 1838 Dr G W Little received his degree in 1858, after completing the requisite course at the Albany Medical College During this year he was assistant house-surgeon of the Albany City Hospital He came here for one year In 1859 he went to Johnsburgh, in this county, where he remained until 1865 In that year he removed to Fort Edward, in which place he practiced until the spring of 1881 While there he was in partnership with Dr B F Cornell, of Moreau, for the ten years ending in 1877, and served three successive terms as coroner Soon after his arrival in Glens Falls he entered into copartnership with H W Coffin, which lasted until July, 1884 Since January, 1885, Dr Hamilton Holliday has been with him Dr Fred B Streeter is a graduate of Union College, from which he received a degree in 1876, and of the Albany Medical College, which gave him its diploma in 1879 He immediately began to practice here Dr H W Coffin was graduated at the New York Homœopathic Medical College in 1880 He practiced in New York until 1882, and then came here As before stated, he was in company with Dr Little two years, but since July, 1884, has been alone Dr Godfrey

R. Martine was graduated from the medical department of the University of Vermont in 1862, and practiced until 1882 in Johnsburgh, Vt   He came here in 1882, and in the following year associated with himself Dr C A Foster. (See biography herein) Dr C S Barney began to practice in Glens Falls immediately after receiving his degree from the medical department of the Union University at Albany in 1883   Dr C A Foster finished his course in the Louisville Medical College, of Louisville, Ky , in 1879   He was then house-surgeon for the Louisville City Hospital for one year   In 1880 he removed to Lowville, N Y , the place of his father's residence, where he remained for three years   In 1883 he came to Glens Falls, and entered into partnership with Dr Martine, which has continued to the present   Dr G W Nyce dates his graduation from the medical department of the University of Philadelphia in the year 1857   He first practiced in Michigan , second in Chicago, where he was burned out by the great fire, third in Indiana , then in Kansas   From there he went to Greenwich, Washington county, N Y , and thence in 1883, to Glens Falls   Though he is a general practitioner, his specialty is in removing cancers, tumors, etc   Dr W Garfield was graduated at the University of Vermont, at Burlington, in 1874   Until September, 1883, he practiced at Pawlet, Vt , and then removed hither   Dr D J Fitzgerald received his degree from the medical department of Union University in March, 1884, and after three or four months' practice in the Hospital of New York came here   Dr Hamilton Holliday was also admitted to practice in March, 1884, and is also a graduate of the medical department of Union University   For about two months after his admission he remained in the office of Dr John Swinburne, of Albany — the Swinburne Medical Dispensary   After leaving there he practiced for a period of eight months in Gansevoort, Saratoga county   He came to Glens Falls and entered into partnership with Dr Little in January, 1885   Dr C Coté is a graduate of the Montreal College of Physicians and Surgeons, and a Fellow of the Royal College of Physicians and Surgeons of London, England   He came to Glens Falls in 1884

Dental —The first dentist in this town was George McNeil Another dentist who came here very early and remained until a comparatively recent date was James E Cadwell, who is unfortunate in that he has been pronounced insane   George E Knox was here formerly, too, and was bought out by James S Garrett, who came here in 1860   Dr Garrett still practices his profession here He passed his apprenticeship with Dr Knox   J H Foulds was graduated at the Ohio Dental College at Cincinnati, in 1881, and began to practice in Glens Falls immediately   W S Huntington, after an experience of fourteen years in Watertown, Jefferson county, came here in November, 1882   J W Benson began practice as a dentist about the year 1858 in Otsego county   He came to Glens Falls in 1863 and has continued here in successful practice since

Civil Engineer —James W Reed is a graduate from the department of civil engineering at Cornell University. He received his degree in June,1883 He was employed by the United States government on the Mississippi commission for nearly a year, and was afterwards overseer of the work of putting in a system of sewerage at Cape May   He came here in the spring of 1884

Present Mercantile Interests — The village of Glens Falls has always been by far the most important mercantile center of the county, but not until the close of the war did it exhibit significant signs of growth as a manufacturing locality, excepting in the one branch of the manufacture of lumber and lumber products   About that time, however, the manufacturing interest received an impetus which has not lost or lessened its influence down to the present day   The early and defunct business interests have been already sufficiently detailed in the preceding pages of the town history

There are at present no fewer than fifty-four mercantile establishments in the village — all apparently prosperous   The oldest establishment at present conducted is the furniture store of C M Wilmarth, which was started in 1841 by his father and grandfather, M L and Leander Wilmarth   At first it was only a miniature chair factory on Warren street, the first in the section   J L Kenworthy (hardware and crockery) established himself here in about 1842 or '43, in company with Noble Peck   The two remained together until Peck's death in 1862, since which time Mr Kenworthy has been alone   He has been a resident of Glens Falls since 1831   George Ferguson is proprietor of a dry goods and Yankee notions house on Glen street   The business was started about 1850 by his father, Henry Ferguson   From 1856 to 1870 George Ferguson and his father conducted the business together   In February of the latter year Henry Ferguson died, and his son, the present proprietor, assumed, and has since retained, sole control of the establishment   The furniture store of Bullard & Loomis was initiated in 1860 by H Colvin, in Exchange Place Colvin was burned out in 1864, and immediately recommenced business across the street   In 1875 he took Charles E Bullard into partnership with him   In 1876 Henry Swan bought Colvin's interest, and the firm was thereafter Bullard & Swan until 1879   Then Mr Bullard was alone until the fall of 1882, when John R Loomis acquired an interest, which he still retains. The Crandell Block, which they occupy, was built with reference to their business   They occupy about 15,000 feet floor room   They are also furnishing undertakers George H Bassinger opened a jewelry store on Glen street, nearly across from his present store, in 1860   He was burned out in 1864, and immediately reopened, farther south   He came into his present place in 1872   De Long & Sons began the hardware business here in 1861   They were also burned out in the great fire of 1864, after which they came to their present quarters The members of the firm respectively are Z. I De Long, T S De Long and J. B De Long   M Snyder, manufacturing confectioner, started here in 1862,

at 68 Glen street, moved to his present store, 22 Warren street, in 1879   D
Peck & Company conduct a large wholesale and retail grocery business at 85
and 87 Glen street   The business was established in 1864 by D Peck and F
Byrne under the name of Peck & Byrne   Mr Byrne retired in 1871, and Mr
Peck continued alone until 1882, when his brother, H F Peck, came in with
him   In the spring of 1885 W M Peck, son of D Peck, entered the firm
These three gentlemen are now the proprietors   They supplied forty hotels
with provisions during the year 1884   They carry a stock ranging in value
from $20,000 to $100,000   L P Juvet, proprietor of a jewelry store at No
68 Glen street, established himself on the opposite side of the street in 1865
He moved into his present quarters in 1867   He is the inventor of the celebrated Juvet time globe   William Cronkhite & Son first opened their grocery
and dry goods store in October, 1865   William Cronkhite built this store
after the great fire of 1864, and his son, H O Cronkhite, came in with him at
that time   The senior member of this firm came to Glens Falls as early as
1853, and with his brother, Eli P Cronkhite, opened a grocery store here   In
1854 his brother withdrew, and he remained alone until 1865   A Wurtenberg
first established his business, dry goods and carpets, in 1867 at No 18 Warren
street   From there he subsequently moved to 104 Glen street   He came to
his present location, 112 Glen street, in March, 1883   The firm name was
Rothschild & 'Wurtenberg for the first ten years   Crittenden & Cowles,
dealers in books, wall paper, shades and stationery, started in 1868 at No 98
Glen street, and in 1876 moved to 96 Glen street   The members of the firm
are Horace Crittenden and Benjamin S Cowles, jr   Leggett & Bush, druggists, No 109 Glen street, began business in Glens Falls in 1870   The individual members of the firm are George H Leggett and John W Bush   Joseph
W Leggett and Elizabeth H Leggett, father and mother to the senior member of the firm, were in the town of Chester early in the century, the former
reaching there as early as 1798   He died there in 1871   His widow survives
him   S B Whitney and W W Rockwell began dealing in boots and shoes
here in 1871, under the present firm name of S B Whitney & Company, 89
Glen street   D E Peck, dealer in clothing, hats, etc, established his business
here in 1871   He bought out Brown & Hotchkiss a year or two before that
He has always been alone   A White, merchant tailor and dealer in gents'
furnishing goods, began business in the Cosgrove Opera House in 1871, came
to present place in October, 1884   F C Wilson began the sale of green groceries on Warren street in 1871   He came to his present location in 1876
D W Sherman started a furniture here in 1872   In 1877 he changed his
wares to general merchandise   In February, 1885, his sons, William A and
Henry L Sherman established partnership relations with him, the firm name
now being D W Sherman & Sons   W H Robbins and D P De Long
established a dry goods business in 1872 in their present location, 108 Glen

street There has been no change of place or proprietorship. The Vienna
bakery and restaurant, now in the hands of Charles T Sewell, was established
in 1877 by S & M E McLaughlin.   In 1883 Mr Sewell bought out S Mc-
Laughlin, who had been sole proprietor for about two years   S D Kendrick,
proprietor of a large wholesale and retail drug store, and also of a planing-mill,
and sash, blinds and door factory, has been associated at various times with
Levi Wing, C M. Peck and Lyman G Willson   He came here in 1873
Ezra Hartman opened a boot and shoe store here in 1873, having bought in a
half interest with John E Potter   Mr Potter soon went out, and the firm name
became Hartman & Freeman in about 1875   Charles E Everest became associated with Mr Hartman in 1876   The firm style is now Hartman & Everest.
J W Haviland began the manufacture and sale of harnesses in Glens Falls in
1874, having George Wells for a junior partner   Mr Haviland purchased
Wells's interest in 1880   In 1874 T C Stillwell bought an interest in the hardware business of W W D Jeffers   In 1876 Jeffers withdrew and was succeeded in the firm by J W Allen   Jeffers had been in the business since 1868
The firm title is now Stillwell & Allen   E M Silver opened a clothing store
here in 1874   He came into the present building, No 1 Warren street, in
1880   Isaac Smith has been the sole proprietor of an extensive grocery establishment since May 18th, 1875, in the Cosgrove Opera House   He was burned
out in 1884, and immediately removed to his present quarters, 99 Glen street
R N. Peck was in the drug business here first in 1870   The beginning of the
present enterprise, however, dates in 1875   Haviland and Ferriss are the proprietors of a wholesale and retail drug store which was first opened in 1876 by
R F and Willis H Haviland   The latter went out in 1881, and the vacancy
was filled by George M Ferriss   The firm are also largely interested in a
lumber, sash, door and blind factory, and in hardware   M & J Cohen opened
their present clothing store, at 80 Glen street, in 1877   George H Thomas
started a hardware store at No 55 Glen street in Glens Falls, in the year 1877
H Thomas acquired an interest in the business in 1879   After various removals, and after being burned out on April 28th, 1884, they removed into their
present quarters September 1st, 1884   H. Thomas and J L Kenworthy both
learned their trade of Noble Peck   Coolidge & Bentley (F B Coolidge and
W F Bentley), dealers in clothing, hats, caps, etc , began business in 1878 on
the corner of Warren and Glen streets, and removed to their present site in
1880   Mr Coolidge was associated with A J. Pearsall from 1872 to 1878
Stephen Bentley, grandfather to W F Bentley was an early settler in the town,
and now lives about two miles from the village   C A Hovey deals exclusively in fruits   He opened a grocery at No 20 Warren street in 1880.   In
the winter of 1884 he removed to his present location, 101 Glen street, and
abandoned the general grocery business for his present stock   O C Smith, in
company with E C Quinlan, started a grocery trade in 1880, at the present

Henry M. Day.

stand of O C Smith, who has been sole proprietor since the withdrawal of Mr Quinlan in October, 1884 S G Boyd began dealing in books, stationery, wall paper and fancy goods in about 1869 or 1870 The present proprietors, P P Braley and E C Boyd, bought him out, in March, 1880 In the fire of April, 1884, he was burned out, but immediately rebuilt on the same site and commenced their occupation of the new store in the following October J Lieberman established a clothing and " gents' furnishing goods " business here in 1880 In 1883 L Sonn acquired a half interest in the concern and the firm name became Sonn & Lieberman M B Sweency & Bro , groceries In 1880 this trade was established by M B Sweeney and Daniel O'Leary under the firm title of M B Sweeney & Co In June, 1881, Mr Sweeney purchased O'Leary's share in the business and a few days later took his brother, G A Sweeney, into partnership with him The trade in boots and shoes now conducted by Long Bros , was originally established in about 1879 or 1880 by Herrick & Freeman, an Albany jobbing house After about six months experience there they sold out to C W Long who remained alone until March, 1885 In that month he associated himself with his brother, D R Long The building which C W Long formerly occupied on the same site was destroyed by the fire of April 28th, 1884 The present firm of general merchants known as Havilands & Gilbert, and consisting of Charles W and John G Haviland, and F W Gilbert, was formed in March, 1881, being successors to Coolidge & Lee who formerly occupied the same site W F Bissell opened a music store in Bay street, in 1882 James E Thompson, who occupies part of the store of Long Bros commenced dealing in jewelry in November, 1882 J Raub, jr , has dealt in dry goods and fancy goods at No 74 Glen street since June, 1883 The drug store now conducted by C L Doty on Bay street was first opened in 1882, by S W Lambie Mr Doty bought him out in 1883 C. P Schermerhorn, merchant tailor and gents' furnishing goods, has been sole proprietor of the business since April, 1883, when he established it M H Bitely began dealing in groceries in July, 1883, in the store still occupied by him George E Adams, dealer in hardware, bought out J A Underwood in February, 1883 , Underwood had had charge of the business about four years prior to this transfer Powers & Day, grocers, went in together in the spring of 1883 Mr Powers was, the previous year, with C A Hovey, and Mr Day bought the latter out Keene & Hovey established the business about 1881 The members of the present firm are J S Powers and H N Day Calvin Day, father to H. N. Day, came from Massachusetts to the town of Chester about 1845. He moved to Glens Falls in 1852 and died in 1881 The The firm of I. N Scott & Son, general merchants, was formed in January, 1884, succeeding the firm of Holman, Haviland & Co I N Scott was the " Co " The business was first conducted by Holman & Haviland Crandell & Mores, dealers in groceries, bought out Charles A Hovey, Bay street, in 1884 H

D Sanford purchased his store of F A Mitchell in 1884, Mitchell's business was then about a year old   G. F Bayle & Co (dry goods and millinery) began business in March, 1884   The junior member of the firm is W T Marsh, of Saratoga   The Glens Falls crockery store was first opened March 31st, 1884, by the present proprietor, A F Stewart   The Rochester clothing company *alias* Henry Schwartz & Co , began to deal in ready made clothing in November, 1884   Martine, Rice & Co , dealers in teas, coffees and spices, established their business in December, 1884   W H Rice is the active manaager of the trade   N S Cronkhite, dealer in books and stationery, bought out I J Keeler in 1884   Keeler had established the business in the fall of 1883   L F Baker, boot and shoe merchant, bought out E A Stevens, January 1st, 1885   Stevens had been here about two years previous   Willis J Kendrick opened a store for the sale of drugs, chemicals, and medicines, on the 12th day of January, 1885   S A Barrows came here from Troy in April, 1885, and opened his present grocery store at No 57 Glen street

Hotels — Glens Falls, being a convenient station for summer visitors *en route* for Lake George, and having been used therefor "time whereof the memory of man runneth not to the contrary," has always been more or less famous for the number and excellence of its hotels   The early taverns, and, indeed, all those that are now dead, have received sufficient mention a few pages back, and therefore all that is required here is a sketch of the hotels at present receiving guests

The site on which the Rockwell House stands has been occupied for hotel purposes since the opening of the present century   In 1802 John A Ferriss erected the original hotel here, and by the aid of various landlords, most prominent among whom is the well-known Peter D Threehouse, the Glens Falls Hotel became deservedly celebrated among the traveling public as a desirable place to stay   Threehouse was followed, among others, by Rogers & Brown, Richard W Higby, A B Tubbs, and Wait S Carpenter   In the fall of 1852–53, Carpenter, last above named, having purchased the premises, tore down the old structure and erected on its site a large, substantial brick building. Carpenter played well the part of "mine host" until the great fire of 1864 consumed his hotel and effects, when he decamped   The ground for a number of years lay idle.   In 1869, in order to forestall the apprehended occupation of the eligible site by a proposed row of stores, a number of gentlemen procured a contribution of fifteen thousand four hundred dollars for the purchase of the lot and the erection of a first-class hotel   The purchase being effected, the premises were offered to any person or firm who could assume the responsibility of building thereon a hotel which would reflect credit upon the village. The offer was accepted in the spring of 1871, by H J and George H. Rockwell, who redeemed their undertaking in a manner of which they and their fellow-townsmen have reason to be proud   The construction of the building occupied all the *interim* between the 26th of March, 1871, and the 31st of January, 1872   In October, 1871, Mr C L Rockwell took the place of George H Rockwell   On the 12th of the ensuing February the Rockwell House was opened for business, and on the 22d of the same month a grand infair attested to the people of Glens Falls, at once the singular adaptability of the new proprietors to the business they had undertaken, and their enterprising determination to employ their talents most worthily   The hotel in front is four stories high, with a Mansard roof and Swiss towers   It extends one hundred feet in length by forty-five feet in depth   Projecting in the rear is an ell one hundred and forty feet long, forty feet wide, and three stories high   There are several parlors, seventy-two sleeping rooms, and a capacity for about one hundred and fifty guests   When the house is filled, the labor of thirty-seven employees is continually required   In round numbers, the cost of the building was sixty thousand dollars, and of the furniture, purchased in Boston, twenty thousand dollars   The crockery and silver ware was purchased in Albany and the carpets in New York city   The iron work used in the construction of the building was furnished by the American Corrugated Iron Company, of Springfield, Mass   The spacious pleasure grounds in the rear of the building, together with the complete catalogue of all the modern appliances, conspire to make this public house homelike and comfortable   The architect was M F Cummings, of Troy, the carpenters were Krum & Adams, brick masons, Holman & Pike James Camp laid the stone work, and the painter and glazier was S P Jackman   The proprietors for the first six years were H J & C L Rockwell, but in 1878, upon the withdrawal of the senior member of the co-partnership, Mr C L Rockwell, the present manager, assumed the control of the business   According to the exceptionless testimony of those who have been entertained by Mr Rockwell, there is not a better hotel in the country   Hotel proprietors, like poets, are born, not made, and Mr Rockwell has not mistaken his calling

The site of the American House is also of considerable antiquity as the foundation ground for a hotel   The old building was destroyed by fire on the 5th of August, 1879, and the present structure completed in the following July   George Pardo the present proprietor, bought out Noble Clark in November, 1865, and has remained the landlord to the present   Clark had been in this hotel about three months when he sold to Pardo

The Nelson House Bay street, deriving its name from the proprietor, John S Nelson, who has kept the house since 1870, will accommodate about twenty-five guests

McSweeney & Lynch have kept the Mansion House for seven or eight years

The remaining hotel is the Fitzgerald House, near the depot, kept by Daniel Fitzgerald, who fitted up the hotel from a former private residence

Banks —The Glens Falls National Bank was organized as a private banking company in 1851, under the name of the Glens Falls Bank The first officers and directors were. B P Burhans, president, Abraham Wing, vice-president; Billy J Clark, Walter Geer, Keyes P Cool, D G Roberts, Bethuel Peck, James Buell, Pelatiah Richards, Benjamin Ferris, Halsey Rogers, Byron Rice, Dan'l H Cowles. In 1865 it was reorganized under the National Bank Act, as the Glens Falls National Bank, with the following officers and directors B P Burhans, president, Abraham Wing, vice-president, Pelatiah Richards, Benjamin Ferris, Thos S Gray, Zenas Van Dusen, Alonzo W Morgan, D G Roberts, Dan'l H. Cowles, J C Finch, N E Sheldon, Chas Rice, S L Goodman Prior to the reorganization, i. e, May 31st, 1864, the corporation suffered in common with the greater portion of the business population of Glens Falls, from the devastating fire which then visited the village Business continued, however, without any serious interruption, until the re-organization, when, of course, it assumed a new phase

The first cashier was E J Blacke. In 1853 he resigned, and was succeeded by John Alden, who filled the position creditably until 1862, when he died. William A Wait, who was elected to fill the vacancy thus caused, has performed the duties incident to the office with unremitting diligence and distinguished ability to the present time The other changes in office are indicated by the following chronological statement.—

1867, Jeremiah W Finch elected vice president, *vice* Abraham Wing resigned on account of failing health, 1870, January. James C Finch died, Hon Halsey R Wing died, February Pelatiah Richards died, 1873, Abraham Wing, late vice-president, died June 13th, Dr. N. Edson Sheldon died July 3d, 1875, Benj Ferris died Feb 15th, June 16th, death of Hon Benjamin P Burhans, president of the bank from its original organization, Jeremiah W Finch elected president, and Stephen Brown, vice-president The present officers and directors are as follows, the dates of the election of the respective directors following their names —

J W Finch, president, (elected director in 1866), Stephen Brown, vice-president, (elected director in 1873), Dan'l H Cowles, (1851), Alonzo W. Morgan, (1856), Zenas Van Duzen, (1858), S L Goodman, (1863); Henry Crandell, (1870), Joseph Fowler, (1871), Fred O Burhans, (1871), John P Bowman, (1871), Dan'l J Finch, (1873), T S Coolidge, (1873); Dan'l Peck, (1873), William A Wait, cashier, John E Parry, teller

First National Bank of Glens Falls —This banking company was originally organized in January, 1853, under the title of the Commercial Bank of Glens Falls, in what was then known as the Sherwood Building, erected about 1841 or 1842, on the site of the present structure The bank purchased it of W S. Sherwood for $2,800, and lost it in the great fire of 1864 The present building was erected in the same year at a cost of $18,000 Architect, Walter Dickson, of Albany, builders, D. C. Holman, original capital unchanged, $136,400

It was reorganized as a national bank in April, 1865 The officers have been as follows President, William McDonald, from the organization ; Augustus Sherman from November, 1858 to December, 1884 , present president, Jerome Lapham Vice-presidents, Bethuel Peck, from the organization ; Augustus Sherman, from February, 1855 , Linus B Barnes, from November, 1858 , James Morgan, from February, 1861 ; Jerome Lapham, from November, 1873 to 1884 Cashiers, Isaiah Scott, from organization , Fred A Johnson, jr , from April, 1859 , Emmett T Johnson, from January, 1865 to and including the present The original board of directors consisted of Lewis Hunt, James C Clark, William W Rockwell, Bethuel Peck, Keyes P Cool, James Morgan, Hermon Peck, William H Warren, Quartus Curtis, Augustus Sherman, Erskine G Clark, Joseph Russell, William McDonald Other members of the board at various times are as follows ; Jeremy Rockwell, elected September, 1853, William A Fonda, February, 1854 , Isaiah Scott, July, 1854 , Levi Hatch, February, 1855 , Enos Howland, ditto , Henry Ferguson, ditto , Ruliff Kipp, February, 1856 , Ira Harris, ditto , Charles R Richards, ditto , Daniel Sweet, February, 1857 , U G Paris, February, 1858 , Linus B Barnes, August, 1858 ; James Morgan, ditto , Alexander Robertson, January, 1859 , Henry Crandell, February, 1860 , Jerome Lapham, ditto , Samuel Pruyn, Gustavus A Austin, Nathaniel Barker, Charles Fowler, February, 1861 , Lifelet Harris, October, 1861 , William H. Gayger, February, 1862 , Daniel V Brown, February, 1864 , William McEchron, February, 1865 , Martin Coffin, August, 1867 The present directors are Jerome Lapham, M A Sheldon, William McEchron, A B Abbott, Z I De Long, Samuel Pruyn, Ruliff Kipp, D W Sherman, Martin Coffin, W E Spier, William H. Gayger, Jonathan M Coolidge, Byron B Fowler

Glens Falls Insurance Company —The first movement toward the formation of an insurance company in Glens Falls was in 1849, when a number of the prominent citizens of the place united their abilities and energies and secured the corporation of what was called the Glens Falls Dividend Mutual Insurance Company Probably none of those who originally moved in the matter supposed that they were laying the corner stone of a corporation that would ultimately count its property by the hundreds of thousands of dollars, and its business by millions, and make Glens Falls a familiar name throughout the United States

The following were the signers of the original call for the purpose of formation : J H Rice, D G Harris, E H Rosekrans, Abraham Wing, Bethuel Peck, Charles Rockwell, E S Vaughn, A. Sherman, E H. Hopkins, George Cronkhite, A N Cheney, D McNiel, Billy J Clark, J G. Haviland, L B. Barnes, James Hurley, J B Cool, W S Carpenter, H R Wing, D H Cowles, John H Walker, J J Perine On the 15th day of February, 1850, at the first meeting of the company, the following were elected directors F D Hodge-

29

man, E H Rosekrans, Thomas Archibald, Charles Rockwell Stephen Goodman, Bethuel Peck, William Cronkhite, Albert Cheney, Pelatiah Richards, L.
B Barnes, Abraham Wing, William H Wells, Billy J. Clark Following close
upon their election the board of directors held a regular business session on
the 4th of March, 1850, and chose the following officers President, Bethuel
Peck, vice-president, Pelatiah Richards; secretary, R M Little, treasurer,
A N. Cheney; attorney, E H Rosekrans The company then commenced
the prosecution of business in a single room of the old Exchange Building, on
the corner of Glen and Exchange streets They shortly afterward removed to
a single room in D H Cowles & Co's building, on the corner of Warren and
Ridge streets, which they occupied until their final removal to their own building on Glen street Dr Holden, in his excellent history, states that the building had been "twice enlarged to meet the requirements of the constantly increasing business which has accompanied its increase of years During the early
years of this company, while in its swaddling clothes, the transaction of its
business was not necessarily diffused into the hands of as extensive a corps of
assistants as at present, and many of our citizens will recall the fact that for
some years the secretary (now president) was ' boss and all hands, ' not only
transacting all the inside work but the outside business as well Even after
the name of the Glens Falls Dividend Mutual Insurance Company had become
well and favorably known over a large extent of territory as an honorable and
efficient corporation, the whole office work was done by the secretary and one
clerk, and that with the accommodations and palatial surroundings and office furniture which would not have brought twenty-five dollars in the market "

In 1864, by reason, it seems, of the general and increasing prejudice
against State mutual insurance companies, which had almost universally met
with disaster through reckless and unscrupulous management, it was proposed
to reorganize the Dividend Mutual Company into a joint stock company
The plan was accordingly executed and the company started on its auspicious
career with a paid up capital of $100,000, and as much more subscribed So
rapid was the growth of the business that in 1868 the capital was increased by
actual payment to $200,000 Following are the more prominent members of
the boards of directors since the original formation of the company D. H.
Cowles, Hermon Peck, Lewis Hunt, Alexander Robertson, Joseph Parry,
George Clendon, S B Lee, T S Gray, O Cronkhite, James W Schenck,
Alonzo W Morgan, Thomas Potter, Isaac J Davis, Walter Phelps, jr., John
Alden, D G Roberts, F A Johnson, jr, O Richards, Jerome Lapham, B F.
Bancroft, Charles Fowler, Augustus Sherman, J. C Greene, E Andrews, M. W.
Fish, H S Rankin, F O Burhans, H R Wing, Asahel Wing, James Mor-
gan, Isaac G. Parker, R M Little, Stephen Brown, Ruliff Kipp, Samuel Pruyn,
A J Pearsall, T. S Coolidge, J L Cunningham, Harvey Brown, M B Lit-
tle, Joseph Fowler, E Alliger, D C. Holman, Joseph E King, W A Wait,

John A Sheldon   Since the formation of the new company the following
have held the offices prefixed to their names in the order in which their names
are written   Presidents   Bethuel Peck, Pelatiah Richards, A W Morgan and
R M Little   Secretaries   R M Little, A N Locke and J L Cunningham
Treasurers   A N Cheney, F A Johnson, jr, Alexander Robertson, Jerome
Lapham and F A Johnson   The present officers are as follows   president,
R M Little; secretary, J L Cunningham, treasurer, F A Johnson, general agent, R A Little, board of directors: Daniel H Cowles, Frederick A
Johnson, Jerome Lapham, Augustus Sherman (deceased since election), Mo-
ses W Fish, Fred O Burhans, Russel M Little, Stephen Brown, Melville A
Sheldon, Thomas S Coolidge, Harvey Brown, Meredith B Little, Joseph
Fowler, Dewitt C Holman, Joseph E King, William A Wait, Alson B Abbott, B F Bancroft, J L Cunningham, Orange Ferriss   The Western Department is at Chicago, Ill, J L Whitlock being manager   The total premiums
paid to the company since its organization amount to $6,163,069 56, divi-
dends (cash) $350,000, losses $3,332,087 10, stock owned by directors personally $72,180   As Dr Holden justly says, "prudence and firmness have
ever been the predominating traits of this sound old company, its risks have
been carefully selected and a powerful resistance always opposed to fraud"

The foregoing mention of the business interests of Glens Falls would be
scarcely complete if the establishment of S R Stoddard, the widely-known
artist and publisher, was neglected   Mr Stoddard came to Glens Falls in 1864,
having then just attained his majority, from Troy where he had been employed
in the celebrated car works of Eaton & Gilbert, as an ornamental painter   Within
six months from the time he entered that establishment, so great was his artistic ambition and natural genius in that direction, he was engaged upon the
finest work, taking the place of a painter who had received more for a day's
work than young Stoddard did for a week   From the time of his advent to
Glens Falls he followed the business of sign and ornamental painting, giving
his spare hours to landscape and portrait work   He learned the art of photography, with a view of thus securing by his own use of the camera broader
opportunities to study the beautiful in nature, his artistic genius turning naturally more to landscape than to portrait work   As his collection of photographic negatives increased, embracing many of the grandest scenes in the
Adirondack region and about Lakes George and Champlain, the prints began
to be called for by tourists and others, and Mr Stoddard finally gave up shop
work and devoted himself entirely to landscape photography, landscape and
portrait painting, and latterly to the publication of books and maps   His first
publication was called *Lake George*, a historical and descriptive guide,
which appeared in 1873   This was soon followed by *Ticonderoga, Past and
Present*, a similar work on that historic region   In 1874 he published *The
Adirondacks Illustrated*, a work of value as a guide book   Since then the

last named work and the Lake George book have been revised and re-publish-
ed annually, meeting with a large sale   These books are written in a pleasant,
entertaining vein to brighten the common monotony of the guide books, and
have been commended by the press of the country   In 1880 Mr Stoddard
published his *Map of the Adirondack Wilderness*, of which one of the leading journals of the country said   " It is the most complete map of the Adirondack region ever published."   In the fall of 1880 he made a plane table
survey of Lake George, and in the next year issued his map of Lake George,
of which it is sufficient to say that it was approved and adopted by the State
engineer and surveyor to accompany the report on public lands in 1883

   Present Manufacturing Interests — As observed in another page, the manufacturing interests of this place have grown to their present respectable proportions mainly since the late war   Something of an impetus was given to the
lumber trade, it is true, when the feeder was first made a navigable channel in
1832, but this was confined to one branch of industry, and had little or no effect in starting up the other interests which now exist here   Glens Falls has,
however, become not only a village of considerable present importance as a
manufacturing center, but promises more richly of the future than its past ever
indicated would be possible   The difficulties and obstacles to its attaining importance in this respect are transitory, its resources are various and well nigh
inexhaustible, and its water power tremendous   Being the gateway of the
Lake George region, it receives considerable wealth from the open-handed visitors of summer who stop here a day or a night on their way to the waters
which the fancy of J Fenimore Cooper has immortalized   Before the opening of the railroads, the transportation of the products of the various manufactories was greatly facilitated by the Glens Falls Transportation Company,
which was incorporated soon after the opening of the feeder   The president for
the first six years of its existence was John Keenan, who organized, and, it has
been said, almost constituted the company   The capital stock at first was
$50,000.   The object of the formation of the company was the more con-
venient and expeditious shipment of products to New York   The company
owned at first twenty-five canal boats, and did an extensive business   In those
days there was a large tanning interest in the county, and the company was
largely employed in the transportation of hides and leather   The business
naturally suffered something of a decline after the completion of the railroads
Upon John Keenan's retirement from the presidency he was succeeded by S
L Goodman, and the latter by Thomas Coolidge   The present president is
Samuel Pruyn

   The Lumber Industry — The reader has already been given, in Chapter
XVI, a general description of this business as developed in the county at large.
By far the greater part of it centers at Glens Falls and vicinity   Many of the
citizens of this town have devoted their energies to the up-building of the in-

dustry and have secured ample fortunes   Companies have been organized embracing in their composition men of character, influence and force, and enormous mills have been built with all the accessories for carrying on the work on a large scale

The firm to which succeeded the Morgan Lumber Company was organized in the fall of 1865, and was then composed of James Morgan, A M Adsit, William McEchron and Jonas Ordway, under the firm name of Morgan, Adsit & Company   They purchased what were then known as the Cheney mills, comprising all of the milling property on the south side of the river at Glens Falls, including a vast amount of real estate along the river, the limestone and marble quarries of that property and the dock property on the canal   Previous to 1865 Messrs Morgan and McEchron had been doing business for several years, but owned no mill property, hiring their sawing done at the Cheney mills, still earlier Mr Morgan was engaged in lumber operations alone   Mr Adsit died in the spring of 1871, and in the succeeding fall J Underwood bought his interest and the firm name changed to James Morgan & Co   Mr Morgan died August 1st, 1873, and in the following January his interest was sold to what was then the Albany house, who had sold the lumber of the firm (W H Weaver & Co) and William F Spier, and the style was changed to the Morgan Lumber Company, thus it has remained   Mr Underwood's interest was bought by the remaining partners on the first of January, 1880

Extensive improvements were inaugurated from the beginning of the first named firm and continued to recent times, the mills were enlarged and improved until they were practically rebuilt, and are now among the largest in the county, and for years the company have done the largest business   About two hundred and fifty hands are employed, in the manufacture of lumber and lime, the same company owning and operating a marble mill   Their operations include the manufacture of staves, wood for burning lime, and other minor products   Their lumber is sold largely in New York   The original cost of the mill property was $200,000   The present members of the company are William McEchron, Jonas Ordway and William E Spier, of Glens Falls, and W H Weaver & Co, of Albany

Mills similar to those above described are situated on the north side of the river directly opposite and are now owned and operated by the Glens Falls Co, comprising J W Finch, Samuel Pruyn and D W Finch   We are unable to give a further description of these mills, the firm having declined to furnish necessary information

On the north side of the river at the State dam, a little above Glens Falls, are the mills of Zenas and Nelson W Van Dusen, which are the largest under one roof in the county and one of the best in the State   This mill is new, having been finished within the past year, the mills previously occupying the site were taken down to make room for the new ones   There are two hundred and fifty saws, and the property is estimated to be worth $250,000 The output from these mills in 1884 was 150,000,000 feet, which was sold largely in New York A smaller steam mill was erected in 1880 near by the one described, for working up the refuse of the larger mills The Van Dusens also own some 60,000 acres of timber lands in Warren, Essex and Hamilton counties These are now the prominent saw-mills of this town and represent a vast industry

Among those others who have been conspicuous in the lumber industry in this town may be mentioned Augustus Sherman, Abraham Wing, Jerome Lapham, and others whose names appear in connection with the business interests of the town

The Lime Business — The manufacture of lime has for many years been only second in this town to the lumber industry The quantity now manufactured at Glens Falls is equaled in no other place in the country except Rockland, Me , while in point of quality it stands at the head The rock in the quarries here yields when properly calcined from ninety-five to ninety-eight per cent of the purest and whitest lime to be found on the continent. The lime-producing rock is embraced in an area of about one hundred and fifty acres, beginning at the head of the falls and extending in a narrow belt eastward on both sides of the river for about half a mile, the strata dipping slightly towards the south and disappearing Above, below and on the north it breaks suddenly off, giving place to a rock of entirely different character Lime was first burned here as early as 1820 by Pownell Shaw simply for home consumption It was first manufactured for shipment (to Troy) by Keyes P Cool, in 1832 The business was continued by K P Cool and Sons (J B , Hiram M and Alvin) until about 1861, when the Jointa Lime Company, organized in about 1858, purchased all their property, including their canal boats known as Cool's six day line The Jointa Lime Company was first composed of John Keenan and Halsey R Wing, but at this time Leonard G DcMonald was admitted partner and new purchases of lime rock were made The business was continued without change of ownership until 1871 when the Keenan and Wing interest (i e , the ⅔ part of all real and personal property including bills receivable and book accounts) was sold for the sum of two hundred thousand dollars to Leonard G McDonald, Walter McDonald, Joseph Fowler, and S L Goodman, and thus it continued until the spring of 1876, when Leonard G and Walter sold out and a new firm was organized composed of Joseph Fowler, S L Goodman, Charles Fowler and T. S Coolidge Since then there has been no change

The Morgan Lime Company was formed in 1868 and composed of James Morgan & Company, Harmon R Leavens and Thomas S' Coolidge They built two kilns that season and two the next, and thus they ran till 1876 when the two-thirds owned by Leavens and Coolidge was purchased by the then Morgan Lumber Company, and later they built a fifth kiln and have so run

S. L. GOODMAN.

till this time   Since May 1st, 1884, they have been permitted to furnish six-thirtieths of the lime

The Sherman Lime Company was formed about the year 1862 and was composed of Augutus Sherman, D W Sherman and H G Lapham   Augustus Sherman died in the fall of 1884, but his interest remains in the estate; otherwise there has been no change in the company

The Glens Falls Lime Company was formed about the year 1863 and composed of K P Cool and Hiram Wilcox   In 1865 James C Clark was admitted to an interest in the company   He died in 1866 or 1867 and his interest was sold to F W Robinson, The firm continued thus until 1880 when the business was purchased by the Glens Falls and the Jointa Lime companies and the Glens Falls Lime Company was discontinued

The Glens Falls Company was formed about 1866, or 1867, and was first composed of J W Finch, Samuel Pruyn and the Jointa Lime Company   Soon afterward the interest of the Jointa Company was sold to the other members and D W Finch was admitted , thus the firm remains

In 1881 the Lime Companies of Glens Falls purchased the lime works of R W Lowber, at Ball Mouutain, Washington county, and still own them jointly

On the 6th day of April, 1871, the contract then existing under which the Jointa Lime Company, Sherman Lime Company and Glens Falls Lime Company were governed in the sales of lime was abrogated and a new and similar contract was made for ten years from that date, in which all the companies then making lime here were made parties and shared in the lime that should be manufactured and sold in proportion as they owned kilns, as follows to-wit, Jointa Lime Company, ten parts, Sherman Lime Company, six parts, Glens Falls Lime Company, four parts, Morgan Lime Company, four parts, and thus was it continued not only the ten years but by mutual consent it has been recognized as binding during the four years since its expiration   In the spring of 1876 the Jointa Lime Company sold to the Glens Falls Company three kilns, and in the winter of 1880 the Glens Falls Lime Company's kilns and property were purchased by the Glens Falls and Jointa Lime Company, thus leaving but four companies in the combination   In 1884 two kilns were added to the total of twenty-eight and the addition conceded to the proportion of the Morgan Lime Company, and from May 1st, 1884, the proportions have been upon the following basis   Glens Falls Company, ten parts, Jointa Lime Company, eight parts, Sherman Lime Company, six parts, Morgan Lime Company, six parts

In this connection the following letter written to a correspondent by Dr A W Holden, in 1884, will be found of interest and value, even at the risk of some slight repetition —

"Geologically speaking the Glens Falls marbles, of which there are two strata, the upper or gray, which is highly fossiliferous, and averages from about two to four feet in thickness, and the lower or black which ranges about eleven feet in thickness — belong to the Trenton limestone group, and in some places (at Sandy Hill and the Big Dam) are overlaid by the Utica shales, but not here at Glens Falls There are two marble saw-mills, one on either side of the river, their product forming a very considerable item of our industries and exports, in the shape of huge sawed and squared blocks, for canal locks, foundation walls, etc , sawed slabs polished for ornamental inside work for dwellings and public buildings, such as bases, fire jambs, mantel-pieces, etc , also largely for flooring and tiles

" Another product of the various quarries, where about one hundred men are employed, is cut stone for various architectural purposes, such as capitals, friezes, pilasters, plinths, coping, horse-blocks, door-steps, window-sills and caps, etc , the entire product varying according to commercial demand, from $100,000 to $300,000 per annum

" In regard to the lime industry here, we have on both sides of the river thirty kilns, divided between four companies, which for purposes of sale are consolidated much after the manner of a stock company, of which each is expected to produce and place in the hands of their joint factors to sell or put on the market in thirtieths according to the following ratio, the numerators representing the number of kilns owned by each — Glens Falls Company, ten-thirtieths; Jointa Lime Company, eight-thirtieths ; Sherman Lime Company, six-thirtieths , Morgan Lime Company, six-thirtieths.

The kilns are all of the kind formerly called " patent," but the patent having expired, they are now called " perpetual," because the fires, so long as the kilns are operated, are kept going night and day , they are fed from the top daily (or oftener) and drawn from the bottom as often The capacity of the kilns varies from two hundred and fifty to three hundred barrels each. The bulk is not materially changed by burning According to fuel and conditions of temperature, it takes from sixty to seventy-two hours to burn the entire contents of a kiln Under the old method by which the contents of a kiln were first burned, then the fires extinguished and the contents drawn, it took from six to ten days The average daily product of each kiln is one hundred barrels, and the total consolidated product 600,000 barrels per annum. This amount fairly represents the annual proceeds of this industry for the last twenty-five years Of this for the last few years, over one-half, or about 300,000 barrels, are shipped by rail, something like 100,000 barrels being shipped by cars in bulk , the remainder being exported by canal Of this over one-third goes to the New England States, one-third to New York State at large and the west, and the remainder to New York city , the balance to the Middle States and south The number of hands employed is roughly estimated at from four hundred to five hundred, varying largely with the season of

J. L. DIX.

the year and demand   About one thousand barrels per year would cover the home demand and sales.   About thirty thousand cords of wood (the fuel used) are annually consumed in this manufacture   This is principally the waste product of our lumber saw-mills, really little cord wood being used and that of an inferior sort   The barrels and casks, with the exception of putting on the hoops, are all made by machinery, the staves and heading being also furnished from what would be waste material from the saw-mills, the estimated cost being about twenty cents each   Until about twenty-five years ago this industry continued gradually to increase in value and importance from its first inception about seventy years ago

The oldest manufacturing business now in Glens Falls is the foundry and machine shop of J L & S B Dix   The business was established about the year 1844 by James Wells   In 1848 Hopkins & Dix bought out Wells, and continued the business until 1854, when Henry M Lewis came into the firm   In about a year, however, another change altered the firm name to Hopkins, Dix & Clendon   In 1856 Hopkins withdrew, in 1869 Hopkins succeeded Clendon, in 1874 S B Dix, son to J L Dix, succeeded Knox   J L Dix came here about 1820 with his father, Samuel Dix, a lumberman, who died in 1857   (See biographical sketch herein)

The Glens Falls Paper Company was incorporated as a stock company with a capital stock of $24,000 in 1864   The president was Mark A Cushing, the stockholders were E H Rosekrans, Albert N Cheney, Ransom M Hawkins, John P Sherwood, Mark A Cushing, and A T Harris, the last named being the treasurer   They built their first mill of wood, but it was destroyed in July 1883, by a fire caused by the explosion of a boiler, whereupon the present mill was constructed of brick   Just before the fire the company was re-organized and purchased the water-rights of the Morgan Lumber Company, which became stockholders in the paper company   The new mill cost $185,000   The sole product of the factory is the material on which newspapers are printed   Sixty or seventy men are employed   The mill has a capacity for making ten tons of paper daily   The pulp is made at Palmer's Falls and at Ticonderoga   The president is W E Spier

The Glen Shirt Company was formed in 1879, by Joseph Fowler and D L Robertson   The present factory, which is operated by steam, was built in 1881–82   The annual products are about $250,000 in value   About three hundred hands are employed in the shop, while work is sent out to no fewer than five hundred more

A shirt factory which has become one of the prominent manufactories of the place, was started in May, 1876, by W E Spier, and was known as the Glens Falls Collar Company   Two years later James L Libby became connected with the business and the firm name changed to Libby & Spier, this style was changed January 1st, 1883, to James L Libby & Co, the present style, the firm being composed of James L Libby, Charles A Libby, Charles A Gilbert and Theo Franklin About six hundred hands are employed in their extensive building on Park street, while about 1800 people are carried on their pay roll The capacity of the factory is about two hundred shirts and six hundred dozen collars and cuffs daily. Charles A Gilbert is the manager.

The Clark Colored Brick and Terra Cotta Company, a stock company, was formed in the fall of 1879 It received its name from T M Clark, the founder The products of the company's industry were pressed brick and terra cotta and fancy tiles The enterprise was unsuccessful and went into the hands of a receiver, but was re-organized in the spring of 1884 under the name of the Glens Falls Terra Cotta and Brick Company, with a capital of $45,000 Since the reorganization J M Coolidge has been and is now the president of the company, and Charles Scales, secretary and superintendent They manufacture now red and buff brick and tiles

The Glens Falls Company, a partnership composed of J. W Finch, D J Finch and Samuel Pruyn, manufacture lumber, lime and marble This is a large and powerful organization, but we have been unable to obtain details of their operations

The Glens Falls Hub and Spoke Company, under the management and proprietorship of S Williamson and his son, J M Williamson, was purchased by them in 1883 of the Jointa Lime Company and E R Bain The Jointa Lime Company had had a controlling interest in the business since its beginning, but had always been associated with some partner. E R Bain's interest was begun about six years before he parted with it The capacity of the mill, which is contained in seven different buildings, is represented as follows About twenty-five sets of hubs, seven hundred spokes, fifteen thousand staves and ten thousand curry-comb handles daily

D C Holman and D W Sherman, own and conduct a brick-yard and tile-works near the village H R T Coffin has also, in two separate yards, a brick yard and a tile yard

The soil in the vicinity of Glens Falls consists of limestone strata for a depth of twelve feet, and below that an excellent limestone is obtained which is valuable for building purposes Up to 1884 large quantities were shipped to Albany Goodman & Coolidge are and for years have been largely interested in the quarries here

James Palmeter had a carriage-factory many years ago on the site of the Catholic church, and was there for many years

Joubert & White (Edward Joubert and James H White) began the manufacture of light carriages at their present location as early as 1860 Light-work is a specialty They are the inventors and patentees of the celebrated Joubert & White Buckboard, which is shipped all over the country The firm employ about thirty hands

For five years after 1874 Nelson La Salle, in company with three others, manufactured all kinds of wagons and carriages in Glens Falls, under the name of the Union Carriage Works   In 1879 La Salle joined George Ferriss about two years in the same business, after which he came to the present site in company with E J Dickinson   In 1881 Dickinson withdrew, and La Salle now conducts the business alone   Twelve hands are employed

William B Griffin and Freeman E Wood, under the firm name of Griffin & Wood, began to make carriages in 1882, in the old shop of the Morris Brothers   They do light and heavy work

P W , E , M J , J T , and R T. Cashion, under the name of Cashion Brothers, commenced light and heavy work in carriages in 1883   They employ eleven hands

Glens Falls Academy [1] — This academy owes its origin to the enlightened public spirit of the citizens of this village, who, desiring to afford their youth the opportunities for training furnished by the best English and classical academies, took measures to found such an institution, and at a meeting of citizens held on the 24th day of February, 1841, the following named gentlemen were elected members of its first board of trustees   William Caldwell, Halsey Rogers, John J Harris, Hiram Barber, John R Thurman, Walter Geer, jr , Alonzo W Morgan, Russell M Little, Elmore Platt, Billy J Clark, Jonathan W Freeman, George Sanford, Bethuel Peck, Julius H Rice, Henry Ferguson, Enoch H Rosekrans, Alfred Fisher and George G Hawley , the officers of the board being   president, Billy J Clark, secretary, Enoch H Rosekrans, treasurer, George Sanford , collector, Russell M Little

The board of trustees decided to erect at once a suitable building for the accommodation of the proposed school, and the following trustees were appointed a building committee   Alonzo W Morgan, Walter Geer, jr , and Jonathan W Freeman   The present academy site was secured and the academy building was erected during the spring and summer of 1841   This building, with a large addition made in 1870, comprises the structure at present in use

Presidents — During the forty-four years of its existence the academy has had but three presidents, as follows   Billy J Clark, 1841–51 ; Bethuel Peck, M D , 1851–63 , Rev A J Fennel, D D , 1863 to present

Trustees — The institution has been fortunate in the men who have been its guardians, many of the best citizens of this and adjoining towns serving at different times as members of the board   In addition to the gentlemen constituting the original and present boards, the following have served the institution as members of the board of trustees at different times   Jonathan W Fairbanks, Jonathan Burr, Albert N Cheney, Daniel H. Cowles, Sheldon Benedict, Henry Ferguson, Dwight Hitchcock, N E Sheldon, M D , Lewis Hunt, Zabina Ellis, J. R Thurman, Ezra Benedict, William A Fonda, Halsey R Wing, Alexander

---

[1] Contributed by Prof D C Farr

Robertson, Rev A J Fennel, Stephen L Goodman, Daniel V Brown, Isaac Mott, Jerome Lapham, George Rugge, Martin Coffin, Stephen Brown, Z I De Long, William McEchron, Wallace W Rockwell, Austin'W Holden, M D, Henry J Lapham, Frederick A Johnson, Jarvis A. Underwood The board at present (1885) is constituted as follows Rev A J Fennel, D D, Hon Jerome Lapham, Jeremiah W Finch, H S Crittenden, Hon F A Johnson, Rev Fenwick Cookson, Melville A Sheldon, William McEchron, A W Holden, M D, John L Cunningham, William A Wait, and Daniel C Farr

Instructors — The trustees have always endeavored to secure as teachers only such as were liberally educated and were in thorough sympathy with the object of the academy in holding up a high standard of scholarship and culture as the end to be reached by its students Most of its principals have been college graduates and a number of them have been eminent as educators The following is the list of principals who have served the institution since its foundation Thomas S Farnsworth, Elbridge Hosmer, L R Satterlee, George Rugge, William McLaren, sr, Rev Jason F Walker, Edson Fobes, Warren P Adams, Rev John Babcock, James A Russell, Alson B Abbott, Charles W Hall, William A Holman, James S Cooley, and associate principals, William McLaren, jr, and Frances A Tefft

In this connection should be named the very able preceptress, Miss Dora . Wilson, who served the academy with great acceptance during the entire period covered by the principalship of the following Messrs Russell, Abbott, Hall, Holman and a portion of Mr Cooley

Students — The value of any educational institution is shown by the character of its students as exhibited in after life; judged by this standard Glens Falls Academy can truly be considered a successful institution, since it can number upon its roll of students such names as Algernon Paddock, late United States Senator from Nebraska, together with his brother, Frank Paddock, esq, an eminent lawyer of New York city, Hon Frederick Johnson, Member of Congress from New York, the late Rev Edgar Goodspeed, D D, of Chicago, pastor at the time of his death of the largest Baptist Church in America, and his brother and successor, Rev Thomas Goodspeed; Hon Daniel E Sickles, former Member of Congress and major-general in United States army, Lemon Thompson, a prominent business man of Albany, a graduate and trustee of Union College; John Bentley, esq, a leading lawyer of Denver, Col, and former United States commissioner of pensions, Charles Hendley, who has been one of the secretaries of the last five presidents, Rev Sheldon Jackson, D D, for many years district secretary for the Presbyterian Church of the Rocky Mountain District, and at present in charge of an educational institution at Sitka, Alaska Territory, where he holds an important position under the government, Herbert S Underwood, one of the editors of the Springfield *Republican*, and a large number of others, who either in professional or business life have secured an enviable reputation

Donors — Besides the liberal donations at the founding of the academy in 1841 and its enlargement in 1870, it has received substantial gifts from many of its generous friends either in the form of contributions to its general fund or in establishing scholarships or prizes, among whom are the late Augustus Sherman, Hon Stephen Brown, Mrs Halsey R Wing, Hon A B Abbott, Dr A W Holden, Daniel J Finch, Hon F A Johnson, Daniel Peck, S A Parks, Samuel Pruyn, Joseph Fowler, and B B Fowler

Alumni Association — Its graduates have ever manifested a commendable interest in the prosperity of their *alma mater*, and in 1882 formed an alumni association to which one day of commencement week is regularly devoted The orations before this body have been in 1883 by Rev F M Cookson, in 1884 by Dr John E Bradley, of Albany, in 1885 by Hon F A Johnson

The presidents of the association have been John A Dix, class of '79, James A Holden, class of '80, George M Watkins, class of '81

Present Condition — Since 1878 the academy has been under the joint management of Daniel C Fair and Frances A Tefft, during this time there have been fifty-six graduates During the same period it has prepared students for Williams, Cornell, Wells, Vassar, Wellesley, and Smith Colleges Others of its graduates are filling important positions in the professional and business worlds The standard of scholarship has been steadily raised and it is believed that its course of study both as regards completeness and thoroughness will compare favorably with that of the very best academies of the country

The library and apparatus, to which additions are constantly being made, are intended to meet the needs of the institution in the varied departments of literature and science The two literary societies afford good opportunities for literary culture in addition to the regular instruction in those subjects While the institution is in no sense sectarian, it aims to be eminently Christian and its managers believe that sound morality and practical Christianity are grand essentials in any course of training

The field from which its students are drawn is increasingly large, while it has a large home patronage, a goodly number of its students are from widely different localities A very large proportion of its students pursue their entire academic course here, covering from four to five years, which enables them to obtain a solid and symmetrical training Judging from its present outlook this academy is destined to a long and substantial career, holding a position among the very first of the successful academies of the day

Young People's Christian Union of the M E Church — This association, which promises to be of great benefit to the community, was organized June 1st, 1884. Its design may be generally stated as the advancement of the cause of religion, the assistance of the pastor in his work, the promotion of social and literary culture among young people, and the making of the church a home to all who come Rev H C Sexton is president of the Union, and the following are the other officers C B Thompson, first vice-president ; Miss Margaret McEchron, second vice-president , N R Courley, recording secretary , Mrs C W. Long, corresponding secretary , C F West, treasurer ; Miss Maggie Sexton, editress Executive committee, C W Haviland, chairman, Rev H C Sexton, Miss Margaret McEchron, Mrs C W Long, Miss Maggie Sexton, Fred H Bullard, C B Thompson, N R Gourley, C F West, Sherman Williams, Hollis Russell

The Rockwell Corps — This military organization, otherwise the 18th Separate Company, N G S N Y, was originally organized in Saratoga county as the 5th Separate Company of the 10th Brigade, November 17th, 1876 It then embraced no Warren county members The first captain was Fred Gleesettle, of Saratoga county (South Glens Falls) He held the office until January 17th, 1880, when he resigned, and Dr J S Garrett, of Glens Falls, was elected to fill the vacancy on the 2d of February In 1881 the original term of service of the company expired, and Dr Garrett recruited a new company from Warren county, and the organization and headquarters were transferred accordingly in January, 1882 The present officers of the corps are : Dr J S Garrett, captain , Willis F Bentley, 1st lieutenant, commission dated January 29th, 1884 , John F Morehead, assistant surgeon with rank of 1st lieutenant, February 12th, 1884 , John H Leonard, 2d lieutenant, April 30th, 1879 The membership is now fifty-eight men and the organization is in an efficient condition

Public Buildings — The growth of the village in population and the increase in the wealth of the population, created a demand for a public hall or place of popular amusement which met with a response in 1869 Daniel Keefe and Mr Amer then erected a beautiful building and called it the Cosgrove Opera House, but afterwards (about 1876) re-christened it the Cosgrove Music Hall It retained this title until 1884, when it was burned D. F Keefe and D C Holman rebuilt on the site after the fire, giving the new structure the name of the Armory Block It is three stories high, fifty feet front and seventy-five deep and is of brick The ground floor is occupied by stores, while the basement is used for corporation purposes The second and third floors are occupied by the armory and quarters of the Rockwell Corps, a billiard parlor, etc.

Prior to the erection of this building the only hall in the place was the Union Hall, adjoining the site of the Cosgrove Music Hall· It was built soon after the great fire of 1864

The Glens Falls Opera House was erected in the summer of 1871 by Coffins & Lasher, of this place, on the old Daniel Peck estate Its front on Warren street is occupied by the village post-office and stores, the second and a part of the third stories are devoted to offices, while the rest of the third story contains two large halls elegantly furnished. The Opera House proper extends back in the rear, and has besides the usual appurtenances of a hall arranged for the reception of theatrical and operatic troops, all the conveniences for parties and festivals. It has a seating capacity for sixteen hundred persons

The Fountain — The fact that the village is provided with a handsome fountain is due more, perhaps, to Meredith B Little than to any other one person In 1872 he circulated a petition to the village trustees, to which he obtained about two hundred signatures, asking that they, in their capacity of commissioners of the water-works, would erect a fountain in the center of the village, at the expense of the corporation, or its taxable property, which should be both a credit and ornament to the place This was presented to the board of trustees, who thereupon authorized the said Little to act as a committee to select and report a design This was done in the winter of 1872 and '73, and the trustees, acting as commissioners, accepted such plans and estimates and made an appropriation from the proceeds of the sale of water bonds to cover its cost In the mean time a new election took place and Mr Little was chosen one of the new board of trustees In the spring of 1873 the work was commenced, and being vigorously pushed, was completed about the time of the commencement of summer travel in the month of June following, Messrs Little and William Wait of the board of trustees acting as a committee of construction It is situated at the central part of the village, near the intersection of Ridge, Warren and Glen streets, and when in full play, is a most conspicuous object of attraction The diameter of the basin is twenty-one feet, the rim being of iron, the bottom of cement Its depth is about three feet The base of the pedestal is of Glens Falls marble, two and a half feet in height, octagonal, with three projecting buttresses The fountain proper, with ornaments, is about fifteen feet high above the water level There are a number of jets and attachments, which give a pleasing variety to its play The entire outlay expended in its construction was nineteen hundred dollars The cost was considerably enhanced by its being built over a nest of five immense cisterns, into which the waste material of the fountain flows, thus creating a large reservoir of water, which can be resorted to in case of great emergency, such as a fire, or obstruction in the water-works

Horse Railroad — The subject of a street horse railroad to connect Glens Falls with Fort Edward has been more than once agitated In December, 1862, the project was discussed and measures adopted for its consummation A meeting of citizens of the villages directly interested was held at Sandy Hill, at which committees from each village were appointed to further the object The gentlemen selected for Glens Falls were Augustus Sherman, Jerome B Lapham and Isaac Mott A stock subscription was opened at the meeting and about $5,500 subscribed within half an hour The first estimated cost of the line was about $33,000 Consent of the villages was obtained to lay the track, and a company organized with the following board of directors Z Van Duzen, Augustus Sherman, Jerome B Lapham, D V Brown and Alex Robertson, of

Glens Falls, William Colman, U. G. Paris, Charles Stone, jr, and O Richards, of Sandy Hill, George Harvey, Daniel Underwood, F D Hodgeman and George Bradley, of Fort Edward The officers chosen were Daniel Underwood, president; Jerome B Lapham, treasurer, Isaac Mott, secretary.

Further estimates of the cost of the road reached $45,000 Of this amount $31,500 was finally subscribed, largely in the town of Queensbury This subscription was still further increased and everything indicated the early completion of the enterprise But the condition of general financial affairs and other local causes, led to the abandonment of the project During this present year (1885) however, the subject is receiving such renewed attention as promises its early accomplishment [1]

Plank Road — In the year 1847 the Glens Falls and Lake George Plank Road Company was organized, the object being clearly indicated by its name The first board of directors and its officers were as follows· Billy J Clark, president, D H Cowles, secretary and treasurer, Abraham Wing, Cyrus Burnham, D G Harris, W S Carpenter, George Sanford, Pelatiah Richards, Thomas S Gray, and John R Thurman The capital stock has always been $24,000 The road has been well maintained and of great utility. The present officers are Joseph Fowler, president, A B Abbott, vice-president, L S Coolidge, secretary and treasurer, D. H Cowles, superintendent The board of directors embraces the above names with those of Daniel Ferguson, F O Burhans, Thomas Cunningham, H G Lapham and William B Gurney

The Fire Department — The *Glens Falls Messenger and Advertiser* of Friday, January 2d, 1835, contained the following brief description of a disaster which gave the first impulse to the organization of a force to protect the citizens of this village from the ravages of fire —

"FIRE — On last Friday evening, about 8 o'clock, the Marble Mill, belonging to N Nunn & Co, together with the machinery, was destroyed by fire. Loss estimated at $2,000" This fire, no doubt, created in that early period much excitement, and stimulated the citizens to some exertion in the right direction, for soon afterward the following notice appeared in the *Messenger and Advertiser*.—

"GLENS FALLS, January 8th, 1835

"At a meeting of the inhabitants of this village at Messrs Rogers & Brown's for the devising and adopting of measures to prevent damage and loss by fire, John A Ferriss was chosen chairman, and Thomas Cotton secretary

"On motion, *Resolved*, That a vigilance committee of three be appointed to examine the apparatus of stoves and fire-places of the whole village, and to

---

1 While this work was passing through the press, during the summer and autumn 'of 1885 a street railway company was organized (the subject having been previously agitated at various times), and the line opened between Glens Falls and Fort Edward on Saturday, September 26th, 1885 This event occurred at so late a day that this mere mention is all that can here be given of the enterprise

cause such alteration as safety may require, and that *J A Ferriss, Henry Spencer,* and *Lewis Numan,* be said committee

" *Resolved,* That three fire-wardens be appointed, who shall take command (in case of fires), in the order following, viz · *Alonzo W Morgan,* first; but in his absence *Bethuel Peck,* second, and *Abram Wing,* third of said fire-wardens

" *Resolved,* That a committee of three be appointed to convey the hooks and ladders when and where useful in extinguishing fire, and that *J L Curtenius, Sidney Berry,* and *K P Cool* be said committee

" *Resolved,* That a committee of three be appointed, whose duty it shall be in case of fire alarm, to provide axes to be used at buildings on fire, and that A T Prouty, H J Cool, and Hermon Peck, be said committee

" *Resolved,* That Dilwin Gardner, Henry Spencer, and Walter Geer be a committee to take charge of property for safety, when exposed to loss by fire.

" *Resolved,* That every house owner be earnestly requested to furnish a ladder to ascend his building in case of fire

" *Resolved,* That the interest and safety of the village require that each householder procure one or more fire buckets

" *Resolved,* That J L Curtenius, A W Morgan and Abram Wing be a committee to superintend the making of a reservoir for a supply of water to extinguish fires

" *Resolved,* That we pledge ourselves to each other to carry the foregoing resolutions into effect, and that the same be published in the *Warren Messenger*   JOHN A FERRIS, Chairman

" THOMAS COTTON, Secretary "

As before suggested, this little incoherent organization, with its committee laboring under duties prescribed by resolutions, with its lack of penal sanction for neglect of duties, and with the willing hearts and ready hands of its members and " committees," constituted the rudimentary germ of a fire department of which Glens Falls is justly proud   Just how much active services they rendered cannot be told, but the movement had begun, the perils of fire realized, and the means of defense against it compassed   On the 20th of July, 1839, only a few weeks after the original incorporation of the village, a resolution was adopted by the " city fathers " that in addition to the $150, which by law they were entitled to raise, the sum of $200 be taken " to defray the expenses of making preparations to guard against fire," etc   Under date of October, 1841, in the village records is found a statement that David Roberts was ordered to get two good pumps for wells, and Henry Spencer to procure such hooks, ladders, etc , as might be needed.   In November, 1841, the wells were deepened   Thus we see that the people in those days were alive to the overruling necessity of guarding in every way against losses by fire   The records are full of similar resolutions and enactments precautionary against this dreaded element   30

The first meeting to organize a company was held in the basement of the building now owned by Judge Rosekrans, and formerly known as the Brick Row, and the following is the article of organization adopted at this place —

"The undersigned, citizens of the village of Glens Falls, in the county of Warren, for the purpose of organizing an efficient fire engine company in said village, hereby enlist and associate ourselves together for such purpose, and stipulate and agree, that we will conform in all respects to such rules, regulations and ordinances as from time to time may be passed and ordered by the board of trustees of said village for the regulation and government of such company

"(Signed) L S Steele, William Briggs, E C Crosby, David Redington, Charles Carpenter, L C Hamilton, M L Wilmarth, George J Tillotson, D G Roberts, Hiram Roberts, J R Taylor, Abel Corbin, J H Hitchcock, George A Swain, Merritt Griffin, Gardner Corey, Ira Scott, R R Tierce, H Holbrook "

Of the nineteen persons who signed the above call, only six are now living Of that number three are now residents of Glens Falls — M L Wilmarth, D G Roberts, and Abel Corbin　The other survivors are located as follows: Charles Carpenter, at Newark, N J; George Tillotson (brother of John Tillotson, of this village) at Muskegan, Mich, and L C Hamilton, at Argyle, Washington county

On the 19th of May, 1842, a village meeting was called for the purpose of raising funds to buy an engine, or engines, and buckets　On the 26th of the same month the sum of $350 was voted, and each house owner requested to furnish two good buckets for use at fires　Dwight Hotchkiss was appointed a committee to secure the purchase of an engine　On the 26th of August, 1842, a resolution was adopted to buy an engine of Button & Co, of Waterford, at $300, and two joints of hose at seventy cents a foot, that a fire company be formed with an initial membership of twenty, and the power of increasing the number to thirty-two, on the approval of the village trustees　The resolution further provided that the proposed company should convene for practice at least once a month for seven months in each year

The First Fire Company was organized June 27th, 1842, and was called " Glen's Falls Fire Company, No 1 "　The following are the names of the original members　William Briggs, Lewis Steele, Henry E Fickett, L C Hamilton, M C Wilmarth, D G Roberts, E Fitch, Abel Corbin, George A Swain, Merritt Griffin, Ira Scott, H Holbrook, Enos C Crosby, David Redington, Reuben Pike, Charles Carpenter, George J Tillotson, Hiram Roberts, J R. Taylor, J H Hitchcock, H M Cool, Gardner Long, R R Tearse, Henry Spencer　The following were elected as the first officers of the company Foreman, William Briggs, first assistant, Lewis S Steele ; second assistant, D G Roberts, engineer, E C Crosby, first hoseman, L C. Hamilton ; second hoseman, C Carpenter, third hoseman, J H Hitchcock, axmen, D Redington, A Corbin

The following persons were shortly afterwards added to the list of original members: K P Cool, George G Hawley, D V Brown, L L Arms, H R Wing, O Ferriss, Jerome Lapham, C M Gilchrist, Rufus Boyd, J H T Norris, Isaac Buswell, Alexander Robertson, Benjamin C Starbuck, Frederick A. Johnson, jr, Daniel Peck, B F Lapham, George Norton, W W Weed, D M Jenkins, A N Locke, S P Jackman, O L Baldwin, Herman Goodman, Isaac Crandell, John H Austin, David Norton, Joseph Mead, Jacob Daggett, A M H Pierson, M B Little, W H Norris, Levi Lord, Eugene E Norris, Zabina Ellis, J H Martin, Daniel H Cowles, Henry Gaygei, John M Clements, Albert T Harris, William Doty, Albert Hall, A Welch, G T Lewis, William T Norris, A F Smith, Gideon T Mead, Marcus C Rich, Marvin J Seymour, O B Smith, J C Eastwood, Henry Knox, Martin Eastwood, L M Burpee, Charles Loveless, George Willard, Legrand Spooner, Ed Brown, Daniel G Norris, 2d, M W Arnold, M L Buswell, Sanford Martindale, Joseph Darby, A L Stoddard, Orville Adams, James Johnson, A Spooner, C H White, H D Spicer, W M Fish, William A Wait, T S Wait, T S De Long, Oscar S Kenworthy, Frank James, H Holcomb, Edward Joubert, Levi J Groom, James Bullard

The First Engine came from Salem, N Y, June 29th, 1842, but not working satisfactorily it was rejected by the trustees of the village   July 25th an engine arrived from Button's Works, Waterford at a cost of $400, and working to the entire satisfaction of all, was accepted and placed on duty   It was a small, insignificant looking affair, had brakes on the ends, the water being supplied with buckets, but did good service on many occasions

In a few years this machine was thrown aside and the engine afterwards in possession of " Jerome Lapham No 3 " was received from Button & Son, Waterford   The first engine, after remaining in obscurity for several years, was again brought out, and a company of boys formed to run with it, under the name of " Young America No 3," and the old machine used more for a plaything than for actual service   In speaking of this engine the Glens Falls *Republican* says in connection with a notice of a fire at Luzerne, December 31st, 1873 —

" While the fire was in progress we learn that inquiries were made for the fire engine once owned by the village   Investigation revealed the fact that the pumping power of the engine had been taken out and used by a citizen to force water to his residence, two of the wheels did duty for a while on a cannon carriage, and the cannon having burst one day, the disabled gun, wheels and all, was dumped over the falls, the other two wheels served as running gear for a cart, but the fate of the box, brakes, ropes, hose-cart, hose nozzles and other appurtenances and attachments of the defunct machine is enveloped in painful mystery

" This engine once belonged to the fire department of this village, and was the first machine used for ' Old Defiance Engine Company No 1 ' Some fourteen years ago it was sold to Luzerne for $125, and the citizens of that place repaired their prize, formed a company, built an engine house, and for nearly four years kept the ' department ' in good working condition Then one or two leading members of the force moved away, the owner of the land upon which stood the engine house concluded he would use the building for his individual benefit, and so turned the old engine out of doors, where its venerable frame stood exposed to the blistering summer sun and the chilling blasts and frosts of winter until the disintegration above recorded occurred — and then came the end "

The records show that on the 28th of May, 1845, a hook and ladder company was formed, to contain not more than thirty members, and to assemble once a month for practice, etc The members were Orange Ferriss, James C Clark, L G McDonald, D McNeil, B F Shattuck, L B Palmeter, W Geer, jr , John C Higby, L L Armes, Thomas J Strong, E S Vaughn, Charles Rockwell, M W Perine, Abijah Western, Henry Spencer, jr , Marvin R Peck, William Rogers, George Champlain, O Cronkhite, H M Cool, D C Hoyt, William R Locke, Sidney T Rogers, A C Geer

Although the first above described company was the first organized effort of the village authorities, *ex-officio*, to incorporate a fire department, the resolutions set forth were in direct response to a movement set on foot by private citizens as such, in the preceding June

The Second No 1 had side brakes, could work about twenty-six men, and threw two streams For several years this was the only machine in the village and was considered a sacred property.

The writer is permitted to make extracts from a speech delivered by Mr M L Wilmarth, at a firemen's supper on New Year's eve, 1861, in which many of the following facts occur —

The first engine house was a barn (to use a Dutchman's expression) then owned by Mr Lewis Pixley, Bridge street, on the site now occupied by Leavens's livery The second was likewise a barn, on the premises of Mrs D V Brown, Elm street The third was built expressly for an engine house, and was located on Warren street, and now used by George Champlain as a boot and shoe store This building being entirely too small, the company was again called upon to change its quarters to Exchange street, and from thence to Church street, where the great fire of 1864 found it, and did not leave it. The first uniform consisted of a painted coat and patent leather cape hanging down over the neck and shoulders, and was one of the most contemptible things of the kind ever invented by mortal man for a fireman's rig

By the great fire of 1864, which laid the greater part of the village in ashes, the old engine quarters were destroyed For a year afterwards meetings were held here and there, and the engines were placed in horse-sheds and store-houses   In 1865 the engine-house on Ridge street was erected

The first foreman was that estimable citizen, William Briggs, who served us four years, second, D G Roberts, one year, third, Hiram Roberts, one year, fourth, Lewis C Hamilton, one year, fifth, G T Lewis, two years, sixth, Lyman Gates, one year, seventh, William T Morriss, three years, eighth, M J Seymour, one year, ninth, Daniel Peck, one year, tenth, B F Lapham, two years, eleventh, M B Little, one year, twelfth, the present incumbent, Mr J H Norriss

The Third No 1 — Finally, in 1862, the new "Defiance" was received from Waterford and cost $1350   Built for a prize engine, it received the well-merited encomiums bestowed upon it   At a fireman's muster at Whitehall, August 20th, 1873, this company received the first prize of $200   This company was badly crippled by the enlistment of its members in the army in 1861   Moreover, the company was located in 1865 in a remote part of the village, which had the effect of diminishing its numbers   A majority of the members of this company met November 13th, 1874, and reorganized under the name of —

J L Cunningham, Hose Company No 1 — The officers of this company were as follows —Foreman, John H Leonard, first assistant, Ed F Clark, second assistant, Joseph W Suprennant, secretary, E T Spencer, treasurer, Aaron F Pike, first pipeman, Ransom S More, second pipeman, Hiram W Norris, third pipeman, Fred E Knox, fourth pipeman, Herbert W Austin; first hydrantman, Charles L Taft, second hydrantman, James W Schermerhorn, propertymen, Enos Traver, Albert Trew

A new hose carriage for this company was built by Button & Son, of Waterford, N Y, at a cost of $700   It was received January 20th, 1874

The company's meeting room in the South street engine house has been newly papered and painted   It is prepared to purchase new furniture and a carpet some time during the coming winter   The organization now numbers twenty-six members   John Suprennant is foreman, J T Sprague, first assistant, John Leonard, secretary and treasurer

Cataract Engine Company No 2 was organized October 1st, 1852, with William Briggs as foreman and L C Hamilton as first assistant   "Cataract" was sold to parties in Whitehall in 1873   A couple of months later this company received "old Defiance" engine from Company No 1, and subsequently the name was changed to M B Little Company No 2   John Feeney was the first foreman after this change of name, and John Morris was first assistant   In the early part of 1873 M B Little Hose Company was organized   Andrew Robillard is the present foreman of the Engine Company, and Daniel McCarthy holds a similar office in the Hose Company

Jerome Lapham, Engine Company No 3 was organized September 13th,

1865, with Henry Wicks as foreman and Charles Roberts as first assistant After the introduction of the water works in 1873, this company disbanded and organized as a hose company with the same name   S B Whitney was the first foreman and William H Van Cott first assistant

In April, 1875, the *James McDonald Jr Hook and Ladder Company* was organized   B S Cowles was the first foreman , first and second assistants, Fred Chitty and T S Barnes, respectively, secretary, Frank G Hicks , treasurer, C W Cool   On the 6th of January, 1881, the name of the organization was changed to D J Finch Hook and Ladder Company No 1, at which time W F Bentley was chosen foreman, and William Manley, assistant   The company disbanded on the 20th of April, 1882, and reorganized forthwith with W F Bentley, as foreman , Erving Simmons and Charles Clements as first and second assistants, respectively   The " Hook's " truck and ladders are stored in the South street engine house

In 1879 a brick hose tower was erected in the rear of the brick engine house, which constitutes a valuable addition to the appliances of the department   Measures are in the initial stage of prosecution to procure for the use of the department a new chemical, new grenades, etc , and looking toward the completion of and embellishment of all the contrivances of the department, especially for the extinguishment of fires in the beginning of their progress

Following is a list of the chief engineers of the department since its organization, effected in 1872   William McEchron, for one year ending 1873, D C Holman, Henry Nesbitt, George Conery, M B Little, George Conery, S D Kendrick, George Cokey, and the present chief, W H Van Cott   The present officers of the several companies are as follows . —

Hook and Ladder : Foreman, Charles H Clark , first assistant, C E Perry , second assistant, Beecher West , secretary, Charles J Clements ; treasurer, John E Parry

Lapham Hose   Foreman, W H Van Cott , first assistant, George Roberts , second assistant, James Knight , secretary and treasurer, John Wandell

Cunningham Hose   Foreman, William O Capron , assistant, William B Stevens , secretary, George H Orton , treasurer, George Thomas

M B Little Engine · Foreman, Lewis Robillard , first assistant, Michael Murphy, second assistant, Patrick Cronin , secretary, William Roach , jr , treasurer, Louis Vancelette , foreman hose, James Moran , assistant, Daniel Mulcahy

In 1861 M L Wilmarth delivered an address (from which we have drawn liberally), in which he gave the following statement of the capital invested in the fire department at that date : —

" In engine house, $1,800 , in engine Defiance No 1, $900 , in engine Cataract No 2, $1,200 , in Hook and Ladder Company No. 1, $150 , in 1,100 feet leading hose, $1,000 , cistern in front Presbyterian Church, $250 ; in three large wells, $400, in five small wells, $200, in articles not enumerated, $100, making the sum total of $6,000 — a sum sufficient to purchase and stock a small farm."

A comparison of the capital invested with the value represented by the department property to-day would dwarf the figures in the above extract into insignificance   The water-works alone, although utilized for various purposes now, were built with a view to subdue the fiery element, and cost about $90,-000   A computation of the amount of water which can be thrown on a burning building in a certain time to-day would show an equally ludicrous disparity between what could be done in 1861 and in 1882

The fire wardens of 1861 were superseded by the chief engineer and assistants in 1874, when the new village charter was adopted   William McEchron was chosen first chief of the department

Water-Works — According to the natural precepts of municipal economy, the water supply of a village or city is always intimately associated, not only with the daily duties of the housewife, but with the sterner and more imperative demands, in emergencies, of the fire department   Glens Falls is not exempt from the action of this law   Through apprehension of possible conflagrations it was that the water-works were ever constructed, and through the action of the same motive power have the continual improvements been superadded until the system has attained almost its maximum approximation to perfection   The primitive water-works, of course, consisted of a village well, just as the primitive fire department consisted of the men and women of the entire village, armed with buckets and home-made ladders

The first indication discovered of a movement for the building up of a water supply system, is the publication of an item in the *Glens Falls Messenger and Advertiser* of the 16th of January, 1835, which read as follows: —

" A meeting of the subscribers for making a ' Village Well' is requested at Rogers & Brown's Hotel this evening, to choose a committee to superintend its construction "

On the 11th of June, 1839, at the second meeting of the first trustees of the village subsequent to its assumption of corporate privileges, it was resolved to construct one public well in front of the Glens Falls Hotel, where the public fountain now stands, and one near Allen's tavern   Furthermore, a meeting of the taxpayers was held at the former hotel, on July 20th, when an appropriation of $200 was voted for the purpose   From this time until 1860 the village authorities increased by annual resolutions, etc , the water supply of the place, and prosecuted the construction of cisterns, wells and culverts with aldermanic iteration   In 1861 there had been invested in a cistern "in front of the Presbyterian Church, $250, in three large wells, $400, and in five small wells, $200 "   In 1864 the trustees were empowered to proceed under the act of the Legislature, passed in 1863, to take steps toward procuring pure water and to petition the Legislature for an increase of the sum devoted to the construction of water-works from $30,000 to $60,000 In the following year a surveyor was appointed to ascertain the practicability of obtaining water from Half-way Brook, and $300 voted to make a similar investigation relating to Forge Pond These ever renewed investigations indicate the state of the public feeling in the matter for years before the consummation of their projects was achieved In January, 1866, it was voted to build nine cisterns and a reservoir in the rear of Cronkhite's store, at a cost of $2,985 00 The cisterns and the Forge Pond water-works were thereupon immediately constructed But the system was not yet satisfactory During all these years the village had been rapidly growing in population, in the number and beauties of its buildings, and in the extent and wealth of its business enterprises and public institutions Meanwhile, while the number of inhabitants was continually on the increase, the danger from fire, the need of water for domestic purposes, and consequently the demand for a modern and improved water supply system, were increased and multiplied The call was too imperative to be resisted In 1871 H M Harris was appointed a committee to investigate the Holly Water-Works system, of Peoria, Ill , another committee visited Greenfield, Mass , on a like errand, the conclusion from these and other reports being that a supply of water two hundred and fifty feet above Glens Falls, with pipes of proportionate size, would afford ample protection against fire

The Glens Falls Water-Works Company was incorporated by legislative sanction May 10th, 1871, with a capital of $100,000 The first members of the company were as follows . Augustus Sherman, Enoch H Rosekrans, William H Rockwell, Daniel H Cowles, L G McDonald, Thomas S Coolidge, Ruliff Kipp, James Morgan, Charles M Gilchrist, Stephen Brown, Daniel Peck, F A Johnson, jr , Stephen L Goodman, George Conery, Joseph Fowler, and Martin Coffin The first meeting of this corporation was held in July following Action was delayed ten days after the beginning of that month to enable the citizens to organize a company, and subscriptions to the stock were obtained to the amount of $21,500 John Salter was employed as engineer at a stipulated salary of $400 a month for all help, etc In October, however, he was superseded by J P Coleman In November Messrs Keenan and Lapham were appointed to purchase land, water courses and rights. The work progressed without interruption, and in 1872 rules for the government of the company and the conducting of the works were adopted At the present time the village is bountifully supplied with pure water, an ample system of mains and hydrants, and a thoroughly efficient organization

Police — At the time of the re-incorporation of the village (1874) it was divided into three police districts Number one embraced all that portion west of Glen street , number two, all of Glen street above Park, Ridge street from Glen, and all between Ridge and Glen streets , number three, all east of Glen

and Ridge streets   On the 15th of June, 1874, a special election was ordered
held on the 29th, to vote upon the question of raising the sum of $1,800 to pay
a police force   The vote was in the negative , and in the report of the board of
trustees for that year it is stated that " soon after your board assumed its duties,
a police force was organized and maintained until the money ran out "   Upon
the decision of the special election, police duty was ordered stopped and the
equipments returned to the clerk   Another meeting was held on the 13th of
July, at which a resolution was passed that $500 be raised for police purposes
This appears to have been a temporary arrangement on the part of the trustees   At the election of March 16th, 1875, it was voted that the sum of $2,200
be raised for police purposes   An effective force has been maintained ever
since and now comprises four officers

French Mountain — This hamlet could hardly be dignified by the title of
community prior to 1825   At that time there was but one tavern there, kept
by Udney Buck   There were no stores   There were no factories of any kind
There was no post-office, and there were only two dwelling houses   Of these
two, one was occupied by John Devine, and the other by a Mr Pulver   Valentine Brown, grandfather of George Brown, was the eldest of the five sons of
Benedick Brown   They located between Glens Falls and French Mountain
Valentine Brown built the first saw-mill in the county north of Glens Falls
They were Quakers   There are not now many descendants of Benedick
Brown in the county, though they were formerly so numerous as to furnish the
name Browntown to a settlement between the outlet of Glen Lake and the village of Glens Falls   Another early settler hereabouts was one Eggleston, who
lived before 1800 within a mile west of the site of French Mountain on the
farm now occupied by James Hillis   Eggleston built a frame-house of very
singular construction, having a chimney in the center built of 199 loads of
stone, and containing a fire-place for each of the four rooms on every floor of
the house   This house was torn down about 1855   Simeon Jenkins, another
early settler, came before 1810 to a farm east of French Mountain   He has
many descendants in town at the present day   Jacob Odell settled in the first
decade of the century on a place just east of French Mountain   Descendants
of his are also living in town   Indeed, his grandson, Jacob Odell, now lives
on the old homestead

The tavern kept by Udney Buck came into the possession of David Vaughn
about 1831   George Brown succeeded Vaughn in 1846, and remained a famous landlord until 1884, when, on his removal to Caldwell, Louis Brown (no
relation), the present proprietor, became his successor   The hotel formerly,
in the days of stages and tally-hos, did a great deal of business   The old
building was torn down about the time the new plank road was built and the
present one erected in its place   For seven years the County Fair Association
held their meetings at this place   (See biography of George Brown herein)

All but three of the houses now standing in the village of French Mountain were erected by George Brown He built in 1857 the store now occupied by Merritt Codner, and kept it himself until 1884 He had a tin shop in the upper part of this building all the time he kept the store, and in connection with his dealing in general wares and merchandise kept a hardware and iron store in connection with it His son Valentine Brown did a considerable business in the manufacture and sale of gloves in that building, too The tannery of Pearsall, Little & Hall was erected by Brown in 1877 This company purchased it of him in 1882. There was a saw-mill run in connection with it This firm now owns all the hotel and factory property formerly held by George Brown The brush-back factory was started in 1882 by Charles Steinburgh, who used the building for the manufacture of spools He was followed by Olef Abel, who was in turn succeeded in the summer of 1882 by the Messrs Reed They immediately converted the establishment into a brush-back factory.

The post-office was established here in 1852, when George Brown received the appointment as postmaster He held the position until the winter of 1882, when he was succeeded by the present postmaster, John N Hall

CHURCHES

The early religious influences of the town having been referred to in previous pages of this work, it will only be necessary at this point to give the continuous records of the various church organizations For these we are again indebted largely to Dr. Holden's *History of Queensbury*, supplemented by statistics of the different religious societies since the production of his work

The Orthodox Friends — The society of Orthodox Friends is said to have organized and erected the first church building in the town, some time previous to the beginning of the present century, to which allusion has already been made The primitive meeting-house was of logs and located on Bay Road near Half-way Brook, about one and a half miles north of the present village After a series of years the log meeting house was abandoned and a large frame building was put up on Ridge street, about two miles north of the village In this they conducted worship until 1875, when the present brick church was built at an expense of about $1,300

The church is governed by thirteen elders who serve one year. No regular pastor was established until about 1879, when John Henry Douglass began his ministry, which continued for two years, when David Douglass succeeded him, remaining in charge for two or three years In November of 1884, Luke Woodard entered upon the pastorate, and at present, with Nelson Hill, conducts the regular meetings The duties of sexton have been performed since about 1877 by S I Stone Among the present trustees are P T Haviland, Harris G Haviland, Charles Eddy and C R Mott Conspicuous among the early members of this society was Roger Haviland, who came from Durham county Of a large family none of the sons are residents here, although there are other branches of the family in the town Hannah Haviland, who is about eighty-five years of age, resides with her daughter, Mrs Calvin Mason, on Ridge street The Dean family, consisting of Caleb, Isaiah and several other brothers were also pioneers in this faith Miss Hannah Moser, also, who is living at the age of ninety-five, has always resided here Her home is in Ridge street near Half-way Brook Jonathan Potter was born in Granville, Washington county, in 1814, and married to Mary Ann Haviland, a native of Queensbury, in 1842 In 1856 he moved into the town and became a resident These are mentioned merely as having been prominent in the councils of this church society

The Baptist Church — Quoting from Dr Holden, we find that the Baptists " were among the earlier inhabitants of this town and have always formed a considerable element of its population It has been impossible to obtain all the facts requisite to a complete record of their several organizations In some instances the minutes have been destroyed by fire, in others, they have been removed beyond reach, or lost through carelessness and indifference, while, with one or two exceptions, those who could have furnished reliable information concerning the annals of this denomination, are now numbered with the dead So far as can be ascertained, the Baptists of Queensbury are, and have been of that class, distinguished as regular, or close communion Baptists By diligent and patient research, and investigation, we are enabled to present the following historic record concerning them Until the year 1795, it is believed that no effort had been made to organize a church within the limits of this town

" On the south side of the river, which was then embraced in the town of Saratoga, a society had been formed on the 19th of August, 1794, over which, according to existing records, Elder Calvin Hulbert presided as pastor for a number of years Among its members were some residing at what is known as the Big Bend of the Hudson River, four miles west of the village of Glens Falls, and it is quite possible that some of the number were residents on the Queensbury side of the river At the eastward a number of Baptist families were among the earliest settlers, by whom a society was organized at Kingsbury street in 1797, with Elder Ebenezer Willoughby as pastor This was connected with the Vermont Baptist Association, formed at Manchester, Vt, 1780, and which met at Middletown, Vt, October 4th, 1797, as shown by existing printed minutes At the northeast, in the town of Westfield, a church had been built up as early as 1789, under the pastoral care of Elder Sherman Babcock This is now designated as the First Baptist Church of Fort Anne; its place of meeting being at Comstock's Landing Being thus surrounded on three sides, as it were, by Baptist influences, it is nothing surprising that the town of Queensbury should have had a plentiful leaven of that element among its inhabitants at an early day.

"From this small beginning, an outgrowth of four distinct churches has been developed in process of time, each of which have had a separate house of worship, in three distinct localities, at distances of five or six miles apart For convenience of reference these might be classified as follows, viz .—

"1st, The Baptist Church of the Round Pond

"2d, The First Queensbury, or Oneida Church

"3d, The Second Queensbury, or West Mountain Church

"4th, The Baptist Church of Glens Falls "

The Baptist Church of the Round Pond. — This church was one of the first fruits of the faith in this section, and had an entirely independent existence, having no connection during its organization with any association It was located on the south edge of the Round Pond, in a pine grove, about five miles distant from Glens Falls in a northerly direction The structure was of logs, and during the week did duty as a school-house, on Sundays the worshipers meeting there for divine service It was founded by Elder Rufus Bates, a native of Coventry, R I, where he was born in April, 1753 He established the church and began his labors about 1794, in 1795 the church was built In the latter year Elder Hezekiah Eastman, of Danby, Vt, made a tour doing missionary work, and visited Round Pond, performing the rites of baptism while there upon several candidates In 1796, the church society was formally organized, Elders Amasa Brown, of Hartford, and Sylvanus Haynes, of Middletown, Vt, officiating in the ordination services This church was known as "Elder Bates's Church," and during his ministry of thirty-four years he was a daily laborer for his bread, his yearly salary never exceeding, and rarely reaching the sum of $100 In the early years of his ministry his parish embraced Harrisena, West Fort Anne, Bolton, Caldwell and Durkeetown, the total membership of which counted but a few over two hundred persons In June, 1808, his house was burned and his aged father-in-law, Abner Goffe, perished In this conflagration whatever records of the church had been kept were consumed In 1828, at the age of seventy-five, Elder Bates retired from active ministerial duties, and passed his remaining years among his people, dying at the opening of the 1840 aged eighty-six After his death, the church over which he had so long presided was bereft of its counsellor and head, and began to scatter, so that in a few years it ceased its existence

From 1802 until 1816 the Baptists of Durkeetown were considered as members of the Queensbury Church, transacting church affairs within themselves as an auxiliary, Elder Bates preaching for them occasionally, as also did Elder Clark In 1832 they organized themselves as a church, being the first Fort Edward church

The First Queensbury or Oneida Church — " The interest which built up this congregation originated in a series of meetings held at Dunham's Bay, in the years 1831 and 1832 These were instituted by Elder Phineas Culver, for a long period pastor of the Fort Anne and Kingsbury Churches, who, on a visit to his brother-in-law, William Lane, found a few faithful brethren living around the head waters of Lake George A revival ensued, several were added to the church, and after a period the meetings were removed to the Vaughn school-house, not far from the present residence of Reuben Seelye, esq The meetings were continued here, and in various adjacent school-houses, until the house of worship at the Oneida was erected The church organization is here given from their own record book in the following language

" ' Be it remembered that on this 13th day of November, 1832, the following brethren and sisters met according to previous appointment, and entered into Church Covenant with each other, at the house of William Lane, in Queensbury, viz James Fuller, Franklin Guilford, Aaron Kidder, Isaac Nelson, A M Odell, Eli Pettis, Betsey Fuller, Samantha Guilford, Amanda Kidder, Amy Nelson, Marian Odell, Lucy Pettis, William Niles '

" It is further recorded that they " adopted, as a brief summary of their faith, the articles of faith and covenant of the Kingsbury Church, while they received the New Testament in common with the Old, as their only rule of faith and practice Elders William Grant and Phineas Culver being present, assisted in the organization, giving them fellowship and hearty approbation, and Elder Culver preached the constituting sermon

" Austin M Odell was chosen clerk and Aaron Kidder their first deacon, who, with Ansel Winchip, was formally ordained on the 20th of February, 1834 Having no regular pastor nor house of worship for years, the organization increased but slowly In September, 1833, they united with the Lake George Baptist Asociation, which at that time held its 17th anniversary at Hague, Warren county, N Y The association then reported eleven churches, seven pastors, and 988 members in their whole body While this new interest, of nineteen members only, was not identical in organization with Elder Bates's church, it was its successor on nearly the same territory, and among many of the same people No doubt some of his flock came into the new church, since it is recorded that Elder Bates and his wife joined by letters from the second Fort Anne church, at Welch Hollow at South Bay, on the 9th of August, 1834 Although an octogenarian he was chosen a delegate to the association which met that year at Caldwell His associates were A M Odell, Ansel Winchip, William Niles, and F Guilford

" The necessities of the people had called for Baptist preaching about this period, and various ministers had come into town, preached and baptized their converts, thereby adding them to their respective churches in adjacent towns Among this number Elder John C. Holt, of Moreau, had officiated here, and in a powerful revival of religion during the years 1832–33, he added about eighty to his church, a large proportion of whom lived in this town, and afterwards helped to swell the ranks of its rising churches   On the west, Elder Stephen Call, pastor of the Luzerne Church, made frequent inroads, and baptized converts into his church, who subsequently aided in establishing the West or Mountain Church   During the first four years there were comparatively few accessions to the church at the Oneida

" In the fall of 1835 there was reported a membership of thirty-five, with Elder John Scofield as pastor, who served in that capacity until the spring of 1837   During his pastorate the house of worship near the Oneida was erected, and although the humble edifice was not entirely finished, the Lake George Association held its twentieth anniversary there on the 7th and 8th of September, 1836   The venerable Elder Bates, then eighty-four years of age, with Elder Scofield, Deacon Ansel Winchip, J Winchip, and E Sargeant, were the delegates on that occasion   The meeting was one of unusual interest, and was followed by a revival in which twenty-five converts were added and eighteen members joined by letter, thus increasing the membership to seventy-four. Elder Jeremy H Dwyer assisted the pastor during the season of revival

" In the spring of 1838, Marvin Eastwood, who had been reared in the west part of the town, and licensed to preach by the Mountain Church, began to labor with this congregation, and on the 11th of September following was ordained to the ministry   A revival soon followed and by the ensuing spring fifty-five converts had been added to the church, which, with those who joined by letter, swelled the membership to 127   During this pastorate the church was increased to its maximum number of 140 members   Elder Eastwood removed to Waterford in 1841 and was succeeded by Elder Simon Fletcher who had charge of the church for one year   Elder John Duncan, who had been pastor of the church at Kingsbury street, served the church another year

" The next in order in charge of this church was Elder O H Capron, from Galway, N Y, who remained three years, during which period an interesting revival season was held, in which about twenty-five were added to the church. Its total membership at this time was reported at 131   He left in 1846, and subsequently returned for another term of labor in 1851–52, with small results in the way of church growth."

In 1853 he removed to Hebron, Washington county, and Elder John H Barker became pastor to the church, remaining in charge two years   During the interval between the years 1846 and 1851, Elder Ira Bentley officiated for about two years, dating from 1859   Since 1853 no regular pastor has been settled over the church, although from 1858 until about 1861, occasional services were held, which were conducted by Elders C R Green and Ransom O. Dyer   During the years between 1833 and 1839, it was a connection of the Lake George Baptist Association , after that date it became a part of the Washington Union

The Second Queensbury, or West Mountain Church — " In the southwestern part of the town, in the earlier days, were a small number of Baptists who were probably connected with the Moreau Church for a while These were afterwards united to the Luzerne church over the mountain, which, from 1813 to 1827, was attached to the Saratoga Association Since that period the progress and history of this interest can be traced by the aid of the minutes of the Washington and Washington Union Baptist Association, with which it has been connected In June, 1827, at the first anniversary of the association above named, the Luzerne church was represented by Elder Stephen Call and Allen Seymour, who reported 108 members in the fellowship The next year it was designated as the Baptist Church of Luzerne and Queensbury, and Elder Call, D Fairchild, and Henry Moses were the delegates How many of this church were residents of Queensbury, there are no present means of determining Elder Call continued his pastorate as late as the year 1837 When the Washington Union Association was formed at Hartford, N Y, in June, 1835, by the consolidation of the Washington and Bottskill bodies, this church went into the new organization, reporting at that time thirty-four baptisms and a total of one hundred and twenty-seven members

"The digest of the state of the churches for 1836 says of this church 'They are inconveniently situated, being separated by a rugged mountain, in consequence of which the members on either side have but little intercourse, and they think of becoming two separate churches' In 1838 the Luzerne Church was present with returns of only forty-nine members, and Deacon Moses Randall, who had been recently licensed, as their preacher The Second Queensbury was represented in the association the same year by Elder Charles Williams, Deacon David Barber, Lewis Wood, Henry Moses and David Williams They reported no aggregate membership, but we find the following in the digest of that year 'The Second Baptist Church in Queensbury has been constituted since our last session, have enjoyed a powerful revival of religion, and have received an addition of forty or fifty by baptism Have a Sabbath-school and bible-class, and are in union Elder J H Dwyer preaches to them one-fourth part of the time' With those set off from Luzerne they must have numbered about eighty members The germ of this new church was called Elder Williams's Conference, and Elder A Wait, of Fort Edward, Norman Fox, residing at Glens Falls, and supplying the Kingsbury church, and John Scofield of the Oneida, preached and baptized here occasionally Elder Williams was reported as pastor from 1838 to 1841, during which period the meeting-house at the foot of the mountain was erected and dedicated "[1]

The site was given by Abraham Van Duzen and the house was built by contributions from David Burnham and son and other Baptist friends After

[1] HOLDEN'S *History of Queensbury*

Missing Page

Missing Page

who established *The Messenger* and also published a Baptist periodical during the time   In August, 1858, Elder Daniel T Hill, of Carmel, N Y, became pastor and remained with the church one year, when he became interested in the South Glens Falls Church, across the river, and aided in the erection of a house of worship, which was built about 1861   From autumn 1859 to 1860, Elder L H Purington, of Rensselaerville, filled the pulpit, but ill-health obliged him to resign the charge and he removed from the place   In October of 1860 the pulpit was supplied by D C Hughes, who was ordained in November, and remained with the church for two years and a half, in addition acting as pastor to the church at Sandy Hill   In September, 1863, Elder C ·A Skinner took charge of the fold, remaining with them one year, during which time twenty-seven were baptized by him   He afterwards removed to Massachusetts   In October, 1864, Elder James M Ferriss, of Preston Hollow, N Y, began the pastorate of the church, remaining four years, in which time the church membership increased until it numbered two hundred and eighty-four   In 1866 the church building was repaired and furnished with cushions carpets and gas fixtures   The thirty-second anniversary was held in the church in June, 1866   Elder Ferriss resigned in October, 1868, and in November following, Elder Charles H Nash was engaged to supply the pulpit until spring, when he was settled as pastor, remaining until 1879   During his ministrations, a debt of $1,400 on the church was removed   In 1879 Elder H B Warring became the pastor, remaining until 1883, when the present pastor, Elder George B Gow, entered upon the duties of the ministry of this church   In the spring of 1885 the church was rebuilt on the site of the old edifice, at a cost of about $25,000.   The present membership is three hundred and thirty-four   The church officers are R J Winchip and Noah Washburn, deacons, Benjamin S Cowles, jr, church clerk; Simeon T Barber, treasurer, and Charles B Ide, Sunday-school superintendent

The Presbyterian Church — On the 1st day of October, 1876, the Rev A J Fennel, the revered pastor of the Presbyterian Church of Glens Falls, preached a sermon embodying a history of the church, it being the thirtieth anniversary of his pastorate   From that sermon we have condensed the following sketch —

We come now to the time when the Presbyterian element, which had come in with new settlers, began to make itself manifest   Except the Rev. Anthony Paul — supposed to have been educated by President Wheelock, and duly licensed in Connecticut — who preached around the shores of Lake George, there had never been a Presbyterian minister resident in the county, and is presumed that there had never been heard, except from this Christian Indian, but few Presbyterian sermons   The Methodists had a flourishing society on the Ridge, which had grown out of the preaching of Lorenzo Dow, and in Johnsburgh they had a society watched over by the local preacher David Noble   Nearly forty years had passed since the settlement of the town, and as yet we had here no name   Moreau already had a Congregational Church, with two houses of worship, and was just settling a pastor, the Rev Lebbeus Armstrong   This may have somewhat interested and aroused the people here   The village occupying this spot, then called Pearl Village, had become a place of considerable trade, had a good hotel, mills on the falls, and a somewhat larger number, in proportion to the whole population, of intelligent and enterprising citizens   The movement for a house of worship seems to have been spontaneous and general, and there being as yet no church organization, it took both the form and name of a Union — and the house thus built was for many years occupied by different denominations   A subscription "to build a house of publick worship in the Town of Queensbury, County of Washington, somewhere near the Four Corners," was drawn up on the 4th of March, 1803   On the first day of June following the number of subscribers having reached thirty-eight and the aggregate amount $974, "a majority of the subscribers being met," a committee of seven[1] was appointed to collect the sums subscribed and erect the church   With this inadequate amount it could not have been expected that the house would soon be finished   It was probably soon raised and enclosed   Three years afterward, June 1st, 1800, the number of subscribers had reached eighty-one and the amount $1292 50   Afterward we find names increasing the whole number of contributors to ninety-nine   The society elected trustees[2] and effected a legal organization on the 23d day of July, 1807, under the name of the "Union Church of Pearl Village," which name was changed to "First Presbyterian Church of Glens Falls" in 1848   A year following (July 30th, 1808) the trustees made a contract with Parsons Ranger, who had been the builder thus far, and who now associated with him Lester Stebbins of Lake George, to complete the house of worship for $750   The work specified as then remaining to be done shows that the whole five years had elapsed without the building reaching a proper condition to be occupied   It was now completed according to the contract "within the space of five months," and within a few days, December 18th, 1808, a church was organized by Rev Jonas Coe, of Troy, consisting of nine members, all of whom now sleep   They were John Folsom, Solomon P Goodrich, Elizabeth Folsom, Ann Goodrich, Glorianna Folsom, Mary Folsom, John Moss, jr , Naomi Ranger, Amy Sanford   The pews in the new church were sold subject to rent, and this was probably the way by which the money was raised to pay for the finishing work

Undoubtedly before this time Presbyterian or Congregational ministers must have occasionally been here and preached — Mr Armstrong had already

---

[1] This committee consisted of Micajah Petit, William Robards, John V W Huyck, Peter Peck, John Mallory, Warren Ferriss, and John McGill

[2] The first trustees were William Robards, Daniel Peck, John Folsom, William Hay, Micajah Petit and John A Ferriss

been the pastor of the Congregational Church in Moreau for five years and at least three years before had organized the Congregational Church of Kingsbury — but with a single exception I cannot learn that any one had ever been employed here to statedly preach the Word   The Rev William Boardman was the first resident minister of the church   Commencing his labors in the spring of 1809 and closing them in the fall of 1811, he was here about two years and a half   It is not probable that he was installed   He came here from Duanesburgh, near Schenectady, where he commenced his ministry in 1803, and where he had been pastor therefore for six years   He was a native of Williamstown, Mass, and a graduate of Williams College   Yet a young man only twenty-eight years of age, scholarly, earnest, a good preacher, very genial and kindly in all social relations, there is evidence existing here yet that he was greatly beloved, and that his departure to take charge of a church in Newtown, Long Island, was much regretted   During a portion and perhaps all of the time that Mr Boardman preached here, he also supplied the church at Sandy Hill   Indeed, it was probably during the time that he was here that the two churches became consolidated, forming the "United Church of Kingsbury and Queensbury"   These two churches, harmoniously uniting in one, and dividing between them the services of one minister as they did for about twenty years, that together they might be able to support the Gospel without missionary help, afford an example to many small churches now that are near each other, which it might not be amiss for them to appreciate and practice   Mr Boardman's salary was $350 in this village, how much it was in Sandy Hill I have not learned

From the time of Mr. Boardman's leaving, September, 1811, to the coming of Mr Rodgers, in March, 1820, there were eight years and a half, during which, with a single exception, it does not seem that the church enjoyed the stated services of any minister.   This exception is in the case of Mr. Sears, who seems to have been here for at least six months, embracing the latter half of 1812.

January 8th, 1813, the trustees purchased of Henry Spencer for $25, "an acre and a quarter and one rod, as glebe for the use of the church"   This became what we now know as the "Old Burial-place"   That it was designed for such use is not learned from the deed, but from the fact that it was immediately put to this use, and the next spring, May 10th, 1813, Mr. Folsom, who was collector and treasurer of the society, was authorized to "contract with some one for fencing the burial-place"   Previous to this time the village burying-ground was on the bluff now occupied by the old stone church   Also, at the same date Mr Folsom was authorized to "purchase a bell for the church, provided he can obtain money for the purpose"   It is evident that he succeeded, for in his account as treasurer we find the items, "Cash for bell, $306," and "Cash for fetching up the bell, $3"   And the next November, 1813, Mr. J. Cunningham was employed to "ring the bell three times a day for the use of

the village, and Sabbath days for the use of the church, for $40, payable every
six months" During the next few years we only get glimpses of the church
through the records of the session and the trustees, and the account of the treasurer We find the name of Dr Coe, of Troy, as many as seven times, nearly
or quite every time he administered the ordinances of the United Church, the
name of Dr Blatchford, of Lansingburgh, of Mr Furman, Mr Clark, Mr
Tomb, of Salem, Mr Hardy (three Sabbaths), Mr Brownell, Mr Griswold,
Mr. Armstrong, of Moreau Occurring as these names do, scattered along
through this whole period, we find in this fact evidence of the weak condition
of the church, that it was not able to command stated preaching It should,
however, be recorded, as yet in the remembrance of some now living, that religious services were maintained much of this time by Mr Folsom and Mr
Goodrich — Mr Folsom preaching the Word There seems to have been much
more than ordinary interest and life in the church, especially at Sandy Hill, in
1816–17 At a communion administered by Dr Coe, November, 1816, twenty-five persons were admitted to the church, and the next March thirteen by
Mr Armstrong And as though Providence was preparing the way for a pastor, and at the same time showing that he could work and give a measure of
prosperity without one, at the beginning of the year, just before Mr Rodgers's
arrival, the session, which for almost the whole time of the church's existence
had consisted of the two original members, was increased by the addition of six
persons — John Thomas, Luther Johnson, S P Goodrich, Samuel Cranston,
Daniel Beaumont, and Edward Moss — who were ordained by Dr Coe in the
court-house at Sandy Hill, January 30th, 1820

We come now to the first regular pastorate of the church — one extending
over considerable time and having a good degree of success Ravaud K Rodgers, a grandson of one of the early and prominent ministers of New York, and
a licentiate of the Presbytery of New York, was spending the winter of 1819–20
as a missionary in the bounds of what was then the Presbyteries of Columbia
and Champlain In the course of his evangelistic work and on his way northward, he spent a couple of Sabbaths at Sandy Hill and Glens Falls The people
of the United Church were so pleased with him and his preaching, that on his
return in March he was invited to remain for a year as stated supply, in the
hope that by that time they might be in a situation to give him a call for a
permanent settlement His acceptance of this invitation, and how the hope of
the church was realized, may be easily inferred from the following minute on
the fly-leaf of the church register, in Mr Rodgers's own fine handwriting "On
Wednesday, the 14th day of March, 1821, Ravaud K Rodgers was ordained
to the gospel ministry, and installed pastor of the United Church of Kingsbury
and Queensbury On this occasion a sermon was delivered by the Rev Jonas
Coe, D D, of Troy, from II Timothy, 4 1, 2 The Rev Samuel Tomb, of
Salem, presided and made the consecrating prayer The Rev Nathaniel S

Prime, of Cambridge, gave the charge to the pastor; and the Rev Ethan Smith, of Hebron, addressed the people " Mr Rodgers's farewell sermon to the congregation at Glens Falls, was on the eighth anniversary of his settlement, March 14th, 1829, although the dissolution of the pastoral relation did not take place till the 28th of April following, at Pittstown His entire ministry to the church, therefore, it will be seen extended through nine years The United Church, on petition of the members, had already been divided by the Presbytery into two distinct churches, August 27th, 1827, to be known as " The Presbyterian Church of Sandy Hill," and " The Presbyterian Church of Glens Falls " Mr Rodgers continued pastor of the church at Sandy Hill till February, 1830, nearly another year During the nine years of this ministry to both congregations there were received to the church on profession of faith one hundred and ninety-two persons, only about three-eighths (seventy-three) of them however belonged to the branch of Glens Falls. During the year 1824 there was a very deep religious interest in both places It is no doubt to the communion on the 14th of March, of this year, that the doctor refers in his *Fifty Years in the Ministry*, where he says: "We had some seasons of delightful refreshing from the Lord I can never forget one of commanding interest, when nearly one hundred persons came out from the world and took the vows of God upon them " Nine years ago, in my *Historical Sketch*, the first discourse delivered in this house, I took occasion to refer to the great amount of discipline which was administered in 1828 It astonished me that a session should have occasion for so much of that unpleasant duty I have now re-read with some care the records of the session for the last five of the nine years of which I am now speaking, and with special reference to this subject I find that in these five years thirty-two were under discipline, several of them more than once No doubt so many coming into the church at one time, borne upon a current of enthusiasm which must soon somewhat abate, and many of them not having been well instructed in religious truth and duty under an established ministry, which they had not then long enjoyed, may in a measure account for not a few of the errors into which they fell — many of the charges against them seem to have been errors in regard to duty rather than immoralities of life And it is not impossible that the session, nearly all of whom, including the pastor, were without experience, may have entertained such views of their proper work and office that they were led to a minuteness of supervision and watchcare over the membership, too nearly like that required by the church in her childhood under the old dispensation, and not exactly in accordance with the manhood and liberty contemplated under the Gospel Although this pastorate is remembered now by the few of the aged members yet remaining with a great deal of satisfaction, and on the whole was certainly a wise and successful one, it is nevertheless too plain that at its close the church was far from being happy or harmonious The membership in this village when Mr Rodgers came could not have been much over thirty, when he left it was about ninety.

The next three years and a half, till the coming of Mr Newton, in September, 1832, while we find the names of quite a number of clergymen on the sessional records, mentioned simply as moderators, there were but two who supplied the church for any considerable time — these were Edwin Hall and Caleb B Tracy Each of these gentlemen preached here about six months — Mr Hall beginning in August, 1830, and Mr Tracy the latter part of 1831 The church, which had become almost dilapidated, was undergoing repairs when Mr Hall arrived; so he was obliged to preach for a time in the session house. The repairs, including a new bell in the place of the old one, which had been cracked, were completed on the 1st of December, and a protracted meeting of considerable interest immediately followed Mr Hall, a native I believe of Granville, in Washington county, supplied also, during the time that he was here, the church in Sandy Hill, preached occasionally at Fort Edward, and acted as a general missionary throughout Warren county

A call was made out for Ephraim H Newton on the 3d day of September, 1832 His service commenced immediately, though he was not installed till the 28th of February following He had already been a successful pastor and teacher for nearly twenty years in Marlborough, Vt, which was his native State He was forty-five years of age, a man whose life from youth had been largely devoted to teaching, of cultivated scientific tastes, and of marked and strong character He was not a brilliant, but a sound and instructive preacher He was the first minister of this congregation, except Mr Tracy for a few months, whose services were not divided with Sandy Hill Being to the manner accustomed, and his support being inadequate, he taught a very excellent select school during a portion of the time that he was here He was dismissed by the Presbytery on the 25th of August, 1836, "in consequence of the embarrassed state of funds for his support," after a ministry here of just four years What his salary was I have not ascertained This ministry had been eminently successful , there had been added to the church sixty persons on profession, and a large number by certificate There had been but one case of discipline, and there was general prosperity and concord

The church now remained without a stated minister for nearly a year — from September 1st, 1836, to August 1st, 1837 — and yet at the two communions which were observed (April and July) there were eleven new members admitted on profession of their faith

On the 10th of August, 1837, Mr Scovill's name occurs as moderator of the session. He no doubt came on immediately after his graduation at Auburn, where he studied theology On the 11th of September following the congregation made out a call for him to become pastor, at $500 a year, and in November of the same year he was installed It is interesting to observe, as belonging to the history of the Presbytery of Troy, that within three days it ordained and installed three pastors, adjourning from one parish to the other

—Lewis Kellogg at Whitehall, John F Scovill at Glens Falls, and A Bordman Lambert at Salem   Mr Scovill's pastorate here continued about five years—he offered his resignation in April, 1842, and I conclude was dismissed by the Presbytery at Sand Lake on the 28th of June following   Within these five years there were fifty-three additions to the church by profession, and fourteen persons were under discipline   It was the period during which the contest between the old school and the new school, between the old mode and the new measures, waxed hottest, and culminated in the unhappy division of the Presbyterian Church   For a time this particular church endeavored to avoid being drawn into the strife   In June of 1838 and in February of '39 the session declined to send any delegate to presbytery, and also in October, '39, to send any delegate to synod, expressly resolving for the time to remain neutral   How could the church or the session know what to do ?   The two former pastors, with their churches, went with the old school, the pastor they then had went with the new   And when in August, 1839, the session rescinded their resolution of neutrality, and sent a delegate to the New School Presbytery at Lansingburgh, it is not at all strange that the strain on the church was so strong that a fissure for a time was quite observable   We wonder now that such feelings and prejudices should have existed as prevailed in those days, but the division of a great and intelligent church into two opposing bodies is not a trifling event to those who are immediately separated   We rejoice now in the reunion of the church, consummated in 1870, after a schooling and cooling of thirty-two years, which brought the parties to respect and trust each other, and to come back and shake hands where they had parted, neither one making any confession, neither one gaining any precedence by forgiving the other

John W Ray commenced preaching to this church in August, 1842 — almost immediately after his graduation at the Union Theological Seminary, New York city, and almost literally, without any period between, joining his ministry to that of his predecessor   His call from the congregation to the pastorate was voted on the 31st day of October, 1842, at $500 a year   When he was ordained and installed is uncertain, but probably it was on the 16th of November, as that was the day chosen by the congregation, if it should be convenient for the Presbytery   He offered his resignation in July, 1845, and it was accepted on the 6th of August   No doubt his term of service was just three years   Mr Ray was young and ardent   He entered into his work with zeal and enthusiasm, if not always with the best taste and judgment   He aimed at immediate effect, and was successful in what he undertook   Sixty-five were admitted to the church by profession during his ministry.   He is remembered by many of the members, to the present day, with interest and esteem

From the 1st of October, 1845, the Rev John Gray was minister of the

church for nine months, to July, 1846 Two years afterward he was preaching in Newburgh, and in the vicinity of that city he died in 1860

I come now to the ministry[1] to which this present service belongs Thirty
years ago this morning, the first Sabbath of October, 1846, I[2] preached for the
first time in the house which then occupied the spot on which this edifice now
stands I had, from my graduation at Auburn three years before, been
preaching as stated supply to the Congregational Church of East Groton,
Western New York Seeking my annual recreation, I had been for several
weeks with friends in Vermont, among the scenes of my childhood, and was
nearly ready to return to continue my service to the people, whom till to-day
I remember and bless as the people of my first love A mere accident—what
appears such—sometimes changes the place of one's home, and determines
where and with whom he shall live and perform his life's work So it was
with me On the apparently unpremeditated invitation of an uncle, I rode
with him to Glens Falls, and was here staying with his friends and mine over
the Sabbath This church was without a minister, and as Elder Benedict and
Elder Tallmadge could not do any better, they invited me to preach And
here I have been preaching ever since

The Rev Mr Fennel has continued in his pastorate until the present time
to the eminent satisfaction of his congregation, and has merited and won the
unqualified esteem of the entire community

The Sunday-school of this church was organized by the village school-
master, Mr Solomon P Goodrich, about the year 1815, in the old academy on

[1] Mr Fennel was born in the town of Ira, Rutland county, Vermont, June 21st, 1815 The first
seventeen years of his life, except the winter terms at a district school, were spent in somewhat hard
work upon the farm He commenced teaching when seventeen, and divided that occupation with
study—privately, at the Poultney Seminary, but mainly at the Castleton Seminary—for the next eight
years He entered the Auburn Theological Seminary in 1840, and graduated in 1843, was honored
with A M by Middleton College in 1847, was licensed and ordained by the Rutland County Association, preached the first three years of his ministry as stated supply for the Congregational Church in
East Groton, Tompkins county He was married October 18th, 1843, at Little Falls, to Miss Racillia
A Hackley, daughter of Hon Philo M Hackley, of Herkimer His call to the church in Glens Falls
was made the 12th of October, 1846, and it was subscribed by A N Cheney, Ira A Paddock, Stevens
Carpenter, Orville Cronkhite, A C Farlin and Halsey R Wing, trustees The installation did not
take place till the 25th of January, 1847 The sermon was preached by the Rev John Todd, D D,
of Pittsfield, Mass, the charge to the pastor was by the Rev Charles Doolittle, of North Granville,
and the charge to the congregation by the Rev Lewis Kellogg, of Whitehall Although never enjoying vigorous health, the thirty years' labor here, with one exception, has only had now and then very
slight interruption The winter of 1850-51—from the 12th of December to the 20th of March—was
spent in the South, a considerable portion of it on the island of Cuba.

Mr Fenner's salary at first was $600, in 1853 it was raised to $800, and in 1867 to $1,500 He
has never alluded to the matter of his salary in the pulpit, nor has he ever anywhere asked for its increase In accordance with a promise made at every pastor's installation, to continue not only the
maintenance which the people have pledged, but "whatever else they may see needful for the honor
of religion, and his comfort among them," his watchful congregation has not only paid the salary in
full, but in observance of a New England custom has made him *twenty-five* visits, which, on the average, were worth $200 each

[2] Rev A J Fennel

Ridge street, which Mr Goodrich occupied for his school during the week After some years it met in the session house on Glen street It was the first Sunday-school in the town, and indeed in the county, and continued to be the only school for many years It was in fact and in name a union school, and remained so for more than forty years Mr Elias Hawley succeeded Mr. Goodrich, and was superintendent till his removal to Binghamton in 1833 Its first two superintendents were elders of the church, as is the one now in office, and two others were elected to be, but declined to serve John L Curtenius was the next superintendent, with George G Hawley for assistant After Mr Curtenius's removal, it is thought that Mr Fordyce Sylvester acted as superintendent for a few months, when George G Hawley was elected probably in May, 1837 Except for a few months, during which Ira A. Paddock served, Mr Hawley continued in office, annually re-elected, for twenty-three years His work in the Sunday-school was, and is, intelligent, earnest and efficient Since he was succeeded in 1860 by F A Johnson, he has much of the time been superintendent of the district Sunday-school of Queensbury, under appointment of the Warren County Sunday-school Union, an organization formed in 1841 greatly through his instrumentality Mr Johnson was superintendent between four and five years, till his removal to New York In May, 1865, J A Freligh was chosen and continued in office for six years, till 1871, when Mr Johnson, having re-established his residence here, was re-elected to superintend the school, and has continued in office to the present time Thus the school, now more than sixty years old, leaving out only a few months, has been the whole time under six superintendents—a fact to the credit of both them and the school

The Sunday-school, ever since its adoption as a department of instruction in this church, has enlisted much of the best talent of the membership, and has done much to promote the intelligent piety of a large share of those who now belong to our communion

In the year 1848 the " Old White " Church as it was known, was demolished and a handsome brick edifice erected at a cost of about $9,000 The building committee consisted of Bethuel Peck, Albert N Cheney and George C Hawley The dedication services were held in March, 1850, Mr Fennel delivering the dedicatory sermon On May 31st, 1864, the church was destroyed by the great fire, and services were held during the building of a new edifice in the Baptist Church

In 1865, the next church building was begun and was completed in 1867 The first sermon was preached by the pastor on June 16th, 1867, at which time the church was free from debt and valued, with furniture, at $25,000 The trustees were S. L Goodman, Henry Crandell, Jerome Lapham, A C Tearse, and Daniel Peck The church was dedicated June 19th, 1867, by the Rev Dr Hickok, the president of Union College An organ was afterward purchased at a cost of $3,000

Trustees —Elected in 1807, William Robards, John A Ferriss, Daniel Peck, William Hay, John Folsom, Micajah Pettit, 1811, Uzziel Stevens, William Robards, John Folsom, John Thomas, Edmund Peck, William Wing, 1812, John A Ferriss, Uzziel Stevens, 1813, John Thomas, John Folsom, 1814, Asahel Clark, Elnathan Parsons, 1815, Stephen Clark, John A Ferriss, 1816, Thomas Colton, John Folsom, John Thomas, 1817, Solomon P Goodrich, Hezekiah Leavens, 1818, Elias Hawley, John A Ferriss, Royal Leavens, 1820, J Lyman Arms, Solomon P Goodrich, John Thomas, B F Butler, 1821, Horatio Buell, Elias Hawley; 1822, J Lyman Arms, Solomon P Goodrich, 1823, John Thomas, Luther Johnson, Bogardus Piersons, Samuel Cook, 1824, Elias Hawley, Alpheus Hawley, 1825, Solomon P Goodrich, Elnathan Parsons, 1826, Bogardus Piersons, Roswell Weston, 1827, Charles G Jones, Sidney Berry, 1828, Horatio Buell, Moody Ames, 1829, Sidney Berry, Lewis Numan, Samuel Estabrook, 1830, John L Curtenius, Sheldon Benedict, John Van Pelt, 1831, Lewis Numan, Sidney Berry, 1832, Moody Ames, Jonathan W Freeman, Fletcher Ransom, 1834, Sidney Berry, Lewis Numan, Sheldon Benedict, George G Hawley; 1835, Jonathan W Freeman, Alexander Folsom, 1836, Lewis Numan, Sheldon Benedict, 1837, Sidney Berry, George G Hawley, Billy J Clark, 1838, Billy J Clark, Jonathan W Freeman

The church was again destroyed by fire April 28th, 1884, and at the present writing is in process of rebuilding

Following is a list of the ruling elders and trustees from the organization of the church to the present time —

Ruling Elders — Elected in 1808, John Folsom, died 1839, John Moss, jr, dismissed, 1822 1809, Jonathan Harris, Matthew Scott, Joseph Caldwell 1819, Solomon P Goodrich, died 1831, Samuel Cranston, dismissed 1832 1827, Charles G Jones, dismissed 1829, Gridley H Packard, dismissed 1830 1830, Levi Hamilton, dismissed 1833, Samuel S Tallmadge, dismissed 1848 1831, Sidney Berry, died 1839, Elias Hawley, dismissed 1833 1834, Albert Blakesley 1838, Sheldon Benedict, Linus B Barnes, Miron Osborn, died 1850 1851, Orville Cronkhite, John J Miller, 1855, Henry Wing, William T Norris 1857, Linus B Barnes, Orville Cronkhite, Sheldon Benedict 1870, Linus B Barnes, Sheldon Benedict, Henry Wing, John J Miller, William Hotchkiss, Frederic A Johnson, jr, Joseph Fowler 1839, Lewis Numan, Abraham Wing, George Cronkhite 1840, George G Hawley, Linus B. Barnes 1841, Billy J Clark, George Sanford 1842, Lewis Numan, George Cronkhite 1843, George G Hawley, Linus B Barnes 1844, Halsey R Wing, Alfred C Farlin 1845, Stevens Carpenter, Albert N. Cheney 1846, Ira A Paddock, Orville Cronkhite 1847, Linus B Barnes, Thomas J Strong 1848, James C Clark, Benjamin F Shattuck Number of trustees reduced to five 1849, Frederic A Johnson 1850, Charles Rockwell, Linus B Barnes 1851, George Cronkhite, George G Hawley, Halsey R Wing

1852, George Cronkhite Frederic A Johnson 1853, Linus B Barnes 1854, Halsey R Wing, George G Hawley 1855, George Clendon, jr, Fred A. Johnson, jr 1856, Linus B Barnes, Fred A Johnson 1857, Halsey R Wing, George G Hawley 1857, George Clendon, jr 1859, Linus B Barnes, Fred A Johnson, jr 1860, Halsey R Wing, George G Hawley 1861, George Clendon, jr 1862, Lewis L Goodman, *vice* George Clendon, jr, Linus B Barnes, Fred A Johnson, jr 1863, Ezra Benedict, Archibald C Tearse 1864, Stephen L Goodman 1865, Daniel Peck *vice* Ezra Benedict removed from the place, Henry Crandell, Jerome Lapham 1866, A C Tearse, Daniel Peck 1867, Stephen L Goodman 1868, Henry Crandell, James A Freligh 1869, A C Tearse, Thos S Coolidge 1870, Stephen L Goodman, to present 1871, Henry Crandell, James A Freligh, Martin Coffin, *vice* A C. Tearse, removed from the place 1872, Martin Coffin, M L Wilmarth, Thomas S Coolidge, to present

Present Trustees — Stephen L Goodman, Samuel Pruyn, Thomas S Coolidge, Byron Lapham, Daniel H Delong Elders Eleazer Goodman, Frederick A Johnson, J L Cunningham, John J Miller, Byron B Fowler, Joseph Fowler, A B Abbott Sunday-school superintendent, J L Cunningham Membership, 350

Union Church of East Lake George, or East Lake George Presbyterian Church — In 1864 C L North, of Brooklyn, N Y, and several ladies and gentlemen who were spending the summer in East Lake George organized a Sunday-school in one of the school-houses The summer of 1865 a second school was organized and church services were held, either in the open air or in the school-houses of the neighborhood From this beginning grew the desire for a house of worship, and Mr North circulated a subscription paper for the purpose of raising a sum of money, the land being given by Mr Mattison The 5th of November, 1867, the corner stone was laid, and on July 12th, 1868 the church was dedicated It was organized under the Congregational form of government and was called the Union Evangelical Church of East Lake George, Rev W B Lee, of Brooklyn, N Y, officiating The church consisted of forty members at that time A parsonage was also built and Rev James Lamb became the pastor Mr Lamb was followed successively by Revs Jacob Fehrman, Isaac M See, Harry Brecket and Sidney M Stray Under Mr Stray's ministry the organization became Presbyterian, and on April 25th, 1877, was identified with the Troy Presbytery, and has since been known as the East Lake George Presbyterian Church After the retirement of Mr Stray, the church was served by the Revs William Bryant, John J Munroe and John H Pollock, the last named gentleman being the present pastor. A school-house has been added to the church, which with the church property is estimated as worth about $10,000 Each summer an anniversary picnic is held at which the neighboring Sunday-schools are expected to be represented

Bay Road Presbyterian Church — The Bay Road Presbyterian Church was organized September 12th, 1850, by the Rev David W French, as the First Associate Presbyterian Church of Queensbury The pulpit was supplied by the Presbytery of United Presbyterians until 1855, when the Rev Chauncey Webster was installed as pastor He remained with the church for two years when failing health interrupted his work The church was then closed and remained so until 1868, when the Rev James Lamb, of East Lake George, began holding services The building was repaired and a request made to the Troy Presbytery to receive them, which was done in February, 1869, and the church was enrolled as the Bay Road Presbyterian Church Mr Lamb ministered to them for a time, when the pulpit was supplied successively by the Revs Rood, John H Parkins, Sidney M Stray, William Bryant, John J Munroe and John H Pollock, who will all be recognized, Mr Rood excepted, as the pastors of East Lake George Church The present church property is valued at about $1,200

Methodist Episcopal Church — Methodism was introduced into Warren county about 1796, when two lay preachers Richard Jacobs and Henry Ryan, explored the northern portion of the county, then known as Thurman's Patent Mr Jacobs was drowned while attempting to ford the east branch of the Hudson near the outlet of Schroon Lake, the same year Mr Ryan was afterward known as one of the most successful itinerant preachers of this district Quoting from Dr Holden " In the same year the Rev David Noble, of Ireland, who had been connected with the John Street M E Church of New York, for some years, removed into Warren county and purchased four hundred acres of land at two and a half dollars per acre, upon which he and his sons soon made a clearing and built them up a log-house, which to them was a dwelling, a school-house and church Here, at this out-post of civilization, they were visited from time to time by those men of God, Elijah Hedding, Martin Rutter, Elijah Hibbard, Samuel Howe, David Brown, and others, and, with the numerous families of Nobles, Somervilles, and Armstrongs as a nucleus, a strong and flourishing church was built up, whose influences are still manifest to the present day The services were held for a long period of years in private houses, and afterward in school-houses, being supplied as long as he lived by the Rev David Noble, and afterward by other leaders who sprang up among them This was the extreme wilderness limit of what was then known as the Ash Grove (since Cambridge), or six week's circuit

" Here as elsewhere in the work of evangelizing the world, the operations of the Spirit and the progress of Divine truth, were met with opposition, obloquy and reproach In reference to this a writer in the *Troy Conference Miscellany* states as follows: ' The persecution in Thurman's Patent was truly grievous Many young people that experienced religion were turned out of doors by their parents

" ' Some of them were whipped cruelly, two young women were so whipped by their father that the blood ran down to their feet, and he then turned them out of doors, and they walked fifteen miles to a Methodist Society. That father was a church member

" ' Two younger brothers having been converted, were often severely beaten for attending Methodist meetings It astonished me that the father of ten children, eight of whom had experienced religion, should drive six of them from the house, and whip these two boys for no other crime, in reality, than that of worshiping God with the Methodists '

" About this time the eccentric and widely-known Lorenzo Dow and his admirer, Timothy Dewey, were sent into this region by the authorities of the church Dow officiated in a school-house in the northern part of the town and in a barn at the east of the Oneida Traditions are yet extant of the power of his sermons, and of the numbers awakened and converted by his preaching Soon after his coming the Methodist society was organized at the Ridge, a settlement then containing more dwellings and inhabitants than the village of Glens Falls As previously stated, Queensbury was at this distant period of time included within the boundaries of what was then called Ashgrove circuit, so named from the locality, which was first planted by Philip Embury, the renowned pioneer of the faith, previous to the Revolutionary War Having previously organized the first society of the denomination in New York, about the year 1770, he removed to the town of Cambridge, and in that portion of the township known in the local annals as Ashgrove, within the present limits of the town of White Creek, established a society and continued as its pastor until his death in 1775 From that time until 1788 they were supplied by traveling and lay preachers During this year the Rev Lemuel Smith was inducted as their pastor, and a chapel was built, the first place of worship north of Albany erected by Methodists to the service of the Most High This church was the center from which northward and westward a Godly influence radiated to the extreme confines of civilization In 1795 it contained sixty members

" Soon afterward the Cambridge circuit was formed. In 1799 Billy Hibbard and Henry Ryan, the itinerants on this circuit, traveled about five hundred miles and filled sixty-three appointments every four weeks, one of their stations at this time being Sanford's Ridge, in the town of Queensbury Among the first Methodist ministers who visited Glens Falls were the Revs. Friend Draper, Daniel Brayton, Andrew McKean, Samuel Howe and others, earnest and vigorous men, ' valiant for the truth ' Not satisfied with the already extended range of country traversed by these men, Revs Tobias Spicer and Sherman Miner made occasional visits to this village, then only a hamlet, and held religious services in the old academy building, then on Ridge street, on the site of Mr Jerome Lapham's residence The building, since removed, is now occupied by Messrs Joubert & White as a carriage manufactory, on the corner of Warren and Jay streets

" The late Dr Spicer was a clear thinker, shrewd debater, catholic spirited and resolute Mr Miner was a man of mild and lovely spirit and abundant in works Both have passed to their reward The first Methodist class, a name by which the branch societies are known and into which for greater activity and efficiency all these churches are divided, was formed in this village in 1824 by Rev John Lovejoy, in the dwelling known as the General Pettit place, situated between the canal and the river, in the rear of the old stone store on the east side of Glen street and near the river bridge The building was removed in March, 1874 The original number of the class was twelve, eleven being women

" From this early date to 1832 this whole northern region was embraced within the New York Conference, and was traversed by heroic men, zealous for the conversion of the scattered inhabitants to Christianity We can only name the active and earnest John Clark, the first regularly appointed preacher to the societies in Sandy Hill and Glens Falls, Seymour Landon amiable and popular, Julius Fields, characterized for administrative and financial ability, under whose auspices the first church edifice (the old stone building) was erected at a cost of about $1,500 in 1829, the land having been given by Mr J Pettit, nephew of the general This structure is still standing, and has been for several years used by the Roman Catholics Mr Fields was followed by Rev Robert Seeney and Coles Carpenter, of precious memory

" In 1832 the territory now known as the Troy Conference, of which Glens Falls is nearly the center, north and south, was set off from the New York, both because of the numerical increase of the churches and for their better cultivation by the ministerial forces within the territory The societies in Glens Falls and Sandy Hill being at about this time somewhat weakened, they were attached to others and entered into what for several years was known as the Fort Anne circuit, to which three preachers were sent, and who alternately supplied the several societies with religious services This itinerant system peculiar to Methodism was established by Wesley as, and history shows, not less adapted to old and populous countries than to new and sparsely settled ones, continued until 1849 — a period of seventeen years — under such men of diversified talents as Elisha Andrews, assisted by P M Hitchcock and L Phillips, Joseph Avres and D P Harding as colleagues, J B Houghtaling, aided by J W B Wood, late of New York, Henry Stewart and G Y Palmer, Russell M Little, with William Chipp and Asa Fenton as colleagues, C P. Clark, under whose administration the parsonage was erected in 1840, A M Osborn (now Rev Dr Osborn, of New York), a clear thinker and able preacher, James Covel, the student and scholar, Seymour Coleman, a war-horse, with James Quinlan assistant, E B Hubbard having William Amer and C. Devol, M D (now of Albany), as colleagues

" In 1847–48 began a new era for the church under the pastorate of Rev C R Morris, in the erection, at a cost of about $5,000, of a new and commodious brick church edifice on Warren street, but which was destroyed by fire in 1864 In 1849 this society was erected into a separate station, having the services of Rev J F Walker as preacher At the time the number of members was 166, of probationers fifteen, making in all 181 The Sunday-school consisted of ten teachers and 125 scholars Owing to the eccentricities of Mr Walker, whose scholarly attainments and preaching abilities are acknowledged, the church did not greatly flourish After his term of two years Rev J H Patterson, M D, transferred from the Vermont Conference, took the pastorate, from which time the society began to take on shape and efficiency that have continued more or less till the present Then followed in succession Revs B O Meeker, George C Wells, Merritt Bates, H W Ransom, M D, W A Meeker, W J Heath, each for the term of two years, except Mr Wells, during which period of thirteen years the church, with slight variations, grew and prospered, less in the number of communicants than in character In 1864 Rev J K Cheesman was, on invitation, appointed to the pastorate, and by his energy and hearty co-operation of his parishioners secured the erection of a church building in 1865 at a cost of $16,000 He was succeeded by the Rev M. B. Mead, under whose charge the church reported a membership of four hundred In 1869 the Rev. B Hawley, D D, took charge of the church society, which consisted of four hundred and thirty-seven members, three Sunday-schools and a library During this year a brick chapel, costing about $1,600, was built in South Glens Falls

" Among the pioneers in this church were Elmore Pratt and wife, Hiram Wells and wife, Joseph Wells, Isaac Cole, Linus Bishop, Rev R. M Little, the Swartout family, the Burnhams, Isaac Hill, Alexander Robertson, William McEchron, D C Holman and others "— *Holden* Irregular service had been held for many years in private houses, or school-houses of adjacent settlements, being conducted by pastors or people as circumstances determined Sunday-schools were organized and class meetings held

" The Rev J W Alderman, who was the next pastor, in 1872, was a native of Ohio, where he was a licensed exhorter and a circuit preacher He was a chaplain in the army during the civil war Afterward he held several charges in Ohio and Wisconsin, after which he removed to New York, and was assigned to the Glens Falls Church In 1873 a protracted revival season added many to the church As the membership increased, the need of more room in the sanctuary was felt and the church building was enlarged This made the purchase of more land necessary, and a lot was purchased of H M Harris On this lot, which was on Warren street west of the church, an addition was built which was finished and open to the public February 12th, 1874 The cost of the improvements was about $21,000, and the church property is estimated at $45,000

"From the M E class of twelve persons in Glens Falls in 1824, the growth of the church has been steady, until now the membership is large and the society in a flourishing condition

"At West Mountain, a brick church was completed in 1871 This has been in charge of the Rev J F Crowl who has also ministered to the church at the Ridge, which stands on the borders of Kingsbury "

Ministers of M E Church stationed at Glens Falls — 1824, John Lovejoy, 1824–25, John Clark, 1826–27, Seymour Landon, 1828–29, Julius Fields, 1830–31, Robert Seeney, 1832, Coles Carpenter, 1833, Elisha Andrews, P M Hitchcock, 1834, Elisha Andrews, Zebulon Phillips, 1835, Joseph Ayers, Doren P Harding, 1836, J B Houghtailing, J W B Wood, Henry W Stewart, 1837, J B Houghtailing, J W B Wood, Gilbert Y Palmer, 1838, Russell M Little, William M Chipp, 1839, Charles P Clark, Asa F Fenton, 1840, A M. Osborn, David Osgood, 1841–42, James Covel, William Amer, 1843, Seymour Coleman, O E Spicer, 1844, Seymour Coleman, James Quinlan, 1845, Elijah B Hubbard, James Quinlan, 1846, Elijah B Hubbard, Charles Devol, 1847, Christopher R Morris, William N Frazer, H W Ransom, 1848, C R Morris, William Frazer, S S Ford, 1849–50, Jason F Walher; 1851–52, J W Patterson, 1853–54, B O Meeker, 1855, George C Wells, 1856–57, Merritt Bates; 1858–59, William H Meeker, 1860–61, Halsey W Ransom, 1862–63, William J Heath, 1864–65–66, J R Cheeseman, 1867–68, M B Mead, 1869–70–72, Bostwick Hawley, D D, 1872–75, J W Alderman, D D., 1875–78, J F Clymer; 1878–81, D W Gates, 1881–84, S McLaughlin, 1884, H C Sexton

Official Board — President, D C Holman, W C Haviland, John W Bush, A J Pearsall, Wm McEchron, R A Little, Jonathan M Coolidge, Hollis Russell

Stewards — C B Thompson, George H Leggett, Chas A Bullard, C W Long, J S Morgan, D L Robertson, John R Loomis, C H Carson, H Colvin, Wm B Griffin, E L Mills, A W Thompson

Class leaders — F Wood, H Russell, D B Ketchum, G B Greenslet, R A Little, J F Craig

The Episcopal Church. — The services of this church were first held in the county by the Rev. Philander Chase (afterward Bishop of the Diocese of Illinois), who made an itinerating tour about 1796, following the Hudson River settlements to Queensbury, and then visiting the more remote settlements in the north At Thurman (now Warrensburgh) an effort was made to found a church, and a subscription paper was circulated among the inhabitants The land was given for the purpose and timber was delivered upon the premises, but with no clergyman to guide the movement the effort failed The timber remained upon the ground until unfit for use and the site was finally appropriated for other purposes.

32

About the year 1800 the Rev Ammi Rogers made a journey through the vicinity, holding services in the counties of Essex and Warren, beside establishing several church societies in Saratoga county   Later on the Right Rev George Upfold, D D, Bishop of the Diocese of Indiana, at that time rector of the parishes in the thriving villages of Waterford and Lansingburgh, at the earnest solicitation of some personal friends, visited this section and contributed to the establishment of Zion Church, of Sandy Hill, which had been organized a short time previously through the zeal and persevering efforts of Dr Zina Hitchcock, of Kingsbury   The services were held in the court-house, which, for a long period, many years later, was still used for the same purpose

Some years afterward the Rev Mr Pardee officiated for a short time in the Beach neighborhood of Kingsbury, and about the same time the Rev Reuben Hubbard came to Glens Falls with the intention of founding a church, but the effort failed   In 1840 several families of the Episcopal faith made another attempt toward establishing a church, and the Rev John Alden Spooner, of St Albans, Vt, was requested to assist in the endeavor   Their efforts were successful, and for a year services were held in the M E Church, which then was the old stone building   The original record was in the following terms, as given by Dr Holden —

"*Act of Incorporation* — To all to whom these presents may come, we, whose names and seals are hereto affixed, do certify that in pursuance of notice duly given according to law for that purpose, at the time of Divine service on two Sunday mornings now last passed, the male persons of full age belonging to such congregation or society worshiping in the village of Glens Falls, in the county of Warren and State of New York, to wit, at the house of W C Carter, for the purpose of incorporating themselves under the act entitled an act to provide for the incorporation of religious societies and acts to amend the same   At which meeting and by a majority of voices the undersigned, John Alden Spooner, being a deacon in the church, was called to the chair and presided, and the undersigned, Keyes P Cool and William C Carter, were nominated to certify the proceedings of said meeting in conjunction with the chairman, and by a majority of votes William C Carter and N Edson Sheldon were elected church wardens; and William McDonald, Abraham Wing, Keyes P Cool, Nehemiah Sheldon, Henry Philo, Walter Geer, jr, George Sanford, and Orange Ferriss were elected vestrymen of said church   And Easter Monday in the week called Easter week was, in like manner fixed on as the day on which the said officers, church wardens and vestrymen shall annually thereafter cease, and their successor in office be chosen   And the name or title of the 'Rector, church wardens, and vestrymen of the Church of the Messiah in the village of Glens Falls,' in like manner fixed on and agreed to as that by which the said church, congregation or society shall be known in law

" In testimony whereof, we, John Alden Spooner, together with the underdersigned Keyes P Cool and William C Carter, have hereunto subscribed our names and affixed our seals this tenth day of February in the year of our Lord, one thousand, eight hundred and forty

"JOHN ALDEN SPOONER, [L S]
"KEYES P COOL,   [L S]
"WILLIAM C CARTER   [L. S]

" Signed and sealed in presence of,
                "Orange Ferriss,
                "Nehemiah Shelden

" On the twenty-fourth day of February, in the year of our Lord, one thousand eight hundred and forty, before me, Hiram Barber, first judge of the Court of Common Pleas in and for the county of Warren, personally appeared Orange Ferriss of Queensbury, one of the subscribing witnesses to the above instrument, who being duly sworn, did depose and say, that he was present and saw John Alden Spooner, Keyes P Cool, and William C Carter, whose names are affixed to the foregoing certificate, sign and seal the same, and that the deponent, together with Nehemiah Shelden, did, in their presence, and at their request, subscribe the same as witnesses   HIRAM BARBER

" I certify the preceding to be a true record of the original certificate with the acknowledgment thereof, and examined and compared with the record being this 11th day of March, A D , 1840   THOMAS ARCHIBALD, Clerk
" State of New York   } ss
    County Clerk's Office }

          I, Thomas Archibald, clerk of said county, do certify that I have
[L S] compared the foregoing copy of a certificate now remaining on record
          in this office, and that the same is a correct transcript of the record, and of the whole of said record   In testimony whereof, I have hereunto set my hand, and affixed the seal of the said county, this 19th day of May, 1857
                    "THOMAS ARCHIBALD, Clerk "

The history of the Episcopal Church is continued by the following account of the present

Church of the Messiah, Glens Falls — In August, 1840, the Rt Rev Benjamin T Onderdonk, Bishop of the Diocese, accompanied by several clergymen, visited the parish for the purpose of confirmation and ordination   The services were held in the "old white" Presbyterian Church, where John Alden Spooner was ordained to the priesthood, and fourteen persons were confirmed   The parish of St James, at Fort Edward, was established, and Zion Church, at Sandy Hill, was revived and reorganized, and with the church at Glens Falls given to the care of Rev Mr Spooner, who held alternate services in the different parishes

Unpleasant circumstances arose soon after this and the society diminished in number   The meetings were held for a time in the Ladies' Seminary, which was afterward the school-house of district No 19, the Sunday-school meeting in the basement of the building, after that being held in an old school-house on Park street. For about a year following, services were held in private dwellings, the rector's salary being derived from the missionary fund and the Sunday collections. In 1843 money was raised and a piece of ground on Ridge street purchased, on which a small chapel was begun, and nearly completed in 1844. In Mr Spooner's report for that year he said. "By the blessing of God, a church edifice at Glens Falls is so nearly completed, that it has been occupied with comfort most of the year past. It is the first and only church edifice in Warren county. Its sittings are *free*, and its font, which is near the porch door, is so constructed as to admit of immersing either children or adults "

A plan to establish parochial schools was perfected about this time, and one was opened at South Glens Falls, and another at Fort Edward. Dissensions in the diocese at this time affected the welfare of the church, and the controversies finally resulted in the suspension of Bishop Onderdonk from the Episcopate and ministry in January, 1845. From that time until the election of the Rt Rev Jonathan M Wainright as provisional bishop of the diocese, September, 1852, no returns were made from the parishes, as all reports are required to be sent to the bishop, and the suspension of Bishop Onderdonk left them with no head. The fire of 1864 also destroyed the church records, thus leaving the church without authentic history.

In the spring of 1846 the Rev Samuel B Bostwick and Henry McVickar were appointed adjunct or assistant ministers of the three parishes. Some little time previously to this event the Rev Mr Spooner had removed to Fort Edward, where, for two or three years, his indefatigable energies found occupation in the management of a parish school, the purchase of a very desirable plot of ground, and the erection of a substantial church edifice.

In pursuance of the plan already indicated, Mr Bostwick made his home at Sandy Hill, and there commenced the instruction of a classical school, which was maintained for a period of nearly twenty years, with a wide-spread repute for superior excellence and usefulness. The school previously established by Mr Spooner, at South Glens Falls, passed at the same time into the hands of the Rev Henry McVickar. The services in the three parishes were held alternately by the three clergymen associated in the mission. As an evidence of their devotion to the work, it may be stated that this laborious interchange of duties was mainly performed on foot, and often at unpropitious seasons and inclement weather.

The relations subsisting between the three parishes continued until the spring of 1847, when the Sandy Hill and Fort Edward churches dissolved their connection with that of Glens Falls, and extended a call to the Rev S B Bostwick to become their pastor. For nearly a quarter of a century he retained this charge, with the unabated respect and affection of his people. The same year

(1847) the Rev John A Spooner is returned in the records of the convention as rector of St Luke's Church, Mechanicsville, and the joint missionary station of Glens Falls and Luzerne is reported as vacant

Notwithstanding this rectorship at Mechanicsville, and his subsequent charge of Grace Church, in Albany, Mr Spooner retained a *quasi* relation and charge over this virtually vacant parish, until the month of September, 1851, when he formally tendered his resignation, which was accepted by the vestry

Continuing, we quote as follows from Dr Holden "On Easter Monday (12th April), 1852, the Rev Mr Bostwick, by invitation, officiated at morning prayers in the chapel, and, due notice having been previously given, a new election, the first for six years, was held for wardens and vestrymen On the 18th of May following a vestry meeting was convened, at which it was 're-solved that the Rev William George Hawkins be engaged as minister of this parish for the ensuing year,' at a salary of three hundred dollars a year, and a donation in addition to the missionary stipend When the connection be-tween the Rev Mr Spooner and this parish was discontinued he declined to surrender the possession of the chapel and other church property on the score of arrearages of salary The congregation was consequently obliged to look elsewhere for a place of worship This state of affairs resulted in hiring for the time being the use of the house of worship belonging to the Universalists, a building since destroyed in the great fire of 1864, and which then stood on a plot of ground now owned and occupied by Judge Rosekrans, facing Warren street Legal proceedings were promptly instituted by the vestry for the re-covery and possession of the church property The points in the controversy were finally referred to the Hon Alonzo C Paige, of Schenectady, and his de-cision, which was rendered in June, 1853, and which was final as regarded further litigation, was substantially in favor of the parish During the same season the old chapel was repaired, and in the autumn following, and until Mr Hawkins's connection with the parish ceased, the services were continuously held therein

"Mr Hawkins remained in charge of the parish until the first of December, 1855 During that period of time the chapel was repaired, a church lot con-tracted for and secured, and the work of building the new church commenced. The corner stone of this substantial and costly structure was laid on Monday, the 12th of June, 1854, by the Right Rev Jonathan M Wainright, Bishop of the Diocese, Bishop Otey, of Tennessee, being present and delivering an ad-dress on the occasion In this time Mr Hawkins made two extended visita-tions to the larger cities of the diocese in solicitation of funds with which to carry forward the church work In this way several thousand dollars were realized with which to strengthen the slender resources of the parish This laborious enterprise, which had been undertaken by Mr Hawkins in addition to the ordinary parochial work, added to the arduous responsibilities of the

school, which under his management speedily attained a magnitude and prosperity both flattering and remunerative, bears cumulative testimony both to
Mr Hawkins's efficiency as a pastor and devotion to the work in which he was
engaged

"About this time Mr. James E Kenney, a resident of this place, and communicant of the church, commenced studying for the ministry with Mr Hawkins, being also associated with him in the instruction and management of the
school

"Early in the fall of 1855 Mr Hawkins tendered his resignation, to take
effect on the first of December following   The interim was passed in negotiations which resulted in the call of the Rev Louis Legrand Noble, a clergyman
of distinguished talents and ability   He assumed charge of the parish about
the first of January, 1856   At that time work had been suspended on the new
church building, the walls having been carried up a short distance only above
the basement story

"Heavy debts had been incurred in the prosecution of this undertaking.
These remained like an incubus upon the feeble parish, paralyzing all efforts.
Through Mr. Noble's active personal solicitations, chiefly made in New York
city, the greater portion of these debts were liquidated, or means and methods
provided for their extinguishment during the short period of his incumbency
Trinity Church alone contributed two thousand dollars at this time, taking a
lien upon the church for security, with a view to insure its perpetuity, and
that the benefaction should not be diverted to other uses

"The dilapidated condition of the old chapel rendered it imperatively
necessary that it should be thoroughly overhauled and repaired   A new roof
was put on, the walls papered, the seats and other wood work painted, and
other necessary repairs effected.   In the mean time, before this renovation
was completed, the Universalist church was again rented for another year, and
the services were conducted therein until the condition of the chapel, improved
by the repairs above named, was such that the congregation was enabled to
resume devotions there, and from that time forward until the completion of
the new church, and the sale of the old one, the services were held with but
slight interruption in this revered and time-honored place

"The costs of these repairs was defrayed by the Ladies' Aid Society of the
church, to whose self-sacrificing efforts and laborious zeal much of the success
of the church enterprises in this parish have been due   During a period of
about fifteen years, dating from the reorganization of the church in 1852, an
energetic and devoted band of women, scarcely a dozen in number, but brave
with a spirit of Christian devotion, earned in various ways of hard-working industry a sum amounting to nearly, if not quite, five thousand dollars, which,
whenever and whatever the financial pinch might be, was always promptly
available and forthcoming to meet the needs of the pastor, the vestry, or the

church, whenever a call was made or the occasion demanded   Deficiencies in ministers' salaries, repairs of chapel, delinquent bank notes given by the building committee for work or material, and finally a large amount expended in finishing the interior of the new church, were among the channels of usefulness to which this steady and unfailing stream of endeavor was applied   A passing tribute to the worth and excellence of these Christian women is without doubt worthy of commemoration in the annals of the church they helped to build   During the greater proportion of the period of Mr Noble's ministrations here, and at his request, the Rev John H Babcock, a minister of the church, who was at the same time principal of the Glen's Falls Academy, was called by the vestry to the position of assistant minister of the parish   In this capacity he aided the rector in his services, besides officiating as missionary in visiting and conducting worship at several contiguous points "

Mr Noble and Mr Babcock severed their connection with the church in June, 1857, and nearly a year elapsed before the parish was regularly supplied   Mr Kenney and other clergymen, however, supplied the pulpit occasionally   In May, 1858, the Rev Henry H Bates, of the diocese of Connecticut, responded to a call and remained with the church for three years, during which time the debt was cleared from the church, and progress made in the building of the new church edifice   June 7th, 1859, the Rev James Kenney was called by the vestry as assistant minister of the parish, without salary save such as was derived from the missionary fund   He added to his income by services in the school already referred to

During Mr Bates's ministry the parish was associated with the missionary station of St James's Church, Caldwell, where he was also assisted by Mr Kenney

In 1860 the chapel was repaired, and but little progress was made in the new church building   In 1861 the church at Caldwell associated itself with the church at Warrensburgh, severing the relations with this parish   In 1861 Mr Bates accepted the position as chaplain of the Twenty-second Regiment N Y Volunteers   During the ensuing fall the Rev Mr Van Antwerp, who was a candidate, officiated   Mr Bates tendered his resignation which was considered by a special meeting in June, 1861   Resolutions of regard were adopted, but the resignation was not accepted   Mr Bates, feeling that the vestry might be hampered by the relations continuing between them while he was in the field, again offered his resignation, which was accepted in June, 1862, and in July the Rev Edwin E Butler was called to the vacancy   He responded, and remained until 1871, when he retired from the rectorship of the parish   During the occasional absences of Mr Butler during his ministry the Rev J A Russell, a presbyter of the church, who was at the time principal of the Glens Falls Academy, officiated, also assisting at times in the services   For two years after Mr. Butler's retirement the church was without a pastor, occasional services being held by visiting and neighboring clergymen

During the ministry of Mr Butler the church, which had been slowly building since 1854, was finished, and the first service in the new edifice was the marriage of Mr James W Schenck, one of the building committee and vestry The church was formally consecrated in June, 1866, by the Rt Rev. Horatio Potter, Bishop of the Diocese, assisted by a large number of visiting and neighboring clergy

" In 1867, a committee was appointed at the diocesan convention, which reported in favor of a division of the diocese The following year the preliminary steps were taken, and the act of separation finally consummated, by which the Diocese of Albany was erected It is greatly hoped that this act will work salutary results for the smaller and feebler parishes.

"On the 29th of May, 1869, the Hon Stephen Brown, in behalf of the executors of the estate of John J Harris, deceased, offered the vestry a deed of gift of a fine stone chapel, situated near his late residence at Harrisena, in the north part of Queensbury This structure was built up in a great degree of the beautiful Ottawa limestone, imported by the founder, specially for the purpose, from Canada Its erection and completion was one of the last acts of the testator's life, his funeral the first service held within its walls (Sunday, March 14th, 1869) On the 3d of July following the gift was formally accepted by a vote of the vestry Six days later the building was consecrated by the Bishop of the Diocese, several of the neighboring clergymen being present and assisting in the ceremonial Since that date up to the 1st of July, 1871, services have been held regularly during the summer months on every alternate Sunday afternoon, in this little chapel, by the rector in charge of the church at Glens Falls

"On the 17th of July, 1869, the vestry passed a vote relinquishing the missionary stipend, of which this parish had been nearly a constant beneficiary from the beginning, and in addition to which, large appropriations have been received from time to time from the Parochial Aid Society, and the Northern Convocation, for the maintenance of the services

"Thus for the first time, during all these years, and without any appreciable increase in the wealth, resources or membership, the church became self-supporting, and though still feeble and weak, yet with a substantial if not attractive church edifice, and no debt to hamper or impair its energies, it is to be hoped that its day of grace and prosperity is not far removed "[1]

The vestry had been looking in this interval for a suitable minister for the church, and finally extended a call to the Rev Russell A Olin, of Manlius, N. Y, who accepted, and in the summer of 1873 established himself at Glens Falls At the first confirmation after his ministry began, March, 1874, twenty-seven were confirmed

In 1881 the Rev F M Cookson assumed charge of the church and is the present minister

[1] Holden's *History of Queensbury*

In 1879–80 the church building was improved at an expense of $2,000 The chapel at Harrisena is in charge of the Church of the Messiah   The present officers (1885) are   Senior warden, William A Wait , junior warden, L S McDonald , vestrymen, Dr A W Holden, Henry Crandell, L P Juvet, William H Robbins, George H Barringer, Isaac C Burwell, R F Haviland, and John L Dix   The rector is superintendent of the Sunday-school

St Alphonsus's Catholic Church (French) —The first French families which settled at Glens Falls came nearly half a century ago   The Poissons (Fish), Jettes (Stay) and Montees were of the number   They were the grand-parents of the heads of the families now bearing the same name in the village

For a number of years there was no French pastor residing among them, but they were visited periodically by clergymen from Troy or Albany, who held services in private houses   It was only in the year 1853 that a frame church was built on the corner of West and Pine streets, under the care of Rev Father Turcotte, residing in Troy

The congregation, having increased sufficiently, applied to the Bishop of Albany for a resident pastor and Father Des Roches was sent in July, 1855 He was succeeded in 1866 by Father J C Theberge, who attended the congregation until April, 1870, when ill health obliged him to resign temporarily

Rev A Payette, of Whitehall, held services twice a month until the middle of July, when Rev Charles Bousquet, who was an invalid, took charge of the church until Father Theberge could return to his post, which he did in October, 1871   But death had marked him for his own and he died a few weeks later, and Rev F X Langie was sent to attend to the wants of the congregation until February, 1872, at which time Rev G Huberdault was sent as permanent pastor

During the preceding year the church had been enlarged and finished, and in 1873 a gallery was added, giving four hundred and sixty-five sittings   A large brick school-house was built next to the church, where the parish children can get a Catholic education

In 1875 Rev Huberdault being called to the Troy church, Father L N St Onge was appointed to the pastorate and is yet in charge   The congregation has increased and numbered 1,497 persons on January 1st, 1885

The parish possesses considerable property   They own besides the church property, the pastor's residence, the brick school, three stories high, a two story frame building for meetings of societies, and a story and a half brick tenement house on a lot adjoining the church grounds, and finally, a large cemetery outside the village, occupying about twelve acres of land   The whole of this property is free from debt , the last mortgage having been paid last year

The members of the church have decided to build a new church edifice on the site occupied by the old church   The new church will be built of brick and will be made large enough for the present wants of the congregation and for many years in the future

The present pastor, Rev L N St Onge, is of French descent, born in Canada near Montreal His ancestors came to America in 1699 from France They were known under the name of *Payen de Saintonge*, but like most all French Canadians, they have abbreviated the name to *St Onge*

He was educated in St Hyacinthe, where he graduated in 1862 at twenty years of age (being born in 1842) Having requested his bishop to send him on to an Indian Mission, he left for Oregon in 1864 and was stationed among the Indians as soon as he was ordained. During the first years of his missionary life he had occasion to preach to the Indian tribes of Washington Territory, the Rocky Mountains, Montana, and Idaho Territory

He perfected himself in the knowledge of two of the principal Indian languages and learned besides several dialects He published a guide for the missionaries in Chinook, and a catechism and spelling book in Yakama for the use of the Indian children

After being in the mission for nearly ten years, exposure and the privations which always attend the life of a missionary who lives actually in the lodge with the Indians, broke down his health and he was sent east for treatment

As he never recovered enough to resume the hard life of a missionary, he accepted a call to the Glens Falls French Church, after having spent a year and a half in a Montreal hospital

His brother, the Rev J B St Onge, assists him in the parochial work and has been with him since 1880

The Roman Catholic Church in Glens Falls — In the year 1848 the Rev M. Olivette, who at that time resided at Whitehall, purchased a small stone building, which had been used as a Methodist Church, for the sum of $800 It was dedicated and opened for worship the same year Before that time there were a few Catholics living in Glens Falls whose spiritual wants were ministered to by the pastor residing in Sandy Hill The names of these pastors were Fathers Guerdet, Coyle, Doyle, and Kelly, each of whom in succession was placed in charge of that village and of an extensive surrounding district The first resident pastor in Glens Falls was the Rev John Murphy, whose ministerial duties were performed from the year 1848 until 1865 His successor was the Rev James McDermott, who is still the pastor

On the 28th of August, 1867, the corner stone of a new church, located on Warren street, was laid, the edifice was completed and dedicated 19th January, 1869 The church is in the Gothic style of architecture ; its length is one hundred and fifty-two feet, width sixty-four feet It is surmounted by a spire whose height from the base is two hundred feet The interior of the building is richly decorated in fresco ; many of the scenes in the life our Redeemer being represented in life-sized figures There are three beautiful altars, a high altar

and two side altars, all exquisitely carved and gilt   It contains a large organ
and bell, the latter weighing 4,500 pounds   After the completion of the
church the present pastor has also erected magnificent schools capable of accommodating 1,000 children, with an actual attendance of 700 , and a convent
in which there are nine Sisters of St Joseph having charge of the schools
There is also a beautiful pastoral residence adjoining the church, recently completed   At a short distance from the town a cemetery containing twenty-four
acres is located   The aggregate cost of the church property is $200,000

CHAPTER XXVI

HISTORY OF THE TOWN OF LUZERNE

THE township of Luzerne lies in the southern extremity of the county, west
of Queensbury and Caldwell   Its western and southern boundary is
formed by the Hudson River, which separates it from Saratoga county   The
town of Warrensburgh bounds it on the north   The surface is extremely
mountainous, two branches of the Luzerne Mountains extending through the
town and occupying respectively the northern and southern portions   These
branches are separated by the valley which lies to the southwest from the southern end of Lake George, which is filled with a chain of small lakes   Two small
streams, rising among these lakes, find their way, the one to Lake George and
the other to the Hudson River   It is stated that about one-half of the surface
bordering upon the river is broken by high hills, but is susceptible, nevertheless,
of cultivation   The highest and most conspicuous mountain peak in the town
is Potash Kettle, in the northern part, which lifts its symmetrical proportions
to an elevation of about 1,735 feet above tide, and from the summit of which
can be obtained broken glimpses of the beautiful Valley of the Hudson   The
soil in some parts is pure sand, and in others is relieved by a slight intermixture of loam.   Some of the farms are quite productive

" History has been enriched somewhat by leaves from Luzerne   It was on
the regular Indian trail from the great villages of the Mohawks to the head of
Lake George   Here King Hendrick and his braves encamped when on their
way to join Johnson at the lake in 1775, and it was also the route taken by
Sir John Johnson when he came from Canada for his buried treasures at Johnson Hall " [1]

The town was taken from Qeeensbury on the 10th of April, 1792, and until
April 6, 1808, was known as Fairfield   On the 30th of March, 1802, a strip

---

[1] S R Stoddard's *The Adirondacks*, p 180

of territory one mile wide was set off to Queensbury   The town records have
no minutes of the proceedings which were had in the year 1792, nor of the
officers which served during that year   The minutes for 1793 are, however,
complete, and as the first officers were probably nearly identical with those
for 1793, a list of the latter will be of interest   They are as follows   (Elected
at an annual town meeting held on April 2d, 1793)   Sepervisor, Jeremiah Russell, town clerk, Benjamin Cowles, assessors, John Price, Gersham Darling,
Daniel Ashley, constable and collector, Thomas Horton (with Jeremiah Russell and John Price as bondsmen), constable, James Kilborn, overseers of the
poor, Gersham Darling and Daniel Ashley, commissioners of highways, Hendrick Loop, John Price and Benjamin Cowles, poundmaster, Daniel Mills;
pathmasters, John Austin, Asa Durham, Philo Dexter, Thomas Holdridge,
and Jeremiah Darling, fence viewers, John Austin and Asa Durham

The records of this and subsequent meetings for a number of years are
quaint and instructive   Quaint in the manner of expression, penmanship and
orthography, and instructive in that they reveal the difficulties with which
these daring pioneers had to contend, the novelty of adjusting themselves to
their new surroundings, and the courage and perseverance which they exhibited in removing or surmounting all the obstacles which lay in their path   In
the record of the meeting at which the above named officers were elected, appear minutes from which the following is an extract —

" Vote Past by this Meting that Hogs may Run on the common with lawful yokes "   .

It was further resolved that a lawful fence must be four feet and six inches
high; that there should be a pound built for this town thirty feet " squire "
and seven feet high, that this pound should be built " at the lowest bid,"
whereupon it was found that Russell Durham was the lowest bidder, at thirty-
eight shillings   He was to build the pound of white-pine logs, and to have it
finished before the first of June, 1794   The account closed with the following
words . " The above Writen Town officers were this day Qualified before Jeremiah Russell, Esqr "

At the annual town meeting held in the spring of 1794 it was, among other
things, resolved · —

" Vote past that Hogs may run from the first of may to the first of September, with yokes the width of the neck above the neck, and half the width below and each side of the neck "

It seems that the pound which Russell Durham built was not constructed
according to specifications   " The report of the committee that was chosen to
inspect the pound, viz . That the Pound was not built according to agreement
and that Russell Durham should return the money again to the town or build
a good, sufficient Pound "—*Town Records of* 1795   Which of the alternatives
Russell Durham complied with, if either, does not appear

By reason, probably of the very early settlement of Glens Falls, it is found that even at this early date a number of rude mountain roads radiated from that place to Lake George and different parts of the Hudson, one coming to Luzerne or Fairfield The following item is from the records of 1795 "By a Request of the Inhabitants of the Town of Fairfield by a Petition sined By twelve Freeholders Dated April 29, 1793, We, the Commitioners of Highways of the Town of Fairfield, Have Viewed the Road at the Eastward of this Town to Queensborough We find that is exceeding Difficult passing From the top of the East Mountain to Queensborough Line We therefore think it Necessary to turn the Road from the first Pitch on the East side of the Mountain and Running a North East Cours to the first water and thence Running a Due East Course By Glans saw mill to Queensbury Line Said road Laid By us

" JOHN PRICE
" BENJAMIN COWLES "

During this and the following years seven roads were laid and four were altered

In these early times nearly every house in remote and pioneer settlements aspired to the dignity of a tavern, where the wayfaring stranger might receive lodging and food and a nameless quantity of the beverage that cheers as well as intoxicates It would be hard, therefore, to designate this or that house as being peculiarly fitted for the purposes of an inn until a few years later, when travelers became too numerous to be conveniently accommodated at private houses This early custom might, even without the aid of ulterior evidence, be inferred from some of the records of the period, in which it seems that nearly every inhabitant of the town must have applied for an innkeeper's license In 1797, in this town, though the names are not numerous, it is more than likely that the applicants were not the owners of establishments which could be classed in the same category with Rockwell's Hotel, The Wayside, or the Riddell House Benjamin Cross paid six shillings and eight pence (English money) for permission to retail spirituous liquors in his house during the months of January and February, 1797, and for the same privilege for the ensuing year he paid two pounds Richard Hempstraught paid the first named sum for the same privilege for the months of January and February, 1797 On June 5th, 1797, Medad Bostwick paid for the privilege for one year one pound and ten shillings

In 1801 there were nine road districts in town and two new roads were laid The work of laying out and altering roads was in constant progress from year to year In 1802 two were laid out

The courts were more strict then than now, perhaps because by reason of the sparseness of population and the near approach to unanimity of sentiment among the inhabitants, the laws were more easily enforced Witness the following records of convictions and methods of punishment —

"Washington county,[1] Be it Remembered that on the Seventeenth Day of
November, In the year of our Lord one thousand eight hundred and two, Noah
Hatch was convicted Before me, Mark A Childs, one of the Justices of the
Peace of said County, For Taking one profane oath   Given under my hand
and seal the Day and year above said   MARK A CHILDS, J Peace "

A conviction is likewise recorded against Samuel Washburn and his wife
Hannah, of Hadley, Saratoga county, for frequenting a tippling house on Sunday, December 6th, 1802, at the house of Richard Hempstraught in Fairfield.
A few years later at the annual town meeting held in April, 1810, it was
"Voted, That there should be a pair of stocks built in the town of Luzerne,
not far from William Johnson's now dwelling house, in order to punish disorderly persons, and to be erected by the poormasters, and on the expense of
the money of the said Town "

Down to a comparatively recent date the mountains and woods of the vicinity were infested by sheep-killing beasts, such as wolves, wild cats, and even
panthers   Premiums or bounties were annually offered to persons who should
succeed in killing any of these troublesome brutes, and were continued down to
nearly the middle of the present century

The method of caring for the poor was greatly different from that at present in vogue   The poor were not a county, but a town charge   Money was
appropriated from the funds voted for the support of the poor to remunerate
persons who had cared for, or should care for one or more paupers for a stated
length of time   This was continued until 1826, when the county-house was
erected and the system became what it is to-day

Of the original settlers here before 1800, their places of residence and their
occupations, it is impossible to say anything   The records reveal nothing but
their names, and the memory of living man does not extend to a period so remote in the past   But it is certain the division of labor was not very marked
in those days   Many of the pioneers were at once inn-keepers, blacksmiths,
farmers, and merchants   The names of the settlers as they appear on the records
may, however, be of some interest   Some of them have already appeared.
Among them are   Jeremiah Russell, Benjamin Cowles, Ebenezer Sprague,
Benjamin Cross, George Loveless, Aaron Vandebogart, Gilbert Caswell, Peter
Mallory, Elijah Buttolph, Silas Dibble, John Cleveland, Henry Schaff, Eliph-
alet Lindsley, Isaac Washburn, Medad Bostwick, John Vanduser, Joel Read,
James Mosher, Thomas Orton, Jabesh Gray, Abijah Adams, Daniel Ransom,
Joseph Stone, Grant Towsey, Jonathan Beebe, John Ferguson, Elijah Brace,
and Hezekiah Weatherby

"Among its early settlers was Edward Jessup, after whom the landing below was named, and odd old Ben Barrett, who was noted for his practical jokes,
and to this day, in that region, if a 'joke' comes to light whose paternity is

---

[1] It will be remembered that Warren county was not organized until 1813

unknown, it is at once ascribed to old Ben   He once rode a horse into Rock-well's bar-room, took a drink, then rode out again   At another time he saw a peddler with a basket of extracts, and at once offered to bet a small sum that he could beat him across the bridge, carrying his basket at the time   The bet was taken, they started, and Ben fell, breaking many of the bottles, then sol-emnly admitting that he had lost, paid the bet, and left the brilliant peddler calculating how much he had made by the operation

"Mr Rockwell gives some very interesting reminiscences of earlier times When a boy he saw an old soldier who, in 1777, with others, was captured by the Indians near Lake George, stripped of their clothing, their hands tied to stakes, and fires built around them, while the savages gathered near to enjoy the sport   He soon managed to slip his hands out of the thongs that bound them, sprang through the flames, seized a little boy who appeared to be the son of a chief, and before the astonished natives could help themselves, sprang back within the circle of flames once more   A rush was made to save the child, and in the confusion the white man, dashing through the lines, made for the woods, with the yelling pack at his heels   Being a good runner, he kept away from them, going through the valley, where the road now runs towards Lake George, past the lake, past Rockwell's, and down the steep bank back of the Wilcox House to a place just below the falls, where he jumped on a rock near the cen-ter of the river, thence to the opposite side, and climbing up the rocks, gained the cover of the bushes on top as the yelling savages appeared on the other side   They then gave up the chase, and he succeeded in reaching his friends in safety "[1]

One of the oldest and most prominent of the men still living who can give valuable and interesting reminiscences of the early part of this century is the venerable George T Rockwell, known more familiarly among his hosts of guests as " Uncle George "   He was born in the town of Hadley, Saratoga county, on the 9th day of March, 1807   His father, Jeremy Rockwell, was a prominent business man in Hadley, just across the river from Luzerne, and hence our present interlocutor's early experiences were connected almost as in-timately with Luzerne as with Hadley   His memory of persons and events as far back as 1815 is quite clear   Of the residents of Luzerne at about that time he gives the following information   William Leavens, some of whose descendants are now living at Glens Falls, was a prominent man here, and a farmer   He lived on the River road about two and a half miles from the vil-lage   Joel Orton kept tavern about the same distance away on the road to-ward Glens Falls, in the same building now occupied by Mr Blackwood   John Cameron, a Methodist preacher, resided six miles north of the village of Lu-zerne on the Hudson   He was an intimate friend of the Rockwell family Nathan A Wells, a lumberman, dwelt in the building now occupied by Peter

---

1 *The Adirondacks*, by S. R Stoddard, (pp 180, 181)

Pulver George T Rockwell became his son-in-law on the 12th of September, 1831 William H Wells and Reuben Wells were sons of Nathan A Wells Marlborough Ball, who came to this vicinity soon after 1815, was a Quaker He kept a farm on what is called the Hog's Back, a mountain ridge in the south part of the town Descendants from him reside there now Joseph Varney, another Quaker, was engaged in the same business with his near neighbor last above mentioned, and worshiped with equal silence at the same shrine His brother (?) Nathaniel Varney, lived near him Another member of this Quaker farming settlement was George Murray John S St John, physician, came here before 1820 He had an office just opposite the present site of Rockwell's Hotel Nathan A Wells, in addition to his lumbering business proper, owned a saw-mill and grist-mill on the site of Burnham's grist-mill, the saw-mill being a few rods farther east or up Wells's Creek At about 1815 Daniel Bocker kept a general store on the corner by the grist-mill. Jeremy Rockwell kept store on the other side of the river It may be stated here that he came from Ballston to Hadley in 1802, and was originally a Connecticut man In 1815 the whole country hereabouts was covered with almost impervious forests of pine Settlements were formed slowly and painfully There were not more than six dwelling houses of any description on either side of the river at the village of Luzerne or Hadley Azariah Scofield began, about the year 1818, to keep a store where Edward C Young now keeps one A portion of the old building is still standing A man named Allard used to visit the various families scattered through this vicinity and mend their boots and shoes He was the only shoemaker known to the community Descendants from him are now living in Greenfield, N Y.

The lumber business here for a number of years prior to 1820 was very extensive Jeremy Rockwell, Artemus Aldrich, Nathan A Wells, Samuel and Benjamin Rogers, Abijah Adams and a man named Powers were all quite largely interested The two first named were undoubtedly the most prominent lumbermen here There were ten or twelve saw mills running in town Jeremy Rockwell had two mills on the falls below the village Artemus Aldrich had another near by The mill of Nathan A Wells has already been mentioned. Thomas Lee owned a large mill about two miles up Wells's Creek from the village Abijah Adams had two above Lee Ware Sherman owned and ran one on Leavens's Brook between two and three miles below the village and about a quarter of a mile from the Hudson, and his son, Augustus Sherman, owned one a few years later At a distance of about six miles up Wells's Creek John Ferguson had two mills Very few logs were in those days floated down the Hudson, as these mills just mentioned did all the sawing for home consumption, and even more — enough to keep the choppers at work.

There was more or less of farming conducted in a general way, corn, oats,

potatoes and rye being then as now the principal products   In the north part
of the town (on the north side of Potash Kettle), Gage, Gay, Bartlett, Benedict Putnam, and John Stanton all owned farms   One grist-mill, and one
alone, owned by Nathan A Wells, flourished in town in 1815, and Jeremy
Rockwell "kept up his end" on the other side of the river   No tannery as yet
existed   Joel Orton kept tavern on the Queensbury Road, and Samuel Van
Tassel kept another about six miles from Luzerne village on the Lake George
Road — where Joseph Ferguson now lives   There was no distillery about
here until 1848, when Jeremy Rockwell built one in Hadley

The lives of these early settlers were not devoid of incident, both of tragedy
and comedy   One of the former kind is related as having taken place about
the period of which we are speaking   Jeremiah Russell, who lived in the
north part of the town, on the late John Cranell place, was justice of the peace
for many years   One Fairchild was charged before him at one time of com-
mitting an unnamable crime, and public indignation ran so high against him
that Russell was upheld in issuing a warrant for the offender's arrest containing
the illegal words, " to be taken dead or alive "   Clothed with the supposed
authority over life, suggested by this phrase, the officer went to Fairchild's
residence, near Ira Lindsey's present home, and seeing Fairchild attempting
to escape, shot him dead   The officer was arrested, taken to Albany, tried
and acquitted

Many are the stories told also about "old Ben Barrett," the practical joker
He was a lumberman and merchant in the village of Luzerne—was in partnership for a time with George Cronkhite   He lived on the site now occupied by
the house of the widow of Andrew Porteus   It is related that one day, while
on a spree, Barrett made a bet of three dollars with a fellow-lumberman that
the former could throw the latter across the Hudson at Albany   The wager
was made with punctilious sobriety of demeanor   After repairing to the place
where the money was to be won or lost, and making due preparation for the
effort, Barrett seized his opponent, held him out over the water, and relinquishing a laughably feeble attempt to throw him, dropped him into the river below.
When the fellow came up all dripping and demanded his money, Barrett made
a plunge for him, with the exclamation that he'd " try it a thousand times before he'd give up the money," whereupon the fellow, as frightened as wet, left
the vicinity with all possible speed, while Barrett and his comrades consumed
the money in " drinks for the crowd "   Another anecdote told of him is that
when rafting logs one evening he and his fellows came to a place on shore
where a wedding party were cooking delicacies in an open oven   None of the
party happening to be near the oven at the time, the jolly lumbermen ran
ashore and lifted oven, sweetmeats and all on the raft and pushed on their way
down the river   They had not gone far before they could hear the splashing
of oars behind them, and prudently concluding that they were pursued, they

33

hid the delicacies in the raft and quietly dropped the oven overboard   In a few minutes a man rowed alongside, peered with most inquisitive scrutiny into every nook and corner of the raft, and finally rowed reluctantly back under the impression that they had done the " honest " lumbermen injustice in their suspicions   It is needless to say that the aforesaid " honest " lumbermen immediately " fell to " with ocular manifestations of appetites which would make a giant anaconda hang his glittering head with humility

Among the other early settlers was Joseph W Paddock, a lawyer, who came here about 1816, married a daughter of Nathan A Wells, lived until about 1832 opposite the site of Rockwell's Hotel, and then went West   He died in about 1837 or 1838 at Rondout, N Y, of cholera   His brother, Ira Paddock, came here several years after the advent of Joseph, and practiced law with him for a number of years   Before 1830 he removed to Glens Falls, the place of his death

John S St John, an early physician already mentioned, lived after 1811 for some years on the site of Rockwell's Vanderbilt cottage [1]

William Johnson, town clerk in early days, lived where John Gladhill now does   He is mentioned in the town records as early as 1806

Another early physician was Dr Truman B Hicks   He married a sister of George T Rockwell   He lived for a time—and died—in what is now known as the Riddell house

Dr James Lawrence, whose history is given in greater detail in the chapter devoted to the past of the medical profession in Warren county, practiced here from about 1825 to January, 1861   His son is the present postmaster of Luzerne

John Cornwell was an early farmer and lumberman   He came before 1800 and lived near John Ferguson's, about six miles north of the village   Elijah Buttolph settled before 1810 at Jessup's Landing on the Luzerne side of the the river   Isaac Washburn, a contemporary with Buttolph, lived on his farm about a mile south of Luzerne village on the bank of the river   Isaiah Parmenter " farmed it " on the premises which now constitute the George T Rockwell farm   John Austin, farmer, lived more than two miles north of the village on land now occupied by Joseph Gailey   His grandson now lives in town. George P Cronkhite had an ashery on the place now belonging to Rockwell's Hotel

In the beginning of the century there was a flourishing school on this side the river   The school building stood right near the site of the present schoolhouse in the village   Daniel Gill taught there before 1815, and was followed by a Mr Harwood   There was an attendance at times of nearly or quite a hundred pupils   There was formerly but one district in the villages of Hadley and Luzerne, but about 1838 the district was divided and a school established

1 So named because formerly rented of Mr Rockwell by the famous Commodore himself

in Hadley   The fiast mention of school matters in the town records appears
in 1813, when Willard Leavens, Daniel Wagar, John S St John, were elected
superintendents of school districts, and Jeremiah Russell, Edward Cornwell,
John Lindsey, William B Colson, and David Bockes, inspectors of schools.
There were then seven school districts in town

Religious meetings were held in the school down to about 1815   Rev
Tobias Spicer, a Methodist itinerant, preached here about 1810 or 1812 During the War of 1812 intense excitement prevailed at times in this remote wilderness   Drafts were made here to fill the American ranks   Several men
from here took an active part in the battle of Plattsburg, among them one
Wells (no connection of Nathan A Wells), carried the last plank from the
bridge at that famous engagement

The "cold season of 1816" affected Luzerne badly   Rye and corn went
up that summer to two dollars a bushels and pork to fifty dollars a barrel
There was a great amount of suffering   Grinding used to be done at the mills
without undergoing the usual process of separating the bran from the kernel
Many people became so destitute that they would come to the mills from miles
away and sweep the beams for flour dust with which to make their bread
Even then many families went for a month without bread

Having viewed the town and village during their early struggles it will be
of some interest to tiace their growth down to a more recent date   A minute
made in the year 1835 states that the village of Luzerne then had one grist-
mill, three saw-mills, clothing works, two taverns, three stores and about thirty
dwellings   The grist-mill was still owned by Nathan A Wells   It was originally built by David Bockes, already named   An old Tory had had one on
the same site in Revolutionary times, but it became too hot for him here and
he left without ceremony   Abijah Adams still ran a grist-mill and saw-mill on
the Lake George road   He died not far from 1840   Jeremy Rockwell and
Ben Barrett owned a double saw-mill in the village on the east end of the dam
It was carried away by a freshet in 1832 or 1833   Nathan A Wells also run
a saw-mill at this time   The clothing works were situated just below the grist-
mill and were owned by Jeremy Rockwell and Orry Martin   They had been
here for a number years, but went down before 1840   The two taverns mentioned referred to George T Rockwell's, which he built in 1832, and Luke
Fenton, who kept one where the Riddell House now is   Before Mr Rockwell bought his hotel premises Luke Fenton run a similitude of a tavern there
He was there several years and was preceded by Edward Scovil, uncle to P
C Scovil   Azariah Scoville preceded Edward Scovil as early as 1815   A
store was kept in one part of the house   The three stores in the village in 1835
were that of Daniel Stewart and William H Wells, who, under the firm name
of Stewart & Wells, kept a store just across from Rockwell's Hotel , that o
Henry Rockwell, brother to George T Rockwell, which was situated on the

site of the store now kept by Walter P Wilcox, and which he kept from about 1820 or 1825 for many years; and that of Barrett & Cronkhite (Ben Barrett and George P Cronkhite), which stood just north of the present Riddell House Soon after 1830, however, Zina H Cowles and William B Martindale succeeded Barrett & Cronkhite George W Ruggles succeeded Cowles in the partnership in a few years, and about the year 1840 Martindale & Ruggles failed

John Durham and Ira St John were at this period wagon-makers on the creek in the village Jeduthan Lake was then a farmer in the south part of the town where he still lives, Isaac Barrows was a neighbor to Lake, Ebenezer Martin ran a farm in the north part of the town These are only a few of the many names that might be mentioned of this date, but they are important

From the town records of the period covering the year 1840 and the following ten years it is learned that at the former date there were twenty-eight road districts in town In 1843 statements reveal the fact that there were then fourteen school districts, three hundred and thirty-five pupils, and four hundred and eighty-eight books (school property) This was a period of temperance agitation, undoubtedly, for there was considerable opposition to the granting of any licenses In 1845 the commissioners of excise granted tavern licenses to William A Pierson and Stephen Lake In the spring of 1846, the town resolved by a vote of 133 to 37 that no licenses should be granted The resolution was re-enacted in the following year At the annual meeting of the excise board on the 31st of May, 1849, the following applications were presented Grocery licenses, T D Stewart, and Taft P Town; tavern licenses, Stephen Lake, Orlin Pember, Carmi Lindsey, and George T Rockwell I. P Wilcox applied for a temperance license Among the various resolutions passed by this honorable body was one to the effect that no grocery licenses be granted, that three tavern licenses be granted, viz. to Stephen Lake, George T Rockwell, and Orlin Pember, that a temperance license be granted to I P Wilcox, and that " no rot-gut be sold in the town "

When the War of the Rebellion broke out, the town of Luzerne responded promptly and heartily to the imperative demand for men and money to preserve the Union from dissolution The first item in the town records appears under date of November 6th, 1862, when the town auditors allowed to Newton Aldrich the sum of $15.38 for the relief of soldiers' families, and $225 for the payment of balances due to the soldiers themselves On the 5th of November, 1863, the sum of $130 71 was allowed to Daniel Stewart for soldiers, and for relief to the families of soldiers, and Morgan Burdick, appointed by the auditors a committee of relief, as required by statute, reported that he had received from the town $25 00, out of which he had paid for the relief of the families of soldiers the sum of $14 61

On the 6th of July, 1864, the following document was presented to the town clerk —

"Call for Special Town Meeting to raise Bounty Money to pay Volunteers
"*To the Town Clerk of the Town of Luzerne* —

"We, the undersigned, citizens of Luzerne, request you to call a special meeting of said Town, to vote upon the question whether a tax shall be raised upon said Town to pay bounties to volunteers under the call to be issued by the President of the United States   Dated July 6th, 1864

"Henry McMaster, Orrin Moore, Perry C Scovil, W W Rockwell, A Hemstreet, O Dean, A J Cheritree, Daniel Stewart, J B Burneson, George T Rockwell, George Eddy, George W Inman "

Whereupon, William H Wells, town clerk, gave notice of such meeting to vote upon the question as to whether or not the sum of $5,000 should be raised   The result was that out of 141 votes cast upon the question, 89 were in the affirmative, and 52 in the negative   At the same meeting it was determined that not more than $100 was expedient to be voted to each volunteer   On the 5th of August following this last measure was rescinded, and the sum made $200 for each volunteer, or person furnishing a volunteer   The aggregate sum, however, was not to exceed $5,000   On the 23d of August, 1864, it was resolved by a vote of 70 against 30 that the additional sum of $3,000 be raised to pay bounties   On September 12th it was decided to raise a still further sum for bounties, but the additional amount is not named

Between the 23d of August and the 5th of October, 1864, bonds were given aggregating $11,125

At a Special Meeting held on February 11th, 1865, called to decide whether or not sufficient money should be raised by tax to pay volunteers and prevent a draft under the president's call for 300,000 men, and to defray the expense of enlisting men and mustering them into service, it was resolved by a vote of 74 to 31 that the necessary amount be raised   Subsequently Andrew J Cheritree, in his capacity of supervisor, was authorized by the auditors to enlist men with money which had been placed in his hands to pay bonds not due, said obligations to be met when due by a sale of town bonds.

Under all these enactments and measures, men enlisted freely and fought bravely   Homes were deserted and hearts broken, but the grand object of saving the Union was accomplished

Following is a list of the town supervisors from the first annual meeting to the year 1885   1793–1800, Jeremiah Russell, 1801 and 1802, Mark A Child, 1803, Willard Leavens; 1804, Jeremiah Russell, 1805–1808, Erastus Cross, 1809–1811, Willard Leavens, 1812 and 1813, John S St John, 1814, Willard Leavens, 1815–1817, John S St John, 1818, Joel Orton, 1819, John Cameron; 1820, Willard Leavens, 1821–1823, John Cameron, 1824, Willard Leavens, 1825–27, Nathan A Wells, 1828, Willard Leavens, 1829–1831,

William H Wells, 1832–1836, Reuben Wells, 1837 and 1838, Daniel Stewart; 1839–1841, James D Weston, 1842–1845, George T Rockwell; 1846, William H Wells, 1847, Jonas Selleck, 1848, Daniel Stewart, 1849'and 1850, Thomas Butler, 1851–1853, George T Rockwell, 1854, William H Wells; 1855 and 1856, Newton Aldrich, 1857, Thomas Butler, 1858, Ira Lindsey; 1859, Newton Aldrich, 1860, Thomas Butler, 1861, William H Wells, 1862–1869, Andrew J Cheritree; 1870–1872, J C Porteus; 1873 and 1874, H P. Gwinup, 1875 and 1876, Benjamin C Butler, 1877, Wilson Smead, 1878, Clark Hall, 1879, James G Porteus, 1880 and 1881, Andrew Porteus, 1882, J B Burnison, 1883–1885, John Peart, jr

The following are the present officers-elect of the town : {Supervisor, John Peart, jr, town clerk, James H Lawrence, assessor, Eugene D Howe, justices of the peace, Charles Trumbull, William Anderson, H. W Lindsey, Perry C. Scovil, L E Stearns, commissioner of highways, W W Ramsay; collector, John L Burneson, overseer of the poor, Alexander Fisher, inspectors of election, E K Thomas, Perry C Scovil, constables, John L Burneson, Thomas H Taylor, Ira H Putnam, Wallace Bullice, W C Howe, game constable, Fred Rorder, commissioners of excise, John Batter, one year, George W Beadmore, two years W H Putman, three years

The population of the town of Luzerne has varied since 1850 as follows: 1850, 1,300, 1855, 1,286, 1860, 1,328, 1865, 1,136; 1870, 1,174, 1875, 1,303, 1880, 1,438

MUNICIPAL HISTORY

The village of Luzerne, as has already been learned, consisted, in 1810, of a saw-mill, a grist-mill, and not more than half a dozen dwellings   In 1835 there was a grist-mill, three saw-mills, clothing works, two taverns, three stores, and about thirty dwellings   The village had grown to reasonable proportions It has grown since then, though not, perhaps, in the same proportion, but it has acquired a reputation for healthfulness and salubrity and unrivaled beauty, which has made it the favorite resort of a large class of people from Troy and Albany, and New York, and other cities, which cannot be diminished by any comparison with other resorts more loudly advertised, and more fervently described by artists and pleasure seekers.   On the northeastern boundary of the village, on a more elevated plane, and yet concealed from view until the approaching traveler is almost upon it, lies Lake Luzerne, imbedded in the hills and slopes covered with evergreens, like a gem of pearl in a setting of emerald, and bearing on its tremulous bosom a solitary island so small that it seems to float   On the other side of the village, separating it from its sister village, Hadley, tumbles the historic Hudson among boulders that stubbornly resist the course of the waters and often retard the progress of the logs that float upon its surface   Out in every direction — over mountains to Glens Falls and Stony

Creek, through mountains to Lake George, and between mountains along the Hudson River, lead roads that carry the admiring sight-seer through an endless and unrepeating succession of pleasing surprises Luzerne is peculiar " It has no brother and is like no brother," and these beauties and this peculiarity crowd its excellent hotels each summer to overflowing

Mr George T Rockwell says that until perhaps 1835 the post-office which had been established at Hadley received mail for the inhabitants of Luzerne About that year the post-office was established and Harmon Wells received the appointment He held the office for a number of years and was succeeded by his brother, Reuben Wells, who remained in office until 1856 Then John B Burneson was appointed In 1861 he was superseded by Andrew J Cheritree, now county judge of Warren county Charles Schermerhorn was appointed in 1862, and performed the duties incident to the position until 1866 In that year Augustus H Cross was empowered to control the distribution of mail to the good people of Luzerne In 1871 he gave place to Thomas Butler, who remained until 1878 James P Darling then took the position, but in 1882 was replaced by the present incumbent, James H Lawrence

Hotels — In preceding pages it has been stated that the present site of Rockwell's Hotel is the oldest hotel site in the village For years before 1832 Luke Fenton had kept a tavern here In that year the venerable proprietor, George T Rockwell, purchased the property of Nathan A Wells, rebuilt the old structures, and on the first of May opened his hotel In 1852 he rebuilt the house a second time, and from that time has occasionally made such additions, attractions and repairs as the vigilance of the owner suggested were necessary The hotel proper, with the four cottages attached, and the barbershop and grounds, covers an area of about four acres One hundred and fifty guests can be comfortably accommodated A farm of six hundred acres provides many of the substantial and wholesome articles of food which load the deservedly famous table of mine host Rockwell Mr George T Rockwell claims, with a strong probability of truth, that he is the hotel proprietor of longest standing of any in the United States He certainly knows the business, and has taught his sons the art with equal success His son and partner, George H Rockwell, went in 1866 to Lake George and assumed the proprietorship of the Lake House, in company with his brother, H J Rockwell In the fall of 1867 he bought out his father in Luzerne and remained here until 1879, when he went to Glens Falls as part proprietor of the Rockwell House at that place In 1881 he came back to Luzerne and has remained here until the present They set one of the finest tables in this part of the country

The Riddell House, E E Riddell proprietor, was originally built about 1810 by Josiah Fuller Luke Fenton kept it until about 1825 Mr Riddell's predecessor was Charles Wilcox, who gave place to the present genial proprietor in 1884 The house can accommodate eighty guests

The Wayside was built in about 1869 by B C Butler, and kept by him for a while The present proprietor, H J Rockwell, son of George T Rockwell, opened the house in 1882 for summers only He was formerly[1] of Rockwell's Hotel, Luzerne ; of the Rockwell House at Glens Falls; of the Lake House and Fort William Henry, at Lake George, and present proprietor of the American House at Troy The hotel is built in the Swiss style of architecture There are nine cottages on the grounds About two hundred persons can be accommodated

Mercantile Interests — The oldest store in town is the drug store and pharmacy of George Y Miller Mr Miller resigned from the U S Navy on the 7th day of April, 1865, and on the 10th of May opened his store in Luzerne He moved into his present store building in May, 1866 James H Lawrence has kept a general store here since 1867 He began in the lower part of the village, but himself erected his present store building in 1875 and immediately occupied it Mr Lawrence, besides his experience as postmaster, served as town clerk from 1867 to 1879 and since 1882 E Dayton, jeweler, began business here in 1871 He started on the corner now occupied by Morton's store, and moved to his present location in the spring of 1884 Walter P Wilcox started a grocery here in the spring of 1873 He began operations in the store now occupied by T C Stillwell, and moved to his present quarters in the spring of 1883 C W Wagar first commenced dealing in general merchandise here in 1873 He went out in a short time and W H Ives occupied the building for a general store About 1876 he removed to Glens Falls and Webster & Co opened a hardware store in the building In 1878 M C Wagar bought them out and placed the management of the business in the hands of C W Wagar In 1882 the latter bought out his brother and has since that time conducted the business alone He now has both a hardware and a general department Stephen V Morton opened a grocery and meat-market in his present location in 1878. W T Garnar started a dry goods and grocery business in Luzerne in the spring of 1880 in company with W S Porteous Since the latter withdrew in 1881 Mr Garner has conducted the business alone Edward Young has had a tin-shop here about three years and a half He came into his present building in 1885 David Frank, dealer in dry goods and ready-made clothing, came here on July 1st, 1882 J J Parker, general merchant, began business in Luzerne on the 1st of May, 1885

Lumber — The only lumber business extensively carried on here at present is controlled by P H Pulver, L E Wait and George H. Rockwell, under the firm style of Pulver, Wait & Rockwell They own tracts of timbered land on both sides of the river towards Lake George, aggregating about four thousand acres Logs are floated down the Hudson to Glens Falls They

[1] S R STODDARD's *Adirondacks*, p 178

have peeled as many as four thousand cords of hemlock bark in a year   The firm of Pulver, Wait & Rockwell is of recent formation, though Pulver & Wait have been together for years

Leather Business — The business now carried on under the title of The Garnar Leather Works was established in 1867, by Raymond & Ely   Thomas Garnar bought from them in 1869 and conducted the business without a partner until 1879, when he associated with himself J V Walsh and E M Garnar, and changed the firm name to Thomas Garnar & Co   In 1869 the concern employed six hands and turned out about six hundred dozen sheepskins per month   The business has been so enlarged that at present forty hands are constantly employed and three thousand dozen sheepskins are prepared per month   The goods are used for book binding

Attorney. — The only practicing attorney at law in Luzerne is H P Gwinup, who was admitted in January, 1876, at Albany, after passing a clerkship with Judiah Ellsworth, late of Luzerne   He has practiced here ever since his admission

Physicians — Dr J B Burneson was graduated at the medical college of Castleton, Vt , in June, 1852, and came at once to Luzerne   Dr James Seth Cooley obtained his medical education in the medical department of the University of New York, and received his diploma in February, 1877   He practiced in Sandy Hill until 1880, when he came to Luzerne   Before entering upon his medical career he had unusual experience as an instructor   Graduated from Williams College in 1869, he became professor of ancient languages at Fort Edward Institute, which position he held for three years   He was vice-principal and professor of the natural sciences there for the scholastic years 1872 and 1873   He was also principal of the Glens Falls Academy from 1873 to 1876 inclusive.

Churches — The first church organization in the town of Luzerne was of the Methodist denomination, who were largely predominant at the time of the building of the first church edifice in town   This edifice is the old Union or Methodist Church still standing, on the River road about three miles north of the village   It was raised on the 10th of June, 1807   The services for many years were conducted by various denominations working together   The Methodists, however, maintained their ascendency in numbers, and, consequently, in influence   The Rev Tobias Spicer and the Rev Henry Coleman were about the first preachers in town   In 1837 the several denominations, still united, removed to the village of Luzerne and erected the house of worship on the site of the present Presbyterian Church   In 1852 the Methodists became a distinct and separate body, and erected their present edifice   It was built by James Hegeman, now of Glens Falls, and Silas Dayton, now in the West   Owing to the destruction of the old records by fire, the figures showing the cost of erection, etc , cannot be obtained.   At the time of the building of this edifice, the Rev

Henry Williams was in the pastorate, the Rev Stephen Stiles came in before the edifice was completed   Since 1841 the pastors, so far as their names could be learned, have been as follows · Revs Adam Jones and Solomon H Foster; Albert Champlin and Abel Ford, Alanson Richards and John L Robertson, Ezra Sayre, Joseph Connor, L D Sherwood, Henry Williams, Stephen Stiles (1852), Chester Chamberlain, C C Bedell, P M Hitchcock, G W S Porter, Bennett Eaton (1861), E Morgan, W H Tiffany, E A Blanchard, Joseph Cope, F K Potter, Edwin Genge, R J Davies (about 1879), J B. Wood, 1881   In 1882 came the Rev J B Searles, the present pastor   About 1864, during the pastorate of Rev E Morgan, the parsonage was burned and the church records lost   The church property is now valued at $3,000 including the parsonage   The present membership is one hundred and eighty-five, with twenty-seven probationers   The present officers are   Orrin Moore, H Burnham, M L Willard, R N Ramsay, Charles Thomas and William Wagar, trustees , Orrin Moore, H Burnham, George Crannell, William Wagar, Linus Wendell, Edwin Kerr, James Taylor, Orson Ball, Myron Selleck, George Anderson, and M L Willard, stewards

The old church on the River road (Call street) is supplied from the pulpit of the Methodist Church at Luzerne, and has a membership of about forty

The first Sunday-school held in Luzerne was started in 1817 by Mrs Ann C Dunham at the old Ira St John house that stood near the present residence of P C. Scovil   There was then no resident minister nor church edifice here. In 1818 Nathan A Wells and Josiah Fassett led the Sunday-school in the old school-house   Mrs McUmber and a Miss Jones had charge of it   In about the year 1822 Mrs Henry Coleman, wife of the Methodist clergyman, superintended one in the old Shearer house, where Mr Garnar now lives   From that time until 1837 no record can be found throwing any light on the history of this school   The first Sunday-school superintendent in the Union Church in the village was Zina Cowles   He was followed by Ira St John, William H. Wells, Reuben Wells, D B Ketchum, James Taylor, Sylvanus Scovil, Newton Aldrich, C R McEwan, W H St John, W S Taylor, Orrin Moore, M L. Willard, W S Taylor, and R N Ramsey, the present superintendent   The average attendance at present is about 125

The Rockwells Falls Presbyterian Church was organized on the 17th day of January, 1856, by a committee of the Albany Presbytery composed of Dr Woodbridge, of Saratoga, Rev Tully, of Ballston, and Rev Lyon, of Fish House   The first elders were William Scofield and Charles Rockwell   The first members were Mr and Mrs Charles Rockwell, Mrs Anna Younglove, Miss Susan Benedict, Mr and Mrs. William Scofield, Mrs Catharine Wells, and Miss Jane Ann Barnes   A few days afterward the following were added to the church : Mr. and Mrs Robert Ramsey, Mr and Mrs. William Ramsey, Mr and Mrs John Dougherty, Mr and Mrs Samuel Gayley   Before the formal organization of the church the Rev —— Benedict, who came in 1852, and was the first Presbyterian clergyman resident at Luzerne, Rev —— Myers, who came in 1854, and Rev Charles H Skillman, who came in 1855, and remained five years, preached to the Presbyterian congregation of this place. In the summer of 1860 Rev J H McLean, of Washington county, began a stay here of four months Rev C A Patterson came in 1861 and remained about a year as minister In February, 1862, F B Hall was ordained and installed as pastor In November, 1862, he entered the army, and did not return to active labor here The church was then for three years without regular supply During the summer of 1864, however, Rev Dr Duryea, then of Brooklyn, occupied the pulpit During this period of the church's history it became greatly reduced in numbers and efficiency, but began to recover in 1866 On August first of that year Rev Elihu T Sanford came to act as stated supply He remained one year, and was succeeded by Rev Walter Nichols He in turn was followed in May, 1868, by Rev George Craig, who remained three years In the summer of 1871 Rev William Durant filled the pulpit Rev —— Whittlesey favored the church with frequent pulpit ministrations during the following fall and winter Rev Alexander Rankin has been the minister here since 1872, and is at present

The building first used by this church as a house of worship was the old Union Church erected in 1837 In about 1855 the ground and edifice became the sole property of the Presbyterians, who reclaimed it from its dilapidated condition, refitted and almost remodeled it at an expense of about $500, and on the 17th of January, 1856, solemnly dedicated it to the worship of God In 1881 the question as to the feasibility of building a new edifice was agitated The present edifice was begun March 20th, 1882, and by December first following was so far completed as to be fit for occupancy It was not dedicated, however, until July 28th, 1883 The cost of the building, in round numbers, was $10,000 The present value of the church property, including the parsonage, is about $13,000 — a low estimate The membership of the church is now eighty-four The present officers are Elders, Charles Rockwell, who has been elder from the beginning, Clark Hall and J S Cooley, M D, trustees, Clark Hall, J S Cooley, M D, George H Rockwell, William Snell and Alexander Fisher

There has been a Sunday-school connected with the church since the organization of the latter The first superintendent was Charles Rockwell The present superintendent is Dr J S Cooley The average attendance of pupils is about 110 [1]

The Roman Catholic Mission at Luzerne was formerly attended from Saratoga It was attached to Warrensburgh in 1874, and under the suspervision of the new pastor, Rev James A Kelley, a handsome little edifice was erected

[1] The old church, built in 1837, is now used as a store by Walter P Wilcox

in July, 1876   The lot was donated to the society by the late Colonel B C Butler.   The building cost, when completed, about $2,500   The society was liberally aided in the work by summer visitors and non-Catholic residents [1] The number of adult communicants is now about one hundred and thirty Since the erection of the edifice a Sunday-school has been organized, and is superintended by the pastor

The first pastor of the Church of the Infant Jesus, as it is titled, was Rev James A Kelley, who resigned in 1881, and after the interval of a year was regularly succeeded by the present pastor, Rev William O'Mahoney, of Warrensburgh [2]

CHAPTER XXVII

HISTORY OF THE TOWN OF THURMAN

THURMAN lies south of Johnsburgh on the west side of the Hudson, and north of Stony Creek   The western part is a high, broken, upland almost unknown except to hunters   The eastern part is a hilly plateau containing peaks which rise in some instances 1,000 feet above the level of the sea   The surface of the whole town is dotted with numerous small lakes   The soil is sandy with numerous intermixtures of loam

The old town of Thurman was formed on the 10th of April, 1792   Bolton and Chester were taken off in 1799, Johnsburgh in 1805, and a part of Caldwell in 1810   The earliest records have been lost, and none are accessible until 1812, the last year before the old town was divided into Athol and Warrensburgh [3]   The officers of Thurman for that year were as follows —

Supervisor, Duncan Cameron , town clerk, Thomas Pattison , justices of the peace, John Cameron, James L Thurman , overseers of the poor, Duncan McEwan, Stephen Griffing and Isaac Woodward   The same officers served in 1813   In 1814 Duncan Cameron was supervisor from Athol, Holden Kenyon was town clerk, and John Cameron, justice-elect

One of the oldest living inhabitants of the town is D Aldrich, who has rendered us valuable assistance in our researches, and whose recollection

---

[1] Rev William O'Mahoney, of Warrensburgh, is authority for this statement, and, indeed, through his kindness the whole matter concerning this church was obtained

[2] We regret our inability to insert a sketch of the Episcopal Church parish here, but we visited the rector several times, and received each time a promise of answer to the questions which we left with him, and were each time disappointed   We finally left our address with him, and came away with his promise to mail us the sketch   We wrote to him for it, but could get no answer

[3] The town of Thurman derived its name from John Thurman, the original patentee. See Johnsburgh History

reaches back unmistakably to 1820   Speaking of the condition of the town of Athol at that time, he says that there was only one road in the town then, which stretched along the west bank of the Hudson, and was so primitive in construction that only foot and horseback travel was attempted upon it   In many places it was positively dangerous   People used to take their grain down the river in canoes to the grist-mill at Luzerne, or the Patent   West of this road the few inhabitants had erected their rude log huts, on the highest and dryest land, and cut out footpaths and saddle-roads to the Hudson   Wagons, and consequently wagon-roads, were as yet undreamed of   It was deemed an encouraging innovation indicative of bold and radical genius, when, a few months later, Amos Bowen and Stephen Griffing bought each a two-wheeled ox-cart, and John McEwan, regardless of his youthful training, purchased a one-horse wood-spring buggy !

The town then possessed but one framed school-house, which stood near the center of the town, about a mile west of the present depot   There were two or three log school-houses in the western part of the town   The inhabitants were very poor, and had not the money to keep the school in operation more than two or three months in a year   One small church edifice was built about this time by the Presbyterians, near the present depot   A large proportion of the inhabitants were Scotch and Presbyterians   Indeed, Athol derived its name from the circumstance that the town of Athol, Scotland, was the birth-place of many of the early settlers here

Between 1835 and 1860 there was no regular church in town, all religious meetings being held in the school-house

There never were any distilleries in town, and only two potash factories   These were built about 1820 by David Cameron and John McEwan   They were kept running eight or ten years, and then allowed to run down   The market was at Waterford, N Y , to which place the proprietors of these asheries had their potash hauled and bartered for household necessaries   It was in the neighborhood of 1820 that the first lumbering was done in Athol   Norman and Alanson Fox, of Chester, began the business in Athol and Johnsburgh, by running pine logs — for pine grew hereabouts in great abundance — down the Hudson to Glens Falls   More or less lumbering has been carried on in town from that time down to the present day, the most prominent lumbermen being Abraham Wing, Walter Geer, Halsey R Wing, Zenus Van Duzen, James and Jeremiah Finch, James Morgan & Co , and Henry Crandell, all of Glens Falls   It has been said that these men have made more money going over the ground a second time and utilizing the spruce and hemlock which followed the "forest primeval," than they did in felling and selling the aboriginal pines   The old town of Athol had a frontage on the Hudson of about fifteen miles, as it comprised the territory now included in Thurman and Stony Creek   The first permanent settlements were made from 1825 to 1830, although of

course the town had been thinly inhabited for years   Commencing at the
south end of the town, Mr Aldrich gives the following names of those who
came here in this period   Alexander Murray, John Murray, James McDonald, Peter McDonald, Peter Woolley, James Cameron, Daniel McMillan, Oliver
Ryley, William Cameron, Benoni Aldrich, Simeon Warren, Daniel Bowen,
David Cameron, Stephen Griffing, (1st), William Griffing, Nathaniel Griffing,
John McMillan, Benjamin A Potter, Stokes Potter, Gideon Lanfear, Calvin
Baldwin   Of these Gideon Lanfear and Nathaniel Griffing are still alive, and
many of the others have descendants residing in either Thurman or Stony
Creek

The first post-office in Athol was established not far from 1820 by the appointment of Duncan McEwan, postmaster, and James Dow to carry the mail
once a week to Glens Falls and back by the way of Luzerne   Mr Aldrich
says " I remember well the old-hero Dow, mounted on horse and saddle-bags,
with a long tin horn in his hand, to sound the glad tidings to the inhabitants
along the river that we were connected with the far off village of Glens Falls
by a mail route   Now we have a daily mail, and any day we can get aboard
a public conveyance at our own door and ride around the world by the same
conveyance, if we desire   When I commenced keeping store in 1836, we had
not one , now we have half a dozen   For two years I hauled my goods on a
wagon from Albany, making the trip in four days   Now we have only a mile
to draw our goods   In 1840 the house I now live in was the only one in town
which was painted white , now you can count them by scores   In 1830 the
old town of Athol used to have three days of election and polled fewer than
200 votes , now, either division, Thurman or Stony Creek, can poll 350 "

Athol was divided into Stony Creek and the present Thurman on the third
day of November, 1852

The first officers of the town of Thurman ware as follows   Supervisor, Hiram P Williams, town clerk, David A Green, assessors, William Johnson,
Daniel Bowen, commissioners of highways, Lorenzo Pasco, Charles S Drull,
justices of the peace, Ichabod Aldrich, John Loveland, inspectors of elections,
A Burdick, Aaron Hall, George Russell, collector. John V Kenyon, overseers of the poor, John Wilsey, James Coyle , constables, Alanson S Orritt,
Jacob L Daggett, Daniel Wilcox, John V Kenyon, John K Thistle

The Rebellion — The first enrollment of men for the army in 1861 was made
by George P Wait, of Johnsburgh   About 150 men enlisted and very few
were drafted   (See chapter on military history of the county)

Churches — The oldest church organization in town is the Baptist which,
was formed in 1833   Preaching had been done here for a number of years
The first sermon ever preached in town was at the house of a Mr Parker, by
Rev —— Green   Down to 1822 occasional sermons were heard from Elders Fox, Grant, Faxon, and Mott   In 1822 the professed Baptists in town

numbered but twenty-nine   At that time they were associated with the Johnsburgh church with Elder Blakeman as pastor   In 1829 there was a great revival throughout the neighborhood, and twenty-six were converted to the true
faith   Elder Cobb preached in 1830   In October, 1833, the Thurman society
organized a distinct church and separated from the Johnsburgh church   The
first officers were   Eben Johnson, clerk, Daniel Pasco and Samuel Barber, deacons   In 1838, under the ministry of Elder Ward, the church attained a membership of ninety-one   Since then the following pastors have resided here
1840, Sherman Farnham was ordained and made pastor , 1846, after a brief
interregnum, Rev W S Bush was pastor , there was no pastor in 1850 , 1851,
Elder Caleb Smith , 1853, Elder G Harrington , 1858, Elder Joseph Brown ;
1863, after an interregnum of two years, Elder William Dickens , 1865, E W
Burdick , 1872 built house of worship , 1873, Elder Burdick, the present pastor, again   The Methodist church was erected here soon after the Baptist edifice, and immediately after the organization of the church, Rev M Wynan,
pastor   Almyron Cameron is class leader, and Hiram Truesdell, Thomas Needham and Asahel Albro, deacons

About 1860, too, a Baptist Church was built in the west part of the town
called Kenyontown

Athol Hotel — There is but one hotel in the town of Thurman, now kept
by John Loveland, at Athol   There was formerly a tavern on the farm now
owned by Loveland, which was built soon after 1820, and first kept by Guy
Brooks   He was followed by Elisha Pendell , then Luman Pendell, and finally,
for about one year, Alanson Kenyon kept it, when Loveland tore it down

The present hotel was erected by a stock company, in 1851, and first occupied by Duncan Cameron, who leased it for five years at a total rental of
$200   In 1856 his brother, William J Cameron, succeeded him, and was soon
in turn succeeded by Myron Griffin   In 1863 Calvin Frost became proprietor   In 1864 William J Cameron again came into possession, and with the
exception of the year 1869–70, when Marvin Parker kept it, remained until
1875   In that year the present proprietor, John Loveland, came, and remained two years   From 1877 to 1880 he was in Caldwell, but he returned
in 1880   The store which he runs in connection with the hotel, he started in
the summer of 1884

Mercantile Interests — The oldest store now open in Athol is that of David
Aldrich, who first dealt in merchandise here in 1836   With the exception of
two years — 1853 and 1854 — when he was at Luzerne, and three — 1870 and
1873 — at Riverside, he has kept the store ever since   Mr Aldrich was born
about one and a half miles south of his present home, September 9th, 1814
John N Elwell has kept store most of the time since 1859   His present store
between the upper and lower villages has been in operation since 1880   C
Y Kenyon opened his general store May 1st, 1881, a little way below his

present place of business   He moved in July, 1884   Asahel Albro's store was first opened in 1882   Albert Covey started his store opposite the hotel in the fall of 1884

Post-office — The establishment of the first post-office in town, about 1820, with Duncan McEwan as postmaster, has been mentioned.   The present incumbent at Thurman post-office is Delilah Parker, successor to John Parker, who was appointed more than thirty years ago   The postmasters at Athol since 1856 have been Michael Byrnes, James Gilpin 1862, Abiel Pendell 1864, Morgan Kenyon 1867, John L Gilpin 1870, and the present official, John L Frest

Following is as complete a list as can be obtained of supervisors from this town or Athol   *Athol* — 1813–16, Duncan Cameron , 1817, David Cameron , 1818–23, Elisha Pendell , 1824, Henry Allen , 1825, Elisha Pendell , 1826, Duncan Cameron , 1827–29, Elisha Pendell , 1830–33, James Cameron , 1834, '35, Richardson Cameron , 1836, '37, Luman Pendell , 1838, '39, Elisha Pendell , 1840, John Parker ; 1841, '42, Luman Pendell , 1843, Peter McDonald ; 1844, James Cameron , 1845, Elisha Pendell , 1846, Ebenezer Johnson , 1847, Elisha Pendell , 1848, David Aldrich , 1849, Simeon Warren , 1850, '51, Clayton L Kenyon , 1852, John McMillen   *Thurman* — 1853, '54, Hiram P Williams, 1855, William J Cameron , 1856, Elisha Pendell , 1857, 58, Marvin Parker , 1859, William J Cameron , 1860, '61, David Aldrich , 1862, Elisha Pendell , 1863, Sandford Johnson , 1864, '65, David Aldrich , 1866, James Warren , 1867, '68, John Loveland , 1869, John T Parker , 1870, Marvin Parker , 1871, John L Loveland , 1872, '73, M W Bowen , 1874, '75, David A Green , 1876, Miles Frost , 1877, '78, William H Kenyon , 1879, Fred E Aldrich , 1880, James Warren , 1881, '82, Luman Pendell , 1883, '84, Andrew McGee , 1885, Charles H Baker

The present town officers, elected on April 7th, 1885, are as follows   Supervisor, Charles H Baker ; town clerk, Frederick Kenyon , commissioner of highways, Warren Harris , assessor, Judson Williams , justice of the peace, H J Truesdell , overseers of the poor, Henry Smith, Stokes R Potter , inspectors of election, James D Smith, Seward Archer; collector, William Needham , constables, George Taylor, Levi S Trumbell, John Covey, Judson Farnham, William Needham

The population of the town in 1855 was 1,259 , in 1860, 1,084 , in 1865, 1,007 , in 1870, 1,084 , in 1875, 1,095 , in 1880, 1,174

CHAPTER XXVIII

HISTORY OF THE TOWN OF BOLTON

THIS town lies on the eastern boundary of the county, between Hague on the north and Caldwell on the south   A part of Lake George forms its eastern boundary and the Schroon River separates it from Warrensburgh on the west   The surface is occupied principally by the lofty mountain ridges — a part of the Kayaderosseras range — which rest between Lake George and the Schroon River   The three prominent peaks of this range are   Tongue Mountain, on the peninsula between the lake and Norwthest Bay, rises to an elevation of about 2,000 feet above tide, Pole Hill, in the northern part of the town, 2,500 feet high, and Cat Head, in the center, from 1,500 to 1,800 feet above tide water   The mountains generally rise abruptly from the lake, but toward the west the surface assumes the character of a high, rolling upland High up among the hills are a variety of lovely lakes, embosomed in the very summits of the mountains   The principal among these are Trout Lake, Marsh Pond, and Edgecomb Pond   Trout Lake is 1,000 feet above the surface of Lake George   The soil, which is a light, sandy loam, is not wholly unproductive, especially along the lake, where fruits are successfully cultivated   The general surface of the town, however, is so stony and broken, that not more than one-half of it is susceptible of cultivation

Bolton was formed from the old town of Thurman on the 25th of March, 1799   It originally comprised, in addition to its present territory, all of Hague, which was taken off in 1807, a part of Caldwell, until 1810, and a part of Horicon until 1838   Among the early settlers who survive to tell of the wilderness days of yore, is Mrs Arabella Anderson, who was born in Shelton, Massachusetts, in 1793, and came here with her father, Daniel Nims, in 1802   Her husband, Allen Anderson, was born in the same town of Shelton in 1787   His father, David Anderson, and Daniel Nims both fought in the Revolutionary War, and Allen Anderson himself was a soldier in the War of 1812, and was within hearing of the guns that were fired at the battle of Plattsburg, being a little too late to take part in that famous engagement   For his services in this war his widow, Arabella Anderson, now draws a pension   He died in 1867. Orlando Anderson, son of Allen and Arabella, now lives in the serenity of old age with his widowed mother, and recounts adventures which would be dated antique but for the reminiscences of his mother, which modernize his earliest memories   He was born here on January 7th, 1813   When Arabella Nims came here in 1802, the inhabitants were fewer even than they are at present The mountains and valleys were covered with trackless forests   Indians roamed about the vicinity in considerable numbers   There were only four or five

34

framed houses in town — all the rest being rudely but not uncomfortably con-structed of logs   James Ware, a prominent man in early days, one of the first town assessors, and supervisor from Bolton for the years 1801–1803, and 1805–1807, then lived where Stephen Braley now dwells   His daughter, Lydia Ware, was the first white child born in town.   David Nash lived on the farm now occupied by Reuben Wells   James Tuttle lived on the north and south road west of the village, and Hezekiah Moody lived a little north of Mr Nash's, on the top of the hill   Jonathan Coolidge, grandfather of T S Coolidge, now of Glens Falls, settled here about 1805   Jonathan Coolidge, 2d, father to T S. Coolidge, was born here soon after   There was no church edifice in town so early As was customary in the pioneer days of all these towns, religious meetings were held in barns and in the houses of neighbors   The first church in town was a union house, erected about 1811   Rev Reuben Armstrong was the first preacher

There was one school-house in this vicinity — situated about three miles north of Bolton Landing   After a few years (about 1804 or 1805) a new one was built just south of the site of the Mohican House

The primitive and wild condition of the country can scarcely be imagined The hills and woods were full of Indian relics, tomahawks, knives, pipes, etc The mountains were mantled to their very summits with pine forests, which were felled so rapidly after the arrival of the first settler, that before 1820 they had become a memory   The farming implements used by the settlers were rude enough, axes and scythes being just as they came from the hammer Abel Walker, the venerable centenarian still living, was here then and was in the battle of Plattsburg   He draws a pension for his services there

In 1802 there was no regular tavern in this vicinity, but at every house the doors were open to guests, and liquor was dispensed with intoxicating liberality It was so pure, however, that there was proportionately less drunkenness then than now   On the site of the Mohican House, Roger Edgecomb had a frme house, from an ell of which he sold liquor   He soon enlarged the building and converted it into a professed tavern   Myrtle Hitchcock came in there in 1807.   The first store in town stood on the point off the Mohican House   It was built by Myrtle Hitchcock and kept by Samuel Brown   About where the Mohican House dock now is was a little stone dock, and in the floor of this primitive mercantile house was a mysterious trap door, opening into a cellar wherein were bestowed goods which had been smuggled from Canada Samuel Brown soon after owned a factory for the manufacture of potash near the Mohican House.   Another ashery stood near the site of the Bolton House By 1815 Reuben Smith had one on the hill north of the "Landing," and Thomas Wright ran one on the site of "The Huddle"   Wright also owned a store and carding-machine here, and about 1830 started the only forge that was ever run in the town   Lumbering, however, was the principal business

here   The pine logs were constructed into immense rafts which were floated
to the head of the lake, and the material from these taken south to points along
the Hudson   The woods were full of wolves, bears, panthers and deer   The
latter would follow the brooks down to the lake, where they fell an easy prey to
the venison lovers of those early days   It was not safe to leave sheep out of
doors all night   In 1802, to return to early settlements, Timothy Stow built
a house on the site of the Bolton House   John Vanderbergh was the owner
The Huddle was not entitled then to the dignity of the name "hamlet "
About one and a half miles to the west of it was a grist-mill, on the brook that
flows through The Huddle   Mr Squires was the miller   Near the mill stood
a small tannery run by David Lockwood   Near by lived John Moss, the first
judge of Washington county   At this time he was the proprietor and conductor of a small saw-mill on the stream last mentioned   One or two saw-mills
were also run by Samuel Brown some distance up Edgecemb Pond [1] Brook
There were several saw-mills, too, at Northwest Bay   Men used to come
across the lake from Easttown, Washington county, to carry on the lumber business   As early as 1820 John J Harris, of Queensbury, built three mills there
and carried on an extensive business   Harris sold to one Barnard, of Albany
A short time before the war these mills were closed because of the scarcity of
lumber   .

Of the four churches now in town, the Presbyterian Church was erected
originally as a Congregational Church, and was torn down about 1845 or
1850, and the present edifice built on the Lake Road nearly two miles towards
Hague from the Landing   There have been no regular services there for
several years   The only stated pastor they have had is the Rev Eldad Goodman, who was also the first preacher in the new building   The Episcopalians
have held summer services in the little chapel on the Lake Road for ten or
twelve years past   The Baptist Church was erected about 1833 or 1834, and
the Methodist edifice followed some eight or ten years later

During the War of 1812 the brawn and bone of Bolton left their homes to
defend their country , and when it was learned that Plattsburg was threatened,
men flocked from the entire region round about to Chestertown whence they
moved in a body rapidly toward the menaced village   In due time news came
that a battle had taken place there and that all the patriots were killed   Mrs
Anderson remembers most vividly the following Sunday, when the meeting
house was filled with women and a few old men   She remembers their sad
faces, and their constrained attempts to cheer each other

The cold season of 1816 affected Bolton about as might be expected
There was a great deal of suffering, and the people used to cross the lake into
Washington county to procure game and food

The first town meeting of Bolton was appointed to be held on the 2d of

---

1 Edgecomb Pond derived its name from the pioneer inn-keeper, Roger Edgecomb

April, 1799, at the house of John Clawson, but "for want of accommodation" said meeting was adjourned to Captain Stow's grist-mill The following town officers were elected   Supervisor, Asa Brown , assessors, Samuel Bigelow, Oliver Pettys, James Ware , commissioners of highways, James Ware, Oliver Pettys, Starbling Waters , poormasters, Asa Brown, John Clawson , constable and collector, Starbling Waters , constable, Samuel Bigelow , poundmasters, Samuel Begelow, Isaac Lyman (their yards pounds), fence viewers, Simeon Fuller, Jeduthan Dickinson , pathmasters, No 1, John Hall, No 2, Rufus Roberts, No 3, Henry Babcock, No 4, Benjamin Hays, No 5, Daniel Beswick, No 6, Samuel Dickinson, No 7, John Squires, No 8, Daniel Lamb, No 9, Stanton Brown   On the lake shore   No 1, Andrew Edmunds, No 2, Sherbael Fuller, No 3, James Sturdevant, No 4, James Tuttle, No 5, Eleazer Goodman, No 6, John McKnight, No 7, Elisha Belden

Among the resolutions passed by this august body was one to the effect that "swine shall not run at large the ensuing season ," that any person that shall receive or take the charge of cattle belonging to people of other towns to run upon the commons in this town shall pay a fine of $2 50, and that cattle driven or left promiscuously shall be treated as strays, one-half of the money to go to the prosecutor, and one-half to the use of the poor Thirty dollars was voted to the support of the poor   Two dollars and fifty cents bounty was offered for each " painter " or wolf killed in the town

The proceedings of subsequent annual town meetings were of the same character   Roads were surveyed, laid out and altered, and internal improvements were gradually commenced   In 1840, for example, a committee, consisting of Roger Edgecomb, James Ware and James Wood, was chosen to look out a road to " Scroon Lake "   In 1811 it was voted " That the poor be sold at vendue to the lowest bidder "   In 1817 the road to Brandt Lake was surveyed

When the War of the Rebellion threatened the destruction of the Union, Bolton, with her scant population did, nevertheless, her duty. It is a notable fact that all the towns in Warren county were remarkably prompt in answering the president's call for volunteers   Unfortunately the town records contain no minutes of the action taken to furnish volunteers

The present postmaster at Bolton post-office is J S Gates, who received his appointment in 1880   His predecessor, George W Seaman, entered upon his duties about 1871   Elam B Miller preceded Seaman for about three years Before Miller, Stephen Pratt, who was appointed in 1862, officiated   Hiram Philo was appointed in 1857, and Stephen Piatt in 1856   Before that Gilbert M Gale held the office for a long time   The post-office of Bolton Landing was established in 1882, and the first postmaster was Frederick W Allen, who still officiates   Its purpose was to accommodate the summer guests who were grouped in greater numbers about the Landing than elsewhere

There are only two stores at the Landing and one at The Huddle   The latter is kept by Gates, Tanner & Co , consisting of J S Gates, Morgan H. Tanner and George S Gates   The partnership was formed on April 16th, 1884   Before that J S Gates had kept store there for ten years   The same firm began a like business at the Landing at the same time   For two years preceding April, 1884, Sidney W Mead had kept store in the same building, and was himself preceded by E E Riddell, now of the Riddell House at Luzerne, who was merchant here three years   This building has been used for a store for a period of not less than fifty years   Stephen Pratt used to keep store here, and about 1845 or 1850 Truxton Pratt was proprietor of the same concern   The other stores in town are, that kept by F W Allen in connection with the post-office , of A A Tanner, who has had a store for over twenty years about two miles north of the Landing , of George Bentley, who for not less than fifteen years has run a store four miles north of the Landing, and John Ormsby, who has had a store for three years near the Landing

The only manufacturing done in the town is done by the saw-mills owned respectively by Isaac Streeter and Davin Putney   They have conducted each his business for ten or fifeen years

There are no practicing attorneys in the town, and but one physician — Charles Robbins, M D ,— who received his degree at the University Medical College of New York city in March, 1852   He came to Bolton about 1860

Hotels — The peculiar thing about Bolton is its splendid situation between mountains and lake   Although not strictly within the technical province of history, a passage or two written in description of Bolton, as it is known to the tourist and summer visitor, will not, perhaps, be deemed entirely inappropriate   In order to be as brief as possible, a description of a single view will be given as presenting a good idea of the general impression formed upon the mind of the susceptible lover of nature who looks from the same point of view   Within a short walk northward from the Mohican House, a characteristic view is found, looking across the mouth of the Northwest Bay to the Narrows   From the eminences, or from the line marked by the gentle waves of the Horicon, the landscape here is of wonderful simplicity, breadth and grandeur   As an enthusiastic writer said more than thirty years ago, it is seen most justly as the morning sun peeps over Black Mountain and its attendant peaks   Looking southward from various points yet further on, fine views of the head of the lake are obtained, terminating a pleasant stretch of lawn, hill and islanded water   It is while the eye is filled with such scenes as these modest hill-tops offer, more, perhaps, than when lost in the musical solitudes of the island shades, or than when meandering by the murmuring shore, that the soul becomes conscious of the subtle nature of the charms which make us cling to and even to dwell forever on the shores of Lake George   The sublimity of the mountains, the quiet beauty of the wooded islands,— neither of these qualities can alone satisfy the soul and sense without a change or feeling of *ennui*   But the insinuating, blending of all in nature that is sweet to the sight and pleasing to the ear, a grandeur which does not terrify, and a beauty which does not clog, is found on the bosom and along the shores of the historic and the romance-inspiring Horicon

Mr S R Stoddard, in his entertaining and instructive guide-book entitled *Lake George*, says (p 77, et seq)   " Strangers are sometimes at a loss to locate ' Bolton ' properly   To the guests it means the hotels   A little further north the ' Huddle,' — where the post-office is situated — is Bolton   It is also gathering around the churches , and the shoemaker, pegging industriously away in the north part of the town, fondly imagines that *that* will be the spot where, at some future day, will gather the *élite* of this highly diffused village   From a point in the steamer's course, after rounding Recluse Island, is obtained the finest general view of Bolton and of the lake also "

From the same source is obtained the information best stated in the same order of detail which Mr Stoddard himself has employed   " Bolton Bay " is the name generally applied to that portion of the lake on the west, between Recluse and Green Islands

Belvoir Island is near Recluse Island on the west, and separated from the main land at its southwestern extremity by a narrow strip of water   Its owner is Rev G W Clowe, of White Plains, who may often be seen swinging the axe or piling brush as energetically as the most enthusiastic votary of muscular Christianity could desire   Hiawatha Island, west of Clay, and farther down in the bay, is owned by Dr Jacobi, of New York   Leontine Island is a charming bit of verdure north of Hiawatha Island   Huddle Bay is the local appellation of the deeper portion of the bay reaching south

Among the numerous and various hotels of Bolton the oldest is the Mohican House   Over thirty years ago people used to come here summers from New York and Philadelphia   Before that the place had only a local or limited reputation as a good point for hunting and fishing   We have seen that Roger Edgecomb kept tavern and Samuel Brown (uncle of M O Brown, now manager of the Sagamore), kept store on the site and grounds of the present Mohican House, at the beginning of the present century   Just how long Edgecomb remained here is not known   About 1820 Thomas Archibald bought the tavern and considerable land with it for three hundred dollars   Before 1830 Truman Lyman purchased it of Archibald for $600, and kept the house until after 1840   Gilbert B Gale followed Lyman and remained a number of years, becoming locally famous for the excellence of his table.   A writer in 1853 says: "Bolton, in the vocabulary of the stranger, is nothing neither more nor less than the ' Mohican House,' whose esteemed commandant is Captain Gale, a name next to that of ' Sherrill,' most gratefully interwoven with the carnal history of Horicon   Yes ! the Mohican House is Bolton, and Bolton is the Mohican House , even as Bardolph was his nose, and his nose was Bardolph Great are both!" Captain Gale was the man who erected the flagstaff surmounted by the wooden effigy of an Indian warrior, which has ever since been used as the trade-mark of the house After Gale came Hiram H Wilson, and next his son Hiram S Wilson, and M O Brown was proprietor for years prior to the time when Mrs E B Winslow took it in the spring of 1883 " The Mohican House has two cottages connected with it, both being directly on the shore of the lake, The larger one, only a few steps from the hotel, has rooms *en suite* The cottages are tastefully furnished, adding considerably to the attractions of the place, and affording altogether accommodations for about eighty guests "

The next most ancient house is the Wells House, so named because Dorcas Wells used to take boarders there nearly twenty years ago The house stands back a few rods from the Mohican House, on the road that leads up the mountain side It will provide for about forty guests The present proprietor is H A Dearstyne

The Bolton House, at Bolton Landing, just north of the Mohican House, is three stories high and is topped with a French roof and two observatories A portion of the building was erected in 1870 Seven years later it was enlarged to double its original size and remodeled, so that now it will conveniently accommodate 125 guests The first proprietors, Norton & Phillips, ran the house for five years Hiram Wilson conducted the business for the four succeeding years Barton & Phelps then assumed possession and remained four years M O Brown followed them, one year In 1883 the present proprietor, H H ,West, entered upon the performance of his duties here. Other hotels or summer boarding-houses are the Locust Grove House, about midway betweeen the Mohican House and The Huddle, J H Vandenburgh, proprietor, the Lake View House, just south of the Locust Grove House, capacity for 100 guests, R J Brown, proprietor; the Vandinberg House, north of the Bolton House, capacity for thirty, Jacob Vandinberg, proprietor

The Sagamore, the proudest hotel on the lake, perhaps, excepting the Fort William Henry, was first opened in the spring of 1883 As Mr Stoddard says " The Sagamore is not a savage, although representing in its title the proudest chieftain of a vanished tribe, and like its distinguished prototype standing a head and shoulders above its fellows, but the new hotel on Green Island, at a point for years looked upon as the hotel site par excellence of this section, now utilized through the energy of Philadelphia capitalists and one of Lake George's most popular landlords, together forming a company possessed not only of a knowledge of what the best people have at home, and naturally desire at a hotel, but also the skill and experience necessary to successfully manage the innumerable details in the business of a great hotel

" The hotel building stands on high ground, and commands, on every side, extended views of the lake and mountains   It is built in the style popularly supposed to belong to the sixteenth century, its varied porticos, balconies and gables all admirably displayed by the harmonious colors with which it is painted   Within will be found every hotel convenience and comfort, including hydraulic passenger elevator, electric bells, telegraph office, etc   It is supplied with an abundance of pure running water, brought through pipes from a mountain on the mainland two miles distant   Many of the rooms are arranged *en suite* with outside entrances, and all rooms are illuminated with the Edison electric light   The interior finish is in the best of taste, the furniture being of native hard woods, polished " [1]   The house will accommodate 300 guests   Lessee and proprietor, M O Brown

Following is a list of the supervisors from Bolton from the beginning to the present: 1799 and 1800, Asa Brown, 1801–1803, James Ware, 1804, Timothy Stow, 1805–1807, James Ware, 1808, Edward Reese, 1809, James Archibald, 1810, Thomas M Wright; 1811–1815, Frederick Miller, 1816–1818, Allen Anderson, 1819, Frederick Miller, 1820–1826, Allen Anderson, 1827 and 1828, Thomas McGee, 1829, William Hammond, 1830 and 1831, Allen Anderson; 1832–1834, Truman Lyman, 1835, Stephen Pratt, 1836, Allen Anderson, 1837 and 1838, Rufus Anderson, 1839, Samuel C Goodman, 1840, Aaron L Judd, 1841 and 1842, Asa C Winter, 1843, Orange Colton, 1844, Homer Davis, 1845, Warren Thomas; 1846–1849, Luther Brown, 1850, Louie Charette, 1851, Stephen Pratt, 1852, John B Coolidge; 1853, Allen Anderson; 1854, George B Reynolds, 1855–1857, Layton Wells; 1858, Jonathan Coolidge, 1859, Sidney W Tuttle, 1860 and 1861, E B Miller, 1862, Layton Wells, 1863, E B Miller, 1864, Jonathan M. Coolidge; 1865, W M Coolidge, 1866 and 1867, George W Seaman, 1868, T N Thomas, 1869, George W Seaman, 1870 and 1871, E W Phillips, 1872, Truman N Thomas, 1873–1875, M O Brown, 1876, H A Dearstyne, 1877, Truman N. Thomas, 1878, Myron O Brown, 1879, Elbridge Cilley, 1880, Myron O Brown, 1881, Harvey Robinson, 1882, Truman H Thomas, 1883, Elbridge Cilley, 1884, Myron O Brown, 1885, Frederick Allen

The present officers are as follows Supervisor, Frederick Allen, town clerk, George Gates, commissioner of highways, H A Dearstyne; collector, Chauncey Murch, assessors, Marvin Truesdell, Asa Dickenson, Hosea Barber, overseers of the poor, William J Griffin, David Putney, commissioners of excise, Dodge S Gates, Oscar G Finkle, Edwin Norton, constables, E La Gay, Chauncey Murch, Wilber Bentley, sealer of weights and measures, William Taylor

According to the census reports since 1850 the population of the town has been as follows 1850, 1,147, 1855, 1,167, 1860, 1,289, 1865, 1,221, 1870, 1,135, 1875, 1,121, 1880, 1,132

---

[1] STODDARD'S *Lake George*, page 85–86

CHAPTER XXIX

HISTORY OF THE TOWN OF CHESTER

THE town of Chester is situated on the northern border of the county, laterally central Its eastern and western boundaries are formed respectively by the Schroon and Hudson Rivers It is bounded on the north by Essex county, on the south by Warrensburgh On the east lies Horicon, and on the west Johnsburgh The surface is broken by precipitous mountains, and covered with huge boulders The Kayaderosseras Mountains extend through the southern part, and the Schroon Range occupies the north The valley of Schroon Lake extends in a southwesterly direction to the Hudson and contains a chain of small lakes, the principal of which are Loon Lake and Friends' Lake Schroon Lake itself is about 1,000 feet above tide, while the surrounding hills rise from 500 to 800 feet above its surface The soil is everywhere light and sandy, and not very productive "The Stone Bridge is a great natural curiosity and gives its name to the stream passing beneath it This stream enters Chester from Essex county, about thirty rods above the bridge, where it falls over a rocky ledge into a natural basin, whence turning east it seeks a subterranean passage by two branches, the north one passing under an arch of massive granite forty feet high, and about eighty feet chord, diminishing in capacity as the stream descends — which may be followed 156 feet from the entrance The southern and greater branch has a passage which may be explored with much difficulty, being in some places much confined, in others opening into caverns thirty or forty feet in diameter, and filled to a great depth with water At 247 feet from the entrance the waters disembogue in one current, having united in the vault, beneath a precipice fifty-four feet high, which terminates the bridge The arch on this side is about five feet high and ten wide The creek enters the river about three-fourths of a mile below the outlet of Schroon Lake "[1]

The early history of Chester is unfortunately involved in almost impenetrable obscurity The most trustworthy and complete resource of the county historian, the town records, have been twice destroyed by fire, and the writer is therefore forced to rely solely on the memory of the oldest inhabitant One of the oldest inhabitants now living in town is Otis Collins, who was born in Massachusetts in December, in 1801, and is therefore eighty-four years of age He was brought to Chester in February, 1805, by his father, Joseph Collins, who settled about half a mile east of the site of Chestertown, on the place now occupied by Mr Russell The town was then about six years old, having been formed from Thurman on the 25th of March, 1799 To complete Mr Collins's biography — he married. in 1833, Melissa Leavens, a Chester girl, who was

---

[1] This description is taken from GORDON'S *Gazetteer*, in the possession of Dr A W Holden

also born in Massachusetts   Joseph Collins was a blacksmith by trade, and plied this vocation for a few years after he came, but devoted the greater part of his time, nevertheless, to farming   When he came, in 1805, new and rudimentary roads had been opened about where they now lie   The main travel was up the Schroon River   The land was thickly covered with maple, spruce, beech, pine, and some oak timber, which was soon after utilized by the pioneer lumbermen   As is usual, in the entire Adirondack region, the custom was to float the logs down the rivers to the lumber marts below   Norman and Alanson Fox, brothers, were extensively interested in the lumber trade   At first they lived about a mile west of the site of Chestertown, but in 1809 or 1810, they moved to the plot of ground now covered with Downs's Hotel, and ran a tavern   Soon after they added to their interests a store, which stood where James McAveigh's store now is   They sold the property, eventually, to Charles Fowler, father of the people of that surname in Glens Falls   It remained in the hands of Fowler and his heirs until a few years ago

There were no distilleries about here in 1805, but five or six years later Harvey Powers started one about a quarter of a mile west of the village of Chestertown, where Demond Gould[1] now lives

A grist-mill was built here before 1815, and was the only one in town Potash was made here in considerable quantities   The Fox brothers had an ashery near their tavern — about where the Downs's Hotel barns now stands, Harvey Powers had one near the site of Mr Faxon's tannery, and Seth Fuller owned one a little over a mile east of the village   Two small tanneries were built in this period — one " hand-tannery," situated about a quarter of a mile north of the village, and owned by Simeon Doty, and one of the same kind owned by one Stearns, which was afterwards made over to a leather factory, since defunct

In 1805 there were only two buildings—log-houses—where now is the village of Chestertown, one on the site of Rising's Hotel, the dwelling place of Joshua Eaton, and the other just east of the site of Downs's Hotel, occupied by Rice Eaton   The only clearings here were around these houses   But within a year or two immigration directed its current to the spot, and before 1820 the wilderness had been broken and a thriving settlement had taken up its abode here

The earliest settlers in the town were undoubtedly the Meads, who were a numerous family   Titus Mead lived on the outlet of Loon Lake, and Jabez Mead lived near him   They built the first, or about the first, grist-mill and saw-mill in town—near their houses   Levi Mead also had a grist-mill and saw-mill near his house about a mile and a-half south of Chestertown, where his son Royal Mead now lives   Gideon Mead lived on a farm adjoining that of Joseph Collins   His family are all gone.   Enos Mead was the son of Levi

---

[1] Grandson of Willard Gould, an early resident here

Mead, and lived with him. His son, also named Levi, lived on the farm after them, and subsequently enlarged his possessions by the purchase of the adjoining lands. Jonathan and David Mead lived in the western part of the town, and devoted themselves exclusively to farming. Mr Beman, a farmer, lived near Loon Lake, and was a neighbor to John Haskins. Obadiah Knapp, a blacksmith, lived about four miles north of Chestertown. His brother Benjamin, a farmer, lived near him. A brother-in-law, Noel Wightman, ran a farm in the same neighborhood. James Starbuck conducted a farm about one and a-half miles east of the village, on the ground now occupied by his grandson, Samuel Starbuck. He has kin in Glens Falls of that name. D Punderson and J Punderson ran separate farms near Loon Lake. Indeed Loon Lake and Friends' Lake were originally the most thickly settled portions of the town

There was no church edifice in town in 1805, the first one, Baptist, being erected about 1810. This church was organized by Rev Jehiel Fox, the founder, he was here called, of Chestertown. The Presbyterians held their meetings in the old school-house, which stood on the site of the Methodist parsonage. Miss Roby Simmons taught there in 1806. It was then just built—in that year,—and replaced a log school-house which formerly stood about a mile further north

The War of 1812 strongly interested the sympathies of the settlers here, and quite a number voluntarily bore arms in that struggle. A few were drafted. Joseph Collins fought in that war, and was at the battle of Plattsburgh

The cold season of 1816 did not so seriously affect the people of Chester as as would naturally be inferred. Most of the inhabitants succceded in getting enough to eat though they were forced to go to Washington and Saratoga counties to get food

Otis Collins removed from the homestead of his father to his present residence in Chestertown in about 1835,—soon after his marriage. It was then quite a village. The Fox brothers were then keeping store here, as also was one Lewis Newman, who afterward went to Glens Falls. There were two hotels here, the same that now hold open their doors to guests. Shadrach Mead, son of Titus Mead, before named, kept the hotel now run by Joel Rising. It was a smaller building then. A man named Smith, from Bolton, kept the other. Levi Mead ran a grist-mill then about a mile and a-half south of the village, and Jabez and Titus Mead still ran the one two miles to the west

Owing to the loss of the town records, before mentioned, which occurred in 1876 or 1877, the measures adopted by the town during the Rebellion cannot be given in that detail which would be interesting. Special meetings were called, and votes passed which reflect great credit on the town, and reveal the loyal patriotism which glows in the bosom of the inhabitants thereof. Generally speaking, however, it is safe to say that the town furnished about three hundred men for the Union, and to many of her volunteers awarded a bounty of $800

In internal improvements Chester has not been slack The roads which pass through its territory have been improved, the bridges that span its streams have been built according to the most approved pattern Especially is this true of the bridge across the Hudson at Riverside It was built in 1872 at an expense of $15,000, and in the spring of 1884 the wooden portion was rebuilt at an additional cost of $2,300 The work was under the supervision of a stock company of which the officers are Edwin A Bush, of Adirondack, president, E D Locke, of Pottersville, secretary, and C H Faxon, of Chestertown, treasurer The directors are the foregoing and C E Benedict, of Pottersville, David Aldrich, of Sherman, John D Burwell and C P Leland of, Schroon Lake [1]

Following is a list of the supervisors from Chester, as far as they could be obtained —

1813, 14, Seba Higley, 1815–17, Norman Fox, 1818–20, Hobby Mead; 1821, Norman Fox, 1822, Hobby Mead, 1823, '24, Norman Fox, 1825–28, Alanson Fox; 1829, Seba Higley, 1830–34, Hobby Mead, 1835, '36, C J. Starbeck, 1837, Hobby Mead, 1838, William Hotchkiss, 1839, '40, Orrison Mead, 1841, '42, Thomas A Leggett; 1843–45, William Hotchkiss, .

1860, William Hotchkiss, 1861, '62, R C Clapp, 1863, '64, R P Fuller; 1865, J H. Walker, 1866, '67, T J Carpenter, 1868, Joseph Fowler, 1869, Robert S Hall, 1870, Charles H Faxon, 1871, L R Locke, 1872, Gideon Towsley, 1873, L R Locke, 1874, R P Fuller, 1875, L R Locke; 1876, R P Fuller; 1877, Robert S Hall, 1878, Joseph A J Smith, 1879, Milo D Knapp, 1880, F A Griswold, 1881, John H Remington, 1882–84, James A Skiff, 1885, Joseph B Mills

The present officers of Chester are as follows Supervisor, Joseph B Mills, town clerk, Oren Birge, commissioner of highways, John H Remington, assessors, Ira M Fish, Willard Wells, Alfred Scott, justices of the peace, Stan-'ley H Bevins, Martin F Byrne, John S Pasko and Cyrus F Kipp, excise commissioners, Royal P Mead, Howard Dunn, Hiram Towsley, superintendents of the poor, Myron Tripp, Hiland Hicks; constables, Courtney C Collins, John F Bryant, Dana Jenks, Irwin Smith, Rollin Russell, auditors, Andrew C Thurston, Frederick A Whitney, James L Tripp, inspectors of election, District 1, James Potter, Marcus U Mitchell, Charles S Leggett, District 2, Jesse B Smith, Charles Hicks, James Mills

The population of the town as shown by the census from 1850 to 1880,

---

[1] To the south of the bridge on the east bank of the Hudson, and completely hidden from view by the trees is the encampment of the Riverside Camp-meeting Association There stand in two circles —a wheel within a wheel — about one hundred handsome cottages and a hotel of comfortable dimensions The Methodists from this part of the country hold their annual camp-meeting there a week every August, and have done so for the past twelve or thirteen years

has been as follows In 1850, 1,850, 1855, 1,936, 1860, 2,411, 1865, 2,274, 1870, 2,329, 1875, 2,193, 1880, 2,247

MUNICIPAL HISTORY

Chestertown — Of the two villages in this town, Chestertown and Pottersville, the former is of greater antiquity, dating its origin as a village back to the period intervening between the years 1805 and 1820 In 1835 the place contained one Presbyterian and one Baptist Church, one grist-mill, one saw-mill, clothing works, an academy, two taverns, three stores, and about one hundred and fifty dwellings It is of late attracting considerable notice as a desirable resort for the summer months Two and a half miles to the north-east lies Loon Lake, three miles to the southwest is Friends' Lake, four miles to the east, Brant Lake, and one mile to the south, Lake Fathomless, of which Mr Stoddard pithily says that it "has recently bounced into public notice as the haunt of some monster of the deep, whose continued ravings have carried consternation to the breasts of all children, and who stirred up the mud 'like all git-out,' (to quote), and whether the shadowy form was that of the sportive ichthyosaurus, the agile plesiosaurus, or the savage bullhead, is unto this day a profound mystery" His description of Panther and Spruce Mountains is so apt that it is best quoted here Panther Mountain is southeast of the village, an abrupt, dark-wooded hill, from which a grand sweep of mountains and forests can be seen, with lakes and ponds, and the strong Adirondacks away to the north and west Spruce Mountain is passed over — or rather *up*, for the village is at nearly the same elevation — through a narrow defile, on the road from Lake George, with a gradual ascent for some ways that is very wild and broken in places Once it was covered with a heavy growth of spruce, but in the summer of 1854 a fire swept through our northern forests For days the smoke hung thick and stifling over the entire land, and Spruce Mountain was stripped of its glory In some places a thick growth of poplar, which seems to spring spontaneously in place of heavier timber burnt or cut away, is growing, in others the mountain side is almost without life, the white, bleached stones gleaming among the blackened trunks of trees still standing, or piled together in inextricable confusion, suggesting the ghastly ruins of a dead world"

The first post-office in town was at the village of Chestertown It was not established until some years after Mr Collins came in 1805 It was at first situated on the site of Rising's Hotel Obadiah Mead was probably the first postmaster, and Sharach Mead his successor Clark Rawson, of Schroon Lake, used to carry the mail on horseback from Sandy Hill, stopping at various points along the route He came once a week Shadrach Mead's successors are not remembered until William Hotchkiss, who served some time before 1847, and

---

[1] *The Adirondacks*, p 183

until 1857 John L Weatherhead then received the appointment In 1862 William Scofield secured the position, but gave it up again in 1868 to John L. Weatherhead In 1870 Nelson B Mallery succeeded Weatherhead, and in June, 1873, gave place to the present incumbent, Robert S Hall

Hotels — It has been stated in former pages of this chapter that the first tavern in town stood on the site of Downs's Hotel as early as 1810

In the present hotel of this name M H Downs followed John L Weatherhead in 1869, the latter having kept it a number of years before In the spring of 1885 he was succeeded by the present proprietors, George Ferris & Son (Charles Ferris) The building is pleasantly located on the highest land in the village It is three stories high, and will provide for one hundred and twenty guests

Rising's Hotel has had an intermittent career Hobby Mead first kept a tavern there in the second quarter of the century, and the house relapsed into the seclusion of a private dwelling until about 1881, when Milo Graham reconstructed it into a hotel In March, 1882, Joel W Rising took possession, having just arrived from Hague, and refitted the house to its present condition. It will accommodate seventy five guests, is neatly furnished and kept, and a toothsome, wholesome table prepared three times a day for guests

Mercantile Interests — Robert S Hall, the merchant of longest standing still in active business here, began his mercantile career in April, 1865, when he and M D Knapp bought out the business of C H Faxon & Co (the "company" being H S Crittenden, now postmater at Glens Falls) Knapp remained with Mr Hall one year E N Scofield established his drug store here in 1872. N B Mallery had formerly had a drug store in the same building for a short time W H Remington commenced a clerkship in the general store of his brother, J H Remington, in 1875 In 1879 he acquired a half interest in the business In 1880 they sold out to George H McDonald and M S Graham, who conducted the business under the firm style of McDonald & Graham W H Remington was clerk for them until 1882, when he purchased the interest of M S Graham, and the business was continued under the name of McDonald & Remington In the spring of 1883 Mr Remington set over his title to McDonald and went to North Creek, where he bought out E O Jaynes & Co. He stayed there but one year, and in the spring of 1885 returned to Chestertown and bought out the entire interest of George H McDonald Before J. H Remington began here in 1875, he had been clerk for Robert S Hall M. C Drake bought in with Hall in the spring of 1872 In 1873 Drake bought out Hall's interest and continued alone until the spring of 1874, when J H. Remington acquired a one-half interest with him The general mercantile business now conducted by James McAveigh was established in 1877, when Thomas and James McAveigh purchased the property of Benjamin Pickens and S G Brayley, who had been doing business for about seven years before

under the name of Pickens & Brayley, and had failed   The firm of McAveigh
Bros continued until 1883, since which time James McAveigh has been the
sole proprietor

Frederick Vetter bought, on the 1st of September, 1881, the hardware
business of J R Dunn & Co, who had been here about eighteen months pre-
ceeding   The business was originally established, in 1864, by Morgan Tripp
and Charles Loy, who continued until the spring of 1880 under the style of
Tripp & Loy   Oren Birge, general merchant, succeeded Robert Hall in the
occupancy of this building for store purposes in May, 1882   The building was
erected by Uri Young, who, in company with his son George, kept store here
for not less than thirty years prior to Hall's occupancy.

Manufacturing Interests — The grist-mill (most properly classed under
this head), now owned by C H Faxon, was originally built here, Mr Faxon
thinks about 1800, by Rev Jehiel Fox   It was twice repaired and rebuilt up
to 1841, at which time it was burned, while under the ownership and operation of Alonzo Towsley   In the following year it was built up again by John
Ransom   The present occupant and owner, C H Faxon, bought the property in 1849 of John Ransom   The mill was enlarged, remodeled, and a new
foundation put in in 1872   The mill, which has three run of stone and the
"appurtenances thereto," can grind 30,000 bushels of wheat per year

The tannery now owned by C H Faxon & Son was built in 1849, by
Alexander Robertson   C H Faxon went in with him from the beginning,
and up to 1856 the business was conducted by these two gentlemen and James
Crandall, under the firm name of Robertson, Faxon & Co   In 1856 Crandall
withdrew and Milton Sawyer became a partner, the new firm name being Sawyer, Faxon & Co   In 1860 Mr Faxon bought out Mr Robertson, and in
company with Sawyer, continued until June 10th, 1865   Mr Faxon then
purchased Sawyer's interest and continued alone until July 1st, 1882   At that
time his son, William H Faxon, became associated with him and the present
firm title was adopted   The capacity of the tannery may be placed at about
24,000 to 30,000 sides of leather annually   About fifty hands are employed
in all   The bark is brought chiefly from Essex county

The marble works of J M Stone & Son (J H Stone) were established in
1872 by H Hanchett   He remained but a few months when the present firm
succeeded him (1873)

William B White began harness-making here in 1874   Charles F May
came here on April 1st, 1884, from Pottersville, where he had made harnesses
for three preceding years

Attorneys — Adam Armstrong, jr, was admitted to the bar in 1869, and
undergoing a thorough course of study with Judge Stephen Brown, of Glens
Falls, passed a year of study in the Albany Law School (1865)   In 1865
he was unanimously nominated for district attorney, but declined   He practiced in Glens Falls until 1871, when, in October, he removed to Chestertown

Charles P Coyle was graduated from the law department of Albany University, and admitted to the practice of law in March, 1883 He did not begin to practice until April, 1875, when he came to Chestertown, remaining, in the mean time, in the office of U G Paris, of Sandy Hill. The first year of his practice here was in partnership with Adam Armstrong, jr Mr Coyle is a young man of vigorous and aggressive intellect, and has already built up an extensive and increasing practice Stanley H Bevens was admitted in 1879, after studying the requisite period, as a partner of Adam Armstrong, jr He began to practice here at once Before he commenced studying law he was exclusively in the insurance business He is one of the justices of the town

Physicians — Of the two physicians practicing in Chestertown, Dr Alfred Mallery is the eldest, and we would gladly give an extended sketch of his long and honorable career as a physician, but were unable to obtain from him the necessary data (See chapter on the Medical Fraternity) Dr F E Aldrich was admitted to the practice of his profession on the 29th day of October, 1878, at the medical department of Dartmouth College He has practiced in Chestertown since October, 1879, and has acquired an enviable reputation, and an extensive ride

Chester Water Works — This system had its origin in 1834, when Jonathan Fish laid a few pipes and conducted a part of the present supply to a few of the dwellings here The water came from springs on the west side of Oak or Panther Mountain The present owner and manager, the enterprising C H Faxon, purchased the springs, fixtures and right of way of Fish in July, 1848, and in the succeeding autumn he reconstructed the works and supplied about every family in the village. In 1856 he bought a spring on what is known as the Leggett farm (now owned by John Cunningham) Mr Faxon didn't bring the water from this spring to the village, however, until the fall of 1880 The two sources now used will afford ample water supply for Chestertown for the next fifty years The mountain water contains valuable mineral properties, particularly iron, which is held in solution to an extent which renders the water wholesome without injuring it for any purpose. The water from the Cunningham farm contains lime enough to make it also an unmixed benefit In 1848 Mr Faxon built the reservoir in the rear of McAveigh's store About two-thirds of all the water used in the village comes through this reservoir Its capacity is 5,000 gallons The reservoir at the foot of Panther Mountain has a capacity for 11,000 gallons About $2\frac{1}{2}$ miles of $1\frac{1}{4}$ inch pipe are laid Mr Faxon intends soon to enlarge the pipe from the Leggett or Cunningham farm

The Chester Academy — This was a private school built in 1845 by Rev T J Haswell In 1847 Rev R C Clapp came to the village when it was nearly as large as it is at present and took charge of the academy It remained a private institution, having an average attendance of from twenty-five

to thirty pupils Mr Clapp remained at its head until 1860, when it was discontinued In 1868 it was sold to George W Mead, the present owner, who enlarged it and converted it into a dwelling-house The schools in the town are now conducted under the district system

Churches — Concerning the history of the older churches in Chestertown information is singularly meagre The oldest church is the Baptist, which is also the oldest in the Lake George Baptist Association It was organized in 1796 by the Rev Jehiel Fox, to whose energy and watchful administrative capabilities is due many of the thriving interests of Chestertown to-day The earliest records are gone, but it was under the pastorate of Rev Jehiel Fox that the edifice was erected It has been repeatedly remodeled How long Mr Fox remained is not known In 1825 the pastor was Rev C W Hodge. Rev Henry Faxon served in that capacity from about 1827 to 1829 The last regular preaching was done by Rev Mr Muller, of Warrensburgh Prior to his labors Rev M L Bennett was pastor for several years and was preceded by Rev A C, Nichols, who remained a year Before him Rev A B Palmetier filled the pastorate for about three years The present trustees are D R Gould, Moses Hedges, B W Mead , deacon and clerk, Amasa F Mead

The first Methodist preaching in Chestertown was by Rev Tobias Spicer in 1807

The West Church edifice, one and a half miles west of the village, was erected before 1830, that in the village about 1835 It is now owned by the Catholics The present edifice was built in 1867 at a cost of $6,000 The present officers are Pastor, Rev Joel Hall, who succeeded Rev. L L Lawrence in April, 1884 ; stewards, J M Stone, T J Carpenter, Lorenzo Thurston, Norman Perry, Arthur Smith, Philander Baldwin, Charles Leggett, W. W Emerson and Charles Thurston , class-leader, T J Carpenter , trustees, Richard Little, C J Noxon, F C Gould, Charles Leggett The present membership of the church is 155, with two probationers There are three church edifices in this charge, one called the Horicon Church, and the old West Church, both of which have fallen into permanent disuse, and the house at Chestertown Including all these and the parsonage the church property is valued at $5,000 There are three Sunday-schools, having a total membership of 148, besides thirty-three officers and teachers The Sunday-school superintendent at Chestertown for a number of years has been William Mundy, who still holds that position

The Presbyterian Church here was organized in 1825 as a Dutch Reformed Church, but was subsequently changed to the Presbyterian denomination The first elders were Bingham Eaton, Benjamin Knapp, Ezra B Smith, Benjamin Eaton, Obadiah and Hobby Mead, and William Hotchkiss There was no regular pastor and no trustees for many years Mr Kitchell, of Bolton, preached occasionally, and Rev Courtney Smith, of Warrensburgh From

35

1847 to 1849, and again from 1877 to 1882, Rev R C Clapp served in the pastorate of this church   From 1842 to 1847, Rev Thomas J Haswell preached   Rev John Newbanks came in 1852 and remained one year [1]   Rev. M C Bronson served from 1868 to 1875

The first and present house of worship was erected in 1833, and was thoroughly remodeled and enlarged in 1872 and 1873   The present value of the church property is about $2,500   Rev E B Mead is pastor   The Sunday-school was organized about 1828, and for the first thirty years of its existence Ezra B Smith acted as superintendent   From 1858 to 1866 Rev R C Clapp performed the duties incumbent on that office   From 1866 to 1875 the superintendent was Charles Loy, and was followed by the present superintendent, Rev R C Clapp

The Roman Catholic Church of Chestertown was formed in 1867   The first pastor was the Rev De Rouch   He was succeeded by Rev Father Kelly, who remained seven years, and was followed in turn by Rev Father O'Mahoney, who served two years   The present pastor is Rev Father Flood, of North Creek   The old Methodist Church was purchased at the time of organization and converted into a Catholic house of worship   The cost of remodeling the edifice was about $1,000, and $1,500 has been expended on improvements since that time   The present value of the property is estimated at $3,500

The first church trustees were Patrick McAveigh, John McPhillips and Timothy Murphy   The present church trustees are Patrick McAveigh and Timothy Murphy   The membership numbers about thirty families   A Sunday-school was formed six years ago, Lizzie McAveigh and Anna Cohen acting as superintendents

The Episcopal Church or Mission was formed here in 1876   The first rector was Rev Aubrey Todrig, the second, Rev C B Flagler, and the third and present, Rev C J Whipple, who came on June 16th, 1882   The first house of worship consisted of the former dwelling house of Charles Fowler, re-modeled, and adapted to the purposes of its consecration   The present edifice was consecrated in June, 1884, and cost in erection about $2,500   The entire property is worth about $3,000   A Sunday-school was organized at the time of the formation of the mission, the rectors being the superintendents   At present, however, those duties and the duties of warden are preformed by Ralph Thurman   There are twenty communicants in the mission

Pottersville — This village derived its name from Joel F Potter, the first business man who started the movement which resulted in the building up of the village   In 1839 he built a store (just south of the present hotel), which burned in 1876, and has never been rebuilt   Potter went from this place to Glens Falls years ago   From there he removed to Schroon Lake where he died

---

[1] He became deranged, and is now hopelessly insane

three or four years ago   He left no descendants in Pottersville   In 1835 there was nothing on the site of this village except a log house which stood on the ground now covered by Daniel Virgil's house   James Danley owned this log house   His grandson, C F Kipp, now lives in the village   The principal business in early times was lumbering   All the inhabitants were more or less interested in it

There never were any extensive mills here   One of the earliest industries here was the old tannery, which formerly stood about ten rods north of the present residence of C F Kipp and which was erected by Milton Sawyer, during the infancy of the village   He conducted the business about eight years, and was followed by Fay & Co, of Greene county, who ran the concern ten or fifteen years and then failed   Fraser & Co, of New York, who now own the Mill Brook tannery, were then at the head of the establishment for about ten years   Finally C F Kipp bought it and converted it into a cider-mill   On the 15th of October, 1882, it burned, and, according to Mr Kipp, the fire remained in the tanbark which covered the ground several inches deep, for a space of eighteen months.

The hotel was built in about 1845 by Joseph Hotchkiss and Joshua Collar   L H Jenks, the present postmaster, worked on this, as indeed, he has on almost every building in the village   Hiram Towsley was one of the oldest proprietors, Isaac Beebe came after him, then Marcus H Downs came into the house, enlarged it, and kept it from about 1860 to 1869   In the last named year L R Locke came into possession and remained until 1879, when his father, R L Locke, the present proprietor, became his successor   The house is nicely kept, and does its principal business in providing dinners for guests bound to and from the resorts around Schroon Lake and farther north and west

The first postmaster here was Joel F Potter, who received the appointment in 1839   He had the office five or six years, and then gave place to Michael Codman, in whose name the office was conducted, by himself and his daughter, Sarah Ann Codman, until 1860   James Wallace then served until 1865, and was succeeded by William R Codman   In 1867 William G Leland was appointed, Charles Brown then performed the postal functions for Pottersville for a short time, and was followed by Livingston H Jenks, the politically-moribund incumbent of the present day

The condition of the vicinity in 1840, in addition to what has already been inferentially described, may be deduced from the fact that the State road, so-called, which John Thurman constructed, was then in good condition, all the other roads now used about here have been opened since   Among the early residents here may be mentioned C F Kipp, L H Jenks, Joseph Hotchkiss, B Vandenthuyzen, Garrett Vandenthuyzen, and Jacob Vandenthuyzen, three brothers   Jacob Vandenthuyzen has a number of descendants living here and about here now

Business Interests — S B Morey has had a general store in Pottersville since 1858 or 1860 He began in the same building which he now occupies, though he has enlarged it considerably beyond its original proportions J H Griswold, M D, began preparing and dispensing drugs and medicine in the village in 1860 He came to the present location in 1880 He was admitted to the practice of medicine in 1845, and has been a licentiate of the Warren County Medical Society since 1876 Silas Daimon has kept a general store here for about twenty years Edgar Wilcox established his hardware and grocery business here in the spring of 1879 He has occupied the buildings he now owns since September, 1883 P M Griswold, brother to J H Griswold, has been the latter's partner and conducted the dry goods department since 1880 R S Pritchard has kept a general store here since the fall of 1881 Frank A Griswold, son of J H Griswold, was licensed to practice pharmacy in December, 1884, by the State Board of Pharmacy, and as dentist in August, 1879, under the act of the Legislature passed on June 20th, of that year

B. S Phelps has run the steam saw-mill, planing-mill, and grist-mill in the south part of the village since 1878

James A Skiff has practiced law in Pottersville ten or twelve years His business is done chiefly before the Departments at Washington

Dr E J Dunn was graduated from the medical department of the University of New York, on March 3d, 1883 He has been practicing medicine in Pottersville for the past seven years, after completing a course of study in the office of Dr F L R Chapin, of Glens Falls

Churches — The oldest church in Pottersville is the Methodist, which was organized in 1810, while all this tract was as yet a thinly peopled and inhospitable wilderness Indeed, the community had been edified by preaching for years before even that date, as tradition and the records concur in saying that the lamented Rev Richard Jacobs exhorted and preached about here as early as 1796 The first class-leader of the class formed in 1810 was Eli Beebe A Sunday-school was organized in 1835 by T S Burnet The house of worship was erected in 1847, and repaired and beautified in the interior in 1884 Following is the list of pastors· 1811, Lansing Whiting, 1812, Gersham Price, 1813, Tobias Spicer; 1814, Gilbert Lyon, 1815, Elijah Hibbard, 1816, Daniel Braton, 1817, Daniel J Wright, 1818, Sherman Miner, 1819, Daniel Braton, 1820, Jacob Hall, 1821, C Silliman, 1822 and 1823, Phineas Doane, 1824, John Clarke, 1825 and 1826, Roswell Kelley, assisted by Joseph Ames, 1827, Jacob Beeman, 1828, Nathan Rice and Alexander Hulin

In 1828 the Luzerne and Warren circuits were divided, leaving a large circuit on the north to be traveled by two preachers In 1830 and '31 Seymour Coleman and Seth Eyres traveled the circuit; 1832, '33, Joseph McCheney, Henry Coleman, and Chester Chamberlain, 1834, Reuben Wescott and James Cobet, 1835, Joel Squier and John Fitch, 1836, William Richards and Horace

Campbell, 1837, '38, (the circuit was divided in 1837) B Pomeroy, 1839, Alonzo Richards, 1840, '41, Ezra Sayre, assisted by William Hull and Reynolds, 1842, '43, I D Burnham, assisted by Ira Holmes and L S Mott, 1844, '45, Joseph Connor, and Warren Fox; 1846, 47, Chester Lyon, 1848, '49, Samuel Hughes; 1850, '51, G H Townsend, 1852, '53, David Noble, 1854, '55, Daniel Rose, 1856, '57, A Stevens, 1858, no record kept; 1859, '69, H M Munsee, 1862, '63, A Shurtliff, 1864, F. F. Hannah, 1865, '66, Z Picket, 1867, '68, G D Rose, 1870, '71, '72, R Campbell, 1873, J C Walker, 1874, '75, P M Hitchcock, 1876, '77, J W Coons, 1878, 79, E· Comstock, 1880, R Patterson, 1881, H S Allen, 1882, '83, Joel Hall, 1884, '85, R E Jenkins

The Episcopal Church was organized, and the edifice erected soon after the construction of the Methodist house of worship No services are held here now

CHAPTER XXX

HISTORY OF THE TOWN OF JOHNSBURGH

JOHNSBURGH is the northwestern town of Warren county, being bounded on the north by the town of Minerva, in Essex county, on the east, across the Hudson, by Chester, on the south by Thurman, and on the west by the town of Wells, in Hamilton county Its surface is everywhere broken by lofty and precipitous mountains, composed for the most part of solid rock The northern and central part is occupied by the Schroon range of mountains, and the south by a spur of the Kayaderosseras Crane Mountain, the highest peak of the latter range, attains an altitude of 3,289 feet above sea level Its name is derived from the circumstance that a small pond which nestles in a concavity near the summit of the mountain is much frequented by cranes [1]

The greater part of the town is too rough and stony for cultivation, the arable land being thus confined to the narrow valleys formed by the Sacandaga and other small streams which find their devious ways from source to mouth. The soil is a sandy and gravelly loam. Kaolin, serpentine iron ore, and a few other minerals are found in small quantities

The early history of the town has been so well written by Dr Holden for the Warrensburgh *News*, from matter furnished him by David Noble, of Weavertown, that we cannot refrain from drawing largely from this storehouse in the compilation of this chapter

[1] Seen from Warrensburgh, eleven miles away, the mountain presents a remarkable similitude to the profile of the human face

The town was taken from the old town of Thurman on the 6th of April, 1805 The records for the first two years are not to be found The officers for 1807, however, are given, as it gives a good partial list of the early settlers here: Supervisor, John Richards, assessors, Norris Hopkins, Archibald Noble, Henry Allen, highway commissioners, Joseph Wilcox, Edward Noble, Nathaniel Trumble; constable and collector, Joseph Hopper, constable, Lyman Lee; fence viewers, Andrus Weaver, William Leach; overseers of the poor, Robert Armstrong, James Parker, committee to build pound, Joseph Hopper, Lemuel Humphrey, John Thurman, pathmasters, Job Wood, Reynolds Weaver, Joseph Wells, Lemuel Harndon, Charles J Wetmore, Edward Noble, Samuel Morehouse, David Kibby, Samuel Somerville, Samuel Ross, Samuel Baxter, John Pasco, Richard Stratton, Archibald Washburn, Archibald Noble, Abiram Galusha.

The old town of Thurman included the present Thurman, Bolton, Chester, Warrensburgh, Stony Creek, a part of Caldwell and all of Johnsburgh It derived its name from John Thurman, the original patentee, who purchased it in about 1778 Its present name was derived from his given name He made the first clearing in the twelfth township of Totten and Crossfield's Purchase on Elm Hill, one mile southeast of the site of Johnsburgh Corners, in about the year 1790 Mr Noble says that Mr Thurman named the place Elm Hill from a large and beautiful elm tree standing on a prominent knoll on this plateau, and that for many years the territory west of the Hudson River and north of Athol was known among the friends in England, Ireland and America as Elm Hill, and letters to the inhabitants here were so addressed The nearest post-office was Thurman, now Warrensburgh About the same time, 1790, Thurman began to clear land on Beaver Brook, nearly a mile west from Elm Hill, and in 1790 or soon after he erected a saw-mill and grist-mill on the falls of of the brook Settlers then began to move in from England, Scotland, Ireland and New England They took up farms varying in size from fifty to one hundred acres In 1794 Thurman built the first framed barn in town It extended thirty by forty feet and was laid by Enos Grover, a cooper, by the scribe, or "cut and try" rule, the method of framing buildings in those days This barn, which has been resilled once and reshingled twice, still stands on the Elm Hill farm, and is in good repair About this time Thurman also opened a store and put up a distillery to create a market for the large quantities of rye which the newly-cleared lands produced In those days the grain was malted for distillation, hence a store, malt-house and kiln was built for the purpose It is said that most of the whisky made was used in the town French's *Gazetteer* states that in 1795 Thurman erected a woolen factory, which was soon changed to a cotton factory, and that as early as 1797 he erected his calico printing works, the first, it is believed in America Mr Noble differs from it in that he does not mention the woolen works, and dates the construction of the cotton factory and calico printing factory between 1800 and 1804   These last two stood about thirty rods above his saw and grist-mill. As early as 1800 this mighty pioneer also erected ash works, and made large quantities of potash, which at that time and for thirty years after brought good prices   Farmers were paid one shilling a bushel for ashes, while potash brought from $2 00 to $3 50 per ton

Thurman had his cotton factory machinery made and put up on the spot by an English machinist named Joseph Holden   The spinning and weaving department was under the superintendence of Daniel McGinnis, an Irishman   The calico printing was done by James Smalley, an Englishman, of enormous height, size and strength   The stones in Thurman's grist-mill were made by Jeremiah Harrington from granite which was found in the vicinity   David Noble well remembers the old man and has often seen those granite mill-stones   John Thurman, the founder and operator of all these industries, was killed at Bolton Landing in September, 1807, by a vicious bull, and was buried on his own premises, on ground now included in the Methodist cemetery at Johnsburgh Corners   So closely identified was he with the business which he conducted that at his death they all, except saw and grist-mills, closed and have never since been operated

— The first death in town was that of Enos Grover, father of the cooper before mentioned   It occurred in about the year 1795   He was buried in the plot of ground just above described   The attendants at the funeral were his family and four of Thurman's men   The first marriage was that of Calvin Washburn and Elizabeth Waddell, daughter of Robert Waddell   The first white child born in town was Polly, daughter of Robert and Julia (Hodgson) Waddell   Polly was married, when a young lady, to Bishop Carpenter, and was the mother of Jordan Carpenter, now of Chestertown   The first tavern in town was kept by Joseph Hopper, in about the year 1800, at now Johnsburgh Corners   The first post-office was established in 1817 or 1818 in the same neighborhood   The postmaster was Dr Martin Gillett, who remained in office until about 1830, when he went West, and was succeeded by Clark Burdick

The first settlers prior to Thurman's death were Robert Maxham and family, Samuel Hamden and family, Robert Waddell, son and daughter, Joseph Hopper, first hotel-keeper, Joseph Robinson, William Leach, Timothy Johnson, Reuben Washburn, Archibald Washburn, Samuel Morehouse, a Revolutionary soldier, and family   John Pasco, Thomas Morehouse, John Ward, Samuel Ross, David Kibber, Philaster Purney, Nehemiah Grover and Samuel Millington were also all Revolutionary soldiers, and settled here with their families   Others were   John Jones, a Welsh cloth manufacturer, and family, Samuel Baxter (Welsh) and family, George Hodgson (English) and family, John Armstrong (Irish) and family, Adam Armstrong (Irish) and family, David Noble (Irish) and sons, Archibald, Edward, William and John , Thomas

Somerville (Irish) and sons, John, Samuel, Archibald and Thomas, John Richards (Welsh surveyor), Assemblyman and Member of Congress from Warren
county, and supervisor from Johnsburgh many years; Levi Hitchcock and
family, Jeremiah Harrington and family, Calvin Crawford, Ebenezer Fish and
family, Lemuel Humphrey and family, Henry Allen and family, John B Gage,
Stephen Scripter, Silas Harrington, Enos Grover, Enos Grover, jr, Daniel
Stratton, Benajah Putnam, Silas 'Sheffield, John G Brewer, Andrew Weaver
and family, William Weaver, John Weaver, Jonathan Barney, Archibald Wilcox, Joseph, Isaiah and Jacob Wilcox, James Parker and family, Daniel Robertson and Alexander Robertson (Scotch), Alexander, Nathaniel and Norman
Trumble, Samuel Barber, J P., John Williams, Charles Wilson, Benjamin L
and Charles C Thomson, Hiram, Elisha and Elijah Ross, Josephus Lee, Jeremiah Bennett, Nathan Raymond and family, John Monell and family, Norris
Hopkins and family, Abiram Galusha (a Revolutionary soldier) and family,
Job Wood, Nathaniel Barber, Martin Gillett, M D, the first physician in town

The first religious societies in town were of the Baptist and Methodist denominations, the New England settlers being for the most part Baptists, and
the English and Irish portion Methodists   The first Baptist preachers who
visited the town were Elder Jehiel Fox, of Chestertown, and Elder Bateman
At this time the Baptists were the most numerous denomination in town   Although this people for the last seventy years have had most of the time a pastor settled here, yet they erected no house of worship until within three years
they built a neat little chapel at North River   Their present membership is
less than it was forty years ago

David Noble, a local preacher, and father of the first Methodist family in
Johnsburgh, was the son of Archibald Noble, of English descent, and Eleanor
(Jamison) Noble, of Scotch extraction, was born in Ireland in December, 1734
The Noble family were Episcopalians, or members of the English Church, as it
was then styled   When a young man David Noble was converted under the
preaching of John Wesley, who, in his early ministry, often visited Ireland,
and together with his sons and daughters united with the Methodist societies
In 1795 he, a widower, and his four sons and three daughters, all adults and
unmarried, came to America and settled in the city of New York, where, with
his eldest son Archibald, he labored as a stone and brick mason   The family
attended the old John street Methodist Church   In 1798, under the persuasive
influence of John Thurman,[1] he came to the wilderness lands of Thurman Patent, now Johnsburgh, and purchased four hundred acres in a body—one hundred for each son—and, in 1800, moved upon the tract and began to clear the
land   He put up log buildings near Beaver Brook, which intersected each of

[1] The story is told of Thurman that in his efforts to colonize his patent he was in the habit of exhibiting beech nuts to the natives and immigrants in New York and observe that that was the kind of
buckwheat that could be raised on Elm hill   Let the reader weigh the probabilities of the story for
himself

the four parcels   He then inaugurated a series of meetings at his own house and at the mills of Mr Thurman—now Dunn's mills, near Johnsburgh Corners The Methodist preachers of Cambridge Circuit immediately followed, and preached at Mr Noble's house once in six weeks   The first of these preachers were Samuel Howe, Martin Rutter, Elijah Hedding (afterward a bishop), David Brown and Mitchell B Bull   The members of the first Methodist class in town were David Noble, his sons and daughters, Thomas Somerville, a brother-in-law and an elder in a Presbyterian church in Ireland, and his wife , William Leach and wife, Adam Armstrong and wife (who afterward lived and died in Albany), Elizabeth Somerville, Elsee Robinson, Rachel Hitchcock, Mrs Enos Grover, Mrs A   Edwards, John Armstrong, Rebecca Armstrong, and Dyer Burdick, of Athol   The first class-leaders were David Noble, Adam Armstrong and William Leach (an exhorter)   From that time to the present Methodist preaching has continued here without interruption

In July, 1807, David Noble went on horseback to Arlington, Vt , on a visit to his eldest daughter, Jane, wife of Richard Empey   On the 10th day of the month, while attending a Methodist meeting in a school-house, at the conclusion of the sermon he delivered an impassioned exhortation, sat down and died without a struggle   He had attained the age of seventy-three years   His last words were " And may this be our happy lot till Heaven "   He was buried at Ash Grove Church — the first Methodist Church erected north of New York city — beside the graves of the Revs David Brown and Philip Emburg, in the town of Cambridge   In June, 1876, his grandson, David Noble, of Weavertown (who furnishes much of the information contained in this chapter), exhumed his remains and re-interred them in the cemetery of the Methodist Church of Johnsburgh   He also removed with the body the marble slab which marked his resting place at Cambridge [1]

Following is a list given by Mr Noble, of aged persons who have died in town   Thomas Somerville, died October 13th, 1815, aged 81 years , Mary Somerville, his wife, died —— —— 1825, aged 83 years , Elizabeth Somerville, a sister, died August 12th, 1837, aged 90 years , Archibald Noble, died August 14th, 1848, aged 78 years , Elisha Ross, died October 3d, 1865, aged 80 years , Hiram Ross, his brother, died October 9th, 1869, aged 88 years , Elijah Ross, also a brother, died May 9th, 1870, aged 85 years , John Ward a Revolutionary pensioner, died June 3d, 1854, aged 101 years , Samuel Somerville, died April, 1872, aged 99 years; Thomas Somerville, died June 2d, 1877, aged 94 years , Edward Noble, died March 12th, 1857, aged 84 years , Mahala Richardson, died —— ——1883, aged 92 years ; Margaret Hodgson, died May 23d, 1884, aged 92 years

---

[1] David Noble, now of Weavertown, is a grandson of the subject of the above sketch, son of Archibald Noble   He was born July 11th, 1804, about three miles west of his present residence   He first came to Weavertown in 1833, soon after the tannery was built   In 1843 he bought a lot and erected thereon the building in which he now lives and does business   He opened his store in the fall of 1844

Johnsburgh responded with alacrity to the demand for volunteers during the War of the Rebellion Her foremost men at once engaged themselves in the work of procuring enlistments, and so well did they do their work, and so patriotic were the sentiments of the inhabitants, that out of a population containing perhaps not five hundred men, one hundred and fourteen found their way to the battle-field

For many years Johnsburgh suffered from great and manifold disadvantages Being a northern town of the county, and abutting on the Northern Wilderness, no commerce and very little travel passed through it For years the inhabitants carried their grain and butter to Glens Falls and Waterford for sale, in return purchasing and bringing home family supplies, such as tea, tobacco, molasses, rum (for the hay and harvest season), sole leather, cotton and woolen clothing. At times somebody would make a spasmodic effort at keeping a store — falsely so-called — by dealing in small quantities of rum, tobacco, salt, etc In 1832–33, the Weavertown Tannery was built by William Watson and James Wasson, of Blandford, Mass The enterprise stimulated the dormant energies of the inhabitants, giving employment to the men, creating a market for bark and farm produce, and awakening hopes of other industries yet to come Several stores were soon established [1] A few years later a tannery was built at The Glen It burned not long a after, was rebuilt, operated a few years and abandoned, having proved a source of loss to everybody interested in it In 1852 Milton Sawyer and Wheeler Mead built the tannery at North Creek In 1875 a Boston company erected a tannery on the Sacandaga River in the west part of the town, which is still in operation [2]

The first church edifice built in town was erected at Weavertown about 1822, by the Dutch Reformed Church, having a membership of ten persons As the society were unable to procure a pastor, some of its members joined other societies, while others moved away In 1835 the Baptists finished the church, which had not yet been plastered, and occupied it a few years, but finally, for want of unity among the members, it was abandoned, and recently torn down The next house of worship was the Methodist Church at Johnsburgh Corners, which was begun in 1838 and completed in 1843 It has been in use since it was repaired in 1879, and is now in good condition Its value is placed at $2,000 The next edifice — Methodist — was built in the Fourteenth Township, or North River, in about 1847, at an expense of about $1,200, and is yet in use The fourth is the Free-will Baptist Church of North Creek, which was built in 1853 It cost about $2,000, and is still in use by that denomination The sixth [3] was the Methodist Church built at North Creek in

[1] It it a noteworthy fact that Weavertown, North Creek and Creek Center in Stoney Creek, date the origin of their existence as villages immediately subsequent to the erection of the tanneries which now keep them alive

[2] The Weavertown Tannery will be closed in the fall of 1885 because of the scarcity, and distance from headquarters, of bark

[3] See Catholic Church given below

1879   It cost about $2,500   The seventh is also a Methodist Church, erected
in Weavertown in 1879–80, at a cost of $2,500   It is very neat and commo-
dious   Its dimensions are thirty-two by forty-eight feet   The Catholic
Church of North Creek was organized in 1875, and the edifice erected in the
same year at an expense of $2,300   The first pastor and Sunday-school su-
perintendent was Rev J. A Kelly   Father Lynch followed him, and was
followed by Father Green   Next came Father O'Mahoney, now of Warrensburgh, and in the fall of 1884 the present pastor, Father Flood, was settled as
pastor

Following is a list of the names of the supervisors from 1807, to the present time, and a list, also, of the present town officers   1807–17, John
Richards (in 1811 he was elected unanimously); 1820, '21, John Boyd, 1822,
John Richards, 1823–27, Archibald Noble, 1829–32, Nicholas Rosevelt,
1833, Thomas Somerville; 1834, 35, Jacob Wilcox, 1836, '37, John D Dunn,
1838, Thomas Somerville, 1839, David Noble, 1840, '41, John Richards,
1842, Nicholas Rosevelt, 1843–46, John Hodgson, 2d, 1847–50, John Noble,
2d; 1851, John D Somerville; 1852, Nicholas Rosevelt, 1853, John Hodgson; 1854, Hugh Waddell, 1855–57, Samuel Somerville, jr, 1858, John
Noble, 2d, 1859, John Hodgson; 1860, George P Wait, 1861, John Hodgson, 1862–65, Robert Waddell, 1866, Charles W Noble, 1867,'68, Godfrey
R Martine, 1870, William Waddell, 1871, '72, Barclay Thomas, 1873, John
Straight, 1874, Barclay Thomas, 1875–77, James C Eldridge, 1878, '79,
William Waddell, 1880, '81, James C Eldridge, 1882, A C Hall, 1883,
'84, Charles W Noble, 1885, Taylor J Eldridge

The present town officers are   supervisor, Taylor J Eldridge, town clerk,
Archibald R. Noble, justices of the peace, Charles W Noble, William H
Waldron, Samuel Somerville, Thomas Eldridge, assessors, Seymour C Armstrong, John A Straight, George S. Bennett, commissioner of highways,
Harry Richards, overseers of the poor, William Dillon, Samuel Rexford;
collector, Robert T Armstrong, constables, Robert T Armstrong, George
Wells, William Johnston Luther Waldron, game constable, Seth T Thomas,
inspectors of election, district No. 1 John T Somerville, Thomas W Armstrong, Delbert Pasco, district No 2, William H Waldron, J B Randall, Patrick Collins

The population of the town has been recorded as follows —1850, 1,503;
1855, 1,983, 1860, 2,188, 1865, 2,286, 1870, 2,599, 1875, 2,577, 1880,
2,742

Municipal History —We have departed, for the sake of convenience, from
the usual method of writing town histories, and have already included much
that might have properly come under another head   We could not adopt a
different here without lessening the value of the matter so well compiled by
Mr Noble, and edited by Dr Holden   There are some sketches, however,

which we believe we can use better than by inserting them under the head of municipal history

As has already been indicated the first settlement in the town was in the near vicinity of the site of Johnsburgh Corners It is now a village of the same proportions that it had gained years ago The oldest mercantile business in the place is that now conducted by Mrs E A Phillips, whose husband, Henry Phillips, now deceased, started it in the stone store opposite to the present location, in 1860 He first went into partnership with John Noble At the expiration of two years this relation terminated Mr Phillips bought the building now occupied by his widow, and associated himself with John W. Armstrong Two years more brought a further change, this time Albert Wills, a brother-in-law of Phillips, succeeding Armstrong They dissolved in 1871, and Phillips carried on the business alone until his death in 1874, since which time his widow, Mrs E A Phillips has been her husband's successor

The building in which she plies her trade was built about 1830, by Hiram Truesdell, and used by him as a store Charles W Noble has had a general store here also since the spring of 1879 Before that he was a merchant in Weavertown In September, 1881, Mrs S Martine and E G C Smith, wife of A W Smith entered into partnership and continued on a large scale, a business theretofore carried on by Mrs Martine alone They bought the building which they use of William Lackey A W Smith occupies a part of the building for the purpose of dealing in hardware William Lackey & Son (Edmund) opened a store on May 1st, 1885, having purchased the stock of Theodore Barrett, who had run a store in the village for a year before.

Johnsburgh Corners boasts of one hotel, which is said to be sixty-three years of age Its first proprietor was John Fuller His successors have been numerous, being in order as follows —Samuel Morgan, Dr G R Martine, now of Glens Falls, John Loveland, Lorenzo Pasco, O Hitchcock, —— Drake, William Lackey, John A Rose, William Eldridge, and the present proprietor, Luke Martin, who assumed control May 1st, 1885 The house has a good reputation It will provide for about twenty-guests

The medical profession alone is represented in this little hamlet by Dr M. C Gill, who finished his medical studies in the Dartmouth Medical College on the 29th of June, 1882, and within two months thereafter displayed his sign to the invalid portion of this neighborhood

It has already been stated that the first postmaster here, Dr Martin Gillet, served from 1817 or 1818 until about 1830 Clark Burdick succeeded him. In 1855 John Noble was in office, but how long he had held it is not positively known Henry Phillips was appointed in 1862 and retained the office until 1874 Since then his widow, Mrs Eunice A Phillips has been postmistress.

Weavertown began its regular growth as a village immediately after the opening of the tannery in 1833 There are now two hotels and three stores, besides the tanning interests   The oldest hotel is that now kept by B Mc-Laughlin, who has been its proprietor since 1860   His predecessor, Ira Russell, built the house some years before and kept it until he took it   J M Waddell became proprietor of the other house in 1867, when he succeeded Robert Lee   Lee had been connected with the house since about 1860   It was erected by John Eldridge and John Loveland   Prior to Lee's occupancy it had been used as a tavern and store together

David Noble was a general merchant in Weavertown from 1869 to January, 1884, when his son, Archibald R Noble, succeeded him   It is now principally a drug store   William Waddell and Robert Waddell, brothers, built in 1865 the store now occupied by the former   Robert Waddell died in 1878 The building which has been used by E & W Moston for mercantile purposes since May 1st, 1881, had been before that closed about a year   A B Humphrey kept store there for two years before the suspension   It had been used as a store for a number of years

There are no lawyers in Weavertown, and but two physicians, Dr W W Aldrich, who was graduated from the medical department of Dartmouth College in 1877 and began to practice here in 1878, and Dr C J Logans, who was admitted at Burlington, Vt , in 1871, and came to Weavertown from Chestertown in December, 1883

The first postmaster at Weavertown was John Hodgson, who was appointed before 1850   In 1869 he was succeeded by the present official, David Noble

North Creek — This village owes its origin to the introduction of the tannery here in 1852   T J Converse, who came here in 1854, informs the writer that at that time there was practically no village here   There were a few roughly-constructed boarding-houses, and one store kept by Russell Fuller in the building now occupied by Taylor Eldridge   There was no post-office here, though very soon after that Russell P Fuller received the appointment [1] In 1857 Mr Converse was appointed , in 1860, Moses Ordway , in 1862, Wheeler Mead , in 1863, Lyman West , in 1865, Thomas J Converse again , in 1870, William H Waldron , and in 1872 the present incumbent, Samuel Richardson

Mr Converse, in continuation, states that the religious meetings in 1854 were held in the old school-house, that there was no saw-mill, nor grist-mill, nor ashery, nor distillery here

Mercantile Interests — The oldest mercantile establishment at North Creek is the one now conducted by T J Eldridge, who bought out William Remington in September, 1884   Remington's predecessor was Elihu Janes   James Wilson was the second one in the store and the first was John Straight   P

---

[1] Mr Converse states that he was the first postmaster, and that he held the office eleven years   If so, the legislative manuals have been in error   We have followed them

Moynehan established a general trade in North Creek in 1877. In May, 1844, he sold out to the present proprietors, M Crehore & Co The B A Martine Pharmacy was first opened in the fall of 1880 by B A Martine Since his death in 1881 A A Skinner carries on the business under the same name

The North Creek tannery, already mentioned, was erected in 1852 by Milton Sawyer and Wheeler Mead The partnership between them terminated about 1865, and Milton Sawyer conducted the business alone until 1876, when the present proprietor, John Reed, took possession William H Healy, of Boston, had some connection with the business up to 1876 He furnished the money with which to build the tannery and afterwards furnished it with hides The tannery has been built over twice since 1876 About twenty men are now kept busy in the building and as many more furnish the bark, though they are not always in Mr. Reed's employ The tannery turns out 30,000 sides of leather per annum

Hotels — There are two hotels at North Creek — the American Hotel, kept by John McInerny since May 1st, 1872, when he came here from Chestertown and built it The house will accommodate thirty guests, and the Adirondack House, of which J J Lyons has been proprietor for four years William Waldron was his successor

Physicians — J L Fuller, M D, received his degree at Dartmouth Medical College in 1881, and came to North Creek in the summer of 1882 Dr F W Spoor was graduated in medicine at the New York Homeopathic Medical College, March 15th, 1884, and bought his brother's practice at North Creek in the same spring

North River. — This is a small hamlet in the north part of the town, containing one hotel, of which Danforth Eldridge has been proprietor for nearly fifteen years; and two stores, kept respectively by Mr Amidon and Samuel Towne

In 1855 Schuyler Fuller was postmaster at North River; he was succeeded in 1867 by Lincoln M Root In 1861 Henry W. Wilson was appointed, in 1863, James M Ordway, 1864, Warren W Gleason, and in 1866, Danforth Eldridge, the present postmaster

CHAPTER XXXI

HISTORY OF THE TOWN OF HAGUE

HAGUE is situated in the northeast corner of the county, along the northern shore of Lake George The surface is mountainous in the extreme, so that not more than one-fourth of it is capable of cultivation Along the shore

of the lake the mountains generally descend much more abruptly to the edge of
the water than in Bolton   They are parts of the ridge and spurs of the Kayaderosseras Mountains, and are separated from each other by the narrow valleys
of Trout and Northwest Bay Brooks   In the northwest part of the town lie the
Trumbull Mountains, and a little to the south therefrom is Ash Grove Hill rising
to an elevation of 2,000 or 2,500 feet above the level of the sea   On the lake
shore in the extreme northeast corner of the town and county is Rogers's Slide,
a mountain nearly a thousand feet in height, with smooth summit and steep
sides   It is said to be singularly rich in minerals, beautiful specimens of garnet
having been discovered on its top, and graphite abounding in its bosom   The
name is derived from the following historical circumstance   Robert Rogers was
sent in the winter of 1757–58, with a small party of followers, to make observations at Ticonderoga and Crown Point, where he met a party of the enemy,
and after a sharp skirmish, was defeated   Rogers, pursued by the savages, directed his eager footsteps to the summit of this mountain

"Arrived at the brow of the precipice he threw his 'luggage' down the
steep walls, and, *reversing himself* on his snow-shoes, made his way down
through a ravine, at the southwest, to the lake, thence around to the foot of
the slide   The savages, following to the edge of the mountain, where the track
of the snow-shoes seemed lost in the path made by a falling body, expecting,
of course, that whoever had attempted it could not have reached the bottom
alive, must have been considerably surprised to see the brave major making off
on the ice toward the head of the lake " [1]   They desisted from further pursuit

Sabbath Day Point is a headland projecting into the lake near the southern
border   The soil is a light, sandy loam, and where the surface admits of cultivation produces average crops of oats, corn, potatoes, and buckwheat   Iron ore
has been found in some parts of the town, but in quantities too slight to encourage the opening of mines   Black lead exists near the center of the town

The town of Hague was formed from Bolton, February 28th, 1807, and
was at first known as Rochester   Its name was changed to Hague on April
6th, 1808   A part of Horicon was taken off in 1838   Settlement was begun
here in the latter part of the eighteenth century   Among the first settlers in
town were Abel Rising, Abner Briggs, Elijah Bailey, Samuel Cook, Ellis Den-
ton, Samuel Patchin, John Holman, Isaac and Uriah Balcom, and Uri Waiste
Probably the most influential family, as a whole, in town, is the Rising family,
although their progenitor, Abel Rising, jr, did not come to Hague until 1811
Abel Rising, sr, lived and died in Suffield, Connecticut   He was twice married, and had five children by his first wife, and one by his second   His second
son was Abel Rising, jr, who removed to Hague in March, 1811, and died here
in 1822   His wife, formerly Lucinda Kent, of Suffield, died in Hague, in October, 1832   They had seven children   One of these seven was Zeno, born in

---

[1] STODDARD'S *Lake George*, pp 119, 120.

Suffield, in 1802, and came here with his parents when he was nine years of age He first married Roxie Balcom, of Hague, who died in 1846 He afterward married Cynthia Balcom, who died in 1862 They had nine children, of whom probably the best known here is Joel W Rising, now proprietor of Rising's Hotel, at Chestertown The present supervisor from Hague is nephew to Abel Rising, jr, and son to Rufus Rising Another well-known family are the Balcoms Isaac Balcom was born in Massachusetts in 1777. He married Sally Green, of his native place, and removed, a little before the beginning of the present century, to a place-about one and a half miles from the lake, in what is now Hague, now being the farm occupied by Mr Moss Two of his brothers, Uriah and Caleb, came with him and settled on farms almost adjoining Mrs Hosea Remington, the writer's informant, was the youngest of the thirteen children of Isaac Balcom, all but four of whom are now dead She was born on the 9th of September, 1823 Of the other early settlers named, the following brief statements have been ascertained as true Elijah Bailey lived until about 1840 or later, at Sabbath Day Point, with Captain Sam Patchin (of whom more will be said) Uriah Balcom lived about two miles south of Hague post-office, where Miles E Morehouse now lives Uri Waiste lived about a mile south of the village on Law's Patent, on property now owned by L Burgess Rufus Rising lived in the west part of the town, where his son, Rufus Rising, now lives

A lead mine has been worked for the past ten years about five miles west of Hague village It is said that the mine was discovered by Samuel Ackerman while he was skidding logs The mine is owned by New York parties, and superintended by George Hooper, of Ticonderoga

The richest portion of the town in historic incident is Sabbath Day Point On this sandy point, in 1756, a party of Provincials, under Generals Putnam and Rogers, defeated a superior force of French and Indians Here, on the 5th of July, 1758, Abercrombie employed the successful ruse of landing with his army of fifteen thousand men, resting until near midnight, and then moving north — leaving behind a hundred blazing piles to delude the enemy into the belief that they were still there In September, 1759, General Amherst landed with a force of twelve thousand men and passed the Sabbath with saintly punctilio [1]

One of the most important personages who inhabited Sabbath Day Point in early times was Captain Sam Patchin An anecdote related of him in Mr S R Stoddard's excellent descriptive guide book of *Lake George*, and verified as thoroughly as may be by ourselves, can be told no better than in Mr. Stoddard's own language (p 106 *et seq*) —

"Vicar's Island is just north of the Harbor Islands Here on its northern

---

[1] Although it is generally believed that this event gave the Point its name, there is really little ground for the belief, as the point is mentioned by that name in Rogers's *Journal* June 28th, 1758, the preceding season

border an affecting incident transpired once, of which Captain Sam Patchin, who lived at Sabbath Day Point at the time, was the hero   One winter's day he conceived the idea of sailing his grist to Bolton mill on the ice   So, piling the bags of grain into the old cutter, with a pitchfork held firmly in his hands for a rudder, he hoisted sail and sped away before a strong north wind

" The ice was ' glare' and the cutter sailed well, remarkably well , but there was not so much certainty about the satisfactory behavior of the steering apparatus   The old man, it is said, was given to spiritual things occasionally, and had, on this occasion, evidently hoisted in rather too much rye in the liquid form to conduce to the safe transportation of that in the bags   The craft insisted on heading directly for the island, and could not be diverted from its course — it was of the kind called 'jumper' — a mettlesome old jumper at that, and the captain had a great deal of confidence in its ability to do whatever it undertook   So he decided to jump the island — he tried it , it was not, strictly speaking, a success   The cutter reached the shore and hesitated — a part of it   Sam was anxious to get along, and continued on , then *he* got discouraged, and paused — in a snow-drift

" Captain Sam was *always* dignified, and on this occasion it is said his manner of resting on that snow-drift was remarkably impressive   Even the snow felt moved, and the island itself was touched   He felt persuaded that he had made a mistake in leaving his cutter, and attempting the underground route for Bolton, so he came out and set his radiant face homeward—not a Sam of joy or a Sam of thanksgiving exactly, but a Sam abounding in such language as would set a mule-driver up in business, or even do credit to the boss canvasser of any circus traveling "

The present owner of the house which the hero of the above narration kept is now, and for years past has been, Samuel Westurn

There is a tradition, supported by more or less equivocal evidence of the nature of records, to the effect that one Samuel Adams lived here as early as 1765   The most authentic evidence is the undeniable fact that, in 1767, a patent of five hundred acres called the Sabbath Day Point Patent, was granted to Samuel Adams   It is said that the road from Bolton to Sabbath Day Point was built by him, in consideration of which he received the patent of five hundred acres of land

Among other patents granted was the Ellice Patent granted to James Caldwell, Robert McClelland and Robert Cochrane   Its date was probably but little later than the one to Adams   It included an extensive tract lying north, west, and south of the site of Hague village, and extended into Essex county   Another parcel, comprising the site of Hague village and about one and a half miles south thereof, eight hundred and fifty acres, was granted to James Caldwell and entitled the J Caldwell or Law's Patent   The George Trimble Patent included one thousand four hundred and forty acres in the northern part of the town and projected a little into Essex county   36

A patent was granted also to George Robinson and others, seven hundred and fifty acres, and to Thomas Ford and others, two hundred and seven and one-half acres, comprising the strip along the valley of the south branch of Beaver Creek The Hague tract was the most extensive piece, including more than six thousand two hundred and forty-five acres of the western part of the territory forming the town

The town records of Hague up to 1822 have unhappily been lost, and the writer must therefore content himself with a list of officers elected in that year, and a survey of the history of the community from that time to the present. The officers elected in the spring of 1822 were as follows . —

Supervisor, William Cook , town clerk, Thomas Gaige, assessors, Elijah Bailey, jr , Archibald McMurphy, Noah Woodard, constable and collector, Calvin Barnard , overseers of the poor, Amisa Burt, John Holman , commissioners of highways, Nathan Taylor, Titus French, Isaac Balcom , poundmaster, Nathan Taylor , school commissioners, Nathan Taylor, Nathaniel Garfield, jr , Leonard Holman , inspectors of schools, William Cook, Joseph Glazier, Thomas Gaige The following officers were chosen by the uplifted hand Overseers of highways 1, John Patchin , 2, John Holman , 3, Dillon Stevens , 4, Isaac Balcom , 5, Seth Johnson , 6, William Woodard , 7, William R Cleaveland , 8, Phineas W Reed , 9, Uriah Balcom , 10, Nathan Taylor ; 11, Noah Woodard , 12, Ira Griggs , 13, James Olna

- These names undoubtedly represent the best families extending throughout the township at the date of the election. Many of them had lived here since the opening of the century, and many others lived here almost until the breaking out of the Civil War There has been, indeed, but little change, either of growth or decline, in the population or business interests since 1820 or 1830. In 1835 there was at Hague village one grist-mill, one saw-mill, one store, one tavern and six or eight dwellings In 1860 there was probably as much business here as there ever has been Rufus Rising, sr , then owned a grist-mill up Quaker Brook, about eighty rods west of the store now owned by L Burgess , H H Harris ran the mill for Mr Rising Just above it was a saw-mill run by Charles F Bevins, and above that, another, run by Newton Wilcox The grist-mill and upper saw-mill are now gone, the latter going down in 1862, and the former being torn down about four years ago by Lyman Bruce. The other saw-mill was rebuilt about 1870, and is now owned by Edwin C Rand and Oliver Yaw [1]

Although the population of the entire town of Hague did not reach the sum of seven hundred at the breaking out of the Rebellion, she furnished one

---

1 The town of Hague is more rich in history than her neighbor Bolton, and less rich than her northern friend Ty In addition to the "feats of broil and battle" performed at Sabbath Day Point in colonial days, may be related the burning of the steamer *John Jay* off Friends' Point, just north of Hague village, on July 29th, 1856 The captain at the time of the fire was J Gale, and the pilot, Captain E S Harris Six lives were lost

hundred and six volunteers, and but one man was drafted   The town records do not contain any account of the public action taken, but the people must have been nearly unanimous in order to furnish so proud a contingent   The men enlisted chiefly in the 118th Regiment, the 5th N Y Cavalry, and the 23d Independent Battery

In 1860 the lumber business was " booming,' no fewer than 10,000 logs being floated on the lake to " Ty," and there sawn   Among the residents of Hague most largely interested were Samuel Ackerman and Stephen Hoyt Nearly all the farmers were engaged during the winter in chopping logs   Such unremitting industry, while it added to the wealth of the laborers then, could not fail in speedily clearing the surface of the country of all the valuable timber   In the last few years scarcely any lumbering has been done, excepting the cutting and hauling of poplar to Ticonderoga and Mechanicsville, for the pulp-mills

There has probably been no potash made here since 1820, though as late as 1860 the remains of an old ashery could be seen in the south part of the town, about three miles from Hague village   There has never been any tannery in town that pretended to the dignity of the name

There was a Union church here in 1860, which had probably been erected about 1835, or soon after   In 1860 the pastor was a Wesleyan clergyman named Leard   The building remained the only church in the village until 1879, when a division took place, and the Wesleyan Methodists erected a separate building   The pastor of the new church is the Rev John Quay   The old church is without a pastor, the last one being a Free Will Baptist, named Lister

The earliest record found of a post-office at Hague is in 1855, when Alvah Bevins was postmaster   In the following year John B Jenkins was appointed. Henry H Harrison succeeded him in 1858   In 1860 the office had been discontinued, but within a few months was re-established with Lewis Burgess in almost supreme control   At that time forty per cent of the stipend allowed to the office went to the mail carrier and the residue to the postmaster

In order to accommodate the people of the town by affording the mail carrier reward enough to induce his bringing the mail twice a week instead of once, Mr Burgess yielded to him the sixty per cent which was the postmaster's due, and worked for nothing himself   He has been postmaster ever since his first appointment   He has run a store in connection with the office since 1865, when he bought out the business of Henry Newton   About ten years before Lewis Burgess began to sell goods, Henry Newton purchased the stock and good-will of Alvah Bevins, who had kept a store here for years   Calvin Barnard was Bevins's predecessor, and one of the first store keepers (if not the first) in town

There is but one regular hotel in town besides the one kept by Samuel

Westurn, at Sabbath Day Point, namely, the Phoenix Hotel, under the management of Mr Gilligan   The site has been covered by a hotel for many years, and, indeed, it is said that some sort of inn has stood there ever since Hague has had a local habitation and a name   Nathaniel Garfield kept an inn there in the thirties, and probably earlier   He built a more pretentious tavern about 1840, and remained there for years, acquiring in the mean time an enviable reputation as "mine host"   In a magazine article published in 1853, T Addison Richards spoke of him in the following language.   "Three miles onward [from Sabbath Day Point] we make the little village of Hague, if village it can be styled   The visitor will remember the locality as Garfield's — one of the oldest and most esteemed summer camps   Judge Garfield would seem to have an intimate acquaintance with every deer on the hill-side, and with every trout in the waters, so habitually are these gentry found at his luxurious table   An excellent landing facilitates the approach to Garfield's, and the steamboat touches daily up and down"   His son, Hiland Garfield, was associated with him during the latter part of his reign   In the spring of 1861 they sold out to William A G Arthur   While he was the owner, in 1863, it was destroyed by fire   William Miller then secured title to the property and at once erected the present house   He kept the house for a time, and then leased it to various persons, notably Edwin Norton and Alonzo Russell   He died in October, 1873   The hotel was then in the hands of Joel W Rising, now proprietor of Rising's Hotel at Chestertown, who remained until 1883   Mrs Marilla Miller, widow of the deceased proprietor of former days, and present owner of the house, then leased it to Alvah E Grimes   The new landlord remained about eighteen months and then left, and Mr Gilligan, in the fall of 1884, took an assignment of the lease, and now conducts the business   He has had considerable hotel experience at Fort Ticonderoga, and knows how to keep, what in fact he does keep, an excellent hotel.   The rooms are neatly furnished and ventilated, and the table cannot be surpassed   The house has a capacity for fifty guests

In the past few years other boarding-houses have been opened for summer guests, and are making Hague a well known and much liked resort   Just north of the Phoenix Hotel a few rods is the Hillside House, having a capacity for thirty-five guests, and owned and supervised by John McClanathan   Farther north still is the Trout House, kept by C. H Wheeler, and providing for twenty-five   Next is the Island Harbor House, which will accommodate twenty-five guests   The proprietor is A. C Clifton

Below is printed the names of the supervisors from Hague, as far as they could be obtained from the records   1813–16, William Cook, 1817–19, Thomas Gaige, 1820–24, William Cook; 1825, Nathaniel Garfield, 1826, Thomas Gaige, 1827, Stephen Pratt, 1828, Warner Cook, 1829, Stephen Pratt, 1830, Nathaniel Garfield; 1 831–1833, William Cook, 1834, 35, Calvin Barnard, 1836, Nathaniel Garfield, 1837–39, William Cook, 1840, '41, Alvah

Bevins, 1842–44, William Ward, 1845, Luma Wing, 1846, Thomas C Brown, 1847, John J Patten, 1848, Alonzo Morris, 1849, Martin Ward, 1850, Alonzo Morris, 1851, John McClanathan, 1852, '53, Alvah Bevins, 1854, Josiah C House, 1855, Ephraim Ward, 1856, '57, Samuel Westurn, 1858, Curtis Allen, 1859–61, H H Harrison, 1862, Lewis Burgess, 1863, W A G Arthur, 1864, H H Harrison, 1865, William M. Marshall, 1866, Lewis Burgess, 1867, John McClanathan, jr, 1868, C F Bevins, 1869, John Mc-Clanathan, jr, 1870–72, H H Harrison, 1873, John McClanathan; 1874, W P Gannon, 1875, John McClanathan, 1876, Lewis Burgess, 1877, '78, John McClanathan, 1879, James A Balcom, 1880, '81, John McClanathan, 1882–84, James A Balcom, 1885, Rufus Rising

At an annual town meeting held on the 7th of April, 1885, at Phoenix Hotel, the following were elected officers for the ensuing year —

Supervisor, Rufus Rising, town clerk, William M Marshall,[1] justice of the peace, Rufus Rising; justice of the peace to fill a contingent vacancy, A C Clifton, assessor, E T Ackerman, commissioner of highways, William Baldwin, constable and collector, Nathan E Yaw, constables, Nathan E. Yaw, William Sexton, Wilson Ward, Eugene Doolittle, James Leach, game constable, William H Garfield, inspectors of election, H G Phillips, Joseph Leavitt, Albert C Clifton (appointed), sealer of weights and measures, William C Evins, commissioners of excise, Nathan Holman, —— ——, Hollis Spaulding, overseer of the poor, Silas B Ackman

Population since 1850 has been as follows 1850, 717, 1855, 615, 1860, 708, 1865, 685, 1870, 637, 1875, 678, 1880, 807.

CHAPTER XXXII

HISTORY OF THE TOWN OF CALDWELL

THIS township was organized March 2d, 1810, and was composed of parts of Queensbury, Bolton and Thurman It was named from General James Caldwell, an Albany merchant, who, in 1787, became the patentee of 1,595 acres of land in this region, in four parcels, by grants dated September 18th–29th of that year The southern extremity of Lake George pushes nearly into the center of the town from the northeast corner Caldwell is bounded on the north by Bolton, on the east by Lake George and Queensbury, on the south by Queensbury, and on the west by Luzerne and Warrensburgh The Schroon River barely touches the northwest corner on its way to

---

[1] To whom we are grateful for valuable assistance

the Hudson   From the lake westward the surface rises abruptly, rendering the central portion of the town broken and hilly, the elevation culminating in the steep and sightly Prospect Hill, which rises about two thousand feet above tide.   South of it a low valley is spread southwest through Caldwell and Luzerne to the valley of the Hudson, near the mouth of the Sacandaga River, and is undoubtedly a continuation of the valley which forms the basin of Lake George   The soil among the elevations in the center is a sandy loam, and in the lowlands a dark, rich mixture of clay and sand with loam   Settlement had commenced here years before the War of the Revolution, but in common with the other pre-Revolutionary communities of Northern New York, it was totally exterminated during that fierce struggle between powers and principalities   Soon after the close of the war, however, the fertility of some portions of the territory, and the natural beauty of the whole, attracted immigration, and settlements were recommenced   General James Caldwell, from whom the town was named, the father of William Caldwell, who is well remembered by the settled residents of the town, used to pass a considerable portion of his time in the village of Caldwell [1]   He built the stone structure now used as the post-office, and for a number of years used it as his office   He lived near the site of the Mansion House, which he built   His will was made in 1841, and he died a few years later   He owned nearly all the ground now covered by the village of Caldwell, and the title to the greater part still resides in his heirs   A small portion only has been sold   Among the early settlers was Daniel Shaw, who located about a mile and a half north of Lake George, on the place now owned by Henry H Haden on the Bolton road   After his death one son, Nathaniel, lived on the farm for years   Another son was David Shaw   His lineal descendants are now all dead   Jehoicham Staats, another pioneer, lived at the beginning of this century on the place now called the Price Manor, two miles north of Lake George on the lake road   His grandson, John J Staats, is one of the present highway commissioners of the town   A son of Jehoicham, named Boynton Staats, practices law in Albany   Eli Pettis, who came here as early as 1800, lived where the Crosby House now is   Two of his great-grandchildren are now living in the town   About the year 1810 a man named Carter lived near the village of Caldwell in the house at present occupied by Fred B Hubbell   None of his descendants lives here now   Samuel Pike dwelt in a house on the site of Daniel Ferguson's new residence   He was a mason and helped build a number of the oldest houses in Caldwell, among them being the old " stone store "   His many children are all dead   Miles Beach was an early cabinet-maker here, and had a shop where Mr Gleason now keeps a meat-market in the village of Caldwell   His children, too, are all gone   John Beebe was one of the first lawyers in the town, and lived in the house now

---

[1] This village is by many called Lake George, and that is the name of the post-office, but we have preferred to abide by the old name in the text

occupied by the county clerk, David V Brown   He was supervisor from 1823 to 1829 or '30 inclusive   He left three children   Joseph Whitley, another lawyer, went from here in early times to Black Brook, Clinton county, where he remained until his death   Daniel Nichols was about the first blacksmith   He moved into the western part of the State a long time ago   One of the most prominent men in this whole vicinity was Thomas Archibald, uncle to S R Archibald, who now resides at Caldwell   He held the office of county clerk for forty-two years, longer than any other person in the State has held that position   He died in Warrensburgh without a family   Samuel Payne came from Albany, where he had been proprietor of the Northern Hotel, and built and ran the Lake House at the head of Lake George   A small part of this old tavern was standing in 1810, and courts held sessions there before the erection of the court-house. Luther Stebbins, farmer and carpenter, immigrated to the town before 1825, and located about two miles north of Caldwell village   Hon William Hay was a very prominent lawyer here before 1820   Nathan Brown lived about a mile south of the village   A son, Alphonso Brown, now resides at Caldwell   Early physicians were Drs Tubbs, Bugbee, Hicks and Cromwell   S R Archibald, of Caldwell village, to whom we are indebted for a considerable of the foregoing information, was born in Salem, Washington county, N Y, in March, 1819   Upon the death of his mother, in 1821, he was taken to an uncle, James Archibald, who lived in Bolton and afterwards in the northern part of Caldwell on the Schroon River   The infant Archibald was next placed in the care of Asa Wilson, who lived three miles north of the village of Caldwell on the farm now occupied by Sylvanus Taylor   In 1823 he was brought to the village of Caldwell, his uncle, Thomas Archibald, being then county clerk, and was adopted by Hiram Hawley, a shoemaker   Hawley was probably the first shoemaker in the place   Mr Archibald remained with his guardian until he attained his majority, and then, having learned the shoemaking trade, he entered into business for himself   In 1841 he purchased the property which forms the site of his present home   The lot was then covered with several old buildings, among them a dilapidated old tannery which David Alden had built in the beginning of the century and run for years [1]   Mr Archibald rebuilt this tannery (in 1842 and again in 1852), and conducted it until 1864, when he tore it down   He is now, and for thirty-four consecutive years has been, a justice of the peace   Among the other early settlers in the town were Benoni Burtch, —— Tierce, Andrew Edmonds, Reed Wilbur, Obadiah Hunt, Thaddeus Bradley, Elias Prosser, Nathan Burdick, George Van Deusen, —— Butler and Christopher Potter   General Caldwell erected the first iron and the first grist-mill

The first town meeting was held on Tuesday, April 3d, 1810, and the records are introduced in the following language —

---

[1] Alden died about 1826   No descendants left   He was supervisor for nine years succeeding 1814.

"Agreeable to a law that was passed by the Legislature of the State of New York, for the purpose of establishing a new town in the County of Washington, known by the name of Caldwell, the inhabitants of the town of Caldwell met on Tuesday, the third day of April for the purpose of holding their first annual town meeting at the house of Samuel Allen, when the following persons were chosen for office ' James Archibald was elected supervisor, John B Prosser, clerk, assessors, Daniel Nichols, Jesse Bishop and William Peffers, commissioners of highways, Pardon Crandall, Asa Wilson, Michael Harris; overseers of the poor, Halsey Rogers, John Simpson; constable and collector, Pardon Crandall, constable, Joseph Gibbs, poundkeepers, Daniel Shaw and Nathaniel Smith. Two weeks later a special meeting was held at the house of Samuel Allen, and the following persons were chosen overseers of highways for the eight districts then in the town —Samuel Cole, Michael Harris, John Simpson, Gilbert Worden, Pardon Crandall, Ezra Fuller, Nathan Crandall, Aaron Gates The early records are full of measures adopted by the board of supervisors and voted upon by the citizens relative to the laying out and opening of new roads, e g, in 1817 a new road was constructed from the foot of the hill south of Fort William Henry to the State road Other curious and interesting facts are hidden in the thumb-worn and dust covered volumes in the county clerk's office In 1818 a bounty of twenty-five cents was offered for every crow killed in the county In 1819 the town was divided into three school districts, and district No 1, according to a report of the commissioners, had had six months and six days of school, the sum of $16 90 school money was received, and there was an attendance of fifty-three children The entire school fund was $163 03 In 1820 a penalty of $1 00 was laid for every hog found on the common without a yoke In 1821 the town was divided into four school districts, and had a school fund of $165 05 With the exception of one or two short roads, all the roads were laid out between 1825 and 1850.

By virtue of its situation at the head of Lake George, the village of Caldwell was formerly the emporium of the county, and indeed of the whole Lake George region There was a large lumber business done The water power in the vicinity was not considerable and consequently the manufacture of lumber was not so great as the shipment of logs to Ticonderoga A few "thunder shower" mills, as Mr Archibald calls them, were in the town The inhabitants, he further states, lived largely " on fish and strangers," the locality being even in these early days, a favorite summer resort. Old men tell now about catching a barrel of trout in a single day The business importance of the place, however, was practically destroyed by the construction of the Glens Falls Feeder, which was surveyed in about 1823, dug through in 1824, and enlarged and completed between 1828 and 1832, at which latter date it was made navigable for canal boats and became a thoroughfare of inland commerce The lumber which had been shipped down the lake was thereafter drawn in

GEORGE BROWN.

wagons to Fort Edward and Glens Falls   These villages thus grew as Caldwell declined, and were fed by the nourishment that had formerly sustained the
importance of the latter

Owing to the destruction of the town records by fire we are unable to give
the first officers of the town, other than the supervisor, who was James Archibald, it is probable that he held the office until 1813   Since that date the
supervisors have been as follows   Halsey Rogers, 1813, David Alden, 1814
to 1822 inclusive, John Beebe, 1823 to 1830 inclusive, Thomas Archibald,
1831 to 1836 inclusive, John F Sherrill, 1837 to 1843 inclusive, Seth C
Baldwin, 1844, Perry G Hammond, 1845, (from 1845 to 1860 we have been
unable to obtain the town records,) W W Hicks, 1860–61, F B Hubbell,
1862 to 1864 inclusive, W H Moshier, 1865–66, Fred B Hubbell, 1867 to
1869 inclusive, Hiram Wood, 1870 to 1872 inclusive, E S Harris, 1873, F
B Hubbell, 1874 to 1876 inclusive, Jerome N Hubbell, 1877–78, Elias S
Harris, 1879, Leander Harris, 1880–81, George W Bates, 1882–83, Elmer
J West, 1884

The present officers of the town are as follows — Supervisor, Elmer J
West, town clerk, James H Carpenter, assessors, Dwight Russell, Edwin
White, O F Nichols, justices of the peace, Charles E Hawley, John Van
Dusen, James T Crandall, Samuel R Archibald, collector, Edward D Smith;
constables, Ebenezer Wilde, George Stanton, C J Bates, K Burlingame, Jesse
M Sexton, game constable, C J Bates, overseers of poor, Ebenezer Wilde,
Hiram Vowers, auditors, Alonzo Brown, C E Weatherhead, R D Gleason;
inspectors of election, C S Wood, F H Worden, C M Smith, excise commis-
sioners, John Caldwell, Dennis Lyons, Sidney Nichols

Caldwell was a valuable and willing contributor to the cause of the Union
during the Rebellion   The number of men furnished to the army between
June 1st, 1861, and the president's call for 600,000 was twenty-three, number
under the call for 600,000 was twenty-four, making a total of forty-seven   S
R Archibald, of the village of Caldwell, is authority for the statement that the
town furnished forty-seven volunteers   He remembers well the drilling and
discipline to which they were subjected in the streets of his village during the
dark days of the war

But the place had, years before, been the theatre of bloody events, human
blood had flowed in rivulets, and men had gone to their shallow graves like
beds   Near the site of Caldwell, Colonel Ephraim Williams, the founder of
Williams College, had fallen while defending the frontiers of his native State,
and General Johnson and Baron Dieskau crossed swords "which smoked with
bloody execution"   The battle of Bloody Pond was fought on September 8th,
1755, and immediately afterward Johnson built Fort William Henry   Fort
George was built four years later by General Amherst   The former fort is
covered by the hotel which bears its name, and the latter is a heap of moulder-
ing and scarcely distinguishable ruins

MUNICIPAL HISTORY

The condition of the town of Caldwell at this time may be inferred to some extent from the reminiscences of George Brown, proprietor of the Central Hotel He was born in the town of Queensbury, September 3d, 1815, and remembers distinctly the Lake George region as far back as 1830 The village of Caldwell was then as now the county seat An old tavern where the Central Hotel now stands was kept by Lyman Jenks, and another on the site of the Carpenter House was kept by a Mr Russell, and known as the Caldwell House The Lake House, then about half its present size, was kept by John F Sherrill There were two stores in the village then, the store which Halsey Rogers built in 1819, was kept by Charles Robarts He had succeeded Halsey Rogers about 1828 The other store stood on the site of Zebee's drug store, and was in the hands of Hiram Wood Charles Robarts also ran a saw-mill on the first stream north of the village, and a grist-mill was kept running near it Pelatiah Richards owned a distillery several miles northwest of the settlement, near Warrensburgh The district school stood on the site of the present building, and a church edifice, probably Union, used now as a residence by Jesse Saxton, attested then the religious energies of its builder, William Caldwell On the site of Fort George stood 'Nathan Brown's lime kiln That potash was made in greater or less quantities is probable, but is not remembered by those now remaining to tell about it Sugar-making was carried on in a general way The principal business, however, was, as has been stated, lumbering The land had not been extensively cleared and was teeming with most valuable timber The only road of much importance was the old State road from Albany to Montreal, occupying the same bed now filled by the plank road The head of Lake George was then a great fishing tract Many suckers would run up the books every spring, and the place seemed to have a greater local celebrity, and less fame abroad, than it has to-day There was one boat running on the lake, viz a steamboat called *The Mountaineer*, commanded by Captain Laribee, and built about 1824,[1] and run until 1836 It was the second boat on the lake, the first being the *James Caldwell*, commanded by Captain Winans It was built sometime between 1816 and 1820, and was disabled by lightning and afterwards entirely destroyed by fire before she had long plied the waters of Lake George In 1838 the *William Caldwell* was put on the lake and ran until 1850 In that year the *John Jay*, commanded by Captain J Gale, superseded her and ran until 1856, when she took fire in her engine room off Friends' Point, and in an effort to reach shore, struck a rock on Waltonian Isle, and sunk Six lives were lost The *Minnehaha* was built at the northern end of the lake in 1857 and ran for twenty years The *Horicon* displaced her in 1877 There are now running, besides the *Hor-*

---

[1] The matter concerning early boats is taken from S R STODDARD'S *Lake George*

Eugene L. Seelye.

icon, the *Ticonderoga*, the *Ganouskie*, and *Lillie M Price* The principal smaller steamers are the *River Queen*, the *Julia*, the *Ed D Lewis*, and the *Meteor*

Postmasters — The first postmaster at Caldwell of which there is any recollection was William Williams, who remained in office until after 1825 He was succeeded, probably, by Charles Robarts, who held the appointment until about 1840, when Hiram Wood came in Wood did not go out until about 1861, when S R. Archibald succeeded him The present postmaster, E S Harris, followed Archibald in 1875 The post-office is Lake George

Present Business — The Central Hotel is kept by George Brown, formerly proprietor of the Half-way House at French Mountain He has been proprietor of the Central Hotel since February, 1884 Before that his son, Clark J Brown, conducted the business four years His elder son, Benjamin O Brown, built the hotel in the winter of 1875–76 and kept it until succeeded by Clark J Brown It will accommodate one hundred guests, and is open the year round

The Carpenter Hotel has just been leased by Messrs Hamilton & Craig, who are successors to Sullivan & Madden Next before them J H Carpenter ran the house for twelve years It will now, after having been twice enlarged, accommodate one hundred guests

The Lake House, just north of the Central House, on the opposite side of the street, is built on the oldest hotel site at the lake It is three hundred feet long The Harris House, south of it, belongs to the same proprietor, who makes use of it only during the busy season F G Tucker is the proprietor.

The Fort William Henry Hotel was rebuilt from an older hotel, in 1868, by T Roessle & Son, who are also proprietors of the Arlington, at Washington It is from four to six stories in height, and fronts three hundred and thirty-four feet on the lake It covers the site of the old Fort William Henry, hence its name

The Prospect Mountain House is built at an elevation of nearly 1,800 feet above the lake. The Mount Ferguson House is on a point which though really lower than the main mountain, appears from Caldwell to be higher W J Ferguson, proprietor Fort George Hotel was completed and ready for occupation in 1874 It is on the east side of the lake, near the head, and has a capacity for nearly three hundred guests E L Seelye is proprietor

Crosbyside, formerly known as the United States Hotel, is across the lake from Caldwell It will accommodate about two hundred guests Proprietor, F G Crosby The Carpenter and the Central Hotels are the only ones which are kept open winters as well as summers

To S R Stoddard's little hand-book entitled *Lake George* we are indebted for much of the information concerning the hotels above mentioned, and we cannot do better than quote a few words from the same interesting chapter concerning the Indian emcampment —

"'A remnant of the once mighty race of Mohicans still lingers,' they are given to lingering, they prefer it to anything else, their wigwams are found in the borders of the forest, just west of the entrance to the Fort William Henry grounds Six or seven families in all, from the home of the St Francis Indians, in Lower Canada, coming in the spring and usually returning with the frosts, descendants of the Abenakis — ' *O-ben-ah-keh* — they will tell you, and pure blood at that "

Mercantile.— Dennis Lyon, successor to Charles E Hawley, keeps a grocery store in Caldwell E A & C J West have been running a general store since 1883 They were preceded by Coolidge & Lee, and they by Sylvester Lewis, who started the business Dr William R Adamson has kept a drug store on Main street for about six years A Wurtenberg has for the last ten years opened regularly every season a dry goods store in the village He occupies the old stone store Julius Tripp, in the fall of 1884, succeeded Adolphus Brown in the hardware business George Smith has had a grocery store at the upper end of the village since the fall of 1884

John R Potter and S R Archibald are the shoemakers of the locality.

Physicians — Dr William R Adamson was graduated from the Bellevue Medical College in 1873, and came to Caldwell in 1875 Dr F H Stevens was graduated from the Medical College at Castleton, Vt (now the Burlington Medical College), in 1849 He practiced first with his preceptor at Crown Point Came to Caldwell in December, 1884

Churches — The oldest church in Caldwell is the Presbyterian, which had a predominating influence in the ecclesiastical councils of the old Union Church before mentioned The present structure was built in 1855, and took the place of the old one The pastor at that time was the Rev Eldad Goodman, successor to Rev Eastman He was followed in 1858 by Rev S Huntington, who remained until 1861, and was replaced by the Rev Eldad Goodman In 1870 Rev James Lamb was called and remained until 1884 Then Rev S. Huntington came in until 1878 In that year the present pastor, Rev Robert Barbour, accepted his call The church was organized in 1830. The records the first year or two were signed by Amos Savage In 1848 the church dissolved, and in 1851 reorganized The present officers are: Elders, F G. Crosby, G W Tubbs, G. W Smith, deacon, Edwin White, trustees, A S. Harris, M N Nichols, G W Tubbs The present membership is forty-one The pastor acts also as Sunday-school superintendent

St James Parish (Episcopal) was organized in 1855, and a frame church edifice at once erected. The clerk at the first meeting was Austin W Holden. The first wardens were James Cromwell, M D, and William H Smith, the first vestrymen, John N Robinson, Horace Welch, Samuel R Archibald, John J Harris, Hiram Wood, Henry M Norman, F G Tucker, and William Vaughn. The first rector was the Rev Robert Locke His successors have been consecutively, Revs Robert F Crary, John F Potter, James A Upjohn, and the present rector, Rev Charles H Lancaster, who commenced his labors here in March, 1874 In May, 1866, the first frame church was blown down by a mighty wind and the present edifice immediately begun on the same site In 1879 the rectory was built at a total cost of $3,183 45, by Thomas Fuller, the original designer of the State capitol at Albany, and now chief architect of the Dominion of Canada The present value of the church and lot is $10,000, and of the rectory and lot, $5,000 There are ninety-one communicants in the parish, and the Sunday-school, with the rector as superintendent, has forty-eight pupils and six teachers The present officers are Rector, Rev Charles H Lancaster, wardens, H H Hayden, and George H Cramer, vestrymen, S R Archibald, F G Tucker, Le Grand C Cramer, Walter J Price, James Crandall, Kleber Burlingame, Galloway C Morris, and Charles M Schiefflin Samuel R Archibald has been clerk of the vestry since 1869

In 1884 a Methodist Church was organized, and a chapel erected in 1885 The Rev. Webster Ingersoll supplied the pulpit for several months The Rev Mr Potter was the first pastor Membership thirty E J West is the Sunday-school superintendent

Water-Works — The first water-works were built in Caldwell in 1879, but proved inadequate and were abandoned In 1883 new works were built by a stock company on Prospect Mountain, which afford an abundant supply of water for fire and domestic purposes

Hill View Post-office — This post-office was established in 1877, four miles north of Caldwell. E L Patrick, M D, has been the postmaster from the beginning

---

CHAPTER XXXIII

HISTORY OF THE TOWN OF WARRENSBURGH

THE town of Warrensburgh lies upon the east bank of the Hudson River, and is formed of a long strip of territory extending north and south It is bounded on the north by Chester, on the east by Caldwell and Bolton, on the south by Luzerne, and on the west, upon the other side of the Hudson, by Thurman, Stony Creek, and a small part of Saratoga county The Schroon River, which forms the northeast boundary of the township, flows southerly for some distance and then turning abruptly from a southerly to a westerly course, divides the town into two nearly equal parts, and flows into the Hudson, the Hudson itself, and the numerous small tributary streams which feed these rivers, constitute the principal drainage   Along the Hudson and Schroon Rivers the soil is alluvial and sandy, elsewhere it is stony and difficult to cultivate, excepting in small strips consisting of a light loam

The peninsular portion is a rolling plateau varying in altitude from six hundred to one thousand feet above the river   The southwestern part is occupied by an immense mountain mass, containing several peaks which rise to an elevation of from two thousand four hundred to three thousand feet above tide. It has been estimated that nearly two-thirds of the land is arable

Warrensburgh was formed from the old town of Thurman, on the 12th day of February, 1813   The territory which it comprises had been partly reclaimed from a savage state for many years, though even in 1813 it might be called a sparsely peopled tract   Indeed, as late as 1836, Gorden's *Gazetteer* describes the town as being mountainous and wild, covered with woods and abounding with iron ore [1]

The earliest settler in the town was William Bond, who moved in 1786 on to a tract of land situated about two miles southwest from the site of the village of Warrensburgh   Bond's Pond was named from him   He had passed away before the present town was formed, of course, and the records have no mention of his name   From an article in the *Warrensburgh News*, under date of January 15th, 1885, corroborated by living witnesses whose memories reach back nearly to the beginning of the present century, and who are conversant with the traditions of early days, we are able to give a tolerably good account of the early settlers of this interesting region   The immigration of William Bond was quickly followed by the coming of other pioneers who forsook, oftentimes, the more plodding and less laborious life of New England, for the rough and even perilous struggle for existence in this unpeopled wilderness   In 1787 Joseph Hatch moved on to what is known as the Duncan McDonald farm, now owned by Stephen Griffin, 2d   In the same year Joseph Hutchinson, and Gideon and Stokes Potter came here   Josiah Woodward moved here also in 1787 from Connecticut, and like the others, brought his family with him   They were the seventh family that settled in the section of the country north of the head of Lake George   He lived on the same ground now covered by the new house of John L Russell   Judge Joseph Woodward, still living, is his grandson, and the son of Isaac Woodward, who was fourteen years of age when he came here with his father in 1787   Aaron Varnum came here in 1788   In 1789 James Pitts built a tavern on the site of the Warren House, and in the same year Timothy Stow moved on to the farm now owned by Samuel Judd   Pelatiah Richards came in 1802   He was born on the 19th day of February, 1786, and was a prominent merchant in the village of Warrensburgh for many years   He was town clerk in 1825, and supervisor from Warrensburgh in 1830, and again in 1838   He died February 11th, 1870

---

[1] No iron has ever been worked in the town

In 1804 James Warren came to Warrensburgh   He was for years proprietor of the tavern kept by John Heffron, and also kept store for a number of
years in the building now used for the same purpose by James Herrick   He
built and conducted quite an extensive potash factory or "ashery" on the
north side of the Schroon River about where Mrs James Fuller now lives   It
was customary in those early days to hold the annual elections at different
points in the town for three consecutive days, it being practically impossible
to establish any central point which would enable all the voting population of
the town to cast their vote and return home on the same day   In 1811 James
Warren, while returning from an election held on the farm now owned by
Nathaniel Griffing, of Thurman, was drowned by the upsetting of a skiff in the
West River   Nelson Warren, then a boy ten years of age, was with his father
at the time, and it is said that the excessive fright caused his hair to turn
white   Two years after this fatality Warrensburgh was organized, and named
after this prominent man   After his decease his personal representatives carried on all the branches of his business for several years

Soon after James Warren arrived here in 1804, Kitchel Bishop settled on
the ground now covered by the dwelling-house of Dr E B Howard   He
was a farmer and owned all the land at present owned by Mrs Minerva King
Judge Bishop represented the county thirteen years in the Legislature   About
the year 1810 or 1812 he established a small tannery, the first in the town

Another early settler of prominence was Dr McLaren, who must have
come here before 1790   He lived and practiced medicine on the site of the
present dwelling house of Stephen Griffin, 2d   He married Susan Thurman,
daughter of Richardson Thurman   Richardson Thurman was a nephew of
John Thurman, the original patentee of all this part of the county and the
owner of nearly all of what was known as Hyde Township, including the
greater part of all the territory now covered by the towns of Chester, Warrensburgh and Thurman   Dr McLaren's wife inherited from the Thurman family
a lot of 500 acres, called Lot 22 of Hyde Township, running along the west
side of the Schroon River in the west part of the village of Warrensburgh
Dr McLaren died in the first decade of years in the present century

In the early part of the nineteenth century the population along the rivers
and on the more fertile tracts of lands in the surrounding county began per-
ceptibly to increase   Stephen Griffing, who is still alive and of keen and
accurate memory, gives an excellent picture of the natural and business condition of the community as early as the period between 1800 and 1810 or 1812
He was born in Duchess county on the 6th of June, 1796, and came here in
March, 1800, with his father, Stephen Griffing, sr, who had served in an
official capacity for five years in the Revolutionary War and drew a pension
for his services   When he first came here he settled where his son, Nathaniel
Griffing, now lives, and three miles and a half southwest of the site of the vil-

lage of Warrensburgh He began at once to clear the land and conduct a farm there At that time William Hough, a blacksmith, was living on the Chester road, a mile from Warrensburgh He went away soon after 1820 Myron Beach boarded in the tavern (now the Warren House), and kept a store where James Herrick now does He afterwards went to Lake George, where his death occurred He was a brother of Mrs James Warren (Melinda Warren), and it was not until after Mr Warren's death that he kept the store as his successor He was captain of a company of artillery that took part in the battle of Plattsburg Joseph Harrington, a farmer, lived about a mile south of Warrensburgh The farm was afterwards divided, and his sons, Israel and Warren, now live on the several halves James Lucas occupied a farm about four miles up the Schroon River, near where his son now lives Jonathan Vowers, another farmer, lived near him Nathan Sheerman, farmer and plow-maker, lived about four miles up the Schroon River from Warrensburgh He has no descendants now living in town Abel Matoon ran a farm about a mile north of Sheerman's David Millington, a farmer also, lived on the Hudson River about three miles westerly from the village Duncan McDonald worked a farm near Millington Daniel Geer, a mechanic, lived four miles south of the village. In 1801 Jasper Duell kept a tavern on the site of the Warren House He was predecessor to James Warren In the upper part of the present village (proper) of Warrensburgh there was, in 1800, but one building, an old school-house, which stood near where Judge Joseph Woodward's house now stands Being the only school within a circle of a number of miles, it was well attended There was no church edifice in town As is usual in the early history of all the towns in the State, the first religious meetings were held in the school-house A Methodist Church was organized about here in 1796, and the first pastor was the Rev Henry Ryan The first store kept in town was that conducted by James Warren before mentioned There was no manufacturing done here so early as 1800 The roads through and from Warrensburgh to Lake George, Chester, Bolton and Thurman were then quite traversable

Among other early settlers were William Lee and William Johnson, the latter being the first white person to die in this town

Coming down to a period a few years later, we find it expedient and interesting to write something more concerning the Woodward family

Judge Joseph Woodward was born on September 20th, 1804, in this town, about three miles and a half north of his present residence on premises now owned and occupied by his nephew, William F Woodward Judge Woodward's father and grandfather have been mentioned in preceding pages On the 5th day of March, 1828, Joseph Woodward married Julia, daughter of Lucius Gunn, a clothier, whose works were just east of the present tannery. She died in 1832, and in 1836 Judge Woodward married Charlotte, daughter

R. P. Burhans

of Duncan McDonald On the 24th of September, 1844, the subject of this sketch moved to his present residence Judge Woodward has a keen recollection of Warrensburgh as it was when he was a boy, and has given the writer much valuable and interesting information During the period between 1810 and 1820, lumbering became quite a prominent industry The surface of this town not only, but of the whole county, and the counties to the north and west, was covered with forests of splendid pine, the demand for which gave a great impetus to the hitherto unaroused activities of the region At this time and for years before there were a greater number of saw-mills in town than there are at present, though they were usually old-fashioned and small Every brook large enough to turn a wheel was brought into requisition Before 1810 Albro Tripp had a mill on a small brook north of the village Dudley Farlin came soon after the organization of the town, and built the mills now operated by Emerson & Co He continued proprietor of them until 1834, when he sold out to Nelson Warren The logs were brought to his mills from all the surrounding country — large quantities floated, as now, down the Schroon River Up to nearly 1820 Dr McLaren had a small saw-mill on the north side of the river Pine logs were then worth twenty-five cents, where now they would bring four or five dollars In 1822 Joseph Woodward bought of James L Thurman a saw-mill about four miles north of the village, on a little tributary of the Schroon

The ample water power afforded by the two large rivers and their numerous tributaries occasioned the springing up of a number of mills and factories of various descriptions Dr Harmon Hoffman built and owned a grist-mill on the site now occupied by the Burhans Mills He sold out to Dudley Farlin about 1816, after an explosion of powder had destroyed the store which he kept near the mill A short distance above this mill were the ruins of a former mill which had been abandoned Farlin rebuilt the structure which is still used as a grist-mill by the Burhans brothers These were the only grist-mills in town Potash was made hereabouts quite extensively The ashery of James Warren has already been mentioned Simon Hough ran a small factory north of the village a year or two in the second decade of years

Even as late as 1810 the farms were all small Josiah Woodward's clearing was probably the largest one in this part of the county, and it did not comprise an area of more than forty acres Kitchel Bishop's clearing was nearly as large, and James Warren's was about of equal size with Bishop's

The only tannery built in early days here was the one owned by Kitchel Bishop about 1810 Its only successor is the extensive tannery owned by the firm known as B P Burhans & Son. The schools of this period were a sort of a community school, without much organization The largest one in town stood where the stone store owned by Lemuel Woodward and the estate of A G Woodward now is In 1811–12 Samuel Lake, of Chestertown, taught

37

there Subsequently Samuel Stevens, who afterwards achieved prominence as a lawyer in Albany, taught this school It was a framed building The attendance was usually quite large, numbering often as many as sixty or seventy pupils

Before 1810 the Methodists had erected a small church edifice on the site of their present church, and worshiped there in goodly numbers Besides the Rev Henry Ryan, already mentioned, the Rev Tobias Spicer was well known here, and indeed, throughout the county The Presbyterians had a meeting-house in the present town of Thurman, on the west side of the Hudson River, and a Rev Whipple, from Chester, preached to them Many people from Warrensburgh were prominent members of this church These were the only churches then about here

After further mention of the earlier settlers of Warrensburgh, we will look a little to the organization of the town

One of the most prominent of the men still living, whose memory reaches back nearly seventy years, is Stephen Griffin, 2d [1] He was born on October 18th, 1812, about two miles west of the village of Warrensburgh on the bank of the Hudson River His father was John Griffing His mother's maiden name was Catharine J McEwan John Griffing came to the town in 1798 He ran the farm summers and "lumbered it winters He died in 1827 at the age of forty-seven years Stephen Griffin, 2d, came from the old homestead in October, 1838, and began keeping the hotel in the village now known as the Adirondack House After he had bought this property he married, on a Wednesday of this October, Maria Coman, of Luzurne, and on the following Saturday he and his bride began to keep the Adirondack House Bradford Tubbs had preceded Mr Griffin as proprietor of this tavern The latter continued in possession until 1847, when he leased the property to Lewis Person In 1874 Mr Griffin was elected Assemblyman from this district In 1884 he was appointed by Comptroller Chapin State agent for State lands — a position which he still holds

Among the early settlers whom he remembers are James L Thurman, a well-to-do farmer who lived in the house now occupied by Samuel Judd He came from the town of Thurman (or Athol) He has two sons, Samuel and Charles, and one daughter, Mrs James Woodward, still living in the village of Warrensburgh John McMillen lived on the road which leads along the west bank of the Schroon River, about one and a half miles from the village He moved to Thurman about 1820. He was a farmer A grandson, Wallace McMillen, now resides in North Creek Joseph Norton, like nearly all the others, a farmer, lived north of Spruce Mountain, on the road to Chester While living here, in addition to his farm labors, he kept an inn, but about 1820 he moved over to the south of the mountain and devoted himself exclusively to

---

[1] This name is spelled differently by different members of the family, sometimes *Griffing* and again *Griffin* being deemed preferable

farming   He died in Caldwell   Albro Tripp, casually named hereinbefore, was a farmer, and in what was formerly a part of Warrensburgh, on the Chester road, where the mile strip was taken off and added to Chester , he thereupon became perforce an inhabitant of the last named town   None of his descendants now lives here   He was captain of a company of militia, and went to Plattsburg during the war of 1812, but reached there too late to participate in the famous battle at that place

Samuel Stackhouse, a carpenter and joiner and millwright, lived on the south bank of the Schroon River, on premises now owned by the peg company

The town was not without its coterie of physicians in those days   Dr Harmon Hoffman lived in the village in the house now occupied by John Stone and David Woodward   Although a practicing physician he owned a grist-mill and saw-mill on the premises now occupied by A C Emerson & Co   About 1816 he and Abraham Wing, who afterwards went to Queensbury, built a store near the iron bridge   After a few months it burned and was never rebuilt   Dr Hoffman moved to Saratoga about 1820 and remained there until his death

Dr Thomas Pattison, a sketch of whose life appears in the chapter devoted to the history of past physicians, came to the village of Thurman in 1805 and boarded with the family of Richardson Thurman   He married that gentleman's daughter, Elizabeth, on the 4th day of February, 1810, and removed at once to the farm now occupied by John and James McGann   He practiced medicine here until about 1850 or 1855   He died February 6th, 1867   He has, now living, four sons — Elias, of Hammondsport, Steuben county , Thurman, of Wellsboro, Pa , Augustus, of Williamsport, Pa , and James, of Ballston, N Y , and two daughters, Mrs Sarah Carpenter and Miss C E Pattison, both residing in the village of Warrensburgh

The reader now has some idea of the condition of the country, and the names and the occupations of the residents of the town at the time of its organization in 1813   He is therefore prepared to read with keener interest an account of some of the early town meetings, and of the quaint and self-explanatory resolutions passed thereat

The first town meeting of the town of Warrensburgh was held on the 4th day of April, 1813, at the house of Mrs Melinda Warren [1]   The following persons were elected the first officers of the town   Supervisor, James L Thurman ; town clerk, Myron Beach , assessors, Dr Harmon Hoffman, John McMillen and Joseph Norton , commissioners of highways, Dr Thomas Pattison, Whitman Cole, Albro Tripp, overseers of the poor, Dr Harmon Hoffman and Dr Thomas Pattison , constable and collector, Samuel Stackhouse , fence

[1] It will be remembered that for a number of years after the death of James Warren, his widow, Melinda Warren, and his son Wilson, carried on the business   The house of Mrs Melinda Warren is undoubtedly, therefore, the present Warren House, kept by John Heffron

viewers, Myron Beach and Dr Thomas Pattison, poundmaster, William Hough; pathmasters: District No 1, Myron Beach; No 2, Joseph Harrington; No 3, Silas Mills, No 4, Dr Thomas Pattison, No 5, James L Thurman, No 6, James Lucas, No 7, Sylvester Saturley, No 8, Thomas Newbury (lived near Bolton), No 9, Joseph Smith, No 10, Nathan Sheerman, No 11, Abel Matoon, No 12, David McCansey, No 13, Albro Tripp, No 14, Solomon Thurston, No 15, Nathaniel Norton, No 16, Solomon Munsil, No 17, Duncan McDonald, No 18, David Millington, No 19, Alexander Robertson: No 20, Daniel Geer, No 21, Samuel Bennett, No 22, Shadrach Newton

At this meeting the sum of fifty dollars was voted for the support of the poor, ten dollars was offered as a bounty for each wolf killed within the town limits, and the meeting was adjourned with a resolution that the next annual meeting be held at the same place At the next meeting, 1814, the wolf bounty was increased to fifteen dollars, and a resolution was passed that a fine of five dollars be levied upon every man who should neglect to destroy the Tory weed on his own farm and in the highway opposite his farm Among the new names that appear are Peleg Tripp, Isaac Woodward, James Griffing, Royal P Wheeler, Aaron Priest, Jonathan Vowers, Henry Lewis, and Philip Baker The third annual meeting was also held at Mrs Melinda Warren's, and for the first time the offices of inspectors, and commissioners of schools were created Seventy-five dollars raised for the support of the poor, indicates that the increasing population did not necessarily bring to the town a proportionate increase of wealth. The wolf bounty was voted at ten dollars and a coon bounty of twelve and a half cents offered The sum of ten dollars was voted to purchase a standard of weights and measures, and the town clerk was directed to copy all the resolutions and post them up in conspicuous places In 1816 it was resolved that twenty-five cents be paid for every crow killed in the town, conditioned upon the presentation of the proper "certifficut" from a justice of the peace

In 1817 the sum of $200 was voted for the support of the poor. By this time the care of the poor of the town had become something of a problem, for in addition to the increased sum raised for their support, James Pattison and Lucius Green, overseers of the poor, and Seth C Baldwin were appointed, pursuant to resolution, a committee to procure a "sufficient and proper establishment" for the employment of the paupers of the town Furthermore, a special meeting was held on the 15th of April, 1817, at which the sum of two hundred dollars was raised for the relief of the poor, and the poormasters were authorized to borrow that amount on the credit of the town, and with it to purchase provisions for the poor No action of any importance was recorded after this until the year 1822, when the extremely significant and peculiar resolution was passed that "a fine of ten dollars be inflicted on any ram running at large from the 12th of September until the 20th of November" Another resolution passed in 1825, reads to the effect that "hogs, horses and sheep shant be free commoners" In 1826 a bounty of five dollars was offered for every wild cat killed During all these years we find indications of improvement in all things, roads were in constant process of construction, alteration and repair Bridges were built and rebuilt School-houses were erected, and there was going on a perpetual readjustment of the existing conditions to the changes wrought by growing population and the increasing importance of business activities But the face of the country did not lose its original grim wildness for years During winters the farmers turned their attention to lumbering and the pine forests that mantled the earth were gradually felled and converted into lumber or floated down the river to the lumber market at Glens Falls Wolves, panthers, lynxes and wild cats infested the neighborhood down to a comparatively recent date, for until 1846 bounties were annually offered for the death of one or all of the kinds of beasts named Nevertheless, improvements were continually going on As we have seen, the roads to Chester, Thurman, Caldwell, and Bolton were all here in a rude state at the beginning of the century They were scarcely traversable, however, except by persons on foot or horseback, being full of stumps and insurmountable rocks The road to The Glen was built about the year 1825 A plank road was built from Warrensburgh to Chester in 1850, and one from Warrensburgh to Caldwell in 1849 The leading men in the company which constructed the former of the plank roads were Pelatiah Richards and Joseph Woodward, who, in connection with B P. Burhans and Thomas S Gray, were also chiefly instrumental in the construction of the plank road to Caldwell Both these roads have been since converted into turnpikes

The bridge across the Hudson between the towns of Warrensburgh and Thurman has also something of a history On the 20th of April, 1836, the Legislature appropriated $4,000 for the construction of a bridge at this place, or "between Warrensburgh and Athol" George Pattison and Stephen Griffing, of Warrensburgh, and Richard Cameron, of Athol were appointed commissioners This was the occasion of the building of the old wooden bridge On the 4th of April, 1871, $2,500 was appropriated by the Legislature " for the relief of Warrensburgh and Thurman towards the building of a bridge between the towns near the mouth of the Schroon River" The construction of the present bridge followed hard upon this action

Warrensburgh, in common with the other towns of the county, did well for the country during the late "misunderstanding between the two sections As the general military history of the county is given in a former chapter, it is unnecessary to do more here than point out a little the action of the town in relation to volunteer service According to the records, a special meeting was called April 4th, 1864, at the house of Duncan Griffin, at which it was voted unanimously that the sum of $1,700 be raised immediately for each volunteer. This was an encouragement to the male inhabitants to fill the quota under the call of the president for men At another special meeting held on August 9th, 1864, it was decided by a vote of sixty-three to twelve to raise $8,000 to fill the quota under the president's call for 500,000 men At the same meeting the town auditors were authorized to borrow money (exclusive of the $8,000 before mentioned) on an issue of bonds for the purpose of paying volunteers, and Thomas Cunningham, F C Burhans, Hiram McNutt, Samuel T Richards and Henry Herrick were appointed a committee to raise the money on these bonds On the 29th of the same month, at another special meeting, it was resolved by a vote of 149 against nine to raise $12,000 additional to fill the quota under the call for 500,000 men, and the sum of $800 was voted as a bounty for each volunteer This was not of course all that the town did during the last war It answered promptly the call for men and money, and a goodly number of those who form the bulk of the population to-day can remember with gratification the part they took in defense of the menaced Union [1]

Following is a list of the supervisors of the town from the date of its formation to the present 1813, James L Thurman, 1814 and 1815, Harmon Hoffman, 1816 and 1817, James L Thurman, 1818–20, Dudley Farlin, 1821–23, Duucan McDonald, 1824, Richardson Thurman, 1825 and 1826, James L Thurman, 1827 and 1828, Dudley Farlin; 1829, Joseph Russell; 1830, Pelatiah Richards, 1831–34, Joseph Russell, 1835, John Thurman, 1836 and 1837, Stephen Griffing, 1838, Pelatiah Richards, 1839, Joseph Russell, 1840, Alton Nelson, 1841, Thomas S Gray, 1842, Asa Crandall, 1843, Abial Burdick, 1844, Nelson J Warren, 1845, Joseph Woodward, 1846, Nelson J Warren, 1847, James R Berry, 1848, Abial Burdick, 1849, John Moon, 1850, Nelson J Warren, 1851 and 1852, James R Berry, 1853, Abial Burdick, 1854, Myron H Shaw, 1855, John S Berry, 1856, Nelson J Warren, 1857 and 1858, Stephen Griffin, 2d; 1859 and 1860, Stephen Griffing; 1861 and 1862, Thomas Cunningham, 1863, Duncan Griffing, 1864 and 1865, Thomas Cunningham, 1866 and 1867, Abial Burdick, 1868, Charles H Ho-

---

[1] The town history should not be closed without a mention of the old block house of tradition, which Dr A W Holden, of Glens Falls, described in a recent number of the Warrensburgh *News* He says in effect that the traveler approaching the "lower borough,' as the residents of Warrensburgh in former days called the lower village, after crossing the ii on bridge which spans the Schroon River, will discover at about forty rods distance a huge boulder whose front overtops the highway There is a tradition connected with it In 1790–91, during the troubles between the government and the Indians along the frontier, the old Indian trail leading from the Mohawk River past the base of Crane Mountain to the lake being yet open, and the memory of former raids being yet fresh in the minds of the inhabitants, they gathered from the surrounding wilderness homes to the hill at the rear of ths big rock, speedily cleared away the forest which hid its summit, and erected from the logs a two-storied blockhouse, with port-holes and fastenings sufficient for the purposes of protection against an ordinary Indian attack It is not recorded that they were called upon to employ it for the purpose of its construction, and even the vestiges of its ruins have been obliterated for years

gan, 1869, Stephen Griffin, 2d, 1870, John Mixter, 1871, Charles M Os-
born, 1872–1877, Thomas Cunningham, 1878, Lewis C Eldridge, 1879,
Stephen Griffin, 2d, 1880, Joel J White, 1881, Thomas Cunningham, 1882,
Joel J White, 1883, Thomas Cunningham, 1884, Henry Griffing, 1885,
Henry Griffing

The present officers of the town (1885,) are as follows Supervisor, Henry
Griffing, town clerk, L C Aldrich, justices of the peace, James Herrick,
elected in 1882, F R Osborne, 1883, Daniel Aldrich, 1884, and B W Sherwood, 1885, assessors, Sylvanus Smith, Jamon H Harrington and John H
Stone, commissioners of highways, Charles H Colvin, Albert H Alden and
John W Wills, collector, Sheridan E Prosser, overseer of the poor, Nathaniel F Mathews, constables, Eugene F Prosser, Charles W Taber, Moses R
Herrington, Edgar T Hayes, game constable, Fred O Hammond, inspectors of election, George W Matthews, John McElroy, Elmer E Whitman,
excise commissioners, George Woodward, Daniel Varnum, Elijah Pratt

According to the various census reports, the population of the town of
Warrensburgh in 1850 was 1,874, in 1855, 1,946, in 1860 1,704, in 1865,
1,585, in 1870, 1,579, in 1875, 1,660, in 1880, 1,725

MUNICIPAL HISTORY

In the preceding pages of this chapter, much that has been deemed of
broad enough application to be placed in the general history, has yet a decided reference to the early condition of the village Although since the arrival
in this vicinity of the earliest settlers, the population has centered, by a natural
law, about the site of this village, yet the community could hardly claim title
to the name village during the first ten or fifteen years of this century Gordon's
Gazetteer [1] describes the place in 1836, as containing one Methodist and one
Presbyterian church, two taverns, five stores, a large tannery, a grist-mill, two
saw-mills, carding and cloth-dressing works, and " about fifty dwellings, *mostly
new* " Considerable business had been done here, however, every year after
about 1815, and many of the important industries which now go to make up the
thrift and prosperity of the village, date their origin back to a period not long
posterior to this time

The first post-office here was kept about where the Warren House now
stands It was established about the year 1806, with Kitchell Bishop as the
first postmaster He was succeeded in a short time by James Warren After
Mr Warren's death, his son, Nelson J. Warren, succeeded to the position, and
kept the office for a number of years After he gave up the office, various
postmasters succeeded In 1856, we find Frederick A Farlin in the office In
1862, Captain M N Dickinson received the appointment, but went at once to
take a prominent part in the Rebellion, and Miles Thomas performed the duties

---

[1] In possession of Dr Holden

incident to the position until 1866, when Captain Dickinson returned, and from that time until July, 1885, he served in that office   On the last named date, C E Cole received the appointment

Various causes have co-operated to make Warrensburgh a thriving village. The excellent water power of the Schroon and of some of the smaller streams in the vicinity afforded the more energetic inhabitants the opportunity of erecting mills with a fair chance of realizing a comfortable profit from the outlay. In earlier days the great quantities of hemlock in the surrounding country attracted hither persons desirous of establishing a prosperous tanning business. When the railroad was opened nearly twenty years ago an additional impetus was given to business by reason of the increase it created in the shipping facilities of the place   Before the road was built all the exports had to be drawn with teams a distance of fifteen miles to Glens Falls, and thence shipped via the feeder to their destination   As Mr A C Emerson expressively says : " Many think that the road takes travelers by, but probably no resident of Warrensburgh would like to see it torn up "

In addition to the advantages of railroad communication, a telephone line connects Warrensburgh with Thurman station, Saratoga and Glens Falls, and stage routes have long been established between this village and Thurman station, Glens Falls and Chestertown   These are at once results and evidences of a continual growth from an infinitesimal beginning   This growth can best be described by giving a brief historical sketch of each of the prominent business establishments and educational and religious institutions at present existing

Hotels — The Warren House was built and first used as a tavern by James Pitts in 1789   In a few years it passed into the hands of Jasper Duel   In 1804 James Warren purchased it of Duel, and kept it until his death   Although the property was leased to various persons, it remained in the hands of the Warren family until 1866, when it was sold to Russell and Chapman   In three or four years Henry Chapman bought out Joseph Russell and in the spring of 1878 he sold to the present proprietor, John Heffron   He has thoroughly renovated, remodeled and repaired the house, and has made it a most commodious and comfortable resting place for tourists and travelers of every name and nature   He sets an excellent table.   The house can conveniently accommodate forty guests

The construction of the Adirondack House, the only other hotel in the village, was commenced by Alton Nelson and John McLaren, but finished in 1825 by Edmund Richards, brother to Pelatiah Richards   He ran the house for a number of years and was followed by Alton Nelson and the latter by Joseph Woodward who bought the property   John McLaren rented it of Mr Woodward a few months, and was succeeded by Bradford Tubbs, who kept the house nearly two years   Stephen Griffin, 2d, acquired title and possession of the hotel in 1838, and kept it until about 1847, when he sold out to

Lewis Persons R C Smith, the present proprietor, came into the house in 1867 as successor to Lewis Persons He can accommodate about forty guests, and has the reputation of keeping a good house

Mercantile Interests — The oldest mercantile establishment in town is that of A T Pasko & Son (E D Pasko), who are engaged in making and selling harnesses and the appurtenances thereto The senior member of the firm began the business here in 1851, in the same building which he at present occupies It is well to state, however, that for two or three years before that he had carried on the business in a small way at his residence About the year 1860 he removed his business to the building which he now occupies as a dwelling, and in 1876 came back to his present quarters At that time his son, E D Pasko, became his partner, and since then the firm name and *personnel* has remained the same, A T Pasko & Son In January, 1863, O F Hammond started a general store in the building which he still occupies as a drug store In 1864 he changed the business from the sale of general merchandise to the preparation and sale of drugs and chemicals It was the first drug store in town Robert Jarvis first kept store in Warrensburgh in 1865, after acting two and a half years as clerk for Henry Herrick, whom he bought out In 1866 he sold again to James and Halsey Herrick This store was where Mr Dickinson's drug store now is In 1867 Mr Jarvis bought out the old James Warren stand, of James Fuller, and for six months had with him a partner, Dennis Stone He then bought out Stone's interest and transferred it to his brother, Walter Jarvis This relation subsisted for about two years, since the termination of which Robert Jarvis has remained alone In 1871 he sold out to the present owner of that store, James Herrick After a partial suspension of business for five years, Mr Jarvis, in 1876, erected his present store, and has since then continued there in the mercantile business Captain M N Dickinson, for so many years postmaster here, began the hardware business in the building now used as the printing office, in 1865, being the pioneer dealer in this description of goods in Warrensburgh In 1871 he sold out to John G Hunt In the fall of 1881 he went into partnership with A H Thomas, in the store they now occupy, and from the commencement of this relation they did business under the firm name of A H Thomas & Co They deal in general merchandise, clothing, however, being a specialty Captain Dickinson has also had the agency for the sale of the Royal St John sewing machine since 1884 A H Thomas began his mercantile career here in 1868, going in with his father, Miles Thomas, who had been a Warrensburgh merchant since 1854 The firm name in 1868 became, therefore, Miles Thomas & Son In May, 1872, Miles Thomas retired, and his son, Charles A Thomas, entered into partnership with his brother. He left, however, in December, 1878, and A H Thomas remained alone until Captain Dickinson went in with him, as above stated When Charles A Thomas left his brother in 1878, he immediately started another store in the stone building which he still occupies   Until January 10th, 1884, he conducted the business in company with M N. Noxon, but since then has been the sole proprietor of the business   In 1866 James Herrick first began to keep a general store in the building now occupied by G W Dickinson as a drug store   In about two years he removed to the building now occupied by E Osborn   In 1871 he went into his present store, at which time he bought the stock of Robert Jarvis, who, as before stated, had been a general merchant here a number of years before   James Fuller, also named before as the predecessor of Robert Jarvis in this building, himself succeeded Nelson J Warren, the son of James Warren, so that this house can probably lay claim to the distinction of being the oldest store building in the village   E S Crandall and his father, J Crandall, entered into co-partnership relations in 1867, under the firm name of Crandall & Son   They occupied the present drug store of G W Dickinson until about 1876, when they moved into the building still occupied by E S Crandall   The partnership was dissolved in 1878   John G Hunt bought out the hardware store of Captain M N. Dickinson in 1871   In 1882 he added the general mercantile department   The business now conducted by E Osborn was founded by his father, C W Osborn in 1872   He died in March, 1885, since which time the present proprietor has continued the business   The building, though unoccupied for some years before 1872, is an old store, being formerly used as such by James Herrick (see above)   Warren Potter established a dry goods business in the building which he still uses, in January, 1877   In October, 1883, Alphonso Young purchased a half interest in the store, and the business is now conducted under the style of Potter & Young   S E Prosser opened a miniature general store at his residence in 1879   In 1883 he increased his stock and removed to his present location   H Herrick opened his store in Louisville in 1879   He originated the business which he now conducts   G W Dickinson opened a drug store in the " upper village " in 1879, taking a one-half interest with L C Charette   In 1880 he purchased Charette's interest   He came to his present location in May, 1883   J W Wills commenced dealing in general merchandise in August, 1881   He has also been wagonmaker and blacksmith in the building which he still uses for the same purpose, since 1860   D. W Bean, jeweler, came here in the spring of 1881, from Chestertown, where he had been engaged in the same business for ten years previously   In 1881 James H Mixter began the hardware business in the same building now used for a like purpose by his brother, F R Mixter. The transfer of the business was effected in 1882   F W Herrick buys and sells furniture now in the same building in which he began, on January 1st, 1883, when he bought out the stock of Bullard & Hunt

Manufacturing Interests — The first grist-mill in town was built by Joseph Hutchinson on the Stow place, at the point which is now known as the south end of the Judd bridge   At low water the remains of the old dam are yet

visible   The first grist-mill erected on the site of that now known as the Burhans mill was built by Dr Michael Hoffman,[1] about the year 1806, and sold
by him to Dudley Farlin in 1816   In 1824 Farlin erected the present mill, and
soon after sold it to Nelson J Warren, who ran it for a term of years and sold
it to William B Farlin on the 4th of August, 1845   In the following December Burhans and Gray bought it   They extensively repaired the mill in the
following summer   On the 1st of May, 1860, Colonel Burhans purchased the
interest of General Gray   In August, 1862, Colonel Burhans placed in a run
of stone — making four in all   Since his death the business has been conducted by his heirs   The mill will grind fifteen tons of produce in twelve
hours

The mills now operated by A C Emerson & Co were built about 1818
or 1820 by Dudley Farlin, who remained sole proprietor of the business until
about 1834   He then sold out to Nelson J Warren, who, after conducting it
for a time, sold his entire interest to Joseph Russell   The latter transferred a
one-fourth interest to Stephen Griffin, 2d, and soon after another one-fourth
interest to Joseph Woodward   Then Mr Griffin purchased a third part of
Russell   In 1855 Joseph Woodward bought of Russell the remaining fourth
In the same year A C Emerson, who is now the senior member of the company, became grantee of one-half of Joseph Woodward's interest   They ran
a store in connection with the mill   In 1858 James McDonald secured an interest in the concern, which he retained until 1865   In the mean time — 1859
—I S Woodward purchased the entire interest of his uncle, Joseph Woodward, and in 1865 he and A C Emerson secured title to McDonald's share
It should be stated that Griffin's interest was distinct and separate from that
possessed by the others   He ran the mill a part of the time alone, and the
rest conducting the business jointly the remainder of the time   Griffin carried
on, also, a separate store   In 1866 I Starbuck & Brothers (George E and
Edward S) bought out Griffin's interest in the mill alone   The next change
in the complex relations between the members of this *quasi*-company consisted
in the formation of a partnership between A C Emerson and I S Woodward
of the one part, and I Starbuck & Brothers of the other part, under the firm
name of Starbucks, Emerson & Co   On the first of December, 1866, the
Starbucks, who had acquired of Thomas S Gray title to the Horicon tannery,
put it in the stock, as they did also the Pharaoh property, which consisted of
nearly 7,000 acres of land and included the lake of that name   Another
change was effected in 1868 when George Harvey and Lewis M Baker bought
out the Starbucks, and the firm name assumed the form of Harvey, Emerson
& Co   Harvey purchased Baker's right in 1869, and on the 13th of February,
1872, Hawley, who by that time owned one-half of the entire property, dis-

---

[1] Judge Woodward has said in previous pages that the Harmon Hoffman named in the town
records was " Dr " Hoffman   The persons may be identical

posed of his interest to S W Johnson and David M. Woodward (brother to I S Woodward)   This relation still subsists

The capacity of these extensive saw-mills may be stated at about 3,000,000 feet of lumber annually, in a good run of water. It is a gang-mill, containing seventy saws and four gates   A shingle and lath-mill is connected with the saw-mill, and in all from twenty to twenty-five men are kept busy   The logs come from a point above Schroon Lake down the river, a distance of about forty miles   About two miles above the mill is a large boom, and near the mill is another, both of which have been in use ever since the original construction of the mill   The lumber, which is made from, perhaps, 15,000 market logs a year, is shipped almost exclusively by the Adirondack Railroad

Until within a few months past this company have had what they call the best tannery in the State of New York, situated at Horicon   It has a capacity for tanning 30,000 hides a year   The building is built largely of stone, the stone part being 400 feet in length by twenty high, and surmounted by a wooden loft reaching ten feet above the stone   Connected with it are ten tenement houses and a store   The entire Horicon concern was closed in 1884, because of the increasing scarcity of bark   The Pharaoh property, mentioned a few lines above, was sold a few years ago for $10,000 to Wilhelm Peckhart, of New York city, who expresses his intention of converting it into a park.

The Warren tannery was built by H. S. Osborn & Co, who began work on the 3d of October, 1831.   It was the first sole-leather tannery built in Warren county   On May 31st, 1832, they first put hides in water   The original proprietors not succeeding in the business, were superseded in the 'spring of 1834 by H J Quackenbosh.   A year later he associated with himself Thomas S Gray, forming the firm of Quackenbosh & Gray   On the 4th of May, 1836, Benjamin P Burhans purchased Quackenbosh's interest in the business, and the new partners conducted affairs under the style of Burhans & Gray   On the 1st of April, 1854, Fred O Burhans became associated with them and the firm style was changed to Burhans, Gray & Co   Colonel Burhans bought out Gray May 1st, 1860, and formed the firm of B P Burhans & Son   Since the death of Colonel Burhans on the 16th of July, 1875, the business has been conducted by his heirs under the same name   The capacity of the tannery is about 3,500 sides per year   From twenty-five to thirty hands are employed [1]

The Empire Shirt Company was formed, and the business established in the fall of 1879, by L Weinman and L W. Emerson   In 1882 J I Dunn had an interest in the concern, but in 1883 he and L W Emerson sold their interests — one-half of the whole — to J A Emerson, then but nineteen years of age   The building which they occupy is the one erected at the time the busi-

---

[1] The facts here stated concerning the tannery and grist-mill were obtained through the kindness of Henry Griffing, esq

ness was started   They manufacture nothing but shirts, but they make about 25,000 dozen of these per year, and employ about one hundred hands in the building

Wyman Flint, of Bellows Falls, Vt , started the peg factory still running in January, 1882   The buildings were erected at that time by I J Brill   The capacity of the factory is indicated by the statement that it turns out about twenty barrels of pegs daily   White, yellow and black birch are used exclusively, and are drawn from the forests in the vicinity   Charles White is the foreman   Two sets of hands are employed, one numbering fifteen and the other about twenty-seven or twenty-eight

The planing-mill and sash factory of S Pasco & Bro. (Walter Pasco), was built in 1881 by John Brill on the site of an old pulp-mill and planing and sawmill which were destroyed by fire   S Pasco had rented this property of Brill since 1875, but in June, 1884, he and his brother, Walter Pasco, purchased the property   The lumber comes from Whitehall and sometimes from Canada

The clothing works of Whitby (R J), Emerson (L W), and Eldridge (T J), were established in the spring of 1885, in a building owned by A C Emerson & Co   Their power is obtained from the same dam that feeds the mills   Twenty-five hands are kept at work, and about sixty-five pairs of pantaloons can be made daily

Warrensburgh News — The first issue of this weekly paper was dated January 17th, 1878   The first owners, publishers and editors were J A Morris & Son (A H Morris)   The prsent editor and proprietor, L C Dickinson, purchased it in January, 1881   Since January, 1885, C E Cole has been associate editor and has performed the greater part of the labor of editing the paper with unusual ability   The paper, which is issued every Thursday, is an eight paged sheet, containing six colmns to the page   It is independent in politics, and its leading articles are distinguished at once for their dispassionate and liberal tone, and their clear elucidation of argument, while the mechanical arrangement of the paper is hardly capable of improvement   It is the only newspaper in Warren county outside of Glens Falls

The banking house of Emerson & Co was founded in January, 1884, by A C and L W Emerson   The latter is cashier   The deposits sum up about $50,000

The Warrensburgh Water-works, owned and conducted by Samuel Bates and Ira Cole under the firm name of Bates & Co , were established in September, 1884   Their method is to lay pipes on all the streets of the village and sell the privilege of using them to the various families   The water is taken from the John McLaren Brook, two miles south of the village, and has a descent of from two hundred and thirty to three hundred feet according to the location of its destination   Hydrants are in process of construction, looking to the formation of a fire company

The Warrensburgh Academy — At present the district school system pre-
vails at Warrensburgh, though the schools are well attended   But the history
of the village would not be complete without some mention of the old Warrensburgh Academy, which has graduated so many men who have since attained prominent positions in the county and elsewhere   It was conducted
by a stock company which was incorporated about the year 1857   The first
trustees were Stephen Griffin, 2d, George and Samuel Richards, Dr H Mc-
Nutt, Dr E W Howard, M N Dickinson, Miles Thomas, Thomas Cunningham, Thomas S Gray, F O Burhans, and three others   In the fall of 1854
the school building, which is still in use, was erected   The first principal was
the Rev Robert C Clapp, of Chestertown   He came, in fact, before the incorporation of the company, and before the second department had become a
feature of the school   He was succeeded in 1857 by Frank Shepherd   The
building when completed, had cost about $4,500   There are now three de-
partments in the school   No principal has been employed for the ensuing
year   The general attendance varies from seventy-five to one hundred and
thirty pupils   The present trustees are as follows   Miles Thomas, Captain M.
N. Dickinson, John W Wills, Harvey White, Lemuel Woodward, A C. Emerson, Dr E W Howard, John P Cole, James Herrick, F O Burhans, and
Thomas Cunningham

Churches — The first church organization formed in the town — or what is
now the town — of Warrensburgh was Methodist, and dates its origin back to
Christmas, 1784, though it did not in reality contain members residing in this
as yet unpeopled region   The present Methodist Church of Warrensburgh,
however, is the same organization, being merely settled in a different locality.
The beginnings must have been extremely small   No appointments were made
north of New York city, 1785, when "Salem appears"   In 1790, this region
was embraced in the Albany circuit   James Campbell was then preacher.
Lorenzo Dow, also, the famous local preacher, was an early "exhorter" hereabouts   From 1799 to 1810 the vicinity formed a part of the Cambridge
Circuit   In 1810 the Thurman Circuit appears on the minutes, with Lansford
Whitney in charge   The circuit then had one hundred and seventy-seven
members   In 1811 Gershum Seaver had charge, and 1812 Tobias Spicer.
At this period local preachers came around once in four weeks   In 1813 Gil-
bert Lyon was preacher, in 1814, Elijah Hibbard; 1815, Daniel Brayton and
Stephen Joyce, in 1816, Daniel I Wright, 1817, Sherman Minor   In 1818
the name was changed to Warren Circuit   Daniel Brayton preached then.
Daniel I Wright came again in 1819, and was followed in 1820 by Jacob Hall.
The following preachers were in charge of the circuit during the following
named years   1821, Cyrus Stillman, 1822, Phineas Owan, 1823, John Clark;
1824 and 1825, Roswell Kelley; 1826, Jacob Beeman and Joseph Eames, 1827,
Nathan Rice and A Hulin, 1828, Nathan Rice and Merritt Bates, 1829,

Seymour Coleman and another, 1830, Seymour Coleman and Joseph Ayres, 1831, Joseph McCreary and Henry R Coleman, 1832, J R McCreary The list of preachers from this time to 1844 was not accessible

The first church edifice was erected about 1802 or 1803 Judge Kitchel Bishop gave the land whereon the building stood, — a tract embracing the present plot and considerable more Major Richardson Thurman gave fifty dollars in money, Josiah Woodward and Isaac Woodward contributed the work and timber

In 1840 the old edifice was removed bodily to the place now owned by Sanford Johnson, just west of John G Hunt's hardware store, and the present edifice was built on the old site by Joseph Woodward and his brother, John Woodward "Mr Woodward" (the records do not say *which* one) gave $200 in money, Joseph Woodward paid a debt of $60, and Peter Cameron, Asa Crandell, Josiah Crandell, Aaron Phillis and one other ten dollars each The church was dedicated by the Rev S Covell, the Rev William Armer being the regular preacher at the time The first class-leaders were Josiah Woodward and Isaac Woodward Among earliest families were those of Josiah Woodward, Daniel Robinson and Nathan Sheerman The list of pastors from the dedication of the church to 1871 has not been found In the latter year, the Rev D Brough was the regular pastor, and was succeeded to the present as follows 1873–75, Rev R Campbell, 1876–78 Rev M M Curry, 1879, Rev William A Groat, 1880, Rev C J Mott, 1881–83, Rev Anthony Wolford; 1883–85, Rev Webster Ingersoll, 1885, Rev W R Winans The present officers are as follows· stewards, J W Wills, district steward, Frederick Herrick, Lemuel Woodward, recording steward, Truman Brown, Edward Wood, trustees, J W Wills, Miles Thomas, Lemuel Woodward, Joseph Woodward, Robert Jarvis, Frederick Herrick and Daniel Aldrich

The Warrensburgh charge includes the churches at Thurman Hollow and Potter School-house, making a territory of about twelve miles in diameter, the total membership amounting to about one hundred and sixty-five The history of the Sunday-school, as far as it could be gathered, is nearly covered with that of the Warrensburgh Church proper The present average attendance is about fifty The superintendent is J W Wills

The next church organization effected here was of the Presbyterian denomination, and dates its beginning in the year 1804 It was originally intended to include a membership extending over a spacious territory, and was known as the Presbyterian church of Warrensburgh and Athol The first pastor was the Rev —— Kloss Among the first members were John McDonald, and Emily, his wife, William Murry, and Margaret, his wife, Kitchell Bishop, and Anna, his wife, Peter Bratt, and Vrontye, his wife, John McEwan. and Christiana, his wife, James Cameron, and Christine, his wife, John McDonald, 2d, and Christiana, his wife, George McDonald, and Jane, his wife, Alexander

Murry, and Molly, his wife, John Moon, and Mary, his wife, John Murry, John Bratt, Derrick Bratt, James Dow, James McDonald, 2d, William Cameron and Duncan McEwan The first elders were John McDonald and Kitchel Bishop The first church edifice was erected at Thurman at the time of organization The present structure was built between 1836 and 1840 by Joseph Woodward. Its cost was about $3,000 It has undergone the repairs that a building of that age would naturally require

In 1805 Rev —— Williams succeeded Mr Kloss in the pastorate, and in 1806, the Rev Jonas Coe, to whom belongs the credit of consummating the formation of the church, was pastor Following is a list of pastors who have served since 1806 1807–12, Rev Matthew Harrison, the first pastor who was duly installed according to the rites of the denomination, 1817, Rev Nathaniel Prime, 1819, Rev Cornelius Bogardus, 1826, Rev Jonas Coe, 1822, '23, Rev John K Davis, 1830, Rev Jonathan Kitchell, 1861, '32, Rev James W Farlin, 1832, '33, Rev John K Davis, 1833, Rev Amos Bingham, 1834–37, Rev James W. Farlin, who died in charge, 1837–39, Rev. Azariah L Crandall, 1839–42, Rev Thomas J Haswell (preached once in two weeks), 1839 (with Mr Haswell), Rev Courtney Smith; 1857, Rev Thomas Riggs, 1859, Rev Henry A Post (died Nov 12th, 1861), 1863, Rev Albert C Bishop, 1870–72, Rev Alexander E Smith, 1876, Rev William M Machette, 1881, Rev. D O Irving, 1884 and at present, Rev James F. Knowles

The present membership of the church is forty, and the elders are as follows John Moon, A C Emerson, W H Wilcox, D B Howard, M D

The Sunday-school, which owes its organization to the efforts of Mrs Sarah Farlin, has now an average attendance of about forty-five Henry Wilcox is the present superintendent

The Baptist church of Warrensburgh was organized on the 26th of December, 1807, and was the result of the labors of the church at Thurman, which was organized at Chestertown in 1796 The first members were Richard Truesdell, Nathaniel Streeter, Asa Smith, Gideon Putney Joshua Kellum, David Smith, Simeon Fuller, Asa Twichel, John Skiff, Elizabeth Fuller, Eda Smith, Lucretia Putney, Desire Burlingame, Mercy Griffis, Eunice Hough, Delight Skiff and Sarah Otis, consisting, as will be seen, of nine male and eight female members Rev Jehiel Fox, the pastor of the church at Chestertown, preached here at the first The first deacons were Asa Smith and Simeon Fuller A frame building owned by Nathaniel Smith and standing on the farm now occupied by Simeon Hall was fitted up for a school-house and meeting-house. In about 1825 they built a house of worship which they used until 1877, when the present edifice, which was commenced in 1876, was dedicated (June 10th) The cost of the present building, lot and fixtures was about $6,500

The following is a list of the successive pastors which have served this church On the 6th of September, 1809, came the first regular pastor, Rev Daniel McBride He remained until December 8th, 1813, when he went West, and in 1814, his successor, Rev Parker Reynolds, began his labors here He too left in 1815, and from that time until 1820, it is not supposed that they had a settled pastor, but were supplied by Elders Harris, Swain, Henry Faxon and Grant On the 24th of June, 1820, Justin Eastwood assumed the duties of the pastorate until his ordination in June, 1821 In 1822 there was a membership of one hundred and six but the records for the next forty years are lost Between 1822 and 1832 two licentiates preached here, Artemus Arnold in 1825 and G Brooks in 1826 In 1836 George B Wells was made a licentiate, and in 1838 was ordained Just previous to 1842 Rev Charles Williams became pastor, and soon after his labors began Aaron Gates, jr , was licensed to preach The membership at this time was 135 A D Milne, afterwards prominent in the county, was licensed to preach here in 1843 In 1844 William S Bush was licentiate and pastor 1846,'47, Walker Stilson, licentiate At this time the church was divided and four new churches organized according to territorial location But the division did not prove a blessing to any of the churches, and on the 5th of July, 1852, eight of the old members dedicated themselves to the work of reviving the old Warrensburgh and Caldwell church. The first clerk after the revival was Truman Chapman, and the first deacon was Warren Potter By the month of September, 1862, the reorganized church had a membership of twenty-four. The pastor then was Rev R O Dwyre, who remained one year, and saw the house of worship remodeled and built almost anew. In 1864 Revs E W Burdick and W Stilson both served in the pastorate, and the membership rose to 101 Rev Caleb Smith followed in 1866 In the following year came Rev W Stilson again, who remained until 1868 Then Rev Stephen Wright followed From December, 1869 to May, 1872, Rev W Stilson resumed this pastorate, during which time Matthew W Burdick was licensed to preach The pastor in 1872 and 1873 was Rev A B Palmatier In December, 1873, Charles H Wyman, a licentiate, became pastor and was ordained on March 19th, 1874 The pastors since 1875 have been 1876, '77, Rev Jacob Gray, 1877–80, Rev Joshua Wood ; 1880–85, Rev George M Muller (ordained here October 6th, 1880) The church is at present without pastor The present officers are as follows :—

Deacons, Warren Potter, Warren Harrington, Dr D E Spoor, and Charles B Hill, clerk and treasurer, S W Johnson , trustees, Warren Potter, Ira Cole, Charles B. Hill, Israel Harrington, Nathan B Sharp, and Sanford W Johnson. The present membership of the church is one hundred and eighty-seven.

The Sunday-school was organized some time before 1860 The superintendent is Ira Cole The average attendance is not far from sixty or seventy persons

38

On the first Sunday in Advent, December 1st, 1861, at two o'clock in the afternoon, the Rev Robert Fulton Crary, missionary at Caldwell, read evening prayer in the Presbyterian house of worship at Warrensburgh, and such services were soon after regularly conducted by him

On the Sunday evenings of the 13th, 20th, and 27th of March, 1864, by the permission of the Bishop of New York, a notice was read which called a meeting for the purpose of incorporating the parish of the Holy Cross of Warrensburgh   The notice proving defective no organization was then effected

On Wednesday in Whitsuntide, May 18th, 1864, the corner stone of the church was laid by the Rev Robert F Crary, priest and missionary in charge of the station   From this time until February 1st, 1865, work was continued upon the building, which, with the exception of the tower and porch, was completed   On the fifth Sunday after Epiphany, February 5th, 1865, the building was opened for Divine service   On Palm Sunday and Easter Day in 1865, a notice was read calling a meeting on April 19th, 1865, for the purpose of incorporation, in pursuance of which the following persons assembled in due time   Rev Robert F Crary, Frederick O Burhans, Duncan Griffin, George A Schneider, Robert Stewart, Charles Braley, John Hochaday, Moses Sutton, and Henry Griffing

Benjamin P Burhans and Stephen Griffin were duly elected wardens, and Frederick O Burhans, Duncan Griffin, Charles Braley, Henry Herrick, Samuel T Richards, James Farrar, Moses Sutton, and Henry Griffing, vestrymen

In the spring of 1865 the porch and tower of the church edifice were completed

On the ninth Sunday after Trinity, August 13th, 1865, the Rt Rev Horatio Potter, Bishop of New York, made his first visit to the parish   The following is taken from his official report   " Aug 13th, 9th Sunday after Trinity, evening, in the Church of the Holy Cross, Warrensburgh, I preached, confirmed four persons, and addressed them   This is a new and beautiful church in a charming situation, and the parish, recently organized, is in a prosperous condition under the ministry of the Rev R F. Crary "

A new pipe organ was placed in the church in May, 1866, and first used on Whitsunday, May 20th, of that year, completing, with the previous cost of the church edifice and ground, an expenditure of $7,792 87   On June 13th, 1866, the Bishop of New York consecrated the church.   In the fall of 1867, Rev R F Crary was appointed to the rectorship of the Holy Comforter, of Poughkeepsie, N Y, and from that time this parish was left in charge of missionaries until November 8th, 1869, when Rev Henry H Oberly was appointed by the Bishop of Albany rector of the parish   He resigned on the first of November, 1872, and was succeeded by Rev James E Hall, who remained until September 29th, 1874   The present rector, Rev William M Ogden, was appointed April 1st, 1875   In the fall of 1874 lands adjoining the church lot of one and one-half acres were purchased, and on July 16th, 1885, ground was broken for the erection of a rectory, parish house and public reading room [1]

The Roman Catholic Church Society of Warrensburgh was regularly organized by Rev James A Kelly, its first resident pastor, under the title of St Cecilia in 1874 This was Father Kelly's first mission after he was ordained in Troy Seminary Before that time the Catholic families in this vicinity were attended at varying intervals by priests from Glens Falls and Minerva The corner stone of the first church edifice was laid on the 23d of July, 1875, and the church, by virtue of the zealous efforts of its young pastor, was dedicated on the 5th of September, 1877, the cost of the building having been $6,000, and of the furniture, $2,000, making a total expenditure of $8,000, its present value The number of communicants is one hundred and twenty-five Since Rev James Kelly resigned, after building and paying for four churches in different towns in the mission, viz At north Creek, Luzerne, Weavertown, and Warrensburgh, the following clergymen have had charge Rev James Greene attended the mission from September, 1881, to November of the same year, and was transferred to Cleveland Rev James Lynch from November 19th, 1881, to February 19th, 1882 Rev James Muldoon, from February 19th, to June 20th, 1882 Rev W O'Mahoney, the present pastor, came July 1st, 1882 The Sunday-school attached to the church was organized in 1874, and Rt Rev Bishop McNierney has conferred confirmation here twice since that year It is stated on good authority that this is the finest and largest church edifice in the Adirondacks, north of Glens Falls and Saratoga

Attorneys and Counselors — Thomas Cunningham, the attorney of longest standing in Warrensburgh, was born in Chesterfield, Essex county, in 1826 He studied law with Kellogg & Hale, of Elizabethtown, and was admitted to the bar at Plattsburg, on the fourth of July, 1854 He has practiced here ever since his admission

Lewis C Aldrich was born on May 13th, 1852, in the town of Thurman He was admitted to the bar on April 9th, 1875, at Albany, after passing a clerkship with Thomas Cunningham of Warrensburgh, which he commenced in the spring of 1871, He was town clerk of Warrensburgh in 1874–77, 1881–85 inclusive; supervisor of Warrensburgh in 1878, and clerk of the Board of Supervisors of Warren county in 1875, '80, '83 and '84

When Mr Cunningham came here in 1854, George Richards was a practicing attorney here He had always been here, he and his brother, Samuel T Richards, being extensively engaged in lumber interests George Richards lived here until 1866 or 1868 He is now is the custom house at Rouse's Point About 1870 Randolph McNutt did a little legal practice here He moved away about 1880

---

[1] We are indebted for the above to Mr Henry Griffing, who kindly sent us the sketch, which we have here inserted almost verbatim

Physicians — Dr E W Howard, longer in Warrensburgh than any living physician, was born January 2d, 1808, in Fort Anne, Washington county He received his general education mainly in common and graded schools He began his medical studies in April, 1830, under Dr Nelson Porter, of Fort Anne In the summer of 1832 and the following winter he studied in the office of Dr Fletcher Ransom, of Glens Falls He attended, also, three courses of lectures at Castleton, Vt, and was graduated from that institution in December, 1833 Thereupon he commenced practicing in the town of Queensbury, four miles north of Glens Falls He came to Warrensburgh in April, 1837 From 1838 to the spring of 1867 he lived in the house now occupied by Captain F A Farlin At the latter date he removed to his present residence

Dr. Louie Charette was born about June, 1820, at Leech Lake in Minnesota, then called the Northwest Territory In the fall of 1841 he was graduated at the Albany Medical College, and at once began to practice in Bolton He came to Warrensburgh in 1854

Dr. Daniel B Howard, son to Dr E W Howard, was born in Warrensburgh January 17th, 1841 He studied medicine with his father, and was graduated from the Albany Medical College on the 7th of December, 1865 He has practiced ever since that time with his father

Dr. W D Aldrich was born in Thurman on January 15th, 1851 He received his medical education in the medical department of Dartmouth College, being graduated November 1st, 1871 He began to practice in Stony Creek, but moved to Warrensburgh in 1878

Dr. D E. Spoor was born in Hartland, Niagara county, N Y, in 1846 He studied medicine in Medina, and received his diploma from Hanneman Medical College in Chicago in 1878 He started his practice in Orleans county, coming from there to this county in September, 1881 He came to Warrensburg in April, 1884

CHAPTER XXXIV.

HISTORY OF THE TOWN OF HORICON

H ORICON is situated on the northern border of the county, east of Schroon Lake and Schroon River It is bounded on the north by Essex county, on the east by Hague, on the south by Bolton, and on the west by Chestertown The two branches of the Kayaderosseras Mountains, separated by the valley of Brant Lake, extend in a northeasterly and southwesterly direction through the town and render the surface uneven and precipitous in the ex-

treme   In the north and east these ranges rise in a number of sharp, rocky
peaks, which attain an elevation varying from 1,600 to 2,000 feet above sea
level, but in the south and west they descend into an uneven plateau   The
soil, like the entire county around it, is a sandy loam, and the surface so thickly
studded with rocks and boulders as to render cultivation a labor of considerable difficulty   Not more than one-third of the surface is arable, and there are
good authorities in the town who hold that not one-tenth part of the surface is
really cultivated   The principal products are buckwheat, corn, oats and potatoes   Among the mountains are a great many small lakes lying imbedded in
more or less huge and towering amphitheatres of rocky slopes and precipices.
The largest of these, Brant Lake, is ten miles long, and has for years been a
favorite resort of the hunter and fisherman   But the most famous and the
most beautiful of all the waters that indent her territory is the lovely Schroon
We cannot do better than to insert here, almost bodily, an article written by
Dr A W Holden for a recent number of the *Warrensburgh News* —

Conspicuous among the myriad lakelets and ponds with which the northern
wilderness abounds is the Schroon   Lying partly in the town of Schroon, in
Essex county, and partly in Horicon, Warren county, it forms with its associate river a beautiful contrast to the fringe of forest bordering on the great
waste of woods and waters known to the Iroquois by the term *Conchsachraga*,
" the great dismal wilderness "

It is but an expansion of the river to which it imparts its name, and lies
embosomed between the sloping hillsides, once wooded to its very brink, but
now, by the industry of man, changed to a civilized aspect, with tilled fields,
pasture lands, and here and there an old-time farm-house, or rustic cottage, or
more pretentious summer hotel

Prior to the voyages and discoveries of the French navigator, Jacques Cartier, and only forty-two years subsequent to the first voyage of discovery of
Christopher Columbus, all of the great peninsula, bounded by Lakes George
and Champlain on the east, and the St Lawrence River on the west, was
claimed and occupied by a powerful tribe of the great Odjibway family, known
to the French as the Algonquin nation, and to the Iroquois as the Adirondack
tribe   A family of this tribe, according to tradition, had its seat on the shores
of this beautiful lake   The derivation of the name Schroon rests in obscurity
A mythical correspondent, mentioned by Da Costa in his *Schroon Lake and
the Adirondacks*, is credited with saying " that a few years ago a Sappho-like
origin of the name was derived from Scarona, a squaw, who, like Winona and
many others, had leaped over a precipice into the lake and was drowned "
Whether from blighted affections is not recorded   Another legend, referring
perhaps to the same maiden, states that the name was conferred in honor of
the beautiful daughter of a distinguished Algonquin chief, the name signifying
" the child of the mountains "   According to Gordon's *Gazetteer of the State*

of New York it is a corruption of the Indian word " Skanetaghrowakna," " the largest lake " An unauthenticated derivation is attributed to Madame Scarron, wife of the French poet Scarron, who lived in the time of Madame de Maintenon — named by a party of French officers who visited the lake " In an effervescence of sentimental gush the ceremony of dedication and claim of discovery has been embellished with formal declarations and the breaking of a bottle of wine on the occasion It might be worth the while of some antiquarian to drag the lake in search of the bottle I have not the least doubt but what success would attend the experiment if the drag was drawn near the shore of the beautiful island, and so a long, vexed question put to rest "

Whatever the conclusion, it is certain that the name is recorded as Scaron on several of the earlier maps of this region, notably Sauthier s *Chronological Map of the Province of New York*, published in 1779 and reprinted in the first volume of the *Documentary History of New York*, and on a map engraved and published in 1777 by Matthew Albert Lottier

Undoubtedly there have been sporodic settlements in Horicon since the earlier years of the century, but industry never was organized here before the formation of the town, and as late as 1831, as will be seen, the aspect of the territory was, even in comparison with its present condition, wild and apparently untenantable

One of the most intelligent and well informed of the residents of Horicon, J N Barton, came here in 1831 from Warrensburgh He was born on the 7th of October, 1820, on the mile strip that was afterward transferred from Warrensburgh to Chester When he first came to the territory which seven years later became Horicon, he lived in the little farming settlement called Hayesburgh Among those who then lived here was Bishop Carpenter, a prominent farmer and lumberman, residing at the outlet of Schroon Lake. One of his sons, Sylvester, now lives in Horicon, and another, Thomas J Carpenter, is a resident of Chestertown Timothy Bennett, another of the original settlers, lived then in Hayesburgh He has no descendants now in Horicon Howard Waters carried on a farm at Hayesburgh Harvey S Waters, now living here, is his son Nathan Hayes, senior and junior, were also farmers at Hayesburgh, four or five miles east of South Horicon They leave no descendants. Benjamin Hayes, sr , — brother to Nathan Hayes, sr , — and Benjamin Hayes, jr , were neighbors of their relatives, and have descendants here now James Hayes, another son of Nathan Hayes, sr , moved away from his farm in Hayesburgh thirty-five years ago Another resident of that neighborhood was John Robbins, farmer and laborer As Mr Barton figuratively observed, " he was a moving planet " James Frazier and Benjamin Wright were also farmers in Hayesburgh, and both have descendants still living hereabouts

In 1831, Mr Barton says, the country was all new There were only two or three frame-houses in what is now the town of Horicon   No tavern, nor store, nor ashery, nor distillery, nor church in the whole town   There were three school districts in the territory, and religious meetings were occasionally held in one of the log school-houses, which were then wont to serve the public in all capacities

There was no post-office in town in 1831   The first one was established at Hayesburgh under the name Horicon about 1840, and Howard Waters had the honor of first distributing the mails   Charles Osborn followed him until about 1862, when Alonzo Davis was made postmaster   In 1865 Homer Davis was made postmaster   In 1867 Charles W Osborn succeeded Davis, and remained until 1869, when Oren Burge took the oath of office   In April, 1882, the present postmaster, Scott Barton, was appointed as successor to Oren Burge   In the mean time the post-office had been removed from Hayesburgh to South Horicon, or more familiarly "The Pit," and from there to the Emerson tannery, and soon after to its present location at Bartonville

When Mr Barton came here in 1831, the principal business of the inhabitants, besides farming, was lumbering   About their only occupation winters was logging   Glens Falls lumbermen made money by floating logs down the Schroon to the Hudson, thence direct to Glens Falls   Pine timber grew here in great abundance, but is now about all gone   Moses Stickney then had a saw-mill at Bartonville, on the site of Smith Barton's present mill   All the little streams in town had one or more "mud mills" as they were called   The practice of these primitive lumbermen was to "stock up" in winter, and saw the timber in the summer, as well as to draw logs to Ticonderoga   Of these small mills one was owned and run by John J Harris at the head of Brant Lake ; near him was the saw-mill of Jonathan Griffin , east of The Pit were two owned severally by Arnold Young and Henry Hopkins   The same grist-mill now operated by L D Waters was then the only one in town, and was the property and under the management of Moses Stickney   In 1865 J N Barton bought him out and ran the mill until 1880, when Thomas J Smith purchased the property   His grantee and successor was Smith Barton   L D Waters bought it in the spring of 1885

Horicon was formed from Bolton and Hague on March 29th, 1838   It is impossible to give the list of first officers because the records were destroyed by fire in 1868.   In addition to what has been incidentally given of the present business interests, may be stated the milling, mercantile and hotel interests of the town   It has been stated that in 1831 Moses Stickney owned the grist-mill and saw-mill at Bartonville   He built them both   The latter, as well as the former, became in 1865 the property of J N Barton, who retained his title until June, 1885, when his son, Smith Barton, bought it, and now operates it   The capacity of the saw-mill is given at 2,500 market logs a year

The store now at Bartonville, under the management of Scott and John

Barton, was started in 1869   J. Barton had had for a partner in the grist-mill Albert Rand   In 1869 they opened the store   In 1871 E B Bentley succeeded Albert Rand and in 1874 Scott Barton succeeded Bentley   J N Barton sold his interest, in 1882, to John Barton   The stock which is owned by the managers, Scott and John Barton, is valued at about $4,000   The building is the property of J N Barton

The tavern now kept in Bartonville by J B Smith was erected by him in 1882, and is the first and only hotel in the place   There was one at South Horicon (The Pit) soon after 1840, kept first by F B Coolidge, and afterwards by Walter Pritchard   It stood on the site of R P Smith's residence, and was burned a short time before the war while under the management of Caroline, widow of Loren Davis.   There is now a hotel just across the road from the old one, kept by Marcus Granger, who bought a private house and fitted it up for a tavern   In 1880 he kept a hotel where R P Smith now lives and moved from there to his present location   There is no store at The Pit now   Harmon A Brace kept one there for about two years but stopped in May, 1885

The place called Starbuckville derived its name from Isaac Starbuck, who started a large tannery there about two and a half miles west of Bartonville in the vicinity of 1845   His brothers, Edward and George, were associated with him for some time   They finally suspended the tannery and began to operate a wholesale shoe manufactory there   In 1870 it burned   Isaac Starbuck is now in St Lawrence county, and Starbuckville is a name alone

Mill Brook or Adirondack —This hamlet can trace its origin back to about 1850   In 1849, when Benjamin T Wells, father of J F and Thomas Wells, came to the site from the south part of the town, the place was, as J F Wells says, a dismal wilderness   There were no roads nor buildings here   Benjamin T Wells erected the first tannery on the site of the present establishment, and so fast did the community grow that in five years it had attained almost its present proportions   The old road to Chester had not been extended to Mill Brook until about 1851   The road connecting this place with Pottersville was constructed about 1875

The tannery now owned by Fraser, Major & Co , of New York, was, as above stated, erected in 1849   Benjamin T Wells was the mechanic who built it, under the supervision of Joseph Russell and a Mr. Leet   After numerous changes it became before 1860 the property of Thomas Fraser & Brother (James)   The individual names of the present members of the firm are James, George and William Fraser, and William K Major   The superintendent, E A Bush, has held his present position since 1860   In 1864 the property was destroyed by fire, but was immediately rebuilt   The tannery has now a capacity for producing 20,000 finished sides of leather annually.

The general store of J M Bush has been in his hands since 1872, when he bought out Thomas Wells, who had conducted the business for some time before   Mr Bush carries about $2,500 of stock

The Wells House was erected in 1872, and opened on the 28th of June in that year   The proprietor now is and always has been Thomas Wells   The dimensions at first were three stories in height, and sixty-five feet in length by thirty-five feet in depth   In 1875 Mr Wells added forty feet to the length, and in 1878 erected an ell extending seventy-four feet to the east   The house with a cottage built in 1878 will accommodate one hundred and fifty guests, and is open from June 1st to October 1st in each year   The two other cottages are occupied each summer by Judge John K Porter and G W Cotterill, of New York, who take their meals at the Wells House

The churches of Horicon have not been uniformly blessed with ostensible prosperity   The first church in town was the Baptist Church in the south part of the town, organized in 1831, under the name of the Baptist Church of Brant Lake   The original membership numbered twenty-five   Revs Norman Fox, of Chestertown, and William Giant, of Bolton, filled the pupit from time to time for the first two years   The first regular pastor was Jonathan Trumbell, a licentiate, who was ordained in 1841   He preached here from 1840 to 1842.   Then occurred a vacancy which lasted several years, the name in the the mean time being changed to the Horicon Baptist Church   The second pastor was the Rev D A Cobb   There is no regular pastor of this church now   They have no house of worship except the one at Mill Brook

The Methodist Church of South Horicon was organized and the edifice erected in about 1850   The first pastor was Rev H L Taylor, then of Warrensburgh   There is no society here now

At Mill Brook, in 1881, an association was formed, containing members of the Baptists.and Methodists denominations, and non-sectarian members   A board of trustees was elected comprising two Baptists, two Methodists and two of neither denomination   The Baptists and Methodists had each a separate organization   Under this arrangement the present union edifice was erected at an expense of $1,700   Preaching has always been done one Sunday by a Baptist clergyman, and on the following Sunday by a Methodist— a member of some other denomination preaching also occasionally   The preaching is now done by Rev I C Hill, of the Baptist denomination, and Elder Town of the Methodist   There are now in the society about thirty-five Baptist members, and the same number of Methodists, making, with the members from outside, a membership of about eighty   The present trustees are Riley Nichols, S B Carpenter, Edgar Hawley, James Floyd, E A Bush and Orange B. Ingraham   Before the present association was formed there had been for ten or twelve years both a Baptist and a Methodist church organization   Meetings were held in the school-house   The first preacher here was Rev Spears, a Methodist clergyman

There is a regular steamship line in Schroon Lake which makes three trips daily the whole length of the lake, by the steamer *Effingham*, owned by Mrs

P S Russell, of Schroon Lake village   Mrs Russell also owns the excursion steamer, *Gypsie*   Other steamers are the *Wilhelmina*, by Wilhelm Pickhardt, and the *Ellen* by E A Bush.

The first post-office established at Mill Brook dates its origin sometime between 1850 and 1855, when the name of the office was Mill Brook   The first postmaster was John A Russell   In 1856 he was followed by Edwin A Bush   In 1865 the office was discontinued, and remained in suspension until 1872, when it was re-established under the name of Adirondack, and the present incumbent, J M Bush, was appointed postmaster

The following is as nearly complete a list of supervisors as in the absence of town records, can be obtained   1838–40, John H Smith, 1841, Benjamin T Wells, 1842, John Ransom, 1843, Benjamin Culver, 1844, '45, F B Coolidge, (not obtained between 1840 and 1860), 1860, Powell Smith; 1861, Thomas Wells, 1862, Joseph A J Smith, 1863–65, Judson N. Barton, 1866, Lemuel Stafford, 1867, S B Carpenter, 1868, J N Barton; 1869, '70, Charles Hill, 1871, S B Carpenter, 1872, Lemuel Stafford, 1873, C P. Hill, 1874, George Carpenter, 1875, Owen Burge, 1876, Walter P Smith, 1877, '78, Oren Burge; 1879, Judson N Barton, 1880, J Freeman Wells; 1881, Thomas J Smith; 1882 '83, Scott Barton, 1884, '85, J Freeman Wells

The present town officers are as follows   supervisor, J Freeman Wells, town clerk, John Barton, assessors, Lemuel Stafford, Edwin R Smith, A J. Barton, highway commissioner, Austin A Ross, justices of the peace, Charles W Gregory, J N Barton, Starling Walters, J Freeman Wells, overseers of the poor, John Streeter and Orange B Ingraham, collector, R E D Paige, constables, R E D Paige, John McLaughlin, A J. Huntington, Richard Bolton, game constable, E Morris Sexton, inspectors of election, district No. 1, Newton Church, George Walters, 2d, William Ovens, No 2, Joseph F Anderson, Austin A. Ross, George Hawley

The population of the town of Horicon since 1850 has been as follows: 1850, 1,152, 1855, 1,246, 1860, 1,542, 1865, 1,398, 1870, 1,500, 1875, 1,539; 1880, 1,633   The diminution in between the years 1860 and 1865 is due to the noble effort put forth by the town to aid in crushing the Rebellion It has been said that Horicon, in proportion to her population, furnished more men for the war than any other town in the State of New York   The town paid $3,500 in bounties in one year, when her population did not exceed one thousand five hundred   It is estimated that two hundred volunteers went from Horicon into the various regiments made up in this county, principally the One Hundred and Eighteenth, Twenty-second, Ninety-third and One Hundred and Forty-second   Only one man was drafted

CHAPTER XXXV

HISTORY OF THE TOWN OF STONY CREEK

STONY CREEK lies just south of Thurman, and is bounded on the east (across the Hudson) by Warrensburgh, on the south by Saratoga county, and on the west by Hamilton county It is even now nearly all a wilderness A mountain range extends through the center of the town, and contains some peaks which reach an altitude of two thousand feet The valleys of the East and West Stony Creek are narrow ravines between the more extensive valleys of the Hudson and the Sacandaga The soil is a light sandy loam

As the town was formerly a part of Athol, and originally of the old town of Thurman, its earliest history, dating back to the beginning of the century, and which is from the nature of the case, very meagre, has already been given in the history of Thurman

Stony Creek was formed by the division of Athol, on the 3d of November, 1852 The condition of the town at that time has been well described to us by Mr James A Brooks, who removed from Greenfield, Saratoga county, to a farm seven miles west from Creek Center, in 1849[1] Creek Center was then scarcely visible as a village The tannery, which has made the place, had not yet been erected, and there were only a few buildings scattered about the place in a somewhat unneighborly manner There was but one post-office in town (or what is now the town), and that was on the Hudson Of the inhabitants of the town at that time Mr Brooks says in effect Alexander McDonald lived about six miles up Stony Creek from Creek Center His son James and John still live in town James Thompson lived on the Hudson River near the present station, Curtis Nolton lived about " half a mile " north of Alexander McDonald's Abram Fry, like the rest, a farmer, lived about one and a half miles southeast of Creek Center, Daniel McMillen occupied a log house on the old main road Columbus C Gill lived near the grist-mill, a mile and a half south of the Center His sons, Charles, Daniel and Dudley, still reside in town Daniel M Cameron owned a farm on the Hudson His daughter, Mrs Allen Wood, is now living here Joseph Hull, a farmer, too, lived just west of the Center, on the place now occupied by his son, Matthew Hull. Parley Gray lived then where he does now, about three-quarters of a mile north of the Center The place of Mr Brooks's residence was called Harrisburgh, from the fact that three brothers named Harris came there some years before 1850 and built a saw-mill It had run down before Mr Brooks came

There were a number of saw-mills in town Alexander McDonald ran one near his house Campbell & Taylor operated one up at Len's Lake on the Roaring Branch Francis G Drake soon after 1850 became its proprietor Horace

[1] He was born in Townsend, Mass , October 8th, 1814

L Hall had a small one on the site of the tannery Lyman Kenyon started one at Harrisburgh in 1854, and ran it several years Theodorus Hall owned and operated one about one-half of a mile southeast of the Center John Walsh had one nearly two miles west of the village, and Gardner Adams had one about five miles west of the village Columbus Gill operated one near his grist-mill, though he devoted the greater part of his time to the latter D. W. Cameron now runs the grist-mill The only store in this part of Athol was kept near the present station by James Fuller Fuller also manufactured the only potash made in the town There was no distillery here Luke Fenton kept an inn on the Hudson. In 1851 or 1852 a broom factory was built about two miles west of Creek Center. Other inhabitants were Joel Dayton, James Robison, Almon Swears, and Edward Stevens, who all lived five or six miles west of the Center, and James and Stephen Kathan, brothers, Alexander Murray and Reuben H Kidder, who were almost the only ones living right at the Center The whole town including Creek Center was a dense forest Deer roamed fearlessly and in great numbers through the woods, and were hunted not alone by man, but by beasts of prey which haunted the forest and mountain fastnesses in profusion The roads had been opened nearly as they are now, but were rough and in places nearly impassable

The first officers of Stony Creek were as follows Supervisor, James McDonald, town clerk, John P Bowman, assessors, James Thompson, Harry Scofield, justices of the peace, C W Davis, Curtis Nolton, Abram Fry, commissioners of highways, Alexander McDonald, Columbus C Gill; overseers of the poor, David M Cameron, Joseph Hull, collector, Parley Gray, inspectors of election, Silas H Cameron, William Green, James Green, constables, Parley Gray, Robert McMillen, James Green, Lyman Wheeler, sealer of weights and measures, Columbus C Gill Pathmasters. 1, John A Cameron, 2, Moses Murray, 3, Theodore Hall; 4, Daniel McMillen; 5, Levi Goodman, 2d, 6, James Wheeler; 7, Henry Cornish, 8, James Kathan, 9, John Deen, 10, Parley Goodman, 11, Parley Gray, 12, William Glassbrooks, 13, Sears Harris, 14, Gardner Adams, 15, Harry Scofield, 16, Lyman Kenyon, 17, Abram Baker; 18, Joseph Walsh, 19, John Leet, 20, Curtis Nolton, 21, Reuben H Kidder; 22, Erastus Smith, 23, Armon E Mores, 24, Olive Chamber, 25, Ira Weaver.

Of the present business interests of Stony Creek, the most important is the tannery of John P Bowman at Creek Center Mr Bowman erected this tannery in 1852, and has operated it without cessation ever since The tannery will turn out 40,000 sides of sole-leather per annum About twenty-five men are employed in and about the building, besides the men in the woods Mr Bowman has 6,000 or 7,000 acres of timbered land from which to take his bark He has done business with the firm of Allen, Fields & Lawrence, or its predecessor, for thirty-three years He has built a boarding-house which will

John P. Bowman

provide for twenty-five men, and houses for sixteen families, in which the tannery men and their families reside

Mercantile Interests — Charles Gill is proprietor of a general store at the Center which his father, Columbus Gill, started in 1858 In 1872 Charles Gill acquired an interest in the concern, and in 1882 bought his father out G N Yarrington began dealing in merchandise at the Center in 1875, A J Aldrich, in 1884, and formerly from 1867 to 1872 W R Clayton started his drug store at the same place in 1882 In 1884 M L Messenger succeeded D M Dunlap, who had kept a general store here for about six years before

The wooden ware manufactory of H L Hall, in which are made peck measures, four-quart measures, barrel covers, etc , was started about four years ago Before that Mr Hall manufactured brush backs there, and originally he was a wagon maker He has been a manufacturer here for about twenty-five years

Hotel — The Creek Center House was built in the winter of 1869–70, by William H Lewis After keeping it a short time, Lewis rented it to C H Nims for two years George Kathan kept it a year and was succeeded by John J Winslow, who remained two years Albert N Day kept the house a year, and was followed one year by Richard Rhodes From the spring of 1877 to the spring of 1879, D M Dunlap was proprietor His successor, M L Messenger, after keeping it a year associated with himself Dudley Gill, who, however, remained in the business but one year and withdrew D M Dunlap, the present proprietor, succeeded Messenger in the spring of 1884 He sets a very good table and has neatly kept and neatly furnished rooms for the thirty guests which he can accommodate

There are no attorneys in town, and but one physician, who, however, is reputed a man of unusual ability and skill in his profession Dr G H Aldrich was admitted to the practice of medicine in 1877, when he was graduated at the Dartmouth Medical College He came to Creek Center in the winter beginning the year 1878

At Harrisburgh Oscar Ordway keeps a hotel and store He has been there about a year They were built by Thomas Wakeley in 1877 Wakeley also started a large saw-mill and wooden-ware factory there in 1877, but it was destroyed by fire in March, 1885, and has not yet been rebuilt

Churches —There are five churches in town, three of the Methodist Episcopal denomination, one Baptist and one Wesleyan Methodist One Methodist Church, besides the Wesleyan, is in Creek Center The Methodist Episcopal Church of Creek Center was organized about 1855 Among the first members were Freeman Holmes, Alexander Kennedy, James Kathan, John A Cameron and Benoni Aldrich The first regular pastor was Rev Z C Pickett, who was succeeded in 1856 by H M Munsee , 1858, Rev Edward Turner, 1860, Rev Joel Hall, 1862, Rev E A Blanchard, 1863, Rev A Champlin, 1866, Rev J Baxley ; 1868, Rev R Washburn; 1870, Rev. F K Potter; 1872, Rev. William H Tiffany; 1873, Rev J W Coons, 1875, Rev D. C Hall; 1877, L W Rhodes and F Cameron, local preachers, and Rev J S. Gould, pastor, 1878, Rev A J Haynor, 1880, Rev J C Walker, 1881, Rev W W Whitney, 1883, Rev J W Coons, 1885, Rev S W Snow. The edifice was erected about 1857   The present value of the church property is about $1,200   The Sunday-school was organized at the same time as the church   Wallace Hemstreet is the present superintendent   The church trustees are E M Black, Wallace Hemstreet and James W Wait

Post-Office —The first postmaster at Creek Center was Thomas Apley, who was replaced in 1863 by Columbus Gill   In 1867 his son, Charles Gill, succeeded him, and still retains the position

The supervisors from Stony Creek have been as follows· 1853, James McDonald; 1854, '55, Thomas Ackley, 1856, '57, James Fuller, 1858–60, Lyman T. Fuller, 1861, '62, Columbus Gill, 1863, John A Cameron, 1864,'65, Columbus Gill, 1866, '67, David Potter, 1868, '69, A J Aldrich, 1870, '71, James McDonald; 1872, '73, Charles Gill, 1874, '75, William D Aldrich, 1876, Wallace Hemstreet, 1877, Almon Swears, 1878, '79, Dudley Gill; 1880, James McDonald, 1881, '82, Henry A Brooks, 1883, '84, Gilbert H. Aldrich, 1885, Dudley Gill

The present town officers are Supervisor, Dudley Gill ; town clerk, James H Gray,[1] justice of the peace, Joseph White; assessor, Charles Murray; commissioner of highways, Alvin Winslow, collector, John Glassbrooks, overseers of the poor, Joseph E Fuller, William E Baker, inspectors of election, James E Stearns, John J Clayton, Charles Robinson, constables, Frederick Corlew, Jonathan W Nolton, Elroy Tripp, Titus Codner, Frank Cudney; game constable, Martin U B Coon, excise commissioners, Samuel Robison, Wm H Walsh

The population of Athol in 1850 was 1,590. of Stony Creek in 1855, 913 ; in 1860, 960, in 1865, 935 , 1870, 1,127 , 1875, 1,253 ; in 1880, 1,253.

CHAPTER XXXVI

BIOGRAPHICAL.

CHARLES HENRY FAXON —Thomas Faxon, ancestor of the Faxon family in the United States, born in England about 1601, came to America before 1647 with his wife, Joane, and three children. His first purchase of land was made May 14th, 1656, in Braintree, Suffolk county, Mass , the tract

---

[1] May 6th, 1885, M L Messenger was appointed Town Clerk vice James H Gray resigned

consisting of about 450 acres, which, to the present time, after many divisions and subdivisions, has continued in part in the family possession, and till recently in the family name A portion of this tract is still known as the "Faxon Meadows" The esteem in which he was held by his fellow-citizens is sufficiently attested by the fact that he was often appointed to transact business of importance for the town of Braintree

When it became necessary to secure from the Indians a deed, extinguishing their title to some of the land of the town, he was one of the commissioners for that purpose He was a representative from Braintree in 1669, and one of the selectmen in 1670–72 George L Faxon, in his *History of the Faxon Family*, closes his notice of him as follows —

"If the record of Thomas Faxon does not place him above a respectable mediocrity in wealth and social standing, it gives him a life without reproach, an ability capable of success in worldly affairs, and a character adapted by its worth and quality to secure the esteem of men "

He died November 23d, 1680 The children of Thomas and Joane Faxon were Joanna, Thomas and Richard The latter born in England about 1630, married, about 1644, Elizabeth —— Thirteen children were the issue of this marriage, of whom Josiah was the fifth and the eldest son He was born in Braintree, September 8th, 1660, married Mehitable (born March 20th, 1665), daughter of Edward and Lydia Adams, of Medfield, Mass He inherited most of his father's estate, and was one of the selectmen in 1722 He died 1731, his wife March 1st, 1753 They had eight children of whom Thomas was the second, born in Braintree, February 8th, 1692, married May 22d, 1716, Ruth Webb They had six children of whom Thomas was the fifth and eldest son He was born in Braintree February 19th, 1724, married, August 24th, 1749, Joanna, daughter of Abijah and Joanna (Bolter) Allen He was a man of small stature, being only five feet two inches in height, but he made up in activity what he lacked in stature During the War of the Revolution he was private in Captain Joseph Stebbins's company of Colonel David Wells's regiment in an expedition in the Northern Department, from September 28th to October 18th, 1777, and again his name appears on a muster roll of six-months' men for pay, belonging to the town of Deerfield, Mass, agreeable to a resolution of court of October 5th, 1781 Time of marching July 29th, 1780. Time of discharge December 15th, 1780 Born in Braintree, he afterwards moved to Pembroke, Mass, then back to Braintree, in 1771 to Leicester, and soon after to Deering, where he died June, 1792 His wife died in Bennington, Vt, June 19th, 1814 Of their eleven children, Jacob Allen was the fourth, and their second son He was born in Braintree September 25th, 1757 Married, February 4th, 1781, Lydia, daughter of Captain Henry and Ruth (Wells) Stiles, of Whately, Mass He was a mason by trade "In personal appearance he was tall, fine looking, of dignified and commanding presence." He was a Revolutionary soldier, and in his latter days received a pension from the United States government   Soon after his marriage he removed to the eastern part of the State of New York, living first at New Canaan, Columbia county, afterwards at Hoosick, Rensselaer county, and finally at Kingsbury, Washington county   He died May 5th, 1828, his wife two or three years prior.   Henry Faxon was the second child and eldest son of their thirteen children   He was born January 1st, 1783, in Hoosick, married, March 20th, 1804, Annis (born 1779 in Bennington, Vt), daughter of David Dodge   She died August 10th, 1857, in Chester, Warren county, N Y   He died February 3d, 1829, in the same place.   He was a mason by trade   After his marriage he removed to Hoosick and thence to Troy, N Y, where he worked at his trade   He was licensed and ordained to preach by the First Baptist Church of Troy, and removed to Chester, Warren county, N Y, in 1820   In April, 1821, he became the pastor of the Baptist Church at Schroon, where he remained until April, 1827, then returned to Chester and was pastor of the Baptist Church in that place until his death

Charles Henry Faxon is the youngest in a family of five children of Henry and Annis Faxon   He was born in Troy, N Y, December 26th, 1816   His education was received in the district schools of Schroon and Chester and a private school for boys in the latter place, taught by Professor Josiah Beebe At the age of fifteen he became a clerk in the store of Ezra B Smith, where, with the exception of intervals of attendance at school, he remained until he was of age   On reaching his majority, in 1837, he became a partner in the store, the firm name being Smith & Faxon   This copartnership continued for two years and four months   In 1840 he formed a copartnership with Alexander Robertson, firm Robertson & Faxon, for the purpose of carrying on a store of general merchandising, which business was conducted by this firm until 1854, at which time Robertson withdrew, and the business was continued by Mr Faxon and his brother, Walter A Faxon, firm name C H Faxon & Bro, until 1861, when W A Faxon withdrew and was succeeded by Horace S Crittenden, under the firm name of C H Faxon & Co, and thus continued until the spring of 1865, when they sold out to Hall & Knapp   The business has been conducted in the same building by different parties to the present time (1885), the present proprietor being William H Remington   In 1849 the firm of Robertson & Faxon united with James Crandall in building the tannery at Chester, and tanning was carried on by them under the firm name of Robertson, Faxon & Co from 1849 to 1856, when Crandall withdrew and Milton Sawyer became a partner, under the firm name of Sawyer, Faxon & Co, a partnership which continued until 1860, when Faxon purchased Robertson's interest, and thereafter until 1865 the business was conducted under the firm name of Sawyer & Faxon   In order to supply their tannery with bark large tracts of timber lands were purchased from time to time, amounting in the aggregate to about 100,000 acres   The manufacture of lumber becomes almost a necessary adjunct to the tanning business   About 1850 the firm of Robertson & Faxon built a saw-mill on the Glens Falls Feeder, known as the " Feeder Mill," which was run by them until 1860, when a division was made between them, Faxon taking Robertson's interest in the Chester tannery, and Robertson Faxon's interest in the saw-mill   Ever since Mr Faxon became interested in the tanning business he has at the same time been largely interested in the manufacture and sale of lumber.   In 1865 Mr Faxon purchased from his partners their interests in all partnership properties, real and personal, and until 1882 he carried on the entire business in his own name   In 1882, July 1st, his son, William H Faxon, was admitted as a partner in the tanning business, firm C H Faxon & Son   The extent of the business may be gathered from the statement that an average of 400,000 pounds of sole leather per annum is produced at their works

In politics Mr Faxon has been a lifelong Democrat, and has been an active supporter of the principles of his party   He was its candidate for Member of the Assembly in 1862 and 1863   He was supervisor of his town in the Board of Supervisors in 1869 and 1870   In 1850 he was the contractor for building the plank road from Warrensburgh to Chester and has been president of the company since the death of Charles Fowler, who had filled the office from the time of its first organization   In 1848 he built the water works of Chester village, has owned and superintended the works ever since

Mr Faxon married, November 18th, 1844, Caroline Adelia, born February 4th, 1821, in Schroon, N Y , daughter of Ezra B and Laura (Barnes) Smith. She died November 10th, 1858   He married, April 25th, 1860, Sophia Smith, born March 2d, 1829, in Bolton, N Y , daughter of Howard and Laura (Putnam) Waters   Children are William Henry, born August 18th, 1846   Catharine Elizabeth, born July 6th, 1849, , died August 8th, 1859   Emma, born October 17th, 1863 , died March 16th, 1865, and Alice, born February 25th, 1866

DANIEL PECK —The subject of this sketch is a representative man, and descendant of one of the oldest families of the town   He is the son of Hermon and Martha (Kenworthy) Peck, and was born in the village of Glens Falls on the 25th of February, 1831   William Peck, the pioneer of the family in this country, was born in London, Eng , in 1601   With his wife Elizabeth, his then only son Jeremiah, he emigrated to this country in the ship *Hector*, arriving at Boston, 26th June, 1637, in the company of Gov Eaton, Rev John Davenport and others, and was one of the founders of the New Haven colony, in the spring of 1638   He was a merchant by occupation, a man of high standing in the colony, and a deacon of the church in New Haven from 1659 to 1694 when he died   His son, the Rev Jeremiah Peck, was the first teacher
39

of the Colony Collegiate School in New Haven, and afterwards settled|minister at Saybrook, Conn, in the fall of 1661, in Elizabethotwn, N J, in 1670, in Greenwich, Conn, in 1674, and in Waterbury, Conn in 1690, where he died in 1699 in his 77th year   His son Samuel settled in Greenwich, Conn, where all his children were born   His grandson Peter, son of Peter, one of nine sons, was the pioneer of the family in Queensbury   He was the oldest of six children, and was born in Greenwich, Conn, in January, 1746   The father dying in 1759, his mother with her little family removed to New Milford, Conn, where on the 7th of December, 1768, Peter married Sarah, daughter of Paul Terrill   He with his family removed to Queensbury in 1786, settled on the Ridge road about a mile from "the corners," where he remained until his decease, June 17th, 1813   According to the family tradition, the family were two weeks on the route , the boys trudging along afoot, driving two yokes of oxen attached to strong, rude wagons, loaded with household stuff, while the father rode on horseback   They brought along with them a large, powerful watch dog, which one night, soon after their arrival, was destroyed and eaten by wolves, troops of which then found their covert in the big Cedar Swamp At that time there were only three dwellings at Glens Falls, a foot path to the Ridge, and a rude wagon rode up Bay street as far as the log Quaker Church by the Half-way Brook   Peter Peck had three sons, all of whom were born in New Milford, Conn, viz Reuben, Daniel, and Edmund   Reuben, the eldest, was born 8th February, 1772, and married 1st, Tryphena Bishop, and 2d, Jane Haight   Hermon, his eldest child, was born 19th of April, 1800, and married 1st, Nancy Quin in 1825 , 2d, Martha Kenworthy in 1830   Seven children were the fruit of this union of whom Daniel is the eldest.   Hermon died at Glens Falls, 27th July, 1865

A few seasons at the district school, four terms at the Glens Falls Academy, and at the early age of thirteen, we find the subject of this sketch, with true Yankee grit and perseverance, at work on a farm, for small wages to be sure, in Sandgate, Vt   At the age of sixteen he went to Union Village, where for six months he was employed in the manufacture of tin-ware   He returned home, and was sent by his father to run and manage a saw-mill of four gates on the Sacandaga River, at what is now known as Conklinville, Saratoga Co, N Y. Here he remained for four years, during which time he had accumulated nearly a thousand dollars by overwork of the roughest kind   He th n returned to the paternal roof, and for a year or niore was employed as a clerk in his father's hardware store   At the end of that period, being little niore than twenty-one years of age, he bought out his father's store, enlarged the business, importing a portion of his stock from England directly, and with characteristic enterprise, built up a large and flourishing business   To this, as is seen above, was added the cares and responsibilities of a large post-office in 1856, which continued for four years   In 1860 Mr Peck disposed of his business to De

Long & Son, and in the latter part of the same year embarked with his cousin, Charles Peck, in a lumber, grain and feed trade for which a new store was erected by them   They were burnt out in the great conflagration of May, 1864, when Daniel alone suffered a loss of upwards of twenty thousand dollars

In less than a week, and while the charred ruins were yet smoking, he had bought out his partner, and established a street bazar for the sale of grain and lumber During the season he rebuilt the store, and continued in the trade for a year, when he formed a co-partnership with Mr Frank Byrne, to carry on the wholesale and jobbing grocery business on the north corner of Glen and Ridge streets   Bringing to this enterprise the same tact, energy and judgment which has characterized his efforts through life, the undertaking was attended with unprecedented success A new store, one of the finest in the place, was erected and completed the following season   Here for eight years was conducted the largest grocery establishment north of the cities, the sales of which soon reached half a million dollars annually   In 1874 this establishment was transferred to H F Peck (brother of Daniel) and C J De Long, and Mr Peck associated himself with Messrs Byrne, Keenan & Wing in developing a lime business at Smith's Basin, on the Northern Canal Two years later he sold his interest in this business to his partners and returned to the grocery house he had founded, forming, in the year 1882, with his brother, H F Peck, the firm of D Peck & Brother   In 1885 Walter M Peck, son of Daniel, was taken into the partnership and the firm style is now D. Peck & Co

Mr Peck has served a term as county treasurer , has been several times elected treasurer of the corporation of Glens Falls   He has also been chosen trustee of the village three or four times, and has served one year as president of the village   In these several positions he has fully met the anticipations of his fellow citizens   He is a man of great public spirit, liberality and energy, takes an active interest in all desirable public improvements and hence enjoys the general respect of the community

JOHN P BOWMAN was born in the year 1816 in the town of Clarendon, Rutland county, Vermont   His grandfather was one of three brothers who came to this country from England and settled near Lexington, Mass Soon after the War of the Revolution he moved to Vermont, where the father of the subject of this sketch was born   Mr Bowman's father was John Bowman, and his mother's maiden name was Lorinda Hart   He received limited educational advantages, but was well schooled in the practical ways of industry and thrift   In the spring after reaching the age of fifteen years he went to Rutland, where for four or five years he worked at the tanning and currying trade   At the end of that time he went to Hunter, Greene county, N Y , for the purpose of better learning the sole leather manufacturing business   He worked there for one season at eight dollars per month   He next found employment with Col B P Burhans at his tannery in the town of Saugerties, Ulster county, N Y Mr Bowman's habits of economy find illustration in the circumstance that while his wages for the first year at Saugerties were only twelve dollars a month, at the year's end one hundred and forty dollars were due him, he having drawn but four dollars during the whole year The acquaintance formed here between his employer and himself ripened into a firm friendship which continued through after years and until the death of Col Burhans

After remaining about four years at Saugerties Mr Bowman went to Warrensburgh, Warren county, N Y Col Burhans had formed a co-partnership with Gen T S Gray and they bought a sole leather tannery in that town Mr Bowman continued in their employment at Warrensburgh for some three years, when he moved to Cuttingsville, Rutland county, Vt Here he carried on the business of upper and sole leather tanning and currying and dealing in rough calf-skins, occupying for the purpose the tannery now operated by Huntoon & Son For a time he engaged in the manufacture and sale of boots and shoes in addition to his other business

In 1851 he was elected a member of the State Legislature and served as such with credit to himself and to the satisfaction of his constituents

In January, 1852, Mr Bowman having disposed of his business in Vermont, came to Stony Creek, Warren county, N Y , where he has since resided and carried on business At that time where the village of Creek Center now stands there was a small tannery, then uncompleted, a saw-mill and three houses. The surrounding country was an almost unbroken forest. Mr Bowman saw the advantage of the location for the prosecution of sole leather manufacturing and set himself with determination to conquer the difficulties of the situation and make the most of its advantages

He at once completed the tannery and put it in operation Hemlock bark was plenty and for years was delivered at the tannery for two dollars and two dollars and fifty cents a cord The nearest accessible railroad point was Saratoga Springs, thirty miles distant All the hides and leather were carried over this road by teams Mr Bowman pushed on his business with the greatest energy, working early and late, and giving his personal attention to the whole work in all its details The sole leather from Stony Creek Tannery soon came to have a reputation and none better was to be had in market The requirements of the growing business made necessary an increase of facilities The tannery was enlarged and improved by the erection of additional buildings in 1856, 1864, and again in 1867 It now has a capacity of forty thousand sides of leather per year

In 1857 Mr Bowman built a pleasant residence, which he still occupies. For years he has carried a large stock of bark usually from five to seven thousand cords When in full operation the number of men employed in the tannery is about twenty-five Mr Bowman has bought extensive tracts of land, covered largely with hemlock trees and now owns some eight or ten thousand acres He has cut and disposed of large quantities of hemlock and spruce logs

In addition to his residence, barns and carriage-house, he has a boarding house with accommodations for twenty persons and houses for sixteen families He has also a convenient office building and a storehouse at the railroad station The Adirondack Railroad now affords transportation facilities, its station being three miles from the tannery Much has been done in grading the grounds around the buildings and making such improvements as add both to appearance and convenience A noticeable feature of the premises with their surroundings is neatness and order Probably no tannery in the State excels this in clean and uniformly neat appearance

Mr Bowman has done his banking and general business at the village of Glens Falls, where he is widely known and greatly respected He is and for years has been a director in the Glens Falls National Bank For thirty-two years he has done all his hide and leather business with one house, the well-known one of Field, Converse & Co , of Boston, and its successor, Allen, Field & Lawrence All his business dealings have been characterized by promptness and strict integrity

Hard work, persistent attention to his own affairs and uncompromising honesty, added to an intelligent aptitude for business have made Mr Bowman's success in life well marked and deserved His upright, sterling character commands for him the entire confidence of all who know him Always averse to ostentatious display, he has accomplished many charitable and beneficent ends in a quiet way The remains of his grand-parents, parents and brother, are buried in the cemetery at East Clarendon, Vt Mr Bowman has erected a stately monument over the place of their interment and made the spot a pleasant one by tasteful improvements

In 1849 he married Jennie E Gates, daughter of Franklin Gates, of Warren, Herkimer county, N Y., and the youngest of seven sisters This marriage proved a wise and fortunate one Mr Bowman found in his wife a companion who excelled in every womanly virtue Possessed of rare judgment and the most estimable traits of character, she made the home over which she presided a model one Mr Bowman recognizes that a large measure of the success that has come to him is due to the faithful endeavors and wise counsel of her whom he chose for a life companion Her influence extended beyond the home circle and they are many who have been made better and happier by her example and kindly assistance She made a large number of friends and attached them to herself by the strongest ties In religious faith she was an Episcopalian and was a member of the society of that denomination at Glens Falls

There were born to Mr and Mrs Bowman two daughters, Addie, who died in early infancy, and Ella H , who lived until just reaching young womanhood Growing up as an only child, she naturally had the full affection of her parents She was of a more than usually sweet and affectionate disposition and naturally gentle and refined in manner. The fondness of her parents was reciprocated and she found her highest enjoyment in their company. Altogether this household was exceptionally happy in its membership and surroundings Mr Bowman's business kept him closely at home and his domestic tastes rendered him peculiarly appreciative of his pleasant home and family But these dearest associations were destined to be rudely broken

In June, 1879, the peace and joy of these parents gave way to the deepest grief when they were called upon to bid a final earthly farewell to their beloved daughter Ella In this trying hour of bereavement the Christian encouragement and faith of the wife and mother yielded strong support to the sorrowful husband and father This comfort was not long accorded him After a few short months and in January, 1880, the death of his faithful and devoted wife left Mr Bowman alone to bear what seemed an insupportable grief

The remains of wife and daughter were taken to Vermont for interment, and in the early summer following Mrs Bowman's death, Mr Bowman commenced at Cuttingsville, in his native county of Rutland, the building of a magnificent tribute to the memory of his loved ones He enlarged and beautified Laurel Glen Cemetery amd erected there a stately mausoleum The structure is of Vermont granite, the interior stone being the finest Rutland marble. The whole is characterized by solidity and elegance which unite to make it one of the grandest, as it is one of the costliest, tombs in existence

Near the tomb is an extensive green-house built and equipped in the most approved manner and liberally stocked with choice and rare plants

In plain view of the mausoleum Mr Bowman has erected a beautiful summer residence He has made walks, set out shade trees and otherwise embellished the grounds at and around the cemetery and his residence Thousands of people from neighboring and distant States have visited this spot, now made famous in monumental grandeur by the munificence of Mr. Bowman

COLONEL BENJAMIN PECK BURHANS — Colonel Burhans was born near Rensselaerville, Albany county, N Y , October 9th, 1798 His mother was Clarissa and his father John C Burhans, he being their eldest child He received an academical education at Litchfield, Conn , and soon after, at the age of sixteen, entered the store of Whittlesey & Co , general merchants, in Greene county, N Y A little later he was employed as clerk with Palen & Co , in the same county, extensive manufacturers of sole leather He soon became a partner in the firm, which continued until about the year 1831, when the firm was dissolved and Mr Burhans formed the firm of Burhans & Townsend, at Palenville, Ulster county, N Y

In 1824 he was married to Rebecca Wickes, whom he survived many years, they had six children, four of whom are living

In March, 1836, Colonel Burhans disposed of his property in Ulster county and came to Warrensburgh, Warren county, N Y Here he purchased the interest of Mr Quackenbush in the leather manufactory of Quackenbush & Gray, his partner being General Thomas S Gray, the firm style was Burhans & Gray In 1854 he transferred one third of his interest in this tannery to his son, Frederick O Burhans, and in 1860 they took General Gray's remaining interest and formed the firm of B P. Burhans & Son, which continued to the time of the former's death

Notwithstanding Colonel Burhans's aversion for the official honors which make the chief aspiration of many men and the ambition of many lives, he has a few times been forced out of his persisted-in adherence to a strictly private, business life He was at one time Colonel of the Third Regiment of Rifles N Y S M, in the days of its glory and efficiency. He was nominated for Member of Assembly in 1838, and although defeated with his party then, he was elected in 1842. He was also the Democratic nominee for Member of Congress in 1862 He was a lifelong Democrat, quietly but always and certainly acting with that party He was at the time of his death and for many years had been the president of the Glens Falls National Bank.

Strict attention to his extensive business — to a business of which he had made himself the master and with which he had from his youth been familiar — gave him an estate unusual to this region He was one of the wealthiest men in Northern New York, and every dollar of his fortune was his own by honorable right and legitimate acquisition No man has been made poor or unhappy by his gain In business life he made friends of all who had dealings with him Invariably pleasant, prompt and courteous, and especially so to his employees, many of whom have been in his employ for over thirty years A leading feature of Colonel Burhans's character was his complete mastery of himself Under any and all circumstances he was always cool, collected, reasonable Those who have known him in his own hospitable home — met him socially at his own fireside — have the largest appreciation of his large and generous heart, his genial sociability, his undemonstrative yet hearty manhood

He was public spirited, loved his adopted village and contributed to all desirable improvements The Episcopal "Church of the Holy Cross" at Warrensburgh, a beautiful edifice of stone, is largely indebted to his generous gifts for its erection and present maintenance He was elected senior warden at the formation of the parish in 1864, and was confirmed at the consecration of the church in 1866 "His works do follow him," and "being dead he yet speaketh "

At the time of his death he was, as stated, president of the Glens Falls National Bank, a position he had filled since the bank was founded, in 1851

The board of directors passed a series of eulogistic resolutions, from which the following is an extract —

Resolved, That the whole history of this bank has been intimately identified with the prudence, sagacity, inflexible integrity, financial ability and large business experience which its lamented chief officer has brought to the councils of its directors He was ever ready to give the weight of his influence and fortune, if necessary, to preserve the highest standard of reputation and credit for this corporation, and his active watchfulness over its interests for nearly twenty-five years slackened only with the physical ability to maintain it By personal endowment and dignity of manner he was eminently fitted to preside By his genial spirit, friendly disposition, courtesy and Christian graces he won and retained the affectionate regard and esteem of hosts of people of all classes, who will long mourn his departure from among them

Colonel Burhans died on the 16th day of July, 1875, his wife having died May 16th, 1863 The surviving children are as follows. Julia, married William B Isham, of New York, a leather dealer, and member of an old Ulster county family Frederick Osborne, who still carries on the business at Warrensburgh Sarah Hine Burhans, now living on the homestead, and Charles Hiram, living in Warrensburgh

Those of the children who are deceased were Mary P, who married General Samuel T Richards, and died in 1864 Clarissa Amelia, died in 1844

CAPTAIN M N DICKINSON —Myron Nelson Dickinson was born in the town of Bolton, Warren county, N Y, on the 14th day of August, 1829 His father, John Dickinson, came to Bolton with his parents from Duchess county when about six months old, in February, 1800 His mother, Lucy Winter, was born in Shutesbury, Mass, August 10th, 1795, and came with her parents to Bolton in 1802 M N Dickinson's grandfather, the pioneer, was also named John Dickinson, and bore arms in the Revolutionary War The name of his mother's father was Jesse Winter M N Dickinson's boyhood was passed in Bolton until he reached his twentieth year, his surroundings, circumstances and school advantages not differing materially from that of other young men of that period When twenty years old he visited Western New York, Pennsylvania and finally the State of Iowa The straitened circumstances of his parents left him without anticipation of any aid from them in beginning his career, he felt that he must depend solely upon his own powers and ambition for success in life While in Allegany county, N Y, and Bellefonte and Snow Shoe, Center county, Pa, he learned the millwright's trade, which he followed until the close of 1857 During this period (in 1854) he returned home from Pennsylvania, and in 1855 went to Maquoketa, Iowa, where he continued working at his trade. In the winter of 1855–56 he saw the necessity of a more thorough education in order to rise above his humble circumstances, and accordingly, although then twenty-six years of age, attended the State Normal School in Albany, N Y , a full term

In the year 1857 Mr Dickinson built the saw-mill at Warrensburgh, N Y , and during that fall and winter he selected his home in that place   The same fall he was elected to the office of school commissioner of Warren county, being the first candidate *elected* to that office, his predecessors having been appointed , that office he held until the close of 1860 when he engaged in mercantile business, and was appointed postmaster at Warrensburgh in the succeeding spring

Now came the sounds of oncoming war from the misguided South and Mr Dickinson was not the man to sit idly at home when his country needed strong arms for her defense   Resigning his position as postmaster in February, 1862, he enlisted in the 118th Regiment, whose gallant services are chronicled in these pages   His enlistment dated from July 16th, 1862, and he aided materially in recruiting Company G, to the second lieutenancy of which he was immediately appointed   On the 20th of January, 1863, he was promoted to first lieutenant of the company, and shared the campaigning of the regiment until December of that year, when he was detailed in the " department of negro affairs south of the James River," with headquarters at Norfolk, Va   He remained on duty there until October 17th, 1864   For a portion of this period he was ordered to Bermuda Hundreds by Captain O Brown, to take charge of quartermaster's stores and hospital transportation   He returned to his regiment October 17th, and on the 25th was placed in command of the Ninety-second Regiment, N Y V , which participated in the battle of Charles City Road, Va (near the Fair Oaks battle-field), on the 27th of October   In this engagement he received a canister shot an inch and a quarter in diameter and weighing a quarter of a pound, in his right shoulder , the shot was subsequently cut out near the spine   He was left on the field for dead, taken prisoner and confined in Libby Prison until February 21st, 1865, when he was paroled   Returning northward to Annapolis, Md , he was there declared exchanged and returned to his regiment in April following   For gallant and meritorious services he was brevetted captain

The war ended and Captain Dickinson resigned in May, 1865, and returned home to engage in the hardware business in Warrensburgh, the first establishment in this line in the place   He was reappointed postmaster January 26th, 1866, and retained the office until August 5th, 1885   In 1871 he retired from the hardware trade, and took up the book and stationery business, which he successfully conducted until November, 1881, when he formed a co-partnership with A H Thomas, under the firm name of A H Thomas & Co , which still continues   Mr Dickinson's life though not a long one, will be seen to have been a busy one   He has, moreover, always taken an active interest in politics, for which field he possesses excellent natural qualifications   These are

well understood and have been repeatedly recognized by his fellow citizens.
He has on several occasions represented the county in Senatorial, Congressional and State Conventions, and in the fall of 1885 was elected delegate to
the State Convention recently held in Saratoga He has frequently declined
the request of his party to represent the county in the Assembly of the State
and other positions of honor and trust in the county It need scarcely be said
that he is a Republican at all times and in all places In the various positions
he has held, as well as in his every day relations, he has shown a degree of ability and those manly and straightforward attitudes that have won him the respect
and esteem of all who know him He has, by industry, economy and abstemi-
ous habits acquired a limited competency and may look forward to many years
of usefulness He espouses every project that has a tendency to promote the
best interests of the town, giving material aid when necessary to success His
benevolence, though marked, is never ostentatious, while he dispenses with liberal hand of his means to alleviate the sufferings of the worthy poor, he re-
jects with firmness the supplications of the wandering beggar Captain Dickinson was married on the 1st of July, 1858, to Betsey Coolidge, of Bolton,
who is connected with the prominent Glens Falls families of that name They
have two living children — Lester Coolidge Dickinson, born August 25th,
1860, now editor and proprietor of the Warrensburgh *News,* and a graduate
of Union College, class of 1881, and Grace Cordelia Dickinson, born April
5th, 1870

JOSEPH HAVILAND, 2d — The father of the subject of this sketch was
also named Joseph Haviland, and was born in the town of Queensbury,
near the feeder dam, on the 12th day of September, 1793 He was married
to Lydia Sisson May 3d, 1814 She was a daughter of Nathaniel Sisson, who
was of New Bedford, Mass, and of English ancestry In the spring of 1826
he purchased his farm on Sanford Ridge, where he lived until his death,
November 26th, 1875 He was one of the most extensive and successful
farmers of the town, acquired ample means and invested largely in farming
lands near his home He was the father of three children, Daniel S, Joseph
and Lydia Ann His long life was one which reflected only the most honorable traits of character and deeds worthy of an honest man.

The original ancestors of the Havilands were from France, the name in
that country being De Havery The earliest records are of three brothers,
who emigrated from France to England, having previously agreed that the
first one of the three who discovered land from the vessel should exclaim
"Haviland," which afterwards became the family name The ancestors of
Joseph Haviland, 2d, are traced backward as follows —

Roger Haviland, father of Joseph, 1st, and grandfather of the subject of
this notice, was a son of Benjamin Haviland, 3d The latter was born in 1698

JOSEPH HAVILAND.

and died in 1757 at the age of fifty-nine years   He was the first of the name
to settle in this section, and had four sons, David, Solomon, Joseph and
Roger.   They were all Quakers of the orthodox faith, and have been among
the foremost and most numerous of that denomination in the town of Queensbury

Benjamin Haviland, 3d, was born in 1698 and died in 1757 at the age
of fifty-nine years ; his wife was Charlotte Parks, and they had thirteen children, seven sons and six daughters, as follows Benjamin, Roger, Thomas,
Daniel, Solomon, Isaac, John, Sophia, Charlotte, Althea, Sarah, Abigail and
Mary

Benjamin Haviland, 2d, was born in 1654 and died in 1724, aged seventy
years   He had three sons, Benjamin 3d, John and Isaac

Benjamin Haviland, 1st, was born in 1623, and emigrated from England in
1647   His wife, Abigail, gave birth to five children, as follows Benjamin 2d,
Adam, Abigail, Bathia and John   They settled in Flushing, Long Island

Benjamin Haviland, father of Benjamin 1st, was a son of John Haviland,
mayor of Bristol, England, and married Mary Knightly   His father was
Christopher De Haviland, who married a daughter of John Mason, esq   His
father was James De Haviland, esq , who married a daughter of King Edward
the IV   His father was Thomas De Haviland, who was distinguished at the
recovery of Mount Orgal, Jersey

The grandfather of the subject of this notice married Hannah Wing, daughter of Edward Wing, who was a son of Daniel J , and born July 10th, 1687 ,
he died in Glens Falls at an advanced age , his occupation was that of saddler
and harnessmaker   Daniel Wing, jr , was son of Daniel 1st, and was born
November 28th, 1664, died in March, 1790   Daniel, 1st, was the oldest son
of John and Deborah (Batchelder) Wing, of Sandwich, Mass , and came with
his father from England early in 1600   The late Abraham Wing, of Glens
Falls, and Daniel Wing, of Fort Edward (father of Halsey R Wing, of Glens
Falls, all now deceased), were sons of Abraham and grandsons of Abraham 1st,
who came to Glens Falls from Duchess county , the latter was a brother of
Edward, father of Hannah, as above stated   This shows the connection of
Joseph Haviland's grandmother, and consequently of himself, with Abraham
Wing, the pioneer of the Queensbury patent

Joseph Haviland, 2d, was born October 25th, 1826, on Sanford Ridge,
about three miles north from Glens Falls   His education was confined to what
he could by diligence acquire at the common school and the Glens Falls
Academy   His school days ended when he was about twenty-one years old,
his last instructor having been Leroy R Satterlee   He immediately engaged
in farming, which has constituted the greater part of his life work   He was
married on the 5th of February, 1849, to Eliza Staples, of Pawlet, Vermont,
and left the homestead to occupy a farm about a mile from where he was born,

and known as the Harvey farm Eliza Staples was the daughter of Jonathan and Sylvia Staples (the latter a daughter of Stephen Rogers), who were noted for their energy and success as managers of a large dairy in the State of Vermont Mr Haviland was on this farm until 1859, when he purchased the farm that he now owns and occupies, known as the Reuben Newman farm from the fact that it was deeded to Israel Newman, father of Reuben, in 1799 Mr Haviland's title came through Daniel Newman, son of Reuben As we have intimated, the whole of Mr Haviland's life has been given up to agriculture, in which occupation he has reached the most unqualified success

He is now the owner of three hundred and eighty-five acres of land in three valuable farms, including the old homestead of his father He has made something of a specialty of breeding and raising superior blooded stock, and is at present giving much of his attention to Holstein cattle He has held all of the offices in the Warren County Agricultural Society and was president for three years In his daily walk he has gained the good will and esteem of his fellow-townsmen

Mr and Mrs Haviland have four children, namely, Willis J , born January 1st, 1852 , Merritt E , born April 11th, 1855 ; and two daughters, twins, Elma S and Emma L , born April 21st, 1858 The latter was married February 26th, 1885, to J Corwin Jacks, of Batavia, N Y Willis J Haviland now lives on what is known as the Sanford farm, on Sanford Ridge, which was one of the earliest settled farms in the town He married Belle Andrews, whose mother was Sarah Jane Wing, daughter of Richard Wing, a cousin of Halsey R Wing, on the 22d of February, 1876 , they have two children, J Bernard and Wing Harrold Mr Haviland is one of the successful farmers of the town. The second son, Merritt E , is a graduate of Cornell University (June, 1877), studied law with Brown & Sheldon, and entered the Columbia Law School in September, 1878 , left it in May, 1879, and was admitted to the bar in May, 1879, as attorney and counselor He is now in practice in New York city

A BRAHAM WING —The subject of this sketch was the youngest of seven children, and was born in Glens Falls on the 17th of August, 1791 His mother, Polly McKie, was nearly related to the family of that name in the eastern part of Washington county His father, Abram, was the youngest son of Abraham Wing, the pioneer, a sketch of whose career is given elsewhere The settlement, which in the slow progress of years has expanded to the proportions of a large and populous village, was originally known by the name of Wing's Falls, a name which has a better claim to our speech than the one it bears

With such scant facilities as the sparsely settled country then afforded, Mr Wing succeeded in acquiring the elements of a sound business education, which served him through a long and busy life in the management of a vast

Abraham Wing.

and complicated business, and the widely extended relations of a large and continually increasing estate

Among his first ventures was a co-partnership with the late Josiah L Arms, in the mercantile business at Emerson's Corners in the town of Wilton, Saratoga county, New York   He was afterwards, at various times and for a series of years, associated in different business enterprises with the leading men of the place , such names as Walter Geer, jr , George Sanford, William McDonald, and others gone before, but whose thrift, enterprise, and energy have left their impress upon our local affairs and contributed largely to the growth and prosperity of our village   With the opening up of the Northern Canal, and the construction of the Glens Falls Feeder, a rare opportunity presented for utilizing the resources of the neighborhood and county   Mr Wing had the forecast and judgment requisite for improving the golden chance, by bringing to market the splendid pines with which the great Brant Lake tract abounded   This rich and extensive lumber region, previously operated by the Fox Brothers, Alanson and Norman, had come into possession of parties in Troy, who, in casting about for some one to manage the business, were referred to Mr Wing as the most suitable and competent person in all this region for the undertaking   To his sagacity and clear sighted judgment do we owe the present system of river-driving and booming which annually replenishes our mills, furnishes employment to a vast array of labor, and which has substantially helped in building up our village to its present urban proportions   When he first took hold of the Brant Lake property, the cry here was that the lumbering business was finished

The plains of Queensbury, to the foot of the West Mountain, had been stripped and denuded of the towering white and majestic yellow pines which once stretched their massive boles in rich profusion from the Pitcher Place to the Round Pond of the Oneida   The magnificent water power of our falls was looked upon as next to worthless, and certainly not warranting the outlay required in the erection of such costly mills as now adorn our water front   No one dreamed that the forest of the far northern wilderness would ever become tributary to our industries   No sooner, however, had Mr Wing taken hold of this enterprise, than a new impulse was given to the whole lumber business of the Hudson River and its affluents   The obstructions in the outlet of Brant Lake were removed, a dam and sluice way were constructed and a new field of labor was inaugurated   The novel sight was witnessed of sluicing and driving the pine logs of that wilderness region, and its wealth has been poured down the breast of the majestic Hudson, building up colossal fortunes and giving impetus and vitality to a thousand ceaseless industries   From a trusted business agent Mr Wing speedily became a partner, and ultimately sole proprietor of this and other large lumber interests   About the year 1853 he disposed of his business and retired from the more active pursuits of life   He was then accounted one of the wealthiest men in the vicinity   From that period up to the date of his decease his time was principally devoted to the management of his large estate.

Mr Wing was a life long Democrat, an earnest and energetic politician   In the days of his active manhood he exerted a controlling influence in his party, both in town and county, and although no office-seeker himself, those who were, generally took the precaution to insure his kind offices and powerful influence in order to achieve their aims

Like most self-made men, Mr Wing's character had its rugged sides and salient points   He was a strong, earnest, untiring friend, a bitter, uncompromising and unyielding opponent, opinionated, self-reliant, and self-willed. Public spirited and liberal, every church in the village received his benefaction, every public enterprise his handsome contribution   At the outbreak of the Rebellion he was among the heaviest subscribers to the relief fund for the benefit of the wives and children of the soldiers, and contributed all along in various ways towards the raising of recruits and bounties, in order that his native town might maintain its credit in the great struggle for the preservation of the Union.   He was married three times   His first wife was Abigail Barnard, of Townsend, Vt   His second was Angeline B (Vail) widow of Alexander Robertson, of New York   His third Mrs Francis A. Glass (*nee* Bowman). He had no issue except by his first wife   Two children only reached adult age, both daughters and both married   He was for years subject to painful and frequently occurring attacks of illness, resisted by a powerful and well preserved constitution, until at last, like a strongly rooted oak, exposed to the the storms of years, he fell, and the places which knew him on earth shall know him no more   He died at his own house on the morning of the 13th of June, 1873   His deeds of generosity and kindness have embalmed his name in the memory of many still living, and in the hard and trying winter of 1874 there are poor, and destitute, and suffering families, who will miss the kind charities of Abraham Wing

———

HALSEY ROGERS WING [1] — The subject of this sketch was the oldest son of Daniel W and Rhoda A (Stewart) Wing, and was born in a building occupying a part of the site of the Middleworth House, at Sandy Hill, N Y, then one of the most flourishing villages between Albany and Montreal. His father was, at the date named and for some years subsequently, an innkeeper in a building (since burned) known as the Eagle Hotel   In 1814 he removed to the lower part of the village of Fort Edward, where he resided for a number of years   Here Halsey had the benefit of the local schools, and the experience acquired by rendering such assistance as he was able in the management of his father's business   His aptitude for study and persevering application to his

1 From Dr HOLDEN's *History of Queensbury*, p. 66

books, undoubtedly determined the direction of his career, and the choice of a profession. At the age of sixteen he was sent to the celebrated academy at Lenox, Mass After three years of a thorough academic course under the supervision of Professor Hotchkiss, its very able principal, he went first to Yale, and subsequently to Middlebury College, Vt, where he entered the sophomore class, graduated in course and took his baccalaureate degree on the 15th of August, 1832 He had probably already commenced the study of the law, for his license shows that he was admitted to the bar as an attorney in October, 1834 His legal studies was pursued in the office of the eminent jurisconsult, the Hon Samuel Cheever In the interim of student life he served for a brief period as assistant district attorney of Albany county

Soon after his admission to the bar he was awarded a gold medal by the Young Men's Association of Albany, for an essay of distinguished merit (afterwards printed) which was read before that body The following are the inscriptions copied from the medal, now in possession of the family —

<table>
<tr><td>OBVERSE</td><td>REVERSE</td></tr>
<tr><td>The Huygen's Premium,</td><td>For the</td></tr>
<tr><td>Awarded,</td><td>Best Essay on</td></tr>
<tr><td>Nov 1st, 1834,</td><td>the influence of the</td></tr>
<tr><td>by</td><td>Study of the Physical and</td></tr>
<tr><td>The Young Men's</td><td>Mathematical Sciences</td></tr>
<tr><td>Association for Mutual Improvement,</td><td>On the Character of Man</td></tr>
<tr><td>In the City of Albany,</td><td>and the usefulness and application</td></tr>
<tr><td>To Halsey R Wing</td><td>of these sciences to the</td></tr>
<tr><td></td><td>Common purposes</td></tr>
<tr><td></td><td>of life</td></tr>
</table>

In December following his name was inscribed upon the rolls as solicitor in chancery, and about the same time he removed to Brockport, Monroe county, where he opened a law office, with E B Holmes as partner He remained but a short time at this place, but removing to the larger and more prosperous village of Buffalo, whose coming greatness and importance were already casting shadows before, he formed a new partnership with Judge Frederick F Stevens Here, with the dawn before him of a lucrative practice and a widespread popularity among the laboring classes, we find him fairly launched upon the swift current of life

On the 31st of August, 1835, he was married with Harriet N , daughter of General E P Walton, and sister of the Hon E P Walton, of Montpelier, Vt, who has lately represented that district for two consecutive terms in Congress Of this union, it is not improper to say that it has been one of the most perfect accord and harmony The chivalric and devoted respect with which he always regarded the gentler sex, found an apotheosis in his wife, whom he reverenced and loved with a devotion which few have equaled, and none excelled Through all his life he seems to have made it a special study to spare those he loved from all care, trouble, anxiety or apprehension

He came to Glens Falls in 1841, in which year he was admitted as counselor at law, and the following year, as solicitor in the United States Courts and counselor in chancery   He became, from the first, prominently identified with the interests of the Democratic party, of which he has been a lifelong and unvarying supporter   In the fall of 1843 he was appointed, by the Board of Supervisors, to the position of county superintendent of common schools   In 1845 he became the first judge of the county, having previously been elected to the office of justice of the peace and inspector of common schools   In all these multiplied relations he invariably fulfilled the trusts and discharged the duties belonging to them with fidelity and conscientious thoroughness   His legal practice, built up in the face of a sharp and eager competition, was always respectable and remunerative, and that he did not descend to do the dirty work of a venal bar, will be no reproach to his memory in the estimation of those whose opinions are worth the having

In 1851 one of those rare opportunities presented, which now and then prove the turning point in a man's fortunes   He was offered a partnership in an already established business, and the celebrated Jointa Lime Company was formed, consisting of himself and Mr John Keenan, to whose indefatigable industry and shrewd management this company is largely indebted for its success   In 1852 Mr Abraham Wing sold out his large lumbering interest, together with the saw-mill near the dam on this side of the river to Halsey R Wing, and his brother-in-law, Lansing G Taylor   After Mr Taylor's death (which occurred in 1856), and the settlement of the estate, Mr Wing became sole proprietor of the lumbering business and the mills connected with it   After assuming these varied business cares and responsibilities, Mr Wing gradually withdrew from the practice of law, throwing his legal business into the hands of Isaac J Davis, esq , with whom he formed a law partnership in 1854, and who has since made his mark in the legal world as a sharp, astute counselor, and a brilliant and successful advocate

Later on, Mr Wing became one of the firm known as The Glen's Falls Company, and of another called The Glen's Falls Transportation Company, in both of which large financial and industrial interests were represented, and whose extended operations have proved eminently successful and remunerative   He was also a stockholder and director in the Glen's Falls National Bank, and the Glen's Falls Insurance Company   In all public matters, connected with education or morality, Mr Wing was an earnest and zealous worker   He was a regular attendant upon the ministrations of the Presbyterian Church, and acted as one of its trustees at a moment of peculiar embarrassment and difficulty   He was an ardent and faithful laborer in the field of temperance, formerly a worthy patriarch of the old Glen Division, one of the charter members of Billy J Clark Division, and a contributor to its exchequer

Mr Wing was a ready promoter and advocate of the interests of education, contributing to its maintenance, and encouraging its elevation and advancement

At the time of his decease, he was one of the trustees of the Glens Falls Academy   He was also elected president of the Young Men's Association at its organization and served it faithfully in that capacity, until his term of office expired, giving the embryo organization much of his valuable time, with the hope and aim of giving it permanence and stability

He always manifested the greatest respect for the observance and ceremonials of religion, tenderly regardful of the feelings of others, and, although he made no verbal professions of piety, his was that broader catholicity of doctrine and example, which holds to the belief in

> "The Gospel of the Golden Rule,
> The New Commandment given to men,
> Thinking the deed, and not the creed,
> Would help us in our utmost need "

With the outbreak of the Rebellion, Mr Wing immediately became identified with the war movement, earnestly and faithfully laboring to further the interests of the Union   He was an ardent Democrat, zealous in the interests of that party, but his devotion to his whole country and its constitution as he believed it should be interpreted, cannot be justly questioned

Mr Wing was a public spirited man, and a hard, efficient worker   To his energetic labors we owe many of our public improvements, and the development of our industrial resources, of which we have no further space to speak

His last appearance in public was on the occasion of a great public festival given at the Cosgrove Opera House, for the benefit of the poor.   He was emphatically a friend to the friendless, and few appeals for help were ever turned unanswered away

His professions were sincere, his friendships enduring, and in his possession was as kind a heart and a soul full of tender emotion, as ever animated a human being   Surrounded abundantly by the comforts and luxuries of life, and the tender, assiduous care of kind and affectionate friends, he passed peacefully to his final rest on the morning of Wednesday, the 26th of January, 1870   His widow still survives him

---

J L DIX — The subject of this sketch was born in Saratoga county, town of Moreau, September 19th, 1816   His father was Samuel Dix, an early settler, who came from Wilmington, Vt   His other children were Samuel B and Harriet   Samuel Dix died in Glens Falls, in 1857, after a long life of usefulness; his principal occupation having been lumbering

J L Dix lived in Moreau until he was five years old, when his father's family crossed the river to Glens Falls   He acquired his education in the common schools and the old Ridge Street Academy   In 1835, when he was nineteen years old, he was employed as clerk in the post-office under Jabez Briggs's administration   Here he continued three years, and then acted as clerk in the stores of Mead & Sanford and Dwight Hitchcock for about six months   Fol-

40

lowing this he spent about fourteen months in various occupations in the States of Illinois, Missouri, and Ohio   Returning to Glens Falls in ill health he remained idle about a year and a half, after which he engaged with Julius H Rice, taking charge of his general business for two years   He then formed a copartnership with H A Hopkins, George Foster and Byron Rice, under the style of Hopkins, Dix & Co , in the manufacture of the well-known " black marble," as it is termed   This firm continued about three years and operated a store at South Glens Falls in connection with their manufacturing business In 1846 he joined Thomas Reynolds in large contracting operations, on the plank road, railroads and canals, at the same time continuing the store with Mr Hopkins   About the year 1848 this store was removed to Glens Falls, and Dix and Hopkins purchased the foundry and machine shop under the hill, of James Wells   In the operation of this establishment Mr Dix has been prominently interested ever since, the firm at the present time being J L & S B Dix, brothers   The contracting business with Mr Reynolds was continued to 1854, and for the past twelve years Mr Dix and Mr Reynolds have carried on the marble business   Since Mr Dix assumed an interest in the foundry it has grown from a small affair to very large proportions   A new building of brick was erected for the foundry in 1855, and other additions have been made, steam power put in, etc

This is the business record of a busy life, and it has been one which has brought with it an enviable reputation for industry, energy and integrity, resulting in the acquirement of a competence from a beginning without means

Mr Dix is a Democrat in politics, but has never sought to make his creed or action a stepping-stone to office   He held the office of deputy sheriff in Moreau for three years   In 1866 he erected his handsome brick residence where he is surrounded by all the comforts of life   He has, during his entire life since reaching manhood, engaged considerably in the purchase and sale of real estate   He was married in 1856 to Laura Stevens, daughter of Lewis Stevens, of Moreau   Their children are, Walter L , married Julia Whedon and lives in Glens Falls , Anna, wife of Dr H W Coffin, of Glens Falls , John A , and Charles, who live with their parents

FRANCIS LE ROY CHAPIN, M D — The subject of this sketch is a son of Joel Chapin and Honor Frances Buckley, and was born in Oxford, Chenango county, on the 30th day of May, 1824   His father was born in Bainbridge, Chenango county, and subsequently followed the business of cabinetmaking in Oxford until the latter years of his life and died at Saratoga   The grandfather of F L R Chapin was also named Joel and served as a surgeon in the Revolutionary army, for which he afterwards received a section of land in Bainbridge, Chenango county   Later he became a Presbyterian minister of that place, and died there

F. L. R. CHAPIN, M. D.

From the age of twelve years he supported and educated himself and on arriving at a proper age he entered the Oxford Academy, then one of the foremost institutions of learning in the State Here his naturally active mind enabled him to advance rapidly, and in 1845 he graduated fully prepared to enter college Choosing Union College for his further studies, he entered that institution soon after leaving the academy, in the junior class Four terms only enabled him to graduate with honor He had already settled upon the medical profession as the field for his life work and at once began his studies in the Albany Medical College From this institution he graduated with his diploma in 1851 Remaining idle for a short time at Saratoga Springs, he began practice in Albany, associating himself for about a year with Dr Robert Lay

In 1853 he was was appointed demonstrator of anatomy in the Albany Medical College; a high compliment to the position he had attained in the esteem of the faculty He continued in successful practice until the outbreak of the war, when he was appointed surgeon of the Thirtieth Regiment N Y S Volunteers, one of the organizations that went out under the call for seventy-five thousand troops for two years This regiment saw hard service as a part of the famous " Iron Brigade," and Dr Chapin remained with it, sharing in its hardships until it was mustered out of service Here his success in practice was almost wonderful, for the first five months of the term there were no deaths in the organization, though there was an unusual amount of sickness, and there were but twelve deaths in the regiment during its term of service outside of battle, and seven of these were purely accidental

Returning to Albany, he remained but a short time, when he became one of a number of volunteer surgeons under a call sent out after the battle of Cold Harbor After a few months' service in this capacity he returned again to Albany and resumed his practice He was soon given charge of a ward in the Soldiers' Home in that city where his already extended practice in surgery was still further contributed to His practice continued in Albany until 1866, when he removed to Glens Falls and was associated one year with Dr James Ferguson, since which time he has continued alone

This constitutes a mere outline of Dr Chapin's life work thus far His excellent natural qualifications for his profession and his thorough education therein have made him a successful practitioner, while his genial social characteristics and sterling goodness of heart and sound common sense have contributed to his general popularity in the communities where he has resided He was elected president of the Warren County Medical Society in the year 1868, and read an able address before that body He was president in 1871 of the Union Medical Association of the counties of Saratoga, Washington and Warren, and delegate from the Warren County Society to the Medical Society of the State of New York, of which body he was elected a permanent member

He was president of the Alumni Association of the Albany Medical College in 1881, and read an address before that body

Dr Chapin has held no political office nor has he any ambition in that direction, or for any public station, his chief desire having been to win and merit the approbation of his fellow practitioners, and the esteem and confidence of his patients   In this he has succeeded to a gratifying degree

He was married first, in 1853, to Lurinda Dodge, daughter of Amos Dodge, of Owego   She died in 185–, and he was married to Matilda Rockfeller, of Albany, daughter of William T Rockfeller, in July, 1863   He has a daughter Lula, by his first wife   A son by his second wife died in infancy   They now have an adopted daughter, Carrie W Chapin, who lives at their home

GEORGE BROWN — One of the earliest permanent settlers on the Queensbury patent was Benedick Brown, who probably arrived there as early as 1772, as his name appears in the ancient records as overseer of the poor for 1773 One of his sons was Valentine Brown, who had a son Richard   Valentine settled at the outlet of what is now called Glen Lake (formerly known as Valentine's Pond), and Richard Brown located about one and a half miles from the site of the Half-way House, which is on the road from Glens Falls to Lake George Richard Brown's children were George (the eldest and the subject of this sketch), Clark J , Daniel V , and Stewart   His wife was Sarah Vaughan, of Washington county, a descendant of one of the Rhode Island pioneers   Descendants of this family are very numerous in Northern New York

George Brown was born on the paternal homestead, September 3d, 1815 His younger days until he was twelve years of age were passed at home and most of the time in attendance at the district schools   When he reached the age of twelve his father died   The family were very poor and the boy, being the eldest son found the burdens of caring for his younger brothers and widowed mother upon his shoulders   But he proved himself equal to the task, and heroically assumed it   He began working out by the month at whatever he found that would pay him best, devoting his earnings to bettering the situation of the family   He continued this course until he reached the age of nineteen, when he returned to the family homestead and assumed the charge of the farm   Here he remained until the year 1846, when he found his proper vocation in catering to the public as a landlord   He began first in a small building that stood opposite the Half-way House, where he remained three years, meanwhile building the famous old hostelry on the opposite side of the road   From the day Mr Brown entered this hotel, situated as it was about midway on the long popular thoroughfare from the outer world to the famed lake and surroundings, he gave it a reputation for comfort and hospitality that was recognized by all who ever had occasion to enter its doors   This popularity continued unabated while Mr Brown remained at the head of the house, a period of nearly forty years, and only waned after the building of the railroad diminished the highway travel

Mr Brown's business operations were not confined to keeping the hotel, for he was the founder of the hamlet of French Mountain, and erected nearly all the buildings Among these was a store where he carried on a general trade until his removal from the place, this business was started in 1849 He also carried on a tin-shop in connection with this store He built a saw-mill in 1852 which he operated until 1876, and erected a tannery in 1867 and ran it until 1874, in partnership with James T Crandell He built seven or eight dwellings also, and during the period named carried on the homestead farm He was postmaster at French Mountain from 1850 to 1880, and, in short, was almost the proprietor of the entire settlement With the necessary decline of business here incident upon the building of the railroad, Mr Brown sold out his entire possessions, except thirty acres or farming land, and removed to Caldwell in March, 1884, where he assumed charge of the Central Hotel, which he had owned since 1880, it having, between those two dates, been in charge of his son, Clark J. Brown, the latter died in March, 1884 This house Mr Brown has rendered very popular among hundreds of his old guests and many new ones

Mr Brown has been a Democrat in politics until about ten years ago, when he espoused the principles of the Greenback organization He held the office of town assessor three successive years, and was pathmaster of his district for twenty successive years In 1856 he was nominated for the Assembly, but defeated, as he expected to be, by the combined vote of the Republican and Know Nothing parties. In 1882 he was nominated on the Greenback ticket for sheriff

Although now seventy years old, Mr Brown is active and energetic to an astonishing degree, and superintends his business with all the enthusiasm and success of his earlier years and enjoys the respect and esteem of his fellow townsmen

Mr Brown was married in 1843 to Silvia Odell, who was born November 22d, 1824, and is descended from one of the pioneer families, a daughter of Benjamin Odell Their children have been as follows Valentine, the eldest, born March 26th, 1845, died in February, 1875 Sarah Jane, born July 30th, 1847, is the wife of James T Crandell, of Caldwell Benjamin O, born November 26th, 1849, died November 11th, 1883. Clark J, born March 23d, 1854, died March 14th, 1884. Mary Ann, born January 2d, 1856; is the wife of A P Scovill, of the town of Queensbury. Kate, born January 25th, 1859, is the wife of William D Buckbee, of Queensbury Stewart D, born January 5th, 1861, now lives with his parents in Caldwell; married Ida Worden, daughter of Isaac Worden Virginia, born July 18th, 1866, died November 12th, 1874

MERRITT AMES —One of the early settlers of Poultney, Vt, was Elijah
Ames, one of the sons of whom was Oramel Ames, who was born July
22d, 1800, and died June 2d, 1870   His wife was Maria Spaulding, of Middletown, Vt   Their children were Merritt, the eldest and the subject of this
sketch, Eliza, Morris, Ellen, Milo and Mary   Oramel Ames was a farmer, but
also learned the shoemaker's trade and was a competent veterinary surgeon

Merritt Ames was born in Poultney, Vt , December 22d, 1825   His boyhood passed in laudable and successful efforts to obtain a good English education in the Vermont common schools, combined with considerable hard work
at home between terms   This continued until he reached his majority, during
which period he had lived with his parents in Poultney, East Dorset, Granville
and Middletown, and acquired a far better education than was common among
his associates who enjoyed only similar facilities

In the year 1846, when he was twenty-one years old, the young man left
home came to Glens Falls and began an apprenticeship as a moulder with
James Wells   Here he remained two years, in which time he became profi-
cient in his chosen occupation   He next went to Fort Edward, where he
worked at his trade in all about five years, separated at intervals with shorter
periods of labor in Philadelphia, Troy and Whitehall   His entire period of
work at his trade extended over about ten years, at the end of which he returned to Glens Falls richer in experience than in money

Mr Ames is a man not only of good natural qualifications, but of broad
views, extensive reading and careful thought , he is moreover a natural orator
of more than ordinary ability   To these characteristics may undoubtedly be
credited the impulse which led to his next occupation   Beginning in 1846
he went on the road with an entertainment embracing at different periods a
series of paintings delineating scenes in the arctic explorations of Dr Kent
Kane and those in Africa by Dr Livingstone, Bible and astronomical scenes,
etc   These were accompanied by appropriate explanatory and descriptive lectures prepared by Mr. Ames himself   This entertainment was an unqualified
success, its popularity, without a doubt, arising more from the interesting character of the lectures and from the energy and business ability infused into the
enterprise by the proprietor than from any other feature   This occupation
was followed for ten years, during which period several States were traveled
over, reaching as far west as Chicago, in the churches of which city the lectures
were last given

Returning permanently to Glens Falls in 1866 Mr Ames entered upon an
entirely new field of labor   He began the work of refining photographer's
residues (silver waste, etc) and manufacturing nitrate of silver and chloride of
gold, for the use of photographers, dry plate manufacturers and wholesale druggists   Under his skillful and energetic management this business has been
developed to splendid proportions   The sale of the manufactured products

M. Ames.

and the refining of residues has extended from the provinces to the Gulf of Mexico and into more than twenty-five States   Men are employed on the road and in the work at home two assistant chemists are engaged in the practical part of the business   The building up of such an establishment in a small inland location leads one to question how it has been accomplished   To this Mr Ames replies, " I have never sought to cheapen my products nor to undersell others   My success is directly traceable to promptness in return of refined goods, and the quality and quantity of the same "   So potent have been these principles that he has become a larger refiner of photographers' residues and manufacturer of nitrate of silver and chloride of gold than any other single person, and he has been honored with refining the waste from five of the photographic departments of the United States government   This success in such a work needs no comment, it merely shows what has been accomplished by energy, perseverance, and integrity   In these years Mr Ames has gained the highest good will and esteem of all his fellow citizens

He was baptized into the first Baptist Church of Middletown, Vt, on the 5th of March, 1843, and has ever since been a zealous and faithful member of that sect   His earnest and consistent church work and his thorough knowledge of the Bible have given him much prominence in the church as a teacher and occasionally as a preacher   He has for the past twelve years taught an adult Bible class in which are many leading church members

Mr Ames was married in 1847 to Celia Gould, daughter of George Gould, of Albany, a union that has brought nothing but peace and contentment with it   Their children are Adelbert M, born April 26th, 1848, died in infancy   Emma M, born December 29th, 1851, married W W Buckingham and lives in Brooklyn   Lina V, married William E Baldwin, of Saratoga, who is now associated with Mr Ames in the chemical works

LEONARD GANSEVOORT McDONALD was born in the town of Queensbury, Warren county, N Y, in 1821, and is now a citizen of Glens Falls, in said town, and has one of the finest and most desirable residences in that place, which he built and finished in 1869, and has occupied ever since

He received a liberal education in the common schools and academies, and in 1844 engaged in the mercantile business in company with his brother, William H, in which he continued until 1849, when he went to California, and after his return became one of the largest manufacturers of the celebrated Glens Falls lime, in which business he continued for about twenty years, and its introduction and general use is largely due to his personal effort and perseverance

He is one of the prominent men in Warren county, and is well-known throughout the State as one of the leading men in his devotion to, and earnest advocacy by his writings, and otherwise, of the financial and main principles of the so-called Greenback party, having been twice nominated and placed upon the State ticket of that party

His father, William McDonald, came into this town from New Milford, Conn , where he was born in 1792, when but eight years of age, and resided here about seventy years   He was installed a Mason in 1805 by Dewitt Clinton and others, and in 1821 was elected a member of the Legislature in this State, and was twice afterwards elected to the same position   To him, and his personal effort, more than to any other man in Warren county, is due the success and prosperity of the village of Glens Falls   As Governor Dewitt Clinton is said to be the father of the Erie Canal, equally, if not more so, was William McDonald the father of the Glens Falls Feeder Canal, for by his own effort, while a member of the Legislature, he procured the passage of a bill, and a survey was ordered and made, which he personally attended and assisted, to change the location which had been previously made for the building of the Feeder Canal, from the river at Sandy Hill to the river about two miles west of the village of Glens Falls, and from there to the summit level of the Champlain Canal, and from that time the growth and future prosperity of Glens Falls became firmly established and assured

Doctor Charles McDonald, the father of William McDonald, and the grandfather of Leonard G , was a physician of considerable eminence, who emigrated from Scotland during the old French war, and as a surgeon served in the American army during the Revolutionary struggle   After the war ended he resumed the practice of his profession at New Rochelle, Westchester county, N Y , where he died at the age of eighty-five years, and his son William McDonald died at Glens Falls in the year 1870 at the age of eighty-six and a half years, leaving eight children, the oldest, Mrs Jane Maria Clark, wife of Dr E G Clark, of Sandy Hill , Richard D , Leonard G , William H , Walter, Mrs Julia A Arms, wife of Lewis L Arms, of Glens Falls , Mrs Helen Cool, wife of Alvin F Cool, formerly of Glens Falls, and Edward McDonald   His mother's maiden name was Mary Sanford, daughter of —— Sanford, and sister of David Sanford, of New Milford, Conn , who came into this town in 1785, and settled on Sanford's Ridge, where he carried on a large farming, mercantile and lumber business

The mother of Leonard G McDonald, before she was married to William McDonald in 1809, was Maria Jane Davis, daughter of Richard Davis, son of Harry Davis, who was one of the early settlers in Poughkeepsie in the seventeenth century, and her mother (the maternal grandmother of Leonard G) was the daughter of —— Geer, who was killed by the Indians while defending his home at the massacre of Wyoming during the French and Indian war

Leonard G McDonald was first married in 1854 to Helen Webster, daughter of Charles Webster, of Stockbridge, Berkshire county, Mass , and she died

D. V. Brown, Sr.

in April, 1871, and in 1872 he married his present wife, Clara M Twinning, daughter of Thomas Twinning, of Lenox, Berkshire county, Mass , having no children by either wife

He is a prominent member and one of the wardens of the Episcopal Church in Glens Falls, and for over twenty years has regularly attended as a delegate the Diocesan Conventions of that church

In politics he was formerly a Democrat, but for the past seven or eight years, after much study and investigation, he firmly adopts and earnestly advocates the general and leading principles of the Greenback party as advocated and maintained by such men as Peter Cooper, Warwick Martin and others, whose lives have ended in advancing and maintaining the leading and financial principles of that party or faction

DANIEL V BROWN, SR — The reader of the history of the town of Queensbury in early days has learned that among the earliest settlers in what is now Warren county was Benedick Brown, whose name is found among the town officers of 1773, when he was made overseer of the poor   He had a son, Valentine Brown, who settled near the outlet of what is now called Glen Lake (known for many years as Valentine's Pond)   One of his sons was named Richard, who located about one and a half miles from the site of the Half-way House, between Glens Falls and Lake George   His children were George (see biographical sketch herein), Charles J , Daniel V , the subject of this notice, and Stewart   Richard Brown's wife was Sarah Vaughan, of Washington county, a descendant of one of the old Rhode Island families, now numerously represented in the Eastern States

Daniel V Brown was born in the town of Queensbury on the 29th of May, 1821   His boyhood was passed at home and he was given such educational advantages as then offered in country districts   Of these his active mind availed itself to the utmost, and he secured a groundwork which, with his later study and experience, enabled him to step into the foremost rank of business men About 1843 he left his home and located permanently in Glens Falls, where he engaged extensively in the forwarding business on the canals, and also interested himself at various times in other ventures of trade or manufacture   His distinguishing characteristics in his business career, were cool and accurate judgment, capacity to deal promptly with large interests and problems, and unflinching integrity

Mr Brown was a zealous and active politician of the Democratic school and was honored by his fellow townsmen with various positions of trust and responsibility   He was collector in 1848, '49, supervisor in 1859, and sheriff in 1861–64, was president of Glens Falls in 1861, and trustee for five years theretofore In these public offices he exhibited the same zeal and fidelity that made his private business successful, and enabled him to acquire a competence before his early and lamentable death

When the war broke out and the government was threatened by traitors, no person came forward with more alacrity than Mr Brown to offer whatever aid lay in his power   So it occurred that when the president made his call for 500,000 troops and there was some difficulty in filling the quota for Queensbury, Mr Brown was selected as one to go into the Southwestern States and purchase voluntary enlistments to apply on the home quota   The work was, of course, well performed, which led to his selection the second time for a similar duty, under the succeeding call for 300,000 men   On this occasion he was associated with Edward Riggs, one of the ablest attorneys of the county   They left New York on Thursday, January 8th, 1865, by steamer *Melville*, for Hilton Head, whence they expected to sail for Savannah   They had with them a large sum of money belonging to the town   When off Staten Island the vessel broke some part of her machinery, and she was taken back to Atlantic Dock, Brooklyn, whence she sailed the next morning at six o'clock   Mr Riggs sent back a brief letter to his sister, by the pilot, dated on Friday morning and on board the ship   They had pleasant weather until Saturday noon, when they encountered one of the terrible gales of our southeastern coast   It was severely cold, and the decks and rigging were soon covered with ice   About nine o'clock in the evening, it was found that a large hole had been stove in the bow, and that the water was running into the forward cabin   The fires were soon put out , and supposing the ship to be sinking, one of the two life-boats was immediately filled , but before it was lowered the weight of the persons and the lurching of the ship broke off the railing to which the boat was attached, and against which the captain was at the time leaning, endeavoring to restore order, precipitating all into the sea, including the captain ; and in the darkness and howling of the winds, nothing was seen or heard of them afterward

The remainder of the night, drenched and shivering, they spent in bailing the vessel — one young lady for a time reading the Bible to the men as they worked   They burned the mails and other combustibles to signal a schooner which was in sight   Sunday morning the storm abated , and about ten o'clock they launched the remaining boat, and putting the ladies into it with a few others, they were manning it with seamen, hoping that they might reach the schooner yet in sight, and bringing back an additional boat, take off the remainder of the passengers and crew — when the steamer suddenly went down, capsizing the boat, and thus leaving all in the surging sea together   The only persons saved were a mate, an engineer, and one passenger, picked up that night about ten o'clock in the boat, by the schooner *Harriet* — and a Mr Boyden taken from a piece of the wreck about three o'clock on Monday morning, by the bark *Rechabite*   The mate of the vessel thinks that he knew our friends; and that, on account of exhaustion and cold, with their life-preservers on, they were waiting in the cabin when the steamer almost instantly went down   Thus these men came to their death, about two hundred miles from New York, and about seventy from the Virginia shore

This calamity cast a shade of sadness over the entire county, and the bar and the people generally united in paying the tribute of sympathy to their memory   A large meeting was held on the 8th of January, under the auspices of the Town War Committee, at which several of the leading men of the village spoke of the virtues of the deceased, and eulogistic resolutions were passed. From these we select the following as applying to Mr Brown —

Resolved, That the fatal event which cost our community the life of Daniel V Brown has inflicted an irreparable loss, not only on the beloved ones of his pleasant domestic home and the many dear friends whom he has left behind, but on this his native county, and especially on this his native town

Resolved, That the value of such a man's example is beyond calculation . Beginning his career as he did without any, or but very few of the advantages of an early education, and with no individual source of reliance except his own strong arm and irreproachable character, backed by an indomitable will and a cheerful temper, whose sunshine could never be shaded, his work-day youth began in our midst, to be crowned as time passed on with an enviable success in business, and with the highest public honors and most responsible public positions of our village, our town and our county, — all the legitimate and just rewards of a life of industry, probity and ever of " good will " towards all men

Upon the presentation of the resolutions, Isaac Mott, esq , was among the speakers, and referred in the following language to Mr Brown's life and characteristics —

" Daniel V Brown was emphatically a man of the people   I have known him in private, social and public life, always frank, genial, generous, he was the friend of all, and all were his friends

" I will not invade the precincts of private grief to speak of his worth as a husband and father , the family circle but too keenly feel the great calamity and irreparable loss which now overwhelms them

" In the social circle he was always a welcome guest, adding much to the good cheer of all around him   As a business man he was active, prompt, energetic, faithful and true , no one ever doubted the word or honesty of Daniel V Brown   His activity, generosity and honorable bearing had won for him a high position in business circles   By the partiality of the people he was often called to positions of honor and trust, and ever discharged the duties with credit to himself and fidelity to the public   He had barely closed his term of three years as the first executive officer of the county when he started on his ill fated mission.   In the discharge of the requirements of law, as sheriff, he was often called to perform unpleasant duties, yet they were always met promptly and efficiently — always mingling with the severities of the law that kindness and consideration to the unfortunate which characterizes a noble and generous soul "

Mr Brown was married in 1840 to Eliza J Case, who still survives him
Their children were Daniel V Brown (of whom a sketch succeeds this), Richard
T., Sanford C., George S , Alida, Helen, Minnie and Jennie   All of these are
still living   Sarah died in infancy

DANIEL V BROWN — Daniel V Brown is a son of the subject of the
foregoing sketch, and was born in Glens Falls, February 23d, 1844.   His
youth was passed with his parents, who gave him excellent advantages for acquiring a good English education in the schools and academy of his native
place, which was supplemented by a full course in Eastman's Business College
at Poughkeepsie, N Y   Previous to his attendance at this school, however,
he had served as clerk and bookkeeper for Brown & Byrne   Returning from
the business college at about the time of the formation of the Glens Falls
Transportation Company (1864), a powerful organization comprising the Jointa
Lime Company and the Sherman Lime Company, he was immediately employed as bookkeeper, which position he occupied one year

In the year following (1865), as narrated in the foregoing sketch, his father
was lost at sea, just as the young man reached his majority   Giving up his
position with the Transportation Company, he engaged in the coal trade and
kindred operations, continuing about a year, and then taking up the clothing
trade with his uncle, Clark J Brown, in 1866   They carried on this business
about four years   In the spring of 1872, when the construction of the feeder
dam was commenced, just above Glens Falls, Mr. Brown was employed first as
foreman and soon after as assistant superintendent, a position in which he in
reality had principal control of the work   When the dam was finished he
entered the office of M B Little, general insurance agent, where he remained
about one and a half years

The reader has learned that Daniel V Brown, sr , was an active and successful politician   His son seemed to have inherited or acquired similar qualifications in this direction which have already enabled him to take the front rank
among the rising politicians of the county, in the Democratic school.   His
popularity in this respect and his adaptation for the office resulted in his election to the office of county clerk in 1879, which position he still retains, discharging its responsible duties with eminent success and unvarying fidelity.

Mr Brown has also been otherwise honored by his fellow-citizens ; he was
under-sheriff under W. W Hicks in 1870, and when Mr Hicks resigned, was
appointed by Governor Hoffman as sheriff for the unfinished term.   He was
treasurer of the corporation of Glens Falls two years (1866, '67), and collector
three years (1868–71) , and again elected in 1879

Personally, Mr Brown is a man of pleasant address, ready speech, active
mind and unimpeachable integrity   His judgment of men and grasp of whatever task he assumes is broad and fair , qualifications that must always give
him prestige and value in political counsels

DANIEL V. BROWN.

Mr Brown was married in September, 1865, to Miss Mary McGinn, of Sandy Hill, N Y   They have two children — Sanford S , and Walter D Brown

EUGENE L SEELYE —The family from which the subject of this sketch is descended was among the earliest settlers in the present county of Warren   Going back three generations we find the settlement of the family of which David Seelye was a member, at what has always been known as " the Oneida" (the site of the present post-office of Queensbury)   One of David Seelye's sons was Reuben Seelye, whose name is found among those who held town offices as early as 1813   His children were Lemuel C P Seelye, Reuben Seelye, and three daughters, named Emilia, Mahala and Saloma   The children of Lemuel C P Seeley are Eugene L (the subject of this notice), Fanny, Cynthia, Belle, Lettie and L J Seelye

Eugene L Seelye was born at his paternal home on the 2d day of December, 1845   He was given facilities for securing a good English education in the common schools of his native town and the Clinton Institute, which was supplemented with a full business course in Eastman's College at Poughkeepsie   Thus fitted for the business of life he left home at the age of eighteen to accept a position as bookkeeper and cashier with F B Gardner & Co , heavy lumber dealers of Chicago   After one year of satisfactory work in their office, he was sent by them to their extensive mills and store in Wisconsin, where for eight years he served them with mutual satisfaction as financial manager   In the mean time his father, who had purchased a tract of timber land (two hundred acres) on the eastern shore of the head of Lake George, opposite the village of Caldwell, had also erected threon a small hotel, having removed the soft wood timber   At the end of his term of service in Wisconsin, E L Seelye was offered gratuitously a half interest in this land and improvements if he would come and conduct the hotel   This proposition was accepted and one year later he assumed the entire property, his father retiring   Here he found a business undertaking requiring all the business skill and energy of which he was master   Assuming charge of the hotel in 1874, he immediately began making extensions and improvements which have not ceased from year to year to the present time , until now the hotel proper, with its eight near-by cottages, offer accommodations to about four hundred guests and receives every summer hundreds of families, the majority from New York, Brooklyn and Philadelphia, with others from all parts of the country   This popular resort, called Fort George Hotel, and its beautiful grounds, occupies a commanding situation a short distance up the hillside from the lake shore and with its surroundings forms an earthly paradise   The eight different and separated cottages, ranging in cost from $2,500 to $6,000, are every summer occupied by families who prefer this manner of living and take their meals at the hotel

The latter building has, with its repeated additions and improvements, become an imposing and picturesque structure, with grand piazzas and lofty, commodious rooms, while the table is bountifully supplied with fresh vegetables, milk, etc, from the surrounding farm   When it is considered that all this has been built up from almost nothing and within the comparatively brief period of ten years, it speaks clearer than words of the business tact and ability, the persevering energy and the natural qualifications for the business of hotel-keeping, of the proprietor

Mr Seelye was married in February, 1873, to Josephine Lawrence, daughter of Philip Lawrence, of Green Bay, Wisconsin, a lady who is in every way fitted to be the companion of her husband   Their children are Lawrence Copeland, born January 3, 1874, Bryan Lorimer, born August 1, 1875; Cynthia Maud, born October 11, 1878, and Mabel Louise, born July 17, 1882

JOHN C MONTY —The subject of this sketch is of French descent, his grandfather, Abraham Monty, senior, having been born in France, whence he emigrated and settled in Clinton county, N Y   He was a soldier in the War of 1812   His son Abraham was born in Clinton county and married Harriet Wait   At their death they had eleven children, eight of whom are now living

John C Monty was born in Plattsburg, Clinton county, N Y, in 1828. His youth until he was sixteen years old, was passed at home in the acquirement of such education as his native place afforded   In 1844 he went to Sandy Hill, where he was engaged in various occupations until 1866   At this date he settled in Glens Falls, where he has since resided

In this community he soon assumed the front rank among the successful business men of the place   He erected, soon after his arrival, his present large saw-mills, a little below the village of Glens Falls   This mill furnishes employment to about eighty hands   He also occupies the position of vice-president of a stone quarrying company of Sandy Hill, which has a capital of $80,000 and employs from one hundred and fifty to two hundred hands

Mr Monty is a man of naturally retiring disposition, never thrusting himself forward for political or other notoriety, but his eminent business qualifications have led to his having been often selected for local positions of trust and responsibility   His chief ambition has been to deserve the esteem of his fellow citizens as a successful and honorable business man   In this he has succeeded in a flattering degree   •

In the year 1853 Mr Monty was married to Miss Mary E Stowell, of Schroon Lake   She died in 1869 leaving five children—Harriet M, William H, Benjamin F, Mary E and Julia A   In 1870 he married Miss Mary E. Nulty, who is still living

J. C. MONTY.

STEPHEN LEWIS GOODMAN — Among the earliest pioneers of War-
ren county was Eleazer Goodman, who came with his family from South
Hadley, Mass, in 1799, and settled about two miles from the shore of Lake
George in the town of Bolton   His children were Eleazer, the eldest, Nathan,
Allen, Samuel, Origen, Rebecca, Holyoton and Eldad W   All of these spent
the greater portion of their lives in the county, respected by their neighbors
Samuel was the father of the subject of this sketch and born June 25th, 1789,
and died in March, 1861, at his son's home in Glens Falls, after a long life of
unpretending usefulness   His wife was Mrs Sarah (Boyd) Tuttle, of Bolton
Their children, besides the subject of this notice, were two daughters, Hannah
B and Sarah Helen   Stephen Lewis Goodman was born in Bolton, June 25th
(the same month and day of the month of his father's birth), 1817   His boyhood was passed at the parental home in the manner common to American
lads in that period   A good deal of hard work and some privation, alternat-
ing with attendance at the common schools of the neighborhood until such
time as he was competent to set out in life for himself   This time seemed to
have arrived in the year 1836, when the young man removed to Chester, in
the town of the same name, Warren county, where he began teaching school
This was but temporary occupation, however, which he continued but one winter,
when, following the natural inclination of his mind for mercantile pursuits, he
entered the store of N & J W Tubbs, in Chester, as clerk, beginning in June,
1838   Remaining here until May, 1839, he soon after entered the store of
Charles Fowler in the same capacity   It may be presumed that this association was eminently satisfactory, for in March of the following year he formed
a co-partnership with his employer, which continued for almost twenty years,
indeed, the business connection of these two men was broken only by Mr
Fowler's death in July, 1884   The mercantile business, combined with large interests in the lumber trade, was continued until 1859, when the firm dissolved
partnership and Mr Goodman removed to Glens Falls   Soon after this date he
associated himself with D G & H Roberts in mercantile business, which partnership was successfully continued to November, 1862   With this mercantile
business was connected, also, the manufacture of lumber   In the year 1873
Mr Goodman purchased an interest in the Joınta Lime Company   Down to
this date a business connection in ownership of lands, etc, had been continuously maintained with his old partner, Mr Fowler, while after 1862 Mr Goodman pursued the lumber business by himself   The purchase of 1873 included
a portion of the stock of the Glens Falls Transportation Company (a powerful organization formed for canal freighting), which was the property of the
lime companies of Glens Falls   In 1876 Mr Goodman, associated with Mr
Fowler and Thomas S Coolidge, purchased the entire property of the Joınta
Lime Company, thus acquiring the interests of L G McDonald, his brother
Walter, while Joseph Fowler retained his former interest   Mr Goodman and

Charles Fowler became by this transaction owners of a one-fourth interest each in this organization, which is retained to the present time, Mr Fowler's interest standing in his estate since his death   The entire stock of the Transportation Company is now the property of three of the four lime companies doing business here, namely, the Jointa Company, the Sherman Lime Company, and the Glens Falls Company, which has acquired the interest of the former Glens Falls Lime Company.   With the exception of his interest in these organizations, Mr Goodman has not devoted himself to active business for several years, he is now superintendent and has nearly entire management of the Jointa Lime Company's business   The reputation he has acquired in this vicinity during an active career for more than a quarter of a century, for sterling integrity, excellent business judgment and foresight and sound common sense, has been fully recognized by his fellow citizens   Upon the death of John Alden, late of Glens Falls, he was entrusted with the management of his estate, which he has carefully and successfully fulfilled from 1862 until quite recently   He has also had the care of other smaller estates during this period He has been a director of the Glens Falls Bank (now the National Bank) for about twenty years, during which period he has been continued by his associates as one of the examining committee   He was a trustee of the Glens Falls Academy for several years   He was a faithful and consistent member of the Presbyterian Church for more than forty years, and was one of the building committee for the erection of the church edifice in Glen Falls, and now on the committee for rebuilding the same on the site where the former one burned He was trustee in the church at Chester and has been church trustee in Glens Falls about twenty-four years   He was also the committee for building the handsome structure of the Glens Falls Bank   All this speaks clearly of Mr Goodman's general practical business ability and the confidence imposed in him by his fellows

Mr Goodman is a Republican in politics, and while he has always been somewhat prominent in the local counsels of that party, especially in all efforts looking to the purity of the primaries and the nomination of worthy men, still he is not and never has been an office-seeker in any sense, but his general character has not been overlooked in this direction   He declined nomination for town offices before he left the town of Chester, but in Queensbury has been induced to act as supervisor for two terms (1882–83), and was made president of the village of Glens Falls in 1865, he has also held the office of loan commissioner   Perhaps this is sufficient to show that Mr. Goodman is entitled in the broadest sense to be classed among the leading men of Glens Falls, where he certainly enjoys the respect of all with whom he has been brought in contact   He was married on the 1st of September, 1842, to Juliette Gould, daughter of Willard Gould, a respected citizen of Chester They have one child, a son, Samuel B Goodman   He was married to Jenny

Stephen Griffin 2ond

Smith, daughter of Isaac Smith, of Glens Falls, and lives with his father   In Glens Falls in the fine residence erected by Mr Goodman in 1860–61, surrounded by all that makes life desirable, the united family now reside

STEPHEN GRIFFIN, 2d — The subject of this sketch was born in Warrensburgh, Warren county, N Y, on the 18th day of October, 1812   The first one of the name, in this branch of the family, to settle in this country was Jasper Griffin   His third son was John Griffin, who was the father of John, jr.   The latter had a son Stephen (the first), who was the grandfather of Stephen, 2d   The father of the latter was named John

Jasper Griffin came to Southold, L I, about the year 1675, from Wales   He was born in 1648   At the Southold Landing he purchased a small farm   His wife's name was Hannah, and they were probably married in Manchester in either New Hampshire or Massachusetts   They had a large family, four of whom were sons, named Jasper, jr, Robert, John and Edward

John, the third son named, removed, when of age, about twenty miles west of his father's residence   He met his death from exhaustion succeeding a fall through the ice in the winter of 1741

John, jr, his son, was born in 1710   His first wife was Sarah Paine, by whom he had thirteen children   After the death of his first wife he married the second time

Stephen, grandfather of the subject of this sketch, was the tenth of the thirteen children, and was born in 1754, in Riverhead   He served honorably in the Revolutionary War and was first lieutenant   After the war he married Elizabeth Uhl, of Clintonville (now Staatsburgh), Duchess county, N Y, and settled there on a farm, and there, in the year 1784 was born John Griffin, father of Stephen, 2d   He removed to Thurman, Warren county, N Y, on the 1st of March, 1800, and settled on the west side of the Hudson River across from its confluence with the Schroon   He married Catherine J McEwen in about the year 1808

Stephen Griffin, 2d, was the third child and first son of John and Catherine Griffin, and on the date given at the beginning of this sketch, was born on the banks of the Hudson, in Warrensburgh, on the place now owned and occupied by William J Raymond   His father died on the 1st of June, 1828, and Stephen remained with his mother until he was nearly twenty-eight years old, taking charge of the farm and working by the month in the woods after he was fourteen years old and bearing a large share of the family burdens

In October, 1838, he was married to Maria Coman, of Luzerne, Warren county   In the same week of his marriage they moved into the hotel now kept by Royal C Smith   For about eight and a half years they successfully conducted the house   In 1846 he purchased an interest in the saw-mill and store of Russell & Woodward, and in the spring of the next year he gave up the

41

hotel business and devoted his time and energy to the mill, in acquiring the mill property he had bought the interest of Joseph Woodward, and continued several years in partnership with Joseph Russell In 1852 he bought out Mr Russell and continued in the business alone until 1865 He then sold the mill to Isaac Starbuck, and kept the store until 1867

In the year 1866 Mr Griffin began lumbering in the town of Newcomb, Essex county, where he continued until he had cut the timber from a tract about six miles square Selling out his lands there he was enabled to purchase in Johnsburgh, Warren county, and Wells, Hamilton county, about 43,000 acres In 1877 he had erected a tannery in the southwest part of Johnsburgh, known as the "Oregon Tannery," and in 1880 another in the northeast part of Wells, which became the nucleus of a settlement called Griffin, from his name In 1882 he sold his interest in both these enterprises to the Morgan Lumber Company, of Glens Falls, returned to Warrensburgh and retired from active business pursuits

Mr Griffin's wife died on the 2d of February, 1882 They have one child, a daughter, named Mary E, who became the wife of Dr Cyrus S Merrill, of Albany, where she now resides

It will be observed that this brief sketch indicates a very busy life, it has been one of Mr Griffin's characteristics to constantly occupy his mind with business that would not only improve his own circumstances, but inure to the general benefit of the community The advantages thus gained he now enjoys in the comfortable serenity of his later life

Mr Griffin has never pushed himself before the attention of his fellows, either politically or socially, but his eminent practical business qualifications and sterling sense and judgment were recognized by his election to the Assembly in 1875, an office which he honored and made his administration satisfy his constituents He has also held the office of supervisor three times, and in 1884 was appointed State agent for the timber lands of Hamilton and Warren counties, a position he still occupies

Mr Griffin's business career has been characterized, not only by success, but by the sturdiest integrity, even in the smallest transactions It follows that he gained, years ago, the respect and esteem of all with whom he had business relations

HENRY M DAY—The subject of this brief sketch was born in Pottersville, Warren county, N Y, on the 1st day January, 1852 His maternal grandparents were Martin and Emily (Day) Vosburgh The former was born near Red Hook, Duchess county, N Y, about 1793, and the latter at Sandy Hill, Washington county, N Y about 1803 They were married about 1821, and died, the former in April, 1882, and the latter in November, 1879 The parents of Martin Vosburgh moved from Duchess county to Warren county and settled at Pottersville when he was only ten months old   Here he spent his life following the business of farming   Martin and Emily Vosburgh had eleven children as follows   John H , Mary M , James E , William, Caroline, the mother of our subject, James 2d, Elizabeth, Helen, Charles, Julia and Eunice, four of whom are now dead, viz , James E , Mary M , William and Eunice

Henry, our subject, is the son of Calvin and Caroline (Vosburgh) Day. The former was born in Massachusetts in 1818, and died in March, 1877   He came to Warren county and settled at Pottersville in 1849, and married Miss Vosburgh about 1850   They had five children, Henry M , Ella, Minnie, Abby and Amelia, all now living except Abby, the mother is still living in Glens Falls   Henry, our subject, lived at home with his parents till he was twenty-one years old   His educational advantages were such as the schools of his native village afforded, and he attended one term at the Fort Edward Institute and two terms in the Glens Falls Academy   Before attaining to his majority he was employed in the store of R P Fuller in Pottersville about two years, and with his father in general merchandizing in the same village, under the firm name of C Day & Son   In 1873 he came to Glens Falls and was engaged by Peck & Delong, grocers, one year, he then engaged with Hollis Russell, with whom he remained as head salesman seven years, he then was employed by D W Sherman as buyer and head salesman in the dry goods department of his store and filled that position for eighteen months. After the close of the latter engagement he commenced business for himself by purchasing the interest of C A Hovey, of Hovey & Powers, wholesale and retail grocers   This firm, Powers & Day, was continued until September 3d, 1885, when Mr Day purchased the interest of Mr Powers and now continues at the old stand, No 20 Warren street

About the time Mr Day started business for himself he was united in marriage with Jennie H , daughter of George and Mary (Hodgson) Bibbey The father of Mrs Day was born in Warrington, England, in 1812, and her mother in the town of Ingleton, England, in 1814   They were married in 1848 and moved to this country in 1859, settling at Glens Falls   The father died November 5th, 1880, the mother is yet living   They had four children, Hannah, Leonard, Jennie and Alice, all living but Alice who died in infancy

A
USTIN WELLS HOLDEN, A M , M D , was born on the 16th of May, 1819, in the town of White Creek, Washington county, N Y   His parents were Jonas and Elizabeth (Holden) Holden (cousins german), both natives of the town of Barre, Worcester county, Massachusetts, and lineal descendants of Richard Holden, who, with his brother, Justinian, embarked at Ipswich, England, in the ship *Francis*, for America, in April, 1634, and settled in Watertown, Mass   It is traditionally stated that his paternal grandfather, Benjamin, served as one of the minute men at the action of Bunker Hill

He lost his mother in infancy   When but four years old he removed with his father to Potsdam, St Lawrence county, in the same State, which in that early day was but a sparsely-settled wilderness region   Here, under the fostering care of a kind stepmother, he acquired the rudiments of an education, afterward matured at the St. Lawrence Academy, a classical institution of deservedly wide reputation   In 1836 his father again removed, this time to Glens Falls, Warren county, N Y , which, with brief interruption, has been from that time forward the abiding place of the subject of this sketch   The same year he commenced the study of law with the Hon William Hay, whose office, at the foot of Elm street, is now used as a business office by the extensive manufacturing firm of Libby & Co   This pursuit was followed for something over a year, when adverse circumstances compelled him to resort to manual labor for a maintenance   He entered his father's shop and learned the trade of cabinet-making, which he followed industriously until his twenty-second year   Failing health, acting upon a feeble constitution, made it imperative that he should seek some other avocation   Accordingly he sought and obtained employment as a teacher of a common school at Doe's Corners, Saratoga county, where he taught two terms of five months, and the following year at Fort Edward for a like period   The succeeding winter he secured a satisfactory engagement at Glens Falls   It was during this period of school teaching that he commenced the study of medicine with Dr Tabor B Reynolds, now of Saratoga Springs   During all the preceding years the doctor had been an omniverous reader, snatching the few spare moments at morning or meal time, he always had a book in readiness to consume the time, and thus his mind became stored with gems of classic literature, the recondite facts of science, and the speculations of the old Grecian philosophers, as well as the more pleasing and congenial narrations of ancient and modern history   Thus broad and deep were made the foundations of his self-acquired education   In the winter of 1844 he attended his first course of lectures at the Albany Medical College   The ensuing autumn he was appointed county superintendent of common schools for the county of Warren, in which capacity he served for two years with credit and popular approval, at the same time continuing his medical studies as opportunity afforded   His term of office having expired, he resumed his attendance upon medical lectures at Albany and graduated with distinction from that time-honored institution in January, 1848   The ensuing spring he opened an office for the practice of medicine at Warrensburgh, the central town of Warren county, where he remained for the next four years, with about the average success which attends beginners in practice   On the 24th of April, 1851, he was joined in marriage with Elizabeth, daughter of the late Hon Horatio Buell of Glens Falls and sister of the late eminent financier James Buell, president of the Importers' and Traders' National Bank and of the United States Life Insurance Company, both of New York city   Of this union three children have been born, viz   Horatio Buell,[1] Pauline Eliza-beth, who died in infancy, and James Austin, only surviving child, who recently graduated with honors from Williams College, Mass

In the month of May, 1852, Dr Holden with his little family removed from Warrensburgh to Glens Falls, taking the place and practice of Donald B McNiel, M D , a medical practitioner of great ability and wide repute, who, the same spring, had removed from Glens Falls to New York   In 1857 the doctor, through the advice and importunity of his friends, was induced to investigate the claims of homœopathy, and he accordingly made a thorough examination of its theories, testing the application of its doctrines during a prolonged visit to several of the most eminent physicians and dispensaries of that school in the metropolis   On his return home, he finally adopted that system of practice, and ultimately with such satisfactory results that he has never had reason to regret the change

With the fierce tempest of wrath, which, upon the fall of Fort Sumter in 1861, aroused the north like a giant from its sleep, Dr Holden was the first man in Warren county, to tender his services to the State   The offer was promptly accepted and he was authorized to enlist a company of volunteers (Co F), which, with another from the same place, and others from neighboring towns, was incorporated into the 22d Regiment of New York Volunteers   This, with three other early-formed New York regiments, were consolidated immediately after the first battle of Bull Run into the First Brigade of the First Division of the First Corps of the Army of the Potomac, that army which, for three long years, was " a pillar of cloud by day and a pillar of fire by night," in its hourly protection and defense of the National Capital   This brigade afterwards, by its dash and endurance, its steadiness and bravery, became known as the " iron brigade," a name well-earned and merited by its gallantry in action and terri-ble losses in the sanguinary engagements of the second Bull Run, South Mountain, Antietam and Fredericksburgh

At the expressed wish of many officers and men of his regiment, Dr Hol-

---

[1] Horatio Buell Holden, M D , eldest child of Austin W and Elizabeth (Buell) Holden, was born at Warrensburgh, Warren county, N Y , on the 4th of March, 1852   The following May he accom-panied his parents to Glens Falls   Here, with trifling exception, he passed the remainder of his days   His education was acquired at the primary schools and academy of this place   He studied medicine with his father   In 1872 he attended his first course of lectures at the medical department of the Vermont University at Burlington   In the summer following his return home, he received the ap-pointment of medical assistant of the Homœopathic Dispensary at Albany, and the following season attended a course of lectures in the medical college of that city   In the spring of 1873 he re entered the medical college at Burlington, Vermont, from which institution he graduated at the following com-mencement   The same year he commenced practice at Mechanicsville, Saratoga county, N Y   The ensuing spring he removed to Stillwater, where he secured a fine practice   Failing health and other discouragements induced his return home, where he died at the early age of 27 years   Possessed of great natural abilities and uncommonly fine intellectual powers, he gave early promise of a career of usefulness, which, unhappily, was not destined to fruition   The summer of his days was cut short be-fore its fruitage had escaped the bloom of its flower

den was transferred in August, 1862, to the medical staff as first assistant surgeon, acting, in the absence of the surgeon, most of the time as chief medical officer of the command, which relation was maintained with general satisfaction until the regiment was mustered out of the service at Albany in June, 1863, its term of enlistment having expired Within six weeks of his discharge, Dr Holden received an appointment as acting assistant surgeon of the U S army, in which capacity he performed active duty until Lee's surrender, being stationed consecutively at the United States general hospitals at Frederick City and Cumberland, Md , and Troy, N Y On finally quitting the army he was honored by Governor Fenton with the commission of brevet major of New York volunteers for meritorious service On returing home the doctor resumed his practice, and has continued in the active discharge of its humane and beneficent ministrations to the present time A well-deserved success has followed his efforts in behalf of the sick and suffering In 1869 he was elected a permanent member of the New York State Homeopathic Medical Society, of which body he has ever since been an active and influential member, holding at different times its most important offices, viz Censor, vice-president, president, delegate to the National Institute, and is at present, and has been for several years, its necrologist In addition to these varied labors and duties, its volumes of transactions have been frequently enriched by his ably-prepared contributions In 1879 he was elected a permanent member of the American Institute of Homeopathy, and has been an acceptable contributor to its transactions In the same year he was one of four members of the State Society who were recommended for and received (in due course) the honorary degree of M D from the regents of the University of the State of New York, an honor that only once before has been accorded to Warren county since its organization Late in the winter of 1876–77, at the instance of several eminent physicians of New York city, Dr Holden accepted the appointment of chief of staff of the Homoeopathic hospital, Ward's Island, New York, a position which he held with great ability, receiving testimonials of satisfaction from the Commissioners of Charities and Corrections, the Board of Visiting Physicians, officials, nurses and attendants He remained in the discharge of these onerous and multiple duties for nearly two years, when failing health compelled his retirement and return home to the health-giving breezes of Warren county, once more to resume the broken thread of his practice

A life-long Democrat in politics, but never in any sense an extremist or partisan, he was elected by a majority of sixty-two, in a county strongly, overwhelmingly Republican, to the Assembly of 1874. In local politics he has often been chosen to places of trust and responsibility One of these, in which he takes much pride, is that of member of the board of education, to which he has been elected a second term He is also a trustee of the Glens Falls Academy. In 1877 he received as an honorarium the degree of A M from Union

College   In January last a medical board for the examination of pension claimants was created at Glens Falls by order of the commissioner of pensions, The board consists of Drs A W Holden, Godfrey R Martine and Buel G Streeter, the first named being president, the second secretary, and the third treasurer   The weekly examinations prove the confidence reposed in their judgment

Much of Dr Holden's time during the past forty years, except when occupied by professional and other cares and duties, has been devoted to literary pursuits   His researches and labors in the domain of local history have been fruitful in rescuing from oblivion many detached facts and incidents of the past that in another generation would have been irremediably lost   His chief and lasting monument, which will bear his name down to posterity, is a work entitled, *A History of the Town of Queensbury, N Y*   This was brought out in 1874 in Munsell's superior typography and style   It is an octavo volume of upwards of 500 pages, profusely illustrated, and covers an important era and section of country in relation to American history   In recognition of his literary abilities he has received, in addition to the honorary degree of master of arts already mentioned, appointments as corresponding member of the Oneida County Historical Society, the New York, Wisconsin and Rhode Island Historical Societies, and the New York and New England Genealogical and Biographical Societies

Dr Holden has been a communicant of the Protestant Episcopal Church since 1841, since when he has held various positions in its vestry most of the time, from warden to collector   Besides being a member of the vestry he at present holds a commission as lay-reader from the bishop of the diocese   He and his family are noted for their zeal and efficiency, and readiness to enter into and co-operate in every good work tending to advance the interests of the church, and the service of his Lord and Master

BRIEF PERSONALS.

ABBOTT, Hon Alson B , Queensbury, p o Glens Falls, was born in New Hampshire in 1844, and reared in Andover, Mass Was a graduate of Phillips Academy at Andover in 1862 and a graduate of Dartmouth College In 1866 he settled in Glens Falls, and read law with Judge Brown He graduated from the Albany Law School, and was admitted to the bar in 1872 In 1878 he was elected member of Assembly Was principal of the Warrensburgh Academy from 1866 to 1868, and principal of the Glens Falls Academy for four years President of the County Agricultural Society for four years, and director in the Glens Falls Insurance Co , also director in the First National Bank of Glens Falls. In 1874 Mr Abbott married Mrs Sarah Morgan Reynolds, daughter of the late James Morgan and widow of the late Dr John H Reynolds She has two children, James B Reynolds and Alson M Abbott.

Ackerman, E T , p o Hague, was born in Hague June 5th, 1840 Is a prominent farmer His estate comprises 235 acres, he is also an assessor of the town Was married to Miss Carrie Irish, daughter of H S Irish, who located in Hague in 1860 They have eight children, Orpha J , Eugene H , William W , Luella, Edmund H , Ettie, Frank and John Mr Ackerman was a soldier of the late war, a member of the 23d N Y Independent Vol Battery He enlisted in 1861 and was discharged July 14th, 1865 Mr Ackerman's father, Abraham Ackerman, is one of the oldest living natives of Hague His wife was Malinda Damon, of Vermont.

Adamson, Dr William R , Caldwell, p o Lake George, was born in the county of Durham, England, in 1852 Is a physician and surgeon, spending his winters in New York and his summers at Lake George In 1873 he graduated from Bellevue Hospital Medical College, and the same year commenced the practice of his medical profession at Richmond, Va In 1876 he settled at Lake George, where he continues his practice during the summer season Has been president of the County Medical Society, and has crossed the Atlantic several times , was married to Miss Emily Jane Jackson, of Yorkshire, England, and they have a family of two children Dr Adamson's parents were William and Martha Adamson, natives of England, who settled in Virginia in 1874

Aldrich, William D , p o Warrensburgh, was born in Thurman in 1851 Read medicine with Dr McNutt Is a graduate of Warren Academy, and also of Dartmouth Medical College, N H He settled at Stony Creek in 1871, and in 1878 removed to Warrensburgh, where he continues his profession, having a large and increasing circle of business. Was supervisor two terms at Stony Creek , was married to Miss Clara Cudney of that place in 1873 Dr Aldrich was a son of Squire Daniel and Catharine Aldrich They have a family of six children Daniel has been a recipient of most of the town offices as well as local governmental appointments Was a justice of the peace for eighteen years

Allen, Frederick W , Bolton, p o Bolton Landing, was born in Corinth, Saratoga Co , in 1850 He settled in Bolton with his parents in 1864 Was appointed postmaster in 1862, and elected supervisor in 1885 Has been collector and excise commissioner and held other minor town offices , was married in 1875 to Miss Helen Finkle and they have one child, Hugh A. Allen Mr Allen's parents were Daniel and Anna (Lake) Allen

Anderson, John, Johnsburgh, p o Weavertown, was born in Ireland Aug 15th, 1834, son of John and Jane (O'Neil) Anderson He emigrated to Canada with his parents in 1836, and came to Johnsburgh in 1850 Is a farmer and lumberman, and owns 215 acres of land , was married to Katharine McKenney, daughter of James and Catherine McKenney, and they have four children, John, jr , Jennie, Edward and Katharine Mr Anderson is a Democrat.

648

Archibald, Samuel R, Caldwell, p o Lake George, was born in Salem, Washington Co, in 1819 While he was yet young his mother died and he went with his two brothers to Bolton to live with James Archibald, and afterwards with his Uncle Thomas Thomas apprenticed Samuel to Mr Hiram Hawley to learn the boot and shoe trade, where he remained until 1840, when he was of age He then purchased the business, which he still holds, giving employment to several hands In 1841 he purchased his present homestead, on the bank of Lake George, and built his present fine dwelling in 1883 He also carried on the tannery business He has been one of the representative men of the county Has been justice of the peace for thirty-four years in succession, elected the last term in 1884 He was postmaster under Lincoln and held the office for fifteen years. He has been county loan commissioner two terms, side judge for two terms and has held minor town and county offices, was married in 1849 to Miss Catharine Nelson, daughter of Lieut Alton Nelson, and they have five children, Mary Elizabeth, Charlotte, Clara, Thomas, and Robert E Robert is telegraph operator at Lake George and Lotta is a music teacher, married to George O Eddy and resides in Bristol, Rhode Island

Armstrong, James W, p o Johnsburgh, was born in Johnsburgh, Aug 14th, 1815 He is a farmer and owns 92 acres of land, has been twice married, first to Katharine McMillan in 1846 She died and for his second wife he married Laura A. Brown in 1849 They have six children living, viz Mary, John B (M E minister), Ella J, Catharine E, William J and Jabez E Mr Armstrong has been a member of the M E Church 48 years

Armstrong, Robert, p o Johnsburgh was born in Ireland March 4th, 1792 Is a farmer, and the owner of two farms, one of 200 and the other of 247 acres Has always been a Democrat in politics and is at the age of 93 hale and hearty He was the son of John and Betsey (Somerville) Armstrong, who emigrated to America in 1807 and settled in Johnsburgh Robert was married in 1816 to Rebecca Armstrong, and they have six children living James, Robert, Eleanor, Ann, David and Thomas

Austin, Chas A, Queensbury, p o Glens Falls, was born in Queensbury, Warren Co, April 10th, 1843 Is a general farmer and dairyman, purchasing his present farm in 1872, in 1869 he was married to Miss Sarah F Smith, of Glens Falls, and they have five children, Walter, Edgar, Ethie Lewis and Bessie Mr Austin's parents were Phineas and Athalinda Austin Phineas's parents died when he was young and he was reared by a Mr Murray By a close application to books he fitted himself for a teacher Later he became a hotel proprietor, and still later purchased a farm on which he settled and died in 1881 His mother, Hannah (German) Austin, lived to be 102 years old Mr Chas A Austin enlisted in Co H, 93d N Y Vol Regiment in 1862 Was discharged for disability at one of the Philadelphia hospitals His brother, William H, served three years, enlisting from a Western State

Austin, John H, Queensbury, p o Glens Falls, was born in Queensbury Was in early life a carpenter, and later a professional painter and jobber Was born in Queensbury Sept 23d, 1821, and married to Miss Hannah Willard, of Saratoga Co, in 1847 They have four children, Herbert W, Maud L, Ida B, and Jessie May They have also one adopted daughter, Mary J, now married Herbert W married Miss Sarah E Hall, and they have two children Mr Austin's grandparents were Phineas and Hannah (German) Austin Hannah lived to be 102 years old,

Baker, Chas H, Stony Creek, p o Athol, was born in Stony Creek in 1855 Is a farmer and owns 100 acres, only about twenty-five of which are under cultivation He is now supervisor of the town, and is probably the youngest man who has ever filled that office since the formation of the town He has also been town clerk and inspector of election was married in 1879 to Alma Evarts, a native of the same place They have one daughter, Gracie Mr Baker's parents were Silas and Roby (Kathan) Baker His mother died when he was very young and his father was killed in the late war Mrs Baker's parents, Duncan and Mary (Harris) Evarts They had five children

Baker, Walter, p o Warrensburgh, was born in Thurman in 1837 He is the owner and proprietor of the Baker House, adjoining the fair grounds He also gives attention to the professional training of valuable horses He purchased his present hotel in 1884, was married to Miss Adaline Herrick November 28th, 1875 Mr Baker was a son of William K and Mary (Belou) Baker They had eight children, six of whom are now living

The Balcom family first located in Hague about 1796, when Isaac and Sally (Green) Balcom came from Hubbardstown, Mass, and made a settlement in West Hague They were the grandparents of the somewhat numerous family of Balcoms now living in the town James A Balcom is a grandson, and a son of Uriah Balcom who led the life of a sailor until about 1848, when he located in Hague His son James A was born Aug 21st, 1840 He has been an active man in public matters, having held offices of town clerk, commissioner of highways, supervisor several terms, and justice of the peace for four years, he entered the army Sept

28th, 1861, and served until 1864, a member of the 23d Independent Vol Battery, was married Nov 28th, 1868, to Olive P, daughter of Thomas Newton, of Hague, and they have one son, Harvey

Balcom, Stephen, was another son of Isaac and Sally Balcom   Was born in 1802   He spent his life in Hague, married Miss Saloma, daughter of Edward Doolittle   They have several children   Myron is a thrifty farmer of Hague and married to Lucina Ackerman   They have three children, Leroy, Carrie W, and Elmer A   Harrison Balcom, who occupies the homestead, is the youngest son of Stephen and Saloma   The other children are Orrin, Evaline, Orpha, Laura and Orrison

Barney, Dr Chas, Queensbury, p o Glens Falls, was born in Otsego county in Feb, 1859 Read medicine at Albany and graduated at the Albany Medical College in 1883   The same year he settled in Glens Falls, where a fine practice is in prospect.   In 1884 he was elected president of the county medical society   Was a graduate of Hartwick Seminary in 1879   Dr Barney's parents were Elery and Mary (Spencer) Barney   They had three other children, William, Fred and Kent

Barton, Judson N, p o Horicon, is a native of Warrensburgh, born about three miles south of Bartonville, Oct 7th, 1820   Has devoted most of his business life to lumbering farming, and of late years merchandizing, but has now practically retired from active business, was married to Lucretia, daughter of Joseph F Smith, of Horicon, and they have five children all living — Jane, now Mrs Austin A Ross, Scott, John, Julia (now Mrs Thomas Smith), and Smith, proprietor of the saw-mill at Bartonville   Mr Barton s grandfather Jonathan came from Whitingham, Mass., and with a brother, Timothy, located in Bolton in 1796   They were ancestors of the somewhat numerous family of Barton of Horicon and vicinity

Barton, Scott, was born Feb 27th, 1854   He is of the firm of Barton Bros, merchants, and also postmaster of Horicon, was married Dec 20th, 1875, to Miss Laura, daughter of Hon R P Smith, of Horicon, and they have two children, Lena and Nellie

Barton, John, son of J N Barton, was born Aug 29th, 1860   He is of the firm of Barton Bros, was married to Minnie, daughter of Captain L G Hall, of Warrensburgh, and they have two children, Walter and Orren   The business of Barton Bros was organized in 1872, by J N Barton & Son   In 1882 Scott Barton purchased his father's interest   Their stock comprises everything found in a first-class general store   With their extended and favorable acquaintance with the public wants, their business is successful and gradually increasing

Bates, George W, Caldwell p o Lake George, was born in Caldwell, Feb 22d 1843   Is a carpenter and builder   Has been collector, town clerk and supervisor for his town, was married in 1866 to Miss Elizabeth Alston, daughter of William and Sarah (Bell) Alston   They have one child, a daughter, Sadie   Mr Bates was a son of Winslow and Sarah (Bennett) Bates   They had four sons and one daughter — viz, Harvey, Christopher J, Samuel, George W and Emily   All the sons are practical mechanics and are among the leading successful men of the town

Bates, Harvey C, Caldwell, p o Lake George, was born in Caldwell in 1832   He learned the general smithing trade of Mr G W Shay, and commenced the business in its various branches in 1850   He still continues it in connection with wagon manufacturing and repairing, he was married to Miss Celestia Ellsworth in 1861, and they have one daughter, Cladia, born in 1871   Celestia was daughter of James Ellsworth and Louisa (Monroe) Ellsworth   Her grandparents, from Massachusetts, settled in Warren county about 1800   Mr Bates was a son of Winslow and Sarah (Bennett) Bates, natives of Warren county   They had five children

Bates, Samuel, Caldwell, p o Lake George was born in Caldwell in 1839   He commenced his early life as a carpenter and joiner and soon became a contractor and builder   In 1883 he joined his brother Christopher in boat-building, in which business Bates Bros are extending their shops   Samuel conceived the idea of supplying the village with fine spring water, and in 1878 he put in pipes and conducted water from one of the mountain streams in pipes of cast and wrought iron of four inch bore, at a cost of about $1,200   It proved so valuable to the town that others joined him in the enterprise with capital   The firm is Bates, Ferguson & Harris, and they have extended the supply to all the principal hotels and residences of the village.   The stream is clear and cold, but never freezes until it enters Lake George   Mr Bates arranged with the property owners for privilege of the springs and stream with head of 250 feet   No one can doubt that Mr Bates has proved himself to be a benefactor to his town, he was married in 1867 to Miss Hattie Staats, of Caldwell, and they have two children, Edith C. and Lena R   His brother Christopher Bates married Sarah Hoag, of Warrensburgh, in 1865 They have one daughter, Emma J   Christopher and Samuel were sons of Winslow and Sarah (Bennett) Bates

Bayle, G F, Queensbury, p o Glens Falls, son of Luke and Adaline (Lee) Bayle, was born at Bald Mountain, Washington county, in 1860 The family settled in Glens Falls in 1870 G F started his business life as a clerk for Messrs Robbins & DeLong in 1872 He was then cashier and book-keeper for B B Fowler for six years, after which he was solicitor for an importing house in New York until he settled in the dry goods and millinery trade at 111 Glen street, on March 10th, 1884, having a fine attractive store and a very inviting stock of domestic and fancy goods, linens, dress goods, silks and a full assortment of haberdashery Mr Bayle married Miss Louisa Bienvenu in 1882 They have one daughter, born Jan 13th, 1884

Bean, John H, p o Warrensburgh, was born in Corinna, Maine, in Nov, 1844 He is a dental surgeon and fitted himself for his profession in Boston In 1870 he opened an office in Boston, where he remained several years In 1879 he removed to Warrensburgh He was a soldier in the late war, enlisting in the 6th Maine Regiment, Co H, under Col Burnham He served until the close of the war Was taken prisoner and held ten months — part of the time in Andersonville prison, and quartered on the race course grounds at Charleston for six weeks and then taken to Florence, S C War married in 1871 to Miss H J Bean, of Plymouth, Mass Dr Bean was a son of Henry W and Eliza A (Kelly) Bean of Maine

Beatie, John, p o Luzerne, was born December, 1859, in Washington county, and settled in Luzerne in 1882 Is a general liveryman, farmer and lumberman Was married to Miss Polly Rice in 1881, and they have a family of two children, James and Lottie Mr Beatie was a son of James and Susan (Patterson) Beatie They had seven children, four now living Mrs Beatie was daughter of Elder E and Lottie (Scoville) Rice

Bennett, Ashael, p o Warrensburgh, was born in Warrensburgh in 1816, was married in 1835 to Miss Sally Dickenson, of Bolton, and they have three children, Edwin, Alice and Paulina Mr Bennett was a son of Caleb and Sally (Harrington) Bennett, natives of Rhode Island, who settled in Warrensburgh in 1797 They had a family of five children, of whom Ashael is the only surviving one

Bennett, Dennis, p o Warrensburgh, was born in Warren county in 1833 He was an early farmer in 1871 Engaged in the stage, express and mail business He now owns, in company with Mr Palmer, an extensive livery, firm is Bennett & Palmer Was married in 1861 to Miss Anna Bennett Mr Bennett was a son of Robert and Phoebe (Merrick) Bennett The grandfather, James Bennett, with his family, settled in Warrensburgh about 1790

Bently, Stephen V, Queensbury, p o Glens Falls, born in Queensbury, March 24th, 1810 Parents, Richard and Dianah (Vaughan) Bently The latter was born in Rhode Island in 1784, came to Washington county in 1793 with his parents, David and Hannah Vaughan Richard and Dianah had seventeen children ten of whom are living Richard was son of Joseph and Jane Bently who settled before the Revolution Stephen V married Miss Thankful S Austin, of Queensbury, in 1833, who died Aug 21st, 1855, leaving four children, Charles N, George M, Eliza A and Mary J Charles N married Maria Hendrix in 1855 and died August 22d, 1870, leaving five children, Willis F, Sanford L, Elroy C, Hattie and Emma S Second wife, Julia Goodman, of Bolton, parents, Oton and Lucy Stephen Was highway commissioner three terms, constable, collector one term, and a general farmer

Bentley, Willis F, Queensbury, p o Glens Falls, was born in Queensbury, Warren county, in 1857 In 1877 he commenced trade in the merchant and tailoring business, having in stock a fine assortment of cloths and cassimeres of the most desirable patterns and the latest styles He deals largely in custom and in ready-made garments, gents' underwear, gloves hosiery, hats, caps, shirts and collars, and all fancy goods for gents' use The firm is Coolidge & Bentley, 92 Glen street, Glens Falls Was married to Minnie Brown, daughter of Daniel and Eliza Brown Were married in 1880, and have one child, Elroy W

Bibby, Leonard, Queensbury, p o Glens Falls, was born in 1853 in England He commenced his present business in 1874, the manufacturing and bottling of soda and all light drinks, and in 1884 he purchased his location on Maple street and built a large factory He admitted Mr Ferguson as partner in 1881 They have also a bottling establishment at Riverside, and their business gives employment to fifteen or twenty hands as well as that number of horses Their location is No 62, 64 and 66 Maple street, Bibby & Ferguson Mr Bibby was married to Ellen Kelly, of Glens Falls, in 1876, and they have one daughter, Minnie Mr Bibby's parents were George and Mary (Hodson) Bibby, natives of England

Black Lawrence B, Caldwell, p o Lake George, was born in Fairfield county, Conn, in 1820 He settled on his present farm in Caldwell in 1850 Gives his attention to civil engineering and general farming and lumber producing He was assessor for five terms, highway commissioner two terms, and notary public for many years, appointed last in 1885 Has had charge of the United States Coast Survey Station, Spruce Mountain, in 1878 He surveyed part of the non-resident lands of the county in 1880 He was married to Miss Mary Pember, of Rutland county, Vt, in 1848, and they have five children James S, Truman A, Orlin P, George W,

Charles F and one daughter, Mary A (deceased) and Alonzo T Black   Alonzo is now in the employ of the State employed in the fine inside paneling of stone, marble and wood work, where he has been engaged for nine years   James B is a farmer in Vermont, and Orlin a large dairy farmer in Rupert, Vt, with a dairy of seventy cows   Mr Black was first employed as a coast surveyor under President Van Buren

Blumenauer, Henry, Queensbury, p o Glens Falls, was born in Ulster county in 1850 and settled in Glens Falls in 1872   He apprenticed himself to Mr Snyder to learn the confectionery business   In 1878 he opened a shop of his own on Glen street and moved in 1884 to No. 8 South street, where he commenced the general baking business in connection with his confectionery trade   He furnishes the finest of goods in his line to parties as well as private families   In 1884 Mr Blumenauer married Miss Fannie Works, of Essex county   Mr Blumenauer's parents were Jacob and Rose Blumenauer, natives of Germany

Bolton, Richard and Hannah (Beadwell) Horicon, p o Brant Lake, were both natives of Yorkshire, England   He was born in 1809 and she in 1819   Were married in 1835, and emigrated from England in 1846   Mr Bolton was accidentally drowned in the Schroon River, and for her second husband Mrs Bolton married Thomas, brother of the deceased   He was also a native of Yorkshire, England, and a soldier of Co A, 93d N Y Vol Infantry   He died in 1881 and his widow now resides with her son Thomas   Thomas was born June 6th, 1838, and married Sarah E, daughter of Henry Jordan, in 1861   They had five children, Effie J, John, Frederick, Thomas J and Harry   Richard Bolton, son of Richard, sr., was born in Stockton, England, in 1845   Is a farmer and owns 440 acres of land   Has been commissioner of highways   Was married in 1868 to Laura, daughter of John Waters, of Hague, and they have three children, Ellis V, Richard and Ella   Valentine, another son of Richard Bolton, sr, was born in Warrensburgh, N Y, March 1st, 1849   He owns a good farm of 329 acres   Was married to Rosetta, daughter of Rodney Horse, of Milwaukee, Wis, in 1871, and their children are William Burt, Valentine, jr, Grace, Martha and George   John Bolton, another son of Richard, was a soldier of the 118th N Y Vol Infantry, and died in the service at Fort Ethan Allen, December 24th, 1862

Bolton, Joseph, son of Thomas E, was born February 14th, 1856, in Chester   Is a farmer and owns 190 acres of land   Was married to Lovina, daughter of Ephraim Bien, of Vermont, in 1882, and they have one child, Cora

Bradley, Thaddeus, Caldwell, p o Lake George was born in Caldwell in 1812   In 1832 he married Miss Mercy Bennett, and they have several children   One son Thaddeus, enlisted in 1862 and served until the close of the war   Marvin was married to Miss Leonora Bennett in 1885   Mr Bradley was a son of Nathaniel and Eunice (Shaw) Bradley   They had a family of three children, two of whom are dead   Thaddeus is the only child living   Thaddeus's grandparents were among the earliest settlers in Caldwell   Mr Bradley's wife, Miss Mercy Bennett, was a daughter of Abel and Jemima (Harrington) Bennett   He was formerly of Vermont, and when he came here there was but one block-house at Lake George, used as a government store-house and treaty was made that year in the fall of Mr Harrington's settlement.

Braley, Pliny P, Queensbury, p o Glens Falls, commenced his business in 1879 and is now located in the Opera House Block   Is a dealer in books stationery, wall paper, wool yarns, zephyrs and all fancy goods of that order   He was born in Bolton, Warren county, in 1854, son of Stephen and Philomela Braley   Miss E C Boyd, partner of Mr Braley in his business, was born in Bolton, Warren county, a daughter of Rufus and Eliza Goodman Boyd, who settled in Glens Falls in 1848

Brayton, George W, Queensbury, p o Glens Falls, jobbing butcher and farmer, born at East Lake George, 1832, wife Caroline Beadleston, married in 1854, seven children, two sons and five daughters.   Parents, Asa W., and Polly (Phelps) Brayton, the former born in 1805 in Queensbury, the latter in Washington in 1805, married in 1826, died in 1856, children four now living Silvia J, Mariah, George W, and Danford   Grandparents, John and Mary (Harris) Brayton   The former was born in Washington county, and settled in Queensbury about 1790   Eleven children, six now living Lois, William, Asa, Orlin, Polly, Diantha   John died 1826 and Mary died 1853

Brooks, Landon W, Stony Creek, p o Creek Centre, came to this town from Maine when only a year and a half old, and has lived here ever since   He is a farmer and owns 129 acres of very fine land, most of which is under cultivation   Has filled the offices of collector and commissioner of highways in the town, was married in 1874 to Mary E Glassbrook   Their two children both died in infancy

Brown, Asahel C, Queensbury, p o Glens Falls, was born in Queensbury, Warren county, in 1826   He was a son of Richard and Mahitabel (Teft) Brown   They had two children, Asahel C and Justus S, Asahel was married in 1865 to Hester Brown, of Queensbury, and they have two children Hollis R and Hattie M Mr Brown's grandparents were Justus and Desire Brown They had a family of eleven children A portion of their land is still in possession of Asahel

Brown, Dolphus J , Caldwell, p o Lake George, was born at Lake George in 1862 He engaged at Lake George in the hardware trade until 1885, when he sold out his stock and is now completing an extensive general meat market , in 1884 he was married to Miss Nellie Lewis daughter of Hamilton Lewis of Warrensburgh Mr Brown's parents were Alphonso and Eunice (Mead) Brown

Brown, George, Caldwell, p o Lake George, was born in Queensbury, Sept 3d 1815 He has been one of the prominent and active business men of the county, engaged in various branches of business He has, for over forty years, been identified in the hotel business of Warren county Has always had room and board for the poor, and is to-day one of the most popular landlords of Northern New York He is proprietor of the Central Hotel at Lake George, in 18— he was married to Miss Sylvia Odell, of Queensbury They had eight children, four of whom are now living Sarah, Annah, Katie D and Stewart D His grandparents, Valentine and Margaret (Haight) Brown, settled in Queensbury before the Revolutionary War Mr Valentine Brown commenced the manufactory of sawed lumber and built the first saw-mill in Queensbury

Brown, Myron O , Bolton, p o Bolton Landing, was born in Bolton in 1837 He is one of the founders and proprietors of the Green Island Improvement Association on Lake George He is the lessee of the Sagamore Hotel, embracing 75 acres, and having ample accommodations for 350 guests It is one of the finest summer resorts in the United States The building, furniture, and the manner in which it is conducted is a credit to the State Mr Brown has held the office of supervisor six terms at Bolton He was an early merchant, in 1862 he was married to Miss Mary E Wilson, daughter of Captain Wilson, of Sandy Hill, and they have two sons Willard W and Frank B Mr Brown's father Luther Brown, was sheriff of the county, and supervisor several terms

Brown, Richard J , p o Bolton, was born in 1846 in New York city, and settled with his parents in Bolton in 1860 By profession he is a civil engineer Has been justice of the peace one term, and appointed notary public in 1885 In 1874 he purchased his present site and erected his hotel "The Lake View House," which he continued to improve until it will give ample accommodation to 100 guests In connection with his hotel he has a small steamer for the pleasure of the guests of his house Was married in 1870 to Miss Helen J Allen, of Saratoga His parents were Richard F and Elizabeth (Lee) Brown He was the only son

Bullard, Chas E , Queensbury, p o Glens Falls, was born in Northville, Fulton county, in 1851, and settled with his parents in Glens Falls in 1860 Was a graduate of the Canandaigua Commercial School in 1872 He then clerked it for Mr H Colvin in the furniture business and in 1875 became a partner In 1876 he, with Mr Henry Swan, purchased the business of Colvin & Co , forming the partnership of Bullard & Swan In 1880 he took the entire business, which he conducted alone until 1882, when he sold part interest to John R Loomis The firm is now Bullard & Loomis, having a complete stock of the most desirable patterns in the furniture and upholstery line in which they are extensive dealers as well as manufacturers They also have a large undertaking department in which all grades, patterns and prices can be found at No 118 and 120 Glen St In Oct , 1879 Mr Bullard married Mary Thomson, of Johnsburgh, Warren county Have a little girl born February 27th, 1885

Bullard, David H , Dr , Queensbury, p o Glens Falls, was born in Schuylerville, Saratoga county, N Y , in 1812 He read medicine at West Troy and finished his studies at the Albany Medical College under Drs March and Armsby in 1849 He commenced practice in Fulton county in 1853, and settled in Glens Falls in 1860 In 1838 he married Julia Spier, of Fulton county They had seven children Julia E , Emma A , Sarah F and Harriet A , Charles E , Frederick H , and William R Dr. Bullard's parents were Alpheus and Hannah (Fitch) Bullard

Burdick, Jas P , Queensbury, p o Glens Falls, was born in Saratoga county in 1843, and settled with his parents in Glens Falls in 1846 His father, Allen Burdick, was engaged in the manufacture of lumber, and James commenced business with him and for several years shared it Their mill was destroyed three times by fire, Mr Burdick was married in 1874 to Miss Kate Rugge, daughter of George Rugge, of Glens Falls

Burgess, Lewis, p o Hague, born Aug 14th, 1834, is a native of Dresden, Washington county , he commenced as a school teacher and afterwards occupied a position as chief clerk for ten years at the Fort William Henry Hotel In 1860 he entered the merchandizing business, and from that date has been the postmaster of his town , has held the office of supervisor of his town for two years and is serving his thirteenth year as justice of the peace Of later years he has spent his winters in Florida, where he has heavy real estate interests His success in life is entirely due to his personal efforts throughout and prompt business methods, Mr Burgess was married Jan 2d, 1862, to Charlotte, daughter of John McClanthan, of Hague Mr Burgess's grandfather was a Hessian soldier   Was pressed into the British army and sent to America, arriving in New York city in 1777   He soon became convinced of the worthiness of the American cause and deserted to the American army   He married a Miss Bennett and located in Putnam, Washington county, N Y

Burhans, Frederick O, p o Warrensburgh, was born in Ulster county in 1832   He is extensively engaged in the tanning business in Warrensburgh, and is also a large land owner and capitalist, was married in 1855 to Miss Helen E Barton, of Le Roy, Genesee county, they have but one child now living, Charles F , Mr Burhans's parents were Benjamin P and Rebecca (Wicks) Burhans   They had six children, four now living   Charles H, Frederic O, Julia and Sarah H   Julia is now Mrs William B Isham   Mr Burhans, senior, early engaged in the tanning business, first in Ulster, then in Greene, and finally in Warrensburgh, where he made a financial success   He was an extensive land owner and dealer of Northern New York, a man of influence and integrity, and liberal in his views and gifts

Burhans, Miss S H, p o Warrensburgh, was a daughter of Colonel Benjamin (Peck) and Rebecca (Wicks) Burhans   They with their family settled in Warrensburgh in 1836   Mrs Burhans died in 1864, and Mr Burhans in 1875   They left a family of six children, four of whom are now living

Burnham, Cyrus (deceased), son of Josiah and Betsey Burnham, was born in Queensbury in April, 1808   Mr Burnham was a well disciplined business man   While he was seventeen years of age his parents lost by fire nearly all their possessions, and from that time Cyrus developed a decided taste for business   At an early age he ranked among the first business men of Warren county   He became an extensive lumber dealer, connected with George G Hawley in its manufacture at Glens Falls, and afterwards with Orin Mead and George Sanford as wholesale lumber dealers at Albany, N Y   He was Member of Assembly in 1850 and a director of the Glens Falls National Bank from its incorporation until his decease   He was married in 1841 to Sophia Rice   At the age of forty-nine he died leaving three children, Sophia R , Glen F , Julius R , an older son, Cyrus, died at an early age   Post-office, Glens Falls

Burneson, John B, p o Luzerne, was born in Schoharie county, N Y, in 1830   Was a graduate of Castleton Medical College, Vt, in 1852   Read medicine at Davenport with Dr. John Ferguson, and settled in Luzerne, where he still resides in his practice of medicine and surgery, was married in 1854 to Miss Frances Stewart, of Warren county and they have one son, John S   Dr Burneson was a son of Andrew and Jane (Granby) Burneson

Bush, John W, Queensbury, p o Glens Falls, was born in Glens Falls in 1850   He commenced the drug business in Glens Falls in 1869, under the firm of Leggett & Bush, establishing a wholesale trade, also a retail, dealing in all classes of drugs, medicines, paints, glass, and a full stock of all the leading patent medicines of recognized value   They make a specialty of fine fancy goods at 109 Glen street   Mr Bush was married to Miss Emily Derrick, of Rensselear county, in 1878, and they have one child

Butler, William H, Queensbury, p o Glens Falls, born in Queensbury in 1818, wife, Zadie Ann Snyder, born in Moreau, Saratoga county, in 1824, married in 1844, children ten   Mary J , Mary J , Emma L , Augusta C, William H , Joseph L , Harley G , Charles A   Walter J and Clinton J   Mary J married James Joseph Whiting, Emma L married Hiram Brown, Augusta C married James Viele   Zadie A was daughter of George and Patience (Carr) Snyder, of Duchess county, who settled in Saratoga county and died in Warren county   Parents, Abraham and Mary (Slot) Butler, born and married in Duchess county, settled in Queensbury with six children   Abraham died in 1868, aged 93 , wife died in 1858, children two, now living.

Cadwell, James E, Dr, Queensbury, p o Glens Falls, was born in Manlius, Onondaga county, in 1820, and settled in Glens Falls in 1850   He engaged in the dental profession, which he still continues   In 1882 he retired from active attention to dentistry, having numerous assistants, and gave his attention to the manufactory of sash, doors, blinds, etc , he having purchased an interest with L G Wilson & Co   It is now run by his son-in-law, Mr S D Kendrick   As a factory it has just been increased in capacity, where the manufacture of all builders' supplies by orders or contract is attended to   Mr Kendrick is also a dealer in drugs, medicines, oils, etc , at No 51 Glen street   Dr Cadwell was married to Miss (nee Doty) Mary A. Wilson, of Glens Falls, in 1854, and they have three daughters, Elizabeth E , Gertrude L and Bertha   Elizabeth E married Mr S D Kendrick of St. Lawrence county, and they have one child, Ethel G   Dr Cadwell was a son of Rowland Cadwell, a native of Springfield, Mass. Besides James E he has eight other children

Cady, J Fletcher, Chester, p o Pottersville, was born in Chester, May 6th, 1853   He is engaged in farming and the livery business, has held the office of collector about four years, deputy sheriff three years, and was constable from 1875 to 1885, is much esteemed by all who know him, was married to Julia Sherman February 1st, 1872, and they have one child, Mattie Mr Cady's father was Dr John W Cady, a native of Burlington, Vt He came to Chester when a youth He studied medicine with Dr Potter, and practiced at Pottersville about thirty years

Cameron, Allen C, Stony Creek, p o Creek Center, was born in 1838 in the town then called Athol Is a farmer and expressman in Creek Center Was married in 1861 to Emily A Everts, daughter of Horace and Orilla (Williams) Everts, natives of this county Mr Everts is still living, over seventy years of age Mr Cameron's parents were George N and Cynthia H (Coman) Cameron, natives of this county, who died several years since

Carpenter, James H, Caldwell p o Lake George, was born in Washington county, Vt, in 1832 In his early life he worked as a carpenter and builder for twelve years He had charge of a steamboat on Lake Michigan one year In 1858 he became a photographer, and in 1872 he purchased his present hotel It is one of the old popular stands at Lake George, called for many years the Caldwell House He enlarged and called it the Carpenter House He has just been enlarging and re-furnishing it. Mr Carpenter married Elizabeth M Edwards of Essex in 1861 His grandfather, David Johnson, was a body guard of General Washington during the Revolution He was taken prisoner by the English and held on board a vessel off New York At the close of the war he settled in Vermont, where he died Mr Carpenter's mother, Julia Carpenter, died at Glens Falls, leaving three children, James H, Ira and Jerome

Carpenter, Thomas, p o Horicon, was born in Chester, June 14th, 1808 He is a miller by trade, which trade he learned at Rochester, N Y He conducted the Horicon grist-mill for about eighteen years Was married to Ann A, daughter of Stephen A Evarts of Thurman, Warren county, and a cousin of William M Evarts They have one son, George, now married to Carrie, daughter of Hon R. P Smith and they have three children, Winfield Scott, Thursah, and an infant unnamed Mr Carpenter's parents were Joseph and Fannie (Crandle) Carpenter

Cashion, Patrick W, Queensbury, p o Glens Falls, was born in 1854, and in 1875 he started the manufacture of carriages and sleighs as successor to Mr Morris From that time to the present four of his brothers have joined him The firm is now Cashion Bros In 1882 they built a large factory, 100 feet by 32, and three stories, and have now developed an extensive business, manufacturing and finishing complete from their several departments under their own supervision The Cashion Bros are sons of Edward and Ann Cashion, natives of Ireland, who came to America and settled in Glens Falls in 1854

Champlin, Lynn D, Queensbury, p o Glens Falls, was born in Glens Falls in 1856 January 1st, 1880, he formed a partnership, and under the firm name of Champlin & Cameron commenced dealing in hides, leather and findings, sheep pelts, calf skins, tallow and sheep-skin moccasins. at wholesale, at No 73 Glen street, Glens Falls The partnership was dissolved in April 1885, and Mr Champlin continues the business In 1882 he married Flora Snedeker, of Warren county, and they have two children, Llora G and Mabel E Mr L D Champlin's parents were George and Esther A (Sisson) Champlin Besides Lynn D they have four children, Egbert, Eliza, Hattie and Helen S

Charette, Dr Louis, p o Warrensburgh, a physician and surgeon of Warrensburgh, was a graduate of the Albany Medical College in 1842 He settled in Bolton the same year, and in 1854 removed to Warrensburgh, where he enjoys an extensive practice in his medical profession Has been supervisor, town clerk, in Bolton, and coroner in Warrensburgh Was married in 1842 to Miss Margaret Smith, of Bolton, and they had two children, George B and Louis C George B enlisted in the 22d Regiment in 1861, was wounded, and died September 14th, 1862, at the hospital in Washington Dr Charette was born in the Northwest Territory at Leach Lake, now the State of Minnesota He attended the Waterford Academy and the Medical College, Dartmouth, two terms, 1837 and 1838 Studied medicine with Dr Timothy Upham, of Waterford, N Y

Clifton, Albert C, p o Hague, was born January 28th, 1842, and came to Hague in 1874 Is proprietor of the Island Harbor House, which is one of the most quiet and picturesque retreats on Lake George It was built in 1882 and accommodates thirty guests Is located one mile north of Hague wharf, and three-fourths mile from the post-office at Hague Mr Clifton was married to Augusta L Severance, of Shoreham, Vt., and they have four children, Bernard, Alice, Bessie and Grace

Coffin, Harvey R T, Queensbury, p o Glens Falls, was born in Glens Falls in 1854 He commenced the manufacture of brick in the old stock company known as the Glens Falls Brick Co In 1883 he purchased the entire interest of the Glens Falls Brick Co, and the works are now known as the H R T Coffin Brick Works, he being proprietor of the Glens Falls Brick

Co It was first organized in 1849 In 1882 he organized the Jointa Tile and Brick Co in connection with the Jointa Lime Co, and in 1883 he formed a company, firm of Coffin, Zimmer & Co & Alfred Sweet, and established poultry yards on an extensive scale, introducing an incubator, capacity of 1,000 eggs His stock of fowls are all pure breed land and water fowls Any one can order or send for circular and price list They also breed blooded stock and deal in dogs of fine imported stock, hunting and house pets, p o address Coffin & Zimmer, Glens Falls, Warren county He was married in 1876 to Catherine J De Long and they have three children, Theodore D, Mildred N and Earl B Mr Coffin is son of Sanford and Catharine (Wing) Coffin

Coffin, Dr Henry W Queensbury, p o Glens Falls, is the son of Sanford and Catherine (Wing) Coffin Was born in Glens Falls in 1859, and read medicine with Dr S T Birdsall, of Brooklyn, N Y In 1881 he graduated from the New York Homeopathic Medical College, where he practiced his profession until 1883, when he settled in Glens Falls Was married in 1882 to Anna Dix, of Glens Falls, and they have one son, John Dix Coffin Dr Coffin's grandparents were early settlers in Warren county

Cole, Chas, p o Warrensburgh, was born in 1861 Since Jan, 1885, he has been assistant editor of the Warrensbugh News He is a son of John B and Amy (Tucker) Cole His mother died in 1883 leaving five children Adaline, Ira, Rachel, Belle and Charles Mr Cole's grandparents were Ira and Lydia (Prosser) Cole, and were among the early settlers of Caldwell

Conkey, George W, Queensbury, p o Glens Falls, son of John and Hester Conkey, was born in New York city in 1837 Is an artist. He learned his profession of S A Holmes and C D Fredericks, of New York city In 1861 he came to Glens Falls to instruct in his art, and there made the first photograph in the county He has so well pleased with his success that he remained, and now has one of the best galleries in the county, opposite the post-office on Warren street, in 1860 he married Miss Mary E Leonard, of Albany

Cook, William, Hague, p o Ticonderoga, is one of the most extensive agriculturists and land-holders of Warren county, was born Sept 21st, 1819, was married to Miss Caroline Moses of Ticonderoga, and they have two children, William A and Carrie C Mr Cook's parents were William and Sophia (Morse) Cook

Coolidge, Jonathan M, Queensbury, p o Glens Falls, was born in Bolton in 1832 He resided with his parents until 1865, engaged in farming and lumbering, and afterward settled in Glens Falls in the firm of Coolidge, Lee & Co, doing a wholesale and retail business in dry goods, groceries and provisions, in 1873 T S Coolidge retired from the mercantile business, which was continued until 1881 under the firm name of Coolidge & Lee. In 1879 the firm engaged in the manufacture of ground wood pulp at Ticonderoga, N Y Mr Coolidge has been supervisor two terms in Bolton, and member of the town war committee, supervisor of Queensbury three terms, president of the corporation one term and director of the First National Bank and Glens Falls Paper Mill Co In 1884 was elected president of the Glens Falls Terra Cotta and Brick Co Mr Coolidge was married in 1870 to Miss Hannah McEchron

Coolidge, Thomas S, Queensbury, p o Glens Falls, was born in Bolton, Warren county, February 8th, 1839 Has been an active business man of the county In 1853 he became a clerk in a country store, and in 1861 he engaged in the mercantile business in Chester. He sold out and went to Glens Falls in 1865 and started a new store, firm of T S Coolidge & Co In 1866 he formed a company which still exists of T S & Jonathan M Coolidge and George W Lee, firm of Coolidge, Lee & Co In 1873 he sold his interest in the mercantile business to his partners, but continued with them in some real estate and other investments Since 1868 he has been interested in the manufacture of Glens Fall lime, and since 1869 continuously engaged in its sale for his own and all the other companies located there Mr T S Coolidge was one of the founders of the present Morgan Lumber Co, and in 1868 he purchased one-fourth interest in the Jointa Lime Co, and is now agent for four lime companies that have consolidated He is also treasurer of the Ball Mountain Co, and director of the Glens Falls National Bank Has been trustee of the corporation, director of the Glens Falls Insurance Co and of the Terra Cotta M'f'g Co In 1867 he married Miss Georgiana Palmer, of Saratoga, and they have one daughter, Gertrude

Cooley, James S, A M, M D, p o Luzerne, was born in Hartford, Washington county, in June, 1845, and fitted for College at North Granville Academy and Fort Edward Institute He was graduated from Williams College, Mass, with the class of 1869, and afterwards taught for four years at Fort Edward Institute as professor of ancient languages and natural science, under Rev Joseph E King, D D, holding the position of vice-principal one year In 1873 he was chosen principal of Glens Falls Academy, where he remained until 1876, when he resigned and completed his medical studies at Burlington Vt., and at the Medical Department of the University of the City of New York, from which he received his diploma in Feb, 1877 He commenced the practice of his profession at Sandy Hill, Washington Co, but in June, 1880, removed to Luzerne, where he is now in the enjoyment of a good practice as the successor of Dr James G Porteous For nearly three years he has held the office of coroner, and is the present health officer of the town, and one of the representative men of the county He was married in 1872 to Miss M Reba Clark, of Willsborough, Essex Co, and has a family of two children Mary Hope, and Ernest Grenville

Cooper, John, p o North Creek, was born in England Feb 14th, 1822, son of Thomas and Sarah (Broughton) Cooper He came to America in 1841 and settled in Johnsburgh, where he has been engaged in farming He owns 100 acres of land, was married to Sarah Aldens, of Washington Co, N Y, and they have two children John W and George

Cote, Dr C, Queensbury, p o Glens Falls, was born in the Province of Quebec, Canada, in 1855 Is a graduate of the Montreal College of Physicians and Surgeons, and of Victoria University, Cobourg, Ontario, and a Fellow of the Royal College of Physicians and Surgeons, London Dr Cote settled at Glens Falls in 1884, No 68 Glen St Was married in 1880 to Miss Agnes Bonde

Cotton, Orange, p o Bolton, was born in Bolton in 1805 Was formerly a successful farmer and lumberman, but has now retired from business Has been a supervisor of the town, was married in 1839 to Miss Ann Brown She died in 1881 leaving four children Calista, Julia, Silas, and Arthur L Arthur L married Miss Amanda Burton, and they have one daughter Silas married Miss Delia George and they have one daughter, Annie Mr Cotton was a son of Luther and Ann Cotton They had but two children

Coty, Peter, jr, p o Luzerne, was born in Canada in 1843 and with his parents settled in Troy, N Y, in 1855 He removed to Luzerne in 1875, and is now the leading blacksmith of the town He is also a carriage and wagon manufacturer, was married in 1867 to Miss Matilda Gilber of Glens Falls She died in 1882, leaving a family of nine children

Covel, Henry, Horicon, p o. Brant Lake, is a native of Chesterfield, and was born in 1838 Has been a resident of Horicon since 1859 Is a farmer and owns 75 acres of land, was married to Harriet, daughter of Leonard Wood, of Horicon, and they have one daughter, Ida May Mr Covel was a soldier of the 118th N Y Vol Inf'y, Co D Entered in August, 1862 and served until the close of the war His father, Daniel, was a native of Keeseville, and was a contractor by occupation

Cowles, Benjamin Sedgewick, Queensbury, p o Glens Falls, born in Saratoga county, Nov 6th, 1841, settled in Glens Falls in 1864, and engaged in the book and stationery trade in 1868, wife, Harriet A Faxon, daughter of Hon W A and Mary (Foster) Faxon, married in 1867, one daughter, Mary Cornelia, born in 1880 Parents, Benjamin and. Cornelia (Van Sanford) Cowles, of Saratoga county, the former born in 1805, the latter born in Saratoga county, April 29th, 1804, married in 1825, the latter died in 1862 leaving six children Grandparents, Benjamin and Rosanna (Boardman) Cowles, children, nine Greatgrandfather, Nathaniel, whose father, John came from the west of England and settled in Connecticut in 1634

Cowles, Daniel H, Queensbury, p o Glens Falls, was born in Hadley (now Corinth), Saratoga county, January 1st, 1810 Settled in Glens Falls in 1833, and commenced business as a general merchant, of the firm of Rogers & Cowles In 1835, his partner died and he changed the firm name to D H Cowles & Co, which remained until 1875 when he retired from the business, but not from active life He is a man interested in all public enterprises of city and county, and his advice is sought by many people

Crandall, Emerson S, p o Warrensburgh, was born in Warrensburgh in 1846 In 1859 he succeeded his father in the mercantile business Has been justice of the peace one term and county treasurer two terms, in 1872 he was married to Mary Mixture, of Warrensburgh, and they had three children, Minnie F, Chas S (deceased), and an infant Mr Crandall was a son of Josiah and Mary Ann (Stead) Crandall Mr Crandall, senior, settled in Warrensburgh in 1832 and learned the tanning business, also manufactured boots and shoes He continued this business until 1867, when he embarked in the mercantile business in which he has been succeeded by his son

Crandall, Harvey, Caldwell, p o Lake George, was born in Caldwell in 1829, and married Miss Eveline Hubbell, daughter of Frederick and Betsey Hubbell They have one son, William E Crandall Mr Crandall commenced his business life as a blacksmith in 1860, and is still engaged in that business He is also a machinist and practical engineer, and carries on the plumbing, gas-fitting and heating business His son William E now owns and runs the pleasure excursion steamer, D W Sherman, and is also a practical engineer Mr Harvey Crandall's grandparents were from Scotland and among the early settlers of this town He has two children now living, Seth W, who is father to Harvey, and Gideon

42

Crandell, Isaac, Queensbury, p o Glens Falls, born in Queensbury August 14th, 1836, wife, Elizabeth Newton, daughter of John and Maria Newton, born in Kingsbury, Washington county, May 23d, 1837, and married September 17th, 1861, two children Herbert L, born July 7th, 1867, and Lillian, born July 31st, 1870   Parents, Peter and Fielove (Cole) Crandell, born in Warren county, Feb 17th, 1803, the latter born in 1816, married in 1833, two sons, Isaac and John, the latter born 1839, died August 21st, 1873, leaving widow and daughter, Carry   Isaac Crandell has been engaged in many different enterprises, first, carpenter and builder, gun-smith, a photographer, thirteen years a machinist for fine work   Erected his present dwelling, office and extensive green-house   Deals extensively in plants and gives his entire attention to the floral business

Crandal, Sela W, Caldwell, p o Lake George, was born in Caldwell in 1825   Has been a farmer and lumber manufacturer   Has been justice of the peace and held several minor town and district offices; was married to Miss Sally A Wilcox, of Caldwell, in 1854, and they had two children Jay and Mary Jane   Mr Crandal was a son of Benjamin and Mary (Tucker) Crandal, natives of the New England States   She died in 1839 leaving eleven children four of whom are now living Seneca, Luana, Sela W, and Mary   Benjamin was justice of the peace for many years and filled a prominent position in town   One of his ancestors was chaplain in Washington's army

Cunningham, Thomas, p o Warrensburgh, was born in Essex county in 1826   He read law with Messrs Kellogg & Hale, of Essex county and graduated at Plattsburg in 1854   He then settled in Warrensburgh where he still resides following his old profession, but devoting a portion of his time to the management of his farm   He also has charge of the Lake George and Warrensburgh Plank Road, in which he is a large stock owner   It is one of the finest roads of the State   Mr Cunningham has been supervisor for fifteen years, also appointed deputy revenue collector, and district attorney   He is one of the leading political and influential men of his town, was married in 1858 to Mary E Burdick of Warrensburgh, and they have a family of seven children   Chas B, Frank, Fred, Harry, Robert, Maude, and Alice   Chas B was a graduate of Dartmouth College in 1881, and now a teacher

Cushion, John, Queensbury, p o Glens Falls, was born in Ireland in 1841   He commenced as a hand on the canal in 1857, is now engaged in saloon, boarding and boating, his wife was a daughter of Dennis and Mary (Sheehan) Linch   They were natives of County Cork, Ireland, and settled in Glens Falls in 1860   He died in 1861, leaving a family of five children, three sons and two daughters, who reside in Glens Falls   Mr Cushion's parents were Edward and Bessie (Brownlow) Cushion.   Mrs Cushion died in 1844, leaving the one child, John, and Edward married for his second wife Ann Noonan   They came to America, settling in Glens Falls in 1850   They had six children

Dalrymple, Luther, Caldwell, p o Lake George, was born in Bolton, Warren county, in 1820   Is a son of Luther and Sally (Hammond) Dalrymple   Luther was married to Huldah Sexton, of Bolton, in 1845, and they have a family of four children   Brigham H, Mary M, Erskine L, Elmer E   Mary is now Mrs Royal Potter   Erskine married Miss Mina Griffin, and Elmer E married Miss Julia Wood   Mr Dalrymple's father, Luther Dalrymple was in the War of 1812   He settled at Northwest Bay about 1800   Luther has two brothers, Harrison and Edgar, who are Morman ministers at Utah

Davis, Ransom, Bolton, p o Bolton Landing, was born at Hinesburgh, Chittenden county, Vt., in 1814   Is a general farmer, and settled in Bolton in 1837 on his present farm of 200 acres, has been assessor, excise commissioner, and highway commissioner, and has held other minor offices for his town, was married in 1835 to Miss Anna Remington, of Wallingford, Vt   They had a family of twelve children, six of them now living Almaria, Diadama, Rebecca, Lucina, Alma, and Charley   Alma was formerly a teacher   They all reside in Bolton. Mr. Davis was a son of Luther and Susanna (Rounds) Davis

Davis, William Henry Harrison, Bolton, p o Bolton Landing, was born in 1839   Has been justice of the peace several terms, and assessor two terms, also has held other local offices, was married in 1862 to Miss Editha A Robinson, and they have had four children Stella, died 1878, aged 15, Carson, Benton, and Belva   Mr Davis was a soldier in the late war, enlisted in 1861 in Co F, 22d N Y Vol. and was discharged for disability   He now receives a merited pension. Four of his brothers also served in the war   One brother, A J Davis, was killed at the Second Battle of Bull Run   Mr Davis's parents were Lensey and Esther Davis

Davison, William H, p o Johnsburgh, was born in New York city, June 20th, 1809, and settled with his mother in Johnsburgh, on the farm he now occupies, in 1817. Has been a member of the Methodist Episcopal Church fifty-five years, and local preacher forty-eight years, was twice married, first in 1836 to Nancy Somerville, and they have three children Sally A, John F, and Samuel A   His first wife died and in 1845, he married Christa Ann Russell, and they have four children James, Jefferson C, Charlie L, and Willie L

Day, Henry M, Queensbury, p o Glens Falls, was born in Chester, Warren county, N Y, in 1851 His parents were Calvin and Caroline (Vosburgh) Day Mr Day, sr, was a merchant and miller His son, Henry M, settled in Glens Falls in 1872, spending several years as clerk for the leading merchants of that place In 1882 he purchased an interest with Mr John S Powers in the general grocery and provision business, wholesale and retail, dealing in all fancy goods, fruits, cigars tobacco and country produce, he married Jennie H Bibby of England Her father, Mr George Bibby, of England, settled in Glens Falls

Dearstyne, Howard A, p o Bolton, was born in Bolton in 1837 In 1865 he opened a summer hotel, and with the help of his mother conducted it in a successful way They continued to increase its capacity and now have ample accommodations for 100 guests The hotel, called the Wells House, is located south of Bolton Landing, on the west side of Lake George, having a private steamboat dock and a variety of small sail-boats There is also a fine livery attached to the hotel accommodations Mr Dearstyne has held the offices of town clerk, superintendent of the poor, highway commissioner, and supervisor, was married in 1860 to Miss Chloe Underwood She died in 1875, and he married his second wife, Miss Fanny C Palmeter They have one daughter, Sarah Mr Dearstyne was a son of John and Dorcas (Potter) Dearstyne They had a family of three children, but one now living

De Long Daniel P, Queensbury, p o Glens Falls, was born in Conklinville, Saratoga county, in 1850 In 1872 he engaged in trade as a general dry goods merchant— firm name, Robbins & De Long They are dealers in domestic goods of all kinds, dress goods, cloaks, shawls, and a full and inviting line of fancy goods and embroideries They are among the leading stores of Northern New York Nov 18th, 1873, Mr De Long married Emily P Tearse, of Grand Rapids, Mich They have four children Walter J, Archy Z, Robert T, and Chester S

De Long, Theodore S, Queensbury, p o Glens Falls, was born in Saratoga county in 1839 His parents were Zopher 1 and Catherine (Scott) De Long They were married in 1838, and settled in Glens Falls in 1860 Eight children Theodore S, John B, Cutler J, Daniel P, George P, Ione E, Margaret E, and Catharine J. Zopher I De Long was an early merchant in the town of Day, and has been trustee and supervisor for Glens Falls He commenced the hardware business in 1860, firm then Dan'l Peck, Z I De Long, T S De Long, under firm name of Peck, De Long & Co In 1862 it was changed to De Long & Son, Z I De Long and T S De Long, and later to De Long & Sons, John B De Long having been admitted as partner Theodore S De Long, in 1869, married Miss Caroline A Roosa, of Sullivan county, and have one daughter, Roosa The firm of De Long & Sons are extensive dealers in all classes of shelf hardware, cutlery and carpenters' and builders' material, stoves and house furnishing goods, 94 Glen street

Dickenson, Asa W, Bolton, p o Bolton Landing, was born in Bolton, Warren county, in 1831 Has held office of assessor for seven years, and was elected for the last term in 1884, was married in 1856 to Miss Betsey Griffin, of Bolton, and they have two children Elmer G, and Victor W Mr Dickenson was a son of John and Lucy (Winters) Dickinson

Duell, Richard, Horicon, p o Brant Lake, was the ancestor of the Duell family in Horicon, he came from Vermont at a very early date and located on a portion of Alphonzo Duell's present farm The family is represented in Horicon by Alphonzo, grandson of Richard Duell He was born August 25th, 1832 He is a farmer and owns 50 acres of land Was a soldier of the Rebellion a member of the 142d N Y Vol Inf'y, entered in 1864 and served one year, was wounded in the knee at the battle of Fair Oaks, and is a pensioner His wife was Phebe J, daughter of Isaac Hill, deceased, and they have one child, Ella

Duell, Joseph R, a member of the same family, was born in Horicon January 13th, 1844 He was also a soldier of the late war, enlisting in January, 1862, in the 93d N Y Vol Infantry, he served until August, 1865, was at the battle of Fair Oaks, Yorktown, Williamsburg and others, was married to Maria, daughter of Jacob Duell, January 7th, 1861, and they have one son, Bertie

Duell, Richard H, another grandson of Richard, was born in Horicon September 18th, 1814, is a farmer, owner of 65 acres of land and is engaged in the jobbing lumber business, was married in September, 1864, to Henrietta Stannard, and they have six children Chauncey R, Herbert, Norman H, Addie A, John F, and Alice A

Dunlop, James W, p o Bolton, was born in Scotland, was married in 1857, at Morristown, N J, to Miss Mary Thomas, and in 1862 they purchased a summer residence on the bank of Lake George He died in 1870, leaving four children, one now deceased Those living are James W, Mary, and Christine Mrs. Dunlop's parents were of English descent

Emerson, Albert C, p o Warrensburgh, was born in Newberry, N H, Aug 13th, 1829 Removed to Warrensburgh in 1837 where he has since resided Commenced his business life as a clerk, and became a successful merchant In 1855 he entered into the lumber business, and holds a large interest in that branch of manufacture   He is also engaged in the manufacture of leather, firm A C Emerson & Co   Was married in 1855 to Miss Abigail Woodward, daughter of Hon Joseph and Julia Woodward   They have two children, Louie W and James Alfred   In Jan , 1884, Mr Emerson in company with his son Louie W organized a banking house   He also visited and invested largely in the Northwest, Puyallup, Washington Territory

Enches, Calhoun S , Queensbury, p o Glens Falls, was born in Glens Falls Oct 31, 1848   He read law in the office of Armstrong & Keefe, finishing with Judge Davis   Was admitted to the bar Jan 14th, 1876, and commenced practice in Glens Falls   Was elected justice of the peace one term, and town clerk one term , was married Sept 11th, 1877, to Miss Katie E Barbour, of Thurman   Mr Enches's parents were Gideon S and Charlotte (Hammond) Enches   Besides the subject of this, they had three other children, C Josephine, Herbert L and Ada I

Farr, Prof Daniel C , Queensbury, p o Glens Falls, of Glens Falls Academy, was born at Ashby, Middlesex Co Mass , in 1847   Graduated in 1868 from the Lawrence Academy, Mass , also a graduate of Williams Colllege, class of 1872, settling in Fort Edward as instructor in Latin in the Fort Edward Institute   He afterward took charge of the public schools of the town and in 1877 founded what is known as the Island Grove School   In 1878 he accepted the office of principal of the Glens Falls Academy, where he still remains the institution being one of the first in the State   Prof. Farr's parents were Marshall and Lois (Wheeler) Farr, the former a native of Chesterfield, N H , and the latter of Acton, Mass

Fennell, A H , Caldwell, p. o Lake George, was born in Groton, Tompkins Co , in 1837   In 1870 he engaged in the drug business, firm Petit & Fennell   He relinquished the business in 1873 and became acting agent for the Glens Falls and Lake George Stage Co , until the opening of the R R when he was appointed general freight and depot agent at Lake George , was married in 1868 to Eliza Freeleigh, of Greene Co , and they have three children, Fred S , Maud H and Helen F   Mr Fennel's parents were Rev Andrew J and Racilla (Hackley) Fennel   They had three sons, Andrew H , George H , and Charles H

Fennel, Rev Andrew J , Queensbury, p o Glens Falls, was born in Rutland Co , Vt., in 1815   He was a graduate of the Castleton Seminary, Vt., and also of the Auburn Theological Seminary in 1843, when he became stated supply at Groton, Tompkins Co , for three years   Was called to Glens Falls in 1846 and installed over the First Presbyterian Church, where he still remains   He has a large and influential congregation   Since he has been there two brick edifices have been built, both destroyed by fire   The third now being erected, if completed according to plans, will be one of the imposing structures of the State   In 1843 he was married to Miss R Augusta Heckley, of Herkimer Co , N Y   They have had five children, three of whom are now living   Mr Fennel's parents were Calvin and Abigail Gorham Fennel

Ferguson, George, Queensbury, p o Glens Falls, son of Henry and Rosana (Harris) Ferguson, was born in the town of Queensbury, July 10th, 1831   In 1850 he became a partner with his father in the mercantile business, and at the death of his father in 1869, he took the business and continues it at present, it being the oldest mercantile house in the town , in 1856 he married Miss Marietta Hawley of Glens Falls   She died in 1868, leaving three children, H Dudley, G Frederick, and Anna M   In 1869, he married for his second wife, Miss Mary E Knox of Glens Falls, born in Elizabethtown, Essex Co , and they have one daughter, Gertie B   Mr Ferguson was supervisor for three years in succession, and town clerk for eight years, excise commissioner for six years and treasurer of corporation for one year   Besides George, his parents had three other children—Ann, Hiram and Henry A.   Hiram resides in Albany, Ann is Widow Phillipps, and Henry A resides in N Y city

Ferguson, Dr James, was born June 29th, 1818, at Kortright, Delaware county, N Y , his parents being John and Margaret (Skellie) Ferguson   He read medicine at Davenport, N. Y , with Dr John Ferguson and in the town of Bovina, N Y , with Drs Green and Ferguson   Attended his first course of medical lectures at the College of Physicians and Surgeons of Western New York at Fairfield and received his diploma in June, 1841, from the Academy of Medicine at Castleton, Vermont   From 1841 to 1852 he practiced his profession at North Blenheim, Schoharie county, N Y , where on December 27th, 1843, he married Miss Cornelia Hager of that place, by whom he has two living children, Walter J and Margaret E   In 1852 he removed to Glens Falls, where he has since resided and is still practicing   In 1877 Dr Ferguson purchased Prospect Mountain (now Mount Ferguson), situated one mile and a half from the village of Caldwell   The house was remodeled and opened as a summer hotel   In 1880 this hotel with the surrounding forest was destroyed by a forest fire caused by the negligence of a neighboring farmer   Relying upon the statements of certain eye witnesses Dr Ferguson sued Frederic B Hubbell, of Caldwell, for $8,000 damages caused by the fire, but owing to clever legal management was defeated after two trials and various appeals to higher courts   The litigation was one of the most famous in the county   The Mountain House has since been rebuilt and now stands on the summit of the mountain some 1,800 feet above the waters of Lake George and commands one of the most magnificent views in America

Ferriss, George W, Queensbury, p o Glens Falls, was born in Glens Falls, N Y, in 1836 Was a graduate of the Glens Falls Academy In Jan, 1867, he commenced the general wholesale and retail drug business in Glens Falls under the firm name of Haviland & Ferriss, and have continued until the present time They were successors to George W Sisson, who established the business in 1860 Their business has been largely increased and in 1882 they opened a second store for all builders' wants, hardware, carpenters' tools, sash, doors and blinds Mr Ferriss was clerk for G W Sisson before his purchase His parents were Benjamin and Sarah (Cooper) Ferris They had two other children besides George W

Finch, Daniel J, Queensbury, p o Glens Falls, was born in Kingsbury, Washington Co, in 1834 He commenced business with his brother in Washington Co in 1854, manufacturing and shipping lumber, and in 1866 they engaged with Mr Samuel Pruyn in that business, and settled in Glens Falls, where they still reside, engaged in the manufacturing and shipping of various products, lumber, lime, lath, timber, and flour, was married in 1867 to Miss Isabella Weston, of Davenport, Iowa, and they have five children, Charles M, Daniel J jr, Weston, Isabella, and Henry A Finch

Fish, George R, p o Bolton, was born in 1834 He is now the proprietor of the Locust Grove Hotel of Lake George It is one of the attractive points on the west shore of the lake for boating and fishing The hotel has ample accommodations for 150 guests, with cottages adjoining, Mr Fish was married to Miss Mary Ann Odell of Queensbury, in 1851, and they had two children, Delia A and Inez B, one only living, Inez B Mr Fish was a son of John and Delia (Shaw) Fish They had three sons and one daughter, George R, John R, Montgomery and Ellen Montgomery was a soldier in the late war

Fitz Gerald, Dr David J, son of Daniel and Mary Kearney, was born in Ireland in 1858. Came to the United States in 1864 with his parents, who settled in Fort Edward, Washington Co, N. Y, in 1865 after remaining a short time in Glens Falls Dr Fitz Gerald received his education at Fort Edward Union School and Fort Edward Institute where he graduated in 1876 He afterwards taught school for three years, studying medicine in the meantime with Dr Linendoll, of Fort Edward Entered Albany Medical College in 1881 and graduated in the class of 1884 After spending some months in the hospitals at New York, settled in Glens Falls in medical practice May 1st, 1884, he entered into a co-partnership with Dr Ferguson, who is the oldest practitioner in the place

Fortune, James, p o Essex, was born in Northumberland, England, March 29th, 1803 He received a liberal early education, acquiring some knowledge of farming pursuits With his parents he came to America in 1819 He is a retired farmer, was married in 1830 to Harriett, daughter of Elisha Royce They had nine children of whom six are living, all residents of Western States but one John, the eldest, continues to reside in Essex Mr Fortune continued upon his farm in Westport until 1860 He soon after removed to Essex village where he has since resided He has been a life long Democrat in politics and with his wife has been a member of the Presbyterian Church for over 55 years

Foster, Dr Chas A, Queensbury, p o Glens Falls, was born in Martinsburg, Lewis Co in 1845 Was a graduate of St. Stephen's College, Annondale, in 1869 For two years he was professor of history and English literature, a teacher of Latin and Greek one year and in 1879 graduated from the Lewisville Medical College He practiced as house surgeon of the city hospital for one year, and in June, 1882, settled in Glens Falls in his profession Was married in 1880 to Miss Catherine R Wetsell of Glens Falls Mr Foster was a son of A and Jane (Scoville) Foster His grandfather was Aaron Foster, a pioneer of Lewis Co, who served in the war of 1812

Fowler, Byron B, Queensbury, p o Glens Falls, was born in Chester, Warren Co, in 1846 He established his present business in 1869 under the firm of Fowler Bros (Byron B and Joseph), dealing in general domestic and all staple and fancy dry goods, making a specialty of fine dress goods, silks, &c From that time to the present they have done a successful trade In 1871 Mr Byron B took the entire business, in 1870 he married Julia A Cheney of Glens Falls, daughter of Albert and Anna (Hunt) Cheney They have one son, Albert N Mr Fowler's parents were Chas and Elizabeth (Baker) Fowler

Fowler, Joseph, of Glens Falls, was born in Chester, Warren Co in 1840 He became an early merchant and is now engaged in different manufacturing interests He organized the Glens Falls Shirt Co, which gives employment to many, also the Lime Co, and Brick and Tile Co, has been supervisor of Chester, and trustee and president of the Glens Falls corporation In 1865 Mr Fowler was married to Miss Mary Coolidge, daughter of Jonathan and Mary (Wright) Coolidge, of Bolton, and they have five children Mr Fowler's parents were Charles and Eliza (Baker) Fowler

Fraser, Dr Ira G, p o Horicon, although a resident of Lansingburgh, N Y, has for many years been prominently identified with the growth of Horicon He was born in Horicon in 1811, and has attained a national cputation as a successful physician and especially in the treatment and ultimate effectual cure of cancer He acquired his secret of treating cancers of the Seminole Indians in Florida, and having made many scientific improvements on their methods, which accounts for his unparalleled success. He has an office in Lansingburgh, also a home in the same place and spends his summers in Horicon, has been three times married, first, to Sarah daughter of Thomas Green She died leaving one son, Harvey His second wife was Eunice Webb, she had two daughters, Adilaide and Katie His present wife was Mrs Gaylord of Oneida Co Dr Fraser's grandfather, James Fraser, came to Horicon in 1798, from Cherry Valley, Otsego Co, N Y

Gage, Nathaniel, p o Luzerne, was born in Luzerne in 1832, was married in 1862 to Miss Rowena Kingsley, of Warren Co, and they have a family of six children, three sons and three daughters Mr Gage was a son of Garret and Dorcas (Adams) Gage Besides Nathaniel they had nine other children, viz, Abijah, Walter, Warren, Adelbert, Priscilla, Myron N, Janet, Betsey, and Lela

Gailey, Joseph I, p o Luzerne, was born in Vermont in 1839, and settled in Warren county with his parents in 1840 He is one of the successful farmers of the town Has been excise commissioner, was married in 1863 to Miss Glory Ann Taylor, and they have four children Willie A, Martha J, Ida B and Crosby A Mr Gailey was a son of Alexander and Catherine (Ramsey) Gailey Besides Joseph they had three other children Mrs Gailey was a daughter of Elias and Sarah (Mosher) Taylor

Garrett, Dr Jas S, Queensbury, p o Glens Falls, was born in Ballston, Saratoga county, N Y, Sept. 19th, 1835 He early fitted himself for the dental profession Settled in Glens Falls in 1860 as a dentist where he still remains, in 1860 he was married to Jennie H Haight, of Ballston His wife died in 1873, leaving one daughter In 1876 Dr Garrett was married to Annetta B Millington, of Glens Falls, and they have three children Edith G, Walter L and Frank A In August, 1862, Dr Garrett enlisted in Co A, 118th N Y Vols, under Col Samuel T Richards Served three years and was discharged He went out as first sergeant of Co A, and was twice promoted He was mustered out as first lieutenant of Co B, 118th N Y Vols Lieut Garrett was present with and participated in all of the actions in which his regiment was engaged until after the capture of the works around Petersburgh, Va, in the fall of 1864, when by reason of physical disability he was sent to Chesapeake general hospital, Fortress Monroe and from there as convalescent to Camp Parole, Md, from which place he was ordered for duty as commander of provost guard, of Annapolis, Md and was serving as assistant provost marshal and ordnance officer of the post and district of Annapolis, Md, when the war closed and he received orders from the War Department to be relieved from duty, when he returned to his native State and was finally mustered out at Albany, N Y, August, 1865, three months after the muster out of the regiment after which, in the fall of 1865, he resumed the practice of dentistry at Glens Falls, where he has since resided and practiced His parents are Anson B and Julia (Styles) Garrett, now living and residents of Ballston, N Y

Gates, Charles, Caldwell, p o Lake George, was born in Caldwell in 1837 Is a farmer and lumberman, was married in 1854 to Miss Alice Bennett, daughter of Asahel and Sally (Dickenson) Bennett Their family consisted of three children Ella Idella, Myron J and Minnie Maria. Charles has been assessor and highway commissioner several terms His parents were Kellum and Rozella (Dickenson) Gates, of Caldwell Besides Charles they had five other children, two of whom are still living Henry enlisted in the 96th Regiment, and served three years He afterwards married Miss Mary Potter Another daughter, Jane Ann Gates, is now Mrs George Hall

Gates, Dodge S, p o Bolton, was born in Bolton, Warren county, in 1851 Is a farmer and blacksmith Has been excise commissioner and held other town offices, was married in 1877, to Mary E Fowden, of Johnsburgh, and they have a family of two children Wallace and John. Mr Gates was a son of John and Hannah (Streeter) Gates

Gates, Franklin, Queensbury, p o. Glens Falls, was born in Kingsbury, Washington county, in Dec 1834, in 1882 he settled at East Lake George, at Van Wormer's Bay and purchased his farm and a large boarding house called the East Lake George House It has ample accommodation for forty or fifty guests, and has various points of interest for one seeking rest and quiet home comforts, with good fishing and mountain scenery Mr Gates was married to Miss Calista Vaughan, daughter of Russell Vaughan Married in 1857 and have six children Etta, Belle, Anna, Fannie M, Alma, Milford R and Bertha.

Gates, Jonathan S, p o Bolton, was born in Bolton in 1847 He is a prominent merchant of the town, in which business he embarked in 1874, and formed the present firm of Gates,

Turner & Co in 1884   Was appointed postmaster in 1880   Was married in 1873 to Miss Zilpha Reynolds, of Bolton, Warren county, and they have one son, Walter E   Mr Gates was a son of John and Hannah (Streeter) Gates, of Bolton   They had seven children, five now living   The names of brothers and sister are as follows   John D Gates lives in Warrensburgh, Warren county, N Y , Joseph H Gates, lives in Bolton, Warren county, N Y   Dodge S Gates, lives in Bolton, Warren county, N Y , George S Gates, lives in Bolton Warren county, N Y , Lydia D Beswick, died in Bolton, Warren county, N Y , Isaac S Gates, lives in Bolton, Warren county, N Y

Gibbs, Nelson J , p o Westport, was born in Westport, May 10th, 1840   Is a dealer in stoves, etc , and a manufacturer of foundry facing   He also owns a mill at Wadham's Mills   Mr Gibbs was a soldier in the late war, enlisting in Co F, 118th Reg N Y Vols   Was promoted to second lieutenant, then to first lieutenant, and was brevetted captain Nov 2d 1864, by Maj Gen Butler, for gallant conduct at the battle of Fort Harrison   Was discharged with his regiment on the 13th of June, 1865, in the city of Richmond, Va , and has since resided at Westport   Mr Gibbs has been twice married, first to Theresa A Clark, daughter of Aaron and H P Clark   She died in 1877, and for his second wife he married Jennie M Richards, daughter of James and Sarah Richards, of Westport   Mr Gibbs's parents were Warren and Abigail C (Morell) Gibbs

Gilbert, Chas A , Queensbury, p o Glens Falls, was born in Livingstone county, Michigan, in 1848   In 1876 he settled in Glens Falls in the employ of the Glens Falls Shirt Manufactory, as book-keeper   He remained in their employ until 1879, when he became foreman for W E Spier & Co, or Libby & Spier   In Jan , 1883, he became active partner of the present firm of Jas L Libby & Co , having their office at No 497 Broadway New York   Mr Gilbert is general superintendent   Was married to Elizabeth S Wright, in 1878, and they have one child, Irene Wentworth   Mr Gilbert's parents were Norman M and Elizabeth C (Wyman) Gilbert.

Gill, Christopher Columbus, was born in Castleton, Vt , May 5th, 1809   His father having moved to Saratoga county while he was yet very young, his youthful days were spent in that county   In 1833 he was married to Miss Lorany Kathan, of the town of Day, Saratoga county, with whom he lived nearly fifty-one years, the most of those years at Creek Center, Warren county, N Y   They have had eight children   John, the eldest son, a very promising young man, having died at the age of twenty years   There now remains only seven   They are Lodema Cudney, Daniel, Charles, Rinda Aldrich Miles, Dudley and Mary   Dudley is the present supervisor of the town   Mary received a music teacher's diploma in 1883 and is now teaching   They all reside in the town with the exception of Miles, who is a practicing physician in the town of Johnsburgh, Warren county   Mr Gill was one of the younger members of a family of sixteen children   He was very active in early life, therefore made a thorough business man   He was among the first settlers of the town   Built one of the first grist and saw-mills and worked them for a number of years   Later was engaged in the mercantile and lumber business   Mr Gill took a prominent part in local affairs, always ready to respond to the call of the poor and distressed, and many to-day thank him for his kindly advice in time of affliction   He filled nearly all the offices of the town, and was supervisor for many years in succession   He was the first regular appointed postmaster   Filled the office until it became burdensome to him whereupon he resigned   His son Charles, held the office from that time until a change came in the administration of our government in 1885, and then his son-in-law, A J Aldrich, was appointed to that office   During the late war Mr Gill and Mr John McMillen (then of the same town), were engaged procuring recruits   They worked harmoniously together, making many sacrifices and in this manner helped to preserve the Union   In 1866 he was elected assemblyman of Warren county, and was one of the committee on roads and bridges   Like a majority of the prominent men of the times he was a self-made man   His father was a native of England and came to this country to do battle for the British, but after witnessing the unreconcilable brutality recorded in history, where a British officer pins the American officer to the ground with his own sword, which he only a moment ago surrendered to him, he, together with a comrade, deserted the British forwith, taking an active part in favor of his adopted country   After the close of the war he was engaged teaching school and was familiarly known as Master Gill until his death in 1844   The subject of this sketch completed his family vault in 1872   In 1882 he prepared the lumber for the making of caskets for himself and wife and in 1883 he had them made   The same year he sickened and on March 29th, 1884 he passed peacefully away from earth to his reward in heaven   She is only waiting the call "It is enough, come up higher "

Goodspeed, Gideon, Chester, p o North Creek, was born in Queensbury, Jan 27th, 1823, son of Hosea and Polly Goodspeed   Mr Goodspeed has been a resident of Warren county for over fifty years, and of Chester since 1876   Is a farmer and owns 150 acres   Was married to Mary, a daughter of Henry and Anna Hewitt of Johnsburgh, and they have four children   Charlie, William, George, and James   Mr Goodspeed was a soldier in the late war, serving in the 175th N Y V, Co D, was honorably discharged on June 30th, 1865, at Savannah, Ga Is a Republican in politics.

Goodspeed, William E, Johnsburgh, p o North Creek, was born in Johnsburgh, Jan 2d, 1837 He located in Chester in 1857 Is a farmer and owns 150 acres of land Was married April 25th, 1861, to Emily, daughter of Frederick and Ellen (Martin) Barss They had two children both deceased Mr Goodspeed's parents were Hosea and Mary Goodspeed

Goodwin, James B, Queensbury, p o Glens Falls, born in Castleton, Vt, 1828 Parents, David and Mary (Johnson) Goodwin, natives of Vermont, the former died 1856, the latter died at Glens Falls 1871, leaving five children, two now living James B and Roland C James B enlisted in Co A, 118th N Y Vols, August 8th, 1862, discharged June, 1865, settled in Glens Falls 1859, and commenced his present freighting and express business added the ice business in 1871 The firm is now Goodwin & Wilmott, general draymen Wife, Anna B Cowles, born in Corinth, Saratoga county, 1838, married Jan 1856, one son (adopted) Floyd C, born May 19th, 1880 Parents of wife, Henry E and Lovina (Cressey) Cowles

Gould, Demon R, Chester, son of Willard and Deborah (Russell) Gould, was born in Chester, Warren county, N Y He at first learned the carpenter trade and engaged in business for himself in 1849 In 1879 Mr Gould went into the cabinet and undertaking business at Chester, in which he is engaged at present He was married in 1849 to Mary J, daughter of Benjamin R. and Almira (Smith) Knapp Children one, Minnie S Mr Gould is a member of the Baptist Church

Granger, Marcus E, p o Horicon, was born June 12th, 1845, at Rockford, Ills, where his parents, Martin, jr and Mary M (Prosser) Granger, lived about three years They were natives of Bolton, Warren county, and returned to Bolton, N Y, in 1847, and located on the Schroon Lake in Horicon in 1874 Marcus is proprietor of the Horicon House Was married March 31st, 1867, to Miss E Viola, daughter of Platt Smith They have had several children, viz Claud C, Gordon L, Ethel V, Mary L, Reginald M, Teressa M and Clinton R

Graves, Amos, Queensbury, p o Glens Falls, was born in Rutland county, Vt, in 1820 He has been an extensive farmer, dairyman and stock-grower He retired from active labor in 1868 and settled in Glens Falls, where they now reside In 1846 he married Miss Mary Rose. of Maryland, Otsego County, N Y, and they have one daughter, Lovina, now married to Mr Warren J Potter, of Queensbury Mr Graves's parents were Amos, sr, and Betsey Rose, natives of Connecticut. He was a descendant of Lord Baltimore Graves, of England, and died in Saratoga county Of their eight children three sons are now living, Horatio, Alexander and Amos

Gregory, Levi, Horicon, p o Adirondac, was born May 12th, 1799, and located in Horicon, then Bolton, about 1811 His father Joseph was a soldier of the Revolution Levi was married to Irene Hayes, and they had twelve children, Matilda (now Mrs Nathan Nichols), Lydia (now Mrs Henry Orton), Nancy (now Mrs James Alexander), Benjamin Charles, Elsie (now Mrs Benager Robbins), Jane (now Mrs Norman Bennett), Emory, Allen and Harmon Matilda lives in Glens Falls and Lydia and Nancy now live in the State of Michigan Joseph and Henry are deceased, and the remainder all live in Horicon Emory was a soldier of the 118th N Y Vol Infantry, served three years, and was wounded at Fair Oaks Allen married Laura, daughter of Henry Wood, and they have six children, Charles, George, Ella (now Mrs Frank Hart, of Chester), Walter, Wesley and Warren Their farm is 130 acres L L Gregory was born February 10th, 1853 He owns and occupies the homestead formerly belonging to his grandfather, to which he has added, making a total of 225 acres Was married June 30th, 1879 to Susan, daughter of Benjamin Hayes, of Horicon

Griffin, William J., Bolton, p o Bolton Landing, was born in Bolton, February 15th, 1822 Was formerly a carpenter and builder, but is now a farmer Was married September 23d, 1842, to Miss Louisa Norton, of Warren county They had four children, Erastus E, William H, Charles J and Thirza Erastus E. enlisted in September, 1864, in the 23d N Y Battery, and died December 2d of the same year of fever at the hospital Mr Griffin, sr, was also a soldier in the 93d N Y Regiment, Company H Was dismissed for general disability from Fortress Monroe hospital He receives a pension Mr Griffin was a son of Charles B and Locinda (Kinney) Griffin They had a family of thirteen children, seven of them now living

Griffing Henry, p o Warrensburgh, was born in Thurman, son of Nathaniel and Susan (Boyd) Griffing They had a family of five children, Stephen, James, Helen, Elizabeth and Henry Helen is now Mrs Frederick Osborn Mr Griffing, sr, was a son of Stephen and Elizabeth (Uhl) Griffing, who settled in Thurman in 1800 They had ten children, but three now living, viz Nathaniel, Stephen and Elizabeth Elizabeth is now Mrs Bowens Stephen was an officer in the Revolutionary War

Gurney, William B, Queensbury, p o French Mountain Born in Claverack, Columbia county, January 7th, 1822 First wife, Ann Robison, of Washington county, married in 1849 Died in 1853, leaving three children, Edgar B, Mary J and Belle Second wife, Mary Alston, married in 1855, children four, Ella, Abbie H, Elizabeth R, Helen A and George E William J has been highway commissioner for twenty-one years, justice of peace two terms Parents Joseph H and Abigail H Gurney Married in Columbia county Settled in Queensbury in 1828 The former died in 1863, the latter in 1862 Children, four

Gwinup, Hon Henry P, p o Luzerne, was born at Plattsburg, N Y in 1825 He settled in Luzerne in 1846, and for several years adapted himself to such occupation as presented At the same time he applied his leisure time to his books and fitted himself for a teacher He taught several terms, afterward read law in the office of Judiah Elsworth, and was admitted to the bar in Albany in 1876 In 1858 he was an active lumber dealer, but in 1862 he disposed of his interest and enlisted in Company G, 118th N Y Vol, under Colonel Samuel Richards He was soon promoted to first sergeant and in March, 1864 to second lieutenant. In March, 1865, he resigned, from disability He has been justice of the peace, justice of sessions, and supervisor, and in 1879 was elected Member of Assembly Was married in 1849 to Miss Martha Hays She died in 1859, leaving two children, Herbert W and Alma. For his second wife he married Maria Peer in 1860, and she has six children, Willie, Clarence, Charles, Edith, Grace and Le Roy Mr Gwinup's parents were Richard and Sarah (Jones) Gwinup

Hack, Roland, Stony Creek, p o Creek Centre, came from Bolton to this town about nineteen years ago, and has lived on his present farm eleven years. In connection with his farm he has a large saw-mill, built eleven years ago by himself It is the largest one in the town Was married in 1848 to Mariah Bennett of Warrensburgh Of their nine children only one is deceased, four are married, and the rest live at home All the children live in the town except Julia, who resides at Johnsburgh

Haley James, jr, p o Warrensburgh, was born in Warrensburgh in 1852 Was a graduate of Warrensburgh Academy, and in 1879 embarked in the mercantile business, dealing in all the staple goods In June, 1883, he was married to Miss Julia Collins, and they have one son, Henry A Mr Haley is the son of James and Mary Haley They were married in Ireland and settled in Warrensburgh in 18— Have had eight children, six of whom are now living, viz Patrick, Mary, Maggie, James, jr Julia and Annie Maggie is a popular teacher of her own town and county

Hall, Clark, p o Luzerne, was born in Luzerne in 1827 Commenced business as a farmer and purchased a mill in 1853 From that time he has been advancing as a lumber manufacturer, and timber contractor and dealer Has been supervisor one term, also commissioner of highways Was married in 1850 to Miss Mary Hall, of Hebron, and they have a family of seven children, Etta, Wilson J, Ella, Emma, Fred, George and Frank Etta is now deceased Mr Hall's parents were Ira and Eleanor (Ferguson) Hall

Hall, Warren, p o Luzerne, was born in Luzerne in 1823 Was married in 1847 to Miss Lucinda Spaulding, of Crown Point They had four children of whom two are now living, viz Harvey G and Willard W Mrs Hall died March 27th, 1881 She was an early teacher at Crown Point High School Of their two sons, Harvey G is a carpenter at Luzerne Mr Hall's parents were Royal and Rachel (Truesdell) Hall

Hammond, Samuel, Caldwell, p o Lake George, was born in Caldwell in 1817 Is a general farmer and lumberman Has been commissioner of highways three terms In 1840 he married Miss Sarah Jane Prosser, of Caldwell She died in 1851, leaving three children, Julia, Arthur and Courtney For his second wife Mr Hammond married Sally Enches, a native of Rhode Island, in 1853 They had seven children, four of whom are now living, viz Ira, Ella, Lida and Sheridon Lida and Ella graduated from Warrensburgh Academy and are now teachers Mr Hammond is a son of Nathaniel and Esther (Hodge) Hammond

Harris, Albert T, Queensbury, p o Glens Falls, was born in Massachusetts in 1816, and settled in Glens Falls in 1843 Commenced the manufacturing of lime, firm of Harris Lime Co, also engaged in various other branches of industry until 1866, when he was made secretary and treasurer of the Glens Falls Paper Co with a present capital of $192,000 He still holds the office In 1840 Mr Harris married Frances Amanda Sherman, of Rhode Island, and they have three children, George R, Susan G and Annie Caroline Mr Harris's parents were Daniel G and Mary H (Tillinghast) Harris, natives of Rhode Island and direct descendants of Thomas Harris, who settled in Rhode Island in 1637

Harris, Captain Elias S, Caldwell p o Lake George, was born in Kingsbury, Washington county, in 1828 He commenced his business life at about fifteen years of age at which time he had the care of a pleasure boat on Lake George, he was also employed on the steamer *Wm Caldwell*, the latter part of the season of 1844 The landings were made with a yawl or small boat He was put in charge of the landing of passengers on account of his skill in handling a boat on such occasions   In 1845, he became a pilot on the steamer *John Jay*, which was built and owned by his brother, John J Harris, which place he held until 1856, when she burned at Hague   In 1857 he had the *Minnehaha*, a new steamer which he had charge of for several years, was afterward captain of the *Ticonderoga* and the *Horicon*   Mr Harris has been supervisor of Caldwell two terms, justice of the peace two terms, was appointed postmaster in 1875, in 1860 he was married to Miss Elizabeth Fisher and they have two children, George B and Walter W   George B is now deputy postmaster

Harris, Veniah W, p o Queensbury, was born in Warren county in 1815, was married Oct 3d, 1839, to Phebe Ann Beadleston, and they have one son, Frelon G Harris, born Sept 6th, 1845   Frelon is now married to Miss Mary E Hubbell and they have three children — Edwin W, Clarence L and Lee L   Mr Veniah Harris was a son of Henry and Margaret (Brown) Harris   They had a family of eight children, four of whom are now living, Veniah, Brayton, Mrs Amy Allen and Mrs Betsey Ann Elms

Hartman, William P, Luzerne, p o Glens Falls, was born in Luzerne in 1839 and was reared on a farm   In early life he built a saw-mill, and in 1870 built his present mill, then a water-power mill, and in 1884 he extended its capacity, and added a steam engine of twenty-five horse-power and a boiler of thirty-five horse-power for sawing planing, and the manufacture of lath, shingles, etc, which he sells at wholesale and retail   He is now thinking of building a store in which he will deal in general groceries   Was married in 1860 to Miss Elvira M Varney, of Queensbury, and they have a family of eight children, Delvin G   Melford T, Norman V, Effa Jane, Edwin, James B, Milton and Elwood S   Delvin G was married in 1874 to Miss Mary Potter of Luzerne   Mr William Hartman was a son of Conrad and Mary Hartman

Haviland, Charles Willard, Queensbury, p o Glens Falls, was born in Glens Falls, N Y, in 1857   In 1880 he was married to Miss Anna Streeter, and they have one child, Florence L   Mrs Haviland is a daughter of Dr Buel G Streeter, who settled in this county in 1865 after the close of the war   Mr Haviland's parents were Roger and Harriet E (Haight) Haviland

Haviland, Daniel S, the subject of this sketch, was born in the town of Queensbury, March 24th, 1819, his father, Joseph Hamilton, senior, being one of the largest land owners in Warren county, owning and operating at one time upwards of 700 acres, his son Daniel S, assisting in its management until the year 1840, when he married Miss Margaret V Otis, daughter of Stephen Otis of Danby, Vt, and soon after located at his present home on Sanford's Ridge in the town of Queensbury, where he has continued to pursue his early calling   He is a prominent member of the Society of Friends, whose present flourishing condition in their new location at Glens Falls, is largely due to his efforts in connection with a few others   He has three children living, Harris G, S Josephine and Joseph D   Harris G married Miss Adelia Winchip, daughter of Remsen J Winchip, S Josephine married Dr S T Budsall of Brooklyn, who has now located in Glens Falls, and Joseph D married Miss Margaretta De Long, daughter of Z I De Long of Glens Falls

Haviland, George E, Queensbury, p o Glens Falls, was born in Queensbury, Warren county, in 1825   Is an extensive farmer and dairyman, was married in 1847 to Laura Jane Barker, of Middletown, Vt   They have four children   Ellen, Ida, Edson and Jay   Ellen is now Mrs Byron Jacobs, and Ida is Mrs Chas. Ford   Mr Haviland is a son of David and Anna (Hoag) Haviland   Four of their children are now living   George E, Lavina, Charlotte and Sarah A

Haviland, Harris G, of Queensbury, p o Glens Falls, was born February 12th, 1842   Is a graduate of the Fort Edward Institute and also of Union Springs   Is a general farmer and breeder of blooded cattle, sheep, swine and poultry   He has the Shropshire sheep, Jersey cattle, and his swine are proving the most valuable in the known market   At present he is giving considerable attention to fruit-growing, was married in 1866 to Miss Adelia Winchip of Queensbury, and they have two children, Walter W, and Gertie K   Mr Haviland's parents were Daniel and Margaret (Otis) Haviland

Haviland, John G, Queensbury, p o Glens Falls, son of John M and Almira (Thompson), was born in Queensbury in 1843   Was formerly a farmer, but in 1881 he, with C W. Haviland and F W. Gilbert commenced the general mercantile trade dealing largely in dry goods, groceries, provisions and farmers' supplies, as well as a class of goods for the most exquisite taste of town or city   The firm is "Havilands & Gilbert" No 100 Glen Street   Mr Haviland still continues to superintend his stock and dairy farm, was married in 1870 to Harriet E Haviland, who was a daughter of Roger and Harriet (Heigth)   She died in May 27th, 1884, leaving two children, Bernice G, and Isabella D

Haviland, Roger Augustus, Queensbury, p o Glens Falls, was born in Queensbury, Warren county, October 14th, 1844   In early life he became a general market dealer, was chief of police in 1876, and in 1882, he with Mr Herbert H Bush, purchased a general stock of dry goods, groceries and provisions, fancy goods, boots and shoes Their location is No 23 Glen street, in 1871 he was married to Miss Helen M Madden of Glens Falls and they have a family of three children Bertha E, Helena Maud, and Anna Elma. Mr Haviland's parents were Roger and Harriet (Haight) Haviland

Haviland, Roger F, Queensbury, p o Glens Falls, was born in Queensbury, Dec 19th, 1838 Is a descendant of Benjamin Haviland, who emigrated from England in 1647, and settled at Flushing, L I In early life Roger gave his attention to farming, which was the profession of his ancestors, but in 1865, he embarked in a mercantile trade at Peekskill, N Y In 1857, he sold out his business and returned to Glens Falls. where he with Mr G M Ferris purchased the drugs and general house of the old house of George Sisson under the firm name of Haviland & Ferris They are among the leading drug houses of New York State, dealing in all classes of drugs, patent medicines, paints, oils sash, doors and blinds. In 1882 they were induced to add another store in which they keep a full assortment of builders' hardware and carpenter tools, for which a wholesale as well as a retail department is found in their store, in 1860 Mr Haviland married Mary Jane Lane of Westchester county, and they have two children, Foster L and Florence L Mr Haviland's parents were Solomon and Lydia (Otis) Haviland

Hawley, A Goodrich, Queensbury, p o Glens Falls, was born in Moreau, Saratoga county, in 1833, was married in 1861 to Miss Harriet Taylor, daughter of Lansing G Taylor, they have two children, Harry Goodrich and Caroline Lizzie Mr Hawley's parents were George G and Eliza (Goodrich) Hawley They had three children, A G George K, Gertrude E Gertude E is now Mrs James McDonald, George E died March 2d, 1882, and Eliza (Goodrich) August 3d, 1885

Hawley, Chas E, Caldwell p o Lake George, was born in Caldwell, March 4th, 1837 Is a practical painter by trade, also a farmer and a member of the Lake George band Has held the office of justice of the peace, town clerk and other offices, was married in 1865 to Miss Sarah E Fairman of West Troy, and they have three children, Fred F, Stuart H and Bertha M Mr Hawley's parents were Hiram and Clara (Chapman) Hawley

Hayes, Orlin S, p o Hague, was born July 14th, 1849, and is a native of the town of Horicon Was married May 18th, 1879 to Stella, daughter of Samuel Ackerman, of Hague, and they have three children, Charles Edith and Mildred Mr Hayes's parents were Samuel and Mahitabel (Howe) Hayes The grandfather, Nathan, was from Rensselaer county and a soldier of the Revolution

Hayes, Stephen, p o Horicon, is a native of Hayesburgh, Warren county, where he was born July 28th, 1831 Is a farmer and lumberman Has a farm of 240 acres Was married in August, 1853, to Delina, daughter of Seely Mallory, of Corinth, Saratoga county, and they have five children, Josephine (Mrs A J Burgess), Fred Melvin, Alice and Rebecca Benjamin Hayes, brother of Stephen, was born in Horicon, March 17th, 1833 He located on his present place in 1860 In 1883 he rebuilt, making one of the finest summer hotels on Brant Lake It is finely located three miles north of Horicon post-office Daily mail, excellent tackle, and accommodations for twenty-five guests Mr Benjamin Hayes was married September 3d, 1853, to Miss Elexcy, daughter of William Baker, of Horicon, and they have three children, Edison, Susan (now Mrs L L Gregory), and Emma (now Mrs. Albert Griffin)

Heffron, John, p o Warrensburgh, was born in Ireland Oct 16th, 1846, and came to Warrensburgh from that country in 1857, two years after the arrival of his parents at Fort Anne, Washington county, was formerly a farmer and lumberman and has now become a popular landlord He is the owner and proprietor of the Warren Hotel at Warrensburgh It is an old popular stand, and dates back in history over ninety-six years He purchased and remodeled, and generally improved it in 1878, and is still adding to its comfort and capacity for his many guests Mr Heffron was married in 1876 to Miss Bridget Ashe, daughter of James and Joanna Ashe, of Thurman

Herrick Frederick W, p o Warrensburgh, was born in Warrensburgh in 1848 He experienced some vicissitudes in his early business life, which only increased his energy, and in 1883 he embarked in his present retail and wholesale business He is an extensive dealer in all classes of furniture, carpets, and undertaking In 1883 he was married to Mary E Reynolds, of Chester Mr Herrick is a son of Robert Geere Herrick, and Hannah P (White) Herrick, natives of Warrensburgh

Hills, James, Queensbury, p o French Mountain, born in Queensbury in 1861, son of James and Eliza (Blackburn) Hills, married in Warren county, the former died at his residence in 1875, at the age of 47 years, the latter died in the same year, at the age of 39 years, leaving five children, two now living Sarah and James. Sarah married John Chapman, James married Rosa Titus, children two

Hillis, Mrs Margaret, Queensbury, p o French Mountain, born in Ireland in 1828, settled in Warren county in 1848, daughter of Andrew and Margaret (Stewart) Lattimore, who were married in Ireland and had five children, settled in Queensbury in 1850, children Ellen Jane, Margaret, Matilda, Mary, and Stewart Margaret married Mr William Hillis, born in Ireland in 1834, enlisted in 1862 in the 153d Regiment and died at Finley Hospital in 1864, leaving two children Mary Jane and William Mary Jane married Robert Chapman in 1882, one child

Hitchcock, Chas H, Queensbury, p o Glens Falls, was born in Salem, Washington county, N Y, Nov 4th, 1849 He settled in Glens Falls in 1879 as the manager of the Wheeler & Wilson sewing machine He has one of the finest offices of Northern New York, and a flourishing business He is also trustee of the Glens Falls corporation In 1882 he was married to Miss Ella R Perry, of Lansingburgh N Y, she died in October, 1883 Mr Hitchcock's parents were Rev P N, and Phebe (Pierson) Hitchcock Rev P N Hitchcock has been a member of the Troy Conference for over fifty years Besides Chas H they had three other children. Adelia M, Hattie A, and Frank Frank enlisted from Saratoga in the 77th N Y Vol Regiment, served three years and was discharged

Hogle, Valentine, p o Luzerne was born in Luzerne, December, 1819, was an early merchant, has been assessor six years, justice of the peace eight years, and commissioner one year, was married in 1840 to Miss Mary E Moore, of Fort Edward, Washington county, of their ten children, six are living, viz Barney B, Frances, Hortense Emma E, Salina L and Addie A Mr Hogle was a soldier in the late war, enlisting in Co C, 118th Regiment, was discharged in 1863 for disability His son enlisted in Co A, 2d N Y Cavalry, in 1863 and was discharged in 1865 Mr Hogle was a son of Barney P and Sally (Sprague) Hogle

Hooper, George H, p o Hague. was born in Warren, N H, March 30th, 1862 He is superintendent of the Dixon Graphite Works at Hague, was married June 2d, 1885 to Miss Lena Woodard, daughter of Elijah Woodard, of Ticonderoga Mr Hooper is a son of William Hooper, of Ticonderoga The mining of graphite in Hague has developed into an important industry at Hague, and under the management of Mr Hooper is very successful

Howard, Eliakim W, p o Warrensburgh, was born in Fort Anne, Washington county, in January, 1808 He read medicine with Dr Porter, of Fort Anne and with Dr Ransom, of Glens Falls, and graduated at Castleton, Vt, in 1833 He settled in Queensbury in practice and in 1837 settled in Warrensburgh where he now resides In 1835 he married Miss Ann Rebecca Brown, of Queensbury, she died in 1860 leaving a family of two children Julia, and Daniel B For his second wife E W Howard married Mrs Adelia Cameron Fenton Dr. Howard's son, Dr Daniel B Howard, was a graduate of the Albany Medical College in 1865, and became partner with his father

Howard, Henry A, Queensbury, p o Glens Falls, was born in Windsor, Windsor county, Vt, in 1845, was a graduate of the Kimball Union Academy, of New Hampshire, in 1862, and of Norwich University in 1865, he also graduated from the Albany Law School, and was admitted to the bar in 1867, the same year he settled in Glens Falls as a lawyer, and in 1879 and 1882 he was elected district attorney In 1875 he was married to Mary E Robbins, daughter of Samuel E Robbins, of Boston, and a descendant of the Buckinghams of Massachusetts Mr. Howard enlisted in Co G, 60th Mass Regiment, and served nearly a year before being discharged

Howe, Clark, jr, Queensbury, p o Glens Falls, was born in Greenfield, Saratoga county, in 1831, in 1851 he settled in Queensbury with all his worldly goods in a handkerchief, he commenced the blacksmith trade which he has continued to the present, reared his family, and has a homestead of 85 acres There is but one person living in the neighborhood who was there at the time of settlement. Mr Howe has served as constable, and was elected assessor of the town in 1884 He is a general blacksmith, carriage and wagon ironer and practical horse-shoer He married Miss Jennett Stanton, of Caldwell, in 1856, and they have nine children Delbert S, Nellie L, Jennie F (now Mrs Edward A Moore), Elmer C, Willie O, Mabel, Erwin, Byron, and Thekla Delbert S married Miss Minnie Brown, and Nellie L is now Mrs George A Moore Mr Howe's parents were Clark and Matilda (Swears) Howe.

Howe, Melvin, p o Luzerne, was born in Vermont in 1842, and settled with his parents in Luzerne in 1849 He enlisted in Co K, 2d N Y Vet. Cavalry, and served until the close of the war, was married in 1866 to Miss Helen Moore, daughter of Alfred and Laura Moore, and they have one child, Fred M Howe Mr Howe's parents were Charles and Orpha (Goodspeed) Howe They had ten children, seven now living

Hubbell, Frederick B, Caldwell, p o Lake George, was born in Queensbury in 1822, he is a farmer and extensive lumber manufacturer, commenced his business life in 1855 by building a saw-mill on Mill Brook He built several saw-mills and in 1867, he, with Mr L C Seelye, built a steam mill at Lake George, which was sold and removed In 1876 he built his present large steam mill at Lake George, having fifty horse power, circle and gang, lathe, planing, moulding and wood sawing, using the saw-dust for fuel, in fact it is one of the substantial mills of the county, having dockage on the lake for shipping and receiving logs Mr Hubbell has been supervisor of Caldwell for about fifteen years, was nominated for Assembly in 1878 on the Democrat ticket, his wife was Miss Susan Smith, daughter of John Smith, of Horicon They were married in 1847 and have a family of eight children, viz Diana, Jerome N, Smith, Richard, Walter, Sarah P, Mack B, and Florence B Mr Hubbell's parents were Frederick and Betsey (Jenkins) Hubbell

Hubbell, Frederick S, Queensbury, p o Glens Falls, was born in Queensbury, April 15, 1818, he is a farmer and lumber dealer and owns and resides on the homestead of his parents, was married in 1839 to Miss Harriet West, and they have five children Mary Jane, Jerome E, Job, Zillah, and Carolina, all of whom are now married Mr Hubbell is a son of Isaac and Hannah (Prey) Hubbell They settled in Queensbury in 1814 and had twelve children, seven of whom are now living

Hubbell, John Pray, Queensbury, p o Glens Falls, was born in Queensbury in 1827, was married in 1853 to Miss Phoebe Anna Jenkins, of Queensbury, she died July 10th, 1875, leaving six children Eugene, Louisa, Ira, Hannah, Allen, and Byron Eugene married Miss Bessie Wood, of Ohio, and Hannah is Mrs Fred Walker, of Flint, Mich Mr Hubbell's parents were Isaac and Hannah (Pray) Hubbell, who settled in Warren county in 1815 They had ten children, of whom seven are now living, four in the town of Queensbury and three in Wisconsin

Hull, Joseph, Queensbury, p o Glens Falls, was born in Granville, Washington county, N Y, in the year 1855, he removed to Queensbury, Warren county, in 1866, is a farmer and resides on his parents' homestead, is also a dealer in blooded stock — Ayrshire and Jersey cattle, Cotswold and Oxfordshiredown sheep, was married in 1882 to Josephine L Staples, daughter of Anson R and Lydia A (Haviland) Staples. They have one child, Anson Hull Mr Hull is a son of Rev Nelson and Hannah R (Dillingham) Hull Besides Joseph they have four other children, the eldest, Otis D Hull, was born in 1853, is now engaged in the orange growing business in Florida, was married to Carrie Norton, and they have two children, George and Lulu Hull

Hunt, Edgar W, Caldwell, p o Lake George, was born in Rensselaer county, N Y, in 1836, he settled in Warren county with his parents in 1840, is an active man of his town, having been deputy county clerk nine years, justice of the peace two terms, and justice of sessions.

Hunt, John G, p o Warrensburgh, was born in New York city in 1846, he is a merchant of Warrensburgh, dealing in hardware, stoves, tin, crockery, stone and hollow wares, and a full line of farmers' supplies, builders' materials, paints, oils, etc., he settled in Warrensburgh in 1871 with a small but well selected stock to which he has consistently added, and now has one of the most well ordered stores of Northern New York, was married in 1867, to Miss Kate W Williams, of Rahway, N J They have a family of five children Maggie G, Kate M, Helen H, Alice, and Charles W

Hurd, Chas W, Queensbury, p o Glens Falls, was born in New Hampshire in 1844, in 1871 he settled in Glens Falls as a machinist and in 1873 commenced his present business on Ridge street, is a jeweler and silversmith, dealing in solid and plated gold and silver ware, rings, watches, clocks, and all fancy goods. In 1879, he purchased his present store and dwelling on Glen street where he has largely increased his stock and business. he makes a specialty of diamonds, spectacles, etc., was married in 1869 to Sarah M Fox, she died in 1872 leaving one son, Albert For his second wife Mr Hurd married Julia Abbott, of New Haven, Vt They have one daughter, Lena, born in 1881

Jarvis, Robert, p o Warrensburgh, was born in Glasgow, Scotland, in November, 1830 He removed with his parents to New York city in 1832, and in 1844 settled in Thurman His parents died leaving four children In 1864 Robert settled in Warrensburgh and embarked in the mercantile trade He still prosecutes this business in its various branches, was married to Miss Julia Kennedy, of Hadley, in 1859 They have a family of three children Robert Gilchrist, Mary, and Myra Mary married Mr Chas Cunningham in 1884 Robert G read medicine and is now in Albany Medical College Myra is a teacher

Jenkins, Gamaliel, Queensbury, p o Glens Falls, was born in Queensbury in 1824 Is a general farmer and lumberman and owns a flour and feed mill which was originally built about 100 years ago Mr Jenkins has repaired it and increased its capacity Has been justice of the peace for several years Mr Jenkins's parents were Palmer B and Lois (Brayton) Jenkins, who settled in Queensbury in 1795 Mr Jenkins, sr, was a soldier in the War of 1812

Johnson, Nathan B, p o Warrensburgh, was born in Thurman in 1850, and settled in Warrensburgh, in 1877, was married to Miss Bessie E Mead, of Johnsburgh, in 1874, and they have one child Mr Johnson's parents were Ebenezer H and Caroline (Baldwin) Johnson They were married in 1847 and have a family of four children Nathan B, Ettie M, William H and Bessie Mr Johnson, senior, was assessor two terms, highway commissioner two terms, and a farmer

Joiner, Fletcher, Queensbury, p o Glens Falls, born in Mira, Franklin Co, N Y, 1825. Parents John W and Hannah (Beatty) Joiner, first wife Mary Ladd, of Franklin, married in 1852, died 1864, leaving eight children, Mary A, Frank L, Fletcher E, Edgar D, Eliza, Alice C, Minnie E, and Addie Second wife Catharine Sailes, of Pine Valley, Chemung Co Son, Edgar D, born 1856, partner of his father, Fletcher Joiner & Son, The Messrs Joiner came to Glens Falls and commenced the building of various patterns of sail and fancy boats Wife Alida Truesdell, of Bolton, married in 1883, one child Ethel

Joslyn, Calvin, jr, Saratoga, p o Glens Falls, born in Lancaster, Mass, in 1816, wife, Hettie Maria Spicer, born in 1824, married in 1844, children five Eber J, Ai, Fordice, Sanford, Clara Belle, Parents, Calvin and Hannah (Robbins) Joslyn, of Massachusetts, married and settled in Hadley, Saratoga county, in 1818, the former died in 1870, the latter in 1860, children four, three now living Calvin, Loria and Sarah

Juvet, Louis Paul, p o Glens Falls, was born in Chaux-de-Fonds, Switzerland, August 4th, 1838 Mr Juvet's parents were Charles L and Augustine Juvet, of Switzerland He received the education to which all young Swiss are entitled and learned the art of watch-making He landed in New York in 1864, on the very day which saw Glens Falls, his destined home, reduced to ashes For the purpose of mastering the English language, then entirely un-known to him, he left the city at once and resided for a few months in Ballston Spa and Sara-toga Springs On the 2d day of January, 1865, he located in Glens Falls and commenced busi-ness as a watchmaker and jeweler, dealing in diamonds, watches, jewelry and a variety of the best quality of silver ware In 1867 he completed the first models of his famous Time Globe, a combination of a globe and a clock by means of which the time of every place on earth is de-termined and which shows the earth in its correct and relative position to the sun at any mo-ment. In 1869 he married Miss Eloise Cameron, of Glens Falls, and lost her by death in 1871. In 1876, at the request of the Philadelphia Exposition committee, two time globes made almost entirely by hand were produced and exhibited This exhibit received the Centennial medal of merit and attracted the attention of scientific men of all nations, prominent among them Gen. John Eaton U S Commissioner of Education, who ordered one built at once for the U S Gov-ernment exhibit This last model was constructed on new and much improved plans for which new patents were issued In 1879 the firm of Juvet & Co, of Canajoharie, N Y, was founded. It was and is now composed of Mrs L P Juvet, James Arkell (senator), W J Arkell (now of the Albany *Evening Journal*) and A G Richmond, cashier, of Canajoharie The purpose of this firm was to manufacture time globes, as well as school globes of all descriptions, their produc-tions have since been shipped to all parts of the world and are found in the libraries of most of our leading men In 1881 Mr Juvet became one of the originators of the Mount McGregor Improvement Co, and with his associates in the globe business became the nucleus of the Sara-toga, Mount McGregor and Lake George R R Co, owners of the Mount McGregor property lately made notable by the sufferings and death of Gen Grant.

Keeffe, Daniel F, was born in 1841 Was educated in the common schools and Glens Falls Academy Read law in the office of Davis & Harris, and was admitted to the bar at a general term of the Supreme Court at Schenectady in 1869, and has since practiced his profession in Glens Falls Mr Keeffe is the present supervisor of the town of Queensbury

Keenan, John, Queensbury, p o Glens Falls, was born in Ulster, Ireland, in 1811 In 1831 he emigrated with two of his sisters to Quebec, and they went to Scranton Falls, where a half brother resided and remained for one year In 1832 John settled in Kingsbury, Washington county, where he was several years engaged in boating, and in 1838 he went to Glens Falls and commenced the manufacturing and shipping of lime to the New York market His partner was the Hon Judge Halsey R Wing of Keenan & Wing, which firm continued until his death In 1860 Mr Keenan's interest was sold to Mr McDonald Mr Keenan has been an active man in his town, president of the corporation for several terms, and prominent in supplying the town with mountain water and fine sidewalks, also president of the Glens Falls and Fort Edward R. R, was married in 1843 to Ann O'Connor, of Kingsbury, Washington county, and they have five children living, viz: Mary, now Mrs. Peck, Angeline, Margaret, Henry and John, jr

Kendrick, Willis J, Queensbury, p o Glens Falls, was born in Stockholm, St Lawrence county, in 1860 He first settled in Glens Falls in 1879, as clerk for Messrs Wilson & Ken-drick Afterward he spent three years in Boston learning the drug trade Returning he be-came partner with his brother, Mr S G Kendrick, and closing his interest he opened one of the fine drug and prescription stores of the town in the Opera House Block in Jan, 1885 Mr Kendrick's parents were Jason M and Esther (Ellis) Kendrick

Kerr, Edward, p o Luzerne, was born in Luzerne, Sept 17th, 1834 He is a general farmer and dairyman, having a farm of 300 acres, was married Oct 6th, 1863, to Miss Isabella Harper, daughter of Arthur Harper, of Canada, and they have two children Arthur W and Margaret S   Mr Kerr has been poormaster three terms Is a son of William and Lovina (Greene) Kerr They had a family of five children, two now living

Kenworthy, John L, Queensbury, p o Glens Falls, was born in Bellows Falls, Windham county, Vt, Dec 8th, 1818 and settled in Glens Falls in 1833 He was apprenticed to Harmon Peck to learn the tin trade, where he remained for six years In 1842 he formed a partnership with Mr Noble Peck, which remained unchanged until Mr Peck's death Mr Kenworthy then took the entire business. Was burned out and then took his present store on Warren St, where he still remains His stock consists of all useful house furnishing goods, from the simplest kitchen article to a parlor ornament with stoves tin and crockery, he was married to Laura L Stour, of Glens Falls, in 1841, and they have four children

King, Frederick W, p o Warrensburgh, was born in Warrensburgh in 1851 Is a farmer Was married, in 1883, to Miss Minerva J Woodward, daughter of Hon Joseph and Jane (Judd) Woodward They have one child, Julia E Mr King was a son of Hesden and Minerva (Richards) King They had six children, George R, Horace P, Frederick W Hesden P, Samuel T and Chas F George R enlisted in Co G, 31st Wisconsin, in 1862, and served until 1865, was a prisoner at Libby Prison Hesden P and Charles F are lawyers, Samuel T is a physician and George is postmaster at Wilcox, Arizona. Horace is a merchant

King, Hesden Prior, Queensbury, p o Glens Falls, was born in Warrensburgh, N Y, in 1853 Read law at Warrensburgh and with Judge Davis, of Glens Falls, and was admitted at Albany Jan 11th, 1878 Was clerk of the Surrogate Court He also graduated in civil engineering in 1873, in 1879 was married to Anna E Cowles, of Glens Falls They have one daughter, Jennie R Mr King's parents were Hesden and Minerva (Richards) King They had six sons George R, Horace P, Frederick W, Hesden P, Samuel T, and Chas F George R served three years during the late war Was a prisoner for a short time in Libby Prison Samuel T is a graduate of Dartmouth and a physician and surgeon in Brooklyn Charles I, also a graduate of Dartmouth College, is a lawyer

Kingsley John S Queensbury, p o Glens Falls, was born in Washington county, in 1827, in 1851 he was married to Miss Margaret M Harris, Queensbury They have four daughters Adelia, Sarah Louise, Ida and Matilla Adelia A married Mr Daniel Sweet, Sarah is now Mrs Allen Brown, Ida is a teacher in the Glens Falls Seminary, and Matilla is a teacher at the Albany Normal School Mrs Kingsley was a daughter of John J and Sarah (Welch) Harris Besides Margaret they had six other children Mr John J Harris built and donated the Episcopal church at Queensbury and it was consecrated in 1869 at a cost of $13,000 He was one of the leading business men of the county, active in all large business enterprises, and an extensive lumber dealer and builder

Kipp, Ruliff, Queensbury, p o Glens Falls, was born at Schaghticoke, Rensselaer Co, in 1811, son of Tunis and Eliza (Van Antwerp) Kipp He settled at an early date at Schaghticoke with his parents In 1840 he removed to Queensbury and became one of the largest farmers of the county, owning over 2 000 acres of land He was an early lumberman and dealer and also engaged in the general grocery and provision trade, from which he retired in 1865 He has been a director of the First National Bank for over thirty years and also director of the Gas Light Co, and Glens Falls Insurance Co, of which institution he is a stock owner Was married in 1834 to Miss Maria Yates She died in 1854 leaving four children For his second wife, he married Miss Mary Flood, of Queensbury, Warren Co

Kirkbride, William A, Queensbury, p o Glens Falls, was born at Rego, Canada, in 1849, and settled in Essex Co in 1865 In 1878 he removed to Glens Falls and commenced business as a journeyman marble and granite worker In 1884 he became a partner of Mr William S Tuttle. The firm is now Tuttle & Kirkbride, and they make a specialty of all classes of the best cemetery work, house marble, ornaments and mantels They handle all of the fine grades of granite and marble, and are competent to execute the finest of work, Mr Kirkbride was married in 1879 to Miss Mary E Rivers, of Vergennes, Vt, and they have two children Mary and Mabel Mr Kirkbride was a son of Robert and Elizabeth (Stevens) Kirkbride

Lapham, Henry G, Queensbury, p o Glens Falls, was born in Queensbury, son of Benjamin and Lydia (Langdon) Lapham, was married to Lydia Sherman in 1862 Mr Lapham is the only representative of a large family, having had seven children The grandparents were Stephen and Rachel (Hussey) Lapham They had a family of thirteen children, nine girls and four boys, all of whom are dead

Lapham, Hon Jerome, Queensbury, p o Glens Falls, was born in Queensbury, Warren Co, in 1823 Has been one of the representative men of his county Has been supervisor several terms and all minor town offices   He was member of Assembly in 1865 and president of corporation   Trustee, and also president and director of County Agricultural Society   Was chairman of the county war committee, was married in 1846 to Hannah Hoyt, and they have two children, Helen and Byron   Byron married Miss Minnie Spencer of Glens Falls in 1870 and they have one son   Helen is now Mrs C L Rockwell, and has three children.   Hon Jerome Lapham's parents were Jonathan and Elizabeth (Healy) Lapham   Besides Jerome, they had two other sons, Benjamin F and Fletcher   Fletcher enlisted in the 22d Regiment under Col Phillips   Served three years and was discharged   He died in 1883, leaving a widow and three children

Langworthy, Myron B, p. o Bolton, was born in Warrensburgh in 1847, and settled in Bolton in 1876   He is an extensive farmer and lumber dealer, owning 300 acres of land and timber, was married in 1869 to Miss Lorinda Bennett, of Warrensburgh, and they have two daughters, Bertha J and Daisey M   Mr Langworthy was a son of Walter and Mary E. (Bennet) Langworthy   They had six children

La Salle, Nelson, Queensbury, p o Glens Falls, was born in Canada in 1828, and settled in Glens Falls in 1851, as a journeyman mechanic in the manufacture of fine work in carriages.   In 1873 he commenced on his own account, establishing a factory, and building fine light work in buggies, and double carriages.   All hand work of the best grades   His smith work, painting and polishing are all done under his immediate supervision, in 1850 he married Miss Maria B Dean, a native of Scotland, and they have four children, Walter H, Minnie I (now Mrs Edwin C Hart, of Wisconsin), George W, and Fred L   Mr La Salle's father was Louis La-Salle

Latham, Lawton, p o Warrensburgh, was born in Greenwich, Washington Co, in 1814, and settled with his parents in Bolton in 1816, moved to Warrensburgh April, 1845   Has been a general farmer and now owns 574 acres   Was married in 1840 to Miss Lucy A Gould, and they have a family of five children, three now living, John J, Lawton W, and Elizabeth M   Elizabeth M is new Mrs Rev Chas F Wilcox, John J married Miss Emma Greenow, and Lawton married Miss Abby D Lewis   They had one son, Sylvester, who enlisted in Co I, 96th N Y Reg, and after an engagement fought at Charles City Road, Oct 27th, 1864, no clear account of him was ever heard   Mr Latham's parents were John and Polly Latham, natives of the New England States

Lawrence James H, p o Luzerne, was born in Luzerne in 1830   In Sept, 1861, he enlisted in Co D, 93d N Y V, under Col Butler   Was discharged at the close of the war from Philadelphia hospital, having lost a leg at the engagement at Spotsylvania Court House   His limb was amputated on the field   In May, 1862, he was appointed postmaster   Was town clerk 13 years, and embarked in the mercantile trade in 1868   In June, 1885, Mr Alexander Dean became his partner, firm of Lawrence & Dean, was married in 1869 to Miss Celinda Rist, and they have a family of three children, Edwin H, James and Oscar   Mr Lawrence's parents were Dr James and Judith (Wells) Lawrence.

Lee, George W, Queensbury, p o Glens Falls, was born in Queensbury, Warren Co, in 1827, commenced his business life as clerk for A Sherman in 1853   He embarked in the mercantile, lumber and real estate business at Horicon and in 1866 he settled in Glens Falls in company with the Messrs. Coolidge in the general merchandise, lumber and real estate business   In 1881 they retired from the mercantile business, but still continue in the lumber and real estate trade, was married in 1857 to Sarah Mead, of Chester, Warren Co, she died in 1863, leaving one child, Forest   In 1884 he married for his second wife, Miss Kate Cowles, of Glens Falls   Mr Lee's parents were James and Polly (Witherell) Lee

Leggett, Charles S, Chester, p o Chestertown, was born in Chester Jan 25th, 1847   Is a farmer and a member of the M E Church, was married to Jannette, daughter of Elijah and Mary (Carr) Hall, and they have four children, Carrie E, Clarkson H, Katie F, and Arthur G   Mr Leggett's grandfather, Charles Leggett, was a native of Westchester Co, N Y, and in 1795 settled on the place now occupied by our subject.

Leggett, George H, Queensbury, p o Glens Falls, was born in Chester, Warren Co, in 1844   In 1863 he settled in Glens Falls as clerk with Mr Sisson in the drug store, and in 1870 he formed a partnership with Mr John W Bush, firm Leggett & Bush, located at 103 Glen St.   In 1884 he erected his new store at 109 Glen St., where they are now located with an extensive stock of drugs, medicine, paints, oils, and all desirable patent medicines of value, Mr Leggett was married in 1869 to Mary H Burdick, of Glens Falls   Mr Leggett's parents were Joseph and Elizabeth (Mead) Leggett.

Little, Dr George W, Queensbury, p o Glens Falls was born in Burlington, Vt, in Nov 1836   Graduated from the Albany Medical College in 1858   He practiced as assistant in the Albany hospital and read medicine with Dr James Ferguson, of Glens Falls, where he practiced until 1860 He then removed to Johnsburgh, and in 1867 he settled in Fort Edward The same year he was married to Miss Helena Dewey, of Kingsbury. For ten years he was a partner of Dr. B F Cornell at Fort Edward In 1881 the doctor built his present beautiful residence at Glens Falls, where he settled in his profession Dr Little's parents were Rev Russell M and Nancy (Blair) Little

Little, Richard, Chester, son of Robert and Catherine Little, was a native of Fermanagh, Ireland He located at Johnsburgh in the year 1848, and engaged in the tanning business He subsequently removed to Chester and was engaged as superintendent or foreman in the tannery now owned by C R Faxon, of Chester Has been a member of the M E Church for a number of years Is a member of the Order of Good Templars, also of the Sons of Temperance, was married to Mary J, daughter of Benjamin Thompson She died in 1865 and for his second wife Mr Little married Sarah J, daughter of Jno Kanwell, and they have six children, Katie, Satie M, Willie (deceased), Richardson, Clara B, and Lettie

Little, Rev Russell M, Queensbury, p o Glens Falls, was born in Middletown, Mass, in 1809, was licensed in Berkshire in 1828, and united with the N Y Conference in 1829 His first charge was at North Adams, Great Barrington, Stuyvesant, Williamstown, Mass, St Albans, Burlington, Waterbury, Vt, and at last to Glens Falls, where in 1838 he resigned on account of poor health He then engaged in the mercantile business but in 1840 was again compelled to give up his work on account of his health and removed to Easton, Pa In 1842, he again returned to Glens Falls in the same mercantile trade, connected with the insurance business He was active in organizing the Glens Falls Insurance Co, and was chosen its secretary in which capacity he remained until 1867, when he was elected president, which office he now holds Mr Little's parents were Russell and Sarah (Mack) Little They had five children, three of whom are now living Rev Russell M Little, was chosen State senator in 1861, also member of the Chicago Convention in 1880 and U S elector in 1876, but with all his pressing business engagements, he has ever been ready to give counsel to the afflicted as a Christian can only do Was married to Nancy Blair, of Cambridge, N Y, and they have six children

Lockhart, Mr William, Caldwell, p o Lake George, was born in Scotland in 1826, a son of Walter and Mary (McKenzie) Lockhart, and emigrated with them for America in 1842 Mr and Mrs Lockhart settled in Queensbury, where they died, leaving eight children William settled in Caldwell, on the east side of Lake George, where he now resides He spent three years in California and is a man of culture, and a gentleman of rare gifts, a man of original thought and a happy turn of mind In his early married life, when first elected path-master, his first thought was to caution his excellent companion "not to be lifted up above her old friends, as he might not win at his next election" Mr Lockhart was married in July, 1852, to Esther, daughter of William and Polly (Sanders) Bates.

Lockwood, John H, p o Warrensburgh, was born in Warrensburgh in 1847 He commenced his early business life as a farmer and lumberman which business he still continues In 1883 he purchased an interest in the stage-coach, mail and express business from Warrensburgh to Glens Falls The firm is Lockwood Bros Mr Lockwood was married in 1880 to Miss Diana Hubbell, daughter of Frederick B and Susan P (Smith) Hubbell Mr Lockwood is a son of George and Eliza (Taylor) Lockwood Two of their three children are now living, John H and George T

Loomis, John R, Queensbury p. o Glens Falls, was born in Cambridge, Washington county, in 1846 In 1882 he removed from New York city to Glens Falls, and purchased an interest in the furniture, undertaking and upholstery business of Charles E Bullard The firm is now Bullard & Loomis, 118 and 120 Glen street Mr Loomis is also a professional accountant. Was married in 1868 to Sarah Emma daughter of the Hon R M Little They have three children, Russell M, John R, jr, and George L Mr Loomis's parents were Ezekiel and Ann (Rice) Loomis

Loveland, John, Thurman, p o Athol, was born in this town in 1826, is a farmer, merchant and hotel-keeper, has been sheriff in his county for two terms, and has also held various local offices in his town, viz Supervisor, justice of the peace, commissioner of highways Was married in 1850 to Sarah Wiltsey, a native of this county They have two children Cordelia and Eloise Loveland

Lyons, Dennis, Caldwell, p o Lake George, was born in Maine in 1841 He settled at Lake George in 1868, and in 1879 embarked in the grocery and provision business at Lake George, where he is having a large trade He is a son of Jeremiah and Ann (Murphy) Lyons They had three children, Dennis, John and Margaret Margaret is now Mrs John Caldwell The father, Jeremiah, was an extensive railroad and canal contractor

43

MacGregor, Duncan, Queensbury, p o Glens Falls, born in Witton, Saratoga county, in 1808 Wife, Harriett G Cornell, of Witton, born in 1813, married in 1844, and died in 1868 One adopted daughter, Anna L Sprott. Mr MacGregor settled in Glens Falls in 1867, where he now resides Parents, James and Elizabeth (Cameron) MacGregor, the latter born in Scotland, came to Saratoga county in 1775 or '77, the former came with her parents on the same ship They were married about 1790, settled and lived in Witton until their death Children, eleven, two living

Macomber, Albert W, Chesterfield, p o Clintonsville, was born in Chesterfield, February 26th, 1826 Is a son of Wesson and grandson of John Macomber, known better as Judge Macomber, being one of the first judges of Essex county Is a farmer and owns 300 acres of land Was married to Sarah Beardsley, daughter of I and Sarah (Day) Beardsley, of Port Jackson, Clinton county, children, five Eunice B (now Mrs Rev Charles A Bradford, of Peru), Adelaid (now Mrs James Wardner, of Brighton, Franklin county), Lillian M, Edmund K and George N, a doctor of Syracuse

Macomber, George N, M D, of Syracuse, was born in Essex county, N Y, May 13th, 1854 His father being a farmer, he was reared to agricultural pursuits His early education was obtained at the Keeseville Academy His scientific knowledge, for which he always had a great desire, was acquired by his own exertions Most of his time for two years was spent in teaching, to obtain means to pursue his studies, having from childhood an inherent passion for medicine He entered the office of Dr H A Houghton, a very able physician of Keeseville, now of Burton, Mass After three years of study he entered Pult Medical College, of Cincinnati, Ohio, from which he graduated in 1878 Immediately after graduating he located in Norwood, St. Lawrence county, where he remained in active practice for four years Not being satisfied to remain longer in so small a town, in the spring of 1882 he sold out to a young physician who was desirous of purchasing an established practice, and at once moved to Syracuse, N Y He entered the office formerly occupied by the late Dr Bigelow, 110 South Salina street, and by his close application to business, and courteous and gentlemanly treatment, he has not only built up a large and lucrative practice, but enjoys the confidence of the entire community, and the respect of the medical profession, who recognize in him a young man of very marked ability In the treatment of chronic diseases he has been especially successful often being called in consultation on difficult cases in preference to older practitioners

Mason, Calvin, Queensbury, p o Glens Falls, was born in Kingsbury, Washington county, in 1822 Is a general farmer and agent for the Bradley mower, reaper and rake Was married in 1848 to Miss Phebe Shepard, of Washington county She died in 1871, leaving one son, Charles E Mason In 1874 Mr Mason was again married to Abbie A Haviland Her parents were David and Hannah (Anthony) Haviland He died in 1862 and left two children, Abbey and Roger E

Mason, Thomas Freeman, Queensbury, p o Glens Falls, born in Roxbury, Litchfield county, Connecticut, January 5th, 1804, and settled in Fort Ann, Washington county, October 28th, 1814 Wife, Chloe Shattuck, born in Pittford, Vt, June 2d 1806 Married June 14th, 1827 Two children, Harriett M and Arabella. Arabella married Mr Dillon P Smith, two children, Charles F and Lucy B Lucy B married Mr E E Winchell, have one daughter Constance C Winchell, born 1884 Charles married Miss Emily Knight, January 22d, 1884

Mattison, Charles, p o Horicon, is one of the respected citizens of Horicon Is a native of the place and was born August 5th, 1845 He is engaged in the lumber business Has held town office of commissioner of highways. Was married March 28th, 1868, to Perthena, daughter of Abram Whitaker, of Weavertown, N Y, and they have nine children, Anjuletta, Ann Melha, Cora, Nora, John, Leonard, Nellie, Albert and Louise Anjuletta Mattison was thirteen years old when she died Mr Mattison's parents were George and Emeline (Hayes) Mattison

McClanathan, John, p o Hague, was born in Hague, November 13th, 1838 He is a farmer and the proprietor of the Hillside House of Hague It is a new house, handsomely located on a sightly eminence overlooking Lake George, and accommodates thirty-five guests Mr McClanathan has held the office of town clerk five years and has been supervisor nine years Was married December 23d, 1872, to Martha A, daughter of Aaron Lyon Mr McClanathan's grandfather, John, came from Connecticut, and located in Hague about 1812 He located about one and a half miles west of Hague on 111 acres of land and raised a family of ten children, of whom one only is now living

McDermott, Rev James, Queensbury, p o Glens Falls, was born in Ireland in 1836, where he received a liberal education In 1854 he went to Baltimore, where he completed his classical education, and on August 22d, 1862, he was ordained at the Albany cathedral by Bishop McCloskey August 27th, 1862, he was sent to Glens Falls, where he has since labored, and has caused the erection of a fine church edifice and large school buildings and dwelling

McDonald, Leonard G, Queensbury p o Glens Falls, was born in Warren county in 1821, son of William McDonald and Mary Jane Davis He was born in Duchess county, N Y, and she in Connecticut in 1784 They married at Schuylerville in 1809 and settled in the village of Glens Falls in 1818 They died in the county, he September 11th, 1870, and she September 16th, 1862 They had eight children, six now living, five sons and one daughter, Richard S, Leonard G, William H, Walter and Edward, and Mrs Julia A Armes The father, William, settled in Warren county in 1795 on what is known as Sanford's Ridge in Queensbury His father was Dr Charles McDonald, was born and educated in Scotland, and after the Revolution settled at New Rochelle, and died at the age of eighty-five years Mr Leonard G McDonald married Miss Clara M Twining, born in Sandersfield, Berkshire county, and married in 1872 She was a daughter of Mr Thomas Twining, of Massachusetts Mr William McDonald was member of Assembly two terms, 1822 and 1826 He was one of the prominent leading men of the State, and was the influential man in locating the feeder of the Champlain and Erie canals at Glens Falls, as it was the early intention to have it at Sandy Hill It is proper here to state that the great growth of this corporation is due to Mr William McDonald or his early influence in legislation

McEchron, William, Queensbury p o. Glens Falls, was born in Saratoga, Saratoga county, in 1831 Mr McEchron is a self-made man, having by persistent effort reached an enviable height in financial success He boated, chopped and lumbered from his childhood until 1846, when he went to Argyle and assisted as errand boy in a store, and attended school at the academy for two terms He then became assistant at the Fort Edward railroad baggage department In 1851 he entered into the employ of a lumbering firm at Fort Edward (Bradly & Underwood), and worked for them thirteen years as foreman and agent, and in 1864 he took the interest of Mr Lapham in the firm of Morgan & Lapham, and the firm name became Morgan & McEchron The firm is now the Morgan Lumber Co, and is one of the large lumber and lime companies of the State Mr McEchron was married in 1858 to Sarah E Carswell, of Fort Edward, and they have three daughters, Margaret, Caroline and Elizabeth Mr McEchron's parents were David and Hannah McEchron David died in 1862, leaving five children, William, Elizabeth, Hannah M, Cornelia and Ruth Ruth still resides with her mother, now aged 82 years

McGuire, Patrick J, Stony Creek, p o Creek Center, came to this town in 1868 and engaged in lumbering Has held several of the minor town offices Was married in 1872 to Miss Julia Murray, daughter of Alexander Murray, an old resident of this town Mr McGuire settled on his present farm about eight years since They have one child

McLafflin, Bartlett, Johnsburgh, p o Weavertown, was born in County Roscommon, Ireland September 27th, 1828, is a son of John and Ann (Kelly) McLafflin He left Ireland when three years of age with his mother, and located in Quebec, Canada. He came to Johnsburgh in 1850 and in 1861 engaged in the hotel business at Weavertown, has remained there ever since, he has two farms, one of 63 acres and the other of 165 acres, was married in 1861 to Ann J Little, and they have six children William, James, John, Minnie Anna, and Maggie Mr McLafflin is a member of the Catholic Church

McMaster, Charles H, p o Luzerne, was born in Luzerne March 17th, 1849, is a carpenter and builder, is an active member of St. Mary's Episcopal Church, was married in 1872 to Miss Minnie Myers, of Schenectady county, of their four children, but two are now living Mr McMaster is a son of Henry and Mary (Bovee) McMaster

Mead, James J, Queensbury, p o Glens Falls, was born in Chester, Warren county, N Y, in 1859, was a graduate of Warrensburgh Academy in 1880 The 1st of February, 1881, he entered the office of Isaac J Davis (now deceased), and commenced the study of law where he remained until the spring of 1882 He then entered the law department of Union University at Albany, graduating from that department in May, 1883, at which time he was admitted to the bar at Binghamton and settled in his profession at Glens Falls The spring of 1885 he was nominated by the Democratic party for justice of the peace, and defeated by a majority of 23 running ahead of his ticket 175 He married Miss Nellie O'Connor in 1883, and they have one child, J Carlisle She was a graduate of Cohir Convent and of Clonmel Model School with full honors of her province, Ireland Mr Mead's parents were Francis and Lurania (Houghton) Mead Besides James J, they had two other children, Lillian E, and Orpha

Merrill, Caleb, (deceased), Bolton, p o North Bolton, was born in Arlington, Vt., was married to Miss Hannah Watson, a native of Rhode Island, in 1840 Mr Merrill died in 1868, leaving four children Mahala, Eugene, Marlow C, and Alvinus Mrs Merrill and her family then settled in Bolton But two of her children are now living The others died in the war Mrs. Merrill's parents were Joseph, and Susan (Clark) Watson, of Rhode Island

Middleworth, Henry V, Bolton, p o Hill View, was born in Greenwich, Washington county, in 1813   In early life he learned the trade of a wagon manufacturer, and in 1831 he became proprietor of a shop   He afterward dropped his trade and commenced purchasing land in Washington county, and erecting buildings   He is now the owner of the Middleworth House at Sandy Hill, and several of the other prominent buildings   He purchased his present summer residence on Lake George and is now erecting a hotel on the west shore of Lake George, five miles from the head of the lake   When finished it will accommodate 100 guests.   Mr Middleworth was married to Miss Orril Bliss, of Massachusetts, in 1838   They have two children, Ella Josephine, and Warren H

Miles, W R , Stony Creek, p o Creek Center, was born in the town of Jay, Essex county, in 1836, and came to Stony Creek in 1858   He was at that time engaged in blacksmithing, he being one of the first blacksmiths in the town   On the breaking out of the war, he went to Springfield, Mass , in the employ of the government, manufacturing arms   In the fall of 1862 he enlisted in the 1st Conn Heavy Artillery as artificer, and served until 1864, when he was discharged for blindness caused by sun-stroke   He returned to Stony Creek and remained until 1871 when he removed to Albany and served on the new capitol as a tool-maker until 1876   He then engaged as a practical salesman with a Philadelphia and New York house, Ely & Williams, and still remains with them.

Miller, Francis L , Stony Creek, p o Creek Center, has lived in Stony Creek about fourteen years   He formerly came from Clinton county, and was a farmer until two years since   He is now a storekeeper and the owner of a grist-mill, was married in 1872 to Acena Hach of Stony Creek   they have two children   Mr Miller was a soldier in the late war, serving in the 96th N Y Regiment   He took part in fifteen general engagements

Miller, George Y , p o Luzerne, was born in Day, Saratoga county, in 1836   He is a general druggist and prescriptionist at Luzerne, dealing extensively in drugs, medicines, paints and oils, also stationery goods, papers, and all fancy and ornamental goods   Mr Miller was a soldier in the late war, enlisting in 1864   He was appointed ensign in the U S Navy, and transferred from the *Savana* to the *Dictator*   In September, 1864, he went on the *Juanita*, and after the explosion of a two-hundred-pounder, they went to Beaufort for repairs   They entered an engagement at Fort Fisher on December 24th and 25th. 1864   On January 12th and 13th was the second bombardment and success   The fort surrendered January 15th, at 2 P M , orders sent to cease firing and the rebels surrendered at 10 P M to the 5,000 troops, mostly of colored soldiers   Mr Miller was married May 31st, 1864, to Miss Lillie A Lindsey, and they have one son, George   Mr Miller is the commander of Post B C Butler, No 316, and grand master of the A O U W   He was a son of David C and Martha (Yerrington) Miller

Miller, John, J , Queensbury, p o Glens Falls, was born in Ireland in 1818, and settled in Queensbury with his parents in 1830, is a general farmer and owns 300 acres of land, was married to Miss Eunice Brainard in 1847   She died in 1881, and for his second wife he married Helen Van Husen, of Queensbury, in 1884. Mr Miller's parents were Samuel and Sarah Miller, natives of Ireland   They had ten children, three only of whom are now living   John J , William, and Susan

Miller, Samuel H , p o Hague, was born June 26th, 1836, in Putnam, Washington county, N Y , is a farmer and owns 183 acres of land, has held the office of highway commissioner five years, and collector of taxes four years, was married September 16th, 1858, to Sarah M , daughter of Anson Elthorp, of Vermont, and they have six children   Willis J , Estella, Elburta, Herbert N , Jennie, and Samuel H , jr   Mr Miller's parents were John and Clarissa (Hutchinson) Miller   They had fourteen children

Miller, William, Queensbury, p o Glens Falls, was born in Monahan, Ireland, in 1827 , is a farmer and owns the farm of 185 acres formerly belonging to his father, was married in 1866 to Eliza M Barker, of South Glens Falls, and they have six children   William S , Lizzie M , Frank B , John E , and twins, Harriet L , and Arthur L   Mr Miller has held several minor town offices   Mr. Miller's parents were William and Sarah Miller, natives of Ireland who settled in Queensbury in 1830

Millington, Levy, p o Warrensburgh, one of the present old settlers, was born in Warrensburgh in 1807 , is a general farmer, has been school commissioner three years, and assessor one term , was married in 1845 to Miss Charity Wilcox, of Johnsburgh, they had a family of three daughters Ella, Mary, and Christine   Ella married Mr Charles Featherson, leaving one child, Ella   Mr Millington's parents were David and Charity (Potter) Millington   They had a family of six children, four now living

Mills, William F , Bolton, p o North Bolton, was born in Castleton, Vt., in 1803   Is a retired farmer , has been assessor several terms, and highway commissioner, was married to Miss Clarissa M Goodman, of Bolton, in 1834   They have seven children   Orlin C , Julia, Marion, Clara, Ellen, Mary, and Sarah   Julia has been a teacher and the sons are merchants   Mr

Mills's parents were Stephen and Polly (Cushman) Mills They had three children, of whom William is the only surviving one

Monroe, Dr A D, p o Horicon, is a native of Smyrna, Chenango county, N Y, born October 18th, 1843, has been a resident physician of Bolton and Horicon since 1867 He first studied with Dr Stanbro, of Otselic, N Y, three years He commenced practice independently in 1866, and has the confidence and esteem of the community He has an extensive practice in Warren and Essex county, is a member of the Central New York Electic Society, in 1872 he was married to Miss Julia T, daughter of Mr Jesse Merrill, of Bolton, and they have one son A B Carlton Monroe

Morand, James, Queensbury, p o Glens Falls, was in born County Carlow, Ireland, in 1826 He came to America and settled in Glens Falls in 1853, was married in 1854 to Miss Ann Timmens, a native of Ireland, and they now reside on the Ridge Road, having a pleasant homestead of six acres Mr Morand's parents were James and Mary (Timmens) Morand, natives of Ireland, who came to America in 1855 and settled in New Orleans

Moore, Andrew, Queensbury, p o French Mountain, born in Londonderry, Ireland, Oct, 1822, son of Archibald and Mary Moore Andrew came to America and settled in Warrensburgh in 1844, married Mary Jane Cardle, born in Vermont in 1827, married in 1852, children three John Henry, George Archibald, and Wilhiem George A married Nellie Howe, of Queensbury, one son Wife was daughter of John and Ann Cardle, born and married in Iceland, settled in Warren county in 1831 Andrew was a tanner and currier for twenty-four years In 1858 he settled on his farm of 225 acres, where he now resides He was collector one term and highway commissioner seven years

Morehouse, Chauncey, Johnsburgh p o Chester, was born in Johnsburgh, May 1st, 1835 Is a farmer Was married in 1863 to Susan, daughter of Thomas and Perthuna Smith of Chester, and they have two children Eva and Arthur Mr Morehouse was a son of Samuel and Betsey Morehouse, both natives of Johnsburgh They had nine children, of whom six are living

Moorhead, Dr John F, Queensbury, p o Glens Falls, was born in New York, Aug 26th, 1855 Graduated from the Fort Edward Institute in 1872 Read medcine with Professor Polk, of New York, and Dr G W Little, of Glens Falls, and graduated from the University Medical College of New York, in 1876 From 1877 to 1883 he served in Bellevue Charity Hospital, New York Settled in Glens Falls in 1883

Morgan, Col A W, Queensbury, p o Glens Falls, was born in St Albans, Vt in 1799 He served an apprentice in the harness and saddlery trade with Judge Spencer, and in 1820 commenced the harness business on his own account He continued in this business until 1835 During this time he had purchased 11 acres of land for $800, near the center of the town After that he commenced laying out, improving and selling his land He continued in the real estate business until 1870 Was active in laying out and adorning many of the streets of Glens Falls, such as Elm Park, Maple, Oak and Walnut In 1840 he purchased the farm of 200 acres where he now resides Has been supervisor several times, assessor, superintendent of the county poor and many other local offices. He was appointed colonel of the Northern New York Regiment, by Gov DeWitt Clinton Has served as canal and railroad appraiser under State appointment Was an elector in 1864 when Lincoln was made president the second term His father was a lawyer and a graduate of Yale College, and his brother was was a graduate of Williams College In 1826 Col Morgan was married to Miss Emma Warren and they had four children His wife died in 1870

Morgan, Freeman M, p o Bolton, was born in Bolton, Warren county, June 27th, 1827 He is a farmer and owns the homestead purchased by his father in 1816 Was married to Electa E Dickenson, October 20th, 1850 She died Jan 21st, 1863, and for his second wife he married Miss Margaret Stockton July 23d, 1863 She was born at Warrington, Cheshire county, England, January 13th, 1835 They have one adopted daughter, Minnie Morgan Mr Morgan's parents were Jonah and Sarah (Brown) Morgan, They had a family of nine children Mahetable, born Sept 9th, 1811, Ephraim, born Oct 1st, 1812, James born Aug 21st, 1814, Anna, born Dec 16th, 1815, Joseph W, born July 22d, 1818, Hannah B, born Jan 14th, 1820, Mary M, born March 3d, 1822, Jonah S, born March 3d, 1824, and Freeman M Morgan, born June 27th, 1827 But three now living, viz Mahetable, Jonah S, and Freeman M

Mosher, Miss Hannah A, Queensbury, Warren county, p o Glens Falls, was born in Saratoga, Saratoga county, 1789 She is a daughter of Jonathan Mosher and Patience Hoag She is the only one living of ten children, and aged ninety-six years She was in early life a teacher in Stephentown, and came to Queensbury in 1830, where she has resided, and is one of the Society of Friends, whose life record will long be remembered by all that know her

Mundy, William, p o Chester, was born in Wiltshire England, June 19th, 1823 Was reared and educated in Wiltshire and learned the tanner's trade, serving an apprenticeship of six years He came to America in 1843, settled in Hudson and in 1848 was married to Angelina Reynolds They have six children Fred, William, Robert, Sarah, Andrew, and Jessie Mr Mundy located in Chester in 1859, and established his present business, building, 70 by 40 feet, with a capacity for turning out 3,000 hides per year

Murray, Alexander, Stony Creek, p o Creek Center, was born in Stony Creek in 1826 He is a farmer, and has held some of the most important offices in the town Was married in 1850 to Julia Goodenow, and they had one daughter (now Mrs P J McGuir) Mrs. Murray died in 1851 and Mr Murray married her sister, Emily Goodenow They have several children Mr Murray was a son of Moses Murray, also a native of this town, who died about fourteen years ago

Murray, Chas W, Stony Creek, p o Creek Center, was born in Thurman in 1852, and removed to Stony Creek when a small boy Has been engaged in farming and working at the carpenter trade, also in lumbering, and is now extensively engaged in the manufacture of barrel material He employs from five to eight hands Was married in 1877 to Miss Ida M Fuller, daughter of Joseph E Fuller They have two children Mr Murray is assessor this year and has held other offices for his town

Needham, William, Thurman, p o Athol, was born in this town in 1856 Is a farmer, is now constable and collector for his town Was married in 1879 to Elizabeth Bennet, they have one son, Orley Needham

Nelson, Homer S, Queensbury, p o Glens Falls, was born at Sandy Hill, Washington county, in 1860 He is proprietor of the Nelson House formerly owned by his father His parents were John and Sarah Nelson, formerly proprietors of the Nelson House and through the assistance of Mrs Nelson the hotel has become a financial success, and to-day is one of the popular houses of the town, is strictly on the temperance plan Mrs Sarah Nelson was a daughter of Nicholas and Abigail (White) Newton, early settlers in the town of Warrensburgh Mr Newton was in the War of 1812 He had a family of eight children, seven of whom are now living, four in this county.

Nelson, John, Caldwell p o Lake George, was born in Warrensburgh in 1827 Has been in the employ of the government in custom house and mail agent Is also a hotel keeper and proprietor of the Nelson House at Troy and St. Albans, Vt He was married to Maria Dupont, of Rouse's Point, in 1863 She died in May of the same year Mr Nelson was a son of Alton and Charlotte (McLaren) Nelson Alton served in the war of 1812, enlisting from Stillwater, Saratoga county

Newton, Leander, p o. Hague, son of Ithamer Newton, was born June 16th, 1833 Was married to Louisa Bevins, and they have four children Andy E, Nellie A., Carrie E and Dema P Mr Newton's grandfather, Joel Newton, came from Hubbardstown, Mass, about 1802, and located near Lake George

Nichols, Riley, Horicon, p o Adirondac, is a native of the town of Schroon, and was born in 1832 He is a blacksmith by trade and has also been engaged in lumbering for about forty years Was married to Martha A. Huntley, of Schroon, and they have three children Eleanor (now Mrs J F Holly), Mary, and Seth, who is a member of the firm of Prouty & Nichols, livery, having purchased his interest of Mr Wells, in 1882 Mr Nichols's father was Levi Nichols, who came from Vermont and lived in Horicon about three years He died in 1875 Mr Nichols and his son own a farm near Adirondac of 83 acres

Noble, Hon David, Johnsburgh, p o Weavertown, son of Archibald and Margaret (Somerville) Noble, was born in Johnsburgh, N Y, July, 1804 Was educated as a farmer, receiving such education as the common schools afforded From the age of twenty to thirty years he taught school in his native town and the surrounding country In 1833 he took charge of a store connected with a large tanning establishment in Johnsburgh, and was book-keeper and general agent until May, 1843, being for a time a partner in the mercantile business In 1843 he purchased 20 acres of land and opened a store at Weavertown where he still resides Has held most of the offices of the town, and commissions up to captain in the militia of the State, and has held many of the offices of the county From 1846 to 1848 he was one of the side judges of Warren county In 1851 and 1854 he was a Member of the Assembly of the State of New York In 1869 he was appointed postmaster, which position he has retained to the present time He was a Democrat until 1859 when he became a Republican Is an active member of the M E Church Was married Feb 7th 1841, to Miss Jane Gunn (a former pupil), who died March 1st, 1884, aged seventy-two years, leaving four married daughters, one unmarried daughter and one son, Archibald R aged thirty, Mr Noble, sr, resides with his son with whom he is engaged in the drug and stationery business

Norcross, Derias, Queensbury, p o Glens Falls, was born at Fort Edward, Washington county, in 1827 Is a master carpenter and builder and architect and has built many of the extensive buildings in Glens Falls, the old opera house, Presbyterian church, and many fine dwellings and hotels on Lake George Is also a manufacturer of sash, doors, blinds, and a stair builder, in fact a general contractor and designer for all fine work pertaining to his art Was married to Miss Margaret Van Derwalker, in 1853 She died in 1865 leaving three children Albert H , Augusta M and Estella For his second wife Mr Norcross married Mrs Olive J Moss They have one child living, Willard D Mr Norcross's parents were Shepherd and Ariy (Stearns) Norcross They had eight children, only four of whom are now living Isaac M, Bethuel, Dellas and Sarah now Mrs Rufus White

Numan, Charles P , Queensbury, p o Glens Falls, was born in Queensbury, Warren county, in 1848, married Miss Carrie Devol of Schaghticoke, in 1872 They have one child, Herbert O Numan Mr Numan is a general farmer and dairyman Mr Numan was a son of Orange and Sarah (Peck) Numan Besides Charles P , they had one other son, George R , and daughter Delia A

Nyce, Dr George W , Queensbury, p o Glens Falls, was born in Sussex county, N J , in 1835 Is a graduate of the Medical University of Philadelphia Was in the late war, enlisting in the 11th Regiment and serving three years He served in the hospitals at Columbus, Nashville and Louisville, and was discharged at the close of the war Was married in 1877 to Mrs Elizabeth Waite, of Indiana They have two children living, John and Bertie Di Nyce is making a specialty of the treatment of cancer and scrofulous diseases His place of business is 17 Ray street, Glens Falls

O'Mahoney, Rev William H , p o Warrensburgh, was born in New York city in 1832 Was a graduate in 1875 of the Assumption and Free Academies in Utica, N Y , also of Niagara College and Troy Seminary where he was ordained in 1879 He was first sent to Watertown, N Y , and from there to Albany in 1881 In 1882 he was put in charge of Warrensburgh Chestertown, Johnsburgh and Luzerne In 1884 the mission was divided the northern half being erected into a separate parish, and Lake George which had previously been under the care of the Paulist fathers, of New York, being added to Warrensburgh, where he still remains

Ordway, Jones Queensbury, p o Glens Falls, was born in Stratford, Vt , Jan 1812 In 1832 he came on foot from Vermont and settled in Glens Falls, bringing all his worldly goods on his back He commenced chopping cord-wood, then boating, but not content with his success in serving others, he resolved to establish himself in business In 1840 he opened a hotel at North River, running a farm and lumber business at the same time He afterwards disposed of his hotel and continued his general lumber business He, with Mr James Morgan as partner, was the founder of the well known Morgan Lumber Company of Glens Falls They now own one-fourth interest in the Glens Falls Paper Mill Mr Ordway purchased an interest in the gas company of which he is now president He is also a large real estate owner in three or four counties as well as in Glens Falls corporation, in 1835 he was married to Miss Clarissa Chambers, of Caldwell, Warren county They had two children, Helen and James James is now dead and Helen also Mr Ordway's parents were James and Arsenath (Perchfield) Ordway They had twelve children, four now living

Ordway, Moses T , Johnsburgh, p o North Creek, was born in Strafford, Vt , Nov 28th, 1835 Is a farmer of North Creek, and owns 230 acres of land , married in Aug 1859, to Jerusha, daughter of Samuel and Mary Richardson, and they have six children Josephine, Frederick, George, James, Emma and Arthur Mr Ordway was a son of James and Sarah Ordway

Orcutt, Joseph, Caldwell, p o Lake George, was born in Hartford, Washington county, in 1808 He settled in Caldwell in 1844, and on his present homestead in 1862 He gives accommodation to picnic parties on the bank of Lake George He furnishes boat accommodations and has a valuable mineral spring which is of great benefit to invalids, in 1833 he married Miss Elizabeth Davis of Vermont She died in 1836 leaving one child, Franklin For his second wife, Mr Orcutt married Miss Emily Dean in 1838 His son Franklin married Miss Harriet Williams Mr Orcutt's parents were David and Polly Orcutt In the later years of their life they came to Joseph and he cared for them until their death

Ormsby, Silon A , p o Horicon, was born in Poultney, Vt , May 14th, 1841 Is a contracting carpenter of Horicon and owns a farm of sixty-five acres, was married to Chloe M , daughter of Steward Weller, of Horicon, and they have one son, Clayton A Mr Ormsby was a soldier in the late war serving in the 123d N Y Vol Infantry, Co B Was at Chancellorsville, Atlanta, in Sherman's march to the sea, was wounded in the left shoulder, was discharged in 1865 and is a pensioner His parents were Lucius and Sarah Elizabeth (Hyde) Ormsby They had eleven children

Osborn, Edwin, p o Warrensburgh, was born in Horicon in 1854 Settled in Warrensburgh in 1868, and in 1872 commenced business as a merchant, selling dry goods, groceries and notions He was a son of Charles W and Ann E (Griffin) Osborn Charles W was a merchant, and had two children, Edwin and Kate

Paige, R E D p o Horicon, is a native of Horicon, born Jan 6th 1850 Is a farmer and owns a house at Bartonville, was married to Mary, daughter of Abijah Bevins, of Ticonderoga, and they have two children Clarence A and Clemma A Mr Paige was a soldier of 1865, 3d N Y Infantry, and served until the close of the war His parents were Cyrenus and Martha (McIntyre) Paige, old residents of Warren county They were married in 1835 and have had nine children, five now living

Palmatier, Rev A B, Horicon, p o Brant Lake, was born in Catskill, Greene county, in 1836 His parents, Peter and Deborah Palmatier, died when he was quite young and he was reared by an older brother He studied in the Catskill graded schools and entered the ministry in 1864, an expounder of the Baptist faith, was married in 1874 to Lucy J, daughter of Deacon John Brown, of Johnsburg, N Y, and they have three children, Gertrude L, Herbert A and Wayland P Mr Palmatier was a soldier in the late war, serving in the 162d N Y Vol Infantry, Co H Was wounded at the battle of Mansfield and discharged in 1865 He is a pensioner Is pastor of the Brant Lake Society and also of the church at Horicon

Palmer, Richard, p o Warrensburgh, was born in Saratoga county, in 1808 He was by trade a mill-wright and settled on his present farm of 67 acres in 1865, was married in 1828 to Miss Clarinda Pratt, of Bolton She died in 1859, leaving three children, Mary A (now Mrs L Potter), Dennis and William, now practical sawyers at Glens Falls For his second wife, Mr Palmer married Mrs. Alice (Bennett) Lamb, in 1865 Mr Palmer was a son of Jesse and Catharine (Hilton) Palmer, natives of Hadley, Saratoga county.

Parks, Solomon A, Queensbury, p o Glens Falls, was born in Saratoga county in 1827 He commenced his business life in a paper mill at Milton, and in 1853 he became interested in the manufacture of printing paper He settled in Glens Falls in 1872 where he purchased one-fourth interest in the Glens Falls Paper Mill Company He was elected superintendent of the organization and still continues in that capacity His son is now his assistant and the company represent a capital of $192,000, and manufacture 200 tons of newspaper per month, Mr Parks married Miss Harriet A Hewitt of Stillwater, Saratoga county, N Y, in 1852 She died in 1881, leaving seven children Fred H George H, Lee A, Julia A, Ella K, Harriet E and Ruth M Mr Parks's parents were Brazilia and Susan Parks

Pasko, Alexander T, p o Warrensburgh, was born in Chester Warren county in 1826 He learned the harness and saddlery trade, and settled in Warrensburgh in 1849 Is a dealer in all harness and horse furniture, trunks, whips, etc Was married in 1848 to Cynthia F Capron, of Broadalbin Fulton county, and they have one son Emerald D, born in 1850 In 1872 Emerald married Miss Margery A Stewart, of Caldwell Mr Pasko has been superintendent of the county poor for nine years. His father was Levy Pasko

Patrick, David E, Bolton, p o Hill View, was born in Hebron, Washington county, in 1842 He purchased his present homestead in 1885 Has enjoyed a large practice for many years and has the respect of the community in which he lives. Was appointed postmaster of Hill View in 1880, was married in 1872 to Miss Sarah Jane Chapman, and they have three children, Eva I, Mary E and John E Dr Patrick is a son of Dr E L Patrick and Nancy (Thomas) Patrick They were married in 1834 and have a family of four children, Mary A, David E Nancy J and Henrietta

Patrick, Dr E S, Caldwell, p o Hill View, was born in Springfield, Mass, 1811 Moved from there to Hebron, Washington county Was married in 1834 to Miss Nancy Thomas, of Hebron, Washington county, and have four children living, Mary Ann David Edwin, Nancy Jane and Henrietta Emma died in infancy He purchased his present homestead in 1865 in Caldwell, Warren county has enjoyed a large practice for over forty years and has the respect of the community in which he has and now lives He was appointed coroner for a number of years Was appointed postmaster of Hill View in 1877 and holds that office yet Dr E L Patrick is a graduate of the Homeopathic Society of New York David E Patrick is a son of Dr E L Patrick and Nancy (Thomas) Patrick Born in Hebron, Washington county, 1842. Was married in 1872 to Miss Sarah Jane Chapman, daughter of John W Chapman and Eliza Chapman, of Hartford, Washington county They have three children living Eva, Eliza and John Edwin Delbert died in infancy Moved to Caldwell, Warren county, 1877 He purchased his present homestead in 1885 in Bolton, Warren county His occupation has been a farmer

Patterson, Charles R, Queensbury, p o Glens Falls, was born in Albany county in 1855 Read law in the office of W S Kelly, of Albany, was a graduate of the Albany law school, and was admitted to the bar in 1878 In 1879 he settled in Glens Falls, where he practices his profession Has been elected corporation clerk two terms. His parents were Rev R and

Sarah J (Annesly) Patterson They now reside in Washington county They had five children, Mary M , Charles R , Robert E , James M and William A Mary is now Mrs Joseph E Sawyer She resides in Glens Falls, also her brothers, Charles R and James

Pearsall, Augustus J , Queensbury, p o Glens Falls, was born in Wilton Saratoga county, in 1830 He commenced business in Iowa as a dealer in grain and stock and a general merchant He remained there from 1855 to 1863, when he sold his business and settled in Glens Falls as a general merchant He retired from this business in 1878 In 1875 he purchased an interest in the Glens Falls Paper Co , and was elected vice president He is a stock owner in the Glens Falls Insurance Co , also a large stock owner in the Terra Cotta Brick Co In 1875 he purchased an interest in the Lake George Yachting Co , of which he is president Is now one of the prominent owners and dealers in real estate of Glens Falls Their yacht is one of the popular excursion boats on Lake George Mr Pearsall was married in 1875 to Miss Susan L Cox, of Schuylerville, and they have four children, Virginie L , Sarah E , Howard C and Lilian Augustus Mr Pearsall's parents were A H and Mary (Reed) Pearsall

Peart, John, jr , p o Luzerne, was born in Clinton Co , in 1842 Has been elected supervisor three terms, and has held several positions of trust in corporations and companies Was a soldier in the late war, enlisting in Company A, 21st Regiment, the Griswold's cavalry, in 1863, under Col W B Tibbits, of Troy He was wounded in the leg at Ashby's Gap and had it amputated below the kneee Was detained at the hospital and finally discharged in 1865, and now receives a sergeant's pension Was married in 1874 to Miss Juliet C Havens, of Saratoga county She died in 1877, leaving one son, Harry W For his second wife he married Miss Julia Guyett, of Luzerne, and they have one son, Rollin D Mr Peart was son of John and Catharine (Taylor) Heart

Peck, Daniel, Queensbury, p o Glens Falls, was born in this corporation Was postmaster of Glens Falls under Buchanan for four years, county treasurer for three years, president of the corporation several terms, which he now represents Has been one of the representative men of town and county In 1865 he established his present general wholesale and retail grocery business The firm then was Peck & Byrne, and in 1870 they sold their business and engaged in the manufacturing of lime and shipping to the N J Market In 1873 he sold out his lime interests to his partner He again went into his former mercantile business Was married in 1858 to Abby Mayo, and they have two sons, Walter M and Hairy M

Peck, Daniel E , Queensbury, p o Glens Falls, was born in Glens Falls in 1849 In 1870 he succeeded Brown & Hotchkiss in the general ready-made clothing business, dealing in all goods in that line, hats, caps and fancy goods Mr Peck's parents were Charles and Charlotte (Elnore) Peck Besides Daniel E they had one other child, Charlotte A

Peck, Reuben N , Queensbury, p o Glens Falls, was born in Glens Falls, Warren county, in 1840 In 1862 he succeeded his father in the drug business, which was first established by his grandfather about the year 1800, it being one of the old land marks to furnish physicians as well as patients In 1868 Mr Peck married Helen M Littlewood, of Columbia county, and they have one child, Helen Pearl Peck Mr Peck's parents were William and Hannah (Newman) Peck

Perkins, Elisha H , Stony Creek, p o Creek Center, is and has been for many years engaged in cabinet-making and undertaking in the village of Creek Center, his being the only shop of the kind in town His business has rapidly increased during the past few years He was married in 1858 to Melinda Uhde and they have had six children, five now living Mr Perkins's father was David C Perkins, one of the first settlers of the town He is now seventy-seven years of age, and has lived here ever since he was a mere boy His aged mother is still alive, aged ninety years

Phelps, Orrin, Horicon, p o Adirondac, was born in Windsor county, Vt., July 10th, 1809 He emigrated to Schroon, Essex county, in 1830, where he lived until 1862, when he located in Horicon He is a farmer and owns 160 acres of land Was married to Alvira Woodard in Vermont She died in 1858, leaving four children, Rollin W , Esther, Augusta (now Mrs L Murdock), and Orpha (now deceased) His present wife was Miss Sarah Wilson, of Clairmont, New Hampshire

Potter, Warren, p o Warrensburgh, was born in Queensbury in 1821 He commenced business as a sawyer and lumberman at the age of seventeen ; at the age of 38 he embarked in the mercantile trade which he followed for ten years and then sold out , in 1878 he again entered the dry goods and general trade, and October 20th, 1884, the firm of Potter & Young was formed He has been assessor three terms, collector three terms, constable three terms, and highway commissioner three terms , his first wife was Miss Charlott Scott, whom he married in 1842, she died in 1852 leaving four daughters Sarah A , Elenor, Charlott, and Alma In 1853 he married his second wife, Miss Phoebe Barton, and they have two children Josephine and James The children of his first wife were all teachers until the death of Charlott, in 1881

Potter, William F, p o Warrensburgh, was born in Warrensburgh in 1847 He is a farmer and owns the homestead formerly belonging to his grandfather, to which he has added until it now amounts to 235 acres, was married in 1874 to Miss Sarah C Wood, of Thurman, and they have a family of four children, Bertha, Oiley, Ethel, and John Mr Potter is a son of William and Mary (Noble) Potter They had a family of six children, four now living

Powers, John S, Queensbury, p o Glens Fall, son of Edwin and Eliza Powers, was born in Queensbury, Warren county, N Y, in 1859 When but eleven years old he commenced his successful business life by working on the State dam, by his industry and economy he soon laid by a small sum of money From that time until 1882 he engaged in various occupations on the river, in 1882 he commenced the general grocery and provision trade on Warren street, is a wholesale and retail dealer in all domestic and foreign staple and fancy goods, the firm name is Messrs Powers & Day, opposite the post-office

Pratt, George, p o Warrensburgh, was born in Warrensburgh in 1848 He occupies his parents' homestead of 60 acres to which has been added 230 acres making in all a farm of 290 acres, was married in 1876 to Eliza Bennett, daughter of Sullivan Bennett of Chester They have two sons, Dennis and Clarence Mr Pratt was a son of Dennis and Olive (Reynolds) Pratt, natives of Bolton

Prosser, Sheridan, p o Warrensburgh, was born in Caldwell in 1852, is a boot and shoe maker by trade and is engaged in the green-house business, also the boating business to accommodate the fishing and pleasure seeking people In 1883 he commenced business as a grocer and fruit dealer, has been constable and collector two terms, was married to Miss Luthera Latham, of Caldwell, and they have a family of three children Mr Prosser was a son of Elias and Lucretia (Colburn) Prosser They had a family of five children

Pulver, Peter H, p o Luzerne, was born in Luzerne in 1837 Is a lumberman and land dealer, being interested as partner in over 7 000 acres of farming and timber land, was married to Miss Belle M Batchelor, of Saratoga county, town of Edinburgh, in 1868, and they have four children Susan Harry, Alice, and Walter Mr Pulver has been commissioner, sheriff deputy sheriff, and deputy sheriff of Saratoga county for ten years Is a son of Henry and Susan (Evans) Pulver

Putney, David T, p o Bolton, was born in Bolton in 1839 He commenced the lumber business at an early age and by constant application has become a successful business man Mr Putney is a son of Joseph and Maria (Beswick) Putney They were married in 1838 and have four children David T, Caleb, Rebecca A, and Esther A

Ranger, Fred E, Queensbury, p o Glens Falls, was born in Queensbury, Warren county, in 1833 He served in the late war, enlisting in Company F, 22d Regiment, and served two years, went out lieutenant and was promoted to captain In 1874, '78, and '82 he was elected justice of the peace Graduated from Glens Falls Academy in 1853 and in 1854 embarked in the book and stationery business which he continued for about twelve years, in 1857 he was married to Miss Agnes H Evens, and they have a family of four children Florence E, Caroline A, Gertrude E, and William F

Rawlins, John, Chester, son of Charles and Anna (Nicholson) Rawlins, was born in the County Tipperary, Ireland, in October, 1837, and came with his parents to this county in 1851 They located in Chester township and Mr Rawlins, sr, took up a tract of 100 acres of land in the town of Chester John has been a successful farmer and business man, and now owns 500 acres of land, has good buildings, and a portion of his land is in a fine state of cultivation He has engaged quite extensively and successfully in the lumber business, is enterprising and progressive and a man of good business tact He is one of the most prominent and wealthy farmers in the county, has held the offices of town auditor and commissioner of highways, was married in March, 1865, to Emeline C, daughter of Marlin and Eliza (Kipp) Mead, and they have two children, Sheridan R, and Ella E

Remington, Daniel C, p o Chester, was born October, 1857, at Darby, Vt', learned the carpenter trade, and subsequently carriage manufacturing business, is now engaged in the manufacture of carriages, wagons, etc, at Chester, and has several hands in his employ, he does quite an interesting business, was married December, 1869, to Anna W, daughter of Harvey S, and Caroline Waters They have three children Harvey W, Lina W, and Willie Mr Remington is a member of the I O O F, No 514, Chester, N Y

Remington, John H, p o Chester, son of John Remington and Maria (Baxter) Remington, was born in the town of Chester, Warren county, N Y, in 1849, he is of English descent, has been engaged for several years in mercantile pursuits, and is at present a lumber manufacturer, was elected to the office of supervisor in the spring of 1881, and the present spring to the office of commissioner of highways, has been successful in his business pursuits, was married October 25th, 1876, to Alice M Stackpole, daughter of Nathaniel and Hannah (Gilmore) Stackpole, and they have two children, George and Bertha Remington

Richmond, Joseph, p o Hague, was born in Ticonderoga July 23d, 1839, has been a farmer of Hague since 1861, he owns a fine landed property, and is classed among the best citizens of the town, was married in 1860 to Louisa M Catlin, of Ticonderoga, and they had three children Ella A. (now Mrs John Gale), of Goshen, Freeman J, of Hague, and Hobert C, of Goshen, Vt Mrs Richmond died and for his second wife Mr Richmond married Sarah J Hays, of Horicon They have four children Alfred H, Almeron J, Louis A, and Carrie M

Ripley, Ruben S, p o Queensbury, was born in Queensbury in 1829, 1851 he was married to Miss Sarah Helen Phelps Their three children are all dead Mr Ripley is a retired farmer, a son of James and Amy (Fuller) Ripley In 1810 Mr James Ripley purchased the Ripley Point, 124 acres on Lake George It was then in nearly a wild state, but he cleared and improved the same, and in 1865 gave title to his son, Ruben S It has become an important place for summer resort, and boarding houses and cottages are fast covering the point

Rising, Rufus, p o Hague, was born in Suffield, Conn, Aug 17th, 1796 Is a descendant of one of the first settlers of Hague His parents were Abel and Lucinda Rising Besides Rufus they had six other children, viz Horace, Abel, Zeno, Joel, Lucinda and Arabella, all now deceased A son of Zeno, Joel W Rising, now keeps the public house in Chestertown, known as the 'Rising Hotel" His sister Jane married H H Moses, a wealthy farmer of Ticonderoga A daughter of Horace married a Mr Harris, and resides in Queensbury Rufus, the subject of this sketch, was married to Joannah, daughter of John and Marcy Hayford, of Old Plymouth, Mass They had two children, Rufus, jr and Arabella The former is a prosperous farmer of Warren county, is the present supervisor of the town and has held other local offices He has been twice married His first wife was Mary, daughter of Ambrose Clancy, of Chester She died July 9th, 1876, leaving one son, Henry R and a daughter, Minnie (now Mrs E S Ross), also a daughter, Ella Bell, now deceased For his second wife Mr Rising married Mrs Henry Ross They had one daughter, Edna M Mrs Ross had two sons, Amos and Eddie who are now married, and residents of Hague, also a daughter, Emma, now Mrs. Russell, of Fort Edward Joel Rising (deceased) was born March 4th, 1814 Was a thrifty farmer and an active upright citizen Was married to Mary, daughter of Isaac and Sally (Green) Balcom, Dec 5th, 1840 Their children are as follows Addie (now Mrs Silas Ackerman), Alice (deceased), Roxie (deceased), Amey A (now Mrs George Marshall), Byron, Jennie (deceased), and Edwin R Mr Rising died Dec 2d, 1867

Robbins Harvey R, p o Horicon, was born in Horicon July 18th, 1841 He enlisted in the United States Army in June, 1861, in the 22d N Y Vol Infantry, Co F, in which he served his time, two years, and re-enlisted in the 2d N Y Vet. Cavalry and served as sergeant in said Regiment three years, was wounded in the thigh at Fredericksburg, April 9th, 1863, and had an ankle broken at Antietam He was honorably discharged in November, 1865, was married April 12th, 1871, to Helen C Kimball, of Huntington, Vt, and they have one daughter, Lela A, and own a residence near Horicon p o Benager Robbins, brother of Harvey, was born in Horicon, May 6th, 1819, he owns a farm of 160 acres and is a trustworthy citizen He served his country three years a soldier in the 118th N Y Vol Infantry, Co D, and is a pensioner, was married to Elsie, daughter of Levi Gregory, and they have five children Susan, (Mrs R Hayes), Irene (deceased), Evangeline, (Mrs M Kingsley), Lewis, and Harvey

Robbins, William H, Queensbury, p o Glens Falls, was born in Maysville, Kentucky, in 1848, in 1869 he settled in Glens Falls as clerk for Messrs. Fowler Bros, and in 1872 formed his present firm of Robbins & De Long They are dealers in general dry goods, dealing extensively in domestic and imported goods, silks, and fancy dress goods, in 1875 he was married to Miss Blanche Cool, of Glens Falls, daughter of H M Cool Mr Robbins's parents were William Hunt and Anna (Scudder) Robbins, natives of New Jersey, and settled in Kentucky in 1846 They now reside in Indiana The firm of Robbins & De Long are located at 108 Glen street, and are one of the leading firms of Northern New York

Roberts, David, Bolton, p o Bolton Landing, was born in Washington county in 1820 and settled with his parents in Warrensburgh in 1821, has been assessor two terms, highway commissioner three years, and excise commissioner six years, and has held other town and district offices, was married in 1851 to Miss Malinda Duel and they have seven children Jerusha, Asa Nathaniel, Hannah, Charles H, Annetta, and Phebe Two of his children were early teachers M Roberts's parents were Nathaniel and Jerusha (Chapin) Roberts

Roberts, George, Queensbury, p o Glens Falls, was born in Glens Falls in 1851 He is his father's successor in the flour and feed, hay and grain business, in February, 1880, he was married to Miss Mary J Hall, of Glens Falls, his father was David G Roberts, who settled in Glens Falls in 1832 He was a ship carpenter and builder, and came here as superintendent of the

Glens Falls Company, the stock then owned in New York city, later he purchased an interest and continued the supervision until 1866, then formed a partnership with Fowler & Goodman in the lumber business, which afterwards became Roberts & Goodman, they became wholesale and retail merchants in Glens Falls, in 1862 they sold out but continued their lumber and shipping interest until 1866 In 1867 Mr Roberts commenced a lumber, feed, flour, and grain business on Ridge street, where his son George is now located, and the father is retired

Robison, Samuel, Stony Creek, p o Creek Center, is a farmer of Stony Creek, and owns his farm jointly with his brother he was collector of the town in 1880, and is now an excise commissioner, his duties as an excise commissioner have been called into service this year for the first time in eleven years, there having been no license in the town during that period, was married in 1872 to Polly, a daughter of Isaac Goodnow, and they have five children

Rockwell, Chas L, p o Glens Falls, was born in Luzerne on the 22d day of March, 1849. His brothers, George and Hiram Rockwell, began the construction of the Rockwell House at Glens Falls, in 1871 Before the building was completed Charles Rockwell bought out the interest of George Rockwell, and in company with Hiram finished the house and in 1872 opened it for the reception of guests In January, 1878, he became sole manager of the business His father, George T Rockwell, is the venerable and widely known proprietor of Rockwell's Hotel in Luzerne The mother of Charles L Rockwell was, before her marriage with George T Rockwell, Miss Eunice Wells In 1870, Charles L married Miss Helen Lapham, of Glens Falls They have three children Bertha E George T, and Helen Rockwell

Rockwell, George H, p o Luzerne, was born in Luzerne in 1842; in 1869 he became a partner with his father in the general farming business and his already extensive hotel or summer resort In their hotel they have ample accommodation for from 150 to 175 guests, having over 100 rooms The house is pleasantly located on the Hudson River near the rapids, was married in 1869 to Miss Miriam Kipp, of Glens Falls, and they have two children Edna W, born in 1870, and Bessie R, born in 1874

Rockwell, Hiram J, p o Luzerne, was born in Luzerne, Warren county, in 1832, in 1875 he, with his brother, built the Rockwell House at Glens Falls, in 1877 he disposed of his interest and became landlord of the Fort William Henry House at Lake George, in December of the same year, he purchased the lease of the American House, Troy, which he has improved and made an attractive hotel, in 1883 he leased the Wayside Hotel with nine cottages at Luzerne, having ample accommodations for from 175 to 200 guests Mr Rockwell is well and favorably known among the pleasure seekers of New York, Philadelphia, and Washington, as well as the traveling public, was married in 1861 to Miss Harriet Wing, of Fort Edward, she died in 1881 leaving two children, Frederick and Caroline E Rockwell Mr Rockwell is a son of George T. and Eunice (Wells) Rockwell He is a grandson of Mr Jeremy Rockwell, who was an early merchant and one of the leading business men of Saratoga county, he was one of the framers of the State constitution in 1821

Ross, Austin A, proprietor of the Ross House and a prominent farmer of Horicon, has from early boyhood been a resident of Warren county His parents, Lensey and Cordelia (Kimball) Ross, having emigrated from Chittenden county, Vt, to Bolton in 1845 They were born in Rutland county, he Feb 24th, 1813, and she Oct 17th, 1808 He was a farmer by occupation, brought with him three children, Sylva A, who is Mrs Morgan Smith, Austin A and Cassius, of Horicon, two others Leonard and Orpha A (Mrs R S Waters), were born in Bolton In 1848 he removed to the present home of the subject, where he died Sept 23d, 1863 Mr Ross was married, Feb 21st, 1864, to Miss Jane, daughter of J N Barton (see sketch), she was born July 25th, 1847, and they have one son Harry, born Dec. 30th, 1864 Married Miss Minnie, daughter of Norman T and Laura (Hayes) Duell, Dec 30th, 1883 Mr Ross was a soldier of the 142d N Y Vol Inf'y, Co C Entered the Rebellion in 1864 Sept 1st, served until the close of the war, taking part in the battles of Fair Oaks, Fort Fisher and minor engagements He is serving his second term as commissioner of highways and been twice collector of taxes He is located at the head of Brant Lake, where there is excellent bass fishing and owns a boat on Lake Pharaoh where there is abundance of trout. Mrs Ross is post-mistress of Brant Lake post-office located at the Ross House

Russell, Dwight, Caldwell, p. o Lake George, was born in Minerva, Essex Co, in 1829 He is one of the representative men of the town A retired farmer, and has held the office of assessor twelve years, besides other local offices, was married in 1858 to Miss Almira Gleason, of Luzerne She died Dec 22d, 1865, leaving two daughters, Helen and Cora For his second wife he married Miss Alma Bartholomew, of Whitehall, Washington Co, they were married in 1868 Mr Russell was a son of Harry and Almira (Hollister) Russell Of their eight children Dwight alone survives

Schneider, Anthony, Horicon, p o Adirondac, was born in Warrensburgh July 23d, 1861.

Is a tanner by trade and foreman of the Frasier & Mayor tannery at Adirondac Is also leader in the brass band, was married May 23d, 1885, to Ann, daughter of E Roberts, of Horicon Mr Schneider's parents were George A and Margaret (Hafner) Schneider, natives of Germany, who emigrated to America and settled in Schroon, Essex Co

Sexton, Ebenezer M, p o Horicon, was born Jan 21st, 1811, in the town of Kingsbury, Washington Co, N Y, and has been a citizen of Warren Co for about 60 years He served in the Rebellion a member of the 118th N Y Vol Infantry Co D entering in 1862 Was wounded in the left knee, and received his discharge July 10th, 1863, is a pensioner, has been twice married, first to Ann Kenyon, of Bolton. She died leaving seven children, Malissa, Edgar, Hiram, Wildman, Huldah, Evaline and Richard Mr Sexton's second wife was Emily A Walker, of Bolton, and they have one child, Jennett

Sexton, Jesse M, Caldwell, p o Lake George, was born in Saratoga Co, in 1844 In 1868 he settled in the village of Lake George and in 1866 married Miss R W Bartlett, of Horicon She died in 1880 leaving six children, Lewis E Fred W, Harry H, Henry E, Cloyd J and Mable E, for his second wife Mr Sexton married Jennie M Prosser, of Warrensburgh, in 1882 Without means or knowledge of his present trade he built his blacksmith shop, and commenced driving his first horse nail, in which art he has become the expert of his town He also added plumbing and does all general repairing His institution has become one of the important institutions of Lake George Mr Sexton was in the late war He enlisted in Jan, 1862, in Co I, 96th N Y Vol under Capt Charles Burhands of Warrensburgh, served until 1865 when he was discharged at Troy Was several times wounded Lost one thumb and at the battle at Chapin's Farm, Va, he had four balls penetrate his body One ball is still in his leg He draws a pension of only four dollars a month His parents were Morris E, and Ann (Kenyon) Sexton, and they had nine children Morris E and Hiram M, brothers of Jessie, enlisted in the late war and served until its close

Shay, George Washington, Caldwell, p o Lake George, was born Sept. 9th, 1815, in Charlton, Saratoga Co, and settled in Caldwell in 1835 At that time he commenced his trade, blacksmithing, horse shoeing and general repairing, and still gives some attention to the business in connection with his farm, was married to Miss Nancy Bennett, of Caldwell, and they have four children, Cynthia, Caroline, George A, and Chas E Mr Shay has been justice of the peace for twelve years His grandparents Shay were natives of Rhode Island His grandfather Wheeler kept a hotel where Saratoga now stands and was burned out

Sheldon, Melville A, Queensbury, p o Glens Falls, was born in Essex, Essex Co, N Y, in 1829 Read law in the office of Judge Hand of Elizabeth, and was admitted to the bar in 1852 He commenced practicing law at Ticonderoga and in 1868 settled in Glens Falls in company with Hon Stephen Brown In 1882 they dissolved and Mr Sheldon opened his present office over the First National Bank on Glen St, is regarded as one of the leading lawyers of the State In 1874 he was made district attorney of his county, was married in 1863 to Miss Glori Anna Arthur They have two children, Arthur and Melville Sheldon

Sherman, A C T, Queensbury, p o Glens Falls, was born in Luzerne, Warren Co, Oct 11th, 1810, and married Miss Caroline Call, daughter of Elder Call of Luzerne They were married in 1838 and she died in 1862, leaving nine children For his second wife he married Miss Sarah Putnam, of Glens Falls, in Oct, 1865, and they have six children He was a son of Ware and Anna (Canfield) Sherman, who settled in Luzerne in 1807 They had five sons and four daughters, but two now living, A C T and Anna

Sherman, Darwin W, Queensbury, Glens Falls, was born in Luzerne, Warren Co in 1837 In 1856 he commenced the general mercantile trade firm of Weed & Sherman and in 1862, Weed, Sherman & Co, Jan 1st, 1881, he commenced his present successful business, doing an extensive trade at 62 Glen St. Mr Sherman is a man of large business experience, few men of his age in the State having had the experience which he has Hotel, merchandizing, and lumbering being some of the various industries in which he has been engaged In 1858 he was married to Marion Robbins of Glens Falls They have two sons, William and Henry

Shurtleff, Darwin, p o Bolton, was born in 1822 He has been assessor one term, also commissioner, was married in 1847 to Miss Betsey Brown, daughter of Caleb and Ellis (Smith) Brown They have one daughter, Alma, who is now married to Alexander Moon, and they have three children Mr Shurtleff's parents were Lothrop and Sarah (Fenton) Shurtleff They had a family of seven children, six now living Charles enlisted in the late war and died at the hospital at Washington

Simmons, Thomas, p o Warrensburgh, was born in Warrensburgh in 1847 Is a farmer Was married in 1875 to Miss Frances Brown, of Warrensburgh She died in 1881 Mr Simmons was a soldier in the late war — enlisted in Co D, 118th N Y Vol, in August, 1862, under Col Richards Was wounded and discharged June 15th, 1865, and now receives a pension

His brother William enlisted in Co I, 91st Regt and died in the service Feb, 1862, aged 16 years Mr Simmons was the son of James and Julia (Bennett) Simmons They had seven children, but two now living, Thomas and Mary Mary and her father reside with Thomas on his farm

Simons, Simeon, Stony Creek, p o Creek Center, was one of the first settlers in the village of Creek Center, having removed there from New Hampshire in May, 1843 He has continued to reside on the same farm since that time, was married to Miss Phoebe Perkins in 1855 and they have had eight children, all of whom are married and scattered through different parts of the United States

Simpson, John H, p o Bolton, was born in Queensbury in 1814 He is a successful farmer; was married in 1842 to Miss Eunice Hall, of Easton, Washington Co She died in 1866, leaving three children — Oscar E, Delia R, and Mary A. For his second wife, Mr Simpson married Ann Smith, of Queensbury in 1871 Mr Simpson's parents were Peter and Amy (Mills) Simpson

Slyter, George S, Caldwell p o Lake George, was born in Essex Co in 1863 In May, 1885, he settled at Lake George and embarked in the general furniture upholstery, and undertaking business He is located on the main street of the town Mr Slyter was a son of Alexander and Rachel (Jackson) Slyter They had a family of six children

Smead, Wilson, p o Luzerne, was born in Edinburgh, Saratoga Co, in 1843 He is, by trade, a stone mason Has been a teacher Has been justice of the peace four years, and supervisor one term He enlisted in Co G, 118th N Y Vol in 1862 and served to the close of the war Was promoted to sergeant and brevetted to captain for meritorious conduct Was wounded three times in the service, in 1873 was married to Miss Mary D Howe and they have a family of two children, Walter Scott, and Gilford W Smead Mr Smead is one of the representative citizens of Warren Co

Smith, Edward A, Caldwell, p o Lake George, was born in Caldwell in June, 1832, was married in 1857 to Miss Maret Moore, of Bolton She died in 1859, and for his second wife he married Nancy Taylor, of Mass, they have one daughter, Ida Mr Smith's parents were Thomas J and Electa (Dickinson) Smith They had three children, two of whom are yet living, Edward A and Martha (now Mrs Lemuel Griffin) Third wife Mary Johnson, of Canada Died June 27th, 1885 age 47

Smith, Frederick Horicon, p o Adirondac, was born in Warrensburgh Sept 16th 1830. Removed with his parents, Frederick and Nancy (Middleton) Smith, to Horicon in 1870. Was married in 1873 to Miss Eleanor Fleming, of Horicon, and they have three children Lee O, Tessa V and Esmond Mr Smith is a farmer and owns 160 acres of land

Smith, George W, Caldwell, p o Lake George, was born in Dorset, Vt, in 1840 and settled in Caldwell in 1858 Was formerly in company with his brother as carpenters and builders, but in 1884 he engaged in the general grocery and provision trade He was married to Miss Sarah J Latham, of Lake George Oct 17th, 1867, and they have one daughter, Nellie J Mr Smith's parents were Robert B and Julia (Morgan) Smith Besides George they had four other children Charles M, brother of George, enlisted in Sept 1864, in Co F, N Y 91st Vols He served until the close of the war Was discharged at Washington in 1865 Chas. married Miss Jennie S Ormsby of Washington county in 1866 They have one son, Franklin H George W was also a soldier in the late war Enlisted in Co H, 5th N Y Vols under Col O DeForest Served eighteen months and was discharged for disability He enlisted again in Sept, 1863, in Co K, 2d N Y Vet. and served throughout the war

Smith, Joseph F, p o Horicon, is a native of Warrensburgh Was a prominent farmer and merchant of Horicon Was married to Miss Eliza Warren, and they raised a large family of children

Smith, Edwin R., was born in Horicon, July 12th, 1832 Married Susan, daughter of Abraham Harp, of Horicon, and they had four children Laura (now Mrs. Edgar Holley), Alice, formerly Mrs Julius Kimbal (deceased), Orville and Dewitt He was assessor of the town of Horicon for twelve years

Smith Judson B, son of Joseph F and Eliza (Warren) Smith, was born in Horicon, Jan 15th, 1850 Is a successful hotel keeper and proprietor of Smith's Hotel, Horicon Was married July 4th, 1868, to Martha, daughter of Oliver Persons, of Bolton, and their children are Elizabeth and Cordie Mr Smith has been constable and collector of taxes

Smith, Oliver M Caldwell, p o Lake George, was born at Fort Ann in 1848, and settled with his parents in Glens Falls in 1849 In 1873 he settled in Lake George and commenced the building of fine fancy sail and row boats He is a skillful workman and has already received many orders from New York for his superior productions. He has built a fine cottage opposite the Lake House Was married to Miss Mary Alston, daughter of William Alston and Sarah Bell Alston Mary Alston was a granddaughter of John and Elizabeth Richardson, natives of Scotland, who settled in Queensbury in 1844 They died leaving a family of four sons and four daughters William enlisted in the 17th N Y Vols in 1861, was killed in the battle of Bull Run

Smith, Hon R P , p o Horicon, was born May 17th, 1823 Is a prominent citizen of the town and has been identified with its business growth, lumbering, merchandizing, etc Has been supervisor of Horicon four terms, supervisor seventeen years, member of the State Legislature in 1852, '53, sheriff of the county three years He owns about 4,000 acres of land in Horicon Married, Oct 27th, 1842, to Mariah, daughter of Howard and Laura (Putnam) Waters Their children are Caroline, now Mrs Geo Carpenter, Orville C , Thomas J , Richard P , jr , Laura (now Mrs Scott Barton), Seneca M , Eunice A and Ella M Mr Smith was a soldier in the late war, captain of Co D 118th N Y Vol Inf'y Went out in 1862 but owing to disability resigned his position Mr Smith's grandfather, Joseph, emigrated from Rhode Island to Hebron, Washington county, thence to Chester and died at the house of a son in Horicon He raised a family of thirteen children, of whom John was the oldest and became a civil engineer and farmer of Horicon Married Sally, daughter of Richard and Mary (Jeffreys) Prichard They are the parents of the subject of this sketch Richard R Smith, jr , son of Hon R P Smith, was born Aug 4th, 1855 Was married to Marion, daughter of Isaac Mills, of Potterville, and they have two children, Ada M and J Pearl

Smith Stephen H , Caldwell, p o Lake George, was born in Horicon, in 1838 Is a general farmer, jobbing contractor, and stone mason, and settled on his present homestead in Caldwell in 1844, consisting of 140 acres Has been justice of the peace four years, also collector In 1862 he enlisted in Co G, 118th Reg and went out as first lieutenant He was discharged for disability, having a paralytic attack of the right arm His first wife was Miss Mary C Hubbell, whom he married in 1862 She died in 1865 leaving one son, John H In 1866 Mr Smith was married to Mrs Mary J Loudon Haggert, of Argyle, Washington county Mr Smith was a son of John H and Sarah (Pritchard) Smith They had a family of eleven children, eight now living

Smith, Walter P , Horicon, p o Adirondac, was born in the town of Horicon, May 3d 1843 Is a farmer and owns 135 acres of good land Was married June 27th, 1865, to Malissa E daughter of Martin Granger, of Horicon, and they have six children living Powell, Henry W , Ellen M , Sophia M , Minerva and Delena Mr Smith's father, Powell Smith, was one of the prominent farmers of the town Was born in Horicon in 1818, and married Minerva Howard, daughter of Howard and Laura (Putnam) Waters They had nine children

Smith, Charles P , is a son of Powell and Minerva Smith Married Josephine, daughter of Joseph De Marse, of Plattsburg, June 22d, 1881, and they have two children, Grace D and Lester C

Smith, Warren J , p o Queensbury, was born in Queensbury Dec 11th, 1841 Was married July 21st, 1877, to Miss Catherine Lockhart, of Queensbury They have three children Anna C , born July 15th, 1878, Marion G , born Aug 30th, 1879 Agnes, born March 10th 1885 Mr Smith's parents were Major and Anna (Clements) Smith, who settled in Queensbury about 1825

Snow Henry E , Queensbury, p o Glens Falls, was born in Wilmington, Windham county, Vt , in 1841 In 1865 he settled in Glens Falls connected with the Putnam Stage Co , has been in the employ of the Del & C Co as conductor, and express messenger for many years In 1884 he was appointed agent for the National Express Co , at Glens Falls In 1862 Mr Snow married Miss Sophronia B Willard of Westminster They have one daughter, Gertrude Mr Snow's parents were Daniel and Maria (Smith) Snow

Spier, William E , Queensbury, p o Glens Falls was born in Northville, Fulton county, N Y , in 1849 and came to Glens Falls as a student attending the academy in 1864 In 1865 he entered the store as clerk for Messrs Lasher & Freeleigh, where he remained for five years He then engaged as book-keeper with the James Morgan Lumber Co In 1871 he became interested in the lumber business, still retaining his position in their office In the fall of 1873 the Glens Falls Morgan Lumber Co was formed and Mr Spier became an active partner, manufacturing and shipping lime and lumber In 1875 he started a new enterprise, the manufacture of collars and cuffs, which institution is now called the Glens Falls Co in 1883 he sold out his interest in that business Mr Spier is one representative business men of Glens Falls Is a director in the First National Bank and was elected president of the Glens Falls Paper Mill, which was organized in 1881, and represents a capital of $192,000 He has also been president of the Glens Falls corporation In 1873 Mr Spier married Miss Ida A Morgan, of Glens Falls, and they have one son, Lester Morgan Spier Mr Spier's parents were William E and Harriet Spier of Fulton county

Spoor Dr. David E, p o Warrensburgh, was born in the town of Harland, Niagara county, in 1846 He fitted himself and practiced several years as a dental surgeon Afterwards read medicine with Dr Bishop and graduated at the Hannemann Chicago Medical College in 1878 He settled in Warrensburgh in 1884 in his practice of medicine Was married in 1868 to Miss Libbie Carnier, of Hartwell, Niagara county, and they have two children Ada L. and Walter D Dr Spoor was a son of Garret and Roxana Spoor

Stafford, Charles B, Caldwell, p o Glens Falls, was born in Caldwell in 1845. He is a general farmer, and now owns a mineral gravel bed, which he is working Its equal can hardly be found in the country for various uses Has been collector two terms, also commissioner two terms In 1875 he was married to Miss Carrie Mead, of Caldwell. They have one child, Libbie Mr Stafford's parents were Byron T and Mary Ann (Crandall) Stafford They had two children, Elizabeth L and Charles R Mr Stafford, sr, was a cloth-dresser, and on settlement in 1333 rented a carding and cloth-mill on the bank of Lake George, near the steam-mill of Mr F B Hubbell This factory or mill is fast passing out of remembrance

Staples, Anson R, Queensbury, p o Glens Falls, was born in Danby, Vt., October 25th, 1825, and settled in Queensbury in 1850 The same year he married Miss Lydia Ann Haviland, and they have two children, John H and Josephine L John H. married Miss Etta P Hull, of St. Lawrence county, and Josephine L married Mr Joseph Hull, of Queensbury, Warren county Mr Staples was a son of Jonathan and Sylvia (Rogers) Staples, of Rutland county, Vt

Stark, Stephen, p o Hague, was born in Saratoga county, Jan 30th, 1807, and has been a resident of Hague since 1830 Has been twice married, first to Hannah, daughter of Asa Pratt She died in 1854, leaving six children, Henry, Jane, Betsey, Eunice, Eliza, Laura, Irene, William, Lorenzo For his second wife Mr Stark married Miss Delight Dunn in 1856, daughter of Thomas Dunn Second wife's children, Ida and Hattie

Stearns, Edward L, Queensbury, p o Glens Falls, was born in Granville, Washington county, N Y, in 1858 His parents were Samuel and Clarissa A (Prentice) Stearns, natives of Warren county, who settled in Warren county in 1874 Mr Stearns, sr, was an inventor, millwright and machinist, and erected several of the large wood and pulp-mills of the East as well as in Wisconsin He invented and patented the perfect water motor for all light machinery, printing and church organs He died in September, 1884, at the age of sixty-one, leaving two sons, George W and Edward L Edward L Stearns attended the Albany law school, and was admitted to the bar at the general term of the Supreme Court at Saratoga in 1879 The same year he commenced the practice of the law at Glens Falls, N Y In 1881 he was elected justice of the peace for four years He now owns the entire interest of the water motor patent.

Stewart, Archibald F, Queensbury, p o Glens Falls, was born May 2d, 1854, in Meadville, Pa Settled in Glens Falls in 1880 He has the only exclusive crockery house in the county, where a full and complete assortment can be found at all times Was married in 1878 to Elizabeth Johnson, of Meadville, Pa They have two children, Louise and Clay Mr Stewart's parents were Archibald and Rebecca (Reynolds) Stewart He died in 1867, leaving a family of seven children. He was a merchant.

Stewart, Horace, Bolton, p o Bolton Landing, was born at Union Village, Washington county, in 1833 He was in early life a merchant of Bolton, also the postmaster and town clerk of that village He is now the owner and proprietor of the Stewart House It is capable of accommodating about forty guests, and has a good livery attached Was married October 20th, 1858, to Miss Ellen Norton, of Bolton, daughter of Philip and Huldah Norton, and they have four children, Fred, Amy, Bessie and Jessie

Stoddard, S R, Queensbury, p o Glens Falls, was born in Saratoga county in 1843, and came to Glens Falls in 1864 He at first engaged in sign and ornamental painting, but soon after gave his attention to the painting of portraits and landscape He has published several valuable books and maps of Lake George and the Adirondack wilderness, which has become of great value to the tourist Was married March 3d, 1868, to Helen A, daughter of Thomas and Judith (Mosher) Potter They have two sons, Charles H and Le Roy

Stone, John H, p o Warrensburgh, was born in Warrensburgh in Sept, 1834 Was an early farmer and practical sawyer The firm of Stone & Bennett are contract lumber sawyers. In 1855 Mr Stone was married to Miss Nancy Collar, of Pottersville, and they have four children Mr Stone has been assessor and held other town and district offices He was a son of Samuel and Sally (Ford) Stone They had a family of ten children, six only of whom survive

Stone, Walter, p o Luzerne, was born in Warrensburgh in 1841, and settled in Luzerne in 1866 At the age of sixteen he commenced the lumber business, and in 1869 he purchased his present mill in Luzerne, where he resides The mill was built by Mr Hall in 1830, but many improvements have been added, and Mr Stone is engaged largely on contract building Mr Stone was a soldier in the late war, enlisting in Company E, 123d Regiment, under Col Van Dougal He was discharged in 1863 for disability His brother, Dwight, enlisted at the same time, died in the service, and is buried at Warrensburgh Mr Walter Stone has been assessor one term Was married in 1860 to Miss Minerva Bennett, of Warrensburgh She died in November, 1861, leaving one son, Byron For his second wife Mr Stone married Miss Abigail Fuller, of Johnsburgh, and they have a family of three children, Herbert D, Eben N and Bernard Mr Stone's parents were Cyrus and Laura (Bennett) Stone

Stronge, Rev L N, Queensbury, p o Glens Falls, was born in the Province of Quebec in 1842, and educated at St. Hyacinth College Graduated in 1864, and was granted permission to go among the Indians as mission worker in Washington Territory and the Rocky Mountains, where he spent ten years among the Yakama and other tribes He was stationed over twelve tribes and learned to converse in nine languages He published several books in their tongue, and his account of the country and tribes is truly very interesting He considers the field one of great interest to missionaries In 1875 he settled in Glens Falls as pastor of the St Alphonsus Church They have a membership of 1,495, 289 families and 928 communicants They as a church organized about 1855, under Rev Father Turcotte

Straight, David, Stony Creek, p o Creek Center, was born in Warrensburgh in 1854 He settled in this town in 1884, near the southeastern part, close to the town line, was married in 1875 to Eliza Ross, of Johnsburgh, whose grandfather was among the first to settle in that town Mr Straight's father was born in Washington Co Removed while young to Johnsburgh, afterwards settled in Warrensburgh, where he lived for several years At present he is residing at Johnsburgh

Streeter, Asa, p o Horicon, was born in Horicon April 13th, 1830 Is a farmer and owns 110 acres of land, was married to Miss Freelove Smith, daughter of J F Smith, of Horicon, and they have six children, Porter, Elmer, Emma (now Mrs A Durfee) Minerva, Roxie, and Gertrude Mr Streeter was a soldier in the late war, enlisted in the 142d N Y Vol Inf'y and served until the close of the war His grandfather, Nathaniel Streeter, was a native of Wales and a soldier of the Revolution Was married to Miss Sarah Dix, a member of the old Gov Dix family, and after the Revolutionary war he became a clergyman He located in Bolton, now Horicon, in 1794, where he followed the ministry They had seven children

Streeter, Buel C Dr, Queensbury, Glens Falls, was born in Wyoming Co, N Y, in 1832 Graduated from Castleton Medical College in 1853, and located at Granville, Washington Co In 1862 he was appointed assistant surgeon in the 9th N Y Cavalry In 1863 he was promoted to surgeon of the 4th N Y Cavalry and resigned in 1864 He was then appointed acting staff surgeon of the U S army, and assigned to duty as surgeon in chief of Gen Powers' Division At the close of the war he settled in Glens Falls, where he is now engaged in active practice, in 1853 he was married to Lavinia Hotchkiss, daughter of Captain Hotchkiss, of Washington They had three children, Fred B, Frank H, and Anna D Fred B is a graduate of Union College, also of Albany Medical College Frank H was a graduate of Union College and has been admitted to practice law at Albany in 1880 Both sons are now practicing at Glens Falls. Anna D is now Mrs C W Haviland Dr Streeter's parents were Jacob and Sophia (Wheat) Streeter He has been coroner for six years

Swan, Franklin, p o Warrensburgh, was born in Warrensburgh in 1857 Is a lumberman and farmer Is a son of John P and Mary (Ferry) Swan Mr John Swan was an extensive lumber dealer, also a land dealer They had ten children, six sons and one daughter still living Two sons, James and William, enlisted and served in the last war James died while in the service and William was discharged at the close of the war

Sweet Alfred, Queensbury, p o Glens Falls, born in Queensbury Warren Co, August 13th 1865, parents Jacob and Betsey (Gage) Sweet, born in Queensbury Feb 12th, 1840 Married Oct 13th, 1862 Six children, Lela, Alfred, Mary, Deborah, Jethnian and Agnes. Grandparents Dodge and Mary (Nelson) Sweet The former born in Beekman, Duchess Co, 1790, latter born in Stillwater, Saratoga Co Two sons, Nelson born in Saratoga Co 1818, and Jacob born July, 1827, in Queensbury Dodge settled in Queensbury in 1820, died April 7th, 1861, wife died Oct. 24th, 1864, the former was an early physician in the county, and had a large practice Dr Dodge was son of Percis Sweet, of Duchess Co, father Elnathan, son of Jonathan, from England Jacob and Nelson Sweet own a farm of some 200 acres, on which the son and nephew Alfred Sweet is engaged in breeding Jersey cattle Is also partner in the firm of H T Caffen, Zimmer & Co

Taylor, Robert T, p o Bolton, was born in Warrensburgh in 1858, and learned the trade of wagon and carriage manufacturing In 1881 he purchased the interest of his employers, Messrs. Pettys & Johnson, and conducts a general smithing and wagon repair and manufacturing business He is also in company with his father in the undertaking business, married Miss Clara B

44

Gates, and they have two children — John G and Lewis E Mr Taylor is a son of William and Mary Taylor

Terrien, Antone, jr , Queensbury, p o Glens Falls, was born in Chateaugay, Franklin Co , Nov 11th, 1844, and settled in Glens Falls in April, 1869   Was married to Miss Victoria Commelia Robilaird in 1869   They had four children, Nettalie C , Lilian May, and Eva Josephine Mr Terrien worked as journeyman until 1873, when he commenced his business, manufacturing horse collars a specialty for jobbing trade as well as to order   He made some changes but returned to Glens Falls in 1881 at the same business Mr Terrien's father was Antone Terrien, sr. His mother died while he was yet an infant

Thomas, Albert H , p o Warrensburgh, was born in 1851 at Bolton and settled at Warrensburgh in 1854   In 1868 he became his father's partner in the general merchandise business In 1881 he changed his interest and joined Mr. Dickinson, firm of A H Thomas & Co , merchants, Mr Thomas was married in 1870 to Mary, daughter of James and Mary Fuller. They have one daughter   Mr Thomas's parents were Miles Thomas and Sarah (Brown) Thomas.

Thomas, Miles, p o Warrensburgh, was born in Bolton, Jan 28th, 1825   He was a farmer and in 1854 he commenced business as a merchant at Warrensburgh , was county treasurer for seven years — from 1873 to 1880   Was postmaster for four years   He retired from active business life in 1880   Was married in 1849 to Miss Sarah Brown, of Bolton, and they had a family of two sons and one adopted daughter, Albert H , Charles A , and Addie Mr Thomas was a son of Simon and Elizabeth (Baker) Thomas   They had three children, Miles, Henry and Ezekiel.

Thomas, Stephen, Queensbury, p o Glens Falls, was born in Queensbury in 1848 Is a general farmer and dairyman , was married in 1872 to Miss Emma M Kenyon, a native of Saratoga Co   They have two children, Mabel A , and Clayton Paul Mr Thomas was son of Paul and Elizabeth (Dillingham) Thomas. His great grandfather, Israel Thomas was a captain in the Revolutionary army A photograph copy of his commission is still in the hands of his great grandson, Stephen

Thomas, Truman N , Caldwell p o Lake George, was born in Bolton in 1829 He commenced life as a farmer which business he has always followed , he was in the late war, enlisting in 1862 in Co G, 118th N Y Regiment, under Colonel S T Richards , was promoted to lieutenant, and resigned in 1863 , he then connected the stone mason work with his farming and in 1881 was appointed keeper of the county house, which position he has held for two years   He was supervisor of his native town (Bolton) three terms, assessor three terms (nine years), and elected sheriff of the county in 1882 , was married in 1850 to Miss Esther Herrick, daughter of Captain William Herrick of Bolton Of their five children, three are now living His wife died in November, 1882 , was buried just a week after the day of his election Mr Thomas's parents were Joshua and Mollie (Streeter) Thomas She was his third wife, and all left families, but two now living, Ormand and Truman N , of a family of thirteen children

Thompson, Charles B , Queensbury, p o Glens Falls, was born in Glens Falls in 1842, and was married in 1870 to Miss Sarah Ellen Haviland, daughter of Roger and Harriet (Haight) Haviland , they have two children, Elizabeth and Fred Mr Charles was a son of John S and Annis (Tearse) Thompson He died in 1884 and left a widow and three children Chas B , Lucretia, and Emma   Lucretia married Mr Jerome Haviland, and Emma married Mr John De Long The grand parents were Anson and Lucretia Thompson, from Norwalk, Conn Charles B Thompson was supervisor of Queensbury in 1881

Thompson, Lewis, p o Warrensburgh, was born in Warrensburgh in 1852 , is a stock dealer and butcher , was married May 17th, 1882, to Phoebe A Sisson, of Fort Anne, and they have one daughter, Pearl Mr Thompson's parents were Benjamin and Eliza (Clipper) Thompson, of Warren county, of their eleven children eight are now living Maria, Laney, Caroline, Lewis, Eliza L , George H , Sarah, John C   The grandfather was an Englishman

Thurston, Richard L , of Mountclair Terrace, Lake George, was born in New York city in 1858 1881 he settled in Caldwell on the east shore of Lake George, and in 1882 he purchased his present homestead on Lake George, of Mr N Bishop, who commenced the building in 1875 It was completed last year by Mr Thurston The design and finish, especially the fine varieties of wood as well as general taste displayed, makes it one of the most attractive residences on the lake Its elevation commands a fine view Mr Thurston was married to Miss Josie E Bumstead, of New York city, in 1881 Mr Thurston's parents were Joseph and Lotetia Thurston of New York city

Titus, Abraham J G , Queensbury, p o Glens Falls, was born in Rensville, Rensselaer county, in 1827 His mother died while he was yet an infant and he was taken into the family of his grandfather, Mr Abraham Gurny, of Duchess county Mr Titus cared for his grandparents until their death and became owner of their homestead of 50 acres. He became an extensive farmer and lumber dealer, owning over 500 acres of land with several cottages for summer resort, and some twenty boats on Long Lake, in 1849 Mr Titus was married to Miss Mary Jane Griffith, and they have four children Harriet, Eliza, Haviland G, Rosa A, and Eber

Tripp, Jas L, p. o Chester was born in Warrensburgh August 12th 1816, is a farmer, settled in Chester in 1846, and married in 1845 to Phoebe A Palmer, she died leaving two children, Hiram L and Josephine M For his second wife Mr Tripp married Dorathea Mills, she was born February 8th, 1816, they have two sons, Isaac and Thomas B Mr Tripp's grandfather was Peleg Tripp, a pioneer of Warrensburgh His maternal grandfather was William Bond, a native of England, born in 1740 He came to Westchester county, N Y, 1760 and located in Warrensburgh in 1784 He purchased a tract of 500 acres where the present fair grounds now stand and later bought a tract of land where Chester village is now situated

Tripp, Julian W, Caldwell, p o Lake George, was born in Caldwell September, 1859 He embarked in the hardware trade in 1884, dealing in all leading articles, shelf hardware, carpenters' and builders' wants, and farming implements He also carries a well assorted stock of gents' clothing, in 1884 Mr Tripp married Miss Marian B Stanton, of Caldwell Mr Tripp's parents were Henry and Lydia E (Hale) Tripp They had ten children George H, Julian W, Franklin G, Mary, Mahala, Eleanor, Florence, Georgia, Simeon R, and Frederick

Tucker, Frederick G, Caldwell, p o Lake George, was born in Worcester, Mass Is the present popular owner and proprietor of the Lake House, Lake George, Mr Tucker's wife was Miss Julia Sherrill, daughter of the Hon Jno F Sherrill, of Lake George Mr Sherrill was a native of Washington county, and purchased the hotel property at Lake George about 1840 The Lake House is one of the oldest hotels and has long been a popular resort for those seeking a pleasant location During the time Mr Sherrill conducted the hotel, he improved and largely increased its capacity He was, during his residence in Warren county, one of the influential prominent business men of the town He represented his district in the Assembly, was supervisor several times, and held other prominent positions The hotel was erected about 1800 The present building, as well as the grounds, show the great growth of business of that section Lake George has become one of the most popular summer resorts in the United States

Van Cott, William Henry, Queensbury, p o Glens Falls, was born in Albany in 1839 Has been a manufacturer of cigars, settled in Glens Fall in 1868, continuing in his manufacture and sale of cigars, in 1881 he was appointed postmaster under Garfield, was excise commissioner three years, in 1860 he married Miss Ellen M Adams, of Suffield, Conn, and they have two children, Augustus C and Helen L Mr Van Cott's parents were David and Mary (Brewster) Van Cott Besides William H they had eight other children Augustus C, Philip T, John H, William H, Sarah J, Caroline E, Martha J, and Mary T Philip T died in 1880, aged 57 years

Vandenburgh, Jacob, Bolton, p o Bolton Landing, was born in Fulton county in 1822 He has been a successful farmer, and in 1882 he built a summer boarding house on the bank of Lake George, opposite Green Island Landing It has capacity for 35 guests This hotel is superintended by his own family, and supplied with vegetables from his farm and garden, and cream from his dairy, was married to Miss Eliza Van Evera, of Saratoga, in 1858, and they have seven children Mr Vandenburgh was a son of Cornelius and Catherine (Norton) Vandenburgh, who settled in Bolton in 1824

Van Denburgh, John, Bolton, p o Bolton Landing, was born in Bolton in 1825 Is a farmer and lumberman, and in 1869-70 he erected the Bolton Hotel, at Bolton Landing, was married in 1858 to Miss Editha Shurtliff, of Bolton, and they have five children Sarah, Catherine Lewis, William, Frank, Swetson and Orlin Mr VanDenburgh has been commissioner of highways three terms

Van Dusen, John R, Queensbury, p o Glens Falls was born in Queensbury in 1827 He, with his brother purchased their present farm and rebuilt their fine dwelling in 1873 They also own their father's homestead Mr Van Dusen's parents were David and Mary (Robinson) Van Dusen; he was born in Queensbury, and she at Nassau, Rensselear county Of their six children, four are now living They are Bethuel, Dewitt, John and Carmi David was a soldier in the war of 1812 and drew a pension until his death

Van Dusen, Nelson W, Queensbury, p o Glens Falls, was born in Queensbury in 1844, was married to Mary E Metcalf, of Worcester, Mass, in 1863, and have one son, Alfred E Mr Nelson Van Dusen was Member of Assembly in 1882, supervisor from 1881 to 1884, and has held minor town offices His parents were William and Betsey (Ward) Van Dusen William died leaving a family of four children, only two of whom are now living, Nelson, and Sarah, now Mrs. Sarah Rice

Van Dusen, Robert, Queensbury, p o Glens Falls, born in Queensbury, in 1790, first wife, Abigail Cross, born in 1798, married in 1816, children eleven, nine now living Hiram, born in

1819, Abner in 1821, Archibald in 1823, Halsey in 1825, Sidney in 1833, Ransom in 1836, Chloe in 1816, Lydia in 1827, Harriet in 1831 Robert was in the War of 1812, served as musician, is now in his 96th year, second wife, Miss Serinda Dayton. Parents, John and Lydia (Slye) Van Dusen, married in Cambridge, settled in Queensbury in 1785, children nine, Robert is the only surviving one Robert and wife now reside with his son, who married Mary Ann Finch, of Johnsburg, born in 1838, married in 1873, children two Jennie L and George W Van Dusen

Van Dusen, Warren, Queensbury, p o Glens Falls, was born in Queensbury in 1820 Is a farmer. He with his brothers owns the farm of 210 acres which has been in the family for 97 years Mr Van Dusen's parents were Abraham and Martha (Orton) Van Dusen Besides Warren, they had nine other children, all of whom are living except Lewis who died in his country's service

Van Dusen, Zenas, Queensbury, p o Glens Falls, was born in Queensbury in 1809 In 1842 he commenced his present business, general lumber manufacturing, and purchased his present site on the Upper Hudson at the feeder dam In 1884 Mr J. W Freeman became his partner and the firm so remained until Mr Freeman's death Mr Freeman's son then became the successor and they are known as heavy lumber dealers, shippers and producers His wife, Mrs Ann Van Dusen, died March 8th, 1881, aged 68 years She was Mrs Betsey (Ward) Van Dusen and was married in 1851 Their only son is Zenas Van Dusen, jr

Vermilha, Albert, Queensbury, p. o Glens Falls, was born in Brooklyn, L I, N Y, in 1824, and settled in Warren county in 1842, and in Glens Falls, in 1845 His occupation is a general market and provision dealer, in which he has made a success by his strict application to business and gentlemanly manner to all, in May 1848, he married Miss Mary Salter, of Glens Falls. Of their two children, one is dead and the other, Emma, is Mrs J W Hunting In 1883 Mr Vermilha was elected assessor of Glens Falls He was the only son of George and Maria Vermilha, of New York city

Vetter, Frederick, p o Chester, son of Jacob and Elizabeth (Hensler) Vetter, was born in May, 1857 at Chester, Warren county, N Y Was educated at Payne's Business College, and graduated in the fall of 1875 He first engaged in the carriage manufacturing business at Chester, but subsequently sold out and is now a hardware merchant. Is a member of the I O O F, and has held the office of town clerk for one year, was married in May, 1884, to Jennie, daughter of Rease and Eliza Braley, and they have one child, Earl A

Wagar, Charles W, p o Luzerne, was born in Schagticoke, N Y., in 1847, and settled in Luzerne in 1871 He is one of the most extensive merchants of the town, dealing in all classes of goods wanted by his many customers He commenced his business in 1873, has been justice of the peace and other minor offices, was married in 1871 to Miss Mary E Cross, youngest daughter of Halsey and Selina Cross, one of the oldest families in the town, also step-daughter of Morgan Burdick, for twenty-four years justice of the peace in the town of Luzerne They have one son, Wilbur A Wagar Mr Wagar was a son of Jonas and Nancy (Cole) Wagar. Of their four children, two are now living, Merritt C and Charles W, James H enlisted in 1861, served three years and was discharged, enlisted again in 1864 in the 125th Regiment and was wounded in service, April 2d, 1865, died the 10th inst, Charles W enlisted in the same company in 1864, and served until the close of the war

Wakley, John, p o Johnsburgh, was born in Washington county, N Y, Aug 15tb, 1815. Is a farmer and owns 160 acres, was married in 1842 to Susan, daughter of Charles C and Susanna (Harris) Thompson They had ten children of whom six survive Benjamin, Susan, Nancy, Charlie, Edward and Nettie. Mr Wakley's parents were Joseph and Nancy (Liddell) Wakley They settled in Johnsburg in 1823 and of their family of six children, four survive

Ward, Elisha, Crown Point, was born in the town of Crown Point, Essex county, February 20th, 1818 His early manhood was passed in farming and lumbering pursuits At the age of twenty-five he was united in matrimony to Harriet Stone They had six children, of whom there are now living, Mary E (now Mrs Alpheus Heustis), Lestina M (now Mrs Charles Talbot, of North Hudson), and George M of Crown Point. Mr Ward's first wife died in 1858, and in 1861 he was married to Mrs Underhill Mr Ward is a genial and intelligent old gentleman

Warren, Nathaniel D, Queensbury, p o Glens Falls, born in Essex county in 1836, wife, Ida M Stevens, daughter of Frederick W and Maria Stevens, married in 1867, parents, Oliver and Clarissa (Robinson) Warren, born in Warren county, the former died in Essex county Children nine, seven now living Three brothers served in the war Nathaniel enlisted in 1861 in the 22d Regiment, served two years, enlisted in the Vet Cavalry in 1863, served until close of war, was wounded and now draws a pension

Waters, Howard, Horicon, was the father of a large family, many of whom with their descendants live in Horicon He was a farmer by occupation and lived in Bolton Married Laura A , daughter of Parks Putnam, a millwright by trade, and for several years a miller at Glens Falls Of their family Harvey S Waters, a respected farmer of Horicon, is the second Was born in Bolton in 1816, and married Caroline Smith, of Horicon, in 1842 They had seven children, Sarah (Mrs. Hugh McCloskey), Joanna (now Mrs D C Remington), Smith (deceased), Susan (deceased), Leoland D , Frank, Caroline (now Mrs C B Coleman, of Chester) Mrs Waters died in 1885 at the age of sixty years Leoland D Waters, son of H S Waters, was born in Horicon in 1852 In February, 1885, he purchased the Horicon mills of Smith Barton Was married to Miss Sarah Vandenburgh, of Bolton, in 1884 Starling Waters, esq , a native of Horicon, was born May 30th 1825 Is a farmer, and owns 124 acres comprising a portion of the homestead Has held the office of commissioner of highways, and is justice of the peace Was married to Elizabeth, daughter of John Cardle, of Horicon, and their children are Stephen, in Dakota, Cora (now Mrs. Garret Smith, of Bolton), and George, at home

Waters, George 3d, was born September 20th, 1860, and married Hattie, daughter of J F. Pritchard, in 1883 They have one son, Morgan, born October 8th, 1884

Wells, Benjamin T , (deceased) Horicon, p o Adirondac, was a native of Bolton, Warren county Born May 7th, 1810 Was a farmer, lumberman and contractor by occupation Was married to Thankful, daughter of George Waters, of Horicon, and they had a family of five children Thomas Wells, proprietor of the Wells House at Adirondac, is the oldest of his children Was born June 7th, 1833 He first entered into the hotel business in 1872 His hotel then accommodated but fifty guests, but he has improved and enlarged it, and it will now accommodate 130 guests It is finely located on the east shore of Schroon Lake, and he has several adjoining cottages Was married January 1st, 1845, to Helen P Weatherhead She is of Scotch descent

Wells, J Freeman, son of Benjamin T Wells, was born September 10th, 1844, in Horicon Is a farmer and owns a farm of 125 acres, comprising the homestead Is prominently identified with the public affairs of Horicon Is serving his second term as justice of the peace and is supervisor of his town He owns the finest livery on Schroon Lake March 1st 1865, he married Helen Jaise, of Glens Falls, and they have two children, Benjamin T and Cora

Wells, Henry, p o Bolton, was born in Queensbury, June 21st, 1826, and settled in Bolton on his present homestead in 1875 Was married in 1856 to Miss Sybil A Black, and they have two children, Frederick and Nelson Frederick was married in 1882 to Miss Ella Gates, and they have one son, Charles H Mr Wells was a son of Benjamin and Anna (Dean) Wells

West, Elmer J , Caldwell, p o Lake George, was born in Fort Ann, Washington county, in 1857 In 1877 he settled in Caldwell as superintendent of a branch store of Messrs Coledge & Lee, and in 1882 he and his brother purchased an interest, and as partners E J & C A West run the business as general merchants, dealing in all classes of goods found in an extensive country store The firm have just purchased their present store and dwelling and are the most extensive dealers in the town Elmer is the present supervisor Was married in 1882 to Miss Dora Brown, daughter of Alphonso and Emma (Mead) Brown His brother, Chandler A West, was married in 1874 to Harriet Bullard, daughter of Dr Bullard, of Glens Falls, and they have a family of four children

West, Henry W , Bolton, p o Bolton Landing, was born in Queensbury, Warren county, in 1847 He is an express agent and hotel-keeper He obtained a lease of the Bolton House in 1882, located at the Bolton landing on the bank of Lake George It has capacity for 125 guests and possesses a fine view of the lake and many islands It is considered a first-class summer resort Mr West was married in 1877 to Miss Orpha Anderson, of Bolton, and they have two children, Maude and Freddie Mr West was a son of Ebenezer and Lovisa (Hubbell) West

Wheeler, John, p o Hague, was born in Bolton, June 2d, 1818 His father, also John, was born in Connecticut in 1778 Was a farmer and lumberman by occupation and a soldier of the War of 1812 After the death of his father John came to Hague and made fishing his occupation until about 1865, when he opened his house for summer boarders Was married to Miss Betsey Roin, daughter of John Roin, and they have one son living, Charles H , who is the proprietor of the Trout House The Trout House is finely located on the west shore of Lake George Has been recently enlarged and refitted throughout It has a capacity for accommodating about thirty guests The proprietor being an experienced fisherman, makes a valuable guide for all lovers of the sport. Was married to Ella, daughter of John Walters, Dec 1st, 1871

Whipple, James N Queensbury, p o Glens Falls, was born in Moreau, Saratoga county, March 14th, 1852 Was a farmer in his early years. He received his education by his own energy and perseverance in the common schools of the county and in the Glens Falls Academy, where he afterwards spent two years as teacher In 1876 he became principal of the Elmwood Seminary, which position he held until January 1st, 1885, when he resigned to attend his office of county school superintendent. His parents were Archibald and Mary (Jackson) Whipple, of Saratoga county Besides James N they had four other children, Holdridge, Julia M , Chas R and Wesley W Holdridge enlisted in Company A, 118th N Y Vol Regiment, served three years, and was discharged with his regiment Received slight wounds at the battle of Drury's Bluff Mr Whipple senior, was a farmer and timber contractor, having a river privilege

White Chas C, p o Warrensburgh, was born at Bellows Falls, Vt, in 1862 He succeeded his father as superintendent of the shoe peg mill He is now a general superintendent of the Flint peg mill which gives employment to about fifteen hands, and produces about 100 bushels per day, mostly shipped to Germany In 1883 he was married to Miss Cora E Sutton, of Cincinnati, Ohio, and they have one son, Alfred H White Mr White's parents were Lysias and Mary (Graves) White, natives of New Hampshire

White, George C, p o Horicon, a native of Saratoga, owns and occupies the finest cottage on Brant Lake It is situated on a romantic and finely wooded projection of land from the east bank, about midway between the Horicon and Brant Lake post-offices He attended school at Concord, N H , four and one half years, and later at the Troy Polytechnic Institute He located in Horicon in 1881 where he lives in complete retirement

White, James Hyler, Queensbury, p o Glens Falls, was born in Greenfield, Saratoga county in 1836 In 1856 he commenced his trade as apprentice in Glens Falls, and in 1864 he formed a partnership with Mr Edward Joubert The firm was and still remains Joubert & White, manufacturers of fine light and heavy carriages They also manufacture a specialty known as the Joubert & White combination buck board It is one of the substantial novelties for comfortable traveling Their carriages are all completed from the wood to the polish under their own supervision, smithing and painting Mr White was married to Miss Susan Smith, of Washington county, in 1861, and they have two children Beecher J , born in 1867 and Lottie, born in 1871

White, Joel J , p o Warrensburgh, was born in Warrensburgh in 1841 He became the successor of his father in the blacksmith business, and conducts an extensive shop and iron supply store, and is termed an expert in horse shoeing, and carriage and heavy work completed on short order Was married to Miss Elizabeth Gilpin in 1868, and they have two daughters Lizzie and Ethel Mr White has been supervisor and held other minor offices Mr White's father was Josiah and his mother Hannah (Potter) White They had nine children, of whom six are now living They were very early settlers in this part of the county

Whitney, Walter Scott, Queensbury, p o Glens Falls, was born in Essex county, N Y , in 1842 His education was chiefly obtained in the county schools He afterward, in 1865 and 1866, took a course at the Albany Commercial College and in April, 1861 he enlisted in Co I, 22d N Y Regiment. Was discharged after serving two years He then enlisted in Co D, of the 2d N Y Vet Cavalry Was promoted to sergeant-major, then to lieutenant, in which capacity he served until the close of the war He settled in this county in 1869 Was elected county clerk for 1877, '78 and '79 In 1882 he embarked in the stock business in Colorado, but returned to Glens Falls in 1883 and in 1884 purchased an interest in the general insurance and real estate business of Mr Ketchum Firm is Ketchum & Whitney, No 62 Glen St. In Oct, 1871, he was married to Lovina Van Tassel, of Glens Falls They have two children Josephine M. and Harry S Josephine M. is deceased

Wills, Joseph W , Horicon, p o Adirondac was born in Chelson, Jan 27th, 1840 Is a native of Orange county, N H , and came to Horicon in 1866 Is a farmer and owns 180 acres of land Was married in 1868 to Nellie, daughter of Robert McKee, of Horicon, and they have two children Minnie and Cordelia Mr Wills is son of Parley G Wills, a Vermont farmer and wagon maker

Wilmarth, Clarence M , p o Glens Falls, born in 1852 in Glens Falls, Warren county, N Y , son of Martin L Wilmarth and Mary S Reed, he was born in New York city in 1821, she was born in Brattleboro, Vt , in 1830 They married at Glens Falls in 1847, have two sons George L. and Clarence M Martin L settled in Glens Falls, Warren county, in 1841, with his parents, Leander and Catharine They had but the one son (Martin L) Leander, born in New Hampshire, 1798 , died Glens Falls 1848 Catharine, born in New York city 1801, died in New York city 1885 Leander and son, Martin L , on settlement in Glens Falls engaged in the manufacture of chairs which they continued until the death of Leander Martin L afterwards added a general line of furniture to his business, including undertaking, continuing until Dec , 1873, when his son, Clarence M , was admitted as partner The business was continued successfully until Feb , 1885, when Martin L retired, the business being taken by Clarence M who now has one of the most complete stocks in Northern New York of choice designs in woodwork and upholstery In the undertaking business it would be sufficient to say that the house is to-day the oldest in that branch in all Northern New York, supplying any grade of goods wanted Clarence M Wilmarth married Miss Kate Finch DeWolfe, daughter of William S and Mary De-

Wolfe, of Marshall, Mich , in 1874   They have four children   James C , Martin L , Bertha C and Mable E   Clarence M Wilmarth commenced his business life as book-keeper in the Glens Falls Nat. Bank in 1868, where he remained until he engaged in his present business in 1873   Martin L has been assessor of corporation two terms, trustee of corporation four terms and member of Board of Health and is now one of the retired early business settlers of the town

Wilmott, Morris T , Queensbury, p o Glens Falls, was born in Ulster county, N Y , in 1851   He formed a partnership in 1875 with James B Goodwin in the carting, lumber and ice business, giving employment to several hands   Was married in 1872 to Miss Lovina Eddy, of Alleghany county   They have one child   Blanche, born in 1881   Mr Wilmott's parents were William and Louisa Wilmott, natives of England   He was a carpenter and ship builder in England and was employed in that capacity in Brooklyn for many years before he died   Besides Morris they had eight other children

Winslow, Alvin, Stony Creek, p o Creek Center, was born in Fort Anne, Washington county, in 1853, and came to Stony Creek with his parents in 1865, settling about a mile from where he now lives   Is commissioner of highways.   Was married in 1872 to Miss Martha Hull, and they have had five children

Winslow, Mrs C , p o Bolton, is the owner and proprietress of the Mohican House   It was among the first summer hotels built on Lake George, and has always been a popular hotel   Was purchased by Mr W Rodman Winslow in 1879   The hotel grounds and property embrace 38 acres, and it has ample accommodations for eighty guests.   It has a private dock, where the largest steamers, as well as the smaller crafts land regularly

Wood, Benjamin, p o Horicon, was born in Rutland county, Vt , Nov 5th, 1840, and came to Horicon with his parents about 1842   He is now a thrifty farmer   Was married to Lura, daughter of Sylvester Ross, July 5th, 1869, and they have three children   Forest, Sylvester and Joseph   Mr Wood was a soldier in the late war, a member of the 22d N Y Vol Inf'y, Co I   He entered in 1861 and served two years   Was wounded at the second battle of Bull Run, in the left arm   He had three other brothers in the war   Joseph, who was in Co A, 93d N Y Inf'y, lost his life in the battle of the Wilderness   Wesley in the same company and regiment, returned at the close of the war and now resides in Glens Falls   Henry was in the 118th N. Y Inf'y, served until the close of the war and now resides at North Hudson   His father, Leonard O Wood was born July 11th, 1806, and his mother, Betsey (Signor) Wood, was born July 9th, 1810   They were married July 9th, 1828   Betsey Wood died April 2d, 1857 and Leonard O Wood died August 22d, 1871

Wood, Epenetus, Caldwell, p o Lake George, was born in Saratoga county, in 1831, and settled in Caldwell in 1861   He is a farmer, stock grower, and lumberman, in 1861 he was married to Miss Eunice P Ripley, daughter of John H and Sarah (Pritchard) Smith   They have five children, Chas S , Julia S   Smith H , William L , and Epenetus J   Julia is now Mrs Elmer Dalrymple   Mr Wood was a son of Epenetus H and Jane (June) Wood

Woodward, David M , p o Warrensburgh, was born in Warrensburgh in 1840   He is one of the firm of A C Emerson & Co , in the manufacture of lumber, they having a mill of sixty gang saws on the Schroon River   He is also one of the firm of J S Woodward & Co , in the tanning business, was married in 1868 to Miss Rebecca Z Edwards   They have one child, Ella E   Mr Woodward's parents were John and Margaret (Summerville) Woodward

Woodward, Hon Joseph p o Warrensburgh, was born in Warrensburgh Sept 20th, 1804   Was Member of Assembly in 1872, and side judge of county five years   Was supervisor one term   In early life he was a merchant and manufacturer and shipper of lumber   His sons succeeded him in the merchant business   Judge Woodward, in company with Mr Burhans and others, owned 30,000 acres of timber and farming land which they purchased from Beverly Robertson, of New York, and sold to others   At one time Judge Woodward was connected in business with many different companies   Has been four times married   First in 1828 to Miss Julia Gunn, she died in 1832 leaving three children, two now living   For his second wife he married Miss Charlotte McDonald in 1836, she died in 1847 leaving four children, but one now living   In Dec., 1857, he married Miss Jane Judd, she died in 1859 leaving one daughter   His fourth wife was Charlotte Kennedy, whom he married in 1861   Four of his children are now living   Leander, Abigail, Lemuel and Minerva

Woodward, William F , p o Warrensburgh, was born in Warrensburgh in 1847.   Is a general farmer and lumberman   He owns the original homestead of 131 acres to which he has added 106 acres making in all 237 acres, was married in 1885 to Mrs Melvina F Shaw, of Warrensburgh   Mr Woodward's parents were Francis and Harriet (Beswick) Woodward   Mr Francis Woodward met his death by the attack of a furious bull

Woodward, Isaac S , p o Warrensburgh, was born in Warrensburgh   Is now engaged with his brother David in the manufacturing of sole leather   Firm name I S Woodard & Co   Mr Woodward was married in 1866 to Miss Cordelia C Sentenne, of Warrensburg   They have four children, viz, Clarence S, Ernest G, Rolland T and Archy J   Mr Woodward was son of John and Margaret (Summerville) Woodward.   They were married in 1833, and had seven children, four sons and three daughters, viz   Isaac S, Samuel A, David M, Thomas W, Emma J, Nancy Orrilla and Ella M   Samuel A and David M enlisted and served in the late war, Nancy Orrilla is now Mrs Shepard F Smith, Ella M is now Mrs Jacob Saylor. The grandparents of Isaac, were Isaac and Ann (Empy) Woodward   They had a family of ten children, of whom Joseph is the only surviving one

Woodward, Leander, p o Warrensburgh, was born in Warrensburgh in 1832   He commenced business as a merchant and lumberman, and in 1863 he retired to farming which business he still continues, was married in 1858 to Miss Susan Brannack of Warrensburgh   They have three children, Fred, Joseph and Berry   Mrs Woodward was a daughter of George and Jane (Wadsworth) Brannack   Mr Woodward was a son of Hon Joseph Woodward

Yaw, Oliver, p o Hague, was born June 28th, 1818, and is a native of Menden, Rutland county, Vt   Is a farmer and owns 180 acres of land and also one-half interest in the Rand and Yaw saw-mill   Has lived in Hague since 1851 and is prominently identified with public affairs in his town   Has held the office of constable, collector of taxes, commissioner of highways, assessor and auditor of town accounts, overseer of the poor, and is now serving his second year as justice of the peace, was married Sept 15th, 1840, to Sarah, daughter of William Fish, of Fort Ann, N Y   Mr Yaw's father was Oliver Yaw, a farmer of Clarendon, and soldier of the War of 1812   His wife was Sarah Ford, of Middletown, and they had 13 children

Cole, Chas., p o Warrensburgh, was born in Warrensburgh in 1861   Since Jan, 1885, he has been associate editor of the *Warrensburgh News*   He is a son of John P and Amy (Tucker) Cole.   His mother died in 1883 leaving five children   Adeline, Ira, Rachel, Belle and Charles   Mr Cole's grandparents were Ira and Lydia (Prosser) Cole, and were among the early settlers of Caldwell   Mr Cole was appointed postmaster of Warrensburgh late in July, 1885, which position he now occupies

Combs, John, Thurman, p o Athol, was born in this county in 1829, is a farmer, was in the last war, serving in the 186th N Y Regiment   Was married in 1848 to Abigail Bennet, and have eleven children   Mr Combs's grandfather, Joshua Combs was a soldier in the Revolution and an early settler in this county

Frost, Calvin, Thurman, p o Athol, was born in this town in 1841, is a farmer, has been commissioner of highways for his town two terms.   Was married in 1861 to Helen E Aldrich, and they have six children

Frost, Enos, Thurman, p o Athol, was born in this town in 1826, is a retired farmer, is excise commissioner for his town, has been commissioner of highways and assessor   He was in the late war, serving in the 96th N Y Regiment.   Was married in 1850 to Emily Williams and they have one son, Eugene Frost

Hitchcock, Chas H, Queensbury, p o Glens Falls, was born in Salem, N Y, Nov 4th, 1849, and settled in Glens Falls in 1879, as manager of Wheeler & Wilson Manufacturing Co's branch at this place   He was elected a trustee of the village corporation in 1883 and served two years as such   On Sept. 1st, 1885, he formed a copartnership with Geo R Harris for the purpose of carrying on a general insurance and real estate business together with the sale of Wheeler & Wilson sewing machines, etc   Their office is the finest in Northern New York in all respects, and they do an extensive business   Mr Hitchcock's parents were Rev P M Hitchcock and Phebe (Pierson) Hitchcock   Rev P M Hitchcock has been a member of the Troy conference (M E Church) for over fifty years   Besides Chas H they had three other children   Adelia M, Hattie A and Frank S   Hattie A died in 1879, the others are still living   Frank enlisted from Saratoga in the 77th N Y Vol Regiment, served three and was discharged

Kendrick, Willis J, Queensbury, p o Glens Falls, was born in Stockholm, St Lawrence county in 1860   He first settled in Glens Falls in 1879 as clerk for Messrs Wilson & Kendrick   Afterward he spent three years in Boston learning the 'drug trade   Returning he became a partner with his brother, Mr S D Kendrick, and closing his interest he opened one of the fine drug and prescription stores of the town in the Opera House Block in Jan, 1885   Mr Kendrick s parents were Jason M and Esther (Ellis) Kendrick

Rawson, Charles E, Queensbury, p o Glens Falls, was born in Queensbury, Warren county   Is an extensive dealer in fruit trees and shrubbery   Was married in 1880 to Delia L Sweet, and they have two children, Leland R and Lulu May   Mr Rawson's parents were Jason R and Emeline (Turner) Rawson   Besides Charles E they have four other children   They have all been teachers   Lavrinda M is now Mrs Dudley Peabody   Francis E married George S Murray, M D, and they reside at Crescent, N Y   Alice L is now Mrs John L Bond   A brother of Charles is engaged with him in business   Mr Rawson, sr, was an early clock manufacturer and dealer

INDEX.

CPSIA information can be obtained
at www.ICGtesting.com
Printed in the USA
BVHW042027010920
587849BV00008B/52

9 781297 763311